D1465643

THE LAW SOCIETY'S CONVEYANCING HANDBOOK
17TH EDITION

THE LAW SOCIETY'S CONVEYANCING HANDBOOK
17th Edition

General Editor

Frances Silverman

LLM Solicitor

Consultant Editors

Annette Goss
Russell Hewitson
Peter Reekie
Anne Rodell
Michael Taylor

Editorial Board

Helen Davies, *Solicitor, Peters Langsford Davies*
Kenneth Edwards, *Solicitor*
Philip Freedman LLB, *Solicitor, Mishcon de Reya*
Emma Slessenger, *Solicitor, Allen & Overy LLP*

*nominated by the Law Society's
Conveyancing and Land Law Committee*

The Law Society

The author has asserted the right under the Copyright, Designs and Patents Act 1988 to be identified as author of this work.

First published January 1992
2nd edition 1993
3rd edition 1994
4th edition 1995
5th edition 1996
6th edition 1997
7th edition 1999
8th edition 2001
9th edition 2002
10th edition 2003
11th edition 2004
12th edition 2005
13th edition 2006
14th edition 2007
15th edition 2008
16th edition 2009
17th edition 2010

ISBN-13: 978-1-85328-869-2
ISSN 1350-1852

Copyright in the Standard Conditions of Sale and the Standard Commercial Property Conditions of Sale (Appendices III.5 and III.6) is jointly held by the Law Society and the Solicitors Law Stationery Society Ltd.

Material in Appendix VII is Crown copyright. Crown copyright material is reproduced here with the permission of the Controller of HMSO and the Queen's Printer for Scotland.

The guidance in Appendix VI appears with the kind permission of HM Revenue and Customs.

This 17th edition published in 2010 by the Law Society
113 Chancery Lane, London WC2A 1PL

Typeset by Columns Design Ltd, Reading
Printed by TJ International Ltd, Padstow, Cornwall

Contents

C.   EXCHANGE

D.   TITLE

E.   PRE-COMPLETION

F. COMPLETION

G. POST-COMPLETION

H. LENDERS

I. NEW PROPERTIES

J. SALES OF PART

K. LEASEHOLDS

CONTENTS

VIII.   DIRECTORY

Preface to the 1992 edition

Conveyancing is a much maligned art – an easy option in the eyes of many practitioners. If this is true, why is it that the Legal Practice Directorate and Professional Ethics Department of the Law Society have a constant stream of telephone calls and letters from practitioners anxious to know how to solve conveyancing problems? The idea of this book originated from the Law Society's Land Law and Conveyancing Committee who felt that the time had come to publish a work which attempted to deal with and resolve the many problems encountered on a daily basis by practitioners. The aim of this book, therefore, is to present in readable form a ready reference handbook of the practice of conveyancing. The book does not pretend to be a comprehensive guide to the law – for this the reader is, at various points throughout the text, referred to specialist works dealing with particular areas, but it does seek to deal fully with the practice of conveyancing and to provide guidance on resolving problems which may be encountered by practitioners. The text is, therefore, divided into sections which deal with the conveyancing transaction in chronological sequence. Chapters have been included on matters which, although peripheral to the main issue, nevertheless impinge on it, e.g. advertising, property selling, costs, undertakings and remedies. Although the book does contain some specialist sections, e.g. the purchase of licensed premises, milk quotas in agricultural land, it is intended as a handbook for the general practitioner and does not, therefore, cover in detail specialist areas pertaining to commercial transactions. It does, however, seek to gather together some information which is not found either in other conventional conveyancing texts or in some cases at all, this aspect particularly concentrating on the resolution of practical problems and provision of checklists and guidelines. Precedents are not included within the text since the practitioner has ample scope for finding precedents in many other published works. Some commonly encountered practical areas are no longer dealt with by trainee solicitors during their Finals course, and in such areas, e.g. residential security of tenure, the book aims to provide the solicitor with a brief résumé of the law with reference to a specialist work on the subject should that be required.

It is hoped that this book will form the practitioner's first point of reference and to that end extensive appendices include the text of many of the matters to which a practitioner has cause to refer during the course of each working day, e.g. HM Land Registry Practice Notes, addresses of authorities for the purpose of making searches, stamp duty tables, the Formulae for exchange of contracts.

It is of course vital that any book which purports to be an essential working tool in the hands of a busy practitioner should be up to date with both law and practice. The decision has, therefore, been taken by the Law Society that this book will be completely revised and updated regularly in order to ensure that the practitioner has available to him in one volume the very latest information relating to conveyancing.

No offence is intended to female members of the profession by references in the text to the solicitor as 'he', for which please read 'he or she' as appropriate. To include the words 'he or she' on every occasion where such reference appears would have the effect of extending the text by a considerable amount which in turn would have adverse repercussions on the publication price of the book.

I would like to acknowledge with thanks the permission of HM Land Registry and the Inland Revenue for publication of their various leaflets and guidance notes which appear in the appendices to the book.

I would also like to thank Linklaters and Paines for their help with sections on milk quotas and VAT, Withers for their assistance in preparing the text on agricultural land, Chris Jowett of the Halifax Building Society for his help in relation to mortgages, Martin Wood of HM Land Registry for his assistance with points on registered land, and Tony Donell who read through each section of the manuscript before publication.

I should also record my appreciation to the staff of the Law Society, in particular Joanna Davies-Evitt and Carl Upsall who have been responsible for the co-ordination of the text, preparation of appendices and index and eventual publication of the text itself.

Finally my thanks go to Trevor Aldridge, Margaret Anstey, Murray Ross, Philip Freedman, and Kenneth Edwards who comprised the Editorial Board for this book. They had the unenviable task of sitting through monthly meetings to discuss and correct my indecipherable manuscript. Without their constant help, support and encouragement this book might not have seen the light of day.

The law is stated as at 1 December 1991.

Frances Silverman
Rowfold Grange
West Sussex

Preface to the 17th edition

The announcement of the abolition of home information packs was made just as this edition was being prepared for press, but fortunately leaving enough time to amend the text to excise references to this unloved and bureaucratic procedure. The Budget which followed the general election then created a new round of amendments to taxation issues at proof stage.

At the time of writing Equality Act 2010 had received Royal Assesnt but had not yet been brought into force and as yet many of the regulations which will accompany the new consolidated provisions (which in the conveyancing context mainly affect leasehod property) have not been made. Thus this edition retains references to the previous legislation in this area but with references to the provisions of the new Act where it has been possible to do so.

Another major change this year has been the introduction of the Building Societies Association Mortgage Instructions which now stand alongside and as an alternative to the CML Handbook. This edition has been fully updated to include references to both sets of lenders' instructions.

My thanks go to the consultant editors who have updated the various sections of the book: Annette Goss, Russell Hewitson, Peter Reekie, Anne Rodell and Michael Taylor; and also to the editorial board: Helen Davies, Kenneth Edwards, Philip Freedman and Emma Slessenger for their continuing support and help with this edition.

At the Law Society my thanks go to Diane Latter and Emma Oettinger; and at the Solicitors Regulation Authority, thanks to Angela Doran, Derek Mitchell, Tracey Calvert, Anne Philpot, Bronwen Still and Chris Brammall.

For their help with the updating of this edition, I would also like to thank Trevor Hellawell (environmental issues), Peter Camp (financial services, mortgage fraud, money laundering), Birketts Solicitors (agricultural land and agricultural tenancies), Allison Broadey (VAT), Alan Riley (stamp duty land tax), and Jane Hanney (licensing).

For their help with permissions and updating this edition, I would like to thank the following organisations: the Land Registry, National Radiological Protection Board, and the Rural Payments Agency.

Any errors which remain in the book are my responsibility alone.

The law is stated as at 1 August 2010.

Frances Silverman
Rowfold
West Sussex

About the authors

Chris Baker is a partner with Davies Arnold Cooper. He has experience in a wide variety of commercial, retail and residential property transactions, particularly development projects. Prior to coming to the UK Chris practised law in Australia for a number of years. Chris has particular expertise with commonhold. He is the author of *A Practical Guide to Commonhold* (Legalease) and is the Home Builders Federation representative on the commonhold consultative working group.

Allison Broadey has over 22 years' experience as a VAT practitioner, initially as a VAT Inspector with HM Customs and Excise, and then as 'gamekeeper turned poacher' in commercial practice. Having qualified as a chartered tax adviser specialising in VAT with Coopers & Lybrand, she is now the Technical VAT Director with The VAT Consultancy. Allison has a diverse range of clients in the professional and private sector and specialises in planning for land and property. She lectures to associations, practitioners and private businesses on all VAT matters.

Peter Camp is a solicitor and is visiting professor (Chair of Ethics) at the College of Law. He is also principal of Educational & Professional Services, which provides training and consultancy services to the solicitors' and accountants' professions. Peter is a former member of the Law Society's Financial Services Taskforce. His publications include *Solicitors and Money Laundering: A Compliance Handbook* (Law Society, 3rd edn, 2009); *Solicitors and the Accounts Rules: A Compliance Handbook* (Law Society, 2nd edn, 2009); and *Companion to the Solicitors' Code of Conduct 2007* (Law Society, 2nd edn, 2009). He is also general editor of the Law Society's *Legal Compliance Bulletin*.

Helen Davies is a solicitor and partner at Peters Langsford Davies and Law Society Council Member for Gwent and the South West. Helen specialises in residential and small scale commercial property, business transfers and some agricultural property. She is also chair of the Regulatory Affairs Board, governor of Plymouth University, and chair of County Environmental Trust.

Kenneth Edwards was admitted as a solicitor in 1961 and from 1965 practised at Cardens in Brighton specialising in building society law. Kenneth also acted as external Head Office Solicitor to the former Alliance Building Society. He continued in that capacity until the 1980s and played a significant part in the merger with Leicester Building Society. As a member of the Law Society's Conveyancing and Land Law Committee, Kenneth was involved in the bringing together of the Law Society's Standard Conditions of Sale and National Conditions of Sale and the documentation for the Law Society's TransAction scheme (he wrote part of the text for the Buyer's Guide).

Philip Freedman is a solicitor and senior property partner at Mishcon de Reya. He is a member of various committees at the Law Society, including the Conveyancing and Land Law Committee, the Standard Conditions of Sale Working Party, the Joint

Advisory Committee of the Land Registry and the Law Society, the Local Searches Joint Working Party of the Law Society and the Local Government Association. Philip is also chair of the Commercial Leases Working Group, a member of the RICS Working Party on the PACT Scheme and a member of the British Property Federation Working Party on Short Leases. His publications include *Service Charges: Law and Practice* (Jordans, 2002).

Annette Goss is a solicitor and worked in private practice as a conveyancer and property lawyer before joining the Government Legal Service. She has worked as a solicitor for the Crown Estate and as a Land Registrar for the Land Registry. Annette has been involved in designing and developing a professional training course with Michael Taylor on land registration law and practice for Land Registry staff. She has also co-authored the fourth edition of *Conveyancing Forms and Procedures* (Law Society, 2009). Annette currently prepares and delivers lectures and seminars for legal practitioners.

Jane Hanney is a solicitor and director of Magna Law Ltd, a niche firm of solicitors specialising in food law, licensing, health and safety, and environmental law with particular emphasis on the food and drink/agriculture sector. Jane is a member of the Law Society Food Law Group, an associate member of the Chartered Institute of Environmental Health and co-author of *Licensing for Conveyancers* (Law Society, 2005). She also lectures regularly in her areas of expertise.

James Harbottle is a solicitor and head of the Agriculture and Equine Unit at Birketts LLP operating from three offices across the east of England. James specialises in agricultural and equestrian properties and advises national and international private clients on long-term ownership strategies as well as disputes arising under Agricultural Holdings Act 1986. James is a member of the Agricultural Law Association and a professional member of the Country Land and Business Association, and sits as a council member of the Essex Agricultural Society.

Trevor Hellawell is a solicitor and legal training consultant with 20 years' experience training in environment law. He works with BPP, the College of Law, lawyers and other professionals, Landmark Information Group, the Ministry of Defence and several other clients, particularly in the engineering sector. Trevor was formerly a member of the Law Society's Planning and Environmental Law Committee and is the author of the *Environmental Law Handbook* (7th edn, Law Society, due 2010) and *Blackstone's Guide to Contaminated Land* (OUP/Blackstone, 2000).

Russell Hewitson is a solicitor and worked in private practice specialising in commercial and residential property and licensing law matters before joining Northumbria University, where he is a principal lecturer in property law and conveyancing. He is property law consultant to BHP Law, a member of the Law Society's Conveyancing and Land Law Committee and represents the Law Society on the NHBC Council. Russell is general editor of *Precedents for the Conveyancer* (Sweet & Maxwell) and *Practical Conveyancing Precedents* (Sweet & Maxwell), and has written a number of other books including *Licensing Law Handbook* (Law Society, 2006), *Conveyancing Searches and Enquiries* (Jordans, 2006), and *Business Tenancies*

(Cavendish Publishing, 2005). He has also devised and presented many continuing professional development courses.

Professor Peter Reekie is a property training consultant with Penningtons and visiting professor at the College of Law. Peter was admitted as a solicitor in 1976 and spent some years in private practice dealing with residential and commercial property work. He is director of Peter Reekie Associates Co. Ltd, which provides legal training and related services to lawyers and other professionals, and was formerly managing director of Legal Network Television. He writes for publication and lectures extensively at property law conferences, seminars and related events, and is consultant materials editor for the College of Law's Structured Commercial Property Programme.

Alan Riley is a solicitor and property law consultant, formerly with Halliwells LLP and the College of Law (Chester) as a senior lecturer. He now provides legal training, professional support and property law information services to law firms throughout the country. He runs a property information website for lawyers at **www.propertypsl. co.uk** and writes and publishes the *Commercial Property Information Update* (a monthly property newsletter for law firms). He has co-written *Leasehold Liability – A Guide to the 1995 Act* (Jordans) and *Commercial Property and Business Leases* (Jordans).

Anne Rodell is an associate director of design at the College of Law, currently teaching property law and practice at the College's Guildford and Moorgate centres. She qualified as a solicitor in 1989 and from 1989 to 1998 was an assistant solicitor in the real estate department of Linklaters, specialising in commercial property matters.

Frances Silverman is a solicitor and formerly a Reader at the College of Law. She has been author of the Law Society's *Conveyancing Handbook* since first publication in 1992. Frances is also author of several other books on conveyancing, sits as a part-time Chairman of Employment Tribunals and of the Leasehold Valuation Tribunal, and is a founder member of the Institute of Expert Witnesses.

Emma Slessenger is a solicitor and real estate professional support lawyer at Allen & Overy LLP. She has been a member of the Law Society's Conveyancing and Land Law Committee since 1998 and a member of the editorial board of the *Conveyancing Handbook* since 2002. She is a founder member of the London Property Support Lawyers Group and was closely involved with its development of the Commercial Property Standard Enquiries. She was co-editor of the *Landlord and Tenant Factbook* (Sweet & Maxwell) from 1996 to 2004 and co-author of *Leasehold Liability: the Landlord and Tenant* (Covenants) Act 1995 (Jordans). Emma is a member of the editorial board of the *Landlord and Tenant Review* (Sweet & Maxwell) and in 2004 was appointed as the precedents editor of the *Conveyancer and Property Lawyer* (Sweet & Maxwell). She writes and lectures widely on real estate issues.

Michael Taylor is a solicitor and the Senior Assistant Land Registrar at the Land Registry, Birkenhead (Rosebrae) office. Michael spent some years as a conveyancing and property lawyer in private practice before joining the Land Registry. Michael has been involved in designing and developing a professional training course with Annette

Goss on land registration law and practice for Land Registry staff, and has also prepared and delivered lectures and seminars to Land Registry staff, legal practitioners, academics and other members of the legal profession.

Table of cases

TABLE OF CASES

Table of statutes

Table of European and international law

(a)   where to act would involve the solicitor in a breach of the law, e.g. a fraudulent conveyance;

(b)   where the solicitor would be involved in a breach of the rules of conduct, e.g. dealing with more than one prospective buyer without disclosing this to all prospective buyers;

(c)   where a conflict of interest exists or is likely to exist;

(d)   where the solicitor lacks the expertise to carry out the client's instructions competently;

(e)   where the solicitor does not have sufficient time to devote to the client's affairs;

(f)   where the instructions are tainted by duress or undue influence, e.g. an elderly client is 'persuaded' by her relatives to sell the family home;

(g)   where the solicitor, one of his partners, employees or close relatives holds some office or appointment the holding of which might lead the client or the general public to infer that the solicitor had some influence over the outcome of the matter, e.g. a solicitor who is a member of the local planning committee should not accept instructions to act in a planning appeal against the authority of which he is a member;

(h)   where another solicitor has already been instructed in the matter and that other solicitor's retainer has not been terminated;

(i)   where the client's freedom of choice to instruct the solicitor of his choosing has been impaired in some way, e.g. the client has received a discount from a builder on the condition that a certain solicitor is instructed.

1.2.2.   Subject to the exceptions outlined above the solicitor cannot decline to act on the basis of the colour, race, national or ethnic origins of the client[1] nor on the basis of the client's sex or sexual orientation, marital status,[2] disability,[3] religion, belief or age.[4]

1.2.3.   Instructions which have been obtained through a referral from an estate agent, mortgage broker or other third party may be accepted provided there is compliance with Rule 9 Solicitors' Code of Conduct 2007 (referrals of business). The solicitor may pay referral fees to introducers provided that the arrangement complies with Rule 9.02 Solicitors' Code of Conduct 2007 (financial arrangements with introducers).

1.2.4.   If instructions are received indirectly through a third party, confirmation of the instructions must be obtained directly from the client in order to clarify the client's exact requirements and to ensure that the instructions are not tainted by duress or undue influence.

1.2.5. The solicitor should be alert to the possibilities of mortgage fraud and refer to the Law Society's Mortgage Fraud Practice Note (15 April 2009) (see Appendix II.4).

1. Race Relations Act 1976; Rule 6 Solicitors' Code of Conduct 2007 (equality and diversity).
2. Sex Discrimination Act 1975; Rule 6 Solicitors' Code of Conduct 2007 (equality and diversity).
3. Disability Discrimination Act 1995; Rule 6 Solicitors' Code of Conduct 2007 (equality and diversity).
4. Employment Equality (Age) Regulations 2006 (SI 2006/1031); Rule 6 Solicitors' Code of Conduct 2007 (equality and diversity).

1.3. Taking instructions in person

1.3.1. The client's name and address and the identity of the other party to the transaction should be requested before, or at the start of, the first interview, in order to check for possible conflicts of interest. At the interview the client should be provided with written information regarding the cost of the transaction and details of whom to contact if the client has a complaint. The client should be asked to sign a copy of the document thereby acknowledging receipt.

1.3.2. Wherever possible instructions should be obtained from the client in a personal interview. This will enable the solicitor to clarify areas of doubt concerning the transaction, enable the client to ask questions about matters which worry him, and establish a confident working relationship between the solicitor and his client.

1.3.3. Where the solicitor is instructed by one person to act on behalf of that person and another, e.g. as co-sellers, the non-instructing client's authority to act and consent to the transaction should be confirmed directly with the person concerned.

1.3.4. If the interviewer is not the person who will conduct the transaction on the client's behalf, the client should be introduced to or at least told the name and status within the firm of the person who will be effecting the client's business and of the person whom he may contact should the need arise and whom the client should contact in the event of a problem or complaint arising about the solicitor's services.[1]

1.3.5. Where the client has been referred to the solicitor under an agreement authorised by Rule 2.02 Solicitors' Code of Conduct 2007, the client must be given, in writing, all the relevant information concerning the referral, including the existence of the financial arrangement with the introducer and the amount of any payment to the introducer. Where the introducer is paying the solicitor to provide services to the introducer's customers, the client must also be informed of the amount the introducer is paying for the solicitor's services and the amount the client is required to pay the introducer. The written notice must also contain a statement that the advice given to the client will be independent and confirm that the information disclosed by the client will not be disclosed to the introducer unless the client consents.[2]

1. See Rule 2.02 Solicitors' Code of Conduct 2007.
2. *Ibid.*

1.4. Instructions taken by telephone, etc.

1.4.1. Where instructions are received by telephone the solicitor must still carry out the conflict of interest enquiries referred to in A1.3.1.

1.4.2. If instructions are received by telephone, e-mail or by any other non-face-to-face method, consideration must be given to Consumer Protection (Distance Selling) Regulations 2000 (SI 2000/2334) (as amended by Consumer Protection (Distance Selling) (Amendment) Regulations 2005 (SI 2005/689)).

1.4.3. The regulations apply where a 'supplier' (the solicitor) is providing services to a 'consumer' (an individual instructing the solicitor on personal business). Corporate clients instructing a solicitor on company business are not consumers within this definition.

1.4.4. A 'distance contract' is one which is concluded under 'an organised sales or services provision scheme', e.g. in response to an advertisement or where there is no physical communication up to and at the moment when the contract is concluded. Instructions received by letter or e-mail may fall within this definition of a distance contract.

1.4.5. Contracts relating to financial services are exempted from the regulations but contracts to provide conveyancing services are not currently exempt.

1.4.6. Where the regulations apply certain information must be supplied to the client in writing (regs.7 and 8). Most of the information required would be contained in a client care letter (e.g. name of solicitor, price, description of service to be provided) but in order to comply with the regulations it is suggested that, in cases where the regulations do or might apply, a clause is included in the client care letter to state that the contract between the solicitor and client will not be concluded until the client signs and returns a copy of the client care letter to the solicitor.

1.4.7. Further, the client care letter must provide the client with information as to how the client's right to cancel may be affected if the client agrees to performance of the services beginning less than seven working days after the contract was concluded (reg.8 as amended by SI 2005/689). Where the solicitor provides this information before the solicitor provides the services and the client agrees to the performance starting before the end of the cooling-off period, the client has no right to cancel under the regulations. Where, however, the information is provided 'in good time' during the performance of the services, the client will have a cooling-off period of seven working days starting on the day the contract is concluded and ending seven working days later or when the performance is completed, whichever is the sooner (regs. 12 and 13 as amended).

1.4.8. It is also essential for the client care letter to obtain the client's agreement to exclude reg.19 which states that if the services provided under the contract are not performed within a maximum of 30 days from the date of the contract, the contract is treated as if it had not been made.

1.4.9. Where the client has been referred to the solicitor under an agreement covered by Rule 9 Solicitors' Code of Conduct 2007, the client must be told the details of the agreement and the level of payment made by the solicitor.

1.5. Identity of the client

1.5.1. A solicitor who purports to act on behalf of a client impliedly warrants to third parties with whom he has dealings (e.g. the other party's solicitor) that he has the client's authority to act. If he does not have the client's authority he may be liable to the third party for breach of warranty of authority.[1] A solicitor must check the identity of a client with whom he is not familiar.

1.5.2. Checking the client's identity may serve as a precaution against mortgage fraud (see A24) and money laundering (see A23) and establishes that the client is the person who he says he is, thus ensuring that the solicitor has the client's authority to act in the transaction.

1.5.3. The Law Society's Anti-Money Laundering Practice Note (29 October 2009) sets out good practice for solicitors in complying with their obligations under Proceeds of Crime Act 2002, Terrorism Act 2000 and Money Laundering Regulations 2007 (SI 2007/2157). The Money Laundering Regulations affect conveyancing. The Regulations require solicitors to take a risk based approach to client due diligence including the obligation to obtain satisfactory evidence of their client's identity (see A23).

1.5.4. Proceeds of Crime Act 2002 includes an extended offence of money laundering and as a result solicitors should:

- enquire of the client how their transactions are to be funded; and

- consider whether they will accept cash payments for property and if so, to what limit.

Lender's requirements

1.5.5. When acting for a lender under the terms of either the CML Lenders' Handbook (**www.cml.org.uk**) or the BSA Mortgage Instructions (**www.bsa.org.uk**), the identity of the client must be verified in accordance with the requirements of paragraph A3.3. of the CML Lenders' Handbook or paragraph B.13 of the BSA Mortgage Instructions, as appropriate.

Land Registry requirements

1.5.6. A solicitor must consider whether the Land Registry's confirmation of identity requirements will apply, and if so, what will be required to satisfy them. Land Registry forms AP1, DS2 and FR1 require the applicant to give details of the conveyancers acting for each party and, where a party is not represented, to provide appropriate evidence of that party's identity. Full details are set out in Land Registry Practice Guide 67.

1. See *Penn* v. *Bristol & West Building Society* [1997] 3 All ER 470.

1.6. Using checklists

1.6.1. Although checklists cannot be expected to cover every eventuality in every transaction they are useful in standard transactions to ensure that all necessary information is acquired during the course of the interview.

1.6.2. Checklists focus the interviewer's mind on the relevant information, which minimises preparation time and ultimately saves time in the interview itself, but do need to be used sympathetically so that the client does not feel he is being processed in an impersonal way.

1.6.3. Where checklists are used it is helpful to have them printed on a distinct colour of paper so that they are easily located in the file either by the solicitor himself or by another member of his staff who has to work on the file.

1.6.4. A reminder of the matters which will be raised at a first interview with a client is set out in A1.7–1.9. Standard checklists for sellers and buyers may be compiled from these guidelines to suit the individual requirements of particular firms.

1.7. Acting for the seller

1.7.1.

Item	Reason for question	Further reference
(a) Date instructions taken.	Record keeping.	
(b) Full names, addresses of seller(s) and buyer(s) and home and business telephone numbers.	Needed in contract and for contact with client.	

	Item	Reason for question	Further reference
(c)	Name and address of person at estate agents	For contact.	
(d)	Find out where title deeds are and obtain client's authority to obtain them if in the hands of a third party.	To deduce title.	Deducing title, D1.
(e)	Ask clients for title number (if known).	To obtain official copies of the title.	Investigation of title, D2.
(f)	Name of other parties' solicitors or representatives.	For contact.	Dealing with non-solicitors, A5.
(g)	Do we act for the other party also?	Conflict of interest, breach of Rule 3.	Acting for both parties, A10.
(h)	Full address of property to be sold.	Needed in contract.	
(i)	Situation of property – position of footpaths/ railways/rivers, etc.	Need for plan or special searches.	Pre-contract searches and enquiries, B10.
(j)	Tenure: freehold/leasehold.	Needed in contract.	
(k)	Price.	Needed in contract, Stamp Duty Land Tax (SDLT) considerations.	
(l)	Has any preliminary deposit been paid? If so, how much? Receipt obtained?	Take account in calculating deposit on exchange.	Preliminary deposits, A12.
(m)	Which fixtures are to be removed?	Needed in contract.	Fixtures and fittings, B22.
(n)	Which fittings are to remain? Additional price for fittings?	Needed in contract and may affect SDLT.	Fixtures and fittings, B22.

	Item	Reason for question	Further reference
(o)	Anticipated completion date.	To advise client on likely duration of transaction and to assess urgency of matter. To discuss redemption of present mortgage, i.e. interest charges up to end of month.	
(p)	Present/proposed use of property.	Planning aspects/restrictive covenants.	
(q)	Does the transaction attract VAT?	May be needed in contract and client may need advice.	VAT, A16.
(r)	Who is resident in the property?	Occupiers' rights, overriding interests.	Seller's investigation of title, B3.
(s)	Is the transaction dependent on the purchase?	Synchronisation.	Exchange, section C.
(t)	Any other terms agreed between parties?	Needed in contract.	
(u)	Any correspondence between the parties?	Existence of a contract, or other terms agreed.	Form of contract, B11.
(v)	Vacant possession/ details of tenancies.	Needed in contract.	
(w)	Advice as to costs.	Required by Rule 2.	Estimate of costs, A8.
(x)	Interest on deposit.	Deposit interest considerations.	Deposit, B17.
(y)	Do a financial calculation, including costs.	To ensure the client can afford the transaction.	
(z)	Time taken in interview.	Time costing/ recording.	
(aa)	Did we act on purchase?	Look at old file prior to interview to gain relevant information.	

Item		Reason for question	Further reference
(bb)	Are there any outstanding mortgages? How much and to whom?	Calculation of financial statement and will normally need to be redeemed on completion.	
(cc)	Ask for seller's mortgage account number or reference.	Needed in order to obtain deeds from lender and to obtain a preliminary redemption statement.	
(dd)	Advise seller not to cancel mortgage repayments or insurance until completion.	So that redemption figure obtained on completion is not higher than presently anticipated.	
(ee)	How much deposit required?	Advise client on dangers of reduced deposit, use of deposit in related purchase.	Deposit, B17.
(ff)	What is to happen to the proceeds of sale?	Accounting to the client, investment advice.	Financial services, A4. Post-completion, section G.
(gg)	Does the sale attract CGT?	Advise the client.	Capital Gains Tax, A15.
(hh)	Discuss making a local search and enquiries and any other relevant searches.		Pre-contract searches and enquiries, B10.
(ii)	Check identity of client.	A precaution against mortgage fraud and money laundering.	A1.5. Money laundering, A23. Mortgage fraud, A24.

1.8. Acting for the buyer

1.8.1.

	Item	Reason for question	Further reference
(a)	Date instructions taken.	Record keeping.	
(b)	Full names and addresses of seller(s) and buyer(s) and home and business telephone numbers.	Needed in contract and for contact with client.	
(c)	Name and address of person at estate agents.	For contact.	
(d)	Name of other parties' solicitors or representatives.	For contact and Land Registry requirements.	Dealing with non-solicitors, A5. See also A1.5.6 where a party is not represented.
(e)	Do we act for the other party also?	Conflict of interest, breach of Rule 3.	Acting for both parties, A10.
(f)	Full address of property to be bought.	Needed in contract.	
(g)	Situation of property – position of footpaths/railways/rivers, etc.	Need for plan or special searches.	Pre-contract searches and enquiries, B10.
(h)	Tenure: freehold/leasehold.	Needed in contract.	
(i)	Price.	Needed in contract, SDLT considerations.	
(j)	Has any preliminary deposit been paid? If so, how much? Receipt obtained?	Take account in calculating deposit on exchange. May need to advise lender.	Preliminary deposits, A12.
(k)	Which fixtures are to be removed?	Needed in contract.	Fixtures and fittings, B22.
(l)	Which fittings are to remain? Additional price for fittings? Apportionment of purchase price?	Needed in contract and may affect SDLT.	Fixtures and fittings, B22.

Item	Reason for question	Further reference
(m) Anticipated completion date.	To advise client on likely duration of transaction and to assess urgency of matter. Effect of date on first payment under mortgage.	
(n) Present/proposed use of property.	Planning aspects/ restrictive covenants.	
(o) Does the transaction attract VAT?	May be needed in contract and client may need advice.	VAT, A16.
(p) Who is resident in the property?	Occupiers' rights, overriding interests.	Seller's investigation of title, B3.
(q) Is the transaction dependent on the sale of another property?	Synchronisation.	Exchange, section C.
(r) Any other terms agreed between the parties?	Needed in contract.	
(s) Any correspondence between the parties?	Existence of a contract, or other terms agreed.	Form of contract, B11.
(t) Vacant possession/ details of tenancies.	Needed in contract.	
(u) Advice as to costs.	Required by Rule 2.	Estimate of costs, A8.
(v) Interest on deposit.	Deposit interest considerations.	Deposit, B17.
(w) Do a financial calculation, including costs.	To ensure the client can afford the transaction.	
(x) Time taken in interview.	Time costing/ recording.	
(y) How will the deposit be funded?	Is bridging finance needed? Need to give notice if funds invested? May need to advise lender. Client's authority if undertaking to be given.	Deposit, B17.

Item	Reason for question	Further reference
(z) How is the balance of the price to be funded? Has the client obtained a mortgage certificate or offer? Does client have outstanding mortgage on any other property?	Advice on sources of finance and/or tax relief on interest. Lenders may insist that all outstanding mortgages are repaid as a condition of the new loan.	Financial services, A4.
(aa) Survey arrangements.	Advise the client.	Surveys, A13.
(bb) Insurance: Property? Life? Contents? Other? e.g. employee liability.	Advise the client.	Insurance, C3.
(cc) How is property to be held by co-owners?	Advise the client.	Joint purchasers, A9.
(dd) Custody of deeds.	Instructions needed if property not mortgaged.	Post-completion, section G.
(ee) Client's present property?	Need to give notice to determine tenancy? Penalty on mortgage redemption.	
(ff) Check client's identity	A precaution against mortgage fraud and money laundering and required by the CML Lenders' Handbook.	A1.5. Money laundering, A23. Mortgage fraud, A24.
(gg) Stamp Duty Land Tax	Advise client of responsibility to complete Land Tax Return.	Post-completion, section G.

1.9. Instructions in special cases

1.9.1. Additional information will be required where the transaction concerns a newly constructed property, is leasehold, or is a dealing with part only of the seller's property. Further checklists to deal with these situations are contained in sections I (new properties), J (sales of part), and K (leaseholds).

1.9.2. If it appears that the property (or part of it) comprises a flying freehold, the client should be warned of the possible difficulties in obtaining finance for the property as many lenders are reluctant to accept a flying freehold as security for a loan.[1]

1.9.3. If the client is to act as a guarantor to another client's debts (e.g. on a mortgage or as surety to a lender), it may be necessary to consider separate representation for the guarantor in order to avoid any conflict of interests (see A10).

1.9.4. If the seller intends to sell the property by organising a competition in which participants can pay for the opportunity to win the property, reference should be made to the Law Society's House Competitions Practice Note (30 October 2008). This Practice Note provides advice for solicitors who are asked to advise or assist with such transactions, and highlights risks relating to illegal lotteries, fraud and money laundering.

1. See paragraph 5.5 of the CML Lenders' Handbook (**www.cml.org.uk**) and paragraphs D.24 and D.25 of the BSA Mortgage Instructions (**www.bsa.org.uk**).

1.10. **After the interview**

1.10.1. Instructions should be confirmed to the client in writing.[1] The letter should include:

(a) information relating to the name and status of the person who will be carrying out the work for the client and the name of the person who has overall responsibility for the matter;

(b) details of whom the client should contact in the event of a complaint about the solicitor's services;

(c) an explanation of how the client will be kept informed of progress;

(d) information as to costs and disbursements including liability for third party costs;

(e) a repetition of the advice regarding any agreement under Rule 9 Solicitors' Code of Conduct 2007 (referrals of business) (where relevant);

(f) information regarding the payment of Stamp Duty Land Tax, see A1.10.4;

(g) advice regarding the evidence of identification needed under money laundering legislation and information about the acceptable means of payment;

(h) a résumé of the information received and advice given at the interview in order to ensure that no misunderstanding exists between solicitor and client;

(i) confirmation of any action agreed to be taken by the solicitor;

(j)   a reminder to the client of anything which he promised to do, e.g. obtain service charge receipts; and

(k)   a request for a payment on account in relation to disbursements.

1.10.2.   Provided that the checklist used contains a note of the time expended on the interview, and that a full written record of the interview exists in the form of a follow-up letter to the client, a detailed attendance note may be dispensed with.

1.10.3.   If not already done, contact should be established with the representatives of the other parties involved in the transaction, e.g. other solicitor, estate agent, lender. If the identity of the other party's solicitor is not known, his or her status should be checked with the Law Society. If a licensed conveyancer, their status can be checked with the Council for Licensed Conveyancers. This is also a requirement of paragraph A3.2 of the CML Lenders' Handbook (**www.cml.org.uk**) and paragraph B.12 of the BSA Mortgage Instructions (**www.bsa.org.uk**).

1.10.4.   The client care letter sent to the buyer following the interview should also make the following points regarding the completion of the Stamp Duty Land Tax return form:

- that it is the client's duty to submit the form within the time limit of 30 days, although the solicitor may send the form on behalf of the client;

- that there are penalties for a failure to submit the form on time (£100 for up to three months delay, and thereafter £200 together with a tax related penalty of up to the amount of tax chargeable if there is a failure to file within twelve months of the 30 day time limit);

- if the firm does complete the form on behalf of the client, that the form will be completed based on information provided by the client and that the client is responsible for the accuracy of the information and for any penalty which may be incurred if the form is returned for correction;

- that failure to submit the form on time may result in delays in registering the purchase of the property;

- that the client is liable for the payment of any tax due and, where there are co-buyers, that the liability is joint and several;

- that if the solicitor is named on the form as 'tax agent' the solicitor will not accept any responsibility for the form, he will merely be the person with whom HM Revenue and Customs will communicate and to whom the land transaction return certificate will be sent;

- that HM Revenue and Customs may enquire into the transaction and the client may be liable to pay additional tax after any enquiry;

- that should an enquiry take place, any costs incurred by the solicitor will be additional to those paid for the conveyancing transaction;

- that the client should keep any documents relating to the transaction for a minimum period of six years;

- that any documents in the solicitor's possession will be available for a minimum period of six years and what will happen to them after that period has expired.

1.10.5. For the seller:

(a) obtain title deeds;

(b) send for official copies of the title (registered land);

(c) ask estate agent for copy of the particulars;

(d) requisition local search and enquiries and other searches (if so instructed by the client);

(e) investigate title before drafting contract;

(f) prepare abstract or epitome of title (unregistered interest in land);

(g) make Land Charges Department search against seller;

(h) check seller's replies to pre-contract enquiries.

1.10.6. For the buyer:

(a) make search applications appropriate to the property and its location (if not to be supplied by seller);

(b) deal with buyer's mortgage and survey arrangements if required;

(c) check the identity of the buyer(s);

(d) check the identity of the seller's representative if not known;

(e) obtain estate agent's particulars;

(f) consider draft contract when received from seller.

1. See guidance to Rule 2.02 Solicitors' Code of Conduct 2007; this information must be given in a clear and readily accessible form. See also the Law Society's Client Care Letters Practice Note (10 March 2010).

1.11.   Lost title deeds

1.11.1. If it appears that the client's title deeds to unregistered land have been lost or destroyed, it may be possible to obtain voluntary registration of the title at the Land Registry.

1.11.2. An application for first registration made by a person who is unable to produce a full documentary title must be supported by satisfactory evidence of the applicant's entitlement to apply, together with, where appropriate, evidence to account for the absence of documentary evidence of title.[1]

1. See Land Registration Rules 2003, r.27; and Land Registry Practice Guide 2. See also G3.4.5.

1.12. **Adverse possession**

1.12.1. If it appears that the land or any part of it may have been acquired by adverse possession it may be possible to obtain voluntary registration of the title at the Land Registry. Land Registration Act 2002 has not changed the substantive law as to what constitutes adverse possession, for example the requirements of factual possession and the intention to possess. Where appropriate, reference should be made to the relevant specialist texts. Reference may also be made to G3.4.4 and G3.10 and Land Registry Practice Guides 4 and 5.

A2. Property selling

2.1.   General principles

2.1.1.   Property selling may be carried out by a solicitor:

- as part of his practice, either through the solicitor's own office or through a separate Solicitors Estate Agency Ltd (SEAL);

- through an individual practice formed for property selling;

- through a joint property selling practice (formed with other firms of solicitors and distinct for all purposes including indemnity rules, accounts rules, practice rules and conflict provisions through a recognised body).

2.1.2.   In selling property the solicitor is still acting as a solicitor and therefore remains bound by Solicitors' Code of Conduct 2007, Solicitors' Accounts Rules 1998, and all other rules, regulations and principles of conduct which affect solicitors in practice.

2.1.3.   A solicitor may carry out such valuation as may be necessary to give advice to the client on the price at which the property should be sold, and to prepare the sale particulars. The solicitor may provide structural surveys and formal valuations through the firm but must ensure that the relevant staff have the appropriate level of competence; see Rule 18 Solicitors' Code of Conduct 2007.

2.1.4.   Property selling may be carried on either as part of the solicitor's business or as a separate business but in the latter case Rule 21 Solicitors' Code of Conduct 2007 (separate businesses) must be observed (see A2.13 and Appendix I.1).

2.1.5.   Fees earned by the solicitor through property selling which is carried on through the solicitor's practice or a SEAL must be included in his gross fees return.

2.1.6.   Paragraphs A2.2–2.12 apply where property selling is carried on as part of the solicitor's business.

2.2.   Advertising

2.2.1.   Subject to compliance with Rule 7 Solicitors' Code of Conduct 2007 (publicity), a solicitor may advertise that he undertakes property-selling work and/or may advertise a specific property which he has been instructed to sell.

2.2.2.   An entry or advertisement of a solicitor who undertakes a property-selling service may appear in a directory or 'Yellow Pages' under the heading of 'estate agents' or 'solicitors'.

2.2.3.   Unsolicited approaches in person and by telephone may be made to a current or former client, another firm or its manager, an existing or potential professional or business connection, or a commercial organisation or public body. Unsolicited approaches in person and telephone calls to a member of the public are expressly prohibited by Rule 7.03 Solicitors' Code of Conduct 2007.

2.2.4.   Solicitors may place 'for sale' boards outside properties which they have been instructed to sell provided that the boards comply with current statutory requirements and with Rule 7 Solicitors' Code of Conduct 2007.

2.3.   Employment and remuneration of unqualified staff

2.3.1.   Unqualified, i.e. non-solicitor, staff may be employed to deal with property selling but they cannot enter into partnership with the solicitor (with the exception of a legal disciplinary partnership which can include up to 25% non-lawyers in its membership).

2.3.2.   Fee sharing with a genuine employee is permitted by Rule 8 Solicitors' Code of Conduct 2007 as is fee sharing with an estate agent who is acting as a sub-agent on the sale of a property. But this must not be used to disguise a 'partnership' by a solicitor with a non-qualified person.

2.4.   Premises used for property selling

2.4.1.   A department or branch office which is used mainly for property selling may be described as an 'estate agency' or 'property centre' or by any other suitable description, provided that the description is not misleading.

2.4.2.   Rule 5 Solicitors' Code of Conduct 2007 (business management in England and Wales) relating to the supervision and management of a firm applies equally to property selling.

2.4.3.   A 'property display centre' is a separate office or premises where a solicitor alone or in association with other firms of solicitors, displays or disseminates information relating to the selling of property, but where no other business of a solicitor's firm, particularly negotiating, is conducted. See paragraph 3 guidance to Rule 18 Solicitors' Code of Conduct 2007 (property selling).

2.4.4. The firms operating a joint property display centre may establish a joint service company to carry out the necessary administrative functions concerned with the running of the centre, but the service company cannot carry on any legal practice nor have any dealings with the actual selling of property.

2.4.5. A joint property display centre cannot be used to carry on any part of the solicitors' professional practice. Any stationery used for writing to the property buying and selling public must be the stationery of the individual property selling firm, and not the notepaper of the joint property display centre. However, the centre's name and logo may appear on the notepaper. The words 'regulated by the Solicitors Regulation Authority' must also appear.

2.5. SEALs

2.5.1. A SEAL is a joint solicitors' property-selling practice. It must be a registered body which is a company. It must be owned by at least four firms of solicitors with no managers or owners in common and none of which has a controlling majority of the shares. It must not itself undertake conveyancing work and must be physically separate from its participating practices.

2.5.2. A SEAL may provide a full range of estate agency services, i.e. act as agent for the seller and provide mortgage services for the buyer.

2.5.3. If the SEAL is acting for the seller on the sale of a property, and

(a) the SEAL is providing mortgage related services to the buyer; or

(b) a participating firm is doing the conveyancing for the buyer;

the buyer and seller must give their written informed consent, and different individuals must deal with the work for seller and buyer; see Rule 3.11–3.14 Solicitors' Code of Conduct 2007 and paragraphs 79–80 guidance to Rule 3.

2.6. Written agreement as to remuneration

2.6.1. When accepting instructions to act in the sale of a property, a solicitor must, at the outset of communication between the solicitor and the client, or as soon as is reasonably practicable, and before the client is committed to any liability towards the solicitor, give the client a written statement setting out the agreement as to:

(a) the identity of the property;

(b) the interest to be sold;

(c) the price to be sought;

(d) the amount of the solicitor's fee or the method of its calculation;

(e) the circumstances in which the fee is to become payable;

(f) details of any payments to be made to others and charged separately, including: the amount, or the method by which they will be calculated and the circumstances in which they may be incurred;

(g) the incidence of VAT.

Within the written statement, the solicitor must also:

(a) state whether or not the solicitor is to have 'sole agency' or 'sole selling rights'. The statement must also include a clear explanation of the intention and effect of those terms, or any similar terms used; and

(b) if the statement refers to a 'ready, willing and able' buyer (or similar term), include a clear explanation of the term.

2.6.2. See paragraphs 15 to 18 guidance to Rule 18 Solicitors' Code of Conduct 2007 (property selling) which set out the detailed information requirements to help a solicitor comply with the above.

2.7. Amount of remuneration

2.7.1. The amount of commission charged by the solicitor for selling a property is a matter for agreement between the solicitor and his client.

2.7.2. The client may have a right to object to the commission by making a complaint to the Legal Complaints Service or the Office of Legal Complaints, and/or by applying to the court for an assessment of the bill under Part III Solicitors Act 1974.

2.7.3. A composite fee for both property selling and conveyancing may be quoted or advertised, but must be clearly expressed.

2.8. Application of Estate Agents Act 1979

2.8.1. Estate Agents Act 1979 does not apply to solicitors who are engaged in property selling, but Property Misdescriptions Act 1991 does. This latter Act makes it an offence for a person selling property to attach a misleading description to the property which is being sold. The liability is similar to that incurred under Trades Descriptions Act 1968. Solicitors' Code of Conduct 2007 imposes on solicitors similar duties and obligations to those to which estate agents are subject under regulations made under the 1979 Act.

2.9. Insurance

2.9.1. Property-selling activities must be covered by the terms of the solicitors' insurance policy.

2.10. Declining instructions to act

2.10.1. Instructions must be declined where there would be a breach of Rule 1 or 2 Solicitors' Code of Conduct 2007.

2.10.2. Where the solicitor is asked to sell a property of a type which he is unused to handling he should either decline the instructions or place the property with a subagent who is experienced in that type of property.

2.10.3. There may be occasions when a conflict of interest arises between the solicitor and his client when the solicitor is engaged in selling the property as well as undertaking the legal work. As in any situation where a conflict arises or is likely to arise, the solicitor must decline to act or should cease to act further in the transaction. Attention is also drawn to the Law Society's Mortgage Fraud Practice Note (15 April 2009) (see A24 and Appendix II.4).

2.11. Introductions and referrals

2.11.1. Provided there is compliance with Rule 9 Solicitors' Code of Conduct 2007 (referrals of business) a solicitor may have an arrangement with an estate agent in relation to the sale of property (see A7).

2.12. Commissions from third parties

2.12.1. Any commission received by a solicitor as a result of the client having entered into, e.g. an endowment mortgage, is subject to Solicitors' Financial Services (Scope) Rules 2001 where the law firm is not authorised by the Financial Services Authority and the commission arises in connection with financial services and, more generally, with Rule 2.06 Solicitors' Code of Conduct 2007 (client relations).

2.13. Property selling as a separate business

2.13.1. Rule 21 Solicitors' Code of Conduct 2007 permits a solicitor to control, actively participate in or operate (in each case alone, or by or with others) a separate business, including a property-selling business, provided that there is compliance with the provisions of Rule 21 which are summarised below.

2.13.2. If the property-selling business shares premises, office accommodation or reception staff with a solicitor's practice, the areas used by the solicitor's practice must be clearly differentiated from the areas used by the property-selling business and the customers of the property-selling business must be informed that, as customers of the property-selling business, they do not enjoy the statutory protection afforded to clients of a solicitor and that the property-selling business is not regulated by the Solicitors Regulation Authority.

2.13.3. The property-selling business must not be held out or described in such a way as to suggest that the property-selling business is carrying on a practice regulated by the Solicitors Regulation Authority or another approved regulator.

2.13.4. All paperwork, documents, records and files relating to customers of the property-selling business must be kept separately from those relating to the solicitor's practice. Money held for the property-selling business and its customers must be held in a client account separate from that used for the solicitor's practice.

2.13.5. If the solicitor's practice refers a client to the property-selling business, the client must first be informed of the solicitor's interest in the property-selling business, that the property-selling business is not regulated by the Solicitors Regulation Authority, and that the statutory protections attaching to clients of a lawyer regulated by the Solicitors Regulation Authority are not available to them as customers of the property-selling business.

2.13.6. If the only services provided to the seller are property-selling services through a SEAL, the solicitor may act for the buyer in the purchase of the property provided that the conditions listed in Rule 3.13 Solicitors' Code of Conduct 2007 are complied with. In particular, the buyer and the seller must give their written and informed consent to the arrangement and different individuals must deal with the work on behalf of the seller and buyer. Alternatively, the solicitor may do conveyancing work for the seller where the separate business has provided mortgage services to the buyer provided Rule 3.13 is complied with.

2.14. Acting for a buyer

2.14.1. Neither the solicitor nor the firm may act in the conveyancing for a buyer of any property sold through the estate agency unless the conditions set out in Rule 21.05(f) Solicitors' Code of Conduct 2007 have been complied with:

(a) the firm must share the ownership of the estate agency with at least one other business in which neither the individual solicitor nor the firm has any financial interest;

(b) no person in the firm has dealt with the sale of the seller's property for the separate business; and

(c) the buyer has given written consent to the firm acting after the firm's financial interest in the sale going through has been explained to the buyer.

A3. Advertising

3.1. Solicitors' Code of Conduct 2007

3.1.1. A solicitor may publicise his practice provided that the publicity complies with Rule 7 Solicitors' Code of Conduct 2007 (publicity). The main points of Rule 7 are summarised in A3.3–A3.8.

3.2. Compliance with Consumer Credit (Advertisements) Regulations 2004

3.2.1. The contents of advertisements relating to the provision of credit and related services must comply with Consumer Credit (Advertisements) Regulations 2004 (SI 2004/1484) which are summarised below. These regulations apply in circumstances where, e.g. the solicitor is advertising his services and indicates that he can obtain mortgage finance for a client. These regulations do not apply to advertisements for mortgages which are a first charge on the borrower's home but they will apply to advertisements for second mortgages. If the firm publishes a credit advertisement it must ensure that the advertisement complies with the regulations.

3.2.2. *Summary of the Regulations*

1. Every credit advertisement must be written in plain and intelligible language; be easily legible (or, in the case of any information given orally, clearly audible), and specify the name of the advertiser.

2. Unless one of the exceptions in Regulation 4(1)(b) applies, e.g. the advertisement is published on the radio, the advertisement must specify a postal address at which the advertiser may be contacted.

3. Where security will be required the advertisement must specify the nature of the security and, where the security required is a mortgage over the debtor's home, the advertisement must contain the following warning: *Your home may be repossessed if you do not keep up repayments on a mortgage or any other debt secured on it.* Where the loan is being used to pay debts due to

other creditors, the advertisement must also contain the following warning: *Think carefully before securing other debts against your home.*

4. Where the advertisement relates to loans under equity release schemes secured on the debtor's home, the advertisement must contain the following statement: '*Check that this mortgage will meet your needs if you want to move or sell your home or you want your family to inherit it. If you are in any doubt, seek independent advice.*'

5. The warnings must be given greater prominence in the advertisement than is given to any rate of charge other than the typical APR, or any indication or incentive of a kind referred to in Regulation 8(1)(c) or (d), and no less prominence than the other issues required in the advertisement.

6. The APR must be specifically mentioned and given greater prominence than the mention of any other charge.

7. The advertisement must also include the issues listed in Schedule 2 of the Regulations:

   (a) The amount of credit which may be provided under a consumer credit agreement or an indication of one or both of the maximum amount and the minimum amount of credit which may be provided;

   (b) a statement of any requirement to place on deposit any sum of money in any account with any person;

   (c) in the case of an advertisement relating to credit to be provided under a debtor-creditor-supplier agreement, where the advertisement specifies goods, services, land or other things having a particular cash price, the acquisition of which from an identified dealer may be financed by the credit, the cash price of such goods, services, land or other things;

   (d) a statement as to whether an advance payment is required and if so the amount or minimum amount of the payment expressed as a sum of money or a percentage;

   (e) in the case of an advertisement relating to running-account credit, a statement of the frequency of the repayments of credit under the advertised transaction and of the amount of each repayment stating whether it is a fixed or minimum amount, or a statement indicating the manner in which the amount will be determined;

   (f) in the case of other credit advertisements, a statement of the frequency, number and amounts of repayments of credit;[1]

   (g) a statement indicating the description and amount of any other payments and charges which may be payable under the transaction advertised;

   (h) in the case of an advertisement relating to fixed-sum credit which is repayable at specified intervals or in specified amounts, the total amount payable by the debtor, being the total of any advance payments, the amount of credit repayable by the debtor, and the amount of the total charge for credit.

1. In subparagraphs (e) and (f) 'amount' can be expressed as a sum of money or a specified proportion of a specified amount (including amounts outstanding from time to time).

3.3. Matters prohibited by Solicitors' Code of Conduct 2007

3.3.1. Rule 7.01 provides that publicity must not be misleading or inaccurate.

3.3.2. Rule 7.03 generally prohibits unsolicited approaches in person or by telephone to a member of the public.

3.3.3. Unsolicited approaches in person and by telephone may be made to a current or former client, another firm or its manager, an existing or potential professional or business connection, or a commercial organisation or public body (subject to any legal requirements such as those under Data Protection Act 1998).

3.4. Application of Solicitors' Code of Conduct 2007

3.4.1. Rule 7 (publicity) applies to all forms of publicity including the name or description of the firm, stationery, advertisements, brochures, websites, emails, directory entries, media appearances, press releases promoting a practice and direct approaches to potential clients and other persons, and whether conducted in person, in writing or in electronic form.

3.5. Property selling

3.5.1. Publicity in relation to any other business or activity carried on by the firm (e.g. property selling) must comply with Rule 7 Solicitors' Code of Conduct 2007.

3.5.2. The solicitor would be able to describe himself as a 'solicitor', 'estate agent' or 'solicitor and estate agent' in an advertisement which relates to his property-selling activities, and may be listed under the heading of 'solicitors' or 'estate agents' in a directory.

3.6. Advertising the solicitor's charges

3.6.1. Any publicity relating to the solicitor's charges or basis of charging must be clearly expressed.

3.6.2. All publicity relating to charges must make it clear whether disbursements and VAT are included.

3.7. Advertising placed by third parties

3.7.1. Where advertisements are placed by third parties which advertise the services of solicitors to whom work may be referred, the solicitor remains responsible for the advertisement. Such advertisements should therefore be checked carefully by the solicitor before publication. If the solicitor becomes aware of a breach, the solicitor must take steps to have the publicity changed or withdrawn. Solicitors must not authorise any other person to conduct publicity for the solicitors' practice in a way which would be contrary to Rule 7.

3.8. Professional stationery

3.8.1. Requirements for professional stationery are set out in Rule 7.07 Solicitors' Code of Conduct 2007. All firms are required to put 'regulated by the Solicitors Regulation Authority' on their letterhead, website and emails and either the firm's registered name and number if it is an LLP or company, or, if the firm is a partnership or sole practitioner, the name under which it is recognised by the Solicitors Regulation Authority, and the number allocated to it by the Solicitors Regulation Authority.

A4. Financial services

4.1. Activities within Financial Services and Markets Act 2000

4.1.1. Financial Services and Markets Act 2000 (FSMA) made major changes to the regulation of the financial services industry. Of necessity, these changes affect solicitors and since the consequences of providing investment services (referred to in the FSMA as 'regulated activities') without authorisation can amount to a criminal offence, solicitors must ensure that any activity caught by the Act is undertaken in an appropriate manner. The FSMA came into force on 1 December 2001.

The following activities may involve a solicitor in regulated activities:

(a) arranging and/or advising a client about obtaining regulated investments such as regulated mortgage contracts, regulated home purchase plans, regulated home reversion plans and regulated sale and rent back agreements; an insurance contract (e.g. endowment, mortgage protection, defective title, household contents or building policies); an ISA (other than a cash-only ISA) or a pension mortgage;

(b) where a property sale is linked to the sale of a business in the form of a sale of company shares;

(c) where shares in a management company are transferred on completion;

(d) where the sale of a property for a client leads to the client looking for advice on how to invest the proceeds of sale.

4.1.2. It is a criminal offence to carry on 'regulated activities' as defined in Financial Services and Markets Act (Regulated Activities) Order 2001, without authorisation unless the activity is the subject of an exclusion or exemption as defined in the Order or FSMA. Since 1 December 2001, authorisation must be obtained from the Financial Services Authority (FSA). However, the majority of firms of solicitors fall outside the requirements to be authorised provided they undertake regulated activities strictly in accordance with the statutory exclusions or exemptions under Part XX of FSMA.

4.2.   **Regulated activities**

4.2.1.   'Regulated activities' are defined in Financial Services and Markets Act (Regulated Activities) Order 2001 (RAO).

4.2.2.   A regulated activity is potentially undertaken when a solicitor is involved in any one of the activities referred to in articles 5–61 RAO and relating to any one of the specified investments listed in articles 74–89. The most common activities will be advice on the merits of buying or selling a specified investment or arranging on behalf of a client the sale or purchase of a specified investment. Shares, endowment policies and other insurance contracts, and regulated mortgage contracts constitute common specified investments.

4.2.3.   Advising the client on or arranging the following products does not constitute a regulated activity:

(a)   a bank or building society account;

(b)   unregulated mortgages;

(c)   a cash ISA.

4.2.4.   Generic investment advice is not within the definition of regulated activities in the RAO. Generic advice is advice about general categories of investment, as opposed to specific investments. Recommendations to the client that 'it would be wise to invest capital in equity shares/unit trusts' or 'you should take out a life insurance policy' are both examples of generic advice. A recommendation to the client that he should 'invest £5,000 in x unit trusts' or to 'take out a regulated life insurance policy for a 15-year term with y insurance company who do a very good policy' is, however, specific investment advice falling within the definition of a 'regulated activity'.

4.2.5.   'Arranging deals in investments' is a regulated activity within the RAO. A solicitor who is involved in arrangements which lead to a client taking out a regulated life insurance policy, or in entering into a regulated mortgage contract, is potentially carrying on a regulated activity even if he has given no advice about the policy or mortgage.

4.2.6.   Solicitors who arrange deals in investments may be able to avoid the need for authorisation by showing that certain exclusions contained in the RAO apply. There are a number of exclusions in the RAO which are relevant to solicitors; if the activity falls within one of these exclusions, and the solicitor is able to satisfy all the conditions attached to it, then the activity will not be subject to financial services regulation. The most important are as follows:

(a)   Arrangements made with or through an authorised person (i.e. one authorised by the FSA under the FSMA) where:

(i)   the transaction is entered into on advice given to the client by an authorised person; or

(ii) it is clear in all the circumstances that the client, in his capacity as an investor, is not seeking and has not sought advice from the person as to the merits of the client entering the transaction (or if the client has sought advice the solicitor has declined to give it but has recommended the client to seek advice from an authorised person).

It is important to note, however, that the above exclusion does not apply to an insurance contract nor does it apply if the solicitor receives from any person other than the client any pecuniary reward or advantage, for which he does not account to the client, arising out of his entering into the transaction. The Solicitors Regulation Authority (SRA) has taken the view that retaining commission with the informed consent of the client in accordance with Rule 2.06 Solicitors' Code of Conduct 2007 does represent 'accounting to the client' and the benefit of the exclusion will still apply in these circumstances.

(b) Introductions: where a person introduces a client to an authorised or exempt person and the introduction is made with a view to the provision of independent advice. Note that like the exclusion in (a) above this exclusion does not apply to insurance contracts.

4.2.7. Solicitors should note that the exclusion arising from the use of an authorised person only applies to arranging; it does not apply to investment advice. Further, none of the exclusions apply to the advice or arrangements where the investment product is an insurance contract (see A4.1.1 for examples of such contracts). Where the activity involves advice or the exclusion for arranging is not available for any reason, an alternative means of avoiding the need for authorisation is to use Part XX FSMA which contains provisions relating to 'exempt regulated activities' carried on by members of a profession which is supervised and regulated by a designated professional body (DPB). The Law Society is a DPB.

4.2.8. Section 327 FSMA provides that the prohibition against carrying on regulated activities contained in the Act does not apply to the carrying on of a regulated activity by a member of a profession if certain conditions apply:

(a) the person must be a member of a profession or controlled or managed by one or more such members;

(b) the person must not receive from anyone other than his client any pecuniary reward or other advantage, for which he does not account to his client, arising out of his carrying on of any of the activities;

(c) the manner of the provision of any service in the course of carrying on the activities must be incidental to the provision by him of professional services;

(d) only regulated activities permitted by the DPB's rules may be carried out.

4.2.9. The SRA is responsible for the Solicitors' Financial Services (Scope) Rules 2001 covering the requirements of (d) above. These rules limit the scope of solicitors benefiting from Part XX. The prohibited activities in rule 3 include:

    (a)   market making;

    (b)   buying, selling, subscribing or underwriting as principal where the firm holds itself out as engaging in the business of buying investments with a view to selling them;

    (c)   acting as a trustee or operator of a regulated collective investment scheme (CIS);

    (d)   acting as a stakeholder pension scheme manager;

    (e)   entering into a regulated mortgage contract as lender or administering a regulated mortgage contract unless this is in the firm's capacity as a trustee or PR and the borrower is a beneficiary;

    (f)   entering into regulated home reversion plasn, home purchase plans, or sale and rent back agreements as plan or agreement providers (see A4.4).

4.2.10. There are further restrictions on using Part XX where the investment is a packaged product. These are defined as long term insurance contracts (including endowment policies but excluding 'pure protection policies' such as term assurance), units or shares in regulated Collective Investment Schemes (e.g. unit trusts or shares in Open Ended Investment Companies) or an investment trust savings scheme, whether or not held within an ISA or PEP or a stakeholder pension scheme. Where such investments are acquired, firms cannot use the exemption in Part XX FSMA but, where possible, should use an authorised person. Firms may, however, pass on the advice of an authorised person.

4.3. **Mortgages**

4.3.1. Under article 61(1) RAO, entering into a regulated mortgage contract as lender is a regulated activity. Further, under article 61(2), administering a regulated mortgage contract where the contract was entered into by way of business is also a regulated activity. A regulated mortgage is one where:

    (a)   the lender provides credit to an individual or trustees;

    (b)   the obligation to repay is secured by a first legal mortgage on land in the UK;

    (c)   at least 40% of that land is used or intended to be used as or in connection with a dwelling by the borrower, a beneficiary of the trust or related person.

Note, purely commercial mortgages, second charges on residential property or mortgages on overseas property will be unregulated.

4.3.2. Financial Services and Markets Act 2000 (Regulated Activities) (Amendment) (No.1) Order 2003 amended the RAO with regard to regulated mortgages. It extended the definition of regulated activities to 'arranging regulated mortgage contracts' and 'advising on regulated mortgage contracts' in addition to entering into as lender and administering a regulated mortgage. The changes relating to regulated mortgages came into force on 31 October 2004.

4.3.3. Solicitors' Financial Services (Scope) Rules 2001 have been amended to prevent solicitors from using Part XX FSMA in relation to the activity of advising on a regulated mortgage (rule 5(7)). Consequently, it will not be possible to use the exempt regulated activity route to avoid authorisation. It will, however, be possible for solicitors to endorse the advice of an authorised person where such endorsement is incidental to other work.

4.3.4. Arranging regulated mortgages will be excluded from the definition of regulated activities in the RAO where the arrangement is with or through an authorised person (the same conditions as noted above will apply) or where the arrangement consists of an introduction to an authorised person with a view to the provision of independent advice.

4.3.5. A further exclusion has been added where an introduction is made to an authorised lender or broker. To benefit from this exclusion, before the introduction the following must be disclosed to the client:

(a) details of any fee or commission to be received or commission to be received for introducing the client; and

(b) an indication of any other reward or advantage to be received arising out of the introduction.

This additional exclusion does not require the introduction to be made with a view to the provision of independent advice.

4.3.6. Enforcing mortgages falls within the definition of 'administering' a mortgage. If the mortgage is regulated this will potentially be a regulated activity. However, there is an exclusion where the administration is pursuant to an agreement with an authorised person. Enforcing mortgage terms on behalf of an authorised commercial lender should, therefore, be excluded.

4.3.7. A solicitor who is involved in obtaining mortgage finance for a client will be acting as a mortgage broker under Consumer Credit Act 1974. For this activity, the solicitor needs to hold a licence under the 1974 Act. The Law Society holds a group licence from the Director General of Fair Trading which covers all solicitors acting within the ordinary course of practice. Normally, therefore, a solicitor does not need to hold an individual licence.

4.4. Regulated home reversion plans, regulated home purchase plans and regulated sale and rent back agreements

4.4.1. A 'regulated home reversion plan' is a form of equity release arrangement under which a person buys all or part of a qualifying interest in land (other than timeshare accommodation) in the UK from an individual who is entitled under the arrangement to occupy at least 40% of the land in question as or in connection with a dwelling. The arrangement specifies one or more qualifying termination events, on the occurrence of which that entitlement will end, e.g. death or permanent residence in a nursing home.

4.4.2. A 'regulated home purchase plan' is an arrangement under which a purchaser buys a qualifying interest or an undivided share of a qualifying interest in land (other than timeshare accommodation) in the UK and the interest is held on trust for the purchaser and other individual(s) as beneficial tenants in common. The arrangement provides for the obligation of the individual(s) to buy the interest bought by the purchaser over the course of or at the end of a specified period. The individual(s) or a related person will be entitled under the arrangement to occupy at least 40% of the land in question as or in connection with a dwelling during that period.

4.4.3. Regulated home purchase plans are forms of Islamic financing arrangements designed to enable the purchase of a home in a way that is acceptable under Islamic law.

4.4.4. Financial Services and Markets Act 2000 (Regulated Activities) (Amendment) (No.2) Order 2006 (SI 2006/2383) amended the RAO with regard to home reversion and home purchase plans. With effect from 1 April 2007 these are specified investments and activities such as arranging and advising on such plans are now regulated. Entering into and administering such plans will also be regulated activities.

4.4.5. Regulated sale and rent back agreements were introduced as specified investments by way of an amendment to the RAO by Financial Services and Markets Act 2000 (Regulated Activities) (Amendment) Order 2009 (SI 2009/1342). These are arrangements under which a person buys all or part of an interest in land (other than timeshare accommodation) in the United Kingdom from an individual seller and the seller (or a related person) is entitled to occupy at least 40% of the land in question as or in connection with a dwelling, and intends to do so. Such an arrangement is not a regulated sale and rent back agreement if it is a regulated home reversion plan. Activities such as arranging and advising on such arrangements are now regulated. Entering into and administering such arrangements will also be regulated activities.

4.4.6. Solicitors' Financial Services (Scope) Rules 2001 have been amended to prevent solicitors from using Part XX FSMA in relation to recommending particular plans and agreements (rules 5(8), 5(9), and 5(10)) but solicitors can endorse the advice of an authorised person where such endorsement is incidental to other work.

4.4.7. Similar exclusions to those available for regulated mortgages apply (see A4.3.4 and A4.3.5).

4.5. Insurance contracts

4.5.1. As a result of the Insurance Mediation Directive, financial services regulation extends to all activities relating to the selling and administration of insurance contracts. Advice on and arrangements made for the acquisition or disposal of all insurance contracts are now caught as regulated activities. Further, assisting in the administration and performance of such contracts (including claims handling) will also be caught as a regulated activity. These provisions came into force on 14 January 2005.

4.5.2. Conveyancers are affected by this change where, as part of their conveyancing, they give advice on or make arrangements for a client to acquire a life policy as part of mortgage arrangements (e.g. endowment or term policies) or where they arrange indemnity policies such as defective title insurance, contaminated land insurance, lender/title insurance, household contents insurance or building insurance. Further, solicitors who assist clients in claims handling will also potentially be involved in regulated activities (although acting in relation to claims handling for an insurance company will generally be excluded).

4.5.3. None of the general exclusions in the RAO will apply (the authorised person and the introductions exclusions expressly cannot apply to insurance contracts). Consequently unauthorised solicitors who wish to be involved in insurance mediation (advice on, arrangements for or administration of insurance contracts) will need to do so as 'exempt regulated activities' under Part XX FSMA. However, if the insurance involves 'long term insurance contracts excluding pure protection policies' (e.g. endowment policies or pension policies) there are restrictions on the use of the exempt regime (see A4.2.10). No advice should be given where such a product is to be acquired (rule 5(1) of the Solicitors' Financial Services (Scope) Rules 2001) except where solicitors pass on or endorse the advice of an authorised person, or where the acquisition is by means of assignment. Arrangements should be limited to purchase by means of an assignment or 'execution only' arrangements (i.e. where it is clear on reasonable grounds that the client is not relying on the firm as to the merits or suitability of that transaction).

4.5.4. For other insurance products (e.g. term assurance policies or indemnity policies) advice, arrangements or administration can be undertaken by a firm if these activities are incidental to the conveyancing transaction. Solicitors' Financial Services (Scope) Rules 2001 have been amended at rule 5(6) to require solicitors who wish to undertake insurance mediation services to:

    (a) appoint a compliance officer, and

    (b) be registered in the register maintained by the Financial Services Authority.

4.6. Trustees and personal representatives

The solicitor who is a trustee or personal representative

4.6.1. If a solicitor, in his capacity as a trustee, buys or sells investments for the trust or estate the activity may be excluded under the RAO, provided he is acting as a principal. Where a solicitor who is a trustee or personal representative advises his fellow trustees or personal representatives or makes arrangements for the acquisition or disposal of investments for his co-trustees or personal representatives or a beneficiary, the RAO provides further exclusions (article 66). These exclusions only apply if the trustee is not remunerated for the arranging or advice in addition to any remuneration received for acting as trustee or personal representative. Article 66 expressly provides that a person is not to be regarded as receiving additional remuneration merely because his remuneration is calculated by reference to time. Article 66 does not apply to insurance mediation activities where such activities are undertaken for reward. This means that solicitors are unlikely to be able to use article 66 for activities relating to insurance contracts.

4.6.2. Trustees or personal representatives will 'manage' the investments belonging to the trust or estate. The RAO makes it clear, however, that only 'discretionary management' will be caught as a regulated activity. Non-discretionary management will not be a 'regulated activity'. Non-discretionary management will occur when either the firm acts for outside trustees or where a solicitor or employee of the firm is a joint trustee or personal representative with someone from outside the firm. Discretionary management is only likely where a solicitor is a sole trustee or personal representative or where the solicitor is jointly acting as such with someone from within the firm. Article 66 excludes 'discretionary management' where such is undertaken by a person acting as a trustee or personal representative. In addition to the condition relating to 'no additional remuneration' noted above for advising and arranging, solicitors must not hold themselves out as providing a management service if they wish to benefit from this exclusion.

4.6.3. If the article 66 exclusion does not apply, it is open to solicitors who are trustees or personal representatives to show that their activities fall within the general exemption contained in Part XX FSMA as noted above.

The solicitor who is acting for trustees or personal representatives

4.6.4. It should be noted that the exclusion contained in article 66 only applies where a solicitor is a trustee or a personal representative – it does not apply if the solicitor merely acts for trustees or personal representatives. In these circumstances, arrangements can be excluded by using the authorised person exclusion noted in A4.2.6 or arrangements and advice may fall within the incidental exemption contained in Part XX FSMA.

4.7. Commissions

4.7.1. Life assurance companies and the providers of some other types of investment product pay commissions to intermediaries on the sale of their products. A solicitor who relies on an exclusion in the RAO and introduces a client to an authorised person will usually receive a commission for the introduction.

4.7.2. Any commission received by the solicitor is subject to Rule 2.06 Solicitors' Code of Conduct 2007 (see Appendix I.1 and N1.8). As noted above, a number of the exclusions from the need for authorisation require solicitors to account for any commission. If a solicitor retains commission without the client's consent these exclusions in the RAO and the Act will not apply. Solicitors risk committing a criminal offence if they undertake regulated activities without being authorised and without the benefit of an appropriate exclusion.

4.7.3. Solicitors who rely on Part XX FSMA to carry on exempt regulated activities, and receive a 'pecuniary reward or other advantage' (such as commission from a third party) must ensure that they comply with rule 4(c) Solicitors' Financial Services (Scope) Rules 2001 and account to the client. Accounting in these circumstances means that the commission must be held to the order of the client and the solicitor must obtain the client's informed consent to keep it. Unlike rule 2.06 of the Code which contains a £20 de minimis provision, the requirement under rule 4(c) is to account for all of the pecuniary reward.

4.8. Compliance

4.8.1. The SRA is responsible for the Solicitors' Financial Services (Conduct of Business) Rules 2001 applicable to solicitors seeking exemption under Part XX to carry on exempt regulated activities.

4.8.2. The Rules include obligations relating to:

- *Status disclosure.* Requiring firms to indicate in writing that they are not authorised by the FSA but are regulated by the SRA (rule 3). Where insurance mediation is undertaken a compulsory statement indicating that the firm's name is included on the FSA register is required (rule 3(3)).

- *Execution of transactions.* Requiring firms to carry out instructions as soon as possible and to keep records of instructions received and instructions given (rule 4).

- *Record of commissions.* Requiring firms to keep records of commissions received and records of how such commission has been accounted for (rule 6).

- *Execution only transactions – packaged products.* Requiring firms to give written confirmation of execution only transactions involving packaged products (rule 8).

- *Insurance mediation activities.* Requiring firms to inform clients whether or not any recommendation is given on the basis of a fair market analysis of the type of product and requiring firms to give clients a demands and needs statement setting out the client's demands and needs and an explanation of why a particular insurance contract was recommended (rule 8A and Appendix 1).

Where a buyer insists upon a seller obtaining an insurance product, e.g. defective title insurance, the solicitor acting for the seller will have to comply with these requirements if the solicitor is involved in insurance mediation. This will be so even if the policy is to be taken out in the buyer's name. However, if the buyer's solicitor advised upon and arranges the insurance at the cost of the seller, the buyer's solicitor will be involved in insurance mediation and as such will have to comply with the Solicitors' Financial Services (Conduct of Business) Rules.

4.8.3. Breach of the Solicitors' Financial Services (Scope) Rules can amount to a criminal offence where firms undertake unauthorised regulated activities. Further, the FSA can order the firm to cease undertaking any regulated activities. Breach of the Solicitors' Financial Services (Conduct of Business) Rules, whilst not amounting to a criminal offence, can lead to disciplinary action by the SRA or Legal Complaints Service (or, after 6 October 2010, the Office for Legal Complaints).

A5. Dealing with non-solicitors

5.1.   Independent licensed conveyancers

5.1.1.   When dealing with a licensed conveyancer who is not known personally to the solicitor, a check on the identity of the conveyancer should be made with the Council for Licensed Conveyancers (see Appendix IX.2 for address).

5.1.2.   The solicitor should ensure that he deals either directly with the licensed conveyancer or with a person working under the immediate supervision of such a person.

5.1.3.   Licensed conveyancers are bound by rules relating to conduct, discipline, insurance and accounts which are similar to those which bind solicitors. It is therefore normally possible to deal with a licensed conveyancer as if the conveyancer was a fellow solicitor subject to the best interests of the solicitor's client.

5.2.   Law Society Formulae and undertakings

5.2.1.   The Law Society Formulae for Exchange of Contracts and the Code for Completion by Post (see Appendix IV.11 and Appendix IV.12) may be used in dealings with licensed conveyancers. Licensed conveyancers have no equivalent sanction to the court's control over the conduct of solicitors, but the Law Society recommends that they are nevertheless treated by solicitors as being on an equal footing with themselves. It is therefore normally possible to rely on undertakings given by such persons.

5.3.   Employment of licensed conveyancers by solicitors

5.3.1.   A solicitor may employ or enter into partnership with a licensed conveyancer. Work done by the licensed conveyancer must be done as an integral part of the

solicitor's practice and is subject to all the practice rules. The licensed conveyancer may be named in the solicitor's publicity (including stationery) provided
that his status is made clear.

5.3.2.   As with any transaction, the overriding concern is for the best interests of the
client. In any situation where there is doubt over the conduct of the matter,
guidance should be sought from the Professional Ethics Guidance Team.

5.4.   Unqualified conveyancers

5.4.1.   The Legal Services Act 2007 provides that it is an offence to carry on reserved
legal activity through a person not entitled to do so. This includes certain
conveyancing services such as preparing a contract for the sale of land or a
transfer or charge for the purposes of Land Registration Act 2002.

5.5.   Dealing with unqualified persons

5.5.1.   The Law Society has published guidance for solicitors who are asked to deal
with unqualified conveyancers which is summarised below. See further Appendix IV.4.

5.5.2.   A solicitor should refuse to have any dealings with an unqualified person unless
he has clear evidence that no offence under the Legal Services Act 2007 will be
committed.

5.5.3.   At the outset of a transaction which apparently involves an unqualified person
the solicitor should write to the unqualified person drawing attention to the Law
Society's guidelines and asking for satisfactory evidence that no offence will be
committed. The solicitor's client should also be informed of the situation.

5.5.4.   Drafts of suitable letters are set out in the guidelines.

5.5.5.   A letter from a qualified person confirming that he will prepare the relevant
documents will be satisfactory evidence that no offence will be committed and
the solicitor may proceed with the transaction.

5.6   Identity evidence for the Land Registry

5.6.1.   Land Registry application Forms AP1, DS2 and FR1 require appropriate
evidence of identity to be included on many applications. Such evidence relates
to those conveyancers[1] acting for other parties in the transaction and to any
unrepresented parties involved.[2]

5.6.2.   A solicitor will need to consider the Land Registry's identity requirements at an
early stage. Additional preliminary enquiries or contractual provisions may be
appropriate to obtain the necessary details and identification evidence.

1. Land Registration Rules 2003, r.217 as amended.
2. See Land Registry Practice Guide 67.

5.7.   Undertakings

5.7.1.   Undertakings should not be accepted from unqualified persons since there is no method of enforcing them. Thus where, e.g. a seller who is represented by an unqualified person has a mortgage subsisting at completion, the buyer's solicitor must require the seller to produce a signed Form DS1 at completion and must not accept an undertaking for its discharge. This may mean that the seller has to obtain bridging finance to repay the loan before completion or that the seller's lender will have to attend at completion. A solicitor who accepts an undertaking from an unqualified person may be in breach of his duty of care to his own client and thus liable to make good to the client any loss sustained as a result of a dishonoured undertaking.

5.8.   Completions and agency work

5.8.1.   There is no duty on a solicitor to undertake agency work by way of completions by post or to attend to other formalities on behalf of third parties who are not clients and who are represented by an unqualified person. A solicitor who does undertake such work should only do so after having agreed in writing with the unqualified person the precise extent of the solicitor's duties and agreed fee for such services. Where a considerable amount of work is undertaken on behalf of the unqualified person's client there is a danger of the solicitor being in breach of Rule 3 Solicitors' Code of Conduct 2007 since he may effectively be acting for both parties in the transaction.

5.9.   The contract

5.9.1.   It will be necessary for special provisions to be inserted in the draft contract to take account of the fact that the other party is not represented by a qualified person.

5.9.2.   Clauses to deal with the following matters should be inserted in the contract:

(a)   personal attendance by an unrepresented seller at completion to take up the deeds and purchase price because Law of Property Act 1925, s.69, only applies when a document containing a receipt for the purchase price is handed over by a qualified person or by the seller himself;

(b)   payment of the deposit either to an estate agent who is a member of a recognised professional body, or to the buyer's solicitor in the capacity of stakeholder. An alternative to these arrangements would be to insert a condition in the contract providing for the deposit to be placed in a bank or building society deposit account in the joint names of seller and buyer.

(c) the provision on or before completion of sufficient evidence of the seller's identity to satisfy the Land Registry's requirements.[1]

1. See Land Registry Practice Guide 67.

5.10. Pre-contract enquiries

5.10.1. The answers to pre-contract enquiries and any other enquiries (including requisitions on title) given by an unrepresented seller should be signed by the seller in person. Although an unqualified person may have the seller's express authority to answer such enquiries on his behalf, an action in misrepresentation (should such become necessary) will more easily be sustained if the answers have been signed by the seller personally.

5.11. Powers of attorney

5.11.1. Any power of attorney which purports to give the unqualified person power to deal with a matter on behalf of his or her 'client' should be carefully checked to ensure its validity and effectiveness for its purported purpose (see B23).

5.12. Acting for the lender

5.12.1. A solicitor acting for a lender where the borrower is represented by an unqualified person is under no obligation to undertake work which the buyer's solicitor should normally assume (e.g. drafting the purchase deed) and should not render the unqualified person additional assistance. However, in such a situation the solicitor must bear in mind that the interests of his lender client in obtaining a good title to the property are paramount. The advance cheque should be drawn in favour of a solicitor, licensed conveyancer or person properly authorised to receive the money by the borrower. On redemption of a mortgage similar principles apply.

A6. In-house solicitors

6.1.   Acting for the lay employer

6.1.1.   A solicitor who is employed by a non-solicitor employer must comply with Solicitors' Code of Conduct 2007 (see in particular Rules 12 and 13) and all the other rules of professional conduct.

6.1.2.   Under Rule 20 (requirements of practice) a practising certificate is required by any person who is practising as a solicitor (including as an in-house solicitor).

6.1.3.   If an employed solicitor uses his employer's stationery it must be clear that the stationery is being used by a solicitor on legal professional business and that the solicitor is responsible for the contents of the letter.

6.1.4.   Rule 13 Solicitors' Code of Conduct 2007 (in-house practice) places restrictions on the type of work which an employed solicitor may undertake. In general he is prohibited from doing work for anyone other than his employer.

6.2.   Acting for work colleagues

6.2.1.   An employed solicitor may carry out conveyancing on behalf of an employee, a manager, the company secretary, a board member or a trustee of his employer provided that the work is permitted by his contract of employment and is done free of charge to the work colleague. The conveyancing must also relate to or arise out of the work of the work colleague, i.e. it must be a job-related move. Before accepting the instructions to act the employed solicitor must ensure that the work colleague does not wish to instruct another solicitor or licensed conveyancer (see Rule 13.02 Solicitors' Code of Conduct 2007).

6.3.   Acting for third parties

6.3.1.   If his contract of employment permits him to do so an employed solicitor may undertake work on behalf of private clients in his own time. In this respect he will be treated as a principal in private practice and must comply with Solicitors' Code of Conduct 2007, Accounts Rules and Indemnity Rules. If he practises from home, compliance with Rule 20 Solicitors' Code of Conduct 2007 (requirements of practice) will be required and he may need to register his home address with the Solicitors Regulation Authority as a practising address.

Because of the danger of conflict of interests private work must not be undertaken for clients and customers of the employer.

6.3.2. Where acting in a conveyancing transaction for a work colleague (see A6.2.1) an employed solicitor may also act for a joint owner/buyer and for a lender. A lender may require an indemnity from the employer or insurance cover similar to that required under Solicitors' Indemnity Rules 2007.

A7. Introductions and referrals

7.1. Rule 9 Solicitors' Code of Conduct 2007

7.1.1. A solicitor may have an arrangement with a third party for the introduction of clients to the solicitor by the third party, or the referral of clients to the third party by the solicitor. Such arrangements are permitted by Rule 9 Solicitors' Code of Conduct 2007 (referrals of business) provided that there is no breach of any of the rules of conduct.

7.1.2. Rule 9 applies to any arrangement made by a solicitor with, e.g. an estate agent, bank, building society or mortgage broker for the introduction of clients to the solicitor from such third parties or the referral of clients to the third parties by the solicitor but not to introductions and referrals between firms of solicitors.

7.2. Maintaining the independence of the solicitor

7.2.1. It is of paramount importance that the solicitor should remain independent of any third party to or from whom referrals are made so that the client may be given impartial and objective advice by the solicitor. A solicitor should not enter into a referral arrangement with an introducer whose overall scheme or arrangement will not be in the best interests of the clients referred to the solicitor.

7.2.2. It should also be noted that Rule 19 Solicitors' Code of Conduct 2007 (financial services) prevents a solicitor from acting as an appointed representative in respect of introductions and referrals made in the field of investment business, other than by having a separate business which is the appointed representative of an independent financial adviser.

7.2.3. A solicitor must ensure that an arrangement with an introducer does not compromise his duties to act in the best interests of the client, to be independent and to provide a good standard of service. If a client is entering into or has already entered into a scheme or arrangement with an introducer which is not in the client's best interests then the solicitor must advise the client accordingly. Schemes or arrangements which involve the client paying unnecessary or unreasonable fees will not normally be in the client's best interests.

7.2.4. Where the solicitor is being paid for his services by the introducer rather than by the client there is a danger of conflict of interests arising, and the solicitor must decline to act if such a conflict arises or is likely to arise.

7.3. Reliance by the solicitor on limited sources of business

7.3.1. If a solicitor allows himself to become reliant on a limited source or sources of business from introducers there is a danger that the advice given by him to his introduced clients will be influenced by the solicitor's need to maintain his source of business, to the extent that the advice will not be impartial and may not be in the best interests of that particular client.

7.3.2. Solicitors are advised to review their referral arrangements at regular intervals (see guidance to Rule 9 Solicitors' Code of Conduct 2007), to ensure that the solicitor remains compliant.

7.3.3. In addition to the core duties (see Rule 1 Solicitors' Code of Conduct), whenever a solicitor reviews a proposed or existing referral arrangement he should also consider:

(a) whether the arrangement enables him to comply with Rule 9;

(b) whether the arrangement involves confidential client information being disclosed to an introducer (see Rule 4.01 Solicitors' Code of Conduct) and what authority he should seek from his client;

(c) whether the introducer's publicity is appropriate (see paragraph 14 guidance to Rule 9 Solicitors' Code of Conduct 2007);

(d) whether his advice to the client includes the relevant information regarding the arrangements with an introducer in respect of any limitations placed upon him (see Rule 2.02(2)(e) Solicitors' Code of Conduct 2007) and if the outcome sought justifies the costs involved (see Rule 2.03(6) Solicitors' Code of Conduct 2007); and

(e) whether he retains control of the work he does for clients. No arrangement with an introducer should affect a solicitor's duty to communicate directly with the client to obtain or confirm instructions in the process of providing advice and at all appropriate stages of the transaction.

7.4. Referral agreements

7.4.1. All referral arrangements must be in writing and available for inspection by the Solicitors Regulation Authority.

7.4.2. Under the agreement the introducer must undertake to comply with Rule 9 Solicitors' Code of Conduct 2007.

7.4.3. Where an introducer wishes to publicise the services of solicitors to whom the introducer will refer work, the publicity must comply with Rule 7 Solicitors' Code of Conduct 2007 (publicity). The solicitor remains responsible for any publicity which should therefore be checked carefully by the solicitor before publication.

7.4.4. The agreement with the introducer must not include any provision which would compromise, infringe or impair any of the solicitor's duties set out in Solicitors' Code of Conduct 2007 or allow the introducer to influence or constrain the solicitor's professional judgement in relation to the advice given to the client.

7.4.5. The agreement must provide that before making a referral the introducer must give the client all relevant information concerning the referral, in particular:

    (a) the fact that the introducer has a financial arrangement with the solicitor; and

    (b) the amount of any payment to the introducer which is calculated by reference to that referral; or

    (c) where the introducer is paying the solicitor to provide services to the introducer's customers:

        (i) the amount the introducer is paying the solicitor to provide those services; and

        (ii) the amount the client is required to pay the introducer.

7.4.6. If the solicitor has reason to believe that the introducer is breaching any of the terms of the agreement the solicitor must take all reasonable steps to ensure that the breach is remedied. If the introducer continues to breach the agreement the solicitor must terminate it.

7.4.7. Potential introducers should be made aware of the terms on which the solicitor will accept instructions from an introducer and the fees that will be charged to an introduced client.

7.5. Confirming the client's instructions

7.5.1. Any instructions received from or through an introducer must be confirmed directly with the client by sending or giving the client written terms of business. If the client was referred to the solicitor under a financial arrangement with an introducer covered by Rule 9 Solicitors' Code of Conduct 2007, the client must be informed of the agreement between the introducer and the solicitor and must be given the information specified in Rule 9.02(g) Solicitors' Code of Conduct 2007.

7.5.2. Before accepting instructions to act for a client referred under a financial arrangement with an introducer under Rule 9 Solicitors' Code of Conduct 2007, the solicitor must give the client, in writing, all relevant information concerning the referral, in particular:

(a) the fact that the solicitor has a financial arrangement with the introducer; and

(b) the amount of any payment to the introducer which is calculated by reference to that referral; or

(c) where the introducer is paying the solicitor to provide services to the introducer's customers:

(i) the amount the introducer is paying the solicitor to provide those services; and

(ii) the amount the client is required to pay the introducer;

(d) a statement that any advice given by the solicitor will be independent and that the client is free to raise questions on all aspects of the transaction; and

(e) confirmation that any information disclosed to the solicitor will not be disclosed to the introducer unless the client consents; but that where the solicitor is also acting for the introducer in the same matter and a conflict of interests arises, the solicitor might be obliged to cease acting.

7.5.3. In addition to disclosing the above information, the solicitor must disclose any other 'relevant information' concerning the referral. This would include a summary of the overall relationship with an introducer if this involves consideration other than the payment of specific fees. If the solicitor provides legal services to an introducer free of charge on the understanding that the introducer refers clients to the solicitor, then the client should be informed of this relationship.

7.5.4. This disclosure is required as soon as the referral is made and the solicitor will normally be expected to write to the client with the information before the first interview. If, due to lack of time, the disclosure is made at the first interview, it should be made at the start of the first interview and confirmed in writing.

7.6. Fees and commissions

7.6.1. Rule 9 Solicitors' Code of Conduct 2007 also applies to agreements which constitute 'financial arrangements'. A financial arrangement includes any payment to an introducer in respect of a referral, and any agreement under which the solicitor is paid by the introducer to provide services to the introducer's customers. 'Payment' includes any consideration but does not include normal hospitality, proper disbursements, or normal business expenses.

7.6.2. Any commission received by the solicitor who has referred a client to a third party is subject to Rule 2.06 Solicitors' Code of Conduct 2007 (client relations) under which rule the solicitor must account to the client for any commission which exceeds £20 unless the client, having been informed of the amount of the commission, consents to the solicitor keeping the commission.

7.6.3. Clients must be charged the correct amount for local searches. Any discount or rebate offered to a solicitor on a disbursement amounts to a reduction in the cost of that disbursement and must be passed to the client. This is irrespective of the amount of the rebate or 'commission'. If the full amount is charged to the client, the solicitor will have misled the client by overstating the cost of the disbursement and effectively will have overcharged (see *Law Society* v. *Adcock and Mocroft* [2006] EWHC 3212 (Admin), [2007] 1 WLR 1096).

7.7. **Referrals by the solicitor to a third party**

7.7.1. A solicitor who recommends a client to a third party must do so in good faith, judging what is in the client's best interests. Any agreement entered into whereby the solicitor recommends clients to a third party must not restrict the solicitor's freedom to recommend clients to other third parties if this would be in the best interests of the client.

A8. Estimate of costs

8.1. Duty to give estimate

8.1.1. A solicitor must, at the outset and as the matter progresses, give a client the best information possible about the likely costs of the transaction including the cost of compliance with SDLT requirements. See Rule 2 Solicitors' Code of Conduct 2007 (client relations).

8.1.2. If it is not possible to give an estimate, a general forecast of the approximate costs should be given.

8.1.3. A solicitor must explain at the outset any payments the client is likely to have to make, e.g. search fees and Land Registry fees. Where possible the solicitor must give details of the probable costs.

8.1.4. Any information about costs must be clear and confirmed in writing. See Rule 2.03 Solicitors' Code of Conduct 2007.

8.2. Residential conveyancing

8.2.1. In residential conveyancing it is normally possible to give the client an estimate of the costs of the transaction.

8.3. Commercial transactions

8.3.1. A precise estimate of costs may not be possible in the context of commercial transactions; nevertheless the client should still be given a general forecast of likely costs and the method of calculation of those costs at the outset of the transaction, and informed if that figure is likely to vary substantially.

8.4. Bills payable by a third party

8.4.1. Where the client is or will become liable to pay a bill presented by a third party, e.g. to a landlord's solicitor for consent to assignment, the solicitor should obtain an estimate of the third party's bill at the outset of the transaction and should inform the client of the amount of the estimate. If the estimate appears to be an unreasonably high figure, negotiations to attempt to reduce it should be undertaken before a substantial amount of work in the transaction has taken place. Money should be obtained from the client on account of the third party's costs before an undertaking to pay is given.

8.4.2. If the client is entitled to be indemnified by a third party, e.g. by a tenant seeking a licence to assign, an estimate of the costs should be given to the third party's solicitor. Such an estimate should be as firm as possible in the circumstances, but may be qualified by a statement to the effect that the estimate has been given on the basis that the matter proceeds without unforeseen complications.

8.5. Giving an estimate

8.5.1. Any information about costs must be clear and confirmed in writing (Rule 2.03 Solicitors' Code of Conduct 2007). In order to avoid misunderstandings it is preferable only to give an estimate in writing or, if oral, confirm the estimate in writing immediately.

8.5.2. In residential conveyancing it is frequently not possible to avoid giving an estimate over the telephone. In such circumstances it should be made clear to the prospective client that the estimate is given on the basis of information supplied by the client and may be subject to variation if unknown factors later emerge which complicate the transaction.

8.5.3. The estimate should be as comprehensive as possible and should be clear as to whether VAT and/or disbursements are included in the given figure.

8.5.4. The client should be warned that if unforeseen complications arise, the estimate may be revised.

8.5.5. Minor expenses, e.g. postage and telephone, which are part of the solicitor's overheads, are to be included in the estimate and must not be added as a disbursement.

8.5.6. The estimate should state whether or not it covers the cost of completing the SDLT form.

8.5.7. Charges specified in the estimate for local and other searches must be as accurate as possible. The client must not be charged more than the cost of obtaining the search from the local search agency. Any attempt to recover a higher payment from the client or for the solicitor to take a commission from the agency will be a breach of Solicitors' Code of Conduct 2007 (see A7.6.3).

8.6. Change in circumstances

8.6.1. If events occur which cause the original estimate to become inaccurate the solicitor must immediately inform the client in writing of the change in circumstances and should revise his estimate accordingly.

8.6.2.   Failure to advise the client of a change in the likely level of fees may render the solicitor liable to prosecution for giving misleading information relating to charges under Consumer Protection Act 1987, s.20.

8.7.   Quotations for costs

8.7.1.   The solicitor should make it clear to the client that an estimate for costs is not a fixed price ('a quotation') for the work unless it is the solicitor's intention to charge a fixed price which will not be altered in any circumstances.

8.7.2.   Where a quotation is given the solicitor is not at liberty to charge the client more than the fixed fee even if the transaction turns out to be more difficult or complex than had been anticipated. Petty expenses such as postage and telephone must not be added as disbursements to the fixed fee.

8.7.3.   It is recommended that if a fixed fee is quoted the client is informed of that fee in writing and told that the quotation will be valid for a stated period, e.g. three months. If the solicitor has not been instructed by the client within this period he will then be entitled to issue a revised quotation.

8.7.4.   Money received for or on account of an agreed fee must not be paid into a client account.[1] It must be paid into an office account.

8.7.5.   A quotation for costs which has been accepted by the client may be subject to Solicitors Act 1974, s.57, which provides that it must:

(a)   be in writing;

(b)   embody all the terms of the agreement;

(c)   be signed by the client or his agent;

(d)   be reasonable in amount and in lieu of ordinary profit costs.

8.7.6.   Where a section 57 agreement has been made, the client may seek court assessment of the bill in the normal way. The agreement is enforceable by the solicitor under the ordinary principles of contract law.

1.   See Rule 19(5) Solicitors' Accounts Rules 1998.

8.8.   VAT on solicitors' charges

8.8.1.   Where a firm is registered, VAT will be chargeable to the client on the solicitor's bill and on some disbursements paid by the solicitor on the client's behalf, depending upon the 'place of supply' for the VAT purposes.

8.8.2.   Where the services are 'closely related to land' such as conveyancing, the 'place of supply' is the place where the land/building is situated (regardless of where the customer is). This could mean that VAT registration in another member state of the EU is required.

8.8.3. Where any other legal services are provided, the 'place of supply' is where the customer is domiciled. For UK customers and individuals in other EU member states, UK VAT at standard rate is therefore chargeable. For businesses registered in another member state, no VAT is charged provided the customer's VAT registration number is quoted on the firm's invoice, and for customers outside the EU, no UK VAT is chargeable.

8.8.4. When giving an estimate or quotation of costs to the client the solicitor should make it clear whether or not that estimate or quotation includes VAT. If no mention of VAT is made the client is entitled to assume that the quoted figure is inclusive of VAT.[1]

8.8.5. Where an individual or firm is registered for VAT, the firm's VAT registration number must appear on the bills issued by the firm or, if a separate tax invoice is issued, on the tax invoice.

8.8.6. Where the client's bill is reduced by the amount of commission which the solicitor has earned, e.g. on an endowment policy taken out by the client, VAT may be charged on the net amount of the bill, providing that the commission set off is correctly shown on the face of the invoice. Customs' VAT Notes No.1 1988/89, item 6, published in April 1988 states the following:

> 'Many traders when charging fees to their clients reduce the amount by taking into account commission they receive from third parties. For example, a financial adviser provides guidance on insurance to a client; the insurance company pays the adviser a commission and the adviser passes on the benefit to the client by charging a lower fee.
>
> In the past, traders have accounted for output tax on the full value of their supply before any deductions for commission. HM Revenue and Customs have reviewed this ruling, and from now on you need only account for output tax on the fee shown on the invoice.'

8.8.7. In March 1990 Customs issued an agreed statement setting out two methods which may be used in respect of the format of invoices for set-offs of commission:

Method 1

Fee	110.00
Rebate equivalent to commission received	10.00
Fee	100.00
VAT @ 17.5%	17.50
Total	117.50

(Note: commission must be described as a rebate when using this method.)

Method 2

Fee net of £10 commission	100.00
VAT @ 17.5%	17.50
Total	117.50

8.8.8.   HM Revenue and Customs are currently reviewing the treatment of commissions and whether the value of the supply is the gross amount chargeable before set-off of commissions, with VAT being calculated on that value, and any commission being set off against the gross fee.

8.8.9.   The Law Society issued the following in the *Gazette* ([1992] *Gazette*, 9 September):

> **'VAT and commission**
>
> The question of the effect on the application of VAT to a bill for professional services rendered to a client on the receipt of commission from a third party has recently been the subject of correspondence between the VAT subcommittee of the revenue law committee and HM Revenue and Customs.
>
> Until agreement can be reached and revised guidance is published, Customs have advised that members could continue to rely upon the practice outlined in item 6 of VAT Notes No.1 1988/89, namely to charge VAT after netting off any commission using one of the methods [set out in A8.8.7 above].'

8.8.10.   Rule 2 Solicitors' Code of Conduct 2007 (client relations) obliges solicitors to account to their client for any commission they receive, subject to a *de minimis* threshold of £20.

1.   Value Added Tax Act 1994, s.89.

A9. Joint purchasers

9.1. Advising the client

9.1.1. When acting for joint purchasers, it is essential to clarify their intentions as to the method by which they are to hold the property. The solicitor should explain the different methods of co-ownership to the clients in language appropriate to their level of understanding and should advise as to the most suitable type of co-ownership to meet the particular situation. A separate trust deed should be completed to express the clients' wishes. Also a note of the clients' wishes should be made on the file so that appropriate steps may be taken to implement the clients' instructions in the purchase deed (see E1).

9.1.2. Instructions should be obtained from both (or all) co-purchasers.[1]

9.1.3. Where the intending co-purchasers are not married to each other nor in a civil partnership[2] it may be necessary to advise each party independently about their rights in the property to be purchased. Solicitors should be alert to the possibility of a conflict of interests arising between the two clients in this situation (see A9.8).

1. See *Penn* v. *Bristol & West Building Society* [1997] 3 All ER 470.
2. Civil Partnership Act 2004.

9.2. Co-ownership or sole ownership?

9.2.1. In the vast majority of cases a husband and wife or civil partners should be advised to hold a property as co-owners and this is usually a requirement of any major lending institution. This requirement by lenders for co-ownership by spouses, civil partners and co-habitees is irrespective of the contribution which each party will make to the mortgage repayments. A contra-indication to co-ownership by a married couple, etc may exist where one or both of the parties is individually wealthy and where consideration must be given to the equalisation of estates for inheritance tax purposes. Sole legal ownership may be considered prudent if one of the parties is in a 'high-risk' category of unincorporated business where the potential consequences of bankruptcy may need to be considered.

9.2.2. A non-owning spouse/civil partner will have rights under Family Law Act 1996 (see A9.2.3) and may have a beneficial interest through contribution to the purchase price of the property (see A9.2.4). But neither of these methods of protection is as secure as co-ownership of the legal estate.

9.2.3.   Where one spouse or civil partner owns the matrimonial home in his or her sole name the non-owning party has a statutory right of occupation under section 30 Family Law Act 1996. The non-owning party cannot be evicted without the leave of the court and, if not in occupation, the court can enforce the non-owning party's right by ordering that they be allowed into occupation of the property (section 33 of the Act). To ensure that the Family Law Act right of occupation can be enforced against a person buying or taking a mortgage from the owning party, the right should be protected by registration of either a Class F land charge under Land Charges Act 1972 or a homes rights notice at the Land Registry. If the right has been protected by registration the court's powers under section 33 Family Law Act 1996 may be exercised against the new owner of the property. Under section 33(5) the court has the power to order that the right of occupation should extend beyond the termination of the marriage as a result of the death or divorce of the owning spouse, or the termination of the civil partnership.

Co-owners

9.2.4.   Where two or more persons buy property together, each contributing to the purchase price and/or mortgage repayments, and the title to the property is held in the name of only one of the buyers, the non-owning party may have a beneficial interest in the property under a resulting or constructive trust.[1] The non-owning party has a right to occupy the property under Trusts of Land and Appointment of Trustees Act 1996, s.12, which can be enforced against the owner by court order under s.14 of that Act. In addition, the court has power to make an occupation order under Family Law Act 1996, s.33 in cases where the applicant does not have home rights but does have a beneficial interest in the property. Where the title to the property is registered, a sale or mortgage will be registered free from the beneficial interest unless registration is prevented by a restriction in the proprietorship register.[2] If, however, the owner of the beneficial interest is in occupation of the property at the time of the purchase or mortgage, the beneficial interest may override the disposition of the registered title under the provisions of Schedule 3 paragraph 2 Land Registration Act 2002. If the title to the property is unregistered the buyer or lender will be bound by the beneficial interest if they had notice of it at the time of the disposition.[3] However, whether the title is registered or unregistered the beneficial interest can be overreached if the sale or mortgage is entered into by all the trustees being at least two in number or a trust corporation.[4] In most cases where a buyer or lender becomes aware of a beneficial interest he will insist that the seller appoints a second trustee to enter into the disposition with him. When the interest is overreached, the person with the beneficial interest will no longer be able to enforce it against the property.

9.2.5.   Unmarried purchasers, whether co-habitees, brother and sister or merely friends who are joining together to purchase a property, should normally be advised to hold the property as co-owners since the existence of a beneficial or overriding interest may be costly and difficult to establish in the event of a dispute between the parties. Many lenders will insist that the legal estate is held jointly in these circumstances.

Civil partners

9.2.6. Civil Partnership Act 2004 which provides for registration of a civil partnership for same-sex couples came into force on 5 December 2005. If a couple choose to register their partnership their property rights both during the partnership and in the event of the partnership being dissolved will be governed by the Act.

9.2.7. With regard to the initial purchase of the property the couple should consider whether or not both partners will appear on the legal title in the same way as any other co-owners and, where appropriate, a trust deed should be drawn up. Once the partnership has been registered, the provisions of Chapter 3 of the Act relating to property and financial relations will come into effect. Under section 65 a civil partner making a substantial contribution in money or money's worth to property, which is either co-owned with the other civil partner or owned entirely by the other civil partner, will acquire a share or an enlarged share in that property. When dealing with a purchase from a sole owner who is in a civil partnership there is a possibility that the other partner has acquired a beneficial interest in the property by direct or indirect contributions.

9.2.8. The provisions of section 30 Family Law Act 1996 apply to civil partners (Civil Partnership Act 2004, s. 82). See A9.2.3.

9.2.9. When a civil partnership is brought to an end the provisions of Chapter 3 and Schedule 5 provide for the adjustment of property rights similar to the rights available on divorce. The ex-partners' ownership of any property will be determined in accordance with the provisions of the Act and not in accordance with any agreement or trust deed entered into before the partnership was registered.

9.2.10. Consideration should always be given to the question of taking out a joint life policy to protect the mortgage over the lives of both spouses/co-habitees even where the property is held in one name alone or where the mortgage repayments are made by one party alone. The joint lives policy will protect the repayments of the mortgage even in the event of death of the non-owning or non-earning spouse/co-habitee.

1. The claimant must be able to prove that he or she made a contribution to the property and the size of that contribution; see *National Westminster Bank plc* v. *Malhan* [2004] EWHC 847 where the court decided that the claimant had failed to prove that she had savings of £31,000 in 1986 which, she alleged, she had used to pay the balance of the purchase price of the house.
2. Land Registration Act 2002, s.26. See also Land Registration Rules 2003, r.94(1) which requires the registered proprietor to apply for a restriction in Form A where the estate is subject to a trust of land.
3. 'Notice' includes actual notice, constructive notice and imputed notice. See *Hunt* v. *Luck* [1902] 1 Ch 428; *Kingsnorth Finance Co. Ltd* v. *Tizzard* [1986] 1 WLR 783.
4. Law of Property Act 1925, s.2(2). See also *City of London Building Society* v. *Flegg* [1988] AC 54.

9.3. The choices

9.3.1. In law co-ownership of land can usually only exist through the medium of a trust of land. The legal estate will thus be held by joint tenants on trust for themselves (and possibly other persons) in equity. The legal joint tenancy is not severable and there must be a minimum of two trustees (and maximum of four) in order to deal with the legal estate.[1]

9.3.2. In equity there is a choice between holding as joint tenants or as tenants in common.

9.3.3. The capacity of the buyers, whether as joint tenants or tenants in common, must be expressly stated in the purchase deed or in a separate trust deed. Panel 10 of Form TR1 (transfer of whole registered title(s)) contains a declaration of trust to be completed where there is more than one transferee.[2] A transfer containing such a declaration of trust must be executed by the buyers. An express declaration of trust may also be made in the additional provisions panel of the Land Registry form (e.g. panel 11 of TR1). In this event, the form must be signed or executed by the buyers.[3] Details of the trust will not appear on the register.[4]

1. Law of Property Act 1925, s.1(6) and s.34.
2. See *Huntingford* v. *Hobbs* [1992] EGCS 38 and *Stack* v. *Dowden* [2007] UKHL 17 as to the effect of declarations in earlier forms of transfer that the survivor of the transferees was entitled to give a valid receipt for capital money.
3. Law of Property Act 1925, s.53(1).
4. Land Registration Act 2002, s.78.

9.4. Joint tenants

9.4.1. Where co-owners hold the beneficial interest as joint tenants, none of the co-owners will be entitled to a distinct or separate proportion of that interest: each one owns all of it. The main distinguishing feature of the joint tenancy is the right of survivorship which leads to the interest accruing to the ultimate sole surviving joint tenant. Because no distinct part of the interest belongs to any individual tenant, no part of it will belong to the estate of a deceased joint tenant and, where the co-owners were married to each other or in a civil partnership, will not attract inheritance tax. An interest in a joint tenancy cannot be left by will, the deceased's share passing automatically to the surviving joint tenant(s). A beneficial joint tenancy can be severed which has the effect of converting it into a tenancy in common if there were only two joint tenants.

9.4.2. An express declaration of joint tenancy will result in the joint owners being given equal shares in the event of a severance: *Goodman* v. *Gallant* [1986] Fam 106. Where there is no express declaration a transfer into joint names will infer both a legal and beneficial joint tenancy. Cases where the court will hold that the parties intended that their beneficial interests would differ from their legal interests would be very unusual: see *Stack* v. *Dowden* [2007] UKHL 17. The presumption of joint beneficial ownership where domestic property is transferred into joint names can apply to personal relationships other than cohabiting couples but does not apply to investment property. See *Laskar* v. *Laskar* [2008] EWCA Civ 347.

9.5.   Tenants in common

9.5.1. Where a tenancy in common exists, each co-owner holds a quantified proportion of the beneficial interest which is capable of being disposed of *inter vivos* or by will or passes on the intestacy of the deceased tenant in common. The proportionate share in the property which belonged to a deceased tenant in common is subject to inheritance tax rules.

9.5.2. Unless the contrary is stated or evidence to the contrary is proved, a court will assume that tenants in common hold the beneficial interest in proportion to the parties' original contributions to the property.[1] In order to avoid subsequent disputes and litigation it is desirable that the proportionate shares of each tenant in common are expressly agreed and recorded in a deed of trust (or certified copy transfer) which is signed by the co-owners. In unregistered land an express declaration as to the proportionate shares may be included in the purchase deed. If the parties cannot agree on the amount of their respective shares separate advice for one or all of them is necessary. Unless the proportions in which the beneficial interest is held are clearly stated, it may be difficult to determine the ownership of the proceeds of sale when the property is ultimately sold. This will present problems for the solicitor if, e.g. the property is sold and the proceeds are to be divided as a result of a matrimonial or civil partnership breakdown. See the Law Society's practice information on conflicts of interest post *Etridge* in Appendix IV.7.

9.5.3. One drawback to an express statement of the beneficial interest is that it cannot be changed except by deed. If, for example, a deed of trust stated that a husband owned 70% of the equitable interest and his wife 30%, but the wife subsequently paid off the whole mortgage on the house using money which she had inherited on the death of one of her parents, the wife might feel that she had become entitled to a larger proportion of the beneficial interest through her contribution to the mortgage but, unless a new deed of trust is drawn up, redefining the proportionate shares of the parties, on sale of the property, the wife would still be entitled only to her original 30%. An alternative solution is that the whole or part of one joint owner's beneficial interest can be transferred to the new owner in writing, signed by the person transferring.[2]

9.5.4. A tenancy in common can be devised by will or will pass on intestacy. Where property is held by this method the parties should be advised as to the desirability of making a will.

9.5.5. Where a tenancy in common is created the deed should make specific provision relating to the appointment of a new trustee in the event of the death of one co-owner. In the absence of such a provision the provisions of Trusts of Land and Appointment of Trustees Act 1996, s.19 may operate to give beneficiaries who are of full age and competence the right to nominate a new trustee.

1. *Springette* v. *Defoe* [1992] NPC 34; *Savill* v. *Goodall* [1992] NPC 153.
2. Law of Property Act 1925, s.53.

9.6.   Suitability of each method

Joint tenancy

9.6.1.   The automatic right of survivorship may make this method of co-ownership both suitable and attractive to prospective co-owners who are married to each other or in a civil partnership. However, a joint tenancy may not be appropriate for a married couple or civil partners where one or both of the buyers is individually wealthy, where equalisation of estates for inheritance tax purposes is a consideration or where one or both of the parties has children from a previous relationship who might expect to inherit on their parent's death. Survivorship rights may well not be intended by co-owners who are not married to each other or not in a civil partnership, and would not normally be considered suitable when dealing with property held in a business partnership.

Tenancy in common

9.6.2.   Prospective co-owners who are not married to each other or not in a civil partnership will usually be advised to hold by this method. This is also the most appropriate method by which partnership property can be dealt with. Consideration should be given to this method where the contributions made by each of the co-owners to the purchase price are in unequal proportions and where the parties are married to each other but one (or both) of them has children from a previous relationship whom the parent might reasonably expect to inherit on the death of their natural parent.

9.7.   Gifts

9.7.1.   Where the purchase price of the property is supplied by one party alone, but the property is purchased in the joint names of the person who paid the purchase price and another, equity generally deems the property to be held on a resulting trust on behalf of the buyer, unless there is an indication to the contrary (such as an express declaration of trust in the transfer), or the circumstances are within the limited cases where a presumption of advancement applies.

9.8.   Co-habitees

9.8.1.   All co-habitees whether they are spouses, civil partners, co-habitees or joint purchasers may need to be advised independently about their respective rights in the property to be purchased. Solicitors should be alert to the possibility of a conflict of interests arising in this situation.

9.8.2. It is advisable for co-habitees who are to be co-owners to enter into a separate deed of trust which sets out their respective interests in the property. The rights and obligations conferred by this document can only be altered by the execution of a further deed of trust but this disadvantage is outweighed by the advantage of having certainty as to the parties' rights and interests.

9.8.3. In *Oxley* v. *Hiscock* [2004] EWCA Civ 546, the Court of Appeal provided guidance on the steps to be taken when acting for co-habitees:

- the solicitor should always enquire about the source of the funds for the purchase and the future liability for the repayment of the mortgage;

- if there is evidence that the purchase is actually a joint acquisition or that others may be acquiring rights under a potential constructive trust, the client(s) should be advised either to purchase the property as legal co-owners and/or to record their arrangement in a trust deed;

- when drafting the transfer and/or trust deed decisions have to be made as to whether the equitable interest is to be held as joint tenants or tenants in common.

9.8.4. If the property is to be purchased in the sole name of one co-habitee, the other should be advised (where appropriate) to protect his or her interest by lodging an application for registration of an appropriate restriction at the Land Registry.[1]

1. Land Registration Rules 2003, r.92 and Sched.4 (e.g. Form A and Form II restrictions).

A10. Acting for both parties

10.1. Conflict of interests

10.1.1. As a general principle of professional conduct a solicitor or firm of solicitors should not accept instructions to act for two or more clients in the same transaction where there is a conflict or a significant risk of a conflict between the interests of those clients.[1]

10.1.2. Neither should a solicitor nor his firm continue to act for two or more clients if a conflict of interests arises between those clients.[2]

1. See Rule 3 Solicitors' Code of Conduct 2007 (conflict of interests).
2. *Ibid.*

10.2. Rule 3 Solicitors' Code of Conduct 2007 (conflict of interests)

10.2.1. Subject to certain exceptions, acting for both parties in a conveyancing transaction at arm's length is generally prohibited by Rule 3.07 Solicitors' Code of Conduct 2007. The rule should be considered carefully before a decision is taken to act for more than one party.

10.2.2. In most circumstances, therefore, a solicitor who is asked to act for both parties to a transaction will decline to act for both either because of the potential conflict of interest between the parties or because of the application of Rule 3.07 Solicitors' Code of Conduct 2007.

10.2.3. A solicitor must not act for both parties in a conveyancing transaction where the prohibitions in Rule 10.06(3) and (4) Solicitors' Code of Conduct 2007 apply, that is where a contract race is being run.

10.2.4. Provided there is no conflict of interest the same solicitor may act for both seller and buyer where the transaction is not at arm's length (e.g. a transaction between parties who are related by blood, adoption or marriage or living together: see paragraph 72 guidance to Rule 3 Solicitors' Code of Conduct 2007).

10.3. **Exceptions to Rule 3**

10.3.1. A solicitor must not act for seller and buyer:

    (a)   without the written consent of both parties;

    (b)   if a conflict of interest exists or arises; or

    (c)   if the seller is selling or leasing as a builder or developer.

If a builder or developer acquires a property in part exchange, and sells it on without development, they are not selling as a builder or developer for the purpose of Rule 3.

10.3.2. Subject to A10.3.1, a solicitor may act for both seller and buyer, but only if:

    (a)   both parties are established clients (the test here is an objective one, i.e. whether a reasonable solicitor would regard the person as an established client. A person who is related by blood, adoption or marriage to or who is living with an established client counts as an established client. A seller or buyer who instructs the solicitor for the first time is not an established client. A person who is selling or buying jointly with an established client counts as an established client); *or*

    (b)   the consideration is £10,000 or less and the transaction is not the grant of a lease (the value of any property taken in part exchange must be taken into account in calculating the consideration); *or*

    (c)   seller and buyer are represented by two separate offices in different localities and

        (i)   different solicitors who normally work at each office, conduct or supervise the transaction for seller and buyer; and

        (ii)   no office of the practice (or an associated practice) referred either client to the office conducting his or her transaction; *or*

    (d)   the only way in which the solicitor is acting for the buyer is in providing mortgage related services; *or*

    (e)   the only way in which the solicitor is acting for the seller is in providing property selling services through a SEAL.

10.3.3. When a solicitor's practice (including a SEAL) acts in the property selling for the seller and either acts for the buyer on the purchase or provides mortgage related services to the buyer, the following additional conditions must be met:

    (a)   different individuals must conduct the work for the seller and the work for the buyer; and if the individual conducting the work needs supervision, they must be supervised by different individuals who are authorised to do the work; *and*

    (b)   the solicitor must inform the seller in writing, before accepting instructions to deal with the property selling, of any services which might be offered to a buyer, whether through the same practice or any practice associated with it; *and*

(c) the solicitor must explain to the buyer, before the buyer gives consent to the arrangement:

   (i) the implications of a conflict of interests arising; *and*

   (ii) the solicitor's financial interest in the sale going through; *and*

   (iii) if the solicitor proposes to provide mortgage related services to the buyer through a SEAL which is also acting for the seller, that the solicitor cannot advise the buyer on the merits of the purchase.

10.4. Mortgages

Standard mortgages

10.4.1. A mortgage is a standard mortgage where:

   (a) it is provided in the normal course of the lender's activities;

   (b) a significant part of the lender's activities consists of lending; and

   (c) the mortgage is on standard terms.

10.4.2. A solicitor may act for both lender and borrower in a standard mortgage provided there is no conflict of interests, the mortgage instructions do not go beyond Rule 3.19 Solicitors' Code of Conduct 2007 (which sets out details of the type of instructions which can be accepted) and, where the property is to be used solely as the borrower's private residence, the approved certificate of title set out in the annexe to Rule 3 is used.

10.4.3. The provisions in Rule 3 also apply to non-residential mortgages but the certificate of title can be in any form recognised by the Solicitors Regulation Authority Board or in any form which complies with Rule 3.19 (e.g. the City of London Law Society Certificate of Title).

Individual mortgage

10.4.4. An individual mortgage is any mortgage other than a standard mortgage (see A10.4.1). The lender and borrower must be separately represented and the grant of an individual mortgage at arm's length; see Rule 3.16(b) Solicitors' Code of Conduct 2007.

Acting for seller, buyer and lender

10.4.5. A solicitor, or solicitors practising in associated practices, must not act for seller, buyer and lender in the same transaction unless no conflict of interest exists or arises, and, in the case of a standard mortgage, the solicitor has given written notification of the circumstance to the lender.

10.5. Contract races

10.5.1. If the transaction involves a contract race the same firm may not act for two or more prospective buyers, nor may the firm act for both the seller and one of the prospective buyers. See Rule 10.06 Solicitors' Code of Conduct 2007 (relations with third parties).

10.6. Merger of firms

10.6.1. As a result of a merger or amalgamation a firm may find that it is acting for both seller and buyer in the same transaction. Unless the circumstances of the transaction fall within one of the exceptions to Rule 3, see Rule 3.09 and Rule 3.10 Solicitors' Code of Conduct 2007, the firm should cease to act for one or both of the parties from the date of the merger. If none of the exceptions apply, the firm may continue to act for one party only if the duty of confidentiality to the other is not at risk (see Rule 3.15 Solicitors' Code of Conduct 2007).

10.6.2. The merged firm may continue to act for both established clients if both clients have been informed of the situation and consented to the merged firm continuing to act. For informed consent the client must be aware that the firm might hold material information in relation to their matter which the firm cannot disclose. In addition it must also be reasonable in all the circumstances of the case for the firm to continue acting.

10.6.3 Where the firm has been acting for two or more clients in compliance with Rule 3 (conflict of interest) and can no longer fulfil the requirements of Rule 3, the firm may continue to act for one client with the consent of the other, provided that the firm complies with Rule 4.04.

10.6.4. New instructions received for clients of the merged firm will be subject to the provisions of Rule 3 Solicitors' Code of Conduct 2007.

10.7. Solicitor who moves to another firm

Client's pending business is taken over by the new firm

10.7.1. In these circumstances the solicitor may find that his new firm is already acting for the other party to the transaction and a situation analogous to that which occurs on a merger of firms pertains. The provisions of Rule 4.04 must be complied with.

10.7.2. On moving to the new firm the solicitor may find he is now acting for the buyer in a transaction where he had previously been acting for the seller in the same transaction (or vice versa). Although in this situation there is no question of the same solicitor or same firm acting for both parties, the solicitor, while working for his previous firm, will have acquired information which is confidential to his (now) former client and which may affect or prejudice the way in which he handles the transaction for the client of the new firm. In order to preserve his duty of confidentiality to his former client the solicitor should not act for the client of the new firm in this transaction, but there is no objection to the matter being handled by another fee-earner in the solicitor's new firm provided that adequate safeguards are put in place in accordance with Rule 4.04 to ensure that the confidential information is safeguarded.

10.8. Property selling

10.8.1. See A10.3.3 where the solicitor conducts property selling as part of the firm's own solicitor's business.

10.8.2. Where the solicitor conducts property selling through a separate jointly owned business and the solicitor does not do the seller's conveyancing or does the seller's conveyancing under one of the exceptions in Rule 3.11 Solicitors' Code of Conduct 2007, he may do the buyer's conveyancing. Alternatively the solicitor may do a seller's conveyancing where the estate agency business provides mortgage services to the buyer. The buyer and the seller must give their written informed consent and different individuals must deal with the work for seller and buyer; see Rule 3.13.

10.8.3. If any of the circumstances in Rule 3.09 apply (established clients; consideration of £10,000 or less; representation by two separate offices) the firm may sell the property, provide mortgage related services, and act for the seller and buyer in the conveyancing provided that Rules 3.10 and 3.13 are complied with. This does not apply where there is more than one prospective buyer: see Rules 10.06(3)–(4) Solicitors' Code of Conduct 2007.

10.9. Joint borrowers

10.9.1. Where joint borrowers are obtaining a mortgage for the purchase of property, there is no objection to the same solicitor advising both of them, provided that their interests coincide. Where, however, one party is acting as surety for the other's debts, e.g. a wife who is guaranteeing her husband's mortgage of the matrimonial home to secure the husband's business debts, the parties' interests will almost certainly be in conflict with each other. In these circumstances, separate and independent advice must be given to each party. It may be possible for the same solicitor to advise both clients in these circumstances, but each client should be seen separately and the advice given to each party must be consistent with that party's interests.[1] When instructions are being carried out under the terms of the CML Lenders' Handbook, paragraph 8 of the Handbook will normally prohibit the same solicitor from advising any borrower who does not benefit personally from the loan or any guarantor or any non-owning occupier. Such persons must have independent advice (also see A10.4). The BSA Mortgage Instructions contain similar provisions in paragraphs B.24 and B.25.

1. See *Barclays Bank plc* v. *O'Brien* [1993] 4 All ER 417; *Midland Bank plc* v. *Serter* [1994] EGCS 45; *Clark Boyce* v. *Mouat* [1993] 3 WLR 1021, PC; *Banco Exterior Internacional* v. *Mann* [1995] 1 All ER 936, CA. Also see *Bank Melli Iran* v. *Samadi Rad* [1995] 2 FLR 367, where the court said that a wife who had been advised separately by a different solicitor in the firm which was also advising her husband had not received 'independent' advice. See also Law Society's guidance on undue influence – solicitors' duties post Etridge (Appendix IV.7).

A11. Mortgages: acting for lender and borrower

11.1. General principles

11.1.1. The buyer's lender will frequently instruct the buyer's solicitor also to act for him in connection with the grant of the mortgage. The same situation commonly occurs in relation to the discharge of an existing mortgage when acting for a seller client.

11.1.2. As soon as the solicitor accepts instructions to act for the lender he is acting for both parties in one transaction (i.e. for both lender and borrower) and owes a duty to both clients.[1] Their respective interests are not necessarily identical and need to be separately considered.

11.1.3. Subject to A10.4, acting for both parties is permissible provided that no conflict of interest arises between the two clients.

11.1.4. The lender's instructions to act and (in the case of a purchase) terms of offer must be carefully scrutinised to ensure that there is no conflict or potential conflict between the interests of the lender and the buyer/seller.

11.1.5. In many cases the lender's instructions will require the solicitor to observe the terms of the CML Lenders' Handbook (which is certified for compliance with Rule 3 Solicitors' Code of Conduct 2007 (conflict of interests)). Where the lender is a member of the Building Societies Association, the BSA Mortgage Instructions may be used instead (these are also certified for compliance with the Solicitors' Code of Conduct 2007).

11.1.6. A solicitor may not act for a lender where the terms of the lender's instructions exceed the limitations imposed by Rules 3.19 and 3.20 Solicitors' Code of Conduct 2007.

1. *Mortgage Express* v. *Bowerman & Partners* [1995] 2 All ER 769, CA.

11.2. Conflict of interests

11.2.1. If a conflict should occur the solicitor must decline to act (or to continue to act) for both parties unless he can, with the consent of one party, continue to act for the other.

11.3. Examples of conflict

11.3.1. Conflict may arise if, for example:

    (a) the terms of the mortgage offer are inequitable;

    (b) instructions reveal that the buyer would be in breach of one of the terms of the offer;

    (c) the buyer/seller is unable to comply with the lender's terms;

    (d) the buyer is offering inadequate security.

11.3.2. A conflict will also arise if the buyer's solicitor becomes aware that the buyer is misrepresenting the purchase price to the lender, e.g. where the buyer and seller have agreed that the actual purchase price of the property will be lower than that shown in the contract and purchase deed, or where the buyer receives an inducement such as a free holiday to persuade him to buy the property. Solicitors have a duty of confidentiality to their clients, but this does not affect their duty to act in the best interests of each client. Subject to the instructions received from the particular lender concerned, any information regarding variations to the purchase price should be forwarded to the lender with the consent of the buyer. If the buyer will not consent to the information being disclosed to the lender the solicitor must cease to act for the lender and must consider carefully whether he is able to continue to act for the buyer. Any attempt to defraud the lender may lead to criminal prosecutions of both the buyer and the buyer's solicitor. The solicitor would also be guilty of unprofessional conduct. If a solicitor is aware that his client is attempting to perpetrate fraud in any form he should immediately cease to act for that client.

11.4. Confidentiality

11.4.1. If a conflict does arise between the borrower and his lender where the same solicitor is acting for both parties it should be borne in mind that all information received by the solicitor from his client is confidential and cannot be disclosed to the lender without the client's consent. Knowledge acquired in the course of acting for the client is not imputed to the lender.[1] Where, for example, the solicitor is told by his borrower client that the client intends to breach the terms of the mortgage offer by letting the premises to a tenant, the solicitor, when informing the lender that he can no longer act for him, must tell the lender that the reason for the termination of the retainer is because a conflict of interests has arisen, but is not at liberty to disclose the nature of the conflict without the borrower client's consent.

1. *Halifax Mortgage Services Ltd.* v. *Stepsky*, *The Times*, 27 June 1995.

11.5. Individual mortgages

11.5.1. The solicitor must not act for both lender and borrower in an individual mortgage at arm's length; see Rule 3.17 Solicitors' Code of Conduct 2007.

11.5.2. An individual mortgage is defined by Rule 3.17 Solicitors' Code of Conduct 2007 as any mortgage other than a standard mortgage. A standard mortgage is one on standard terms provided in the normal course of the lender's activities.

11.5.3. Subject to the general principles of conflict of interests it would be possible to act in an individual mortgage which is not at arm's length (e.g. a loan between father and son), but it is advisable to ensure that the borrower receives independent advice about the terms of the loan.

11.6. Lender's costs

11.6.1. See N1.

11.7. Sureties

11.7.1. Where the lender requires a surety to enter into the transaction, the surety should be advised to take independent advice before signing the security document. This is of particular importance where the intended surety is the wife of the borrower since the courts take the view that a security should not be enforced against a married woman unless the lender can show that he has taken reasonable steps to show that she understood the transaction.[1] Under the terms of the CML Lenders' Handbook (paragraph 8) a solicitor cannot act for both the borrower and a surety without the lender's consent and the surety must have independent advice. The BSA Mortgage Instructions contain similar provisions in paragraphs B.24 and B.25.

11.7.2. If the proceeds of a life policy fall into the deceased's estate (e.g. because the policy was not formally assigned to the lender) the surety has no claim against the deceased's estate.

1. See *Barclays Bank plc* v. *O'Brien* [1993] 3 WLR 786, HL; *CIBC Mortgages* v. *Pitt* [1993] 3 WLR 802, HL.

11.8. Mortgage fraud

11.8.1. Mortgage fraud can occur in either a residential or commercial transaction and can assume many different guises. Solicitors must be alert to the possibility of fraud and should be careful not to participate, even unknowingly, in a transaction where such a fraud is being perpetrated (see A24 and Appendix II.4).

11.9. Ownership of documents and confidentiality

11.9.1. The following guidance relates to the position where the same firm of solicitors acted for the buyer/borrower and for the lender on a contemporaneous purchase and mortgage and the lender asks to see documents on the 'conveyancing file'.

11.9.2. Where all the documentation is kept on one file, the solicitor will have to sort through the file to determine ownership of the various papers.

11.9.3. The documents which the lender will be entitled to see fall into two categories. The first category is documents prepared or received by the solicitor on behalf of the lender. The second category is documents prepared or received by the solicitor on behalf of the borrower which, it is considered, the lender is nonetheless entitled to see. The rationale is that these documents relate to that part of the solicitor's work where the lender and borrower can be said to have a common interest, i.e. the deduction of title, the acquisition of a good title to the property and ancillary legal issues, such as the use of the property. Examples of the most common items in these two categories are set out below.

11.9.4. Documents held by the solicitor on behalf of the lender are:

    (a)   the lender's instructions to the solicitor;

    (b)   copy mortgage deed;

    (c)   copy report on title;

    (d)   any correspondence between the solicitor and the lender or between the solicitor and a third party written or received on the lender's behalf.

11.9.5. Documents held by the solicitor on behalf of the borrower which the lender is entitled to see include:

    (a)   contract for sale;

    (b)   property information form/enquiries before contract;

    (c)   official copies of the title/abstract or epitome of title;

    (d)   requisitions on title;

    (e)   draft purchase deed;

    (f)   draft licence to assign (where appropriate);

    (g)   Land Registry application forms.

11.10. The CML Lenders' Handbook for England and Wales

11.10.1. The CML Lenders' Handbook forms the contract between the solicitor (or licensed conveyancer) and lender where the solicitor (or licensed conveyancer) is representing a lender who has agreed to be a party to the CML Lenders' Handbook. A number of major lenders have agreed to be parties to the CML Lenders' Handbook and other mortgage lenders may instruct solicitors to act on the terms of the CML Lenders' Handbook. The instructions apply whether or not the solicitor is acting for both borrower and lender or for the lender only.

11.10.2. Modifications of the instructions specific to the transaction in hand will be notified to the solicitor in the lender's written instructions to the solicitor and/or in Part 2 of the CML Lenders' Handbook.

11.10.3. It is the solicitor's responsibility to ensure that the property has a good and marketable title which can safely be accepted by the lender as security and that the property is validly charged to the lender to secure the advance made to the borrower.

11.10.4. Communications between the solicitor and the lender must be in writing (or confirmed in writing) and must quote the mortgage account or roll number, the borrower's name and initials, the address of the property and the solicitor's reference.

11.10.5. Documents contained in the 'joint file' (as defined in the CML Lenders' Handbook) must be retained by the solicitor for at least six years from the date of the mortgage. The borrower is not permitted to have documents from the file without the lender's consent. Equally, the lender is not permitted to have documents from the file without the borrower's consent. Each would be entitled to certified copies, but the lender only to those documents relevant to its retainer because of the right of the borrower to confidentiality (see A11.9.4 and A11.9.5).

11.10.6. The solicitor must use the lender's standard documentation the wording of which must not be varied without the lender's consent.

11.11. BSA Mortgage Instructions

11.11.1. The BSA Mortgage Instructions form the contract between the solicitor (or licensed conveyancer) and lender where the solicitor (or licensed conveyancer) is representing a lender who is a member of the Building Societies Association and who has agreed to use the BSA Mortgage Instructions. A number of building societies and other lenders have agreed to use the BSA Mortgage Instructions. The instructions apply whether or not the solicitor is acting for both borrower and lender or for the lender only. The instructions comprise two sections: a core set of mortgage instructions; and specific requirements setting out individual lenders' policies.

11.11.2. Modifications of the instructions specific to the transaction in hand will be notified to the solicitor in the lender's written instructions to the solicitor and/or in the lender's specific requirements.

11.11.3. It is the solicitor's responsibility to ensure that the property has a good and marketable title which can safely be accepted by the lender as security and that the property is validly charged to the lender to secure the advance made to the borrower.

11.11.4. Communications between the solicitor and the lender must be in writing (or confirmed in writing) and must quote the mortgage account or roll number, the borrower's name and initials, the address of the property and the solicitor's reference.

11.11.5. Documents contained in the 'joint file' (as defined in the BSA Mortgage Instructions) must be retained by the solicitor for at least six years from the date of the mortgage. The borrower is not permitted to have documents from the file without the lender's consent. Equally, the lender is not permitted to have documents from the file without the borrower's consent. Each would be entitled to certified copies, but the lender only to those documents relevant to its retainer because of the right of the borrower to confidentiality (see A11.9.4 and A11.9.5).

11.11.6. The solicitor must use the lender's standard documentation the wording of which must not be varied without the lender's consent.

A12. Preliminary deposits

12.1.	General law	12.3.	New properties
12.2.	Payment to estate agents	12.4.	Action by solicitor

12.1. General law

12.1.1. There is no requirement in law for either party to pay a preliminary deposit since neither party is committed to the sale and purchase until contracts have been exchanged.

12.2. Payment to estate agents

12.2.1. An estate agent will sometimes ask a prospective buyer to pay a preliminary deposit as an indication of the buyer's good intentions to proceed with negotiations. The buyer should be advised to resist pressure from the agent to make such a payment since no advantage to the buyer derives from it.

12.2.2. If a preliminary deposit is to be paid the buyer should ensure that the agent has the seller's authority to take the deposit. Without such authority the buyer has no recourse against the seller if the agent misappropriates the money.[1]

12.2.3. A signed receipt must be obtained in respect of any preliminary deposit which is paid, a copy of which should be placed on the solicitor's file for reference. The terms of the receipt should be scrutinised before signature to ensure that the deposit will be refundable if the transaction does not proceed.

12.2.4. Any preliminary deposit paid is normally fully refundable to the buyer if the transaction does not proceed.

12.2.5. Preliminary deposits are usually paid to the estate agent who will hold the money in the capacity of agent for the seller. Interest on a preliminary deposit which exceeds £500 may be payable under Estate Agents Act 1979.

12.2.6. Where a preliminary deposit is taken by a solicitor who is acting as an estate agent, consideration should be given to holding that deposit in the capacity of agent for the buyer.

1. See *Sorrell* v. *Finch* [1977] AC 728.

12.3. New properties

12.3.1. A seller who is a builder or developer will invariably require a prospective buyer to pay a preliminary deposit. In this situation the payment of the deposit may operate as an option to purchase a numbered plot at a stated price, the seller promising that he will not sell that plot elsewhere nor raise the price provided that contracts are exchanged within a stated period. Here the buyer may have little choice but to pay the deposit, but a receipt should always be obtained and a copy of it placed on the buyer's solicitor's file for reference. The terms of the receipt should be scrutinised to ascertain whether the deposit is refundable to the buyer if he later changes his mind and withdraws from the transaction. Since this type of preliminary deposit often buys an option on a numbered plot it is not unusual to find that the deposit is not returnable to the buyer in any circumstances, although it will be credited as part of the purchase price if the matter proceeds.

12.3.2   The Consumer Code for Home Builders, which sets out requirements that builders who are registered with NHBC, Premier Guarantee and LABC New Home Warranty must meet, provides that the builder must clearly explain how the buyer's contract deposits are protected and how any other pre-payments are dealt with.

12.4. Action by solicitor

12.4.1.   The solicitor should always enquire whether a preliminary deposit has been paid, and if so how much and to whom. A copy of the receipt should be obtained and a note of the amount of the deposit made on the file so that this may be taken into account when calculating the balance of deposit needed on exchange.

12.4.2.   The solicitor should also enquire whether the prospective buyer has signed any authority or other documents held by the estate agent which may be relevant to the contract.

A13. Surveys

13.1. **When should a survey be**
     commissioned?
13.2. **Reasons for a survey**
13.3. **Advice to the client**

13.4. **Types of survey**
13.5. **Surveyor's liability**
13.6. **CML Lenders' Handbook**
13.7. **BSA Mortgage Instructions**

13.1. When should a survey be commissioned?

13.1.1. Ideally the buyer should always have a survey carried out before exchange of contracts, but many buyers, particularly first-time buyers for whom the expense of a survey is a major consideration, do not commission an independent survey, preferring to rely instead on the valuation undertaken by their lender. Most lenders disclose their written valuation reports to their customers.

13.1.2. In the case of commercial premises a buyer will have much more detailed concerns relating to the structure, use, and floor loading capabilities of the property. Compliance with statutory requirements must also be checked. The comments contained in the following paragraphs do not reflect the detail required in a commercial transaction.

13.2. Reasons for a survey

13.2.1. The *caveat emptor* rule places on the buyer the onus of discovering any physical faults in the property agreed to be sold. For this reason alone, a survey is always advisable in order to discover physical defects which are not readily apparent on inspection of the property by the lay client, except perhaps where a property in the course of construction is being purchased with the benefit of structural defects insurance.

13.2.2. In addition to the above the surveyor's report should:

    (a) confirm whether or not the value of the property equates with the price agreed to be paid for it;

    (b) point out any major structural defects which exist;

    (c) give the buyer early warning of potential structural problems or major repair work which will be required in the foreseeable future so that these may be taken into account in deciding whether the buyer is able and/or prepared to undertake the responsibility for such future expenditure;

    (d) bring to the attention of the buyer's solicitor the existence of factors which may be indicative of third party rights or overriding interests over the property and which need to be the subject of further enquiries by the solicitor;

(e)   point out minor matters which may need remedial work in the near future;

(f)   confirm whether or not the boundaries on the ground correspond with those shown in the title deeds.

13.3.   Advice to the client

13.3.1.   If the client has not already instructed a surveyor, the reasons for having a survey done and the limitations of the home condition report (if one has been provided) should be explained to the client. A note should be made on the file that the client was so advised and of the client's decision following the receipt of the advice. The advice given should include information relating to the different types of survey available and their relative cost.

13.3.2.   The client should be advised to commission a survey as soon as a firm offer has been accepted by the seller. The results of the survey must be obtained before exchange of contracts since once exchange has taken place the client will no longer have the right to withdraw from the transaction on the grounds of a physical defect in the property. The results of the survey may reveal matters which will require further investigation by the buyer's solicitor, or even give grounds for the negotiation of a reduction in the purchase price, both of which must, where appropriate, be concluded before a binding contract is entered into.

13.3.3.   Although there is no reported decision on the point, it is possible that a court might hold that a solicitor who had not advised a client to have a survey done was in breach of his duty of care towards his client or in breach of Supply of Goods and Services Act 1982, s.13 which implies an obligation to perform a contract for services with reasonable skill and care.

13.3.4.   If the solicitor does go through the surveyor's report prepared for the client, he is expected to exercise his own judgment and expertise in relation to the interpretation of the report and should emphasise to the client the limitations on the advice which can be given by the solicitor about the report (i.e. that he is looking at the report as a lawyer and not as a surveyor).

13.4.   Types of survey

13.4.1.   In broad terms the client has three options open to him:

(a)   to rely on the valuation made by his lender;

(b)   to commission a 'Homebuyer' report;

(c)   to instruct an independent surveyor to do a building survey.

Valuation

13.4.2.   This will be undertaken by the buyer's lender in order to establish whether the property being purchased will be adequate security for the amount of the loan. The buyer pays the cost of this valuation and is usually permitted to see the valuer's report, but the report will not necessarily reveal sufficient information about the state of the property to allow the buyer to make a reasoned judgment as to whether or not to proceed with his purchase. Where the amount required by the buyer on mortgage represents a high percentage of the purchase price of the property, the interests of the buyer and his lender in the valuation broadly coincide, in that if the value of the property does not provide adequate security for the loan, then neither does it represent a wise investment for the client. In these circumstances therefore it may be considered that a lender's valuation report alone will provide sufficient protection of the client's interests, although he should be advised that it will not necessarily safeguard against unknown or undisclosed lack of repairs that may be expensive to remedy, even if they do not constitute structural defects. A valuation alone may also be considered adequate in circumstances where the client is purchasing a property in the course of construction which is to be covered by a structural defects insurance scheme.

'Homebuyer' report

13.4.3.   This option represents a compromise between the mortgage valuation and the building survey and is thus an attractive option for a client who, for reasons of expense or otherwise, is reluctant to commission a building survey. In many cases the buyer's lender will agree (for an additional fee) to instruct the lender's valuer to undertake the survey concurrently with the mortgage valuation with consequent savings in time and expense for the client. This type of survey may provide adequate information for the client who is purchasing an ordinary suburban residential property built within the last 100 years, but the client should not be misled into thinking that the survey result is an absolute guarantee of the state and condition of the property. Although of much more value to the client than a mere valuation, this type of survey is still relatively superficial in scope.

Building survey

13.4.4.   The potential expense of a building survey (formely called a structural survey) deters many clients from choosing this option. The client might be reminded that £500 abortive expense on a survey is preferable to discovering that £30,000 worth of structural repairs needs to be done to the property he has just purchased without the benefit of a survey. This option is undoubtedly the most expensive of the three on offer, the exact expense and value to the client depending on what the surveyor has been instructed to investigate. A building survey will only reveal the true state and condition of the entire property if the surveyor is correctly instructed to investigate all aspects of the property.

Guidelines

13.4.5.   The need for a building survey may be indicated by the presence of one or more of the following factors:

(a)   the property is of a high value;

(b)   the amount of the buyer's intended mortgage represents a low proportion of the purchase price, e.g. less than 70%;

(c)   the property is more than 100 years old;

(d)   the buyer intends to alter or extend the property after completion;

(e)   the property is not of conventional brick and mortar construction;

(f)   the proximity of the property to features which may cause subsidence or other structural problems, e.g. mines, filled-in gravel pits, rivers, vibration damage from aircraft or railways;

(g)   the property is not detached.

Surveys in special cases

13.4.6.   A surveyor, even when instructed to carry out a building survey, will not normally investigate drainage or electrical systems. A property which does not have the benefit of mains drainage will require a separate drainage survey from an expert in that field, since the cost of repair or replacement of a private drainage system can be prohibitive. Liability for escaping effluent can also involve civil and criminal penalties. If the electric wiring system in the property has not been inspected during the past five years a report on the adequacy and safety of the electrical installations may also be desirable. Where environmental issues are relevant, e.g. on purchases of development land, a separate environmental survey may also be desirable to ensure that the land does not harbour any hazardous substances which may incur liability on the landowner under Environmental Protection Act 1990 or Environment Act 1995. The local authority for the area can supply information relating to the presence of radon in the area. The Radiation Protection Division of the Health Protection Agency publishes definitive maps, provides information on radon, and offers a written report on the radon potential for a property (see B25.6.6).

Flats and other attached properties

13.4.7.   Where the property to be purchased is a flat or is a property which is structurally attached to neighbouring property, a building survey is desirable. The structural soundness of the property being bought is in these circumstances dependent on the soundness of the neighbouring property also, and the surveyor must therefore be instructed to inspect the adjoining property (if possible) as well as the property actually being purchased.

Water supply pipes

13.4.8. The owner or occupier of land may be responsible for the maintenance of a water supply pipe which crosses privately owned land before joining the publicly maintained mains supply pipe. A building survey may not deal with the water supply system (particularly where the pipes supplying the property being surveyed pass through or under adjoining property). The client may be advised to obtain a separate survey of the water supply pipes from his water supply company. A fee may be payable for this service.

13.5. Surveyor's liability

13.5.1. The surveyor owes a duty of care to his client to carry out his survey with reasonable skill and care. This common law duty is reinforced by Supply of Goods and Services Act 1982, s.13 which implies into a contract for services a term that the work will be carried out with reasonable skill and care.

13.5.2. Where a client suffers loss as a result of a negligent survey an action can be sustained against his surveyor, subject to the validity of any exemption clause which may have formed part of the surveyor's terms of work. The normal rules relating to remoteness of damage apply; thus the client will not sustain a successful action unless the area of the client's complaint lies within the scope of what the surveyor was instructed to do, and hence the importance of giving full and explicit instructions when the survey is commissioned.

13.5.3. An exclusion clause which seeks to limit or to exclude the surveyor's liability in contract or tort will be subject to the reasonableness test in Unfair Contract Terms Act 1977, s.11. Where a lay client has suffered loss the burden of showing that the clause satisfies the reasonableness test will be a difficult one for the surveyor to discharge,[1] but the clause may give some protection where the client who commissioned the survey was experienced in the property field.[2]

13.5.4. Where the client suffers loss after having relied on a lender's valuer's report an action in tort may lie against the surveyor. No action in contract can be sustained because, the survey having been commissioned by the lender, there is no contractual relationship between the buyer and the surveyor. The success of such an action may again depend on the validity of any exclusion clause contained in the valuation; however, it was held by the House of Lords in *Smith* v. *Eric S Bush (a firm)*; *Harris* v. *Wyre Forest District Council*[3] that a valuer instructed by a lender to carry out a mortgage valuation of a modest house, in the knowledge that the buyer would rely on the valuation without obtaining an independent survey, owed a duty of care to the buyer to exercise reasonable care and skill in carrying out the valuation. Similarly in *Beresforde* v. *Chesterfield Borough Council*,[4] where the lender presented the valuer's report to the buyer on its own headed notepaper, the Court of Appeal allowed the buyer to proceed with a claim based on loss arising out of an allegedly negligent valuation directly against the lender. However, the court's decision in this case was interlocutory and as no trial took place it cannot be assumed that a lender will always be liable in such circumstances. The decisions in these cases may assist lay purchasers of ordinary modestly priced houses or small businesses,[5] but may not assist in other circumstances where it would be reasonable to assume that the buyer would commission his own independent survey.

13.5.5. A complaint about a negligent valuation/survey made in-house by a lender may be investigated by the Financial Ombudsman Service provided the complainant is an existing borrower from that lender.[6]

1. See *Yianni* v. *Edwin Evans & Sons* [1982] 1 QB 438.
2. See *Stevenson* v. *Nationwide Building Society* (1984) 272 EG 663.
3. [1990] 1 AC 831, HL.
4. [1989] 39 EG 176.
5. See *Qureshi* v. *Liassides* (unreported 22 April 1995). See commentary in *Estates Gazette*, 11 November 1994, p.123.
6. See *Halifax Building Society* v. *Edell* [1992] Ch 436.

13.6. CML Lenders' Handbook

13.6.1. Paragraph 4.1.2 of the CML Lenders' Handbook[1] requires the solicitor to check that certain assumptions made by the valuer in his report are correct.

13.6.2. The solicitor is recommended by the CML Lenders' Handbook to advise the buyer client that the valuation may contain omissions or inaccurate information.

1. The CML Lenders' Handbook is reproduced at **www.cml.org.uk**.

13.7. BSA Mortgage Instructions

13.7.1. Paragraph C.4 of the BSA Mortgage Instructions[1] requires the solicitor to check that certain assumptions made by the valuer in his report are correct.

13.7.2. Paragraph C.5 recommends the solicitor to advise the buyer client that the valuation may contain omissions or inaccurate information.

1. The BSA Mortgage Instructions are reproduced at **www.bsa.org.uk**.

A14. Stamp Duty Land Tax

14.1. Introduction

14.1.1. Stamp Duty Land Tax (SDLT) replaced Stamp Duty in relation to transactions completing on or after 1 December 2003.[1]

14.1.2. SDLT is a tax on transactions (not on documents) and applies, with minor exceptions, to all transactions affecting land within the UK.

14.1.3. The tax applies irrespective of where the transaction was completed (i.e. offshore completions are no longer exempted) and whether or not the transaction was evidenced by a document.

14.1.4. The purchaser (as defined in Finance Act 2003, s.43(4)) is responsible for the payment and the submission of the self-assessment land transaction return form to HM Revenue and Customs. Unless it is submitted online, the purchaser (or his attorney) must personally sign the form.

14.1.5. Where there are joint purchasers the liability for payment is joint and several.

14.1.6. The 'purchaser' will normally be the buyer in a land transaction or the tenant under a lease but note that a landlord who pays a premium on surrender of a lease will also fall within the definition of a purchaser.

14.1.7. The SDLT form and payment must be submitted within 30 days of the date when the charge to tax arises.

14.1.8. Penalties and interest are payable for late payment and criminal penalties including imprisonment and fines exist for tax evasion and fraud. The investigation powers of HM Revenue and Customs last for a period of up to 20 years.

14.1.9. The document evidencing the land transaction is not required to be submitted with the land transaction return.

14.1.10. Unlike its predecessor, stamp duty, SDLT is not always a single one-off payment. For example, in the case of a lease, a further charge to tax can arise on the exercise of a rent review. It is therefore essential that a copy of the SDLT return and associated papers are safely retained.

14.1.11. Where ownership of land is transferred by means of a transfer of shares in a limited company, the maximum tax payable by the purchaser is 0.5% stamp duty on the shares transferred.

14.1.12. If the transfer of the ownership of a company is made within the triggers for withdrawal of acquisition, group or company reconstruction relief, the company which is the subject of the transfer of ownership must make an amendment return within 30 days of the transfer and pay any tax previously relieved (Finance Act 2003, Sched.7).

1.   See A14.32 for transitional provisions and examples of transactions which may still be subject to stamp duty.

14.2. Time of payment

14.2.1. Payment of SDLT is due within the same timescale that a land transaction return is made; namely within 30 days of the 'effective date' of the relevant land transaction (Finance Act 2003, s.86).

14.2.2. Although the effective date will normally be the date of completion, the charge to tax arises when the purchaser has 'substantial benefit of the contract'. In the following circumstances this will give rise to a charge to tax before actual completion:

    (a)   payment of (normally) at least 90% of the purchase price;

    (b)   the purchaser or a connected person having the right to occupy the land, including under a licence;

    (c)   the purchaser or a connected person having the right to receive rents;

    (d)   payment by the purchaser or a connected person of rent.

14.3. Chargeable transactions

14.3.1. For SDLT purposes a land transaction is a transaction which consists of the acquisition of a chargeable interest in land in the UK. An acquisition of a chargeable interest includes its creation, the surrender or release of a chargeable interest, and the variation of a chargeable interest.

14.3.2. Chargeable interests in land are defined in section 48 Finance Act 2003 and comprise:

(a) an estate, interest, right or power in or over land in the UK; or

(b) the benefit of an obligation, restriction or condition affecting the value of any such estate, interest, right or power;

other than an exempt interest.

14.3.3. Section 48(2)–(5) Finance Act 2003 provides details of exempt interests, which include any security interest (such as a mortgage or charge), a licence to use or occupy land, and a tenancy at will. The acquisition of an exempt interest is not a land transaction and therefore does not involve SDLT.

14.3.4. For a land transaction to be chargeable to SDLT, there must be chargeable consideration. This is consideration in money or money's worth given for the subject matter of the transaction directly or indirectly by the purchaser (Finance Act 2003, s.50 and Sched.4).

14.3.5. Certain land transactions, although involving the acquisition of a chargeable interest, are specifically exempt from payment of SDLT (see A14.6 and Finance Act 2003, Sched.3).

14.3.6. Transactions where no money passes may still be chargeable, where non-monetary consideration is given. This may include the provision of services, goods or works, or the assumption of debt. Where the consideration consists of services, goods or works, the market value of such items will be attributed as the consideration on which SDLT will be levied.

14.3.7. The transfer of land where no money consideration passes, but where the land is subject to a mortgage or other financial charge, continues to be treated as a transfer for consideration. The consideration is taken to be the amount of debt assumed and is charged to SDLT accordingly. Where jointly owned land is subject to a mortgage and there is a transfer of equity, the amount of debt assumed is taken to be a proportion of the outstanding mortgage corresponding to the proportion of the equity share acquired.

14.3.8. The value of chattels is not liable to SDLT (see A14.14).

14.4. Notifiable transactions

14.4.1. Under Finance Act 2003, s.76, in the case of every notifiable land transaction, the purchaser must deliver a land transaction return form to HM Revenue and Customs within 30 days of the effective date of the transaction.

14.4.2. The land transactions that are notifiable are:

(a) The grant, for a chargeable consideration, of a lease for a term of seven years or more (running from the date of the grant).

As from 12 March 2008, there is no requirement to notify HM Revenue and Customs of the grant of such a lease if the chargeable consideration (other than rent) is less than £40,000, and the annual rent is less than £1,000.

(b) The grant of a lease for less than seven years (running from the date of the grant) where the chargeable consideration (either in the form of rent or a premium) would, ignoring the availability of any relief, be chargeable to tax at 1% or higher.

(c) An acquisition of a freehold interest that is not exempt.

As from 12 March 2008, there is no requirement to notify HM Revenue and Customs of such an acquisition if the chargeable consideration for the acquisition is less than £40,000.

(d) An acquisition of a leasehold interest that is not exempt where the lease was originally granted for seven years or more. An acquisition of a leasehold interest includes a surrender.

As from 12 March 2008, there is no requirement to notify HM Revenue and Customs of such an acquisition if the chargeable consideration for the acquisition is less than £40,000.

(e) An acquisition of a leasehold interest that is not exempt where the lease was originally granted for less than seven years, but only if the chargeable consideration for the acquisition would, ignoring the availability of any relief, be chargeable to tax at 1% or higher. As above, an acquisition of a leasehold interest includes a surrender.

(f) An acquisition of a chargeable interest other than a freehold or leasehold interest (e.g. the grant or release of an easement, the release of a restrictive covenant, or the grant of an option) where the chargeable consideration for the acquisition would, ignoring any relief, be chargeable to tax at 1% or higher.

14.5. Linked transactions

14.5.1. Where transactions are linked (whether or not there is a gap in time between them) the chargeable consideration is aggregated and charged to SDLT at the rate applicable to the total combined price paid.

14.5.2. Where an earlier linked transaction has been notified to HM Revenue and Customs, credit is given for the amount of tax already paid and only the top-up tax is payable on each subsequent linked transaction.

14.5.3.   It is therefore always necessary to keep records of SDLT returns to provide evidence of tax paid.

14.6.   Exempt transactions

14.6.1.   The principal exemptions from SDLT are:

(a)   transfers on divorce or dissolution of a civil partnership;

(b)   gifts;

(c)   other transfers for no chargeable consideration.

The last category would include a transfer to a beneficiary out of a trust where, but for the trust, the beneficiary would otherwise be absolutely entitled to the land (Finance Act 2003, Sched.16), and a partition of jointly owned land where there is no consideration paid between the participants (Finance Act 2003, Sched.4).

14.6.2.   Transactions where the consideration does not exceed the zero-rate band (see A14.12) are not exempt from SDLT and may still be required to be notified to HM Revenue and Customs on a land transaction return form.

14.6.3.   A land transaction that is exempt is not chargeable to SDLT and does not need to be notified to HM Revenue and Customs on a land transaction return form.

14.6.4.   Note that if a transaction is 'relieved' rather than exempted (see A14.7) an SDLT return must be made together with a claim for relief.

14.7.   Relieved transactions

14.7.1.   In the following cases the transaction may be relieved from SDLT but it is still necessary to make an SDLT return and to claim relief expressly:

(a)   alternative property finance mortgages effected by resale or sale and leaseback (Finance Act 2003, ss.72 and 73);

(b)   group, reconstruction and acquisition reliefs which apply to companies either at least 75% subsidiaries of one another, or both of another company. Qualifications apply in various circumstances and in all cases clawback of relief applies for three years from the transaction or longer where an agreement to transfer out of the group is made within three years, but the company leaves the group more than three years later (Finance Act 2003, Sched.7);

(c)   residential properties in Disadvantaged Areas (DA) (i.e. those areas defined as 'Enterprise Areas' by the Chancellor in his 2002 Pre-Budget Report). The 2003 Budget announced and from 10 April 2003 brought into effect the full reliefs sanctioned by the EU for Disadvantaged

Areas. The same provisions are re-enacted under Finance Act 2003, s.57 and Sched.6. Since 17 March 2005 this relief applies only to residential property (see A14.13.5);

(d) registered charities acquiring land for charitable purposes may claim full relief from SDLT. However, the relief is subject to clawback if the land ceases to be used for charitable purposes (Finance Act 2003, s.68);

(e) compulsory purchase and for performance by public bodies of planning matters (Finance Act 2003, ss.60 and 61);

(f) sale and leaseback (or lease and leaseback): the leaseback element is relieved where full SDLT has been paid on the sale and the property leased back forms all or part of the land that was the subject of the sale (Finance Act 2003, s.57A).

Residential property relief

14.7.2. A series of reliefs relating to residential property is granted by Schedule 6A Finance Act 2003. Subject to qualifications, these allow various classes of property trader to take property into stock or in part exchange without payment of SDLT. In all cases, the property taken in part exchange must be second-hand and must have been the main or only residence of the seller at some time in the two years prior to the date of purchase. In the case of a sale by personal representatives the qualifying period is the two years prior to the date of death. The amenity land surrounding the second-hand house should not normally exceed 0.5 hectares. If the curtilage is greater than 0.5 hectares, the value of the property will have to be apportioned between the value of the property comprising 0.5 hectares and the excess. Full relief will be granted on the qualifying area and SDLT charged at the normal rate on the excess. In each case the buyer must be a company genuinely trading in the relevant sector. A house building company or an associated company taking a property in part exchange will have to insert its Construction Industry Scheme number on the land transaction return when claiming Schedule 6A relief.

14.7.3. House builder's relief on second-hand houses bought in part exchange is only available where there is a related sale of one of the builder's new houses which is intended to be the only or main residence of the buyer. A new house is a building (or part of a building) which has been constructed or adapted for use as a single dwelling. Once the property is acquired, a house building company is free to deal with the property as it sees fit, but on re-sale, the buyer will be liable to SDLT at the normal rate. A buyer of a new house from a house builder in part exchange for his own second-hand property will not receive any relief from SDLT on the purchase.

14.7.4. Under Finance Act 2003, Sched.6A, paras.2–4, property traders, chain breaker companies and traders buying from personal representatives may all claim relief from SDLT on their purchases. Under Finance Act 2003, Sched.6A, paras.5 and 6, employers and relocation companies may buy an employee's existing house to facilitate relocation for a new job with either the same or a new employer or at a new location to which the employee cannot reasonably travel from the existing house. The purchases under Finance Act 2003, Sched.6A, paras.5 and 6 must be made by companies in the relevant business and do not permit directors or others to occupy the properties. Before reselling the properties, the relieved buyers may only carry out such work to make them clean and safe and may not normally spend more than £10,000 on those works. In default, the relief is lost. Where 3% of the value of the property exceeds £10,000, this amount may be spent on the permitted works, up to a maximum of £20,000.

14.7.5. Certain acquisitions by registered social landlords (Finance Act 2003, s.71) and certain leases granted by registered social landlords (Finance Act 2003, s.128) are exempt.

14.7.6. Certain right-to-buy transactions (Finance Act 2003, Sched.9) are exempt for qualifying purchases by sitting tenants.

14.7.7. Collective enfranchisement by leaseholders (Finance Act 2003, s.74), where the transferee is a person nominated or appointed by the leaseholders for the purposes of enfranchisement, may result in a zero charge to SDLT. Section 74 enables the right-to-buy tenants to divide the purchase price by the number of flats in respect of which the right is being exercised. This lower figure determines the rate of SDLT (which may be 1% or zero) that is then applied to the gross price.

14.7.8. As from 1 October 2007 (and until 2012) relief is available on the acquisition of a new zero-carbon home. Full relief from SDLT is available where the purchase price does not exceed £500,000 provided the home satisfies a zero-carbon requirement. Where the purchase price exceeds £500,000, relief is available to reduce the 4% charge to SDLT by £15,000. The relief is available for new homes only. It is not available on second and subsequent sales, or on existing homes.

First time buyer's relief

14.7.9. From 25 March 2010 (and until 24 March 2012), relief is available on the purchase of property by an individual, or by individuals, for not more than £250,000, where the individual (or all of them) intends to occupy the property as his or their only or main residence, and the individual (or any of them) has not previously acquired a major interest in land which includes residential property, or an equivalent interest in land, situated anywhere in the world.

Non-residential property relief

14.7.10. Finance Act 2003 provides the following reliefs for non-residential property:

(a)   where both parties are public bodies (section 66);

(b)   where land is acquired by bodies for national purposes, including historic buildings, museums etc. (section 69);

(c) transactions resulting from alterations to parliamentary constituency boundary changes (section 67);

(d) transactions as a result of the demutualisation of insurance companies and building societies (sections 63 and 64);

(e) the initial transfer of assets to a limited liability partnership (section 65);

(f) public/infrastructure projects where a public body transfers to a private body;

(g) public projects exempted from stamp duty.

14.7.11. The provisions of Finance Act 2003 should be checked to ensure that the transaction meets the requirements for relief.

14.8. Option agreements

14.8.1. Agreements granting options and rights of pre-emption are chargeable transactions in their own right.

14.8.2. SDLT is payable on any fee for the grant of an option or right of pre-emption. A further liability arises on the exercise of the option or right and the two transactions are normally linked (see A14.5).

14.8.3. On submission of each land transaction return, the buyer must determine the consideration for the land transaction concerned and calculate the SDLT due, deducting the tax already paid and paying any balance of tax, penalties and interest due to accompany the return forms.

14.9. Sub-sales

14.9.1. Care needs to be taken not to incur SDLT on the first limb of a sub-sale (Finance Act 2003, ss.45 and 45A). For example, B enters into a contract to purchase land from A (the 'main contract'). B then enters into a second contract (the 'sub-sale contract') to sell the same land to C, so that either A transfers direct to C, or there are simultaneous transfers from A to B and from B to C. Provided the two contracts complete (or are 'substantially performed') at the same time, B will incur no liability for SDLT. In such cases, completion of the main contract, or its substantial performance, will be disregarded for the purposes of SDLT (see Finance Act 2003, s.45(3)). C will incur a liability for SDLT on the aggregate of the amount B is obliged to pay to A under the main contract, and the amount C is obliged to pay to B for the benefit of the sub-sale contract.

14.9.2. However, if the main contract is substantially performed prior to its completion (e.g. where B enters into occupation of the property before transfer to C), or the completion of the sub-sale contract is delayed beyond completion of the main contract, the main contract will give rise to a land transaction, and B must submit a land transaction return and pay any SDLT due. Both purchasers will become liable to submit a land transaction return and to pay any SDLT due on the consideration payable under the relevant contract.

14.9.3. Group companies cannot claim relief on sub-sales by one to another (Finance Act 2003, s.45A(9)).

14.9.4. Care needs to be taken with sub-sales not to infringe SDLT avoidance regulations contained in section 75A Finance Act 2003.[1] In a case where the sub-sale contract is made at a price that is lower than the consideration payable under the main contract, the sub-purchaser will nevertheless be charged to SDLT at the higher main contract price.

1. Finance Act 2007, s.71.

14.10. Exchanges of land

14.10.1. Both parties to an exchange of freehold and leasehold interests in land are liable to SDLT at the appropriate rate on the market value of the interest in land each acquires (Finance Act 2003, s.47).

14.10.2. The tax will be payable on the full market value of the interest regardless of the amounts specified in the documentation if they do not represent the market values.

14.10.3. Reliefs are available for house builders acquiring second-hand houses in part exchange for new ones of their own construction (see A14.7).

14.11. Contract and conveyance

14.11.1. Despite particular provisions for option agreements and sub-sales, the general rule is that SDLT will not be payable on contracts for the sale of land where the transaction is perfected by conveyance (Finance Act 2003, ss.44 and 45).

14.12. Rates of SDLT

14.12.1. SDLT is calculated in accordance with the rate tables contained in Finance Act 2003, s.55 for capital payments. Schedule 6 gives the rates applicable to property in a Disadvantaged Area (DA) and Schedule 5 gives the charge on lease rents. Solicitors can perform a post code and ward search on the HM Revenue and Customs website to determine whether land falls within a DA (see B10 for more information on this search). From 25 March 2010 (and until 24 March 2012), relief is available on the purchase of property by an individual, or by individuals, for not more than £250,000, where the individual (or all of them) intends to occupy the property as his or their only or main residence, and the individual (or any of them) has not previously acquired a major interest in land which includes residential property, or an equivalent interest in land, situated anywhere in the world. The level of this temporary relief for certain purchases of residential property is above the current Disadvantaged Area Relief threshold of £150,000.

Rate for residential freehold property

14.12.2. SDLT is calculated as a percentage of the whole of the consideration paid. The following rates apply:

Not more than £125,000	0% (outside a DA)
Not more than £150,000	0% (within a DA)
More than £125,000 but not more than £250,000	1%
More than £250,000 but not more than £500,000	3%
More than £500,000	4%

14.12.3. The increase in the higher rate of SDLT from 4% to 5%, announced in the Budget of 24 March 2010, only applies to purchases of residential property over £1M, and only where the effective date of the transaction is on or after 6 April 2011. However, the higher rate will not apply to any transaction effected pursuant to a contract (not including an option or pre-exemption right) made before 25 March 2010, unless the contract has been varied or assigned on or after that date.

14.12.4. Where the property is partly within a DA, the zero-rate band threshold applicable to the part within the DA is £150,000.

Rate for non-residential or mixed freehold property

14.12.5. SDLT is calculated as a percentage of the whole consideration paid:

Not more than £150,000	0%
More than £150,000 but not more than £250,000	1%
More than £250,000 but not more than £500,000	3%
More than £500,000	4%

14.13. Calculating SDLT

14.13.1. Several methods of calculation of tax are available to solicitors:

    (a) longhand from the rate tables;

    (b) on-screen software tools either free-standing or embedded in SDLT forms software;

(c) online calculation tools available on the Stamp Office website at **www. hmrc.gov.uk/so**.

14.13.2. Solicitors should take care to ensure that the calculation and result are accurate and correct and that the buyer checks the return and figures before signing the land transaction return form.

14.13.3. Calculation of SDLT depends not only on the price, value or consideration for the land but also on which current tax rates apply, the type of property, and whether or not the land lies in a DA.

14.13.4. It is important to distinguish between residential and non-residential property because different rates of SDLT apply (Finance Act 2003, s.116):

(a) a residential property is property which is used or has been adapted for use as a single dwelling, even if the single dwelling is part of a larger building;

(b) amenity land forming part of the garden or grounds of the building, a garage (detached or integral), parking space and (domestic) garden shed are all included within the definition of residential property;

(c) a single transaction involving six or more dwellings is not residential;

(d) institutional property used as residential accommodation for school pupils, students, the armed forces or as a principal residence for more than 90% of the occupants is residential property;

(e) institutional property used as accommodation for higher education halls of residence, children's homes, care and/or treatment and psychiatric homes, hospitals, prisons and hotels is not residential;

(f) where land is used for residential purposes no account shall be taken of any other use;

(g) where land is not used, but is suitable for a particular residential or non-residential use, it will be treated as within that class.

14.13.5. For contracts for the acquisition of non-residential land made or varied on or after 17 March 2005, DA relief is abolished (see A14.7.1(c)).

14.13.6. Mixed use land is land which combines both residential and non-residential property. Where that land is situated outside a DA, non-residential tax rates apply (Finance Act 2003, Sched.6). When mixed use land is within or partly within a DA a just and reasonable apportionment has to be made as between the use and as to the location.

14.13.7. When land is outside a DA and is either wholly non-residential or mixed use, the whole property is treated as non-residential and the £150,000 zero-rate threshold applies.

14.13.8. Where non-residential land is partly within a DA, the value of the property which is not exempt must be taken as a just and reasonable apportionment of the whole. The SDLT rate bands then apply to that value.

14.13.9. Where land within a DA is residential then the £150,000 zero-rate band applies to it.

14.13.10. Where ownership of land is transferred by means of a transfer of shares in a limited company, the maximum tax payable by the purchaser is 0.5% stamp duty on the shares transferred.

14.13.11. If the transfer of the ownership of a company is made within the triggers for withdrawal of acquisition, group or company reconstruction relief, the company which is the subject of the transfer of ownership must make an amendment to its original return within 30 days of the transfer and pay any tax previously relieved (Finance Act 2003, Sched.7).

14.14. Fixtures and fittings

14.14.1. All those buildings, plants and fixtures which common sense and the doctrine of annexation dictate are part of the land, remain so under SDLT. Those fittings which are easily and obviously portable are not annexed to the land.

14.14.2 HM Revenue and Customs has clarified the types of fixtures that it will regard as annexed and not susceptible to an apportionment of the price for chattels, and gives a list of similar items usually regarded as fittings (see SDLT Manual at Appendix VI.3).

14.14.3. The guidance provided in SDLT Bulletin 6 is neither conclusive nor finite. While the examples given relate principally to residential property, the same principles apply to non-residential property.

14.14.4. A buyer should consider whether the apportionment between price and chattels can be justified to HM Revenue and Customs on enquiry and whether any tax saved justifies possible enquiries, tax-related penalties, and interest.

14.15. Leases

14.15.1. The duty payable on a premium and on the lease rent are calculated separately (Finance Act 2003, Sched.5).

14.15.2. The duty payable on a premium paid for the grant or transfer of a lease is calculated in the same way as on a capital payment for a freehold, but the operation of the zero-rate band on the grant of a lease depends on the type of property and the level of rent under the lease. If the property is non-residential or mixed use, and the lease rent is more than £1,000 a year, all the premium is charged to SDLT at 1% or above, the zero-rate band being inapplicable. The £1,000 rule does not apply to residential property leases.

14.15.3. Although the premium may be taxed at 1% or more of the price paid, the rent under the lease will not necessarily give rise to further charge to SDLT. Lease rents continue to be separately taxed and SDLT charged either alone or as well as the SDLT levied on the premium paid.

14.15.4. Payment of a reverse premium is not chargeable consideration and is ignored for calculation of tax.

14.15.5. The total SDLT payable on grant of a lease is the sum of tax payable on premium and on rent.

SDLT on rents

14.15.6. The relevant zero-rate band (for either residential or non-residential property) may be used twice in determining the actual SDLT payable for any one lease. This will occur when the zero-rate band is applied first to calculating the tax on the premium, where either the property is wholly residential or, if the property is non-residential or mixed use, where the rent is less than £1,000 a year; and second to establish whether the Net Present Value (NPV) of the lease rents exceeds the relevant threshold. If the NPV does exceed the threshold, SDLT is charged on the rent.

14.15.7. SDLT on the excess of NPV of the rent over the relevant zero-rate band thresholds (£125,000 for residential property leases and £150,000 for non-residential property leases) is all charged at 1%.

14.15.8. As SDLT is rounded down, the excess of NPV needs to exceed £100 before the first £1 of tax is payable on lease rent. The calculation of 1% of less than £100 produces less than £1 and is therefore rounded down to nil.

Net Present Value of the lease rents

14.15.9. The Net Present Value (NPV) of a lease is the product of multiplying the rent in pounds sterling by the term in years and discounting the result by the current Treasury Discount Rate. The current Treasury Discount Rate is 3.5%. NPV is an accepted mathematical formula for calculating on principles of compound discount.

14.15.10. There are several ways of working out the NPV for rents under a lease:

    (a)   longhand, using pen, paper and HM Revenue and Customs Individual Year Factor and Cumulative Factor tables or calculator;

    (b)   using the NPV function on Microsoft Excel spreadsheet software;

    (c)   using the lease tax calculator tool on the HM Revenue and Customs website at **www.hmrc.gov.uk/so**.

14.15.11. The NPV of a lease will only be accurate if the correct number of years and rent levels are entered into the formula:

    (a)   no account is taken of either break options or rights to extend the term (Finance Act 2003, Sched.17A, para.2);

    (b)   if the term is known and is a fixed number of years, enter the number of whole years during which rent is paid;

    (c)   if the term is indefinite (e.g. a periodic tenancy), the term is deemed to be one year (Finance Act 2003, Sched.17A, para.4).

14.15.12. Calculation of the NPV of a lease involves ascertainment of the annual rent throughout the term. Rents may be unascertained, ascertainable, or certain for any period (Finance Act 2003, Sched.17A, para.7). The way in which rents are treated for the purpose of the NPV calculation varies accordingly. If the annual rent is a fixed amount, calculating the NPV should be relatively straightforward. If all or part of the rent is uncertain at the outset, complications arise.

14.15.13. Only the first five years' rental payments are relevant to the NPV calculation, since the rent for year six and beyond is taken to be equal in all cases to the highest rent payable in any consecutive 12-month period in the first five years.

14.15.14. Complications arise when the rent payable within the first five years is either uncertain, or unascertained at the outset. Where rent varies in accordance with a provision in the lease (whether by way of a fixed increase, or by the operation of a rent review), or is contingent, uncertain or unascertained (whether fixed, subject to review, or turnover), the following rules apply:

    (a)   rent for the first five years. As regards calculating the rent payable for the first five years of the term, there must be added to any fixed amount of rent made payable by the lease a reasonable estimate (as under Finance Act 2003, s.51) of any rent that is contingent, uncertain or unascertained (e.g. because the rent is wholly or partly a turnover rent, or there is an open market rent review within the first five years);

    (b)   rent for years six, seven, eight etc. As regards calculating the rent payable after the end of the fifth year of the term, the rent is to be taken in every case (even where there are later fixed increases) as being equal to the highest amount payable during any consecutive period of 12 months during the first five years of the term.

No account is to be taken for these purposes of any provision for rent to be adjusted in accordance with the retail price index.

14.15.15. HM Revenue and Customs regard the term of a lease to be its contractual term or, if shorter, the time running from the date of the grant. However, rent review dates which, as a result of this interpretation, fall within the final three months of the fifth year running from the date of the grant can be ignored (see Finance Act 2003, Sched.17A, para.7A). The commonplace backdating of the term commencement date to the quarter day immediately preceding the grant of the lease will not therefore normally result in the rent for the fifth year being partly unascertained.

14.15.16. The amount of rent used in the calculation must be increased by VAT on the rent if the landlord has made a valid option to tax prior to the effective date of the transaction, otherwise the rent is entered net into the NPV calculation. Where service charge under a lease is stated separately from the rent, only the rent is entered in the NPV calculation. Where a single figure is specified in the lease for rent, service charge and any other sums, the whole amount is included as rent for determining the NPV of the lease.

14.15.17. Using the appropriate numbers, NPV can be calculated using one of the methods suggested above to establish whether or not any lease duty is payable. Where longhand or manual calculation of NPV is preferred, the tables provided by HM Revenue and Customs for Individual Year and Cumulative Year Factors should be used:

(a) the Individual Year Factor table is used for calculating NPV during the first five years of the term where rent is unascertained at the time of the return. Rent changes for each year should be calculated separately by multiplying the rent for the year by the Individual Year Factor for that year. The results for each year are then added together to give the NPV for the period;

(b) the Cumulative Factor table is used for both fixed rent during the first five years of the term and where NPV is being calculated for the period from year six to the end of the term at a certain rent. Multiply the fixed rent by the Cumulative Factor for the appropriate number of years to give the NPV required.

14.15.18. The tables and detailed instructions for their use are given in SDLT Bulletin 6.

14.16. Further returns of SDLT on leases

14.16.1. Where the rent for any period within the first five years of the term is not certain at the outset, the NPV of the lease will initially have been calculated (and any SDLT paid) on the basis of an estimate of that rent. In such cases, a further return may need to be made within 30 days of the earlier of the date when the rent becomes certain or the fifth anniversary of the commencement of the term (Finance Act 2003, Sched.17A, para.8). A new determination of the NPV under the lease will be made in exactly the same way as for the original return, inserting the ascertained rent into the calculation. If the outcome is that the original NPV calculation was correct (because the ascertained rent matches the original estimate) nothing further is required to be done. If the outcome of the new determination is that SDLT becomes payable where none was before (e.g. because the NPV now exceeds the zero-rate threshold), or that additional SDLT becomes payable (because the actual NPV exceeds the original estimate), a further return must be filed. If the outcome results in SDLT having been overpaid on the original return (because the original estimate was excessive) a claim for a repayment can be made.

14.16.2. After the fifth anniversary of the commencement of the term, it should not normally be necessary to make further returns in respect of the original grant of a lease. However, an exception is made for abnormal rent increases occurring after the end of the fifth year of the term (Finance Act 2003, Sched.17A, para.14). Abnormal increases of rent may be due to a scheduled rent review, or may be systemic (because of, e.g. a turnover rent or royalty rent), or may simply arise because the lease is varied by agreement. In broad terms, an abnormal increase is one which sees the rent increase by more than 20% each year (so that, over a five-year period, the rent doubles). Although long rent-free periods and stepped rents may also mean that smaller increases are treated as 'abnormal', Schedule 17A, para.15 sets out a formula to determine whether a rent increase is abnormal. The effect of there being an abnormal increase is that a new lease is deemed to have been granted in consideration of the rent increase. It is treated as being linked with the original term. HM Revenue and Customs has provided an abnormal rent increase calculator at **www.hmrc.gov.uk/tools/ stamps/abnormalrentcalculator.htm**.

14.16.3. Further returns may be required after the end of the term. Special provisions under paragraphs 3 and 4 Schedule 17A Finance Act 2003 deal with leases that are granted for a fixed term and then until determination, and those granted for fixed terms that are extended by operation of law.

14.16.4. Where a lease continues after its contractual expiry date (e.g. because the tenant enjoys statutory security of tenure), it is treated as if it were a lease for the original term of years plus one year (hence a six-year lease will become a seven-year lease). If it continues beyond the first extra year, it is treated as if it were a lease for the original term of years plus two years (hence a six-year lease will become a seven-, then an eight-year lease). At the start of each additional year, a new determination of the NPV of the lease (with its added year(s)) needs to be made. If the outcome of the new determination is that the NPV of the lease now exceeds the zero-rate threshold (£150,000 in commercial property cases), SDLT becomes payable within 30 days of the start of the year. If the NPV of the lease had originally exceeded the threshold on grant (so that tax had been paid), additional tax becomes payable by virtue of the additional year(s). Where tax, or additional tax, becomes payable as a result of these rules, a tax return must be made within 30 days of the date on which the lease is treated as being for a longer term. Where a lease has been assigned, it is the assignee's responsibility to pay the additional tax, and to comply with the requirement to file returns arising out of the holding over. These rules only apply to leases that were originally subject to SDLT.

14.16.5. A lease for an indefinite term (such as a periodic tenancy) is treated at first as a lease for a term of one year. However, if the tenancy remains in place beyond the first year, it is treated in the same way as if the lease was for a fixed term that had been extended by operation of law.

14.16.6. Certain transfers and assignments of leases will trigger either a clawback or the end of relief enjoyed since grant (Finance Act 2003, Sched.17A, para.11). In those circumstances, either the transferor or transferee or both may need to make returns (Finance Act 2003, Sched.17A, para.12):

(a) the transferor will need to make an amendment return if the transfer triggers withdrawal of a relief claimed (such as a group relief or charities relief);

(b) the transferee will need to make a full return (as on grant of a lease) when on the transfer the property ceases to be entitled to the relief claimed since grant of the lease (such as charitable use or social landlord relief);

(c) a transferee's return will require a full land transaction return as at grant of lease and calculation of SDLT on both premium paid on transfer and on the lease rents. However, the NPV calculation is only for the period from the effective date of the transfer to the end of the term.

Tax is not chargeable retrospectively for the period when the tenant was eligible for the relevant relief.

14.17. Surrenders

14.17.1. The surrender of a term of years is treated as an assignment of a lease and will therefore only be a notifiable transaction if:

(a) a consideration is paid (by the landlord) exceeding the relevant zero-rate band; or

(b) the lease was originally granted for seven or more years, and a consideration is paid (by the landlord) of £40,000 or more.

In either case, the landlord will then need to make a land transaction return within 30 days of the effective date of the surrender (Finance Act 2003, Sched.17A, para.16).

14.17.2. Payment of a reverse premium by the tenant does not count as chargeable consideration (Finance Act 2003, Sched.4). A surrender made for no consideration is not a notifiable land transaction.

14.17.3. In the case of a surrender and re-grant (whether express or implied), a full land transaction return is required in relation to the re-grant as for any new grant. However, in calculating SDLT payable, a form of allowance (overlap relief) is given for the SDLT already paid in respect of the unexpired term surrendered (Finance Act 2003, Sched.17A, para.9). Overlap relief works so that, when calculating the NPV of the newly granted lease, the tenant is able to reduce the amount of rent to be brought into the calculation by deducting rents that would otherwise have been payable during the overlapping period of the surrendered and new terms. Such rents have already effectively been taxed as part of the surrendered lease and so should not be taxed again. Overlap relief only applies where the surrendered lease was itself subject to SDLT.

14.18. Leases as linked transactions

14.18.1. Leases may be linked transactions in the same way as any other land transactions and will then be subject to the aggregation of premiums paid and of rents used in calculating NPV. Only the aggregation of premium will be subject to an increase in the relevant rate of tax, since rents are taxed at a flat rate of 1%.

14.18.2. New grants of lease between the same or connected parties may be treated as linked transactions, if they form part of a single scheme, arrangement or series of transactions. Where successive leases of the same or substantially the same premises are treated as linked transactions, the successive terms take effect as a single lease (Finance Act 2003, Sched.17A, para.5).

14.19. Agreement for lease

14.19.1. An agreement for lease is a notifiable transaction if the agreement is substantially performed (e.g. the tenant takes up occupation). The date of substantial performance is the effective date of the transaction. A notional lease is treated as having been granted on the effective date on the terms of, and at the rent payable under, the actual lease. A land transaction return relating to the notional lease must be made, and tax paid, in the standard way (Finance Act 2003, Sched.17A, para.12A).

14.19.2. When completion of the lease takes place, the actual lease may need to be notified, a further return may be required, and any additional tax may be payable. The actual lease operates as a notional surrender of the notional lease. The tenant can use overlap relief (see A14.17.3) to reduce the NPV of the actual lease as if an actual surrender and re-grant had occurred. In some cases, the operation of overlap relief may reduce the NPV of the actual lease to nil, in which case the actual lease is not a notifiable land transaction.

14.20. Partnership property

14.20.1. An acquisition of land by a partnership is chargeable to SDLT in the usual way. However, measures were introduced by Finance Act 2004 to apply SDLT to certain partnership transactions which had initially been excluded from the scope of the tax. As from 23 July 2004, SDLT became chargeable in the following additional circumstances:

(a) where an interest in land is transferred into a partnership, either by an existing partner or by some other person in exchange for an interest in that partnership;

(b) where partnership property includes an interest in land and arrangements are in place so that either an existing partner transfers (for money or money's worth) all or part of his partnership interest to a person who is or becomes a partner, or a person becomes a partner and an existing partner reduces his partnership share (or ceases to be a partner) and withdraws money or money's worth from the partnership; and

(c) where a partnership transfers an interest in land to a partner or former partner.

In those circumstances, a share of the relevant partnership property is taken to have been acquired.

14.20.2. Provision is made in each case for calculating the value of the relevant share of partnership property acquired (Finance Act 2003, Sched.15, Part 3). That value is based on the proportion of market value transferred making allowance for a share already held. Formulae for calculation of tax liability according to circumstance are specified.

14.20.3. As from 19 July 2006, the provisions of A14.20.1(b) only apply to transfers of partnership shares in property investment partnerships (i.e. partnerships whose sole or main activity is in investing or dealing in interests in land). This means that transfers of partnership shares in ordinary professional partnerships are no longer chargeable to SDLT.

14.20.4. For most transfers of partnership property, general exemptions and reliefs apply, but may be subject to special rules on calculation of value.

14.21. Land transaction returns

14.21.1. Every relevant notifiable transaction must be reported to HM Revenue and Customs and the details provided in standard form.

14.21.2. Reporting transactions may be conducted in handwritten paper form only by delivering a land transaction return to HM Revenue and Customs, or electronically through the online SDLT filing service.

14.21.3. Returns comprise four separate forms for buyers to use[1] and an HM Revenue and Customs certificate. Forms SDLT1–4 comprise the self-assessment return.[2] The forms are accompanied by explanatory notes, which can be viewed and downloaded from **www.hmrc.gov.uk/so**.

14.21.4. Original paper forms SDLT1–4 and SDLT6, payslips and explanatory leaflets may be obtained from the HM Revenue and Customs order line:

HMRC Contact Centre
PO Box 37
St Austell
PL35 5YN

Tel. 0845 302 1472
Fax. 01726 201015

14.21.5. Electronic versions of SDLT1–4 and SDLT6 are also available. Alternatively, proprietary software is available for firms to generate their own forms to file online using the online filing service.

14.21.6. Except where the online service is used, the form must be signed by the buyer personally (not by his solicitor) or by the buyer's attorney. The latter must be duly appointed in writing for the specific purpose of signing SDLT declarations.

14.21.7. No documents are sent with the form.

14.21.8. The form submitted, if on paper, must be an original (not a photocopy) with a unique identifier number.

14.21.9. If the land transaction return is one of those statistically or otherwise sampled (normally within nine months of the submission of the return), it is important that the taxpayer and any agents concerned in the transaction are able to provide any requested information and documents called for by the Board of HM Revenue and Customs. For this reason alone it is important to retain workings and calculation results on file with all other documents relevant to any tax calculation for the mandatory period of six years.

1. HM Revenue and Customs have also provided non-statutory schedules for transactions involving multiple properties or subject to multiple leases which are available from their website or the Manchester Complex Transactions Unit.
2. Stamp Duty Land Tax (Administration) Regulations 2003 (SI 2003/2837).

14.22. Subsequent returns

14.22.1. Where circumstances or facts come to light after the original land transaction return has been made, as many subsequent land transaction returns as necessary must be submitted. For example, a further return must be submitted for each subsequent linked transaction or for the draw down of each parcel of land. Each subsequent return must be signed by the buyer declaring its truth and completeness (Finance Act 2003, s.81A).

14.22.2. On each occasion, tax must be recalculated and consideration for all elements of the series of transactions aggregated: total tax recalculated, credit given for tax already paid and the balance tendered.

14.23. Price unascertainable

14.23.1. Where the price to be paid under a chargeable transaction is uncertain or contingent and all or some part of the price will not be paid until more than six months after the effective date, the buyer may apply to HM Revenue and Customs to defer payment (Finance Act 2003, s.90). While application to defer is pending, the buyer should make a return, but need not pay SDLT on the deferred amount. On notification of the decision by HM Revenue and Customs, payment should be made in accordance with the decision unless an appeal is lodged against the decision. Otherwise the terms of the decision should be complied with in all respects for original and amendment or further returns.

14.24. The forms

14.24.1. Form SDLT1 is required for every notifiable transaction. For most residential and simple non-residential land transactions comprising freehold only or not reporting a new lease, only form SDLT1 will need to be completed. On form SDLT1, financial statistics for the transaction are given and the self-assessed tax is declared.

14.24.2. Form SDLT2 is required where there are more than two sellers or two buyers. A separate form SDLT2 is required for each additional party. Form SDLT2 must be signed by the buyer named in it. Additional sellers do not need to sign, although their details must be supplied to HM Revenue and Customs.

14.24.3. Form SDLT3 may be required to provide full information about the land transferred and a separate form SDLT3 will be required for each additional parcel of land after the first. The first parcel is reported on SDLT1, but may be continued in form SDLT3 if space is insufficient.

14.24.4. SDLT4 is the form on which further details of complex and commercial transactions are reported, including sales of companies where part of the price is apportioned to land. The form is also used for reporting details of new leases granted and for additional data for corporate buyers.

14.24.5. A SDLT payslip and payment of tax must accompany any land transaction return. If payment is made by cheque, the cheque must state the SDLT1/payslip unique identifier number.

14.24.6. SDLT6 is the explanatory notes booklet which accompanies the forms to assist in their completion. Online guidance is also available.

14.25. Submission of the forms

14.25.1. The completed land transaction return, comprising SDLT1 and such of forms SDLT 2–4 as are necessary, is sent to the HM Revenue and Customs Data Capture Centre (see Appendix IX.2 for address). Returns should be submitted only to the address specified on form SDLT1 and in accordance with those instructions.

14.25.2. For the data capture facility to work, SDLT forms, payslips and cheques should not be folded or stapled. Only original form SDLT1 and payslips may be submitted, although forms SDLT2–4 may be copied. Data should be aligned within the boxes in the forms to ensure forms can be scanned and to avoid automatic rejection of the return.

14.25.3. When HM Revenue and Customs is satisfied that a land transaction return has been made and the details are not manifestly inaccurate or the tax incorrect, the taxpayer or his agent will be issued with an HM Revenue and Customs certificate in form SDLT 5. This certificate acknowledges receipt of the return, but is not conclusive evidence either that the return is correct or that liability to SDLT has been satisfied. Certificates are issued without prejudice to the HM Revenue and Customs enquiry and enforcement powers available to the Board.

14.25.4. Where the online filing service is used, HM Revenue and Customs issue an electronic SDLT 5 certificate. Online filing of a tax return generates a receipt which is sent online within a few minutes. This can be printed for submission to HM Land Registry with the application for registration.

14.25.5. The buyer may stipulate that the HM Revenue and Customs certificate is returned to him, or to the property address, or to a specified agent.

14.25.6. It is important that both taxpayer and agent retain copies of land transaction return certificates and forms for future reference and in case of requests for production.

14.26. **Amendment returns**

14.26.1. When a taxpayer or any other person concerned in the preparation or submission of a land transaction return becomes aware of a factual inaccuracy in a return (e.g. that the return is incorrect, incomplete, or that the tax has been overpaid or underpaid or assessed), the taxpayer must make an amendment return within 30 days. Compliance, penalty and enforcement provisions apply to amendment returns as for original land transaction returns (Finance Act 2003, s.80).

14.27. **Keeping records**

14.27.1. From the outset of the transaction, it is advisable to ensure that full records of transactions are maintained. There is a duty to keep and preserve records to enable a complete and correct land transaction return or claim[1] to be made and delivered.[2] The documents which should be retained include:

    (a)   all materials relating to valuation and/or price;

    (b)   all documents and information relating to apportionments for chattels;

 (c) accounts records for funds received and disbursed;

 (d) documents demonstrating allowable costs;

 (e) calculations for assessment of SDLT.

14.27.2. All documents relevant to a SDLT transaction and necessary for determination of value and assessment of the tax may be required by HM Revenue and Customs for enquiry purposes.[3] The required records must be retained for a minimum of six years after either any enquiry has been completed or HM Revenue and Customs no longer has the power to enquire into the return, usually nine months after the SDLT filing date.

14.27.3. Once completed, the land transaction return forms should be copied and the copies retained. On-screen and online forms lend themselves to electronic archiving.

14.27.4. All documents relevant to a SDLT transaction and return must be retained for a minimum of six years. This duty applies to all persons concerned with the relevant land transaction. Even in a straightforward purchase of a residential property, there may be issues of valuation and apportionment of chattels which necessitate the retention of specific information. A paper record of all monetary movements within the transaction or a confirmed electronic accounts record should be included in the retained documentation.

14.27.5. In practice, retention of the whole file, including accounts records and copies of the land transaction return forms, payslip and certificate, may be an easier alternative.

14.27.6. The duty to retain documents, in either paper or electronic form extends to all persons concerned in a transaction. The duty extends to specifically proscribing destruction of documents.

14.27.7. The penalty for failure to keep records is £3,000 unless HM Revenue and Customs is satisfied that the information contained in the destroyed documents can be proved by other documentary evidence (section 93).

1. Finance Act 2003, Sched.11A, Part 3.
2. Finance Act 2003, Sched.10, para.9 and Sched.11, Part 2.
3. Finance Act 2003, Sched.10 and Sched.11, Part 2.

14.28. Refunds

14.28.1. Claims for refunds not made in a return can be made by letter and the claimant must maintain all supporting evidential and transactional records to substantiate the claim (Finance Act 2003, Sched.11A, para.2).

14.29. Acting as the buyer's agent and acting for the lender

14.29.1. The taxpayer must consent to the appointment of an agent and for HM Revenue and Customs to conduct correspondence about the land transaction return with the agent. This consent is given on form SDLT1.

14.29.2. The question of agency has several implications for solicitors:

(a) does the solicitor necessarily know enough about the buyer's affairs to be able to conduct correspondence with HM Revenue and Customs for SDLT purposes?

(b) can the solicitor be sure that he acts for the client in all relevant transactions?

(c) has any necessary disclosure been full and frank?

If the answer to any question is not an unequivocal affirmative, it may be sensible for the solicitor to decline to act as the client's agent.

14.29.3. Where there are multiple buyers, deciding whether or not it is appropriate to act as an agent may be even more difficult.

14.29.4. Where the solicitor acts only for the lender and not for the buyer, a decision must be made concerning the administration of submitting the land transaction return, receiving the certificate and submission of any Land Registry applications. The options open to the lender and the lender's solicitor are:

(a) lender's solicitor acts as buyer's agent;

(b) lender permits buyer's solicitor to act as its agent for making the land transaction return, obtaining the certificate, with or without also making the Land Registry application;

(c) lender's solicitor acts as buyer's agent only for limited purpose of submitting the completed land transaction return and obtaining the certificate.

14.29.5. Whichever of the alternatives is adopted by the lender, the lender's solicitor will need to ensure that the buyer and/or his solicitor fully understand(s) what is required of each party and gives any necessary undertakings. In particular, the lender's solicitor will need to ensure that he undertakes no obligation or liability in connection with any tax affairs of the buyer and that this is clear to both the buyer and his solicitor and to HM Revenue and Customs.

14.30. Land Registry applications

14.30.1. No document effecting or evidencing a notifiable land transaction may (unless exempt from certification) be registered at the Land Registry, recorded or reflected in an entry in the register without a certificate as to compliance with SDLT (Finance Act 2003, s.79). See Land Registry Practice Guide 49 for details of the Registry's cancellation policy.

14.30.2. The Land Registry does not require any evidence as to compliance with SDLT in respect of the registration of any matter relating to a land transaction completed on or after 12 March 2008 if the transaction is not a notifiable land transaction. The former practice of submitting a SDLT60 form (self-certificate as to compliance) with the application for registration was discontinued on that date.

14.30.3. The fact that a transaction is not registrable at the Land Registry does not preclude a subsequent HM Revenue and Customs enquiry into the transaction. In such a case, it is advisable for the buyer to retain records in relation to the transaction for at least six years.

14.31. Enforcement and penalties

14.31.1. HM Revenue and Customs may enquire into any land transaction return. To instigate an enquiry it must give notice of the enquiry to the buyer within nine months after the actual date of filing the return or within nine months after the last amendment was made.

14.31.2. The enquiry may extend to whether tax is chargeable or whether the transaction was chargeable or notifiable and to the amount of tax chargeable (Finance Act 2003, Sched.10, para.12).

14.31.3. On at least 30 days' notice, HM Revenue and Customs can require the buyer to produce documents for the purpose of the enquiry, but the documents must be within the taxpayer's possession or power and may normally be copies unless HM Revenue and Customs, by notice, requires originals. HM Revenue and Customs may specify the information and form as it reasonably requires. However, the buyer is not obliged to provide information or documents relating to any pending appeal by him or referral to the Special Commissioners to which he is a party.

14.31.4. The penalty for failure to produce documents on notice is £50 and either £30 a day determined by an officer of the Board or £150 a day if determined by the Court (Finance Act 2003, Sched.11, para.16).

14.31.5. During an enquiry the taxpayer may amend his land transaction return. The amendments will take effect unless HM Revenue and Customs in its notice of closure of enquiry states that the amendments have been taken into account. If so, the notice of closure specifying liability of the buyer applies.

14.31.6. Authorised HM Revenue and Customs officers have the power to call in writing for documents and information which are reasonably required to establish tax liability or the amount of tax due from a taxpayer (Finance Act 2003, Sched.13). Documents and information may be required from:

(a) the taxpayer, including companies which have ceased to exist and deceased taxpayers (within six years after the death);

(b) a third party (but not more than six years after the taxpayer's death);

(c) a tax accountant in relation to clients' tax affairs (if the tax accountant has been convicted of a tax offence or had a SDLT penalty imposed);

(d) an auditor or tax adviser when acting as tax accountant (disclosing advice to or identity of client/taxpayer and not disclosed to HM Revenue and Customs elsewhere).

14.31.7. HM Revenue and Customs must adhere to the limitations of its power to call for information so that:

(a) notices to barristers, advocates and solicitors must be made by HM Revenue and Customs Board (not an authorised officer) where information is required from them as a third party or tax accountant;

(b) the person must be given a reasonable opportunity to make documents and information available before HM Revenue and Customs applies to Commissioners for consent to issue notice;

(c) where notice is served on any other person, a copy must be given to the taxpayer.

14.31.8. Documents and information outside the scope of an HM Revenue and Customs notice (Finance Act 2003, Sched.13, Part 4) include:

(a) personal and journalistic material;

(b) documents relating to a pending tax appeal;

(c) documents more than six years old at the date of the notice;

(d) documents subject to legal privilege;

(e) auditors' and tax advisers' own papers in connection with acting under a statutory appointment.

14.31.9. To obtain information relating to the tax liability and amount of tax due, the Board of HM Revenue and Customs may:

(a) give any person written notice (in prescribed form) requiring delivery of documents and information;

(b) obtain a court order for delivery of documents where reasonably believing a serious fraud has been committed; or

(c) on oath obtain a warrant (expiring after 14 days) to enter and search premises, with force if necessary.

Offences and penalties

14.31.10. Contravening the provisions of the Finance Act is a criminal offence.

14.31.11. The most serious of the offences created under Finance Act 2003 is fraudulent evasion of tax for which the sanctions are:

    (a)   on summary conviction – imprisonment for a maximum of six months or a fine up to the statutory maximum or both; and

    (b)   on conviction on indictment – imprisonment for a maximum of seven years or an unlimited fine or both (Finance Act 2003, s.95).

14.31.12. There is a lesser offence of assisting preparation or delivery of incorrect information, return, or other document knowing that it is incorrect and likely to be used for tax purposes. This does not need to result in non-payment or under-payment of SDLT and the penalty is a maximum fine of £3,000 (Finance Act 2003, s.96).

14.31.13. The offences relating to documents are:

    (a)   falsification, concealment or destruction of documents or information; and

    (b)   causing or permitting falsification, concealment or destruction.

14.31.14. The sanctions for offences relating to documents are:

    (a)   on summary conviction – a fine of up to the statutory maximum;

    (b)   on conviction on indictment – imprisonment for a maximum of two years or an unlimited fine or both.

14.31.15. Defences for document related offences are:

    (a)   acting more than two years after notice or order was made and HM Revenue and Customs has not notified of unsatisfactory compliance; and

    (b)   acting more than six months after HM Revenue and Customs requested information and the HM Revenue and Customs Board has refused consent to serve notice.

Tax payments, tax underpayments and penalties

14.31.16. There is a regime of penalties for various failures by the taxpayer unless with reasonable excuse, in which case HM Revenue and Customs may allow extra time to effect the necessary act (Finance Act 2003, s.97). The defaults within the scope of the penalties include: late delivery of returns, non-payment or under-payment of tax, or failure to amend. Penalties are without prejudice to any criminal proceedings and civil penalties and criminal sanctions are cumulative (Finance Act 2003, s.99).

14.31.17. The penalties for late submission of land transaction returns (Finance Act 2003, Sched.10) are as follows:

    (a)   up to three months late: £100;

    (b)   more than three months late: £200;

    (b)   more than 12 months late: flat-rate penalty and tax-related penalty up to amount of tax due (so the total may be double tax and flat-rate penalty).

14.31.18. The penalty for submitting an incorrect return applies where the land transaction return is incorrect or is not corrected. If the original return is fraudulently or negligently made or correction is not made in a reasonable time, the buyer is liable to a tax-related penalty not exceeding the amount of the underpayment.

14.31.19. Interest is payable both by the taxpayer on late payments and underpayments, but also by HM Revenue and Customs on repayments of SDLT. The tax must be paid at the time of making a land transaction return, whether the original return, an amendment return, a return on withdrawal of relief or a further return in respect of lease rents (Finance Act 2003, s.86). Penalties to which the buyer is liable must also be paid when submitting the return. Payment is treated as having been made on the day it was received by HM Revenue and Customs where a cheque is tendered and is paid on first presentation to the paying bank (Finance Act 2003, s.92).

14.31.20. Interest is payable at the applicable rate on unpaid tax and penalties for the period from 30 days after the latest date for submission of the relevant return until the date of payment (Finance Act 2003, ss.87 and 88). HM Revenue and Customs pays interest at the applicable rate on repayment of tax and penalties for the period from the date the funds were lodged with it to the date of repayment (Finance Act 2003, s.89).

14.32. Stamp duty

14.32.1. There are only two occasions when land transaction documents must still be produced to HM Revenue and Customs:

    (a)   documents witnessing a transaction subject to stamp duty and completing after 1 December 2003 under Stamp Act 1891 as amended; and

    (b)   documents which should have been stamped under the Stamp Act regime and are required to be produced in evidence and/or where the court does not exercise its discretion to admit.

14.32.2. Finance Act 2003 does not repeal the former stamp duty legislation nor is it superseded for all transactions. Those transactions which were historically stamp duty transactions at the making of the contract do not become transactions subject to SDLT merely through the passing of time.

14.32.3. Transactions which were not completed before 1 December 2003 and which are the culmination of contracts entered into under the stamp duty regime remain so, unless some action is taken to alter or novate the contract. This action only affects SDLT liability if taken on or after the first relevant date for contracts on sale, or on or after 17 April 2003 for grants of options or rights of pre-emption.

14.32.4. Documents evidencing those transactions still subject to stamp duty remain subject to submission to HM Revenue and Customs for adjudication, production or impress. Submission of documents for stamping should be accompanied by forms L(A)451 delivering particulars of the transaction, Stamps 61 and payment. Where the transaction comprises land and other assets, the declaration of apportionment of price between the land and other assets continues to be made on form Stamps 22 (see Appendix VI.2).

14.33. Certificates of value

14.33.1. Transitional documents still requiring production to the HM Revenue and Customs (see A14.32) whose consideration is below the zero-rate band threshold still require the relevant certificate of value.

14.33.2. Transactions still subject to stamp duty (see A14.32) will also be subject to the rate bands relevant for the date of the contract when calculating stamp duty payable.

14.33.3. Where the transaction is subject to SDLT, a certificate of value will not be required. The land transaction return will contain all the information required to ascertain the value and appropriate rate of tax, even if this is 0%. A certificate will still be issued by HM Revenue and Customs in the usual way.

A15. Capital Gains Tax

15.1. Liability to CGT	**15.4.** Business premises
15.2. The principal private dwelling house exemption	**15.5.** Charities
15.3. Chargeable gains	**15.6.** Time of disposal

15.1. Liability to CGT

15.1.1. A liability to CGT may arise on the disposal of an interest in land. A seller's solicitor should be aware of the possibility of potential liability and advise his client accordingly. Similarly, a buyer who is purchasing property other than for use as his principal private dwelling should be made aware of potential tax liability which may be incurred in his subsequent disposal of the property.

15.1.2. The definition of 'chargeable assets' within Taxation of Chargeable Gains Tax Act 1992 includes an interest in the proceeds of sale of land held by co-owners. Thus a disposition by a beneficial joint owner of his equitable interest in land could give rise to a charge to CGT.[1]

15.1.3. Some transactions which are incidental to the sale of land also give rise to a charge to CGT, e.g. where a separate payment is made for the release or modification of an easement or covenant.

15.1.4. For the purposes of the Act, a sale and leaseback transaction is technically treated as two separate disposals, but in practice HM Revenue and Customs may regard them as one, namely the part disposal of land by the seller of the freehold.

15.1.5. Subject to certain reliefs, gifts fall within the meaning of 'disposal'.

1. *Kidson* v. *Macdonald* [1974] Ch 339.

15.2. The principal private dwelling house exemption

15.2.1. The disposal of an individual's principal private dwelling house including garden or grounds is exempt from CGT. Up to 0.5 hectare (including the site of the house) is within the exemption.[1]

15.2.2. To qualify for the exemption the seller must have lived in the dwelling house as his only or main residence throughout his period of ownership. A degree of permanence and expectation of continuity is required for the exemption to be claimable. A short period of residence (e.g. of a few months) may not qualify for relief.[2]

15.2.3. Certain periods of absence are disregarded when deciding the question of residence:[3]

(a) the last 36 months of ownership;

(b) by extra-statutory concession, the first 12 months of ownership (in order to facilitate the sale of another property). If there are good reasons for this period exceeding one year, which are outside the individual's control, it will be extended up to a maximum of two years;

(c) any period(s) not exceeding three years in total throughout the period of ownership. Absence within this exception may be for any reason, e.g. an extended holiday and can be made up of several separate periods of absence provided that the total under this exception does not exceed three years;

(d) any period(s) during which the individual was working outside the UK. This exception applies to employees only, not to self-employed persons;

(e) any period(s) not exceeding four years in total during which the individual was prevented from living in his dwelling house because he was required by his conditions of employment to live elsewhere. This exception would be applicable, e.g. to a headmaster who was required to live in accommodation provided by the school, or to an employee who was temporarily seconded to a branch office beyond commuting distance from his home.

15.2.4. The periods of absence outlined above are cumulative, and if exceeded a proportion of the exemption relative to the length of the absence in proportion to the length of ownership of the property will be lost and the non-exempt part chargeable to CGT.

15.2.5. Where a dwelling house has grounds of more than 0.5 hectare, the excess is prima facie taxable, but HM Revenue and Customs have a discretion to allow land in excess of 0.5 hectare to be included within the principal private dwelling house exemption if the extra land can be shown to be necessary for the reasonable enjoyment of the house.

15.2.6. The sale of land alone, where the ownership of the house is retained, enjoys the benefit of the exemption so long as the land sold does not exceed 0.5 hectare. It should be noted that if the house is sold and land retained, a subsequent sale of the land will usually attract CGT.

Duality of user

15.2.7. Where part of a principal private dwelling house is used for business purposes, e.g. a doctor who has a consulting room in his home, a proportion of the exemption may be lost, relative to the area of the 'business premises' in relation to the total area of the dwelling house. If, however, a 'duality of user' can be shown, the full exemption may be available. Thus a person who works from home, but who does not have a separate room for his business which the other members of the family are prohibited from entering, may still take full advantage of the principal private dwelling house exemption.

15.2.8. Only one exemption is available to married couples. Where a married couple own more than one house an election must be made as to which property is to take the benefit of the exemption. An election in respect of one property is not irrevocable and can be switched, e.g. if it appears that one property is increasing in value at a faster rate than the other.

15.2.9. The principal private dwelling house exemption is available where the disposal is made by trustees provided that the person in occupation of the property was a person who was entitled to be in occupation under the terms of the settlement, e.g. a tenant for life.[4]

15.2.10. Tenants in common may be liable for CGT on their respective shares in the equitable interest in the property.

15.2.11. An individual who buys his dwelling house in the name of a company will not be able to claim the principal private dwelling house exemption.

1. Taxation of Chargeable Gains Act 1992, s.222.
2. *Goodwin* v. *Curtis*, *The Times*, 14 August 1996.
3. Taxation of Chargeable Gains Act 1992, s.223.
4. Taxation of Chargeable Gains Act 1992, s.28(1) and (2).

15.3. Chargeable gains

15.3.1. Any gain is chargeable at the highest rate at which the individual pays income tax, subject to the availability of proper relief. Corporations pay CGT at the corporation tax rate applicable to them, subject to roll-over relief. Separate taxation is applied to married couples; each spouse therefore has his or her own annual allowance for CGT purposes.

Guidelines

15.3.2. When taking instructions from an individual in relation to the sale of a dwelling house, the answers to the following four questions will indicate to the solicitor whether there is likely to be a CGT liability on the property. If the client's answers to all the questions set out below match the suggested answers, there is unlikely to be a CGT liability arising out of the transaction. If any of the client's answers differ from those suggested, further enquiries should be raised with the client.

1. Question: Did you move into the house immediately after you bought it?
   Answer: Yes.

2.   Question: Have you lived anywhere else since moving into this house?
     Answer: No.
3.   Question: Does the house and the garden cover more than 0.5 hectare?
     Answer: No.

(The answer to this question may already be apparent from the estate agent's particulars of the property.)

4.   Question: Do you own another house?
     Answer: No.

15.4.   Business premises

15.4.1.   Subject to certain reliefs, business premises are subject to CGT. The matter should be referred to the client's accountant for him to check the correct apportionment of the purchase price as between the property and any goodwill paid for the business.

15.5.   Charities

15.5.1.   Generally charities are exempt from CGT.

15.6.   Time of disposal

15.6.1.   The time of disposal of the property affects the year of assessment for the calculation of gains and losses for CGT purposes. A disposal of an interest in land is made at the time of the contract and not at the later time of completion.[1] However, no charge to tax arises unless the contract is completed, since until completion there will have been no disposal within the tax. Where a contract is conditional, the disposal is made at the time when the contract becomes unconditional, or in the case of an option, when it is exercised.[2] See Taxation of Chargeable Gains Act 1992, s.144 for more about options and in particular the treatment of a payment for the grant of an option.

1.   Taxation of Chargeable Gains Act 1992, s.28(1).
2.   Taxation of Chargeable Gains Act 1992, s.28(2).

A16. Value Added Tax

16.1. VAT on property transactions

The charge to tax

16.1.1. VAT at standard rate has been chargeable on certain commercial property transactions since 1 April 1989. Non-compliance with the legislation (where relevant) will involve the client in heavy penalties and interest payments, as well as unforeseen VAT liability. An exempt transaction can have implications for recovery of input tax incurred up to 10 years prior to the transaction. It is therefore essential that the relevance of VAT to a transaction is considered at an early stage and the client advised accordingly.

16.1.2. Generally VAT will not be chargeable on transactions involving residential property but may be relevant to both freehold and leasehold commercial property and to land. This chapter does not deal with problems associated with the self-supply of services.

16.2. Residential property

16.2.1. The sale of an existing building (i.e. not new) which is a dwelling or is used for a qualifying residential purpose or qualifying charitable purpose is generally exempt from VAT. However, zero-rating may apply if it:

- has been empty for 10 years or more and has just been renovated; or

- has just been converted from a non-residential building; or

- is a protected building and has undergone a substantial reconstruction; or

- is a first grant of a major interest (freehold or lease if over 21 years) in a new dwelling, or a building for use for 'qualifying residential purposes' or 'qualifying charitable purposes'.

The detailed conditions for zero-rating must be met. The benefit of zero-rating is that VAT on costs may be recovered, whereas with an exempt transaction, it may not.

16.2.2.   The Standard Conditions of Sale provide that all sums payable under the contract are exclusive of VAT, and in the case of residential property no further provisions as to VAT are normally necessary.

16.2.3.   'Qualifying residential purposes' include premises which are used as a hospice; accommodation for the armed forces; a children's home; a care home; and the accommodation element of a residential school, a monastery or nunnery and any other residential premises which is the sole or main residence of at least 90% of its residents. Specifically excluded from this category are hospitals, prisons and hotels or similar accommodation. 'Qualifying charitable purposes' include use as a village hall or similar, or use by a charity otherwise than in the course or furtherance of a business.

Supply of construction work

16.2.4.   The construction or development of new dwellings, qualifying residential or qualifying charitable property is zero-rated. A garage built at the same time as the dwelling for use with it will usually also benefit from zero-rating. Services supplied to a registered housing association for the conversion of a non-residential building are also zero-rated. Work of converting a non-residential property into residential property and of converting, for example, a house into flats, and renovation of a dwelling which has been empty for two years or more, is chargeable at the 5% rate.

16.2.5.   Holiday, and other similar accommodation, can fall within the zero-rated category, even where there are restrictions on its occupation. However, care needs to be taken and if the property is not designed as a dwelling then the construction will be standard-rated.

16.2.6.   A residential developer, building new houses and flats for sale, will be able to recover his input tax (e.g. on agents', solicitors', architects' and other professional fees) since the sale of a major interest in his property to a private buyer will be zero-rated. The buyer pays no VAT on his purchase. The same position applies to sales of substantially reconstructed listed buildings and the first sale of buildings converted into residential from non-residential property. It should be noted that certain purchases, including white goods, fitted furniture except in kitchens, and carpets, are specifically blocked for input tax recovery purposes in the hands of a developer. The builder must charge VAT at standard rate to the developer on these types of goods, even if the project is otherwise zero-rated.

16.2.7.   Subsequent sales by private individuals or commercial organisations will be exempt from VAT.

16.2.8. Owners of residential accommodation who did not construct the building in question, and who subsequently sell the building in the course of a business, will be making an exempt supply with no right to opt to tax.

Change of use

16.2.9. If the use of a building designed as a dwelling is subsequently changed to non-residential use, this has no immediate VAT consequences. In the case of a building intended for a qualifying residential purpose as defined above (i.e. a communal residential building) or qualifying charitable (non-business) use, then HM Revenue and Customs will require the owner to satisfy them that qualifying non-residential or non-charitable use is intended, at the time of purchase or construction, for the following 10 years. HM Revenue and Customs announced on 1 July 2009 that they were withdrawing an 'extra statutory concession' which previously allowed 10% business use of a charitable property and that from 1 July 2010, if a property is not used at least 95% for non-business purposes then a self supply charge will arise. See Business Brief 08/09 issued by HM Revenue and Customs.

16.3. Mixed developments

16.3.1. Where only part of a building qualifies for zero-rating, e.g. a shop with a residential flat above, the non-zero-rated element of the building construction (in the example given, the shop) will be standard rated and a supply of the property will either be exempt or standard rated, subject to an option to tax, or if the building is under three years old and the transaction is the freehold sale. The proceeds received from the development must be apportioned between the two differently rated parts of the building on a fair and equitable basis. There is no set method for determining apportionment of common areas of the building, e.g. foundations and roof, although any fair and reasonable method will usually be accepted.

16.4. Land

16.4.1. The sale of a freehold interest in land (without buildings or civil engineering works on it), grant of a lease, or of a licence is generally exempt from VAT, subject to the right in most cases (except outright sales of freeholds in new buildings or civil engineering works under three years old which are standard rated in any case) to exercise the option to tax. The grant of certain short term rights over land, such as car parking, mooring of boats, storage of aircraft, sporting rights over land, or the right to fell and remove standing timber and certain other supplies listed in Item 1, Group 1, Schedule 9 VATA 1994 attract VAT at the standard rate.

16.5.   Commercial property

16.5.1.   The freehold sale of a new building (within three years of the date of completion) is standard rated (see A16.6). Other dealings with commercial property are exempt subject to the option to tax. If the option to tax has been exercised and notified to HM Revenue and Customs within 30 days the standard rate will apply, or if the property is a new freehold to which the compulsory standard rate charge applies on a mandatory basis. The sale of a let property by a VAT-registered seller to a VAT-registered buyer may be treated as the sale of a business as a going concern, so that VAT will not be chargeable, provided that the buyer opts to tax the property and notifies HM Revenue and Customs prior to the tax point for the transaction. In addition, the buyer must notify the seller that his option to tax is not subject to the statutory block under paragraph 12, Schedule 10 VATA 1994. Clearance for transfer of a going concern transaction is not generally provided by HM Revenue and Customs for straightforward transactions and reference should be made to HM Revenue and Customs VAT Notice 700/9. It is advisable for the seller to ensure the buyer provides evidence of having opted to tax by the relevant date, and the buyer will also require to see that the seller has opted to tax.

16.5.2.   The Standard Commercial Property Conditions, Second Edition, provide as a standard provision that the sale of the property is exempt from VAT and that the seller will not exercise the option to tax. However, optional provisions are also included enabling the contract to provide for the sale to be standard-rated for VAT or to be treated as a transfer of a going concern (see A16.16).

16.6.   Freehold sales of new commercial buildings

16.6.1.   Every freehold sale of a new commercial property (including civil engineering works) before it is completed and within the first three years after its completion attracts VAT at standard rate unless a sale as a transfer of a property letting business as a going concern can be arranged – see A16.16.

16.6.2.   'Completion' of the building is either the date of the architect's certificate of practical completion or the date when the building was first fully occupied, whichever first occurs.

16.6.3.   The buyer of such a building must therefore raise additional enquiries of the seller in order to ascertain whether the transaction (and any subsequent disposal of the building by the buyer) will attract VAT and the parties must agree on the contractual provisions which are to be inserted relating to the payment of VAT.

Guidelines

16.6.4.   (a)   Matters to be considered on taking instructions:

        (i)   will the sale be a standard rated supply so that VAT will be chargeable (whether as a 'new' commercial building or as a result of the option to tax having been exercised)?

(ii) if not, what evidence (if any) is needed to satisfy HM Revenue and Customs that the sale will be an exempt or zero-rated supply or a transfer of a going concern?

(iii) if the sale is exempt from VAT, is the building subject to the Capital Items Scheme (was the building purchased, constructed, renovated or fitted out by the seller, or predecessor, within the last 10 years at a cost in excess of £250,000 plus VAT)?

(b) Additional enquiries:

(If the contract requires the buyer to pay VAT he will want to be certain that VAT is chargeable and will also wish to have evidence to establish whether or not there is a mandatory charge to VAT on a subsequent sale. If the contract does not require the buyer to pay VAT he may be inclined not to raise the issue with the seller, but he should still ensure that the supply is in fact an exempt supply and that he has sufficient evidence to establish that a future sale by him will be exempt.)

(i) why does the seller consider that the sale is a standard-rated supply?

(ii) please provide a copy of the architect's certificate of practical completion;

(iii) when was the building first fully occupied?

(iv) what evidence is available to verify the date when the building was first fully occupied?

(v) please confirm that if VAT is paid on completion the seller will at that time deliver a VAT invoice to the buyer;

(vi) has the seller previously opted to tax or does he intend to do so before completion?

(vii) if the answer to question (vi) is 'yes', please confirm that the exercise of the option to tax has been or will be notified to HM Revenue and Customs within 30 days of its being made. The buyer's solicitor should request a copy of the option to tax document and of the letter of notification to ascertain the extent of the land to which the option will apply and to check that it is valid. It should also be noted that it is HM Revenue and Customs' policy to acknowledge receipt of an option to tax and this can therefore be acceptable evidence;

(viii) if the purchase is by way of a transfer of a going concern, is the building subject to the capital items scheme? If so, please provide details of the initial deduction or subsequent adjustments, if any. See also A16.8.20.

(Note that if the seller agrees not to charge VAT, the contract should either specify that the price stated is inclusive of any VAT or should expressly provide that the seller has not opted to tax in respect of the property and agrees not to do so.)

(c) The deposit:

If the seller's solicitor receives the deposit in the capacity of 'agent for the seller', a VAT tax point arises on exchange of contracts in relation to the amount of the deposit. If the deposit is held as 'stakeholder' the tax point for both the deposit and the balance of the purchase price will not arise until completion. This can be particularly important when dealing with the transfer of a going concern rules (see A16.16), or purchase of a property at auction.

16.6.5. A special condition on the printed version of the Standard Conditions of Sale Form provides that the sale is exclusive of VAT (see Appendix III.5).

16.7. Commercial leases

16.7.1. Commercial leases are normally treated as giving rise to exempt supplies by the landlord to the tenant, and no VAT will be payable on the premium or rent unless the landlord has exercised his option to tax in respect of the building on or before completion or before rent is paid (or invoiced if earlier). If the landlord exercises that option, he must account to HM Revenue and Customs for VAT on the rent from all tenants of the building whether or not he obtains that VAT from the tenant. The landlord will normally want the tenant to pay the VAT, but whether the tenant will be liable to do so depends upon the date and wording of the lease. If the landlord makes the option to tax after the grant of the lease, he can compel the tenant to pay VAT in addition to the rent unless there is anything in the lease to the contrary (and for this purpose a contrary provision must expressly refer to VAT; a general reference to the tenant not being liable to pay for tax on rent will not preclude the landlord from holding the tenant liable to pay the VAT).[1] Conversely, where a lease is granted after the landlord has opted to tax the building, the rent specified in the lease will be inclusive of VAT unless the lease states otherwise.[2] If the landlord exercises his option to tax during the term of a lease which expressly exonerates the tenant from paying VAT, or exercises his option and then grants a lease which is silent as to VAT, the landlord will have to account to HM Revenue and Customs for VAT as if the rent payable by the tenant was inclusive of VAT, i.e. with VAT at 17.5%, seven forty-sevenths of the rent will be regarded as VAT.

16.7.2. Any lease which might be subject to VAT should contain a covenant by the tenant to pay to the landlord any VAT chargeable on the rent or on any payment made under the lease in addition to the rent. The clause should also provide that in any situation where the tenant is required by the lease to reimburse the landlord for expenditure incurred by the landlord, e.g. for insurance premiums or service charge, the tenant should also reimburse any VAT paid by the landlord in respect of those payments unless VAT on those payments is recoverable by the landlord. Generally the VAT treatment of the service charge follows the rent, i.e. if the rent is standard rated, so is the service charge.

16.7.3. Where in a lease a landlord has covenanted not to opt to tax during the currency of the lease, that covenant, being personal in nature, may not be binding on a subsequent purchaser of the reversion unless a direct covenant has been entered into by that purchaser. It is therefore safer for the tenant to negotiate a lease which includes a covenant given by the landlord that he will undertake to obtain a non-opting covenant from any buyer.

Exempt tenants

16.7.4. If the tenant of a lease makes exempt supplies he will be seriously disadvantaged by having to pay VAT on his rent (since he will not be able to recover some or all of that VAT). An exempt tenant in a market dominated by taxable tenants should consider taking a valuer's advice about the consequences of the VAT implications in his lease.

Guidelines

16.7.5.   (a) 'Options to tax' checklist for landlords:

Consider:

(i)   how much irrecoverable VAT has the landlord incurred/does the landlord incur?

(ii)   the VAT status of tenants/potential tenants/purchasers;

(iii) the short- and long-term consequences of exercising an option which is only revocable in limited circumstances (generally within six months, provided that no input tax has been recovered or output tax charged or after 20 years in both cases with the written permission of HM Revenue and Customs – with effect from 1 June 2008 the option to tax will automatically be revoked if a relevant interest in the land or property has not been held within the last six years);

(iv)   the consequences of agreeing a premium rent with an exempt tenant;

(v)   the costs of any additional administration which would be incurred in collecting VAT and issuing VAT invoices.

(b) Reminders for tenants:

(i)   check whether or not VAT is included in the rent;

(ii)   remember that if the lease is silent section 89 VATA 1994 could apply;

(iii) if the tenant makes taxable supplies only, the main adverse consequence of paying VAT on his rent may be a cash flow disadvantage, set against which there may also be cash benefits for the tenant, e.g. the recovery of VAT on his service charge payments;

(iv) if the tenant makes exempt or mainly exempt supplies he may be seriously disadvantaged by having to pay VAT on his rent since he will not be able to recover some or all of that VAT.

Purchases subject to leases

16.7.6. The leases to which the property is subject should be checked to discover whether the buyer will be able to charge VAT should he wish to exercise his option to tax. The following matters should also be considered:

(a) does the lease expressly provide that VAT is payable in addition to rent and other payments made or consideration given by the tenant or if not will section 89 apply?

(b) will the landlord be able to recover from the tenant VAT on supplies received from a third party? or

(c) is the landlord under an obligation to attempt to recover VAT from HM Revenue and Customs before he can look to the tenant for indemnity?

(d) are all other sums referred to in the lease expressed to include any VAT which will be chargeable?

(e) are the rent review provisions adequate if the landlord decides to opt to tax?

1. Value Added Tax Act 1994, s.89(1).
2. Value Added Tax Act 1994, s.89(2).

16.8. **The option to tax**

16.8.1. Where a transaction involving a commercial building or land is exempt from VAT the seller or landlord normally has the right to opt to tax the building, with a result that VAT will be chargeable both on the rents received from lettings and on the proceeds of any sale (see A16.5).

16.8.2. The option to tax relates to the landlord's interest in an entire building. Thus an option made by a landlord who owns a whole office block affects all his tenants. Buildings which are linked by covered walkways or internal access are treated as one building as are complexes consisting of a number of units grouped around a fully enclosed concourse. If a tenant wishes to sub-let premises the VAT treatment does not depend upon the landlord's option to tax. The tenant must himself opt to tax if he wishes to charge VAT to the sub-tenant and retain the right to recover input tax charged to him by the landlord.

16.8.3. An option to tax cannot be exercised retrospectively. When ownership of the building changes hands, the new owner must make his own option to tax. A transfer by one company to a subsidiary or holding company will be a change of ownership giving rise to a fresh option to tax so long as the transferee company is not in the same VAT group as the transferor. Normally such a transfer would have to be at the market price, that price being subject to VAT, so that the VAT on the purchase would be irrecoverable by the transferee if it did not itself make the option to tax unless the transferee was occupying the building for the purposes of its taxable business.

16.8.4. A common problem encountered is where the owner of the property has charged VAT on rent but there is no formal option to tax in place. Where the option to tax was exercised prior to 1 March 1995 and the total rental income was under £20,000 pa, then there was no requirement to notify the option to HM Revenue and Customs. In cases where the option took place subsequent to that date and VAT has been charged, HM Revenue and Customs will generally accept that the option was exercised but there was a failure to notify it, and a belated notification will usually be accepted. Alternatively it could be argued that as no notification was made, the option is invalid and the supply should be exempt from VAT.

16.8.5. Written notice of an option must be given to the Commissioners not later than 30 days from the date that a decision was made to opt to tax or such later date as may be agreed with them. This has to be done by submitting Form VAT1614A (available from the HM Revenue and Customs website – see address at Appendix IX.2). Form VAT1614A must include a clear description of the property involved including the building name and postcode. Plans or maps should be supplied where available, particularly if these are necessary to identify the land and buildings. Form VAT1614A should be signed by an appropriately authorised person, for example, a director, a partner (or trustee), an authorised administrator or by a sole proprietor.[1] In cases where any other person notifies the option, it must be accompanied by a letter of authority signed by the 'taxable person'. There is a specialist Option to Tax National Unit, at Cotton House, 7 Cochrane Street, Glasgow, G1 1GY.

16.8.6. An option to tax which is under six months or over 20 years old can be revoked upon application by Form VAT1614C (for six months) and VAT1614J (for options made more than 20 years ago) to HM Revenue and Customs and obtaining their agreement in writing. If the election is under six months old, no output VAT must have arisen, conditions relating to input VAT recovery must be met and no 'transfer of a going concern' treatment must have been applied to the land in question. The first revocations of elections exercised in 1989 only became possible in August 2009. If an option to tax has been made on a property or land in which the opter has not had a relevant interest for the past six years then the option is automatically revoked. HM Revenue and Customs do not need to be notified of this revocation but the taxpayer will need to retain extremely good records of their property portfolios and their respective opted interests.

16.8.7.   A buyer who has had to pay VAT on his purchase may wish to charge VAT on a letting or a subsequent disposal of the property by him in order to recover the VAT which he incurred on his purchase. VAT incurred before the date of option is irrecoverable (except with the consent of HM Revenue and Customs) unless no exempt supplies have been made in the meantime; thus the buyer's option to tax must normally be made before or at least within 30 days of completion, particularly where the building is bought subject to existing tenancies.[2] Similar considerations apply to developers who have incurred substantial input tax as a result of construction work on the building.

16.8.8.   Exempt or partially exempt tenants, e.g. those whose business is in the financial sector, banks, building societies, etc., will be reluctant to pay VAT on their rent because they cannot usually recover the tax in full.

16.8.9.   Persons who wish to make an option may need to seek permission from HM Revenue and Customs *before* they elect when the land or buildings concerned have *already* been the subject of an exempt supply by them, usually an exempt letting. If HM Revenue and Customs are satisfied that there would be a 'fair and reasonable' attribution of input tax between the exempt supplies already made and the taxable supplies to be made following the option, then the requested option to tax will be granted from the date that the permission was submitted. All requests for permission to opt to tax have to be made on a Form VAT1614H. Alternatively, prior consent is not needed provided the conditions for automatic consent published by HM Revenue and Customs are met (see VAT Notice 742A, para.5.2, and VAT Information Sheet 06/09 issued on 1 May 2009). Under the capital items scheme, recovery of some of the VAT incurred on the land or buildings may then follow by means of annual adjustments and, usually, a 10-year period beginning with the time the VAT was incurred.

16.8.10.   The option to tax applies only to commercial buildings. It does not therefore apply to dwellings: relevant residential buildings; relevant charitable buildings (other than use as an office); pitches for residential caravans; facilities for mooring a residential houseboat; sales of land to a DIY housebuilder; or sales of land to a housing association where the housing association has provided a certificate (a Form VAT1614G) that it intends to use the land for residential development.

16.8.11.   In addition, the option to tax is disapplied in the case of a commercial building sold to either a buyer who intends to convert it into dwellings or to a buyer who intends to sell to another party for them to convert into dwellings, i.e. the sale of the property to a 'relevant intermediary'. In both cases the seller, and where an intermediary is involved, the buyer, will need to receive a certificate (Form VAT1614D) before the price is fixed in order for the option to tax to be disapplied. There are conditions attached to the issuing of a certificate (see VAT Notice 742A, para.3.4).

Statutory block to the option to tax

16.8.12.   A statutory provision intended to counter tax avoidance in this area (e.g. lease and leaseback between associated traders) can catch 'innocent' transactions.

The provisions are complex and the following is only a summary. If it appears that a transaction may be caught by the provisions, reference to the detail of the legislation is essential and specialist advice may be necessary. The disapplication of the option to tax could have serious effects on the viability of a development as it may result in the recovery of input tax incurred on the project being forfeited.

16.8.13. Paragraphs 12 to 17 of Schedule 10 VATA 1994 apply to supplies made on or after 19 March 1997. These paragraphs provide that where the grant of an interest in property is between connected parties, and the recipient is unable to recover at least 80% of their input tax under the partial exemption rules, then the option to tax is disapplied and the grant is exempt. Paragraph 12 provides that where an option to tax has been made a supply will not be treated as a taxable supply in situations where:

(a) the grant giving rise to the supply was made by a person ('the grantor') who was a developer of the land; and

(b) the exempt land test is met.

The exempt land test is met, if at the time when the grant was made the relevant person intended or expected that the land:

(a) would become exempt land; or

(b) would continue, for a period at least, to be exempt land.

16.8.14. Land is exempt land if, at any time during the 10-year capital items scheme adjustment period (see A16.8.20):

(a) a relevant person is in occupation of the land; and

(b) the occupation is not wholly, or substantially wholly, for eligible purposes.

16.8.15. A relevant person is each of the following:

(a) the grantor;

(b) a person connected with the grantor;

(c) a development financier; and

(d) a person connected with a development financier.

A development financier means a person who has provided finance for the grantor's development of the land or has entered into any arrangement to provide finance for the grantor's development of the land, with the expectation that the land will remain or become exempt land.

16.8.16. A person does not occupy for eligible purposes unless he is a taxable person. A taxable person must also occupy the land for the purpose of making supplies which are in the course or furtherance of his business and the supplies are taxable supplies (whether zero-, reduced- or standard-rated) such that any input tax of his which was wholly attributable to those supplies would be input tax for which he would be entitled to a credit. HM Revenue and Customs will treat the property as being used 'substantially wholly' for taxable activities providing that at least 80% of the person's supplies are taxable. With effect from 1 April 2010 a further concession was granted by HM Revenue and Customs to enable a development financier or a person connected with the financier to occupy a minor part of the building without the option to tax being disapplied. 'Minor' is considered to be occupation of less than 10% of the building (see HM Revenue and Customs Information Sheet 02/10 dated March 2010).

16.8.17. Occupation of land by a body to which section 33 VATA 1994 applies (local authorities and various other statutory bodies) is occupation of the land for eligible purposes to the extent that the body occupies the land other than for the purposes of a business. Occupation of land by a government department (within the meaning of VATA 1994, s.41) is also occupation of the land for eligible purposes.

16.8.18. References to the funding of the grantor's development of the land include:

    (a) providing funds for meeting the whole or any part of the cost of the grantor's development of the land;

    (b) procuring the provision of any such funds by another;

    (c) providing funds for discharging (in whole or in part) any liability that has been or may be incurred by any person for or in connection with the raising of funds to meet the cost of the grantor's development of the land; and

    (d) procuring that any such liability is or will be discharged (in whole or in part) by another.[3]

Transitional provisions

16.8.19. The rules above apply to supplies made on or after 19 March 1997 unless the supply arises from a 'relevant pre-commencement grant'. A 'relevant pre-commencement grant' is a grant which was either made before 26 November 1996; or made after 26 November 1996 but before 30 November 1999 in pursuance of an agreement in writing entered into before 26 November 1996 on terms fixed in that agreement.[4]

Capital items scheme

16.8.20. The following types of land are covered by the capital items scheme (all figures are to be taken as net of VAT):

    (a) land or a building or part of a building, or a civil engineering work or part of a civil engineering work, where the value of the interest supplied to the owner, by a taxable supply is £250,000 or more (excluding any part of that value consisting of rent);

(b)   a building or part of a building where the owner's interest in, right over or licence to occupy it is treated as self-supplied to him. The value of the supply must be £250,000 or more;

    (c)   a building where the aggregate value of the land on which the building is constructed and the goods and services in connection with the construction supplied to the owner by way of taxable (reduced or standard-rated) supply is £250,000 or more;

    (d)   a building which the owner alters, or an extension or an annexe which he constructs, where additional floor area is 10% or more of the original floor area before the work was carried out. The value of all taxable (standard-rated or lower-rated) supplies of goods and services, made or to be made to the owner on or after 3 July 1997 for, or in connection with, the alteration, etc., must be £250,000 or more;

    (e)   a refurbishment of property costing more than £250,000 where the goods or services involved are supplied to the landlord on or after 3 July 1997. Refurbishment includes fitting out but is otherwise undefined. This gives rise to a practical difficulty in distinguishing between refurbishment and repair.

16.8.21.   Where a buyer inherits the balance of the seller's capital items scheme adjustment period, as is the case where a building is acquired under the transfer of a going concern rules, the method of scheme adjustments for that balance of the adjustment period must be agreed in advance with HM Revenue and Customs. Enquiries should therefore be raised with the seller as to whether there is an existing capital items scheme adjustment period. If so, the seller must be asked to supply details of the cost of the property, of the VAT initially recovered by the seller, any subsequent adjustments to that recovery and the timing of the intervals in the adjustment period.

1.   See Business Brief 17/99, dated 5 August 1999.
2.   But, see the decision in *Higher Education Statistics Agency Ltd* v. *Customs and Excise Commissioners* [2000] STC 332 where it was held that the relevant date when an election had to be made by is the date of payment of the deposit. In the case of HESA the option to tax was made after the deposit was paid at auction but prior to completion. HESA were found liable to pay VAT on the purchase price.
3.   VATA 1994, Sched.10, para.14(3).
4.   VATA 1994, Sched.10, para.12(7).

16.9.   Surrenders

16.9.1.   Surrenders in the course of a business are exempt from VAT. They may be taxable if the tenant has exercised his option to tax in respect of his leasehold interest.[1]

16.9.2.   If the tenant has exercised his option to tax in respect of his leasehold interest, and if the landlord is paying the tenant for the surrender, the tenant is making a standard rated supply of an interest in the land. Where the consideration for the surrender is other than in money VAT is payable on the value of the interest surrendered. Thus if the landlord in return for the surrender grants a long lease to the tenant, VAT is payable on the value of the surrendered lease, but a precise value may be difficult to assess. If a proposal involves a surrender by operation of law, liability to VAT should be agreed in writing before the surrender is made.

16.9.3. Variations to a lease will be treated as being part of the supply of the lease. Variations will therefore be exempt unless the landlord has opted to tax, in which case the lease and the variations will be subject to VAT at the standard rate. A variation of a lease is regarded as the surrender of the lease and the grant of another in its place. HM Revenue and Customs have published a revised Statement of Practice which will apply in circumstances where a deemed surrender and re-grant occur by operation of law (see Appendix VI.4).

1. *Lubbock Fine & Co.* v. *Commissioners of Customs and Excise* (Case C-63/92) [1994] STC 101.

16.10. Charities

16.10.1. The construction or first grant of a major interest in a building which is constructed or converted from non-residential use for use for a 'relevant charitable purpose' is zero-rated. Where the charity is using the premises for the purpose of a business carried on by it (e.g. a shop run by the charity where goods are sold to the public or a school where fees are charged for attendance), the rules for commercial property apply as this is not a use for a relevant charitable purpose.

16.10.2. A landlord is prevented from exercising the option to tax where the building is to be occupied for a charity solely for a relevant charitable purpose, other than as an office.

16.10.3. Legislation also provides for zero-rating of the construction of a charitable use 'annexe', providing that the annexe is capable of functioning independently from the existing building and the main access to the annexe is not through the existing building or vice versa. The main difficulty in this area is whether the building constitutes an 'annexe' or is rather an 'extension' or 'enlargement', in which case standard-rating applies. There has been considerable case law on this issue and it is recommended that professional advice be sought before the charity issues the necessary certificate for zero-rating to the builder. In the case of both purchase and construction of qualifying buildings, for zero-rating to apply the supply must be to the charity which will use the building for qualifying purposes and must be supported by a certificate.

16.11. Conversions and renovations

16.11.1. The cost of reconstruction, alteration or enlargement of an existing building generally attracts VAT at the standard rate. However, the sale by a developer of a major interest in a building which has been converted to a dwelling or for residential use from a non-residential building is zero-rated. A 'major' interest is a freehold sale or the grant of a lease for over 21 years. However, there are problems in applying the zero rate where the non-residential premises contained residential accommodation prior to the conversion, such as in the case of a converted public house. In such cases the zero rate only applies to the extent that an additional dwelling is formed not containing any part of the pre-existing residential accommodation.

16.11.2. The reduced rate of VAT (5%) is chargeable on works for the conversion of a property into a different number of dwellings; conversions of dwellings into residential communal homes; and the renovation of dwellings that have been empty for at least two years (prior to 1 January 2008 the property had to be empty for at least three years). This covers the qualifying conversion/renovation services, and building materials supplied with those services. In addition, from 1 August 2001 the sale of the freehold, or the premium or first payment of rent on a lease in excess of 21 years, in a renovated dwelling which has been empty for 10 years or more prior to the sale is zero-rated.

16.12. Listed buildings

16.12.1. Alterations to residential listed properties and other protected buildings (scheduled monuments) which required and have received listed building consent are zero-rated, whereas repairs and maintenance to such buildings are normally standard-rated. A reduced rate of VAT will, however, apply to repairs and maintenance where the property has been empty for two years or where a qualifying conversion is taking place (see A16.11.2.). The grant of a major interest in a substantially reconstructed residential building is zero-rated. If a building is simply in a conservation area it does not qualify for the zero rating.

16.13. Agricultural land

16.13.1. The option to tax applies to agricultural land in a broadly similar way to other kinds of land whereas before 1995 an option to tax agricultural land affected adjacent land. Marshland and moorland which is used for grants of sporting rights comes within the definition of agricultural land in this context. Agricultural dwelling houses are exempt and no option to tax can be exercised in respect of them, but an apportionment of their value will have to be made where they are part of a sale of agricultural land. See also B8.

16.14. Real estate election

16.14.1. From 1 June 2008 a 'real estate election' (REE) allows a 'blanket' option to tax to take effect on all land and buildings where an interest is acquired after the REE is made. The REE binds the VAT registered entity for at least 20 years from the date of making the option but individual properties can be removed from the option to tax by seeking permission from HM Revenue and Customs. The REE can be made on Form VAT1614E. Care should be taken when land or buildings are subject to a REE as the VAT registered entity will need to retain evidence to show when the land and buildings were acquired, as otherwise there will be little to demonstrate whether a valid option to tax is in place over a particular parcel of land or agricultural building (the REE does not bind land or property held before the date that the REE is made).

16.15. Sporting rights

16.15.1. Where sporting rights are sold as part of the sale of freehold land, the whole supply is treated as exempt subject to the option to tax, unless the value of the sporting rights is more than 10% of the total value in which case an attribution must be made and standard rate VAT accounted for on the sporting rights. In the case of supplies of sporting rights where the freehold of the land over which they are to be exercised is not sold to the same person, VAT at standard rate applies.

16.16. Property sold as a going concern

16.16.1. Where property is sold as a transfer of a going concern (TOGC), the transaction will only be outside the scope of VAT if the buyer satisfies all the criteria for relief. If he does not do so, the seller will be liable for VAT.

16.16.2. To qualify for relief there simply needs to be a transaction involving the sale of assets which puts the buyer in a position to carry on the business previously conducted by the seller. The relief may therefore be lost if the buyer contracts a sub-sale or re-sells the property within a short period.

16.16.3. It should be noted that there are special provisions relating to the sale of a 'new' or opted property, in that the buyer must also opt to tax in order for the transaction to be treated as the transfer of a going concern.

16.16.4. In addition, in order for the property to qualify as part of the transfer of a going concern, the buyer must also provide a notice to the seller, confirming that the buyer's option to tax is not subject to the statutory block (see A16.8.10). This notice is normally included as a clause within the contract. If the option to tax is not exercised or this notice is not provided, then the property must be treated as standard-rated, outside the 'transfer of a going concern' provisions, although a transitional period, effective to 30 June 2004, allowed transfer of a going concern treatment if the notice was not provided but the conditions were otherwise met – i.e. the option to tax was not blocked.

16.17. Summary checklist of application of VAT to property transactions

Type of dealing	Rate of tax
A. Freehold sales	
Buildings designed as dwellings built or converted and sold by developer.	Zero.[1]
Communal residential buildings sold by developer.	Zero.[1]
Non-business charitable buildings sold by developer.	Zero.[1]
Domestic and other non-commercial buildings sold by others.	Exempt.
New commercial buildings.	Standard.[2]
Other commercial buildings.	Exempt subject to option.
B. Leases[3]	
New dwellings or dwellings converted from non-residential buildings, communal residential buildings or non-business charitable buildings if for more than 21 years where built by and granted by developer.	Zero on premium or first payment of rent, exempt thereafter.[1]
Similar to above but lease for 21 years or less.	Exempt.
Domestic and non-commercial buildings granted by other than developer.	Exempt.
New commercial buildings.	Exempt subject to option.
Other commercial buildings.	Exempt subject to option.
Assignments.	Exempt subject to option.
Surrenders.	Exempt subject to option.
Reverse surrenders.	Exempt subject to option.
C. Listed buildings	
Approved alterations to dwellings, communal residential and non-business charitable buildings.	Zero.
Other work on similar buildings.	Standard or 5%.
Freehold sales by developer of substantially reconstructed similar buildings.	Zero.[1]

Type of dealing	Rate of tax
Leases for more than 21 years from developer of substantially reconstructed similar buildings.	Zero on premium or first payment of rent, exempt thereafter.[1]
Any works to commercial listed buildings.	Standard.
Sales and leases of substantially reconstructed commercial listed buildings.	Exempt subject to option.

D. Building land

Sales and leases.	Exempt subject to option.[4]

E. Refurbished buildings

Sales and leases of residential buildings.	Exempt.[5]
Sales and leases of non-residential buildings.	Exempt subject to option.

F. Conversions

Freehold sale by developer of conversion from non-residential building into dwelling or communal residential building.	Zero.[1]
As above but grant of lease for over 21 years.	Zero on premium or first rent, exempt thereafter.[1]
Construction services supplied to registered housing association on conversion of non-residential building into a dwelling or communal residential building.	Zero.
Conversion of a property into a different number of dwellings (e.g. house into flats or vice versa) or of a dwelling into residential communal homes.	5%

G. Building services

Construction of new buildings designed as dwellings (including sub-contractors' services).	Zero.
Construction of communal residential and non-business charitable buildings provided an appropriate certificate is obtained from the customer, and the customer is the person using the building for qualifying purposes.	Zero.

Type of dealing	Rate of tax
Construction of new commercial buildings.	Standard.
Repairs and alterations.	Standard.
Demolition.	Standard unless part of a single zero-rated construction for new build dwellings, etc.
Professional services.	Standard.
Renovations of dwellings which have been empty for at least two years.	5%

H. Civil engineering work

New work.	Standard (zero-rated for dwellings).
Repairs, maintenance and alteration of existing buildings.	Standard (zero-rating may apply to alterations to listed dwellings).

I. Options

Option to undertake a transaction which itself is chargeable to VAT.	Standard on option fee.

1. Zero on first grant, subsequent supplies exempt.
2. All freehold sales are taxable at standard rate while building remains 'new'.
3. In relation to leases, 'grant' includes assignment.
4. Except for sales to housing associations where a certificate for residential development is supplied or sales to DIY housebuilders, where the option to tax is not available.
5. Unless the property has besen empty for 10 or more years when freehold sale, or lease over 21 years is zero-rated.

A17. Tax relief on mortgages

17.1. Introduction

17.1.1. Tax relief on the interest element of mortgage repayments relating to the purchase of an individual's private dwelling house ceased to be available as from 6 April 2000.

17.2. Business premises

17.2.1. Where a loan is taken out in respect of the purchase or improvement of business premises interest on that loan may qualify as an allowable expense of the business for tax purposes and thus some element of tax relief will be obtained against an individual's income tax liability or a company's corporation tax liability.

17.3. Companies

17.3.1. A company which takes out a loan for the purchase or improvement of business premises may obtain corporation tax relief on the interest element of the loan provided it is an allowable business expense.

A18. Transfers on breakdown of marriage or civil partnership

18.1. Introduction

18.1.1. Special considerations apply to the transfer of property between husband and wife on the breakdown of a marriage. This chapter does not deal with giving advice on the terms of the settlement between husband and wife, only on its implementation (see the guidance on Undue Influence in Appendix IV.7). Similar considerations are relevant on the breakdown of a civil partnership.

Conflict of interests

18.1.2. Even in cases where the settlement is amicable and is not made pursuant to a court order in matrimonial proceedings, the parties must be independently advised because of the inevitable risk of conflict of interests which arises in this situation.

18.2. Acting for the transferor

Mortgages

18.2.1. The solicitor acting for the transferor should ascertain the extent of existing mortgages over the property to be transferred. It must be decided whether the property is to be transferred free of the mortgage to the other spouse, and if so, whether the transferring spouse will redeem the mortgage or will continue to make repayments. If the property is to be transferred free of the mortgage, steps must be taken to discharge those charges before completion of the transfer. This may involve advising the transferor about refinancing and taking a new loan secured over another property in order to discharge his indebtedness over the property to be transferred. The lender's consent to the transfer will be required if either the mortgage deed requires it or if the borrower-spouse is to be released from his or her covenant under the mortgage. The borrower's continuing liability under the mortgage may affect his or her ability to obtain another loan on a different property. Arrangements must be made for the continuation of payments under the mortgage. Any life policy taken out in connection with an existing mortgage should be checked to ascertain the name(s) of the person(s) insured under the policy. If the property is to be transferred free of the mortgage to which the policy related, a re-assignment of the policy should be effected on discharge of the mortgage. If the benefit of the policy is to be transferred, the consent of the lender should be obtained and the insurance company notified of the change. The transfer of the benefit of the policy may attract CGT liability (see A15).

Outstanding discount on purchased local authority housing

18.2.2. A disposal of property which had been bought from a local authority under the provisions of Housing Act 1985, Pt. V made in pursuance of an order under Matrimonial Causes Act 1973, s.24 does not trigger the repayment of discount provisions under Housing Act 1985.[1] Thus no discount is repayable where the property is transferred under a court order for the transfer or a property adjustment order made under section 24. Where the court order is for the sale of the property under Matrimonial Causes Act 1973, s.24A a proportion of the discount may be repayable if the property is sold within three years after its purchase from the local authority.

18.2.3. Similar provisions are relevant on the breakdown of a civil partnership.

1. Housing Act 1985, s.160(1)(*c*).

18.3. **Acting for the transferee**

18.3.1. The transferee's solicitor should undertake the normal pre-contract searches and enquiries to ensure that no entries exist which might adversely affect the property or its value (see B10).

18.3.2. Any charge which had been registered to protect the spouse's rights of occupation under Family Law Act 1996 ceases to be effective on issue of a divorce decree absolute unless an order under section 33(5) of the Act has been made and registered.

18.3.3. In appropriate cases advice should be given in relation to raising finance to purchase the share in the property to be transferred.

18.3.4. If the property is to be transferred subject to an existing mortgage, the lender's consent to the transfer must be obtained if the borrower is to be released from the covenant and/or if the mortgage so requires and arrangements made for the continuance of payments under the mortgage. If the benefit of a life policy is to be transferred, the lender's consent may be necessary and notice of the transfer must be given to the insurance company after completion.

18.3.5. Where the transferred property is mortgaged, consideration should be given to the protection of the mortgage by either an endowment policy or a mortgage protection policy. A lender may also insist that a policy to insure against the transferor's subsequent insolvency is acquired.

18.3.6. Transfers made in connection with divorce settlements do not attract Stamp Duty Land Tax (see A14.6.1).

18.3.7. A transfer of land between spouses for which 'value' is not given, that is, full consideration or something like it, in some form may be set aside by the court, under Insolvency Act 1986, ss.339–342 at the request of the trustee in bankruptcy if the transferring spouse becomes bankrupt within five years of the transfer. The solvency of the transferring spouse at the time of the transfer may be a material factor in the decision whether the transfer can or should be set aside, so the transferee spouse may wish to get a declaration of solvency from the transferor at the time when the transfer is made. The transferee might also consider the possibility of insuring against the risk of the transferor's becoming bankrupt within five years. Should the transferee want to mortgage or sell the property within five years, this should not cause difficulties because of the amendments made to the 1986 Act by Insolvency (No.2) Act 1994 (see Appendix IV.3).[1]

18.3.8. Transfers of shares of property between joint owners are subject to Land Registry identity requirements and the applicant for registration will have to give details of the conveyancers acting for all the other parties to the transaction and, where a party is unrepresented, provide appropriate evidence of that party's identity.'

1. See *Hill* v. *Haines* [2007] EWCA Civ 1284; [2008] Ch 412 where the ability of one spouse to apply to the court for an order under the Matrimonial Causes Act 1973 s.23 to s.24D had value as its exercise might lead to court orders entitling one spouse to property or money from or at the expense of the other, and the value of that right was the value of the money or property.

18.4. Public funding

18.4.1. The cost of conveyancing work necessary to give effect to the terms of a court order will usually be covered by the client's public funding certificate. This applies equally to consent orders and the work which is undertaken to implement such orders.[1]

1. See *S* v. *S* (*Legal Aid Taxation*) [1991] Fam Law 271; *Copeland* v. *Houlton* [1955] 3 All ER 178.

18.5. Mentally incapacitated party

18.5.1. Where a property adjustment order or an order for sale has been made and one of the adult parties lacks mental capacity, the provisions of the Practice Note, 'Ancillary relief orders: conveyancing for mentally incapacitated adults', issued by the Official Solicitor on 3 January 2006, must be followed (see Appendix VII.1). This Practice Note has not yet been updated to reflect Mental Capacity Act 2005 and should be read accordingly.

18.5.2. Before the property can be sold, either the authority of the Court of Protection must be obtained or, where the incapacitated party is a trustee of a jointly owned property, an order appointing a substitute trustee must be made. Where the party is a sole owner of the property and a deputy has been appointed, the deputy will apply for authority to sell the property. Where no deputy has been appointed, the Court of Protection may authorise someone to act on the owner's behalf.

18.5.3.   If the incapacitated party is a co-owner, section 22(2) Law of Property Act 1925 prevents the disposition of the legal estate in land so long as one trustee lacks mental capacity. The sale can only take place if there is another person authorised to act under an Enduring or Lasting Power of Attorney, or if another trustee is appointed by the High Court (or the county court where the estate fund does not exceed the county court limit or there is consent to the jurisdiction). A copy of the order appointing the new trustee should be produced to the Land Registry with the application to register the transfer (see generally B7).

18.6.   Lenders' instructions

18.6.1.   The provisions of paragraph 16.3 of the CML Lenders' Handbook and paragraphs F.4 to F.9 of the BSA Mortgage Instructions must be observed in appropriate cases (see **www.cml.org.uk** and **www.bsa.org.uk**).

A19. The National Conveyancing Protocol

19.1.   Aim of the Protocol

19.1.1.   The Protocol for domestic conveyancing was first introduced by the Law Society in March 1990 in an attempt to standardise and streamline the procedures involved in domestic transactions. The fifth edition took effect on 30 November 2004.

19.1.2.   The fifth edition of the Protocol is currently under review by the Law Society.

19.2.   Use of forms

19.2.1.   While the Standard Agreement for Sale (front and back pages of the printed form) may be reproduced on a solicitor's word processor, the text of the Conditions themselves, for copyright reasons, may not (see A21).

19.2.2.   The following TransAction forms have been published by the Law Society to support solicitors using the protocol:

- TA6 Property Information Form (2nd edition)
- TA7 Leasehold Information Form (2nd edition)
- TA8 New Home Information Form
- TA9 Commonhold Information Form
- TA10 Fittings and Contents Form (2nd edition)
- TA13 Completion Information and Requisitions on Title

19.2.3.   A general licence has been granted to solicitors to reproduce the TransAction forms using a word processor.

19.2.4.   Any form which is reproduced under the general licence outlined above, which applies to solicitors only, must be presented in a format as close as possible to the original form with no textual alterations. It must also state in a prominent position 'This form is part of the Law Society's TransAction Scheme' where this appears on the printed form. The forms may not be photocopied except for the purpose of taking a file copy.

A20. Interest on clients' money

20.1. Solicitors' Accounts Rules 1998

20.1.1. A solicitor who holds money on behalf of a client may be required to pay the client interest or a sum in lieu of interest on the money he is holding. The circumstances when the client is entitled to interest and the amount of that interest are governed by Solicitors' Accounts Rules 1998 a summary of which is set out below.

20.1.2. The Rules can be varied by agreement in writing between the solicitor and his client, but contracting out is never appropriate if it is against the client's interests (Rule 27 Solicitors' Accounts Rules 1998).

20.1.3. If a solicitor pays a lender's cheque into his client account in anticipation of completing the mortgage and completion is postponed, the mortgage instructions may make the solicitor liable to pay interest at the mortgage rate if the money is not returned to the lender within the time stipulated in the lender's instructions.

20.2. Deposits in conveyancing transactions

20.2.1. The Rules apply to all money held by a solicitor on behalf of a client, including a deposit held by a solicitor whether as agent for the seller or as stakeholder.

20.2.2. Where the Rules apply, interest must be paid to the client irrespective of whether the money was held in a deposit or current account.

20.3. Stakeholder deposits

20.3.1. A deposit which is held in the capacity of stakeholder does not belong to either client until completion, but an entitlement to interest on that deposit arises under Rule 26 Solicitors' Accounts Rules 1998.

20.3.2. In the absence of express agreement to the contrary the interest will follow the stake.

20.3.3. Standard Condition 2.2.6 provides for the seller to receive the interest earned on a stakeholder deposit, provided the contract is completed but not if it is rescinded (see Appendix III.5).

20.4. Designated accounts

20.4.1. Where client money is held in a separate designated client account, the solicitor must account to the client for the interest actually earned on that account. A separate designated client account is a deposit or share account for money relating to a single client.

20.5. General client account

20.5.1. If the money is held in a general client account the duty to pay interest depends on the amount of money held and the period for which it is held, but there is no requirement to pay interest if the amount calculated is £20 or less.

Table of minimum balances

20.5.2. No interest need be paid if the money held does not exceed the amounts set out in the table below for times not exceeding the periods shown.

Time in weeks	Amount
8	£1,000
4	£2,000
2	£10,000
1	£20,000

20.6. Sums exceeding £20,000

20.6.1. If a sum exceeding £20,000 is held for one week or less, a solicitor is not required to pay interest unless it is fair and reasonable to do so in all the circumstances. Although this part of the rule allows some discretion to be exercised by the solicitor in deciding whether or not to pay interest, such discretion should be exercised in the client's favour. Thus, if a sum of £1,000,000 were held on behalf of a client for two days, the considerable amount of interest which would accrue during that short time should be paid to the client.

20.7. Intermittent amounts

20.7.1. There will be occasions when the solicitor either holds money intermittently for the client, or when the amount being held varies from time to time. In these circumstances the solicitor must account to the client for interest where it would be fair and reasonable to do so, having regard to the amounts of money held and to the length of time for which it is held. The discretion permitted by this rule should be exercised in favour of the client.

20.8. Rate of interest

20.8.1. The rate of interest (for money not held in a separate designated client account or held on a general client account) is the same rate as would have been payable if the money had been kept in a separate designated client account. Where money is held in a separate designated client account (which should be a deposit account with a major clearing bank or a deposit or share account with a building society) the amount of interest payable is the sum actually earned on that money while on deposit. However, for money held in a general client account, Rule 25(2) Solicitors' Accounts Rules 1998 requires payment (if higher) of the rate of interest payable on money placed on deposit on similar terms by a member of the business community.

20.8.2. Accrued interest on a contractual deposit held under the terms of the Standard Conditions of Sale is defined by Standard Condition 1.1.1.(a) (see Appendix III.5). The difference between a fair sum in lieu of interest and any higher rate payable in respect of a much larger general account may be retained by the solicitor.

20.9. Trustees

20.9.1. Money held by a solicitor which belongs to a trust of which the solicitor is a trustee, where the solicitor is acting for the trust, is client money and the interest provisions described above apply. If interest arises under a controlled trust (see Rule 2(2)(h) Solicitors Accounts Rules 1998), all of the interest must be paid to the beneficiaries (see Rule 15, note (vi) and Rule 24, note (x) Solicitors' Accounts Rules 1998).

20.10. Client's right to complain

20.10.1. A client who feels that he ought to have been paid interest on money held on his behalf by his solicitor may apply to the Legal Complaints Service for a determination as to whether or not interest ought to have been paid and, if so, the amount of that interest.

20.11. Tax on interest

20.11.1. In some circumstances deduction of tax at source may be applicable to interest which is paid on clients' money. The Law Society guidance on this matter is set out in full in Appendix IV.5.

A21. Reproduction of standard forms

21.1. **Standard Conditions of Sale and Standard Commercial Property Conditions**
21.2. **TransAction forms**

21.3. **Enquiries of Local Authority forms**
21.4. **Land Registry forms**

21.1. Standard Conditions of Sale and Standard Commercial Property Conditions

21.1.1. Solicitors may reproduce on their own word processors the agreement for sale which incorporates the Standard Conditions of Sale or Standard Commercial Property Conditions by reference but are not permitted to reproduce (whether on a word processor or by other means of reproduction) the text of the General Conditions of Sale without express permission from the copyright holder. Copyright is jointly held by the Law Society and the Solicitors' Law Stationery Society (OYEZ). Enquiries relating to copyright should, in the first instance, be addressed to Law Society Publishing (see Appendix IX.2). The Conditions are reproduced in Appendix III.5 and III.6.

21.2. TransAction forms

21.2.1. It is in the interests of both the solicitor and his client that uniformity of presentation should be maintained where forms form part of the TransAction scheme.

21.2.2. The forms are Law Society copyright but may be reproduced by a solicitor on a word processor in a version which resembles the printed form as closely as possible. No additions, deletions, adaptations or alterations of the text of the printed version must be made. Additionally each word-processed copy must bear in a prominent position the following phrase: 'This form is part of the Law Society's TransAction Scheme', where this appears on the printed form.

21.3. Enquiries of Local Authority forms

21.3.1. A general licence has been granted to solicitors to reproduce CON 29R Enquiries of Local Authority (2007) and CON 29O Optional Enquiries of Local Authority (2007) on word processors provided that the quality of the form produced is of a standard acceptable to local authorities.

21.3.2. As a general guideline, reproduction on paper which weighs no less than 80gsm, at a resolution of no less than 300 dpi, in 12 point Roman typeface should satisfy these requirements. The local authority has the right to reject a form which does not meet an acceptable standard of reproduction.

21.3.3. The forms may be reproduced on separate sheets of A4 paper. Permission has been granted for practitioners to reproduce and submit to the local authority only the front page of the printed CON 29R and CON 29O. The local authority may insist that the format of the printed form is followed as closely as is possible and in particular that the boxes which appear on the front page of the printed form are reproduced in the word-processed version.

21.4. Land Registry forms

21.4.1. Land Registry forms may be downloaded free of charge from the Land Registry website **www.landregistry.gov.uk** and may be freely reproduced for use within the firm. They may also be obtained from a law stationer or commercial software organisation.

21.4.2. All Land Registry forms are Crown copyright and all rights are reserved. The forms may not be sold to a third party in hard copy or machine readable format.

21.4.3. Schedule 1 forms may be reproduced in accordance with Rule 210 Land Registration Rules 2003 and must be printed on durable A4 size paper.

21.4.4. Electronically reproduced forms need to comply with the requirements of Rule 211 but are more adaptable. For example, the guidance notes outside the panels can be omitted and the width of the panels expanded. Similarly, inapplicable certificates and statements may be omitted.

21.4.5. Documents for which no form is prescribed must be in such form as the registrar may direct or allow.[1]

21.4.6. Any queries about adaptation of forms and the Registry's checking and approval service or reproducing forms electronically should be made to the Forms Unit, Land Registry, Head Office, Lincoln's Inn Fields, London, WC2A 3PH. Telephone no. 0207 166 4405.

21.4.7. Detailed guidance on reproduction of Land Registry forms can be found in Land Registry Practice Guide 46.

---

1. Land Registration Rules 2003, r.212.

A22. Electronic conveyancing

22.1. **Introduction**	22.3. **E-conveyancing:**
22.2 **E-conveyancing: the**	**implementation**
statutory framework	22.4. **Electronic services**

22.1. Introduction

22.1.1. Land Registration Act 2002 (the Act) provides the statutory framework for the development and regulation of a system of electronic conveyancing (e-conveyancing) and subordinate legislation provides the necessary supporting detail.

22.1.2. The fundamental objective underpinning the Act was set out in paragraph 1.5 of the Law Commission Report 'Land Registration for the Twenty-First Century' (Law Com. No.271):

> '... the register should be a complete and accurate reflection of the state of the title of the land at any given time, so that it is possible to investigate title to land online, with the absolute minimum of additional enquiries and inspections.'

22.1.3. E-conveyancing is being developed incrementally. As part of that development, the Land Registry plans to continue to improve and extend its existing electronic services. New services will generally be introduced as pilots and/or trials to test the systems and procedures before extending and rolling out such services.

22.1.4. Up-to-date information about developments in e-conveyancing and electronic services is available on the Land Registry's website at **www.landregistry.gov. uk**.

22.2 E-conveyancing: the statutory framework

22.2.1. The Act provides the statutory framework for a system of e-conveyancing in which the transfer and creation of interests in registered land will be made by electronic means.

22.2.2. The provisions set out in the Act, Part 8 and Sched.5, provide for:

    (a)   electronic dispositions being deemed to comply with statutory and common law requirements as to deeds and documents;

    (b)   the creation of and access to a secure electronic communications network;

    (c)   power to require the use of electronic conveyancing; and

(d)   the provision of a system of electronic settlement in relation to transactions involving registration.

22.2.3.   The Act also provides that an electronic document when lodged will record the time and date when it takes effect and bear the electronic signature of each person who needs to authenticate it. Each electronic signature will need to be certified.

22.3.   E-conveyancing: implementation

22.3.1.   The Land Registry is planning a staged approach to the implementation of an e-conveyancing system in which documents created by practitioners and 'executed' electronically will result in automatic changes to the register.

22.3.2.   Land Registration (Network Access) Rules 2008 (SI 2008/1748) provide for network access agreements (NAAs) which regulate the terms on which access to the network is authorised and the procedures under which a NAA can be terminated.

22.3.3.   The Land Registry has introduced two forms of NAA

- a full NAA is required for the creation and lodgement of electronic documents;

- a signature access NAA allows for the application of an electronic signature to a document.

A technical manual forms part of a NAA. This is regularly updated to take account of technical developments and security aspects of the e-conveyancing network. Further information is available on the Land Registry website at **www.landregistry.gov.uk**.

22.3.4.   Network Access Appeal Rules 2008 (SI 2008/1730) regulate appeals from a decision of the Registrar concerning the entry into, or termination of, a NAA. Appeals are made to the Adjudicator to HM Land Registry (see G3.13).

22.3.5   The Land Registry is currently developing an electronic transfer (e-TR1) which will initially be limited to transfers on sale of the whole of a registered title involving private individuals. The Land Registry intends to provide a system that will also enable conveyancers to evidence the submission of an SDLT return to HM Revenue and Customs.

22.3.6.   Further consultation exercises will deal with the remaining secondary legislation required to operate an e-conveyancing system. Full details of the proposals will be set out in the respective consultation papers. Details will also be available at **www.econsultations.e-conveyancing.gov.uk**.

22.3.7.   The Land Registry anticipates that the paper-based and electronic systems of conveyancing will co-exist for a period. Before introducing rules to make e-conveyancing compulsory the Act provides that a draft of such rules must be laid before and approved by resolution of each House of Parliament after appropriate consultation.

22.4.   Electronic services

22.4.1.   The Land Registry portal provides a single point of access to its information, network and lender services. The portal conditions of use contain the terms, conditions and obligations of its business users. See **www.landregistry.gov.uk** for details of the electronic services available and portal guidance notes.

22.4.2.   The Land Registry has also introduced a business gateway service which enables conveyancers to use case management software to lodge applications direct to the Land Registry.

Information services

22.4.3.   The Land Registry portal provides the facility to view registers of title and to obtain register information from the Land Registry database via instant online access. It enables account holders to view registers and title plans from their own computers, make searches online, view online documents referred to on the register and print official copies. All Land Registry portal users have access to information services.

Network services

22.4.4.   A NAA is required for access to the Land Registry's network services which allow for the creation and lodgement of electronic documents. This service provides the facility to use electronic signatures, where appropriate. An application can also be supported, where necessary, by an electronic attachment of a conveyancer's certificate of compliance or any required documentary evidence.

22.4.5.   An electronic charge in standard form (e-CSF) has been introduced by the Land Registry enabling certain mortgages of registered land to be prepared, signed and submitted for registration electronically.[1] Further information is available in Land Registry Practice Bulletin 15.

Lender services

22.4.6.   This service enables lenders and their appointed agents to lodge electronic applications to discharge registered charges. A lender must enter into an appropriate arrangement with the Land Registry to access such services.

22.4.7.   The electronic discharges (EDs) system involves a lender's computer sending an electronic message to the Land Registry's computer instructing the removal of the relevant charge entries. On receipt of the message, and if electronic validation is successful, the Land Registry computer will automatically remove the relevant entries from the register of the title. For further information see G1.10 and Land Registry Practice Guide 31.

22.4.8. The Land Registry has introduced an electronic submission of discharge (e-DS1) for use by corporate lenders and their agents. An e-DS1 provides both the application to cancel a registered charge and the necessary evidence of discharge. For further information see G1.11 and Land Registry Practice Guide 31.

22.4.9. For further information on electronic services see Land Registry Practice Guide 71.

1. See Land Registration (Electronic Conveyancing) Rules 2008 (SI 2008/1750).

A23. Money laundering

23.1.   What is money laundering?

23.1.1.   Money laundering is the process through which criminals attempt to conceal the true origin or ownership of the proceeds of their criminal activities so as to retain control over them and ultimately make it appear as though the proceeds come from a legitimate source. Solicitors should be alert to the possibility of their clients using them to launder money, which may expose the solicitors themselves to criminal offences. Failure to report a client where there is a suspicion that a money laundering offence may be, or has been, committed can result in the solicitor being prosecuted, as can assisting a money launderer.

23.1.2.   Solicitors are advised to study the Law Society's Anti-Money Laundering Practice Note (29 October 2009) (available at **www.lawsociety.org.uk/antimoneylaundering**). HM Treasury has formally approved this Practice Note which means that the Solicitors Regulation Authority and the courts will need to have regard to the note when considering whether a solicitor's conduct was reasonable in relation to allegations of money laundering, failure to report and failure to comply with Money Laundering Regulations 2007. See also *Solicitors and Money Laundering: A Compliance Handbook* by Peter Camp, published by Law Society Publishing (3rd edition, 2008).

23.2.   The offences

The current offences relating to money laundering are contained in Proceeds of Crime Act 2002. References to section numbers in the following paragraphs are references to Proceeds of Crime Act 2002. The offences carry a penalty of between two and 14 years' imprisonment. The offences divide into three categories.

Offences where the firm is involved in a client matter or transaction

23.2.1.   It is an offence:

(a)   to acquire, use or possess the proceeds of criminal conduct (section 329);

(b)   to conceal, disguise, convert, transfer or remove from the UK the proceeds of criminal conduct (section 327);

(c) to be concerned in an arrangement which facilitates the acquisition, retention, use or control of another person's criminal property, where there is knowledge or suspicion that this is the case (section 328).

23.2.2. Criminal property is defined as the benefit (or representation of the benefit) of a person's criminal conduct, i.e. any conduct which constitutes a crime in the UK, or if undertaken abroad, would have constituted a crime if committed in the UK. It is necessary for the alleged offender to know or suspect that it does constitute or represent such a benefit (section 340). A defence came into effect on 15 May 2006 and applies where there are reasonable grounds for believing the conduct occurred abroad and it was not unlawful conduct in that overseas jurisdiction (and was not of a description proscribed by Order).

23.2.3. A defence is available where disclosure of knowledge or suspicion is made to the Serious Organised Crime Agency (SOCA) or to a Nominated Officer, i.e. a firm's Money Laundering Reporting Officer (MLRO) (section 338).

Offences following a disclosure report made to the SOCA or to the firm's Nominated Officer (section 333A)

23.2.4. It is an offence to disclose to any person (including your own client) that a report has been made to the SOCA or to the firm's MLRO in circumstances where this is likely to prejudice an investigation (tipping off). There is a defence available to professional legal advisers who may make a disclosure to a client for the purpose of dissuading the client from engaging in criminal conduct.

23.2.5. Further, once a report has been made to the SOCA or to the MLRO it may be an offence to continue to act for the client without the consent of the SOCA or the MLRO. The MLRO can only give consent where he knows of or suspects money laundering if he has disclosed details to the SOCA and the SOCA has, in turn, either given consent for the firm to continue to act or the SOCA has not, before the end of seven working days of the MLRO's disclosure, refused consent to continue to act.

Offences involving a failure to disclose knowledge or suspicion of money laundering (section 330)

23.2.6. It is an offence for a person who knows or suspects or who has reasonable grounds for knowing or suspecting that another is engaged in money laundering not to disclose that information where the information came to him in the course of business in the regulated sector. On 15 December 2007 the definition of the regulated sector was amended. The definition includes participation in financial or real property transactions concerning (*inter alia*) the buying or selling of real property. Conveyancing transactions will therefore be within the 'regulated sector' for these purposes. The section provides that a person does not commit an offence if he is a professional legal adviser and the information came to him in privileged circumstances.

23.3. Money laundering and conveyancers

23.3.1. Solicitors involved in property transactions are at particular risk – many of the typical day-to-day transactions in the property department could, potentially, bring a solicitor within the ambit of the legislation. The Law Society's Practice Note contains specific examples involving property work.

23.3.2. The following are specific areas of concern.

(a) **Use of client account**

Money launderers will find it difficult to pass money through banks and financial institutions without providing a good reason. Passing money through a solicitor's client account with repayment on a 'clean' client account cheque or electronic banking transfer is a useful laundering transaction. Solicitors should take particular care where property trans-actions are aborted after the payment of substantial sums into client account (i.e. payments made for a deposit or purchase price) or where costs are paid twice (particularly if the second payment is from a third party indicating that they had agreed to pay the client's costs).

(b) **Purchase of property with suspect funds**

Once money has been cleaned as a result of passing sums through a number of transactions, the money launderer will wish to invest the laundered funds in such a way that no one will suspect the asset to be the indirect benefit from crime. Property purchase is an ideal investment – particularly commercial property which will bring in a rental income as well as potentially giving rise to a capital gain. Solicitors acting on the conveyancing will be facilitating the acquisition, use, retention and control of criminal property in these cases and can be guilty of an offence if they do so with knowledge or suspicion. Solicitors who defend clients charged with criminal offences should be particularly alert to the danger of money laundering if their firms also undertake property work.

(c) **Tax evasion and welfare benefit fraud**

The notional proceeds of tax evasion or welfare benefit fraud (i.e. the amount of money equal to the savings in tax or benefit received) are criminal property. Information regarding tax evasion and/or welfare benefit fraud may come to light during a conveyancing retainer. Where there is knowledge or suspicion that assets (including bank balances) have been acquired after the date of any such evasion or fraud, solicitors should be cautious and consider possible money laundering implications. Real property itself may be criminal property if it has been purchased using funds which are criminal property or purchased using a mortgage which is subject to monthly payments from a bank account containing the notional proceeds of a crime. Any subsequent sale of the property would amount to money laundering. Abuse of the Stamp Duty

Land Tax procedure may also give rise to money laundering implications, e.g. through misleading apportionment of the purchase price.

(d) **Mortgage fraud**

The proceeds of a mortgage fraud will be criminal property. A solicitor
who assists a client in mortgage fraud will be facilitating the acquisition
of criminal property within section 328. It is not necessary for the
solicitor to know that the client is committing a mortgage fraud. The
solicitor can be guilty under section 328 if he suspects that the circumstances will lead to fraud. Further, even if a solicitor is not involved in
the mortgage application, completing a purchase using the proceeds of
a mortgage fraud will facilitate the retention, use or control of criminal
property. A solicitor who therefore proceeds to completion suspecting
that the client has been engaged in mortgage fraud is at risk of prosecution under section 328.

23.4.   The conduct issues

23.4.1.   Note (ix) to Rule 15 Solicitors' Accounts Rules 1998 warns solicitors that they
should not provide banking facilities for third parties (including clients of the
firm) as this might lead to assisting money launderers. In the case of *Wood and
Burdett*,[1] the Solicitors' Disciplinary Tribunal said that it is not a proper part of a
solicitor's everyday business or practice to operate a banking facility for third
parties, whether they are clients of the firm or not. Solicitors should not,
therefore, provide banking facilities through a client account. Further, solicitors are likely to lose the exemption under Financial Services and Markets Act
2000 if a deposit is taken in circumstances which do not form part of a solicitor's
practice. It should also be borne in mind that there are criminal sanctions
against assisting money launderers.

Disclosure and legal professional privilege

23.4.2.   Legal professional privilege may prevent solicitors from reporting their
suspicions. The Court of Appeal in *Bowman* v. *Fels* (2005) EWCA Civ 226
confirmed that common law legal professional privilege is not overridden by
the authorised disclosure defence. Consequently, before making a disclosure to
the authorities, a solicitor must consider whether any knowledge or suspicion
arises as a result of legal professional privilege. If it does, no disclosure can be
made without a client waiver, and before that waiver can be obtained, the
solicitor would have to consider the tipping-off offences. However, privilege
does not extend to information communicated in order to further a criminal
purpose.

1.   *Wood and Burdett* (Solicitors' Disciplinary Tribunal, case number 8669/2002 filed on 13 January 2004).

23.5. Money Laundering Regulations 2007

23.5.1. The Regulations (SI 2007/2157) implement the Third European Money Laundering Directive (Council Directive 2005/60/EC of 25 November 2005) and came into force on 15 December 2007.

Scope of the 2007 Regulations

23.5.2. The Regulations apply to the following persons acting in the course of business carried on by them in the United Kingdom ('relevant persons')

    (a)   credit institutions;

    (b)   financial institutions;

    (c)   auditors, insolvency practitioners, external accountants and tax advisers;

    (d)   independent legal professionals;

    (e)   trust or company service providers;

    (f)   estate agents;

    (g)   high value dealers;

    (h)   casinos.

The obvious activities affecting solicitors will be in the case of (c) where they are providing tax advice or (d) when acting as independent legal professionals. Solicitors will also be caught by the Regulations if they act as estate agents as in (f).

23.5.3. Regulation 3(9) defines an 'independent legal professional' as a firm or sole practitioner who by way of business provides legal or notarial services to other persons, when participating in financial or real property transactions concerning, *inter alia*, the buying and selling of real property or business entities; or the managing of client money, securities or other assets. Conveyancing services will be within the scope of the Regulations.

Systems and training to prevent money laundering

23.5.4. The 2007 Regulations impose a requirement that solicitors establish procedures relating to:

    (a)   customer due diligence and ongoing monitoring;

    (b)   reporting;

    (c)   record-keeping procedures;

    (d)   internal control;

    (e)   risk assessment and management;

(f) the monitoring and management of compliance with, and the internal communication of, such policies and procedures.

The Regulations also require provision of training on anti-money laundering to all relevant employees. Failure to comply with the Regulations is a criminal offence.

Customer due diligence

23.5.5. Part 2 of the Money Laundering Regulations 2007 deals with the requirements relating to 'customer due diligence' (CDD) and replaces the identification procedures required by the 2003 Regulations. Significant changes have been made to a solicitor's obligations and changes to internal systems will be required as a result of these obligations.

Meaning of customer due diligence

23.5.6. Regulation 5 defines customer due diligence (CDD) as meaning:

(a) identifying the customer and verifying the customer's identity on the basis of documents, data or information obtained from a reliable and independent source;

(b) identifying, where there is a beneficial owner who is not the customer, the beneficial owner and taking adequate measures, on a risk-sensitive basis, to verify his identity so that the relevant person is satisfied that he knows who the beneficial owner is, including, in the case of a legal person, trust or similar legal arrangement, measures to understand the ownership and control structure of the person, trust or arrangement; and

(c) obtaining information on the purpose and intended nature of the business relationship.

This is probably the most onerous of the obligations applicable to solicitors who are subject to the regulations. It requires firms to have in place procedures which ensure that satisfactory evidence of clients' and beneficial owners' identification is obtained.

23.5.7. Solicitors must determine the extent of CDD measures on a risk-sensitive basis depending on the type of customer, business relationship, product or transaction and must be able to demonstrate to the Solicitors Regulation Authority that the extent of the measures is appropriate in view of the risks of money laundering.

Beneficial owners

23.5.8. In addition to verifying a client's identity, regulation 5(b) requires solicitors to identify any beneficial owner who is not the client and to verify the beneficial owner's identity. Unlike the requirements relating to the verification of a client's identity (i.e. document, data or information obtained from a reliable and independent source), the verification of a beneficial owner need only be undertaken by taking 'adequate measures on a risk sensitive basis'. This means in many cases, verification of a beneficial owner's identity can be satisfied by information provided by the client.

23.5.9. For conveyancers, identifying beneficial owners will commonly be relevant when acting for a body corporate, trust, partnership or other similar legal arrangement. It will be necessary to take measures to understand the ownership and control structure of the client. Regulation 6 identifies and defines six different classes of beneficial owner. These are:

1. **Body corporate** (including a LLP). Regulation 6(1) provides that, except in the case of a company whose securities are listed on a regulated market, a beneficial owner will be any individual who ultimately owns or controls more than 25% of the shares or voting rights in the body, or who otherwise exercises control over the management of the body.

2. **Partnership** (other than a LLP). Regulation 6(2) provides that a beneficial owner will be an individual who ultimately is entitled to or controls more than a 25% share of the capital, profits or voting rights or any individual who otherwise exercises control over the management of the partnership.

3. **Trusts**. Beneficial owners will only arise in circumstances where the trust administers and distributes funds. However where a trust does administer and distributes funds, regulation 6(3) defines a beneficial owner as any individual who is entitled to a specified interest (i.e. a vested interest in the capital of the trust property) in at least 25% of the capital of the trust property. If no beneficiaries (or only some, not all) fall into this category, the beneficial owner is the class of persons in whose main interest the trust is set up or operates. Further, any individual who has control over the trust will be a beneficial owner (this will catch the trustees where a solicitor is acting, e.g., for a beneficiary).

4. **Legal entities or arrangements not falling within regulation 6(1) to (3)**. This could apply when acting for a club or other unincorporated association but only to such bodies who administer and distribute funds. Under regulation 6(6) a beneficial owner is, where the persons who benefit from the entity have been determined, any individual who benefits from at least 25% of the entity's property. If there is no determination as yet, a beneficial owner is the class or persons for whose main interest the entity is set up or operates. Further, anyone who exercises control over at least 25% of the property of the entity or arrangement will be a beneficial owner.

5. **Estates of deceased persons**. Regulation 6(8) provides that the beneficial owner will be the executor, original or by representation, or administrator for the time being of the deceased person, during the administration of the estate.

6. **Agency.** Regulation 6(8) provides that a beneficial owner will include any individual on whose behalf the transaction is being conducted.

Timing of CDD

23.5.10. CDD must be undertaken before a business relationship is established or before an occasional transaction is carried out. A business relationship is defined as a relationship which is expected to have an element of duration. Conveyancing transactions should be treated as business relationships.

23.5.11. If CDD cannot be completed in time, transactions cannot be carried out through a bank account, business relationships cannot be established and any existing business relationship must be ended. However, CDD can be completed during the establishment of a business relationship where it is necessary not to interrupt the normal course of business and there is little risk of money laundering.

On-going monitoring

23.5.12. Unlike the 2003 Regulations, under the 2007 Regulations a solicitor's obligations relating to CDD are not discharged once CDD has been completed at the outset of the retainer. The 2007 Regulations contain obligations relating to on-going monitoring. Ongoing monitoring means:

    (a) scrutiny of transactions undertaken throughout the relationship to ensure transactions are consistent with knowledge of client, their business and risk profile; and

    (b) keeping documents, data or information obtained for CDD up to date.

In addition to applying CDD at the outset of a transaction, CDD must also be applied when money laundering is suspected or when there is doubt over the veracity or adequacy of documents, data, or information previously obtained for CDD purposes. Chapter 4 Law Society's Practice Note contains detailed advice on how CDD can be carried out.

Policies and procedures

23.5.13. Firms must establish and maintain appropriate and risk sensitive policies relating to, *inter alia*, reporting and record keeping. Records should be kept of CDD material and supporting evidence and records (reg.21).

23.5.14. Internal reporting procedures are necessary and there must be a person within the firm to whom all information about known or suspected money launderers is to be given, 'the Nominated Officer' (usually known as the MLRO). The Nominated Officer will probably be a partner. Anyone in the firm must disclose to the Nominated Officer any information or matter which comes into his possession in the course of relevant business, as a result of which he knows or suspects or has reasonable grounds for knowing or suspecting that a person is engaged in money laundering. Where such disclosure is made, the Nominated Officer must determine whether it does give rise to such knowledge or suspicion and, if so, must report to the SOCA.

Training

23.5.15. All relevant employees must be made aware of the law relating to money laundering and regularly be given training in how to recognise and deal with transactions which may relate to money laundering (reg.21).

Reporting to the SOCA

23.5.16. All reports are dealt with nationally by the SOCA. Section 339 Proceeds of Crime Act 2002 allows the Secretary of State by order to prescribe the form and manner of disclosure reports. At the time of writing no such order has been made. It is therefore recommended that reports are made on the standard form which can be found at **www.soca.gov.uk**.

23.6. Summary

23.6.1. The law and regulations on money laundering are complex and far-reaching.

23.6.2. In the context of conveyancing, the solicitor must ensure that he properly identifies his client (and any beneficial owner) at the outset of the transaction, and has in place procedures for recording that information and a 'reporting officer' has been appointed within the firm. Ongoing monitoring under the 2007 Regulations must be undertaken by all fee-earners.

23.6.3. The source of any large cash payments from a client should be verified. It may be prudent to include a sentence in the client care letter to the effect that the solicitor will not accept cash payments from the client in excess of a stated amount (e.g. £500).

23.6.4. The solicitor should also be wary of the client who withdraws from a transaction without good reason after payment of the deposit and requires his deposit to be returned to him. This is one example of how money may be laundered through a solicitor's client account.

23.6.5. Any suspicious circumstance involving the handling of client's money must be reported to the firm's reporting officer.

A24. Mortgage fraud

24.1. Guidance from the Law Society

24.1.1. Solicitors need to be alert to the possibility of a mortgage fraud. The Law Society issued a Mortgage Fraud Practice Note on 18 March 2008, which was updated on 15 April 2009 (see Appendix II.4). Furthermore, the Solicitors Regulation Authority have issued warning cards on fraudulent financial arrangements, money laundering and property fraud. These cards can be found at **www.sra.org.uk/warningcards**. The following paragraphs outline the most common types of fraud and the solicitor's duty in relation to a suspected fraud.

24.2. Solicitor's duty

24.2.1. If a solicitor is aware that his client is attempting to perpetrate fraud in any form, he must immediately cease acting for that client.

24.2.2. Rule 2.01 Solicitors' Code of Conduct 2007 states that:

'... you must refuse to act or cease acting for a client in the following circumstances:

(a)   when to act would involve you in a breach of the law or a breach of the rules of professional conduct;'

24.2.3. Failure to comply with the Rule carries with it the risk of criminal prosecution (for having aided and abetted a fraud) and/or civil action (breach of contract or negligence by, e.g. a lender who suffers loss) and of being disciplined for breach of the Code of Conduct.

24.2.4. A solicitor may be guilty of conspiracy to defraud by undertaking the conveyancing work for a client who is himself engaged in a fraudulent transaction. The solicitor's active knowledge of or participation in the fraud is not necessary; if the work involved in the conveyancing falls below the standard expected of a normal solicitor, this may indicate that the solicitor had no genuine belief in the transaction in which he was acting and imply that the solicitor was involved in the conspiracy. A solicitor who is found guilty of fraud is likely to be struck off the Roll.

24.3.   Types of fraud

Status

Income

24.3.1.   The borrower overstates his income in the mortgage application, usually with the sole aim of securing a higher mortgage. A solicitor who knows that his client is unemployed or that there are substantial arrears owing on the client's current mortgage should be alert to the possibility of mortgage fraud but is not under a duty to inform the lender of these circumstances unless the lender's instructions expressly require him to do so.[1]

Identity

24.3.2.   The borrower conceals his true identity, perhaps to disguise the fact that he has another subsisting mortgage. Fraud can also occur where a husband forges his wife's signature (or vice versa). An indication of this type of fraud is where the solicitor is asked to contact the husband at his business address rather than his home address. Another example in this category is the sale at an inflated price to an individual by a company controlled by him. This device is used to raise additional finance for the company. This type of fraud is sometimes carried out on a large scale and often involves other fraud, e.g. tax, improvement grants. Instructions to purchase or transfer the property into the name of nominees may indicate a fraud of this type. In all cases where the client is not personally known to the solicitor, the identity of the client must be checked. Where there are co-buyers (e.g. husband and wife), instructions must be confirmed from both of them.[2]

Property

Price reduction

24.3.3.   The price to be shown in the purchase deed is less than that agreed to be paid by the buyer, or situations where the client instructs that a reduced price has been agreed to take account of an allowance for 'repairs to the property'. In some cases, the amounts shown in the contract and purchase deed will be identical but fraud occurs because the full amount of the purchase price is never in fact paid, e.g. the buyer says he has paid money directly to the seller, or that part of the price has been set off by the buyer against money owed to him by the seller.

Fraudulent valuations

24.3.4.   Where it appears that the valuation of the property is higher than might be expected for a property of that type or is considerably higher than the figure in a recent (say within the last 12 months) disposal of the property. A solicitor is not an expert in valuations and cannot be expected to advise on the accuracy of a valuation obtained by the client; nevertheless, a valuation which is patently out of line with the apparent value of the property may give rise to suspicion.

Roll-over fraud

24.3.5.   This occurs where the borrower sells a property to an associate at an inflated price. As a result, the associate is able to obtain a higher mortgage. No repayments are made under the mortgage. Before the lender is able to repossess the property, it is sold to another associate for a higher figure, and so on.

Use of sub-sales

24.3.6.   A client instructs a solicitor in the purchase of a property for, say, £100,000. The solicitor is told that the property, currently owned by Y, is to be bought in the name of B who is selling to C at a price of £160,000. B and C are either the same person (using assumed identities) or associated persons. Y may also be a party to the fraud, although in some cases he may be an innocent seller. C obtains a mortgage of £150,000 based on the higher value and secures an immediate profit of £50,000. The balance between the original sale price and the higher sub-sale price is never paid, or is said to be paid direct by B to C, or is allegedly set off by B against money owed to him by C. A simultaneous exchange of contracts followed by a quick completion is often a feature of these transactions. The lender is then left with a property worth only £100,000 as security for the loan.[3] A variation on this theme is where A grants a lease to B at a ground rent; B then assigns the lease to C at a premium. The purpose of this type of transaction is to give C a legal interest on which he can then obtain a mortgage.

Money paid direct

24.3.7.   A deposit or balance of the purchase price which is paid (or said to be paid) direct to the seller from the buyer may indicate a mortgage fraud.

1.   *Penn* v. *Bristol & West Building Society* [1997] 3 All ER 470.
2.   *Bristol & West Building Society* v. *Kramer*, *The Independent*, 26 January 1995.
3.   *Ibid.*

24.4.   **The conduct issues**

24.4.1.   A solicitor must act in the best interests of the client. Where he is acting for both the buyer and his lender, he owes a duty to both. There is a duty to report to the lender any alteration in the purchase price and any other information specifically identified in the lender's instructions.[1]

24.4.2.   The solicitor's duty of confidentiality means that the buyer/borrower must consent to disclosure being made to the lender. This situation may give rise to a conflict of interests between the lender client and the buyer client. The solicitor cannot then continue to act for both clients and cannot continue to act for one client without the consent of the other. The safest course of action to adopt is to cease to act for both clients in these circumstances. Where the solicitor is obliged to cease to act for the lender, he should return the papers to the lender, stating that they are returned 'for professional reasons'. The principles of client confidentiality would usually mean that the lay client would need to waive their confidentiality before the mortgage company could be informed. However, if there was no valid retainer because of the crime/fraud exception, the solicitor can tell the mortgage company without the client's permission. If knowledge or suspicion is formed during the course of the retainer with the mortgage company the solicitor will have a duty to advise the lender because the information is relevant to the lender's decision to make the loan.

24.4.3. Mortgage funds obtained using fraudulent means will be the proceeds of crime. Solicitors must appreciate that knowledge or suspicion of a client's mortgage fraud may require action to be taken under Proceeds of Crime Act 2002 (see A23).

1. *Alliance & Leicester Building Society* v. *Edgestop Ltd* [1994] 2 EGLR 229; *Bristol & West Building Society* v. *May, May and Merriman* [1997] 3 All ER 206.

A25. Rentcharges

25.1. Definition

25.1.1. A rentcharge is generally defined as being a periodic sum issuing out of land which arises other than out of a landlord/tenant relationship.

25.1.2. Since 22 August 1977 rentcharges have not, with limited exceptions, been able to be created (see Rentcharges Act 1977, s.2 and A25.5).

25.1.3. If a rentcharge is created in fee simple or for a fixed term of years it is a legal interest which is binding on a subsequent buyer of the land charged irrespective of notice where the title to the land is unregistered.

25.1.4. A rentcharge for life (e.g. created under a settlement) is equitable only.

25.2. Title

25.2.1. On a sale of unregistered land subject to a rentcharge, in the absence of a provision to the contrary in the contract, the document creating the rentcharge must be abstracted in addition to a 15-year-old good root of title and subsequent documentation.

25.2.2. On first registration of land which is subject to a rentcharge, the rentcharge is noted in the charges register of the title to the land (see Land Registration Rules 2003, r.35(1)).

25.3. Transfer

25.3.1. The benefit of an existing rentcharge must be transferred by deed. Where the rentcharge is registered, Form TR1 should be used and the necessary express assignment of the benefit of the covenant for payment should be inserted in the Additional Provisions Panel of Form TR1. The benefit of a covenant for payment of the rentcharge must be expressly assigned. In the absence of express assignment, the obligation to pay remains, but would be unenforceable by action for its recovery other than by distress or re-entry.[1]

1. *Grant* v. *Edmondson* [1931] 1 Ch 1.

25.4. Extinction

25.4.1. The three main ways in which a rentcharge can come to an end are:

(a) by release by the owner of the rentcharge to the owner of the land charged;

(b) by merger when the owner of the rentcharge and the owner of the land charged become the same person;

(c) by redemption under Rentcharges Act 1977.

25.4.2. Except for rentcharges which are exempted under Rentcharges Act 1977, the 1977 Act provides that every rentcharge will be extinguished at the expiry of the period of 60 years from 22 August 1977 or on the date when it first becomes payable, whichever is later.

25.4.3. On compulsory redemption of a rentcharge and on proof that an applicant has paid the rentcharge price either to the person entitled to payment or into court, the Secretary of State or the National Assembly for Wales will issue a redemption certificate. Where a rentcharge is redeemed by agreement or surrender, a deed of release should be drawn up and signed by the parties. Where the land subject to the rentcharge is registered, an application to cancel notice of the rentcharge should be made to the Land Registry.

25.5. Creation of new rentcharges

25.5.1. Rentcharges Act 1977 prevents the creation of new rentcharges after 22 August 1977, except in the following circumstances:[1]

(a) those which give effect to trusts in the case of family charge under Schedule 1, Trusts of Land and Appointment of Trustees Act 1996;

(b) creation of an estate rentcharge;

(c) a rentcharge created under any Act in connection with works on land;

(d) a rentcharge created under an order of the court.

1. Rentcharges Act 1977, s.2(3).

25.6. Estate rentcharges

25.6.1. An estate rentcharge[1] is a rentcharge created for the purposes either:

(a) of making covenants to be performed by the owner of the land affected enforceable by the rent owner against the owner for the time being of the land; or

(b) of meeting the costs of performance by the rent owner of covenants for the provision of services, the carrying out of maintenance or repairs, or effecting insurance or the making of a payment for the benefit of the land affected by the charge.

25.6.2. Rentcharges created under (a) above represent one method of providing for the effective enforcement of positive covenants. Rentcharges under (b) above are a useful method of reserving service charges out of freehold sales, e.g. where a management company covenants to maintain amenity areas or to provide services, although some lenders are reluctant to lend money on the security of a property which is subject to such a charge.

25.6.3. The rentcharge must represent a payment for the performance by the rent owner of a covenant (e.g. for insurance, etc., under (b) above) which is reasonable in relation to that covenant. If this provision is not complied with, the rentcharge will not be a valid estate rentcharge unless the amount reserved is only nominal.

25.6.4. It appears, however, that the wording of the rentcharge does not have to be expressed to require a reasonable sum, it is sufficient that the actual sum should be reasonable. Where the amount is no more than 100% of the expenditure incurred on behalf of owners of properties on an industrial estate this has been held to be reasonable.[2]

1. Rentcharges Act 1977, s.2(4).
2. *Orchard Trading Estate Management Ltd* v. *Johnson Security Ltd* [2002] 2 EGLR 1.

25.7. Apportionment

25.7.1. By Rentcharges Act 1977, s.4, the owner of land affected by a rentcharge which also affects other land not owned by him may in certain circumstances apply to the Secretary of State or the National Assembly for Wales for a certificate apportioning the rent between the two parcels of land. A similar procedure exists for the apportionment of a rentcharge on a sale of part of land.

25.7.2. By Standard Condition 4.5 and Standard Commercial Property Condition 6.5 the buyer is not entitled to object to an informal apportionment of a rentcharge as being a defect in title.

25.7.3. The Land Registry's requirements are set out in its Practice Guide 56.

25.8. Registration of rentcharges

25.8.1. If a rentcharge capable of subsisting as a legal interest is granted out of a registered title, then, in accordance with the fundamental principles of registration of title, the disposition must be completed by registration to be legally effective.[1] The compulsory first registration provisions do not apply to rentcharges. They may, however, be registered voluntarily.[2]

25.8.2. If it appears to the registrar that a right to determine a registered rentcharge is exercisable he may enter notice of the fact in the register.[3] An application for such an entry must be supported by evidence to satisfy the registrar that the applicant has the right to determine the rentcharge and that the right is exercisable.[4]

1. Land Registration Act 2002, s.27(1) and (2)(b).
2. Land Registration Act 2002, s.3.
3. Land Registration Act 2002, s.64.
4. Land Registration Rules 2003, r.125.

A26. Home information packs

26.1   Suspension and abolition of HIPs

26.1.1.   From 1 August 2007 a 'responsible person' had several duties under Housing Act 2004[1] in relation to marketing a residential property in England and Wales, including:

    (a)   to have in his possession a Home Information Pack (HIP);

    (b)   to provide a copy of the HIP to a potential buyer on request;

    (c)   to ensure the contents of the HIP complied with the HIP regulations.[2]

26.1.2.   On 20 May 2010 the Department for Communities and Local Government announced that 'with immediate effect, Home Information Packs are suspended'.[3] A statutory instrument suspending the duties under sections 155–159 Housing Act 2004 came into force on 21 May 2010.[4] Provisions effecting the permanent abolition of HIPs are likely to be contained in the Decentralism and Localism Bill, announced in the Queen's Speech on 25 May 2010.

26.1.3.   Although the HIP was previously the trigger for commissioning an Energy Performance Certificate and the vehicle for its supply, the EPC is provided for by separate regulations that remain in force, unaffected by the suspension of HIPs.[5] On 21 May 2010 amendments were made to the principal EPC regulations introducing an alternative means of requiring the commission of an EPC and its provision to potential buyers of residential property (see A26.2).

1   Housing Act 2004, Part 5, ss.155–159.
2. Home Information Pack (No.2) Regulations 2007 (SI 2007/1667) as amended by SIs 2007/3301, 2008/572, 2008/1266, 2008/3107, 2009/34.
3. The announcement made by Communities Secretary Eric Pickles and Housing Minister Grant Shapps is reported on the Department for Communities and Local Government website (**www.communities.gov. uk**) in the news item 'Pickles and Shapps announce HIPs are History' (20 May 2010).
4. Home Information Pack (Suspension) Order 2010 (SI 2010/1455) under the power granted by section 162 Housing Act 2004.
5. Energy Performance of Buildings (Certificates and Inspections) Regulations 2007 (SI 2007/991) as amended.

26.2.   Energy performance certificates

26.2.1.   On 21 May 2001 an order[1] amending the principal EPC regulations[2] brought into force duties for the seller and the person acting on behalf of the seller, in place of those duties contained in Part 5 Housing Act 2004 previously in effect. See A27 for more information about these duties and EPCs generally. Broadly, the duties in effect from 21 May 2010 are:

(a) the seller must 'secure' that an EPC has been commissioned before the property is 'put on the market';

(b) 'a person acting on behalf of the seller' must not market the property unless he is first satisfied that an EPC has been commissioned;

(c) both the 'seller' and 'the person acting on behalf of the seller' must make 'all reasonable efforts to secure' that a valid EPC is obtained within 28 days of first putting the property on the market;

(d) the person providing 'written particulars' for the purposes of marketing the property must ensure that these particulars include the asset rating from the EPC or a copy of the EPC is 'attached to the particulars'.

1. Energy Performance of Buildings (Certificates and Inspections) (England and Wales) (Amendment) Regulations 2010 (SI 2010/1456).
2. Energy Performance of Buildings (Certificates and Inspections) (England and Wales) Regulations 2007 (SI 2007/991).

26.3.   Previous content of HIPs

26.3.1. The HIP regulations divided the content of HIPs into 'required' (mandatory) and 'authorised' (optional) documents.

26.3.2. The mandatory documents and information in a HIP previously included:

(a) a home information pack index;

(b) a property information questionnaire;

(c) an energy performance certificate or equivalent for properties being constructed;

(d) a sustainability certificate or a nil-rated certificate (when marketing new homes);

(e) a sale statement;

(f) an official copy of the title register and an official copy of the title plan (or a certificate of an official search of the index map and 'such other documents on which the seller can reasonably be expected to rely in order to deduce title');

(g) replies to enquiries of local authority;

(h) replies to a search of the local land charges register;

(i) replies to standard drainage and water enquiries;

(j) any leases or licences to which the property is subject or will be subject following completion of the sale;

(k) the lease and replies to the leasehold part of the property information
     questionnaire (or for new leasehold interests: the terms of the lease
     proposed and estimates of service charges, ground rent and insurance).

26.3.3. The sustainability certificate or nil-rated certificate for new homes was a
required document in a HIP for residential property in England from 31 March
2008.[1] Unlike the position with EPCs, the requirement to supply a sustainability certificate to potential buyers of residential property remains suspended as a
result of the suspension of the duties under sections 155–159 Housing Act 2004.

26.3.4. The Home Condition Report was a type of survey prepared by a qualified home
inspector and, despite being a central document in earlier draft HIP regulations,
was an authorised (optional) document in the HIP.

1. Home Information Pack (Amendment) Regulations 2008 (SI 2008/572).

26.4.   Further information

26.4.1. Information and links to legislation relating to the suspended regime for HIPs
can be found on the Law Society's website at **www.lawsociety.org.uk/hips** and
the Department for Communities and Local Government website
(**www.communities.gov.uk**).

A27. Energy performance of buildings

27.1. The energy performance of buildings directive

27.1.1. The European Union directive on the energy performance of buildings ('the directive')[1] came into force on 4 January 2003. Its objective is 'to promote the improvement of the energy performance of buildings within the Community, taking into account outdoor climatic and local conditions, as well as indoor climate requirements and cost-effectiveness'.

27.1.2. The directive lays down requirements regarding a general framework for calculation of the energy performance of buildings, the application of minimum requirements for energy performance, energy certification of buildings and the regular inspection of air-conditioning systems and boilers.

27.1.3. The obligations to be met under the directive are to 'ensure that when buildings are constructed, sold or rented out, an energy performance certificate is made available to the owner or the prospective buyer or tenant, as the case may be'.

27.1.4. A proposal to revise the directive to strengthen and extend its scope was presented by the European Commission in 2008.[2] The recast of the energy performance of buildings directive[3] was published in the Official Journal of the European Union on 18 June 2010.

1. Directive 2002/91/EC of the European Parliament and of the Council of 16 December 2002 on the energy performance of buildings.
2. See the consultation document 'Recast of the Energy Performance of Buildings Directive' at **www.communities.gov.uk/publications/planningandbuilding**.
3. Directive 2010/31/EU of the European Parliament and of the Council of 19 May 2010 on the energy performance of buildings (recast).

27.2. The Regulations

27.2.1. Energy Performance of Buildings (Certificates and Inspections) (England and Wales) Regulations 2007 (as amended)[1] ('the regulations') implement Articles

7, 9 and 10 of the directive. The duties imposed by the regulations were subject to a phased implementation.

27.2.2. The regulations create duties for sellers and landlords prior to any agreement for sale or rent, duties on the construction of buildings and on the completion of certain modifications to existing buildings. The regulations apply to both commercial and residential property and affect the majority of buildings in England and Wales.

27.2.3. For the purposes of the regulations a building means: 'a roofed construction having walls, for which energy is used to condition the indoor climate, and a reference to a building includes a reference to a part of building which has been designed or altered to be used separately'.[2]

27.2.4. The regulations include provision for the:

- creation and supply of energy performance certificates (EPCs) and recommendation reports;

- commissioning of EPCs before putting a residential property on the market;

- inclusion of an 'asset rating' or attachment of a copy of an EPC to the written particulars given to prospective buyers of a residential property once a valid EPC has been obtained;

- production and display of display energy certificates (DECs);

- accreditation of energy assessors;

- creation of a register or registers to store certificates and reports;

- inspections of air-conditioning systems; and

- enforcement of duties.

27.2.5. Since 1 October 2008 an EPC has been required on the construction, sale or rent of all buildings subject to minor exceptions.

27.2.6. Articles 3–6 of the directive were implemented in England and Wales by separate regulations[3] and the Building Regulations have been amended to allow for the establishment of standard methods to assess energy performance (see also B24.8).

1. Energy Performance of Buildings (Certificates and Inspections) (England and Wales) Regulations 2007 (SI 2007/991) as amended by Energy Performance of Buildings (Certificates and Inspections) (England and Wales) (Amendment) Regulations 2007 (SI 2007/1669); Energy Performance of Buildings (Certificates and Inspections) (England and Wales) (Amendment No.2) Regulations 2007 (SI 2007/3302); Energy Performance of Buildings (Certificates and Inspections) (England and Wales) (Amendment) Regulations 2008 (SI 2008/647); Energy Performance of Buildings (Certificates and Inspections) (England and Wales) (Amendment No.2) Regulations 2008 (SI 2008/2363); Energy Performance of Buildings (Certificates and Inspections) (England and Wales) (Amendment) Regulations 2009 (SI 2009/1900); Energy Performance of Buildings (Certificates and Inspections) (England and Wales) (Amendment) Regulations 2010 (SI 2010/1456).

2. For further information as to the interpretation of this definition see the guidance available at **www.communities.gov.uk/planningandbuilding/publications/guidance**.
3. Building and Approved Inspectors (Amendment) Regulations 2006 (SI 2006/652).

27.3.   Energy performance certificate and recommendation report

27.3.1.   The EPC must be issued by an energy assessor accredited to produce EPCs for the particular category of buildings concerned (see A27.5). In most cases an EPC is prepared following a physical inspection of the building.[1] The energy assessor's inspection involves the compilation of various details of a building, including size, type, age, construction materials, insulation, roof type, heating systems, and amount and type of glazing. Broadly, an EPC should reflect the energy performance of the space being offered for sale or rent.

27.3.2.   The information gathered during the inspection and the criteria applied to it differs depending on whether the building is or will be a dwelling and whether it is newly constructed.[1] The certificate is generated from this data using a standard software package and must contain the information specified in regulation 11.

27.3.3.   An EPC contains the asset rating, reference information (including the unique reference report number as stored on the central register), date, estimated energy use, details of the energy assessor and his accreditation scheme, details on how to complain, and general advice on energy efficiency. It must also be accompanied by a recommendation report.

Asset rating

27.3.4.   The asset rating is a main element of the EPC. It is a numerical indicator of the amount of energy estimated to meet the needs of a standard use of a building. In some circumstances it may be supplied separately to the EPC (see A27.6.4). The asset rating of a domestic EPC illustrates the energy efficiency rating (how energy efficient the home is) and the environmental impact rating (in terms of carbon dioxide emissions) of the building. The asset rating of a non-domestic EPC uses a carbon dioxide (CO_2) based index.

27.3.5.   The asset rating of a building is calculated according to a government approved methodology. The rating is expressed by a number and graphically, by coloured bands labelled A–G (with A being the most efficient), similar to the ratings given to household white goods.

27.3.6.   The asset rating is calculated by comparing various details of a building to a model of how energy efficient a building of that type and size ought to be. It does not record the actual energy consumption of a building.

Recommendation report

27.3.7. A recommendation report is prepared by the energy assessor who carries out the energy assessment and such a report must accompany the EPC. The report must make recommendations for the improvement of the energy performance of the building. For each improvement the cost of making it and the typical saving gained by making it are given. The asset rating graphs in the EPC show the 'potential' ratings which could be achieved for the building if all the recommendations are acted upon. There is no duty to carry out the recommendations in the report.

Registration and validity

27.3.8. The EPC and recommendation report, and the data collected to generate it, must be entered by the energy assessor on a central register (via the appropriate accreditation scheme) prior to supplying a copy of it to the person who commissioned the EPC. It must remain stored in the register for a period of at least 20 years (reg.31).

27.3.9. An EPC remains valid for a period of 10 years. The most recent EPC will be the only valid EPC.

27.3.10. There are two central registers for EPCs, one for EPCs commissioned for dwellings (the domestic EPC register) and the other for EPCs for non-dwellings (the non-domestic EPC register). Both are operated by Landmark Information Group on behalf of the government (**www.epcregister.com**).

27.3.11. The EPC for a building can be viewed and printed from the appropriate register by entering the unique report reference number that appears on the EPC. Access to the register is restricted in this way. It is a criminal offence to disclose an EPC unlawfully.[2]

27.3.12. Examples of the different forms of EPC used for domestic and non-domestic buildings are available from the Department for Communities and Local Government website at **www.communities.gov.uk/planningandbuilding/theenvironment/energyperformance**.

1. However, an EPC for a flat or a unit in a block may be based on an assessment of another unit in the same block. See the guidance available as to producing EPCs for portfolios of similar residential properties at **www.communities.gov.uk/planningandbuilding/publications/guidance**.
2. A recent DCLG consultation, 'Making Better Use of EPCs and Data', proposes allowing wider access to energy efficiency data and extending the scope of EPCs and DECs.

27.4. Display energy certificate (DEC) and advisory report

27.4.1. A DEC is required for buildings with a total useful floor area over $1,000m^2$ occupied by public authorities or other institutions providing public services to a large number of people. Regulation 16 Energy Performance of Buildings

(Certificates and Inspections) (England and Wales) Regulations 2007 provides for occupiers of such buildings to have a valid advisory report and to display a valid DEC in a prominent place clearly visible to the public.

27.4.2. The DEC and advisory report are created by an energy assessor accredited to produce EPCs for the particular category of building concerned (see A27.5). The DEC illustrates the energy performance of a building based on actual energy used and contains an operational rating (reg.15). The advisory report makes recommendations for the improvement of the energy efficiency of such a building.

27.4.3. A DEC is valid for a period of 12 months and an advisory report is valid for a period of seven years (reg.16). If such a building is to be sold or let it will require an EPC.

27.4.4. Further guidance as to DECs and an example of a DEC is available at **www.communities.gov.uk/planningandbuilding/theenvironment/ energyperformance**.

27.5. Energy assessors

27.5.1. An EPC must be created by an energy assessor who is a member of an accreditation scheme approved by the Secretary of State. The energy assessor must be accredited to produce EPCs for the particular category of building concerned at the appropriate level (reg.25).

27.5.2. A number of accreditation schemes for energy assessors have been approved by the Secretary of State. For details of the accredited schemes see **www. communities.gov.uk**.

27.5.3. Such accreditation schemes must contain adequate provision for indemnity arrangements and for facilitating the resolution of complaints (reg.25).

27.5.4. Energy assessors must carry out energy assessments with reasonable care and skill (reg.27). An energy assessor must also include in an EPC a declaration as to any related party disclosure, if appropriate (reg.26).

27.5.5. A national register of accredited domestic energy assessors and details of those in particular areas is available at **www.epcregister.com**. For details of other energy assessors see **www.ndepcregister.com**.

27.6. Duties of the seller

27.6.1. The seller of a residential property[1] for which no valid EPC is available must ensure that an EPC is commissioned before putting the property on the market (reg.5A(2)). A property is put on the market when 'the fact that it is or may become available for sale is, with the intention of marketing the property, first made public in England and Wales by or on behalf of the seller' (reg.5A(5)(b)).[2]

27.6.2. Before marketing such a property, a person acting on behalf of the seller must be satisfied that an EPC has been commissioned (reg.5A(3)).[3]

27.6.3. The seller of such a property, and a person acting on his behalf, must use all reasonable efforts to secure that a valid EPC is obtained for the property before the end of a period of 28 days starting with the day on which the property was first put on the market (reg.5A(4)).

27.6.4. Once a valid EPC has been obtained, the person giving the written particulars of the residential property to potential buyers must ensure that they include the asset rating of the building or that a copy of the EPC is attached.[4]

27.6.5. The seller of a building must make available to any potential buyer a copy of a valid EPC and recommendation report free of charge at the earliest opportunity and, in any event, before entering into a contract for sale (reg.5(2)). The earliest opportunity will be the sooner of the following events:

- when following a request, written information about the building is made available to the potential buyer; or

- when following a request, the building is viewed by a potential buyer.

27.6.6. The seller's duty to make an EPC and recommendation report available to any prospective buyers does not apply (reg.5(3)) if the seller reasonably believes that the prospective buyer:

- is unlikely to have sufficient means to buy the building; or

- is not genuinely interested in buying a building of a general description which applies to the building; or

- is not a person to whom the seller is prepared to sell the building.[5]

27.6.7. An EPC provided by the seller is valid if it is no more than 10 years old and no other EPC has been created since it was made.

27.6.8. The seller has a duty under reg.5(5) to ensure that the person who ultimately becomes the buyer of the building has a valid copy of the EPC and recommendation report free of charge.

1. 'Residential property' means premises in England and Wales consisting of a single dwelling, including any ancillary land (reg.2(1)).
2. A fact is made public when it is advertised or otherwise communicated (in whatever form and by whatever means) to the public or to a section of the public (reg.5A(5)(c)).
3. An EPC is commissioned when a request is made which is properly addressed to an energy assessor accredited to produce EPCs for that category of building and the request is 'in such form, contains all such information and is accompanied by such payment or undertaking to make such payment as is usually necessary to obtain a certificate' (reg.5A(5)(d)).
4. See reg.6 as to the specific requirements and definition of written particulars.
5. This does not authorise any unlawful act of discrimination.

27.7. **Duties of the landlord**

27.7.1. The prospective landlord of a building must supply to any potential tenant a valid EPC and recommendation report free of charge at the earliest opportunity and, in any event, before entering into a contract to let. The earliest opportunity will be the sooner of the following events:

- when following a request, written information about the building is made available to the potential tenant; or

- when following a request, the building is viewed by a potential tenant.

27.7.2. The landlord's duty to make an EPC and recommendation report available to any prospective tenant does not apply (reg.5(3)) if the landlord reasonably believes that the prospective tenant:

- is unlikely to have sufficient means to rent the building; or

- is not genuinely interested in renting a building of a general description which applies to the building; or

- is not a person to whom the landlord is prepared to rent the building.[1]

27.7.3. The landlord has a duty under reg.5(5) to ensure that the person who ultimately becomes the tenant of the building has a valid copy of the EPC and recommendation report free of charge.

1. This does not authorise any unlawful act of discrimination.

27.8. **Duties on construction**

27.8.1. Where a building is erected, or a building is modified to change the number of parts for separate use, the person carrying out the work shall on completion of the works:

- supply an EPC to the owner of the building; and

- give to the local authority notice to that effect with the report reference number of the EPC.

27.8.2. Such an EPC must be produced by an accredited on construction energy assessor. A final completion certificate for a home will not be issued under the Building Regulations until an EPC has been so provided.[1]

27.8.3. The duty to provide an EPC does not apply to buildings whose construction is not yet complete.

1. See Building and Approved Inspectors (Amendment) Regulations 2006 (SI 2006/652).

27.9. **Exemptions**

27.9.1. Regulation 4 Energy Performance of Buildings (Certificates and Inspections) (England and Wales) Regulations 2007 provides that the following buildings do not require an EPC:

- buildings which are used primarily or solely as places of worship;

- temporary buildings with a planned time of use of two years or less;

- industrial sites, workshops and non-residential agricultural buildings with low energy demand;

- stand-alone buildings with a total useful floor area of less than 50m² which are not dwellings.

27.9.2. Under regulation 7 the duty to provide an EPC and recommendation report may not apply where buildings are to be demolished and the resulting site is suitable for development.

27.10. Inspection of air-conditioning systems

27.10.1. An air-conditioning inspection is required if the effective rated output of systems within a building is more than 12 kilowatts:

- where the system has an effective rated output of 250 kilowatts or more, the first inspection must have been carried out by 4 January 2009, and

- where the system has an effective rated output of 12 kilowatts or more, the first inspection must be carried out by 4 January 2011.

27.10.2. Such systems must be inspected at intervals not exceeding five years. The person who controls the operation of the system is the relevant person with responsibility for ensuring an inspection takes place.

27.10.3. An air-conditioning inspection report must include an assessment of its efficiency and contain advice on possible improvements to the system.

27.11. Enforcement

27.11.1. The local Weights and Measures Authority is responsible for the enforcement of the duties under the regulations (reg.38). An authorised officer of an enforcement authority has power to require the production of documents for inspection (reg.39) and, in the event of a breach of duty, has the power to issue a penalty charge notice (reg.40). The amount of the penalty charge is determined according to the category of building and the breach concerned (reg.43). An appeal against such a penalty charge notice lies to the county court (reg.45).

27.11.2. Regulation 42(1) and (1A) provides a defence where an EPC is unobtainable.

27.11.3. Regulation 50 provides that it is the duty of every person with an interest in, or in occupation of, a building to co-operate with a seller or prospective landlord to allow access to an energy assessor to enable an EPC to be made available.

27.12. Further information

27.12.1. A range of legislation has been introduced by the government with the aim of reducing carbon emissions and securing energy efficiency. Improving the energy performance of buildings is one of the key measures being adopted to reduce such emissions.[1]

27.12.2. The Carbon Reduction Commitment Energy Efficiency Scheme (CRC) was introduced on 1 April 2010.[2] The scheme is a mandatory emissions trading scheme which applies to public sector organisations and large businesses. Further information and guidance is available at **www.environment-agency. gov.uk/business**.

1. See **www.decc.gov.uk** as to other measures proposed to reduce carbon emissions pursuant to the obligations of the United Kingdom under Climate Change Act 2008 and the Kyoto Protocol.
2. See CRC Energy Efficiency Scheme Order 2010 (SI 2010/768).

B. PRE-EXCHANGE

B1. Pre-contract negotiations

1.1. Effect of 'subject to contract'

1.1.1. The phrase 'subject to contract' may no longer be of great importance in view of the fact that Law of Property (Miscellaneous Provisions) Act 1989, s.2, requires the contract for the sale of land to be in writing and signed by both parties. It is unlikely that a contract would inadvertently be entered into by correspondence between the parties (see B1.6.3).

1.1.2. The inclusion of the phrase 'subject to contract' will normally act as a suspensory condition which will prevent the formation of a binding contract until such time as the effect of the condition is removed, e.g. on exchange.

1.1.3. Once introduced, the phrase will continue to govern subsequent correspondence until its effect is expressly or impliedly removed. It is thus not essential that every item of pre-contract correspondence carries the suspensory condition.

1.2. A contract already exists

1.2.1. The phrase 'subject to contract' can only give protection to the parties where no contract exists. If a contract has already come into existence the phrase cannot invalidate or eradicate that contract.

1.3. Removal of suspensory condition

1.3.1. The condition will normally remain in effect until removed with the consent of both parties on exchange. It cannot be removed unilaterally.[1]

1.3.2. However, care should be taken to ensure that the wording of correspondence or telephone conversations does not imply the current existence of a contract which will negate the effect of the 'subject to contract' formula.[2]

1.3.3.   The phrase should thus be used with care and not regarded as a magic formula which will protect the parties in all circumstances.

1.   *Sherbrooke* v. *Dipple* (1980) 255 EG 1203.
2.   See *Griffiths* v. *Young* [1970] Ch 675; *Michael Richards Properties Ltd* v. *Corporation of Wardens of St. Saviour's Parish Southwark* [1975] 3 All ER 416.

1.4.   Protracted negotiations

1.4.1.   In *Cohen* v. *Nessdale*,[1] it was held that the phrase 'subject to contract' continued to govern negotiations despite an interval of some eight months; however, it is unwise to rely on this decision as the continued protection of the phrase cannot be guaranteed in all circumstances.

1.4.2.   Where negotiations for the property have become interrupted or protracted a solicitor should not rely on the continued effect of the phrase 'subject to contract'. When negotiations recommence after an interval the 'subject to contract' formula should be repeated in all subsequent correspondence to ensure its continued protection pending the resolution of the negotiations.

1.   [1982] 2 All ER 97.

1.5.   Contract denied

1.5.1.   Difficulties have in the past arisen over the use of the phrase 'subject to contract'[1] and some solicitors prefer to use the words 'contract denied' in preference to 'subject to contract'. However, there is no reported decision on the effect of the phrase 'contract denied' and the phrase should therefore, for safety's sake, be regarded as being similar in operation and effect to the words 'subject to contract'.

1.   See *Law* v. *Jones* [1974] Ch 112; *cf. Tiverton Estates* v. *Wearwell Ltd* [1975] Ch 146.

1.6.   Need for written contract

1.6.1.   In most cases the requirement for a written contract for the sale of land will be satisfied by the formal exchange of contracts by the parties, following negotiations conducted by their respective solicitors (see B11).

1.6.2.   To ensure that no contract inadvertently comes into existence before the parties are ready to exchange it is customary to qualify all pre-contract correspondence with the words 'subject to contract' or 'contract denied'.

1.6.3.   In exceptional cases an exchange of correspondence may satisfy the requirements of section 2 Law of Property (Miscellaneous Provisions) Act 1989, but only where:

(a) the letters set out or incorporate all the terms of the agreement; and

(b) there is an intention that the exchange of letters will result in a binding contract.[1]

Correspondence which is headed 'subject to contract' cannot fulfil the above conditions.[2]

1. *Commission for the New Towns* v. *Cooper (Great Britain) Ltd* [1995] 26 EG 129, CA.
2. *Ibid.*

1.7. Collateral contracts

1.7.1. Section 2 Law of Property (Miscellaneous Provisions) Act 1989 requires that all agreed terms be incorporated into the written contract. As a result, a contract will be invalid if it omits any of the terms agreed between the parties.

1.7.2. One way around this rule was for the party attempting to enforce the contract to argue that the omitted terms formed a collateral contract, and did not have to be included in the main contract. The courts are increasingly reluctant to accept such argument so care should be taken to include all the terms in the main contract.

1.7.3. In *Grossman* v. *Hooper*,[1] Chadwick LJ used the example of the sale of a house and carpets and curtains. If the parties have agreed that the sale of the house will be without the carpets and curtains and later they enter into a separate agreement for the sale of the carpets and curtains, this later agreement could be regarded as independent of the property contract. However, if the agreement for the sale of the house includes the carpets and curtains, the terms relating to the chattels must be included or incorporated into the property contract. If the terms are omitted, the property contract will not satisfy section 2 Law of Property (Miscellaneous Provisions) Act 1989.

1.7.4. It may be possible to avoid this problem by including a clause in the property contract to the effect that all matters agreed in correspondence between the parties' solicitors should be deemed to be included in that contract.[2]

1. *Grossman* v. *Hooper* [2001] 2 EGLR 82.
2. *Jones* v. *Forest Fencing* [2001] NPC 165.

1.8. Lock-out agreements

1.8.1. A lock-out agreement where the seller agrees not to negotiate with any third party for a specified period of time is capable of being a valid collateral contract and does not need to satisfy the requirements of Law of Property (Miscellaneous Provisions) Act 1989, s.2.[1] A lock-in agreement, i.e. to negotiate with these parties only, is never valid.[2]

1.8.2. Breach of a lock-out agreement does not give rise to a claim for substantial damages nor for long-term injunctive relief.[3]

1. *Pitt* v. *PHH Asset Management Ltd* [1993] EGCS 127; *Walford* v. *Miles* [1992] 2 AC 128, HL.
2. *Courtney & Fairburn Ltd* v. *Tolaini Bros Ltd* [1975] 1 WLR 297.
3. *Moroney* v. *Isofam Investments SA* [1997] EGCS 178; *Tye* v. *House* [1997] 41 EG 160, CA.

B2. Contract races

2.1.	Solicitors' Code of Conduct 2007	2.4.	Acting for seller and buyer
2.2.	Solicitor acting for seller	2.5.	Acting for more than one buyer
2.3.	Disclosure of race to buyers	2.6.	Licensed conveyancers

2.1. Solicitors' Code of Conduct 2007

2.1.1. Where a seller's solicitor is asked by his client to deal simultaneously with more than one prospective buyer he is required to comply with Rule 10.06 Solicitors' Code of Conduct 2007 (relations with third parties).

2.1.2. Compliance with the Rule is mandatory and breach thereof can lead to disciplinary action being taken against the solicitor.

2.1.3. The Rule applies irrespective of whether the prospective buyers are supplied with their contracts simultaneously or whether contracts are issued to different prospective buyers one after the other. The supply of documentation such as a plan of the land or Land Registry title number in order to facilitate the transfer of the premises to a buyer is covered by the Rule. As the Rule prohibits 'dealing' with more than one prospective buyer, it is not necessary for each prospective buyer to be supplied with a 'contract', nor need each contract be in identical terms. The Rule applies to both domestic and commercial transactions. The Rule also applies where the seller's solicitor knows that the second (and subsequent) buyer(s) are being dealt with directly by the seller without the solicitor's involvement.

2.1.4. Where, having supplied a prospective buyer with a draft contract or other documentation, the seller later receives a further offer for the property which later offer he would prefer to accept, the seller may accept the second offer but his solicitor should give notice of withdrawal to the first prospective buyer's solicitor prior to dealing with the second prospective buyer and submitting draft papers to him. If notice of withdrawal is given, Rule 10.06 does not apply. Similarly, if the first prospective buyer's solicitor returns the papers to the seller's solicitor before papers are submitted to the second prospective buyer, only one buyer would be in possession of draft papers at any given time, thus a contract race does not exist and Rule 10.06 does not apply. The Rule does not apply to the distribution of auction papers to potential bidders or their solicitors, but does apply where a prospective buyer by private treaty has been given a draft contract and the seller then decides to put the property into auction.

2.1.5. Where information is provided for an estate agent, the solicitor will not have 'dealt' with the prospective buyers and Rule 10.06 will not apply. However, providing additional information, either directly or indirectly through an estate agent, will normally amount to a 'dealing'.

2.2.   Solicitor acting for seller

2.2.1.   Where a solicitor is acting for the seller he must explain to his client that the solicitor is required to comply with the Conduct Rule referred to above, and if the seller refuses to allow the solicitor to make the notification the solicitor must decline to act; see Rule 10.06(1) and (2) Solicitors' Code of Conduct 2007.

2.3.   Disclosure of race to buyers

2.3.1.   If the seller instructs the solicitor to deal with more than one prospective buyer, other than in a sale by auction or tender, the solicitor must at once disclose the seller's decision direct to the solicitor acting for each prospective buyer or (where no solicitor is acting) to the prospective buyer(s) in person. Such disclosure should be made immediately by the most suitable means but if made face to face, or by telephone, the solicitor should consider confirming the instruction in writing. Prior to making the disclosure the client's authority must be obtained. If the client refuses to give his authority the solicitor must cease to act.

2.3.2.   The solicitor's obligation under Rule 10.06 will also arise where, to the solicitor's knowledge, the seller deals directly with another prospective buyer (or their conveyancer) or the seller instructs another solicitor to deal with another prospective buyer.

2.3.3.   Since buyers are themselves wary of entering into contract races, the seller should also be warned of the danger of losing the prospective buyers altogether if a race is commenced. It is normally preferable to avoid a contract race if at all possible.

2.4.   Acting for seller and buyer

2.4.1.   Even where a solicitor would normally be entitled to act for both the seller and buyer, e.g. because the situation falls within one of the exceptions set out in Rule 3.10 Solicitors' Code of Conduct 2007, the contract race gives rise to a significant risk of conflict of interests between the two clients and the solicitor must not continue to act for both; see Rule 10.06(3) Solicitors' Code of Conduct 2007.

2.5.   Acting for more than one buyer

2.5.1.   Where forms of contract are submitted to more than one prospective buyer, a solicitor must not accept instructions to act for more than one such buyer; Rule 10.06(4) Solicitors' Code of Conduct 2007.

2.6.   **Licensed conveyancers**

2.6.1.   Licensed conveyancers may be regarded in the same light as solicitors; thus, for the purpose of the Rule, disclosure of a contract race to a licensed conveyancer can be treated as disclosure of the race to the client of the conveyancer. Disclosure of the existence of the race must, however, be made directly to the buyer if that buyer is represented by an unqualified person.

B3. Seller's investigation of title

3.1. Seller's investigation of title

3.1.1. Having obtained official copies of the title (registered land) or the seller's title deeds or a copy of them (unregistered land), the seller's solicitor should investigate title before drafting the contract for sale. The manner and method of such investigation is dealt with in D2. Existing land/charge certificates no longer have any legal status and thus their loss/absence is not necessarily a matter of concern.

3.2. Reasons for investigation

3.2.1. The investigation of the title by the seller's solicitor at this stage of the transaction is a precautionary measure to ensure that:

(a) the seller is the owner of or is otherwise entitled to sell the whole of the estate in accordance with the instructions given to his solicitor;

(b) any incumbrances on the title can be revealed in the draft contract in order to satisfy the seller's duty of disclosure;

(c) any defects in the title may be spotted and appropriate steps taken to rectify them before exchange of contracts;

(d) any consents which may be necessary from third parties may be obtained;

(e) any requisitions on title by the buyer can be anticipated, and if necessary an appropriate special condition may be included in the draft contract.

3.2.2. Not all covenants noted on the register at first registration will be binding. The Registrar is not required to check the validity of a covenant on first registration. Rule 35 Land Registration Rules 2003 requires him 'to enter a notice in the register of the burden of any interest which appears from his examination of title to affect the registered estate'. If the applicant for first registration wishes to have a particular covenant omitted from the register he must produce evidence that the covenant is void due to its lack of registration under Land Charges Act

1972.[1] Unless such an application is made the Registrar will enter a notice of the covenant on the register.

1.   See G3.4.7–3.4.9 for further details of Land Registry requirements.

3.3.   Registered titles

3.3.1.   Obtain up-to-date official copies of the title and check to ensure that no entries have been made which will affect the seller's right to sell the property as instructed, e.g. there may be a restriction or a caution against dealings on the register. (Although cautions against dealings were abolished with prospective effect by Land Registration Act 2002, existing cautions were unaffected.)

3.3.2.   On first registration of the title positive covenants may have been omitted from the register; in such a case the seller will need to take an indemnity covenant from the buyer and provide the buyer with a copy of the transfer which imposed the covenants in order to prove the need for indemnity. This latter will involve the inspection of pre-registration title deeds.

3.4.   Unregistered titles

3.4.1.   The solicitor should check when the compulsory registration order came into force in the area and that no dealings which would have induced registration have occurred since that date. The date of compulsory registration for each district is set out in Land Registry Practice Guide 51.

3.4.2.   In most cases the land will require registration after completion of the current transaction. Although this will primarily be the responsibility of the buyer, this factor should be borne in mind by the seller's solicitor in his pre-contract investigation of title so that any areas of difficulty which might be the subject of a requisition by the Land Registry may be clarified.

3.4.3.   If it transpires that the land should have been registered on a previous disposition, an immediate application for late registration must be made by the seller's solicitor, a full disclosure of the situation being made to both the seller and the buyer's solicitor. Title will then need to be dealt with as if the seller's title was awaiting registration at the Land Registry (see B4).

3.4.4.   An index map search should be made to ensure that no part of the land has already been registered without the owner's knowledge and that no caution against first registration affects the land (see B10).

3.4.5.   A Land Charges Department search should be made against the name of the seller to ensure that no incumbrances exist other than those revealed by the title deeds (see B10).

Freeholds

3.4.6.   (a)   Decide which document is to be used as the root of title, and check the validity of the chain of title forwards from that time.

(b)   Does the root document refer to any earlier documents which the buyer may be entitled to call for?

(c)   Are there any pre-root covenants which need to be disclosed to the buyer?

(d)   Are all documents within the chain correctly stamped and executed?

(e)   Watch for change of names, e.g. on marriage or change of a company name. Obtain evidence of the changes if necessary.

(f)   If in doubt as to the effectiveness of restrictive covenants, options or third party rights revealed by the title, a Land Charges Department search should be made to clarify the position.

(g)   Obtain copies of any necessary death certificates or grants of representation.

Existing leaseholds

3.4.7.   Law of Property Act 1925, s.44 limits the right of an intended lessee or assignee of an existing lease to require production of the reversionary title or titles. This limitation, however, does not apply to:

(a)   registered land or a term of years to be derived out of registered land; or

(b)   a contract for the grant of a lease to which the compulsory registration provisions apply.[1]

Where the lease falls outside the compulsory registration provisions and there is little or no premium payable for its assignment the buyer may be content not to insist on deduction of the reversionary title.

3.4.8.   Problems may, however, arise if the title to the freehold was not called for on the original grant of the lease. The following points should be checked:

(a)   Is a marked copy of the freehold title available or can it be obtained? If not, check that the contract excludes the buyer's right to deduction of the freehold.

(b)   Check the chain of title from the lease (or sub-lease) including evidence of surrenders and copies of any necessary consents, e.g. to assignments or alterations.

(c)   Is consent to this assignment required? If so, obtain the names of referees from the buyer's solicitor and forward them to the landlord's solicitor. Obtain a firm estimate from the landlord's solicitor before giving an undertaking for costs.

(d) Is the freehold or superior leasehold title registered? Whether or not this is so can be ascertained by making an index map search. Where the freehold or superior title is registered official copy entries of the title can be obtained by the buyer. This may overcome the limitation posed by the seller being unable to deliver the freehold or superior leasehold title.

1. Law of Property Act 1925, s.44; as amended by Land Registration Act 2002, Sched.11, para.2.

3.5. Title in name of sole owner

3.5.1. Instructions will have revealed whether anyone other than the seller is living at the property. If there is, consideration should be given to the question of whether the occupants have any rights in the property which may impede the seller's intention to sell with vacant possession.

Is the seller married or in a civil partnership?

3.5.2. The seller's spouse or civil partner may have statutory rights of occupation under Family Law Act 1996 and/or a beneficial interest in the property through a contribution to the purchase price. Enquiries should also be made to ascertain whether the non-owning spouse or civil partner has the benefit of an occupation order under Family Law Act 1996.

Homes rights

3.5.3. Current registration of such rights can be verified by inspecting official copies of the title (registered land) or by making a Land Charges Department search against the seller (unregistered land). Even if such rights are not presently protected by registration the spouse or civil partner may still effect a registration at any time until actual completion.

Rights are already registered

3.5.4. It will be a condition of the contract that such registration is removed before completion.[1] Negotiations must be entered into with the spouse's or civil partner's solicitors for the removal of the charge and a satisfactory solution obtained before exchange of contracts.

Rights in existence but not registered

3.5.5. It is unsafe to assume that the spouse or civil partner will not exercise the right to register a charge under Family Law Act 1996 and instructions should be obtained directly from the spouse or civil partner (through a separate solicitor if there is any possibility of conflict of interests) to confirm their consent to the proposed sale. A formal release of rights and agreement not to enforce any such rights against the seller should be prepared for signature before exchange by the non-owning spouse or civil partner.

3.5.6.   A registration under Family Law Act 1996 can be removed on production of:

  (a)   an application made by the person with the benefit of the rights;

  (b)   a divorce decree absolute or dissolution order for a civil partnership;

  (c)   a court order to that effect;

  (d)   the death certificate of the spouse;

unless an order under s.33(5) of the Act has been made and registered.

Beneficial interests

3.5.7.   If it is thought that the spouse or civil partner may also be entitled to a beneficial interest in the property it should be assumed that the property is held by the seller on constructive trust for himself and his spouse or civil partner. The spouse's or civil partner's independent confirmation of agreement to the sale must be obtained and the spouse or civil partner joined as a party to the contract. A solicitor would be well advised to explain to the spouse or civil partner that his/her written consent to the sale is required, that giving such consent may affect his/her legal rights and that the spouse or civil partner should obtain independent advice before signing the release. The dangers of negligence and undue influence should also be noted where the owning spouse or civil partner 'persuades' the non-owning spouse or civil partner to consent to the transaction (see Appendix IV.7).

3.5.8.   Suggested form of wording for release of rights:

  (a)   'In consideration of the buyer entering this agreement I (*name of spouse or civil partner*) agree:

     (i)   to the sale of the property on the terms of this agreement; and

     (ii)   that I will not register rights in relation to the property, whether under Family Law Act 1996 or otherwise, and that I will procure before completion the removal of any registration made by me; and

     (iii)   that I will vacate the property by the completion date.'[2]

  or

  (b)   'In consideration of your today entering into a contract with (*name of owning spouse or civil partner*) for the purchase of the property known as (*insert address of property to be sold*), I agree:

     (i)   to release any beneficial interest which I may have in the property (such interest, if any, being transferred to the proceeds of sale of the property), such release to be effective from the date of completion of the sale of this property;

     (ii)   to procure the cancellation of any registration which may have been effected by me or on my behalf on or before completion, including any registration in respect of rights of occupation which I may have under Family Law Act 1996; and

(iii) to vacate the property by the completion date.'[3]

Sharers and co-habitees

3.5.9. Sharers and co-habitees may be able to establish a beneficial interest in the property through contribution to the purchase price. Investigation must be made of the exact status of each occupier. If necessary a release of rights should be obtained, or they may be joined as parties to the contract. The solicitor should advise the sharer/co-habitee in similar terms to those suggested in B3.5.7. Enquiries should also be made to ascertain whether the non-owning occupier has the benefit of an occupation order under Family Law Act 1996, s.33.

Overriding interests

3.5.10. Persons in actual occupation of registered land may have overriding interests.[4] A formal release of such rights should be obtained. The occupiers may also be joined as contracting parties.

3.5.11. If the existence of a beneficial interest is suspected, the buyer's solicitor may request the appointment of a second trustee to overreach the interest (see B3.6.2).

Tenants

3.5.12. If vacant possession is to be given of the property on completion effective steps must be taken to terminate the tenancies.

3.5.13. If vacant possession is not to be given on completion full details of the tenancies must be obtained since disclosure of the tenancies must be made in the draft contract. Accurate information will be required by the buyer in relation to the amount of rent payable by the tenants, the dates of rent reviews, and the effect of any security of tenure legislation on the tenancies.

1. Family Law Act 1996, Sched.4, para.3(1).
2. This clause should be included in the contract of sale.
3. This clause may either be incorporated in the contract or drawn up as a separate document and attached to the contract. In either case the clause should be signed by the non-owning spouse.
4. Land Registration Act 2002, Sched.1, para.2, Sched.3, para.2 and Sched.12, para.8.

3.6. **Death of a joint proprietor**

Registered land

Registration of restriction

3.6.1. A restriction in either Form A or the earlier Form 62 registered in the proprietorship register indicates that the equitable interest is held on a tenancy in common and two trustees will be needed to transfer the legal estate. A buyer will normally insist that the seller obtains the appointment of a new trustee or the removal of the restriction before taking a transfer from him. If he does not do this then, on lodging his application for registration of the transfer, the buyer would need to produce to the Land Registry such evidence as will satisfy the Registrar that the registered estate is no longer subject to a trust of land.[1] Such evidence might comprise a statutory declaration by the sole survivor that in stated circumstances the declarant has become entitled legally and beneficially to the registered land, that he has not incumbered his undivided share, and that he has not received notice of any incumbrance upon the undivided share of the deceased proprietor. A certificate by the seller's solicitor will be accepted in place of a declaration if the solicitor is able to speak from his knowledge of all the relevant facts.

Appointment of second trustee

3.6.2. The seller's solicitor may be appointed as the new trustee provided that there is no conflict of interest between the instructing client and the other person(s) now entitled to the remainder of the property. The appointment of the second trustee should be dealt with as a matter of urgency so that there are two trustees named in the contract. If there is difficulty over the appointment of a second trustee the contract may include a clause providing that a second trustee will be appointed prior to execution of the purchase deed, the existing trustee contracting alone at this stage of the transaction. This latter situation should be avoided if possible because it is less satisfactory to the buyer who in contracting with one trustee alone has no guarantee that the matter will proceed smoothly to completion.

No restriction registered

3.6.3. Where no restriction is registered the equitable interest may be presumed to have been held under a joint tenancy and the sole surviving joint tenant may sell on production of the death certificate of the deceased.[2]

Unregistered land

3.6.4. Check the document under which the joint owners acquired the property to ascertain whether it was held on a joint tenancy or tenancy in common.

Tenancy in common

3.6.5. The existence of two trustees of the legal estate gives the buyer the assurance that any subsisting beneficial interests will be overreached on completion, thus removing any doubt which may exist as to whether the deceased had disposed of his interest in the property during his lifetime.

Joint tenancy

3.6.6. Check the deed by which the joint tenants bought the property to ensure that no memorandum of severance is endorsed on it and make a bankruptcy search in the Land Charges Department to establish that no bankruptcy proceedings were or are pending against either joint tenant (see B10). Provided that these conditions are satisfied, the sole survivor may sell with a certificate that he is a sole beneficial owner on production of the death certificate of the deceased joint tenant. Again, provided that these conditions are satisfied, the personal representatives of a last surviving joint tenant can convey the land on production of the grant so long as the conveyance contains a statement that the survivor was solely and beneficially entitled to the property. If the joint tenancy has been severed or if bankruptcy proceedings are pending the tenancy must be treated as a tenancy in common and dealt with by the appointment of a second trustee.

1. Land Registration Rules 2003, r.99.
2. Land Registration Rules 2003, r.164.

3.7. Breach of restrictive covenant/other defect in title

Restrictive covenants

3.7.1. If the breach cannot be remedied, e.g. by obtaining belated consent of the person entitled to the benefit of the covenant, consider obtaining restrictive covenant indemnity insurance in an appropriate sum.

Other defects in title

3.7.2. Defects which can be remedied, e.g. the appointment of a new trustee or missing stamp duties should be rectified as soon as possible and in any event before exchange of contracts. Defects which are irremediable will have to be revealed in the draft contract and insurance cover obtained as appropriate (see B6).

3.8. Planning

3.8.1. Although not strictly a matter of title, the seller's solicitor should check at this stage that any necessary planning or building regulation consents have been obtained and complied with. If not with the deeds copies of such consents should be requisitioned from the local authority for the buyer's use.

3.9. Donatio mortis causa

3.9.1. It is possible, although extremely rare, for the seller to have acquired the land through a *donatio mortis causa*.[1] In such a case there will be no documentary evidence of the devolution of title from the deceased to the present seller. Proof of the validity of the seller's title will have to be shown to the buyer; it may be possible to do this by means of a statutory declaration made by the seller.

1. See *Sen* v. *Headley* [1991] 2 All ER 636.

3.10. **Action after investigation of title**

Registered land

3.10.1. Official copies of the title and any other supporting documentation, e.g. evidence of tenancies or overriding interests should be prepared for delivery to the buyer with the draft contract.

Unregistered land

3.10.2. An epitome of title should be prepared for delivery to the buyer with the draft contract.

B4. Seller's title awaiting registration

4.1. The nature of the problem

4.1.1. A seller, after completion of a recent purchase of registered land, may seek to sell the land to a third party before registration of his own transfer has been completed at the Land Registry. As such, he will not at that stage be the registered proprietor of the land.

4.1.2. A similar problem exists where, having bought unregistered land which is subject to compulsory registration, the seller wishes to sell that land before his application for first registration has been completed. In this latter situation he should not sell on his unregistered title to the buyer, leaving the buyer to apply for registration on completion of his purchase, since the seller's title will become void if no application for registration is made by the seller within two months of the completion of his own purchase.[1] A safer course of action is for the seller to submit his application to the registrar for first registration and then to sell on with registration of title pending.

1. Land Registration Act 2002, s.7; and see *Pinekerry* v. *Needs (Contractors)* (1992) 64 P&CR 245.

4.2. Seller's right to deal with land

4.2.1. The seller is entitled to exercise owner's powers in relation to a registered estate if he is the registered proprietor or entitled to be registered as the proprietor.[1]

1. Land Registration Act 2002, s.24.

4.3. Delay

4.3.1. In practice, if the buyer were to insist that completion of his purchase be delayed until the seller became the registered proprietor of the land through completion of the pending application for registration, the transaction might be delayed which would result in adverse practical and financial consequences for both parties. The buyer will normally agree to complete provided that the seller's own title to the land is registered at some time before the buyer's application for registration is completed.

4.3.2. The buyer's lender must be informed of the position and his requirements observed.

4.4. Contractual condition for deduction of title

4.4.1. The seller must prove to the buyer's satisfaction that the seller is a person who is entitled to be registered as proprietor of the land concerned. This is normally achieved by producing to the buyer official copies of the title (which will show the seller's predecessor as registered proprietor), together with a copy of the transfer and a copy of the Land Tax Certificate from the registered proprietor to the seller, appropriate evidence as to those matters upon which the register is not conclusive, a clear Land Registry search against the title, and evidence that the seller lodged a correct application for registration preferably within the priority period afforded by his own search.

4.4.2. Where the land is presently unregistered, the buyer will insist on deduction of the unregistered title together with evidence that the seller has lodged a properly completed application form for first registration of the title. Deduction of title by this method requires the insertion of a special condition to this effect in the contract.

4.4.3. The contract should require the seller to expedite the application and assist the buyer in answering any requisitions which might be raised by the Land Registry in relation to the pending registration.

4.4.4. If the contract requires the buyer to purchase the seller's existing equitable interest in the property (the seller does not have the legal estate until registration is complete), the seller must be required to give an undertaking to transfer the legal estate to the buyer on completion of the seller's registration of title.

4.4.5. Any clause in the contract which relates to obligations that remain in existence after completion will not merge on completion under Standard Condition 7.4.

4.5. Provision for payment of interest by buyer

4.5.1. In order to discourage the buyer from delaying completion by insisting on the seller actually becoming registered as proprietor it is not uncommon to find a contractual provision to the effect that if the buyer does insist on the seller completing his own registration before completion of the sale to the buyer, the buyer will pay interest on the balance of the purchase price at the contract rate for the period between the agreed contractual completion date and actual completion. The Court of Appeal has upheld such a provision.[1]

1. *P & O Overseas Holdings Ltd* v. *Rhys Braintree Ltd* [2002] EWCA Civ 296.

4.6. Protection of the buyer

4.6.1. The buyer may insist that the seller includes a provision in the contract whereby he agrees to expedite his application for registration and that he will assist the buyer by answering any requisitions relating to the pending application which are raised by the Land Registry. Such a condition should be expressed so that it remains extant after completion of the buyer's contract and does not merge with the transfer on completion. Some risks are inherent in this situation and the buyer should protect his contract by registration.

4.7. Protection of the lender

4.7.1. The mortgage, until registration, takes effect only as a charge on the equitable interest and will not comply with the provisions of Building Societies Act 1986. The borrower would, however, be estopped from denying the validity of the charge.[1]

1. *First National Bank plc* v. *Thompson* [1995] NPC 130.

B5. Seller's duty of disclosure

5.1. Reasons for disclosure

5.1.1. It is an implied term of a contract for the sale of land that the seller is selling free from incumbrances. If this is not to be so the seller must reveal the incumbrances to which the property is subject. Failure to disclose incumbrances may give the buyer the right to rescind the contract and to claim damages.

5.2. What must the seller disclose?

5.2.1. As an exception to the *caveat emptor* principle the seller is under a duty to disclose to the buyer latent incumbrances and defects in his title. This duty exists irrespective of whether the buyer raises enquiries about such matters.

Meaning of latent

5.2.2. Legally a defect is latent if it is not apparent, but the distinction between latent and patent defects is, in practice, unclear: see, e.g. *Yandle & Sons* v. *Sutton*[1] where a right of way which was apparent on inspection of the property was nevertheless held to be a latent defect. A seller should err on the side of caution and make a full disclosure of defects and incumbrances.

Law of Property Act 1969, s.24

5.2.3. Although a defect is not latent if the buyer has constructive notice of it under Law of Property Act 1925, s.198, the effect of Law of Property Act 1969, s.24 is to place a duty on the seller to reveal matters which are registered at the Land Charges Department. A buyer who enters into a contract knowing of an irremovable incumbrance impliedly agrees to take subject to that incumbrance (i.e. cannot rescind because of it), but the effect of section 24 is that mere registration under Land Charges Act 1972 is not knowledge for this purpose.

Occupiers

5.2.4. A buyer of an unregistered title who inspects the property will be deemed to have notice of the rights of occupiers.[2] Where the title is registered, the rights of occupiers may be overriding interests. It is uncertain whether the rights of occupiers fall within the duty of disclosure. Following *Williams & Glyn's Bank Ltd* v. *Boland*[3] the accepted view is that a full disclosure of occupiers' rights should be made.

Local land charges

5.2.5. Unless the contract provides to the contrary, the duty of disclosure includes matters which would be revealed by a local land charges search. Where the contract does not contain an effective clause excluding such matters from the duty of disclosure the seller should make a local land charges search before drafting the contract.[4]

Matters outside the seller's knowledge

5.2.6. It was held in *Re Brewer & Hankin's Contract*[5] that the seller's duty of disclosure may extend even to matters of which he was unaware. However, standard contractual conditions will normally exclude the seller's liability for non-disclosure in these circumstances (see Standard Condition 3, Appendix III.5). Knowledge acquired by the seller's solicitor in the course of acting for his client is imputed to the seller.[6]

Overriding interests

5.2.7. The seller is under a duty to disclose latent overriding interests. In practice a disclosure of all overriding interests known to the seller should be made (see G3.11.7–G3.11.9).

1. [1922] 2 Ch 199.
2. *Hunt* v. *Luck* [1902] 1 Ch 428.
3. [1981] AC 487.
4. *Rignall Developments Ltd* v. *Halil* [1988] Ch 190.
5. (1889) 80 LT 127.
6. *Strover* v. *Harrington* [1988] Ch 390.

5.3. **Matters falling outside the duty of disclosure**

Matters known to the buyer

5.3.1. There is no duty to disclose matters which are already known to the buyer, but the seller must ensure that the buyer has actual knowledge of such matters and cannot assume that a matter is within the buyer's knowledge. Even where an incumbrance is contained within one of the title deeds supplied to the buyer with the draft contract or appears on the register in registered land, the buyer's knowledge of the incumbrance cannot be assumed and the seller should take steps, whether by inclusion of a contractual condition or otherwise, specifically to draw the defect to the buyer's attention.

Matters apparent on inspection

5.3.2. Matters which can readily be discovered on an inspection of the property do not fall within the duty of disclosure.[1]

Physical defects

5.3.3. Physical defects, whether latent or patent, do not generally fall within the duty of disclosure, but the buyer may seek a remedy in misdescription if the contractual description of the land is rendered inaccurate through this omission.[2] Rescission may also be available to a buyer who, through the non-disclosure of a physical defect, is unable to use the land for the specific purpose for which it was sold.[3] The deliberate concealment of a known physical defect may give rise to an action in the tort of deceit.[4]

Planning matters

5.3.4. Planning matters are not matters of 'title' and are therefore not strictly within the duty of disclosure. It is, however, considered good practice to make disclosure of such matters.

1. But see *Yandle & Sons* v. *Sutton* [1922] 2 Ch 199.
2. *Re Puckett & Smith's Contract* [1902] 2 Ch 258.
3. It is rare for the contract to state the purpose of the buyer's use specifically.
4. *Gordon* v. *Selico Co. Ltd* (1986) 278 EG 53.

5.4. Non-disclosure by buyer

5.4.1. As a general rule a prospective buyer who is not already in a fiduciary relationship with his seller owes no duty of disclosure to his seller. Exceptionally such a duty may exist, e.g. *English* v. *Dedham Vale Properties*,[1] where the buyer was held liable to account to the seller for profit ultimately received from an undisclosed planning application made by the buyer.

1. [1978] 1 WLR 93.

5.5. Consequences of non-disclosure

5.5.1. The buyer's remedies for non-disclosure will be rescission of the contract if the non-disclosure is judged to be substantial. If the non-disclosure is not substantial the buyer can be forced to complete and will obtain his remedy through an abatement in the purchase price. A substantial non-disclosure is one where its effect is substantially to deprive the buyer of his bargain. A remedy may also lie in misrepresentation since non-disclosure effectively amounts to a misrepresentation by silence.[1]

1. *Pankhania* v. *Hackney London Borough Council* [2002] All ER (D) 22.

5.6. Contractual exclusion clauses

5.6.1. Clauses which purport to exclude liability for non-disclosure and misrepresentation are common, e.g. Standard Condition 7.1 (Appendix III.5), and as far as the latter is concerned are subject to the reasonableness test in Unfair Contract Terms Act 1977.[1] Their effectiveness in protecting the seller cannot therefore be guaranteed. Some restriction of the seller's duty of disclosure may be felt desirable but a total exclusion of liability would probably not be upheld by the courts save in exceptional circumstances. See also the impact of Unfair Terms in Consumer Contracts Regulations 1999, in B11.10.

1. *Pankhania* v. *Hackney London Borough Council* [2002] All ER (D) 22.

5.7. Conclusion

5.7.1. Despite the various recognised exceptions to the duty of disclosure outlined above, a prudent seller will make a full disclosure of all defects and incumbrances to the buyer, protecting himself where necessary by the inclusion of appropriate contractual clauses to prevent the buyer from exercising a right to rescind in respect of the disclosed matters. Some restriction of the seller's duty of disclosure may be incorporated by way of an exclusion clause in the contract, but care must be exercised to ensure that the clause is reasonable in the light of the circumstances of the particular transaction.

B6. Defective title and restrictive covenant insurance

6.1. Discovery of defects

6.1.1. The seller's solicitor should make a full investigation of the seller's title prior to drafting the contract for sale. Any potential defects in that title must be disclosed to the buyer in the contract and accepted by him, otherwise the seller may be called upon to remove the incumbrance.

6.1.2. Where it appears that a defect in title exists which is not remediable, the seller's solicitor may consider obtaining defective title insurance to cover liability arising out of the defect. Many, but not all, defects can be insured against in this way.

6.1.3. Before obtaining the policy the seller's instructions should be obtained, authorising the solicitor to proceed with this course of action. The seller should be fully advised of the problem and of the likely cost of a policy.

6.1.4. Some lenders insist on the borrower obtaining an indemnity policy against the seller's insolvency, for example where it is apparent that a voluntary transaction has been effected within the past five years. A typical policy will cost a minimum of £175.

6.2. Financial Services and Markets Act 2000

6.2.1. Since 14 January 2005, solicitors who advise clients about obtaining defective title insurance may be involved in activity regulated by Financial Services and Markets Act 2000. It is a criminal offence to carry on 'regulated activities' unless authorised by the Financial Services Authority, or unless able to rely on the exemption in Financial Services and Markets Act 2000.

6.2.2. Most solicitors rely on the Part XX exemption in Financial Services and Markets Act 2000. This means that solicitors may advise upon and arrange indemnity policies where the activity is incidental to the conveyancing transaction but the solicitor must comply with Solicitors' Financial Services (Scope)

Rules 2001, i.e. the firm must appoint a compliance officer and be registered with the Financial Services Authority on its Exempt Professional Firms Register. Firms should contact the Solicitors Regulation Authority if they need to be registered (see A4.1.1).

6.3. Obtaining a policy

6.3.1. Many insurance companies issue policies to cover defects in title. To ensure that a proper premium, commensurate with the risk involved, is paid, quotations should be obtained from more than one company.

6.3.2. The defect in title is the seller's responsibility because he will be contractually bound to prove a good title to his buyer. The seller should therefore normally expect to meet the costs of obtaining the policy. If the policy is obtained at the request of the buyer it may be possible to negotiate to share the expense with him. In any event the contract should deal with the liability for the expense of obtaining such a policy.

6.3.3. The policy will be a single premium policy the benefit of which will attach to the land. The policy should be mentioned in the contract (if the policy is available at that time) and handed over to the buyer on completion to be kept in a safe place with the documents of title.

6.4. Information needed by insurance company

6.4.1. Before issue of the policy the insurance company will need to assess the risk involved. As a general rule, defects which have occurred in the recent past, e.g. during the last five years, will be more expensive to insure than those which occurred many years ago. The seller's solicitor should be prepared to provide the insurance company with the following information or documents:

- (a) the precise nature of the defect;

- (b) where relevant, a copy of the document in which the defect appears;

- (c) the date when the defect arose, or date when the problem giving rise to the defect occurred;

- (d) what steps (if any) have been taken to remedy the defect;

- (e) whether any third party has taken steps to assert rights against the land because of the defect;

- (f) an approximate estimate of the amount of cover needed.

6.5. Restrictive covenants

6.5.1. The breach of a restrictive covenant affecting the title is a common reason for needing defective title insurance. In some cases the need for the policy will arise, not because a covenant has been broken, but because some contemplated action with or on the land will cause a breach. For example, it is common to find a restrictive covenant which prevents use of the property except as a single private dwelling house and the client wishes now to convert the property into flats, which action would cause a breach of covenant. In such a case it may be possible to obtain an insurance policy which will cover liability for the future breach of covenant. Where the seller is contracting to sell with planning permission for development, he should obtain and bear the cost of the policy; in other cases this matter will be the buyer's responsibility.

6.5.2.   Apart from the matters listed in B6.4, the insurance company will also need the following information or documents:

(a)   a copy of the document imposing the covenant or, if this is not available, a copy of the exact wording of the covenant;

(b)   the exact nature of the breach which has occurred or details of the action which is contemplated which will cause the breach;

(c)   the date when the covenant was imposed;

(d)   whether or not the covenant is registered on the charges register of the title (or as a Class D(ii) charge in unregistered land where the covenant was imposed after 1925);

(e)   the nature of other properties in the immediate neighbourhood. This is to enable the insurance company to assess the risk of enforcement of the covenant more precisely. Taking the example given above of a potential breach being caused by a conversion of a dwelling into flats, if many of the neighbouring properties have already been converted into flats, the likelihood of this particular covenant being enforced if breached is more remote than if the surrounding properties remain in single ownership. A plan which shows the property in the context of the surrounding locality is often useful;

(f)   a copy of any planning permission which permits the development to be undertaken by the client and copies of any objections which were lodged in respect of the application;

(g)   what steps have been taken (if any) to trace the person(s) with the benefit of the covenant and the results of those enquiries. The identity of the person who has the benefit of the covenant should be revealed if known, but steps should not be taken to approach that person without the prior consent of the insurance company since such an approach may have an adverse effect on the outcome of the situation and the consequent insurance risk;

(h)   details of any complaints which have been received from persons with the benefit of the covenants.

6.5.3.   Before arranging insurance, check that the covenant is binding on the title, either by registration under Land Charges Act 1972 or by the registration of a notice against the title at the Land Registry. Covenants noted on the register at first registration will not necessarily be binding. Under Rule 35 Land Registration Rules 2003, the Registrar is not required to check the validity of a covenant at first registration and covenants will be entered in the register unless the applicant for first registration makes an application to have the covenant omitted from the register (see G3.4.7–G3.4.9 as to the Land Registry's requirements in this respect).

6.6. Accepting the policy when acting for the buyer

6.6.1. Where a buyer is asked to accept a policy taken out by the seller or his predecessor which purports to cover liability for a defect or breach, consideration should be given to the following matters:

   (a) check that full disclosure of all relevant facts was made to the insurer prior to the issue of the policy;

   (b) ensure that the policy enures to the benefit of successors and is not restricted to a named person;

   (c) check that the policy covers the defect or breach in question;

   (d) check that the amount of cover offered by the policy appears to be adequate;

   (e) if the policy is already in existence enquire whether any claims have been made under the policy and the result of those claims;

   (f) ensure that the original policy will be handed over on completion. Where the policy has been taken out by a developer to cover the building of several properties, an examined or certified copy of the policy should be handed over on completion;

   (g) where a policy already exists, consideration should be given to taking an express assignment of the benefit of the policy from the seller and, after completion, giving notice of the assignment to the insurance company;

   (h) obtaining any proposed lender's approval to the policy terms and amount of cover.

6.7. Positive covenants

6.7.1. Similar considerations apply where indemnity has been given in relation to a positive covenant.

6.8. Lenders' requirements

6.8.1. Both the CML Lenders' Handbook and the BSA Mortgage Instructions outline a number of situations in which indemnity insurance will be required by the lender. The terms on which the lender will accept a policy are contained in paragraph 9 of the CML Lenders' Handbook (**www.cml.org.uk**) and paragraph D.57 of the BSA Mortgage Instructions (**www.bsa.org.uk**).

B7. Capacity

7.1. Introduction

7.1.1. In general a seller cannot convey a legal estate unless that estate is vested in him, although in very limited cases he may, under a power, convey a legal estate vested in some other person, e.g. a lender exercising a power of sale.

7.1.2. Although the nature of the seller's capacity no longer affects the extent of the covenants which are implied in the buyer's favour in the purchase deed, certain points relating to the seller's capacity to deal with the interest in land which he is purporting to dispose of still need to be addressed. These points are outlined in the paragraphs below. Implied covenants are discussed in M9.[1]

7.1.3. A registered proprietor has unfettered powers of disposition.[2] A buyer of registered land is concerned only to ensure that any restrictions on the register are complied with. The statutory provisions have effect only for the purpose of preventing the title of a buyer being questioned (and do not affect the lawfulness of a disposition).[3] The seller will in any event be bound to comply with any fiduciary duties he has, but a buyer is not concerned with them unless they are reflected in a restriction on the register. For example, if trustees were to sell land in breach of trust, in the absence of a restriction on the register, the transfer could not be impeached but the trustees would be liable to the beneficiaries of the trust for the breach. Where the title to the property is registered with title absolute, and there is no restriction placed on the proprietorship register, the seller is deemed to have the capacity to transfer the land (subject to provisions relating to alteration of the register) and further enquiry into the seller's capacity is in such cases unnecessary.

1. See Law of Property (Miscellaneous Provisions) Act 1994 and M9.
2. Land Registration Act 2002, s.26(1).
3. Land Registration Act 2002, s.26(2).

7.2. **Provision for capacity in the contract**

7.2.1. For contracts entered into on or after 1 July 1995, it is no longer necessary to state the seller's capacity in the contract.[1]

1. See Law of Property (Miscellaneous Provisions) Act 1994 and M9.

7.3. **Beneficial owner**

7.3.1. A beneficial owner is a single estate owner who owns the whole of the legal and equitable interest in the property for his own benefit. Either an individual or a corporation may satisfy this requirement. No other person must have any beneficial interest in the interest in land if the capacity of beneficial owner is to apply. Co-owners cannot satisfy this requirement since they hold the property on a trust of land.[1]

7.3.2. If it appears that someone other than the seller named in the contract is in occupation of the property, the buyer must make full enquiries about the status of such occupier in order to establish what interest he has in the property and to establish whether or not the seller is in fact a beneficial owner.

7.3.3. An occupier may claim a beneficial interest in the property through, e.g. contributing to the purchase price. In such a case, it will be necessary for a second trustee to be appointed to act with the seller in order to overreach the beneficial interest of the occupier.[2] Alternatively (or additionally) it may be thought desirable for the occupier to sign a release of his or her rights. Such a release may be included as a contractual term, in which case the occupier will need to sign the contract before exchange. The validity of such disclaimers seems to have met with the court's approval.[3]

7.3.4. In registered land the rights of persons in actual occupation may be overriding interests.[4] If so, a buyer will take subject to these rights (including those which are capable of registration but which are not in fact registered). However, where the sale is by trustees, the rights arising under the trust will be overreached provided the capital money arising is paid to at least two trustees or a trust corporation.

7.3.5. In unregistered land a buyer is deemed to buy with notice of occupiers' rights, other than those capable of registration but which are not registered as land charges;[5] thus the buyer needs to inspect the property and to make full enquiries about the rights of any occupiers.

7.3.6. A surviving co-owner may be a beneficial owner (see E6.3).

1. See *Re Robertson's Application* [1969] 1 All ER 257.
2. See *City of London Building Society* v. *Flegg* [1988] AC 54; *Lloyds Bank* v. *Rossett* [1991] 1 AC 107.
3. *Appleton* v. *Aspin* [1988] 1 WLR 410.
4. Land Registration Act 2002, Sched.1, para.2 and Sched.3, para.2.
5. *Hunt* v. *Luck* [1902] 1 Ch 428.

7.4.   Trustees of land

7.4.1.   Where land is held on a trust of land any conveyance or transfer of the land must be made by the trustees, being at least two individuals or a trust corporation, in order to overreach the equitable interests of the beneficiaries.

7.4.2.   Co-owners hold land on a trust of land.[1]

7.4.3.   Where a trust of land exists, whether expressly created or arising under statute (e.g. on intestacy), the trustees are under a duty to consult with, and, so far as is consistent with the general interests of the trust, give effect to the wishes of the adult competent beneficiaries who are entitled to a beneficial interest in possession of the land, when exercising their powers under the trust (e.g. to sell the land).[2] A trust which is created by an *inter vivos* disposition (but not by will) can expressly exclude the duty to consult.[3] A buyer is not concerned to check compliance with the obligation to consult.[4] In registered land the buyer is only concerned to see that the terms of any restriction on the register are complied with.

7.4.4.   Where the trust was expressly created, a power to postpone the sale is implied and cannot be excluded by contrary provision in the trust instrument.[5]

7.4.5.   Where the trust arises under statute (e.g. on intestacy), the trustees have a power (but not a duty) to sell the land.[6]

7.4.6.   Difficulties may arise if there are only two acting trustees who disagree over the decision to sell, since one trustee alone cannot transfer the legal estate. It may therefore be necessary in these circumstances to apply to the court under Trusts of Land and Appointment of Trustees Act 1996, s.14 to resolve the dispute. On an application under this section the court may make any order it thinks fit (including an order for sale), and thus may, but is not obliged to, order the sale of the property.

7.4.7.   In making such an order the court must have regard to the factors listed in section 15 Trusts of Land and Appointment of Trustees Act 1996 including the purpose of the trust and the interests of any secured creditor or beneficiary.

7.4.8.   If a disposition creating a trust of land requires the trustees to obtain the consents of a person or persons before exercising their power of sale, the buyer is only concerned to see that a maximum of two consents have been obtained (even if the trust deed requires a greater number) and is never concerned with the consents of persons suffering mental incapacity. Where a person whose consent is required is not of full age, the buyer is not concerned to see that such consent has been obtained, but the trustees must obtain the consent of a parent or guardian of the under age beneficiary.[7] In registered land the buyer is only concerned to see that the terms of any restriction on the register are complied with.

7.4.9. Trustees' powers to sell, mortgage, and grant leases are the same as those of an absolute owner but they must exercise those powers having regard to the rights of the beneficiaries.[8]

7.4.10. Trusts of Land and Appointment of Trustees Act 1996 has converted existing trusts for sale into 'trusts of land'. From 1 January 1997, co-owners hold land on a trust of land (formerly trust for sale).

7.4.11. Where the purpose of the trust is to sell the land it is still possible to create an express trust for sale. The requirement for the trustees to sell must however be expressly stated since it is no longer implied under the general law.

1. Law of Property Act 1925, ss.34 and 36.
2. Trusts of Land and Appointment of Trustees Act 1996, s.11.
3. *Ibid.* s.11(2).
4. *Ibid.* s.16(1).
5. *Ibid.* s.4(1).
6. *Ibid.* Sched.2.
7. *Ibid.* s.10.
8. *Ibid.* s.6.

7.5. Personal representatives

7.5.1. Personal representatives have all the powers of trustees of land but are only entitled to exercise those powers during the administration.[1] They are not, however, subject to sections 10, 11 and 14 Trusts of Land and Appointment of Trustees Act 1996 (duties to obtain consents, consultation with beneficiaries and the court's power of sale).[2]

7.5.2. Their powers are joint as to land, whether freehold or leasehold; therefore all proving personal representatives must be made parties to the contract and purchase deed (conveyance, lease, etc.).[3] A single proving personal representative may, however, act on his own.

7.5.3. The buyer should always see a copy of the grant to ascertain the names of all of the proving personal representatives.

7.5.4. In registered land a buyer is only concerned to see that the terms of any restriction on the register are complied with.

1. Administration of Estates Act 1925, s.39.
2. Trusts of Land and Appointment of Trustees Act 1996, s.18.
3. Law of Property (Miscellaneous Provisions) Act 1994, s.16.

7.6. Settled land

7.6.1. The following sub-paragraphs should be read in the light of Trusts of Land and Appointment of Trustees Act 1996 which abolished the creation of new strict settlements (with very limited exceptions) on or after 1 January 1997. The Act is not retrospective in effect and existing strict settlements are unaffected by the legislation. Land which is held under Universities and Colleges Estates Act 1925 will continue to be settled land and is unaffected by the 1996 Act.

7.6.2. The tenant for life is the person in whom the legal estate in settled land is vested via the vesting instrument. Where there is no tenant for life, or he is a minor, the legal estate is vested in statutory owners who are usually the trustees of the settlement. The tenant for life (or, if none, the statutory owners) will therefore be the seller of settled land, but the trustees of the settlement must be joined as parties to the purchase deed in order to give a valid receipt for capital moneys arising and thus to overreach the interests of the beneficiaries.

7.6.3. The trust deed itself is generally 'behind the curtain' and thus of no concern to a buyer. The buyer is bound and entitled to assume that the person in whom the legal estate is vested by the vesting instrument is the person rightfully entitled to the legal estate and that the persons named as trustees are the properly constituted Settled Land Act trustees.

7.6.4. A sale or other disposition of settled land can only be made for the purposes of the settlement and must be made for the best consideration in money reasonably obtainable.[1] Unless expressly extended by the terms of the settlement certain restrictions on dispositions are imposed by Settled Land Act 1925. The main restrictions relate to mortgages and leases, e.g. the Act permits leases for building or forestry to be granted for a term not exceeding 999 years, for mining, not exceeding 100 years, and for agricultural or occupational purposes, not exceeding 50 years. Powers to grant options to purchase or to take a lease and to grant easements are limited by Settled Land Act 1925, s.51. A disposition which is not authorised either by the Act or by the terms of the settlement is void, even if the buyer was unaware of the settlement.[2]

7.6.5. Where settled land is registered, the tenant for life (or statutory owners) will be registered as proprietor and appropriate restrictions are entered on the proprietorship register.[3] A buyer is only concerned to see that the terms of the restrictions are complied with.

1. Settled Land Act 1925, s.39(1).
2. *Weston* v. *Henshaw* [1950] Ch 510; *cf. Re Morgan's Lease; Jones* v. *Norsesowicz* [1972] Ch 1.
3. Land Registration Rules 2003, r.186 and Sched.7.

7.7. Mortgagees

7.7.1. In order to sell the property the lender must have an express or implied power of sale and that power must have arisen and become exercisable. A power of sale is implied in every mortgage made by deed unless expressly excluded.[1] A legal mortgage must be made by deed.[2] It therefore follows that a lender who has taken a legal mortgage will always have a power of sale unless (exceptionally) that power has been expressly excluded. An equitable mortgage need not be made by deed;[3] it will therefore be necessary to check carefully the existence of the lender's power to sell. In some cases an equitable mortgage may give the lender an irrevocable power of attorney which would give the lender power to convey the legal estate vested in the borrower in exercise of the power of sale.

7.7.2. Under Land Registration Act 2002, s.52, subject to any entry in the register to the contrary, the proprietor of a registered charge is to be taken to have the powers of disposition conferred by law on the owner of a legal mortgage. Conversely, the owner of a charge which is not substantively registered has no power of sale under the Act.

7.7.3. As far as a buyer is concerned, he need only check the existence of the power of sale and that it has arisen. The power of sale arises on the legal date for redemption of the mortgage which is usually specified to be a date early on in the mortgage term (e.g. one month after creation of the mortgage).

7.7.4. A lender who is exercising his power of sale must ensure that:

(a) his power of sale exists;

(b) the power has arisen; and

(c) the power has become exercisable.

7.7.5. The lender's power becomes exercisable if one of the three following conditions is met:[4]

(a) notice requiring payment of the principal money has been served on the borrower and default has been made in payment of the principal money for three months; or

(b) some interest under the mortgage is in arrears and unpaid for two months after becoming due; or

(c) there has been breach of some other provision contained in the mortgage deed or Law of Property Act 1925.

7.7.6. A lender who sells in a situation where his power has arisen but not become exercisable will nonetheless pass good title to the buyer but may be liable in damages to the borrower.

Borrowers

7.7.7. Subject to any contractual restriction in the mortgage (e.g. restricting further the limited statutory power to grant leases of the property) which may be reflected by a restriction on the register of the title, a borrower may be treated as a beneficial owner.

1. Law of Property Act 1925, s.101.
2. *Ibid.*, s.85.
3. But must be in writing and signed by both parties to satisfy Law of Property (Miscellaneous Provisions) Act 1989, s.2.
4. Law of Property Act 1925, s.103.

7.8. **Charities**

7.8.1. If there is no restriction on the proprietorship register, a buyer may safely deal with the charity as if it were an absolute owner. If there is a restriction on the register, the following subparagraphs should be considered. Reference should also be made to Land Registry Practice Guide 14.

7.8.2. Unless a charity is an exempt charity, no disposition (the term disposition applies to the transfer or conveyance of land and not to the contract for sale)[1] can be made by the charity without an order of the court or the Charity Commission unless all the following conditions are satisfied:[2]

(a) the trustees must obtain a written report about the proposed disposition from a qualified surveyor (FRICS, ARICS, SVA or ASVA);

(b) the property is advertised for the period and in the manner advised by the surveyor;

(c) the trustees decide that in the light of the surveyor's report they are satisfied that the terms of the disposition are the best that can be obtained;

(d) prescribed words are inserted in both the contract and purchase deed.

7.8.3. The prescribed words must be in one of the following forms:

(a) the land transferred (or as the case may be) is held by [(proprietors) in trust for] (charity), an exempt charity; or

(b) the land transferred (or as the case may be) is held by [(proprietors) in trust for] (charity), a non-exempt charity, but this transfer (or as the case may be) is one falling within paragraph (a), (b) or (c) (as the case may be) of section 36(9) Charities Act 1993; or

(c) the land transferred (or as the case may be) is held by [(proprietors) in trust for] (charity), a non-exempt charity, and this transfer (or as the case may be) is not one falling within paragraphs (a), (b) or (c) of section 36(9) Charities Act 1993, so that the restrictions on disposition imposed by section 36 of that Act apply to the land.[3]

Note that when there is no trust (i.e. the land is the corporate property of the registered proprietor charity) the words 'XXXX in trust for' are omitted.

7.8.4. Where the prescribed words are included in the disposition, the buyer and persons who subsequently acquire the property for money or money's worth are entitled to rely on the conclusiveness of the facts stated and rely on a certificate in the purchase deed that the trustees have power under the trusts of the charity to effect the disposition and that they have complied with the provisions of Charities Act 1993, s.36 so far as applicable to it. The buyer may also rely on such a certificate where the land is registered with a restriction in Form 12 or Form E.[4]

Dealing with land owned by a charity

7.8.5.   When dealing with land owned by a charity the following points should be checked:

     (a)   is the transaction authorised by the statute or deed which governs the charity?

     (b)   is the charity exempt? If so, the transaction can proceed without delay.

If not an exempt charity:

     (c)   can the trustees give the certificate referred to in B7.8.4?

     (d)   if not, has an order of the court or the Charity Commission been obtained?

7.8.6.   Where an order is needed it must either be obtained before exchange of contracts or the contract must be made conditional on the order being obtained.[5]

7.8.7.   The purchase deed containing the certificate must be signed by the charity trustees, or by two or more of them acting under an authority given by the trustees.[6] In the case of a corporate charity this usually means the directors. It is not sufficient for the deed to be sealed by the company in the presence of a director and the secretary.

7.8.8.   Land held on charitable, ecclesiastical and public trusts ceased to be settled land and became subject to a 'trust of land' on 1 January 1997 (with the exception of land to which Universities and College Estates Act 1925 applies).[7]

1.   *Osborn and Co. Ltd* v. *Dior; Marito Holdings SA* v. *Borhane* CA [2003] All ER (D) 185 (Jan).
2.   Charities Act 1993, ss.37–40.
3.   Land Registration Rules 2003, r.180.
4.   Land Registration Rules 2003, Sched.4.
5.   See B13.
6.   See Charities Act 1993, s.82.
7.   Trusts of Land and Appointment of Trustees Act 1996.

7.9.   Companies

7.9.1.   A company incorporated after 1 October 2009 may freely deal with land unless there are any restrictions on its objects set out in its articles of association, Companies Act 2006, s.31. A company incorporated before 1 October 2009 may deal with land so long as the transaction is within the scope of the objects clause of its memorandum of association (existing objects clauses in the memorandum of association are now treated as part of the company's articles, Companies Act 2006, s.28). Section 31 also applies to such companies and so an existing company may amend its objects to make them unrestricted. In favour of a person dealing with a company, the validity of an act done by a company shall not be called into question on the ground of lack of capacity by reason of anything in the company's memorandum. The good faith of the buyer is irrelevant and it is no longer necessary to make a company search to ensure that the power to conduct the transaction exists.[1] A company may hold property jointly with another company or individual.[2] Where a company applies to become the proprietor of registered land, details of the company's powers must be supplied to the registrar.[3]

7.9.2. The powers of a company incorporated by Royal Charter are not restricted by the terms of its Charter; it may therefore be regarded as having the same powers as an individual.

7.9.3. The powers of a company which is incorporated by some other statute are governed by the enabling statute which should in each case be checked and the requisite procedures followed. A transaction outside the terms of the statute will be void.

7.9.4. The powers of a foreign company should be expressly checked and the requisite procedures followed. Checks may include confirmation from a lawyer entitled to practise in the jurisdiction in which the foreign company was incorporated that the company exists in law and has power to buy, sell and hold land, etc. (see E7).

Transactions between a company and one of its directors

7.9.5. Companies Act 2006, s.190 applies to arrangements under which a director acquires an asset from the company. The word 'arrangement' will cover freehold and leasehold transactions and options made between the director and the company. Transactions under which the company purchases assets from one of its directors are also covered by section 190(1)(b). A transaction to which the section applies must be sanctioned by a resolution of the members of the company or it must be made conditional on such approval being obtained. The resolution should identify the property, the buyer and the price and may approve the transaction on such other terms as the board of directors may agree. Minor transactions, defined as those which are below £5,000 in value or those with a value of between £5,000 and £100,000 where the value represents less than 10% of the company's assets, do not need approval. The term 'director' includes persons connected with the director so that a transfer by a company to a member of a director's family or to another company with which the director is associated will invoke the provisions of the section. The members of a director's family include the director's spouse or civil partner, the director's children or step-children, someone with whom the director lives as partner in an enduring family relationship (unless that person is the director's grandparent or grandchild, sister, brother, aunt or uncle, or nephew or niece), a child or step-child of the director's unmarried partner if they live with the director and have not attained the age of 18, and the director's parents. The consequences of failure to comply with section 190 are contained in section 195: broadly, the transaction is voidable at the instance of the company. The company is entitled to be compensated for any loss it has suffered as a result of the unapproved transaction and to account for any gain. Where the transaction is affirmed by the shareholders within a reasonable time, the transaction may no longer be avoided (section 196).

Transactions before company formed

7.9.6. A person who purports to act on behalf of a company or as agent for it at a time when the company has not been formed will be personally liable on the contract, Companies Act 2006, s.51(1). This provision can result in the solicitor acting on a sale or purchase for a company in the process of incorporation becoming personally liable for the contract and being entitled to enforce the contract.[4]

1. Companies Act 2006, s.40(2).
2. Bodies Corporate (Joint Tenancy) Act 1899, s.1.
3. See Land Registration Rules 2003, r.183.
4. *Braymist Ltd* v. *Wise Finance Co. Ltd* [2002] 2 All ER 333, CA.

7.10. Minors

7.10.1. A person aged under 18 years cannot hold a legal estate in land but may hold an equitable interest. If, however, there is no restriction on the register of the title, the buyer is entitled to assume that the seller has full capacity. A conveyance to a minor alone takes effect as an agreement to create a trust of land and in the meantime to hold the land on trust for him. A contract for sale to a minor is binding on him unless repudiated by him during minority or within a reasonable time after attaining majority.[1]

1. See Minors' Contracts Act 1987.

7.11. Persons with a mental disability

7.11.1. A contract for the sale or purchase of land, entered into by a person who lacks the mental capacity to understand the nature of the transaction, is voidable at the option of the incapacitated party, provided he can prove that at the time of the transaction the other contracting party was aware of the lack of capacity.[1]

7.11.2. The following persons may deal with the land of an individual who lacks mental capacity:

(a) a deputy appointed by the Court of Protection under Mental Capacity Act 2005;

(b) an attorney appointed under a lasting power of attorney to deal with property and financial affairs where the donor no longer has capacity; or

(c) an attorney appointed under an enduring power of attorney to deal with property and financial affairs where the donor no longer has capacity and the enduring power of attorney has been registered at the Court of Protection.

7.11.3. On the appointment of a deputy a restriction is not normally entered on a registered title unless the deputy or other authorised person requests its entry. Where the deputy is registered as proprietor a restriction is automatically entered.[2] The restriction would usually prevent registration of any disposition unless made pursuant to an order of the court under Mental Capacity Act 2005. On a dealing with registered land, the registrar will require a copy of the order which provides the deputy's authority to act.

7.11.4. Consent of the Court of Protection is not required to sell land if the order or direction appointing the deputy authorises the deputy to make decisions about 'property and affairs' or the lasting power of attorney or enduring power of attorney authorises the attorney to deal with the property and affairs of the person who lacks capacity. In either case the sale must be in the best interests of the person who lacks capacity, and if there is any doubt as to this the deputy or attorney should apply to the Court of Protection for consent (using form COP1/COP9 (within proceedings)).

7.11.5. Consent of the Court of Protection may be required to purchase land. A deputy appointed after 1 October 2007 to deal with the property and affairs of an individual may have general authority to purchase land without obtaining authority from the Court of Protection. The terms of the order or direction appointing the deputy should be checked to see whether such a general authority has been given, and, if it has, whether there is any limitation on the authority. If there is any doubt as to whether the deputy has authority, the deputy should apply to the Court of Protection (using form COP1/COP9 (within proceedings)). An attorney appointed to deal with property and financial affairs under either a lasting power of attorney or an enduring power of attorney may have authority to purchase a property and the power should be checked for such authority.

7.11.6. The Official Solicitor's Practice Note 'Ancillary relief orders: conveyancing for mentally incapacitated adults', should be consulted when transferring land pursuant to a property adjustment order or sale order made on a divorce, nullity or judicial separation in matrimonial proceedings (see A18.5). This Practice Note has not yet been updated to reflect Mental Capacity Act 2005 and should be read accordingly.

1. *Broughton* v. *Snook* [1938] Ch 505.
2. Land Registration Act 2002, s.42(1)(a).

7.12. Universities and colleges

7.12.1. Universities and Colleges Estates Act 1925 confers powers to sell and exchange land and to purchase land as an investment on the universities of Oxford, Cambridge and Durham (and their respective colleges) and on Winchester and Eton Colleges and restrictions are entered in registered land reflecting the limitations on their powers under the statutes governing them. Other universities and colleges may be educational charities and are subject to the rules on charities outlined above.

7.13.   Local authorities

7.13.1.   A local authority may acquire land, inside or outside its own area, for the purpose of any of its functions under any Public General Act or for the benefit, improvement or development of its area. Power to acquire land for the provision of accommodation is given by Housing Act 1985, s.17. Powers of compulsory purchase of land are conferred by many statutes and are outside the scope of this book.

7.13.2.   Ministerial consent is required for certain disposals of land by a local authority. In such a case, consent must be obtained before contracts are exchanged, or alternately the contract made conditional on such consent being forthcoming. A conveyance made without the requisite consent may be void. In certain cases a buyer is entitled to assume that the transaction is within the powers of the local authority and does not have to investigate whether or not ministerial approval has been given. Under Housing Act 1988, s.44 (which does not apply to right to buy sales and leases), any disposal of residential property by a local authority for which the consent of the Secretary of State for the Environment is required is void if made without consent unless:

(a)   the disposal is in favour of an individual or two or more individuals; and

(b)   the disposal comprises only a single house or flat.

7.13.3.   The protection afforded by Local Government Act 1972, s.128 does not apply in respect of residential premises unless both these conditions are satisfied. Where the land is registered, a buyer is only concerned to see that the terms of any restriction are complied with.

7.14.   Parish and community councils

7.14.1.   Land may be acquired by such a council (whether inside or outside its own area) for the purposes of any of its functions under Local Government Act 1972 or any other Public General Act.

7.14.2.   Ministerial consent is required for disposals of land, but buyers from parish and community councils are protected against breach of the consent provisions.[1]

1.   Local Government Act 1972, s.128.

7.15.   Building societies, friendly societies, trade unions

7.15.1.   A building society may acquire and hold land for the purpose of its business or for commercial purposes under Building Societies Act 1986, ss.16 and 17. It

B

will also have power to sell land as a lender where it has lent money on mortgage and the lender's power of sale has become exercisable (see B7.7).

7.15.2. Registered friendly societies and industrial and provident societies have power to buy, sell and hold land, subject to the rules of each individual society.

7.15.3. Property belonging to a trade union must be vested in trustees on trust for the union. Powers of acquisition and disposition are subject to the rules of the union and the general law relating to trustees.

7.16. Fiduciary relationships

7.16.1. Where a fiduciary relationship exists between the parties to the transaction, there is a presumption of constructive fraud which is rebuttable on proof (by the dominant party to the relationship) that the transaction was at a fair price (an independent valuation is highly desirable), that all the circumstances of the transaction were known to the subordinate party, and that each party received, or was given a proper opportunity to take, independent legal advice. The transaction is prima facie voidable at the instance of the subordinate party.

7.16.2. A fiduciary relationship is deemed to exist in dealings between the following persons:

(a) solicitor and client;

(b) trustee and beneficiary;

(c) parent and child (where the influence of the parent over the child may be held to have endured beyond the child's majority);

(d) doctor and patient;

(e) religious advisor and disciple;

(f) teacher and pupil;

(g) fiancés (but not between husband and wife).

7.16.3. A fiduciary relationship may exist in circumstances other than those listed above, but is not presumed to exist, and the dominance of one party over the other would have to be proved before the court would apply the doctrine of constructive fraud.[1]

7.16.4. If a solicitor is asked to act in dealings between any of the parties listed in B7.16.2, or in any other situation where he feels that the relationship between the contracting parties may be classed as fiduciary, he should ensure that:

(a) an independent valuation of the property is obtained;

(b) all the facts pertaining to the transaction are known by and understood by both parties;

(c)   the parties are separately represented (see A10).

1.   See, e.g. *Lloyds Bank* v. *Bundy* [1975] QB 326 (fiduciary relationship proved to have existed between bank manager and customer).

7.17.   One-man companies

7.17.1.   It is permitted for a company to have only one shareholder. That shareholder may also be a director of the company. If he is the only director a second person must be appointed to act as company secretary.

7.18.   Administration procedures

7.18.1.   If a company is in administration, any sale of property will be carried out by either an administrative receiver or by an administrator, depending upon the date of the charge under which the appointment is made. If the charge was entered into before 15 September 2003 (when the relevant provisions of Enterprise Act 2002 came into force and amended Insolvency Act 1986) the creditor may appoint an administrative receiver. If the charge was made after the provisions came into force, an administrator will be appointed. Administrative receiverships still exist for charges created before 15 September 2003 but will become less important as time passes.

7.18.2.   Both administrators and administrative receivers must be qualified insolvency practitioners.

7.18.3.   When buying a property from an administrator or an administrative receiver, the validity of the appointment should be checked, including:

(a)   the validity of the floating charge under which the appointment was made and that the charge is a qualifying floating charge under paragraph 14 Schedule B1 Insolvency Act 1986 amended by Schedule 16 Enterprise Act 2002;

(b)   that the charge covered the whole or substantially the whole of the company's property;

(c)   that the charge is not likely to be invalidated, e.g. for want of registration, or fraudulent preference;

(d)   that the appointment does not exceed any powers in the charge;

(e)   that the administrator or the administrative receiver has power to conduct the transaction in question;

(f)   in a case where two receivers have been appointed, whether they are able to act jointly and severally or jointly only.

B

7.18.4. A certified copy of the appointment should be obtained by the buyer since this is one of the documents that will have to be produced to the Land Registry on registration of the transfer: see Land Registry Practice Guides 35 and 36.

7.18.5. As a matter of practice the administrator or the administrative receiver may decline to give any warranties or covenants and may seek to exclude his personal liability. A buyer may, where appropriate, prefer to take a transfer from the lender in exercise of his power of sale where the buyer will benefit from the limited covenants given by lenders and will also have the guarantee of over-reaching subsequent incumbrances.

7.18.6. An administrator has the same powers as an administrative receiver under Insolvency Act 1986 and he acts as an agent of the company and an officer of the court. His main function is to rescue the company as a going concern, but he does have the power to realise assets in order to make a distribution to creditors. An administrator's appointment will terminate automatically after 12 months unless it is extended by the court or by consent.[1]

1. Insolvency Act 1986, Sched.B1, paras.76–86 as amended by Enterprise Act 2002, Sched.16.

7.19. **Attorneys**

7.19.1. A power of attorney can be general (giving the attorney power to do anything that the donor can lawfully do) or specific (giving the attorney power to sell a specific property).

7.19.2. Where the seller is a beneficial owner he can delegate his power to sell land to an attorney by using a general power of attorney.[1]

7.19.3. Where the land is held by co-owners the land is held on a trust of land. A trustee with a beneficial interest in the land can appoint an attorney using a general power or a general trustee power and can appoint his sole co-trustee to be his attorney. The attorney must make a statement that the donor is beneficially entitled either at the time of the disposition or within three months following the disposition.[2]

7.19.4. A trustee who is not beneficially entitled under the trust should use a general trustee power. He can appoint his sole co-trustee to be his attorney; however, the power will be limited to a maximum period of 12 months.[3]

7.19.5. If a sole co-trustee has been appointed to be an attorney using a general power or a general trustee power of attorney, he cannot give a good receipt for the purchase price and overreaching will not operate. In such a case the donor should appoint a third party to act as attorney.

7.19.6. The buyer must insist on seeing the original or a certified copy of the power of attorney and he must carry out a bankruptcy search against the donor. Provided that the buyer is not aware of any event that would revoke the power, the buyer will get a good title.

7.19.7. At completion the buyer must collect a certified copy of the power of attorney.

7.19.8. Where the property is registered see B23.7 and Land Registry Practice Guide 9 for the Land Registry's requirements on registration of a purchase from an attorney.

7.19.9. When the person who bought from the attorney comes to sell an unregistered property, his buyer will want to ensure that the power had not been revoked prior to the sale by the attorney. He can conclusively presume that it was not revoked if the sale by the attorney took place within 12 months of the power being granted. If the sale took place more than 12 months after the date of the power then the current buyer must obtain a statutory declaration from his seller stating that the seller was not aware of any revocation of the power at the time of his purchase. This statutory declaration must be produced either before the sale to the buyer or within three months of that sale having taken place.

7.19.10. For example, on 1 January 1990, A, an unregistered owner, appointed B to be his attorney. On 1 July 1990, A, through his attorney, sold his property to C. In 2006, C is selling the property to D. D can presume that the power had not been revoked before the sale to C because the sale took place within 12 months of the power having been granted. However, if the sale to C had taken place on 1 July 1991, D would require a statutory declaration from C stating that he, C, had no knowledge of any revocation of the power at the time of his purchase from the attorney. The statutory declaration must be prepared at the time of the sale to D or within three months of that sale having taken place.

1. Powers of Attorney Act 1971, s.10.
2. Trustee Delegation Act 1999, s.1.
3. *Ibid.*, s.5.

B8. Agricultural land

8.1. Introduction

8.1.1. The procedure when buying agricultural land will be similar to that employed when buying any piece of freehold or leasehold land (as appropriate). The following paragraphs merely draw attention to some matters to which particular attention needs to be paid because of the nature of agricultural land. For more detailed information reference should be made to a specialist text on the subject.

8.2. Plans

8.2.1. The boundaries of agricultural land need to be checked carefully so that both parties understand clearly and precisely the extent of the land to be sold or let. The seller and buyer and/or their respective surveyors should inspect the land and agree the boundaries which should be marked on a plan to be attached to the contract and, in due course, the form of lease or transfer. It is essential that the plan should be of sufficiently large scale (e.g. 1:2500) and dimensions to identify the land and its salient features clearly. In order to satisfy Land Registry requirements a large scale up-to-date Ordnance Survey map must be used for this purpose. The route of any services and other easements which cross the land should be identified.

8.2.2. Where possible 'T' marks should be marked on the plan to indicate the future responsibility for maintenance of boundaries with specific reference in the wording of the transfer or lease to those responsibilities. Where no definite indications as to boundaries exist, reference may be made to the common law presumptions, e.g. where there is a hedge and ditch boundary, the boundary lies on the far side of the ditch from the hedge. At common law the *ad medium filum* rule applies to roads and rivers.

8.2.3. Rights of way and access to the property should be checked including individual field access points.

8.3. Pre-contract searches

8.3.1. The situation of the land may indicate that some of the less usual pre-contract searches should be undertaken, e.g. rivers, mining (see B10). It may also be necessary for the buyer's solicitor to require the local authority to answer some of the questions on Form CON 29O Optional enquiries of local authority, including enquiry 22 relating to the existence of any entries on the relevant commons register (see Appendix III.2). Particular attention should be paid to questions relating to public rights of way. The buyer should be made aware of the possibility of future modification orders arising in relation to public rights of way.

8.3.2. If only part of land which enjoys rights of common is being sold, an apportionment of those rights between the two parcels of land should be considered.

8.3.3. Specific enquiries should be raised with the seller about sites of special scientific interest or other environmental designations where the local search replies indicate that such a site is included in the land to be bought.

8.3.4. A search may be made with the relevant utility provider where it is necessary to establish the routes of pipelines and cables passing under, through or over the property.

8.3.5. A chancel repair liability search may be necessary (see B10).

8.3.6. Any index map search made against the property should be supplemented by a search of the index of relating franchises and manors held by the Land Registry.

8.3.7. Geological workings may necessitate searches, e.g. for coal, oil, sand and gravel (see B10).

8.3.8. An agricultural credits search should be carried out where the transaction includes the purchase of agricultural machinery and equipment (see B8.12).

Enquiries of the seller

8.3.9. In addition to the normal pre-contract enquiries, a form of agricultural tenancy enquiries may be required where the land to be bought includes tenanted property and some of the following additional enquiries may be relevant to the purchase:

    (a) planning enquiries concerning agricultural buildings and whether or not they fall within the Agricultural General Development Order (see B8.4.3);

    (b) enquiries concerning listed buildings and scheduling under Ancient Monuments and Archaeological Areas Act 1979;

    (c) information should be sought on all grant or subsidy schemes relating to the property ascertaining whether the conditions applicable to them have been properly observed and ensuring no money will become repayable;

(d) enquiries concerning single farm payment entitlement and other quotas which may benefit the property and whether they are transferable to the buyer;

(e) enquiries concerning boundaries and their maintenance;

(f) enquiries relating to services benefiting the property (especially water supplies);

(g) enquiries relating to sites of special scientific interest or other environmental designations whether or not these come to light in answers to a local search;

(h) enquiries relating to abstraction and discharge licences granted by the Environment Agency under Water Resources Act 1991, Environmental Protection Act 1990 or Environment Act 1995;

(i) enquiries as to the history of the occurrence of notifiable diseases on the property;

(j) specific enquiries relating to sporting rights;

(k) enquiries relating to the existence of standing timber felling licences and grant conditions.

8.3.10. Particular attention should be paid to matters arising in (c) and (d) above in view of the current single farm payment. Most transactions in agricultural land will involve the transfer of single farm payment entitlement units. In normal circumstances a buyer should expect to acquire an entitlement unit for each eligible hectare comprised in the land to be purchased or let. Although the lease of entitlements is possible, the common practice is for entitlements to be transferred to the tenant for the duration of the relevant tenancy term and returned to the landlord on termination.

8.3.11. The buyer should ensure the seller provides an up-to-date copy of the seller's Rural Payments Agency register of entitlement units. Once this has been reviewed by the buyer's surveyor, contract provisions should be agreed to deal with the price for the entitlement units and the mechanics of transfer. It is common to see the price for the entitlement units deducted from the overall purchase price by way of an apportionment. The buyer's surveyor should review and agree the terms of the required RLE1 Form which must be submitted to the Rural Payments Agency not less than six weeks prior to the agreed transfer date. It is essential that the notification timetable is agreed with a view to meeting:

(a) the scheme year application date (normally on or about 15 May); and

(b) the requirement under the scheme for the claimant to occupy the relevant holding on the required date (normally 15 May).

A failure to consider the timing of notification may give rise to a significant loss of support income in the relevant claim year.

8.4.   Planning

8.4.1. The authorised use of the land under Town and Country Planning Act 1990 should be ascertained. This information may be revealed in answers to enquiries of the local authority where planning permissions have been granted or a certificate confirming lawful use has been obtained from the planning authorities. In the absence of these the seller should be asked to disclose detailed information on the use of the property. Any restrictions on the use of the property should be discussed by the buyer's solicitor with his client to ensure that they do not conflict with the client's requirements. It is unusual for a seller to give a warranty in the contract relating to the authorised use of the property.

8.4.2. In most cases a change of use to agricultural use needs no consent. In some cases the erection of agricultural buildings does not require consent.

8.4.3. Particular care should be taken to establish whether any dwelling on the property is subject to any occupancy restriction, requiring occupation by someone employed or last employed in agriculture.

8.4.4. Particular care should also be taken to establish the extent of any listing affecting the property, as outbuildings falling within the curtilage of a listed building may also be affected by the designation.

8.5.   Taxation consequences

8.5.1. If the transaction involves the sale of a business as a going concern, value added tax should not be paid where both the seller and the buyer are registered for VAT. The VAT rules for a going concern transaction are more rigorous where land is included. If the buyer is not registered but the seller is, the seller must charge VAT on the assets which are subject to VAT at the standard rate, unless the buyer registers for VAT and also opts to tax prior to the tax point for the transaction being reached, in which case no VAT is charged. The buyer must also satisfy the seller that their option to tax will not be disapplied (see A16.16.4). This may include the agricultural land if the option to tax has effect in relation to it.[1] In other cases value added tax may be payable on the transaction, in which case an appropriate clause to this effect needs to be included in the contract.

8.5.2. This type of transaction will often raise taxation issues in relation to capital gains tax and/or corporation tax as well as inheritance tax and Stamp Duty Land Tax. Both the seller and the buyer should ensure they take appropriate specialist tax advice before the structure of the transaction is finalised. Ideally, where the purchase is being made by an individual or individuals, making up-to-date wills should be considered as part of the purchasing process, as the value of agricultural property will often be significant and securing any applicable inheritance tax reliefs will be important to the buyer.

1.   VAT (Special Provisions) Order 1995 (SI 1995/1268), para.5.

8.6.   Grants and subsidies

8.6.1.   The buyer should enquire of the seller whether any grants or subsidies have been received or are payable in respect of the land. If any part of these grants or subsidies is repayable on sale of the land, the seller should be required to fulfil this obligation before completion.

8.6.2.   If the buyer is intending to purchase any entitlements from the seller under the single farm payment scheme, the buyer should ask the seller to disclose all information held by the seller relevant to the scheme. Entitlements do not attach to land and, as a result, will not automatically transfer to the buyer on completion of the purchase of the property (see B8.3.10).

8.6.3.   The buyer should take advice from a surveyor on the environmental issues arising under cross compliance, the entry level scheme and the higher level scheme in so far as these relate to the property being purchased. Where completion falls in the middle of a single farm payment scheme year, a seller is advised to seek an indemnity from the buyer to ensure cross compliance obligations are met by the buyer from completion to the following 31 December.

8.7.   Growing crops, livestock, machinery

8.7.1.   The seller must agree with the buyer which items of livestock and/or plant and machinery are to be included in the sale. A valuation of these items is often required and the contract should contain an appropriate clause to cover the valuation issues. A schedule of items to be included in the sale should be annexed to the contract.

8.7.2.   Similarly agreement must be reached between the parties relating to growing crops, i.e. whether the seller is to be entitled to return to the property after completion in order to harvest his crops, or whether ownership of and responsibility for the growing crops will pass to the buyer on completion. Where the buyer is to take over responsibility for livestock and/or growing crops he may require the seller to give a warranty in the contract that the seller will use his best (or reasonable) endeavours to maintain standards of good husbandry and/or cross compliance over the land until completion. The buyer may consider it prudent to employ a veterinary surgeon to inspect livestock and to certify their state of health. The seller may be required to produce current vaccination certificates for livestock (where appropriate) and livestock passports. It should be noted that a contract to fell and remove standing timber is a contract for the sale of an interest in land which is, by Law of Property (Miscellaneous Provisions) Act 1989, s.2, required to be in writing.

8.8. Water

8.8.1. If the land currently has a water abstraction licence under Water Resources Act 1991, enquiries should be raised to confirm that the benefit of the licence is assignable; a condition providing for the licence to be assigned to the buyer must then be included in the contract. The buyer must then notify the Environment Agency promptly of the change of ownership of the land benefitting from the licence. Forms supplied by the Environment Agency (in duplicate and accompanied by a plan of the land) should be used to notify the Environment Agency of the assignment. Assignment of a licence is only possible where the buyer takes over the whole of the land to which the licence applies. If the licence relates to only part of the land sold, no assignment is possible and the buyer will need to apply for an apportionment of the existing licence with the seller's co-operation. The contract and transfer should contain appropriate clauses to deal with any proposed apportionment and ongoing rights to use the supply.

8.8.2. Where the water supply to the property is metered, the relevant water company must, in addition to being notified of the change of ownership, be asked to read the meter on the day of completion, in order that apportioned accounts can be sent to seller and buyer.

8.8.3. Some or all of the following enquiries may need to be raised in connection with the water supply to the property:

(a) does the property have a mains water supply?

(b) if there is a mains water supply, does the mains pipe (which is maintained by the water company) run through the property or immediately adjacent to the property in a public highway?

(c) if there is no direct access to the mains water pipe, how is the property connected to the mains, who owns and is liable for the private spur, and does the property have the benefit of private easements for the continued use of the pipe, its maintenance, repair and replacement and the taking of water through it?

(d) where is the mains water meter?

(e) if the property has a private water supply its source should be identified and enquiries raised as to whether the source supplies this property exclusively;

(f) are special water uses required, e.g. for spray irrigation?

(g) if the property is supplied by a private water source from an adjoining property enquiries should be raised to ascertain the legal rights and obligations of the parties.

8.9. Tenancies

8.9.1. In order to fulfil his duty of disclosure the seller must give the buyer full details of any tenancies or licences which affect the property. Such details having been supplied, the buyer is, by Standard Condition 3.3.2(a) and Standard Commercial Property Condition 4.1.2 (current editions), deemed to enter the contract knowing and accepting the tenancy terms. By Standard Condition 3.3.2(e), it is the buyer's responsibility to check the effects of any security of tenure legislation affecting such tenancies. Some tenant farmers may have significant protection under Agricultural Holdings Act 1986 or some protection under Agricultural Tenancies Act 1995 (see K8) and farm workers living in tied accommodation may be protected by Rent (Agriculture) Act 1976 or Housing Act 1988 (see K6).

8.9.2. If the property is sold subject to existing tenancies, the buyer should covenant with the seller to observe and perform those conditions which remain to be observed and performed by the landlord and to indemnify the seller against them.

8.10. Wayleave agreements

8.10.1. Any wayleave agreements which affect the property (e.g. for pylons, pipelines, etc.) may be expressly assigned to the buyer with the consent of the appropriate authority. Wayleave payments need only be apportioned if they are of substance. Generally a plan of the property sold can be sent to the utility company after completion and they will apportion the wayleave and issue refunds and demands as appropriate.

8.10.2. The utility companies generally offer a pre-contract search where a buyer wishes to establish exactly what wayleaves exist over the property.

8.11. Quotas

8.11.1. Milk quota must be expressly transferred to the buyer. This topic is further considered in B9. The sale of milk quotas is a standard-rated supply of services for VAT purposes if it is done in the course of a business and the seller is VAT registered. If the quota is sold together with the land, HM Revenue and Customs have indicated that they will treat it as a simple supply of the land.

8.11.2. Sugar beet contracts with British Sugar plc are not quotas. They are standard form contracts agreed through the NFU under the industry's Inter Professional Agreement (IPA) the form of which is currently settled to cover beet sown up to

2014. The contract is personal to the grower and, except in limited circumstances provided in the IPA or where special dispensation has been given by British Sugar plc, they cannot be assigned (in whole or in part) or charged or dealt with in any way. All changes are subject to the agreement of British Sugar without which the contract may be terminated. All queries or proposed changes should be referred to British Sugar plc, Sugar Way, Peterborough, PE2 9AY.

8.12. Agricultural credits search

8.12.1. A fixed or floating charge made by a farmer in favour of a bank over agricultural stock or assets is void against anyone other than the farmer himself unless the charge is registered with the Land Registry within seven days of its execution.[1]

8.12.2. A person who is buying farming stock or assets or a mortgagee who is lending money on the security of such items should make an agricultural credits search at the Land Registry in order to check the existence and validity of subsisting charges. The search should be made by the buyer before contracts are exchanged in order to find out whether any charges affect the property; in such a case the seller must be required to provide evidence of their discharge at completion. A further search is advised, to be made just before completion, to ensure that no further charges have been registered since the date of the earlier search.

8.12.3. The search is made by submitting Form AC6 in duplicate to Agricultural Credits, Plumer House, Tailyour Road, Crownhill, Plymouth PL6 5HY (DX 8249 Plymouth 3). No personal or telephone search facilities currently exist.

8.12.4. A certificate of search is conclusive but affords no priority period in favour of the searcher. A copy of the memorandum of an agricultural charge can be obtained on application on Form AC5.

8.12.5. An agricultural credits search can only be made against a private individual. Where the seller is a company, the buyer should make a search at Companies House to establish whether any floating charges exist over the company's farming stock or assets.

8.12.6. For more information see Land Registry Practice Guide 63 (section 9).

1. Agricultural Credits Act 1928, s.9.

8.13. Company search

8.13.1. If buying or leasing land from a limited company or granting a mortgage to a limited company, a company search will normally be desirable. This search should be made before exchange of contracts and updated before completion, particularly where farming stock or assets form part of the sale (see E2.10).

8.14. Post-exchange matters

Mortgages

8.14.1. Appropriate releases should be obtained from the seller or the relevant chargee in relation to any mortgages which affect the property being sold.

8.14.2. Where a floating charge is discovered against a company seller, a certificate of non-crystallisation should be obtained from the relevant lender at completion. In the case of registered land, however, a certificate is only required where the floating charge is noted on the register (see E2.10.1).

Duplicate transfer

8.14.3. When a part only of agricultural land is sold or where the buyer is giving indemnities or other covenants to the seller, it is advisable to have the transfer drawn up and executed in duplicate, the duplicate being kept by the seller. This is essential if the seller's title is not yet registered at the Land Registry. Full consideration should be given to the easements, covenants and other matters the seller may require to preserve the legal integrity and commercial value of the land being retained.

Completion statement

8.14.4. In addition to the normal requirements for a completion statement (see E4) the following may need to be considered on a dealing with agricultural land:

(a) VAT on vatable supplies, e.g. farming stock and assets, sporting or fishing rights, entitlement units and quota;

(b) apportionment of agricultural rents, cottage rents, wayleave payments, sporting or fishing rents;

(c) payment for fittings being purchased;

(d) payment for any seeds, cultivations or labour at valuation (plus VAT if applicable);

(e) allowance for any agreed retentions for holdover;

(f) payment for entitlements (plus VAT if applicable);

(g) where VAT is payable, a separate VAT invoice should be supplied with the completion statement on receipt of the VAT from the buyer.

8.15. Post-completion matters

8.15.1. On the sale of the whole or part of a freehold which is subject to an agricultural tenancy, written notice of the change of ownership should be served on the tenant including details of any rent apportionment.

8.15.2. Transfer forms for the transfer of milk quota must be registered with the Rural Payments Agency after completion (see B9).

8.15.3. Transfer forms for the transfer of entitlements must be registered with the Rural Payments Agency.

8.15.4. If the benefit of a grant is taken over with the granting authority's consent, registration of the new owner must be made in accordance with the granting authority's requirements.

8.15.5. Notice of transfer of a water abstraction licence must be given to the Environmental Agency promptly following completion of the transfer of the property, not least to protect the seller from ongoing liability.

8.16. Environmental aspects

8.16.1. Any discharge which may pollute controlled waters will require a licence/consent from the Environment Agency under Water Resources Act 1991. Discharge from slurry tanks or yard washing may be sufficiently contaminated to require such a consent.[1]

8.16.2. Enquiries should be made as to whether the agricultural processes carried out on the property fall within the scope of the regulations made under Environmental Protection Act 1990 as amended or other statutes governing the environment.

8.16.3. Enquiries should be raised as to whether the property has been the subject of a past land use, such as a farm pit, which has left residual contamination likely to interfere with the buyer's proposed use of the property or which may cause pollution.

8.16.4. Consideration should be given to the Waste Management (England and Wales) Regulations 2006 (SI 2006/937) which regulate the licensing of the disposal of agricultural waste on the property.

1. See Control of Pollution (Silage, Slurry and Agricultural Fuel Oil) Regulations (SI 1991/324).

8.17. Sporting and other rights

8.17.1. Occasionally sporting rights are reserved by the seller. These may include game under Ground Game Acts, deer (not included in Ground Game Acts) and fishing rights for the seller and his licensees. The rights will include rights of access both to exercise the sporting rights and to retrieve fallen game, any damage caused being made good by the seller. The terms of the contract should be checked to see which, if any, of such rights are being reserved by the seller.

8.17.2. If it is likely that minerals are contained under the land being sold, consideration should be given to their reservation to the seller, including, where appropriate, rights to work and take away the minerals. A bare reservation of minerals does not allow either seller or buyer to work them. Alternatively, a restrictive covenant may be imposed on the buyer preventing him from working any minerals in the land. If this is done a buyer who wished in the future to work the minerals would have to seek a release of the covenant from the seller (or his successor in title), but no further transfer of the mineral rights would be needed.

8.17.3. Unless there is a specific reservation in the purchase deed, most incorporeal hereditaments (including a lordship of the manor) will pass with the land. Lordships and manorial rights are sometimes reserved to the seller when land is sold since they are saleable commodities in themselves.

8.17.4. The reservation of sporting rights, minerals and incorporeal hereditaments all impact on the value of the interest being transferred or leased. The buyer should ensure that appropriate valuation advice is taken where the seller requires reservations of this kind.

8.17.5. Certain sporting rights are separately registrable under sections 3 and 27 Land Registration Act 2002: see Land Registry Practice Guide 16. An application for registration of such rights should be made in the usual way.

B9. Milk quotas

9.1.   General principles

9.1.1.   Milk quotas were introduced in the UK on 2 April 1984 to regulate the quantity of milk and milk products being produced in the EU. Farms producing milk and other milk products were given an allocation (a quota) the amount of which was normally based on their production levels in 1983. A levy may be payable if a producer exceeds his quota. Quota attaches to the land and will thus pass to a buyer or tenant of the land. Further information and *A Guide to Milk Quotas* can be found at **www.rpa.gov.uk**.

9.2.   Buying land with quota attached

Pre-contract enquiries

9.2.1.   Additional pre-contract enquiries will be necessary to establish:

(a)   the exact amount of quota attaching to the land;

(b)   the composition of the quota (i.e. does it include direct sales, or wholesale quota?);

(c)   that the seller is the freehold owner of the whole holding to which the quota attaches;

(d)   that the quota does not attach to any land outside the land agreed to be sold;

(e)   that if the seller is not the freehold owner of the entire holding, all other persons with an interest in the holding, such as landlords or lenders, who will be affected by the disposal of the quota have signified their agreement to the disposal on Form MQ/1; or

(f)   if an apportionment of the quota has been made within the previous six months and notified to the Rural Payments Agency by means of Form MQ/8.

9.2.2.   If a third party, other than persons referred to in (e) above, has an interest in the land (e.g. lender or trustee) that person's consent to the transfer of the quota should be required on Form MQ/1.

B

9.2.3. The seller should be required to supply the buyer with his most recent computer print-out from the Rural Payments Agency[1] which will show the allocation of quota and the registration of the quota in the seller's name. The seller will also need to produce his latest statement from his purchaser(s) of milk, showing deliveries to date, to assess the used/unused element of the quota to be sold.

9.2.4. To assist the buyer in dealing with future transfers of quota or claims for compensation from tenants, the seller's records relating to livestock cropping in 1983 and details of the use of the land and buildings, tenant's improvements and rent paid in 1983 should be produced to the buyer and handed over to him on completion.

9.2.5. A seller who sells milk direct to the public must have a licence, a copy of which should be supplied to the buyer and arrangements made for the transfer of the licence to the buyer on completion. Farmhouse cheesemakers are classified as direct sellers if they use their own milk for cheese production within a single business entity. If a farmhouse cheesemaker buys milk directly from a producer or processes his own milk in a separate business entity, the cheesemaker must be approved by the Rural Payments Agency to act as a purchaser. The producer will need to ensure that the quota is registered with the farmhouse cheesemaker to cover deliveries.

The contract

9.2.6. The contract must contain a clause dealing with the transfer of the quota to the buyer (see B1 and B11). Wording similar to that set out below will be appropriate for this purpose:

> 'The seller is the proprietor of wholesale/direct sales quota for [volume] of quota per annum. On completion the seller shall hand over to the buyer an application form for the transfer of the said quota duly signed and completed so far as the seller is able together with a signed statement as required by the Rural Payments Agency and thereafter shall use his best endeavours to obtain the transfer of the said quota to the buyer by providing any further evidence as the Agency shall require.'

The purchase deed

9.2.7. The purchase deed must contain a clause assigning the benefit and burden of the specified amount of quota to the buyer.

Completion

9.2.8. On completion (in addition to normal completion requirements) the buyer must ensure that such of the following documents as are relevant to the transaction are handed over:

(a) completed Form MQ/1 (consent to transfer of quota);

(b) any documentation relevant to an apportionment of quota;

(c) the quota notification from the Rural Payments Agency;

(d) the seller's records for 1983;

(e) a direct seller's licence.

Post-completion

9.2.9. The buyer must give notice of change of occupation to the Rural Payments Agency on a quota transfer form (Form MQ/1). MQ/1 forms must be received by 31 March of the quota year to which the transfer relates.

9.2.10. The buyer should also be advised to keep accurate records of his milk production, use of land, tenant's improvements, etc., for use in future transfers or disputes relating to a tenant's right to compensation.

9.2.11. The buyer can only retain the quota until transfer to another active producer or the end of the quota year in which the quota is transferred, whichever is earlier, unless he is himself an active producer.

9.3. Sales of part of land

9.3.1. Where a buyer buys part of the seller's land he will become entitled to a proportionate amount of the quota attaching to the holding. If the parties (including interested parties) cannot agree on the apportionment of the quota taking account of areas used for milk production then the matter must be referred to arbitration:

(a) where apportionment is to be carried out by arbitration the transferor and transferee may, by arrangement, appoint an arbitrator, and the transferee must give notice of such appointment to the Rural Payments Agency within 14 days of the appointment; or

(b) the transferor or transferee may apply to the President of the Royal Institution of Chartered Surveyors (RICS) for the appointment of an arbitrator. The party which makes the application must, within 14 days of making the application, notify the Rural Payments Agency of the application. The arbitrator will base his award on the areas used for milk production during the last five-year period in which production took place. A fee will be charged by the RICS; or

(c) where neither of the above have taken place, the Rural Payments Agency may make application to the President of RICS for the appointment of an arbitrator.

9.3.2. The provisions in B9.2 will also be relevant to a sale of part of a holding. In particular the contract must contain a clause to deal with the transfer of the quota. Provisions similar to those set out below will be appropriate:

'(a) in addition to the property the seller shall transfer on completion ... litres of wholesale/direct sales quota;

    (b)   on completion the seller shall hand over to the buyer's solicitors an application form for the transfer of the said quota duly signed and completed (so far as the seller is able) together with a signed statement the contents of which are in accordance with the provisions of the relevant regulations.[1] The documentation shall be submitted to the Rural Payments Agency forthwith;

    (c)   if the seller fails to hand over the requisite forms the buyer may rescind the contract and the seller shall repay the deposit money to the buyer;

    (d)   the seller shall supply the buyer and the Rural Payments Agency (or as appropriate) with all necessary evidence required to substantiate the amount of quota transferred with the property and shall use the seller's best endeavours to obtain a transfer of that share of the quota.'

1.   Dairy Produce Quotas Regulations 2005 (SI 2005/465) as amended by Dairy Produce Quotas (Amendment) Regulations 2006 (SI 2006/120), Dairy Produce Quotas (Amendment) Regulations 2007 (SI 2007/106), and Dairy Produce Quotas (Amendment) Regulations 2008 (SI 2008/439); Dairy Produce Quotas (Wales) Regulations 2005 (SI 2005/537) as amended by Dairy Produce Quotas (Amendment) Regulations 2006 (SI 2006/762), Dairy Produce Quotas (Amendment) Regulations 2007 (SI 2007/844), Dairy Produce Quotas (Amendment) Regulations 2008 (SI 2008/685) and Dairy Produce Quotas (General Provisions) (Amendment) Regulations 2008 (SI 2008/438).

9.4. Selling land with the benefit of quota

9.4.1.   The seller should be prepared to supply the buyer with the information specified in B9.2.1 and, on completion, such of the documents listed in B9.2.8 as are relevant. The contract and purchase deed must contain a clause dealing with the transfer of the quota (see B9.2.6).

9.5. Tenancies

9.5.1.   Clauses to deal with the following matters should be considered for inclusion in any tenancy agreement which relates to land which has the benefit of quota:

    (a)   prohibition of alienation of the quota by the tenant;

    (b)   maintenance of milk production on the land to prevent loss of quota;

    (c)   the benefit of the quota on termination of the tenancy;

    (d)   tenant's rights to compensation for loss of quota at the end of the tenancy.

9.5.2.   The quota will revert to the landlord on termination of the tenancy but the tenant may be entitled to compensation for the loss of the quota. Where the quota reverts to the landlord, Form MQ/1 needs to be completed and sent to the Rural Payments Agency. The landlord can only retain the quota until transfer to another active producer, or until the end of the quota year in which the quota is transferred, whichever is earlier, unless he is himself an active producer.

9.5.3.   Where a tenancy expires without possibility of renewal, there is no agreement between landlord and tenant in respect of any quota purchased without land by the tenant, and the tenant intends to continue in milk production, the tenant may give notice to the Rural Payments Agency that the quota is to remain available to him at the end of the tenancy.

9.5.4.   Agricultural tenancies are explained in more detail in K8.

9.6.   Compensation payable to tenants for loss of quota

9.6.1.   Agriculture Act 1986 provides for payment by the landlord to certain agricultural tenants on termination of a tenancy which is subject to the provisions of Agricultural Holdings Act 1986. Agricultural Tenancies Act 1995 applies to farm business tenancies entered into on or after 1 September 1995. The 1995 Act entitles a tenant to compensation at the end of a tenancy for physical improvements made to a holding and for intangible advantages which increase the value of the holding, provided they are left behind by a departing tenant and the landlord's written consent to the improvements has been obtained. Intangible advantages include milk quota obtained during the course of a tenancy. For tenancies covered by the 1995 Act the milk quota provisions in section 13 and Schedule 1 Agriculture Act 1986 do not apply.

Eligible tenants

9.6.2.   To be eligible for compensation under Agriculture Act 1986 a tenant must:

(a)   have the quota registered in his own name (not in the name of a company or partnership through which the tenant carries on business); and

(b)   have been in occupation of the land as tenant on 2 April 1984; or

(c)   have succeeded to a tenancy since 2 April 1984 under the succession provisions of Agricultural Holdings Act 1986, so long as the party from whom the tenant succeeded was himself in possession on 2 April 1984.

9.6.3.   Assignors of tenancies assigned after 2 April 1984 are not eligible, but the assignee is, subject to satisfying the qualifications outlined above.

9.6.4.   The statutory entitlement to compensation relates to only one transfer of occupation. There is no entitlement on subsequent transfers. It is therefore open to a landlord to determine the terms under which new tenants can enjoy the quota attached to the holding, i.e. whether they will be charged for quota at the beginning of the tenancy and whether or not they will be entitled to any payment at the end of the tenancy. If the land being vacated comprises only part of the tenant's holding there is an apportionment of the quota for compensation purposes.

Calculation of payment

9.6.5.   Payment is calculated by taking:

(a) the value of the allocated quota in excess of the standard quota for the land (or if allocated quota is less than the standard quota a proportionate reduction is made); and

(b) the value of the tenant's fraction of the standard quota; and

(c) the value of the transferred quota (this will be the entire value where the tenant has borne the whole cost of the transfer and proportionately where the tenant has only borne part of the cost).

Valuation of quota

9.6.6. Value is defined as the value at the termination of the tenancy taking into account available evidence of the value of the quota including the value of the land with and without quota.

9.6.7. Standard quota is calculated by multiplying the relevant number of hectares by the prescribed quota per hectare.

9.6.8. Prescribed quota is defined by Milk Quota (Calculation of Standard Quota) (Amendment) Order 1992 (SI 1992/1225) as 7,140 litres per hectare. There is a lower figure for land in less favoured areas (areas eligible for hill livestock compensatory allowance) and different figures apply for different breeds.

9.6.9. The relevant number of hectares is the average number of hectares used during the relevant period (the period to which allocated quota was determined, normally 1983) for feeding of dairy cows kept on the land.

Method of assessing quantum

9.6.10. The quantum of compensation (called the 'tenant's fraction') is ascertained by comparing the annual rental value of the tenant's dairy improvements and fixed equipment with the rent paid for the land during the relevant period.

9.6.11. The formula used is

$$\frac{r}{r+R}$$

where r = the annual rental value at the end of the relevant period of the tenant's dairy improvement and fixed equipment and R = the rent of the land.

9.6.12. Liability for compensation does not arise until the termination of the tenancy but either landlord or tenant may at any time prior to termination seek determination of the standard quota or the tenant's fraction by agreement or arbitration.

9.6.13. The procedure for claiming compensation is similar to that for claiming tenant right under Agricultural Holdings Act 1986.

9.7. Quota transfers without land

9.7.1. The notification of a transfer without land is effected on form MQ1 to be received by 31 March in the quota year to which the transfer relates.

9.7.2. The transferee must meet the definition of a producer at the operative date of the transfer.

9.7.3. Notification of a transfer without land is made using form MQ/1 (*Notification of permanent transfer of milk quota*). The form should be received by 31 March in the quota year to which the transfer relates.

Used and unused quota

9.7.4. The transferor and transferee must agree how much quota is used or unused. When calculating how much of the original wholesale quota is used it is necessary to take into account deliveries which have already been made with the butterfat adjustment.

9.7.5. If used quota is transferred with unused quota, the Rural Payments Agency will:

(a) permanently transfer all of the quota, used and unused, to the new owner (the transferee), and

(b) recalculate their ongoing and permanent butterfat bases to take account of the newly-acquired unused quota for the current quota year.

In addition, any unused quota will remain available to the transferor for the remainder of the quota year in question.

Geographical restrictions on transfers

9.7.6. Quota cannot be transferred to or from any of these groups of Scottish islands:

(a) the islands of Orkney, except for the island of Stronsay; or

(b) the islands of Jura, Gigha, Arran, Bute, Great Cumbrae and Little Cumbrae, the Kintyre peninsula south of Tarbert and the areas of land within the Argyll and Bute District comprising those parts of the parishes of Dunoon and Kilmun and Inverchaolain.

9.7.7. These groups of islands form separate units of production and are known as 'ring-fenced areas'. A temporary transfer of quota is permitted where it increases quantities available to dairy enterprises within the ring-fenced areas. Quota may be transferred temporarily or permanently within each ring-fenced area, and may be leased into a ring-fenced area, provided the normal requirements are met. Quota may not be transferred, either permanently or temporarily, outside a ring-fenced area.

Changes in butterfat base after a permanent transfer

9.7.8. 'Permanent' butterfat base is the figure attached to permanent quota, after being adjusted for transfers, permanent conversions and special allocations. If the butterfat base of any wholesale quota transferred in is higher or lower than the transferor's ongoing or permanent butterfat base, the new ongoing or permanent butterfat base will be recalculated as the weighted average of the butterfat base of the quota transferred in and the transferee's existing quota and butterfat base. A quota holder who has leased in quota and then leases/permanently transfers quota out, will have their ongoing butterfat base reweighted after each quota movement.

Confirmation of transfer

9.7.9. The Rural Payments Agency will write to the transferor to confirm:

    (a) that the transfer has been entered on the quota register;

    (b) the changes to the transferor's quota and permanent and ongoing butterfat bases (where applicable);

    (c) the details of the producers and purchaser(s) involved.

9.7.10. They will also notify the purchaser of the change in the amount of quota registered with them and the changes to the producer's permanent and ongoing butterfat bases. The Rural Payments Agency will also write to the transferee (and transferee's purchaser, where appropriate) to confirm the results of the transfer in.

Temporary reallocation of quota

9.7.11. Farmers affected by herd movement restrictions can apply for a temporary reallocation of quota using Form MQ/16. For details see Form MQ/16A Explanatory Notes.

B10. Pre-contract searches and enquiries

10.1. Reason for making searches and enquiries

10.1.1. Subject to the seller's duty of disclosure,[1] it is up to the buyer to make sure of his bargain. Thus the buyer needs to find out as much about the property as possible before he commits himself to a binding contract to purchase the property. At common law the seller is generally under no obligation to disclose physical defects in the property to the buyer; therefore if the seller does not reveal information about the physical aspects of the property the buyer must obtain such information from other sources, much of which can be obtained through making proper pre-contract searches and enquiries.[2] The buyer should also be advised to arrange for a survey to be carried out to discover physical defects in the property. A solicitor's failure to make appropriate searches may give rise to liability in negligence to the buyer if as a result the buyer suffers loss.[3] However, the seller must not fraudulently conceal known defects or reply dishonestly to questions on pre-contract enquiries or information forms.

1. Discussed in B5. The common law duty of disclosure is often modified by contractual condition, e.g. Standard Condition 3.
2. See Standard Commercial Property Conditions of Sale (Second Edition) 3.1.2(d) on 'searches and enquiries which a prudent buyer would have made before entering into the contract'. Reproduced in Appendix III.6.
3. *Cooper* v. *Stephenson* (1852) Cox M & H 627.

10.2. Who should make the searches and enquiries?

10.2.1. The onus of making searches rests with the buyer, but in some cases the seller may make all appropriate pre-contract searches and pass the results of these searches to the buyer as part of the pre-contract package. However the sale will still be on a *caveat emptor* basis. It will frequently assist the progress of the transaction if the seller chooses to instigate pre-contract searches on behalf of the buyer and thus gives the buyer a complete package of documentation at an early stage in the transaction, but he is not obliged to do so. The liability provisions on Forms CON 29R and CON 29O (see Appendices III.1 and III.2) acknowledge a duty of care in negligence by the council to a buyer who relies on replies obtained from another party.

10.2.2. In any case where the seller does not make all the appropriate pre-contract searches, the buyer should do so. Since the risk of buying the property subject to undiscovered defects broadly rests with the buyer, it is up to the buyer to ensure that all necessary pre-contract searches have been made, whether by the buyer himself, or by the seller on the buyer's behalf.

10.3. When should searches and enquiries be made?

10.3.1. Where the searches and enquiries are being undertaken by the seller's solicitor, they should be put in hand in sufficient time to ensure that their results will be available to send to the buyer with the draft contract. Where it is anticipated that delay in receiving the search result will be experienced, this may mean that it is necessary to submit a search application as soon as instructions for the sale of the property are received notwithstanding that a buyer has not at that time been found for the property. In other cases the search application need not be submitted until a buyer for the property has been found since, the more recent the date of the search result, the more benefit it will be to the buyer. If the buyer's solicitor is to make searches, he should put his searches in hand as soon as firm instructions to proceed are received from his client. The buyer's solicitor, on receipt of the pre-contract package from the seller's solicitor, should check which searches (if any) have been made by the seller, and immediately submit additional search forms if he considers that any additional searches need to be made to meet the requirements of the particular transaction. Search applications should always be submitted without delay since some authorities take a long time to reply to them. It is unwise for a buyer to exchange contracts before having analysed the results of his pre-contract searches; thus delay in submitting search applications may result in delay to the transaction itself.

10.3.2. The buyer's solicitor should also check to see whether any of the searches supplied need to be renewed and to check that all appropriate enquiries, including those relating to environmental issues, have been raised (see B25.5).

10.4. Which searches and enquiries should be made?

10.4.1. Details of the searches and enquiries listed below are contained in B10.5.

All transactions

10.4.2. The following searches are regarded as 'usual' and should be undertaken in every transaction:

- search of the local land charges register;

- enquiries of the local authority and, if appropriate, optional enquiries;

- standard drainage and water enquiries of the water service company;

- pre-contract enquiries of the seller.

Registered land

10.4.3.   In addition to the searches and enquiries listed in B10.4.2, official copies of the title must be obtained.

Unregistered title

10.4.4.   In addition to the searches and enquiries listed in B10.4.2, a Land Charges Department search against the name of the seller and prior estate owners whose names appear on the abstract or epitome of title should be undertaken.

Other common searches and enquiries

10.4.5.   Other common searches and enquiries in addition to those listed in B10.4.2 are:

- coal mining search;

- index map search if dealing with unregistered title or an unregistered interest in registered land;

- environmental data search;

- Disadvantaged Areas search (checking relief from Stamp Duty Land Tax);

- any of the less usual searches which may be applicable in the circumstances (see B10.6).

10.5.   **Summary of usual searches and enquiries**

10.5.1.   Local land charges search

- **When to make:** in every transaction.

- **Form:** LLC1 in duplicate (LLC1 is a prescribed form provided for by Local Land Charges Rules 1977, Schedule 1, form C).

- **Search methods:**

  – National Land Information Service Channel or other electronic search provider;

  – post/DX to local authority;

  – electronic search (some authorities only);

– personal search.

- **Plan:** needed if land cannot be clearly identified from postal address.

- **Fee:** yes. Contact the relevant authority for details. Fees will differ between authorities. See Local Land Charges (Amendment) Rules 2009 (SI 2009/2494) for the fee for a personal search: £22.00 (plus £1.00 for each additional plot of land up to a maximum for additional plots of £16.00).

- **Summary of information to be obtained from search:** financial charges affecting the property.

- **Protection given by search:** none. Search result only shows state of register at time when search is made but warning of impending land charges can sometimes be obtained by making an Enquiries of Local Authority search on Form CON 29R (see B10.5.2). A third party can take benefit of search made by someone else (e.g. a seller can make a search to pass the result to buyer or his lender). Local Land Charges Act 1975, s.10 provides compensation in limited circumstances where there is an error on the search certificate, or where a matter is binding on the land but is not revealed by the search, because it was not registered at the time of the search. An entry is binding on the land whether or not it is revealed by the search.

- **Personal search facility:** there is a statutory right to make a personal search, but local authorities do not guarantee the accuracy of the result. It should only be undertaken where time does not permit an official search to be made. Some lenders will not accept personal searches and, if a personal search is undertaken, clients should be warned that it is not guaranteed by the local authority.

- **Special points:** can be made personally or by agent, but the result is not guaranteed. Insurance may be available if exchange has to take place before result of search received.

10.5.2. *Standard and optional enquiries of local authority*

- **When to make:** standard enquiries in every transaction, optional enquiries where appropriate.

- **Form:** the enquiry form CON 29 is split into two forms and both should be submitted in duplicate:

    – CON 29R Enquiries of Local Authority (2007) (Appendix III.1).

    – CON 29O Optional Enquiries of Local Authority (2007) (Appendix III.2).

- **Search methods:**

    – National Land Information Service Channel or other electronic search provider;

–   post/DX to local authority;

–   electronic search (some authorities only);

–   personal search.

In view of local government boundary changes, care should be exercised to ensure that the search forms are sent to the correct local authority.

● **Plan:** always include a plan with search requests. Some local authorities have specific requirements in relation to the submission of forms and plans (e.g. Cornwall County and District Councils). Noncompliance with these procedures may result in delay in receiving the answers to enquiries.

● **Fee:** yes. Contact the relevant authority for details. Fees will differ between authorities and between standard and optional enquiries. VAT is payable on a personal search but not on one made by post. See also the special points below.

● **Summary of information to be obtained:** relates only to the property being searched against. Matters which affect neighbouring properties are not disclosed in the search replies.

–   *from standard enquiries:* planning and building regulations; roads; land for public purposes; land for road works; drainage agreements and consents; road schemes; railway schemes; traffic schemes; outstanding notices; infringements of building regulations; notices, orders, directions and proceedings under planning acts; conservation areas; compulsory purchase; contaminated land; radon gas. See Appendices III.1 and III.2 for the full enquiries.

–   *from optional enquiries:* road proposals by private bodies; public paths and byways; advertisements; completion notices; parks and countryside; pipelines; houses in multiple occupation; noise abatement; urban development areas; enterprise zones; inner urban improvement areas; simplified planning zones; land maintenance notices; mineral consultation areas; hazardous substance consents; environmental and pollution notices; food safety notices; hedgerow notices; common land and town and village greens.

● **Protection given by search:** the buyer is bound by matters even if not discovered by search. The authorities 'do not accept legal responsibility for an incorrect reply, except for negligence. Any liability for negligence will extend to the person who raised the enquiries and the person on whose behalf they were raised. It will also extend to any other person who has knowledge (personally or through an agent) of the replies before the time when he purchases, takes a tenancy of, or lends money on the security of the property or (if earlier) the time when he becomes contractually bound to do so' (extract from the notes to Forms CON 29R and CON 29O, see Appendices III.1 and III.2).

- **Personal search facility:** some authorities permit personal searches, but do not guarantee the accuracy of the result; it should only be undertaken where time does not permit an official search to be made. Even where facilities are granted for personal searches, these may not cover all the matters normally covered by Forms CON 29R and CON 29O and may not be acceptable to the buyer's lender.

  There are limitations on personal searches and some lenders will not accept them. The accuracy of a personal search depends on the ability and diligence of the searcher. It is not guaranteed by the local authority. If a personal search is undertaken, clients should be told of this and advised of the limitations on personal searches and their possible implications.

- **Special points:** can be made personally or by agent, but the result is not guaranteed. Insurance is available if exchange has to take place before result of search received, but check lender's requirements. Where a local authority refuses to answer a question relating to whether or not a property abuts a public highway consideration should be given to enquiry 22 of Form CON 29O Optional Enquiries of Local Authority, relating to common land and town and village greens (see B10.5.7) and to making an inspection of the property.

  The fee requested from the client in respect of the local land charges search and the enquiries of the local authority must accurately reflect the fee charged by the local authority or the local search agents used by the solicitor. It is not acceptable to charge the client an enhanced fee. It is also not acceptable to charge the client an enhanced fee which is paid to the local search agent in exchange for a commission payment from the local search agent to the solicitor.

- **Notes:** both the local search and enquiries of the local authority contain questions relating to planning matters. In most cases the local authority to whom the search application is submitted will also be the planning authority for the area who will therefore answer the planning enquiries on the standard forms. In a few cases, e.g. new town development corporations, the planning authority is separate from the local authority and planning enquiries have to be separately addressed to the planning authority. If in doubt, telephone the local authority prior to submitting the search application in order to check the position.

10.5.3. *Standard drainage and water enquiries*

- **When to make:** standard enquiries in every transaction.

- **Form:** CON 29DW (2007) Standard Drainage and Water Enquiries (see Appendix III.3).

- **Search methods:**

  – National Land Information Service Channel or other electronic search provider;

  – online via relevant company's website (see Appendix IX.2 for URLs);

  – post/DX to relevant company (see Appendix IX.2 for addresses);

  – fax to the relevant company (see Appendix IX.2 for fax numbers).

  Care should be exercised to ensure that the search forms are sent to the correct company. In some cases enquiries will need to be made of more than one company. The website **www.drainageandwater.co.uk** has a postcode search facility that will return the correct company for a property.

- **Plan:** insisted on by some water service companies, always needed if land cannot be clearly identified from postal address.

- **Fee:** yes. Contact the appropriate regional water service company for details or visit **www.drainageandwater.co.uk**. All regional water service companies answer standard drainage and water enquiries (and for a higher fee may answer an expedited standard search). A 'commercial search' may be available at a higher fee. Solicitors should be aware that the Law Society has only been involved in approving the form and content of the CON 29DW Standard Drainage and Water Search. Some areas, such as those served by Dee Valley Water plc, may be subject to further administrative charges – always check with the appropriate water service company before sending fees.

- **Summary of information to be obtained from search:** location of public sewers within boundaries of the property or its vicinity; whether foul water and surface drainage from property drain to a public sewer; whether any sewers or proposed sewers are adopted; location of public water mains and whether the property is connected; the basis of charging for sewerage and water supply to the property (see Appendix III.3 for full enquiries).

- **Protection given by search:** The standard drainage and water enquiries were aimed primarily at residential property but were not intended to exclude commercial properties, however when first launched the liability was limited to £5,000. Following representations from the profession and discussion between the Law Society and the regional water service companies, an interim measure was agreed in September 2002 – an increase in professional indemnity cover maintained by most water companies to £2 million for commercial property transactions. Some companies do not offer the increased level of cover. Solicitors are advised to check the level of liability cover with individual water service companies before making a search.

- **Personal search facility:** none.

- **Special points:** protection extends to the person, company or body who is the recipient of the report with an actual or potential interest in the property. The property may be located where two different water companies separately provide water and sewerage services. Check carefully for this before submitting the search form to avoid unnecessary delays.

10.5.4. *Pre-contract enquiries of seller*

- **When to make:** in every transaction.

- **Form:**

  - TA6 Property Information Form (2nd edition);

  - TA7 Leasehold Information Form (2nd edition) (for use in addition to form TA6 for leasehold property);

  - TA9 Commonhold Information Form (for use in addition to form TA6 for commonhold property);

  - Commercial Property Standard Enquiries (CPSEs);

  - other forms from legal stationers are also available.

- **Search methods:** send to seller's solicitor.

- **Plan:** no.

- **Fee:** no.

- **Summary of information to be obtained from:**

  - *TA6 Property Information Form:* boundaries and boundary features (fences, walls, hedges, ditches or similar); disputes and complaints; notices and proposals; alterations, planning and building control; guarantees and warranties; council tax; environmental matters; formal and informal arrangements; other charges; occupiers; transaction information; services; connection to utilities and services;

  - *TA7 Leasehold Information Form:* the property; relevant documents; management of the building; contact details; maintenance and service charges; notices; consents; complaints; alterations; enfranchisement;

  - *TA9 Commonhold Information Form:* commonhold association; commonhold assessments and reserve fund levies; notices; common parts; insurance; consents; complaints; rights for the developer;

  - *Commercial Property Standard Enquiries (general – for all transactions):* boundaries and extent; party walls; rights benefiting the property; adverse rights affecting the property; title policies; access to neighbouring land; access to and from the property; physical condition; contents; utilities and services; fire safety and means of escape; planning and building regulations; statutory agreements and infrastructure; statutory and other requirements; environmental; occupiers and employees; insurance; rates and other outgoings; capital allowances; value added tax registration information; transfer of a business as a going concern; other VAT treatment; standard-rated supplies; exempt supplies; zero-rated supplies; transactions outside the scope of VAT; notices; disputes; Stamp Duty Land Tax on assignment of a lease; deferred payments of Stamp Duty Land Tax; commonhold.

- **Protection given by search:** none. Seller may be liable in misrepresentation for inaccurate replies. There may also be criminal liability under Fraud Act 2006.

- **Personal search facility:** none.

- **Special points:** Solicitors making pre-contract enquiries of the seller using the TransAction forms may use form TA6. Forms TA7 Leasehold Information Form and TA9 Commonhold Information Form may be used in addition to form TA6, when appropriate.

  Explanatory notes for the seller have been added to forms TA6, TA7 and TA10.

  If TransAction forms are used to make pre-contract enquiries of the seller, the forms should be completed, signed and dated by the seller.

  Use of the TransAction forms by solicitors is voluntary and there are currently no standard procedures or good practice guidance recommended by the Law Society in relation to their use by solicitors.

  There is no requirement for the seller's solicitor to certify the information given on the TransAction forms TA6 Property Information Form, TA7 Leasehold Information Form or TA9 Commonhold Information Form. However, this does not affect the legal responsibility of the seller's solicitor and checking the answers given is part of the solicitor's duty as a prudent conveyancer. Failure to do this may amount to inadequate professional service and may be professional negligence (*McMeekin* v. *Long* [2003] 29 EG 120). Where questions have been answered in the terms 'not so far as the seller is aware', this will imply that the seller and his solicitor have made investigations and have no actual knowledge of any defect (*William Sindall plc* v. *Cambridgeshire County Council* [1994] 3 All ER 932). To be adequate, these investigations must cover the seller's personal knowledge as well as the contents of such files, deeds, etc., as are in the firm's personal possession and any other reasonable investigations.

In addition, solicitors acting for the buyer should not accept a TA6 Property Information Form, TA7 Leasehold Information Form or TA9 Commonhold Information Form if it has not been properly completed. Acceptance of an improperly completed form may amount to a failure to carry out all the usual enquiries and the solicitor will be in breach of his duty to the buyer client and to any lender client for whom he is also acting (see B10.9).

Enquiries additional to those on the TransAction forms should only be raised where relevant and necessary to the particular transaction. Do not raise additional enquiries about matters that can be resolved by a survey or personal inspection of the property. Seller's replies should be factual and accurate and not based on statements of opinion. The seller's solicitor must take his client's instructions before answering the enquiries.

In commercial property cases where CPSEs are used, it is standard practice for the buyer's solicitor to submit the request form to the seller's solicitors (usually via e-mail) while the CPSEs referred to in the request are available to all parties on the Practical Law Company's website (**www.practicallaw.com**).

10.5.5. *Official copies of the title*

- **When to make:** in every registered land transaction.

- **Form:**

  - OC1 Application for Official Copies of Register/Title Plan and/or certificate in Form CI;

  - OC2 Application for Official Copies of Documents Only.

- **Search methods:**

  - National Land Information Service Channel or other electronic search provider;

  - Online at **www.landregistry.gov.uk** for Land Registry account holders;

  - post/DX/fax to the Land Registry (see Appendix IX.1 for addresses);

  - telephone by Land Registry account holders on 0844 892 0307 (English counties) or 0844 892 0308 (Welsh counties and Welsh speaking).

- **Plan:** no (except where the application is for a certificate in Form CI and an estate plan has not been approved).

- **Fee:** yes, see Land Registration Fee Order 2009 (see Appendix VIII.4).

- **Summary of information to be obtained from search:** up-to-date copy of entries affecting seller's title.

- **Special points:** the application is usually made by the seller who supplies the results to the buyer. For more information see Land Registry Practice Guide 11.

10.5.6. *Land Charges Department search*

- **When to make:** in all cases when dealing with unregistered land. Strictly not relevant to land registered with an absolute title but sensible for seller's solicitor to make search against his own client's name to ensure no bankruptcy proceedings pending.

- **Form:**

  – Form K15 Application for an Official Search: not applicable to registered land.

  – Form K16 Application for an Official Search (bankruptcy only).

- **Search methods:**

  – National Land Information Service Channel or other electronic search provider;

  – Online at **www.landregistry.gov.uk** for Land Registry account holders;

  – post/DX/fax to Land Charges Department, Plymouth;

  – personal search at Plymouth address only;

  – telephone by Land Registry account holders on 0844 892 0307 (English counties) or 0844 892 0308 (Welsh counties and Welsh speaking).

- **Plan:** none.

- **Fee:** £1 per name for written applications, £2 per name for telephone, fax and computer searches.

- **Summary of information to be obtained from search:** this is the quickest method of checking that no bankruptcy proceedings are registered against a client (although it must be borne in mind that bankruptcy entries are normally cancelled automatically after five years). In addition, in unregistered land, information relating to incumbrances over the land, e.g. post-1925 restrictive covenants, second and subsequent mortgages, estate contracts, and home rights.

- **Protection given by search:** full search: 15 working days from date of official search certificate provided completion takes place within this period. Where an entry is revealed which appears to be irrelevant to the transaction in hand, the seller's solicitor may be asked to certify that the entry does not apply to the transaction (by endorsing the search certificate to this effect). Such endorsement does not alter the legal significance of the search result, but an unqualified endorsement by the seller's solicitor would commit him to personal liability if loss were subsequently suffered by the buyer resulting from that particular entry.

- **Personal search facility:** at Land Charges Department, Plymouth only, but no protection given by personal search.

- **Special points:** the effect of Law of Property Act 1969, s.24 (by displacing the 'registration is notice' rule contained in Law of Property Act 1925, s.198) is to place the burden of disclosure of incumbrances on the seller and thus renders this search strictly unnecessary at the pre-contract stage of the transaction. Since the search needs to be made against all estate owners of the land whose names are revealed in the evidence of title, it is only possible for a buyer to make proper searches if title is deduced to him before exchange. These points notwithstanding it is advisable for the buyer to make a search at least against the seller's name at this stage in order to ensure that no bankruptcy or other financial charges are pending against the seller and that no Class F charge protecting the seller's spouse's or civil partner's home rights have been registered at that time. Additionally, if the documentation supplied by the seller reveals the existence of restrictive covenants which if valid would impede the buyer's proposed use of the land, a check may be made against the name of the person on whom the burden of the covenants was imposed to check whether the covenants were registered as Class D(ii) land charges (if not the covenants are not enforceable against a subsequent purchaser if entered into after 1925). To take advantage of the protection period afforded by the search it will usually need to be repeated shortly before completion. In registered land, bankruptcy entries or a notice protecting a spouse's or civil partner's home rights will be entered on the register and so revealed by official copy entries of the title so long as those copies are up to date.

- For more information see Land Registry Practice Guide 63.

10.5.7. *Commons registration*

- **When to make:** in any case where the property abuts a village green or common land, where property is newly built on or is to be built on previously undeveloped land, where a verge or strip or other land, not owned by the property, separates the property from the public highway (see also B26).

- **Form:** this information is now obtained by making optional enquiry of local authority, enquiry 22 'Common land, town and village greens', on Form CON 29O Optional Enquiries of Local Authority (2007) (see B10.5.2).

- **Search methods:**

    - National Land Information Service Channel or other electronic search provider;

    - post/DX to local authority;

    - electronic search (some authorities);

    - personal search.

- **Fee:** £14.

- **Summary of information to be obtained:** whether any land is registered under Commons Registration Act 1965 (CRA 1965) or Commons Act 2006 (CA 2006).

- **Protection given:** see B10.5.2.

- **Personal enquiry facility:** see B10.5.2.

- **Special points:** where land has been registered as a common or as a town or village green under CRA 1965 or CA 2006 generally no development over the land will be possible. Third parties may have rights over land that is registered, e.g. rights to graze cattle. CA 2006 provides for the registration of land as a town or village green where the land has been used by a significant number of the inhabitants for sports and other pastimes as of right over a period of 20 years and they continue to do so at the time of the application. Section 15 CA 2006 allows the following periods of grace for such applications for registration where the use as of right has ceased before the application is made:

    - two years from the use ceasing; or

    - five years where the use ceased before 19 July 2006.[1]

    CA 2006 also contains provisions that enable 'missed' commons to be registered and wrongly registered land to be deregistered.

    Section 2 Countryside and Rights of Way Act 2000 provides for the right of access to open country or registered common land as shown on the maps issued by the Countryside Agency. The maps can be inspected at **www.openaccess.gov.uk**.

1. The five-year period of grace may not apply where planning permission was granted and construction works commenced before 23 June 2006.

10.5.8. *Coal mining and brine subsidence claim search*

- **When to make:** in any case when dealing with land in coal mining and brine subsidence claim areas, known as 'affected areas'. To determine whether a coal mining and brine subsidence claim search is required, conveyancers may consult the Coal Authority's gazetteer at **www.coal. gov.uk/services/propertysearch/gazetteer/** and consult the printed gazetteer in *Coal Mining and Brine Subsidence Claim Searches: Directory and Guidance* (Law Society, 2006). This book also contains further guidance from the Law Society and a user guide from the Coal Authority.

- **Form:** CON 29M (2006) Coal Mining and Brine Subsidence Claim Search form.

- **Search methods:**

  – National Land Information Service Channel or other electronic search provider;

  – online via the Coal Authority's Property Search Service (**www.groundstability.com**);

  – fax (an expedited same/next working day service is available for an additional fee);

  – post/DX to the Coal Authority (see Appendix IX.2 for address);

  – telephone to the Coal Authority's customer service team on 0845 762 6848.

- **Plan:** yes.

- **Fee:** Current fees for residential property are £33.87 plus VAT for postal or telephone applications and £27.00 plus VAT for online applications. Fees for non-residential searches up to a maximum extent of 25 hectares are £64.00 plus VAT irrespective of the method of application. An additional fee of £50.00 plus VAT is payable for same/next working day fax service. Fees information is available from the Coal Authority by telephone, 0845 762 6848 and at **www.coal.gov.uk/services/miningreports**.

- **Summary of information to be obtained from search (coal enquiries):** whether the property is in an area where coal mining has taken or is likely to take place; the existence of underground coal workings and mine entries which may cause problems with subsidence; whether compensation for subsidence has been paid in the past or repairs carried out or any claim is current.

  Summary of information to be obtained from search (Cheshire brine subsidence claims): whether the property is in the Cheshire Brine Compensation District or within a Consultation Area prescribed by the Brine Board; an indication of whether there have been any claims for damage made by the owner or a previous owner against the Brine Board for past or suspected past damage; whether the Board has made a 'once-and-for-all' payment commuting the property from any further claim for compensation: such a commutation will usually result in the value of the property being reduced and make it difficult to mortgage. If the search result reveals that a claim for compensation has been lodged but not yet adjudicated the buyer must after completion give notice of the change of ownership to the Board.

- **Protection given by search:** Any liability of the Coal Authority for negligence in giving mining reports shall be for the benefit of not only enquirers but also a person (being a purchaser for the purpose of section 10(3) Local Land Charges Act 1975) who or whose agent had knowledge before the relevant time (as defined in that section) of the contents of the mining report. Such extension of liability to another (who did not purchase the mining report from the Authority) is limited to a purchaser, lessee or mortgagee of the property and not others (e.g. other recipients of reports on title, etc.). Full Terms and Conditions and guidance on liability can be found in the printed book Coal Mining and Brine Subsidence Claim Searches (Law Society, 2006) or online at **www. coal.gov.uk/services/miningreports/**. All residential reports include insurance cover for the property owner of up to £20,000 in respect of loss of value as a result of there being a material change in the mining information in a subsequent residential report. It is intended to cover loss suffered as a result of changes in the coal mining database at any time during the insured person's ownership of the property. Where the search is obtained by the seller, the buyer will receive the benefit of the insurance cover. Similar cover applies to 'residential-search-not-required' certificates.

- **Personal search facility:** none.

- **Special points:** disused mines exist in many areas where coal mining has not been carried on within living memory. The dangers of subsidence exist in any area where mining has at some time taken place. Provisions for compensation for subsidence are complex: in some cases, once a sum has been paid in compensation, no further claim can be sustained despite further subsidence damage to the land.

The Coal Authority also offers an interpretive report service for residential property. Under the service the applicant will be provided with detailed analysis and advice about mine shafts revealed in the initial report, including a risk assessment as to whether, in the opinion of the Coal Authority, the main building of the property is inside the possible zone of ground movement from any reported mine entry. This service will be offered at an additional cost if the initial report discloses a mine shaft.

The Coal Authority also promotes other products including a 'ground stability' report. This report reveals information from the British Geological Survey relating to natural subsidence. It also includes replies to the enquiries made in the CON 29M (2006) Coal Mining and Brine Subsidence Claim Search. The Law Society of England and Wales has not participated in the development of the ground stability search. The Law Society recommends that solicitors make a CON 29M Coal

Mining and Brine Subsidence Claim Search when dealing with land in areas affected by coal mining and brine subsidence.

10.5.9. Index map search

- **When to make:** in all cases when buying an interest in unregistered land. It is also useful when buying an area of land comprised in more than one registered title.

- **Form:** SIM Application for an Official Search of the Index Map.

- **Search methods:**

  – National Land Information Service Channel or other electronic search provider;

  – Online at **www.landregistry.gov.uk** for Land Registry account holders;

  – post/DX/fax/telephone to the Land Registry (see Appendix IX.1 for addresses).

- **Plan:** a suitable plan may be needed, see Land Registry Practice Guide 10.

- **Fee:** see Land Registration Fee Order 2009 (see Appendix VIII.4).

- **Summary of information to be obtained from search:** whether the land is already registered or is subject to a pending application or caution against first registration or existence of a registered rentcharge or affecting franchise.

- **Protection given by search:** none, although if search result is inaccurate, a right to indemnity may arise (see M7.5).

- **Personal search facility:** not available.

- **Special points:** if it is discovered that the land is already registered or that a compulsory registration order came into force before the date of the most recent conveyance on sale on the title the seller must be asked to rectify the situation before this transaction proceeds.

For more information, see Land Registry Practice Guide 10.

10.5.10. Environmental data search

- **When to make:** there is no professional obligation to undertake an environmental data search in the course of property transactions. Solicitors must, however, consider whether contamination is an issue in every transaction and advise clients of the potential liabilities associated with environmental issues, without overstating them. In all commercial transactions, and in residential cases where contamination is considered a potential issue, solicitors may consider making specific pre-contract enquiries of the seller, and other enquiries of statutory and regulatory bodies and if there is a possibility that the site is contaminated, or the buyer or lender requests one, an environmental data search may be made, see B25 and the *Environmental Law Handbook, 6th edition* (Law Society, 2010).

- **Form:** there is no standard form.

- **Search methods:**

  - National Land Information Service or other electronic search provider;

  - online with search providers (see Appendix IX.2);

  - post to search providers;

  - fax to search providers.

- **Plan:** it is essential to confirm the location of the land by reference to a plan (paper or online) or by grid reference.

- **Fee:** From £25 to several hundred pounds (differs for residential and commercial).

- **Summary of information to be obtained from search:** (depending on provider) all information held by regulatory bodies, a detailed land use survey highlighting current and historic uses, floodplain data, risk assessment.

- **Protection given by search:** none.

- **Personal search facility:** none.

- **Special points:** the purpose of this search is to establish that there is no cause for concern regarding environmental issues or, if there is a concern, to inform further enquiries and advice to the client. For further guidance see B25, Appendix IV.1 and the *Environmental Law Handbook*, 6th edition (Law Society, 2010).

10.5.11. *Disadvantaged Areas Search (Relief from SDLT)*

- **When to make:** when acting for the buyer or seller of residential property, a search should be made to determine whether a property is located within a designated disadvantaged area. This will be necessary in every purchase of residential property where the purchase price does not exceed £150,000. However, from 25 March 2010 (and until 24 March 2012), relief is available on the purchase of property by an individual, or by individuals, for not more than £250,000, where the individual (or all of them) intends to occupy the property as his or their only or main residence, and the individual (or any of them) has not previously acquired a major interest in land which includes residential property, or an equivalent interest in land, situated anywhere in the world. The level of this temporary relief for certain purchases of residential property is above the current Disadvantaged Area Relief threshold of £150,000.

From 17 March 2005 Disadvantaged Areas Relief is not available for non-residential land transactions.

The purchase of six or more separate dwellings as a single transaction is classed as a non-residential transaction and SDLT is payable at the appropriate rate.

Section 116 Finance Act 2003 defines residential, commercial, and mixed-use property. In mixed-use property (part residential and part non-residential) the value has to be apportioned and the £150,000 limit applied to the residential part.

The scope of the exemption is such that it applies to property which on 7 May 1998 was situated in specified qualifying wards included in the current indices of deprivation for England and Wales (Indices of Deprivation 2000).

The exemption will apply to a property falling outside a qualifying ward if on 27 November 2001 it had the same postcode as land which on 7 May 1998 was within a qualifying ward.

Where a property is partly inside a qualifying ward, the purchase price must be apportioned and the part outside will be subject to SDLT.

This complicated definition can give rise to a number of problems, not least that searches currently available to establish whether property falls within a qualifying ward for the purposes of disadvantaged areas SDLT exemption are not always conclusive.

- **Form:** not applicable.

- **Search method for properties with a postcode:**

  - check the postcode lies in a disadvantaged area by using the postcode search on the HM Revenue and Customs website (**www.hmrc.gov.uk/so/dar/dar-search.htm**);

  - check in which ward the property was located in England on 7 May 1998 (1 April 1998 for Wales) by visiting **www.neighbourhood.statistics.gov.uk** and searching against the property's postcode;

  - check the ward is listed on the HM Revenue and Customs website (**www.hmrc.gov.uk/sdlt/reliefs-exemptions**). There are separate lists for wards in England, Wales, Northern Ireland and Scotland.

If the results of these three checks are positive, then the property is exempt.

If the postcode search is positive but the ward search shows part or all of the property is outside the relevant ward, the property will still be exempt if the property on 27 November 2001 had the same postcode as land which on 7 May 1998 fell within a qualifying ward.

Warning: The HM Revenue and Customs postcode search is not complete, and is therefore inconclusive. If the postcode search shows that the property is outside a designated area or no postcode is found it may be prudent to follow the steps for properties without postcodes below.

- **Search method for properties without a postcode:**

  – check with the local authority to find out in which ward the property was located in England on 7 May 1998 (1 April 1998 for Wales). Maps showing wards as at 1998 can be viewed as pdf files on **www. neighbourhood.statistics.gov.uk**;

  – check whether the ward is listed on the HM Revenue and Customs website (**www.hmrc.gov.uk/sdlt/reliefs-exemptions**);

  – obtain a copy of the 7 May 1998 (England) or 1 April 1998 (Wales) boundary ward map from the Ordnance Survey Boundaries Service (Tel. 023 8030 5092) and check that the property is within the boundaries shown. The Neighbourhood Statistics website also holds pdf files of the 1998 ward boundary maps.

  If the results of these checks above show the property within the ward, it is exempt. Any part outside the ward is subject to SDLT.

- **Alternative search method:** the procedures to ascertain whether a property qualifies for the relief can be time-consuming and not always conclusive. An alternative may be to contact either HM Revenue and Customs Stamp Taxes Helpline on 0845 603 0135 or the Stamp Office in Birmingham (complex transactions) and seek written advice. However, a binding opinion of the SDLT due can only be obtained if HM Revenue and Customs has been informed of everything it needs to know about the transaction. If advice is sought, HM Revenue and Customs will assist, but any opinion it gives will be an informal opinion and will not bind it.

- **Plan:** a copy of the 7 May 1998 (England) or 1 April 1998 (Wales) ward map clearly showing the property within a ward boundary.

- **Fee:** none.

- **Summary of information to be obtained from search:** an indication of whether the property falls within one of the designated areas that qualify for relief.

- **Protection given by search:** none.

- **Personal search facility:** not applicable. Telephone queries may be directed to the Stamp Taxes Helpline on tel. 0845 603 0135.

- **Special points:** Schedule 6 Finance Act 2003 determines how property situated partly within and partly outside a designated disadvantaged area is to be treated for the purposes of the relief (queries may be referred to HM Revenue and Customs Stamp Taxes Office).

- **Claiming the relief:** For transactions affected by SDLT, relief will be claimed by completing form SDLT1. Box 9 of the form deals with reliefs. No supporting documents or evidence need accompany the return. After the HM Revenue and Customs certificate has been issued, some claims will be checked. At this point the client or solicitor may be asked to provide evidence to substantiate the claim, which may include:

  - the full postcode for the property being transferred;

  - a full photocopy of the transfer document;

  - a copy of the contract or sale agreement;

  - evidence that consideration for the transaction did not exceed £150,000;

  - if the document is a lease, a payment in respect of the rent element;

  - if possible, a copy of the ward map with the location of the property clearly marked.

10.6. Less usual searches and enquiries

10.6.1. The buyer's solicitor must in all cases be alert to the need to make additional searches since his client will normally be bound by any matters which those searches would have revealed if made. If a less usual search is not made, in circumstances where it would have been relevant, and as a result of this omission the client suffers loss, the buyer's solicitor will be liable in negligence.[1] In some cases the seller's solicitor may make the appropriate searches and supply the results to the buyer's solicitor, but it remains the buyer's solicitor's duty to ensure that all the correct searches have been undertaken and that their results are satisfactory. A summary of some of the less usual pre-contract searches appears below.

10.6.2. *Waterways*

- **When to make:** where a river, stream or canal passes through or adjoins the property.

- **Form:** letter.

- **Search methods:**

  - National Land Information Service Channel or other electronic search provider;

- for rivers, streams or brooks post to the Environment Agency (see Appendix IX.2 for address);

- for canals post to British Waterways (see Appendix IX.2 for address).

- **Plan:** yes.

- **Fee:** yes.

- **Summary of information to be obtained from searches:** ownership of river banks and canals; liability for repairs of and maintenance of river banks and canals; fishing rights; licences to abstract water; drainage rights; liability for flooding from rivers; rights of way affecting towpaths along sides of canals.

- **Protection given by searches:** none.

- **Personal search facility:** none.

- **Special points:** The local authority may be responsible for smaller waterways within its own area. Although a search may be requested electronically through an NLIS channel, the response will arrive by post/DX.

10.6.3. *Underground railways*

- **When to make:** land adjoins railway, railway passes through land, property built close to underground railway network.

- **Form:** letter.

- **Search methods:**

- National Land Information Service Channel or other electronic search provider;

- post to appropriate underground authority (see Appendix IX.2 for addresses).

- **Plan:** yes.

- **Fee:** yes.

- **Summary of information to be obtained from search:** ownership of track, routes of underground tunnels.

- **Protection given by search:** none.

- **Personal search facility:** not available.

- **Special points:** although a search may be requested electronically the response will arrive by post/DX.

10.6.4. Overground railways

There is no statutory basis for response to property enquiries by the railway industry in Great Britain. The main infrastructure controller is Network Rail (formerly Railtrack plc) and a variety of train operators use the track, occupy stations and other railway land. None of these bodies has a system to respond to search letters. Network Rail does not respond to enquiries. Network Rail has answered a series of frequently asked questions at **www.networkrail.co.uk**. Information can also be obtained from the reply to enquiry 3.5 'Nearby Railway Schemes', on Form CON 29R Enquiries of Local Authority (2007). This will give details of railways within 200m of the proposed property.

10.6.5. Tin mining

- **When to make:** mainly applicable to land to be purchased in West Devon or Cornwall.

- **Form:** letter.

- **Search methods:**

  - National Land Information Service Channel or other electronic search provider;

  - post to Cornwall Consultants (see Appendix IX.2 for address).

- **Plan:** yes.

- **Fee:** yes.

- **Summary of information to be obtained from search:** presence of disused underground workings which could cause subsidence damage.

- **Protection given by search:** none.

- **Personal search facility:** not available.

- **Special points:** although a search may be requested electronically, the response will arrive by post/DX.

10.6.6. Clay mining

- **When to make:** mainly applicable to land to be purchased in Dorset, West Devon or Cornwall. To determine whether a search is required, conveyancers can use the online postcode search at **www.kabca.org**.

- **Form:** letter.

- **Search methods:**

  - National Land Information Service Channel or other electronic search provider;

  - post/fax to Imerys Minerals Ltd (for china clay searches in Cornwall and Devon) or to Sibelco UK Ltd (for ball clay searches in Devon and Dorset) (see Appendix IX.2 for addresses).

- **Plan:** yes.
- **Fee:** yes.
- **Summary of information to be obtained from search:** presence of workings which could cause subsidence damage.
- **Protection given by search:** none.
- **Personal search facility:** not available.
- **Special points:** although a search may be requested electronically, the response will arrive by post/DX.

10.6.7. Brine

- **When to make:** land to be purchased in Cheshire, Greater Manchester or Droitwich Spa (Worcestershire). The search is made using form CON 29M (2006) Coal Mining and Brine Subsidence Claim Search (see B10.5.8).

10.6.8. Limestone

- **When to make:** land to be purchased in Dudley, Sandwell, Walsall or Wolverhampton.
- **Form:** letter.
- **Search methods:**
  - National Land Information Service Channel or other electronic search provider;
  - post to local, district or metropolitan council.
- **Plan:** yes.
- **Fee:** yes.
- **Summary of information to be obtained from search:** presence of disused underground workings which could cause subsidence damage.
- **Protection given by search:** none.
- **Personal search facility:** not available.
- **Special points:** although a search may be requested electronically, the response will arrive by post/DX.

10.6.9. Rent registers

- **When to make:** land to be purchased is subject to a Rent Act 1977 tenancy.
- **Form:** CON 29E Request for a search of the register kept pursuant to section 79 Rent Act 1977 (in duplicate).

- **Search methods:** post to the relevant Rent Assessment Panel (see Appendix IX.2).

- **Plan:** no.

- **Fee:** £1.

- **Summary of information to be obtained from search:** the form of enquiry is as follows: 'Are there any, and if so what, subsisting entries in the Register in respect of the above property or any part of it kept pursuant to Section 79 of the Rent Act 1977, as amended by Paragraph 43 of Schedule 25 to the Housing Act 1980?'. Such entries will be disclosed by the search.

- **Protection given by search:** the replies are furnished in the belief that they are correct but on the distinct understanding that neither the President nor any member of his staff is legally responsible therefore, except in negligence.

- **Personal search facility:** not available.

- **Special points:** if a rent is registered, it is an offence for the landlord to charge more than the registered rent for the property. Rent charged in excess of the registered amount is recoverable by the tenant. Registration of a revised rent can normally only be made after two years have elapsed since the last registration. There are now five Rent Assessment Panels covering England, and one covering Wales. For details of their coverage, visit the website of the Residential Property Tribunal Service (**www.rpts.gov.uk**). Form CON 29E was agreed between the Law Society of England and Wales and the Department of the Environment, it has not been updated since 1996.

Chancel repair liability

10.6.10. The cost of repairing the chancel of a parish church (Church of England or Church in Wales) is generally met by either the parochial church council, the representative body of the Church in Wales, other ecclesiastical bodies, or educational establishments. In some rare instances, however, landowners are liable for the costs of such repair.[2]

10.6.11. Where the liability is not recorded in the title deeds, consideration should be given as to whether it is appropriate to make enquiries.

10.6.12. Enquiries may be made using commercial products that determine if a property is located in a parish where there remains a potential to enforce chancel repair liability, but these products are not property specific.

10.6.13. Property specific enquiries may be made by conducting a personal search or 'FOI paid for search' of the Record of Ascertainments held by the National Archives. For details, see National Archives Legal Records Information Leaflet

33 and 'Information from the Archive L1', both available from **www. nationalarchives.gov.uk**. It is understood that these records are incomplete.

10.6.14. Insurance may be considered as an option following the results of a search, or as an alternative to searching. Insurers may require confirmation that no enquiries of the local church have been made regarding chancel repair liability. (See A4, B6 and C3.)

10.6.15. Schedules 1 and 3 to Land Registration Act 2002 provide that a right in respect of the repair of a church chancel is an interest which overrides first registration and a disposition of a registered title. This liability will retain its overriding status until 13 October 2013. After this date a purchaser will generally only be bound by the liability if it has been protected by an entry on the register or, in the case of unregistered land, a caution against first registration has been registered or the liability is referred to in the title deeds (see Land Registry Practice Guide 66 as to overriding interests losing automatic protection in 2013).

10.6.16. *Search of the index of relating franchises and manors*

- This search will not be required in most conveyancing transactions but may be appropriate when dealing with agricultural land (see B8.3.6). The application should be made in form SIF.

- For more details see Land Registry Practice Guide 13.

1. See *G & K Ladenbau (UK) Ltd* v. *Crawley & De Reya* [1978] 1 All ER 682.
2. See *Aston Cantlow and Wilmcote with Billesley Parochial Church Council* v. *Wallbank* [2004] 1 AC 546.

10.7.   **Results of searches**

10.7.1. On receiving the results of searches the buyer's solicitor must check the answers given to ensure that the information supplied complies with his client's instructions. Any reply which is unclear must be pursued with the appropriate authority (or seller in the case of pre-contract enquiries) until a satisfactory explanation is received. Failure to pursue an unsatisfactory reply which results in loss being suffered by the client may result in the buyer's solicitor being liable to his own client in negligence.[1] Any reply which is for any reason not satisfactory must be referred to the client for further instructions. Contracts should not be exchanged until satisfactory results of all searches have been received. A summary of the information received from the searches should be communicated to the buyer by his solicitor.

10.7.2. When reporting back to the client it is essential that the client is made aware of the type of issues that cannot be identified from the local search and enquiries.

1. *Computastaff* v. *Ingledew Brown Bennison Garrett & Co.* (1983) 133 NLJ 598.

10.8. Checklist

10.8.1. *Making searches*

(a) Decide which searches need to be made and which method is most appropriate.

(b) Is a plan required, is it accurate, and is it on a sufficiently large scale to identify the property and the surrounding area clearly?

(c) What questions (in addition to those on the printed form) need to be asked?

(d) Correct application form and fee?

(e) Correct address for submission of the search?

(f) Diarise the file and chase up delayed responses.

10.8.2. *Search replies*

(a) Analyse the answer to each question – does it accord with what you would expect to find and with what the client wants?

– If it does: place a tick in the margin against that question.

– If it does not: place a cross in the margin by the question, pursue the question with the relevant authority until a satisfactory reply is received, then replace the cross with a tick, take the client's further instructions if the ultimate reply is not satisfactory.

(b) Where an answer contains information which should be communicated to the client or on which the client's further instructions are needed, place a 'C' in the margin beside that question and contact the client.

(c) Do not exchange contracts until all search replies have been received and all answers are marked with a tick.

(d) Consider whether the results of any searches require an insurance policy to be taken out to cover potential liabilities. Remember that the negotiation of an insurance policy may constitute 'arranging' within Financial Services and Markets Act 2000.

10.9. Liability on searches

Local land charges

10.9.1. Where a person suffers loss as a result of an error in an official certificate of search, compensation may be payable under Local Land Charges Act 1975, s.10.

Pre-contract enquiries of the seller

10.9.2.   An incorrect reply to pre-contract enquiries may lead to liability in misrepresentation. A reply expressed in terms such as 'the seller is not aware (etc.)' may import a warranty that the seller has made reasonable enquiries relating to the matter in question.[1] Any exclusion clause purporting to avoid or minimise liability for misrepresentation will be subject to the reasonableness test in Unfair Contract Terms Act 1977, s.11 and cannot therefore be guaranteed to afford protection to the seller.[2] Even a carefully worded reply to an enquiry, insisting upon *caveat emptor*, may not excuse the seller from a misrepresentation.[3] Where the erroneous reply stems from the seller's solicitor's negligence he will be liable to his own client,[4] he may also owe a duty of care to the buyer under *Hedley Byrne* v. *Heller* principles.[5] Knowledge acquired by the solicitor while acting on his client's behalf is imputed to the client (regardless of whether the client had actual knowledge of the matter in question); thus a seller may be liable in misrepresentation to the buyer for a statement made by his solicitor without his knowledge. In such a case indemnity against the seller's liability could be sought from the seller's solicitors.[6] Where the answers to the enquiries are to be completed by the seller personally (and not by his solicitor), the seller's solicitor should advise his client to complete the form with care, since an inaccurate or misleading reply could lead to liability in misrepresentation.[7] The seller should also be advised of the need to notify the buyer if circumstances change, thus rendering inaccurate the original reply given to a question on the search form.

1.   *William Sindall plc* v. *Cambridgeshire County Council* [1996] 3 All ER 932.
2.   See Standard Condition 7.1. Some forms of pre-contract enquiries also contain an exclusion clause. See also *Walker* v. *Boyle* [1982] 1 All ER 634.
3.   *Morris* v. *Jones* [2002] EWCA Civ 1790.
4.   *Cemp Properties* v. *Dentsply* [1989] 35 EG 99.
5.   *Hedley Byrne & Co. Ltd* v. *Heller & Partners Ltd* [1964] AC 465 and *Wilson* v. *Bloomfield* (1979) 123 SJ 860.
6.   See *Strover* v. *Harrington* [1988] Ch 390.
7.   See *McMeekin* v. *Long* [2003] All ER (D) 124. It was held that the Longs should have answered yes to a question on the Seller's Property Information Form asking whether there were any neighbourhood disputes. See also *Sykes and another* v. *Taylor-Rose and another* [2004] All ER (D) 468. The sellers were not under a duty to disclose to the buyers their knowledge that a murder had occurred at the property.

10.10. Relying on searches made by a third party

10.10.1.   In relation to enquiries of local authorities on Forms CON 29R and CON 29O and those other enquiries whose terms and conditions include similar provisions as to liabilities, the results of searches are not personal to the searcher; thus their benefit may be transferred to a third party. Where the seller makes pre-contract searches and passes their results to the buyer, the buyer and his lender may in such cases take the benefit of the results. The buyer must check that the seller has undertaken all the searches and enquiries which the buyer deems necessary for the transaction in hand and, if not, he must effect the additional searches himself. If the buyer is not satisfied with the results of the searches made by the seller because, e.g. he considers that they are out of date, or that insufficient questions have been raised, he should repeat the search himself.

10.10.2. There are limitations on personal searches and some lenders will not accept them. The accuracy of a personal search depends on the ability and diligence of the searcher. It is not guaranteed by the local authority. If a personal search is undertaken, clients should be told of this and advised of the limitations on personal searches and their possible implications.

10.11. Inspection of the property

10.11.1. Inspection of the property should be undertaken by the client in all cases. There is no obligation on the solicitor, either in law or conduct, to carry out an inspection, but he should do so if his client so requests or if matters reported by the client's inspection give rise to suspicion on the part of the buyer's solicitor. The client should be advised to look for (and to report their existence to his solicitor) any of the following matters:

(a) a discrepancy or uncertainty over the identity or boundaries of the property;

(b) evidence of easements which adversely affect the property;

(c) the existence and status of non-owning occupiers;

(d) discrepancy between the fixtures and fittings which the client understood to belong to the property and those actually existing.

10.11.2. It is useful for the client to take a plan of the property with him in order to check its accuracy. An appointment to inspect should be arranged with the seller. The client's surveyor may be able to obtain the necessary information whilst carrying out a survey, but must be instructed to do so.

10.11.3. A solicitor who carries out an inspection on behalf of his client may be liable in negligence if he fails to discover a matter which he ought reasonably to have discovered,[1] for example, the existence of a right of way crossing the property, but the solicitor should stress to the client that the inspection has been carried out by the solicitor in his role as solicitor, and that he does not profess to have the same knowledge about, for example, structural defects in the property as possessed by a surveyor.

1. *Barclay-White* v. *Guillaume & Sons* [1996] EGCS 123.

10.12. Tithes

10.12.1. Tithes were abolished in 1936. The 60-year annuities which replaced them were themselves extinguished by Finance Act 1977. There is therefore no need to consider any search for tithes.

10.13. **Company search**

10.13.1. Where either the seller or buyer is a corporate body a company search prior to exchange should be undertaken in order to check that the company actually does exist. Company searches are discussed in E2.

10.14. **Assignment of guarantees**

10.14.1. Where the answers to pre-contract enquiries reveal that the property has the benefit of a structural defects policy (for example, NHBC, Zurich, Premier Guarantee) or other guarantee (such as, for woodworm or damp treatment) the benefit of which will pass to the buyer on completion, consideration should be given to whether a formal assignment of the benefit of the policy or guarantee will be needed.

10.15. **Properties without mains drainage**

10.15.1. Some rural properties may not have the benefit of mains drainage. The client's surveyor should be asked to ascertain the type of drainage provided at the property and if necessary a drainage survey may need to be undertaken to ensure that the system is functional and adequate to meet the needs of the property and its occupants. In some cases it will be necessary to obtain the consent of the Environment Agency for the operation of the drainage system (because the system may discharge effluent into the land or into an adjacent watercourse). The seller should be asked to supply a copy of any such consents in his possession. It may be necessary to transfer such consents to the buyer on completion.

Cesspools

10.15.2. A cesspool is a covered watertight tank used for receiving and storing sewage. It has no outlet but must be regularly emptied either by the local authority or by a private contractor. The tank must be, and remain, impervious to the ingress of groundwater or surface water and to leakage. No consent from the Environment Agency is required for a cesspool.

Septic tanks

10.15.3. A septic tank is a sewage system (usually consisting of two or three chambers) in which the sewage is retained for sufficient time to allow it to partially break down (anaerobic decomposition) before the contents are discharged. Discharge may be by soakage into the ground. The effluent cannot be discharged into a watercourse without further treatment. Environment Agency consent may be required for discharge into the ground.

Package sewage treatment plants

10.15.4. Package sewage treatment plants are similar to septic tanks but treat the sewage to a higher standard than the latter before discharging the effluent. Environment Agency consent is required for the discharge.

Environment Agency consent

10.15.5. Under Water Resources Act 1991, Environment Agency consent is required for any discharge of sewage effluent into a watercourse, lake or pond, and may also be required for any discharge into or onto land. Separate consent is required under Land Drainage Act 1991 if the discharge is made into a main river. An administration charge is made by the Environment Agency for an application for consent together with an annual fee to cover monitoring and other costs.

10.16. Lenders' instructions

10.16.1. When acting under the terms of the CML Lenders' Handbook paragraph 5.2 gives details of the pre-contract searches which must be made (see paragraph 5.2.4 for specific details on environmental searches). Note that, except where the search result carries a priority period, the search must not be more than six months old at the date of completion. The lender's specific requirements should also be checked since some lenders will not accept personal searches or search insurance. The BSA Mortgage Instructions contain similar provisions in paragraphs D.7 to D.14.

B11. Form of contract

11.1. Statutory provisions

11.1.1. Law of Property (Miscellaneous Provisions) Act 1989 repealed Law of Property Act 1925, s.40. The 1989 Act requires all contracts for the sale or other disposition of land or an interest in land to be made in writing and signed by the parties. The writing must incorporate all the terms which have been expressly agreed by the parties and the document must then be signed by or on behalf of all the parties. Where contracts are to be exchanged each part of the contract must contain all the agreed terms and be signed by the appropriate party. It is possible for the signed document to refer to another document which itself contains the agreed terms. If the document does not contain all the agreed terms an order for rectification may be sought.[1]

11.1.2. The requirement for a written contract does not apply to contracts:

(a) to grant a lease for a term not exceeding three years taking effect in possession without a fine;

(b) made at public auction.

Joining two documents together to satisfy the section

11.1.3. Where the signed document does not itself contain all the agreed terms it is possible to join two (or more) documents together in order to constitute a complete contract and thus satisfy the statutory requirements. There is little case law on this point under the 1989 Act,[2] but the rules which applied to the joining of documents under Law of Property Act 1925, s.40 (predecessor to section 2) will not necessarily be applied to actions brought under section 2 of the 1989 Act.[3] It is possible, e.g. to draft a contract which incorporates the Standard Conditions of Sale or Standard Commercial Property Conditions[4] by reference without setting out the full text of those conditions. In such a case the Standard Conditions or Standard Commercial Conditions (as appropriate) will be deemed to be incorporated as part of the contract although contained in a different document from that which was signed by the parties. Since the court's interpretation of this aspect of section 2 is as yet unknown, it is not possible to speculate in what circumstances the court will allow documents to be joined together to form a contract. It should be borne in mind that failure to satisfy the requirements of section 2 results in there being no contract at all between the parties, and the court has no equitable jurisdiction to allow the enforcement of a contract which does not meet the statutory requirements.[5] Care should therefore be taken to ensure that the contract does satisfy section 2 and to this end it is recommended that the full text of the general conditions of sale which are being used (e.g. the Standard Conditions of Sale) is set out in the contract itself.[6] See also B1.7 and B1.8.

Resulting, implied and constructive trusts

11.1.4. Section 2(5) Law of Property (Miscellaneous Provisions) Act 1989 states that nothing in section 2 shall affect the 'creation or operation of resulting, implied or constructive trusts'. A constructive trust will arise if there is evidence that the parties had concluded an agreement. In such a case the courts will be able to give effect to the agreement by enforcing the constructive trust. However, if there are any preconditions to the agreement, e.g. the landlord's consent is required to an assignment, then the trust will not come into being until the condition has been satisfied.[7]

Proprietary estoppel

11.1.5. Section 2 Law of Property (Miscellaneous Provisions) Act 1989 will also not apply where claims are based on proprietary estoppel. Proprietary estoppel is often argued as an alternative where it may not be possible to show the common intention needed to establish constructive trusts. An estoppel may arise where a property owner makes a representation to another party which is relied on by that other party and which leads that other party to act to their detriment.[8] The representation usually relates to the current or future ownership of land or of interests in land. If the party to whom the representation has been made acts to their detriment in reliance on that representation, the representation cannot be revoked and the courts will enforce it despite the lack of a written agreement. In *Yeomans Row Management Ltd* v. *Cobbe* [2008] UKHL 55; [2008] 1 WLR 1752 the House of Lords held that the party claiming proprietary estoppel must have an expectation of a 'certain interest in land' and so unconscionable behaviour alone will not be sufficient to give rise to a proprietary estoppel. In *Crabb* v. *Arun District Council* [1976] 1 Ch 179, Lord Denning explained that proprietary estoppel '… will prevent a person insisting on his strict legal rights … when it would be inequitable for him to do so having regard to the dealings which have taken place between the parties'. In various cases the courts have accepted a wide range of 'acts to the detriment' including: the expenditure of money on a property in which the claimant had been led to believe she had an interest,[9] looking after the property owner and working in his house and garden,[10] continuing in the property owner's employment[11] and selling land without reserving a right of way over it.[12]

1. *Wright* v. *Robert Leonard Developments Ltd* [1994] EGCS 69. See also *Oun* v. *Ahmad* [2008] EWHC 545 (Ch).
2. *Raymond Ruddick* v. *Paul Ormston* (2005) (unreported) LTL 24/11/2005. The High Court refused to join two documents written on separate pages of a diary, one signed by the seller and the other by the

buyer. The pages were written as separate, self-contained documents. Even if they could have been joined, the court went on to decide that they would not have complied with 1989 Act, s.2(1) because the completion date, which had been agreed by the parties, was not specified in the written agreement.

3. See *Firstpost Homes Ltd* v. *Johnson* [1995] 1 WLR 1567.
4. See Appendices III.5 and III.6.
5. See however *Pagemanor* v. *Ryan* [1998] NPC 37 where a buyer under contract which did not fulfil s.2 obtained an alternative remedy in quasi-contract. See also *Nweze and another* v. *Nwoko* [2004] EWCA Civ 379, in which the Court of Appeal decided that an oral compromise of a dispute, a term of which was that one party would sell a property at the best price available, was not a contract for the sale of land and was not caught by Law of Property (Miscellaneous Provisions) Act 1989, s.2.
6. See *B. Ltd* v. *T. Ltd* [1991] NPC 47 where it was held that incorporation of the National Conditions of Sale by reference did satisfy s.2 of the Act. See also *Commission for New Towns* v. *Cooper, The Independent*, 15 March 1995, CA where it was held that an exchange of letters did not satisfy s.2.
7. *Representative Body for the Church in Wales* v. *Newton* [2005] EWHC 681; 16 EGCS 145, QBD.
8. See *Taylor Fashions Ltd* v. *Liverpool Victoria Trustees Co. Ltd* [1982] 1 QB 133.
9. See *Pascoe* v. *Turner* [1979] 1 WLR 431.
10. See *Re Basham* [1986] 1 WLR 1498.
11. See *Greasley* v. *Cooke* [1980] 1 WLR 1306 and *Gillett* v. *Holt* [2001] Ch 210.
12. See *Crabb* v. *Arun DC* [1976] 1 Ch 179.

11.2. Satisfying the statutory requirements

11.2.1. The statutory requirements are normally satisfied by the preparation by the seller's solicitor of a formal contract. The contract is usually prepared in two identical parts based on the Standard Conditions of Sale or Standard Commercial Property Conditions as amended to fit the particular circumstances of the transaction. A summary of both sets of Standard Conditions is contained in B12 and the conditions are set out on Appendix III.5 and III.6. The contract comes into being when exchange of contracts takes place. For signature and exchange of contracts see section C.

Collateral contracts

11.2.2. To be enforceable, options, equitable mortgages[1] and side letters issued in connection with sale of land transactions also need to satisfy the requirements of section 2. This will mean that these documents need to be in writing and signed by both parties. An agreement not to negotiate with any other buyer (a 'lock-out' agreement) can be enforceable as a separate collateral contract provided good consideration is given.[2] This type of agreement does not fall within the scope of section 2.[3] A 'lock-in' agreement (i.e. to negotiate with these buyers only) is not an enforceable contract.[4] Also see B1.7 and B1.8.

Variation of contract

11.2.3. A variation of a contract to which section 2 applies must itself comply with the section.[5]

1. *United Bank of Kuwait plc* v. *Sahib* [1996] NPC 12.
2. *Walford* v. *Miles* [1992] 2 AC 128.
3. *Pitt* v. *PHH Asset Management Ltd* [1993] EGCS 127. See also *Chilli Developments Ltd* v. *Commission for New Towns* [2008] EWHC 1310 (QB).

4. *Courtney & Fairburn* v. *Tolaini Bros* [1975] 1 WLR 297.
5. *McCausland* v. *Duncan Lawrie* [1996] NPC 94. An exception to this is a variation of the payments to be made under a mortgage which are not required to satisfy the section: *Target Holdings* v. *Priestly* [1999] *Gazette*, 6 May.

11.3. Contents of the contract

11.3.1. In addition to the formal parts, i.e. date, parties, signature, the contract comprises two main elements:

(a) the particulars, which describe the physical extent of the property to be sold and its tenure; and

(b) the conditions which set out the terms on which the seller is prepared to sell the property.

11.4. The particulars

11.4.1. These must contain a clear description of the physical extent of the property to be sold and whether the estate to be sold is freehold or leasehold. The title number of a parcel of registered land is its sole distinguishing feature and thus must be referred to in the particulars. The class of title under which the land is registered (e.g. absolute) must also be included in order to give the buyer an accurate description of the estate which is being sold. Where the boundaries are well defined and the property has a regular postal address, the postal address may suffice to describe the land itself. In other cases a more detailed description may be necessary, referring where appropriate to the measurements of the property and/or a plan (see B21). Any inaccuracy in the particulars may give rise to an action in misdescription or misrepresentation (see section M).

11.5. Conditions of sale

Open contract rules

11.5.1. Where a contract makes no reference to a particular matter the contract is said to be 'open' on this point and is thus governed by the open contract rules which are laid down either by common law or by statute. Some of the open contract rules are satisfactory in operation, e.g. the rules for deduction of title on the sale of unregistered freeholds, and are invariably used without alteration. Others, e.g. the time for completion, which under the open contract rules is set at 'a reasonable time after the contract', are less satisfactory and are frequently altered by special condition in the contract itself. The Standard Conditions of Sale normally vary the open contract rules, but may themselves require amendment to suit the particular circumstances of the transaction.

Standard Conditions of Sale

11.5.2.   Assuming that the Standard Conditions of Sale have been used to form the basis
of the contract, special conditions will still be needed to deal with any variations
which are required, and any features peculiar to the particular transaction. Even
in the most straightforward transaction special conditions will invariably be
required to deal with the matters listed below.

Checklist of usual special conditions

11.5.3.

Condition to deal with	Reason for inclusion	Standard Condition	Reference
Title	Buyer is entitled to know what title is being offered.	SC 4.1 SCPC 6.1	Section D
Deposit	No provision at common law, variation of general conditions may be required.	SC 2.2 SCPC 2.2	B17
Interest on deposit	Interest is payable under Solicitors' Accounts Rules.	SC 2.2.6	A20
Completion date	Open contract rule and general conditions not satisfactory.	SC 6.1 SCPC 8.1	Section F
Title guarantee	Defines scope of implied covenants for title.	SC 4.6.2 SCPC 6.6.2	M9
Incumbrances	Seller's duty of disclosure.	SC 3 SCPC 3	B5
Fixtures and fittings	To create an obligation and to avoid disputes between the parties.	SC 10 SCPC 12	B22

Condition to deal with	Reason for inclusion	Standard Condition	Reference
Vacant possession	Implied by common law unless stated to the contrary. Normally included for certainty and must deal with requirement for completion to take place at the property if so required.	SC Special condition 4 SCPC Special condition 2	B3

11.6. Full/limited title guarantee

11.6.1. The seller can sell with either full or limited title guarantee irrespective of the capacity in which he could have sold the property under the pre 1 July 1995 law (Law of Property (Miscellaneous Provisions) Act 1994). The guarantees apply to the sale of both freehold and leasehold property and on the grant of a lease. They can also be used on the transfer of personal property including intellectual property and rights in shares. The extent of the warranties given under the full and limited title guarantees is discussed in M9.[1]

11.6.2. On the front of the Standard Contract form the seller should specify whether he sells with full or limited title guarantee. Should the seller fail to specify the nature of the title guarantee, Standard Condition 4.6.2, and Standard Commercial Property Condition 6.6.2, provide that the seller will sell with full title guarantee. In addition, Special Condition 2 of the standard conditions of sale provides that the seller will sell with either full or limited title guarantee as specified on the front page of the contract.

11.6.3. The warranties given under the full and limited guarantees can be amended in the agreement. If the seller is concerned about incumbrances he should disclose them in the contract and ensure that the buyer agrees to take the property subject to them. See also Standard Condition 4.6.2. Under s.6 of the 1994 Act (as amended by Land Registration Act 2002) the sale of a registered title will also be subject to any matters entered on the register of title at the time of the disposition. As a result any such matters will not be covered by the title guarantee.

11.6.4. If the seller is a beneficial owner he will usually provide full title guarantee. If the seller is a trustee, personal representative or mortgagee, he will usually provide a limited title guarantee.

11.6.5. Where the disposition is of an interest the title to which is registered the seller will not be liable under any of the covenants for title for anything which at the time of the disposition was entered in the register in relation to that interest.[2]

1. Land Registration Rules 2003, rr. 67–69, incorporate the provisions as to implied covenants into registered conveyancing.
2. Law of Property (Miscellaneous Provisions) Act 1994, s.6 as inserted by Land Registration Act 2002, Sched.11, para.31.

11.7. Drafting the contract

11.7.1. Although drafting the contract is the prerogative of the seller, the relative bargaining strength of the parties rarely permits the seller to draft a contract which is entirely to his own satisfaction. Contract drafting is therefore an exercise in the art of compromise. The seller must seek to preserve his own interests without misleading the buyer, but will frequently have to include or concede some terms which favour the buyer in order to achieve a prompt conclusion to the transaction. A solicitor, whether acting for seller or buyer, who obstinately insists on the total protection of his own client's interests in the contract terms will at best prolong the transaction unnecessarily or at worst find that negotiations break down entirely and in neither case can he be said to be providing a proper service to his client.

11.8. Style of drafting

11.8.1. The contract must clearly state what the seller is offering to sell and on what terms including price. Use of anachronistic language should be avoided but clarity must not be sacrificed for brevity. Conditions should only be included where they are relevant and necessary and not through force of habit. Bearing in mind that it is the solicitor's duty to draft a contract which will avoid disputes or litigation between the parties, it becomes a matter of judgment as to the extent of the inclusion of clauses which cater for unforeseen eventualities.

Guidelines

11.8.2. (a) Does the contract describe clearly what is to be sold?

(b) Is a plan necessary?

(c) Does the contract accord with the client's instructions as to the conditions on which the property is to be sold?

(d) Are the conditions concise and unambiguous?

11.9. Looking at the contract from the buyer's point of view

11.9.1. No two draftsmen will ever produce identically worded contracts for the sale of the same property. Drafting is a personal skill and the draftsman's choice of words must be respected by the buyer's solicitor. Amendments should not be made to suit the individual whim of the buyer's solicitor but should be confined to those which are necessary and relevant to the particular transaction. The primary questions in looking at the contract from the buyer's point of view are:

(a) does the clause accord with the client's instructions? and

(b) does the clause do what it is intended to do?

11.9.2. If the answers to these questions are in the affirmative – leave the wording alone. If not, alter the clause until it does meet the above criteria.

11.9.3. Amendments should be clearly inserted on both copies of the draft contract in a distinctive colour.

11.10. Unfair Terms in Consumer Contracts Regulations 1999

11.10.1. Unfair Terms in Consumer Contracts Regulations 1999 (SI 1999/2083) affect all contracts (oral or written) made between a seller or supplier and a consumer (this latter expression applies to individuals only). Unlike Unfair Contract Terms Act 1977, the 1999 Regulations do apply to land contracts,[1] including mortgages and tenancy agreements. Agreements for financial services made between an individual and his broker are also potentially within the Regulations. The EU Directive (93/13/EEC), from which the English Regulations derive, intended land contracts to be included within its scope.

Situations in which the Regulations apply

11.10.2. The Regulations do not apply to a contract for sale made between two private individuals but catch contracts made between a corporate or business seller and a private individual. Thus contracts for new houses or plots on a building estate where the seller is a developer and the buyer a private individual are potentially affected since in these circumstances the contract is usually in standard form and there is little or no freedom for the buyer to negotiate terms. Similarly mortgages, where the lender is in business and the borrower is not, are caught, as also are sales by mortgagees.

11.10.3. Tenancy agreements and contracts for financial services are potentially within the scope of the Regulations.

Effect of the Regulations

11.10.4. If a term is held to be unfair, that term is to be treated as void, but the rest of the contract remains binding on the parties, so long as it is capable of continuing without the offending term.

11.10.5. A term will be regarded as unfair if, contrary to the requirement of good faith, it causes a significant imbalance in the parties' rights and obligations arising under the contract to the detriment of the consumer. Various factors, similar to those contained in Unfair Contract Terms Act 1977, are contained in the Regulations to act as guidelines as to whether 'good faith' exists, e.g. the strength of the bargaining position of the parties, the circumstances surrounding the contract, and whether the consumer has received any special inducement, such as a discount, to agree to the term.

11.10.6. The burden of proof will lie on the consumer to show that a term included in the contract which was not individually negotiated between the parties is unfair.

11.10.7. The Regulations also require all contracts to be drafted in plain intelligible language. See also A21 for information on the reproduction of the contract.

1. *Khatun* v. *Newham London Borough Council* [2003] EWHC 2326.

B12. Standard Conditions of Sale and Standard Commercial Property Conditions

12.1. Standard Conditions of Sale

12.1.1. Most contracts for the sale of residential property will be made either on the Standard Conditions of Sale Form or by reference to the Standard Conditions.

12.1.2. The text of the Standard Conditions of Sale (fourth edition) is set out in Appendix III.5. Individual conditions are referred to in context in the text of this book.

12.1.3. The Standard Conditions of Sale (fourth edition) came into force on 13 October 2003.

12.2. Standard Commercial Property Conditions

12.2.1. The Standard Commercial Property Conditions (second edition) are based on the Standard Conditions of Sale (fourth edition) but apply to commercial transactions. The full text of the conditions is set out in Appendix III.6. Many of the conditions in the Standard Commercial Property Conditions are identical in wording to their Standard Conditions counterparts, but there are some notable exceptions. The method of calculating compensation for late completion under Standard Commercial Property Condition 9.3 is not based on the concept of relative fault. The Standard Commercial Property Conditions are intended for use in more complex commercial transactions and the Standard Conditions may be appropriate for simple commercial transactions.

12.3. Incorporating Standard Conditions of Sale

12.3.1. To satisfy Law of Property (Miscellaneous Provisions) Act 1989, s.2 a contract for the sale or other disposition of land must be in writing, incorporating all the terms which have been agreed between the parties. These terms will normally include the Standard Conditions of Sale or the Standard Commercial Property Conditions. Where a solicitor prepares a contract on a word processor or by other duplicated means, incorporation of either set of the Standard Conditions by reference may satisfy the requirements of section 2 (but see B11.1.3). Failure to satisfy section 2 means that no contract exists between the parties.[1]

12.3.2. The Standard Commercial Property Conditions are drafted in two parts. Only Part I will automatically be incorporated into the contract. An express condition is needed if it is desired also to incorporate Part II.

1. See *B Ltd* v. *T Ltd* [1991] NPC 47.

12.4. Using Standard Conditions of Sale

12.4.1. Not all of the Standard Conditions will be appropriate for use in every transaction. Solicitors should, in every transaction, give careful thought to the application of the conditions and expressly amend those which are inappropriate to the particular circumstances of the current transaction. As in all cases, amendments should be restricted to those which are essential to meet the circumstances of an individual case.

B13. Conditional contracts

13.1. **When are conditional contracts appropriate?**	13.4. **Requirements for a valid conditional contract**
13.2. **Desirability of conditional contracts**	13.5. **Withdrawal from the contract**
13.3. **Conditions precedent and subsequent**	13.6. **Waiver of the condition**
	13.7. **Drafting**

13.1. When are conditional contracts appropriate?

13.1.1. Conditional contracts carry with them some risks and uncertainties which make them inappropriate for everyday use, but they may be considered for use in the following circumstances:

(a) where the buyer has not had the opportunity before exchange of contracts to make searches and enquiries or to conduct a survey or where his mortgage arrangements have not been finalised;

(b) where the contract is dependent on planning permission being obtained for the property;

(c) where the sale requires the consent of the Charity Commission under Charities Act 1993 (see B7.8);

(d) where the sale is dependent on permission being obtained from a third party, e.g. ministerial consent, landlord's consent;

(e) where the parties wish to be bound to a contract but there is some other unresolved matter which prevents commitment to an unconditional contract for the time being, e.g. the seller has to get in part of the legal estate.

13.2. Desirability of conditional contracts

13.2.1. Conditional contracts are generally not desirable since they leave an element of doubt as to the very existence and validity of the contractual obligations between the parties. Most of the situations in which conditional contracts are proposed for use benefit the buyer more than the seller (e.g. 'subject to planning permission'), and the seller should resist the suggestion of entering a conditional contract if at all possible. A conditional contract may, however, be inevitable where the seller needs the consent of the Charity Commission to the sale under Charities Act 1993 since an unconditional contract which is entered into without such consent is not lawful.

13.2.2. Conditional contracts should never be used where one or both of the parties has an unconditional sale or purchase contract which is dependent on the conditional contract. In this situation, if the conditional contract were to be rescinded for non-fulfilment of the condition, this would give rise to great difficulties in the fulfilment of the linked unconditional contract and may result in a breach of that contract.

13.2.3. Before agreeing to enter a conditional contract the seller should consider whether there are any viable alternative solutions. Where it has been suggested that the sale is 'subject to planning permission', it may be preferable to delay exchange until the results of the planning application have been received by the buyer, rather than enter into a hastily drafted conditional contract. An alternative solution may be to grant the buyer for a nominal consideration an option to purchase the property to be exercised within a stated period.

13.3. Conditions precedent and subsequent

Conditions precedent

13.3.1. A condition precedent has the effect of suspending the operation of the contract until the terms of the condition have been met. If the condition has not been fulfilled by the appropriate time limit, the party with the benefit of the condition may withdraw and the contractual obligations of the parties never come into existence.

Conditions subsequent

13.3.2. Where the contract is subject to a condition subsequent, the contractual obligations of the parties arise on the creation of the contract and continue to exist until terminated by the party with the benefit of the condition on its non-fulfilment.

13.3.3. If the wording of the condition reads 'subject to x', this indicates a condition precedent.

13.3.4. If the wording of the condition reads 'until x', this indicates a condition subsequent.

13.4. Requirements for a valid conditional contract

Certainty

13.4.1. The terms of the condition must be clear and certain. In *Lee-Parker* v. *Izzet* (*No.2*),[1] an agreement to sell a freehold house 'subject to the buyer obtaining a satisfactory mortgage' was held to be void because the word 'satisfactory' was too nebulous and there was thus no certainty regarding the circumstances in which the buyer would validly be able to withdraw from the contract. It should be noted, however, that not all 'subject to mortgage' clauses will suffer the same fate. A similarly worded clause in *Janmohamed* v. *Hassam*[2] was held to be valid.

Time for performance

13.4.2. It was held in *Aberfoyle Plantations Ltd* v. *Cheng*[3] that the time for performance of the condition is of the essence and cannot be extended either by agreement between the parties or by the court. The same case also laid down the rules relating to the time for performance of the condition which are summarised as follows:

(a) where the contract contains a completion date, the condition must be fulfilled by that date, irrespective of whether time was of the essence of the contractual completion date;

(b) if a time is stated for the fulfilment of the condition, that time limit must be complied with or the contract will fail;

(c) if no time limit is specified the condition must be fulfilled within a reasonable time. This provision is patently unsatisfactory since it leaves room for argument about what is a reasonable time.

1. [1972] 2 All ER 800.
2. (1976) 241 EG 609.
3. [1960] AC 115.

13.5. Withdrawal from the contract

13.5.1. Only the party with the benefit of the condition may withdraw from the contract, and only for reasons connected with the condition. No other reason will justify withdrawal, although there is no obligation on the resiling party to prove that he is being reasonable in exercising his rights to withdraw. It is a question of construction of the condition itself as to whether a party may withdraw before performance of the condition.[1]

1. *Tesco Stores Ltd* v. *William Gibson & Co. Ltd* (1970) 214 EG 835.

13.6. Waiver of the condition

13.6.1. Where the condition benefits one party only, it may be waived unilaterally. In other cases the waiver amounts to a variation of the contract and requires the consent of both parties. If to remove the condition takes away the whole purpose of the contract, the whole contract will fail for uncertainty.

13.7. Drafting

13.7.1. The drafting of a condition requires extreme care to ensure that the requirements outlined in B13.4 have been satisfied. No such provision is included in the Standard Conditions of Sale although a contract to assign a lease may be conditional on the landlord's consent being obtained under Standard Condition 8.3.

Guidelines

13.7.2.   (a) Consider the precise event(s) on which the contract is to be made conditional.

(b) By what time must the condition be fulfilled? (Bear in mind that the specified time limit cannot be extended.)

(c) Consider the precise terms on which the party with the benefit of the condition may rescind.

(d) Ensure that there are no loopholes which would enable one party to escape from the contract other than for the non-fulfilment of the event(s) contemplated in (a) above.

(e) Use an established precedent, tailoring it to fit your exact requirements.

(f) Take your time: a condition which is hastily drafted may contain unforeseen errors.

(g) Having drafted your 'perfect' condition, leave it on the desk overnight and review the wording objectively in the cold light of day. Does the condition achieve its objectives? Is it clear and certain? Do any unforeseen or unwanted consequences flow from the wording?

Precise terms for conditions

13.7.3.   'Subject to searches'

(a) Which searches?

(b) Which adverse entries will give rise to the right to rescind?

(c) By when must the search result(s) be received?

(d) Can buyer rescind if he changes his mind and never makes search applications?

13.7.4.   'Subject to mortgage'

(a) Specify name of lender(s) to whom application made.

(b) Specify amount of required advance.

(c) Specify acceptable interest rates.

(d) Should the buyer be entitled to rescind if the mortgage offer is subject to conditions or a retention – what conditions attached to the offer would be acceptable/unacceptable?

(e) Time limit by which application must be determined?

(f) Can buyer rescind if he changes his mind and never puts in an application for a mortgage?

13.7.5.   'Subject to survey'

    (a)   Named surveyor?

    (b)   What type of survey?

    (c)   Which defects revealed by survey report will entitle buyer to withdraw?

    (d)   Should a financial limit be placed on the entitlement to rescind? E.g. buyer can rescind if survey reveals defects which exceed £x in total. If so who assesses the value?

    (e)   Time limit for obtaining result of survey.

    (f)   Can buyer rescind if he changes his mind and never instructs the surveyor?

13.7.6.   'Subject to planning permission'

    (a)   Form of application to be agreed between the parties.

    (b)   What conditions attached to the consent would entitle the buyer to rescind?

    (c)   Can buyer rescind if he changes his mind and never puts in a planning application?

    (d)   Time limit for result of application (including any challenge to the application by way of appeal).

    (e)   Which party is to make the application and pay the fee?

    (f)   The non-applying party should agree in writing not to oppose the application and to support it.

    (g)   Is the application to be for outline or detailed permission?

    (h)   Which party is to pay the architect's and other professional fees in connection with the application?

B14. Sub-sales

14.1. Definitions

14.1.1. In this section of the text only, the following expressions have the meanings set out below:

  (a)   'the buyer' means the person who has contracted to buy land and who is selling the land under a sub-sale contract before completion of his own purchase;

  (b)   'the seller' means the person from whom the buyer (as defined above) is purchasing the land and in whom the legal title to the property is vested pending completion;

  (c)   'the third party' means the person who is buying the land from the buyer (as defined above) under the sub-sale contract.

14.2. Buyer's position pending completion

14.2.1. A buyer who has exchanged contracts for the purchase of property is the owner of the beneficial interest in the land, but does not obtain the legal estate until registration of the transfer to him (or completion in the case of unregistered land).

14.3. Contractual restriction on sub-sales

14.3.1. Where a buyer intends to sell the property to a third party by way of sub-sale he must ensure that his existing contract to purchase the land contains no restriction which would prevent the sub-sale. Standard Condition 1.5 and Standard Commercial Property Condition 1.5 both state that the buyer is not entitled to transfer the benefit of the contract. As a result the seller cannot be forced to transfer the title to anyone other than the buyer named in the contract. This provision will not prevent sub-sales of freeholds nor sub-assignments of leases. However, the buyer will have to complete the second transaction separately and subsequent to his own purchase. The provision does however provide protection on the grant of a lease as the seller (landlord) cannot be forced to grant the lease to anyone other than the buyer (tenant) in the contract. A seller should resist a buyer's request to remove Condition 1.5 from the contract, because its presence ensures that the seller will take the benefit of the covenants given by the first tenant on grant of a lease.

14.3.2. If a restriction against sub-sales is included in the buyer's contract, he will be able to contract to resell the land to a third party, but will have to complete this second transaction separately and subsequent to his own purchase.

14.3.3. Provided there is no such restriction, the buyer may enter a contract for sale with a third party, prior to completion of his own purchase. In such a case, the buyer may, if he wishes, draft the transfer document to reflect the sub-sale (i.e. the seller transfers direct to the sub-purchaser with the original buyer joining in as a party to transfer his beneficial interest in the estate being transferred). Provided the buyer's transfer is technically correct, the seller cannot refuse to sign even if he had previously been unaware of the sub-sale.

14.3.4. Where there is a restriction on sub-sales in the contract it may be possible for the buyer to assign the benefit of his contract with the seller to the third party and then to complete the purchase as nominee for the third party. Because the buyer will have the right to occupation on completion of his purchase, he will be liable for the relevant Stamp Duty Land Tax (SDLT) and the subsequent transfer to the third party will also be brought into charge to tax. If the assignee fails to complete, the buyer (assignor) may find himself in a position where he is unable to force the seller to transfer the property to the buyer because the assignment is binding on all parties, including the seller (see *Scammell* v. *Dicker* [2005] EWCA Civ 405).

14.4. Special conditions in the sub-sale contract

14.4.1. Special conditions may need to be inserted in the sub-sale contract to deal with the following matters.

The contract

14.4.2. When drafting the sub-sale contract, care must be taken to take account of any relevant provisions in the principal contract, e.g. as to length of a notice to complete; the buyer needs to be in a position to give the third party a notice to complete expiring not later than the date of expiry of any notice to complete which the buyer receives from the seller and vice versa.

Title

14.4.3. The third party should be required by contractual condition to accept the buyer's entitlement to be registered by the production of official copy entries of the seller's registered title, and the contract between seller and buyer. In unregistered land the buyer, having investigated title with his own seller, can usually satisfy Law of Property Act 1925, s.44 by supplying a good root of title and subsequent documentation, but will need to produce his own purchase contract to the third party as evidence that he can compel the seller to convey the legal estate.

The purchase deed

14.4.4. The purchase deed will usually consist of a transfer or conveyance from the seller direct to the third party. The buyer will need to be made a party to the document in order to transfer his equitable interest in the property to the third party.

Apportionment of the price

14.4.5. Where the amount payable by the third party exceeds the consideration due from the buyer to the seller, the purchase deed will need to contain an apportionment of the price as between buyer and seller, with a receipt for their respective portions being given by each.

14.5. Completion

14.5.1. Depending on the arrangements which have been made between the parties, special provisions may need to be considered in relation to actual completion of the transaction, e.g.

    (a)   where completion is to take place;

    (b)   transmission of the money;

    (c)   custody of deeds;

    (d)   undertakings for the discharge of the seller's mortgage(s) over the property.

14.6. Stamp Duty Land Tax

14.6.1. Under the stamp duty regime, an intermediate buyer of land who entered into a sub-sale contract was often able to arrange that completion was effected by the owner/seller conveying land direct to the sub-purchaser and thus saving or reducing his liability to tax. Similar arrangements can be made under Stamp Duty Land Tax (SDLT), but care needs to be taken (see A14.9).

14.6.2. Sections 45 and 45A Finance Act 2003 provide for both the main contract and sub-sale contract to be fully chargeable to tax unless the two contracts complete or are substantially performed at the same time. Finance Act 2003, by introducing the concepts of the effective date of a transaction and substantial performance meant that resting on contracts as a device for postponing the charge to duty has disappeared.

14.6.3. Where an intermediate buyer of land substantially performs the main contract (for example, where he enters into occupation of the land, or commences to develop it), the contract becomes a land transaction and is subject to SDLT. Its effective date is the date of substantial performance. Completion may not take place until the owner conveys the (now possibly developed) land to the sub-purchaser. At such time, a further land transaction occurs. The transfer to the sub-purchaser is a land transaction. Its effective date is the date of transfer. Both purchasers will become liable to submit a land transaction return and to pay any SDLT due on the consideration payable under the relevant contract.

14.6.4. Group relief is not allowable for sub-sales between group companies.

14.7. Registration of third party

14.7.1. Whether the transaction proceeds by way of a direct transfer from the seller to the third party or by two separate purchase deeds, the third party will still be able to effect registration of his own title at the Land Registry without needing to insist that the buyer obtains a registered title in his own name first. Where two purchase deeds have been executed, the third party will need to produce the transfer from the seller to the buyer to the Registry as proof of the devolution of title (see B4).

14.8. Protection of sub-sale contract

14.8.1. The third party is in a more vulnerable position than a normal buyer since completion of his contract is dependent on the buyer's completion of his own contract with the seller. It may therefore be advisable for the third party to protect his contract by registration. Registration of a contract for sale as a class C(iv) land charge can only be effected against the owner for the time being of an unregistered legal estate, i.e. the seller (see C5.3). When the title is registered protection is by the entry of notice in the register of the title.

14.9. Notice to complete

14.9.1. The buyer cannot serve a notice to complete on the third party unless and until he has completed his own contract with the seller. Until this happens the buyer is not 'ready able and willing' to complete within the terms of Standard Condition 1.1.3[1] or Standard Commercial Property Condition 1.1.3. This problem can be overcome by the insertion of a special condition in the contract which allows the buyer to serve a notice notwithstanding that he has not yet completed his own contract. Once a notice to complete is served, time will be of the essence of the contract; the buyer should therefore not serve such a notice unless he is confident that he can complete his own purchase (from the seller) within the time limit which he has imposed on the third party.

1. See generally *Cole* v. *Rose* [1978] 3 All ER 1121.

14.10. Capital Gains Tax

14.10.1. Where a Capital Gains Tax liability is incurred by either the seller or buyer as a result of the sale(s), HM Revenue and Customs treats a sub-sale transaction as being two separate sales (even if completed by one deed), the sale from seller to buyer being regarded as having taken place before the transaction between the buyer and the third party (see A15).

14.11. VAT

14.11.1. The VAT implications of a sub-sale will also need to be considered and provision made in the contract for the responsibility for payment of VAT where applicable (see A16).

B15. Supply of evidence of title before exchange

15.1.	Supply of evidence of title before exchange	15.2.	Registered land
		15.3.	Unregistered land

15.1. Supply of evidence of title before exchange

15.1.1. Having investigated title prior to drafting the contract it will be possible in most cases for the seller to supply the buyer with evidence of title concurrently with the draft contract.

15.1.2. The supply of such evidence of title before exchange enables the buyer to obtain a comprehensive view of the property which he is buying and obviates delays after exchange, since problems which arise on the title will be brought to light and dealt with at an early stage in the transaction.

15.1.3. Where this is done, it is common for the seller to include a contractual condition which precludes the buyer's right to raise requisitions on the evidence of title. Such a condition does not bind the buyer's lender. Such a condition will exclude the normal contractual condition allowing requisitions to be raised within a certain time after exchange of contracts (see Standard Condition 4.2.1 and Standard Commercial Property Condition 6.2). Where such a condition is included in the contract the buyer must obtain satisfactory answers to his queries on the evidence of title before exchange of contracts. He will not be able to rescind the contract after exchange if he discovers a defect arising out of the evidence of title which was supplied to him prior to exchange. The buyer should ensure that any condition excluding his right to raise requisitions should be limited to requisitions upon the evidence of title actually supplied by the seller prior to exchange of contracts. It should not prohibit requisitions being raised on undisclosed matters which are only revealed by pre-completion searches at the Land Registry or the Land Charges Department.

15.2. Registered land

15.2.1. Up-to-date official copies of the title together with supporting documents, e.g. evidence of overriding interests, tenancies, title plan, etc., should be supplied by the seller at his own expense. The copies supplied to the buyer must be *original* official copies. Photocopies of official copies do not satisfy this requirement. Official copies issued electronically are imprinted with a watermark. Official copies in paper form are no longer printed on watermarked paper.

15.3. **Unregistered land**

15.3.1. An epitome of title together with clear photocopies of the documents referred to in it should be supplied to the buyer.

B16. Undertakings for bridging finance

16.1. General points on undertakings

16.1.1. An undertaking is a promise by a solicitor (or a member of the solicitor's staff) to do, or to refrain from doing, something. The promise is enforceable against the solicitor personally, even where the promise was given by a member of staff and not by the solicitor himself. An undertaking given in the firm's name binds all the partners. Undertakings are binding because they are given and no other considerations impinge on their enforceability; thus the normal period of limitation of actions imposed by the Limitation Acts does not apply and an undertaking may be enforced against the giver irrespective of the fact that the normal limitation period has expired.[1]

16.1.2. Failure to honour an undertaking is professional misconduct.[2]

16.1.3. Because of the personal liability which attaches to undertakings it is important that both the giver and recipient of the promise understand precisely what the terms of the promise are. To avoid any misunderstanding it is recommended that undertakings are always given in writing. Any ambiguity in the terms of the promise is construed against the giver of the undertaking. The guidelines contained in the Solicitors Regulation Authority's Undertakings Warning Card should be observed (see Appendix I.3).

16.1.4. An undertaking is enforceable because it has been given and thus needs no consideration for its validity, although in practice consideration will often be present.

16.1.5. A promise to give an undertaking is enforceable as an undertaking.

16.1.6. A solicitor is responsible for honouring any undertaking given by his staff. In order to ensure that no undertaking is given which is outside the control of the solicitor to perform it is recommended that undertakings should only be given by partners in the firm, or by other staff with the prior consent of a partner.

16.1.7. Where an undertaking is given by a member of staff without having obtained or exceeding the requisite authority from a partner, the firm will still be bound to honour that undertaking unless the recipient was aware of the lack of authority on the part of the giver.

16.1.8. Any exclusion of the personal liability of the giver of the undertaking must be clear and explicit. Such undertakings should be regarded with great caution since the primary value of the undertaking, i.e. its enforceability may have been seriously eroded by the exclusion clause. A solicitor may give an undertaking on behalf of a client provided that the wording of the undertaking makes it clear that the primary responsibility for performance of the promise lies with the client and not with the solicitor.

16.1.9. The solicitor must ensure that whatever is promised by the undertaking is capable of performance and is totally within his own control to perform. An undertaking will be enforceable even if the circumstances which prevailed at the time when the undertaking was given subsequently change. Any change in circumstances which potentially affects the fulfilment of an undertaking must be notified to the recipient and, if necessary, the terms renegotiated to ensure that whatever promise has been given is capable of performance.[3]

16.1.10. An undertaking to do something which is not within the direct control of the giver should, if it is appropriate to give such an undertaking at all, only be given in qualified form, e.g. an undertaking to procure the client's signature to a document is not totally within the solicitor's own control since he cannot force the client to sign; thus the undertaking should be worded on the basis that the solicitor will use his best (or reasonable) endeavours to procure the required signature.

16.1.11. Undertakings given by licensed conveyancers are enforceable as if they were given by solicitors.

16.1.12. Undertakings given by unqualified persons who are not acting through a solicitor's practice are only enforceable under the ordinary law of contract and should never be accepted.

Guidelines

16.1.13. (a) Obtain the client's irrevocable written authority before giving an undertaking.

(b) Ensure the wording of the undertaking is clear, unambiguous, and totally capable of performance.

(c) Only give written undertakings, signed or authorised by a partner.

(d) Mark the client's file conspicuously to ensure that the undertaking is not overlooked.

(e) When the undertaking has been fulfilled obtain a written release from the recipient.

1. *Bray* v. *Stuart West & Co.* [1989] EGCS 60.

2. Rule 10.05 Solicitors' Code of Conduct 2007.
3. *Udall* v. *Capri Lighting Ltd* [1997] 3 All ER 262.

16.2. Bridging finance for the deposit

16.2.1. Where bridging finance is being extended for the deposit on the client's purchase the bank or other lender will normally require the solicitor to give an undertaking to repay the loan, usually out of the proceeds of sale of the client's existing property.

16.2.2. Such an undertaking should only be given where:

(a) the solicitor is sure that sufficient funds will be available on completion to repay the loan with interest;

(b) the solicitor knows the client well enough to feel confident of making a binding commitment on that client's behalf;

(c) the client has given his irrevocable authority for the undertaking to be given. If in doubt, obtain the authority in writing.

16.3. When should the undertaking be given?

16.3.1. Until contracts have been exchanged on the client's related sale transaction there is no guarantee that any funds will be available to repay the loan. Ideally, therefore, such an undertaking should not be given until contracts have been exchanged on the sale. In practice it may be necessary to give the undertaking shortly before exchange in order to ensure the availability of funds for a simultaneous exchange on both sale and purchase contracts. The undertaking should not be given until negotiations for the sale contract are close to the point of exchange, with no outstanding unresolved problems.

16.4. Terms of the undertaking

16.4.1. The Law Society has agreed a form of wording for use by solicitors when giving undertakings to banks for bridging finance. The full form of this undertaking is set out in Appendix IV.9.

16.4.2. Even where an undertaking is presented to the solicitor in the standard form or a familiar and frequently used form of wording, the entire wording should be read carefully in the light of the particular transaction to ensure that the wording is appropriate for those circumstances. If the wording is not wholly appropriate to the circumstances in hand, the undertaking should be amended to reflect the particular requirements of the transaction.

16.4.3. Confine the terms of the undertaking to repayment:

(a) of a stated figure, plus interest on that sum if so instructed;

(b) from a defined source, e.g. the proceeds of sale of a named property;

(c) of the net proceeds of sale, having defined what is understood by the word 'net', i.e. after deduction of specified loans, estate agents' commission, solicitor's fees, disbursements on the sale and purchase, and any other known and defined liabilities which will reduce the amount available to repay the loan;

(d) when the proceeds of sale are actually received by the solicitor. This protects the solicitor against having to honour the undertaking in circumstances where the sale of the property is completed but for some reason the funds are never received by him, e.g. the client intercepts the money and absconds with it.

16.5. Change of circumstances

16.5.1. If, having given an undertaking, the circumstances of the client's sale and purchase transactions change, e.g. the consideration for the sale is reduced to take account of a structural defect, the terms of the undertaking must be considered carefully to ensure that they are still capable of performance. The recipient of the undertaking must be informed of the changed circumstances irrespective of whether they affect the obligations covered by the undertaking. Where the undertaking has become impossible of performance because of the changed circumstances the solicitor must renegotiate the undertaking to obtain either a release of his obligations or a form of wording which is capable of performance in the light of the current situation.

16.6. Checklist

16.6.1. (a) Do I know the client well enough to feel confident about giving the undertaking?

(b) Have I got the client's irrevocable written authority to give the undertaking?

(c) Has the client disclosed all subsisting mortgages and liabilities which will or might affect the amount of money which will be available to discharge the loan?

(d) Is there sufficient equity to repay the loan with interest?

(e) Are the terms of the undertaking totally acceptable?

(f) Are negotiations for the client's sale sufficiently firm and advanced to make it safe to give the undertaking?

(g) Has the undertaking been authorised by a partner?

(h)   Has the cover of the client's sale file been clearly marked to show that an undertaking has been given, to whom, and for what amount?

16.7.   Loan guarantees

16.7.1.   A solicitor who gives an undertaking which is effectively a guarantee of a loan being taken out by the client will be bound by that undertaking even if it is not given 'in the normal course of practice'. Such an undertaking may, however, be outside the scope of the solicitors' indemnity insurance.

B17. Deposit

17.1. Is a deposit necessary?

17.1.1. In law a deposit is unnecessary and neither common law nor statute provides for such to be payable. The payment of a deposit is a purely customary arrangement which is expressly incorporated into the contract for the benefit of the seller.

Purpose of deposit

17.1.2. The payment of a deposit acts as part payment of the purchase price, demonstrates the buyer's good intentions of completing the contract, and gives the seller leverage to ensure the fulfilment of the contract since he is usually able to forfeit the deposit if the buyer defaults, thereby recouping part or all of the loss occasioned by the buyer's default.

17.2. How much deposit?

17.2.1. No deposit at all is payable unless the contract expressly makes provision for one.

17.2.2. The Standard Conditions of Sale provide for a deposit of 10% of the purchase price and chattels price. This figure will apply unless specifically amended. The Standard Commercial Property Conditions provide for a 10% deposit of the purchase price and this will apply unless specifically amended.

17.2.3. In recent years deposits of less than 10% have become more widespread in residential transactions due in part to the increase in 95% or 100% mortgage offers to buyers, and to the fact that high property prices, with consequently high deposits, place an unfair financial burden on the buyer whilst over-compensating a seller who forfeits that deposit on the buyer's default.

17.2.4. It is clearly to the seller's advantage to demand a 10% deposit; if, however, he is asked by the buyer to accept a reduced amount the following factors should be considered:

(a) the risk of the sale going off, with the consequent need to forfeit the deposit to compensate for loss;

(b) the buyer's mortgage arrangements – are they firm and settled? Is the offer of advance for the whole of the purchase price (taking into account the amount of the reduced deposit)?

(c) the likely amount of loss which the seller would suffer if the buyer were to default, e.g. cost of bridging finance or interest needed to complete a related purchase, length of time and costs of resale of the property.

17.2.5. The seller's solicitor must explain the consequences of taking a reduced deposit to his client and obtain his client's express authority before agreeing the reduction with the buyer's solicitor or representative. *Morris* v. *Duke Cohan*[1] suggests that it may be professional negligence for a solicitor to accept a reduced deposit without the client's express authority.

17.2.6. If a reduced deposit is taken on exchange, the contract should provide for the balance of the 10% to become immediately payable on service of a notice to complete.[2]

17.2.7. Only in exceptional circumstances should the transaction proceed without any deposit being taken. Examples might include family transactions or sales to sitting tenants.

17.2.8. Deposits in excess of 10% are very rare, and cannot be justified in normal circumstances. The risk is that a defaulting buyer may be able to obtain repayment of the whole of an excessive deposit (not just the amount in excess of 10%).[3]

17.2.9. The amount of the deposit actually payable on exchange will take into account any preliminary deposit already paid, but, unless the contract provides other-wise,[4] is calculated exclusive of the value of chattels which are to be paid for in addition to the purchase price of the land.

1. (1975) 119 SJ 826.
2. See Standard Condition 6.8.3.
3. See *Dojap Investments Ltd* v. *Workers Trust and Merchant Bank Ltd* [1993] AC 573 where the forfeiture of a 24% deposit was held to be a penalty.
4. See Standard Condition 2.2.1.

17.3. How is the deposit to be funded?

17.3.1. The answer to this question should be obtained when initial instructions are taken from the client. It is safest to assume at this stage that the seller will require a full 10% deposit, and if the buyer wishes to pay a reduced deposit the matter will have to be raised during negotiations with the seller's solicitor.

From an investment account

17.3.2.   (a) How much notice does the buyer need to give to withdraw his funds without losing a significant amount of interest?

(b) Ensure sufficient money is transferred to a short-term investment account in time for it to be immediately available on exchange.

Bridging finance

17.3.3.   Bridging finance from a bank or other lender will often be needed in a situation where the purchase is dependent on a related sale:

(a) It should be apparent at an early stage in the transaction that bridging finance will be required and arrangements should be made as soon as possible so that the money is immediately available when required on exchange.

(b) An undertaking to repay the bridging loan out of the proceeds of sale of the client's existing property will often be required from the solicitor. Should an undertaking be given and, if so, are its terms acceptable?

(c) Has the client been properly advised about the costs and risks of bridging finance, e.g. high interest rate payable over an uncertain period if the sale goes off, arrangement fees?

(d) Tax relief on the amount of the bridging finance is available where the loan is taken on a separate loan account, but not where the loan is taken by way of overdraft on a current account. If the client has a high cash flow passing through his current account it may be more cost effective to forgo the tax relief and take advantage of the lower interest rates payable on the current account.

Deposit guarantee

17.3.4.   Check buyer's eligibility – the conditions of the scheme may provide, e.g. that the scheme is not available for first-time buyers, or that the deposit must not exceed either 10% of the purchase price or £15,000, or that the completion date in the contract must not be more than six weeks from the date of exchange.

17.3.5.   The seller's agreement to use of the scheme must be obtained as soon as possible and arrangements put in hand to obtain the guarantee so that it is available to be handed to the seller on exchange of contracts.

17.3.6.   Before agreeing to accept deposit by way of guarantee the seller should consider:

(a) the fact that he may not be able to use the deposit towards the deposit on

B

his own purchase (depending on the scheme used) although this factor will be of no consequence if a deposit guarantee is to be used in that transaction also;

(b) the consequences (including costs and delay) of attempting to enforce payment through the scheme if the reasons for the buyer's ultimate default are either disputed or not covered by the scheme.

Lenders' deposit-free schemes

17.3.7. The terms of these schemes vary from lender to lender. The terms of the particular scheme should be considered carefully by both parties before a decision to use them is taken. In particular the seller should have regard to the possible consequences (including costs and delay) if the reasons for the buyer's ultimate default are either disputed or not covered by the scheme.

17.4. Clearing funds

17.4.1. Under Standard Condition 2.2.4 the deposit is payable by direct credit or by a cheque drawn on the solicitor's or licensed conveyancer's client account. The buyer's solicitor must therefore ensure that he receives the amount of the deposit from his own client in sufficient time to allow the client's cheque to be cleared through the solicitor's clients' account before drawing the cheque in favour of the seller for the deposit or authorising the direct credit.

17.4.2. Under Standard Commercial Property Condition 2.2.2 the deposit is payable by direct credit only. The Conditions require that the direct credit arrive not later than the date of the contract in cleared funds at the bank nominated by the seller's solicitors (see Conditions 1.1.1(g), 2.2.1 and 2.2.2). This may be impossible to fulfil if exchange takes place in the late afternoon. Agreeing between solicitors to send the money the next working day may avoid the buyer's solicitor being in breach of the undertaking implied in Formula B but will not operate to amend the contract because of Law of Property (Miscellaneous Provisions) Act 1989 s.2 – so (a) his client will technically be in breach of contract and (b) is the seller entitled to the overnight interest which his solicitor has forgone?

17.5. Capacity in which deposit is held

17.5.1. The deposit is held in one of the three capacities listed below:

(a) agent for the seller;

(b) agent for the buyer;

(c) stakeholder.

17.5.2. In the absence of contrary agreement solicitors and estate agents hold in the capacity of agent for the seller, but an auctioneer holds as stakeholder.[1] This general rule may be varied by express contractual condition.

17.5.3. The capacity of agent for the buyer is rarely used since in most situations the seller will be reluctant to agree to the deposit being held in this way. It may, however, be necessary to use this capacity where the seller is represented by an unqualified person.

17.5.4. If the deposit is held as agent for the seller, the agent may hand the money over to the seller before completion. In this situation the seller can use the money towards the deposit on his own purchase, but where this occurs the buyer may have difficulty in recovering the money if the seller defaults on completion. The buyer should be advised of the risks involved in agreeing to the deposit being held in the capacity of agent.

17.5.5. A stakeholder is the principal for both parties and where this capacity is used the money may be handed to either party without the consent of the other provided the stakeholder is confident that circumstances exist which justify his decision to make payment. Normally, however, the stakeholder should not part with the money until completion or other resolution of the matter.

17.5.6. Most deposits are paid to the seller's solicitor in the capacity either of agent for the seller or stakeholder.

17.5.7. The Standard Conditions of Sale (Condition 2.2.6) and Standard Commercial Property Conditions (Condition 2.2.2) generally provide for the deposit to be held as stakeholder and this is the capacity recommended by the Law Society.[2] The capacity of agent for the seller will, however, apply if the seller is to use all or part of the deposit towards the deposit on his related residential transaction in England and Wales (Standard Condition of Sale 2.2.5), and may be necessary in some circumstances where an exchange under the Law Society's Formula C is contemplated; see B17.9.7.

17.5.8. Where the seller is represented by an unqualified person the buyer's solicitor should ensure that he or a reputable estate agent holds the deposit (in either case in the capacity of stakeholder) or that it is placed in a deposit account in a bank or building society in the joint names of seller and buyer.

Fiduciary vendors

17.5.9. Where the sellers are selling as trustees the money arising from the sale will be trust money and should never be outside the control of the trustees.[3] This requirement will be satisfied if the deposit is paid to some person in the capacity of agent for the seller.

17.5.10. Where the deposit or any part of it is proposed to be held as agents of the seller, it is recommended that the buyer client should be advised of the risks involved in agreeing to this.

1. *Edgell* v. *Day* (1865) LR 1 CP 80; *Ryan* v. *Pilkington* [1959] 1 All ER 689.
2. [1975] *Gazette*, 184.
3. [1957] *Gazette*, 327.

17.6. Solicitor holding the deposit

17.6.1. The money is client money and must be placed in a client account in accordance with Solicitors' Accounts Rules 1998.

17.7. Interest on the deposit

17.7.1. Whether the money is held in the capacity of agent for the seller or stakeholder interest may be payable under Part C Solicitors' Accounts Rules 1998.

17.7.2. Where the money is held as stakeholder interest is payable on the stake money under the provisions of Solicitors' Accounts Rules 1998. It is up to the parties to decide which of them should be entitled to the interest on the stake money and an appropriate clause must be included in the contract to deal with the payment of interest in these circumstances. The Law Society's recommended form of wording for such a clause is as follows: 'The stakeholder shall pay to the seller/buyer a sum equal to the interest the deposit would have earned if placed on deposit (less costs of acting as stakeholder).' In the absence of an agreement the interest follows the stake under Rule 26 Solicitors Accounts Rules 1998.

17.7.3. Standard Condition 2.2.6 provides that where the deposit, or part of it, is held in the capacity of stakeholder, interest on the deposit will be payable to the seller on completion. If the buyer negotiates an agreement that he is to be credited with interest on the deposit, a special condition must be inserted in the contract to that effect. Standard Commercial Property Condition 2.2.2 contains provisions similar to Standard Condition 2.2.6.

17.8. Deposits paid to estate agents

17.8.1. At common law an estate agent holds the deposit as agent for the seller, but this capacity may be changed to stakeholder by express contractual provision.

17.8.2. In whichever capacity the deposit is held the risk of its loss through the default of the agent generally falls on the buyer.[1]

17.8.3. This risk has been minimised by Estate Agents Act 1979, s.16 which requires agents to carry insurance to cover clients' money. 'Clients' money' is defined by section 12 of the 1979 Act to include any contract or pre-contract deposit.

17.8.4. The money must be placed in a clients' account (section 14 Estate Agents Act 1979), and is held on trust by the agent for the person who is or who will become entitled to the money. Since the money is trust money it will not vest in a trustee in bankruptcy should the agent be made bankrupt.[2]

17.8.5.   An estate agent who holds in the capacity of agent for the seller is under a duty to account to the client for interest on any deposit exceeding £500.[3] It is not clear whether an estate agent who holds in the capacity of stakeholder is subject to the provisions relating to the payment of interest.

1. *Sorrell* v. *Finch* [1977] AC 728.
2. Estate Agents Act 1979, s.13(1).
3. Estate Agents (Accounts) Regulations 1981 (SI 1981/1520), reg.7.

17.9.   Contractual terms relating to the deposit

17.9.1.   Standard contractual conditions will normally provide for the seller's solicitor to hold a 10% deposit as stakeholder, the deposit to be paid by direct credit or solicitor's cheque (see Standard Condition 2.2.1 and 2.2.4 and Standard Commercial Property Condition 2.2.2).

17.9.2.   The standard clauses represent the safest method both of payment and of holding the deposit. Variations of these provisions by express contractual term is possible but should only be done where the substituted term is necessary to meet the circumstances of the individual transaction and sufficiently safeguards the interests of both parties.

17.9.3.   Variation of the standard provisions may be required where the seller is represented by an unqualified person, or where a less than 10% deposit is being taken. In the latter case provision should be included in the contract for the balance of the 10% to become immediately payable in the event of a notice to complete being served so that the seller is able to forfeit the full 10% sum should it become necessary to do so. (See Standard Condition 7.5.2.)

17.9.4.   Any preliminary deposit which was paid to an estate agent before exchange should be handed over to the solicitor who is holding the deposit once exchange has taken place. If this does not occur the seller will technically be in breach of contract because the contract requires the solicitor to hold 'the deposit', and this may in turn cause problems for a buyer who seeks the recovery of his deposit on the seller's default. In practice estate agents are reluctant to part with the preliminary deposit, seeking to retain it in part payment of their commission. The solicitor who is to hold the deposit should check the terms on which any preliminary deposit is held by the estate agent to ascertain if it can be taken into account in the completion statement.

Checklist for contract terms

17.9.5.   (a)   How much deposit is required in total?

(b)   Has a preliminary deposit been paid – if so, how much and to whom?

(c) Who is to hold the deposit and in which capacity?

(d) Method of payment?

(e) If in cash, provide for payment by banker's draft or equivalent.

(f) If less than 10%, provide for balance to be immediately payable on service of a completion notice.

17.9.6. The Standard Conditions of Sale recognise the existing practice in many areas for the deposit received on the sale of the property to be used to pay the deposit on the purchase of another property.

17.9.7. The presence of Standard Condition 2.2.6 may mean that a special condition will be necessary if the Law Society's Formula C is used on exchange of contracts and the person at the end of the chain will not agree to the deposit being held as stakeholder. In this event, it would be necessary for all parties in the chain to be notified and a special condition would be required only in the last contract in the chain. It is suggested that this should be:

> 'The deposit shall be paid to the seller's solicitor as agent for the seller and Standard Condition 2.2.6 is varied accordingly.'

17.10. Methods of payment of deposit

17.10.1. The seller may insist on the payment of the deposit in cash unless he has agreed to accept some other method of payment.[1] Standard Condition 2.2.4 requires payment to be made by direct credit or solicitor's cheque only, except where the contract is made at auction. Standard Commercial Property Condition 2.2.2 requires payment only by direct credit except at sales by auction where other methods of payment are acceptable.

17.10.2. Solicitors should be wary of accepting a deposit in cash because of the dangers of money laundering (see A23).

17.10.3. If a cheque taken in payment of the deposit bounces, this constitutes a fundamental breach of contract which gives the seller the option either of keeping the contract alive for the benefit of both parties, or of treating the contract as discharged by the breach, and in either event of suing for damages.[2] A separate cause of action arises out of the cheque itself. The contract should be drafted to indicate precisely what the rights of the parties are in the event of the dishonour of the deposit cheque.

17.10.4. The option of treating the contract as discharged is of little consolation to a seller who, on the strength of his sale contract, has exchanged contracts for the purchase of another property. Provision should therefore be made in the contract to ensure that the deposit is only payable by a method which will be honoured on presentation, e.g. banker's draft or solicitor's clients' account cheque.

1. *Johnston* v. *Boyes* (1898) 14 TLR 475.
2. *Millichamp* v. *Jones* [1983] 1 All ER 267, and see Standard Condition 2.2.2.

17.11. Using the deposit to fund another transaction

17.11.1. A seller who is a builder or developer, or one who is involved in the purchase of another property, may wish to use part or all of the deposit received from his sale before completion of that transaction takes place.

17.11.2. The deposit may only be used by the seller in this way if it is held in the capacity of agent for the seller.

17.11.3. Although totally satisfactory for the seller, this situation is less than satisfactory for the buyer who may find that he has difficulty in recovering his money if the sale is not completed through the default of the seller or if the seller goes bankrupt or absconds with the money. The buyer should be advised of these risks.

17.11.4. Before agreeing to allow the seller to have use of the deposit pending completion the buyer should try to ensure that the contract contains some protection for him against the seller's default. In an exceptional case it would be possible for the buyer to secure the deposit by taking an equitable charge over the seller's existing and new properties. Such a charge would need to be protected by registration of a notice (registered land) or Class C(iii) land charge (unregistered land) to bind a purchaser and could only be enforced by a court order for the sale of the property.

17.11.5. Standard Condition 2.2.5 allows the seller to use all or part of the deposit to fund his own deposit on a related residential transaction in England and Wales but for no other purpose. No equivalent provision is contained in the Standard Commercial Property Conditions.

17.12. Buyer's lien

17.12.1. From the moment when he pays the deposit to the seller in the capacity of agent (but not stakeholder) the buyer has a lien over the property for the amount of the deposit. The lien is only enforceable by a court order for sale of the property and will only bind another buyer of the land if protected by notice (registered land) or Class C(iii) land charge (unregistered land) or if, in the case of registered land, the buyer is in occupation and the lien takes effect as an overriding interest.[1]

17.12.2. If the buyer defaults on completion he has no right to the return of his deposit. This is subject to the court's discretion to order the return of a deposit under Law of Property Act 1925, s.49(2) (see M3.10).

17.12.3. If the contract is terminated for any other reason the buyer has a lien which may be enforced either by the buyer himself or by a person claiming under him.[2]

17.12.4. When the reason for non-completion of the sale is a defect in the seller's title the lien extends to the deposit, interest, and the costs of investigating title, and where the sale is by auction under the direction of the court, costs incurred by the buyer in connection with the auction are also included.[3]

17.12.5. A buyer who pays a deposit to a stakeholder is not entitled to recover through his lien the costs of an unsuccessful action for specific performance brought against him by the seller.[4]

1. Land Registration Act 2002, Sched.1, para.2 and Sched.3, para.2.
2. *Levy* v. *Stogdon* [1898] 1 Ch 478.
3. *Holliwell* v. *Seacombe* [1906] 1 Ch 426.
4. *Combe* v. *Lord Swaythling* [1947] Ch 625.

17.13. Deposits paid direct to the seller

17.13.1. A buyer's solicitor should be wary of a situation in which the buyer has apparently paid a deposit directly to the seller. This may indicate the existence of a mortgage fraud (see A24).

17.13.2. Solicitors are reminded of the Law Society's Mortgage Fraud Practice Note (see Appendix II.4). In many cases of such fraud, the deposit is allegedly paid direct between the parties.

17.13.3. A solicitor should not confirm to another solicitor that deposit payments have been made or received unless the moneys have been paid into that solicitor's client account or that solicitor has actual evidence that the payment has been made or received by a third party.

17.13.4. Solicitors are reminded of Rule 4 Solicitors' Code of Conduct 2007 (confidentiality and disclosure). Any solicitor with a query about a suspected mortgage fraud should contact the Solicitors Regulation Authority Professional Ethics Guidance Team for advice.

B18. Liquor licensing and food safety

18.1. Introduction

18.1.1. Significant changes were introduced to the licensing laws in England and Wales by Licensing Act 2003, which came into effect on 24 November 2005. This Act created a single integrated scheme for licensing premises which sell alcohol, provide regulated entertainment or provide late night refreshment. This was achieved by amalgamating the six previous licensing regimes – for alcohol, public entertainment, cinemas, theatres, late night refreshment houses and night cafes. Under the Act, the system of separate licences for different activities was replaced by a single licence – the premises licence – which authorises the use of any premises, part of premises or place for any or all of the 'licensable activities'.

18.1.2. The licensable activities covered by the Act are:

(a) the sale by retail of alcohol;

(b) the supply of alcohol by clubs;

(c) the provision of regulated entertainment (including cinemas and theatres);

(d) the provision of late night refreshment.

18.1.3. Licensing Act 2003 also introduced the concept of personal licences. These are portable and allow the licence holder to move from one licensed premises to another without any procedural requirements other than the requirement to notify a change of address.

18.1.4. Under the Act club premises certificates authorise qualifying clubs for qualifying club activities and licensable activities at temporary events are covered by temporary event notices.

18.1.5. The 2003 Act provides that the Secretary of State must issue and, from time to time, may revise national guidance to the licensing authorities detailing how the

2003 Act works and how the licensing authorities should carry out their functions in this respect. This is called Section 182 guidance and was last amended in March 2010.

18.2.   Licensing objectives

18.2.1.   The 2003 Act focuses on the promotion of four fundamental statutory licensing objectives. These are:

(a)   the prevention of crime and disorder;

(b)   public safety;

(c)   the prevention of public nuisance; and

(d)   the protection of children from harm.

These objectives establish the criteria to be used by the licensing authorities in determining or reviewing licence applications.

18.3.   Licensing authority

18.3.1.   The responsibility for authorising licensable activities and the administration of the licensing system lies with the local authorities, which means that determinations reflect local circumstances and take into account local discretion.

18.3.2.   Under Licensing Act 2003, each licensing authority is required to determine and publish a statement of its licensing policy every three years, which must be kept under review and revised when necessary.

18.3.3.   The purpose of the licensing policy statement is to set out the criteria which are used in determining licence applications and provide transparency to all those involved in a licence application. This will thus specify the attitude of the authority on licensing issues and will provide guidance to potential applicants or existing licence holders. As each authority's statement reflects local circumstances there are differences between the different statements. Different local authorities will therefore take different views on similar issues, and those advising in transactions involving licensed premises should accordingly acquaint themselves with the licensing policy of the area in which those premises are located.

18.3.4.   It should be noted that some licensing authorities have adopted cumulative impact policies as part of their licensing policy statement. Such policies create a rebuttable presumption against the grant of new licences or material variations to a licence within a particular area, following relevant representations, because the area is already saturated with certain types of premises. However, in determining applications for premises situated in such areas, the licensing authority must still consider the merits of each individual application and, where grant of a licence or variation would be unlikely to add significantly to the cumulative impact of licensed premises on the promotion of the licensing objectives, the licence should be granted. Furthermore, if there are no representations, the licensing authority must grant the application in terms that are consistent with the operating schedule submitted.

18.3.5. Crime and Security Act 2010 which received royal assent on 8 April 2010 amends Licensing Act 2003 to give licensing authorities the power to make 'early morning alcohol restriction orders' when they consider it necessary to promote the licensing objectives. Effectively this means that local authorities will have the power to restrict late opening across a specified area, banning the sale and supply of alcohol between the hours of 3 am and 6 am. An order may apply to every day of the week or only on particular days; the whole or part of a licensing authority's area; for a limited or unlimited period of time.

18.4. Licensing register

18.4.1. Each authority is required to maintain a licensing register detailing applications made to and authorisations issued by the licensing authority.

18.4.2. The licensing register will contain a record of:

(a) each premises licence issued;

(b) each club premises certificate issued;

(c) personal licences issued for those resident (at the time of application) in the licensing authority area;

(d) all temporary event notices received.

18.4.3. The register will also include a record of:

(a) applications to vary (including minor variations);

(b) applications to transfer;

(c) applications to review;

(d) changes of name and address of licence holders;

(e) surrender of licences.

18.4.4. Every formal application will be recorded in the register. The register will be the starting point for the solicitors acting in any transaction involving licensed premises.

18.4.5. This register is available to the public and the licensing authority must provide facilities for inspection during office hours. Inspection is free and copies of entries are to be provided at a reasonable charge. Many licensing authorities maintain an online licensing register which is searchable.

18.5. Premises licence

18.5.1. A premises licence is required to cover all the licensable activities that take place at an establishment. Once granted the premises licence remains valid indefinitely until such time as it is revoked or surrendered. Practitioners should be aware however that it will lapse in circumstances of the licence holder's death, insolvency or insanity. The licence is not subject to renewal but an annual payment to the licensing authority is required.

18.5.2. A premises licence is required for a wide range of premises, including:

(a) pubs and bars;

(b) restaurants;

(c) nightclubs;

(d) supermarkets, off licences, and shops making retail alcohol sales;

(e) hotels;

(f) late night refreshment premises;

(g) non-qualifying clubs (see B18.9);

(h) cinemas;

(i) theatres.

18.5.3. Applications for a premises licence can be made by anyone over the age of 18 (including companies, partnerships, etc.), who is carrying on, or proposes to carry on, a business that involves licensable activities on the premises. The application form for a premises licence incorporates an 'operating schedule' which sets out the nature and times of the licensable activities being provided together with the steps being taken to meet the licensing objectives outlined above. It is vitally important that the applicant considers these steps very carefully as they will be translated into conditions on the licence.

18.5.4. An application for a premises licence may be made in writing, or electronically via businesslink or the licensing authority's own electronic application facility if they have one.

18.5.5. Where the premises licence specifies the provision of alcohol, the application also needs to specify the 'designated premises supervisor' (DPS) (see also B18.5.15). This person will have to hold a personal licence (see B18.8) and will be the point of contact for the premises for the licensing authorities, or the police or fire services if problems occur at the premises. A designated premises supervisor may supervise more than one premises provided they can ensure that the licensing objectives are met and the licensing law and licence conditions are complied with.

18.5.6. A premises licence application also needs to be accompanied by a set of current floor plans for the premises on a scale of 1:100, unless it has been previously agreed with the relevant licensing authority in writing that an alternative scale is acceptable.

18.5.7. All applications must be advertised in the local press and on the premises and notified to the responsible authorities. Objections (which are referred to as 'relevant representations') to premises licence applications may be made by responsible authorities and interested parties.

Responsible authorities

18.5.8. Responsible authorities are defined as the following in relation to the area in which the premises are situated:

    (a)   the chief officer of police;

    (b)   the fire authority;

    (c)   the health and safety authority;

    (d)   the local planning authority;

    (e)   the environmental health authority;

    (f)   the body recognised as being responsible for protection of children from harm;

    (g)   inspectors of weights and measures (trading standards officers);

    (h)   any licensing authority (other than the relevant licensing authority) in whose area part of the premises is situated.

Interested parties

18.5.9. Interested parties are defined as any of the following:

    (a)   a person living in the vicinity of the premises;

    (b)   a body representing persons who live in that vicinity;

    (c)   a person involved in a business in the vicinity of the premises;

    (d)   a body representing persons involved in such businesses;

    (e)   a member of the relevant licensing authority.

Objections

18.5.10. Any objections raised must relate to one or more of the four licensing objectives.

18.5.11. If relevant representations are received, the licensing authority must hold a hearing, unless all parties agree that a hearing is not necessary, in order to consider the representations and determine the application.

18.5.12. If no relevant representations have been received, then provided the application has been lawfully made and properly advertised and notified, the licensing authority must grant the licence subject only to those conditions which are consistent with the operating schedule.

Conditions

18.5.13. On granting a premises licence a licensing authority may impose conditions. These may be either discretionary or mandatory. Where no relevant representations have been made against the application, no conditions can be imposed (other than mandatory) beyond those consistent with the operating schedule. If relevant representations have been made, then conditions may only be imposed where they are necessary for the promotion of one or more of the licensing objectives.

18.5.14. Where a licence authorises the supply of alcohol, mandatory conditions indicating the following must be attached:

(a)   there must be a designated premises supervisor (DPS) who is a holder of a valid personal licence; and

(b)   any supply of alcohol must be made by a personal licence holder or someone authorised by a personal licence holder.

18.5.15. An exception to the requirements for a DPS or for alcohol sales to be supervised by a personal licence-holder came into force on 29 July 2009 for community premises. This change allows a committee or board of individuals with responsibility for the management of the community premises to disapply these mandatory conditions. An alternative licence condition that every supply of alcohol under the licence be made or authorised by the management committee (which will also be the premises licence holder) is required instead. The applicant must apply to the licensing authority for the alternative condition to be used either on a new application or on a variation to an existing premises licence.

18.5.16. Although there is no legal requirement for this, the Guidance strongly recommends that personal licence holders give specific *written* authorisations to individuals whom they are authorising to sell alcohol.

18.5.17. Three new mandatory conditions where the licence authorises the supply of alcohol came into force on 6 April 2010. These impose a duty on those managing licensed premises to: prohibit irresponsible promotions; prohibit one person from dispensing alcohol directly into the mouth of another; and ensure that free tap water is provided on request to customers. The new mandatory conditions override any pre-existing conditions already included in a licence.

18.5.18. Two further new mandatory conditions relating to age verification policies and ensuring smaller measures are available will come into effect on 1 October 2010.

18.6. Regulated entertainment

18.6.1. Regulated entertainment is defined as the provision of entertainment or entertainment facilities subject to conditions and exemptions as set out in the Act.

Entertainment

18.6.2. The descriptions of entertainment given in the Act are:

    (a) the performance of a play (including a rehearsal if the public are admitted);

    (b) an exhibition of a film;

    (c) an indoor sporting event;

    (d) boxing or wrestling entertainment (indoor and outdoor);

    (e) a performance of live music;

    (f) any playing of recorded music;

    (g) a performance of dance;

    (h) entertainment similar to live music, recorded music or dance;

where the entertainment described takes place in the presence of an audience and is provided in order to entertain the audience.

Entertainment facilities

18.6.3. Entertainment facilities are described as facilities for enabling people to take part in entertainment consisting of:

    (a) making music (vocal or instrumental or both);

    (b) dancing;

    (c) entertainment similar to making music or dancing;

where the facilities are provided for the purpose of being entertained.

18.6.4. The Government has recently consulted on a proposal to clarify the definition of 'entertainment facilities'.

18.6.5. Private entertainment is also licensable if it is provided for 'consideration and with a view to profit'.

18.7. Late night refreshment

18.7.1. All establishments (apart from exempt categories) that provide hot food and hot drinks to the public for consumption either on or off the premises between the hours of 11 pm and 5 am must be licensed.

18.7.2. The following types of late night refreshment are exempt from the requirement for a premises licence:

(a) hot drinks distributed by a machine that is operated solely by the customer;

(b) hot food or hot drink supplied free of charge, where there is also no charge for admission to any premises, or a charge for some other item to obtain the hot food or hot drink;

(c) hot food or hot drink supplied by a registered charity or by a person authorised by a registered charity (registered under Charities Act 1993, or not required by this Act to be registered);

(d) hot food or hot drink supplied on a moving vehicle (for example: trains, coaches, limousines);

(e) hot food or hot drink supplied to members and guests of recognised clubs that hold a club premises certificate;

(f) hot food or hot drink supplied to hotel and bed and breakfast guests;

(g) refreshments in staff canteens, where the staff are required to work between 11 pm and 5 am.

18.8. Personal licence

18.8.1. Personal licences are issued to individuals to authorise the holder to sell or supply alcohol or to authorise the sale or supply of alcohol for consumption on or off premises for which a premises licence is in force. No sale of alcohol can be made except by a personal licence holder or under their authorisation.

18.8.2. A personal licence relates only to the sale/supply of alcohol under a premises licence. It does not permit the holder to sell/supply alcohol from anywhere, only from establishments operating under a premises licence or at temporary events.

18.8.3. A personal licence is not required for other licensable activities such as the provision of regulated entertainment or late night refreshment or for the sale/supply of alcohol under a club premises certificate.

18.8.4. An applicant for a personal licence must fulfil the following qualifying criteria in order to obtain a personal licence:

(a) be aged 18 or over;

(b) possess a recognised qualification;

(c) have not had a personal licence revoked in the previous five years;

(d) either the police have not raised any objections to the grant; or

      (e)   if the police have raised objections, the licensing authority has decided not to act on the objection; and

      (f)   the appropriate fee has been paid.

18.8.5.   As part of the application process, in order to satisfy the police that they do not have a criminal record, the applicant must submit a criminal conviction certificate or a criminal record certificate or the results of a subject access search of the police national computer.

18.8.6.   The licence is valid for 10 years initially, unless it is surrendered by the holder, revoked by the licensing authority, or forfeited or suspended by the court. At the end of the 10-year period, the holder may apply for renewal of the licence which may be renewed at 10-yearly intervals thereafter.

18.8.7.   There is no need to apply for a new licence when a personal licence holder moves as these licences are portable and may be used anywhere in England and Wales.

18.9.   Club premises certificate

18.9.1.   Licensing Act 2003 preserves aspects of earlier licensing legislation as it applied to 'registered members clubs', where technically there are no retail sales of alcohol to club members.

18.9.2.   Clubs which satisfy certain qualifying conditions are classed as 'qualifying clubs' and require a club premises certificate. An application for this certificate is very similar to an application for a premises licence and requires the inclusion of an operating schedule and also needs to be advertised and notified to responsible authorities. However, there is no requirement for a designated premises supervisor to be specified on this type of licence, and also no requirement for those supplying alcohol under the club premises certificate to hold a personal licence.

18.9.3.   Clubs which do not satisfy the requirements to be classed as a 'qualifying club' will need a premises licence in order to provide licensable activities.

18.10.   Transfer of premises licence

18.10.1.   When a business involving licensable activities is sold to a new owner it will be necessary to transfer the premises licence. Any person or company that is eligible to apply for a premises licence may apply to have a premises licence transferred to them. Such a transfer will only change the identity of the licence holder and will not alter the licence in any other way.

18.10.2.   An application to transfer must be notified to the chief officer of police. In exceptional circumstances, where the police believe that the transfer may undermine the crime prevention objective, they may object to the application, but this is expected to be rare. Objections to a transfer cannot be made by other responsible authorities or interested parties. In the absence of police objections, the transfer must be granted.

18.10.3. In order to enable continuity and ensure there is no interruption to business at the premises during determination of the transfer, it is possible to request that the application for transfer be given immediate effect, i.e. from the date it is received by the licensing authority, until formally determined or withdrawn.

18.10.4. An application for immediate effect will normally require the consent of the current licence holder. However, this may be waived if the applicant can demonstrate that he has taken all reasonable steps to obtain the consent and can show that he is in a position to use the premises immediately for the licensable activities authorised by the licence.

18.10.5. To avoid any problems with respect to obtaining the consent of the holder of the premises licence to an immediate transfer, it may be sensible for the contract for sale to include the agreement of the licence holder to the buyer making an application for transfer with immediate effect (Licensing Act 2003, s.43) on or before the completion date.

18.11. Variation of premises licence

18.11.1. The holder of a premises licence may apply to vary the licence by, for example, altering conditions attaching to the licence, or changing the hours of operation, or changing the authorised licensable activities permitted. An application to vary the actual premises may also be made, provided it is a minor change. However, it is not possible to vary substantially the premises to which the licence relates. Any substantial change would require an application for a new licence.

18.11.2. Where the variation required relates to features shown on the plan submitted with the original application for the premises licence which were not legally required to be shown and the variation is not likely to have any impact on the promotion of the licensing objectives, the Guidance advises that individual licensing authorities have discretion to decide whether or not an application to vary is required.

18.11.3. The procedure for an application to vary is essentially the same as for the original grant and must also be advertised and notice of the application given to each responsible authority. Responsible authorities and interested parties may object to the variation on grounds relating to the licensing objectives. In the absence of any objection the variation will be granted.

18.11.4. A simplified procedure for 'minor variations' came into force on 29 July 2009. This process removes the requirements to advertise the variation in a local newspaper and give notice to responsible authorities. However, the applicant is required to display a notice on the premises for 10 days and interested parties may object.

18.11.5. A 'minor variation' is defined as a variation that will not impact adversely on the licensing objectives. These are categorised as minor changes to the structure or layout of a premises; small adjustments to licensing hours; the removal of out-of-date, irrelevant or unenforceable conditions or the addition of volunteered conditions; and the addition of certain licensable activities.

18.12. Provisional statements

18.12.1. Where premises which are intended to be used for licensable activities are constructed, extended or altered, it is possible to apply for a provisional statement. While this does not provide a guarantee that a full licence will be granted once the building work has been completed, it does give a degree of assurance. The provisional statement describes the likely effects of the intended licensable activities on the licensing objectives and what steps the licensing authority would consider necessary for the promotion of the licensable activities if and when an application was made for a premises licence. The provisional statement therefore gives an indication of the prospects of any future application for a premises licence.

18.12.2. The application for a provisional statement must be accompanied by plans, details of the work to be carried out and details of the proposed licensable activities. The procedure for advertisement and hearing of these applications is similar to that which applies to a new premises licence. Accordingly, there will be a hearing if there are objections and the licensing authority can then issue a provisional statement expressing its view. It would indicate, for example, that it would be necessary to attach conditions to the licence or to exclude some of the proposed licensable activities if, in its view, the licensing objectives required those amendments.

18.12.3. The holder of such a statement knows that when he applies for a full premises licence he is likely to obtain a grant in accordance with the statement. There is still however an opportunity for further objection when that application is made. The licensing authority can only entertain such an objection, however, if it is satisfied that it could not have been raised at the provisional stage.

18.12.4. As an alternative to applying for a provisional statement, there is nothing to prevent an application being made for a full premises licence before new premises are constructed or existing premises are extended or changed, provided the relevant information is available. If the licence were granted it would not have immediate effect, but the date when it would become effective would be included in the licence.

18.13. Interim authorities

18.13.1. A premises licence lapses on the death, mental incapacity or insolvency of the licence holder. As there may be a delay before a new premises licence holder can be appointed, there are provisions under Licensing Act 2003 to permit the continuation of the authorisations under a premises licence until a formal transfer can occur. This arrangement is called an 'interim authority' and allows the licensable activities to continue until transfer.

18.13.2. In these circumstances an 'interim authority notice' (IAN) should be submitted to the relevant licensing authority within seven days of the lapse of the premises licence. The effect of giving an interim authority notice is to reinstate the premises licence from the time the licensing authority receives the notice and for the person giving the notice to become the licence holder. The maximum period for which an interim authority notice may have effect is two months. An application for transfer to a new licence holder must, therefore, be made within this time period.

18.13.3. Where a premises licence has lapsed due to death, incapacity or insolvency of the holder or has been surrendered, it is also possible under Licensing Act 2003, s.50, for anyone who is eligible to apply for a premises licence, to apply for a transfer of the licence with immediate effect. Such an application must be made within seven days of the lapse of the licence and can only be made where there is no interim authority notice in force. The effect of this application is to reinstate the licence from the time the application was received by the licensing authority.

18.13.4. A draft order to amend Licensing Act 2003 in relation to IANs has been laid before Parliament and will come into effect later in 2010. Three amendments are introduced. Firstly, the timescale during which the IAN must be submitted is extended from seven days to 28 days and the notice will have effect for three months rather than two months. Secondly, the police will have two working days rather than 48 hours following receipt of the notice in which to object. Thirdly, the maximum period for making a transfer application following the lapse of a licence under s.50 is increased to 28 days from the current seven days.

18.14. Review of licences

18.14.1. The 'review' process allows an interested party or a responsible authority, at any time following the grant of a premises licence or club premises certificate, to apply to the licensing authority for a review of the licence, if they consider that there is an issue relating to one of the licensing objectives occurring at that particular premises.

18.14.2. Licensing authorities are not permitted to initiate their own reviews of premises licences or club premises certificates. However, now that the definition of interested party has been expanded to include all members of local authorities that are licensing authorities, elected councillors can seek a review in their own right.

18.14.3. The licensing authority is required to advertise any application to review it receives for a period of 28 days during which time the licence holder, interested parties and responsible authorities may make representations. A hearing must then be held within 20 working days of the end of this period.

18.14.4. Following a review hearing, the licensing authority has a range of powers. It may decide that no action is necessary for the promotion of the licensing objectives, or it may decide that only informal action, such as informal warnings or recommendations for improvements within a specified time, is the most appropriate way forward.

18.14.5. However, where the licensing authority considers that formal steps are required, it may take any of the following actions:

    (a)   modify (add, alter or omit) the conditions of the licence;

    (b)   exclude a licensable activity from the licence;

    (c)   remove the designated premises supervisor;

    (d)   suspend the licence for a period not exceeding three months;

    (e)   revoke the licence.

18.14.6. Modifications of conditions and exclusion of licensable activities may be imposed either permanently or for a temporary period of up to three months.

18.14.7. The powers for tackling crime and disorder under the Act were extended in October 2007 by the introduction of a summary review process where a premises licence authorises the sale of alcohol. In situations where the police consider that the premises concerned are associated with serious crime and/or disorder, they can apply for an expedited review of the licence, to which the licensing authority can respond, where appropriate, by taking interim steps pending a full review.

18.15. Closure orders

18.15.1. In circumstances where a particular geographical area is either experiencing, or it is anticipated that it will experience, disorder the police have the power to close all licensed premises within that area for up to 24 hours. This power is only exercisable through the courts. In addition, the police have the power to close specified premises for a period up to 24 hours without having to apply to the courts where disorder is actually taking place, is likely to break out or is imminent, or a public nuisance is being caused as a result of noise from the premises. The police can also apply to the courts for an extension of the closure beyond the initial 24 hours if necessary. Where specified premises have been closed under these powers, the licensing authority must review the premises licence following the procedure set out in B18.14.

18.16. **Pre-contract enquiries**

18.16.1. In view of the provisions summarised above, the following enquiries should be made of the seller by those proposing to acquire licensed premises:

(a)   to supply a copy of the premises licence;

(b)   to supply a plan of the premises as incorporated in the licence;

(c)   to supply a copy of any application which has been submitted for a variation of the premises licence;

(d)   to establish that no alterations have been made to the premises since the licence has been granted;

(e)   to supply a copy of any provisional statement which has been issued in connection with the property;

(f)   to obtain confirmation that the designated premises supervisor (as specified in the licence) remains on the premises;

(g)   to provide details of all personal licensees currently working on the premises;

(h)   to confirm that no closure orders or applications for closure orders have been made in relation to the premises;

(i)   to ascertain the outcome of any reviews by the licensing authority in relation to the premises licence, or whether any review is pending;

(j)   to confirm any current capacity limit on the premises;

(k)   to specify the number of temporary event notices held at the premises (including their duration) in the current year and to provide copies of any notifications which have been given on future temporary events;

(l)   to provide a copy of the receipt for the current annual fee;

(m)   to confirm the rateable value of the premises;

(n)   to obtain confirmation that the licence holders have complied with the terms of their licence and any mandatory conditions which apply to the premises; and

(o)   to require copies of any correspondence between either responsible authorities or interested parties that might indicate the possibility of an application to review the licence.

18.17. **Register of interest**

18.17.1. Provision is made for freeholders, licence holders, occupiers and others with prescribed interests in premises situated in a licensing authority's area to register their interest with the licensing authority. On payment of a fee they are then entitled to be notified of any changes made in the licensing register in the following 12 months.

18.18. **Food premises licensing/approval**

Introduction

18.18.1. New EU food hygiene legislation which came into force in the UK in January 2006 introduced a less prescriptive and more risk-based regime based on the application of hazard analysis and critical control points (HACCP) principles. This legislation affects all food businesses including manufacturers, processors, distributors, retailers, caterers and primary producers, and requires food premises to be either registered or approved.

18.18.2. The EU Hygiene Regulations are directly applicable in the UK and therefore do not need to be implemented by national legislation. However, UK legislation (Food Hygiene Regulations (England) 2006 (SI 2006/14), which came into force on 11 January 2006) was required to give effect to the EU regulations by introducing legislation to cover offences, penalties, enforcement, revocations of existing legislation and to enact national measures required or provided for in the EU regulations.

18.18.3. A 'food business' is defined as any undertaking whether for profit or not and whether public or private, carrying out any stage of production, processing and distribution of food. This includes businesses involved in primary production in many cases for the first time.

18.18.4. A 'food business operator' is the natural or legal person(s) responsible for ensuring that the requirements of food law are met within the food business under their control.

18.18.5. The Hygiene Regulations do not apply to all food activities and consequently the following are exempt from registration/approval:

    (a) primary production for domestic use;

    (b) the domestic preparation, handling or storage of food for private domestic consumption;

    (c) the direct supply, by the producer, of small quantities of primary products to the final consumer or to local retail establishments directly supplying the final consumer;

    (d) collection centres and tanneries which fall within the definition of food business only because they handle raw material for the production of gelatine or collagen.

18.18.6. The rules that apply to a food business will depend on the type of food handled or sold. The requirements are therefore different depending on which of the following categories applies to the business:

(a) restaurants, caterers and businesses selling food to the final consumer;

(b) businesses (other than restaurants, caterers and businesses selling food to the final consumer) manufacturing food not of animal origin;

(c) businesses (other than restaurants, caterers and businesses selling food to the final consumer) making or handling foods of animal origin.

Restaurants, caterers, businesses selling food to the final consumer and other food businesses processing or handling foods of non-animal origin

18.18.7. Restaurants, caterers and other businesses selling food to the final consumer must register their food businesses with their local authority. (Where food is sold to the final consumer there is no distinction made between food of animal origin and that which is not of animal origin.)

18.18.8. Other food businesses processing or handling foods of non-animal origin also require registration. The registration requirements are the same as for restaurants, caterers, etc., selling to the final consumer but they are classified separately because other requirements under the EU food hygiene legislation are slightly different.

18.18.9. If the food business establishment is located in more than one local authority area, it must be registered with each authority separately. Moveable establishments such as burger vans and ice cream vans should be registered by the food business operator with the local authority in whose area the vehicle is normally kept. Vehicles and stalls used to transport, prepare or sell food, should register with the local authority where the stocks of food are normally kept.

18.18.10. Registrations are to be made on a standard form and must provide full details of all the activities undertaken. These forms are available from the relevant local authority and are usually available online.

18.18.11. New businesses need to submit their registration forms at least 28 days before food operations commence. Once establishments are registered, the food business operator must ensure that the local authority has up-to-date information on the establishments by notifying it of any subsequent changes such as change of food business operator or change to the food operations undertaken. Such notifications should be made in writing as soon as possible and in any event no later than 28 days after the change occurred.

18.18.12. As well as the registration requirements, food business operators must also comply with general hygiene requirements set out in EU Regulation 852/2004 and establish, implement and maintain food safety management procedures based on HACCP principles.

Other businesses processing or handling foods of animal origin

18.18.13. Foods of animal origin include fresh meat (including game meat), minced meat, meat products, meat preparations, shellfish, fish and fishery products, milk and dairy products, eggs and egg products, rendered animal products and miscellaneous products including frogs' legs and snails.

18.18.14. Food businesses that handle food of animal origin (with some exceptions for wild game meat) must be approved by the competent authority (either the Food Standards Agency or local food authorities). If a food business requires approval it does not require registration as well. Approval replaces both previous approvals and licences.

18.18.15. Food businesses falling into this category include catering and retail butchers supplying to the catering trade and/or other establishments (unless the supply is on a marginal, localised and restricted basis), slaughterhouses, cutting plants, game handling establishments, meat processing facilities, and retail and wholesale cold stores. Premises which make food containing both products of plant origin and processed products of animal origin do not require approval but do need to be registered.

18.18.16. As well as approval of establishments, food business operators must also comply with general hygiene requirements set out in the Regulations and establish, implement and maintain food safety management procedures based on HACCP principles. In addition products of animal origin have to bear an identification mark.

18.18.17. The above requirements apply to these food businesses irrespective of the throughput of the premises.

Butchers' shops

18.18.18. Butchers' shops are subject to the EU hygiene regulations and are required to register with the local authority in the same way as other food businesses selling food to the final consumer.

Register

18.18.19. The local authority is required to keep a list of food business establishments registered with it. This list is available for inspection by the general public at all reasonable times. The list contains the following information:

(a) name of food business operator;

(b)   name of food business;

(c)   address of food business establishment;

(d)   particulars and nature of the food business.

B19. Mortgage offers

19.1.	**Acceptance of offer**	19.5.	**Consumer Credit Act 1974**
19.2.	**Conditions attached to offer**	19.6.	**Discharge of existing**
19.3	**Islamic mortgages**		**mortgage**
19.4.	**Duty of confidentiality**		

19.1. Acceptance of offer

19.1.1. Where the client is purchasing a property with the aid of mortgage finance, the solicitor must ensure that the client has received and (where necessary) accepted a satisfactory offer of a mortgage before advising the client to exchange contracts. The mortgage offer, even if formally accepted, may be subject to a condition allowing the lender to withdraw the offer even after exchange.

19.1.2. Mortgages are regulated by the Financial Services Authority (FSA) under Financial Services and Markets Act 2000. Advice given to the client about the terms of a mortgage offer and/or arranging a regulated mortgage may be regulated activity within the terms of the Act (see A4). Unless a regulated mortgage is arranged by a person who is authorised under the Act or with a (properly authorised) financial institution, it will be unenforceable without the leave of the court (see A4.3).

19.1.3. Giving generic advice regarding different types of mortgage and their suitability for the client is not within the definition of a regulated activity. However, providing specific advice about different providers and mortgage products is a regulated activity (see A4.2.4). Provided the solicitor follows the Scope Rules and Conduct of Business Rules issued by the Law Society, the advice given will fall within the 'exempt regulated activities' provision of Part XX Financial Services and Markets Act 2000 (see A4.2.7).

19.1.4. Financial Services and Markets Act 2000 (Regulated Activities) (Amendment) (No.2) Order 2006 (SI 2006/2383) extends the FSA remit to 'home reversion plans' (where the home owner sells all or part of the home in exchange for a lump sum or income and continues to live in the house rent-free) and to *Ijara* and Diminishing *Musharaka* products (a rental-purchase arrangement compatible with Sharia law – see B19.3).

19.2. Conditions attached to offer

19.2.1. Before acceptance of the offer or committing his client to the purchase, the solicitor should ensure that the client understands the conditions attached to the mortgage offer and the terms of the mortgage and will be able to comply with them. Conditions may be general, e.g. a condition that the property must not be let without the lender's consent, or special, having application to this offer only, e.g. a condition that the buyer obtains an endowment policy as security for the mortgage. The solicitor should check the offer to see whether this is the case and whether or not the lender requires a formal acceptance of the offer.

19.2.2. If the conditions attached to the mortgage offer are not wholly acceptable to the client, e.g. the offer requires the client to take out a new endowment policy when the client would be better advised to extend and re-assign an existing policy, an attempt should be made to renegotiate the terms with the lender. Such a term may be invalid under Part IV Courts and Legal Services Act 1990. In extreme cases an alternative source of finance may need to be investigated.

19.2.3. If the mortgage is being entered into under an equity release scheme, the client may require advice as to the scheme's suitability for the client's particular needs from a specialist financial adviser. These schemes are designed to provide the borrower with a regular income or lump sum secured against property. The loan will be repaid when the property is sold on the borrower's death. They are not generally suitable for a borrower who intends to move house again during his lifetime.

19.2.4. In this situation, where the buyer's solicitor has also been instructed to act for the lender, a conflict exists between the interests of the buyer client and the lender client. Unless such conflict can be resolved to the satisfaction of both clients, the solicitor cannot continue to act for either, unless with the consent of one client he is permitted to continue to act for the other. The solicitor's duty of confidentiality towards his client may prevent him from continuing to act for either client in this situation.

19.2.5. If it comes to the notice of the solicitor that the client will be in breach of the terms of the mortgage offer, e.g. where the purchase price for the property has been misrepresented to the lender, the lender must be informed of the problem (see A11). The duty to inform the lender exists throughout the transaction, not just at the time when the offer is being considered. Failure to inform the lender of circumstances in which it appears that the buyer client is attempting to perpetrate a fraud on the lender may lead to the criminal prosecution of the solicitor and to disciplinary proceedings being taken against him. It may also invalidate the solicitor's indemnity insurance if the solicitor has acted dishonestly.[1] This gives rise to a conflict of interests between the buyer client and the lender client since the lender may, in the light of the information received, choose to adjust the terms of the mortgage offer to the detriment of the buyer client. Attention is drawn to the Law Society's Mortgage Fraud Practice Note (see Appendix II.4).

1. See *Shultari* v. *Solicitors Indemnity Fund Ltd* [2004] All ER (D) 327.

19.3 Islamic mortgages

19.3.1. There are two basic Sharia compliant schemes for providing finance to assist in the purchase of property. The *Murabaha* involves a bank purchasing the property on behalf of the buyer and then reselling it to the buyer at a higher price. The buyer pays for the property by instalments. The repayment term is usually short (around 15 years). *Murabaha* arrangements satisfy the requirements of a regulated mortgage and are therefore regulated by the FSA.

19.3.2. For buyers who require greater flexibility the *Ijara* and Diminishing *Musharaka* schemes permit a bank to buy the property and then to lease it to the buyer. The bank agrees to transfer the property to the buyer at the end of the term of the lease. Both of these schemes came under the FSA regulation on 6 April 2007 when Financial Services and Markets Act 2000 (Regulated Activities) (Amendment) (No.2) Order (SI 2006/2383) came into effect.

19.3.3. Rule 3 Solicitors' Code of Conduct 2007 (conflict of interest) provides that a solicitor may act for both the borrower and the lender in a conveyancing transaction where the transaction is a standard mortgage and no conflict of interest arises (see Rule 3.17). If the mortgage is an individual mortgage, in that material terms of the mortgage have been negotiated separately between the lender and the borrower, the parties must be separately represented (see Rule 3.16(2)(b)). With *Ijara* and Diminishing *Musharaka* schemes some of the terms of the mortgage may be negotiated between the parties which will bring the mortgage within the definition of an individual mortgage. In addition, as both of these schemes operate on the basis that the lender sells the property to the buyer over a period of time, a solicitor acting for both parties may be in breach of Rule 3.07.

19.3.4. It is a fundamental principle of common law, reflected by Rule 3 Solicitors' Code of Conduct 2007, that a solicitor cannot act for both parties where there is a conflict of interests. For so long as, and to the extent that, any property finance product (including Sharia compliant products) gives rise to a conflict of interests, Rule 3 will apply to prevent a solicitor from acting for both parties.

19.3.5. Buyers using Islamic mortgages do not incur multiple payments of SDLT. Individual buyers were exempted from double taxation in 2005 by virtue of Finance Act 2003, s.71A (as amended). Purchases by companies and partnerships were given the same exemption under Finance Act 2006, s.168 which came into effect on 20 July 2006, subject to changes introduced with effect from 12 March 2008 designed to prevent use of the exemption for pure SDLT avoidance purposes.

19.3.6. The Right to Buy scheme introduced by the Housing Act 1980 is incompatible with the use of Islamic mortgages as it requires ownership of the property to pass directly from the seller to the buyer.

19.3.7. See Land Registry Practice Guide 69 for its registration requirements.

19.4. Duty of confidentiality

19.4.1. In any of the above circumstances where a conflict of interests exists between the buyer client and the lender client the solicitor, acting in his capacity of adviser to the buyer, may only disclose the nature of the conflict to the lender with the consent of the buyer client. Disclosure of information without the buyer client's consent will be a breach of the solicitor's duty of confidentiality (see also A11.4).

19.5. Consumer Credit Act 1974

19.5.1. Consumer Credit Act 1974, s.58 may be applicable if the mortgage is:

(a) to be granted to an individual or partnership by a non-exempt lender; and

(b) is not a loan for the purchase of land (see H3.4).

19.5.2. Consumer Credit Act 1974 does not generally apply to loans granted by most major banks, building societies and insurance companies.[1]

19.5.3. The requirements of section 58 will thus not normally be relevant in circumstances where the buyer client is purchasing land with the assistance of a first mortgage from an institutional lender. Where, however, the client already owns the land in question and is refinancing or taking out a second or subsequent mortgage, the provisions of section 58 should be borne in mind, particularly where the solicitor is acting also for the lender.

19.5.4. Where section 58 applies, it provides that the borrower must be given a 'cooling-off' period (normally of 14 days) after the mortgage documentation has been sent to him by the lender. The purpose of this period is to allow the borrower to reflect on and to take independent advice on the terms of the loan without being subjected to pressure from the lender or anyone acting on behalf of the lender. During the 'cooling-off' period neither the lender nor anyone acting on his behalf (which includes the solicitor acting for the lender) may make contact with the borrower, whether by letter, telephone or any other means of communication. During this time the solicitor may speak or write to his borrower client if the client approaches him, but client contact should not be initiated by the solicitor whilst the consideration period is running. Failure to comply with this provision will render the mortgage unenforceable except with leave of the court, which will not automatically be granted. Thus a solicitor who is acting for a lender in circumstances where section 58 applies must establish precisely when the consideration period begins to run and must not prejudice the enforceability of the loan by voluntarily contacting his client during this period.

1. See Consumer Credit (Exempt Agreements) Order 2007 (SI 2007/1168) for the exemption of consumer credit agreements where the debtor is of a high net worth.

19.6. Discharge of existing mortgage

19.6.1. It is usually a term of a mortgage offer for a first mortgage over property that any existing mortgage which the client has should be discharged on or before completion of the new loan. The solicitor must ensure the buyer client is aware of and can comply with this condition.[1]

19.6.2.   Some lenders charge interest on an existing loan until the end of the calendar month notwithstanding that the mortgage is repaid earlier. Since this extra amount of interest can add up to a considerable sum, the solicitor should enquire of the lender whether such interest will be charged on the discharge of the existing mortgage and advise his client accordingly.

1. See paragraph 5.8 of the CML Lenders' Handbook (**www.cml.org.uk**) and paragraph D.5 of the BSA Mortgage Instructions (**www.bsa.org.uk**).

B20. Auctions

20.1. Acting for the seller

20.1.1. Where property is to be sold by auction the contract generally consists of particulars, describing the land to be sold, conditions stating the terms of the sale, and a memorandum of the sale which will be signed by or on behalf of the buyer at the auction itself.

20.1.2. The special conditions of the contract are normally prepared by the seller's solicitor in conjunction with the auctioneer who will prepare the particulars of sale. The contract will frequently incorporate the Standard Conditions of Sale although many auctioneers have their own general conditions of sale and some have adopted the Common Auction Conditions (RICS, third edition, 2009).

20.2. Preparing the contract

20.2.1. In addition to the usual contractual clauses particular attention should be paid to the matters listed below. Most of these matters are normally dealt with either in the auctioneers' general conditions, the Common Auction Conditions, the Standard Conditions of Sale or by the Standard Commercial Property Conditions but it is advisable to check their relevance to the particular property concerned and to ensure that any necessary amendments or additions to the Standard Conditions are included in the special conditions of the contract. Some, but not all, of the matters listed below are included in the Common Auction Conditions, Standard Condition 2.3 and in Standard Commercial Property Condition 2.3.

Reserve price

20.2.2. By Sale of Land by Auction Act 1867, s.5 the contract must state whether or not the property is subject to a reserve price. Unless a reserve is placed on the property the auctioneer will be bound to sell to the highest bidder.

Right to bid

20.2.3. Where the property is subject to a reserve price the seller may, under Sale of Land by Auction Act 1867, reserve the right to bid at the auction. This right when reserved by special condition in the contract may be exercised by the seller or his agent.

The auctioneer's control over the bidding

20.2.4. In order to avoid uncertainty the contract should make it clear whether the auctioneer has the right to refuse a bid; or to fix the amount of bids; and should contain provisions whereby the auctioneer may settle any dispute which arises over the bidding.

Payment of deposit

20.2.5. The contract should provide for the amount of the deposit to be paid, the time when it is to be paid, and the methods of payment which are acceptable. It is usual at an auction to provide for a full 10% deposit to be paid. At common law the deposit must be tendered in cash.[1] Standard Condition 2.2.1 and Standard Commercial Property Condition 2.2 provide for a 10% deposit to be payable but do not limit the methods of payment (Standard Condition 2.2.4 does not apply to auction contracts); therefore unless this condition is amended the seller would have to accept payment by the buyer's own cheque with the attendant risks of that cheque not being honoured on presentation. Under the Common Auction Conditions the deposit must be paid to the auctioneer by cheque or banker's draft drawn on an approved bank. It will be held as stakeholder unless a special condition provides otherwise (Common Auction Condition G2.2).

Seller's right to withdraw from auction

20.2.6. In the absence of a special condition it is uncertain whether the seller is entitled to withdraw the property from auction once bidding has commenced unless the sale is subject to a reserve price. Under the Common Auction Conditions, the auctioneer may, without explanation, refuse to accept a bid.

Retraction of bids by buyer

20.2.7. It is common to include a condition precluding the retraction of a bid once made. Such a condition is probably unenforceable at common law under the general principles of offer and acceptance. A bid made at auction is an offer, and the offeror (buyer) is free to withdraw his offer at any time until acceptance by the auctioneer. Acceptance takes place with the fall of the hammer. It should be noted that auction contracts are excluded from the provisions of Law of Property (Miscellaneous Provisions) Act 1989, s.2 (requiring a contract for the sale of land to be in writing); an auction contract will therefore be binding and enforceable even if oral and no memorandum is signed.

Division of property into lots

20.2.8. If required, an express right to divide the property into separate lots should be included in the contract.

Buyer's right to rescind

20.2.9. Where the buyer has not been given the opportunity to make searches or to inspect copies of searches made by the seller prior to the auction, it may be felt appropriate to include a provision which allows the buyer to rescind within a certain time if the results of his searches are not satisfactory. The inclusion of such a condition will introduce an element of uncertainty into the contract, which is not primarily in the interests of the seller. Any such condition must be carefully drafted to ensure that it will not render the contract void for uncertainty and will not allow the buyer to escape from the contract except in precisely worded given circumstances. Under Common Auction Condition G4.2, where no documents were made available before the auction, evidence of title must be provided within five business days of the contract. The buyer then has seven business days to raise requisitions. If the title is not satisfactory the buyer can withdraw from the contract. Condition G8 deals with the consequences of rescission.

Tenancies

20.2.10. The seller's duty of disclosure requires that accurate details of all tenancies to which the property is subject must be revealed in the contract.

Inspection of title deeds and searches

20.2.11. It is common to include a clause in the auction particulars which entitles any prospective buyer to inspect the title deeds and any searches which have been made by the seller. The clause should provide for a time and place for the inspection.

1. *Johnston* v. *Boyes* (1898) 14 TLR 475.

20.3. **Other preparatory steps by the seller**

20.3.1. In addition to the preparation of the contract the seller's solicitor should, before the auction, undertake the preparatory steps in B20.3.2–20.3.4.

Searches

20.3.2. A buyer will frequently not have sufficient time before the auction in which to make the usual searches and enquiries. In order to avoid having to include a clause in the contract entitling the buyer to rescind if the results of searches are not satisfactory, it is preferable for the seller to undertake such searches himself and to make them available for inspection by prospective buyers both before the auction and at the sale itself. A local authority search and enquiries may be requisitioned by the seller's solicitor, as well as any other searches which are relevant to the particular transaction. The seller's solicitor should also prepare and make available answers to standard enquiries before contract.

Title

20.3.3. As with the preparation of any draft contract, the seller's solicitor should investigate his client's title prior to drafting the contract so that any imperfections may either be disclosed in the contract or put right before the auction takes place. Particular care is needed to ensure that full details of any existing tenancies are obtained.

Inspection of deeds

20.3.4. It is helpful to the buyer if the seller can allow a prospective buyer an opportunity to inspect the title deeds and search results at the seller's solicitor's office or other named place at a convenient time prior to the auction. The deeds and search results should also be available for inspection at the auction itself.

20.4. Attending the auction

20.4.1. The seller's solicitor should attend the auction in order to make the title deeds and search results available for inspection to prospective buyers and to answer any queries which may arise.

20.5. Memorandum of sale

20.5.1. The memorandum of sale is usually annexed to the printed auction particulars and conditions. It is common to include a condition that the buyer will sign the memorandum immediately after the sale. The auctioneer has implied authority to sign on behalf of both seller and buyer. An auctioneer's clerk has no such implied authority but may be expressly authorised to sign for one or both of the parties. As far as the buyer is concerned, the auctioneer's authority is limited to 'the time of the sale' which expression has no legal definition but must be taken to mean either at the sale itself or within a short time afterwards. In *Chaney* v. *Maclow*[1] the auctioneer's signature, effected at the auctioneer's own offices some two hours after the sale, was held to bind the buyer; *cf. Bell* v. *Balls*[2] where a signature made one week after the sale was not effective to bind the buyer. If the buyer refuses to sign and the auctioneer will not sign as the buyer's agent the seller cannot force the buyer to sign, because an oral agreement to put a contract into writing and to sign it cannot be enforced by specific performance, but it seems that damages may be recovered for breach of such a condition.[3] It should be noted that auction contracts are excluded from the provisions of Law of Property (Miscellaneous Provisions) Act 1989, s.2 (requiring a contract for the sale of land to be in writing); an auction contract will therefore be binding and enforceable even if oral and no memorandum is signed.

20.5.2. Under the Common Auction Conditions, before leaving the auction the buyer must sign the sale memorandum and pay the deposit. If he fails to do so, the auctioneer may either sign the memorandum on the buyer's behalf or offer the property for sale again.

1. [1929] 1 Ch 461.
2. [1897] 1 Ch 663.
3. See *Wood* v. *Midgely* (1854) 5 De GM & G 41.

20.6. Acting for the buyer

Searches

20.6.1. In frequent circumstances the buyer may not instruct his solicitor in sufficient time to permit the usual searches and enquiries to be undertaken. In these circumstances the buyer's solicitor should at least attempt to make enquiries of the local authority in the usual way. If there is insufficient time to do this, the buyer's solicitor should make enquiries of the local authority in person or through an agent, unless the results of these enquiries are otherwise available from the seller's solicitor or the auctioneer.

20.7. Survey

20.7.1. Where time permits the buyer should be advised to have the property surveyed prior to the auction.

20.8. Contract and title

20.8.1. A copy of the auction particulars, containing the contract terms, should be obtained and scrutinised prior to the auction. Where searches have not been made by the buyer it should be ascertained whether the contract contains a provision allowing the buyer to rescind if the results of searches undertaken after the auction are adverse. If no such provision is included, the buyer should be advised of the consequences of entering a contract without having made searches and enquiries.

20.8.2. The seller's solicitor will often allow the buyer the opportunity to inspect the title deeds (and sometimes also searches which he has undertaken) before the auction. The buyer's solicitor should inspect the deeds and make such further enquiries as are relevant to the property at the earliest possible opportunity. The buyer may take the benefit of searches requisitioned by the seller, but reliance on such searches is inadvisable if the search results are more than two months old. If inspection of the deeds is not possible prior to the auction the buyer's solicitor should attend the auction and make such inspection before the bidding commences.

20.8.3. The terms of an auction contract are often less favourable to the buyer than would be the case in a sale by private treaty. Auction contract terms are generally non-negotiable as far as the buyer is concerned, and therefore the contract terms need to be carefully scrutinised before the auction and the buyer advised about the consequences of any adverse terms. Occasionally, the special conditions of the contract will be altered by an oral statement made at the time of the auction itself and the buyer should be advised to listen carefully and note the effect of any such amendments. Examples of terms which might be onerous to the buyer include the following:

(a) terms precluding the buyer's right to raise enquiries or requisitions after the auction;

(b) restrictions on sub-sales by the buyer;

(c) obligations on the buyer to pay the arrears of rent or service charge on a leasehold property;

(d) terms requiring the buyer to reimburse the seller for search fees and/or the cost of supplying an engrossment of the transfer deed;

(e) on the sale of a freehold reversion of a block of flats, terms excluding any warranty by the seller that the provisions of Landlord and Tenant Act 1987 have been complied with. See K9.

20.8.4. Any information supplied by the seller to the potential buyers prior to the auction must be accurate. Despite the terms of the contract, inaccuracies in any documents provided by the seller may lead to an action in misrepresentation.[1]

1. *Pankhania* v. *Hackney London Borough Council* [2002] All ER (D) 22.

20.9. Finance

20.9.1. The buyer should be warned of the possibility of abortive expenditure if his bid is not successful. As the contract to purchase will come into existence at the time of the auction itself it is essential that the buyer's financial arrangements have been finalised prior to the auction. Arrangements must be made for the deposit to be available at the auction, in cash (banker's draft) if this is required by the auction particulars.

20.10. Insurance

20.10.1. The buyer should also make arrangements for the property to be placed on insurance cover from the moment of the fall of the auctioneer's hammer since, depending on the terms of the contract, risk in the property may pass to him at this time.

20.11. Rights of first refusal

20.11.1. If the property to be sold at auction is affected by Landlord and Tenant Act 1987 which gives the tenants of some leasehold flats the right to purchase the landlord's reversionary interest (see K9) the landlord must comply with section 5B Landlord and Tenant Act 1987 (as amended by Housing Act 1996). This section requires the landlord to serve notice on at least 90% of the qualifying tenants between four and six months before the auction. Failure to comply with the Act is a criminal offence.

20.12. **VAT**

20.12.1. The auctioneer usually holds deposits for the seller as agent. This means that when the hammer goes down, a tax point is created for the transaction. Therefore, if the property is subject to an option to tax, and it is intended to make the purchase under the TOGC rules (so that no VAT is payable) the buyer must exercise their option to tax and notify it to HM Revenue and Customs at the latest on the day of auction, otherwise TOGC procedures cannot be invoked. If the purchase does not take place, the buyer can then revoke the option to tax (see A16).

B21. Plans

21.1. **When is a plan necessary?**   21.4. **Referring to the contract**
21.2. **Preparing the plan**   **plan**
21.3. **Showing features on the**
        plan

21.1.   When is a plan necessary?

21.1.1.   Before drafting the contract the seller's solicitor should consider whether it is
necessary to identify or describe the property by reference to a plan. On receipt
of the draft contract from the seller's solicitor, the buyer's solicitor should also
consider whether a plan is required. The buyer is entitled to demand a plan on
the purchase deed (at the seller's expense) only if the description of the property
through the contract and evidence of title is inadequate without one; therefore
this matter must be addressed at the pre-contract stage. In other circumstances
the buyer might be able to insist on the inclusion of a plan provided that he
offered to prepare and pay for it. The buyer's solicitor may need a plan of the
property in order to make pre-contract searches and enquiries (see B10).

21.1.2.   A plan must be used on a sale of part of land (which includes the grant of leases
of flats) and may be desirable in other cases, e.g. where the boundaries of the
property are not self-evident, but should not be used indiscriminately (see Land
Registry Practice Guide 40). The sale of the whole of a registered title can
usually be described adequately by reference to its title number and, where
applicable, its postal address.

21.1.3.   Land Registration Rules 2003, r.213, provides that a document lodged at the
Land Registry dealing with part of the land in a registered title must have
attached to it a plan identifying clearly the land dealt with. However, if the land
dealt with is identified clearly on the title plan it may instead be described by
reference to that title plan. On building estates, the seller should normally
submit his estate layout plan to the Land Registry for approval before the sale of
the individual plots is commenced. Any changes in the approved estate layout
plan should be notified by the seller to the Land Registry. See Land Registry
Practice Guide 41.

21.1.4.   Whatever type of plan is used it must be of sufficient size and scale to enable the
boundaries and other features of the property to be readily identified.[1] A plan on
a scale of 1:1250 will suffice for most cases, but a larger scale will usually be
required for sales of flats or the division of buildings into separate units.

21.1.5.   Boundaries shown on the majority of plans prepared by the Land Registry are
general boundaries only and do not therefore show the exact line of the
boundaries.[2] The registered proprietor may apply to the Land Registry for the
exact line of the boundary, or any part of the boundary, to be determined. The

application must be made in Form DB.[3] For further guidance as to the evidence to be lodged in support of the application see Land Registry Practice Guide 40.

21.1.6. A plan will be required where the sale is by reference to a fence line or where the boundaries of the property are otherwise unclear. In such a case the parties should be asked to agree the boundaries (if necessary by a site inspection and with the co-operation of the owner of neighbouring property) and the fence line or boundary should be staked out on the site.

21.1.7. For the possible requirement for a new plan on the first registration of a lease following an assignment where the lease has more than seven years to run, see K11.8.7.

1. See *Scarfe* v. *Adams* [1981] 1 All ER 843; *Gillen* v. *Baxter and another* [2003] PLSCS 235; and *Horn and another* v. *Philips and another* (CA, 18 December 2003).
2. Land Registration Act 2002, s.60. See also *Chadwick and others* v. *Abbotswood Properties Ltd and others* [2004] EWHC 1058; *Derbyshire County Council* v. *Fallon* [2007] EWHC 1326 (Ch), [2007] 3 EGLR 44; *Strachey* v. *Ramage* [2008] EWCA Civ 384; and Land Registry Practice Guide 40.
3. Land Registration Rules 2003, r.118 and Land Registration Act 2002, s.60.

21.2. Preparing the plan

21.2.1. Plans used in deeds may emanate from a variety of sources. Generally, any plan that has been professionally prepared and is drawn accurately to a scale referred to below should be satisfactory for use in a deed. Hand drawn sketches should not be used.

21.2.2. There are some occasions where a professionally drawn plan may be unsuitable, e.g. if it was drawn for an architectural or engineering purpose (large scale) or it was drawn for a location plan or road map (small scale). The most commonly acceptable base plans for use in any deed lodged for registration are copies of Ordnance Survey maps (see B21.2.7) or copy estate layout plans approved by the Land Registry (see B21.1.3).

21.2.3. Where a plan is required for any new deed or for any application lodged at the Land Registry it should be prepared having regard to the following guidelines:

- it should be drawn to and show its actual scale;
- show its orientation (for example, a north point);
- use preferred scales of 1/1250–1/500 for urban properties;
- use preferred scales of 1/2500 for rural properties (fields and farms etc);
- not based on a scale of imperial measurement (for example, 16 feet to one inch);
- not reduced in scale (see B21.2.4);
- not marked or referred to as being for identification only;

- not show statements of disclaimer used under Property Misdescriptions Act 1991;

- show sufficient detail to be identified on the Ordnance Survey map;

- show its general location by showing roads, road junctions or other landmarks;

- show the land of the property including any garage or garden ground;

- show buildings in their correct (or intended) position;

- show access drives or pathways if they form part of property boundaries;

- show the land and property clearly (for example by edging, colouring or hatching);

- have edgings of a thickness that do not obscure any other detail;

- show separate parts by suitable plan markings (house, parking space, dustbin space);

- identify different floor levels (where appropriate);

- show intricate boundaries with a larger scale or inset plan;

- show measurements in metric units only, to two decimal places;

- show undefined boundaries accurately and where necessary, by reference to measurements;

- show measurements that correspond, so far as possible, to scaled measurements.

Note: The Land Registry does not consider it necessary to specify in any deed or on any plan the area of the property described.

21.2.4. Where it is clear that the plan contained in a deed or copy deed is a reduced copy of the original, the reduced plan is acceptable provided:

- the original scale has been deleted; or

- the plan has been endorsed with a statement to the effect that it is a reduced copy (or in the case of a copy deed, a reduced copy of the plan to the original deed); or

- the actual scale is stated in place of the original scale.

21.2.5. The Land Registry will reject any dealing of part or lease application in respect of registered land which contain plans that have been reduced from their original scale that still bear the original scale endorsement.

21.2.6. Any plan attached to a certified copy of an original deed must not be a reduced copy of the original. It must be identical to the original in all respects.

21.2.7. Current Ordnance Survey mapping is only available from authorised Ordnance Survey Stockists (see **www.ordnancesurvey.co.uk** for details).

21.2.8. The Land Registry is not authorised to supply Ordnance Survey maps.

21.2.9. Where the value or complexity of the transaction justifies the expense, an architect or surveyor may be instructed to prepare a plan. The client's authority should be obtained prior to incurring such expenditure.

21.2.10. If there is any doubt as to the size or extent of the property an inspection should be carried out and measurements taken.

21.2.11. Guidance on the preparation of plans can be found in Land Registry Practice Guide 40.

21.3. **Showing features on the plan**

21.3.1. The plan must be clearly drawn so that it is capable of being read in isolation from the accompanying contract or purchase deed. The wording of the contract or purchase deed will, however, need to make reference to the plan and its various features and this point should be borne in mind when the plan is drawn, e.g. a right of way may be more easily described in words in the contract if its beginning and end points are marked 'A' and 'B' on the plan in addition to the demarcation of the route.

Points to note

21.3.2. (a) Markings should be clear and precise.

(b) Land to be sold should be outlined or coloured in red.

(c) Retained land (if any) should be outlined or coloured in blue.

(d) Other land referred to should be coloured or hatched in distinct colours other than red or blue. If possible it is best to avoid the use of green on a plan where red has already been used since the most common form of colour blindness relates to the inability to distinguish between these two colours. See Land Registry Practice Guide 40 as to its preferred practice for colouring plans.

(e) The ownership of boundaries should be indicated by 'T' marks with the 'T' on the side of the boundary line within the land which bears responsibility for the maintenance of the boundary. In the absence of a specific request the Land Registry will only show 'T' marks on the title plan if referred to in a covenant or other provision in the transfer.

(f) Rights of way and routes of services should be tinted or marked with broken or dotted lines of a distinct colour, with each end of the route being additionally identified with separate capital letters.

(g)   Where the plan is to scale the scale should be shown.

(h)   If the plan is not to scale, metric measurements should be shown along each boundary. An imperial measurement can be used in addition to the metric measurement provided that the metric measurement is placed first and the imperial measurement is in characters no larger than the metric figures.

(i)   A compass point indicating the direction of north should be shown.

(j)   A key should be included to explain the meaning of the various colours and lines used on the plan.

21.4.   Referring to the contract plan

21.4.1.   The contract (and subsequent purchase deed) may refer to the plan as being 'for identification purposes only', or will describe the land as being 'more particularly delineated on the plan'. These two phrases are mutually exclusive and a combination of the two serves no useful purpose.[1]

'Identification purposes only"

21.4.2.   Where there is a discrepancy between the land shown on the plan and the contract description and the plan has been described as being for identification purposes only, the verbal description of the land will normally prevail over the plan. The court may, however, refer to such a plan to define the boundaries of the property where the verbal description is unclear.[2] In the case of deeds or applications relating to registered land, the Land Registry will not accept a plan which is described or marked as being for identification purposes only.

'More particularly delineated'

21.4.3.   In the event of a discrepancy between the verbal description of the land and the plan, the plan will prevail over the words where the phrase 'more particularly delineated' has been used. This phrase should not be used unless the plan is to scale.

21.4.4.   A plan which is included in the purchase deed but which is not referred to by use of one of the above phrases may be looked at in order to identify the land only if the description of the property as afforded by the purchase deed and other available evidence (e.g. title deeds) is unclear.[3]

Registered land

21.4.5.   A transfer or lease of part of the land in a registered title must have attached to it a plan identifying clearly the land transferred or leased (unless such land is clearly defined on the seller's title plan).[4] A plan described as 'for identification purposes only' does not meet this requirement.

1. *Neilson* v. *Poole* (1969) 20 P&CR 909.
2. See *Wiggington & Milner Ltd* v. *Winster Engineering Ltd* [1978] 3 All ER 436.
3. *Leachman* v. *L & K Richardson Ltd* [1969] 3 All ER 20.
4. Land Registration Rules 2003, r.213.

B22. Fixtures and fittings

22.1. Distinction between fixtures and fittings

Fixtures

22.1.1. Fixtures are generally items which are attached to and form part of the land and which will therefore be included as part of the property on sale of the land unless the seller expressly reserves the right to remove them.

Fittings

22.1.2. Fittings or chattels do not form part of the land and so are not included as part of the property on sale of the land unless the seller expressly agrees to leave them behind.

Practical distinction

22.1.3. The legal distinction between fixtures and fittings as outlined in the above subparagraphs is quite clear. The practical distinction between the two categories is sometimes less obvious. Movable objects which are not attached to the land, e.g. carpets, curtains and free-standing furniture clearly fall within the definition of fittings, but items which are attached to the land such as gas boilers and satellite dishes are not always classified as fixtures. Case law in this area is unclear and there have been reported cases where items such as greenhouses, garden ornaments, plumbed-in kitchen appliances and even freezers have been held to be fixtures, and other cases where the same items have been held to be fittings.[1]

1. See *TSB Bank* v. *Botham* [1996] EGCS 149, and *Elitestone* v. *Morris* [1997] 2 All ER 513.

22.2. Need for certainty in contract

22.2.1. In view of the uncertainty of the status of some items in law it is essential that in appropriate circumstances the contract deals expressly with:

> (a) fixtures which the seller intends to remove on or before completion (including, where appropriate, the tenant's right to remove tenant's trade fixtures);

(b)   compensation for the buyer if the seller causes damage in the course of the removal of fixtures;

(c)   fittings which are to remain at the property;

(d)   any additional price which the buyer is to pay for the fittings;

(e)   the apportionment of the purchase price to exclude from the total the price paid for the fittings;

(f)   deferment of passing of title to fittings until completion because in the absence of such a condition Sale of Goods Act 1979, s.18 will provide that title to the fittings passes to the buyer on exchange;

(g)   a warranty that fittings are free of incumbrances (e.g. subsisting hire-purchase agreements). Although Sale of Goods Act 1979, s.12 will imply such a warranty its express inclusion in the contract prevents the matter from being overlooked by the seller (see Standard Condition 10).

22.2.2.   Disputes over the unexpected removal of fixtures and fittings are common and frequently cost more to resolve than the value of the disputed items. The buyer may require the seller to supply written confirmation that fixtures and fittings which were seen by the buyer on inspection of the property will not be removed from the property and are included in the sale, or in appropriate cases the contract may contain a warranty given by the seller that he has not removed any fixtures from the property since a stated date.

22.2.3.   The estate agent's particulars should be scrutinised to see which items are listed as being included or excluded from the sale, and checked with the client to ensure their accuracy.

22.2.4.   When taking instructions it will be necessary to ascertain from the client which items are to be removed, which items he expects to remain at the property, and whether any price in addition to the price of the land is required for the fittings.

22.2.5.   The Standard Conditions of Sale contract form provides for a list of items being sold to the buyer to be attached to the contract.

22.3.   Apportionment of purchase price

No SDLT on chattels

22.3.1.   The sale of chattels, including chattels which although attached to the land have not become fixtures, does not attract SDLT unless included in the conveyance. The value of chattels which have been included in the purchase price of the land may therefore be subtracted from the total purchase price and ignored in deciding whether reduced rates of SDLT for transactions not exceeding £500,000 can be claimed in the transfer, thereby effecting a reduction in the value of the land and a possible consequent reduction in the rates and/or amount of SDLT payable by the buyer.

22.3.2. This apportionment of the purchase price between the land and the chattels is of most value to the buyer when the value of the land and chattels together is marginally above one of the current SDLT thresholds.

Consequences of over-valuation

22.3.3. Only the fair value of the chattels may be deducted from the purchase price for this purpose (see the guidance from HM Revenue and Customs SDLT Manual in Appendix VI.3). Any over-valuation of the price of the chattels is a fraud on HM Revenue and Customs which may render both the solicitor and his client liable to criminal sanctions. Such conduct would also be conduct unbefitting the solicitor which could result in disciplinary proceedings being brought against him. A further consequence of the over-valuation is that the contract for the sale of the land would be unenforceable by court action since it could be construed by the courts as being a contract to defraud HM Revenue and Customs, such contracts being unenforceable on the grounds of public policy.[1]

22.3.4. If the draft contract does not make provision for the apportionment of the purchase price in a situation where such apportionment would be appropriate, the buyer should, as a matter of courtesy, seek the seller's consent before making the necessary adjustment to the contract.

1. See *Saunders* v. *Edwards* [1987] 2 All ER 651.

22.4. Guidelines

22.4.1. In order to avoid future disputes between the parties the solicitor is advised to check with the client which items are included/excluded from the sale and whether any additional price is payable for the included items. Items which would normally be considered to be fixtures (e.g. fitted wardrobes) should not be charged for in addition to the contract price nor removed from the property unless there is an express reservation of the right to do so in the contract. Items which are normally removable as fittings, e.g. carpets, will not be included in the contract unless the parties agree to their inclusion, possibly at a price additional to the sum payable for the land. Where there are items which may be regarded either as fixtures or fittings depending on the circumstances, e.g. a greenhouse, the solicitor will need to make further enquiries of his client and should consider express mention of these items in the contract for the avoidance of doubt. In residential transactions use of Form TA10 Fittings and Contents is strongly recommended. This form, the contents of which will be agreed by the parties, will be annexed to and form part of the contract.

22.5. Passing of title to chattels

22.5.1. Under Standard Condition 10 both the risk and title in chattels does not pass to the buyer until completion.

22.5.2. Under Standard Commercial Property Condition 12 title in chattels remains with the seller until completion but risk passes on exchange. It may be difficult for a buyer to obtain insurance over chattels which he does not own.

B23. Powers of attorney

23.1.   When is a power needed?

23.1.1.   The solicitor should consider the preparation of a power of attorney for his client if the client:

(a)   is elderly and/or physically infirm; or

(b)   is likely to be unavailable at the time when it will be necessary to obtain his signature to documents.

23.2.   What type of power?

General power under Powers of Attorney Act 1971

23.2.1.   This type of power will give the attorney authority to deal with all of the donor's assets including the sale or purchase of property.

Special power under Powers of Attorney Act 1971

23.2.2.   A special power will give the attorney authority to deal only with the matters specified in the power and thus may be limited to, e.g. the sale of a named property. Except where it is intended to allow the attorney to assume complete control of the donor's affairs this type of power would be more appropriate than a general power in the context of the sale or purchase of land.

Enduring power under Enduring Powers of Attorney Act 1985

23.2.3.   It is no longer possible after 30 September 2007 to create an enduring power of attorney.[1] An enduring power of attorney created before 1 October 2007 will still have effect. This type of power must have been executed in the form prescribed by the regulations in force at the time it was made.[2] An enduring power of attorney is not revoked on the subsequent mental incapacity of the donor. This power could not be used by a trustee to confer power on his sole co-trustee where, e.g. property is jointly owned by husband and wife and one party wishes to appoint the other as his or her attorney during a period of absence abroad.

23.2.4. A power which was executed under a prescribed form which was not current at the time of execution is probably not valid. A new power, which cannot now be an enduring power of attorney, must be executed. Acts done by the attorney under an invalid power can be ratified by execution of a deed of ratification by the donor, provided the donor is still mentally capable.

Security powers

23.2.5. A security power under Powers of Attorney Act 1971, s.4 may be taken, for example, by a lender who has taken an equitable mortgage in order to give him a power to sell the property if the borrower defaults on the mortgage. Such a power is irrevocable and may be incorporated in the mortgage document or given by another transaction deed.

Trusts and powers of attorney

23.2.6. Prior to 1 March 2000, if a trustee (including a co-owner) wished to appoint an attorney to act in connection with a sale or purchase of a property, he could not use a general power of attorney. The donor had to use a specific power of attorney under Trustee Act 1925, s.25. This was limited in duration to 12 months. In addition the power could not be used by a trustee to delegate to his sole co-trustee, in such a case he would have to use an enduring power of attorney under Enduring Powers of Attorney Act 1985.

23.2.7. From 1 March 2000 a trustee who is beneficially entitled under the trust (e.g. a co-owner) can now use a general power (Trustee Delegation Act 1999, s.1). He can also appoint his sole co-trustee to be his attorney. If the trustee is not beneficially entitled under the trust, section 5 of the 1999 Act states that he can use a general power but that it must be limited to a period of 12 months, and the trustee can appoint his sole co-trustee to be his attorney. In either case, if a sole co-trustee has been appointed, the attorney cannot give a valid receipt for capital money and overreaching will not operate. Where there are only two trustees a third party should be appointed to act as attorney. An enduring power of attorney could not be used by a trustee to appoint a sole co-trustee to act as attorney. A lasting power of attorney cannot be used by a trustee to appoint an attorney to act in his place as a trustee.

Lasting powers of attorney

23.2.8. Lasting powers of attorney have replaced enduring powers of attorney. A lasting power must be executed using the forms prescribed by Lasting Powers of Attorney, Enduring Powers of Attorney and Public Guardian Regulations 2007 (SI 2007/1253) as amended by Lasting Powers of Attorney, Enduring Powers of Attorney and Public Guardian (Amendment) Regulations 2009 (SI 2009/1884). There are two prescribed forms of lasting power:

    (a) a property and affairs lasting power of attorney which gives authority in relation to the donor's property and affairs;

(b)   a personal welfare lasting power of attorney which gives authority in relation to the donor's personal welfare.

The Law Society's Lasting Powers of Attorney Practice Note (24 September 2007) assists solicitors in advising clients wishing to draw up a lasting power, as well as solicitors who are acting as an attorney under a lasting power. The Practice Note also covers ongoing arrangements for enduring powers of attorney. Unlike an enduring power of attorney, a lasting power does not take effect until it has been registered with The Office of the Public Guardian (**www.publicguardian.gov.uk**). Notice must first be served by the person applying for registration of the power. When acting under a lasting power, an attorney must apply the principles of section 1 Mental Capacity Act 2005 and any act or decision made must be in the donor's best interests according to the best interests 'checklist' in section 4 of the Act. An attorney must also have regard to the Mental Capacity Act Code of Practice.

23.2.9.   The Office of the Public Guardian will accept a lasting power that differs in an immaterial way in form or expression from the prescribed form.[3] The Court of Protection also has the power to give effect to a lasting power that is not in the prescribed form, if it is satisfied that the donor intended to create a lasting power.[4]

23.2.10.   An attorney who acts under a registered lasting power which turns out to be invalid will not be liable to the donor or a third party, unless the attorney knew that the lasting power was invalid or he was aware of circumstances that would have brought his authority to act under the lasting power to an end.[5]

23.2.11.   If a lasting power has been registered but no lasting power was actually created, a transaction between the attorney and a third party will, in favour of that third party, be valid as if the lasting power had existed, unless at the time of the transaction the third party knew that a lasting power was not created or was aware of circumstances that would have terminated the attorney's authority to act had a lasting power been created.[6] A purchaser who subsequently buys from the third party in good faith and for valuable consideration can rely on the presumption that the transaction between the attorney and the third party will be valid if either the transaction between the attorney and the third party was completed within 12 months of the date on which the lasting power was registered or the third party makes a statutory declaration, either before or within three months of completion of the purchase, that he had no reason to doubt that the attorney had authority to dispose of the property at the time of the transaction.[7]

1.   Mental Capacity Act 2005, Sched.1, para.3(1).
2.   *Ibid.*, para.3(2).
3.   *Ibid.*, para.3(1).
4.   *Ibid.*, para.3(2).
5.   *Ibid.*, s.14(2).
6.   *Ibid.*, s.14(3).
7.   *Ibid.*, s.14(4).

23.3. Who should be the attorney?

23.3.1. The client should be advised of the consequences of giving a power of attorney, i.e. that the attorney will (depending on the terms of the power) have a wide authority and discretion to deal with the client's affairs. Only a person whom the client trusts absolutely should be considered for appointment as attorney. The solicitor may be appointed as attorney provided that no conflict of interests exists between himself and his client(s). The solicitor should advise the client of his charges in relation to so acting. The limitations on the appointment of an attorney in the case of trust property have been noted above.

23.4. When should the appointment be made?

23.4.1. The power of attorney should be drawn up and executed as soon as the decision to appoint an attorney has been made. This is necessary because it is courteous to inform the other party to the transaction at the earliest opportunity that the documents will be signed under a power of attorney.

23.5. The client who already has a power

23.5.1. Where a client comes to the solicitor with an existing power of attorney, the solicitor should examine the power to ascertain its type and validity for the transaction proposed.

23.6. Informing the other party of the appointment

23.6.1. It is courteous to inform the other party to the transaction at the earliest opportunity that the documents will be signed under a power of attorney. A copy of the power should be supplied to the other party as soon as possible so that its validity and suitability for the transaction in progress may be confirmed.

23.6.2. Except in the case of a security power or an enduring or lasting power which has been registered with the Court of Protection, if the power will be more than 12 months old at the date when it is purportedly exercised, the person who buys from the attorney will need to make a statutory declaration within three months of completion stating that he believed the power to be valid and had no knowledge of its revocation at the time of its exercise. See Powers of Attorney Act 1971, s.5.

23.7. Evidence of non-revocation

23.7.1. Except in the case of a security power or an enduring or lasting power which has been registered with the Court of Protection, if the power was more than 12 months old at the date it was purportedly exercised, Powers of Attorney Act 1971 provides that when the person who buys from the attorney comes to sell the property he must provide a statutory declaration to his buyer stating that he (the purchaser from the attorney) had no knowledge of any revocation of the power at the time he bought the property (see Powers of Attorney Act 1971, s.5).

23.7.2.   In the case of registered land, the fact that the registered proprietor bought the property from an attorney will not be apparent from the register. For this reason, Land Registration Rules 2003, r.62 provides that any required evidence of non-revocation should be produced when the buyer from the attorney applies to be registered as proprietor.

23.7.3.   If the Land Registry does call for evidence of non-revocation it will require the buyer from the attorney to provide evidence of non-revocation in Form 2, being either:

- a statutory declaration or statement of truth stating that the buyer from the attorney was not aware of any revocation of the power at the date of the transaction; or

- a certificate signed by the buyer's conveyancer.[1]

23.7.4.   In all cases it is the buyer from the attorney who must provide the declaration or certificate, not the attorney nor the seller's solicitor. It is the knowledge of the person dealing with the attorney which is relevant under Powers of Attorney Act 1971.

23.7.5.   In all cases the Land Registry will require evidence of the power of attorney which should either be:

- Form 1 completed by the buyer's conveyancer; or

- the original power of attorney; or

- a certified copy of the power of attorney.

23.7.6.   For more information as to the evidential and other requirements when the title depends upon a sale by an attorney, see D2.9.26 to D2.9.37, and Land Registry Practice Guide 9.

1.   Form 2 is set out in Schedule 3 Land Registration Rules 2003.

B24. Planning

24.1. Relevance of planning to the transaction

24.1.1. Heavy penalties may ensue from breach of planning legislation; it is therefore important to check at the start of a transaction that any necessary planning requirements have been or will be complied with. It may also be necessary to check whether any restrictive covenants on the property conflict with the present structure(s) and/or use, and if so whether consent to the buildings and/or their current use/or a release or indemnity insurance has been obtained.

24.1.2. The development of land will normally require the grant of planning permission. Development is defined by Town and Country Planning Act 1990 (as amended) as 'the carrying out of building, engineering, mining or other operations in, on, over or under land, or the making of any material change in the use of any buildings or other land'. This definition encompasses the erection of new buildings, the demolition of and alterations and additions to existing buildings, fish farming and in certain circumstances changing the use of a building.

24.1.3. A house which has been in multiple occupation will need planning permission for use as a single dwelling unless it has been occupied by not more than six residents living together as a single household (including a household where care is provided for residents). See Class C3 Town and Country Planning (Use Classes) Order 1987.

24.2. Acting for the seller

24.2.1. Although planning matters do not necessarily fall within the seller's duty of disclosure, the buyer's solicitor will raise various enquiries about planning matters and will be reluctant to proceed with the transaction unless he can be reassured that the buildings and use of the property satisfy current planning regulations. The following matters should therefore be checked either from the documents in the solicitor's possession, from information obtained from the client, or from the local planning authority (usually the district council):

(a)   the date when the property was first built;

(b)   whether any additions, alterations or extensions have been made to the property or within its grounds since the property was first built and, if so, the date of each addition, etc.;

(c)   if the property has been built or any alteration to it has been made within the past four years, either that planning consent was obtained (either expressly or by virtue of General Permitted Development Order) or was not required. Any conditions attached to the planning consent should, if possible, be checked to ensure that they have been complied with. Proceedings to enforce planning restrictions in respect of development which consists of 'building works' must normally be taken within four years of the breach;

(d)   if the property is leasehold, in addition to (c) above, whether any additions, alterations, etc., have been made since the date of the grant of the lease and, if so, whether any restriction on development contained in the lease has been complied with;

(e)   what the property is used for, whether any material change of use to the property has occurred during the past 10 years and, if so, whether the appropriate consent has been obtained. There is a 10-year time limit on the enforcement of breach of planning control through change of use. If no enforcement proceedings are taken within the 10-year period the previously unlawful use becomes an authorised use. The change of use from one use class to another requires consent, as does the change from use as a single dwelling house to use of the premises for multiple occupation or sub-division into separate units;

(f)   where alterations or additions to the property have been made within the past 12 months, whether Building Regulations consent has been obtained and complied with (see B24.7);

(g)   whether the property is a listed building or in a conservation area. Special provisions apply to such buildings and areas and the restrictions on development are more stringent than those applied in other cases. Where a building is listed, separate listed building consent may be required.

24.2.2.   Any irregularity in the planning situation should ideally be corrected by the seller before contracts are exchanged. Realistically this may not always be possible and the seller may have to reveal the irregularity to the buyer who, depending on the nature of the problem, may be prepared to proceed with the transaction subject to a reduction in the price or an indemnity against liability given by the seller in the contract.

24.3.   Acting for the buyer

24.3.1.   The matters itemised in B24.2.1 should be raised as pre-contract enquiries with the seller. Any irregularity revealed by the seller's answers should either be corrected at the seller's expense or, depending on the nature of the breach, an indemnity taken from the seller in the contract. Liability for breach of planning legislation enures with the land; thus any breach which exists on completion will become the responsibility of the buyer.

24.3.2. Instructions should be taken from the buyer in relation to the following matters:

(a) does the buyer's intended use of the property correspond with its present authorised use? If not, will planning permission be required for the buyer's intended use and is it realistic to expect that consent from the local planning authority would be forthcoming?

(b) is it apparent on inspection of the property that new buildings or alterations have been made within the last four years? If so, check with the seller whether planning consent for the new buildings was needed/obtained/complied with;

(c) does the buyer intend to alter the property in any way after completion? If so, will the proposed alterations require planning consent or consent from the person with the benefit of an existing restrictive covenant against development and is it realistic to expect that such consent(s) will be forthcoming?

24.3.3. The answers to the local search and enquiries should be checked carefully to ensure that no breach of planning law is revealed in those answers. Any matters of doubt should be clarified with the local authority and the seller before the matter proceeds to exchange of contracts.

24.3.4. Where the client's instructions reveal that his proposals for the property will require planning permission to be obtained, it should first be ascertained whether or not the client would wish to proceed with his purchase in the event of an application for permission being refused by the local authority. If the client would not wish to pursue his purchase in such circumstances, he should be advised either to delay exchange until planning permission for his proposed development is obtained, or to ask the seller to make the contract conditional on obtaining such consent (see B13). Even where the client is prepared to take the risk of planning permission ultimately being refused, he should be advised about the procedure for making such application (including the costs) and the consequences of developing the land without permission. The register of planning applications maintained by the local authority under Town and Country Planning Act 1990 may be inspected to obtain an insight into the authority's policy for the area, and thus the likelihood of obtaining permission for the proposed development. Generally an authority will not permit development which conflicts with its development plan documents for the area, e.g. industrial development would not be permitted in an area designated for residential use or vice versa.

24.3.5. Even where the client's proposals will not require planning permission, consideration should still be given to the necessity for building regulation consent (for building works of any description) and compliance with or insurance against any restrictive covenants on the property which would prevent the client's intended development.

24.3.6.   If the seller has made additions or alterations to the property, the local authority has the right to reconsider the council tax banding of the property when it changes hands.

24.4.   Matters which do not require specific planning permission

24.4.1.   Certain matters which would otherwise fall within the definition of development (and thus require planning permission) are specifically excluded from that definition by the Act itself or by General Permitted Development Order. A summary of the main cases where permission is not required either by the statute or by regulation is listed below. In any case of doubt, the Act and the various regulations made under it should be checked, and/or advice sought from the planning department of the local authority:

     (a)   maintenance works to buildings, e.g. painting the exterior;

     (b)   internal works which do not materially affect the appearance of the exterior, e.g. sub-dividing a room by the erection of a non-load-bearing partition wall;

     (c)   the use of buildings or land within the curtilage of a dwelling house for any purpose incidental to the use of the dwelling house, e.g. using an existing outhouse as a playroom. The 'curtilage' of a dwelling house is the land immediately surrounding the house and except where the grounds are large will normally encompass the whole of the garden area;

     (d)   change of use within the same use class as specified by Town and Country Planning (Use Classes) Order 1987 (as amended), e.g. changing from use as a newsagent's shop to an ironmonger's shop. Changing a single dwelling house into two or more units is a material change of use which requires planning permission, as is a change from one use class to another, e.g. changing from use as a shop to use as an office;

     (e)   development which falls within Town and Country Planning (General Permitted Development) Order 1995, e.g. erection of fences (subject to a height restriction), some demolition works, development within the curtilage of a dwelling house. This latter provision will permit the building of a small extension to an existing dwelling house without the need for express planning permission but is subject to strict conditions on the extent and siting of the extension; once the size limit for extensions under General Permitted Development Order has been used, all further extensions to the house require express permission. The conditions attached to General Permitted Development Order must be strictly observed, and if they cannot be complied with express permission for the development is needed. The local authority has power to restrict General Permitted Development Order in whole or in part in relation to its area. Before the client proceeds to effect works which ostensibly fall within the Order it should be confirmed that the relevant part of the Order is in force in the area concerned.

24.4.2. Enquiries of the local authority, which will be undertaken in every transaction, contain several questions relating to planning matters. The answers to these questions should be analysed carefully by the buyer's solicitor.

24.4.3. Special rules apply to listed buildings and the provisions outlined above may not apply.

24.5. Enforcement of planning breaches

24.5.1. The time limits for the enforcement of planning breaches are:

- in the case of building operations, four years from the date that the operations were substantially completed;

- in the case of a change of use to a single dwelling house, four years from the date the change of use commenced;

- in the case of any other breach, e.g. unauthorised change of use or failure to comply with a condition attached to planning permission, 10 years from the date of the breach.

24.5.2. On the expiry of the time limit, if no enforcement action has been taken, the operation or use becomes lawful. The commencement of enforcement actions, i.e. the issue of an enforcement notice, prior to the expiry of the time limit, stops time running and will prevent the breach from becoming lawful.

24.6 Planning rules which apply in special cases

24.6.1. If the land is covered by a Special Development Order, or is within an enterprise zone or a simplified planning zone, special rules apply which alter the general law.

24.6.2. In some cases the rules relating to the need for planning permission are relaxed within these special zones, in others parts of General Permitted Development Order may be restricted. The replies to enquiries of the local authority will reveal whether or not the property is affected by any of these special zonings. If so, the provisions of the relevant Order should be checked before advice is given to the client on the need for planning permission.

24.7 **Building Regulations**

24.7.1. Building Regulations compliance is necessary whenever building works are to be undertaken. The need for this is separate from planning consent and is required even where the development falls within the General Permitted Development Order and does not require express planning permission.

24.7.2. The regulations cover various aspects of the structure including its structural stability, fire resistance and means of escape, weather resistance, sound resistance, ventilation, drainage, heating and energy performance, stairways, ramps and guards and facilities for disabled people and the safety of glazing.

24.7.3. Since 1 April 2002 the regulations have applied to the installation of replacement windows and doors. All replacement windows, roof lights, and glazed doors will have to be covered by either a certificate issued by the Local Authority Building Control or by FENSA. The Glass and Glazing Federation has established a self-assessment scheme, FENSA, and FENSA members must carry out the work to the appropriate standard and can then issue a certificate with the local authority within 10 days of the work being completed. These provisions apply to contracts entered into on or after 1 April 2002. The provisions will apply to orders placed before 1 April 2002 if the work was not completed before 1 July 2002. The solicitor needs to check that the appropriate consents are available.

24.7.4. Since 1 January 2005 certain building works which involve electrical installations and amendments to existing electrical installations require Building Regulations consent unless carried out by a person registered under the appropriate self-certification scheme listed in Schedule 2A, Building Regulations 2000 (SI 2000/2531). Since 1 April 2005 this has also applied to the installation of a central heating system or a renewable energy heating system. On 1 April 2009 the self-certification scheme changed from CORGI to the Gas Safe Register. The registered installer will issue a Building Regulations compliance certificate when the work is complete.

24.7.5. Certain buildings do not need Building Regulations consent, for example, certain detached buildings not used for sleeping and some extensions, provided they are under certain size restrictions. In addition the construction of a greenhouse, porch, conservatory (with transparent or translucent roof), covered yard or car port are exempt from Building Regulations control where the floor area of the addition does not exceed 30 square metres.

24.7.6. A person who intends to undertake building works must make an application for consent before starting work. There are two forms of application, the Full Plans Application and the Building Notice method. For a Full Plans application detailed plans are required and full details of the construction must be submitted. The Building Notice differs from the Full Plans Application in that all that is necessary is the completion and submission of a simple form describing the proposed work. With the Building Notice application the Building Control Surveyor will inspect the work on site and will expect any problems to be rectified immediately.

24.7.7. A key element of building control is the inspections conducted by the Building Control Officer. Statutory inspections have to be carried out at specified stages in the construction and the Building Control Officer may also inspect at other stages in the construction.

24.7.8. The local authority issues a Certificate of Compliance when the building work is finished and the final inspection has taken place. This confirms that the work is in accordance with the regulations. In some cases an independent building inspector will carry out the inspections and issue the Certificate of Compliance to the local authority. It is essential that a copy of this certificate is provided to the buyer on the sale of the property.

24.7.9. The time limit for bringing proceedings in a magistrates' court for breach of Building Regulations depends upon the date when the breach was committed. For breaches committed before 6 April 2008 proceedings must be brought within six months of the date when the offence was committed. For breaches committed on or after 6 April 2008 but before 22 September 2008 the time limit depends upon the particular regulation breached. For certain regulations that deal with conservation of fuel and power or the reduction of greenhouse gas emissions[1] the time limit is six months from discovery of the breach provided that the proceedings are brought within two years of the completion of the offending work. For breaches of all other regulations, proceedings must be brought within six months of the date the offence was committed. For breaches of any regulation committed on or after 22 September 2008 proceedings must be brought within six months from discovery of the breach provided that the proceedings are brought within two years of the completion of the offending work.[2]

24.7.10. However, in some circumstances the local authority may be able to enforce the regulations outside the time limits.[3] A buyer should therefore seek confirmation of compliance with the regulations in respect of works completed since the property was built and if this is not available the buyer should consider insurance against the risk of enforcement.[4] Although enforcement action under section 36(1) or (2) Building Act 1984 cannot be taken outside of the 12-month time limit under section 36(4), the Building Control Department may still be able to obtain an injunction under section 36(6).[5] The buyer could ask the seller to obtain a Regularisation Certificate from the Building Control Department at the local authority. The Building Control Officer will inspect the property and provide a list of work required to bring the building up to the correct standard. Depending upon the level of work required the buyer might choose to ask the seller to carry out the work prior to completion, negotiate a reduction in the purchase price to cover the cost of carrying out the work after completion or withdraw from the transaction. The buyer's lender may also need to be informed.

1. Regulation 4 to the extent that the applicable requirements are those contained in Part L of Sched.1; Regulations 4A and 4B; Regulation 6 to the extent that the applicable requirements are those contained in Part L of Sched.1; Regulations 17C and 17D.
2. Building Act 1984, s.35A.
3. Building Act 1984, s.36(1).
4. See Building Act 1984, s.36(6).
5. *Cottingham* v. *Attey Bower & Jones* [2000] PNLR 557.

24.8   Energy performance certificates

24.8.1.   Energy Performance of Buildings (Certificates and Inspections) (England and Wales) Regulations 2007 (SI 2007/991)[1] amend the Building Regulations and place sellers, landlords and builders under an obligation to provide an energy performance certificate (EPC) to prospective buyers and tenants[2] (see A27 for further details).

1. As amended by Energy Performance of Buildings (Certificates and Inspection) (England and Wales) (Amendment) Regulations 2007 (SI 2007/1669); Energy Performance of Buildings (Certificates and Inspections) (England and Wales) (Amendment No.2) Regulations 2007 (SI 2007/3302); Energy Performance of Buildings (Certificates and Inspections) (England and Wales) (Amendment) Regulations 2008 (SI 2008/647); Energy Performance of Buildings (Certificates and Inspections) (England and Wales) (Amendment No.2) Regulations 2008 (SI 2008/2363); Energy Performance of Buildings (Certificates and Inspections) (England and Wales) (Amendment) Regulations 2009 (SI 2009/1900); Energy Performance of Buildings (Certificates and Inspections) (England and Wales) (Amendment) Regulations 2010 (SI 2010/1456).
2. Reg.5.

24.9.   Environmental issues

24.9.1.   Where a planning application is made for 'environmentally sensitive development' as defined in Town and Country Planning (Environmental Impact Assessment) (England and Wales) Regulations 1999 (SI 1999/293) (as amended), the local planning authority may require the applicant to submit an environmental statement with his application. Some local authorities ask for an environmental assessment to be submitted in connection with all applications for major development irrespective of the above Regulations.

24.10.   Sustainability certificate

24.10.1.   The requirement to supply a sustainability certificate to potential buyers of residential property has been suspended as a result of the suspension of the duties under sections 155–159 Housing Act 2004.

B25. Environmental issues

25.1. Introduction

25.1.1. The issue of the contaminated land regime focused most conveyancing practitioners' minds on environmental matters, and the legislation was brought into effect in England on 1 April 2000 and in Wales on 1 July 2001. It applies to all land, whether residential, commercial, industrial or agricultural. It can affect owners, occupiers, developers and lenders. The legislation, which is contained in Part IIA Environmental Protection Act 1990 (EPA 1990) and in regulations and statutory guidance issued under it, is retrospective. See Contaminated Land (England) Regulations 2006 (SI 2006/1380); Contaminated Land (Wales) Regulations 2001 (SI 2001/2197); and DEFRA Circular 01/2006.

25.1.2. This regime has now been supplemented (but not in any sense superseded or replaced) by Environmental Damage Regulations 2009 which contain similar mechanisms for remediating damage caused by certain polluting events and occurring after 1 March 2009. These Regulations are not retrospective and tend to focus on the environmentally damaging activities of large-scale 'operators' of activities which fall to be licensed under the various legislative regimes referred to below.

25.1.3. The Carbon Reduction Commitment Energy Efficiency Scheme (CRC) (effective from April 2010) will also have significant impacts on commercial property transactions. Effectively a carbon-trading system for larger industrial and commercial consumers of electricity, gas and coal, the CRC will require an assessment to be made about whether the property transaction might have the effect of placing the buyer in a participating organisation (or removing the seller from one) or aggregating its portfolio to the extent that it meets the qualifying criteria for the Scheme. This may be even more of a concern in leasehold transactions than freehold and the property industry is promulgating standard contract and lease clauses to address issues of common concern arising from this legislation. This legislation is complex and is the subject of specialist consideration beyond the remit of this section.

25.1.4.   Moreover, in addition to all these new initiatives, it has always been the case that a number of other environmental legislative regimes affect property transactions and practitioners are required to take the potential effects of those into account too, where relevant.

25.1.5.   Solicitors should be aware of the provisions of the environmental legislation and the contents of the Law Society's Contaminated Land Warning Card (see Appendix IV.1). This section includes an outline of the range of potential liabilities and gives further information on the steps recommended in the Warning Card.

25.2.   Environmental risks

Legal liabilities

25.2.1.   A buyer may inherit a number of legal liabilities on purchasing a property. The liability for the remediation of contaminated land is the most acute, but not the only, risk faced by buyers.

25.2.2.   The full implications of environmental law in property transactions are explained in the *Environmental Law Handbook*, 7th edition (Law Society, 2010). Liabilities may emerge under a number of statutes and in a number of ways. Most of the liabilities mentioned below are more relevant to commercial transactions, but some may also be significant in residential cases.

25.2.3.   Issues may emerge under the following legislation and common law principles:

- the nature conservation regime contained in Wildlife and Countryside Act 1981, Parts I and II as amended by Countryside and Rights of Way Act 2000;

- Pollution Prevention and Control Act 1999 and Pollution Prevention and Control (England and Wales) Regulations 2000 (now subsumed in Environmental Permitting Regulations 2010);

- the waste regulatory regime under Environmental Protection Act 1990, Part II (now subsumed in Environmental Permitting Regulations 2010);

- the contaminated land regime under Environmental Protection Act 1990, Part IIA;

- the statutory nuisance regime under Environmental Protection Act 1990, Part III;

- the water pollution legislation in Water Resources Act 1991 (water discharge consenting and abstraction licensing issues now being subsumed in Environmental Permitting Regulations 2010);

- the sewer discharge legislation in Water Industry Act 1991;

- Environmental Damage (Prevention and Remediation) Regulations 2009;

- the common law torts of nuisance and negligence.

The particular issue of contaminated land

25.2.4. Land may become contaminated as a result of past or present industrial use: leakages of liquids from storage tanks, washings from site plant and equipment, spillages from delivery wagons, or wastes and liquids being deposited (deliberately or inadvertently) on site from a potentially contaminative industrial process or other historic land use.

25.2.5. Contamination is not only a result of industrial waste, it may result from such things as leakages of oil from storage tanks for domestic heating systems, or waste oils from car engines, or other polluting matter disposed of on the land from DIY activities.

25.2.6. Details of which sites are determined as contaminated are available from the local authority (or Environment Agency if a special site). However, a negative reply to the local authority enquiries (in CON 29) does not guarantee that the site is uncontaminated. Such an answer may merely mean that the site has not been inspected or that such pollution as does exist is not so serious as to meet the Part IIA definitions. More specific enquiries may need to be made to ascertain the true position regarding pollution on the site.

25.2.7. An offence is committed if those required to do so fail to remediate contaminated land when so instructed (Environmental Protection Act 1990, Part IIA). The liability to remediate land may arise as a result of substances already in the land at completion, which are giving rise to a risk of significant harm to persons or things nearby.

25.2.8. If the original polluter of the land cannot be found, the current owner or occupier may be served with a remediation notice requiring the land to be cleaned up. An offence is committed if he fails to comply, and the authorities can do the necessary works themselves and recover the costs from the person served with the notice.

25.2.9. A further problem is that a buyer can himself be determined as the 'original polluter'. This is because the original polluter is defined as 'any of the persons who [caused or] knowingly permitted the [contaminating substances] to be in, on or under the land'. Allowing something to remain on land if you could remove it amounts to permitting it to be on the land.

25.2.10. Actual knowledge of the contamination, turning a blind eye to an obvious risk of the presence of contamination, or failing to make enquiries for fear of discovering the truth would all amount to having the required knowledge.

25.2.11. Accordingly, if a buyer knew, or ought to have known, or realised, or could have found out, that there was contamination on the site, he may be liable as an original polluter.

25.2.12. There may also be leakages of substances onto the ground after completion in respect of which the buyer client may be deemed to be the 'original polluter' of the land.

25.2.13. Detailed provisions in Part IIA exclude a seller from any further liability for contamination if a reduction in the purchase price was negotiated to take account of particular contamination and remediation, or if a site is sold with full information about its contaminated history. These exclusions are likely to be relevant in most commercial transactions, the effect being that liability for contamination tends to run with the land.

25.2.14. Where there is no original polluter, the liability will fall on the owner or occupier for the time being.

Non-legal risks and liabilities

25.2.15. In addition to the legal risks mentioned above, environmental issues which may concern a buyer might include:

- flooding (increased information on flood risk will become available as a result of Flood Risk Regulations 2009 imposing on flood agencies an obligation to carry out and publish flood risk assessments by December 2011);

- mining and other extractive industry;

- radon gas;

- other health effects;

- invasive weeds and other pests;

- potential resale value.

25.3.   Contaminated land warning card

25.3.1. Following the implementation of Part IIA EPA 1990 the Law Society issued a Warning Card on Contaminated Land (Appendix IV.1). The advice contained in the Warning Card is intended to conform to best practice and not to constitute a professional requirement for solicitors.

25.3.2. The Warning Card requires solicitors, in every conveyancing transaction, to exercise their professional judgement in each case as to whether environmental liability is likely to be an issue.

25.3.3. The Warning Card also contains a series of steps that can be taken by solicitors to conform with best practice in conveyancing. Steps 1 and 2 should be routinely followed by solicitors acting in all types of conveyancing cases.

B

25.3.4. Steps 3 and 4 are recommended in all commercial conveyancing cases, and in those residential cases where solicitors consider that contamination is likely to be a risk. Steps 5 and 6 are recommended in commercial cases where steps 3 and 4 have revealed a risk of contamination. Steps 7 and 8 are for consideration where there are unresolved problems in any conveyancing case.

25.4. Step 1 – advising the client

25.4.1. In every conveyancing case solicitors should advise the client of:

- the possibility of acquiring an interest in contaminated land;
- the potential liabilities associated with contaminated land;
- the range of other legal and non-legal risks outlined above;
- the steps that can be taken to assess the risks.

25.4.2. Solicitors may consider a standard paragraph added to the client care letter, a leaflet which can be sent at the start of the matter, or a meeting to discuss the issues.

25.4.3. If the client does not wish the solicitor to undertake any environmental enquiries, solicitors should confirm the initial advice (and the fact that no investigations have been requested or made) to the client and any lender. Whatever the wishes of the borrower, some lenders may require such investigation.

25.5. Step 2 – specific enquiries of the seller

25.5.1. The extent and type of enquiries will depend on whether the land and property to be transferred is for domestic residential or commercial use.

25.5.2. The following are examples of some of the enquiries that may be made of the seller in domestic residential transactions:

- whether the seller is aware of any potentially contaminative use of the site or previous accidents, incidents or spillages;
- whether the site has been used for landfill or waste disposal purposes;
- details of previous owners or occupiers and activities carried out by them;
- whether there have been any disputes, or circumstances which may give rise to any disputes with neighbours or regulatory bodies regarding the state of the land;
- what (if any) planning consents have been issued in respect of the site,

what conditions they contained regarding contamination and its remediation, and details of any works carried out to comply with the
conditions.

25.5.3.   It may be possible to check any such information whenever acting for a buyer of
new property from a developer who will offer facilities for inspection of the
documentation. There is an incentive in Part IIA Environmental Protection Act
1990 for the developer to give full and clear information to a buyer to enable
him reasonably to assess the risk of contamination on the site at purchase.

25.5.4.   The Commercial Property Standard Enquiries (CPSE v.2.9) include enquiries
to make of the seller with regard to environmental issues. In general, the
enquiries to make of a seller in commercial transactions include:

- the need for, and compliance with, all consents, licences, authorisations
  and permits in relation to any activities or processes conducted on the
  site, etc.;

- any contact or disputes with the regulatory bodies;

- details of any pollution incidents or accidents affecting the site and
  copies of any reports, correspondence, court orders, notices (including
  in particular remediation, charging or works notices) or recommendations relating to such accidents or incidents and details of any remedial
  work carried out including certificates of satisfactory completion;

- details of any environmental impairment liability insurance or any
  application therefor (whether or not the proposal was accepted by the
  insurers);

- disclosure of any consultants' or other report on the environmental risk
  assessment of the property or the seller's business;

- whether the seller is aware of any potentially contaminative current or
  previous use of the site or neighbouring sites;

- whether the site or any adjoining sites have been used for landfill or
  waste disposal;

- details of previous owners or occupiers and activities carried on by
  them;

- what (if any) planning consents have been issued in respect of the site,
  what conditions they contained regarding contamination and its remediation, and details of any works carried out to comply with the
  conditions.

25.5.5.   The Law Society's Property Information Form 2nd edition (TA6) also makes
enquiries of the seller in relation to environmental matters such as flooding,
radon and cesspools.

25.5.6.   There are two possible responses to these enquiries:

(a) *Replies are forthcoming.* The replies may need specialist interpretation by a surveyor or environmental consultant. Further, more detailed investigation may be needed if there are specific areas of concern.

(b) *The seller resists.* If the seller issues the blanket reply 'not so far as the seller is aware, please rely on own investigations and surveys', the buyer client must consider whether to undertake his own alternative investigations. The seller must also be aware that in giving such a response he may be impliedly warranting that he has himself already undertaken enquiries.

25.6. Step 3 – enquiries of statutory and regulatory bodies

25.6.1. The Warning Card states that Step 3 should be taken in 'all commercial cases, and if contamination is likely to be a risk in residential cases (e.g. redevelopment of brown field land)'.

25.6.2. Solicitors should make full searches of any public registers regarding the site and adjacent land. The main bodies to contact (see Appendix IX.2 for details) are:

- Natural England (and Scottish and Welsh equivalents) (nature conservation designations);

- Environment Agency (licences, registers and prosecutions);

- local authority (registers and information on contaminated land and any relevant planning consents and hazardous substance information);

- Health and Safety Executive (incidents and accidents);

- sewerage undertakers (consents and registers);

- British Coal (mining activities and abandoned mine leakage issues).

25.6.3. Enquiries of these bodies should be made regarding any:

- information held by them about the site, any investigations or inspections made of it or adjacent land, details of any accidents, incidents or complaints and an indication of whether there is any intention to serve any notices in respect of the land;

- accidents, incidents and complaints by regulators or others relating to adjacent land.

25.6.4. Forms CON 29R Enquiries of Local Authority (2007) and CON 29O Optional Enquiries of Local Authority (2007) (see Appendix III.1 and III.2) request information regarding notifications or entries on registers maintained under various statutes and regulations, including Part IIA Environmental Protection Act 1990. However, such notification procedures and register entries need only appear if land is actually identified and determined as contaminated. If land is not formally so identified or determined, no information will be held on the registers nor need be revealed in answer to the enquiries.

25.6.5. Information regarding the actual state of the land (albeit not yet 'contaminated') may be in the possession of the authority and may be of interest to a buyer. In such cases, consideration should be given to widening the scope of the enquiry and the wording of the questions to require disclosure of any 'information relating to the environment' at the relevant target site. Such information must be provided in compliance with Environmental Information Regulations 2004 (SI 2004/3391).

Radon

25.6.6. Radon is a naturally occurring radioactive gas which is present in the ground and is found at low levels in all buildings. The recommended limit for radon in UK homes is called the Action Level. A Radon Affected Area is declared when the estimated percentage of dwellings at or above the Action Level is 1% or more. The answer to question 3.13 of Form CON 29R Enquiries of Local Authority (2007) will reveal whether a property is in a Radon Affected Area. If this is the case, the seller should be asked for the results of any radon measurements made in the property.

25.6.7. The Health Protection Agency (formerly the National Radiological Protection Board (NRPB)) offers an information service to provide information on the radon potential of a dwelling (see Appendix IX.2 for contact details).

25.6.8. Measures can be taken with relative ease to assess the level of radon in any property, and then to vent the property to ensure removal.

25.7.   Step 4 – independent site history investigation

25.7.1. The Warning Card states that Step 4 should be taken in 'all commercial cases, and if contamination is likely to be a risk in residential cases (e.g. redevelopment of brown field land)'. This step may include:

- obtaining a site investigation report from a commercial search company;

- desktop studies of the site involving consideration of old maps, plans, photographs and local physical and anecdotal evidence, to evaluate potential risks;

- consideration of contaminated land profiles available on the Environment Agency website, which outline the usual types of contamination associated with certain types of land use (e.g. landfill, railway yards, gasworks, munitions factories, etc.).

25.7.2. Residential and commercial search products are offered by a number of search providers.

25.7.3. Search providers often offer an initial risk assessment of the information provided in a report. Different providers offer different forms of risk assessment. An assessment might include a professional opinion on whether the property will be determined as contaminated land within the meaning of Part IIA Environmental Protection Act 1990 and whether there is likely to be any effect on the value of the property.

25.7.4. Solicitors should note that any such risk assessment is based purely on the publicly available information. No assessment of the actual site is undertaken. Also, there are matters contained in the report, which may affect a client's decision, which are not taken into account in the risk assessment at all. Moreover, no mapping or information service is able to determine, for instance, whether there had been a spillage of domestic heating oil in the back garden. Enquiries of the seller or the local authority may still be necessary here and practitioners should not assume that a risk assessment that gives the property a clear report means there is no problem. If problems are evident on the search, the providers will usually indicate what further steps should be taken before deciding to buy and these can help the solicitor and client decide how next to proceed.

25.7.5. In most cases, the search will reveal no entries of any concern. Keeping the search with the file or deeds in electronic form will assist if future reference needs to be made in relation to the information disclosed. There would be no need to inform the lender where the search result is clear.

25.7.6. In some cases, the search will reveal entries that may be of some concern to the buyer. The solicitor should discuss these issues with the client to decide how to proceed, if necessary following consideration of any risk assessment, to ascertain the degree of risk posed by a revealed entry.

25.7.7. The mere fact that information reveals an entry, or a potentially contaminative historical use, does not necessarily mean that there is a problem with the land, merely that there may be, and this possibility may require further investigation.

25.7.8. The decision whether to proceed, undertake further investigations or withdraw must be the client's, and it will frequently depend on factors unrelated to the environmental information revealed by the search. Factors such as the cost of the further investigations, the difficulty and delay involved in undertaking them, the accuracy and helpfulness of the further information revealed, the general timescale of the transaction and the client's attitude to risk will all influence the decision.

25.7.9. Often, the next step after obtaining a report is simply to acquire further information (especially as it may be easily obtainable from an obvious source), rather than to consider an actual site inspection at significant additional cost.

25.7.10. Next steps could be to contact the relevant agency or local authority. The local authority will have assessed their area for the purposes of Part IIA and may have records of the steps taken by a developer to make the land safe which in most cases would avoid the need for a site investigation. Enquiries could also be directed towards the developer.

25.7.11. Until the actual extent of a potential problem is investigated and revealed by an intrusive ground investigation, no solicitor can advise fully on its implications, and reports are only designed to provide the information to enable solicitors to identify the next questions. A ground investigation is highly unlikely ever to be undertaken in a routine domestic transaction, and thus the client will ultimately be required to take a view on the basis of information alone. In these circumstances a solicitor cannot provide the client with conclusive answers. If the client wishes to proceed the solicitor should advise the client to seek assistance from a specialist.

25.7.12. If the property which is the subject of the report is to be charged as security for a loan, the solicitor should contact the lender to report the findings and indicate (if it be the case) that further investigations are ongoing. Solicitors should ask the lender whether they require any further steps to be taken. The report should only be sent to the lender with a recommendation that it is referred to the lender's valuer for consideration in extreme cases. The report should be kept with any documentary records along with other important searches.

25.7.13. Similar searches are available in relation to flood risks, extractive industry and ground stability and local planning applications and land uses.

25.8. Step 5 – full site investigation

25.8.1. The Warning Card recommends this step in 'commercial cases where there is a likelihood that the site is contaminated'. It would be very rare to undertake this step in residential cases, in which case the solicitor should consider Step 7.

25.8.2. The scope for detailed surveys of potentially contaminated sites will depend on agreeing the cost with the client and weighing the cost against the potential risks.

25.8.3. The cost of an investigation might be shared between the buyer and the seller as it may be in the seller's interests that the buyer knows the state of the site at completion.

25.8.4. Where there is a substantial risk of contamination, the investigation costs may well be acceptable to an intending buyer or lessee. For sites with a lower degree of prima facie risk, the client may prefer to limit the investigation to a 'desk survey'. If the desk survey reveals problems that need further investigation, then a thorough site survey involving test boreholes and sampling may be advisable.

25.8.5.   The solicitor should be consulted regarding the terms of engagement of the environmental consultant to ensure that the client gets a report which is useful and reliable as a basis for risk assessment. It is important that the client is made aware of the risks of having no survey, or one that does not cover contamination issues.

25.9.   Step 6 – contractual protections

25.9.1.   Step 6 is to consider contractual protections against the seller. These may include:

- requiring the seller to make a specifically quantified and earmarked payment or price reduction, to take account of the potential liability;

- requiring the seller to provide full information about the contamination to the buyer in the contract;

- agreeing a formula whereby remediation costs are shared between potential polluters;

- seeking appropriate warranties as to the state of the site at completion;

- seeking an indemnity against future liabilities or reductions in value due to the state of the land at completion;

- requiring remediation by the seller before completion;

- obtaining assignment of any environmental insurance policies which may cover the site (or obtaining fresh cover).

Specific payments or price reductions

25.9.2.   The buyer may seek a reduction in the price (as opposed to a retention) to cover the cost of remediation or clean-up, or any perceived blighting effect on value. Alternatively, the buyer may want the seller to make a payment towards the cost of remediation. These 'payments for remediation' may affect the allocation of the costs of a clean-up of the site and should be the subject of specialist drafting.

Requiring the provision of full information

25.9.3.   The provision of full information on a voluntary basis is a way in which a seller can establish precisely that full information has been given to a buyer in relation to the presence of contaminants on the site, their nature and concentration.

25.9.4.   The provision of this information would have the effect of removing the seller from the category of person eligible to receive a remediation notice in respect of contaminated land, thus leaving the buyer to foot the seller's share of the cost in addition to any they would already have to bear. There is thus a clear incentive for a seller to give the information and a corresponding incentive for the buyer to know exactly the state of the site and take decisions about whether to proceed and if so, at what price. Contractual clauses providing this information should be the subject of specialist drafting.

Agreements on liabilities

25.9.5. The parties may wish to agree between themselves how they wish to apportion any liability for contamination.

25.9.6. Any such agreement will be honoured by the authority, and all its decisions regarding contaminated land liability will be taken with the intention of effecting the agreement.

25.9.7. Such agreements may need to specify in percentage terms what proportion of any remediation work required or agreed is to be borne by the respective parties.

25.9.8. It is suggested that any indemnities regarding contaminated land which are intended to amount to an 'agreement on liabilities' for the purposes of Part IIA Environmental Protection Act 1990 be kept separate in the documentation from other environmental provisions. In addition, modification may be required of any inconsistent provisions contained in Standard Condition 3.

25.9.9. When considering the extent of any indemnities to be given, not only is it essential to decide who must take the risk of all existing contamination, but also the effect of any future contamination, the effects of any future development of the land, which may release earlier contamination and the risks of changes in environmental legislation. Standards of clean-up need to be agreed, as do the respective contributions. A sliding scale over three to five years may be appropriate as may threshold and cap arrangements for levels of expenditure.

Retention by buyer

25.9.10. Alternatively, the buyer may prefer to complete on the basis of a retention from the price sufficient to cover any likely costs of remediation or clean-up. This will enable the buyer to carry out the remediation works rather than rely upon the seller and this has advantages in terms of quality control and project management.

Indemnities

25.9.11. The seller might be required to indemnify the buyer against the costs of remediation or clean-up or against any damages, loss or injury resulting from any past contamination or pollution of the soil or any water courses or aquifers.

25.9.12. Caps on the level of indemnity are common, and they are only as good as the credit of the person giving them. Moreover, any obligation on the recipient to mitigate any losses must be explicitly built in to the wording of the indemnity, as it will not be implied by the common law.

B

25.9.13. Phased indemnities are becoming more common – an arrangement whereby the seller remains liable for the first year, but the buyer gradually assumes part of the risk as the years go by until after, say, 10 years, the buyer is wholly liable.

25.10. Step 7 – withdrawal from the purchase

25.10.1. This step should be considered in residential or commercial cases when any of steps 1 to 6 above result in 'unresolved problems'.

25.10.2. At any stage in the above process, a buyer must be prepared to walk away from the transaction if:

- the risks are too great;

- the information is too hard to find; or

- the seller is too resistant to negotiation.

25.11. Step 8 – advising insurance

25.11.1. This step should be considered in residential or commercial cases when Steps 1 to 6 above result in 'unresolved problems' and when the client does not wish to withdraw.

25.11.2. In commercial cases, new insurance cover may be available to the buyer against the risks of liability resulting from contamination or pollution. In some (increasingly rare) cases, this may only be granted following an environmental risk assessment by specialist consultants appointed or approved by the insurance companies. It may be a requirement that any contamination found be cleaned up and an annual environmental audit of pollution control procedures carried out, although these requirements are less common than they were. The insurance contract will need specialist negotiation. Some commercial providers will now offer cheaper cover for smaller risks on standard wording which may be sufficient for smaller projects.

25.11.3. Several companies in the insurance market offer cheaper products designed to cover the risk that residential property may be designated as contaminated within the meaning of Part IIA. However, these are limited in scope.

25.11.4. Some insurers offer cover for new, converted and rental homes. It should be noted that this cover is limited in its ambit and application.

Earlier insurance cover: assignment of the policy?

25.11.5. In commercial cases, the availability of insurance cover in respect of past polluting events should also be considered and investigated with the seller in pre-contract enquiries.

25.11.6. Although the current practice of insurers is to limit or exclude liability for such events, older public liability and third party liability policies were wide enough to cover them and there may still be residual cover under old policies.

25.11.7. If this is possible or likely, specialist brokers might be called in to carry out an investigation into past insurance policies. If cover is available to the seller under these older policies, the indemnity clause in the contract should be coupled with an assignment of the benefit of this policy.

25.12. Advice to sellers

25.12.1. From the seller's point of view, achieving a clean break from the liabilities attaching in particular to a commercial site may not always be possible. In particular, liability may continue for:

- breaches of the consents committed while the seller was the site-owner and operator (commercial sites only);

- breaches of waste legislation while in possession (commercial sites only);

- contaminated land (on the person who originally caused or knowingly permitted substances to be on the site pre-sale) (commercial and residential sites);

- statutory nuisances caused or continued (commercial and residential sites);

- water pollution offences caused or knowingly permitted (commercial and residential sites);

- sewage discharge offences (commercial sites only);

- civil liability (as co-defendant for damage caused or continued during the period of ownership (commercial and residential sites).

25.12.2. In respect of most of these liabilities (all save for contaminated land) there is no easy way to shift liability on to a buyer other than by asking for indemnities, which the buyer is unlikely to give. A more important strategy is to ensure (perhaps by incoming and outgoing audits) what the state of play is when the site is sold on, so as to be able successfully to determine who did in fact cause a pollution incident, should there ever be a dispute.

25.12.3. As far as contaminated land is concerned, sellers should take close note of those clauses in the legislation that would exclude a seller from liability if:

- contract documents specifically reflect the payment (often in the form of a price reduction) of a specific sum for remediation;

- the land is sold in circumstances where full information is provided to the buyer about the contamination on the site;

- the seller and buyer agree on a contractual formula for dealing with any liabilities which emerge;

and ensure that the paperwork is drafted in such a way as to maximise the chance of exclusion.

B

B26. Boundaries and easements

26.1. Checking boundaries

26.1.1. The burden of discovering the identity and ownership of boundaries usually lies with the buyer since Condition 4.4.1 Standard Conditions of Sale and Standard Commercial Property Condition 6.3.1 will (unless excluded from the contract) relieve the seller of the obligation to define precisely their route or to prove title to their ownership.

26.1.2. The buyer's solicitor should therefore check the boundaries as shown on the title deeds, accompanying plans, and (where supplied) the estate agent's particulars. Where from investigation of the above documents the boundaries are unclear or a discrepancy exists, further enquiries should be undertaken to clarify the position.

26.1.3. The client should be asked to check the boundaries by a site inspection or the client's surveyor should specifically be asked to undertake this task in the course of his own inspection of the property. The solicitor is not generally under an obligation to inspect the property but may need to do so where a discrepancy or query over the boundaries exists which is not resolved by inspection of the deeds and plans or by other enquiries made by the solicitor. An inspection may be required in the case of the purchase of a newly constructed property to ensure that the site plans accord with the property as it stands on the ground. Where the solicitor does accept the obligation of inspecting the property he will be liable in negligence if he does not carry out that duty with proper care.[1]

26.1.4. The following enquiries and investigations may also assist to determine the extent and ownership of boundaries:

(a) specific pre-contract enquiries of the seller;

(b) application of the common law presumptions (see B26.2.2–B26.2.7);

(c) a site inspection of the property;

(d) an inspection of pre-root or pre-registration title deeds (if available);

(e) an Index Map search at the Land Registry (see B10);

(f) inspection of Ordnance Survey maps.

Ordnance Survey maps

26.1.5. It is the practice of Ordnance Survey maps to show the centre line of boundary features as the boundary. These maps may therefore give a general indication of the placing of a boundary subject to tolerances of scale but will not show the precise delineation of the boundary.

'T' marks

26.1.6. Plans attached to conveyances and transfers may indicate the ownership of boundaries by the use of 'T' marks. The stem of the 'T' should rest on the relevant boundary, the 'T' being on the side of the boundary which is responsible for its maintenance.[2]

26.1.7. The CML Lenders' Handbook, para.6.2 and the BSA Mortgage Instructions, para.C.7 require the solicitor to ensure that the boundaries of the property are clearly defined by reference to a suitable plan or description.

26.1.8. Boundary agreements entered into for the purpose of clarifying the boundary, rather than for the conveyance of land, need not comply with section 2 Law of Property (Miscellaneous Provisions) Act 1989.[3]

26.1.9. In boundary disputes where the definition of the parcels in a conveyance or transfer is not clear, the court will take into account the physical features on the ground when determining where the boundary lies.[4]

1. See *Barclay-White* v. *Guillaume & Sons* [1996] EGCS 123.
2. See *Seeckts* v. *Derwent* [2004] EWHC 1913 (Ch).
3. *Joyce* v. *Rigolli* [2004] EWCA Civ 79. See also *Neilson* v. *Poole* (1969) 20 P&CR 909.
4. *Chadwick and others* v. *Abbotswood Properties Ltd and others* [2004] EWHC 1058.

26.2. **Evidence of boundaries**

Registered land

26.2.1. Provided that provisions relating to the ownership of boundaries were clearly set out in the documentation accompanying the application for registration, these will be recorded on the register of the title. The extent of the boundaries shown on the title plan will usually not show the exact position since boundaries shown on plans drawn by the Land Registry are general boundaries only unless shown on the register as determined.[1]

Common law rebuttable presumptions as to boundaries

The ad medium filum rule

26.2.2. A person who owns land abutting on a private or public highway is presumed to own the soil or sub-soil respectively of the highway up to the middle line. The surface of a public highway is vested in the highway authority. Registered titles do not show ownership of the sub-soil to the centre of an adopted road even where expressly included in the transfer.

The hedge and ditch rule

26.2.3.   Where two properties are separated by a hedge and a man-made ditch, the boundary line is presumed to lie on the far side of the ditch from the hedge.[2]

Foreshore

26.2.4.   In the absence of contrary evidence, the boundary of land adjoining the sea lies at the top of the foreshore. The foreshore is that part of the shore lying between the ordinary high and low water marks. Land below the medium line of the foreshore belongs to the Crown.

Non-tidal rivers and streams

26.2.5.   The *ad medium filum* rule applies so that the owners of properties on either bank of the stream or river own the bed up to the middle of the stream or river. The owner of the river is also presumed to own the right to fish in the river but this presumption may be rebutted and it is common to find that fishing rights have been separately sold to third parties.

Tidal rivers and sea inlets

26.2.6.   The bed and foreshore of a tidal river is prima facie vested in the Crown subject to the public's rights of navigation and fishing. The Crown's rights extend to that point in the river where the tide ebbs and flows, beyond which point the *ad medium filum* rule applies.

Trees

26.2.7.   A tree belongs to the owner on whose land it was planted even if its trunk, roots or branches extend on to a neighbouring property. Where it cannot be established who planted the tree (e.g. because the trunk straddles the boundary of the land) ownership may be inferred from the circumstances. Regular maintenance (e.g. lopping or topping) by one person may be indicative of ownership by that person.

Accretion and diluvion

26.2.8.   Where land is bounded by water the land owner's boundary extends to that land as added to by accretion or lost by diluvion (erosion). This doctrine applies only where the changes in the boundary are gradual and imperceptible in the ordinary course of nature. It does not apply where a substantial and recognisable change in the boundary has suddenly taken place.[3] The doctrine applies to registered land unless an agreement as to its operation has been noted in the register.[4]

1. Land Registration Act 2002, s.60 and see Land Registration Rules 2003, r.118 and Land Registry Practice Guide 40 as to applications for a boundary to be determined. See also *Clements and others* v. *Goodacre* [2004] All ER (D) 120. In cases of difficulty specialist texts should be consulted. See also D2.5.2.
2. See *Alan Wibberley Building Ltd* v. *Insley*, *The Times*, 30 April 1999.
3. *Southern Centre for Theosophy Inc.* v. *State of South Australia* [1982] 1 All ER 283.
4. Land Registration Act 2002, s.61.

26.3.   Party walls

Party Wall Act 1996

26.3.1.   Party Wall Act 1996 in substance re-enacts London Building Acts (Amendment) Act 1939 which previously only applied to London. The provisions of the 1996 Act apply throughout England and Wales.

New party structures

26.3.2.   Section 1 requires a building owner to give at least one month's notice if he wishes to build a party structure where none exists. If the adjoining owner consents within 14 days, the wall is to be built half on the land of each owner or in such position as they agree. The expense of building is agreed between them or in an appropriate proportion considering the use and the cost of labour and materials. If consent is not forthcoming, the building owner may only build on his land. He may, subject to certain conditions, place footings below the land of the adjoining owner. He must compensate the adjoining owner and any occupier for any damage caused. Any dispute which arises is to be determined in accordance with the dispute resolution procedure in section 10.

Existing party structures

26.3.3.   Section 2 gives a building owner wide powers to deal with party structures. A building owner may not cause unnecessary inconvenience and must compensate the adjoining owner and occupier for any loss or damage caused. If he opens any part of the adjoining land or building, he must maintain hoarding or shoring for its security. He must usually make good all damage caused to adjoining premises, internal furnishings and decorations, and may be required to pay expenses in lieu. He must also pay a fair allowance for disturbance and inconvenience.

Procedure

26.3.4.   Section 3 requires a building owner to serve the adjoining owner with a party structure notice stating the building owner's name and address, details of the proposed work and the date on which it is to start at least two months before any proposed work is to start. Section 20 defines 'owner' to include anyone with a tenancy for more than a year and any purchaser under an agreement for purchase or lease. The notice ceases to have effect if work is not started within

12 months and if it does not proceed with due diligence. If an adjoining owner does not consent to the notice within 14 days, a dispute arises and section 10 applies. An adjoining owner may serve a counter notice within one month requiring the owner to build chimney breasts, recesses or other such works. The works must be specified and plans, sections and particulars must accompany the counter notice. In the case of a structure used by the adjoining owner only as a boundary, the works may include the reduction of the height of the wall to not less than two metres or the height of any building of the adjoining owner. A building owner must comply with a counter notice unless this would injure him, cause unnecessary inconvenience or delay. If he does not consent to the counter notice within 14 days, section 10 applies. The procedure differs where a building owner wants to construct special foundations. If the adjoining owner does not consent, they may not be put in.

Dispute resolution procedure

26.3.5.   Where a dispute arises, it is to be settled by surveyors (section 10). Both parties must agree on the appointment of a surveyor or appoint their own surveyor and the two surveyors must select a third surveyor. Either of the other two may then call on him to settle the matter. All appointments must be in writing and cannot be rescinded. Provision is made to deal with the situation where a surveyor dies, becomes incapable of acting, or refuses or neglects to act effectively. An award cannot authorise interference with an easement of light or rights in the party wall but may deal with the right, time and manner of carrying out work and any other matter arising from the dispute. The surveyor's award is conclusive, subject to the right of either party to appeal to the county court within 14 days of the date of the award. The court may rescind or modify the award.[1]

Payment for the work

26.3.6.   The building owner generally pays for all work. Where work is due to lack of repair, required by the adjoining owner or the latter makes use of the work, he must pay or contribute to the cost of the work. The building owner must serve him with an account within two months of completion. If the adjoining owner objects within one month, the matter is to be settled under section 10. Security for costs may be required before any work starts.

Miscellaneous

26.3.7.   A building owner who proposes to excavate and construct a building or structure within three to six metres of any building or structure of the adjoining owner may, and must if required by the adjoining owner, strengthen or safeguard at his own expense the foundations of the adjoining owner if certain conditions are met. Finally, the Act gives rights to enter and remain on land for carrying out works and an occupier who refuses to permit this may be guilty of an offence.

1. See *Young and another* v. *Bemstone Ltd* [2004] All ER (D) 108 for an example of a dispute under s.10(b) which was referred to the county court.

26.4. Hedgerows

26.4.1. Hedgerow Regulations 1997,[1] reg.3 prevents or inhibits the removal of hedgerows growing in or adjacent to common land, a nature reserve, a SSSI, or land used for agriculture, forestry, or the keeping of horses, ponies or donkeys. Optional enquiry 21 on Form CON 29 (Part II) asks: 'if there are entries in the record under reg.10, how can they be obtained, and where can the record be inspected?'

26.4.2. The Regulations apply where a hedgerow has a continuous length of at least 20 metres (or if less than 20 metres must meet by intersection or junction another hedgerow). They do not apply to hedgerows within or marking the boundary of a domestic curtilage.

26.4.3. The local planning authority has power to prevent the removal of an 'important hedgerow' which is defined by regulation 4 as one which has existed for 30 years or more and which satisfies at least one of the criteria set out in Part II of Schedule 1 to the Regulations. These criteria relate to archaeological/historical matters and to wildlife/landscape considerations.

26.4.4. An owner (which includes a tenant) who wishes to remove a hedgerow which is covered by the Regulations must serve a 'hedgerow removal notice' on the local planning authority. The form of notice is specified in Schedule 4 and must include a plan. The local planning authority may then either serve a notice saying that the hedgerow can be removed or serve a 'hedgerow retention notice'. If no notice has been served at the expiry of 42 days, the hedgerow can be removed.

26.4.5. Exceptions, where hedgerow removal is permitted, include:

    (a)   making a new access to replace an existing access;

    (b)   making a temporary access in an emergency;

    (c)   national defence;

    (d)   development for which planning permission has been granted;

    (e)   flood defence or land drainage;

    (f)   work preventing plant or tree pests;

    (g)   felling, etc., to prevent obstruction with electric lines;

    (h)   proper management.

26.4.6. An appeal against a retention notice lies to the Secretary of State for Environment within 28 days. It is an offence to remove a hedgerow without the necessary permission.

26.4.7. As an alternative to prosecution the local planning authority can serve a notice requiring a new hedge to be planted. The local planning authority can apply for an injunction in the county court or High Court to restrain an actual or apprehended offence.

High hedges

26.4.8. Anti-social Behaviour Act 2003 gives the owner or occupier of a domestic property the right to complain to the local authority on the grounds that a high hedge (as defined in the Act) is adversely affecting the reasonable enjoyment of his property. A fee is payable.

26.4.9. If the local authority decides that the complaint is justified, it can issue a remedial notice requiring, for instance, that the hedge owner cut back the hedge. This notice cannot require the hedge to be reduced to a height of less than two metres. Failure to comply with a remedial notice can lead to a fine of up to £1,000 and the court can order the hedge owner to carry out the works with additional fines if the order is not complied with.

26.4.10. For more information, see the relevant sections of website of the Department for Communities and Local Government: **www.communities.gov.uk**.

1. SI 1997/1160.

26.5.   **Checking easements**

Acting for the buyer

26.5.1. During the pre-contract stage, the buyer's solicitor must check the title and all the other documents in his file to ensure that the buyer will have the benefit of all the easements necessary for the enjoyment of the property and that there are no easements existing over the property that might impede the buyer's use and enjoyment of it. The Standard Conditions of Sale and the Standard Commercial Property Conditions provide that the buyer will take the property subject to incumbrances discoverable by inspection of the property (Standard Condition 3.1.2(b) and Standard Commercial Property Condition 3.1.2(b)).

Acting for the seller

26.5.2. From the seller's point of view, he must make sure that the contract discloses all the incumbrances that will bind the buyer after the purchase. To comply with this duty the seller's solicitor must also investigate the existence of easements over the property being sold.

Discovering easements

26.5.3. To discover easements the solicitor needs to:

- inspect the official copy of the register or the title deeds;

- if the title is unregistered, carry out a search at the Land Charges Department to check whether any D(iii) (equitable easement) land charges are registered;

- if acting for the seller, make enquiries of the seller client as to the rights his neighbours and others enjoy over the property being sold and the rights he enjoys over adjoining property;

- if acting for the buyer, instruct the buyer to make a personal inspection of the property to look for evidence of any easements, e.g. rights of way, rights to light, drainage, right to park, both enjoyed by the property and exercised over it.

26.6. Creation of easements

26.6.1. Easements can be created by express grant (either by deed or in writing), by implication on the sale of part of a property, or by prescription. The enforceability of easements depends upon their mode of creation and whether they have complied with the appropriate requirements regarding registration.

Express easements

26.6.2. To be legal, an express easement must be for an interest equivalent to an estate in fee simple absolute in possession or a term of years absolute.[1] It must also be created by deed.[2] If the easement is not granted for the equivalent of a legal estate (e.g. a determinable easement) or it is in writing, it can only take effect in equity. If in writing, the written agreement must comply with Law of Property (Miscellaneous Provisions) Act 1989, s.2.

Unregistered land

26.6.3. An express legal easement is binding on the land. Its existence should be discoverable from the deeds and it may also be obvious on an inspection of the property. If the easement is created in writing it can only be equitable and, to be enforceable against subsequent owners of the property, it requires registration as a D(iii) land charge. A search at the Land Charges Department should reveal its existence. If the D(iii) land charge has not been registered, it will be void against a purchaser of the legal estate for money or money's worth.[3]

Registered land

26.6.4. The creation of an express easement by deed over a registered title is a registrable disposition and must be completed by registration to take effect at law.[4] Prior to the implementation of Land Registration Act 2002 the creation of an easement by deed also needed to be completed by registration. So all express easements created by deed, which were created after the title was registered should appear on the title of the servient property. Equitable easements must be protected by an entry in the register. Under Land Registration Act 1925 protection was either a notice or caution. Under Land Registration Act 2002 an equitable easement should be protected by notice. For more information see Land Registry Practice Guide 62 which deals with the registration of easements under Land Registration Act 2002.

Implied easements

26.6.5. Implied easements come into existence on the sale of part of a property.[5] See J1.3.1 as to the creation of implied easements under the rule in *Wheeldon* v. *Burrows* and Law of Property Act 1925, s.62. Implied easements over unregistered land are legal easements and as such are binding on subsequent owners of the property. Where the land is registered, implied easements do not need to be completed by registration to take effect at law.[6]

Prescriptive easements

26.6.6. Easements created by prescription are legal easements which come into existence as the result of a long period of use. Easements created by prescription over unregistered land are legal easements and therefore are binding on the owner of the land. Where the land is registered, prescriptive easements take effect as legal interests. This is so whether created before or after the implementation of Land Registration Act 2002. Unlike expressly granted easements, prescriptive easements do not need to be registered to take effect at law.

1. Law of Property Act 1925, s.1(2)(a).
2. Law of Property Act 1925, s.52(1).
3. Land Charges Act 1972, s.4.
4. Land Registration Act 2002, s.27(1). The application to register the benefit and/or burden of the easements should be made in Form AP1 (Land Registration Rules 2003, Rule 90).
5. *Wheeldon* v. *Burrows* (1879) 12 Ch 31.
6. Land Registration Act 2002, s.27(7).

26.7. Easements as overriding interests in registered land

First registration

26.7.1. All legal easements existing at the date of first registration are overriding interests to which the land is subject.[1] Under Land Registration Act 1925, equitable easements that were openly exercised and enjoyed could take effect as overriding interests.[2] Under Land Registration Act 2002, only legal easements can be overriding interests. Expressly granted easements, whether legal or equitable, will be entered on the register on first registration in view of the Registrar's obligation to enter the burden of any interest appearing from his examination of the title to affect the registered estate.[3]

Dispositions of registered land

26.7.2. Any easement which was an overriding interest immediately before the coming into force of Land Registration Act 2002 retains its overriding status indefinitely. This will include both legal easements and equitable easements that were openly exercised and enjoyed.[4]

26.7.3. Easements expressly granted on or after 13 October 2003 must be completed by registration to operate at law. If not registered they take effect only in equity. Such equitable easements are not overriding interests and must be protected by way of notice if they are to bind a subsequent owner of the land. Implied easements and prescriptive easements do not require to be completed by registration to be legal easements and will take effect as overriding interests.

26.7.4. The only easements capable of overriding dispositions are:

(a) easements that were overriding interests when the Act came into force on 13 October 2003; and

(b) those arising by implication or prescription.

26.7.5. For dispositions of registered land registered on or after 13 October 2006, a buyer of registered land for valuable consideration will not be bound by an implied or prescriptive easement arising after the Act came into force that is an overriding interest unless:

(a) the buyer knows of it; or

(b) it is obvious from a reasonable inspection of the land; or

(c) it has been exercised within one year of the date of purchase.[5]

26.7.6. Most implied and prescriptive easements will be used on a regular basis and will not be at risk of losing their status. However, if a person has the benefit of an easement that does not meet the requirements above, he should apply for his interest to be protected by the entry of a notice against the servient land.[6]

26.7.7. Where the servient land is unregistered, consideration should be given to making an application for entry of a caution against first registration (see G3.4.10–G3.4.16).

1. Land Registration Act 2002, ss.11(4)(b) and 12(4)(c), and Sched.1, para.3.
2. See *Celsteel Ltd* v. *Alton House Holdings Ltd* [1985] 2 All ER 562 and *Thatcher* v. *Douglas* [1996] 146 NLJ 282.
3. Land Registration Rules 2003, r.35 and Land Registration Rules 1925, r.40.
4. Land Registration Act 2002, Sched.12.
5. Land Registration Act 2002, Sched.3, para.3(1) and Sched.12, para.10.
6. For further guidance see Land Registry Practice Guide 19 on notices, restrictions and the protection of third party rights and Practice Guide 52 as to easements acquired by prescription (both available at **www.landregistry.gov.uk**).

26.8. **Access to neighbouring land**

26.8.1. Access to Neighbouring Land Act 1992 allows the court to grant the applicant a temporary right of access to another person's land for the purpose of carrying out basic preservation work, i.e. work necessary to protect, repair or maintain (but not to improve) the applicant's property. The fact that the repairs would be substantially more expensive to carry out without access to the neighbour's land is not itself a ground for making the order. For an order to be made, the proposed works must be either impossible or substantially more difficult to carry out without an access order. The applicant need not be the owner of the land in question.

26.8.2. The county court must refuse an access order where it is satisfied that the respondent or any other person would suffer interference with or disturbance of his use or enjoyment of the land to such a degree that it would be unreasonable to make the order.

26.8.3. An order, if made, will be binding on successors in title of the respondent, provided it is registered. Although the applicant need not own the land, if he does the Act does not seem to provide for the benefit of the order to enure for the benefit of successors in title to the applicant's land. Where the land is unregistered an application under the Act is registrable as a pending action, an order as a writ and order. Where the land is registered, an application under the Act can be protected by either an agreed or unilateral notice. An order under the Act can only be protected by an agreed notice.[1]

26.8.4. The Act contains provisions for compensation for loss of privacy, inconvenience, pecuniary loss, damage or injury. Except where the dominant land concerned is residential, payment of a fee for the access may be ordered by the court.

26.8.5. Pre-completion searches at the Land Registry (or the Land Charges Department in the case of unregistered land) will identify cases where access orders have been registered under the Act.

26.8.6. It is not possible to contract out of the provisions of the Act.

1.   Land Registration Rules 2003, r.80.

26.9. Vehicular access over land

26.9.1. The driving of a vehicle over common or other land is prohibited by section 193(4) Law of Property Act 1925, and section 34 Road Traffic Act 1988 makes it a criminal offence to drive a motor vehicle over land which is not a road but which is a restricted byway, or land over which a bridleway or public footpath runs. These offences are committed if the vehicle is driven on the land without lawful authority. It was therefore assumed that it was not possible to obtain an easement by prescription to drive over such land as easements by prescription could only be acquired in respect of activities which were capable of being carried out lawfully. However, the House of Lords in *Bakewell Management Ltd* v. *Brandwood*[1] decided that in a situation in which the owner of the land *could* have granted such an easement (i.e. had the legal right to grant it) then it is possible for an easement to drive vehicles over the land to be acquired by prescription provided that there has been a long and uninterrupted use of the right.

26.9.2. Where the benefiting or burdened land is registered, an application to note the benefit and/or burden of the easement should be made to the Land Registry in the usual way.[2] Land Registry Practice Guide 52 deals with easements claimed by prescription and statutory rights of way for vehicles.

1. [2004] UKHL 14.
2. Where the benefiting land is registered the application should be made in Form AP1. Where the benefiting land is not registered the application against the registered servient land should be made in either Form AN1 or UN1.

C. EXCHANGE

C1. Preparing to exchange

1.1. Introduction
1.2. Checklist

1.3. Reporting to the buyer

1.1. Introduction

1.1.1. On exchange a binding contract will come into existence, after which time neither party will normally be able to withdraw from the contract without incurring liability for breach. It is therefore essential to check that all outstanding queries have been resolved and that both parties' financial arrangements are in order before the client is advised to commit himself to the contract.

1.2. Checklist

1.2.1. Although the checklist below largely reflects matters which are of concern to a buyer, many of the items will also be of concern to a seller. The seller should pay particular attention to those items marked with an asterisk.

Searches

(a)   Have all necessary searches and enquiries been made?

(b)   Have all the replies to searches and enquiries been received?

(c)   Have all search and enquiry replies been checked carefully to ensure that the replies to individual questions are satisfactory and accord with the client's instructions?

* (d)   Have all outstanding queries been resolved satisfactorily?

Survey

(a)   Has a survey of the property been undertaken?

(b)   Is the result of that survey satisfactory?

Mortgage arrangements

(a)   Has a satisfactory mortgage offer been made and (where necessary) accepted by the client?

(b)   Are arrangements in hand to comply with any conditions attached to the advance, e.g. in relation to an endowment policy?

(c)   Taking into account the deposit, the mortgage advance (less any retention) and the costs of the transaction (including SDLT, Land Registry fees and other disbursements), has the client sufficient funds to proceed with the purchase?

* (d)   Have arrangements been made to discharge the seller's existing mortgage(s)?

* (e)   If the transaction is a sale of part, has the seller's lender (if any) agreed to release the property to be sold from the mortgage?

Deposit

* (a)   How much (if any) preliminary deposit has been paid?

* (b)   How much money is needed to fund the deposit required on exchange?

(c)   Has a suitable undertaking been given in relation to bridging finance?

* (d)   To whom is the deposit to be paid?

NB: Where Formula C is to be used for exchange, the deposit may have to be paid to someone other than the immediate seller.

(e)   Have the deposit funds been obtained from the client and cleared through clients' account?

NB: Standard Condition 2.4 requires that payment is to be made only by a cheque drawn on a solicitor's or licensed conveyancer's client account or by direct credit. Standard Commercial Property Condition 2.2 requires payment be made by direct credit.

The contract

* (a)   Have all outstanding queries been satisfactorily resolved?

* (b)   Have all agreed amendments been incorporated clearly in both parts of the contract?

* (c)   Has the approved draft been returned to the seller?

* (d)   Is a clean top copy of the contract available for signature by the client?

* (e)   Have the terms of the contract been explained to the client?

* (f)   Has the list of fixtures and fittings been agreed between the parties?

Insurance

(a)   Have steps been taken to insure the property immediately on exchange?

* (b)   If the buyer is to rely on the seller's insurance policy, has the buyer's interest been noted on that policy?

(c)   Have steps been taken to obtain any life policy required under the terms of the buyer's mortgage offer?

Completion date

*   Has a completion date been agreed?

Method of exchange

*   Which method of exchange is most suitable to be used in this transaction?

Synchronisation

*   Where the client requires a simultaneous exchange on both sale and purchase contracts, are both transactions and all related transactions in the chain also ready to proceed?

Signature of contract

*   Has the client signed the contract?

Occupiers

*   Has the concurrence of all non-owning occupiers been obtained?

1.3.   Reporting to the buyer

1.3.1.   When the buyer's solicitor has completed his investigations into the property (including having finalised any amendments to the draft documentation) he should prepare and send or give to his client a report on the proposed purchase which should explain to the client (in language appropriate to the client's level of understanding) the nature of the solicitor's investigations into the property and its legal title, the results of these investigations, the terms of the contract and the mortgage offer, and a summary of conclusions or advice to the client.

1.3.2.   An example of such a report is set out in Appendix III.7. The precise content of the report will vary from transaction to transaction and in the case of commercial property a more detailed report may be desirable. A report on leasehold property should explain the terms of the lease to the client (see K3).

C2. Signature of contract

2.1.   Requirement for signature

2.1.1.   Both parties must sign the contract (or each must sign one of two identical copies) in order to satisfy Law of Property (Miscellaneous Provisions) Act 1989, s.2. Such signature need not be witnessed.

2.2.   Signature by the client

2.2.1.   Ideally the client should be asked to sign the contract in the presence of his solicitor, the solicitor first having ensured that the client understands and agrees to the terms of the contract.

2.2.2.   In cases where it is not practicable for the client to sign in the solicitor's presence, the contract may be sent to the client for signature with an accompanying letter which clearly explains where and how the client is required to sign the document. If not already done, the letter should explain the terms of the contract in language appropriate to the client's level of understanding, and also request a cheque for the deposit indicating by which date the solicitor needs to be in receipt of cleared funds. The client should be asked to return the signed contract to the solicitor as soon as possible. (There is an example report on proposed purchase at Appendix III.7.)

2.3.   Signature by solicitor on behalf of client

2.3.1.   A solicitor needs his client's express authority to sign the contract on behalf of the client.[1]

2.3.2.   Although it is possible for a client to give his authority orally,[2] unless the solicitor holds a valid power of attorney it is recommended that such an authority is obtained from the client in writing. In either case, the client should previously have been informed of the legal consequences of giving such authority (i.e. signature implies authority to proceed to exchange, and exchange creates a binding contract). Failure to obtain authority may render the solicitor liable in damages for breach of warranty of authority.[3]

1.   *Suleman* v. *Shahsavari* [1989] 2 All ER 460.

2. *McLaughlin* v *Duffill* [2008] EWCA Civ 1627.
3. *Suleman* v. *Shahsavari* [1989] 2 All ER 460.

2.4.   **Special cases**

Co-owners

2.4.1.   One co-owner may sign the contract on behalf of all the co-owners, but the solicitor should ensure that all co-owners have voluntarily given their consent to the transaction and have authorised the signature of the contract.

Trustees

2.4.2.   One trustee alone may sign the contract for sale on behalf of his co-trustees. The solicitor should ensure that all co-trustees have voluntarily given their consent to the transaction and have authorised the signature of the contract.

Partners

2.4.3.   Provided that the transaction has been authorised by the partnership, one partner may be given authority to sign the contract on behalf of the partners.

Companies

2.4.4.   Provided that the transaction has been authorised by the company, an officer of the company (usually a director or the secretary) may be authorised to sign on behalf of the company.

Attorneys

2.4.5.   A person who holds a valid power of attorney on behalf of another may sign the contract on behalf of the donor of the power. The attorney may sign either in his own name or that of the donor. The solicitor acting for the other party should be notified that the contract will be signed by an attorney and a properly certified copy of the power supplied to him so that he may satisfy himself as to the validity of the power and that it contains proper authority for the conduct of the particular transaction (see B7.19 and B.23).

Personal representatives

2.4.6.   All proving personal representatives must be parties to the contract and purchase deed.[1]

Occupiers

2.4.7.   A non-owning occupier may be joined as a party to the contract in order to give a release of his or her purported interest in the property. Where this occurs the non-owning occupier must sign the contract.[2]

1. Law of Property (Miscellaneous Provisions) Act 1994, s.16.
2. See B3.5.8 for an appropriate form of wording to release rights.

2.5. Authority to exchange

2.5.1.   It may be appropriate to obtain the client's express authority to exchange at the time of signature of the contract (see C4.2).

C3. Insurance

3.1.   Risk in the property

3.1.1. At common law and unless the contract provides otherwise, the risk in the property passes to the buyer from the moment of exchange; the buyer thus bears the risk of loss or damage, except where it can be shown that the loss or damage is attributable to the seller's lack of proper care.[1] The buyer should therefore normally insure the property from exchange of contracts onwards.

3.1.2. Since it is impossible to predict at which precise moment exchange will occur, it is essential that the buyer's insurance arrangements have been made in advance of actual exchange so that the policy will be effective immediately upon exchange.

3.1.3. Standard Condition 5.1 provides for the seller to bear the risk in the property until completion and permits rescission if the property is substantially damaged between exchange and completion. This condition permits the seller to cancel his insurance policy (except in certain cases related to the sale of an existing lease) and also excludes Law of Property Act 1925, s.47 which would otherwise give the buyer the right, in certain circumstances, to claim off the seller's policy in the event of damage to the property. However, the buyer's lender will frequently insist that the property is insured in the buyer's name from the date of exchange, in which case Standard Condition 5.1 is excluded by special condition.

3.1.4. Standard Commercial Property Condition 7.1.4 passes risk to the buyer on exchange and provides that the seller is under no obligation to the buyer to insure the property, except where Condition 7.1.2 applies (where the contract expressly provides for the seller to insure or where the lease requires the seller to insure the property either as landlord or as tenant). Condition 10.1.3 applies to leasehold property and in this context may require the seller to maintain his policy if so required by the lease.

3.1.5. A solicitor who fails to advise his client of the consequences of failure to insure, or who fails to carry out his client's instructions to insure the property, will be liable in negligence if the client suffers loss as a result of the lack of insurance.

1. *Clarke* v. *Ramuz* [1891] 2 QB 456; *Phillips* v. *Lamdin* [1949] 2 KB 33.

3.2.   Buyer insuring the property from exchange

3.2.1.   Where the buyer's solicitor has in force a block policy which covers all properties currently being handled by the firm, the property should be noted on the policy in accordance with the firm's standard procedures and, at the latest, by the morning of the day on which it is anticipated that exchange will occur.

3.2.2.   If the buyer is financing his purchase with the assistance of a mortgage, the lender will normally attend to the insurance arrangements on being requested to do so by the buyer's solicitor. The lender's standing instructions to solicitors should be checked to ensure that:

(a)   the amount of cover will be adequate;

(b)   the property will be put on cover from the time of exchange;

(c)   the lender's insurance requirements do not conflict with the terms of the contract or of any lease to which the property is subject.

3.2.3.   If neither of the preceding subparagraphs apply the buyer must obtain a policy which will cover the property from exchange.

3.3.   The terms of the policy

3.3.1.   The terms of the policy should be checked to ensure that:

(a)   the amount of cover is adequate;

(b)   the sum insured is index linked;

(c)   the risks insured against are adequate, e.g. is flood damage covered where the property is situated in a low-lying area?

(d)   particular features of the property have been disclosed to the insurance company and are adequately insured, e.g. thatched roofs, garden walls, interior decorative plasterwork;

(e)   where the property consists of a flat within a larger building, or is otherwise attached to adjoining property, the insurance cover extends to damage to neighbouring property where practicable.

3.3.2.   The client should be alerted to possible exclusions under the policy. In particular damage caused by terrorist activity, environmental contamination and flooding may not be covered; in a leasehold context, in the event of damage by an uninsured risk, the tenant or prospective tenant may remain liable under the terms of the lease, including the covenants to repair and pay rent. Similarly, some policies will not cover damage to empty properties (or to blocks of flats where a resident is claiming social security benefits).

3.4.   Property at seller's risk

3.4.1.   In some cases, and commonly with property which is in the course of construction, the contract will provide that the property is to remain at the seller's risk until completion. Standard Condition 5.1 also provides for the seller to bear the risk in the property until completion and permits rescission if the property is substantially damaged between exchange and completion. Except in certain cases applicable to the sale of leaseholds, the seller is not obliged by the condition to maintain his own insurance policy after exchange.

3.4.2. Where the risk in the property remains with the seller the buyer need not take out his own policy until completion but should ensure, before exchange, that:

(a) the seller will maintain his policy until completion and the terms of that policy provide sufficient protection for the buyer;

(b) the buyer receives written confirmation that his interest has been noted on the seller's policy;

(c) the contract contains a provision requiring the seller to transfer the property in substantially the same physical condition as at the time of exchange, failing which the buyer is entitled to rescind the contract (Standard Condition 5.1 contains this type of provision). This type of clause is not necessary where the property is in the course of construction because the contract for such a property will normally contain provisions requiring the seller to complete the building in accordance with specifications, failing which the buyer is under no obligation to complete.

3.4.3. Where the property is in the course of construction and the risk is to remain with the seller until completion, the buyer should clarify with the seller whether the word 'completion' is intended to refer only to completion of the building works, or whether it is intended that the seller will retain the risk in the property until actual completion of the transaction.

3.5. Maintenance of seller's policy

3.5.1. Except where the seller is obliged by a condition of his mortgage or lease to maintain his policy, the seller could cancel his insurance policy on exchange of contracts, but in practice he would be ill advised to do so, e.g. in case the buyer failed to complete.

3.5.2. In practice the seller will not usually cancel his policy until after completion; thus for the period between exchange and completion there will often be two policies in force (one having been taken out by the buyer on exchange), both covering the same property against the same risks.

3.5.3. Should the property be damaged or destroyed during the period when the two policies subsist difficulty may sometimes be experienced in obtaining payment from the insurer, since each insurer may maintain that the responsibility for payment lies with the other.[1] This difficulty may be resolved by including a special condition in the contract which requires the buyer to complete, subject to an abatement in the purchase price, leaving the seller to resolve the dispute with his own insurers.

1. *National Farmers Union Mutual Insurance Society Ltd* v. *HSBC Insurance (UK) Ltd* [2010] EWHC 773 (Comm).

3.6. Damage to the property

3.6.1. Under the common law the buyer will have to bear the cost of any damage caused to the property after exchange unless one of the provisions outlined below can be utilised. Additionally, the buyer's solicitor may be liable to his client in negligence (see C3.1.5).

3.6.2. Law of Property Act 1925, s.47 provides that a buyer may claim his loss from the policy maintained by the seller provided that:

(a) the contract does not exclude the operation of the section;

(b) the buyer pays a proportionate part of the insurance premium; and

(c) the insurance company consents to noting the buyer's interest in the policy.

3.6.3. The contract will normally exclude the operation of section 47, rendering the section ineffective so far as the buyer is concerned. (See Standard Condition 5.1 and Standard Commercial Property Condition 7.1.5.)

3.6.4. Fires Prevention (Metropolis) Act 1774, s.83 allows a person interested in or entitled to a property to require an insurance company to apply the proceeds of the policy towards the reinstatement of the property in the event of its damage by fire. Despite its title, the operation of the Act is not confined to London, but there is no direct authority for the proposition that a buyer under a contract for sale is a 'person interested' under the section.[1]

1. *Rayner* v. *Preston* (1881) 18 Ch 1 suggests *obiter* that a buyer can claim under the Act.

3.7. Other types of insurance

3.7.1. In appropriate cases the buyer should be advised to take out insurance to cover other risks, e.g. house contents, as well as life insurance in accordance with the terms of the mortgage offer.

3.7.2. Steps should be taken before or immediately after exchange to put such policies on foot although they will not normally need to be effective until completion. Advice given by the solicitor to his client about the terms of life insurance policies will be subject to the provisions of Financial Services and Markets Act 2000 (see A4). The seller should be advised not to cancel his house contents or other policies (including life policies linked to his mortgage) until completion.

3.8.   **Insurance mediation**

3.8.1.   If the solicitor is involved in insurance mediation services with regard to any insurance policy, care must be taken to ensure that the provisions of the Law Society's Scope Rules and Conduct of Business Rules are complied with (see A4).

C4. Exchange of contracts

4.1. **The practice of exchange**	4.4. **Standard Conditions of Sale**
4.2. **Authority to exchange**	**and Standard Commercial**
4.3. **Methods of exchange**	**Property Conditions**

4.1. The practice of exchange

4.1.1. The physical exchange of contracts between the parties is not a legal require-ment for a contract for the sale of land but where a contract is drawn up by solicitors acting for the parties it is usual for the contract to be prepared in two identical parts, one being signed by the seller, the other by the buyer. When the two parts are physically exchanged, so that the buyer receives the part of the contract signed by the seller and vice versa, a binding contract comes into existence. The actual time when the contract comes into being depends on the method which has been employed to effect the exchange (see C4.3).

4.1.2. The practice of exchange was given legal recognition in *Eccles* v. *Bryant and Pollock*[1] where Lord Greene in his judgment stated in relation to the then existing law under Law of Property Act 1925, s.40[2] that the three essential ingredients of a contract for the sale of land were:

    (a)   compliance with the requirements of Law of Property Act 1925, s.40;[3]

    (b)   certainty in respect of the existence of the contract; and

    (c)   certainty in respect of the terms of the contract.

4.1.3. All three of the above requirements are satisfied by the practice of exchange of contracts, because where a contract is to come into existence through exchange both parties have the assurance of knowing that no contract exists until that time, i.e. either party is free to change his mind and withdraw from the negotiations until exchange. In the same way, once exchange has taken place, there is certainty for both parties as to the existence of an enforceable contract, and also certainty over the terms which have been agreed since each party retains a copy of the contract signed by the other in identical form to the one which he himself signed. Where contracts are to be exchanged both parts of the contract must be identical. This includes the filling in of the date of the contract and the date of completion. If this requirement is not met no contract will come into existence whether or not the exchange takes place.[4]

4.1.4. Since exchange is not a legal necessity there is no reason why the contract should not be embodied in a single document which is signed by both parties. In such a case the contract becomes binding and enforceable as soon as the second signature has been put on the document.[5] This situation will not frequently occur and in any event the same solicitor is usually forbidden from acting for both parties by Rule 3.07 Solicitors' Code of Conduct 2007.

4.1.5. An exchange of faxes or e-mails is not an exchange of contracts to satisfy section 2 Law of Property (Miscellaneous Provisions) Act 1989.[6] In *Commission for the New Towns* v. *Cooper (Great Britain) Ltd*[7] an exchange of letters was held not to satisfy section 2.

1. [1948] Ch 93.
2. [1948] Ch 93 at 99.
3. Now replaced by Law of Property (Miscellaneous Provisions) Act 1989, s.2.
4. *Harrison* v. *Battye* [1975] 1 WLR 58.
5. *Smith* v. *Mansi* [1963] 1 WLR 26.
6. *Milton Keynes Development Corporation* v. *Cooper (Great Britain) Ltd* [1993] EGCS 142.
7. [1995] 2 All ER 929, CA.

4.2. Authority to exchange

4.2.1. A solicitor who exchanges contracts without his client's express or implied authority to do so will be liable to the client in negligence. In *Eccles* v. *Bryant and Pollock*[1] Lord Greene said that where a contract was to come into existence using the standard form of contract (now the Standard Conditions of Sale or Standard Commercial Property Conditions), it was implicit that the contract would come into existence on exchange, and that the client therefore impliedly authorised his solicitor to effect an exchange. In *Domb* v. *Isoz*[2] it was held that, once the solicitor has his client's authority to exchange, he has the authority to effect the exchange by whichever method the solicitor thinks most appropriate to the situation.

4.2.2. Although *Eccles* v. *Bryant and Pollock*[3] suggests that a solicitor's authority to exchange may be implied, it is better practice to obtain express authority from the client at the time of signature of the contract. Where an exchange of contracts by telephone is contemplated, it is suggested that, for the avoidance of doubt, express authority to use this method should be obtained. Where Formula C is to be used, it is a requirement of that Formula that express authority be obtained, preferably in writing. The Formula contains a suggested form of wording to meet this situation. Formula C is set out in full with notes for guidance in Appendix IV.11.

1. [1948] Ch 93.
2. [1980] Ch 548.
3. [1948] Ch 93.

4.3. Methods of exchange

4.3.1. Whichever method is chosen the exchange is usually initiated by the buyer indicating to the seller that he is now ready to commit himself to a binding contract. Once contracts have been exchanged neither party will be able to withdraw from the contract; it is therefore essential that the parties' solicitors have checked that all necessary arrangements are in order before proceeding to exchange. Also, where the purchase of one property is dependent on the sale of another the solicitor must ensure that the exchange of contracts on both properties is synchronised to avoid leaving his client either owning two houses or being homeless. Failure to synchronise the exchange where the client has instructed that his sale and purchase transactions are interdependent is professional negligence. Even in synchronised exchanges there will be a gap between the sale and purchase and, subject to the client's instructions, it is preferable to exchange contracts on the sale before the purchase.

Telephone

4.3.2. Exchange by telephone is now the most common method of effecting an exchange of contracts. Legal recognition of the practice was given by the Court of Appeal in *Domb* v. *Isoz*.[1] With the exception of personal exchange this method represents the quickest way of securing an exchange of contracts and is thus particularly useful in a chain of transactions. The method is not, however, risk free. Where exchange is effected by telephone, the contract between the parties becomes effective as soon as the parties' solicitors agree in the course of a telephone conversation that exchange has taken place. The telephone conversation is usually followed by a physical exchange of documents through the post in the normal way, but the existence of the contract is not dependent on this physical exchange; the contract already exists by virtue of the telephone conversation. If one party were subsequently to change his mind about the contract there is ample scope with this method for disputing the contents of the telephone conversation and thus the existence of the contract itself. Also, neither party is able to check that other's contract is in the agreed form, incorporates all agreed amendments or has been signed by the other party. To avoid the uncertainties arising out of this method of exchange the parties' solicitors must agree prior to exchange that the telephonic exchange will be governed by one of the Law Society's Formulae which were drawn up by the Law Society in response to the decision in *Domb* v. *Isoz*. The text of these Formulae appears in Appendix IV.11. An accurate attendance note recording the telephone conversation must also be made as soon as practicable.

Using the Formulae

4.3.3. (a) The text of the Formulae with their accompanying guidance notes is set out in Appendix IV.11 and IV.12.

(b) Whichever Formula is used, the client's express authority to exchange must be obtained before the procedure to exchange is commenced.

(c) If any variation to a Formula is to be made, such variation must be expressly agreed and noted in writing by all the solicitors involved before exchange takes place. Any agreement relating to the payment of a less than 10% deposit should be finalised at the preliminary enquiries stage of the transaction and not left until exchange is imminent. Any agreed variation to the Formula which has been made orally must be confirmed in correspondence between the solicitors.

(d)　Subject to (c) above, the conditions attached to the Formula being used must be strictly adhered to. In particular, where an undertaking is given to remit a deposit cheque and/or contract to the solicitor acting for the other party, such undertaking must be complied with on the day on which exchange takes place or, if compliance on the same day is not practicable, e.g. because exchange takes place after normal working hours, at the earliest opportunity on the next working day.

(e)　To ensure compliance with the conditions attaching to the Formulae it is recommended that only qualified staff be authorised to effect an exchange by telephone.

(f)　The Formulae may be used where the other party to the transaction is represented by a licensed conveyancer. The Formulae must never be used where the other party is represented by an unqualified person whose undertaking is not enforceable in the same way as those given by solicitors and licensed conveyancers.

(g)　Extreme care needs to be exercised when using Formula C (for use in chain transactions) where, in certain circumstances, a solicitor is required to give an undertaking, the performance of which is outside his direct control, e.g. solicitor A undertakes to solicitor B that solicitor C will send the deposit cheque to solicitor B. The Standard Conditions of Sale only permit a deposit to be used for an exchange of contracts along the chain if that contract contains similar provisions as to the deposit. This almost inevitably means that the second contract must also be made by reference to the Standard Conditions.

(h)　Under Formula C the ultimate recipient of the deposit must hold as stakeholder. No other capacity is permitted.

(i)　An attendance note recording full details of the exchange by telephone must be made immediately exchange has taken place.

(j)　A solicitor's failure to honour an undertaking given in relation to use of one of the Formulae (e.g. failure to send the deposit cheque on the same day as exchange takes place) is professional misconduct but probably does not affect the validity of an otherwise valid contract.[2]

(k)　Fax can be used to activate the Formulae.

Personal exchange

4.3.4.　By this method the solicitors for the parties meet, usually at the seller's solicitor's office, and the two contracts are physically exchanged. A contract exists from the moment of exchange. Although this type of exchange represents the safest and most instantaneous method of exchange it is frequently not possible to use personal exchange because the physical distance between the offices of the respective solicitors make it impractical to do so. Personal exchange is little used today, but it should be considered for use when the parties' solicitors are located in sufficient geographical proximity to make personal exchange feasible. A personal exchange has the benefit not only of being instantaneous, and thus leaving no uncertainty over the timing of the creation of the contract, but also of enabling both parties to see the other party's part of the contract before exchange actually takes place, so that both may be reassured that the parts of the contract are identical in form and have been properly signed.

Postal exchange

4.3.5. Where exchange is to take place by post the buyer's solicitor will send his client's signed contract and the deposit cheque to the seller's solicitor who on receipt of these documents will post his client's signed contract back to the buyer. Generally a contract does not come into being until the buyer has *received* the seller's contract. Exchange of contracts by post forms an exception to this rule and the contract is made when the seller *posts* his part of the contract to the buyer.[3] Posting the contract means that the seller must actually place the letter in the letter box. Handing the letter to a third party with instructions that it should be posted is not sufficient.[4] The postal rules of acceptance may be displaced by contrary intention in the contract itself.[5] It follows from the above that a contract will be formed even if the seller's part of the contract is lost in the post and is thus never received by the buyer. Using the post as a method of exchange is reasonably satisfactory when dealing with a single sale or purchase which is not dependent on another related transaction, but even in this simple scenario some dangers exist. There will inevitably be a delay between the buyer sending his contract to the seller and the seller posting his part back, during which time the buyer is uncertain of whether he has secured the contract. There is also no guarantee that the seller will complete the exchange by posting his part of the contract back to the buyer. Until he actually does so he is free to change his mind and withdraw from the transaction. Although these dangers are minimal where a single sale or purchase is being undertaken, the risks assume a much greater importance where a chain of transactions is involved; thus, the use of postal exchange is not advisable in linked transactions.

Document exchanges

4.3.6. A document exchange would be used to effect an exchange of contracts in a similar way to the normal postal service and is subject to the same risks as are outlined in the preceding subparagraph. The court has approved the use of document exchanges for the service and delivery of documents in non-contentious matters in *John Wilmot Homes* v. *Reed*.[6] The rules on postal acceptance do not apply to document exchanges and unless the contract contains a contrary provision the contract will come into existence when the seller's part of the contract is received by the buyer.[7] Where the Standard Conditions of Sale in each case are used, Condition 2.1 provides that the contract is made when the last copy of the contract is deposited at the document exchange. Standard Commercial Property Condition 2.1 provides to identical effect. If the Standard Conditions of Sale or Standard Commercial Property Conditions do not form the basis of the contract, the contract probably comes into existence when the last part of the contract is placed in the solicitor's box at the document exchange. There is no decided case on the making of a contract for the sale of land where a document exchange has been used to effect an exchange, and the proposition outlined above would be subject to the rules of the particular document exchange which was being used.

Fax

4.3.7. An exchange of faxes is not a valid exchange of contracts under Law of Property (Miscellaneous Provisions) Act 1989, s.2.[8] The main use of fax is to transmit the messages which activate the Law Society's Formulae. In this context fax is merely a substitute for using the telephone. Standard Condition 1.3.3 and Standard Commercial Property Condition 1.3.3 do not permit fax to be used as a valid method of service of a document where delivery of the original document is essential (as it is with the contract), thus effectively ruling out an *exchange* by this method, although there is no objection to the parties using fax in order to activate the Law Society's Formulae.[9]

E-mail

4.3.8. E-mail can also be used to transmit the messages activating the Law Society's Formulae under both the Standard Conditions of Sale (Condition 1.3) and Standard Commercial Property Conditions (Condition 1.3), provided the relevant e-mail addresses are included in the contract. At present, contracts for the sale of land cannot be entered into electronically via e-mail or the internet.

1. [1980] Ch 548.
2. See *Khan* v. *Hamilton* [1989] EGCS 128.
3. Despite doubts expressed about these rules in *Eccles* v. *Bryant and Pollock*, it is generally accepted that the postal rules as established in *Adams* v. *Lindsell* (1818) 1 B & Ald 681 do apply.
4. *Re London and Northern Bank, ex p. Jones* [1900] Ch 220.
5. *Holwell Securities* v. *Hughes* [1974] 1 All ER 161.
6. (1985) 51 P&CR 90.
7. See Standard Conditions 1 and 2 and Standard Commercial Property Conditions 1 and 2.
8. *Milton Keynes Development Corporation* v. *Cooper (Great Britain) Ltd* [1993] EGCS 142. An exchange of faxes was held not to be an exchange of contracts.
9. See *Hastie & Jenkerson (a firm)* v. *McMahon* [1991] 1 All ER 255 where the court, in a contentious case, approved fax as a valid method of service of a document but said that, to be valid as a method of service, the onus was on the sender of the document to prove that the document, in complete and legible form, had arrived at the recipient's terminal.

4.4. Standard Conditions of Sale and Standard Commercial Property Conditions

4.4.1. Condition 2.1 of both sets of conditions governs the date of the contract where the parties agree to exchange contracts by post or through a document exchange (see Appendices III.5 and III.6).

C5. After exchange

5.1. **The effects of exchange**   5.3. **Protection of the contract**
5.2. **After exchange**

5.1.   The effects of exchange

5.1.1.   A binding contract exists from which normally neither party may withdraw without incurring liability for breach.

5.1.2.   The beneficial ownership in the property passes to the buyer who becomes entitled to any increase in value of the property, but also bears the risk of any loss or damage; hence the need to ensure that insurance of the property is effective from the moment of exchange.[1] Standard Condition 5.1 states that the risk in the property is to remain with the seller until completion. However, Standard Commercial Property Condition 7.1.4 passes risk to the buyer on exchange of contracts.

5.1.3.   The seller retains the legal title to the property until completion, but holds the beneficial interest on behalf of the buyer. During this period the seller is entitled to remain in possession of the property and to the rents and profits (unless otherwise agreed). He must also discharge the outgoings, e.g. water rates until completion. He owes a duty of care to the buyer and will be liable to the buyer in damages if loss is caused to the property through neglect or wanton destruction.[2] This duty continues so long as the seller is entitled to possession of the property and does not terminate because the seller vacates the property before completion.[3]

5.1.4.   From the moment that a binding contract exists between the parties two equitable liens arise, enforceable only through a court order for sale of the property. The seller's lien on the buyer's equitable interest is for the balance of the purchase price and if this is not paid in full on completion the lien attaches to the legal estate in the hands of the buyer. The buyer's lien is on the seller's legal estate for any deposit paid to the seller in the capacity of agent (but not as stakeholder). In the case of unregistered land the lien would not bind another buyer from the seller unless registered as a Class C(iii) land charge under Land Charges Act 1972. In the case of registered land the lien could be protected by the registration of a notice, although this might not be necessary if the buyer was already in occupation of the property as the lien may then constitute an overriding interest within Land Registration Act 2002.[4] Protection of the lien by registration is not normally considered to be necessary, but should be undertaken immediately if problems arise between the parties in the period between contract and completion. (See M8 as to liens generally.)

---

1. In *National Carriers Ltd* v. *Panalpina (Northern) Ltd* [1981] AC 675 it was held that the doctrine of frustration can, in exceptional cases, apply to leases. Thus if a leasehold property were to be totally

destroyed between exchange and completion, it is arguable that the buyer could not be forced to complete. The same case contains dicta to the effect that the doctrine may also be applicable to freehold land, but to date there has been no decided case where the doctrine has been held to apply, and it is therefore unsafe to assume that the buyer will be discharged from his obligations following total destruction of the property.

2. *Clarke* v. *Ramuz* [1891] 2 QB 456; *Phillips* v. *Lamdin* [1949] 2 KB 33.
3. *Lucie-Smith* v. *Gorman* [1981] CLY 2866.
4. Land Registration Act 2002, Sched.1, para.2 and Sched.3, para.2, and see also *London and Cheshire Insurance Co. Ltd* v. *Laplagrene Property Co. Ltd* [1971] Ch 499.

5.2. **After exchange**

The seller's solicitor

5.2.1.   (a)   Inform the client and estate agent that exchange has taken place and enter completion date in diary or file prompt system.

(b)   Where, immediately after exchange, the seller is in possession of both copies of the contract, the seller's solicitor should check that both parts of the contract have been dated and bear the agreed completion date. The copy of the contract signed by the seller should immediately be sent to the buyer's solicitor to fulfil any undertaking given in the course of an exchange by telephone.

(c)   Any deposit received must immediately be paid into an interest-bearing clients' deposit account.

(d)   If any preliminary deposit has been held by an estate agent, the agent should be asked to remit such sum to the seller's solicitor who is normally required under the contract to hold 'the deposit', i.e. the whole of the amount specified in the contract as the contractual deposit (see Standard Condition 2.2 and Standard Commercial Property Condition 2.2). The agent may be reluctant to part with the money, preferring to hold it on account for any commission due to him.

(e)   If not already done, the seller should deduce title to the buyer.

The buyer's solicitor

5.2.2.   (a)   Inform the client and his lender that exchange has taken place and enter completion date in diary or file prompt system.

(b)   Where exchange has taken place by telephone, immediately send to the seller (or as directed by him) the signed contract and deposit cheque in accordance with the undertaking given, having first checked that the contract is dated and bears the agreed completion date.

(c)   Where the buyer is to insure, inform the insurer that exchange has taken place and check that the insurance policy is in force (see C3).

(d)   Where appropriate, protect the contract by registration (see C5.3).

5.3. **Protection of the contract**

Registered land

5.3.1. The contract constitutes an interest which needs to be protected by entry of a notice on the register of the title. The contract will then have priority over any future buyer or chargee of the land, but would not take priority over another buyer or chargee who had made an official search before registration of the contract and who lodged his own application for registration within the priority period afforded by his search. Where a buyer is in possession the contract could constitute an overriding interest.[1] In this case protection of the contract by the entry of a notice may not be necessary.

Unregistered land

5.3.2. The contract is an estate contract within the Class C(iv) category of land charge and will be void against a buyer of the legal estate for money or money's worth if not registered. Registration must be made against the name of the legal estate owner for the time being.[2] Care needs to be exercised when effecting the registration of sub-contracts, where the buyer under the sub-contract needs to register his C(iv) against the current owner of the legal estate who will not be his immediate seller. For example:

> A contracts to sell to B.

> Before completion of this contract B contracts to sell to C.

> If C seeks to protect his estate contract, he must register a Class C(iv) land charge against A who will be the owner of the legal estate until completion of the contract between himself and B.

5.3.3. Options to purchase and rights of pre-emption also require registration within this category.

Registration of the contract

5.3.4. Since the contract is capable of registration, a solicitor who fails to register, thereby causing loss to his client, may be liable in negligence to the client. However, since completion of most contracts occurs within a very short period following exchange, in practice registration of the contract is uncommon. Consideration should always be given to the question of whether or not a particular contract requires protection by registration and the contract should always be registered if any of the circumstances listed in C5.3.5 apply.

Guidelines

5.3.5. Registration of the contract is desirable in any of the situations listed below. The following is not an exhaustive list of all the circumstances in which registration is desirable. If the solicitor is in any doubt, he should err on the side of caution and register the contract in order to protect his client's interests:

(a) there is to be a long interval (e.g. more than two months) between contract and completion;

(b) there is reason to doubt the seller's good faith;

(c) a dispute arises between the seller and buyer;

(d) the seller delays completion beyond the contractual date;

(e) the purchase price is to be paid by instalments, the conveyance or transfer to be executed after payment of the final instalment;

(f) the transaction is a sub-sale.

1. Land Registration Act 2002, Sched.3, para.2.
2. *Barrett* v. *Hilton Developments Ltd* [1975] Ch 237.

D. TITLE

D1. Deducing title

1.1. Time for deduction of title

1.1.1. Historically the seller deduced title after exchange of contracts but this practice had serious disadvantages because the buyer was committed to a contract without knowing the state of the seller's title. This could cause problems, particularly if the transaction was one of a chain.

1.1.2. Only in exceptional cases should deduction of title be delayed until after contracts have been exchanged. In the majority of cases, the seller will send evidence of his title to the buyer with the draft contract and other pre-contract documentation.

1.1.3. Standard Condition 4.3.1 and Standard Commercial Property Condition 6.3.1 which both require evidence of title to be supplied 'immediately after making the contract', reflect the traditional practice of supplying the evidence of title after exchange of contracts. Despite these conditions, in most cases deduction of title will in practice take place before exchange of contracts. Standard Condition 4.2.1 and Standard Commercial Property Condition 6.2.1 preclude requisitions from being raised after exchange on the title shown by the seller before exchange of contracts.

1.2. Seller's obligation

1.2.1. The seller's obligation in relation to the deduction of his title is to supply sufficient documentary evidence to the buyer to prove that the seller is either the outright owner of the land he has contracted to sell or, if not, that he is in a position to compel someone else to transfer the land to the buyer or is a lender whose power of sale has arisen and become exercisable, thus entitling him to sell the land. It is not enough to show that the seller is able to ask a third party to transfer the land to the buyer; the seller must be able to force or oblige the third party to execute the purchase deed, e.g. where the land is held in the name of a company, the seller would need to own a controlling shareholding in that company in order to be able to compel the company to convey to the buyer.[1]

---

1. See *Re Bryant & Barningham's Contract* (1890) 44 Ch 218; *cf. Elliott* v. *Pierson* [1948] Ch 452.

1.3.   Method of deduction in registered land

1.3.1.   Land Registration Act 1925, s.110 contained detailed provisions as to the documents that a seller was required to supply to the buyer. These provisions have not been carried forward into Land Registration Act 2002. The Act does provide that rules may be made about the obligations of a seller to prove or perfect his title under a contract for the transfer or other disposition for valuable consideration of registered land.[1] No rules have been made, however, and the seller and buyer are free to make their own bargain as to the evidence of title to be deduced.

1.3.2.   Standard Condition 4.1.2 and Standard Commercial Property Condition 6.1.2 require the seller at his own expense to supply official copy entries of the title to the buyer. Official copy entries of the title should always be supplied since they usually show the up-to-date position of the register. The official copy entries of the title supplied to the buyer must be originals (not photocopies) and of recent date. Official copies issued electronically are imprinted with a watermark. Official copies in paper form are no longer printed on watermarked paper.

1.3.3.   When making a search at the Land Registry, the buyer will need to search from the date of the official copy.[2]

1.   Land Registration Act 2002, Sched.10, para.2.
2.   Land Registration Rules 2003, r.131.

1.4.   Method of deduction in unregistered land

1.4.1.   The seller will prove his ownership of unregistered land by supplying the buyer with an abstract or epitome of the documents comprising the title. In some cases the evidence supplied will be made up of a combination of these two styles of presentation.

1.4.2.   An abstract of title is in essence a summary of all the documents comprised in the title. The preparation of an abstract in traditional form is a skilled and time-consuming task which has largely been superseded by the practice of supplying an epitome of the title supported by photocopies of all the documents referred to.

1.4.3.   An epitome of title is a schedule of the documents comprising the title. The documents should be numbered and listed in chronological order, starting with the earliest in time. Each document should be identified as to its date, type (e.g. conveyance, assent, etc.), the names of the parties to it, whether a copy of the document is supplied with the epitome, and whether or not the original of the document will be handed to the buyer on completion. Photocopies of the documents which accompany the epitome must be of good quality, marked to show the document's corresponding number on the list shown by the epitome, and any plans included in the documents must be coloured or marked so that they are identical to the original document from which the copy has been made.

Before the epitome and copy documents are sent to the buyer the seller's solicitor should check that all the copies are legible and bear the appropriate markings as outlined in the preceding sentence, and that all pages are complete and assembled in the correct sequence. The paper on which the epitome is supplied must be sufficiently permanent and durable to last in a clearly legible state throughout the likely period of its need as evidence of the title. An epitome which is supplied by means of a faxed copy may not at present satisfy these requirements unless the originals of all the documents referred to are to be handed over on completion. Thus if a seller delivers the epitome by fax, in a situation where all of the original documents will not be handed over on completion, he should deliver a further copy of the epitome to the buyer, by post or document exchange, such further copy being produced on non-glossy A4 size durable paper.

Documents to be included in the epitome

Root of title

1.4.4. The epitome must commence with a good root of title, as specified by a special condition in the contract. A good root of title is a document which, at the date of the contract:

(a) is at least 15 years old;[1]

(b) deals with or shows the ownership of the whole legal and equitable interest contracted to be sold;

(c) contains an adequate description of the property; and

(d) contains nothing to cast any doubt on the title.

1.4.5. A conveyance on sale or legal mortgage which satisfies the above requirements is generally acknowledged to be the most acceptable root of title because it effectively offers a double guarantee on the title. The buyer in the present transaction will be investigating the seller's title for a minimum period of 15 years; the buyer under the root conveyance would similarly have investigated title over a period of at least 15 years when he bought the property. Thus the present buyer is provided with the certainty of the soundness of the title over a period of at least 30 years. If there is no conveyance on sale on the title which satisfies the requirements of a good root, a legal mortgage provides an acceptable alternative. Since a lender will not lend money on the security of a property without investigating the title, a legal mortgage used as a root document provides a similar double guarantee of the title to that afforded by a conveyance on sale. In the absence of both a conveyance on sale and a legal mortgage, title may be commenced with either a voluntary conveyance or an assent dated after 1925.[2] Since both of these documents effect gifts of the land, no investigation of prior title would have taken place at the time when they were executed, and they do not therefore provide the double check on the title which is given by the conveyance on sale or the legal mortgage and for this reason are less satisfactory to a buyer when offered as roots of title. They should therefore only be offered as roots of title (and accepted as such by the buyer) where, after investigation of all the title documents available to the seller, no better root can be found. The nature of the root document will be specified by special condition in the contract, and if the buyer does not consider the root being offered to be adequate he must raise this problem with the seller before contracts are exchanged; once contracts have been exchanged, it is too late to vary the terms of the contract. If, however, it transpired that the seller was ultimately unable to prove his title to the property, the buyer could withdraw from the contract.

Less than statutory minimum title is offered

1.4.6.   Only in very rare cases will it be found that the seller cannot provide the buyer with a root of title which satisfies the statutory minimum period of 15 years prescribed by Law of Property Act 1925, s.44 (as amended). A buyer who is offered a short title should not accept the situation until he has received a satisfactory explanation for the reasons for the short root from the seller and should be advised that, in accepting less than his statutory entitlement under Law of Property Act 1925, he is also assuming the risk of being bound by incumbrances on the title which he has had no opportunity of discovering or investigating. The risk of being bound by undiscovered incumbrances stretches backwards in time, not just to the statutory 15-year period, but to the date of the first document on the title (however old) which would satisfy the requirements for a good root. A short root should not be accepted by the buyer without a full investigation of the circumstances, the agreement of his lender, and investigation of the possibility of obtaining defective title insurance, preferably at the seller's expense. The acceptance by the buyer of a short root of title may also affect his ability to obtain registration with an absolute title at the Land Registry. At best, the Land Registry may only grant possessory title. An entry may also be made in the register as to any subsisting restrictive covenants or easements affecting the registered estate prior to the short root of title.

Documents to be included in the abstract or epitome

1.4.7.   From the root of title, all dealings with the legal and equitable interests in the land down to and including the interests of the present seller must be shown, thus constituting an unbroken chain of ownership stretching from the seller named in the root document to the present day. This includes the following:

   (a)   conveyances on sale and by gift;

   (b)   current leases;

   (c)   evidence of devolutions on death (death certificates, grants of representation, assents);

   (d)   change of name of an estate owner, e.g. marriage certificate, deed poll or statutory declaration;

   (e)   mortgages and discharge of legal mortgages;

    (f)   documents prior to the root which contain details of restrictive covenants which affect the property;

    (g)   memoranda endorsed on documents of title, e.g. recording a sale of part, assent to a beneficiary, or severance of a beneficial joint tenancy;

    (h)   powers of attorney under which a document within the title has been executed.

Documents which need not be included in the abstract or epitome

1.4.8.   Certain documents need not be included in the abstract or epitome, although in some cases their inclusion will be helpful to the buyer and may forestall queries on the title raised by the buyer. They include:

    (a)   documents of record and Land Charges Department search certificates (but it is good practice to include these so that the buyer can see which searches have been correctly made in the past, in which case he need not repeat the search during his own investigation of the title). It is recommended that documents of record should always be abstracted so that the buyer receives a complete picture of the title and one on which he can act immediately. Failure to supply such documents may lead to delay while, e.g. the buyer obtains a document which was not supplied by the seller;

    (b)   documents relating to equitable interests which will be overreached on completion of the current transaction (the buyer may discover these charges when he makes his pre-completion searches and if he has already been supplied with information about them he will not need to raise last-minute queries with the seller or to delay completion while he investigates them; therefore as a matter of good practice some notice of their existence should be given to the buyer);

    (c)   leases which have expired by effluxion of time (but if the tenant is still in possession of the property, possibly with the benefit of security of tenure, evidence of the terms on which the tenant enjoys the property should be supplied). Although leases which have been surrendered should be abstracted, together with evidence of the surrender, it is common practice not to provide evidence of leases which no longer affect the title;

    (d)   documents which pre-date the root of title except where a document within the title refers to the earlier document[3] (note that where a document within the title has been executed under a power of attorney, the power must be abstracted whatever its date);

    (e)   documents relating to discharged equitable interests in the land, e.g. receipted equitable mortgages.

1.4.9.   Standard Condition 4.1.3 and Standard Commercial Property Condition 6.1.3 require the seller to produce to the buyer (at the seller's expense) the original of every relevant document, or an abstract, epitome or copy with an original marking by a solicitor of examination either against the original or against an examined abstract or an examined copy.

1.4.10. If the title documents produced by the seller do not adequately show the physical extent of the property or its title, the seller may have to supplement the evidence of title with a statutory declaration. By Standard Condition 4.4 and Standard Commercial Property Condition 6.4.1 the seller is relieved of the obligation to define precisely the boundaries of the property, or to show the ownership of fences, hedges, ditches or walls, or to identify separately parts of the property with different titles, further than he is able to from information in his possession, but the buyer may, if reasonable, call for a statutory declaration as to the facts of these matters. If the land cannot be properly identified or described from its description in the title deeds and contract, the buyer is entitled to call for a plan, to be prepared at the seller's expense. In other cases if the buyer insists on describing the property by means of a plan, he must bear the cost of preparation of the plan himself.

Documents which will not be handed over on completion

1.4.11. The epitome must specify which documents will be handed to the buyer on completion and which will be retained by the seller. The buyer is entitled on completion to take the originals or marked abstracts or marked copies of all the documents within the title except those which relate to an interest in the land which is retained by the seller, e.g. on a sale of part the seller will retain the title deeds in order to be able to prove his ownership of the land retained by him. Similarly, a general power of attorney will be retained because the donee of the power needs to keep the original document in order to deal with other property owned by the donor, and personal representatives will retain their original grant in order to administer the remainder of the deceased's estate.

1. Law of Property Act 1925, s.44, as amended by Law of Property Act 1969.
2. Before 1926 there was no requirement for an assent to be in writing, and an oral assent alone would not have been capable of satisfying the definition of a good root of title.
3. Law of Property Act 1925, s.45.

1.5. **Sub-sales**

1.5.1. Law of Property Act 1925, s.44 does not appear to apply to a contract for a sub-sale. The buyer of unregistered land will require his immediate seller to deduce title to him as if this section did apply to the transaction, otherwise the buyer will not be sure of purchasing a good title, but the seller, until he completes his own purchase, may not be in a position to deduce such a title to the buyer. In any event the requirements for the deduction of title in these circumstances must be specifically dealt with by a special condition in the contract since there are no common law rules applicable to this situation.[1]

1.5.2. Where the land is registered the requirements for deduction of title must again be dealt with by a special condition in the contract.

1. See also B4 and B14 and see *Urban Manor* v. *Sadiq* [1997] NPC 24, CA.

1.6. Leaseholds

1.6.1. Deduction of title to leaseholds is discussed in section K.

D2. Investigation of title

2.1. Purpose of investigation

2.1.1. The seller having supplied the buyer with evidence of his title, the buyer's task is to investigate that evidence to ensure that the seller is able to transfer that which he has contracted to sell and that there are no defects in that title which would adversely affect the interests of the buyer or his lender.

2.1.2. Any matters which are unclear or unsatisfactory on the face of the documentary evidence supplied by the seller may be raised as queries (requisitions) with the seller within the time limits specified in the contract for raising requisitions (see D3).

2.1.3. Investigation will be carried out by the solicitor on behalf of his buyer and/or lender client. Where the same solicitor is acting for both the buyer and his lender in a simultaneous transaction investigation is carried out only once, bearing in mind the particular requirements of each client (see A11, E3 and section H).

2.1.4. If ultimately the seller cannot show a good title, the buyer is entitled to withdraw from the contract. Prima facie the seller's inability to show title is a breach of contract entitling the buyer to a remedy in damages, but in practice the buyer's right to damages may, in certain circumstances, be curtailed or precluded by express provision in the contract (see D3 and section M).

2.2. Time for investigation

2.2.1. Traditionally investigation of title followed deduction of title as a procedure which is undertaken after exchange of contracts and is subject to time limits imposed by the contract.[1]

2.2.2. In practice the seller will usually supply his evidence of title at the draft contract stage of the transaction and may, by inclusion of a contractual provision to such effect, prevent the buyer from raising his requisitions after exchange, thus compelling the buyer to carry out his investigation at that stage of the transaction.[2]

1. See Standard Condition 4.3.2 (Appendix III.5) and Standard Commercial Property Condition 6.3.1 (Appendix III.6).
2. See Standard Condition 4.2.1 and Standard Commercial Property Condition 6.2.1.

2.3.   Registered land

2.3.1.   Investigation of title comprises:

    (a)   an examination of the official copy entries of the title supplied by the seller (including a copy of the lease where the title is leasehold and documents which are referred to on the register and evidence relating to matters as to which the register is not conclusive);[1]

    (b)   checking for evidence of overriding interests as these are not entered on the register but are binding on the buyer irrespective of notice; and

    (c)   pre-completion searches (see E2).

2.3.2.   Particular points which may arise out of the examination of the official copy entries of the title are dealt with below.

2.3.3.   The existence of most overriding interests can be discovered through:

    (a)   pre-contract enquiries of the seller under which the seller will normally be asked to reveal details of adverse interests and occupiers' rights. A seller who did not disclose such matters might be liable to the buyer for non-disclosure (see B5);

    (b)   a local land charges search (local land charges not protected on the register are overriding interests);

    (c)   inspection of the property before exchange which may reveal, e.g. occupiers, easements, or adverse possession. The buyer may also be advised to re-inspect immediately prior to completion.

2.3.4.   The examination of official copy entries of the title in registered land is a relatively quick and simple process. So long as a note is made of any matters on which requisitions need to be raised the method of investigation to be employed with a registered title is a matter to be decided by the solicitor concerned.

Official copies of the title

2.3.5.   The following points should be checked:

    (a)   on the property register:

        (i)   the description of the land accords with the contract description;

      (ii)   the title number corresponds with that given on the contract;

      (iii)   the estate – is it freehold or leasehold?

      (iv)   easements enjoyed by the property (if they are entered on the register) (see B26.5 and B26.6);

      (v)   has any land been removed from the title? If so, does this affect the land being purchased?

(b)   on the proprietorship register:

      (i)   is the class of title correct?

      (ii)   is the seller the registered proprietor? If not, who has the ability to transfer the land?

      (iii)   the existence and effect of any other entries (restrictions, or pre-Land Registration Act 2002 cautions or inhibitions);

(c)   on the charges register:

      (i)   are there any incumbrances or other entries?

      (ii)   how do these affect the buyer?

      (iii)   which of them will be removed or discharged on completion and how will their removal be effected?

(d)   on the title plan:

      (i)   is the land being purchased included within the title?

      (ii)   check any colourings/hatchings which may indicate rights of way, the extent of covenants or land which has been removed from the title;

(e)   the date of issue of the official copy entries of the title.

Adverse entries in the proprietorship register

2.3.6.   The most commonly found entry on the proprietorship register will be a restriction which regulates the circumstances in which a disposition of a registered estate may be the subject of an entry in the register.[2] The wording of the restriction will indicate what procedure must be followed in order to conduct a valid disposition of the land. The buyer must therefore either follow that procedure (e.g. payment of money to two trustees in the case of land held on a trust of land) or require the seller to procure the removal of the restriction from the register on or before completion. In some cases a pre-Land Registration Act 2002 inhibition will be found on the proprietorship register (usually in connection with the bankruptcy of the proprietor) which will prevent any disposition of the land until it is removed. Similarly, a caution may have been entered on the register before Land Registration Act 2002 was implemented. In the absence of a withdrawal no dealing with the land could be registered until the Registrar has served notice on the cautioner giving him the opportunity to show cause why the dealing to the buyer should not proceed.

1. See Standard Condition 4.2.1 (Appendix III.5) and Standard Commercial Property Condition 6.3.1 (Appendix III.6).
2. Land Registration Act 2002, s.40(1).

2.4. Unregistered land

2.4.1. Investigation of title comprises:

(a) an examination of the documents supplied in the abstract or epitome to check that:

    (i) the root document is as provided for by the contract or, if none is specified, complies with Law of Property Act 1925, s.44 (see D1). The root document will usually have been specified by special condition of the contract. Once contracts have been exchanged it is too late to object to the date or nature of the deed being offered as a root of title. If the wrong document has been supplied, the buyer is entitled to insist on the correct document being supplied in its place. Both parties may agree to substitute a different document as the root of title;[1]

    (ii) there is an unbroken chain of ownership beginning with the seller in the root document and ending with the present seller;

    (iii) there are no defects in the title which will adversely affect the buyer's title or the interests of his lender;

(b) verification, i.e. inspection of the original deeds (see D2.14);

(c) checking for evidence of occupiers (this is normally done by inspection of the property);

(d) pre-completion searches (see E2);

(e) checking the date when the area became subject to compulsory registration to ensure no event triggering registration has taken place since that date (see Land Registry Practice Guide 51 for the relevant date).

1. The substitution of a different document would constitute a variation of contract and will be subject to Law of Property (Miscellaneous Provisions) Act 1989, s.2. See *McCausland* v. *Duncan Lawrie Ltd* [1996] 4 All ER 995.

2.5. Method of investigation (unregistered land)

2.5.1. Examination of an unregistered title can be a complex and time-consuming business. It is essential that each of the documents within the abstract or epitome is carefully scrutinised to ensure that it is in order and a note made of any irregularities which need to be clarified by way of requisitions with the seller (see D2.6).

2.5.2.   To ensure that nothing is overlooked on investigation it is recommended that the solicitor adopts and follows a systematic and thorough method of investigation of an unregistered title and allows himself sufficient time in which to carry out this procedure at an unhurried pace. Except in the simplest cases, written notes of the title should be made while carrying out the investigation so that these notes can be used as the basis for framing requisitions and, if needed, will be available for reference at a later stage of the transaction.

Method

2.5.3.   (a)   Check each document chronologically starting with the root.

      (b)   Is the root as provided for in the contract? (See D2.4.1.)

      (c)   Is there an unbroken chain of title from the root to the present day?

      Then, in each document within the abstract or epitome, check the following points, making written notes of any matter which needs to be clarified or rechecked:

      (d)   **Date**

      A deed is not invalid because it is not dated or is wrongly dated, but the date of the document will:

      (i)   establish whether a root document is a good root (see D2.4.1);

      (ii)   affect the amount of stamp duty payable;

      (iii)   affect its vulnerability under Insolvency Act 1986 in the case of a voluntary disposition;

      (iv)   assist in making a reasoned judgement on an apparent defect in title, e.g. a technical defect in a document which is over 15 years old may be less detrimental to the title than one contained in a more recent document.

      (e)   **Stamp duty and SDLT**

      (i)   For transactions completed under the Stamp Act 1891 regime (as amended) and subject to impress of stamps on documents, ad valorem and Particulars Delivered stamp should be checked. The amount of duty will depend on the nature of the document, the value of the consideration and the date of the document. The seller must be required to rectify any irregularities of this nature. If no certificate of value is included in the document, stamp duty at full rate should have been paid on the conveyance. In the event of doubt, the buyer should insist that the earlier document is adjudicated and any additional duty, penalties and interest paid (see also D2.13.2–D2.13.5).

      (ii)   The majority of unregistered land transactions entered into since SDLT came into force on 1 December 2003 will have resulted in an application for registration of title at the Land Registry. For an unregistered transaction which was subject to SDLT, such as a lease granted for a term not exceeding seven years:

- is the assignment an assignment of a lease that was exempt from SDLT on grant?

- will the buyer become liable to pay SDLT on remainder of term (as if a new grant)?

- has any relief been claimed by seller or connected party? Will this transaction trigger clawback (e.g. group relief or charities relief)?

- does the buyer need seller's warranties in respect of SDLT?

- is there an obligation to file a further tax return following the ascertainment of an uncertain rent?

(f) **Parties**

For example, are the seller's names as shown on the previous document?

(g) **Description of the property**

Does it accord with the contract and is it consistent throughout the epitome?

(h) **Acknowledgements for production of earlier deeds**

Is there one where necessary, e.g. where deeds are being retained by the seller on a sale of part?

(i) **Execution**

Have all formalities been observed?

(j) **Powers of attorney**

Is the disposition by the attorney valid and are subsequent buyers protected?

(k) **Endorsements on deeds**

Are those that are necessary present, and are there any adverse memoranda?

(l) **Incumbrances**

What are they? Are they as expected? Is there a chain of indemnity covenants where required?

(m) **Easements and rights**

Are these as expected? Do they follow down the chain? Have any been added or taken away? (See B26.)

(n) **Receipt clause**

This is evidence (although not necessarily conclusive evidence) that the seller's lien for the unpaid purchase price has been extinguished.[1]

(o) **Searches supplied with the abstract**

Have searches against all previous estate owners been abstracted or are there gaps? Are the names and periods searched against correct? Did completion take place within the priority period?

(p) **Compulsory registration**

Check:

(i) that there has been no conveyance on sale since the area became one of compulsory registration. The date of the compulsory registration order can be checked from Land Registry Practice Guide 51;

(ii) that there has been no dealing of any kind since 1 April 1998.

If necessary the seller should be required to register before completion.

1. See *London and Cheshire Insurance Co. Ltd* v. *Laplagrene Property Co. Ltd* [1971] Ch 499.

2.6. Root of title and interpretation of a conveyance

2.6.1. Documents which are capable of being used as a good root of title are listed in D1.4.4.

2.6.2. The document which is to constitute the root will be specified by a special condition in the contract and once contracts have been exchanged cannot be changed except with the consent of both parties (and, where relevant, the buyer's lender) and provided that the variation of the contract meets the requirements of Law of Property (Miscellaneous Provisions) Act 1989, s.2.[1]

2.6.3. Generally the buyer cannot require evidence of title prior to the root except:[2]

(a) he is always entitled to a copy of a power of attorney under which any abstracted document is executed;

(b) where an abstracted document refers to an earlier document, he may call for that earlier document, e.g. where an abstracted document refers to restrictive covenants imposed by a pre-root conveyance, the document imposing the covenants may be called for;

(c) where an abstracted document describes the property by reference to a plan which is attached to or referred to in an earlier document, that earlier document may be called for so that the plan may be examined;

(d) any document creating any limitation or trust by reference to which any part of the property is disposed of by an abstracted document may be called for even if dated pre-root.

2.6.4. Where the root document is a conveyance, or the epitome reveals a conveyance elsewhere in the chain of title, the following guidance may assist in the interpretation of the conveyance.

2.6.5. The conveyance will start with the words 'This conveyance' followed by the date and the full names and addresses of all the parties to the deed.

2.6.6. Recitals do not form an operative part of the body of the deed but are more in the nature of a preamble, the function of which is to introduce the nature of and to set the scene for the deed which follows, e.g. by explaining the recent history of the title. Although recitals do not form an operative part of the deed, a party is estopped from later denying the accuracy of a statement of fact made in a recital. Recitals of fact which are contained in a deed which is 20 years old are by Law of Property Act 1925, s.45(6) deemed to be correct. Where there is an ambiguity in an operative part of the deed, recitals may be looked at and used to clarify that ambiguity.[3] Where personal representatives are required to give a statement under Administration of Estates Act 1925, s.36(6) that they have not made any previous assent or conveyance, such statement is usually dealt with by way of recital. Similarly a statement that the survivor of joint tenants is solely and beneficially entitled to the property (required under Law of Property (Joint Tenants) Act 1964) is commonly dealt with in this way.

2.6.7. A consideration and receipt clause will be included (see E1.10.6).

2.6.8. The operative word ('convey(s)') is followed by a statement of title guarantee which imports covenants for title (see section M).

2.6.9. The parcels clause must clearly and adequately describe the land being sold. Where the sale is of part of the seller's land, reference will generally be made to the land which is retained by the seller, such land being identified on the plan annexed to the deed.

2.6.10. Express reference may be made to benefits previously enjoyed by the land which are to pass to the buyer.

2.6.11. Clauses may be included to deal with exceptions, i.e. those matters which are excluded from the land and which do not therefore pass to the buyer, and to reservations, i.e. those matters which (usually on a sale of part) are being regranted by the buyer for the benefit of the seller.

2.6.12. Easements which are to be expressly granted to the buyer (usually only on a sale of part) may be included.

2.6.13. The habendum ('to hold') is followed by express references to the estate conveyed (fee simple) and existing incumbrances, e.g. existing restrictive covenants subject to which the property is sold.

2.6.14.   Declarations may be inserted, e.g. on a sale of part to negate the implied grant rules especially in respect of rights of light and air following a contractual provision to this effect (see E1.11.5). Declarations may also be used to define the ownership of party walls.

2.6.15.   Where the property is bought by co-owners a statement of their capacity will be included, i.e. as joint tenants or tenants in common. Where the co-owners are tenants in common the division of the beneficial interest between them may be specified either in the conveyance or by separate deed of trust. Since 1 January 1997 it is no longer necessary to include a clause to extend the powers of the trustees to make them co-extensive with those of an absolute owner because these powers are implied by Trusts of Land and Appointment of Trustees Act 1996, s.6.

2.6.16.   On a sale of part, new restrictive covenants may be imposed (see E1.11).

2.6.17.   Where existing positive covenants or restrictive covenants which are not limited to ownership will continue to bind the land after completion of the sale to the buyer an indemnity covenant will be included in fulfilment of the contractual obligation to that effect.[4]

2.6.18.   If any of the documents of title which the seller had were not to be handed over to the buyer on completion, e.g. a grant of probate or all the title deeds on a sale of part, an acknowledgement for their production and undertaking for safe custody will be included in the document. By Law of Property Act 1925, s.64 the acknowledgement gives a right to production of the named document(s) at the cost of the person requiring production. Production may be required, e.g. to satisfy requisition raised by a sub-purchaser. This right is reiterated by Standard Condition 4.6.5 and Standard Commercial Condition 6.6.5. All sellers will give an acknowledgement for production (where relevant), but only a beneficial owner gives the undertaking for safe custody. The undertaking gives a right of damages (but no other remedy) if the named document(s) is lost or destroyed otherwise than by fire or inevitable accident. Such an undertaking is not appropriate in a situation where the seller is not the true owner of the deeds. If the title deeds which were being retained are not in the seller's possession at the time of completion, e.g. on a sale of part, they may be in the hands of his lender; the seller may give a covenant that he will give an undertaking for safe custody as and when the title deeds come into his possession.

2.6.19.   The document concludes with schedules (if any), e.g. of covenants, etc., testimonium (in witness) and attestation clauses. Since 31 July 1990 the attestation clause should contain the words 'signed as a deed' to comply with Law of Property (Miscellaneous Provisions) Act 1989, s.1.

1. See *McCausland* v. *Duncan Lawrie Ltd* [1996] 4 All ER 995.
2. Law of Property Act 1925, s.45.
3. The converse situation is not true. An ambiguous recital cannot be clarified by a statement in the operative part of the deed.
4. See Standard Condition 4.6.4 and Standard Commercial Condition 6.6.4. Also see E1.10.8.

2.7. Problem areas

2.7.1. The transaction with the seller and any past transactions revealed in the official copies or the epitome should be considered to see if they involve any of the problem areas in D2.8 to D2.12.

2.8. Conveyance by trustees to themselves

2.8.1. If on the title there is a conveyance by trustees or personal representatives to one of themselves, enquiry must be made into the circumstances of the transaction since, on the face of it, such a conveyance is in breach of trust and is voidable by the beneficiaries without enquiry as to fairness.

2.8.2. Such a transaction can be justified if one of the following situations exists:

(a) there is proof of a pre-existing contract to purchase, an option or right of pre-emption in favour of the trustee or personal representative;

(b) the personal representative was a beneficiary under the will or intestacy of the seller;

(c) the consent of all the beneficiaries being legally competent was obtained to the transaction;

(d) the conveyance was made under an order of the court;

(e) the transaction was sanctioned by the trust instrument.

2.9. Particular capacities

Trustees of land

Registered land

2.9.1. In registered land, a Form A (or earlier Form 62) restriction may be entered on the proprietorship register indicating what must be done to overreach the beneficial interests. A further restriction may also be entered reflecting any other limitations on the trustees' powers to dispose of the land. Provided the terms of any restriction are complied with the buyer will get good title. Where trustees hold the land on trust for themselves as joint tenants in equity, no restriction is placed on the register and the buyer may safely deal with the survivor on proof of death of the other trustee.

Unregistered land

2.9.2. Such trustees have a wide power of sale,[1] and if consents are required to a sale a buyer is not concerned to see that the consents of more than two persons are obtained and is never concerned with the consents of persons under disability (i.e. minors, persons under mental incapacity).

2.9.3. A buyer paying his money to the trustees, being at least two individuals or a trust corporation, will take the land free from the equitable interests of the beneficiaries, but not otherwise.[2] Thus a conveyance on the title by a sole individual trustee will require investigation.

Personal representatives

Registered land

2.9.4. Personal representatives may apply to become registered as proprietors of the land. In this case, provided the buyer deals with the registered proprietors and complies with any restriction on the register, he will get good title. Personal representatives would not normally register themselves as proprietors unless they intended to hold on to the land without disposing of it for some period of time, e.g. during the minority of a beneficiary. In other cases the personal representatives will produce their grant of representation to the buyer as proof of their authority to deal with the land. Provided the buyer takes a transfer from all the proving personal representatives and submits an office copy or certified copy of the grant with his application for registration, he will obtain a good title.[3] A transfer or assent made by personal representatives must be in the form prescribed.[4]

Unregistered land

2.9.5. Personal representatives have the wide powers of trustees of land. If there is only one proving personal representative he has all the powers of two or more personal representatives and consequently (unlike a sole individual trustee) can convey the land on his own and give a valid receipt for the proceeds of sale. If, however, the grant is made to two or more personal representatives, they must all join in the assent or conveyance, but a sole proving personal representative of an absolute owner is entitled to act on his own. A buyer must therefore call for the grant to see who have been appointed as personal representatives, and must insist that all the personal representatives named in the grant join in the assent or conveyance, or call for evidence of the death of any personal representative who will not be a party to the purchase deed. However, a sole surviving personal representative cannot give a valid receipt for the proceeds of sale.

2.9.6. An assent made by personal representatives must be in writing in order to pass the legal estate in the land to the beneficiary. The beneficiary who is to take the land must be named in the document, which must be signed by the personal representatives. If the document contains covenants given by the beneficiary (e.g. indemnity in respect of existing restrictive covenants) it must be by deed. Even where the beneficiary is also the sole personal representative (as may be the case where a widow is her deceased husband's sole personal representative and sole beneficiary) a written assent is required.[5] A buyer from an assentee (or a subsequent buyer where there is an assent in the chain of title) must check that a memorandum of the assent was endorsed on the grant; otherwise, there is a danger that a later sale by the personal representatives will have deprived the assentee of legal ownership (see D2.9.7).

2.9.7.   The effect of Administration of Estates Act 1925, s.36 is that an assent in favour of a beneficiary may be defeated by a later sale of the land by the personal representatives in favour of a buyer who takes from them a written statement that they have made no previous assent or conveyance of the land. However, this will not be the case if either there was an endorsement of a previous assent on the grant or there had been a previous sale by the assentee. It follows that a conveyance on sale by personal representatives should contain a section 36(6) statement and that an assentee (and a buyer) should require an endorsement on the grant. This may be done at the cost of the estate. Where the transaction induces first registration (as it almost always will) an endorsement on the grant is not required.

2.9.8.   A disposition by personal representatives should contain an acknowledgement of the right to production of their grant of representation as this is a document of title the inspection of which may be required by subsequent buyers of the land. The grant should be inspected to check for endorsements which have been made on it.

2.9.9.   An assent or conveyance by personal representatives of a legal estate is sufficient evidence in favour of a buyer that the person in whose favour it is made is the person entitled to have the legal estate conveyed to him, unless there is a memorandum of a previous assent or conveyance on the grant. This in effect means that a buyer from an assentee of land, having checked the grant and found no adverse endorsements, does not have to look at the deceased's will to check that the assentee was rightly entitled to the land, but this provision will not protect the buyer if it is apparent from some other source (e.g. the assent itself) that it was made in favour of the wrong person.[6]

2.9.10.   On a sale by the personal representatives of the survivor of beneficial joint tenants, a statement should be included in the conveyance to the effect that the survivor was solely and beneficially entitled so that the buyer has the protection of Law of Property (Joint Tenants) Act 1964. If such personal representatives did not sell the land but made an assent in favour of a beneficiary, the assent should properly include the above statement in order to protect a buyer from the assentee. If the statement was missing from the assent, consideration should be given to joining the personal representatives of the survivor into the conveyance by the assentee in order to give the statement.

2.9.11.   If a sole or sole surviving trustee of a trust of land dies in a case where a buyer cannot rely on the 1964 Act (because the survivor was not solely and benefi- cially entitled), his personal representatives can exercise all the powers of that trustee. If a sole personal representative is appointed in such a situation, he can act on his own in dealing with the deceased's private property (including land), but he must act jointly with another trustee in making a disposition of the trust property under which capital money arises.

Co-owners

2.9.12.   Co-owners hold land on a trust of land and the remarks relating to trustees in D2.9.1, D2.9.2 and D2.9.3 apply.

Registered land

2.9.13.   If the co-owners are tenants in common in equity, there will generally be a restriction on the proprietorship register to the effect that no disposition by a sole proprietor of the registered estate (except a trust corporation) under which capital money arises is to be registered unless authorised by an order of the court. In the event of the death of one or more of the co-owners, so that at the time of sale there is only one surviving trustee, a second trustee must be appointed to join with the survivor in the transfer. Alternatively, the buyer can deal with the survivor alone provided that the restriction is removed from the register, or the survivor provides the buyer with documentary evidence which will enable the restriction to be removed on the buyer's application for registration. Such proof might consist of a statutory declaration by the survivor that in stated circumstances the declarant had become entitled legally and beneficially to the registered estate and that he has not encumbered or dealt with his own share nor has he received notice of any incumbrance on or dealing with the deceased's share. A certificate by the seller's conveyancer will be accepted in place of a declaration if the conveyancer is able to speak from his knowledge of all the relevant facts. In practice, it is better either for the seller to procure the removal of the restriction or to appoint a second trustee to act with the seller.

2.9.14.   If the co-owners are joint tenants in equity, no restriction is placed on the register and a buyer may deal with the survivor of them on proof of the death of the deceased co-owner.

Unregistered land

2.9.15.   Inspection of the conveyance under which the co-owners bought the land will reveal whether they held as joint tenants or tenants in common in equity.

2.9.16.   The sole survivor of tenants in common does not automatically become entitled to the whole equitable estate in the land since a tenancy in common is capable of passing by will or on intestacy. The trust therefore still subsists and a buyer from the survivor should insist on taking a conveyance only from two trustees in order to overreach any beneficial interests which may subsist under the trust. Alternatively, if the survivor has become solely and beneficially entitled to the whole legal and equitable interest in the land, he may convey alone on proof to the buyer of this fact. Such proof would consist of the death certificate of the deceased, a certified or office copy of the grant of representation and an assent made in favour of the survivor.

2.9.17.   The survivor of beneficial joint tenants becomes entitled to the whole legal and equitable interest in the land but a buyer from him will only accept a conveyance from the survivor alone if he can be satisfied that he will gain the protection of Law of Property (Joint Tenants) Act 1964. This Act (which is retrospective in operation to 1925) allows the buyer to assume that no severance of the joint tenancy (turning it into a tenancy in common) had occurred before the death of the deceased joint tenant. To gain the protection of the Act the following three conditions must all be satisfied:

   (a)   there must be no memorandum of severance endorsed on the conveyance under which the joint tenants bought the property;

   (b)   there must be no bankruptcy proceedings registered against the names of either of the joint tenants;

   (c)   the conveyance by the survivor must contain a recital stating that the survivor is solely and beneficially entitled to the land.

   If any of the above conditions is not met, the survivor must be treated as a surviving tenant in common and the procedure in D2.9.16 followed.

Settled land

2.9.18.   Section 2 Trusts of Land and Appointment of Trustees Act 1996 prohibits the creation of new strict settlements (except in limited circumstances). The following sub-paragraphs will generally be relevant only to settlements which were in existence on 1 January 1997.

Registered land

2.9.19.   The tenant for life (or, if none, the statutory owners) will be registered as proprietor of the land and an appropriate restriction entered on the register. This restriction will be in Form G, H or I.[7] Provided the buyer complies with the terms of the restriction he will take a good title.

Unregistered land

2.9.20.   Where land is settled land within Settled Land Act 1925, the legal estate in the land will be vested in the tenant for life under the Act by a vesting instrument, which will be a vesting deed in the case of an *inter vivos* settlement) and may be a vesting assent by the personal representatives of the deceased where the settlement arises under a will. In exceptional cases, e.g. where the person who would otherwise be tenant for life is a minor, the legal estate will be vested in the trustees of the settlement as statutory owners. Both the tenant for life and the statutory owners have a wide power of sale under the Act (which can be extended by the terms of the settlement itself) but it is provided by Settled Land Act 1925, s.18 that where the land is the subject of a vesting instrument and the trustees of the settlement have not been discharged, any disposition which is not authorised by the Act or by the settlement is void. Further, where capital money arises on a disposition of the land, the disposition is of no effect for the purposes of the Act unless the money is paid to the trustees of the settlement, being at least two individuals or a trust corporation.

2.9.21. A vesting instrument under Settled Land Act 1925 must describe the land, name the person in whose favour it is vested and name the trustees of the settlement for the purposes of the Act. Except in exceptional circumstances, a buyer is bound and entitled to rely on these statements and cannot call for the trust instrument.

Lenders

2.9.22. A power to sell the legal estate vested in the borrower, subject to prior incumbrances but discharged from subsequent ones, is given by Law of Property Act 1925, s.101 to every lender whose mortgage is made by deed. Thus unless expressly excluded the power is available to a lender who has taken a legal mortgage and to one whose equitable mortgage is made by deed. In order actually to convey the legal estate of the borrower to the buyer an equitable lender whose mortgage is not made by deed must adopt some conveyancing device such as an irrevocable power of attorney granted by way of security in his favour by the borrower. An equitable lender whose mortgage is made by deed can apply to the court under Law of Property Act 1925, s.90 for an order for sale and an order appointing a person to convey the land.

2.9.23. In relation to registered land, the proprietor of a registered charge is taken to have the powers of disposition conferred by law on the owner of a legal mortgage in the absence of any entry in the register to the contrary.[8] The owner of a charge which is not substantively registered has no statutory power of sale.

2.9.24. The power of sale arises when the mortgage money becomes due under the mortgage, i.e. on the legal date for redemption which is usually set at an early date in the mortgage term. The power only becomes exercisable by the lender when one of the events specified in Law of Property Act 1925, s.103 has occurred (see B7.7.5). A buyer from the lender must check (by looking at the mortgage deed) that the power of sale has arisen, but is not concerned to enquire whether the power has become exercisable.

2.9.25. The sale must be genuine; a sale to the lender's nominee or to a company controlled by him will not be treated as a valid exercise of the power of sale.

Attorneys

2.9.26. The buyer is entitled to a certified copy of any power of attorney which affects the title (even if in unregistered land the power is dated earlier than the root of title). The buyer must check that the power authorises the transaction and that it has not been revoked before the transaction in question.

2.9.27. Where the seller is a sole legal owner he can delegate his power to sell using a general power under Powers of Attorney Act 1971, s.10. A certified copy of the power should be handed over on completion.

2.9.28. Where co-owners are concerned the requirements vary according to the date of the transaction:

> (a) before 1 March 2000 a co-owner who wanted to appoint an attorney to act for him on the sale had to use a specific power of attorney under Trustee Act 1925, s.25. This power was only effective for a period of 12 months. Under a Trustee Act power a co-owner or trustee could not appoint his sole co-trustee to be his attorney. If a co-owner or trustee wished to appoint his sole co-trustee an enduring power of attorney under Enduring Powers of Attorney Act 1985 should have been used;
>
> (b) on or after 1 March 2000 a co-owner who has a beneficial interest in the land can use a general power of attorney and can appoint his sole co-trustee to be his attorney (Trustee Delegation Act 1999, s.1);
>
> (c) under Trustee Delegation Act 1999, trustees who are not beneficially entitled to the land may use a general trustee power (Trustee Delegation Act 1999, s.5). However, the general trustee power is only effective for a period of 12 months. The trustee can appoint his sole co-trustee to be his attorney under the general trustee power;
>
> (d) however, whether a general power or general trustee power is used, if a sole co-trustee has been appointed to act as attorney he cannot give a valid receipt for capital money. Overreaching cannot operate in these circumstances. If one of two owners wishes to appoint an attorney to execute the purchase deed, he should therefore appoint a third party to act as attorney. From 1 March 2000, enduring powers of attorney cannot be used to appoint a sole co-trustee to be an attorney.

Registered land

2.9.29. If any document executed by an attorney is delivered to the Land Registry there must be produced to the registrar either the instrument creating the power of attorney or a sufficient copy of the power or a certificate by a solicitor or conveyancer in Form 1.[9]

2.9.30. If the transaction between the attorney and the buyer is not made within 12 months of the date on which the power came into operation, the registrar may require evidence to satisfy him that the power has not been revoked. This may consist of or include a statutory declaration or statement of truth by the buyer or a certificate given by the buyer's conveyancer in Form 2.[10]

2.9.31. For more information on powers of attorney and registered land, see Land Registry Practice Guide 9.

Unregistered land

2.9.32. A buyer from an attorney holding such a power of attorney under Powers of Attorney Act 1971, s.4 will take good title provided that he had no actual knowledge that the power had been revoked with the attorney's consent.

2.9.33. A person who buys directly from the attorney will take good title under Powers of Attorney Act 1971, s.5(2) provided he buys in good faith without knowledge of the revocation of the power. The power is revoked automatically if the donor dies, becomes bankrupt or becomes incapable of managing his own affairs. Thus the buyer cannot take good title if he is aware of the death, bankruptcy or incapacity of the donor. A subsequent purchaser gains the protection of Powers of Attorney Act 1971, s.5(4) if either:

(a) the dealing between the attorney and his immediate purchaser took place within 12 months of the grant of the power; or

(b) the person who buys directly from the attorney makes a statutory declaration within three months of completion of his transaction to the effect that he had no knowledge of the revocation of the power.

2.9.34. Where a person buys directly from an attorney more than 12 months after the date of the grant of the power, the buyer's solicitor should require his client immediately on completion of the transaction to make the requisite statutory declaration, since this document will be required as evidence of non-revocation on a subsequent disposition of the property. If not made immediately, and the buyer client dies before making the declaration, there will be a defect in title, since the subsequent buyer will not be able to take the protection of Powers of Attorney Act 1971, s.5(4).

2.9.35. An enduring power of attorney is one made under Enduring Powers of Attorney Act 1985. This Act has been repealed and the provisions governing enduring powers are now contained in Mental Capacity Act 2005, Sched.4. Until the incapacity of the donor the enduring power of attorney takes effect as an ordinary power and Mental Capacity Act 2005, Sched.4, Part 6 contains provisions to protect buyers which are similar to those outlined above. On the incapacity of the donor the attorney's authority to act becomes limited to such acts as are necessary for the protection of the donor and his estate until such time as the power is registered with the Office of the Public Guardian. Once registered, the power is incapable of revocation and the attorney's full authority to act is restored. Where a person is buying from an attorney who holds an enduring power he should conduct a search at the Office of the Public Guardian to ensure that no application for registration of the power is pending. If the power has already been registered, the attorney should produce the registration certificate to the buyer. An office copy of the power can be produced as evidence both of the contents of the power and of its registration.

2.9.36. A lasting power of attorney is a statutory power of attorney created by Mental Capacity Act 2005, ss.9–14. The lasting power replaces the enduring power, although existing enduring powers will not be revoked. Where a person is buying from an attorney who holds a lasting power he should check that the lasting power is registered with the Office of the Public Guardian, the attorney is a named individual who is over 18 or a trust corporation, and the attorney is acting within the scope of their authority (i.e. that the authority is not limited by any restrictions or conditions). An office copy of the power is evidence of the contents of the power and the fact that it has been registered. The buyer from the attorney will be protected under Mental Capacity Act 2005, s.14(3) unless he knew that the power was invalid or was aware of the circumstances which would have terminated the attorney's authority to act under the power. A subsequent buyer will be protected under Mental Capacity Act 2005, s.14(4) if either the sale by the attorney to the first buyer was completed within 12 months of the date on which the power was registered, or the subsequent buyer makes a statutory declaration, before or within three months of completion of his purchase, that he had no reason to doubt that the attorney had authority to dispose of the property at the time of his purchase. See also B23.2.8 and the Law Society's Lasting Powers of Attorney Practice Note (24 September 2007).

2.9.37.   Powers granted before 1 October 1971 are governed by Law of Property Act 1925, ss.126–128 and not by Powers of Attorney Act 1971.

1.   Trusts of Land and Appointment of Trustees Act 1996, s.6.
2.   Law of Property Act 1925, ss.2 and 27.
3.   Land Registration Rules 2003, r.162.
4.   Land Registration Rules 2003, r.58.
5.   *Re King's Will Trusts* [1964] Ch 542.
6.   Administration of Estates Act 1925, s.36.
7.   See Land Registration Rules 2003, Sched.4 as to the wording of the restrictions.
8.   Land Registration Act 2002, s.52.
9.   Land Registration Rules 2003, r.61 and Sched.3.
10.   *Ibid.*, r.62 and Sched.3.

2.10.   Discharged mortgages

Registered land

2.10.1.   A mortgage over registered land which has been discharged will be deleted from the charges register of the title and is thus of no further concern to the buyer. As to the discharge of the seller's existing mortgage see F4.2.13.

Unregistered land

2.10.2.   Discharged legal mortgages should be abstracted by the seller and checked by the buyer's solicitor to ensure that the discharge was validly effected. Discharged equitable mortgages will not normally be abstracted and once discharged no longer affect the title.

2.10.3.   Where a sale has been effected by a lender in exercise of his power of sale, the mortgage deed will not bear a receipt.

2.10.4.   In the case of a building society mortgage, provided that the receipt (usually endorsed on the mortgage deed) is in the form of wording prescribed by Building Societies Act 1986, and is signed by a person authorised by the particular society, the receipt may be treated as an effective discharge of the mortgage without further enquiry being made.

2.10.5.   In other cases, by Law of Property Act 1925, s.115 a receipt endorsed on the mortgage deed (even if the receipt is not executed as a deed) operates to discharge the mortgage provided it is signed by the lender and names the person making repayment. However, where the money appears to have been paid by a person not entitled to the immediate equity of redemption, the receipt will usually operate as a transfer by deed of the mortgage. Thus if the person making repayment is not the borrower named in the mortgage or a personal representative or trustee acting on his behalf, the receipt should make it expressly clear that the receipt is to operate as such and is not intended to be a transfer of the mortgage to the person making payment. If the borrower makes repayment of the mortgage debt, but the receipt is dated later than the date of the conveyance by the borrower to a buyer of the land charged, at the date of the receipt the borrower will not be the person immediately entitled to the equity of redemption under the mortgage, because the mortgage had not been discharged at the date of completion of the sale of the land; thus the buyer will technically have bought the land subject to this incumbrance. In these circumstances the receipt operates to transfer the mortgage to the borrower (and not as a receipt) and it is, in theory, undischarged. In reality, any rights which the borrower has under the mortgage are unlikely to be enforced since he may be estopped from setting up the mortgage against the buyer. The borrower's position is at best that of a puisne mortgagee, since the title deeds will have passed to the buyer on completion of the sale, and unless registered as a Class C(i) or C(iii) land charge would be unenforceable against a subsequent buyer of the land for valuable consideration.[1] A buyer should therefore check the mortgage receipt to see who made repayment and also check that the receipt is dated no later than the date of the next transaction in the chain. If the mortgage receipt appears inadvertently to have transferred the mortgage and not discharged it a requisition should be raised to ensure that the seller or his lender is in possession of the title deeds (so that no mortgage supported by deposit of deeds can have come into existence as a result of the transfer) and the buyer should make a Land Charges Department search against the name of the person who bought from the borrower to ensure that no land charge has been registered against his name. Provided that the present seller or his lender has the deeds and the result of the land charges search reveals no adverse entries the defect can be ignored.

1.   See *Cumberland Court (Brighton) Ltd* v. *Taylor* [1964] Ch 29.

2.11.   Transactions at an undervalue

2.11.1.   Dispositions which are made by way of gift or at an undervalue (whether *inter vivos* or by assent) are not generally acceptable as roots of title in unregistered land because no investigation of title would have been made by the donee at the time of the transaction. They do not therefore provide the double check on title which is afforded by an arm's length conveyance.

2.11.2.   Where a prospective buyer or mortgagee of land, whether registered or not, has notice that the land has been the subject of an undervalue transaction, it may be necessary to consider whether the courts' powers to set aside, under Insolvency Act 1986, s.238 or s.339, apply. An undervalue transaction may be the result of a gift, a partial gift (made for a consideration but a substantially below market value one), financial arrangements following a marriage breakdown, or a deed of variation in relation to an inheritance. If sections 238 or 339 do apply, it will then be necessary to see whether the protection provided by sections 241(2) and 342(2) operates. The courts' sections 238 and 339 powers are exercisable for periods of two or five years, respectively, from the date of the transaction (depending on whether the transferor was a company or an individual), but the Act's provisions protect a person acquiring in good faith and for value during those periods (see D2.11.7). For transactions at an undervalue to defraud creditors, see D2.11.10.

Dispositions by companies

2.11.3. If a company has made a disposition at an undervalue within the last two years, the transaction can be set aside on application from the liquidator or administrator on the company's subsequent insolvency if the transaction was with a person connected with the company, or if the present buyer knows that the company was insolvent at the time of the transaction or knows that the company would have become insolvent as a result of that transaction at an undervalue.

2.11.4. In any dealing where a company has made a transaction at an undervalue more than two years ago, a company search must be carried out as to whether the company went into liquidation or administration within two years of the voluntary disposition.

2.11.5. The term 'connected person' includes a director (Insolvency Act 1986, s.249).

Dispositions by individuals

2.11.6. If an individual becomes bankrupt after having made a disposition at an undervalue, the transaction can be set aside by his trustee in bankruptcy if the transaction was made within the last two years. If the transaction was made within the last five years it can be set aside if the present buyer knows that the donor was insolvent at the time of the transaction or knows that he would have become insolvent as a result of the transaction. It can also be set aside if the transaction at an undervalue was made within the last five years and it was made to an 'associate' of the donor. The word associate is widely defined in Insolvency Act 1986, s.435 to include the donor's spouse, ex-spouse, partner, partner's relatives, employers and employees. Buyers must carry out a Land Charges Department search against the donor in a transaction at undervalue to find out if he has become insolvent within five years.

Protection of the buyer

2.11.7. The courts can set aside transactions at an undervalue against subsequent owners of the property if the insolvency occurred within the two- or five-year periods. Insolvency Act 1986, s.241(2) and s.342(3), provide protection for subsequent buyers. For dispositions made on or before 26 July 1994, the transaction cannot be set aside where the buyer:

(a) was not a party to the transaction at an undervalue;

(b) acted in good faith;

(c) provided value for the purchase (i.e. the open market price) and was without notice that the transaction was at an undervalue.

2.11.8. Where the transaction at an undervalue was made after 26 July 1994, it cannot be set aside where the buyer bought in good faith and for value. Insolvency (No.2) Act 1994 amended s.241(2) and s.342(3) to the effect that the clawback will be limited to cases where either:

(a) the buyer is connected with or is an associate of the donor or donee to the transaction at an undervalue; or

(b) the buyer has notice that the transaction was at an undervalue and that the donor has become insolvent or was about to become insolvent.

If one of these two exceptions in section 241(2A) applies the buyer is rebuttably presumed not to have bought in good faith. Provided the buyer does the appropriate searches and has no knowledge of any insolvency and provided he is not an associate he will be protected from the clawback provisions.

2.11.9. Insolvency (No.2) Act 1994 was passed to deal with difficulties caused by those provisions of Insolvency Act 1986 which apply to undervalue transactions. Various questions had arisen about its effect since it came into force in July 1994. As a result, the Law Society obtained the opinion of leading counsel, Gabriel Moss QC, on certain points. Appendix IV.3 sets out his views.

2.11.10. If the transaction at an undervalue was entered into for the purpose of defrauding creditors (to put assets beyond the reach of someone or to prejudice the interest of someone in relation to a claim they may make), a person who is or is capable of being prejudiced by it can make an application under Insolvency Act 1986, s.423 to have the transaction set aside whether or not the donor is subject to insolvency procedures. Unlike applications under sections 238 and 339, there is no time limit for actions. Section 425(2) provides protection for a subsequent buyer who has acquired the property in good faith, for value and without notice of the relevant circumstances.

2.12. Effect of failure to register land charges (unregistered land)

2.12.1. Charges of Classes C(i), C(ii), C(iii) and F are void against a purchaser of any interest in the land for valuable consideration (including marriage).

2.12.2. Charges of Classes C(iv) and D are void only against a purchaser of a legal estate for money or money's worth.

2.13. Checking stamp duties

Registered land

2.13.1. Once the buyer has become registered as proprietor, the transfer and/or preregistration deeds, in general, no longer concern a subsequent buyer.

Unregistered land

2.13.2. Unstamped or incorrectly stamped documents or documents not bearing adjudication or denoting stamps where these are required by the legislation are not good roots of title, nor good links in the chain. They cannot be produced in evidence in civil proceedings and will not be accepted by the Chief Land Registrar on an application to register the title.

2.13.3. A buyer is entitled to insist that all documents within the title are properly stamped at the expense of the seller. If, therefore, on examination of the title stamping defects are found, the buyer or mortgagee should raise a requisition requiring the seller to remedy the deficiency at his own expense.[1]

2.13.4. Stamp duty may be *ad valorem* or fixed duty, the rates of which vary from time to time. Each document in the title should be checked against a table of stamp duties to ensure that it bears the correct duty in relation to the nature of the instrument, its date, and the amount of its consideration. The presence of a certificate of value in a document may have the effect of reducing the liability to duty or of exempting it from duty altogether. Where VAT has been paid on the consideration, stamp duty is payable on the VAT element of the price.

2.13.5. In addition to stamp duty, conveyances on sale and leases granted for a term of seven years or more and assignments of such leases had to be produced to HM Revenue and Customs under Finance Act 1931. On production a Produced Stamp (Particulars Delivered Stamp) was affixed to the document. The consequences of failure to produce a document are the same as for lack of stamp duty and the seller must be required to rectify any deficiency at his own expense.

1. Stamp Act 1891, s.117.

2.14. Verification of title

2.14.1. Verification of title consists of checking the evidence of title supplied by the seller against the original deeds.

2.14.2. In registered land the current state of the register can be confirmed by the buyer when making his pre-completion search at the Land Registry.

2.14.3. In unregistered land, the abstract or epitome should be checked against the seller's original deeds. The buyer's time limit for making this inspection expires with his time limit for raising requisitions. Verification should therefore be carried out as part of the investigation of title procedure. In most cases, where the title is not complex, and the photocopy documents supplied by the seller are of good quality, the buyer's solicitor postpones his verification until actual completion. If, however, he then finds an error on the title it will be too late to query the error since his time limit for raising requisitions will have expired. If there is any doubt over the validity of the title, or it is of a complex nature, verification should be carried out at the proper time. Unless the contract provides to the contrary the costs of verification are borne by the buyer. Standard Condition 4.1 and Standard Commercial Property Condition 6.1 require the seller to produce to the buyer (without cost to the buyer) the original of every document within the title or, if the original is not available, an abstract, epitome or copy with an original marking by a solicitor of examination either against the original or against an examined abstract or an examined copy.

2.15. Acting for the lender

2.15.1. The solicitor will be instructed to ensure that the property has a good and marketable title free from unspecified defects.

2.15.2. The lender may not be prepared to accept as security any property which is registered with a title other than absolute or any property which is a flying freehold.

2.15.3. Where the solicitor has been instructed under the terms of the CML Lenders' Handbook or BSA Mortgage Instructions the provisions of these documents must be observed. See in particular paragraphs 5.4 and 5.5 of the CML Lenders' Handbook relating to a good and marketable title.

D3. Requisitions on title

3.1. Purpose of requisitions

3.1.1. The purpose of requisitions on title is to require the seller's solicitor to clarify and if necessary to rectify matters on the title supplied which the buyer's solicitor finds unsatisfactory. In practice they are commonly used also to resolve administrative queries relating to the arrangements for completion.

3.2. Time for raising requisitions

3.2.1. Where title has been deduced following exchange, Standard Condition 4.3.1 and Standard Commercial Property Condition 6.3.1 require written requisitions on the title supplied to be raised within six working days after either the date of the contract or the day of delivery of the seller's evidence of title, whichever is the later. The buyer will lose his right to raise requisitions if he does not do so within the time limits prescribed by these conditions. If the evidence of title is incomplete and this fact is pointed out to the seller within the above period, under Standard Condition 4.3.1 and Standard Commercial Property Condition 6.3.1, the buyer's solicitor has six working days from the supply of additional evidence to raise requisitions on that additional evidence. By Standard Condition 4.3.4 and Standard Commercial Property Condition 6.3.4, this time limit may be adjusted *pro rata* to fit a completion date which is less than 15 working days from the date of the contract.

3.2.2. Where title has been deduced prior to exchange, Standard Condition 4.2.1 and Standard Commercial Property Condition 6.2.1 prevent the raising of requisitions after exchange, but only in relation to matters disclosed by the seller prior to exchange. The buyer may still raise requisitions on previously undisclosed title problems after exchange, so long as he does so within six working days of the problem coming to his attention.[1]

1. See Standard Condition 4.2.2 and Standard Commercial Property Condition 6.2.2.

3.3. Standard form requisitions

3.3.1. A standard form of requisitions (TA13 Completion information and requisitions on title form) is published by the Law Society. Most law stationers produce a standard form of requisitions on title which includes many commonly asked questions, e.g. confirmation that the seller's mortgage on the property will be discharged on or before completion. The seller's solicitor should be asked to confirm that the answers given to enquiries before contract remain correct. Additionally the printed questions frequently deal with the administrative arrangements for completion itself, e.g. method of payment of money. Queries which are specific to the title under consideration may be added to the end of the standard form or typed on a separate sheet. The buyer's solicitor should send two copies of the form to the seller's solicitor who will return one copy with his answers appended, keeping the other copy on his own file for reference. Standard Condition 4.3.1 and Standard Commercial Property Condition 6.3.1 require the seller's solicitor to reply to requisitions within four working days after receiving them from the buyer's solicitor.

3.4. Further queries

3.4.1. On receipt of replies from the seller's solicitor, the buyer's solicitor should ensure that the answers given to his queries are satisfactory both in relation to the title and to the client's interests. Any replies which are unsatisfactory should be taken up with the seller's solicitor and further written queries raised until the matter is resolved.

3.4.2. Standard Condition 4.3.1 and Standard Commercial Property Condition 6.3.1 govern the time limits for raising observations on the seller's replies to requisitions.

3.4.3. In some cases the replies given to requisitions may be construed as undertakings, e.g. to discharge the seller's outstanding mortgage on the property. Where such an undertaking is given the seller's solicitor should ensure that he has only committed himself to do what is within his power to do; an undertaking to discharge the seller's mortgage(s) on the property or one which is simply worded 'confirmed' or 'noted' will be interpreted as meaning that *all* subsisting charges will be removed. The seller's solicitor should therefore ensure that he is fully aware of the details of all such charges before committing himself to such an undertaking. Alternatively, the seller's solicitor or licensed conveyancer may prefer to undertake to discharge certain named charges only. Similarly, an unqualified promise to send title deeds within a specific time limit should only be given where these deeds are in the possession or control of the seller's solicitor.

3.4.4. From the buyer's point of view, the buyer's solicitor should ensure that he asks the seller's solicitor to supply a list of all outstanding charges and obtains a specific undertaking in relation to each of them. See F4.2.13 to F4.2.15 for further details of the considerations that apply in this situation.

3.5. Restrictions on subject matter of requisitions

3.5.1. The buyer's solicitor is only entitled to raise requisitions on the title which he has, by contractual condition, agreed to accept. Except where Law of Property

Act 1925, s.45 applies, he cannot in the case of unregistered land require production of documents prior to the root of title.[1] The buyer's right to raise requisitions may be curtailed or excluded by a condition in the contract. Such a restriction only takes effect on exchange of contracts and does not preclude the buyer from raising queries in relation to that particular matter before contracts are exchanged. If the seller wishes to curtail or exclude the buyer's right to raise requisitions he must make a full disclosure of all defects in his title. In strict theory, the seller is only obliged to answer requisitions which relate to title, and not those which relate to, e.g. the form of the purchase deed. In practice the distinction between true requisitions on title and those relating to other matters is largely ignored and the seller's solicitor will answer all reasonable queries raised by the buyer's solicitor. Contractual conditions may also require the buyer in certain circumstances to waive a defect in title. At common law the buyer is deemed to accept the seller's title (and thus loses his right to raise requisitions or further requisitions) when he delivers a draft purchase deed to the seller. In practice the draft purchase deed is usually submitted to the seller simultaneously with requisitions and the buyer's right to raise requisitions will be expressly preserved by a contractual condition, e.g. Standard Condition 4.6.1 and Standard Commercial Property Condition 6.6.1.

1. See D2.6.

3.6.   Vendor and purchaser summons

3.6.1.   If the seller's solicitor refuses to answer a proper requisition, the buyer can compel an answer by means of the vendor and purchaser summons procedure under Law of Property Act 1925, s.49 which provides a summary method of resolving disputes between the parties. This procedure is intended to be used to resolve an impasse between the parties where agreement cannot be reached over a specific point in relation to the title and not as a general sounding-board to test the validity of the whole title or of the contract.

3.7.   Right to rescind

3.7.1.   Neither the Standard Conditions of Sale (fourth edition) nor the Standard Commercial Property Conditions (second edition) contain clauses entitling the seller to rescind the contract where the buyer raises a requisition with which the seller is unable or unwilling to comply (see D2.3).

3.7.2.   If the seller has not answered a requisition by the contractual completion date it might be possible for the buyer to treat the contract as discharged by a breach of condition or to serve a notice to complete under Standard Condition 6.8 or Standard Commercial Property Condition 8.8 (see section M).

E. PRE-COMPLETION

E1. The purchase deed

1.1. Who prepares the deed?

1.1.1. It is normally the buyer's duty to prepare the purchase deed (typically a transfer), although the seller may, by Law of Property Act 1925, s.48(1), reserve the right by contractual condition to prepare the deed himself. This right is usually used in estate conveyancing where the seller commonly supplies an engrossment of the purchase deed in standard form, a draft of the deed having been annexed to the contract. If the seller charges a fee for the engrossment, such fee must be reasonable and is deemed to include VAT unless stated otherwise. In commercial transactions the seller often prepares the first draft of the purchase deed, which is then agreed with the buyer and annexed to the contract.

1.2. Time for preparation of deed

1.2.1. Traditionally the deed was prepared after completion of the buyer's investigation of title, but in practice in residential transactions and those commercial transactions where the deed has not been agreed before exchange, the deed is usually prepared shortly after exchange of contracts and submitted to the seller for his approval with the buyer's requisitions on title. At common law the buyer is deemed to have accepted the seller's title when he submits the purchase deed for approval, and thus the submission of the purchase deed simultaneously with requisitions would preclude the buyer's right to raise requisitions on the seller's title. This problem is solved by Standard Condition 4.6.1 and Standard Commercial Property Condition 6.6.1 which both preserve the buyer's right to raise requisitions in such circumstances. By Standard Condition 4.3.2 and Standard Commercial Property Condition 6.3.2, the buyer is required to submit the draft purchase deed to the seller at least 12 working days before the contractual completion date.

1.3. Form of the deed

1.3.1. The purchase deed must be a deed in order to transfer the legal estate in the land to the buyer.[1]

1.3.2. The purchase deed puts into effect the terms of the contract and so must reflect its terms.

1.3.3. Where the property being transferred is registered land the form of the purchase deed is prescribed by Land Registration Rules 2003.[2] Subject to permitted variations, the prescribed form of wording and layout must also be used.[3]

1.3.4. Land Registry forms may be downloaded free of charge from the Land Registry website at **www.landregistry.gov.uk**. Almost all of the standard Land Registry forms are reproduced by law stationers and these may be used as the basis of the purchase deed. Most of the forms (such as TR1 and TR2) can also be reproduced electronically using commercial forms packages or using the firm's own software.

1.3.5. The Land Registry for Wales will accept a document which is prepared in Welsh and does not require a translation to be supplied.[4]

1.3.6. No prescribed form of wording exists for a conveyance of unregistered land. The buyer is thus free to choose his own form of wording subject to the seller's approval and provided that it accurately reflects the terms of the contract. As the transaction will be submitted for first registration after completion, instead of using a traditional conveyance the buyer will usually prepare his purchase deed as a Land Registry transfer suitably amended.

1. Law of Property Act 1925, s.52.
2. Land Registration Rules 2003, r.58 provides that a transfer of a registered estate must be in Form TP1, TP2, TP3, TR1, TR2, TR5, AS1 or AS3 as appropriate.
3. Land Registration Rules 2003, rr.210 and 211. Detailed guidance on the reproduction of Land Registry forms can be found in Land Registry Practice Guide 46 and see A21.
4. Under the Land Registry's Welsh Language Scheme prepared under Welsh Language Act 1993, s.21(3), the Land Registry will ensure that the English and Welsh languages are treated on a basis of equality in Wales.

1.4. Drafting the deed

1.4.1. When drafting the purchase deed the buyer's solicitor needs to have access to:

    (a) the contract – because the purchase deed must reflect the terms of the contract;

    (b) the official copies of the title/title deeds – because the contract may refer to matters on the title which need to be repeated or reflected in the purchase deed;

    (c) except in straightforward cases, a precedent on which to base the deed under preparation.

Using a precedent

1.4.2. Except in the simplest cases it is advisable to refer to a precedent if only to focus the mind on the types of clauses which will be required in the draft deed. Use the precedent as a guide and not as a model to be followed slavishly. Consider whether a clause is really necessary before copying it from a precedent and check that the law has not altered since the precedent was published.

1.5. Seller's approval of draft deed

1.5.1. When the draft has been prepared two copies should be submitted to the seller's solicitor for his approval. A further copy of the draft should be retained by the buyer's solicitor so that amendments can be agreed over the telephone if required. By Standard Condition 4.3.2 and Standard Commercial Property Condition 6.3.2 one of the copies submitted to the seller's solicitor can be of engrossment quality enabling the seller to use this as a top copy for signature in cases where no amendments are needed and where the buyer does not need to sign the deed.

1.5.2. On receipt of the draft, the seller's solicitor should check it carefully to ensure that the document accurately reflects the terms of the contract. Amendments should be confined to those which are necessary for the fulfilment of the document's legal purpose, bearing in mind that the choice of style and wording is the buyer's prerogative. Minor amendments may be agreed with the buyer's solicitor by telephone in order to save time. More substantial amendments should be clearly marked in a distinct colour on both copies of the draft, one copy being returned to the buyer's solicitor for his consideration, the other being retained in the seller's solicitor's file for reference. By Standard Condition 4.3.2 and Standard Commercial Condition 6.3.2 the seller's solicitor is to approve or return the revised draft document within four working days after delivery of the draft transfer by the buyer's solicitor.

1.6. Engrossment

1.6.1. When amendments (if any) to the draft deed have been finalised, the buyer's solicitor should prepare an engrossment of the deed on good quality paper. A deed which is to be submitted to the Land Registry should be engrossed on durable A4 size paper.[1]

1.6.2. The engrossment must be checked carefully (if necessary by comparing the draft document with the engrossment) to ensure the accuracy of the typing and that all agreed amendments have been incorporated. A copy of the engrossment should be kept on the buyer's solicitor's file for reference.

1.6.3. The completed engrossment should then be sent to the seller's solicitor for execution by his client. Where the buyer is required to execute the deed it is common practice for the buyer to execute the deed prior to delivery of the deed in escrow to the seller for his signature. The condition attached to the escrow should be defined. By Standard Condition 4.3.2 and Standard Commercial Property Condition 6.3.2 the buyer must deliver the engrossment of the purchase deed to the seller at least five working days before completion (see also F4.3.8).

1. Land Registration Rules 2003, r.210.

1.7.   Execution

1.7.1.   To be valid in law a deed must be clear on the face of it that it is a deed, signed by the necessary parties in the presence of a witness, and delivered.[1] Use of a seal is no longer required either by individuals or bodies corporate. A company seal may, however, still be used and is a valid method of execution of a document.

1.7.2.   Where land is registered, the form of transfer and certain other deeds affecting the land must follow the prescribed form.[2] The forms of words of execution are also prescribed.[3] Land Registry Practice Guide 8 gives further guidance on the execution of deeds.

1.7.3.   Signature by the seller is always required in order to transfer the legal estate.[4]

1.7.4.   The buyer is required to execute the deed if it contains a covenant or declaration on his behalf. Thus execution by the buyer will be needed where the document contains an indemnity covenant in respect of existing restrictive covenants or a declaration by the buyers relating to the trusts on which they hold the property.

1.7.5.   Where other parties are joined in the deed, e.g. to release the property from a mortgage or to give a valid receipt for money paid under the deed, they should also sign the document.

1.7.6.   Signature by an individual must be made by him in person, preferably in ink and it must be signed in the presence of one witness who also signs his name.

1.7.7.   Where an individual is incapable of signing the document himself, e.g. as a result of illness or disability, another person may execute it on his behalf. If necessary the document should be read over to the individual, or its contents clearly explained to him, before signature. Two witnesses are required to the signature.[5]

1.7.8.   Any responsible person may be a witness to the signature of an individual. There is no legal restriction on one party to a document being a witness to the other party's signature nor on one spouse or civil partner being a witness to the signature of the other spouse or civil partner, but an independent witness is preferable since if the validity of the document was ever challenged in court, the independent witness would provide a stronger testimony. The witness should sign his name, and add underneath the signature his address and occupation. If the name of the witness is not clear from the signature it is sensible to ask the witness also to write his full name in block capitals after his signature. Two witnesses are required whenever the document is signed by one person on another's behalf.

1.7.9. Where an individual is capable of signing the document but cannot read it, e.g. because he is blind or the document is in a foreign language, he should familiarise himself with its contents. It is preferable that a solicitor witnesses the signature to confirm that the correct procedure was followed.

1.7.10. A solicitor should always be satisfied before submitting a document for signature that the client understands the nature and contents of the document. Where the solicitor invites his client to sign the purchase deed in the solicitor's presence the deed can be explained to the client before signature, and actually signed in the presence of the solicitor who can then act as a witness to the signature. If this is not possible, the purchase deed may be sent to the client for signature and return. The letter which accompanies the purchase deed should:

(a) explain the purpose and contents of the document;

(b) contain clear instructions relating to the execution of the deed;

(c) specify a date by which the signed document must be returned to the solicitor;

(d) request that the client leaves the document undated.

Attorneys

1.7.11. A person who holds a power of attorney on behalf of another may execute a deed on that person's behalf. The attorney may sign either in his own name or in that of the person on behalf of whom he is acting, e.g. 'X by his attorney Y' or 'Y as attorney on behalf of X'.

Companies

1.7.12. Since 6 April 2008, when Companies Act 2006, s.44 came into force, a document is validly executed by a company if the common seal is affixed or it is signed on behalf of the company by either two authorised signatories (the company's directors and the company secretary) or by a director of the company in the presence of a witness who attests the signature.

1.7.13. A company may execute a deed by using its common seal which is impressed on the document in the presence of a director of the company and its secretary (who for this purpose must be two separate individuals) or two directors who will then sign the document to witness the execution by the company. If this is done, then a buyer is protected by Law of Property Act 1925, s.74(1) (as amended by Regulatory Reform (Execution of Deeds and Documents) Order 2005 (SI 2005/1906)) against any irregularity in the execution.

1.7.14.   Alternatively, the document may simply be signed by two authorised signatories (a director and the secretary or by two directors), or by a director of the company in the presence of a witness who attests the signature.[6] Use of a common seal is no longer compulsory. If either of these methods is used, due execution by the company may be presumed under Companies Act 2006, s.44(5) and a buyer (but not a volunteer) need not investigate whether the manner of execution is authorised by the company's articles.

1.7.15.   In some cases a company's articles may permit execution of a document by a method different from those outlined above, e.g. signature by an authorised person acting alone. In such a case the procedure prescribed by the articles should be followed and a copy of the signatory's authorisation attached to the deed to prove the validity of its execution.

1.7.16   Land Registry Practice Guide 8 contains detailed information on the Land Registry's current requirements.

1.7.17.   The requirements for execution of documents by companies incorporated outside the UK are dealt with in E7.

Other bodies

1.7.18.   The requirements for execution of deeds by other bodies, e.g. corporations sole (e.g. a bishop), district councils, government departments or statutory undertakings, will vary depending on the body concerned. The precise procedure for execution should be checked well in advance of execution. The document should then be executed in accordance with the prescribed method, and a copy of the authority of the signatory to sign attached to the deed to prove the validity of its execution. The relaxation on the use of corporate seals which was granted to registered companies by Companies Act 1989 does not extend to these bodies.

Patients

1.7.19.   Since 1994, deeds affecting sale and purchase transactions have not been required to be sealed by the Court of Protection.

Delivery

1.7.20.   In addition to signature a deed must be delivered. A deed takes effect on its delivery. When the buyer delivers the engrossment to the seller for execution by him, he does not normally intend the deed to become effective at that time. It is therefore common practice for the buyer to deliver the deed to the seller in escrow, i.e. conditionally, so that the operation of the deed is postponed until completion. In the case of a company, delivery is presumed at the date of execution unless the contrary is proved.[7]

1.   Law of Property (Miscellaneous Provisions) Act 1989, s.1.
2.   Land Registration Rules 2003, r.206(1) and Sched.1.

3. Land Registration Rules 2003, r.206(3) and Sched.9.
4. Law of Property Act 1925, s.52.
5. Law of Property (Miscellaneous Provisions) Act 1989, s.1.
6. Companies Act 2006, s.44(2).
7. Companies Act 2006, s.46(2). The timing of delivery can be expressly postponed by stating in the deed that the document is delivered as at its date.

1.8. Plans

1.8.1. If the contract provides for the use of a plan the purchase deed will also refer to the plan. In other cases the buyer is not entitled to demand that a plan is used with the purchase deed unless the description of the property as afforded by the contract and title deeds is inadequate without one. If the buyer wishes to use a plan in circumstances where he is not entitled to demand one, he may do so with the seller's consent but will have to bear the cost of its preparation.

1.8.2. Where the sale is of the whole of the seller's property use of a plan is not normally considered necessary, and unless very clearly drawn may confuse rather than clarify the deed as well as adding unnecessary expense.

1.8.3. On a sale of part (including flats and office suites) a plan is highly desirable and where the land is registered must be used unless the part is identified clearly on the title plan and is described by reference to that title plan.[1]

1.8.4. The plan(s) to be used with the purchase deed should be checked for accuracy, including all necessary colourings and markings, and firmly bound into the engrossment of the deed which should in its wording refer to the use of the plan(s). Measurements must be expressed in metric values.

1.8.5. In registered land cases the transferor must sign the plan. In unregistered land signature of the plan is not compulsory but is highly desirable. Such signatures need not be witnessed. Where a company seals the purchase deed, it should also seal the plan.

1.8.6. The preparation and use of plans is further discussed in B21.

1. Land Registration Rules 2003, r.213.

1.9. Parties

1.9.1. Anyone whose concurrence is necessary in order to transfer the legal estate or who is to give a valid receipt for capital money arising out of the transaction must be joined as a party to the deed.

1.9.2. The seller and buyer will usually be the only parties to the deed, but in view of the principle outlined in E1.9.1 it may be necessary to join, e.g. the trustees of a Settled Land Act settlement or a non-owning occupier.

1.9.3.   Where the seller is bankrupt, his trustee in bankruptcy will transfer the property
and the seller is not a party to the deed. See E6.7.5 for the situation where one or
more of the co-owners becomes bankrupt.

1.9.4.   If the seller is a company which is in liquidation or under receivership, the
company itself transfers the property with the receiver or liquidator joining in
the deed to give a receipt for the purchase price. In such a case the liquidator
actually executes the deed. Exceptionally, if an order has been made by the
court under Companies Act 1989 vesting the legal estate of the company's
property in the liquidator, the liquidator will be the seller and the company will
not be a party to the deed.

1.9.5.   In a sub-sale transaction, the seller transfers the property directly to the
sub-purchaser, but the original buyer will join in the document to give implied
covenants and, where appropriate, to give a receipt for all or part of the purchase
price.

1.9.6.   On a sale of part of registered land which is subject to a mortgage, the lender
will not be a party to the purchase deed since he will release the part sold from
his charge by using Form DS3. In the same situation in unregistered land the
lender may join in the conveyance in order to release the part sold from the
mortgage and, where appropriate, to give a receipt for such part of the purchase
price as is paid to him. Alternatively, a lender in the case of unregistered land
may give a separate deed of release to the buyer. The seller must ascertain from
his lender which of these methods of release the lender wishes to employ and
inform the buyer accordingly so that the buyer can, if necessary, include
appropriate clauses relating to the lender in the draft purchase deed.

1.9.7.   On a sale by a mortgagee in possession the mortgagee will be the seller and the
owner will not enter into the deed.

1.10.   Transfer of whole

1.10.1.   A transfer of whole must be in Form TR1 (or, in the case of a transfer under
power of sale, TR2).[1] The following paragraphs relate to a transfer to give effect
to one sale.

1.10.2.   The title number and description of the property, i.e. its postal address, may be
taken from the official copies of the title supplied by the seller.

1.10.3.   The date of the document is inserted on actual completion.

1.10.4.   The seller's name should be inserted as it appears on the proprietorship register
of the title. If the seller is not the current registered proprietor, the seller's name
should be inserted as it appears in, for example, his transfer.

1.10.5.   The buyer's full name and address should be inserted. The buyer's address or
addresses for service given in the Transfer Form or AP1 (Application to change

the register) will be placed on the proprietorship register on registration of the buyer's interest and is the address which will be used by the Chief Land Registrar if it becomes necessary for him to contact the registered proprietor of the land, e.g. to serve notices on him. The form allows up to three addresses to be given. The addresses given should therefore be ones at which it is certain that the buyer can be contacted.[2] In the case of residential property where the buyer will be moving into the property on completion, one of the addresses should be the address of the property being purchased and not the address at which the buyer is currently living.

1.10.6. The amount of consideration must be stated[3] in both words and figures in the consideration panel. The receipt in the consideration panel renders any other form of receipt for the purchase price unnecessary and acts as a sufficient discharge to the buyer.[4] The presence of this receipt also gives the buyer authority to pay the purchase price to the seller's solicitor.[5] The receipt is also evidence, but not necessarily conclusive evidence, that the seller's lien over the property for the unpaid purchase price has been extinguished. The purchase price in the transfer should exclude the amount of any consideration attributable to chattels for which a separate receipt should be prepared.[6]

1.10.7. There is provision on the form for the seller's title guarantee, which will imply covenants for title under Law of Property (Miscellaneous Provisions) Act 1994 (see section M). Any modification of the covenants must be set out expressly on the face of the transfer and must refer to the section of the 1994 Act which is being modified or excluded.

1.10.8. Joint purchasers must indicate in the transfer the capacity in which they will hold the equitable interest in the property, i.e. as joint tenants or tenants in common. On registration of the buyers as proprietors a restriction in Form A will automatically be entered on the register unless it is clear that the survivor can give a good receipt for capital monies. Instructions as to the method in which the beneficial ownership is to be held should have been taken by the buyer's solicitor at an early stage in the transaction, and those instructions will now be effected in the transfer. Where the buyers have decided to hold as tenants in common, instructions should also have been obtained in relation to the proportionate shares which each co-owner will hold in the equitable interest. In the absence of evidence to the contrary it will be assumed by the court that they hold the equity in proportion to their original contributions to the property.[7] In order to avoid costly and time-consuming litigation at a later date, it is essential that full details of the beneficial interests of the co-owners are recorded in writing at the time of their purchase. There is provision in the form of transfer to record the respective beneficial interests. Alternatively, a short deed of trust may be drawn up to give effect to the buyers' wishes, in which case it should be referred to in the transfer and kept safely for future reference.

1.10.9. Where the sale is subject to existing covenants the contract will usually provide for the purchase deed to include an indemnity covenant to be given by the buyer.[8] An indemnity covenant will be required in respect of positive covenants and restrictive covenants which are not limited to seisin.[9] Where such a covenant is necessary it should be added expressly to the transfer form, there being no such covenant included on the printed forms. A covenant which gives indemnity only is enforceable in breach by an action for damages. One which is 'to observe perform and indemnify' is enforceable by injunction and damages and thus provides fuller protection for the seller. Standard Condition 4.6.4 and Standard Commercial Condition 6.6.4 provides for the full form of covenant to be given. Where there are joint purchasers, the covenant should be given by both or all of them.

1.10.10. Additional provisions may be required in the deed in accordance with special conditions of the contract. There is a panel in Land Registry forms to include these.

1.10.11. The transfer should provide for execution by all parties in the presence of a witness. The form of attestation is prescribed by Schedule 9 Land Registration Rules 2003 and will vary dependent on the identity of the signatory.[10] See Land Registry Practice Guide 8.

1. Land Registration Rules 2003, r.58.
2. Land Registration Rules 2003, r.198 sets out the requirements as to addresses for service. See also G3.11.6.
3. Stamp Act 1891, s.5
4. Law of Property Act 1925, s.67.
5. Law of Property Act 1925, s.69.
6. The amount of the consideration affects the amount of SDLT payable on the document and, since chattels are not subject to stamp duty, any sum payable for them does not need to be included in the purchase deed. Where VAT is payable the amount of the consideration stated should include the VAT element of the price.
7. *Springette* v. *Defoe* (1993) 65 P&CR 1, CA.
8. See Standard Condition 4.6.4 and Standard Commercial Property Condition 6.6.4.
9. See *Rhone* v. *Stephens*, *The Times*, 18 March 1994, HL; *Austerberry* v. *Oldham Corporation* (1885) 29 ChD 750.
10. Land Registration Rules 2003, r.206(3) and Sched.9.

1.11.   Transfer of part

1.11.1. A transfer of part of a registered title must be in Form TP1 (or in the case of a transfer of part under power of sale, TP2).[1] All of the matters referred to in E1.10 will be relevant to a sale of part but the following will also be required either in addition to or in substitution for the above.

1.11.2. At this stage the sale is made by reference to the seller's existing title number. A new title number for the part being sold will be allocated by the Land Registry on registration of the transaction.

1.11.3. A clear description of the land being sold must be included with reference to the plan annexed to the transfer. When necessary, the land retained by the seller should also be expressly defined and identified on the plan. When the postal address of the property is not yet known, the property may be described by the plot number on the seller's approved estate layout plan. However, it will not then be possible to give the property as the buyer's address for service. In this case a care of address may be inserted in the transfer. If the postal address is available when application is made for registration of transfer, it may be inserted in the application Form AP1.

1.11.4. Where the contract made provision for the grant of easements to the buyer or reservations in favour of the seller, these easements must be expressly inserted into the transfer.

1.11.5. The contract will usually provide for the exclusion of rights of light and air from the transfer. This contractual provision (Standard Condition 3.4 and Standard Commercial Property Condition 3.3) must be implemented by a declaration to this effect in the transfer.

1.11.6. New restrictive covenants are frequently imposed in a contract for the sale of part of land; these too must be expressly set out in the transfer. Except where the land forms part of a building scheme, to be enforceable against subsequent owners of the land sold, the covenants must be taken for the benefit of land retained by the seller and the burden annexed to the land sold. Express words to give effect to these principles are advisable.

1.11.7. Land Registry transfer forms provide sub-headings within the additional provisions panel under which full details of the rights granted and reserved, restrictive covenants, and other matters may be inserted. These sub-headings may be added to, amended, repositioned, or omitted as desired.[2]

1. Land Registration Rules 2003, r.58.
2. Land Registration Rules 2003, rr.210 and 211.

1.12. Conveyance

1.12.1. As a conveyance of unregistered land will lead to first registration, it is common practice to use a registered land transfer. The only amendments required will be the omission of the title number and a fuller description of the property by reference to a document in the chain of title. In the rare cases where a traditional conveyance is to be used, it will contain similar information but is presented in a different format from a registered land transfer. Each conveyance of unregistered land has slightly different requirements and thus each has to be individually drafted to fit the situation in hand (see D2.6 for guidance on the form and contents of a conveyance).

1.13. Assent

1.13.1. Where personal representatives transfer land to a beneficiary they will use an assent. If they sell land to a third party the purchase deed will be a transfer or conveyance depending whether or not the land is registered.

1.13.2.   One exception to the rule that a legal estate can only be conveyed by a deed is an assent by personal representatives which must be in writing but need not be by deed unless it contains a covenant by the assentee, e.g. for indemnity in respect of restrictive covenants.

1.13.3.   An assent of registered land must be in a transfer in Form AS1 or AS3 (prescribed by Land Registration Rules 2003, r.58). An assent of unregistered land is not subject to any restraints on its form or contents except that it must be in writing and must name the person(s) in whose favour it is given.

1.13.4.   On a sale or assent by personal representatives all proving personal representatives must be parties to the document.

1.13.5.   In unregistered land the assent may contain recitals, and will otherwise be similar to an unregistered conveyance. Since the land will be subject to first registration of title following the assent, it may be more convenient to use Form AS1 or AS3 (suitably amended) in preference to an unregistered form of assent. A memorandum of the assent should be noted on the grant after completion, although this is not strictly necessary where the land is to be registered on completion of the assent.

1.14.   Assignment

1.14.1.   An assignment of an existing registered lease is the transfer of a registered estate and the purchase deed will be a Land Registry transfer form. The form is the same as for the transfer of a freehold. An assignment of an unregistered lease is similar in form to a conveyance of unregistered land, subject to some modifications.

1.14.2.   Frequently the contract contains provision modifying the effect of the implied covenants for title in leasehold cases (e.g. Standard Condition 3.3 and Standard Commercial Condition 4) and the purchase deed will contain a provision giving effect to this contractual term. In a transfer, this will appear in the title guarantee panel.

1.14.3.   An express indemnity covenant will be inserted if required by the contract (if any) (see Standard Condition 4.6.4 and Standard Commercial Condition 6.6.4). No indemnity covenant is implied by statute in new leases (granted after 1 January 1996).[1] In leases granted before this date an indemnity covenant is implied except where in unregistered land value is not given by the assignee for the transaction.

1.14.4.   In addition, an unregistered assignment may contain recitals relating to the recent history of the lease, the agreement to sell and, where appropriate, the fact that the landlord has consented to the assignment. The estate transferred will be the unexpired residue of the term, subject to the terms and conditions of the lease itself. The benefit of options should be expressly assigned to ensure that their benefit is transferred to the buyer.

1. Landlord and Tenant (Covenants) Act 1995, s.14.

1.15. Sellers' cashback schemes

1.15.1. These schemes appear to be operated by brokers who, in conjunction with a small number of lenders, participate in enabling a seller to offer an incentive to a buyer. In essence the seller and lender state that, e.g. the property is to be sold for £200,000 but that on completion the seller agrees to pay £25,000 to the buyer. Traditionally the contract discloses the arrangement, but the price inserted in the contract will be the higher figure, e.g. £200,000 rather than £175,000, which is the net price the seller receives from the buyer.

1.15.2. In these schemes the lender is normally aware of the circumstances, and so the schemes do not, in fact, involve a fraud on the lender in the usual sense. Solicitors (whether acting for sellers or buyers) should always check that the lender is aware of the proposed cashback. In relation to new-build, converted or renovated homes, all incentives and discounts offered by the builder/developer must be disclosed to the solicitor acting for the lender in the CML Disclosure of Incentives form before the solicitor can submit his certificate of title to the lender (see I1.8).

1.15.3. As the transfer is a matter of public record, it is a solicitor's duty not to be a party to any mis-statement of the sale price. Inserting the higher price would be a mis-statement. If solicitors are instructed in relation to such schemes, they should make it clear from the outset that the figure they will insert in the transfer will be the net figure, and should decline to act if the client instructs otherwise.

1.15.4. These schemes should be distinguished from cases where the lender gives an incentive 'cashback' to borrowers, as such cashbacks do not affect the price paid to the seller.

E2. Pre-completion searches

2.1. Who makes the searches?

2.1.1. In accordance with the *caveat emptor* principle it is up to the buyer to make sure of his bargain. Therefore it is the buyer's solicitor's responsibility to ensure that such pre-completion searches as are relevant to the transaction are carried out and that the results of those searches are satisfactory to his client.

2.1.2. Where the buyer is purchasing with the assistance of a mortgage, his lender also has an interest in the soundness of the title to the property and some or all of the pre-completion searches may be carried out by the lender's solicitor acting at this stage on behalf of both the lender and the buyer.

2.2. Reason for making searches

2.2.1. The principal reason for making pre-completion searches is for the buyer's solicitor to confirm that information obtained about the property prior to exchange remains correct. In some situations searches additional to those which were made before exchange of contracts will also be undertaken at this stage either to verify information received after exchange or where the circumstances were such that the buyer did not have sufficient time to make the relevant search before contracts were exchanged.

2.3. When to make searches

2.3.1. The searches must be done in sufficient time to ensure that the results are received by the buyer's solicitor in time for completion to take place on the contractual completion date.

2.3.2. Pre-completion searches should generally be made about seven days before the contractual completion date but may be left until closer to the completion date if, e.g. a telephone, computer or fax search is to be made. Searches will need to be done earlier than seven days before completion if some delay in the receipt of replies, e.g. through industrial action, is anticipated.

2.3.3. The principal searches which are made at this stage of the transaction (the Land Registry and/or Land Charges Department searches) generally confer protection on the searcher against later entries (i.e. they give a priority period); thus a balance has to be drawn between making the search at the latest moment before completion in order to gain the benefit of a long priority period after completion, and the risk, if a search is submitted at the last moment, of completion being delayed (and compensation payable by the buyer for the delay) because the search result has not been received by the date of completion.

2.4. Which searches to make

2.4.1. The following searches should be made:

    (a)   for registered land, search against title number at the Land Registry (see E2.5);

    (b)   for unregistered land, including an unregistered reversion to a lease, search at Land Charges Department against names of estate owners of the land (see E2.6);

    (c)   if acting for a lender, a bankruptcy search against the name of the borrower (see E2.8);

    (d)   such other of the searches listed in E2.9–E2.13 as are applicable to the transaction.

2.5. Land Registry search

2.5.1. When acquiring an interest in a registered estate in land, a pre-completion search should be made at the appropriate Land Registry Office.[1] Guidance on making these searches can be found in Land Registry Practice Guide 12. A fee of £8 per title is payable (£4 if made online at the Land Registry). Fees can be paid by cheque (if the application is lodged by post, DX or in person), or direct by a Land Registry account holder.

Official search of the register with priority

2.5.2. An application for an official search with priority can only be made by a 'purchaser'. This term is defined in the Rules as a person who for valuable consideration has entered into or intends to enter into a registrable disposition of a registered estate or registered charge.[2]

Application by post or DX: search of whole

2.5.3. Where the interest being purchased, leased or mortgaged concerns the whole of a registered title, the search application should be made on Form OS1. The application will give details of the title number of the property to be searched, a brief description of its situation, i.e. postal address, administrative area and postcode, and the names of the registered proprietors. The applicant's name must also be given together with his reason for making the search, i.e. he intends to purchase/lease/take a charge on the land. Where a solicitor is acting both for a buyer and his lender the search application should be completed in the name of the lender client. If this is done the buyer may take the benefit and protection of the search and a separate search in the buyer's name is unnecessary.

2.5.4. The form requests the registrar to provide information on any adverse entries made in the register or daylist[3] since a specified date. This 'search from' date can be either:

(a) the date shown as the 'subsisting entries' date on an official copy of the register; or

(b) the date shown as the 'subsisting entries' date when register entries were accessed by remote terminal.[4]

2.5.5. The search result contains the applicant's name but where, for example, the clients are both chargor and chargee and the applicant is chargee, the chargor's name will not be shown. Further, the result does not contain the address of the property, but it does include an applicant's reference of not more than 25 characters (including spaces). It is therefore suggested that the applicant's reference stated on Form OS1 should include sufficient detail (e.g. applicant's or chargor's name and the address of the property or solicitor's file number) to ensure that the incoming search can be returned to its proper file without delay.

Application by post or DX: search of part

2.5.6. Where the interest being acquired comprises only part of a registered title, the search application is made on Form OS2 and must identify the part of the land against which the search is to be made either by the submission of a clearly marked plan of the land with sufficient detail to identify the land in relation to features shown on the Ordnance Survey plan, or by its plot number where the Land Registry has already approved an estate layout plan. Where the application is made on Form OS2 and an accompanying plan is required, the plan must be delivered in duplicate. It is advisable that the same plan is used for the contract, search application and purchase deed. Care should be taken not to search against more land than is included in the contract as the priority conferred by the search may delay transactions in relation to the additional land. In other respects the application is similar to that made on Form OS1.

Application by fax

2.5.7. This facility is available at all Land Registry offices and further information is contained in Land Registry Practice Guide 44. The facility is only open to Land

Registry account holders. No additional fee is charged for this service. Applications may be faxed to the specified fax number at the proper office at any time between 8.00 am Monday and 4.00 pm Friday, except:

- after 4.00 pm on the day before a public holiday; and

- on public holidays; and

- before 8.00 am on the day after a public holiday.

The result of the search cannot be sent by fax but is posted to the applicant in the usual way.

2.5.8. The search must be a search of whole of a title on Form OS1, or a search of part of a title on Form OS2 provided that the applicant can either state the plot number of an approved estate plan and the date of approval of the estate plan or attach a suitable plan. The plan must:

- clearly show the extent of the land to be searched (e.g. by thick black edging, hatching or stippling);

- be drawn to a stated scale of not less than 1/1250;

- be sufficiently detailed to allow accurate plotting to be undertaken on the title plan;

- include a north point; and

- not be endorsed with a statement of disclaimer intending to comply with Property Misdescriptions Act 1991 or stated to be 'for identification only'.

When lodging a search of part of a title on Form OS2 the plan must also:

- adequately depict the extent to be searched on a single A4-sized plan;

- be referred to in panel 6 of Form OS2; and

- be sent in fine mode where possible.

Application by telephone

2.5.9. An application can be made (through Land Registry Telephone Services) by an applicant who is or who acts for an intending buyer (including lessee and chargee) and must be for a search of the whole title. Further information is contained in Land Registry Practice Guide 61. The telephone call, using the special number allocated for this service, will only be accepted between 8.30 am and 6.00 pm (Monday to Friday) excluding Christmas Day, Good Friday or a statutory bank holiday. The application can only be made by a Land Registry account holder. (Official copies can also be obtained by this procedure.) On telephoning the registry the following information must be supplied:

(a) the applicant's Land Registry account number;

(b) name and address of firm holding the account;

(c)   if different from (b) above, the name and address to which the result of search is to be sent;

(d)   title number of the land;

(e)   the name of the registered proprietor (or applicant for first registration);

(f)   (if requested) the administrative area or local authority district in which the land is situated;

(g)   where the land is already registered, the date from which the search is to be made;[5]

(h)   the applicant's reference (maximum 25 characters);

(i)   whether the search is intended to protect a purchase lease or charge;

(j)   the name of the applicant on whose behalf the search is being made;

(k)   the name and telephone number of the person making the search telephone call or the person to be contacted if there is an enquiry.

2.5.10.   A paper result of the search is normally dispatched to the applicant's solicitor on the same or following working day. The priority period commences from the time the application is entered on the day list, usually at the time of the telephone call. If the search is 'clear' (if there are no relevant adverse entries in the register or pending applications), a guaranteed result will be given over the telephone. Several search applications may be made during the course of one telephone call including searches of the Land Charges Registers. Informal disclosure of entries revealed by the search can be made over the telephone if so requested by the applicant. Such information is not, however, guaranteed by the Registry. Further, a result of a search of the Land Charge Registers (including a result that reveals no entries) given over the telephone is never guaranteed.

Application by personal attendance

2.5.11.   A buyer or a person acting for a buyer may apply orally for an official search with priority of the whole of the land in a registered title. Application may only be made by the applicant attending a Customer Information Centre at a Land Registry office. Such applications may be made between 8.30 am and 6.00 pm Mondays to Fridays (other than public holidays).

Application online

2.5.12.   An application can be made online at **www.landregistry.gov.uk** by an applicant who is or who acts for an intending buyer (including lessee and chargee) and must be a search of the whole title. A fee of £4 is charged for this service. The application can only be made by an authorised user.

Application via the National Land Information Service

2.5.13. An applicant can apply via NLIS for any type of search, subject to the usual requirements. An applicant must also provide similar information to that required for an application made online at the Land Registry.

Sub-sales of whole of a registered title or pending first registration title

2.5.14. Where A has contracted to sell to B, and before B completes his purchase he contracts to resell to C, the sub-purchaser (C) will need to make a search against the title quoting A's name as proprietor since at the time of C's application B will not be the registered proprietor of the land.

Sub-sales of part of a registered title or pending first registration title

2.5.15. Where A has contracted to sell part of his estate to B, and before B completes his purchase he contracts to resell that estate or part of it to C, the sub-purchaser (C) will, to reserve priority, need to make a search. The title to be searched will depend upon whether the application to register B's interest is pending in the Land Registry or not. If the application to register B's interest is pending in the Land Registry, the search should be made against the title number allocated to B's application quoting B as the proprietor. If the application has not been lodged, the search should be made against A's title quoting A as the proprietor.

Official search with priority where application for first registration pending

2.5.16. Where an applicant has applied for first registration of his title and has contracted to sell, lease or charge the land to a third party before completion of the first registration, the third party can make a search as if the land were already registered. A search against the whole of the land in a pending application may be made by post, DX or NLIS on Form OS1 or by using the other methods of searching against the whole of a registered title explained above. A search of part can only be made by post, DX or NLIS on Form OS2. The purpose of the search, in relation to a pending first registration, is to ascertain whether any adverse entry has been made in the daylist (i.e. list of applications received by the Land Registry) since the date of the pending first registration application. The date of the pending first registration application does not have to be specified by the searcher. The effect of the result of search will be to give the searcher priority against any other intervening application if he lodges his own application before the expiry of the priority period.

Result of official search

2.5.17. On completion of the application for the official search with priority, a result of search is issued giving the result of the search as at the date and time that the application was entered on the daylist. The information to be included in the result of an official search is specified in Schedule 6 Land Registration Rules 2003.

Priority period

2.5.18. Currently an official certificate of search issued by the Land Registry following an application for an official search with priority gives a priority period to the searcher of 30 business days.[6] A buyer will also take advantage of this protection where a search was made on his behalf in the name of his lender. The searcher will take priority over any entry made during the priority period provided that a correct application for registration of the transaction is received by the appropriate Land Registry office within the priority period given by the search and the application is completed by registration.

2.5.19. The date of expiry of the priority period is shown on the search certificate and should be marked on the outside of the client's file and entered in the solicitor's diary or file prompt system to ensure that it is not overlooked. The application for registration must actually be delivered to the Land Registry before noon on the date on which the priority expires.

2.5.20. The priority period given by an official search cannot be extended. If completion is delayed and cannot take place within the priority period given by the search, a new search application will have to be made. The new search certificate will give another priority period but does not extend the original priority period from the first search. This means that if a third party has made a search or lodged an application in the intervening period, the third party's interest may have priority.

Withdrawal of official search

2.5.21. A person who has made an application for an official search with priority of a registered title or in relation to a pending first registration application, may withdraw that official search by application to the registrar.[7] Such an application cannot be made if an application for an entry in the register in respect of the purchase made pursuant to that official search has been made and completed.

Official search of the register without priority

2.5.22. The searches with priority are only available for use by a 'purchaser' (see E2.5.2). In other situations or where a priority search is not required an application for a search of the register may be made in the following ways:

(a) by post, DX, fax or NLIS – on Form OS3 for searches of whole or part; and

(b) by telephone, online at the Land Registry or by personal attendance for searches of the whole of a registered title.

2.5.23. A search without priority can be used in the following circumstances, e.g.:

    (a) when acting for a buyer of an equitable interest in the land;

    (b) a lender who is selling under a power of sale should make a search to discover subsequent incumbrances (if any).

Lender's search for homes rights

2.5.24. This search is of limited application and may only be used by a lender who has a charge of registered land which consists of or includes a dwelling house. The search is available to any lender regardless of whether or not the charge is registered. The purpose of the search is for the chargee of a dwelling house to ascertain whether any entry has been made on the register to protect a non-owning spouse's or civil partner's homes rights under Family Law Act 1996. A chargee is required to serve notice on such a person before taking action to enforce his security. The search is made in Form HR3 by post, DX, telephone, online at the Land Registry or NLIS.

Outline applications

2.5.25. An outline application can be used to reserve a period similar to a short period of priority for certain interests that cannot be protected by an official search such as a charging order, a homes right notice or a restriction. The interest claimed must be in existence at the time that the application is made.[8] There is no paper form. An outline application can only be made by telephone, personal attendance, online at the Land Registry and NLIS.[9] Guidance on making outline applications and the interests that can be so protected can be found in Land Registry Practice Guide 12.

1. For address see Appendix IX.1.
2. Land Registration Rules 2003, r.131.
3. The daylist is a record of all pending applications and unexpired priority searches kept by the registrar under Land Registration Rules 2003, r.12.
4. Land Registration Rules 2003, r.131.
5. *Ibid.*
6. *Ibid.*
7. *Ibid*, r.150.
8. *Ibid*, r.54(2)(b).
9. *Ibid*, r.54(3).

2.6. Land Charges Department search

Unregistered land

2.6.1. This search is only of relevance to unregistered land. The register is open to the public and can be searched by anyone subject to the payment of the fee (Land Charges Act 1972, s.9).

Applications

2.6.2. The search is made by submitting Form K15 to the Land Charges Department at Plymouth with the appropriate fee (see Appendix VIII.4 for fee). An official certificate of result of search confers a priority period of 15 working days on the applicant (see E2.14). The search application can be made by post, or by telephone, telex or fax by a Land Registry account holder. Applications can also be made online at the Land Registry or NLIS. A personal search of the register can be made but it confers no protection or priority period on the applicant.

Name based system

2.6.3. The register comprises a list of the names of estate owners of land, with details of charges registered against those names. The search is therefore made not against the land itself but against the names of the estate owners.[1] In the case of unregistered land it is necessary for the search to be made against the names of all the estate owners whose names appear on the abstract or epitome of title supplied by the seller, including those who are merely referred to in the bodies of deeds (as opposed to being parties to the deeds themselves) or in schedules attached to deeds which form part of the title. There is no need to repeat searches where a proper search certificate made against previous estate owners has been supplied with the abstract of title.

Variation in names

2.6.4. The register is maintained on a computer which will only search against the exact version of the name as shown on the application form. It is therefore important to check that the name inserted on the application form is identical to that shown on the title deeds and that if any variations of that name appear in the deeds, e.g. if Frederick Brown is variously referred to as 'Frederick Brown', 'Frederick Browne' and 'Fred Brown', all the given variations of the name are separately entered on the search form and a separate fee paid in respect of each.[2]

Periods of ownership

2.6.5. It is only possible for an effective entry to be made against a name in relation to that person's (or company's) period of estate ownership of the land in question. Except as below it is therefore only necessary to search against a name for the period during which the estate owner owned the land. For the purposes of the search form, periods of ownership must be stated in whole years and can be ascertained by looking at the abstract or epitome of title supplied by the seller. If the estate owner's period of ownership is not known, as will be the case when searching against the name of the person who was the seller in the document forming the root of title, the search is in practice made from 1926 (the year when the register was opened).

2.6.6. Where there is a voluntary disposition on the title which is, at the date of the contract, less than five years old, it is necessary to search against the donor's name for a period up to and including the fifth year after the date of the voluntary disposition to ensure that no bankruptcy of the donor occurred during this period. The bankruptcy of the donor during this period could lead to the disposition being set aside by the trustee in bankruptcy. (See D2.11.)

2.6.7. Since it is possible to register a land charge against a deceased estate owner after his death, it is necessary to extend the period of search against the deceased to cover the period between his death and the current date.

Description of the land

2.6.8. Unless a description of the land is inserted on the search application form, the computer will produce entries relating to every person of the given name in the whole of the county or counties specified. In order to avoid having to read through and then reject multiple search entries revealed by the certificate of search, a brief description of the land, which is sufficient to identify it clearly, should be included on the application form.

2.6.9. Although the intention of describing the land is to curtail the number of irrelevant entries produced by the computer, care should be taken in supplying the description, since an inaccurate description of the land may result in a relevant entry not being revealed by the search.[3] Particular care is needed when the abstract shows that the land was formerly part of a larger piece of land, e.g. is one plot on a building estate, since the land may previously have been known by a different description from its current postal address. If the search is limited to the present postal address, entries registered against its former description will not be revealed by the search. In such a case both the present address and former description of the land should be entered on the search application form.

2.6.10. Similarly, there is a possibility that the land was previously situated in a different administrative county from that in which it is now situated. For the above reasons, both present and former county must be included in the description of the land given on the search application form. In some cases the postal address of the property differs from its actual address, e.g. the village of Rogate is in the administrative county of West Sussex, but its postal address is Hampshire. In such cases the search must be made against the actual address of the property and not its postal address. Guidance on the names of counties as used by the Land Charges Department is given in Land Registry Practice Guide 63 (and any Addenda) which also provides advice about land charges applications.

Pre-root estate owners

2.6.11. The buyer is not concerned to search against estate owners who held the land prior to the seller in the root of title supplied to him except in so far as the names of such persons have been revealed to him in documents supplied by the seller.

Conclusiveness of the search

2.6.12. An official certificate of search is conclusive in favour of a 'purchaser' which is defined as anyone taking an interest for valuable consideration.[4] This includes mortgagees, lessees and persons acquiring other legal or equitable interests. The search is only conclusive if it has been correctly made, i.e. it extends over the whole period of the title supplied by the seller and has been made against the correct names of the estate owners for this period, against the correct county or former county, and for the correct periods of ownership of each estate owner. In order to ensure that the buyer gains the protection afforded by the search, and the accompanying priority period, it is vital to check that the search application form is accurately completed.

Priority period

2.6.13. An official certificate of search issued by the Land Charges Department gives a priority period of 15 working days from the date of the certificate. The purchaser will take free of any entries made on the register between the date of the search and the date of completion (except pursuant to a priority notice) provided that completion takes place during the priority period given by the search.[5] The date of expiry of the priority period is shown on the search certificate and should be marked on the outside of the client's file and entered in the solicitor's diary or file prompt system to ensure that it is not overlooked.

2.6.14. The priority period given by land charge searches cannot be extended. If completion is delayed and cannot take place within the priority period given by the search, a new search application will have to be made. The new search certificate will give another priority period but does not extend the original priority period from the first search. This means that if a third party has made a search in the intervening period, the third party may have priority, and that the purchaser will take, subject to any entries from the date the original search was made until the date of the new search.

Previous search certificates

2.6.15. Where the seller provides previous search certificates as part of the evidence of title, it is not necessary to repeat a search against a former estate owner provided that the search certificate supplied by the seller reveals no adverse entries and was made:

(a) against the correct name of the estate owner as shown in the deeds;

(b) for the correct period of ownership as shown in the title deeds; and

(c) against the correct description of the property as shown in the deeds;

and the next disposition in the chain of title took place within the priority period afforded by the search certificate. If any of the conditions outlined above cannot be met, a further search against the previous estate owner must be made.

Sub-sales

2.6.16. Where A has contracted to sell to B, and before B completes his purchase he contracts to sub-sell to C, the sub-purchaser (C) will need to make a search against A's title since at the time of C's search application B will not be the estate owner of the land. B's name should be included on the search (although B will not be an estate owner in the land within the terms of Land Charges Act 1972) because the search may reveal bankruptcy entries against him. If, however, B does become an estate owner before completing the second sale to C, B's name must also be searched against.

1. Land Charges Act 1972, s.3(1).
2. *Oak Co-operative Building Society* v. *Blackburn* [1968] Ch 730 illustrates the importance of searching against all variations of the relevant names. See also *Diligent Finance Ltd* v. *Alleyne* (1972) 23 P&CR 346 and *Standard Property Investments plc* v. *British Plastics Federation* (1985) 53 P&CR 25.
3. *Horrill* v. *Cooper* (1999) 78 P&CR 336.
4. Land Charges Act 1972, ss.10, 17.
5. Land Charges Act 1972, s.11(5).

2.7. **Acting for the lender**

2.7.1. The lender is, like the buyer, concerned to ensure that the property being purchased has a good and marketable title.

2.7.2. Where the same solicitor is acting both for the buyer and his lender, pre-completion searches in the Land Charges Department are normally carried out once on behalf of both clients each of whom is able to claim the protection (if any) afforded by the search certificate.

2.7.3. Where a Land Registry search is being made the buyer is able to take the protection of the search if it is made in the name of the lender but not vice versa. It is therefore important in this situation to remember to complete the search application form in the name of the lender client. If the application form is completed in the name of the buyer client a second search must be made on behalf of the lender. The CML Lenders' Handbook requires the search to be made in the name of the lender.

2.7.4. If the buyer and his lender are separately represented, subject to E2.7.3, the lender will frequently accept the results of searches made by the buyer's solicitor, but in some cases may insist on carrying out the pre-completion searches himself. The lender's requirements in relation to this matter should be ascertained in good time to avoid the duplication of work and expense involved in making two separate sets of searches.

2.7.5. No lender will lend money to a buyer who is bankrupt. The lender will therefore always insist that his solicitor obtains a clear result of a bankruptcy search against the buyer (see E2.8) before releasing the advance.

2.7.6.   Some lenders may also insist that a search is made against the buyer's name in the Register of Voluntary Arrangements (see E2.8.5).

2.7.7.   Where instructions are being carried out under the terms of the CML Lenders' Handbook (paragraph 5.12) or the BSA Mortgage Instructions (paragraph D16), the solicitor must certify that entries revealed by a Land Charges Department search certificate do not apply to the borrower client. If they do, the solicitor must report this to the lender.

2.8.   Bankruptcy search

2.8.1.   Irrespective of whether the transaction relates to registered or unregistered land, a lender will require a clear bankruptcy search against the name of the buyer and also against any guarantor of the buyer for the purposes of the mortgage before releasing the advance.

2.8.2.   Unless a full search of the register has been made on Form K15 (see E2.6) the lender's solicitor should submit Form K16 to the Land Charges Department, completed with the full and correct names (and any known variations of name and spelling) of the borrower(s) and guarantor(s) (if applicable). See Appendix VIII.4 for fee.

2.8.3.   A search certificate will be returned by the Department.

2.8.4.   In the event of there being an adverse entry revealed by the search, the solicitor should seek to establish without delay whether or not his client is the person to whom the search entry relates. For this purpose he can obtain an office copy entry, and enquiries of the Official Receiver's office may assist in this investigation. The lender must be informed immediately if the search entry does relate to the borrower client (or guarantor). If there is any doubt about whether the entry does relate to the borrower or guarantor, the lender's instructions should be obtained. The solicitor should only certify the search entry as not relating to the borrower or guarantor if he is absolutely certain that this is the case. A certification is tantamount to a warranty given by the solicitor. The client's self-certification of the entry may not satisfy a lender client.

2.8.5.   Where a mortgage is being taken out independently from the purchase of unregistered land the lender's solicitor should make a full search on Form K15 (see E2.6) against the names of the borrowers and any guarantor(s) to ensure that there are no bankruptcy entries or priority notices registered against them. A bankruptcy only search will not reveal priority notices or deeds of arrangement under Insolvency Act 1986. In respect of the latter a search should be made at the Register of Voluntary Arrangements. This register is maintained by the Insolvency Practitioners Control Unit and a search can be undertaken, without fee, by letter or by telephone (see Appendix IX.2 for address).

2.9. **Probate and administration**

2.9.1. Where a grant of representation is relevant to the title and it appears from replies given to requisitions on title that the seller cannot produce the original or a marked copy of the grant on completion, the buyer should consider making a pre-completion search at the Principal Probate Registry to ensure that the grant has not been revoked or, in the case of a limited grant, that it has not expired. Alternatively, where the grant forms a link in the chain of title to unregistered land, the buyer's solicitor may ask the seller's solicitor to produce written evidence (i.e. a clear probate search) on or before completion that the grant was valid at the time of the purported disposition. Where the grant was issued by a District Registry there may be some delay before it is noted at the Principal Registry. Therefore a clear search result may not be conclusive. There is a case for saying that the search should be made in all cases where a grant forms a link in the title but in practice this is not the case.

2.9.2. The protection given to a buyer by Administration of Estates Act 1925, s.27(2) that the payment of money to a personal representative in good faith acts as a good discharge to the payer only operates where the grant is valid and had not been revoked at the time of payment. A probate search confers no priority period on the searcher and if where the buyer is buying directly from personal representatives there is doubt as to the validity of a grant, the buyer may consider whether he should require the seller to insist on the registration of the personal representatives as proprietors at the Land Registry before completion takes place.

2.9.3. The search may be made in person by searching the year book for the year of the issue of the grant. If the grant has been revoked, a note of this fact will be recorded next to the entry recording the issue of the grant.

2.9.4. Alternatively an application may be made by letter for a postal search enclosing the appropriate fee (see Appendix VIII.4). The application should specify the full names of the deceased, the date of death, and the last known address of the deceased.

2.10. **Company search**

2.10.1. The effect of Land Registration Act 2002 is that a buyer is not bound by a charge created by a company unless that charge is registered at the Land Registry, or otherwise protected on the register. However, it is suggested that a company search should still be made even in the case of registered land. The company search might reveal, e.g. impending insolvency or that the company had been struck off the register and therefore no longer exists in law.

2.10.2. When buying unregistered land from a company, a company search ought to be undertaken in order to ensure that there are no adverse entries which would affect the buyer. Adverse entries would include, e.g. fixed or floating charges, or the appointment of a receiver or liquidator.

2.10.3. Where the company search reveals a floating charge, it is necessary when buying unregistered land to obtain a certificate of non-crystallisation from the lender on completion. It is also necessary to do this when the transfer is of registered land but the transfer is not for value.

2.10.4. No official search procedure exists for making a company search which must be made either in person or through an agent by attendance at Companies House or online (see Appendix IX.2 for address).

2.10.5. The search is made by requisitioning the company's filed documents. For documents filed prior to 31 December 2002, these are available on microfiche but after that date copies must be obtained online or by applying for hard copies (available by post or fax). The information obtained from the search is thus dependent on both the extent of the instructions given to the searcher and his diligence in carrying out those instructions. The search will only reveal matters registered against companies which are registered in England and Wales (not foreign companies). Equivalent facilities are available in Scotland for Scottish companies. Since company charges need only be registered within 21 days of creation, and are valid in the intervening period, a company search may not reveal a very recently created charge.[1]

2.10.6. Where the search is carried out through an agent, care must be taken to instruct the agent fully as to the information which it is desired to obtain from the search.

1.   See *Burston Finance v. Speirway* [1974] 3 All ER 735.

2.11. Enduring and lasting powers of attorney

2.11.1. Where the purchase deed is to be executed by a person who is acting under the authority of an enduring power of attorney a search should be made at the Office of the Public Guardian to check whether or not registration of the power has been effected or is pending.

2.11.2. If no registration has been made or is pending the transaction may proceed to completion.

2.11.3. If the power has been registered the attorney may deal with the land and thus, provided the donor is still alive, completion may proceed, since the power is no longer capable of revocation without notification to the Office of the Public Guardian.

2.11.4. While registration is pending the transaction may only proceed if it is within one of the limited categories permitted by Mental Capacity Act 2005, Sched.4, Part 1, para.1(2).

2.11.5. Note that no new enduring powers of attorney could be created after 30 September 2007.

2.11.6. Where the purchase deed is to be executed by a person who is acting under the authority of a lasting power of attorney, a check should be made to ensure that the lasting power is registered with the Office of the Public Guardian, the attorney is a named individual who is over 18 or a trust corporation and that the attorney is acting within the scope of his authority (i.e. that the authority is not limited by any restrictions or conditions). An office copy of the lasting power is evidence of the contents of the power and the fact that it has been registered.

2.11.7. The buyer from the attorney acting under a lasting power will be protected under Mental Capacity Act 2005, s.14(3) unless he knew that the power was invalid or was aware of the circumstances which would have terminated the attorney's authority to act under the power.

2.11.8. A subsequent buyer will be protected under Mental Capacity Act 2005, s.14(4) if either the sale by the attorney acting under a lasting power to the first buyer was completed within 12 months of the date on which the power was registered, or the subsequent buyer makes a statutory declaration, before or within three months of completion of his purchase, that he had no reason to doubt that the attorney had authority to dispose of the property at the time of his purchase.

2.11.9. See also B23.2.8 and the Law Society's Lasting Powers of Attorney Practice Note (24 September 2007).

2.12. Local land charges search and enquiries

2.12.1. These searches are invariably made before exchange of contracts and are discussed at B10. Although the local land charges search only shows the state of the register at the time of issue of the search certificate and neither search confers a priority period on the buyer, a repeat of these searches before completion is not normally considered to be necessary provided that completion takes place within a short time after receipt of the search results or (in the case of the local land charges search) adequate insurance has been taken out. Delay in receipt of the replies to these searches also frequently makes it impracticable for them to be repeated at this stage of the transaction.

2.12.2. These searches should, however, be repeated prior to completion if:

(a) there is to be a period of two months or more between exchange of contracts and completion and the search has not been covered by insurance or replaced by insurance;

(b) information received by the buyer's solicitor suggests that a further search may be advisable in order to guard against a recently entered adverse entry on the register;

     (c)   the contract was conditional on the satisfactory results of later searches;

     (d)   required under paragraph 5.2 of the CML Lenders' Handbook.

2.12.3.   In the absence of a special condition in the contract the discovery of a late entry on such a search is not a matter of title and will not thus entitle the buyer either to raise requisitions about the entry or to refuse to complete. Where there is to be a long gap between exchange of contracts and the contractual completion date, the buyer should try to negotiate a special condition enabling him to raise requisitions prior to completion in respect of any local land charges or adverse schemes and proposals revealed by a local search and enquiries made prior to completion and not revealed by the searches and enquiries made before exchange. Such a condition may be resisted by the seller.

2.13.   Other searches

2.13.1.   The buyer's solicitor should check to ensure that all other searches which are relevant to the circumstances of the transaction have been carried out and that their results are satisfactory. A checklist of the most common pre-contract searches appears at B10. These searches should normally have been carried out before exchange of contracts but may be required at this stage of the transaction if either there was insufficient time to make them before exchange or since that time additional information has come to light which indicates that a particular search may be relevant. Arrangements should be made for final inspection of the property if necessary. It should be noted that paragraph 5.2 of the CML Lenders' Handbook requires searches which have no priority period attaching to them to be not more than six months old at the date of completion.

2.14.   Results of searches

2.14.1.   The results of searches must be received by the date when completion is due to take place. Completion cannot proceed until these results have been received and are considered to be satisfactory to the interests of the client.

2.14.2.   In the majority of cases the results of searches will either show no subsisting entries or will merely confirm information already known, e.g. an entry on the register protecting the contract between the buyer and the seller or, in the case of unregistered land, the registration of existing restrictive covenants. In such circumstances no further action on the search results is required from the buyer's solicitor.

2.14.3.   If an unexpected entry (other than a Class D(ii) protecting restrictive covenants, which cannot generally be removed) is revealed by the search result, the buyer's solicitor should:

     (a)   find out exactly what the entry relates to;

(b) if the entry appears adversely to affect the property, contact the seller's solicitor as soon as possible to seek his confirmation that the entry will be removed on or before completion;

(c) in the case of a Land Charges Department search, apply for an office copy of the entry using Form K19 (see Appendix VIII.4 for fee). The office copy consists of a copy of the application form which was submitted when the charge was registered and will reveal the name and address of the person with the benefit of the charge who may have to be contacted to seek his consent to its removal;

(d) keep the client, his lender and, subject to the duty of confidentiality, other solicitors involved in the chain of transactions informed of the situation since negotiations for the removal of the charge may cause a delay in completion.

2.14.4. An application form for the removal of an entry from the register in either registered or unregistered land will generally only be accepted by the Chief Land Registrar if it is signed by the person with the benefit of the charge or a person acting on his behalf. An application form signed by the seller's solicitors or an undertaking given by them on completion to secure the removal of the entry may not therefore suffice unless the seller is the person with the benefit of the entry.[1] In the case of registered land, the cancellation of a registered charge may be made by Form DS1, or by using the EDs or e-DS1 systems. Withdrawals of cautions and restrictions are effected on Forms WCT and RX4 respectively. The application for cancellation of a unilateral notice must be made in Form UN4. An application for the cancellation of a notice (other than a unilateral notice or a home rights notice) must be in Form CN1. As to bankruptcy entries, evidence needs to be lodged that the bankruptcy no longer affects the property.

2.14.5. Charges which are registered at the Land Charges Department can only be entered against the name of an estate owner in relation to the period during which he was the owner of the land in question. Thus an entry which was made before or after this time cannot prejudice the buyer. The computerised system which is used to process these searches will sometimes throw up entries which are clearly irrelevant to the transaction in hand, particularly where the name searched against is a very common one, e.g. John Smith. Having checked that the entry is irrelevant, it may either be disregarded or the seller's solicitor may at completion be asked to certify the entry as being inapplicable to the transaction. Certification by a solicitor is tantamount to a warranty, the consideration for it being completion of the transaction.

2.14.6. The court has a discretion to remove entries which are redundant but which cannot be removed from the register because the person with their benefit will not consent to their removal or cannot be contacted.

2.14.7. Entries protecting a spouse's or civil partner's homes rights under Family Law Act 1996 can be removed on production of the death certificate of the spouse or civil partner or a decree absolute (unless an order under Family Law Act 1996, s.33(5) has been made and registered) or by an order of the court. In the absence of these items, the charge can only be removed with the consent of the spouse or civil partner who has the benefit of the charge.

2.14.8.   An official certificate of search issued by the Land Registry is not conclusive in favour of the searcher who will thus take his interest in the land subject to whatever entries are on the register irrespective of whether or not they were revealed by the search certificate.[2] However, where a person suffers loss as a result of a mistake in an official search he will be able to claim compensation under Land Registration Act 2002, Sched.8, para.1.

2.14.9.   An official certificate of search issued by the Land Charges Department is conclusive in favour of the searcher who will thus take his interest in the land free of any entries which are on the register but which were not revealed by the search certificate. Where a person suffers loss as a result of an error in an official certificate of search he may be able to claim compensation from the Chief Land Registrar, but there is no statutory right to compensation in these circumstances. No liability will attach to the solicitor who made the search provided that a correctly submitted official search was made.[3]

1.   See *Holmes* v. *Kennard & Sons* (1985) 49 P&CR 202.
2.   *Parkash* v. *Irani Finance Ltd* [1970] Ch 101.
3.   Land Charges Act 1972, s.12.

E3. The buyer's mortgage

3.1. Instructions from lender

3.1.1. Instructions from the lender to act will usually be received at the same time as an offer of mortgage is made to the buyer, i.e. shortly before exchange of contracts. Since each lender's requirements will differ slightly, the precise instructions of the lender for whom the solicitor is acting in the present transaction must be noted and strictly observed. The instructions should comply with Rule 3.19 Solicitors' Code of Conduct 2007 (see Appendix I.1). Any queries which arise in relation to those instructions, whether at the outset of the transaction or during its course, must be immediately clarified with the lender. Where the solicitor is acting also for the buyer, the problems of conflict of interests and confidentiality must be borne in mind. Where the same solicitor is acting for both borrower and lender he owes a duty to both clients.[1] These issues are further discussed in A11. Many lenders require their solicitors to obtain and check evidence of the client's identity (e.g. a passport) and to keep a copy of the evidence of identity on file.[2]

3.1.2. Where a mortgage is being taken from an institutional lender over residential property it is likely that the solicitor will be instructed to follow the CML Lenders' Handbook (**www.cml.org.uk**). The solicitor must check which specific variations to the Handbook are required by the lender to suit both the lender's own requirements and the transaction in hand.

3.1.3. Alternatively, the solicitor may be instructed to comply with the Building Societies Association (BSA) Mortgage Instructions, which have been available for use by BSA members since January 2010. If acting for a building society using these instructions, the solicitor must obtain a copy from the BSA website (**www.bsa.org.uk**) as the instructions are not available in printed format.

3.1.4. See also A4 regarding liability under Financial Services and Markets Act 2000 in respect of arranging and advising upon regulated mortgages.

3.1.5. Where the seller has a mortgage to be discharged, see G1.5.2 as to the Land Registry's early completion policy.

1. See *Mortgage Express* v. *Bowerman & Partners* (1994) 34 EG 116; and *Bristol & West Building Society* v. *May, May and Merriman* [1997] 3 All ER 206.
2. See paragraph A3.3 of the CML Lenders' Handbook (**www.cml.org.uk**).

3.2.   Investigation of title

3.2.1.   When instructed to act both for the buyer and his lender, investigation of title on behalf of both clients will be carried out simultaneously, but the particular requirements (if any) of the lender must be considered when carrying out this procedure. Any queries which arise during the course of the investigation should immediately be clarified with the lender client since if they are deferred until a later stage in the transaction some delay in completion may result.

3.2.2.   When acting only for the lender, the lender's solicitor should request the buyer's solicitor to send him copies of the following documents as soon as the buyer's solicitor has completed his own investigation of title:

    (a)   all pre-contract searches and enquiries with their results;

    (b)   the contract;

    (c)   evidence of title;

    (d)   requisitions on title with their answers;

    (e)   the draft and subsequently the approved purchase deed;

    (f)   at a later stage, all pre-completion searches with their results;

    (g)   any other documents which are relevant to the acquisition of a good title by the lender or which are specifically required by the lender's instructions.

3.2.3.   On receipt of these documents from the buyer's solicitor, the lender's solicitor should conduct his own investigation of the title in accordance with instructions received from his client. Any queries on the title should be raised with the buyer's solicitor who will in turn seek an answer from the seller's solicitor. Investigation must be carried out as quickly as possible so that no delay in completion occurs.

3.3.   Report on title

3.3.1.   Investigation of title having been completed, the solicitor will be required to make a report on title to his lender client certifying that he has carried out a full investigation in accordance with the lender's instructions and that the title to the property is good and marketable. In residential transactions the report on title will be in the form of the certificate set out in the annexe to Rule 3 Solicitors' Code of Conduct 2007 (see Appendix I.1); in other transactions the CLLS Certificate and Short Form Report on Title may be used. At the stage when the Report on Title or Certificate is submitted to the lender, there should be no remaining queries on the title, any such queries having been clarified during the course of investigation of title. Notification of queries at this late stage may well result in completion being delayed pending their resolution. If a plan has been supplied by the lender for verification this must be carefully checked before certification. The solicitor may also be asked to advise whether a further inspection of the property by the lender's surveyor before completion will be required. This is usually only required in connection with property which is in the course of construction.

3.3.2. If the enquiries before contract indicate that works have been carried out to the property, paragraph 5.3 of the CML Lenders' Handbook and paragraph D21 of the BSA Mortgage Instructions make it clear that the solicitor must ensure that all the necessary consents are available (i.e. both planning and building regulations consents) and there should be no evidence of any breach of any condition attached to any consent. This should be done before exchange of contracts. Solicitors will rarely be in a position to give an unqualified assurance that all the conditions attached to a planning consent have been complied with.

3.3.3. Local land charge searches on Form LLC1 will reveal if there are any planning charges and proceedings for building regulation breaches. The replies to questions on CON 29R Enquiries of Local Authority (2007) should reveal if proceedings have been authorised for any infringement of building regulations. Enquiries of the seller's solicitors, or the borrower himself if he is in occupation, should reveal whether any notices have been received from the local authority complaining of building regulation or planning breaches.

3.3.4. Any certificate relating to planning matters by the borrower's solicitor should be limited to matters revealed by the usual local searches and by their enquiries of the seller/borrower. It is suggested that reporting solicitors should decline to certify that they are not aware of any matters which would give rise to a breach of planning conditions or building regulation control. Such a statement might lead a lender to assume that the solicitor has undertaken more extensive enquiries than a solicitor would reasonably be expected to make.

3.3.5. A reporting solicitor can properly go no further than confirm to the lender that searches and enquiries do not reveal evidence of any breach. This should be done before exchange of contracts.

3.3.6. A solicitor is liable for a report on title signed by his employee (*Nationwide Building Society* v. *Lewis* [1997] 3 All ER 498).

3.4. **Searches before completion**

3.4.1. Searches before completion are an integral part of the investigation of title procedure and should be strictly carried out before a report on title or certificate is submitted to the lender. If time does not permit this, the report on title or certificate should be qualified by a statement saying that the report is given subject to the results of such searches being satisfactory. The searches which need to be undertaken are identical to those which are conducted on behalf of a buyer, subject to the following modifications, and when the same solicitor is acting both for the buyer and his lender will be carried out once on behalf of both clients. Where two separate solicitors are acting for the buyer and his lender, the lender's solicitor should indicate to the buyer's solicitor whether he will accept the results of pre-completion searches made by the buyer, or whether he wishes to conduct his own searches. Where the title being purchased is registered, the buyer may take the benefit and protection of a search made in the name of the lender; thus only one search application is necessary.[1] The converse is not true, so that if the search application is made in the name of the buyer, a second application must be submitted in the name of the lender. Whether or not the land is registered, the lender will invariably instruct his solicitor to make a Land Charges Department search for bankruptcy against the name of the borrower(s) and to obtain a clear result to that search before releasing the mortgage funds into the buyer's hands. Where the borrower is a company a company search should be made against the borrower both as a safeguard against liquidation, receivership or administration and also for potential incumbrances, e.g. debentures which charge after-acquired property.

3.4.2.   All searches, both pre-contract and pre-completion must be no older than six months at completion (CML Lenders' Handbook, para.5.2.3).

1.   Land Registration Rules 2003, r.151.

3.5.   Life policies

3.5.1.   The lender's instructions in relation to any life policy which is to protect or act as collateral security to the mortgage must be carried out before completion. In a case where a solicitor is acting both for the buyer and his lender, in his capacity as buyer's solicitor and irrespective of whether the lender requires an endowment policy to be on foot by actual completion, or whether his instructions permit the policy to be obtained within a certain period after completion has taken place, the solicitor owes a duty to the buyer to ensure that the policy is on foot at the date of actual completion,[1] failing which the solicitor might be liable to the buyer or his personal representatives in negligence for any resulting loss, e.g. if the buyer died after completion so that the mortgage had to be repaid before the policy became effective. It is also usual in the case of a new policy to check that the first premium has been paid and that it states that the age of the insured is admitted. If age is not admitted and the age of the policy holder turns out to be wrong, this could have the effect either of invalidating the policy or of reducing the proceeds which are payable under the policy.

3.5.2.   Some lenders require a formal assignment to them of the benefit of the policy, in which case such assignment must be prepared (usually on a standard form supplied by the lender) and executed by the borrower. The assignment should be kept with the title deeds to the mortgaged property and after completion sent to the lender for safe custody or otherwise in accordance with the lender's instructions. The deed of assignment is not submitted to the Land Registry when an application for registration of title is made. Where the lender does not require a formal mortgage or deposit of the policy, the proceeds of the policy will fall into the deceased's estate on his death, and may not therefore be available to pay off the mortgage debt. This problem is particularly relevant where one of two unmarried co-owners dies, and the policy taken out by the deceased will fall into his estate and not into the hands of the surviving co-owner. The consequences of non-assignment or non-deposit of the policy should be explained to the policy holder and to potential beneficiaries under the policy at the time when the policy is taken out.

3.5.3.   To preserve the priority of the lender's claim to the benefit of the policy moneys, notice of the assignment of the benefit of the policy should, after completion, be given to the insurance company in accordance with Policies of Assurance Act 1867. If the lender does not supply a standard form on which to make this notification, a letter may be sent to the insurance company informing them of the assignment, the name of the assignee (the lender), and the details of the policy which has been assigned. Two copies of this letter or standard form notice should be sent to the insurance company, requesting them to sign one copy in acknowledgement of its receipt and to return it to the solicitor. The receipted copy must then be placed with the title deeds of the property for safe custody.

3.5.4.   The lender may require that an endowment policy is put on risk on or before completion of the mortgage.

1.   But see *Lynne v. Gordon Doctors & Walton* (1991) 135 SJ (LB) 29.

3.6.   **The mortgage deed**

3.6.1.   Where the mortgage is granted by an institutional lender, e.g. a bank or building society, drafts and engrossment copies of the lender's standard form of mortgage will be supplied to the solicitor for completion and execution by the borrower. In other cases the lender's instructions (if any) as to the form and contents of the mortgage must be followed and his approval obtained to the draft deed before engrossment. A legal mortgage must be made by deed to comply with Law of Property Act 1925, s.87. In registered land cases, the mortgage deed must identify the registered land which is to be charged, i.e. by its title number or by reference to a suitable plan. A legal charge of a registered estate may be made in Form CH1.[1]

3.6.2.   The mortgage deed will be prepared simultaneously with the purchase deed and will be executed by the borrower prior to completion. The borrower is required to execute the deed in the presence of a witness, but in the case of a legal mortgage the lender does not usually sign the deed. If the mortgage is equitable it will generally be a contract for a disposition of an interest in land within Law of Property (Miscellaneous Provisions) Act 1989, s.2 which is required to be in writing and signed by both contracting parties.

3.6.3.   The contents and effect of the mortgage deed must be explained to the borrower before signature to ensure that, e.g. the borrower understands that the lender will be entitled to sell the property if the borrower defaults in his repayments. Any prohibitions contained in the mortgage, e.g. as to letting the property or particular conditions attached to it, must also be explained to the borrower and where the charge is an all-moneys charge the effect of this type of charge should be explained to the client.

3.6.4.   The solicitor acting for the lender should take reasonable steps to check that the security effected over the property will be valid and enforceable. Problems can arise where, e.g. a 'friend' of one of the co-borrowers ostensibly pretending to be the co-borrower's wife signs the mortgage deed in the wife's place thus vitiating the security. It would appear that a solicitor does not generally have a duty to ensure that the mortgage deed is validly executed by the named borrower(s) but he should be alert to the issues involved and should do what he can to ensure proper execution by the correct persons. Execution by the borrower(s) in the solicitor's presence is a sensible precaution to take, although even this will not guard against forgery where the identity of the borrowers is not known personally to the solicitor (see A24). The CML Lenders' Handbook recommends that the mortgage should be signed in the presence of a solicitor but does not specifically require the mortgage deed to be executed in the presence of the solicitor. It does, however, normally require the solicitor to check the identity of signatories to documents and to ensure that the lender is supplied with a fully enforceable first charge by way of legal mortgage over the secured property.

3.6.5.   The lender's instructions may frequently also require the solicitor to discuss repayment of the mortgage with the borrower and may require the solicitor to obtain a signed banker's standing order for repayments from the borrower.

1.   Land Registration Rules 2003, r.103.

3.7.   **Mortgage funds**

3.7.1.   The effect of any retentions from the mortgage advance must be explained to the buyer in advance of completion and, if necessary, the buyer should be advised to seek estimates for any works which are to be effected on the property.

3.7.2.   The lender will not release the mortgage advance to the solicitor until he is satisfied that all conditions attached to the advance have been complied with and he has been requested to release the funds by the solicitor acting for him. Such request is commonly made on the Report on Title Form or Certificate of Title, or on a separate form supplied by the lender. The solicitor should ensure that he is in receipt of cleared funds (in order to avoid any breach of Solicitors' Accounts Rules) by the morning of the day of actual completion. The mortgage advance is clients' money and must be placed in a clients' account. If completion does not take place on the anticipated date, the amount of the mortgage advance must be returned to the lender or dealt with in accordance with his instructions, and a further cheque requested for the re-arranged completion date. If the solicitor pays the advance cheque into his clients' account and completion is delayed the solicitor may be liable to pay interest on the amount of the advance if the cheque is not returned to the lender within the time specified in the lender's instructions. The mortgage advance is held by the solicitor (pending completion) on trust for the lender. If the solicitor deals with the funds during this time, except in accordance with the lender's instructions, a breach of trust will occur.[1]

3.7.3. Any conditions relating to the discharge of the borrower's existing mortgage(s) over the same or another specified property identified by the lender must be complied with before the mortgage advance is released for his use.

3.7.4. If it is not possible to synchronise a sale and purchase transaction or in any other situation where it becomes apparent that the mortgage funds will not be available in time to complete the purchase, the buyer must be advised of the consequences of a delayed completion and of any decision to use bridging finance in order to complete the purchase on the due date.

3.7.5. Where different solicitors are acting for the buyer and his lender, it will be necessary for the two solicitors to liaise in order to ensure that the mortgage funds reach the seller's solicitor's bank account in time for completion.

1. *Target Holdings* v. *Redferns (a firm)* [1995] NPC 136, HL and see *Bristol & West Building Society* v. *May, May and Merrimans* [1997] 3 All ER 206.

3.8. Duty to lender

3.8.1. Solicitors who do not apply the advance in the manner required by their instructions or who release it before the lender's title is complete may be liable to repay the advance. Until the mortgage is completed, the solicitor may hold the advance on the borrower's client account but it must be clearly identifiable as coming from the lender and will be returned to the lender on demand.

3.8.2. Where the lender instructs that separate advice must be given to joint borrowers, the joint borrowers must be seen separately.

3.8.3. Where the solicitor signs a certificate saying that he has independently advised the borrowers,[1] the lender is not under a duty to enquire as to the nature of the advice given.[2]

1. In *Bank Melli Iran* v. *Samadi-Rad* [1995] 2 FLR 367 the court suggested that advice given by a separate solicitor in the same firm was not considered to be 'independent'.
2. *Bank of Baroda* v. *Rayarel* [1995] NPC 6, and see A10.

3.9. Completion of the mortgage

3.9.1. Since it is not possible for the buyer to mortgage a property which he does not own, it follows that formal completion of the mortgage cannot take place until after completion of the purchase, irrespective of the fact that the mortgage funds will have been released to the use of the borrower on completion of the earlier purchase. As soon as completion of the purchase of the property has taken place, the mortgage deed can be completed by insertion of the date of completion and any other formalities which have to be entered in it, e.g. date of first repayment. The lender client may require to be informed that completion has taken place. If there is any doubt over whether vacant possession will be given the client should be advised to inspect the property immediately prior to completion.

3.9.2.   Following completion of the mortgage, the lender's charge must be protected by registration on the charges register of the title. The solicitor acting for the lender should take possession of all the necessary documents on completion and should effect the registration on behalf of his client. Where separate solicitors are acting for the buyer and the lender, it is usual for the lender's solicitor to require the buyer's solicitor to hand over on completion completed and signed Land Registry application forms.

3.9.3.   Charges created by companies must, in addition to any registration at the Land Registry, be registered at Companies House on form MG01 within 21 days of their creation in accordance with sections 860–877 Companies Act 2006. When registering the charge, the company is required to give certain details as set out in Regulation 2 Companies (Particulars of Company Charges) Regulations 2008. These details are the date of creation of the charge, a description of the charging instrument, the amount secured, the name and address of the chargee and short particulars of the charged property. Additionally, evidence must be lodged at the Land Registry that the charge has been registered at Companies House (see G1.6).

3.9.4.   Note that equivalent registration requirements apply under section 862 Companies Act 2006 when the company acquires a property subject to an existing charge.

3.10.   Custody of deeds

3.10.1.   The lender's requirements should be checked to ascertain the precise requirements of the lender in relation to the safe custody of documents.

3.10.2.   On completion of the post-completion formalities, any relevant documents, e.g. life policy and assignments and notices relating to it, should normally be sent to the lender for safe custody. The documents to be sent should be listed in triplicate, one copy of the list being retained on the solicitor's file, the remaining two being sent to the lender with the deeds with a request that one copy of the list is signed by the lender and returned to the solicitor as an acknowledgement of their receipt. The deeds should be despatched by a method which ensures their safe arrival at their destination, e.g. registered post, document exchange or insured post. If there is to be any delay in the despatch of the deeds, e.g. because of delays in registration at the Land Registry, the lender should be informed of the delay, the reason for it and its likely duration.

3.11.   Costs

3.11.1.   The lender's costs in relation to the grant of the mortgage are primarily the lender's responsibility since he is the client who has instructed the solicitor, but the lender commonly seeks indemnity for those costs from the buyer who should be informed of this fact and their likely amount at the outset of the transaction. In other cases the amount to be charged must be agreed between the solicitor and his lender client (see N1).

E4. Preparing for completion

4.1.	Introduction	4.5.	Completion statement
4.2.	Seller's checklist	4.6.	Statement to client
4.3.	Buyer's checklist	4.7.	Money – the buyer
4.4.	Apportionments	4.8.	Completion checklist

4.1. Introduction

4.1.1. In order to ensure that completion proceeds smoothly, both parties need to undertake a number of preparatory steps. Most of these steps have been examined in depth in other areas of this book. The following paragraphs therefore concentrate on summarising the matters to be dealt with at this stage of the transaction by way of checklists with some additional commentary.

4.2. Seller's checklist

(a) Ensure purchase deed has been approved and requisitions answered.

(b) Receive engrossed purchase deed from buyer – has buyer executed the deed (where appropriate) and plan (if used), or has an acceptable undertaking been given that he will execute after completion?

(c) Get seller to execute purchase deed and return it to solicitor in time for completion.

(d) Obtain redemption figure(s) for seller's mortgage(s) and check that they are correct and ensure that the seller's solicitor is aware of *all* the mortgages which need to be redeemed. The redemption figure will be provided by the seller's mortgage company; see the guidance issued by the Council of Mortgage Lenders and the Law Society in 1992 (and updated in 1999) relating to mortgage redemption statements (see Appendix IV.13). Where the redemption figure relates to a 'flexible mortgage', i.e. one where the borrower's savings and income appear in the one account, it may be necessary to ask for the account to be frozen until the redemption figure has been transferred at completion.

(e) Obtain last receipts, etc., where apportionments are to be made on completion.

(f) Prepare completion statement (where necessary) and send two copies to buyer in good time before completion.

(g) Remind client to organise final readings of meters at the property.

(h) Prepare forms for discharge of land charges where necessary (unregistered land).

(i) Approve any memorandum which the buyer has requested be placed on retained title deeds or grant of representation (unregistered land).

(j) Prepare any undertaking which needs to be given on completion (e.g. for discharge of seller's mortgage if also acting for the lender).

(k) Contact lender to confirm final arrangements for discharge of seller's mortgage, method of payment, certificate of non-crystallisation, etc.

(l) Prepare authority addressed to tenants relating to payment of future rent (tenanted property).

(m) Check through file to ensure all outstanding queries have been dealt with.

(n) Prepare list of matters to be dealt with on actual completion.

(o) Locate deeds and documents which will need to be inspected/handed over on completion and prepare certified copies for the buyer of those documents which are to be retained by the seller.

(p) Prepare two copies of schedule of deeds to be handed to buyer on completion.

(q) Prepare inventory of chattels and receipt for money payable for them.

(r) Check arrangements for vacant possession and handing over keys.

(s) Receive instructions from buyer's solicitor to act as his agent on completion and clarify instructions with him if necessary.

(t) Make final arrangements with buyer's solicitor for time and place of completion.

(u) Ensure estate agents are aware of completion arrangements.

(v) Prepare bill for submission to client.

4.3. Buyer's checklist

(a) Ensure purchase deed has been approved and requisitions satisfactorily answered.

(b) Engross purchase and mortgage deeds.

(c) Get buyer to execute mortgage deed, purchase deed and plan (if necessary) and return it to solicitor.

(d) Send (executed) purchase deed to seller's solicitor for his client's execution in time for completion. The submission of the deed should be in escrow subject to the express condition that the buyer may withdraw if the seller fails to complete.[1]

(e) Make pre-completion searches and ensure their results are satisfactory.

(f) Make report on title to lender and request advance cheque in time for completion.

(g) Receive completion statement (where necessary) and copies of last receipts in support of apportionments and check it is correct.

(h) Remind client of arrangements for completion.

(i) Prepare forms for discharge of land charges where necessary (unregistered land).

(j) Obtain seller's approval of the wording of any memorandum which the buyer has requested be placed on retained title deeds or grant of representation (unregistered land).

(k) Prepare and agree the form of wording of any undertaking which needs to be given or received on completion.

(l) Confirm with seller that certificate of non-crystallisation will be given (if appropriate).

(m) Contact lender to confirm final arrangements for completion.

(n) Ensure that any life policy required by the lender is on foot and check with client that any other insurances required for the property (e.g. house contents insurance) have been taken out. Prepare and engross assignments of other insurance policies to the buyer (e.g. for damp treatment) if appropriate.

(o) Check through file to ensure all outstanding queries have been dealt with.

(p) Prepare statement of account and bill for client and submit together with a copy of the completion statement, requesting balance due from client be paid in sufficient time for the funds to be cleared before completion.

(q) Receive advance cheque from lender, pay into clients' account and clear funds before completion.

(r) Receive balance of funds from client and clear through clients' account before completion.

(s) Arrange for final inspection of property if necessary.

(t) Prepare list of matters to be dealt with on actual completion.

(u) Check arrangements for vacant possession and handing over keys.

(v) Instruct seller's solicitor to act as agent on completion if completion not to be by personal attendance.

(w) Make final arrangements with seller's solicitor for time and place of completion.

(x) Ensure estate agents are aware of completion arrangements.

    (y)   Make arrangements for transmission of completion money to seller's solicitor (or as he has directed).

1.   Under Companies Act 2006, s.46(2) execution by a company is rebuttably presumed to be delivery of the deed: this re-emphasises the need for execution subject to an express condition in such cases.

4.4. Apportionments

4.4.1.   Where completion does not take place on a date when outgoings on the property fall due, outgoings which attach to the land may be apportioned between the parties on completion, the calculations of the apportioned sums being shown on the completion statement.

4.4.2.   Uniform business rate and water rates can be apportioned but it is normally considered better practice to inform the relevant authority after completion of the change of ownership and request them to send apportioned accounts to seller and buyer.

4.4.3.   Where applicable, rent and service charge payments may have to be apportioned. These matters are further dealt with in K1 and K5.

4.4.4.   Standard Condition 6.3 and Standard Commercial Condition 8.3 deal with apportionments and allow a provisional apportionment to be made where exact figures are not available at completion (e.g. in respect of service charges).

4.4.5.   The seller must be asked to produce the last demands or receipts for all sums which are to be apportioned so that the calculations of the amounts due or to be allowed on completion may be made. Copies of these receipts should be sent to the buyer with the completion statement to enable him to check the accuracy of the calculation.

4.5. Completion statement

4.5.1.   A completion statement, to be prepared by the seller's solicitor, showing the amount of money required to complete the transaction and how that figure is calculated, will be requested by the buyer when he submits his requisitions on title.

4.5.2.   It is only necessary to provide the buyer with a completion statement where the sum due on completion includes apportionments or other sums apart from the balance of the purchase price.[1]

4.5.3.   If not sent to the buyer with the answers to his requisitions on title, the completion statement should be supplied in good time before completion to enable the buyer to check its accuracy and to make arrangements for the amount due to be available.

4.5.4. The statement should show clearly the total amount due on completion, and how that total sum is made up. Depending on the circumstances it may be necessary to take account of some or all of the following items:

    (a)   the purchase price, giving credit for any deposit paid;

    (b)   apportionments of outgoings;

    (c)   money payable for chattels;

    (d)   compensation if completion is delayed;

    (e)   a licence fee if the buyer has been in occupation of the property.

4.5.5. Two copies of the completion statement should be sent to the buyer together with copies of any receipts or demands on which apportioned figures have been based.

1.   *Carne* v. *Debono* [1988] 3 All ER 485; *Hanson* v. *South West Electricity Board* [2001] EWCA Civ 1377.

4.6.   Statement to client

4.6.1. The buyer's solicitor should prepare and submit to his client a financial statement which shows clearly the total sum which is due from him on completion and how that sum is calculated.

4.6.2. In addition to the matters dealt with on the completion statement, the financial statement should also take account of such of the following matters as are relevant to the transaction:

    (a)   the mortgage advance and any costs and/or retentions made in respect of it;

    (b)   disbursements, e.g. SDLT, Land Registry fees, fees payable for registration of notices or search fees;

    (c)   the solicitor's costs.

4.6.3. The financial statement, accompanied by a copy of the completion statement and the solicitor's properly drawn bill, should be sent to the client in sufficient time before completion to allow the client to forward the required balance of funds to the solicitor in time for those funds to be cleared by completion.

4.7.   Money – the buyer

4.7.1. On being informed of the amount required to complete, the buyer's solicitor should check the figures for accuracy, verifying any apportionments made against the copy receipts or demands supplied by the seller. Any discrepancies must be clarified as a matter of urgency.

4.7.2.   The solicitor should then make a final calculation of the sums due on completion, preparing his financial statement and bill for submission to the client.

4.7.3.   If at this stage it appears that there is any shortfall in funds the client must immediately be informed and steps taken to remedy the shortfall. If bridging finance or a further loan are necessary in order to complete the transaction arrangements must be made to effect such arrangements without delay. An undertaking given by the solicitor to repay bridging finance must only be given where the promise given by the solicitor is wholly capable of performance by him (see B16).

4.7.4.   The mortgage advance requested by the solicitor from the lender should be received in sufficient time to permit the funds to be cleared through clients' account before completion.

4.7.5.   The client must be asked to put the solicitor in funds for the balance of the completion money (over and above the mortgage advance) in sufficient time to permit the funds to be cleared through clients' account before completion. On receipt of the funds from the client, the cheque should be credited to a ledger account in the name of that client.

4.7.6.   On the day of completion arrangements must be made to remit the amount due to the seller's solicitor in accordance with his instructions.

4.8.   Completion checklist

4.8.1.   When preparing for completion the buyer's solicitor should make a checklist of the matters which need to be dealt with on actual completion to ensure that nothing is overlooked. Where the transaction is complex, the list should be submitted to the seller's solicitor for his agreement as to its contents. Where the buyer instructs a person to act as his agent on completion he should, when instructing the agent, send him a copy of the checklist so that the agent is fully informed as to the matters which need to be dealt with.

4.8.2.   Some or all of the items in the following checklist will need to be attended to on actual completion.

4.8.3.   The list should contain an itemised list of the documents which need to be inspected/marked/handed over/received at completion.

(a)   **Documents to be available at completion**

(i)   contract;

(ii)   evidence of title;

(iii)   copy purchase deed;

(iv)   answers to requisitions;

      (v)   completion statement.

(b) **Documents to be inspected by buyer**

      (i)   title deeds where in unregistered land these are not to be handed over on completion (e.g. on a sale of part);

      (ii)   general or enduring power of attorney;

      (iii)   grant of administration;

      (iv)   receipts/demands for apportionments if not previously supplied.

(c) **Documents, etc., to be handed to buyer on completion**

      (i)   title deeds;

      (ii)   original lease;

      (iii)   executed purchase deed;

      (iv)   schedule of deeds;

      (v)   Form DS1/discharged mortgage or undertaking in respect of discharge of mortgage(s), certificate of non-crystallisation (if appropriate);

      (vi)   receipt for money paid for chattels;

      (vii)   authority addressed to tenants relating to payment of future rent and original tenancy agreements/leases (tenanted property);

      (viii)   keys of the property (if these are not available the seller's solicitor should be asked to telephone the key holder to request the release of the keys);

      (ix)   certified copy of any memorandum endorsed on retained deeds;

      (x)   landlord's licence.

(d) **Documents, etc., to be handed to seller on completion**

      (i)   banker's draft for amount due on completion (unless remitted by direct credit);

      (ii)   executed duplicate purchase deed/counterpart lease/licence (where appropriate);

      (iii)   receipted schedule of deeds received from seller;

      (iv)   release of deposit if held by third party in capacity of stakeholder.

(e) **Endorsements on documents if required by buyer**

      (i)   endorsement of assent or conveyance on grant of representation (unregistered land);

      (ii)   endorsement of sale on most recently dated retained document of title (sale of part of unregistered land);

(iii)   mark up abstract or epitome as compared against the original deeds (unregistered land in respect of any document the original of which is not handed over on completion).

E5. The buyer in occupation

5.1.   Introduction

5.1.1.   In many cases the seller will be in actual occupation of the property until completion and thus the question of the buyer taking possession before completion does not arise. The seller is entitled to retain possession until completion unless otherwise agreed.

5.1.2.   The buyer's request to enter and occupy the premises before completion should be regarded with some caution by the seller since once the buyer takes up occupation he may lose his incentive to complete on the contractual completion date and, if ultimately he does not complete the transaction at all, it may be difficult to evict the buyer from the property. Where the seller has a subsisting mortgage on the property, his lender's consent should be obtained before the buyer is allowed into occupation.

5.1.3.   It is essential that the nature of the buyer's occupation is a licence and not a tenancy in order to avoid the possibility of the buyer claiming security of tenure against the seller.[1] Even where a licence is granted a court order will always be necessary to remove a residential occupier who does not voluntarily vacate the property,[2] and may be necessary in non-residential cases where the tenant will not peaceably surrender his occupation.

1.   See K12. An outline of the major statutes affecting security of tenure is given in section K.
2.   Protection from Eviction Act 1977, s.2.

5.2.   Conditions to be imposed on buyer

5.2.1.   Where it is agreed to allow the buyer into possession the seller may consider imposing some restrictions or conditions of occupation on the buyer. If the contract does not make provision for occupation by the buyer (e.g. Standard Condition 5.2), the terms of the occupation should be agreed in writing and signed by both parties prior to the commencement of the buyer's occupation.

5.2.2.   Some or all of the following conditions may be considered:

    (a)   the occupation shall be a licence and not a tenancy;[1]

    (b)   payment of a further instalment of the purchase price as a precondition of occupation;

(c)   payment of a licence fee during occupation (frequently this is calculated by reference to the rate at which compensation for late completion
is payable under the general conditions of the contract);

(d)   the licence should be non-assignable;

(e)   restrictions on who may occupy the property;

(f)   restrictions on the use of the property during the buyer's occupation
(including an obligation to comply with the terms of the lease in the case
of leasehold property);

(g)   payment by the buyer of all outgoings on the property;

(h)   the buyer to be responsible for insuring the property and/or paying the
insurance premium;

(i)   the buyer to be responsible for repairs and maintenance;

(j)   prohibition on alterations and improvements;

(k)   provisions for termination of the licence by either party;

(l)   entitlement to the income of the property (if any).

5.2.3.   Some but not all of the above conditions are provided by Standard Condition
5.2 which restricts the occupation of the property to the buyer and his
household.

5.2.4.   Alternatively, the seller may consider granting the buyer a licence for access
only, e.g. for measuring up for alterations, such licence to be restricted to access
at specified times and for a specific purpose.

1.   See K12. Where the terms of the original contract do not provide for the buyer's occupation, care must
be exercised in drawing up the terms of the licence agreement. Such an agreement does not fall within
Law of Property (Miscellaneous Provisions) Act 1989, s.2 but for certainty should be in writing and
signed by both parties.

5.3.   Delay

5.3.1.   Where there is a delay in completion and the seller sues for specific performance, the court usually gives the buyer the option either of paying the balance
of the purchase price with interest into court or of giving up possession.[1] This
provision is, however, thought not to apply where the buyer takes possession
under a provision to that effect contained in the contract to purchase the
property, e.g. Standard Condition 5.2.[2]

5.3.2.   The seller has an equitable lien over the property which endures until the
purchase price is paid in full (see section M).

1.   This order is known as a 'Greenwood and Turner' order after the case of that name: *Greenwood* v.
Turner [1891] 2 Ch 144.
2.   *Attfield* v. *DJ Plant Hire and General Contractors Ltd* [1987] Ch 141.

5.4. Common law provisions

5.4.1. The seller's position as quasi-trustee of the property on behalf of the buyer, from which stems the seller's duty to take care of the property pending completion, is not affected by the buyer's occupation. Therefore the seller should expressly pass this duty of care (and to do repairs) on to the buyer as part of the licence to occupy.

5.4.2. The buyer becomes entitled to receive the income of the property and is responsible for outgoings.

5.4.3. Unless the contract provides to the contrary, the buyer, by taking possession, will be deemed to have accepted the seller's title and thus loses his right to object to any defects of which he knew at that time (see C5). Standard Condition 5.2.7 reverses this common law rule by providing that the buyer's right to raise requisitions is unaffected by his occupation of the property.

5.5. The buyer

5.5.1. Since the terms of the occupation agreement will normally be construed as a licence and not a tenancy the buyer's position as occupier is somewhat tenuous and he will face certain eviction if he does not ultimately complete the purchase. The buyer should therefore be advised not to spend money on altering or improving the property until completion has taken place. The terms of the occupation agreement will often prohibit the buyer from altering or improving the property pending completion.

5.5.2. If delay in completion is anticipated, the buyer may seek to protect his contract by applying for registration of a notice (registered land) or a Class C(iv) estate contract (unregistered land), although a buyer of registered land may be protected by being in occupation because the buyer may be able to establish an overriding interest under Land Registration Act 2002.[1]

5.5.3. The terms of the occupation agreement should be fully explained to the buyer. In particular his attention should be drawn to the financial provisions since the buyer is often required to pay a further instalment of the purchase price together with a daily licence fee as one of the terms of his occupation. Where the purchase is being financed by a mortgage, the lender's consent to the terms of the occupation agreement should be obtained.

1. Land Registration Act 2002, Sched.1, para.2 and Sched.3, para.2.

5.6. Sitting tenants

5.6.1. Where the property is being sold to a sitting tenant there is ample justification for accepting a less than 10% deposit on exchange of contracts, or even for dispensing with the deposit altogether (see B17).

5.6.2. Although the tenant will already be familiar with the physical condition and structure of the property, he should still consider the merits of a survey of the property. In cases where the landlord is responsible for repairs, the tenant will on completion become responsible for the maintenance and upkeep of the property and will thus need to be aware of any major structural defects in it which might affect his decision to proceed with the purchase or his ability to resell the property at a later date. Even in cases where the tenant is currently responsible for repairs he may still consider it wise to have a survey of the property made.

5.6.3. Even where the tenant is not raising a mortgage to finance his purchase, full deduction of title by the landlord should be required to ensure that the tenant will become registered with an absolute freehold title and thus able to resell the property should he wish to do so. If the title to the tenant's lease is already registered, an application for merger of the freehold and leasehold titles may be made after completion. If the tenant's leasehold interest in the property is subject to a mortgage which is not discharged on completion of the purchase of the reversion, the freehold and leasehold titles cannot be merged.

5.6.4. The landlord should include a contractual provision to the effect that the tenant will remain liable on the tenant's covenants contained in the lease until actual completion. Without such a clause it could be argued that the lease under which the tenant currently holds the property comes to an end on the contractual completion date irrespective of whether actual completion occurs then or later. This would mean that the landlord would be unable to enforce covenants or to recover any rent from the tenant during the period between the contractual completion date and actual completion. Alternatively a contractual condition may be inserted to the effect that the sale of the property is subject to the terms of the lease, the lease merging with the freehold on completion. The landlord should consider the effect of the contract for sale on his insurance policy covering the property.

5.6.5. Standard Condition 5.2 (occupation by buyer) does not apply to a sale to a sitting tenant.

E6. Death and insolvency

6.1. Death of a contracting party

6.1.1. The death of one of the contracting parties between contract and completion does not affect the validity of the contract; the benefit and burden of the contract passes to the deceased's personal representatives who are bound to complete.

6.2. Death of sole seller

6.2.1. The seller's personal representatives are bound to complete the contract, but cannot actually do so until issue of the grant of representation. Executors derive their authority from the will, administrators from the grant, but in either case the grant is necessary in order to make title to the buyer. Even in the case of executors, it is unsafe for a person dealing with them to rely on evidence of their appointment other than by production of the grant.

6.2.2. If completion does not take place on the contractual completion date, a breach of contract will occur (irrespective of whether time was of the essence of the completion date) and remedies, e.g. compensation or damages, will be available to the innocent party (see section M).

6.2.3. A delay in obtaining the grant of representation will have adverse consequences for a buyer who is involved in a chain of transactions since he may be forced to complete his sale, but unable to complete his purchase simultaneously because of the death of the seller and delay in the issue of the grant of representation. Loss suffered by the buyer, e.g. the cost of temporary accommodation may be claimable as a head of damage against the seller's personal representatives.

6.2.4. If time was not originally of the essence of the completion date, it can be made so by service of a notice to complete. Such a notice can be served on the executor(s) named in the seller's will (if any) and a separate copy of the notice served on the Public Trustee.

6.2.5. The practical answer to the problem of the seller's death is for the seller's solicitor immediately to inform the solicitors for the other party (or parties in a chain of transactions) and (with the authority of those concerned) to apply for an expedited grant of probate or letters of administration. Obviously the closer the death to the date of completion, the more acute the problem, but even in a chain transaction the parties may agree in the circumstances to postpone completion until a grant is obtained if assured that this can be done with expedition. In any circumstances where delay in completion is likely, consideration should be given to the protection of the contract by registration by the buyer's solicitor of a notice (registered land) or a Class C(iv) land charge (unregistered land).

6.2.6. Although generally probate cannot issue within seven days of death (administration within 14 days), there is an exception in case of emergency with leave of two registrars. It is considered that leave would normally be granted in this situation where there is a possibility of damages being awarded against the estate and the Probate Registry will assist with quick responses and advice in such a situation.

6.2.7. A possible solution to the problems caused by the death of the seller before completion is for the executors named in the will to negotiate to allow the buyer into possession pending formal completion. On taking possession the buyer would normally be required to pay a licence fee under the terms of the contract (see Standard Condition 5.2 and E5) which could be offset against the compensation payable by the personal representatives for late completion.

6.3. Death of co-owner

6.3.1. Property owned by beneficial co-owners is held on trust and all the trustees must join in any conveyance of the legal estate.[1] The death of one trustee between contract and completion does not, however, affect the validity of the contract.

6.3.2. Where following the death there still remain at least two trustees of the legal estate, the transaction can proceed to completion without delay. It will be necessary to produce the death certificate of the deceased in order to provide the buyer with evidence of the death. The purchase deed will need to be redrawn to reflect the change of parties to the transaction.

6.3.3. Frequently the legal estate is held by only two trustees (e.g. husband and wife) and the death of one of them will leave only one trustee of the legal estate which will prima facie be insufficient to satisfy Law of Property Act 1925, s.27. If the trustees held the property as joint tenants in equity, the surviving joint tenant will become entitled to the deceased's equitable interest through the law of survivorship (*jus accrescendi*) and can deal with the property as a beneficial owner provided that there is no restriction on the proprietorship register of a registered title or, in unregistered land, that the requirements of Law of Property (Joint Tenants) Act 1964 are satisfied.

Surviving beneficial joint tenant

6.3.4.   Where the sole surviving joint tenant is to transfer registered land the buyer should:

    (a)   check that no restriction is entered on the proprietorship register of the title;

    (b)   redraft the transfer to reflect the change of parties and capacity of the seller;

    (c)   require the seller to provide evidence of the death,[2] for example, an official copy of the death certificate of the deceased co-owner.

6.3.5.   Where the land is unregistered the buyer should:

    (a)   check the conveyance under which the co-owners *bought* the property to ensure that no memorandum of severance of the joint tenancy has been endorsed on it;

    (b)   redraft the purchase deed to reflect the change in parties. The deed should recite the death and state that the sole seller has become solely and beneficially entitled to the property;

    (c)   make a Land Charges Department search against the names of both the deceased and the survivor to ensure that no bankruptcy proceedings have been registered against either name.

6.3.6.   Steps (a) and (c) immediately above would be done as a matter of course during the normal investigation of title procedure and thus do not put the buyer to extra inconvenience or expense (see D2).

6.3.7.   If these conditions are not satisfied, another trustee should be appointed to act with the survivor. Where the survivor has become solely and beneficially entitled to the property, delay in completion should be minimal, but normal remedies for delay would in any event be available (see section M).

Surviving beneficial tenant in common

6.3.8.   In all circumstances another trustee should be appointed to act with the surviving tenant in common. This appointment can be effected either by separate deed of appointment or by including the appointment in the purchase deed. In either case the purchase deed will have to be redrafted to reflect the change in parties. The seller's solicitor may act as the second trustee provided that there is no potential conflict of interests between the survivor and other beneficiaries (if any). Alternatively, the other beneficiary (or one of them, being of full age and competence) may be appointed as second trustee of the legal estate.[3] If a dispute arises between the trustees in relation to the sale, delay may occur. The contract is, however, binding and such delay will incur liability to the buyer and the refusal of the new trustee to, e.g. sign the purchase deed will not frustrate the transaction since the buyer could seek specific performance of the contract or serve a notice to complete (see section M).

Settled land

6.3.9. On the death of a sole tenant for life under Settled Land Act 1925 the position depends on whether the land remains settled land after the death. If it does, the trustees of the settlement are entitled to a grant of probate or administration limited to the settled land, and they will be the persons with capacity to make good title. If, however, the settlement ends on the death, the former settled land is included in the grant made to the deceased's ordinary personal representatives who will perform the contract.

1. Law of Property Act 1925, s.27.
2. Land Registration Rules 2003, r.164.
3. See Trusts of Land and Appointment of Trustees Act 1996, s.19 in relation to the appointment of new trustees. See also Land Registry Practice Guides 21 and 24.

6.4. Death of sole buyer

6.4.1. The personal representatives step into the shoes of the deceased and will be bound to complete the contract. Even in the most straightforward case some delay in completion may be experienced because the purchase deed will have to be redrafted to reflect the change in parties and the personal representatives cannot complete until they obtain the grant of representation. Where the purchase was due to be financed by a mortgage, the death of the borrower (the buyer) will usually mean that the offer of mortgage is revoked and the personal representatives may therefore find themselves with insufficient funds to complete unless an alternative source of finance can be found. Where the deceased buyer intended to purchase the house for his own sole occupation the personal representatives may feel that since the purpose of the transaction has been defeated they no longer wish to proceed with the transaction. Unless they can negotiate a written release with the seller they will, however, be bound to complete (and may then attempt to resell the property) or face an action in damages from the seller.

6.5. Death of joint buyer

6.5.1. The survivor remains bound by the contract and can be forced to complete. The joint buyers obtained an equitable interest in the property on exchange of contracts and it is possible that the deceased's share in the property may on his death have passed to a third party (not to the co-purchaser) under his will or intestacy. In order to avoid delay while this matter is resolved it may be advisable to transfer the property into the names of two trustees on completion. In any event the purchase deed will have to be redrafted to reflect the change in parties. Finance may have to be rearranged and a new mortgage deed prepared. Some delay seems to be inevitable and the seller will have a claim against the buyer for loss caused by the delay (see section M). In cases where the surviving buyer (being solely entitled to the benefit of the contract) decides that he/she no longer wishes to proceed with the purchase, an attempt may be made to negotiate a written release with the seller, but he is under no obligation to accede to this request. Failing a negotiated release the buyer will have to proceed with the purchase and then attempt to resell the property.

6.6. Service of notices on deceased estate owner

6.6.1.   If the person serving the notice is at the time of service unaware of the death, service on the deceased at his last known address is valid.

6.6.2.   If at the time of service the person serving the notice was aware of the death, notice should be served on the deceased and his personal representatives at the deceased's last known address and a copy of the notice served on the Public Trustee (Law of Property (Miscellaneous Provisions) Act 1994, ss.10–14).

6.7. Bankruptcy of seller

6.7.1.   A buyer will usually only be affected by the bankruptcy of the seller if there is a bankruptcy entry shown on the result of his official search or on official copy entries of the title. Such entry may reveal either the presentation of the petition and/or the making of a bankruptcy order.

6.7.2.   On the bankruptcy of an individual who is the sole proprietor of the land, the legal estate in the property owned by him passes to his trustee in bankruptcy and the buyer must from that time deal only with the trustee and not the seller. The trustee may be forced to complete the sale by an action for specific performance, subject to his right to disclaim under Insolvency Act 1986, s.315. Under that section the trustee may, by the giving of a prescribed notice, disclaim any onerous property, which is defined as 'any unprofitable contract, and any other property comprised in the bankrupt's estate which is unsaleable or not readily saleable or is such that it may give rise to a liability to pay money or perform any other onerous act'. 'Onerous' does not in this context extend to disclaiming the contract simply because the trustee can realise more money by entering into some other contract. The trustee might in an appropriate case take the view that the contract constituted a transaction at an undervalue or a preference, in which event he might refuse to complete the transaction on this ground. Assuming the matter proceeds to completion, the purchase deed will have to be redrafted to show the trustee as the seller and the bankrupt will not be a party to the deed.

6.7.3.   Between the making of a bankruptcy order and the time at which the bankrupt's estate vests in a trustee, the Official Receiver is the receiver and manager of the bankrupt's estate, but under Insolvency Act 1986, s.287 his powers in this period are very limited and it is doubtful whether in most cases he would be entitled to complete the transaction. The Official Receiver has, under Insolvency Act 1986, s.293, 12 weeks following the bankruptcy order in which to decide whether to convene a meeting of creditors to appoint a trustee. If the Official Receiver decides not to summon such a meeting then he must give notice of his decision to the court and to every creditor of the bankrupt known to him or identified in the bankrupt's statement of affairs and as from the giving to the court of such notice the Official Receiver becomes the trustee of the bankrupt's estate (section 293(3)).

6.7.4. If a creditors' meeting is held then a trustee may be appointed at such a meeting.

6.7.5. Trust property, which includes the legal estate in land held by co-owners, does not vest in a bankrupt's trustee. The making of a bankruptcy order effects a severance of a joint tenancy. The bankrupt's beneficial interest in the property will vest in the trustee in bankruptcy. Consequently, on the bankruptcy of one of the co-owners the legal estate is unaffected and completion may proceed, the bankrupt and the co-owner being entitled to convey the legal estate. If the bankrupt will not co-operate, it is open to his or her co-trustee to replace the bankrupt on the grounds of the bankruptcy under the provisions of Trustee Act 1925. A buyer should attempt to get the trustee in bankruptcy to join in the purchase deed to give his consent to the sale of the beneficial interest and preferably to give a receipt for the part of the purchase money attributable to the beneficial interest, but cannot insist on this happening, nor can the trustee insist on joining in the deed.

6.7.6. See Land Registry Practice Guide 34 as to the evidence to be lodged on registration of a transfer by a trustee in bankruptcy.

6.8. Bankruptcy of buyer

6.8.1. The benefit of the contract passes to the buyer's trustee in bankruptcy who may complete the transaction subject to his right to disclaim onerous contracts. Where the transaction was to be financed by a mortgage the buyer's mortgage offer will have been revoked by the bankruptcy, and there will obviously be no other available funds to complete the purchase. The trustee is in this situation more likely to disclaim, although he would in so doing forfeit the deposit already paid and be subject to an action brought by the seller against the bankrupt's estate to recover loss suffered. Some delay is inevitable pending the appointment of the trustee and while waiting for his decision whether or not to disclaim. Where one of two or more co-purchasers goes bankrupt, the bankrupt's equitable interest will pass to his trustee.

6.8.2. The remaining buyer(s) may have difficulty in completing on the contractual completion date, or at all, since a joint mortgage offer may have been vitiated by the co-purchaser's bankruptcy. If the non-bankrupt buyer can refinance his purchase he may complete the purchase on his own (he is contractually bound to do so) but would hold the bankrupt's equitable interest in the property on trust for the trustee who might at a later stage wish to sell the property in order to realise this asset for the benefit of the bankrupt's creditors.

6.8.3.   A seller who wished to force completion on a buyer's trustee in bankruptcy must give written notice to the trustee requiring him within a period of 28 days (or such longer period specified by the court) in which to perform or disclaim the contract and the property. If the trustee does not disclaim within this period the right to disclaim is lost. The seller may at all times pursue the remedies open to a seller where a buyer defaults, including bringing an action for specific performance.

6.8.4.   If the seller completes the transaction with the buyer between the presentation of a petition but before the bankruptcy order is made, but having effected a priority search on which no bankruptcy entry appears, the trustee cannot reclaim the purchase price from the seller: this is probably the case even if he is able to prove that after the making of the priority search the seller became aware of the presentation of a bankruptcy petition.

6.9.   Appointment of liquidator

6.9.1.   Every disposition of a company's property after presentation of a winding-up petition to the court is void if a winding-up order is subsequently made unless sanctioned by the court. Accordingly where a petition for the compulsory winding up of a company is presented the buyer must insist on obtaining the sanction of the court to the completion of the transaction or he must await the result of the petition. In the case of a voluntary liquidation the directors' powers cease on the appointment of a liquidator whether the liquidation is a members' voluntary liquidation or a creditors' voluntary liquidation. A liquidator can complete a sale on behalf of the company and can bring proceedings to force a buyer to complete a transaction. In the case of a compulsory winding up the liquidator will require the sanction of the court to bring proceedings, but in the case of a voluntary winding up no such sanction is required. When a seller company goes into liquidation the liquidator will normally complete the transaction. The company will normally remain as 'seller' and the liquidator will attest the deed on the company's behalf. The liquidator will only become the 'seller' in the purchase deed if an order vesting the legal estate in him has been made by the court, which happens only very rarely. The formalities of a liquidator's appointment are dealt with by Insolvency Rules 4.100–4.105 and a buyer from a liquidator should ensure that those formalities have been complied with.

6.9.2.   Where a liquidator is appointed to a company which is buying land, the liquidator has the power to complete or to disclaim an onerous contract in which latter case the position is the same as already discussed under E6.7 in the case of an individual buyer becoming insolvent. Non-availability of funds may present practical problems in proceeding to completion. Where the buyer company is in liquidation and does not complete the seller may exercise his contractual rights, including the ability to forfeit any deposit, and in the converse situation the buyer has the right to recover his deposit from any stakeholder. If the matter does not proceed to completion then any damages will be a provable debt in the liquidation.

6.9.3. For the Land Registry's requirements see Land Registry Practice Guide 35.

6.10. Appointment of receivers and administrative receivers

6.10.1. The amendments made to Insolvency Act 1986 by Enterprise Act 2002 came into force on 15 September 2003. With regard to charges completed on or after 15 September 2003 the lender can usually only appoint an administrator.[1] Where a charge was completed before 15 September 2003 the lender can still appoint an administrative receiver. The appointment of an administrator or administrative receiver between exchange of contracts and completion does not affect the validity of the contract. The powers of the administrators or administrative receivers are those contained in the instrument under which he was appointed and in addition he will have the powers conferred upon him by Schedule 1 Insolvency Act 1986. Most of the powers of the directors will be suspended by virtue of his appointment. The administrator or administrative receiver may join in the purchase deed on sale to give a receipt for the purchase price and will execute the purchase deed on behalf of the company. The company normally remains the 'seller' under the contract or purchase deed since if the administrator or administrative receiver enters the transaction in his own name he will assume personal liability for it. The administrator or administrative receiver is the agent of the company (Insolvency Act 1986, s.14(4)). For this reason, any contract entered into in the name of the company will normally contain a clause excluding the receiver's personal liability and excluding the effect of any implied covenants for title from the purchase deed. Where the company is buying land, the administrator or administrative receiver will execute the purchase deed on behalf of the company, but in this situation the financing of the purchase may have to be re-arranged and this may result in some delay. In practice, the administrator or administrative receiver may be unable to complete because of the lack of available funds. Where completion does take place, a certified copy of the document appointing the administrator or administrative receiver should be handed over on completion.

6.10.2. Administrators are appointed by the court, where a company is likely to become unable to pay its debts. Following the administrator's appointment, he will take over the management of the company and will have authority to use the company seal and execute documents in the name of the company. The administrator has much the same powers as an administrative receiver (see Insolvency Act 1986).

6.10.3. Administrative receivers are appointed by, or on behalf of, holders of debentures or floating charges. Their powers are specified in Insolvency Act 1986,

Sched.1 and include the power to sell and to grant or accept the surrender of a lease. The administrative receiver's powers can be contractually extended in the debenture under which he is appointed (Insolvency Act 1986, s.42(1)). If a receiver uses a power of attorney to sell under a contractually extended power, his appointment should be by deed rather than under hand.[2] Conventionally administrative receivers are appointed under hand and the appointment is regarded as merely identifying the receiver upon whom the debenture confers the power of attorney.

6.10.4. Receivers may be appointed by debenture holders under Law of Property Act 1925, s.101(1)(iii). However, the powers of administrative receivers do not extend to receivers appointed under section 101(1)(iii). LPA receivers have very limited powers under the Law of Property Act 1925, s.109. Therefore, even if sales are arranged by receivers appointed under Law of Property Act 1925, it is better practice to arrange for the appointing lender to sign the contract once his power of sale has arisen and thereafter for the lender to execute the purchase deed or to transfer as lender.

6.10.5. An LPA receiver appointed by a debenture holder *in writing* has the power to bind a borrower to a conveyance of the legal estate in the property charged by the debenture.[3] The irrevocable authority for the appointment of the receiver as attorney for the company is contained in a debenture executed as a deed by the company, the common law rule requiring that a receiver should be appointed under seal was satisfied. In other words, provided that the company has executed the debenture under seal, the receiver can then validly be appointed by the debenture holder in writing alone.

6.10.6. If an LPA receiver sells with a power of attorney in place of a lender, he will not be able to sell the property free of incumbrances and a deed of release will also need to be executed by the lender and any other charge holders. In this instance, care should be taken to ensure the deed of release is executed by the lender after the execution of the transfer, as otherwise there is a risk that the receiver has no power to sell the property due to the determination of his power of sale and power of attorney under the debenture. However, if the lender sells as outlined above, the property will automatically be sold free of the mortgage and will remove subsequent charges from the title.

6.10.7. For the Land Registry's requirements see Land Registry Practice Guide 36.

1. See Insolvency Act 1986, s.72 for the limited circumstances in which an administrative receiver can still be appointed.
2. *Windsor Refrigerator Co. Ltd* v. *Branch Nominees Ltd* [1968] Ch 88.
3. *Phoenix Properties Ltd* v. *Wimpole Street Nominees Ltd* [1989] Ch 737.

6.11.   **Signature of documents**

Trustee in bankruptcy

6.11.1. A trustee in bankruptcy should sign a contract using the following wording: 'trustee in bankruptcy of XY a bankrupt [without personal liability]'.

6.11.2. The attestation clause of the purchase deed can be expressed in the following way: 'signed as a deed by CD in the presence of [*name*] (trustee of the estate of XY, a bankrupt)'.

6.11.3. Many insolvency practitioners seek to limit their liability by adding the words 'without personal liability' to the attestation clause. It is understood that these words imply that the trustee can still be sued *qua* trustee, but that liability in him in his personal capacity is excluded. These words do not preclude negligence liability for which most insolvency practitioners will carry indemnity insurance.

Supervisor of voluntary arrangement

6.11.4. The company, individual or mortgagee will execute the document in the normal way unless the scheme is such that the land has been vested in the supervisor or trustee. If this occurs the supervisor must transfer and execute as a trustee.

6.11.5. A contract signed or transfer executed by a supervisor may use the following wording: 'Supervisor of XY acting in the voluntary arrangement of XY [without personal liability]'.

6.11.6. The words 'without personal liability' have the same effect as is noted in E6.11.3.

Administrative receiver

6.11.7. In the absence of any provision to the contrary, Insolvency Act 1986, s.42 and Sched.1 give power to an administrative receiver to execute deeds and other documents in the name of and on behalf of the company using the company's seal.

Company in administration

6.11.8. A deed can be executed using the common seal of the company in the presence of the administrator, or by the administrator signing in the name of and on behalf of the company (Insolvency Act 1986, Sched.1(8) and (9)).

Law of Property Act receiver

6.11.9. A Law of Property Act receiver can sign a contract or execute a transfer provided that the appointing lender delegates this power. The authority from the lender should be in writing but under section 1 Law of Property (Miscellaneous Provisions) Act 1989 does not need to be under seal. A receiver signs a contract as agent for the borrower. It is normal practice in these circumstances for the appointing lender to sign the contract and execute the transfer using his power of sale. The capacity in which the lender sells will affect the nature of the implied covenants for title given to the buyer in the purchase deed.

Debenture holder

6.11.10. A debenture holder can sign in the name of the company provided he holds a valid power of attorney from the company. The attestation clause should read as follows:

'Signed as a deed by [*name of company*] acting by [*name of attorney*] duly appointed to execute as an officer of [*name of bank*] pursuant to clause [of a debenture dated …] in the presence of:	Sign here the name of the company and your own name with details of the resolution appointing you [*example:* John Smith Ltd by its attorney Jane Brown duly appointed officer of … Bank by a resolution of … Bank plc dated …]'

Company in liquidation

6.11.11. A disposition made by a company in liquidation will be executed by the liquidator, who may either use the common seal, in which case he will sign the document to attest that the seal was affixed in his presence, or the liquidator may sign the deed on behalf of the company.

Signature of contracts

6.11.12. To avoid incurring personal liability, any contracts for the disposal of land should be signed by including the extra words 'without personal liability' in order to ensure that a signatory signs as agent and not principal. The following is a suggested example of how agreements should be signed:

'Signed as agent for ABC Ltd without personal liability	Signature of supervisor/ administrator/ administrative receiver/ liquidator/trustee'

6.11.13. After winding up, or after the presentation of a winding-up petition, a better wording may be:

'Signed in the name of ABC Ltd by its [administrator/administrative receiver] JOHN SMITH ESQ. Without personal liability	Signature: ABC Ltd [in liquidation]'

6.11.14. See Land Registry Practice Guides 8, 35 and 36 as to the Land Registry's requirements for the execution of deeds submitted for registration.

E7. Foreign companies

7.1. What is the status of the foreign company?

7.1.1. If it is recognised as a corporation under its foreign law it will be treated as such by English law.

7.1.2. If the status of the company is not clear from its documents, further evidence of status will be needed. This will consist either of an unequivocal certificate by the company's solicitors that it is a corporation validly incorporated under the law of its country of origin or a letter from a lawyer practising in the foreign country confirming that the applicant is a corporation under that law. Confirmation should also be obtained of the corporation's power to enter the particular transaction and of the authenticity of a named person or persons to sign the contract/purchase deed on the corporation's behalf.

7.1.3. The information in E7.1.2 does not apply to companies incorporated in Scotland. Companies registered in the Channel Isles or Isle of Man, however, are foreign companies.

7.1.4. Solicitors acting for the foreign company should ensure that any local consent needed for the transaction is obtained. The documents relating to the transaction should also make it clear which jurisdiction is applicable to the transaction.

7.2. Registration of foreign companies

7.2.1. An application by a foreign company to be registered as proprietor of a registered estate or charge must be accompanied by evidence of the extent of its powers to hold and deal with land. The evidence must include the charter, memorandum and articles of association or other document constituting the company or a certificate in Form 7.[1] If an original document is not in English or Welsh a certified translation should accompany the application.

1. Land Registration Rules 2003, r.183.

7.3. What are the powers of the company?

7.3.1. This question is not usually relevant in the case of companies incorporated in the European Union nor where there is evidence that the law of the country of origin contains provisions equivalent to the powers conferred by the Companies Acts on trading companies. In other cases, where the land is registered, any limitation on the power of the company will be reflected on the register of title by an appropriate restriction. The constitution of the company should be perused to see what its powers are and, if not clear, evidence of the powers must be requested.

7.4. Execution of documents

7.4.1.   From 1 October 2009, the execution of documents by foreign companies must comply with Overseas Companies (Execution of Documents and Registration of Charges) Regulations 2009 (SI 2009/1917). These regulations amend sections 43–48 Companies Act 2006 and state that a foreign company validly executes a document:

- by the affixing of its common seal; or

- by the signature of a person acting under the authority of the company in accordance with the laws of the territory of incorporation; or

- (since many foreign companies do not have a common seal) by any manner permitted by the laws of its territory of incorporation.

In the last case, it will therefore be necessary to provide proof that the execution of the document complies with foreign law.

7.4.2.   Schedule 9 Land Registration Rules 2003 contains a form of execution to deal with execution by overseas companies without using a common seal. The prescribed form of execution in Form E is as follows:

'Signed as a deed on behalf of [*name of company*] a company incorporated in [*territory*], by [*full name(s) of person(s) signing*], being [a] person[s] who, in accordance with the laws of that territory, [is] [are] acting under the authority of the company.	Signature Authorised signatory [*or signatories*]'

7.4.3.   In the case of an overseas company having a common seal, the form of execution appropriate to a company registered under the Companies Acts may be used, with such adaptations as may be necessary, in place of execution by a person or persons acting under the authority of the company. See also Land Registry Practice Guide 8.

7.5. Dispositions by foreign companies

7.5.1.   When a foreign company is disposing of property which it owns the following question is relevant: does the company have power to make the disposition?

This will only be of concern where a restriction is already on the register. Provided the terms of the restriction can be complied with the transaction can proceed.

7.5.2. When applying to the Land Registry to register a charge created by an overseas company, the applicant must either supply evidence that the charge has been registered by the Registrar of Companies under Overseas Companies (Execution of Documents and Registration of Charges) Regulations 2009 or state that the charge, when created, was not required to be so registered. In the absence of such evidence or statement the Land Registry will enter a note in the register that no evidence has been lodged that the charge has been registered under the Regulations or that such registration was not required.[1]

1. Land Registration Rules 2003, r.111A.

F. COMPLETION

F1. Date and time of completion

1.1.	**Date**	1.2.	**Time**

1.1. Date

1.1.1. The date of completion will be agreed between the solicitors for the parties (after consultation with their respective clients) shortly before exchange of contracts.

1.1.2. Where the buyer's purchase is dependent on his sale of another property the completion dates in both contracts must be synchronised. It follows that the completion dates in all transactions in a chain of transactions must also be synchronised if the chain is not to break.

1.1.3. In residential transactions a completion date 28 days or less from the date of exchange is common. Sufficient time must be allowed between exchange and completion for the respective solicitors to undertake the pre-completion steps in the transaction. If it is anticipated that the clients will wish to complete very quickly after exchange, arrangements can usually be made for some of the pre-completion steps in the transaction to be effected before exchange, e.g. preparation of the purchase deed.

1.1.4. In the absence of express agreement Standard Condition 6.1.1 and Standard Commercial Property Condition 8.1.1 provide that completion shall take place on the 20th working day after exchange.

1.1.5. Under Standard Condition 6.1.1 and Standard Commercial Property Condition 8.6.1 time is not of the essence of the completion date (unless a notice to complete has been served). Thus although a delay in completion beyond the date fixed in the contract would give rise to an action in damages at the instigation of the innocent party and would activate the compensation provisions of Standard Condition 7.3 and Standard Commercial Property Condition 9.3, the delay would not of itself entitle the innocent party to withdraw from the contract at that stage (see section M). In the absence of this provision time would be of the essence of the completion date (thus enabling the innocent party to withdraw from the contract if delay occurs) where the common law so provides, e.g. in the case of the sale of a business as a going concern. Since delay in completion can occur for reasons beyond the control of the contracting parties, e.g. due to postal delays, it is not generally a good idea to make time of the essence of the completion date. If exceptionally it is desired to make time of the essence, this may be done by inserting an express provision to this effect in the contract, e.g. by adding the words 'as to which time shall be of the essence' alongside the insertion of the contractual completion date.

1.2. Time

1.2.1. Where a buyer's purchase is dependent on the receipt of money from a related sale, the solicitor must ensure that arrangements are made to complete the sale before the purchase to allow funds received from the sale to be utilised in the purchase.

1.2.2. Where the transaction is part of a chain such arrangements may be complex. Most contracts do not require completion to take place by a certain time, but merely provide that, where the completion money arrives at the nominated bank after a specified time (e.g. 2 pm), it is deemed to have arrived on the next working day for certain purposes (e.g. so as to entitle the seller to compensation). Special conditions may however require completion to take place at a specified time. In practice, particularly if the chain is long, funds will be transferred from the first (time) buyer as early as 9 am and the funds will travel by a series of inter-bank telegraphic transfers until the deadline of 2 pm or even later. Security is maintained in two ways. First, each solicitor will not transmit purchase funds until after the sale proceeds reach his bank. Second, the keys to the property being sold will not be released to the buyer or his agent until the seller's solicitor has received the purchase funds.

1.2.3. Even where a seller has no related purchase, he should ensure that the completion time agreed allows sufficient time for the proceeds of sale to be banked on the day of completion. If the money is not banked or remitted to the lender until the following working day the seller will suffer loss of interest on his money. To this end a completion time later than 2 pm is inadvisable.

1.2.4. Provided each set of funds reaches its destination before bank closing on the day of completion, the strict timetable of 2 pm is unlikely to be enforced. Nevertheless, Standard Condition 6.1.2 and Standard Commercial Property Condition 8.1.2 provide that if completion does not take place by 2 pm on the day of completion, compensation for late completion becomes payable. It is therefore important for the solicitor to ensure that there is as little delay as possible between receipt of the sale proceeds and release of the purchase money so that his client does not become liable to pay compensation at the contractual interest rate for the delay which he cannot, in turn, recover from his buyer. Standard Condition 6.1.2 and Standard Commercial Property Condition 8.1.2 do not apply where the sale is with vacant possession and the seller has not vacated the property by 2 pm on the date of actual completion.[1]

1. Standard Condition 6.1.3 and Standard Commercial Property Condition 8.1.3.

F2. Place of completion

2.1.   **Place of completion**

2.1.1.   By Standard Condition 6.2.2 and Standard Commercial Property Condition 8.2 completion is to take place in England and Wales, either at the seller's solicitor's office or at some other place which the seller reasonably specifies.

2.1.2.   These conditions mirror the convention that the money goes to the deeds.

2.1.3.   Where the seller has an undischarged mortgage over the property and the seller's solicitor is not also acting for the lender, completion may be required to take place at the offices of the seller's lender's solicitors.

2.1.4.   Where there is a complex chain of transactions it may sometimes be convenient for some or all of the solicitors for the parties involved in the chain to meet at a mutually convenient location in order to complete several of the transactions in the chain within a very short interval.

2.1.5.   Under Standard Condition 6.2.2 and Standard Commercial Property Condition 8.2 the choice of venue for completion is given to the seller. If completion is not to take place at the seller's solicitor's office he should give the buyer's solicitor sufficient notice of the chosen venue to allow the buyer's solicitor to make his arrangements for attendance at completion and/or transmission of funds. If possible, the buyer's solicitor should be informed of the venue for completion in the answers given to his requisitions on title.

2.1.6.   Although traditionally the buyer's solicitor attends the seller's solicitor's office in person to effect completion, it is usual (especially in residential transactions) for completion to be effected by using the Law Society's Code for Completion by Post (see Appendix IV.12) with the transmission of funds being made directly to the seller's solicitor's bank account. In such cases the actual place of completion is of little significance to the transaction so long as both parties' solicitors are able to contact each other by telephone, fax or email to confirm the transmission and receipt of funds on the day of completion itself.

2.1.7.   If the sale is with vacant possession and the buyer is in doubt whether or not the seller will comply with this condition (e.g. because of the presence of tenants or other non-owning occupiers in the property) he may consider the benefits of insisting on completion taking place at the property itself following an inspection of the property. The buyer may also wish to complete at the property if he, for other reasons, needs to inspect the property or its contents before completion, e.g. to check an inventory of stock or fittings. In such cases the buyer should have included a special condition in the contract stating that completion shall take place at the property, or, if this was not possible, make his request to the seller's solicitor in adequate time before completion to permit the necessary arrangements to be made. Unless such a term is included as a contractual condition, the seller is under no obligation to accede to the buyer's request since the choice of location for completion is, by Standard Condition 6.2.2 and Standard Commercial Property Condition 8.2, given to the seller.

F3. The money

3.1.   Method of payment

3.1.1.   Standard Condition 6.7 and Standard Commercial Property Condition 8.7 provide that the buyer is to pay the money due on completion by direct credit and, if appropriate, by an unconditional release of a deposit held by a stakeholder. Payment by any other method than direct credit requires express amendment to the Conditions.

3.1.2.   Direct credit is a direct transfer (frequently referred to in practice as a telegraphic transfer (TT)) of cleared funds to an account nominated by the seller's solicitor and maintained at a clearing bank. A clearing bank is a bank which is a shareholder in CHAPS Clearing Co. Ltd.

3.1.3.   In the absence of agreement to the contrary, the seller's solicitor is entitled to refuse payment tendered by any method other than those mentioned in the contract. A special condition in the contract is required if payment is to be made in foreign currency or out of the jurisdiction.

3.1.4.   Notes and gold coins are legal tender up to any amount,[1] but other coins are subject to the limits imposed in Coinage Act 1971, s.2. Currently these limits restrict payment by cupro-nickel or silver coins with a value exceeding 10p (including £1 coins) to a maximum face value of £10. Payment by cupro-nickel or silver coins with a face value not exceeding 10p are limited to a maximum of £5, and bronze coins to a maximum of £0.20. Due to the increased liability under Money Laundering Regulations 2003 and Proceeds of Crime Act 2002, solicitors should be wary of accepting cash unless the legitimate source of the funds has been verified.

3.1.5.   Provided the parties agree, payment of money on completion may be made by a solicitor's clients' account cheque or building society cheque, but in practice payment by such methods is uncommon since there is the danger that the cheque could in theory be stopped. A 'stop' on a building society cheque would in practice be very rare and is generally confined to cases of theft, forgery, or fraud.

1. Currency and Bank Notes Act 1954, s.1.

3.2. Banker's draft

3.2.1. Where completion is to take place in person payment by banker's draft is the most common method of payment.

3.2.2. The buyer's solicitor may have the draft drawn in favour of the seller's solicitor (or as he has directed) or may prefer to have the draft drawn to show the buyer's solicitor as payee. In the latter case, the draft will be endorsed in favour of the seller's solicitor at actual completion, but can easily be paid back into the buyer's solicitor's clients' account should completion for some reason not take place on the due date. The draft should not be marked 'account payee only' or 'not negotiable' since the seller's solicitor may wish to endorse the draft to a third party, e.g. to use towards payment in another transaction.

3.2.3. A banker's draft can be regarded as being analogous to cash. It is therefore sensible to take precautions against forgery and theft of a draft. For this reason it may be considered to be unwise to send a banker's draft through the post and, where completion is to take place through the post or through the attendance of an agent, some other method of transmission of funds should be used.

3.3. Direct credit transfer of funds

3.3.1. Frequently completion will take place using the Law Society's Code for Completion by Post (see Appendix IV.12). In such a case the parties will normally agree to transfer the amount of money needed to complete the transaction through the telegraphic transfer (or similar) system. Payment under a contract governed by the Standard Conditions of Sale or the Standard Commercial Property Conditions must be by way of direct credit (unless the contract has been amended to provide otherwise).

3.3.2. The seller's solicitor should inform the buyer's solicitor of the amount needed to complete the transaction and of the details of the account to which the funds are to be remitted. This information is normally given in response to the buyer's requisitions on title.

3.3.3. The buyer's solicitor should instruct his bank to remit funds from the buyer's solicitor's clients' account to the account nominated by the seller's solicitor. Instructions to the bank must be given sufficiently early on the day of completion to ensure that the funds arrive at their destination before the time limit for receipt of funds, as specified in the contract, expires. Some delay in the transmission of funds may be experienced where the funds are to be transmitted from one bank to another as opposed to transfers between different branches of the same bank.

3.3.4. The seller's bank should be asked to telephone the seller's solicitor to inform him of the receipt of the funds immediately they arrive. Completion may proceed as soon as the seller's solicitor is satisfied as to the arrival of the funds in his clients' account, and it is courteous for him to confirm the safe arrival of the funds to the buyer's solicitor.

3.4. Cleared funds

3.4.1. In order to avoid breach of Rule 22 Solicitors' Accounts Rules 1998, payment of completion money should only be made from cleared funds in client account. This means that the buyer's solicitor must ensure that he is put in funds by his client in sufficient time for those funds to clear through client account before it becomes necessary to draw against them.

3.5. Time for payment

3.5.1. Standard Condition 6.1.2 and Standard Commercial Property Condition 8.1.2 encourage the payment of money on the day of completion by 2 pm in default of which payment is treated (for compensation purposes only) as having been received on the next following working day which may result in the buyer becoming liable to pay compensation for late completion under Condition 7.3 of both sets of conditions. Standard Condition 6.1.2 and Standard Commercial Property Condition 8.1.2 do not apply where the sale is with vacant possession and the seller has not vacated the property by 2 pm on the date of actual completion. See Standard Condition 6.1.3 and Standard Commercial Property Condition 8.1.3.

3.5.2. Where the transaction forms part of a chain of transactions it may be necessary to insert a time limit for the payment of completion money imposing a contractual obligation to complete by this specified time (see F1.2.2). If this is not done, there is a danger that the seller will not receive the funds from his sale in sufficient time to allow him to meet the time limit in his related purchase transaction.

3.6. Chain transactions

3.6.1. As noted in F3.5.2, it will frequently be necessary to insert a special condition relating to the time of completion in order to allow sufficient time for funds to be received by the seller's solicitor and then utilised to complete a purchase transaction later on the same day.

3.6.2. Where it is known that the transaction forms part of a chain arrangements may be made by the solicitors involved for the funds to be sent directly to their ultimate destination. Thus if A is selling to B and buying from C, he may need to use part of the proceeds of sale (to be paid by B) towards payment for his purchase from C. In this case A's solicitor may ask B's solicitor to send a specified part of the sale money direct to C's solicitor, the remainder being sent to A's solicitor in the normal way. C's solicitor must be asked to telephone A's solicitor when he receives the funds from B's solicitor so that the transaction between A and B can be completed. C's solicitor will also be asked to undertake to hold the funds received from B's solicitor to A's order until completion of the transaction between A and C is ready to proceed. Such an arrangement can help to avoid delays in the transmission of funds, since fewer telegraphic transfers are required (particularly in a long chain), and thus it ultimately helps to ensure that all transactions within the chain are completed within their relevant time limits. The solicitors involved must nevertheless be careful to obtain the written authority of the parties since the protection given by Law of Property Act 1925, s.63, only applies where the money is paid to the seller's solicitor. It is a breach of trust for the buyer's solicitor to part with the money without having the title deeds in his possession or without knowing that the seller's solicitor is holding the deeds to the buyer's solicitor's order.

3.7.   Discharge of seller's mortgage

3.7.1.   The seller's existing mortgage over the property being sold will frequently be discharged immediately after completion of the sale using part of the proceeds of sale to make payment to the lender.

3.7.2.   The seller's solicitor may choose to ask the buyer to draw separate banker's drafts for completion, one in favour of the lender for the amount needed to discharge the mortgage and the other, for the balance of the money due, in the seller's solicitor's favour.

3.7.3.   Alternatively, where payment is to be made by direct credit transfer, the seller's solicitor may request that a direct transfer is made to the separately represented lender's solicitor, and a second transfer, for the balance of funds due, to the seller's solicitor. The method for achieving this is broadly similar to the method described in F3.6.2.

3.7.4   If the seller had a 'flexible mortgage' on his property the solicitor should have requested that the account be frozen from the time when the mortgage redemption statement was prepared until completion. This is due to the fact that the amount outstanding on such mortgages can vary depending upon the amount of the seller's savings and income in the account. To ensure that the redemption figure is accurate at completion the account must be frozen at the date of the redemption statement.

3.8.   Undertakings to remit funds

3.8.1.   In exceptional circumstances the seller's solicitor may be prepared to complete the transaction against the buyer's solicitor's undertaking to remit funds within a specified time, the actual transfer of the money occurring after completion has taken place. The seller's solicitor should only do this if he has his client's authority to do so, and the client understands the consequences of completing against an undertaking. The seller may have an equitable lien over the property for money not paid which should be protected against a subsequent buyer (see M8.1).

3.8.2. Such an undertaking given by the buyer's solicitor is binding on him and should therefore not be given unless the buyer's solicitor is absolutely certain that he will be put in funds in sufficient time to comply with his promise to the seller's solicitor.

3.8.3. If completion does take place on the strength of the buyer's solicitor's undertaking, the seller is bound to complete and may not retain possession of the title deeds and other documents even if the money does not arrive when promised. By Standard Condition 6.5.1 and Standard Commercial Property Condition 8.5.1, the seller is not entitled to a lien over the title deeds after completion.

3.9. Release of deposit

3.9.1. A deposit which is held in the capacity of agent for the seller belongs to the seller and does not need to be released on completion.

3.9.2. Where a deposit is held by some person in the capacity of stakeholder, the buyer's solicitor should on completion provide the seller's solicitor with a written release addressed to the stakeholder, authorising payment of the deposit to the seller or as he directs. Where the deposit is being held by the seller's solicitor as stakeholder, a written release is often neither asked for nor provided, the release being given orally once completion has taken place. If the deposit is being held by a third party, e.g. an estate agent in the capacity of stakeholder, a written release will be required. In the absence of a written release the stakeholder, on being satisfied that the conditions under which he holds the money have been fulfilled, may pay the stake money to the party whom he considers entitled to receive it, subject to his becoming liable to account to the other party if he makes the wrong judgment in relation to the handing over of the money.[1]

1. *Hastingwood Property Ltd* v. *Saunders Bearman Anselm* [1991] Ch 114.

3.10. Retentions from the purchase price

3.10.1. Where it has been agreed that a retention should be deducted from the purchase price on completion, e.g. to cover the cost of outstanding works to be done by the seller, the agreement should be expressly clear as to whether interest is payable on the retained sum and to whom, and whether the buyer is to withhold the sum on completion or, e.g. to pay the full purchase price to the seller's solicitor with the amount of the agreed retention being held by the seller's solicitor in a deposit account opened in the joint names of the seller and buyer until the matter is resolved. It is also desirable to agree that if the obligation secured by the retention money has not been performed by a particular date, the retention money would be remitted back to the buyer to deal with the matter instead, and if it costs more than the retention money to do so, the buyer can claim the deficit from the seller.

3.11.   Money laundering

3.11.1.   Where a transaction is being funded by the client in cash, or via a third party (other than a recognised lender) or from a foreign bank, the solicitor should be alert to the possibilities of money laundering and should take appropriate steps to check the identity of the client and the source of the funds (see A23).

3.12.   Banking crisis

3.12.1.   In the event of a bank's collapse, client funds held in that bank may be lost. The Financial Services Compensation Scheme will only cover deposits of up to £50,000 per client. Moreover, a solicitor must honour any express undertaking to pay money, even if the bank in which the client's money is held has collapsed.

3.12.2.   The Law Society's Banking Crisis Practice Note (updated 8 January 2009) gives interim advice to solicitors on how to mitigate any risk of liability for client funds in the event of a bank's collapse. The Practice Note includes advice on updating terms of business to limit liability, complying with the Solicitors' Accounts Rules 1998, dividing money among separate client accounts, distributing a client's money in different banks, moving funds to foreign banks and information to be given to the client.

F4. Completion

4.1.   Introduction

4.1.1.   The date and time of actual completion will be specified in the contract but may be varied by subsequent agreement between the parties. Similarly the place and method of completion will previously have been agreed by the parties.

4.1.2.   Completion may take place by personal attendance by the buyer's solicitor or his agent or through the post using the Law Society's Code for Completion by Post (see Appendix IV.12).

4.1.3.   The Law Society's Execution of Documents by Virtual Means Practice Note (16 February 2010) advises solicitors who deal with the execution of documents at virtual signings or closings where some or all of the signatories involved are not physically present at the same meeting using pre-signed signature pages and the exchange of signature pages by e-mail. The practice note identifies one option (and a method) for the execution of deeds and real estate contracts by virtual means but states that a virtual signing or closing is very unlikely to be suitable for property documents that require registration.

4.2.   Completion by personal attendance

4.2.1.   Personal attendance by the buyer's solicitor on the seller's solicitor or seller's lender's solicitor is the traditional method by which completion takes place but is not commonly used in uncomplicated transactions where, particularly in residential conveyancing, it is now more common for completion to take place through the post.

4.2.2.   If the transaction is complex or of a high value, consideration should be given to the benefits of completing the matter in person since, when this method is employed, the buyer's solicitor is able physically to inspect all the relevant documents prior to handing over the purchase price; he takes possession of those documents immediately completion has taken place instead of having to rely on the seller's solicitor's undertaking to forward the documents to him, and there is therefore absolute certainty that all the documents are in order and that completion has taken place at a specific time. Against these benefits may be set the time and expense involved in the buyer's solicitor having to travel to the seller's solicitor's office in order to attend personally at completion.

4.2.3. A few days before the date arranged for completion the buyer's solicitor should telephone the seller's solicitor to arrange a mutually convenient appointment for completion.

4.2.4. On the morning of completion or on the day before completion, arrangements should be made for completion money to be sent by direct transfer to the seller's solicitor's bank account (or as agreed under the contract). Alternatively, a banker's draft for the amount required to complete the transaction should be drawn by the buyer's solicitor and kept in a safe place until it is needed (see F3).

4.2.5. The representative from the buyer's solicitors who is to attend completion should take with him to the seller's solicitor's office the following items:

(a) the contract (queries which arise may sometimes be resolved by checking the terms of the contract);

(b) evidence of title (in order to verify the title);

(c) a copy of the approved draft purchase deed and of any other documents which are to be executed by the seller and handed over on completion (in case there is any query over the engrossments);

(d) answers to requisitions on title (some queries which arise, e.g. over who has the keys, may be resolved by the answers previously given to requisitions);

(e) the completion checklist and completion statement (see E4);

(f) banker's draft (if this method of payment is to be used);

(g) any documents which are required to be handed over to the seller's solicitor on completion, e.g. release of deposit.

Verifying title

4.2.6. The buyer's time limit for verifying title, i.e. comparing the original deeds against the evidence of title supplied by the seller, expires with the time limit for raising requisitions. Under Standard Condition 4.3.1 and Standard Commercial Property Condition 6.3.1 the buyer must raise his requisitions within six working days after the date of the contract or delivery of evidence of title by the seller, whichever is later. In practice, where title is deduced before exchange of contracts, the right to raise requisitions on certain matters after exchange will be precluded by Standard Condition 4.2.1 and Standard Commercial Property Condition 6.2.1.

4.2.7. Strictly therefore the buyer has no right to verify at this stage. In practice verification is not normally carried out at the requisitions on title stage of the transaction unless the transaction is complicated and the buyer's solicitor will check the evidence of title against the original deeds at completion itself. It should, however, be remembered that since the time limit for verification has now expired, the buyer will have no right to query any defect which he discovers on verification, nor to refuse to complete because of a defect discovered at this stage.

4.2.8.   In the case of registered land verification is unnecessary since official copy entries of the title will show the current position of the register.

4.2.9.   On a sale by a lender under his power of sale, it is not necessary to obtain discharges relating to subsequent mortgages which will be overreached on the completion of the sale by the selling lender.

4.2.10.   When the buyer's solicitor is satisfied as to the title, he should ask the seller's solicitor to hand over the documents necessary to complete the transaction. These documents including the title deeds (in unregistered land) will have been previously agreed in a list drawn up between the parties and itemised on the completion checklist. Except where these documents have recently been checked by verification, the buyer's solicitor should check each document to ensure it is as he expects to find it, and tick each off on his list as he receives it. The purchase deed will be among the documents to be received by the buyer's solicitor and should be dated at completion after being checked by the buyer's solicitor to ensure it has been validly executed and has not been altered since the buyer last saw the document. The seller's solicitor will have prepared a schedule of deeds in duplicate, one copy of which will be handed to the buyer's solicitor to keep; the other should be signed by the buyer's solicitor when he is satisfied that he has received all the documents listed on it, and returned to the seller's solicitor as evidence for his file of the handing over of the deeds.

4.2.11.   Depending on the circumstances it may be necessary for the buyer's solicitor to inspect receipts for, e.g. last payment of outgoings where such items have been apportioned on the completion statement. Copies of these receipts should have been supplied to the buyer's solicitor with the completion statement in order to allow him to check the amount of the apportionments. By Standard Condition 6.6 and Standard Commercial Property Condition 8.6 the buyer is required to assume that whoever gave any receipt for the payment of rent, rentcharge or a service charge which the seller produces was the person or agent of the person then entitled to that rent or service charge. In the absence of this condition from the contract Law of Property Act 1925, s.45(2) requires the buyer to make the same assumptions in respect of rent and rentcharges.

4.2.12.   Where the sale includes fittings or chattels, a separate receipt for the money paid for those items should be signed by the seller's solicitor and handed to the buyer's solicitor. A copy of the receipt should be retained by the seller's solicitor. The receipt clause in the purchase deed only operates as a receipt for the money paid for the land; therefore a separate receipt for the money paid for chattels is necessary.

Discharge of seller's mortgage

4.2.13.   Arrangements for the discharge of the seller's mortgage(s) over the property will have been agreed between the parties at the requisitions on title stage of the transaction. Where the mortgage is a first mortgage of the property in favour of a building society lender, the parties will frequently have agreed to permit the seller to discharge his mortgage after completion takes place by using part of the proceeds of sale to make payment to the lender. In such a case it will have been agreed that the seller's lender's solicitor should hand to the buyer's solicitor on completion an undertaking in the form of wording recommended by the Law Society to discharge the mortgage (F4.2.16) and to forward the receipted deed or Form DS1 to the buyer's solicitor as soon as this is received from the lender. Alternatively an undertaking may be given to discharge the charge by using the Land Registry ED or e-DS1 systems (see G1.10 and G1.11).

4.2.14.   An undertaking to discharge the seller's mortgage should only be accepted from a solicitor or licensed conveyancer because of the difficulties of enforcement of undertakings against unqualified persons.[1] It will not normally be advisable to accept an undertaking if the lender is not a member of the CML, and/or where the amount required to redeem the mortgage exceeds the minimum level of solicitors indemnity insurance (£2 million per claim, £3 million for recognised bodies). In such a case an undertaking should not be accepted and it may be necessary for completion to take place at the lender's solicitors' offices (not the seller's solicitors' offices) or for the lender's solicitor to attend personally at completion in order to discharge the mortgage. If the amount of the mortgage exceeds £2 million consider asking for a warranty from the seller's solicitor that his insurance cover does exceed the amount required to redeem the mortgage. See Appendix IV.6 for practice information regarding accepting undertakings following the Court of Appeal decision in *Patel* v. *Daybells*.[2]

4.2.15.   The Land Registry early completion policy applies to all applications to discharge the whole of a registered charge where other applications are made but no evidence of satisfaction of the charge is supplied. Unless there is a restriction on the register preventing a disposal or the registration of a new charge without the consent of the existing lender, the Land Registry will reject the discharge application but complete the other applications. Accordingly, a buyer purchasing with a new mortgage will be registered as the proprietor, but the seller's mortgage will remain on the title and until evidence of discharge is provided, the buyer's mortgage will rank in priority behind the seller's mortgage on the register. Where there is a restriction on the register preventing a disposal or the registration of a new charge without the consent of the existing lender, proof of satisfaction of the charge or evidence of compliance with the restriction must be provided to the Land Registry within 20 working days (which can be extended to 40 working days on application). If this is not done, the Land Registry will cancel the buyer's applications for discharge, transfer and charge. Further details of the early completion policy are set out in Land Registry Practice Bulletin 16: Early Completion. The Law Society has published a Practice Note: 'Land Registry early completion' (9 July 2009) on how to proceed with completion in the light of the early completion policy. This contains advice to sellers' solicitors and buyers' solicitors on additional undertakings and assurances relating to early completion.

4.2.16. The buyer's solicitor must ensure that any undertaking given mentions every subsisting mortgage on the title. The form of wording recommended by the Law Society for undertakings to discharge building society mortgages is given at Appendix IV.10.

4.2.17. When the buyer's solicitor is satisfied as to the documents received from the seller's solicitor and the documents which he has inspected, he should hand to the seller's solicitor any documents which the seller's solicitor requires in accordance with the list agreed prior to completion, e.g. release of deposit, and a banker's draft for the amount specified on the completion statement or otherwise notified to the buyer's solicitor by the seller's solicitor.

4.2.18. Where the banker's draft has been made out in the name of the buyer's solicitor it will have to be endorsed over to the seller's solicitor or as he directs. An endorsement may be general or special. To effect a general endorsement the buyer's solicitor simply signs the reverse of the draft using the payee's name as shown on the front of the draft. To effect a special endorsement the buyer's solicitor writes on the reverse of the draft 'pay to the order of [*name of seller's solicitor or as he directs*]' and then signs the endorsement. In either case the buyer's solicitor must ensure that his signature is in an identical form of wording to that used on the front of the draft where the payee is named. In default of this the endorsement may not be accepted by the bank when the draft is presented for payment.

Release of deposit

4.2.19. An unconditional written release of deposit should be supplied in any situation where the deposit under the contract has been held in the capacity of stakeholder. In practice, where the deposit has been held by the seller's solicitor in that capacity, an oral release will suffice. A written release is only therefore necessary where the deposit has been held by a third party, e.g. an estate agent as stakeholder.

Endorsement of memoranda

4.2.20. Where in unregistered land a document affecting the title is not to be handed over on completion, the buyer may want the seller to endorse a memorandum of the transaction on the deed(s) retained by the seller. The endorsement of such a memorandum protects the buyer against a subsequent mistaken or fraudulent reconveyance of the same property. This is most likely to be needed on the sale of part of unregistered land where the buyer is entitled to insist on the endorsement of the memorandum on the most recent in date of the seller's retained title deeds under Law of Property Act 1925, s.200 (where the seller enters into new restrictive covenants), or where the purchase is from personal representatives of a deceased seller where Administration of Estates Act 1925, s.36(4) gives the buyer the right to insist on the endorsement of a memorandum on the grant of representation.

4.2.21. The form of wording to be used for the endorsement should be drafted by the buyer's solicitor and agreed with the seller's solicitor at the requisitions on title stage of the transaction. A copy of the endorsement should be given to the buyer's solicitor for retention by him as evidence that this has been done. In registered conveyancing this procedure is not necessary.

4.2.22. If in unregistered land the seller is entering into new restrictive covenants he should either retain a copy of the conveyance which imposes those covenants or a copy of the covenants themselves. The covenants will be contained in the purchase deed which will be handed to the buyer on completion and unless a copy is retained by the seller, he will have no documentary evidence of the covenants to produce to a buyer on a subsequent sale of the retained land. An alternative is for the conveyance or transfer to be prepared and executed in duplicate, the seller's solicitor retaining the duplicate on completion.

4.2.23. In some cases the buyer will only be entitled to have copies of documents relating to the seller's title and not the originals. Chiefly this will occur on a sale of part of unregistered land where the seller is entitled to retain the title deeds which relate to the land retained by him. Other examples would include purchases from personal representatives where they are entitled to retain the original grant and purchases from attorneys who hold a general or enduring power. Where a power is a special power, relating only to the sale of this property, the buyer is entitled to the original power.

4.2.24. In any case where an original document relevant to the title is not being handed over, the buyer's solicitor should call for the original document and examine his copy against the original. The copy should then be marked to show that it has been examined against the original and is a true copy of the original document.

4.2.25. On a sale of part of unregistered land all the documents contained in the abstract or epitome of title will have to be so marked and each examined document should bear the wording:

> 'examined against the original at the offices of [*insert name of seller's solicitors or as appropriate*] signed [*by buyer's solicitor's representative either in his own name or in the name of the firm*] and dated [*insert date of examination*]'.

4.2.26. Where a certified copy of a document will be required by the Land Registry the certification should be carried out by a conveyancer (or such other person as the registrar may permit) by writing on the document clearly and in a conspicuous position the words:

> 'I certify this to be a true copy of the [*insert type of document*] dated [*insert date of document being certified*] signed [*signature of conveyancer*] and dated [*insert date of certification*]'.

The name and address of the signatory should also be endorsed.[3] This will assist in the event of the certification later having to be checked in a subsequent transaction. It should be noted that under Powers of Attorney Act 1971, s.3(1)(*b*)(ii), a copy of a power of attorney must be certified on every page.

1. See *Patel* v. *Daybells* [2001] EWCA Civ 1229 and Appendix IV.6.
2. *Ibid.*
3. See Land Registration Rules 2003, r.217(1) (as amended) as to the definitions of 'certified copy' and 'conveyancer'.

4.3. Completion through the post

4.3.1. In many cases, particularly with simple residential transactions, the buyer's solicitor will not wish to attend completion personally. In such a case arrangements may be made with the seller's solicitor to complete the transaction through the post.

4.3.2. Arrangements to complete through the post should be made at the latest at the requisitions on title stage of the transaction, although it is courteous for the buyer's solicitor to ask the seller's solicitor whether this method of completion will be convenient at an earlier stage so that the seller can if necessary obtain the consent of his lender's solicitor to this procedure.

4.3.3. The Law Society's Code for Completion by Post should be used (see Appendix IV.12). The buyer's solicitor should agree any variations to the Code in writing with the seller's solicitor well before completion is due to take place. He should also send written instructions to the seller's solicitor specifying precisely what the buyer's solicitor requires the seller's solicitor to do on the buyer's solicitor's behalf at completion and agreeing a time on the day of completion itself when completion will take place.

4.3.4. The seller's solicitor will effectively act as the buyer's solicitor's agent for the purpose of carrying out the completion procedure. The instructions given by the buyer's solicitor should therefore encompass such of the matters detailed in F4.2 as the buyer's solicitor would have carried out had he attended personally at completion. If the seller's solicitor perceives any difficulty or ambiguity in the instructions received from the buyer's solicitor, he must resolve that query or ambiguity before completion is due to take place.

4.3.5. The buyer's solicitor must either send the banker's draft to the seller's solicitor to arrive in time for completion and to be held by the seller's solicitor to the buyer's solicitor's order until completion takes place, or, more commonly, remit the necessary funds by telegraphic transfer to the seller's solicitor's nominated bank account to arrive there in time for completion to take place at the agreed time.

4.3.6. On being satisfied as to the proper payment of the completion money, either by draft or telegraphic transfer, the seller's solicitor must carry out the buyer's instructions and effect completion on his behalf. He should then immediately telephone (or fax) the buyer's solicitor to inform him that completion has taken place and post to the buyer's solicitor, by first class post or document exchange, the documents which the buyer is entitled to receive on completion. Where documents are required to be marked, certified or endorsed, the seller's solicitor will carry out these operations on behalf of the absent buyer's solicitor.

4.3.7.   Under the Law Society's Code, the seller's solicitor is not entitled to make a charge to the buyer's solicitor for acting as his agent in carrying out completion.

4.3.8.   In the unusual case where the seller sends the executed deed to the buyer before completion, he should ensure that the deed is to be held to his own order pending actual completion.[1]

1.   *Bank of Scotland plc* v. *King and Okoronkwo* [2007] EWHC 2747 (Ch).

4.4.   Using an agent

4.4.1.   If the buyer's solicitor is unable to attend personally at completion, but does not wish to complete through the post, he may appoint another solicitor to act as his agent, the agent attending completion in person and carrying out the same procedures that the buyer's solicitor would have done had he been present.

4.4.2.   The agent will generally be a solicitor who practises within the vicinity of the office where completion is due to take place and should be given instructions to act in good time before actual completion day.

4.4.3.   The instructions given to the agent should be full and explicit so that the agent is in no doubt as to what he is required to do. Copies of all the documents which the buyer's solicitor would normally take to completion with him should be supplied with the instructions and the agent should be put in funds either by banker's draft or telegraphic transfer so that he has cleared funds in his own clients' account against which to draw the draft for the completion money.

4.4.4.   The agent is entitled to charge a reasonable sum for carrying out his duties as agent. The fee should be agreed in advance between the agent and the buyer's solicitor to avoid any later dispute. The buyer's solicitor is then bound to pay the agent's fee after completion irrespective of whether he has received reimbursement from his own client. It should be made clear to the client at the outset of the transaction that if the employment of an agent is required in order to attend completion, the agent's fee will be added as a disbursement on the client's bill (see A8).

4.4.5.   The agent should attend completion in person and carry out the buyer's solicitor's instructions. As soon after completion as possible he should telephone (telex or fax or email) the buyer's solicitor to confirm that completion has taken place and should send the documents which he has received at completion to the buyer's solicitor by first class post or document exchange.

4.5.   Synchronisation

4.5.1.   Where the client is to complete a sale and purchase of property on the same day, it is essential that the sale actually takes place before the purchase so that the proceeds of sale can be utilised in the later purchase transaction. Sufficient time should be allowed between the times of completion of sale and purchase to permit the funds received from the sale transaction to be transmitted to and received by the seller's solicitor in the purchase transaction within the time limits specified in the purchase contract.

4.6.   Deemed late completion

4.6.1.   By Standard Conditions 6.1.2 and 6.1.3 and Standard Commercial Property Conditions 8.1.2 and 8.1.3, where the sale is with vacant possession and the money due on completion is not paid by 2 pm on the day of actual completion (or such other time as may have been agreed by the parties), for compensation purposes completion is deemed to have taken place on the next following working day unless the seller had not vacated the property by 2 pm (or other agreed time). The buyer's solicitor must therefore instruct his bank to remit the completion money in sufficient time to ensure its arrival at its destination bank within the time limit specified in the contract. In default the buyer may find himself liable to pay compensation to the seller under Standard Condition 7.3 or Standard Commercial Property Condition 9.3 (see also M1.4).

4.7.   Lender's requirements

4.7.1.   The buyer's solicitor will often also be acting as solicitor for the buyer's lender. In such a case the buyer's solicitor should check the lender's requirements for completion when he is preparing his checklist and making arrangements for completion. In most cases the lender's requirements will be identical to the buyer's solicitor's own requirements, but a check on the lender's instructions should always be made to ensure that nothing is overlooked.

4.8.   Problems with vacant possession

4.8.1.   If the buyer's solicitor suspects that there may be practical problems in obtaining vacant possession, he should deal with this matter at an early stage in the transaction. Taking a written release of rights from an occupier and/or joining the occupier as a party to the contract will in most cases resolve the problem, but a signed release is of little comfort if on the day of completion the occupier refuses to vacate the property. If it is suspected that this might happen, the buyer's solicitor may take the precaution of inserting a contractual condition specifying that completion shall take place at the premises themselves so that an inspection of the property can be carried out immediately before completion takes place. Such a condition would have to be inserted into the contract before exchange and it is too late to try to impose such a term just before completion. Standard Condition 6.2.2 and Standard Commercial Property Condition 8.2 give the seller the right to decide where completion will take place.

4.8.2.   In the absence of a term allowing completion to take place on the premises themselves, the buyer's solicitor may, in appropriate cases, either inspect the property himself on the day of completion, or ask the client or the client's surveyor to do so and then to telephone the buyer's solicitor to confirm that the premises are vacant before completion proceeds.

4.8.3.   Accepting an instruction from a lender that the solicitor acting for the lender will ensure that vacant possession is obtained is a breach of Rule 3.19 Solicitors' Code of Conduct 2007. Such an instruction must therefore be deleted from the lender's instructions.

4.9.   Effect of completion

4.9.1.   In unregistered land, title in the property passes to the buyer on completion.

4.9.2.   In registered land, the legal title does not pass until the buyer has become registered as proprietor of the land.[1]

4.9.3.   On completion the contract merges with the purchase deed in so far as the contract and purchase deed cover the same ground; thus after completion it is not possible to bring an action which arises out of one of the terms of the contract unless that provision has been expressly left extant by a term of the contract itself. For this reason it is common for the contract to contain a non-merger clause. Standard Condition 7.4 and Standard Commercial Property Condition 9.4 say that the provisions within the contract do not merge on completion in so far as there is outstanding liability under these provisions.

4.9.4.   In the absence of a non-merger provision an action on the contract may not be possible after completion has taken place, but an action in tort or for misrepresentation would still be available since neither of these actions is based on the contract.

4.9.5.   The principal remedy available to the buyer after completion is an action on the title guarantee or covenants for title, which is further discussed in M9.

1.   Land Registration Act 2002, s.27(1).

G. POST-COMPLETION

G1. After completion

1.1. Seller's checklist

1.1.1. Where appropriate to the transaction the following steps should be taken by the seller's solicitor as soon as possible after completion has taken place:

(a) Where completion has taken place by post, telephone the buyer's solicitor to inform him that completion has taken place.

(b) Telephone the estate agent to inform him of completion and to direct him to release the keys to the buyer.

(c) Inform client that completion has taken place.

(d) Where completion has taken place by post, send purchase deed, title deeds and other relevant documents to buyer's solicitor by first class post or document exchange.

(e) If part of the proceeds of sale are to be used towards the purchase of another property on the same day, make arrangements for the transmission of these funds in accordance with instructions received.

(f) Deal with the discharge of the seller's existing mortgage(s) by sending a clients' account cheque for the amount required (as per redemption statement previously obtained) to the lender together with the engrossment of the Form DS1 (or deed of release relating to unregistered land) requesting him to discharge the mortgage and to forward the receipted Form DS1 to you as quickly as possible.[1] If the mortgage is over unregistered land, the lender will, instead of using a Form DS1, complete the receipt clause on the reverse of the mortgage deed and forward the receipted deed to the seller's solicitor. If in unregistered land the lender is not a building society, the lender should be requested to date the receipt with the date of completion in order to avoid the risk of a transfer of the mortgage under Law of Property Act 1925, s.115. Where necessary, the reassignment of collateral security, e.g. a life policy, should also be dealt with, and a lender who has insured the property will also need to be told to cancel the property insurance cover.

(g) If instructed to do so, pay the estate agent's commission and obtain a receipt for the payment.

(h) Account to the seller's bank for the proceeds of sale in accordance with any undertaking given to them.

(i) Account to the client for the balance of the proceeds of sale in accordance with his instructions.

(j) If not already done, draft and remit bill of costs to the client.

(k) Where money is being held by the solicitor on account of costs, it may be transferred to office account provided that the client has expressly or impliedly agreed to this being done.

(l) If the land is to remain unregistered after completion of this transaction make application for registration of land charges at the Land Charges Department.[2]

(m) On receipt of the completed Form DS1 or receipted mortgage from the lender, check the form or receipt to ensure it is correct, then send it to the buyer's solicitor and ask to be discharged from the undertaking given on completion.

(n) Remind the client of the need to notify the local and water authorities of the change of ownership of the property.

(o) Remind the client to cancel insurance cover over the property (and associated insurances if relevant).

(p) Advise the client about the payment of capital gains tax on assessment.

(q) Deal with the custody of deeds in accordance with the client's instructions. Most, if not all, original deeds will have passed to the buyer's solicitor on actual completion, but the seller will have retained custody of such deeds on a sale of part, or may have, e.g. an original grant of representation or power of attorney.

(r) Check through the file to ensure that all outstanding matters have been dealt with before sending the file for storage.

1. Alternatively a mortgage of the whole may be discharged using the ED or e-DS1 systems (see G1.10 and G1.11).
2. See G3 as to the events giving rise to compulsory first registration.

1.2. Buyer's checklist

1.2.1. Where appropriate to the transaction the following steps should be taken by the buyer's solicitor as soon as possible after completion has taken place:

(a) Inform client and his lender that completion has taken place.

(b) Complete the mortgage deed by insertion of the date and any other information which still has to be completed, e.g. date when first repayment is due.

(c) Complete file copies of the mortgage, purchase deed and other relevant documents.

(d) Ensure that the SDLT return (form SDLT1) is completed and submitted to HM Revenue and Customs, together with the payment of any tax due, within the time limit.

(e) Register any charge created by a company at Companies House within 21 days of its creation in accordance with Companies Act requirements. This time limit is absolute and cannot be extended without an order of the court. Failure to register within the time limit may prejudice the lender's security and will be an act of negligence on the part of the defaulting solicitor.

(f) Account to the buyer's bank for any bridging finance in accordance with any undertaking given to them and ask to be released from that undertaking.

(g) If not already done, draft and remit bill of costs to the client.

(h) Where money is being held by the solicitor on account of costs, it may be transferred to office account provided that the client has expressly or impliedly agreed to this being done.

(i) If the seller's land is to remain unregistered after completion of this transaction make application for registration of land charges at the Land Charges Department within the period given by the previously lodged priority notice, e.g. new restrictive covenants by the seller on a sale of part.

(j) On receipt of the completed Form DS1 or receipted mortgage from the seller's lender's solicitor, check the form or receipt to ensure it is correct, acknowledge its receipt and release the sender from the undertaking given on completion.

(k) Make copies of all documents which are to be sent to the Land Registry to ensure that file copies exist in case requisitions are raised by the Registry or the documents are lost or damaged before registration is complete.

(l) Make copies of any documents where a request is to be made to the registrar for the original to be returned.

(m) Certify copy documents which are to be sent to the Land Registry (see G1.8).

(n) Make application for registration of title within the relevant priority period (land already registered) or within two months of completion (application for first registration).

(o)   Make diary or file prompt entry recording the approximate date when the title information document may be expected to be received from the Land Registry and send a reminder if the document is not received by that time.

(p)   Send notice of assignment of a life policy to the insurance company and place their acknowledgement of receipt with the title deeds.

(q)   Give notice to the landlord's solicitors of an assignment, mortgage, etc., in accordance with a requirement to that effect in the lease or in the mortgagee's instructions and place their acknowledgement of receipt with the title deeds.

(r)   Notify tenants of the change of ownership of the property.

(s)   Make application for the discharge of any entry which was lodged to protect the contract. In registered land this will be combined with any application for registration.

(t)   On receipt of the title information document from the Land Registry, check its contents carefully and ask the Registry to correct any errors which have been made.

(u)   Deal with the custody of deeds in accordance with the client's instructions.

(v)   Check through the file to ensure that all outstanding matters have been dealt with before sending the file for storage.

NB: Where a separate solicitor has been instructed to act for the buyer's lender, the lender's solicitor will normally have taken custody of the purchase deed and other title deeds on completion and he will assume responsibility for the presentation of the documents for SDLT and registration of title in place of the buyer's solicitor.

1.3.   Undertakings

1.3.1.   Failure to honour an undertaking is professional misconduct. Any undertaking given must therefore be honoured and the obligations promised must be fulfilled without delay.[1]

1.3.2.   A solicitor who has performed his undertaking should formally ask the recipient to release the giver from his undertaking so that the giver has written evidence of the fulfilment of the undertaking. The recipient may either acknowledge the giver's release by letter, or return the original undertaking to the giver, and in either case the evidence of release is to be kept on the giver's file.

---

1.   *Angel Solicitors* v. *Jenkins O'Dowd & Barth* [2009] EWHC 46 (Ch) and *Thames Valley Housing Association and others* v. *Elegant Homes (Guernsey) Ltd and others* [2009] EWHC 2647 (Ch).

1.4. Stamp Duty Land Tax

1.4.1. The SDLT return form should be submitted to HM Revenue and Customs as soon as possible after the effective date has taken place to ensure that the land transaction return certificate will be returned to the buyer's solicitor in sufficient time for an application for registration of title to be made within the appropriate time limits. Forms can be ordered via the HM Revenue and Customs website. Single copies of forms, leaflets and guides can be downloaded. The land transaction return certificate or the electronic SDLT5 submission receipt must be sent to the Land Registry with the application for registration of the transaction. The Land Registry does not require any evidence as to compliance with SDLT in respect of the registration of any matter relating to a land transaction completed on or after 12 March 2008 if the transaction is not a notifiable land transaction. The former practice of submitting a SDLT60 (self-certificate as to compliance) with the application for registration was discontinued on that date.

1.4.2. It is not advisable to delay the initial application for registration until the land transaction return certificate is available because in doing so the client might lose the protection of the priority period afforded to him by his pre-completion search. However, the Land Registry's practice is to reject applications for registration where the application relates to a notifiable transaction and is not accompanied by a land transaction return certificate or a submission receipt (electronic SDLT5) where one is required.

1.4.3. In the absence of the above documents, the Land Registry will accept the application if an outline application is pending in respect of the transaction or the application clearly states that a land transaction return form has been sent to HM Revenue and Customs and 20 business days or more have passed since completion. In such a case the original transaction document, e.g. the transfer, must accompany the application to the Land Registry. For further information, see Land Registry Practice Guide 49 and Practice Bulletin 11.

1.4.4. Depending on the nature of his instructions and report on title, a lender's solicitor may be under a duty to pay SDLT and register at the Land Registry even if the buyer has not put him in funds to do so.

1.4.5. Stamp duty and the Produced Stamp procedure applied only to transactions before 1 December 2003 and to some later transactions. See A14.32 for details on which documents may require stamping and producing to HM Revenue and Customs.

1.5. Registration of title

1.5.1. It is essential that the relevant time limits for submission of an application for registration of the client's title are complied with. Failure to make an application for first registration within two months of completion results in the transfer of the legal estate becoming void and may lead to the buyer's title becoming subject to interests from which it would otherwise take free.[1] Failure to make an application for a registration of a transfer or other disposition within the priority period of 30 business days given by a pre-completion Land Registry search may have the consequence of the client's interest losing priority to another application.[2] In either case, if the client suffered loss as a result of the late application, the solicitor would be liable in negligence.

1.5.2.   Under the Land Registry's early completion policy, an application for a discharge of whole is considered substantially defective if evidence of satisfaction of the charge is not lodged either with or in advance of the application. The Land Registry's policy is to reject such an application.[3] Where such a discharge application is made with other applications, e.g. the registration of a transfer of whole and a new charge, the defective discharge application will be rejected and the other applications completed (provided they are in order). The existing registered charge entry will remain on the register of title until an application for discharge accompanied by evidence of satisfaction of the charge is completed.[4] If a restriction has been registered in favour of the existing chargee preventing registration of a disposition without the chargee's consent, the Land Registry will requisition for evidence of discharge or evidence of the chargee's consent.

1.5.3.   Registration of title is further dealt with in G3.

1. Land Registration Act 2002, s.7 and see *Sainsbury's Supermarkets Ltd* v. *Olympia Homes Ltd* [2005] EWHC 1235 (Ch).
2. See Land Registration Rules 2003, r.131 for the definition of 'priority period'.
3. Land Registration Rules 2003, r.16(3).
4. See Land Registry Practice Bulletin 16 and Practice Guide 31. See also the Law Society's Land Registry Early Completion Practice Note (9 July 2009) which provides guidance on how early completion will operate and gives advice on how to proceed with the different applications.

1.6.   Registration of company charges

1.6.1.   Legal charges created by a company are registrable at the Land Registry (or the Land Charges Department in the case of a charge over unregistered land which is not supported by a deposit of title deeds) and, as a separate obligation in relation to any charge on land, at Companies House under Companies Act 2006 (see E3.9.3). Failure to register the charge under Companies Act 2006 within the 21 days following its creation renders the charge void against a liquidator or another creditor of the company. This time limit can only be extended by an order of the court which is not automatically granted. Fixed equitable charges and floating charges must also be noted on the register if they are to affect registered land.

1.7.   Notices of assignment

1.7.1.   Where following completion notice has to be given to a landlord of an assignment or mortgage, or notice given to an insurance company of the assignment of a life insurance policy, such notice should be given in duplicate. The recipient of the notice should be requested to sign one copy of the notice in acknowledgement of its receipt, and to return the receipted copy to the sender. The receipted copy will then be kept with the title deeds as evidence of compliance with this requirement.

1.7.2.   In the case of the assignment of a life policy, the notice of assignment should be given as soon as possible after completion, since the giving of the notice establishes the priority of charges and is required to be given by Policies of Assurance Act 1867.

1.7.3.   Where notice is being given under the terms of a lease, it should be delivered within the time limits specified in the lease together with the appropriate fee.

1.8.   Certifying documents

1.8.1.   Where a certified copy of a document will be required by the Land Registry the certification should be carried out by a conveyancer (or such other person as the registrar may permit) by writing on the copy clearly and in a conspicuous position the words:

> 'I certify this to be a true copy of the [*insert type of document*] dated [*insert date of document being certified*] signed [*signature of conveyancer*] and dated [*insert date of certification*].'

1.8.2.   The name and address of the signatory should also be endorsed.[1] This will assist in the event of the certification later having to be checked in a subsequent transaction.

1.8.3.   It should be noted that under Powers of Attorney Act 1971, s.3(1)(b)(ii), a copy of a power of attorney must be certified on every page.

1.   See Land Registration Rules 2003, r.217(1) (as amended).

1.9.   Custody of deeds

1.9.1.   Instructions relating to custody will have been obtained from the client at an earlier stage in the transaction.

1.9.2.   In many cases the client's lender will not require custody of the deeds after completion and, if this is the case, the client should be advised to deposit the deeds with his bank or in the solicitor's strongroom.

1.9.3.   Where the original deeds are not to be sent to the client himself, it is courteous to photocopy the principal title deeds and send these copies to the client who will thus have immediate access to the relevant information in the case of, e.g. a dispute over a right of way or restrictive covenant.

1.9.4.   Before deeds are sent to a lender (or other third party) for custody, they should be checked for accuracy and a schedule of deeds drawn up in duplicate. The recipient should be asked to acknowledge the receipt of the deeds by signing and returning one copy of the schedule. This signed acknowledgement will then be placed on the buyer's solicitor's file as evidence that the deeds have been sent to the recipient.

1.9.5.   Deeds should normally be sent by recorded delivery, insured post or document exchange to ensure their safe arrival at their destination.

1.9.6.   If deeds are to remain in the solicitor's own strongroom, a schedule of the deeds should be drawn up in duplicate, one copy being placed with the deeds, the other remaining in the solicitor's file. In no circumstances should original deeds be left in the solicitor's file when the file is sent for storage. If deeds are kept in the solicitor's strongroom, the solicitor owes a duty of care to his client and, if the deeds are lost, the solicitor may not charge the client with the cost of replacement.

1.9.7.   Declarations of trust (e.g. relating to co-ownership) should be treated in the same way as documents of title and retained with the title deeds.

1.9.8.   Firms will have different policies on the appropriate time for storing property transaction files. However, where a firm is storing will-related material (including original wills and powers of attorney), consideration should be given to retaining the files regardless of the standard conveyancing policy. In particular, transactions involving deeds of gift, gifts of land, transfers at an undervalue, right to buy where funds come from someone other than the purchasing tenant and lifetime gifts may be open to challenge many years after the transaction in question. For further guidance on good practice in this area, see the Law Society's File Retention Practice Note (11 September 2007).

1.10.   Electronic discharge (ED)

1.10.1.   An ED is an electronic message from a lender authorising the discharge of a registered charge. The ED system enables mortgage lenders to discharge mortgages electronically using a direct link to the Land Registry's computer system. It may only be used for a discharge of the whole of the land charged.

1.10.2.   Lenders will inform the solicitor in their redemption statement if they belong to the scheme. The solicitor will need to agree on a revised form of undertaking to allow for an ED. Suggested forms of undertaking are at Appendix IV.10.

1.10.3.   The borrower's solicitors will remit to the lender the amount required to redeem the mortgage. The lender will then send an ED to the Land Registry. On acceptance, the charge entries will be cancelled automatically by the Land Registry's computer system. The lender will then notify the borrower's solicitors that the charge has been discharged.

1.10.4. For further information see Land Registry Practice Guide 31.

1.11. Electronic submission of discharge (e-DS1)

1.11.1. An e-DS1 is an electronic discharge submitted by lenders or their authorised agents through the Land Registry portal. It is a service that is currently designed for use by corporate lenders and their agents.

1.11.2. The e-DS1 provides both the application to cancel a registered charge and the necessary evidence of discharge. It may only be used for a discharge of the whole of the land charged.

1.11.3. Lenders will inform the solicitor in the redemption statement if they intend to discharge the charge using an e-DS1. The solicitor will need to agree on a revised form of undertaking to allow for an e-DS1. A similar undertaking to that used for an ED may be appropriate. Suggested forms of undertaking are at Appendix IV.10.

1.11.4. On receipt of the required payment the lender will arrange for the e-DS1 to be submitted to the Land Registry. The lender will be able to notify the borrower's solicitor that the charge has been discharged upon receipt of the Land Registry's confirmation of completion of the registration.

1.11.5. For further information see Land Registry Practice Guide 31.

1.12. Electronic notification of discharge (END)

1.12.1. The Land Registry withdrew the END service on 3 January 2010. This method of discharge was an alternative to Form DS1 in registered land transactions. Like the paper form of discharge, an END did not cause the charge to be cancelled, it had to be combined with a formal application to the Land Registry using Form AP1 or DS2 to discharge the charge.

G

G2. Stamping documents

2.1.　Introduction

2.1.1.　The following paragraphs relate to those documents that continue to require stamping. See A14 for an explanation of Stamp Duty Land Tax (SDLT) and for details on which documents may require stamping.

2.1.2.　In circumstances where land transactions remain subject to stamp duty, the relevant instrument must be produced to HM Revenue and Customs for stamping within 30 days of execution or, if delivered subject to conditions, within 30 days of the date when the conditions are fulfilled.

2.1.3.　HM Revenue and Customs do not offer a 'local office' service for stamping documents. Postal applications should be made to the Birmingham Stamp Office, 9th Floor, City Centre House, 30 Union Street, Birmingham, B2 4AR (or, by DX service, to the Birmingham Stamp Office – Stamp Duty, DX15001, Birmingham 1).

2.2.　Effect of unstamped documents

2.2.1.　Unstamped or insufficiently stamped documents are not admissible in evidence and it is the duty of the advocate and the judge to take the point (Stamp Act 1891, s.14(4)). This applies even where the litigant relying upon the document is not a party to it such as a lender seeking to enforce his security. Failure to take stamp objections to the other side's documents is a breach of duty to the client.

2.2.2.　The Land Registry and Companies House will not accept unstamped or incorrectly stamped documents for registration and they may insist that the instrument is presented to HM Revenue and Customs Stamp Taxes Office and adjudicated (Stamp Act 1891, s.17). Duty must therefore normally be paid before an application for registration of title is submitted.

2.2.3.　Unstamped or incorrectly stamped documents cannot be used in evidence in civil proceedings. Such a document is not therefore a good root or link in the chain of title to land and since certain documents, including certain contracts for sale, may be subject to stamp duty, these can affect the title to unregistered land.

2.3.　Avoidance by inserting false information

2.3.1.　An agreement to avoid the payment of the correct duty by inserting false information in a document may be a fraud on HM Revenue and Customs which could result in the transaction being declared void as being illegal on the grounds of public policy. This liability extends to the parties' professional advisers involved in the preparation of the documentation (see *Saunders* v. *Edwards* [1987] 2 All ER 651).

G3. Registration of title

3.1.   Introduction

3.1.1. Registration of title is governed by Land Registration Act 2002 (the Act) and Land Registration Rules 2003 (the Rules), which came into force on 13 October 2003. The Act contains the major principles of law and the supporting details are contained in the Rules.

3.1.2. Section numbers and rule numbers in this section (G3) correspond to Land Registration Act 2002 and Land Registration Rules 2003 unless otherwise stated.[1]

3.1.3. The Land Registry produces Practice Guides and Practice Bulletins which are regularly revised and updated to take account of changes in the law and Land Registry practice. They can be downloaded free of charge from **www. landregistry.gov.uk** or obtained from any Land Registry Office.

3.1.4. Registration guarantees the title to registered land. Thus, a person who suffers loss as a result of a mistake in the register is normally entitled to be indemnified for that loss (see M7).

1. Both the Act and the Rules have been amended since 13 October 2003. The section and rule numbers referred to in the text relate to the sections and rules as amended.

3.2.   Compulsory registration

Extension of compulsory registration

3.2.1. The extension of compulsory registration to the whole of England and Wales became effective on 1 December 1990.[1] The Act extended the events which trigger first registration to include leases granted for more than seven years and leases assigned where they have over seven years left to run (s.4(1)). Most commercial leases are now compulsorily registrable on grant or assignment. The Act also contains provisions enabling the Lord Chancellor, by order, to add to the events that will trigger compulsory first registration (s.5).

When title must be registered

3.2.2. Registration is compulsory on specified types of transfers, leases and mortgages of a qualifying estate, which is defined as either a legal freehold estate or a legal lease with more than seven years to run. Under section 4(1) they are:

(a) a transfer:

    (i) for valuable or other consideration, by way of gift or in pursuance of a court order; or

    (ii) by means of an assent;

(b) the grant of a legal lease:

    (i) for a term of more than seven years; and

    (ii) for valuable or other consideration,[2] by way of gift or in pursuance of a court order;

(c) the grant of a legal lease to take effect in possession more than three months after it is granted;

(d) the creation of a first legal mortgage where the mortgage is protected by the deposit of documents.

Certain disposals under Housing Act 1985

3.2.3. The following disposals under Housing Act 1985 also trigger compulsory registration:

(a) the transfer or grant of a legal lease of an unregistered estate where Housing Act 1985, s.171A applies (a disposal by a landlord which leads to a person no longer being a secure tenant); or

(b) the grant of a 'right to buy' lease under Housing Act 1985, Part 5.

Appointments of new trustees and partitions

3.2.4. Since 6 April 2009,[3] first registration is also compulsory on:

(a) the appointment of a new trustee of unregistered land held in trust where the land vests in the new trustee by deed or by vesting order under section 44 Trustee Act 1925; and

(b) the partitioning of unregistered land held in trust amongst the beneficiaries of the trust.

Transfers not subject to compulsory registration

3.2.5. The compulsory registration provisions do not apply to:

(a) a transfer by operation of law, e.g. the vesting of land in personal representatives (s.4(3));

(b)   an assignment of a mortgage term; or

(c)   a surrender of a lease where the term is to merge into the reversion (s.4(4)).

Duty to apply for registration

3.2.6.   Where registration is compulsory, the transferee, lessee or mortgagor is under a duty to apply for first registration (s.6(1)–(3)). In the case of a mortgage, the mortgagee may make an application in the name of the mortgagor whether or not the mortgagor consents (r.21). The application for first registration must be made within two months. This period may be extended by the registrar if he is satisfied that there is a good reason for doing so (s.6(4) and (5)).

Effect of failure to register

3.2.7.   Where an application is not lodged within the registration period the transfer, lease or mortgage is void as regards the legal estate (s.7(1)). In the case of a transfer, the legal estate reverts to the transferor. A lease or mortgage takes effect as a contract made for valuable consideration to grant the lease or mortgage concerned (s.7(2)). Although the registration period can be extended, a client is at risk of being registered subject to interests which would not have otherwise bound the land.[4]

Liability for making good void transfers, etc.

3.2.8.   If the transaction has to be repeated because of a failure to register, the transferee, lessee or mortgagor:

(a)   is liable to the other party for the costs involved; and

(b)   must indemnify the other party for any other liability reasonably incurred due to the failure to register (s.8).

1.   Registration of Title Order 1989 (SI 1989/1347).
2.   If the estate transferred or leased has a negative value it is to be regarded as transferred or leased for valuable or other consideration. Valuable consideration does not include marriage consideration or a nominal consideration in money. See ss.4(6) and 132(1).
3.   Land Registration Act 2002 (Amendment) Order 2008.
4.   See, e.g. *Sainsbury's Supermarkets Ltd* v. *Olympia Homes Ltd* [2005] EWHC 1235 (Ch).

3.3.   **Voluntary registration**

When title may be registered

3.3.1.   Under section 3 the following legal estates and interests may be registered under their own title numbers:

(a)   a freehold estate;

(b)   a lease for a term of which more than seven years are unexpired;[1]

(c)   a lease for a discontinuous term whatever its length;

(d)   a franchise;

(e)   a profit à prendre in gross.

Reasons for voluntary registration

3.3.2.   The benefits of the registered system of conveyancing, such as simplified methods of deduction of title, are such that a client should be encouraged to make an application for voluntary registration in appropriate circumstances. This might be particularly appropriate where, for example, an unregistered title is complex; or where the title has minor defects, since on first registration the registrar has a discretion to 'cure' such defects (ss.9(3) and 10(4)). Voluntary applications attract a reduced fee.

1.   Where a reversionary lease is to take effect in possession on, or within one month of, the end of the lease in possession, the terms may be treated as one continuous term. If this exceeds seven years, the lease can be registered, see s.3(7).

3.4.   Applications for first registration

3.4.1.   The application for first registration must be made to the proper land registry office. See G3.11 as to the proper office for the receipt of applications and other general matters relating to applications to the Land Registry.

3.4.2.   The application must be made in Form FR1 (r.23). It must be accompanied by (r.24(1)):

(a)   sufficient details, by plan or otherwise, so that the land can be identified clearly on the Ordnance Survey map;[1]

(b)   where the land is leasehold, the lease, if in the control of the applicant, and a certified copy;

(c)   all deeds and documents relating to the title in the control of the applicant;

(d)   a list in duplicate in Form DL of all the documents delivered.

3.4.3.   The registrar needs to investigate title on an application for first registration in order to decide which class of title can be allocated to the title. He therefore needs to have access to all the documents which form the evidence of title to the land. The documents should be individually listed and numbered in chronological sequence in Form DL. They should include:

(a)   all the documents which formed the evidence of title supplied by the seller's solicitor;

(b)   all the buyer's pre-contract searches and enquiries with their replies (including any variations or further information contained in relevant correspondence);

(c)   the contract;

(d)   requisitions on title with their replies;

(e)   all pre-completion search certificates;

(f)   the purchase deed;

(g)   the seller's mortgage, duly receipted;

(h)   the buyer's mortgage;

(i)   where the transaction is leasehold, the original lease and a certified copy;

(j)   a land transaction return certificate where required.

3.4.4.   Limitation Act 1980 continues to apply unamended to adverse possession of unregistered land. A person claiming to be in adverse possession of unregistered land may make an application to the Land Registry for first registration on the basis that, under the provisions of section 15 Limitation Act 1980, the documentary title owner is barred from obtaining possession of the land. The application must be accompanied by one or more statutory declarations or statements of truth in Form ST1 providing evidence of the adverse occupation for a minimum of 12 years to show the applicant's entitlement to be registered (r.27). For further guidance see Land Registry Practice Guide 5.

3.4.5.   Similarly, an application for first registration can be made where the title deeds have been lost or destroyed. The application must be accompanied by one or more statutory declarations or statements of truth in Form ST3 establishing the applicant's title to the land and accounting for the absence of the deeds (r.27). For further guidance see Land Registry Practice Guide 2.

3.4.6.   There is a case for retaining copies of all documents which are to be submitted to the registry on the applicant's solicitor's file pending completion of the registration. The registrar may need to raise requisitions on an application (particularly for first registration) and it assists in the speedy reply to those requisitions if the solicitor has retained copies of the documents which may contain information relevant to the query raised by the registry. A further reason for retaining copies of the documents is so that any queries which arise in relation to the land pending completion of the registration, for example over boundaries or the exercise of a right of way, can be resolved from the copies in the solicitor's possession.

Land charges

3.4.7.   On first registration, the Land Registry does not investigate whether restrictive covenants and other land charges may be void for non-registration at the land charges department. Any land charge appearing on the title is noted on the register. This entry, however, does not mean that the land charge is valid.[2]

3.4.8. Application can be made on first registration (or subsequently) to omit (or cancel) notice of a land charge that is void for non-registration. The application should be accompanied by:

(a) the deed or other instrument creating the land charge;

(b) the subsequent conveyance on sale;[3]

(c) any intervening voluntary conveyances or assents; and

(d) an official certificate of the result of search in the land charges department confirming that the land charge has not been registered.[4]

3.4.9. Before making such an application the following matters should also be considered:

(a) registration at the land charges department is not required for a land charge created by an instrument dated on or after 27 July 1971 which was compulsorily registrable;[5]

(b) before 1 August 1977, a land charge in favour of a local authority was registrable as a local land charge and may only be revealed by a local land charges search;

(c) before April 1976, the Land Registry sometimes cancelled Class D(ii) (restrictive covenants) land charge entries from the land charges register on first registration of the land burdened by the covenants;[6] and

(d) where the burdened land falls wholly or partly within the former Ridings of Yorkshire, a land charges search made prior to 1 April 1976 may not reveal land charges registered at the Yorkshire Deeds Registry.

Cautions against first registration

3.4.10. An application for a caution against first registration must be made in Form CT1 (r.42). However, owners of a registrable estate cannot register a caution against first registration to protect their own interest against third parties (s.15). The most appropriate course is for such an owner to apply for the first registration of his estate.

3.4.11. A caution against first registration merely entitles the cautioner to be notified of an application for first registration. It does not confer any validity or priority on the interest claimed. Where necessary, such interest should be protected by registration at the Land Charges Department. Land Registry Practice Guide 63 provides advice about land charges applications.

3.4.12. It is important to note that a person must not lodge a caution against first registration without reasonable cause (s.77(1)). A duty of care is owed to any person who suffers damage in consequence of its breach (s.77(2)).

3.4.13. An application to alter the caution register, for instance to record the transmission of the cautioner's interest, should be made in Form AP1. The application must give details of the alteration required and the grounds on which the application is made and include any relevant supporting documents (r.50).

3.4.14. The cautioner can apply to withdraw the caution. The application must be made in Form WCT (r.43).

3.4.15. An application to cancel a caution against first registration is made in Form CCT (r.45). The application can be made by the owner of the legal estate to which the caution relates or a person deriving title out of that estate (s.18).

3.4.16. For further information see Land Registry Practice Guide 3.

1. On an application to register a rentcharge, franchise or profit à prendre in gross, the land to be identified is the land affected: see Land Registration Rules 2003, r.24(2). See r.26(1) as to the additional information that may be required on first registration of a flat.
2. Land Registration Act 2002, s.32(3).
3. See Land Charges Act 1972, s.4 and D2.12 as to the effect of failure to register land charges.
4. See E2.6 as to the requirements for the search being correct in every particular.
5. Land Charges Act 1972, s.14(3), and see Land Registry Practice Guide 51 as to the relevant dates of compulsory registration.
6. Enquiry of the appropriate Land Registry office will confirm whether this procedure was carried out in any particular case.

3.5.   Classes of title

3.5.1. On first registration the registrar will decide which class of title should be granted to the estate which is being registered. The class of title granted is shown in the proprietorship register of the title (r.8(1)).

Absolute title

3.5.2. The vast majority of titles are registered with absolute title. An absolute title may be approved if the registrar is of the opinion that title to the estate is such that a willing buyer could properly be advised by a competent professional adviser to accept (ss.9(2) and 10(2)(a)). The registrar may disregard a defect in the title if he is of the opinion that the defect will not cause the holding under the title to be disturbed (ss.9(3) and 10(4)). Where the title is leasehold, absolute title is granted where the registrar also approves the lessor's title to grant the lease (s.10(2)(b)).

Qualified title

3.5.3. A person may be registered with qualified title if the registrar is of the opinion that title has been established only for a limited period or subject to certain reservations which cannot be disregarded (ss.9(4) and 10(5)). A qualified title is very rare in practice. It might be approved where, for example, the title submitted for first registration showed that a transaction within the title had been carried out in breach of trust. In this situation the proprietor would take his interest in the land subject to the interests (if any) of the beneficiaries under the trust and a qualification entered in the register to reflect this. Qualified title can be given to either a freehold or a leasehold estate in the land.

Possessory title

3.5.4. Possessory title may be granted where the registrar considers that the applicant is in possession of the land, or in receipt of rents and profits, and there is no other class of title with which he may be registered (ss.9(5) and 10(6)). In practice, a possessory title will be granted where the applicant's title is based on adverse possession or where title cannot be proved satisfactorily because the title deeds have been lost or destroyed. Possessory title can be given to either a freehold or leasehold estate in the land.

Good leasehold title

3.5.5. Registration with good leasehold title will be granted where the registrar is satisfied only as to the title to the leasehold estate (s.10(3)). Such a title will therefore generally only result where the title to the freehold reversion is unregistered and where the applicant for registration of the leasehold interest does not submit evidence of title to the freehold reversion when making his application. A good leasehold title is regarded by some mortgagees as being unsatisfactory, and for this reason is sometimes difficult to sell or mortgage.

3.5.6. The problems of a good leasehold title are discussed in K11.5.2. See also Standard Condition 8.2.4 and Standard Commercial Property Condition 10.2.4, which require a seller on the grant of a new lease for over seven years to deduce to a buyer such evidence of title as will enable the buyer to obtain registration of his title with an absolute leasehold title.

3.6.   **Effect of first registration**

Freehold estates

3.6.1. On first registration with absolute title, the legal estate is vested in the proprietor together with all interests subsisting for the benefit of the estate, such as appurtenant implied or prescriptive easements (s.11(3)). The registered estate is subject only to the following interests affecting the estate at the time of registration (s.11(4)):

(a) interests which are entered in the register (the only interests entered on first registration will be charges, notices and restrictions);

(b) overriding interests falling within Land Registration Act 2002, Sched.1; and

(c) interests acquired under the Limitation Act 1980 of which the proprietor has notice.[1]

3.6.2. Where the proprietor is a trustee, the estate is vested in him subject to the rights of the beneficiaries under the trust of which he has notice (s.11(5)).

3.6.3. Registration with qualified title has the same effect as registration with absolute title except that it does not affect the enforcement of any estate, right or interest appearing from the register to be excepted from the effect of registration (s.11(6)).

3.6.4. Registration with possessory title has the same effect as registration with absolute title, except that it does not affect the enforcement of any estate, right or interest, adverse to, or in derogation of, the title subsisting at the time of registration (s.11(7)).

Leasehold estates

3.6.5. In general terms the registration of a proprietor with absolute, qualified or possessory title to a leasehold estate has the same effect as registration with the corresponding freehold estate. The significant difference is that a leaseholder is also subject to implied and express covenants, obligations and liabilities incident to the leasehold estate. The registration, therefore, takes subject to interests such as restrictive covenants contained in the lease (s.12).

3.6.6. Registration with good leasehold title has the same effect as registration with absolute leasehold title except that it does not affect the enforcement of any estate, right or interest affecting, or in derogation of, the title of the lessor to grant the lease (s.12(6)).

1. During a three-year transitional period ending on 12 October 2006, a right acquired under Limitation Act 1980 before the coming into force of the 2002 Act was an overriding interest whether or not the proprietor had notice: see Land Registration Act 2002, s.11(4)(b) and (c) and Sched.12, para.7.

3.7. Upgrading title

3.7.1. The registrar has power to upgrade a title in the following circumstances (s.62(1)–(5)):

    (a) from possessory or qualified freehold title to absolute freehold title if he is satisfied as to the title to the freehold estate;

    (b) from good leasehold title to absolute leasehold title if he is satisfied as to the superior title;

    (c) from possessory or qualified leasehold title:

        (i) to good leasehold title, if he is satisfied as to the title to the leasehold estate; and

        (ii) to absolute leasehold title if he is satisfied both as to the title to the leasehold estate and as to the superior title;

(d) from possessory freehold title to absolute freehold title or from possessory leasehold title to good leasehold title if the title has been registered for at least 12 years and he is satisfied that the proprietor is in possession of the land (see s.131 for the meaning given to 'proprietor in possession').

3.7.2. The registrar cannot upgrade a title if there is any outstanding adverse claim under any estate, right or interest whose enforceability is preserved by the existing class of title (s.62(6)). Any adverse claim must be resolved before the title can be upgraded.

3.7.3. An application to upgrade a title must be made in Form UT1 (r.124(1)).

3.8. Dispositions of registered land

Powers of disposition

3.8.1. A registered proprietor is to be taken to have all the powers of an absolute owner unless any limitation of these powers is reflected by an entry on the register (ss.23 and 25), for example, a restriction. The purpose of the statutory provisions is to prevent the title of the buyer being challenged. They do not affect the lawfulness of the sale (s.26). The Law Commission report preceding the Act illustrated the effect of these provisions with the example of trustees who have limited powers of sale, but who failed to enter a restriction on the register to reflect this limitation. If they then sell the land in breach of the terms of the trust they will remain personally liable for this breach. The buyer's title could not be challenged although he might be personally accountable in equity if he knew of the trustee's breach of trust at the time of the sale.

Registrable dispositions

3.8.2. The Act sets out the dispositions that must be completed by registration if they are to operate at law (s.27(1)). These are:

(a) a transfer;

(b) the grant of a term of years absolute of an estate in land:

    (i) for a term of more than seven years from the date of the grant;

    (ii) taking effect in possession after the end of the period of three months beginning with the date of the grant;

    (iii) under which the right to possession is discontinuous;

    (iv) in pursuance of Part 5 Housing Act 1985 (the right to buy); or

    (v) in circumstances where section 171A of that Act applies (disposal by landlord which leads to a person no longer being a secure tenant);

    (c)   the grant of a lease of a franchise or manor;

    (d)   the express grant or reservation of an easement or other right falling within Law of Property Act 1925, s.1(2)(a), other than one which is capable of being registered under Commons Registration Act 1965;

    (e)   the express grant or a reservation of a rentcharge or right of re-entry falling within Law of Property Act 1925, s.1(2)(b) or (e);

    (f)   the grant of a legal charge; and

    (g)   the transfer or sub-charge of a registered charge (s.27(3)).

3.8.3.   The requirement for registration applies also to transfers by operation of law except for:

    (a)   a transfer on the death or bankruptcy of an individual proprietor;

    (b)   a transfer on the dissolution of a corporate proprietor; and

    (c)   the creation of a legal charge which is a local land charge (s.27(5)).

Effect of dispositions on priority

3.8.4.   The general principle under the Act is that the priority of an interest in registered land is determined by its date of creation and not the date on which it is entered in the register or whether or not it is entered in the register (s.28(1)). There is a crucial exception, however, in the case of registrable dispositions (such as a transfer or charge) made for valuable consideration. In such cases, on completion of the disposition by registration, the disposition takes priority to an interest whose priority is not protected at the time of registration. The effect of these provisions is that registration of a disposition for valuable consideration takes effect subject only to:

    (a)   a registered charge;

    (b)   an interest the subject of a notice on the register;

    (c)   an overriding interest under Schedule 3 of the Act;

    (d)   an interest appearing from the register to be excepted from the effect of registration (for example, where the title is less than absolute); and

    (e)   where the land is leasehold, any interest incident to the leasehold estate, e.g. the covenants contained in the registered lease (s.29).

Relative priority of registered charges

3.8.5.   Registered charges rank as between themselves in the order shown in the register (s.48). Any application to alter this priority must be made by, or with the consent of, the proprietor of any postponed registered charge and any other registered charge whose priority is affected by the alteration. But no consent is required from a person who has executed the instrument altering the priority of the charge (r.102(1)). Registration of charges and the priority of further advances are dealt with in more detail in H3.

3.9. Registered land: applications

3.9.1. Applications for registration of transfers, charges and other dispositions of registered land must be made on Form AP1 (r.13). This is the 'default' form to be used when no other application form is prescribed. The application must be delivered to the proper Land Registry office (see G3.11.4).

Transfer of whole

3.9.2. The application for registration of a transfer of the whole of the seller's title (whether freehold or leasehold) should be lodged at the proper office within the 30 business days priority period conferred by the applicant's pre-completion official search certificate (see E2.5.18). It is important to note that the period of protection under the search cannot be extended (although a second search conferring a separate priority period can be made). The application should be accompanied by:

(a) the transfer in Form TR1 (or TR2 if the transfer is under a chargee's power of sale);

(b) the appropriate fee under the current Land Registration Fee Order; and

(c) in appropriate circumstances:

(i) a completed Form DS1 (or reference in the Form AP1 to the use of the ED or e-DS1 systems) in respect of the application for the discharge of the seller's mortgage (see G3.11.18);

(ii) where the seller was the personal representative of a sole deceased proprietor an office copy or certified copy of the grant of representation (rr.163(2) and 214);

(iii) where the transfer has been executed under a power of attorney, the original or a duly certified copy of the power, or a certificate by a conveyancer in Form 1 (r.61(1) and Sched.3); and where the transfer is not made within one year of the power, appropriate evidence of non-revocation by statutory declaration, statement of truth or certificate in Form 2 (r.62 and Sched.3);

(iv) a land transaction return certificate or a submission receipt when one is required;

(v) evidence of identity when required (see G3.11.3).

Transfer of part

3.9.3. The transfer must be in Form TP1 (or TP2 if the transfer is under a chargee's power of sale). The transfer should include a plan signed by the seller identifying the land transferred (r.213). (See B21 for a detailed explanation of the Land

Registry's requirements on plans.) The application should be lodged within the priority period referred to in G3.9.2 accompanied by the transfer and such documents listed in that paragraph as are relevant to the transaction.

Charges

3.9.4. A registered proprietor has power to mortgage the land in any way permitted by the general law but not by a mortgage by demise or sub-demise. He may also charge the land at law with the payment of money (s.23). An application to register the charge should be made within the priority period conferred by the pre-completion official search certificate (see E2.5.18) and be accompanied by the charge and any requisite fee.

3.9.5. Where the charge is by a company registered under the Companies Acts or by an incorporated limited liability partnership, the applicant must also produce a certificate that the charge has been registered under Companies Act 2006 (r.111(1)). In default, the registrar will enter a note in the register that no evidence of registration of the charge has been lodged (r.111(2)). (See E7.5 as to the corresponding requirements for overseas companies.)

3.9.6. The best way of protecting a lender of registered land is by substantive registration of the charge when the chargee will be entered in the register as the proprietor of the charge (Sched.2, para.8). On registration, a registered charge takes effect as a charge by way of legal mortgage and the proprietor of the charge can exercise all the powers of a legal mortgagee (s.51). The priority of registered charges is governed by the order shown in the register (s.48). A registered chargee will also gain priority over any earlier charges not appearing on the register at the date of registration of the chargee (see G3.8.4).

3.9.7. Alternatively, a charge can be protected by the entry of notice in the register and any future buyer of the land would take subject to a charge in this way. However, where a charge is not a registered charge, in order to exercise a lender's power of sale, the chargee would need either to register the charge substantively (if it is capable of being registered in its own right), or to obtain an order of the court under Law of Property Act 1925, s.90 and obtain substantive registration pursuant to that order. It is important to note that, unlike a charge completed by registration, protection of a charge by notice does not confer priority over any earlier unregistered charges (see G3.8.4).

3.9.8. Where a lender wishes the Land Registry to note on the register an obligation to make further advances, an application to enter the obligation should be made in Form CH2 unless the form of the charge incorporating the obligation clause has been approved by the registrar or the application is contained in panel 7 of Form CH1 (r.108).

Third party interests

3.9.9. Third party interests in registered land may now only be protected by the entry of either a notice or a restriction. A person must not apply for entry of a notice or restriction without reasonable cause. A duty of care is owed to any person who suffers damage in consequence of its breach (s.77).[1]

3.9.10. A notice is used to protect interests that will not be overreached on a disposition (for example, restrictive covenants and equitable easements) and will therefore continue to affect the land. A notice may be either an agreed or a unilateral notice. Certain interests are excluded from protection by way of notice (s.33). The main excluded interests are:

(a) an interest under a trust of land;

(b) a lease for a term of three years or less which is not required to be registered; and

(c) a restrictive covenant between lessor and lessee so far as it relates to the property leased.

Where an interest protected by a notice is valid then the notice will protect the priority of that interest. The notice itself does not confer any priority.

3.9.11. Where a restriction is entered on the register, a disposition cannot be registered otherwise than in accordance with the terms of the restriction. A restriction may be used, for example:

(a) to reflect any limitations on the proprietor's powers;

(b) to require that the proceeds of sale of land held on a trust of land are paid to at least two trustees or a trust corporation thus overreaching the beneficial interests under the trust; or

(c) to ensure that any required consents to a disposition are obtained.

A restriction, however, cannot be entered for the purpose of protecting the priority of an interest which could be protected by notice (s.42(2)).

Agreed notices

3.9.12. An application for an agreed notice is to be made in Form AN1 (r.81). The proprietor's consent is normally required for an application for an agreed notice. An agreed notice may also be used without the proprietor's consent if the registrar is satisfied as to the validity of the claim (s.34(3)). In practice, this might be the case where there is, for example, an application relating to a document signed by the registered proprietor, such as a contract for sale or an equitable charge. If the document contains prejudicial information an application could be made to designate it an exempt information document (see G3.12).

3.9.13. There are some special cases (for example, a home rights notice and an inheritance tax notice) which can be protected only by agreed notice (r.80).

Unilateral notices

3.9.14. An application for a unilateral notice must be made on Form UN1 (r.83). The application will be considered on the basis of the statutory declaration or conveyancer's certificate in the Form UN1. The instrument giving rise to the claimed interest need not accompany the application. Where the contents of the instrument are confidential, it is advisable not to lodge a copy in any event, as the Land Registry may file the copy thus making it open to public inspection (see G3.12.1). A unilateral notice is entered without the consent of the registered proprietor. A unilateral notice must indicate that it is such a notice and identify who is the beneficiary of the notice. Where the registrar enters a unilateral notice in the register, notice of the entry will be given to the registered proprietor who may at any time apply for its cancellation using Form UN4. Notice will not be served on the beneficiary of the unilateral notice on registration of a disposition. The unilateral notice remains on the register until such time as it is cancelled or withdrawn in Form UN2.

Restrictions

3.9.15. An application for a restriction is to be made in Form RX1 save where the application is for a standard form of restriction and the application is made in:

    (a)   the additional provisions panel of Forms TP1, TP2, TR1, TR2, TR4, TR5, AS1, AS2 or AS3;

    (b)   panel 8 of Form CH1 or in an electronic legal charge;

    (c)   a charge, the form of which (including the application for the restriction) has first been approved by the registrar;

    (d)   clause LR13 of a Prescribed Clauses Lease (see K1.20); or

    (e)   Form SEV for entry of a Form A restriction.

The standard forms of restriction are those listed in Schedule 4 Land Registration Rules 2003 (as amended). Standard form restrictions should be used where possible to avoid the risk of a non-standard restriction being rejected on the grounds that its form is unreasonable or that its application would not be straightforward (s.43(3)).

3.9.16. An application for a restriction must be accompanied by full details of the required restriction. If the restriction requires notice to be given to a person, requires a person's consent or certificate or is a standard form of restriction that refers to a named person, that person's address for service must be provided (r.92).

3.9.17. The application may be made by the registered proprietor or with his consent. A third party who can show a sufficient interest can also make an application (s.43(1) and rr.92 and 93).

3.9.18. The Rules list persons who are to be regarded as having a sufficient interest for this purpose (r.93). These include a person with a beneficial interest under a trust of land, a person who has applied for a freezing order and a person with the benefit of a charging order over a beneficial interest under a trust of land. The corresponding standard forms of restriction are set out in Schedule 4 to the Rules.

3.9.19. For further information see Land Registry Practice Guide 19.

1. For an example of a declaration by the Court that a notice had been applied for without reasonable cause, see *Anderson Antiques (UK) Ltd* v. *Anderson Wharf (Hull) Ltd* [2007] EWHC 2086 (Ch).

3.10. Adverse possession

3.10.1. Under Schedule 6 Land Registration Act 2002 a squatter on registered land is able to apply for registration if adverse possession has been enjoyed for at least 10 years. The application must be made in Form ADV1 and be accompanied by a statutory declaration or statement of truth meeting the requirements of r.188 Land Registration Rules 2003.

3.10.2. If the application appears to be in order, notice will be served on the owner, chargee and other interested parties. A person in receipt of a notice has the following options:

(a) he can take no action. If no response is received to the notices, the applicant will be registered as the owner of the registered title;

(b) he may object to the application on the basis that the applicant has not been in adverse possession for 10 years. In the absence of agreement the dispute will need to be resolved judicially (s.73);

(c) he may serve a counter-notice on the registrar requiring that the matter be dealt with under Schedule 6, paragraph 5 of the Act.

3.10.3. Where a counter-notice has been served, the applicant can only be registered if he meets one of three conditions. Summarised, these are that:

(a) an equity by estoppel has arisen by reason of which the applicant should be registered as proprietor;

(b) the applicant is for some other reason entitled be registered as proprietor; or

(c) the squatter is the owner of adjacent land and has been in adverse possession of the land in the application under the reasonable but mistaken belief that the land belonged to him.

3.10.4. Where an application is rejected, then, if still in adverse possession, the squatter may re-apply in two years' time. If the owner has not either evicted the squatter or agreed terms within that period then on re-application the squatter will be registered in place of the owner.

3.10.5. Where a squatter has been in adverse possession of registered land for at least 12 years prior to 13 October 2003, he may apply for registration under the transitional provisions in Land Registration Act 2002 (Sched.12, para.18). Such an application is not affected by the provisions of the Act summarised above.

3.10.6.   Further information as to the Land Registry's requirements is contained in Land Registry Practice Guides 4 and 5.

3.11.   Applications generally

3.11.1.   Applications for first registration are dealt with in G3.4. Applications for registration of transfers, charges and other dispositions of registered land are dealt with in G3.9. Applications based on adverse possession are considered in G3.10. This section deals with the more general matters relating to applications to the Land Registry.

Land Registry Forms

3.11.2.   The current prescribed forms are set out in Schedules 1 and 1A Land Registration Rules 2003 (as amended). Except for form CH1 the use of these forms is mandatory. For further information on prescribed forms and their use see A21.4 and Land Registration Practice Guide 46.

Evidence of identity

3.11.3.   Forms FR1, AP1 and DS2 require evidence of identity to be included on many applications. Full details of the Land Registry's requirements are set out in Land Registry Practice Guide 67.

Proper office

3.11.4.   An application for registration must be delivered to the proper Land Registry office. Care must be taken to send the application to the proper office (and within the priority period conferred by any official search). Lodging documents at the wrong office may result in loss of priority for the application or at worst no registration at all. See Land Registry Practice Guide 51 which details the areas served by each Land Registry Office. A search facility is also available online at **www.landregistry.gov.uk**. This enables a search to be carried out by county/district or postcode. The addresses of Land Registry Offices are listed in Appendix IX.1.

Time of delivery

3.11.5.   An application for registration is to be taken as made at the earlier of:

    (a)   the time of the business day that notice of it is entered on the daylist;[1] or

    (b)   (i)   midnight on the day of receipt (if received before 12 noon on that day); or

    (ii)   midnight on the day after receipt (if received after 12 noon) (r.15(1)).[2]

Address for service

3.11.6. A registered proprietor must give the registrar at least one postal address for service, whether or not in the United Kingdom, to which the registrar may send notices and communications. Two further addresses for service may be given. They must be either a postal address, inside or outside the United Kingdom, a Document Exchange address in the United Kingdom (provided that delivery can be made on behalf of the Land Registry under existing arrangements between the Land Registry and the service provider), or an electronic address (r.198). See also Land Registry Practice Guide 55. It is important that addresses for service are kept up to date as these are the addresses to which all formal notices will be sent.

Duty to disclose overriding interests

3.11.7. A person applying for either first registration or registration of a registrable disposition must provide the registrar with information as to certain overriding interests which affect the estate. The Act lists separately those interests that override first registration and those that override registered dispositions (see Land Registration Act 2002, Scheds.1 and 3). The information is to be provided in Form DI. See s.71 and rr.28 and 57.

3.11.8. The provision of this information will enable the interests to be noted on the register and they will, as a result, lose their overriding status.

3.11.9. This disclosure obligation relates only to interests within the actual knowledge of the applicant; and does not extend to, for example:

    (a)   an interest arising under a trust;

    (b)   a lease for a term of three years or less which is not required to be registered;

    (c)   a local land charge;

    (d)   a public right; and

    (e)   on first registration, an interest that is apparent from the deeds and documents of title accompanying the application.

Capacity

3.11.10. Joint buyers are required to state on their application for registration whether they will hold the land as beneficial joint tenants or beneficial tenants in common. In the latter case a restriction in Form A will be entered in the proprietorship register of the title. Where the parties are to hold as tenants in common, a separate document may have been drawn up prior to completion indicating the proportionate shares which each tenant in common holds in the property because the register will not record the beneficial interests. This document is not submitted to the registry with the application for registration of the title but should be retained safely to avoid later disputes over the shares in the beneficial interests in the property (see A9).

3.11.11. On registration of a company the application form needs to be completed with the company's registered number. For overseas companies, the application should also state its territory of incorporation and be accompanied by evidence of the company's powers to hold, sell, mortgage and otherwise deal with the land. The evidence may consist of a certificate in Form 7 or Form 8 (r.183 and Sched.3).

3.11.12. In other situations the solicitor may have to satisfy the registrar as to the capacity of the applicant to enter the transaction, for example, housing associations, charities, building societies.

3.11.13. If the transferee of a registered title dies before registration of his interest has been completed, the deceased's equitable interest in the property passes to his personal representatives who may continue the application in their names on production of the grant of representation to the registrar (r.18).

Applications not in order

3.11.14. If an application is not in order the registrar may raise such requisitions as he considers necessary (r.16(1)). Any requisitions raised will:

    (a)   explain what is needed;

    (b)   state when the application will be cancelled if a full reply is not received (the period for complying with the requisitions will be not less than 20 business days from the date of the requisition); and

    (c)   explain what to do if a reply cannot be made by the cancellation date.

3.11.15. Extensions to the cancellation date can be made, particularly when the cause is outside the applicant's control. The Land Registry will need to know:

    (a)   the reason for the delay;

    (b)   what is being done to resolve the problem; and

    (c)   when it is expected that a full reply to the requisition can be supplied.

3.11.16. If an application appears to the registrar to be substantially defective, he may reject it on delivery or he may cancel it at any time thereafter (r.16(3)). Some examples of where this might occur are:

    (a)   applications where the original transfer, lease, charge or other primary document is not lodged and no reasonable explanation for its absence is supplied;

(b)   dispositions for which a compulsory form is prescribed (for example, TR1 for a transfer of whole) where that form has not been used;

(c)   on an application in respect of a land transaction if not accompanied by a land transaction return certificate or submission receipt where one is required; and

(d)   applications that have been previously rejected or cancelled if the outstanding points remain unresolved.

3.11.17. For more information on the Land Registry's cancellation and rejection policy, see Land Registry Practice Guides 49 and 50. See also Practice Guide 68 as to the Land Registry's requirements and cancellation and rejection policy when amending deeds which effect dispositions of registered land.

The Land Registry's early completion policy

3.11.18. An application for a discharge of whole is considered by the Land Registry to be substantially defective if evidence of satisfaction of the charge is not lodged either with or in advance of the application. The Land Registry will reject such an application.[3]

3.11.19. Where such a defective application is made with other applications, e.g. the registration of a transfer of whole and a new charge, those applications will be completed (provided they are in order) and the defective discharge application rejected. The existing registered charge entry will remain on the register of title until an application for discharge accompanied by evidence of satisfaction of the charge is completed.[4] If a restriction has been registered in favour of the existing chargee preventing registration of a disposition without the chargee's consent, the Land Registry will requisition for evidence of discharge or evidence of the chargee's consent.

Completion of applications

3.11.20. Any entry in, removal of an entry from, or alteration of the register made as a result of an application has effect from the time of the making of the application (r.20) and not from the time of completion of the registration.

3.11.21. A title information document is issued by the Land Registry where an application leads to a change of ownership. The title information document does not constitute a guarantee of title and it does not need to be lodged on the registration of any dealing with the land.

3.11.22. Where panel 8 of the application form AP1 has been completed with the name and address of a third party the Land Registry will send notification of completion of the application to the third party.

Retention and destruction of documents

3.11.23. On completion of any application the registrar may retain all or any of the documents that accompanied the application (r.203(1)). However, if when making the application the applicant or his conveyancer requests the return of any of the documents sent with the application and provides certified copies of those particular documents with the application, the registrar must return the original documents so requested on completion of the application. On an application for first registration, however, an applicant need only provide certified copies of any statutory declaration, statement of truth, subsisting lease, subsisting charge, certificate relating to Stamp Duty Land Tax and the latest document of title (r.203(2)–(5)).

3.11.24. The registrar has power to destroy any documents which have been retained by him, if he is satisfied that either he has made and retained a sufficient copy of the document or that its further retention is unnecessary (r.203(6)).

Objections

3.11.25. Any person may object to an application to the registrar (s.73(1)). The objection must be in writing, signed by the objector or his conveyancer, state the ground for the objection and give the full name of the objector and an address for service complying with r.198 (see r.19). The objection must be delivered to the appropriate office.

3.11.26. A person who objects to an application must not do so without reasonable cause; and owes a duty to any person who suffers damage in consequence of its breach (s.77). If the objection is not groundless and cannot be disposed of by agreement it must be referred to the Adjudicator to HM Land Registry (see G3.13).

3.11.27. See Land Registry Practice Guides 37 (objections and disputes) and 38 (costs).

1. The daylist shows the date and time at which every pending application was made (r.12).
2. See Land Registration Rules 2003, r.15(2) and (3) as to receipt of applications on non-business days and as to the deemed delivery of applications.
3. Land Registration Rules 2003, r.16(3).
4. See Land Registry Practice Bulletin 16 and Practice Guide 31. See also the Law Society's Practice Note 'Land Registry early completion' (9 July 2009) which provides guidance on how early completion will operate and gives advice on how to proceed with the different applications.

3.12. **Access to information**

3.12.1. Section 66 provides that any person can inspect and make copies of:

    (a) the register of title;

    (b) any document kept by the registrar which is referred to in the register of title;

(c) any other document kept by the registrar which relates to an application that has been made to him; or

(d) the register of cautions against first registration.

Excepted documents

3.12.2. The general right to inspect and make copies of documents kept by the registrar does not apply to excepted documents as defined in r.133. These include:

(a) exempt information documents (see G3.12.3);

(b) any document relating to an application for a network access agreement (see A22.3.2);

(c) any documents provided to the registrar as evidence of identity of any person (but not Forms AP1, DS2 and FR1);

(d) certain documents which relate to the prevention or detection of crime.

Exempt information documents

3.12.3. Any person may apply to the registrar for a document to be designated an exempt information document if he claims that the document contains prejudicial information (r.131).

3.12.4. The application must be made in Forms EX1 (the application form) and EX1A (the reasons in support) and be accompanied by an appropriately certified copy of the document which excludes the prejudicial information (r.136(2)). If the registrar is satisfied that the applicant's claim is not groundless and that completing the application would not prejudice the keeping of the register, he must designate the document an exempt information document (rr.136(3) and (4)).

3.12.5. When so designated, the general right to inspect and make copies relates to a copy of the exempt information document from which the prejudicial information has been excluded (this copy is known as an edited information document (r.131)). The exempt information document and Form EX1A are excluded documents.

3.12.6. An application can be made for an official copy of an exempt information document. The application must be made in Form EX2. In most cases the registrar will serve notice of the application on the person who applied to exempt the document before deciding whether or not to issue an official copy of the exempt information document. And exemption does not prevent an application for inspection or an official copy being made under the provisions of Freedom of Information Act 2000.

Historical copies of the register

3.12.7. The registrar may, on application in Form HC1, provide information about the history of a registered title. Historical editions of the register are available where the register is held in electronic form (r.144).

Index of proprietors' names

3.12.8. The Registry maintains an index of the names of the proprietors of registered estates and registered charges (r.11(1)). An application can be made in Form PN1 for a search to be made in respect of:

- the applicant's own name;

- the name of a company or other corporation aggregate;

- the name of some other person in whose property the applicant can satisfy the registrar that he is interested generally (for instance as trustee in bankruptcy or personal representative (r.11(3)).

In other cases, the court has power to allow a search of the index to assist a third party in enforcing a judgment.[1]

Further information

3.12.9. See also Land Registry Practice Guide 57 (Exempting documents from the right to inspect), Public Guide 1 (Information that can be obtained from the Land Registry) and Public Guide 15 (Freedom of Information Act 2000).

1. See *Parkinson* v. *Hawthorne* [2008] EWHC 3499 (Ch).

3.13.   **The Adjudicator to HM Land Registry**

3.13.1. The Office of the Adjudicator to HM Land Registry is established by the Act (Part 11 and Sched.9). The Adjudicator is independent of the Land Registry and is part of the Tribunals Service.

3.13.2. The Adjudicator determines references made to him by the registrar where there is a dispute between a person who has made an application to the registrar and some other person (s.73(7)). The Adjudicator can decide a matter himself or direct a party to commence proceedings in the court to determine the dispute (s.110).

3.13.3. The Adjudicator also hears appeals from a decision of the registrar relating to the entry into or termination of a NAA.[1]

3.13.4. The Adjudicator also has power, on application, to make any order which the High Court could make for the rectification or setting aside of a document which:

(a) effects a qualifying disposition of a registered estate or charge;

(b) is a contract to make such a disposition; or

(c) effects a transfer of an interest which is the subject of a notice in the register.

A qualifying disposition is a registrable disposition or one which creates an interest which may be the subject of a notice in the register (s.108).

3.13.5. Proceedings before the Adjudicator are governed by Adjudicator to Her Majesty's Land Registry (Practice and Procedure) Rules 2003 (SI 2003/2171) as amended by Adjudicator to Her Majesty's Land Registry (Practice and Procedure) (Amendment) Rules 2008 (SI 2008/1731).

3.13.6. A requirement made by the Adjudicator is enforceable as an order of the court.

3.13.7. Further information, appropriate application forms and guidance is available at **www.ahmlr.gov.uk**.

1. See s.108(1)(b) and Network Access Appeal Rules 2008 (SI 2008/1730) and see also A22.3.4.

H. LENDERS

H1. Acting for the lender

1.1. Introduction

1.1.1. Matters relating to the solicitor who is acting for a lender client are dealt with in context in other sections of this book. The following paragraphs draw together some of those points in the form of checklists for ready reference.

1.1.2. In many cases the solicitor acting for the lender will also be acting for the borrower in a related sale or purchase transaction. In such a case the principles of conduct relating to conflict of interests and confidentiality must at all times be observed (see A11).

1.2. Instructions to act

1.2.1. Even where instructions are received from a lender for whom the solicitor acts frequently, it should not be assumed that the instructions in the current transaction are identical to those issued on previous occasions.

1.2.2. Instructions to act must be carefully checked in each particular case and any queries clarified with the lender. If at any time during the course of the transaction it appears that compliance with the lender's instructions will not be possible, further instructions must immediately be sought.

1.2.3. In many cases where the loan is connected to residential property the solicitor will be instructed to act in accordance with the terms of the CML Lenders' Handbook or BSA Mortgage Instructions.[1] Part 1 of the CML Lenders' Handbook and Parts A–F of the BSA Mortgage Instructions contain provisions which are applicable to all transactions. These provisions may be varied by individual lenders according to Part 2 of the CML Lenders' Handbook or the special instructions in the BSA Mortgage Instructions and/or in special instructions supplied to the solicitor with the lender's letter of instruction. Where applicable, the CML Lenders' Handbook or the BSA Mortgage Instructions set out the terms of the contract between the solicitor and the lender and the conditions must be closely observed.

1.2.4. A solicitor may only act for a lender where the lender's instructions do not extend beyond the requirements contained in Rule 3.19 Solicitors' Code of Conduct 2007 (see Appendix I.1).

1. The CML Lenders' Handbook and the BSA Mortgage Instructions are available online at **www.cml.org.uk** and **www.bsa.org.uk**.

1.3. Creation of new mortgage – checklist

(a) Check instructions to ensure that all conditions attached to the advance can be complied with by both the solicitor and the borrower and that the instructions comply with Rule 3.19 Solicitors' Code of Conduct 2007.

(b) If the lender is not a building society, confirm with him the rate of charging for acting for him and who is to be responsible for payment of the solicitor's bill.

(c) Check that the terms of the contract to purchase are acceptable – does the purchase price in the contract accord with that shown on the lender's instructions?

(d) If the mortgage is being granted to a sole borrower, what are the lender's instructions relating to non-owning occupiers? Has any relevant consent form been signed?[1]

(e) Have adequate enquiries been made to ensure that there are no overriding interests over the property which will adversely affect the lender's security?

(f) Inform lender of exchange of contracts and of contractual completion date if necessary.

(g) Check that the property will be properly insured from the moment of exchange or completion (as appropriate).

(h) Has investigation of title been completed satisfactorily (including the results of pre-contract searches and enquiries) – have all the lender's specific requirements been met?

(i) Engross mortgage deed and obtain borrower's signature(s) to it. Where there are joint borrowers one or more of whom is not known personally to the solicitor, precautions should be taken to verify the signature of the unknown borrower(s) in order to guard against forgery, e.g. by requiring the document to be signed in the presence of the solicitor.[2]

(j) Engross and obtain borrower's signature to assignment of life policy (where appropriate).

(k) Ensure that life policy in terms which comply with lender's instructions is in existence.

(l) Are results of pre-completion searches satisfactory, including a clear result of a bankruptcy search against the names of the borrower(s) and a company search against a company seller?

(m) Send a report on title/certificate of title to the lender and request the advance cheque.[3]

(n) On receipt of advance cheque pay it into clients' account – ensure funds have been cleared before completion.

(o) Make arrangements for completion.

(p) If required, arrange for inspection of property immediately before completion to ensure vacant possession will be given.

(q) Arrange for transmission of funds on day of completion.

(r) Inform lender of completion.

(s) Obtain purchase deed and title deeds from borrower's solicitor on completion with cheque for SDLT and Land Registry fees.

(t) Date and fill in blanks in mortgage deed and related documents.

(u) Send notice of assignment of life policy (in duplicate) to insurance company.

(v) Give notice to prior lender(s) (if second or subsequent mortgage).

(w) Attend to payment of SDLT.

(x) Register the creation of the charge on form MG01 at Companies House.

(y) Submit application for registration of title within relevant priority period.

(z) Keep lender informed of the reason for any delays at the Land Registry.

(aa) Prepare schedule of deeds for lender.

(bb) Send deeds to lender (or as instructed) and request return of receipted schedule of deeds.

1. A signed deed or form of consent must be obtained from all occupants aged 17 or over (CML Lenders' Handbook, para.7.3). Also note that the CML Lenders' Handbook states at para.8.3 that the solicitor must not advise anyone who is intending to occupy the property regarding the signing of the consent. Arrangements must be made for them to see an independent adviser.
2. See the requirements relating to identification in the CML Lenders' Handbook, para.3. The signature must be checked against one of the documents specified in the Handbook. Also, see para.11.3 of the Handbook where it states that it is considered good practice if the signature of a document that needs to be witnessed is witnessed by a solicitor, a legal executive or a licensed conveyancer.
3. For special procedure on the completion of a mortgage over a new property see I.1.8.

1.4.   Redemption of mortgage – checklist

(a) Request redemption figure from lender and title deeds if unregistered. If the seller has a 'flexible mortgage' ask for the account to be frozen until after completion (see F3.7.4).

(b) Make a search to check if there is a subsequent chargee to whom the title deeds should be handed on completion.

(c) Check instructions from lender on their receipt.

(d) In the case of a related sale prepare epitome of title and send to borrower's solicitor (if unregistered land and lender's solicitor is not also acting for borrower).

(e) In the case of a related sale keep in touch with borrower's solicitor about arrangements for completion.

(f) Prepare Form DS1[1] (or receipt in unregistered land).

(g) Prepare reassignment of life policy (where relevant).

(h) Prepare undertaking for discharge of mortgage to be given to buyer's solicitor on completion.

(i) Prepare forms for discharge of land charges entries (second and subsequent mortgages of unregistered land).

(j) Obtain final redemption figure from lender and inform borrower's solicitor of the figure.

(k) Arrange with borrower's solicitor for actual payment on completion.

(l) On receipt of repayment money, clear draft through clients' account and account to lender in accordance with redemption statement.

(m) Hand over undertaking for discharge of mortgage to buyer's solicitor.

(n) Send Form DS1 (or receipt in unregistered land) and deed of reassignment of life policy to mortgagee for execution and return. In the case of non-building society lenders, request that documents are dated with the date that completion of the mortgagor's sale took place to avoid problems over inadvertent transfer of the mortgage (see D2.10).

(o) On receipt of executed Form DS1 (or receipt), check it before sending to buyer's solicitor and request to be released from the undertaking given on completion.

(p) Return life policy to borrower.

1. See G1.10 and G1.11 as to electronic discharges (EDs) and electronic submission of discharges (e-DS1s).

1.5. Mortgage not simultaneous with purchase – checklist

(a) Obtain official copy entries of the title/title deeds.

(b) Make relevant pre-contract searches and enquiries including a search to find out whether prior mortgages exist (see B10).

(c) Make enquiries about non-owning occupiers and obtain signature of consent form/release of rights in accordance with lender's instructions (see H1.3).

(d) Investigate title to the property.

(e) Check the state of the prior mortgage account (if relevant).

(f) Ensure compliance with Consumer Credit Act 1974, s.58 where applicable (see H3.4).

(g) Draft, then engross mortgage deed.

(h) Send report on title/certificate of title to lender with request for advance cheque.

(i) Explain the effect of and obtain borrower's signature to mortgage deed.

(j) Make pre-completion searches, including bankruptcy search against name of borrower, and obtain clear results to searches.

(k) Ensure any conditions attached to offer of advance have been complied with.

(l) Arrange to complete.

(m) On completion hand advance money to mortgagor, date and fill in any blanks in mortgage deed.

(n) Protect lender's security by registration at Companies House and the Land Registry.

(o) Give notice to a prior lender (where relevant).

(p) Advise lender of completion of the mortgage.

1.6. Buy to let mortgages

Occasionally a condition is attached to a buy to let mortgage to the effect that the new tenancy must be agreed and the start date set prior to the completion of the mortgage. This is not always possible to achieve.

1.7. Incorrect redemption statements

Guidance has been issued jointly by the Law Society and Council of Mortgage Lenders in connection with problems arising out of incorrect redemption statements supplied by lenders (see Appendix IV.13).

H2. Sales by lenders

2.1. Power of sale

2.1.1. A lender may sell property over which he enjoys a power of sale and convey in his own name provided his power has both arisen and become exercisable. The existence and exercise of the power are discussed in B7.7.

2.1.2. A first lender sells free of all charges registered subsequent to his own; thus a buyer is not concerned with the discharge of second and subsequent mortgages when a power of sale is exercised by a first lender.[1]

2.1.3. If a second or subsequent lender wishes to sell he must either sell the property subject to any prior charges, or redeem them (thus becoming a first lender) but will overreach all charges which are subsequent to his own.

2.1.4. The lender must exercise his power in good faith for the purpose of obtaining repayment; subject to this, he can exercise his powers even if the exercise is disadvantageous to the borrower.[2] There is no wider duty in negligence.[3]

2.1.5. A lender must not sell to himself or to his nominee.[4] There is no rule that he cannot sell to a person connected with him[5] but the correctness of the price must plainly be beyond doubt, and the lender must have taken and acted on expert advice as to the best method of selling, what steps should reasonably be taken to make the sale a success, and what reserve price should be fixed.

2.1.6. It is usually inadvisable for the sale contract to be conditional or for an option to be granted, since there is a risk that the loan might be repaid and the borrower would then be entitled to a discharge of the mortgage. The borrower's equity of redemption, and his ability to redeem, is only destroyed when there is a binding unconditional contract for sale.[6]

2.1.7. If the mortgage is only over the beneficial interest of a joint owner, the lender will have to make application to the court under section 14 Trusts of Land and Appointment of Trustees Act 1996 for an order for sale. This order will not necessarily be granted by the court.

2.1.8. In the case of an equitable mortgage made by deed, there can be a power of sale provided the power has both arisen and become exercisable. However, there is doubt over whether the power relates to the legal estate vested in the borrower as well as the equitable estate vested in the lender and since the buyer usually requires both the legal and the equitable estate, additional conveyancing devices may be necessary. One option is for the borrower to give the lender a power of attorney and a declaration of trust over the legal estate. Also, the lender can apply to the court under section 90 Law of Property Act 1925 for an order conveying the property to the buyer or creating and vesting in the lender a legal mortgage to enable the lender to carry out the sale. See G3.9.6 as to the registration of legal charges relating to registered land.

1. Law of Property Act 1925, s.104 and Land Registration Act 2002, s.52.
2. *Kennedy* v. *De Trafford* [1897] AC 180. See also *Meretz Investments NV and Britel Corporation NV* v. *ACP Ltd* [2006] EWHC 74 where it was held that if a lender had mixed motives for exercising his powers of sale and one of the motives was to recover the debt secured by the mortgage, his exercise of the power of sale would not be invalidated.
3. *Downsview Nominees* v. *First City Corp.* [1993] 3 All ER 626.
4. *Farrar* v. *Farrars Ltd* (1888) 40 Ch 395.
5. *Tse Kwong Lam* v. *Wong Chit Sen* [1983] 3 All ER 54, PC.
6. *Property & Bloodstock Ltd* v. *Emerton* [1968] Ch 94.

2.2. Possession

2.2.1. Before selling the lender will normally take possession in order to be able to sell with vacant possession (or subject to any tenancies which bind him).

2.2.2. In the case of residential property it will be necessary to obtain a court order for possession unless the occupier leaves the premises voluntarily.[1] The court may impose a sanction on a lender that has failed to comply with the Pre-action Protocol for Possession Claims based on Mortgage Arrears in respect of Residential Properties if its failure to do so has resulted in unnecessary costs or proceedings.[2] A borrower who has suffered a temporary loss of income may also be eligible for the government's Homeowners Mortgage Support Scheme enabling him to defer payment of a portion of the interest payments on the mortgage for up to two years (see **www.communities.gov.uk** for further details).

2.2.3. A buyer from the lender is not concerned to see the court order authorising possession.

1. Protection from Eviction Act 1977, s.2.
2. See the Law Society's Mortgage Possession Claims Practice Note (updated 4 June 2009).

2.3. Price

2.3.1. Building societies are under a statutory duty to obtain the best price for the property.[1]

2.3.2. Other lenders must take reasonable precautions to obtain a proper price for the property.[2] Although there is a theoretical distinction between building societies and other lenders in relation to the price which they must obtain for the property, in practice the courts appear to apply similar criteria when applying each test.

2.3.3.   Sales by lenders commonly take place by auction but there is no legal requirement to this effect. A sale by auction does not necessarily constitute evidence
that the lender has obtained the best possible price for the property,[3] and the
lender's duty in this respect is not discharged by placing the property for sale in
the hands of reputable agents.[4]

2.3.4.   A sale at a sum which is sufficient only to pay off the mortgage would be looked
at carefully by the court.[5] Where the mortgage lender fails in its duty and the
property is sold at an undervalue, the mortgage lender will have to reimburse the
borrower for the loss suffered.[6]

2.3.5.   The fact that the property is resold to a third party shortly after the sale by the
lender and at a substantially higher price than that obtained by the lender would
also be viewed with suspicion by the court.[7]

2.3.6.   The borrower can challenge the amount of costs claimed by the lender by
making an application to the court for the taxation of the lender's costs.[8]

1.   Building Societies Act 1986, s.13(7).
2.   *Cuckmere Brick Co. Ltd* v. *Mutual Finance Ltd* [1971] Ch 949.
3.   *Tse Kwong Lam* v. *Wong Chit Sen* [1983] 3 All ER 54, PC.
4.   *Cuckmere Brick Co. Ltd* v. *Mutual Finance Ltd* [1971] Ch 949.
5.   *Midland Bank Ltd* v. *Joliman Finance Ltd* (1967) 203 EG 612; *Predeth* v. *Castle Phillips Finance Co.
Ltd* [1986] 2 EGLR 144, CA.
6.   *Mortgage Express* v. *Mardner* [2004] EWCA 1859.
7.   *Bank of Cyprus (London) Ltd* v. *Gill* [1980] 2 Lloyd's Rep 51.
8.   *Gomba Holdings (UK) Ltd* v. *Minories Finance (No.2)* [1992] 4 All ER 588.

2.4.   The sale transaction

2.4.1.   The sale follows the normal procedures for the sale of land, subject to any
specific requirements or instructions given by the lender client.

2.4.2.   Since the lender will have taken possession of the property (if at all) only shortly
before exercising his power of sale, he will have little or no knowledge of the
condition of the property and may not therefore be able to answer pre-contract
enquiries as fully as the buyer would wish. The buyer should be advised of this
fact and of any other special conditions attaching to the sale, e.g. requirement
for payment of a full 10% deposit. A selling lender will commonly require the
buyer to exchange contracts within a stated period, reserving the right to
withdraw from the sale if this condition is not met. This type of condition is
imposed because of the lender's duty to obtain the best price for the property. If
exchange of contracts became delayed, property values might in the interim
period have altered and the lender might find himself liable in an action for
breach of trust if he continued with a prospective sale in circumstances where
the market price of the property had risen and a better price would be obtainable
elsewhere.

2.4.3.   The lender's duty to both the borrower and to subsequent lenders to obtain the
best or proper price means that the lender is under an implicit duty to preserve

the value of the property by ensuring that it remains in good physical order. For this reason, the buyer should not be allowed access or entry into possession before completion. Standard Condition 5.2 (occupation by the buyer) or any similar provision, should therefore normally be excluded from the contract. If not so excluded a buyer does not have a *right* to occupy; he may only do so with the seller's consent.

2.4.4. The buyer can demand to see the mortgage deed under which the power of sale is being exercised in order to check the existence of the power and that it has arisen, but is not concerned to enquire whether circumstances exist which entitle the lender to exercise the power.

2.4.5. In the case of registered land, the transfer must be in Form TR2.[1]

2.4.6. The lender will need to consider which covenants for title (if any) he is prepared to give to the buyer in the purchase deed.

2.4.7. On completion of a sale by a lender, the mortgage under which the power is exercised is not 'discharged' although the buyer takes free from it. Where the land is unregistered, the buyer will receive the mortgage deed and other title deeds but not a mortgage receipt. Where the land is registered, the buyer will not receive a discharge in respect of the mortgage. Discharges (mortgage deeds and/or receipts in unregistered land) relating to subsequent mortgages (if any) do not need to be handed over on completion since the sale by the lender overreaches these subsequent charges.

1. Land Registration Rules 2003, r.58 and Sched.1.

2.5.   Proceeds of sale

2.5.1. The selling lender will discharge the debt owing to him, including interest and the costs of the sale, from the proceeds of sale.

2.5.2. If any surplus then remains, the selling lender holds the surplus on behalf of and must account to a subsequent lender. It is essential that the selling lender makes a search at the Land Registry (registered land) or the Land Charges Department (unregistered land) to discover whether or not subsequent mortgages exist before accounting to the borrower for the surplus proceeds of sale. In registered land, the selling lender is taken to have notice of anything in the register immediately before the transfer.[1] The buyer from the lender is not concerned to see that the lender deals properly with the surplus.

2.5.3. When considering the application of the proceeds of sale, a lender must have regard to any other security he holds for the mortgage debt (e.g. an endowment policy). The lender who sells in possession may not recover his entire debt (or an unfair proportion of it) from one security rather than another, even if he regards the property as his primary security, where this is to the detriment of a second lender who only has one type of security. So, for example, the lender may not take his entire debt from the property and hand the endowment policy back to the borrower, where this would result in the second lender on the property receiving nothing. The selling lender must recover his debt pro rata against all available security in his hands to achieve fairness between himself and any subsequent lender(s) and between subsequent lenders *inter se*.[2]

2.5.4.   In the event that there is a shortfall, the lender has a 12-year limitation period in which to bring an action against the borrower to recover the shortfall.

1.   Land Registration Act 2002, s.54.
2.   For a more detailed discussion of this rather esoteric doctrine of 'marshalling the assets' see *Fisher and Lightwood's Law of Mortgages*.

2.6.   Administrative receivers and administrators

2.6.1.   A properly appointed administrative receiver of a company (who must be a licensed insolvency practitioner) has power to sell a company's property but is personally liable on all contracts he enters into, unless the contract otherwise provides. He owes a duty to both borrower and lender to take reasonable care to obtain the best price which circumstances permit when selling the assets.[1]

2.6.2.   Where the charge was entered into on or after 15 September 2003 an administrator will be appointed (Enterprise Act 2002). The administrator is appointed by the court and has all the same powers of an administrative receiver and he acts as an agent of the company and an officer of the court in carrying out those duties. An administrator can make distributions to secured and preferential creditors (and with the consent of the court, to unsecured creditors). He can dispose of the floating charge property as if it were not subject to the charge but he must obtain the leave of the court to dispose of other secured property or to acquire property.

2.6.3.   For the Land Registry's requirements see Land Registry Practice Guide 36.

1.   *Gosling* v. *Gaskell* [1897] AC 575.

2.7.   Receiver appointed by lender

2.7.1.   The receiver need not be a licensed insolvency practitioner unless his position is classified as that of an administrative receiver (i.e. his responsibilities extend to substantially the whole of the company's assets and he is appointed under floating as well as fixed charges). The receiver is agent for the borrower company and is personally liable on his contracts unless the contract otherwise provides. The receiver will not automatically take possession of the company's property but is entitled to collect income accruing from it. He must apply that income as directed by section 109 Law of Property Act 1925. Rent collected by and in the hands of the borrower's managing agent may strictly not be classified as 'income' to which the receiver is entitled. To overcome this difficulty the receiver should as soon as practicable after his appointment give notice to all tenants and to the managing agent advising that all rent should be paid to the receiver as from that time. The receiver owes a duty to the borrower to carry out all rent reviews, lease renewals and other acts that a prudent landlord would do.[1] Where a receiver contracts to sell property owned by the borrower, the contract should provide for the purchase deed to be signed by the lender under his power of sale; this procedure will ensure that other interests in the property are overreached on completion.

1. See *Knight* v. *Lawrence* [1991] 1 EGLR 143.

H3. Second and subsequent mortgages

3.1.	**Introduction**	3.4.	**Consumer Credit Act 1974**
3.2.	**Registration of charges**	3.5.	**Tacking**
3.3.	**Power of sale**	3.6.	**Consolidation**

3.1.   Introduction

3.1.1.   The creation of a second or subsequent mortgage will not necessarily occur simultaneously with the purchase of the property over which the mortgage is taken.

3.1.2.   The solicitor acting for the borrower may also be instructed to act for the lender but not infrequently separate solicitors are instructed to act in this situation.

3.1.3.   The procedures to be followed by the lender's solicitor broadly follow the steps to be taken in a normal purchase transaction (except that there is no contract) since full enquiries about the property and its title must be made on the lender's behalf to ensure that he will obtain a viable security for his loan.

3.1.4.   A checklist of the steps to be taken when acting on a mortgage which is not simultaneous with a purchase is set out in H1.5.

3.1.5.   Mortgages sometimes contain a condition prohibiting the borrower from creating further charges over the property without that lender's consent. In such a case the requisite consent should be sought and obtained at an early stage in the transaction. A mortgage created in breach of such a condition is not itself invalid but will render the borrower vulnerable to repayment of the first charge.

3.2.   Registration of charges

3.2.1.   On completion of a mortgage of registered land the charge must be protected by registration at the Land Registry within the priority period afforded by the lender's search.

3.2.2.   The priority of registered charges in registered land depends on the order in which the charges are registered on the title; therefore registration within the priority period given by a pre-completion search certificate is essential.[1]

3.2.3.   An equitable mortgage must be in writing and signed by both parties in order to satisfy Law of Property (Miscellaneous Provisions) Act 1989, s.2.[2]

3.2.4. An equitable mortgage of registered land should be protected by registration of a notice at the Land Registry. If not so protected the lender is at risk of losing his priority to the holder of a subsequently created legal charge.[3]

3.2.5. A charge created by a company, whether fixed or floating and whether over registered or unregistered land, must be registered at Companies House under sections 860–877 Companies Act 2006 within 21 days of its creation (see E3.9.3).

3.2.6. In unregistered land a mortgage which is not accompanied by the deposit of title deeds must be protected by registration at the Land Charges Department by entry of a Class C(i) (for a legal mortgage) or Class C(iii) (for an equitable mortgage) land charge. By Law of Property Act 1925, s.198 registration constitutes actual notice to a third party for all purposes connected with the land; further, the date of registration governs the priority of mortgages. In order to effect registration at the earliest possible opportunity, a priority notice should be lodged at the Land Charges Department at least 15 working days before completion and the application for registration made within 30 working days of lodging the priority notice. This will ensure that registration is effective from the date of completion itself.

3.2.7. Notice of the mortgage should be given to prior lenders in order to ensure that they are actually aware of the existence of the new charge. The proprietor of a registered charge may make a further advance on the security of that charge ranking in priority to a subsequent charge if he has not received notice of the creation of the subsequent charge (from the subsequent chargee).[4]

1. Land Registration Act 2002, s.48 and see *Mortgage Corporation Ltd* v. *Nationwide Credit Corporation Ltd* [1994] Ch 49, CA.
2. *United Bank of Kuwait plc* v. *Sahib* [1996] NPC 12.
3. Land Registration Act 2002, s.29(1) and (2).
4. *Ibid.*, s.49(1).

3.3. Power of sale

3.3.1. Provided that he has a power of sale and that it has both arisen and become exercisable (see B7.7) there is no legal reason why a second or subsequent lender should not sell the property in order to realise his security.

3.3.2. In practical terms he may experience difficulty in selling the property. Although he will sell free of incumbrances ranking in priority subsequent to his own, he cannot sell free of prior incumbrances (although he may be able to redeem these on completion if the proceeds of sale are sufficient). He should therefore obtain an official copy of the register from the Land Registry (registered land) or make an official search at the Land Charges Department (unregistered land) to establish which incumbrances, if any, have priority over his own.

3.3.3. The sale of a property which is subject to a subsisting mortgage is not an attractive marketable proposition and the price attainable on such a sale may be low as a reflection of the existence of the mortgage over the property. The selling lender may therefore either have to persuade his prior lender to join with him in exercising the power of sale (assuming that the price obtainable would then be sufficient to discharge both debts) or discharge the prior mortgage out of his own funds before selling thus placing himself in the position of first lender. A contract for sale by a subsequent lender cannot prevent the prior lender selling the property in the meantime. This would put the second lender in breach of his sale contract. He needs to come to an arrangement with the first lender before exchanging contracts. That could either involve him redeeming the first mortgage beforehand out of his own money, or agreeing to discharge it on completion out of the proceeds of sale.

3.4.   Consumer Credit Act 1974

3.4.1.   Section 58 Consumer Credit Act 1974 is primarily of concern when dealing with the creation of second or subsequent mortgages in favour of finance houses.

3.4.2.   The section applies where:

    (a)   a mortgage is created over land;

    (b)   the mortgage is not taken out to finance the purchase of the land which is being mortgaged, i.e. a bridging loan or mortgage which is simultaneous with the purchase of land is not within this section;

    (c)   the lender is not exempt under Consumer Credit Act 1974, s.16 (most building societies, banks and insurance companies are exempt lenders);

    (d)   the mortgage is not exempt under Consumer Credit Act 1974, s.16A where the debtor is a person of high net worth;

    (e)   the mortgage is not exempt under Consumer Credit Act 1974, s.16B as one which is entered into wholly or predominantly for the debtor's business purposes where the credit provided exceeds £25,000.

3.4.3.   Where this section applies the creditor (lender) must supply the debtor (borrower) with a copy of the prospective mortgage agreement and related documents, e.g. assignment of life policy. Having done this, he must allow seven days to elapse before sending a further copy of the agreement and related documents to the debtor for signature by him. A further period of seven days must then elapse before the creditor is permitted to contact the debtor for any reason. Thus the debtor is given a 14-day 'consideration period' which runs from the date when the first copies of the agreement and related documents are sent to him in which to consider the prospective transaction free of influence from the creditor and if desired to take legal advice. During the whole of this time the creditor must not contact the debtor except to send him the signature copies of the agreement and related documents, although he may speak to or otherwise communicate with the debtor if the debtor contacts him first. Any communication between the creditor and debtor during this period must only be at the instigation of the debtor.

3.4.4. The consideration period can come to an end before the expiry of the 14 days if within that time the debtor signs and returns the agreement to the creditor.

3.4.5. For the purposes of this section, communications sent to or made with the debtor by the creditor's solicitor would be treated as being communications made by the creditor himself.

3.4.6. Failure to comply with the section or breach of its provisions renders the agreement improperly executed. This means that it cannot be enforced without a court order under Consumer Credit Act 1974, s.127. Such a court order would not necessarily be granted.

3.4.7. Because of the seriousness of the consequences of non-compliance with section 58, it is imperative that creditors and their solicitors comply with its requirements and do not contact the debtor while the consideration period is running.

3.4.8. Where it appears that the loan will be subject to the provisions of section 58, it is best for the parties to be represented by separate solicitors in order to avoid the problems outlined in this paragraph. The section causes particular difficulty where the same solicitor is acting for both parties to the transaction since it means that during the consideration period the solicitor is unable to contact his debtor client, even to advise him about the terms of the loan agreement. It is uncertain whether in such circumstances contact made by the solicitor with the debtor about a matter unrelated to the loan would infringe the terms of the section, but it would seem advisable not to contact the debtor client at all during this period.

3.4.9. Where the loan is subject to Consumer Credit Act 1974 a proper default notice under section 87 of the Act must be served before enforcement of the security. The court may then make a time order under sections 129–130 of the Act (these sections are similar in their effect to Administration of Justice Act 1970, s.36).[1]

1. See *Southern & District Finance v. Barnes* [1995] NPC 52.

3.5. Tacking

3.5.1. Tacking is the name given to the process by which a lender makes a further advance to the borrower and claims priority for repayment of both the original loan and the further advance over intervening lenders whose mortgages were created after the first loan but before the further advance.

Registered land

3.5.2. Registered charges are to be taken to rank as between themselves in the order shown in the register.[1] However, this general rule is affected by the provisions contained in Land Registration Act 2002, s.49. Under this section a chargee can make a further advance ranking in priority to a subsequent charge:

   (a) if he has not received notice from another chargee that a subsequent charge has been created;[2]

   (b) if the advance is made pursuant to an obligation and this obligation is recorded in the register;[3] or

   (c) where the parties to the original charge have agreed a maximum amount for which the charge is security and the agreement is entered on the register.[4]

3.5.3.   In other cases, tacking is only possible with the agreement of the subsequent chargee.[5]

Unregistered land

3.5.4.   Section 94 Law of Property Act 1925 allows a mortgagee to tack a further advance in three cases:

   (a) where the intervening lender agrees;

   (b) where his mortgage imposes on him an obligation to make a further advance;

   (c) where he had no notice of the intervening mortgage at the time of making the further advance. The registration of the intervening mortgage (whether legal or equitable) under Land Charges Act is notice for this purpose, except that if the first mortgage was made to secure a current account or other further advances, the mere registration of the intervening mortgage as a land charge is not of itself notice to the first lender to prevent tacking.

3.5.5.   It follows from (c) above that a second or subsequent lender of unregistered land should (as well as registering his mortgage as a land charge) give express notice of his mortgage to any prior lender in order to prevent the tacking of further advances by the prior lender.

3.5.6.   A further reason for giving such notice is to compel a first (or prior) lender to hand the title deeds to the later lender when the earlier mortgage is discharged. The earlier lender is bound to do this where he has notice of the later mortgage, but the mere registration of the mortgage as a land charge is not notice for this purpose.

1. Land Registration Act 2002, s.48.
2. *Ibid.*, s.49(1) and (2), and see Land Registration Rules 2003, r.107 as to when notice shall be treated as received.
3. Land Registration Act 2002, s.49(3).
4. *Ibid.*, s.49(4).
5. *Ibid.*, s.49(6).

3.6. **Consolidation**

3.6.1. Consolidation is the right of a lender to refuse to allow a mortgage on one property to be redeemed unless a mortgage on another property (or properties) is also redeemed. It is an equitable doctrine, based on the principle that it would be unfair to allow a borrower to redeem a mortgage over a valuable property and leave the lender with security on another property which was not worth the amount of the loan.

3.6.2. As it is an equitable doctrine, the borrower must be seeking to exercise his equitable right to redeem, i.e. the legal date for redemption on all the mortgages sought to be consolidated must have passed, and all the mortgages must originally have been created by the same borrower. At least one of the mortgages must expressly reserve the right to consolidate, i.e. it must expressly exclude the effect of Law of Property Act 1925, s.93 which restricts consolidation.

3.6.3. Provided the conditions set out in H3.6.2 are satisfied, a lender may consolidate provided that all the equities of redemption are in one hand (i.e. owned by the same person) and all the mortgages in another, or, that state of affairs having existed in the past, the equities (only) have become separated.

3.6.4. Because a second mortgage of land is in principle a mortgage of the equity of redemption of the first mortgage, the right, where it exists, can be exercised not only against the transferees of the land, but also against subsequent lenders.

3.6.5. A buyer who is taking land subject to an existing mortgage, or a subsequent lender of the land, should make enquiry as to the existence of mortgages on other land created by the same borrower, since the doctrine operates independently of notice and even the subsequent uniting of mortgages in one hand could cause prejudice to such a person.

3.6.6. A chargee who has a right of consolidation in relation to a registered charge on registered land may apply to the registrar for entry of a notice in the individual register of the registered titles affected to show that the specified registered charges are consolidated. The application must be made in Form CC.[1]

1. Land Registration Act 2002, s.57 and Land Registration Rules 2003, r.110.

H4. Certificates of title

4.1.   Definition

4.1.1.   A certificate of title is written confirmation given by a solicitor or other person qualified in the law of the country in which the property is situated as to the ownership of land or any interest in land.

4.2.   When will a certificate of title be required?

4.2.1.   A certificate of title may be used in any case where confirmation as to the title to property is required and is increasingly requested by mortgage lenders (but see H4.3.5). It may be appropriate to require that a certificate of title be given by or on behalf of the person who owns the land. As an alternative to a certificate it may be possible to deal with the title to the property by means of warranties given by the person owning the property or an investigation and report on the title by lawyers acting on behalf of the person who is seeking to ascertain the quality of the title.

4.2.2.   Examples of situations where a certificate may be appropriate:

(a)   the purchase of shares in a company;

(b)   the purchase of assets from a company;

(c)   flotation, mortgage, debenture or other security arrangements made by companies;

(d)   occasionally on a straightforward house purchase, if required by the mortgage lender.

4.2.3.   In order to avoid a possible breach of Rule 3.07 Solicitors' Code of Conduct 2007, where a seller's solicitor is asked to provide a certificate of title to the buyer's solicitor, it must be made clear that in providing the certificate the seller's solicitor is not acting on behalf of the buyer.

4.3.   Contents of certificate

4.3.1.   The person to whom the certificate is addressed is entitled to rely on its contents; thus the person giving the certificate can be held liable for inaccuracies in its contents. It is therefore important for the person giving the certificate to identify the recipient of the certificate and to know for what purpose the certificate is required. The giver may seek to limit his liability on the certificate to named recipients and/or to limit the validity of the certificate for a specified period, e.g. three months from its date.

4.3.2. The object of certification is not to give evidence of a perfect title but to provide an accurate description of the legal character of the property in question. Any material information or irregularities affecting the property should be stated in a schedule to the certificate.

4.3.3. To be of practical use to the recipient the certificate should deal with the following matters:

(a) ownership of the property;

(b) an adequate description of the property;

(c) its tenure with relevant details;

(d) the name of the current owner of the estate in land;

(e) whether the title to the land is good, marketable and unencumbered;

(f) whether there are any statutory orders, schemes or provisions detrimental to the property or its use;

(g) where appropriate, provisions relating to planning, highways, public health, etc., should be referred to;

(h) appropriate searches which have been made at the Land Registry, the Land Charges Department and the district council, and other relevant searches;

(i) which searches have not been carried out in order to give the recipient a complete picture of the title which he is accepting.

4.3.4. Although the certificate should be positive, a solicitor should qualify it to suit the circumstances where it has not been possible to obtain or to verify all the relevant information.

4.3.5. Where a certificate of title has been requested by a mortgage lender and the form has been provided by the lender, care must be taken to ensure that the certificate does not breach Rules 3.16 to 3.22 Solicitors' Code of Conduct 2007. These Rules apply whenever the solicitor is acting for the lender and borrower, or borrower only, in a standard mortgage as defined in Rule 3.17.

4.3.6. An annexe to Rule 3 Solicitors' Code of Conduct 2007 includes an approved certificate of title, which must be used when acting for both lender and borrower in a standard mortgage of property which is to be used as the borrower's private residence only. This certificate is set out in Appendix I.1.

4.4. City of London Law Society certificate of title

4.4.1. The City of London Law Society's (CLLS) standard form certificate of title has been designed to reduce negotiation over the form and content of such certificates. It is designed for use in connection with a number of commercial transactions, including secured loans, acquisitions of companies and businesses, flotations and privatisations. Some lenders insist on the certificate being used.

4.4.2.   The sixth edition of the certificate was updated in 2008 and is available from the CLLS website **www.citysolicitors.org.uk**.

4.4.3.   The Solicitors Regulation Authority has confirmed that the sixth edition of the CLLS certificate is recognised for the purpose of Rule 3.22(2) Solicitors' Code of Conduct 2007.

4.5.   Right to buy certificate of title

4.5.1.   Where land is being purchased under right to buy legislation, the Land Registry is bound to accept a certificate of title supplied by the seller, the seller being obliged to indemnify the Registry if the certificate turns out to be inaccurate.

I. NEW PROPERTIES

I1. New property

1.1.   Introduction

1.1.1.   A sale of a new property is a more complex transaction than the sale of an existing house or building, and some matters additional to those relevant to a sale of an existing house or building must be considered. The following paragraphs only deal with those matters which are exclusive to new properties.

1.2.   Consumer Code for Home Builders

1.2.1.   The Consumer Code for Home Builders is a voluntary code of practice for those involved in the building of residential properties, but is compulsory for builders and developers who are registered with certain home warranty providers (see I6).

1.2.2.   The Code is intended to provide additional consumer protection to individual home buyers who have made a reservation to buy a new or newly converted home on or after 1 April 2010. The Code sets out what information must be provided to home buyers and requires the home builder to monitor customer satisfaction. There is an associated redress scheme (see M6.15). Further information can be obtained from **www.consumercodeforhomebuilders.com**.

1.3.   The contract

1.3.1.   Where the property comprises a plot on a new building estate the contract will often be in standard form and the seller will be reluctant to allow substantial amendments to that form.[1] The buyer's solicitor should ensure that the contract does not impose unnecessarily burdensome terms on the buyer, sufficiently protects his client's interests and complies with any conditions required by the buyer's lender. The seller may require the deposit to be paid to him as 'agent' and not as 'stakeholder'. The consequences of this requirement should be explained to the buyer and the lender's consent to such a contractual condition obtained.

1.3.2.   A contract for the sale of a new property will frequently be a sale of part of the seller's existing property and may comprise a plot on a new building estate. In either case adequate provision must be made in the contract for the grant and reservation of easements to the parties and the property being sold will usually be described by reference to a plan which should be prepared in accordance with the Land Registry requirements (see J1 and B21).

1.3.3.   The contract should require the seller to complete the building works in accordance with the agreed specifications, planning permissions and plans submitted to the buyer. It may also contain a 'long stop' completion date requiring the builder to use his reasonable endeavours to complete the building works within a specified period so that, e.g. in the event of a prolonged strike by the workmen on site the buyer has the opportunity to rescind the contract. The buyer and his lender may wish to have a right to inspect the property during and at the completion of the building works.

1.3.4.   Where the property being sold is in the course of construction it may not be possible for the seller to agree a definite completion date at the time of exchange since he will not be able to guarantee that the building works will be completed by a specified time. In such a case he may prefer to include a condition in the contract providing for completion of the transaction to take place within a specified number of days after completion of the building works.[2] This type of condition may give rise to difficulties from the buyer's point of view since if he is involved in a chain of transactions such a condition will make it difficult to synchronise the chain, unless similar conditions relating to completion are imposed in every transaction in the chain. The buyer should therefore be advised of this difficulty and warned of the possibility that in the event of the transactions not being synchronised the buyer may either have to complete his dependent sale first and move into temporary accommodation pending completion of the new property, or be prepared to use bridging finance for the completion of the new property pending sale of the old one. Where completion is to take place within a specified number of days of completion of the building works, the buyer's solicitor should also ensure that the number of days provided by the contract gives the buyer's solicitor sufficient time in which to carry out his pre-completion searches and to arrange for the purchase price to be obtained and for a final inspection of the building by the buyer's lender's surveyor. In addition, the contract should provide that notice of the completion date cannot be given unless (as applicable) the new homes warranty cover note has been issued (see I1.8.5) and/or a completion certificate has been issued under the Building Regulations.

1.3.5.   Provision may be made for the seller to rectify minor defects in the building within a specified time after completion, although where the property is to be covered by a structural defects policy (see I1.6) this matter will usually be covered by such a policy. A contract to build a building is a contract for services within Supply of Goods and Services Act 1982 which implies a condition that the builder will provide his services to a reasonable standard and within a reasonable time if no time is specified in the contract.

1.3.6. The buyer should consider whether the contract should provide for the builder to remove all builder's rubbish from the site before completion, to leave the property in a clean and tidy condition, for the erection of boundary fences, and if appropriate for the landscaping of the gardens and surrounding areas.

1.3.7. New restrictive covenants will frequently be imposed on the buyer by the contract. From the seller's point of view, the imposition of the covenants will be done to allow the seller to maximise his ability to sell the remainder of the houses in the development. From the buyer's point of view, the imposition of such covenants provides the buyer with the certainty that the estate will be developed and will remain in a saleable condition without having to worry about unsightly or undesirable alterations carried out by neighbours to their properties. The wording of the covenants should be checked to ensure that they do not impose an unnecessary or burdensome restriction on the buyer's use and enjoyment of the property and their significance explained to the buyer (see E1).

1.3.8. The plan attached to the purchase deed should be signed by the seller and by or on behalf of the buyer.

1.3.9. Where there is to be a long delay between exchange of contracts and completion, the buyer's contract should be protected by registration (see C5.3).

1. The terms of the contract may be subject to Unfair Terms in Consumer Contract Regulations 1999 (SI 1999/2083) as amended by SI 2001/1186.
2. The building works will be 'complete' on the issue of a certificate of practical completion or on certification by the seller's architect. Habitation certificates are not generally now issued on completion of a building.

1.4. Planning permission

1.4.1. The erection of a new building will normally require both express planning permission and building regulation consent. Copies of the relevant documents should be supplied to the buyer's solicitor prior to exchange of contracts and should be checked by the client or his surveyor to ensure (as far as possible) that the erection of the building complies with the permissions and with any restrictions or conditions attached to them. If on the face of the planning permission there are reserved matters requiring the further consent of the planning authority, compliance with such matters should be checked by the buyer's solicitor. Where there is a short-term condition attached to the permission which affects the right to occupy the property (e.g. the property shall not be occupied until all estate roads have been completed) the contract must be checked to ensure that the completion date specified in the contract can, if necessary, be adjusted to take account of this restriction on occupation. The contract may contain a warranty given by the seller to the effect that he has complied with all restrictions and conditions attached to the planning permission.

1.4.2. In relation to work completed after 1 June 1992 it may be possible to obtain a certificate of completion of the building works from the local authority. The buyer should enquire whether such a certificate is available.

1.5. Roads and drains

Roads

1.5.1. The buyer's solicitor will need to check whether the roads and street lighting adjoining the property are publicly maintained or are intended to be so. Where the property forms part of a new building estate the seller (or developer) will frequently have entered into an agreement with the local highway authority under Highways Act 1980, s.38 whereby the highway authority will, after a certain period of time, adopt the highway and thereafter maintain it at public expense. Such an agreement should be supported by a bond which will guarantee sufficient money to allow the making up of the road to the proper standards required by the highway authority in case of default by the developer.

1.5.2. Where appropriate a copy of the section 38 agreement and bond should be supplied to the buyer's solicitor with the draft contract and the buyer's solicitor should ask his client whether he wants his surveyor to check the bond to ensure that the amount guaranteed by it is adequate to cover the cost of the outstanding roadworks.

1.5.3. In practice it is difficult to estimate the cost of the outstanding works and the buyer's solicitor may have to accept the bond which is offered without further investigation. The contract should contain provisions allowing the buyer and his employees, and others authorised by him, a right of access over the road pending its adoption. If no agreement and bond has been entered into, the road will remain in private ownership, maintainable at the expense of the owner. In such a case the buyer's solicitor must ensure that his client is given adequate rights of way to provide access to the property, and should ascertain that proper provisions are being made for the maintenance of the road and the likely cost of maintenance. The buyer and his lender must be advised accordingly.

1.5.4. Where the property forms part of a small new estate it is common for the roads to remain in the ownership of the seller (or developer). From the buyer's point of view, the contract should then contain a covenant for maintenance by the road owner (at the shared cost of the buyer and owners of other houses on the estate), with provision for the house owners to carry out the work and recover any charges from other liable contributors in the event of default by the road owner.

Such a provision may be dealt with by the imposition of an estate rentcharge under Rentcharges Act 1977 (see A25.6).

1.5.5. In appropriate cases the client should be advised of any potential liability to road charges arising out of section 219 Highways Act 1980 (where advance payments procedure has not been correctly followed by builder and local authority) or arising from the situation where (as is not uncommon) the local authority has released the builder from his bond in relation to part of the development but without formally adopting the roads in the part released.

Drains

1.5.6. Except where the property is being built in a rural area, the seller will normally have entered into an agreement and bond with the water authority under Water Industry Act 1991, s.104 for the ownership and maintenance of the drains to be transferred to the water authority within a certain time after completion of the building works. Similar considerations apply here as in relation to the maintenance of highways (see I1.5.1). If the drainage system is to remain in private ownership a drainage survey may be desirable to ensure that the system under construction will be adequate to service the property.

1.6. Insurance against structural defects

1.6.1. Most new residential properties will be offered with the benefit of structural defects insurance, which provides the buyer and his successors in title with insurance against structural defects in the property for a number of years after completion of the building. The contract will normally provide for such cover to be obtained by the seller without cost to the buyer and the appropriate insurance policy and other documentation should be supplied to the buyer on or before completion. The cover may not come into effect until the acceptance form is returned to the insurance provider.

1.6.2. The absence of such insurance cover may present the buyer with problems since it will frequently be a condition of the mortgage offer that cover is obtained. Even where the present buyer is not financing his purchase with the assistance of a mortgage, a subsequent buyer who buys the property within the first 10 years after its construction will expect to take the benefit of the policy, and thus the absence of such cover will restrict the potential both to mortgage and to resell the property.

1.6.3. The terms of the policies and their limitations should be examined in each case and their effect explained to the client. The explanatory notes furnished with the scheme documentation should be handed to the client.

1.6.4. It should be noted that subsidence is not generally covered by these schemes and so must be covered by the buyer's buildings insurance policy. The builder's liability under the schemes is often limited to the first two years after completion. After that time, the policy only covers structural defects. A structural survey of the property may be desirable immediately prior to the end of the two-year period.

1.6.5. Where a property is to be covered by a structural defects scheme a full survey may not be necessary, particularly if the property is still in the course of construction so that there is very little for the surveyor actually to survey. However, the usual mining and environmental searches (if applicable) should be undertaken. In some cases a surveyor may be asked to look at the plans for the prospective building to ensure that as far as can be ascertained the building is to be erected in accordance with the client's wishes and expectations.

Assignment of policy

1.6.6. The benefit of the policy can be assigned to a subsequent buyer of the property, although a formal assignment of the benefit of the policy may not always be needed.

1.6.7. Where the property is being constructed under the supervision of an architect (e.g. under a JCT contract), a lender may accept an architect's certificate of completion of the building in place of a structural defects policy, although in such a case it may be desirable from the buyer's point of view for the contract to contain warranties given by the seller as to the proper design and construction of the building. The insurance cover carried by architects will only provide indemnity if the architect has a valid current policy at the time when liability is notified to the insurers. If therefore the architect has died or ceased to practise since completion of the building and before liability is discovered there may be no insurance policy in force to meet the claim and the architect's own assets or estate may be insufficient to cover the liability.

1.6.8. Defective Premises Act 1972 implies a term into a contract to purchase a building in the course of construction that the building when built will be habitable.

1.7. Payment of purchase price

1.7.1. The contract should state clearly whether the buyer is required to pay an additional price for extras (e.g. a coloured bathroom suite) and, if so, how much.

1.7.2. Some builders require the purchase price to be paid in stages as the building works progress. In such a case the buyer's lender must be informed of this fact and his agreement sought to release the mortgage advance in accordance with the builder's requirements. For the buyer's protection, he may seek an equitable charge over the property to the extent of the instalments paid by him. Such a charge must be registered and the contract to purchase should also be protected by registration as an estate contract since completion is unlikely to follow quickly after exchange of contracts in this situation. The lender's consent should be obtained to the form of the contract prior to exchange.

1.7.3. Any retention made by the buyer's mortgagee, e.g. in respect of outstanding roadworks must be discussed with the buyer and arrangements made to cover the resulting shortfall in time for completion.

1.7.4. Where the new property is a single building, i.e. not part of an estate development, it may be advantageous for the buyer initially to enter a contract to buy the site alone, and then to have a second contract for the builder to build the house or other building. In such a case the builder would expect to take a charge over the site to secure payment for the building works.

1.8. Mortgages

1.8.1. In order to increase transparency as to the agreed price of new homes, the Council of Mortgage Lenders has introduced a requirement for a new 'CML Disclosure of Incentives Form' from the builder/developer of any new-build, converted or renovated property.

1.8.2. From 1 September 2008, part 2 of the CML Lenders Handbook (which sets out each lender's specific requirements as to the reporting of discounts and incentives) requires a solicitor acting for a lender to be in receipt of a CML Disclosure of Incentives Form before he can submit the Certificate of Title.

1.8.3. The CML Disclosure of Incentives Form requests information on all incentives and discounts offered by the builder/developer and is available on the CML website **www.cml.org.uk**. The form will be completed by the builder/developer and supplied to the lender's solicitor by the builder/developer's solicitor as part of the initial contract package. The lender's solicitor will then be required to report such information from the CML Disclosure of Incentives Form as the relevant lender requests in Part 2 of the CML Lender's Handbook.

1.8.4. The BSA Mortgage Instructions also require the full disclosure of cash and non-cash incentives for certain new build transactions. The form and guidance on it can be accessed via links on the BSA website, **www.bsa.org.uk**.

1.8.5. The CML Lenders' Handbook, para.6.6.1 and the BSA Mortgage Instructions paragraph C13 require structural defects insurance to be in place before the certificate of title is completed. However, paragraph 6.6.2 of the CML Lenders' Handbook and paragraph C14 of the BSA Mortgage Instructions also provide that where appropriate cover is not in place by this time, a new homes warranty cover note will be acceptable. A copy of this cover note must be obtained before the certificate of title is sent to the lender.

1.8.6. Problems may be encountered when clients want to obtain occupation of the property as early as possible as this procedure may lead to short delays. Clients should be advised at the outset that completion will not take place until this procedure has been carried out.

1.8.7. Problems may also be encountered in view of the fact that the cover note will be issued provided there are no 'red' (serious) defects in the property. This means that the cover note can be issued whilst there are still 'green' (minor) defects in the building. Solicitors should advise the client that completion may take place despite the existence of minor defects.

1.9. Building estates

1.9.1. This section does not deal in detail with site acquisition and development for which the reader should refer to a specialist work on the subject (e.g. *Property Development: a practical guide* (Law Society, 2010)).

1.10. Sustainability certificates

1.10.1. From 1 May 2008 until 21 May 2010, all new homes had to be rated against the standards contained in the Code for Sustainable Homes and where a new home was to be marketed in England, the home information pack had to include information on the sustainability of the home.[1] This was in addition to energy performance certificates (see A27).

1.10.2. On 21 May 2010, the requirement for a seller of a new home to provide a sustainability certificate was suspended.

1. See Home Information Pack (Amendment) Regulations 2008 (SI 2008/572), Explanatory Note.

1.11. Carbon reduction

1.11.1. Builders, developers and buyers of new large buildings will be conscious of the need to ensure that the owners and occupiers can participate effectively in the CRC Energy Efficiency Scheme (see A27).

1.12. Checklist for seller's solicitor

1.12.1. (a) Has the site been inspected to ascertain the boundaries of each plot and the extent of easements and reservations?

(b) Has planning permission been obtained?

(c) Has a section 38 agreement and bond been obtained in respect of the roads?

(d) Has a section 104 agreement and bond been obtained in respect of sewers?

(e) Who is responsible for building regulation control and who will issue the certificate of completion of the building?

(f) Is the seller to make (and regularly update) pre-contract searches or will this be each buyer's responsibility?

(g) Will the property be covered by structural defects insurance? Has the builder registered and handed to his solicitor the appropriate documentation? (See I1.6.) Ensure that an unqualified (i.e. unconditional) certificate will be issued.

(h) Has an estate plan been prepared and approved by the Land Registry?

(i) Has the form of transfer been approved by the Land Registry? This is not essential but may save time and requisitions from the Land Registry at a later stage.

(j) Has all the necessary pre-contract documentation been prepared and duplicated for each plot? (See I1.12.2.)

(k) Have arrangements been made with the seller's lender to release the plots from the charge?

(l) Has the builder complied with Construction (Design and Management) Regulations 2007 (SI 2007/320) (e.g. the appointment of a planning supervisor)?

(m) Has the builder provided a Disclosure of Incentives Form and an energy performance certificate?

1.12.2. Documents to be prepared and sent to the prospective buyer's solicitor for each plot on receipt of instructions:

(a) pre-contract enquiries with answers (may include Form TA8 New Home Information);

(b) pre-contract searches with replies (where the seller is to undertake this task);

(c) draft contract in duplicate (with buyer's name left blank);

(d) draft transfer in duplicate with plan attached (annexed to contract, buyer's name left blank);

(e) evidence of title;

(f) requisitions on title with answers;

(g) copies of relevant planning permissions and building regulation approval;

(h) copies of relevant section 104 and section 38 agreements and bonds;

(i)   structural defects insurance documentation where appropriate;

(j)   a copy of the plan of the property properly marked and coloured in accordance with Land Registry requirements, with a spare copy for search purposes;

(k)   if desired, a general information sheet for the buyer containing *inter alia* addresses of local authorities and other bodies with whom searches may need to be conducted and an explanation of the contract terms (including arrangements for deposit and completion);

(l)   a Disclosure of Incentives Form;

(m) covering letter.

12. Defects in new commercial buildings

2.1. Introduction

2.1.1. The owner or tenant of a new commercial building,[1] not being the party for whom the building was constructed or refurbished, will only be in a position to recover the cost of remedying defects to the building from the contractor or professional team (architect, engineer, etc.) if he has a contractual relationship with them.[2] He would, however, be able to sue the contractor or other professional in negligence for damages arising out of personal injury or damage to other property. To enable the subsequent owner to be able to sue the contractor or other professional for the cost of remedial works to the building, he needs to establish an enforceable contractual relationship with the contractor or professional who is to be sued.[3] This can be achieved either by creating new contracts between the subsequent owner/tenant and the contractor/professionals (these are usually called 'collateral warranties') or, where practical, by taking an assignment from the original owner of the building of his original contract(s) with the contractor/professionals. The subsequent owner/tenant might additionally seek a warranty from the original owner as to the condition of the building even in the current market, which may be difficult to obtain; sellers and landlords of new buildings understandably prefer the liability for defects to rest with the contractor/professionals.

Collateral warranties

2.1.2. A buyer or tenant of a new commercial building should, as a term of the contract, require the seller or landlord to procure that on completion collateral warranties in favour of the buyer/tenant are provided by the contractor and all professionals in the form approved by the buyer/tenant. In these the contractor/professionals warrant that they have to date exercised reasonable skill and care and (where work is unfinished at the time of the contract) agree to continue to do so. Other terms are generally included dealing with professional indemnity insurance, the limitation period, assignment and limitations on the warrantor's liability, for example where the defect was partly his fault and partly the fault of other parties.[4]

Assignment of original contracts

2.1.3. Where the whole development is being sold or let the buyer/tenant should consider requiring an assignment of the original contracts with the contractor/ professionals with a view to putting the buyer/tenant in a position to recover under these contracts for any breaches by the contractor/professionals.

2.1.4. In the following paragraphs references to 'A' are to the contractor, architect or other professional, 'B' is the original owner of the building who entered the construction (or as the case may be) contract with A (the 'A–B' contract), and C is the subsequent owner of the building who, having purchased from B, seeks to enforce a term of the A–B contract.

1. Not covered by a structural insurance policy.
2. *Murphy* v. *Brentwood District Council* [1991] 1 AC 398; *Department of the Environment* v. *Thomas Bates & Son Ltd* [1991] 1 AC 499.
3. *Ibid.*
4. For example, the precedents produced by the British Property Federation.

2.2. Method of assignment

2.2.1. The assignment is a chose in action which, by section 136(1) Law of Property Act 1925 must be in writing (between B and C) and notice of the assignment must be given to A. Notice of the assignment could be given by either B or C, but it is clearly in C's interests to ensure that it is done. A should be asked to sign and return one copy of the notice of assignment served on him in duplicate by C so that tangible evidence exists of the fact that notice was correctly given.

2.3. Types of assignment

2.3.1. The purpose of the assignment is to enable the benefit of the contract between A and B to be transferred to and enforced by C against A.

Novation

2.3.2. Where it is intended that obligations under the A–B contract should be assigned, a novation must take place. The assignment of one party's burdens or obligations can only be done with the consent of the other original contracting party. Therefore, for this to occur, a new contract, made between A, B, and C, will have to be entered into.

Sub-contract

2.3.3. A might enter a sub-contract with D (the sub-contractor) under which D agreed with A to perform some or all of A's obligations to B under the A–B contract. This is effectively an assignment of A's obligations without B's consent, but in this situation A always remains liable to B since the original contract between A and B has been neither novated nor discharged. Any defect in D's performance can therefore be remedied by an action by B against A. The main issue in this situation is whether B is bound to accept D's performance of the contract in A's place. Where the obligations to be performed by A are construed as 'personal services', B cannot be forced to accept performance from anyone other than the original contracting party, i.e. he is entitled to reject D's performance and treat A as being in breach of contract. An obligation to carry out building works has been held to be within the concept of personal services.[1]

Assignment of benefits or rights

2.3.4. Where there is a prohibition against the assignment of the benefit of the contract, that prohibition is effective to prevent the assignment unless the party with the burden of performance consents to it. Thus an assignment by A to C of the benefit of the A–B contract would require B's consent. This applies irrespective of whether the assignment is of accrued rights (e.g. existing breaches committed by B) or of future rights (e.g. the right to sue for breaches as and when they occur in the future).[2]

2.3.5. If assignment is not possible (because B will not consent) C's remedy lies in persuading A to take direct action against B. The contract between A and C should contain warranties to this effect given by A. The damages recoverable by A on C's behalf are not restricted to A's losses (which may be nominal since he will no longer have an interest in the property) but can include reimbursement of losses suffered by C.[3] The contract between A and C should also contain a warranty given by A to hold any damages recovered on behalf of C.

1. See *Southway Group Ltd* v. *Wolff* [1991] EGCS 82, CA.
2. *Linden Gardens Trust Ltd* v. *Lenesta Sludge Disposals Ltd*; *St Martins Property Corporation Ltd* v. *Sir Robert McAlpine Ltd* [1993] 3 WLR 408. See also *Darlington Borough Council* v. *Wiltshire Northern Ltd*, *The Times*, 4 July 1994, CA and *Alfred McAlpine Construction Ltd* v. *Panatown Ltd*, *The Times*, 11 February 1998.
3. *Ibid.*

2.4. Protection of subsequent owners

2.4.1. In view of the uncertainty demonstrated by the general law a subsequent owner of a building needs to ensure that he will have the right to recover his losses in the event of a later defect being discovered.

2.4.2. In residential property transactions, the property will normally be covered by a structural defects insurance policy which should provide adequate protection for the buyer.

2.4.3. In commercial situations a buyer from the original owner should ensure that his contract to purchase contains warranties given by the original owner, and that a valid novation or assignment with the contractor's consent takes place. Protection of the subsequent owner is a matter to which attention should be paid when the original owner is entering the original A–B contracts. If at that stage he can ensure that there is no prohibition against assignment in the A–B contract, the benefit of the A–B contract may more easily be assigned to C at a later stage.

2.4.4.   The distinction between the assignment of obligations and fruits of performance should not, however, be overlooked since the court seems to apply different rules to these two types of benefits.

2.5.   Contracts (Rights of Third Parties) Act 1999

2.5.1.   Contracts (Rights of Third Parties) Act 1999 permits a person or company who is not a contracting party to enforce a term of contract, as if he or it were a contracting party, unless the contract indicates that the actual parties did not intend such right of enforcement to arise. The term must be made for the third party's benefit and the third party must be identified in the contract by name, description or implication. The third party does not, however, have to be in existence at the time when the contract is made (e.g. a company not yet incorporated). The provisions of this Act may therefore provide a simpler method of enforcing warranties than that outlined above. Defences and exclusion clauses which would be available to a contracting party can be used against the third party who is seeking to enforce the contract. The Act can be expressly excluded from a contract. It should, however, be noted that where a third party is to benefit under the Act, the contract between the original contracting parties cannot be varied so as to affect the third party without the third party's consent. This provision, too, may be excluded from the contract.

J. SALES OF PART

J1. Sales of part

1.1. Introduction

1.1.1. A sale of part is a more complex transaction than the sale of the whole of the seller's interest in a particular piece of land, and some matters additional to those relevant to a sale of the whole must be considered. The following paragraphs only deal with those matters which are exclusive to sales of part.

1.2. Description of the land

1.2.1. The description of the land in the seller's existing register and/or title deeds may not suffice to describe the part of the land being sold and a new, accurate description of the property must then be devised to describe the land in the particulars of sale of the contract. It will usually be necessary to identify the land by reference to a plan (see B21.2 and J1.6.1 for the Land Registry's requirements). There may be circumstances in which it is useful for the seller's solicitor to inspect the property prior to drafting the contract.

Retained land

1.2.2. Reference will usually have to be made to the land which is to remain in the ownership of the seller after the sale off, e.g. in relation to easements and reservations; such land must therefore also be defined verbally in the contract and marked clearly on the plan attached to the contract.

1.2.3. Where the sale is of part of a registered title and comprises a plot on a building estate, the seller will frequently have deposited an estate plan at the Land Registry and the official copies which are issued will give a certificate of inspection in Form CI in lieu of a title plan.[1] Where the estate plan procedure is used it is important that it is strictly adhered to in order to avoid difficulties. In addition the solicitor should emphasise to his builder client that if revisions are made on the ground to the layout shown on the approved estate plan, the builder should notify the solicitor immediately so that the solicitor can inform the Land Registry and submit a revised estate plan.

1. Land Registration Rules 2003, rr.134 and 143.

1.3.   Grants and reservations

1.3.1.   On a sale of part of land Law of Property Act 1925, s.62 and the rule in *Wheeldon* v. *Burrows*[1] may give the buyer as easements certain rights over the land which are continuous and apparent, are necessary for the reasonable enjoyment of the land sold, and which had been and are at the time of the sale used by the seller for the benefit of the part sold. Although Law of Property Act 1925, s.62 and the rule in *Wheeldon* v. *Burrows* will give the buyer such easements and quasi-easements as were previously enjoyed by the land before its division, the existence and extent of these implied rights may not be entirely clear and, for certainty, such matters should be dealt with expressly in the contract. Easements which pass by the operation of these provisions cannot give the buyer any right which the seller has no power to grant, and do not create any better title to any right than the seller is able to transfer. It will therefore usually be necessary to grant new express easements to the buyer, e.g. for a right of way or drainage. Express easements which are to arise in the future must comply with the perpetuity rule.

1.3.2.   Section 62 Law of Property Act 1925 and the rule in *Wheeldon* v. *Burrows* only operate in the buyer's favour. There is no reciprocal section or case which entitles the seller to easements over the land being sold off (other than easements of necessity). For this reason it is important to consider what rights the seller will need to exercise over the land being sold, e.g. passage of cables, drainage, etc., and to reserve these expressly in the contract.

1.3.3.   Rights of light and air may pass to the buyer under either Law of Property Act 1925, s.62 or the rule in *Wheeldon* v. *Burrows*. The acquisition of such rights by the buyer may have adverse consequences for the seller since the buyer might be able by exercising such rights to prevent the seller from building on his retained land. It is therefore usually considered necessary to exclude the buyer's right to easements of light and air by an express condition in the contract which provides for the insertion of a provision to this effect in the purchase deed.[2] Standard Condition 3.4 and Standard Commercial Property Condition 3.3 both contain a provision to this effect.

1.3.4.   Standard Condition 3.3 and Standard Commercial Property Condition 3.3 both provide for the mutual grant of easements and reservations on a sale of part, but the rights given by these conditions are limited and will in most cases be inadequate to deal effectively with the parties' requirements on a sale of part of land.

1.3.5.   In registered land, a proprietor who claims the benefit of a legal easement or profit à prendre which has been acquired by implication (or prescription) may apply for it to be registered as appurtenant to the registered estate.[3]

1. (1879) 12 Ch 31.
2. See *Emmet and Farrand on Title*, Chapter 15.
3. Land Registration Rules 2003, r.74.

1.4. Imposition of new covenants

1.4.1. In many cases the seller will wish to impose new covenants on the buyer, e.g. restricting the future use of the land. Provision for the imposition of new restrictions must be made expressly in the contract.

1.4.2. Covenants which are imposed on the sale of a new house on a building estate will usually comply with the terms of a building scheme.[1] In other cases, the enforceability of such restrictions against a subsequent purchaser of the land depends on their being negative in substance, expressly taken for the benefit of the seller's retained land, and protected by the entry of notice in the charges register of the title (or as class D(ii) land charges in unregistered land).[2] Positive covenants may be indirectly enforced through a chain of indemnity covenants but their burden does not run with the land. Where the contract expressly provides for a covenant to benefit a subsequent owner the subsequent owner may be able to enforce the covenant (whether positive or negative) through Contracts (Rights of Third Parties) Act 1999. This Act is not retrospective in operation.

1. See *Re Dolphin's Conveyance* [1970] 1 Ch 654.
2. *Tulk* v. *Moxhay* (1848) 2 Ph 774.

1.5. Consent of seller's lender

1.5.1. Where the land to be sold comprises part of the land which is mortgaged to the seller's lender, the seller must, at the earliest possible opportunity, obtain his lender's consent to the transaction. It should be ascertained from the lender whether the lender requires repayment of the whole or any part of the principal sums owing out of the proceeds of the sale of part and, if part, how much. Arrangements must be made for the lender to discharge the land being sold from the mortgage. In registered land the discharge is in Form DS3 (accompanied by a plan to show the extent of the land being released if not sufficiently defined on the title plan). In unregistered land the lender may either give a deed of release, or he may prefer to be joined as a party to the conveyance in order both to release the land being sold and to give a receipt for the money being paid to him.

1.6. The purchase deed

Registered land

1.6.1. A transfer of part will be drawn up to reflect the contract terms. The transfer must be in Form TP1 or TP2. The seller's title number is used in panel 1 of the transfer form, a new title number being allocated to the land sold off on registration of the sale of part. A transfer of part must have attached to it a plan identifying clearly the land dealt with. However, if the land dealt with is identified clearly on the title plan of the registered title, it may instead be described by reference to that title plan.[1] (See B21 for a detailed explanation of the Land Registry's requirements on plans.) The transfer should be executed by the transferor; and by the transferee if it contains transferee's covenants or declarations or contains an application by the transferee (e.g. for a restriction). In the case of joint transferees, the transfer must be executed by each of them.[2] The transfer plan need only be signed by the transferor.[3] The buyer's pre-completion search at the Land Registry should be made on Form OS2 accompanied by a plan in duplicate or should refer to a Land Registry approved plan and plot number supplied by the seller.

Unregistered land

1.6.2.   The conveyance will reflect the terms of the contract. Although a plan is not essential in unregistered land, it is highly desirable in cases where only part of the seller's estate is being sold and should be signed by both parties. Where the transaction will be submitted for first registration after completion, see B21 for a detailed explanation of the Land Registry's requirements on plans. Since the seller will be retaining the documents of title an acknowledgement for production and undertaking for safe custody (where appropriate) of the deeds should be included in the conveyance.[4] Where the seller is selling other than as beneficial owner, only an acknowledgement will be given. The undertaking is not given by owners who are selling in a fiduciary capacity. Where the land is subject to a mortgage the seller may be required to give a covenant that he will give the statutory undertaking for safe custody of the deeds as and when they come into his possession. Where the buyer is entering into a covenant in the deed (whether for indemnity or to observe fresh restrictive covenants) he must execute the purchase deed.

1.6.3.   Commonly the draft purchase deed will be prepared by the seller and annexed to the draft contract so that the buyer in fact has limited scope for negotiating its contents.

1.   Land Registration Rules 2003, r.213(1) and (4).
2.   See the prescribed forms of transfer in Land Registration Rules 2003, Sched.1.
3.   Land Registration Rules 2003, r.213(2).
4.   See Law of Property Act 1925, s.64 and Standard Condition 4.6.5 and Standard Commercial Property Condition 6.6.5.

1.7.   **Completion and post-completion**

1.7.1.   Where the land is unregistered, the seller will not be handing over his title deeds to the buyer on completion; the buyer should therefore verify his abstract or epitome against the original deeds and mark his abstract or epitome as examined against the original (see F4). Even where the title to the land bought is to be registered immediately after completion this procedure is necessary so that the buyer can produce proper evidence of the title to the Land Registry with his application for first registration. Additionally, a memorandum of the sale off should be noted on the most recent of the seller's retained title deeds to prevent a second sale of the same land by the seller.[1] A note of any restrictive covenants imposed by the conveyance to the buyer (or a copy of that conveyance) should also be retained by the seller. New restrictive covenants will automatically be entered on the register of the new title on first registration.

1.7.2. Where the seller's title is already registered it is not necessary to provide for an acknowledgement for production of the deeds nor for a memorandum to be endorsed on the seller's deeds since the buyer will obtain his own title number on registration of the sale of part. An acknowledgement is needed where the sale is of part only of a lease or where the purchase deed is to be executed in duplicate. New restrictive covenants imposed or rights reserved by the transfer of part will automatically be entered on the charges register of the new title on registration. Similarly, any new rights granted by the transfer will automatically be entered in the property register.[2]

1.7.3. A lender who has custody of the title deeds will give an acknowledgement for their production. Such an acknowledgement may be contained in the deed of release supplied by the lender but is not necessary when dealing with registered land.

1.7.4. In some cases where new covenants are being imposed the contract will require the buyer to prepare the purchase deed in duplicate, the duplicate copy will be handed to the seller as a record of the transaction. An acknowledgement for production is required in this situation.[3]

1. See Law of Property Act 1925, s.200.
2. Land Registration Rules 2003, r.72(2).
3. See Standard Condition 4.6.5 and Standard Commercial Property Condition 6.6.5.

1.8. Checklist of matters to be considered on sale of part

Easements in the buyer's favour

1.8.1. (a) To what extent will Law of Property Act 1925, s.62 and/or the rule in *Wheeldon* v. *Burrows* imply easements in the buyer's favour?[1]

(b) Is it necessary to extend the implied easements by granting express rights to the buyer?[2]

(c) What does the buyer need? For example:

(i) rights of way;

(ii) right to lay new cables/pipelines/drains;

(iii) right to use/maintain existing or new pipelines/cables/drains.

Rights of way

1.8.2.   (a)   Will the right be to pass over the land in both directions or should it be restricted to one way only?

(b)   Should the right be restricted, e.g. to a particular class of user, e.g. pedestrian only?

(c)   Is the exercise of the right to be restricted, e.g. use only for a particular purpose or only at a specified time of day?

All easements

1.8.3.   (a)   Is the route of the right of way/drain, etc., specified on the plan?

(b)   Who is liable for maintenance/repairs?

(c)   Will it be necessary for the buyer to enter the seller's land to inspect the state of repair and/or to maintain?

(d)   Should the buyer's access to inspect be restricted, e.g. a right to inspect on 24 hours' notice except in case of emergency?

(e)   Should the buyer be under an obligation to cause no unnecessary damage and to make good any damage done while inspecting/maintaining?

(f)   Where the buyer is to construct a new pipeline/cable, etc., should he be required to finish the construction works within a specified period after completion?

Reservations

1.8.4.   (a)   Remember the seller generally gets nothing under the implied grant rules.

(b)   After completion will the seller need to continue to use a right of way/drain/pipeline/cable passing through the land being sold?

(c)   If so, express reservations must be included in the contract by way of special condition. The same considerations in drafting apply as above.

(d)   Additionally, to protect the seller, it may be considered necessary to include a general reservations clause in his favour dealing with all easements, quasi-easements, etc., presently enjoyed by the land as a whole.

(e)   Should rights of light and air be expressly reserved in order to preserve the seller's freedom to use the retained land in the future?[3]

Existing covenants

1.8.5.   Is an indemnity clause required?[4]

New covenants[5]

1.8.6. (a) Should new restrictive covenants be imposed?

(b) If so, what type of restrictions will serve to protect the seller's land without imposing unnecessary constraints on the buyer?

(c) Consider:

    (i) erection of new buildings on the land;

    (ii) use of the land;

    (iii) repair/maintenance of buildings or land;

    (iv) general covenant against nuisance.[6]

(d) Will the covenants be negative in nature?

(e) Do the words used ensure that the covenants will create an enforceable obligation?

Description of the property in the contract

1.8.7. (a) Does the wording of the particulars accurately describe the land being sold?

(b) Has the seller's retained land been precisely defined?[7]

(c) Is there reference in the particulars to a plan?

(d) Is the plan of sufficient size and scale to be able to delineate accurately both the area of land being sold and the routes of easements, etc.?

(e) Does the plan comply with the Land Registry's requirements (see B21)?

Seller's lender

1.8.8. (a) Will it be necessary to obtain the lender's consent to the sale – if so has this been obtained?

(b) How will the lender deal with the release of the land being sold from the mortgage?

Registration of title

1.8.9. The seller should consider including a clause in the contract requiring the buyer's solicitor to supply the seller's solicitor with a copy of the buyer's registered title (when registration has been completed) so that the seller's solicitor may check that all new easements, covenants, etc. have been correctly entered on the new title. The seller may also wish to consider requiring the buyer to complete panel 8 in the application form AP1 with the seller's name and address so that the Land Registry will notify the seller when the transfer application has been completed.

1. Section 62 Law of Property Act 1925 may operate to create easements over retained land where at the time of sale the two tenements are in separate occupation. Further, the rule in *Wheeldon* v. *Burrows* (1879) 12 Ch 31 will impliedly grant to the buyer as easements all rights which are continuous and apparent and reasonably necessary to the reasonable enjoyment of the property sold. These provisions will normally have the effect of giving the buyer fewer easements than he requires, but in some cases may give him more than the seller intends. It is therefore considered safer to negate the effect of these rules in the contract and to deal with easements by way of express grant.
2. Since the extent of the implied easements created by the implied grant rules is not always clear, these matters are better dealt with by way of express condition. Standard Condition 3.4 and Standard Commercial Property Condition 3.3 deal briefly with easements but do not normally give adequate rights to the buyer; hence the need for express special conditions.
3. Standard Condition 3.4 and Standard Commercial Property Condition 3.3 reserve rights of light and air to the seller.
4. Standard Condition 4.6.4 and Standard Commercial Property Condition 6.6.4 require indemnity covenants but it is common to include an indemnity clause by way of special condition in order specifically to draw the requirement to the buyer's attention. See E1.
5. See E1.
6. Nuisance is a tort actionable at common law; therefore the imposition of such a covenant may strictly be unnecessary.
7. Inspection of the property may assist with these matters. It may also be desirable to peg out the boundaries to the property or to ask a surveyor to confirm that it is possible to plot the site.

K. LEASEHOLDS

This section deals only with those matters where the considerations applicable to leasehold property differ from the requirements outlined in other sections of this handbook relating to freehold land.

Some problem areas, e.g. licences to assign, are confined exclusively to the context of leaseholds and these are discussed within this section of the handbook.

A summary of the law relating to security of tenure and the right to buy is included, but the handbook does not contain a comprehensive guide to these topics.

The first group of paragraphs within this section deal with matters which are applicable to most leases, whether short or long and whether of business or residential premises. Then follow paragraphs dealing with a specific type of lease or tenancy and, finally, paragraphs on specific points which affect leasehold land such as the right to buy, options, and liability on covenants.

The Land Registry's requirements are set out in the following Practice Guides, which can be viewed and downloaded from the Land Registry's website **www.landregistry.gov.uk**:

- 25. Leases – when to register
- 26. Leases – determination (and addendum)
- 27. The leasehold reform legislation
- 28. Extension of leases
- 64. Prescribed clauses leases

K1. Acting on grant of lease

1.1. Taking instructions

1.1.1. There are a number of key issues upon which thought, advice and instructions will be needed when acting on the grant or acceptance of a lease. There can be no standard approach; instead the details of the property and letting in question must be carefully considered.

1.1.2. Subject to the above, much of the information required by the landlord's solicitor from his client will be similar to that required from the seller in the case of a freehold transaction.

1.1.3. When acting for a landlord or tenant, a solicitor should draw his client's attention to, and explain, lease provisions which may be of importance to the client and influence the client's decision whether or not to accept the proposed terms.

Code for Leasing Business Premises

1.1.4. In appropriate cases, the client's attention should be drawn to the Code for Leasing Business Premises. The latest version of this voluntary code was introduced in March 2007 and contains 10 recommendations for landlords, a guide for occupiers and model heads of terms.[1] In conjunction with the Code the Commercial Landlords Accreditation Scheme has been formed. Landlords who join the scheme agree to be bound by certain rules, which include that they will abide by the Code.[2]

Model leases and model lease clauses

1.1.5. The British Property Federation and the British Council for Offices have produced a set of 'model lease clauses' for possible use in commercial leases.

The clauses cover eight topics: rent, outgoings, repair and maintenance, alterations and signage, disposals, insurance, costs and rent review. They are designed to provide a fair compromise between landlord and tenant.[3]

1.1.6. The Law Society's Standard Business Leases are also available for use as precedents in appropriate cases and are intended to comply with the Code for Leasing Business Premises.[4]

1.1.7. The government has produced precedents and guidance notes for short term lettings to encourage the letting of empty town centre retail premises by, e.g. charitable groups. These are called 'Meanwhile Use' leases.[5]

1.1.8. The use of so-called 'green leases' is now beginning to emerge. These are leases that impose various types of environmental obligations on the parties.[6]

1. A copy of the Code can be obtained from www.leasingbusinesspremises.co.uk. The government commissioned research into the effectiveness of the Code on which it reported in June 2009 (see **www.communities.gov.uk**).
2. For further details and a list of members see **www.clascheme.org.uk**.
3. A copy of the model lease clauses can be obtained from **www.bpf.org.uk**.
4. The leases are available for purchase from law stationers.
5. These are available from **www.communities.gov.uk**.
6. One example is the Green Leases Toolkit produced by the Better Buildings Partnership available from **www.betterbuildingspartnership.co.uk**.

1.2. Demised premises

1.2.1. The lease must clearly define the extent of the demised premises. A detached building standing in its own ground should cause no problems of description but care is needed when letting parts of a building, e.g. flats or suites of offices. See B21, K1.20 and K6.1.2 for the Land Registry's requirements.

1.2.2. As far as possible express provision should be made relating to the ownership of walls, floors, ceilings, etc.[1] In the absence of express provision the following presumptions apply:

    (a) external walls – these are included in the demise even if the landlord is responsible for their repairs;[2]

    (b) internal walls – there is no presumption in respect of the internal boundary walls dividing one flat from another or the flat from common parts;

    (c) floors and ceilings – the flat includes the ceiling at least to the underside of the floor joists to which the ceiling is attached;[3]

    (d) the ownership of the roof area should also be specifically dealt with since if this is not done it may be possible for the tenant of a top floor flat to claim occupation of the roof space and to carry out alterations to the roof space against the landlord's wishes.[4]

1. It is possible to create an 'eggshell' tenancy in which the demise only includes the airspace defined by reference to the area contained within the surfaces of the walls, floors and ceilings. See *Pumperninks of Piccadilly Ltd* v. *Land Securities Ltd* [2002] 21 EG 142.
2. *Sturge* v. *Hackett* [1962] 3 All ER 166.
3. *Ibid.* and see *Phelps* v. *City of London Corporation* [1916] 2 Ch 255. Joists are likely to form part of the structure; see *Marlborough Park Services Ltd* v. *Rowe* [2006] EWCA Civ 436.
4. See *Davies* v. *Yadegar* [1990] 09 EG 67 and *Haines* v. *Florensa* [1989] 09 EG 70.

1.3.   Easements – grant

1.3.1.   Consideration must then be given to whether the tenant will require easements over the landlord's adjoining property in order to use the demised premises. The tenant might, e.g. need the right to use a private road in order to gain access to the premises or to use conducting media on the landlord's adjoining land to bring services from the mains supply to the demised premises. The tenant of a flat or suite of offices will certainly need such rights over the remainder of the building.[1]

1. Where such rights are not granted this will depress the rent in a commercial lease at renewal under Landlord and Tenant Act 1954 – see *J Murphy & Sons Ltd* v. *Railtrack plc* [2002] 19 EG 148.

1.4.   Easements – reservation

1.4.1.   The landlord will need to consider if he or others claiming title under him will wish to exercise rights over the demised premises because, if so, an express reservation should be included. An example would be part of a driveway which is included within the demised premises but which is required to be used by the landlord and his other tenants.

1.5.   Length of the term to be granted and tax consequences

1.5.1.   Apart from the parties' wishes, consideration must be given to the SDLT consequences of the length of the term and also to the possible effect of security of tenure legislation on the lease which may affect the seller's ability to recover possession at the end of the term (see K5, K7 and K8). Where a short lease of a dwelling is to be granted, the effect of the landlord's implied repairing obligations under Landlord and Tenant Act 1985, ss.11–14 must also be borne in mind (see K1.7.2). The term created must be of certain duration but, subject to security of tenure legislation, it may be made determinable on a certain event.[1]

1.5.2.   Rent will usually be taxed as income.[2] Where a premium is charged for the grant of a lease this will be deemed to be a part disposal for Capital Gains Tax (CGT) purposes and liability to this tax may arise. However, where a lease is granted for a term not exceeding 50 years some or all of the premium will be treated as income of the landlord and will therefore be left out of account for CGT purposes. The landlord is treated as receiving rent calculated by reference to a formula that relates the premium to the length of the term.

1. *Prudential Assurance Co. Ltd* v. *London Residuary Body* [1992] 3 All ER 504.
2. Income Tax (Trading and Other Income) Act 2005, ss.276–307 (individuals); Corporation Tax Act 2009, ss.217–223 (companies).

1.6. Amount of rent and rent reviews

1.6.1. The purpose of a rent review is to ensure that the rent payable during the term of the lease reflects changes in the value of the property in the market place, and changes in the value of money itself, e.g. because of general inflation. Rent can be reviewed by a number of different mechanisms, e.g. by a fixed amount, by being linked to a price index or by being valued by a valuer on the basis of the state of the open market at the point of review. The Law Society's Standard Business Leases 2008 provide the parties with two options: a market rent review clause as the default option, or an alternative index-linked rent review clause.

1.6.2. Some statutory limitations on the amount of rent recoverable may be applicable where the lease is an assured tenancy or a protected or statutory tenancy (see K5).

1.6.3. Rent review provisions should be carefully checked by both landlord and tenant. In commercial leases reviews every five years or so are common. A rent review within, broadly, the first five years will require further SDLT returns to be made (see A14.15.14).[1] In long residential leases fixed increment reviews every 25–30 years are more usual. Without an enforceable rent review provision the landlord will not be able to increase the rent during the term of the lease. Rent review provisions in commercial leases are often complex, but they must specify the period at which each review is to take place, and a formula for determining the amount of rent to be paid after each review date with a fall-back procedure (e.g. arbitration) in case of dispute.

1.6.4. A landlord prefers a clause which provides for 'upwards review' only so that the rent payable after the review date can never be less than that which was payable before the review date. The Code for Leasing Business Premises recommends that rent reviews should generally be to open market rent and discourages landlords from automatically inserting upwards only clauses (see K1.1.4). However, the benefit to a tenant of a rent review to open market rent, i.e. one that can fix a new rent more or less than the old rent, can easily be lost if the lease enables only the landlord to initiate the rent review.[2]

1.6.5. It is also common to provide that the new rent, whenever determined, shall be payable as from the review date in question so that where a rent review goes to arbitration and the new rent is not determined until some time after the actual review date, the tenant should be advised to place some money in a deposit account on each rent day so that he will be able to meet the cost of the reviewed rent when it is finally determined. Delay in implementing a rent review generally will not, of itself, be a bar to implementing a rent review in the future. For example, in one case it was held that a period of 12 years delay did not disentitle a landlord from implementing a rent review in the absence of some other factor, e.g. estoppel.[3]

1.6.6. Whilst there is a general presumption that time is not of the essence in rent review clauses, this is subject to any indication to the contrary in the wording of a lease.[4] One indication would be where deeming provisions stipulated that a failure to take a particular step would have certain consequences, e.g. a clause that provided that following the service of a notice by the landlord specifying a particular increase, if no counter notice is served by the tenant by a particular deadline the increase becomes payable.[5] Further, some leases will have break clauses which are operative in the tenant's favour at review dates, thus enabling the tenant to bring the lease to an end before the contractual term date if the rent payable after the review is more than he can afford to pay. A link between a break right and a rent review clause might impliedly make time of the essence in respect of any time limits that may be contained in the rent review clause.[6]

1. Finance Act 2003, Sched.17A, para.7A provides, in effect, that where a rent review falls in the three months before the end of the fifth year of the term this is treated as taking place after the fifth anniversary for the purposes of SDLT.
2. See *Hemingway Realty Ltd* v. *The Clothworkers' Company* [2005] EWHC 299; [2005] 11 EG 181.
3. *Idealview Ltd* v. *Bello* [2009] EWHC 2808 (QB).
4. *United Scientific Holdings Ltd* v. *Burnley Borough Council* [1978] AC 904.
5. See *Starmark Enterprises Ltd* v. *CPL Distribution Ltd* [2001] EWCA Civ 1252 and *Secretary of State for Communities and Local Government* v. *Standard Securities Ltd* [2007] EWHC 1808 (Ch).
6. *Central Estates Ltd* v. *Secretary of State for the Environment* [1997] 1 EGLR 239; *United Scientific Holdings Ltd* v. *Burnley Borough Council* [1978] AC 904.

1.7. Common express covenants

To pay rent

1.7.1. The covenant should be clear as to the amount of rent, the intervals of payment, whether payable in advance or in arrear, whether the rent includes outgoings on the property, provisions for increase of the rent and payment of VAT (see A16.7).

To repair

1.7.2. In certain residential cases the landlord will be obliged by statute to keep the structure and exterior of the premises in repair.[1] In all cases, an express covenant to repair should precisely identify the obligations required of the party responsible for undertaking the repairs including, in the case of redecoration obligations, the intervals at which the work is to be undertaken. Where the demised premises form part of a larger building the landlord (or in the case of a flat perhaps a management company) will usually covenant to keep the structure and common parts of the building in repair. See, for example, Law Society

Standard Business Lease (Whole of Building) (Registered) 2008 clause 5. Note that under Defective Premises Act 1972, s.4 where a landlord has an express or implied obligation for the repair or maintenance of the premises, the landlord may, in certain circumstances, owe a duty to take reasonable care to see that all those who might reasonably be expected to be affected are safe from injury or damage. However, this obligation does not extend to a duty to make safe by remedying potential safety hazards.[2]

Gas and electrical equipment

1.7.3. Gas Safety (Installation and Use) Regulations 1998 require gas appliances to be installed and maintained by competent personnel and regularly inspected. Work should be done by a person registered on the Gas Safe Register which replaced the CORGI scheme.[3] Landlords of relevant residential premises are under an obligation to carry out an annual inspection of such appliances (even where the lease places full repairing obligations on the tenant). These provisions apply to leases for a term of less than seven years (including periodic tenancies) and any statutory tenancy arising out of such a lease. The duty also extends to relevant premises held under a licence. A lease which contains a landlord's break clause, exercisable within the first seven years of the term, falls within these provisions but a lease which contains a tenant's option to renew which, if exercised, would extend the term to seven years or more, does not.

1.7.4. Landlords are also subject to statutory provisions which require them to maintain electrical equipment in a safe condition.[4]

Asbestos

1.7.5. Control of Asbestos Regulations 2006, reg.4 contains a duty relating to the management of asbestos in non-domestic premises. Broadly the duty is imposed on dutyholders (as defined), e.g. those responsible for maintenance of the premises. The duties basically require an assessment as to whether there is asbestos in the premises, a decision as to whether it should be removed or properly maintained, and monitoring. Information has to be provided to those likely to come into contact with the asbestos, for example, contractors and the emergency services.

Fire safety

1.7.6. The Regulatory Reform (Fire Safety) Order 2005 applies to most non-domestic premises. The Order has replaced fire certification under Fire Precaution Act 1971 with a general duty to take fire precautions.

1.7.7. Responsibility for complying with the Fire Safety Order rests with the 'responsible person'. The primary duty falls on employers, if the workplace is to any extent under their control. Otherwise the duty in Article 3 of the Order is on the person who has control of the premises for the purpose of a trade, business or undertaking (whether or not for profit), which may be the tenant in many instances or, if not, the owner. Article 22 of the Order anticipates there could be more than one 'responsible person' for the same premises, for example, the tenant, landlord and the managing agent in so far as each has responsibility for the maintenance and safety of the building. Responsibility for enforcement will be undertaken by the local fire and rescue service authority. Detailed guides have been published in relation to the application of the Order to various types of properties.[5]

General principles

1.7.8.   The extent of the repairing obligations imposed by the lease will vary from lease to lease but the following general principles are relevant:

(a)   the wording of the clause must cover every part of the building and estate which is intended to be covered. Usually this will mean that the clause(s) must cover five main areas (which may overlap): the demised premises, the structure (including roof, main walls and foundations), the common parts, the common conduits, and the exterior;

(b)   the operative words of the clause(s) must be sufficient to cover all foreseeable repair activities. In this respect the wording of the clause should provide for the main areas of maintenance: repairing, cleaning, and decorating. Improvements to the property or major rebuilding effected by the landlord will not necessarily be covered by the wording of a covenant 'to repair' and thus, unless expressly included in the wording of the covenant, a landlord may be unable to recover their cost from the tenants.[6] The word 'repair' is generally regarded as meaning the restoration by renewal or replacement of subsidiary parts of the whole.[7] The courts have drawn a marked contrast between an obligation to 'repair' and one of 'rebuilding' and 'renewal';[8]

(c)   the wording of the covenant(s) must leave no grey areas where liability for repair is uncertain, and should not have areas of overlap. Care should be taken with the liability for repair, etc., of walls, ceilings, floors and joists. Clarity in these areas is largely dependent on the wording of the definition of the ownership of the various parts of the walls, floors, ceilings, etc., in the description of the property demised. The obligation to repair can then be defined in relation to ownership of the various parts. In particular, in multi-let buildings the lease should make it expressly clear whether the windows are part of the structure or of the demise;[9]

(d)   the wording of the clause must clearly specify the apportionment of liability for repairs, etc., between landlord and tenant;

(e)   where the lease requires the premises to be kept in 'good condition' this will require work to be done where the property is in a bad condition even though the property is not in disrepair.[10]

Not to make improvements or alterations

1.7.9. Such a covenant is commonly included in short leases of residential premises and leases of business premises in order to allow the landlord to retain control over his property and to ensure that no alterations are effected in breach of restrictive covenants on the landlord's title, or in breach of planning law or building regulation consent. Some improvements made by a tenant of business premises or agricultural land may commit the landlord to the payment of compensation when the tenant leaves the premises.[11]

1.7.10. The covenant may be absolute, in which case the tenant is totally prohibited from making improvements or alterations unless the landlord grants a deed of variation of the lease. An absolute covenant is usually considered inappropriate in the context of the grant of a long lease (e.g. exceeding 21 years) of an entire building. A qualified covenant is one where the tenant must seek the landlord's prior consent to the alterations or improvements. A fully qualified covenant is one where the landlord's consent cannot be unreasonably withheld.[12] This may be stated expressly, however, a statutory provision will, in most leases, convert a qualified covenant into a fully qualified one where the alteration amounts to an improvement.[13] An example of the wording of a clause can be seen from the Law Society Standard Business Lease (Whole of Building) (Registered) 2008, clause 5.

1.7.11. Even in the case of an absolute covenant a tenant may seek the court's consent to the proposed improvements or alterations in certain circumstances. Thus if the tenant's works amount to 'improvements' within Part I Landlord and Tenant Act 1927, this Act provides a mechanism whereby the tenant may obtain permission for such improvements even in the face of an absolute prohibition. The Act sets out a procedure whereby, broadly, the tenant must serve notice on the landlord, who may refer the matter to the county court if he wishes to object. If there is no objection or the court consents, the tenant can make the improvement and on leaving he is entitled to compensation.[14]

Disability discrimination

1.7.12. Equality Act 2010 consolidates and amends much of the law relating to disability, including that contained in Disability Discrimination Act 1995. Here we are concerned with the legislation as it affects property and the obligations on landlords and tenants.

1.7.13. Equality Act 2010 is to be supplemented by Codes of Practice and non-statutory guidance, much of which is unavailable at the time of writing. Therefore, in what follows the law that applies at the date of publication of this book is set out, principally under Disability Discrimination Act 1995, together with a brief explanation of the position as it will be under Equality Act 2010 when it is fully implemented.

1.7.14. In outline, Disability Discrimination Act 1995 (and Equality Act 2010) impose duties on a number of categories of persons including landlords and employers not to discriminate on the basis of disability.[15] The legislation requires employers[16] to take such steps as are reasonable to alter arrangements or physical features of premises if these put a disabled person at a substantial disadvantage in comparison with persons who are not disabled. The Disability Rights Commission has published various Codes of Practice including 'Rights of Access: services to the public, public authority functions, private clubs and premises'; and one on 'Employment Occupation'. These include details of the obligations to make reasonable adjustments to premises and includes a consideration of how leases are affected by this obligation.

1.7.15.   One aspect of the legisation which has caused concern to owners of property is in relation to obligations imposed on 'service providers'.[17] These include anyone (landlord or tenant) who provides goods, facilities or services to the public or a section of it. It may therefore include landlords who provide services over common parts to tenants. One element of this obligation is a duty to take reasonable steps to remove or alter a physical barrier which makes it unreasonably difficult for disabled persons to make use of facilities or a service, or to obtain goods offered to others. Alternatively, in appropriate cases, the service provider may provide a reasonable alternative method of making the service, etc., available to the disabled person.[18] In relation to the provision of banking services, the Court of Appeal has held, on the facts of the case, that physical alterations to the premises were required because suggested alternative methods of making banking services available (e.g. internet banking and/or using alternative branches) were not reasonable alternatives.[19] A public authority has obligations similar to those imposed on service providers.[20]

1.7.16.   The legislation[21] provides that, irrespective of what the lease may actually provide, the lease is deemed to contain provisions permitting a tenant to make any adjustments required by the Act (whether as employer or service provider) with the landlord's consent and any such consent is not to be unreasonably withheld.[22]

1.7.17.   There are further obligations[23] on landlords and those managing residential and commercial property, which are intended to help eliminate discrimination in the letting of property. It is unlawful for landlords and managers, in relation to premises they wish to let or that are let, to discriminate against a disabled tenant or prospective tenant by failing without justification to comply with a duty to provide a reasonable adjustment for the disabled person.[24] Whilst these duties are not intended to require the making of any alteration to the physical features of premises by a landlord, nonetheless the provisions would, for example, require a landlord or manager to take reasonable steps to provide an auxiliary aid.[25]

1.7.18.   Duties are imposed on private clubs of more than 25 members, in certain circumstances, to carry out physical alterations to property. Where a private club has a physical feature which makes it impossible or unreasonably difficult for disabled persons who are members, associates or guests to make use of a benefit, facility or service, the club may be required to take such steps as are reasonable in all the circumstances to alter the premises accordingly.[26]

1.7.19. Equality Act 2010 contains further provisions that go beyond those in Disability Discrimination Act 1995. In particular where there is a building that includes residential premises (save for 'small premises' as defined) the person responsible for the common parts must make certain reasonable adjustments to the common parts if a request is made by a disabled tenant, in certain circumstances, after consultation, and normally at the tenant's cost.[27]

Covenant restricting user

1.7.20. Some restriction on the tenant's use of the premises is usually considered desirable for the same reasons as are cited in K1.7.9. The covenant may be absolute, in which case the tenant is totally prohibited from changing the use of the property unless the landlord grants a deed of variation of the lease. If the covenant is qualified, a statutory provision implies, in most cases, that no premium can be charged by the landlord for giving consent.[28] There is no implied statutory proviso that the landlord's consent will not be unreasonably withheld. In the context of the lease of a dwelling house it may be appropriate to include an absolute covenant against any use except that as a private residence. In the case of business premises a very restrictive user clause (e.g. a clause which permits one specific type of business only) may have an adverse effect on the marketability of the premises and the amount of rent chargeable for them. A common device to attempt to alleviate the depressive effect on the value of the property for rent review purposes is to provide in the lease for this effect to be disregarded on such a review.

Covenant against alienation

1.7.21. A covenant restricting the tenant's right to dispose of the property must be carefully drafted since such covenants are construed narrowly by the courts, e.g. a covenant preventing assignment alone will not prevent the tenant from granting a sub-lease of the property. The covenant may be absolute in form, in which case no alienation of the property will be possible unless the landlord specifically grants consent usually by granting a deed of variation of the lease. A qualified covenant is subject to the statutory restrictions and modifications which are explained in K11.[29] Except where the lease provides for payment of a premium as a condition of the granting of consent, no premium is payable for such consent.[30] In the context of the long lease of a dwelling house it is unusual to include a general restriction against alienation except during the last few years of the term. The CML Lenders' Handbook and BSA Mortgage Instructions contain detailed requirements for the content of long term residential leases (see K6.6). In other cases such a restriction is common and desirable to ensure that the landlord retains some control over the occupiers of his property. In respect of business premises, quite detailed provisions are common.[31] See the Law Society Standard Business Lease (Whole of Building) (Registered) 2008, clause 7. 'Virtual assignments' are dealt with at K7.11.8.

Covenant to give notice of dealings to landlord

1.7.22. Such a covenant is normally included in order to give the landlord notice of all dealings by the tenant with the property. The obligation for the tenant to give notice of dealings should specify the occasions on which the covenant is to operate, e.g. notice of assignment, sub-lettings, mortgage, change of ownership on death or bankruptcy of the tenant. The tenant is usually required to pay a small registration fee to the landlord with each notice served. See the Law Society Standard Business Lease (Whole of Building) (Registered) 2008, clause 6.

Landlord's covenant for quiet enjoyment

1.7.23. Such a covenant will be implied into the lease by the common law, but it is usual to find an express covenant to this effect. Under this covenant the tenant is entitled to be put into possession of the premises and to remain quietly in possession of them throughout the term. The covenant is broken, for example, by unlawful eviction of the tenant.[32] Damages for mental distress are not recoverable for breach of this covenant.[33]

1. See, e.g. Landlord and Tenant Act 1985, ss.11–14. Exceptionally a landlord may be under a common law implied duty to repair: see *Liverpool City Council* v. *Irwin* [1977] AC 239; *King* v. *South Northamptonshire District Council* [1992] 1 EGLR 53, CA.
2. See *Alker* v. *Collingwood Housing Association* [2007] EWCA Civ 343.
3. See Gas Safety Regulations 1998, reg.3(3) and **www.hse.gov.uk**.
4. See, for example, Consumer Protection Act 1987 and Electrical Equipment (Safety) Regulations 1994 (SI 1994/3260).
5. These can be downloaded from **www.communities.gov.uk**.
6. See *Mullaney* v. *Maybourne Grange (Croydon) Management Ltd* [1986] 1 EGLR 70; *cf. Sutton (Hastoe) Housing Association* v. *Williams* [1988] 16 EG 75.
7. See, e.g. *Minja Properties Ltd* v. *Cussins Property Group plc* [1998] 2 EGLR 52.
8. See, e.g. *Norwich Union Life Insurance Society* v. *British Railways Board* [1987] 2 EGLR 137; *New England Properties* v. *Portsmouth New Shops* [1993] 1 EGLR 84; *Credit Suisse* v. *Beegas Nominees Ltd* [1994] 1 EGLR 76.
9. See *Holiday Fellowship Ltd* v. *Hereford* [1959] 1 All ER 433 and *Irvine* v. *Moran* [1991] 1 EGLR 261. Note also *Sheffield City Council* v. *Hazel St Clare Oliver* (2008) LRX/146/2007 (Lands Tribunal).
10. *Welsh* v. *Greenwich London Borough Council* [2002] 49 EG 118.
11. Part 1 Landlord and Tenant Act 1927; and see K8.5.17.
12. The Court of Appeal set out a series of principles to be applied in determining whether a refusal of consent is reasonable in *Iqbal* v. *Thakrar* [2004] PLSCS 125.
13. Landlord and Tenant Act 1927, s.19(2) and (4); *Lambert* v. *FW Woolworth & Co. Ltd* [1938] 2 All ER 664.
14. See *Norfolk Capital Group Ltd* v. *Cadogan Estates Ltd* [2004] 1 WLR 1458.
15. Thus a refusal to permit the installation of a chair lift for a disabled tenant may be lawful if the reasons for the landlord's refusal do not relate to the tenant's disability; see *Richmond Court (Swansea) Ltd* v. *Williams* [2006] EWCA Civ 1719. In a similar way a refusal to allow a tenant to keep a dog was not discriminatory on the facts, see *Thomas-Ashley* v. *Drum Housing Association Ltd* [2010] EWCA Civ 265. The meaning of disability in Disability Discrimination Act 1995, s.1 is supplemented by the publication, *Guidance on Matters to be Taken into Account in Determining Questions Relating to the Definition of Disability*, which is available from **www.equalityandhumanrights.com**.
16. Disability Discrimination Act 1995, s.4A. A similar duty exists in relation to contract workers in s.4B, and office holders in s.4E: see Equality Act 2010, Part 5, Chapter 1
17. Disability Discrimination Act 1995, s.19; Equality Act 2010, s.29.
18. For details of various codes of practice see **www.equalityhumanrights.com**. Note also the provisions of Disability Discrimination (Service Providers and Public Authorities Carrying Out Functions) Regulations 2005. Equality Act 2010, s.29(7) imposes a similar duty on a service provider to make reasonable adjustments to the property from which they provide their services. The extent of this duty is set out in s.20 and Sched. 2
19. See *Royal Bank of Scotland Group plc* v. *Allen* [2009] EWCA Civ 1213.

20. See Disability Discrimination Act 1995, ss.21B–21F and Disability Discrimination (Service Providers and Public Authorities Carrying Out Functions) Regulations 2005 (SI 2005/2901); see Equality Act 2010, s.29, in relation to a 'person who exercises a public function'.
21. Disability Discrimination Act 1995, s.27; Equality Act 2010, Sched.21, para.3.
22. Further details as to the landlord's consent are contained in Disability Discrimination (Providers of Services) (Adjustment of Premises) Regulations 2001 (SI 2001/3253). Note also that Disability Discrimination Act 2005, s.16 inserted section 49G into Disability Discrimination Act 1995 which contains provisions that apply where a tenant seeks consent to make improvement to a let dwelling to facilitate the enjoyment of the premises by a disabled occupier. Equality Act 2010 contains provisions that allow for similar regulations to be made.
23. See, in particular, Disability Discrimination Act 1995, ss.24A–24L and s.49G; Equality Act 2010, s.36 and Sched.4.
24. See Disability Discrimination Act 1995, ss. 24A–24L; Equality Act 2010, Sched.4
25. Disability Discrimination Act 1995, s.24J. Further detailed provision is made by Disability Discrimination (Premises) Regulations 2006 (SI 2006/887); Equality Act 2010, Sched.4.
26. See Disability Discrimination Act 1995, s.21F, inserted by Disability Discrimination Act 2005, s.12. These provisions are supplemented by Disability Discrimination (Private Clubs etc.) Regulations 2005 (SI 2005/3258). Equality Act 2010, s.29 imposes duties on anyone 'concerned with the provision of a service to the public or a section of the public (for payment or not)'.
27. Equality Act 2010, Scheds. 4 and 5.
28. Landlord and Tenant Act 1927, s.19(3) and (4).
29. See Landlord and Tenant Act 1927, s.19(1) and (4), as amended by Landlord and Tenant Act 1987, and Landlord and Tenant (Covenants) Act 1995.
30. Law of Property Act 1925, s.144.
31. See K7.11.
32. *Miller* v. *Emcer Products Ltd* [1956] Ch 304.
33. *Branchett* v. *Beaney* [1992] 3 All ER 910.

1.8. Service charge

1.8.1. Leases of flats and of commercial premises will often require the tenant to pay a service charge for services provided by either the landlord or a management company, e.g heating or cleaning and repair of the building, of which the demised premises form part, and decoration of the common parts. The service charge is traditionally expressed to be payable as 'additional rent'. The main reason for this is to enable the landlord to distrain for its non-payment. The remedy of distress will be abolished when the relevant provisions of Tribunals, Courts and Enforcement Act (TCEA) 2007 come into force.[1] This Act replaces distress, in the case of commercial premises only with the remedy of 'commercial rent arrears recovery'.[2] This enables the landlord to follow a statutory procedure to recover the rent by taking control of the tenant's goods and selling them to recover that sum. This procedure is set out in Schedule 12 to TCEA 2007. Commercial rent arrears recovery only applies to the rent itself, as opposed to other sums that may be described as rent, e.g. service charges, however they may be described in the lease. Nonetheless, by describing the service charge as being payable as 'rent' it does enable the landlord to recover the sum due without the necessity of serving a notice under Law of Property Act 1925, s.146.

1.8.2. The tenant should ensure that the proportion of the charge which he is required to pay is fair in relation to the amount of the building which he occupies or enjoys rights over, and should ensure that the clause specifies precisely what services are to be supplied in return for the charge. A landlord may wish to provide for an estimate of the service charge to be payable in advance and for there to be a reconciliation at the end of the year.

1.8.3. The landlord may also contemplate setting up a sinking fund to cater for major expenditure on the property. The tenant of a flat may be required to become a member of a residents' association or management company which will have responsibility for providing services and effecting the landlord's repairing covenants under the lease. This allows the tenants to control the expenditure to which they are committing themselves. Membership of a management company is normally restricted to the tenants of the block or estate and the covenant will require the tenant on assignment of his lease to require his assignee to take a transfer of the tenant's share in the management company where this is a company limited by shares. The articles of association of the management company may also require tenants to contribute to the service charge and tenants will need to be aware of obligations as shareholder as well as under the lease.[3] The landlord should be required to assume responsibility for the management company's responsibilities under the lease until the company is set up and shares have been allotted to all the tenants (see further K6.3.5).

1.8.4. Statutory controls over service charges on dwellings are discussed in K6.8. The CML Lenders' Handbook requirements are considered in K6.6 (the BSA Mortgage Instructions contain similar requirements). See also the Law Society Standard Business Lease (Part of Building) (Registered) 2008, clause 3.

1.8.5. Tenants are only obliged to pay for items agreed in the lease. The landlord should therefore be careful to include in the service charge provisions all the necessary expenditure which he may incur on the building.[4] The clause must therefore encompass all the obligations which are covered by the landlord's covenants in the lease, e.g. repairs and decoration, insurance, services such as lifts, cleaning common parts, garden maintenance, etc. If the landlord may need in the future to make improvements to the property, this too should be covered by the clause. From the landlord's perspective, it is advisable to include a sweeping-up clause to cover any omissions of specific items and to take account of any higher expectations in standards which were not anticipated at the commencement of the term. These are commonly called 'sweeper' clauses. These clauses also generally allow landlords to recover other items which, in the future, may be provided. As a general rule the courts will construe these clauses narrowly and will not generally allow the landlord to charge wholly new service charge items to the tenant through such a provision.[5] This may be a particular issue in relation to wholly new matters, e.g. costs of obtaining Energy Performance Certificates or the landlord's relevant costs of the Carbon Reduction Commitment Energy Efficiency Scheme (CRC).

1.8.6. The CRC is a new emissions trading scheme under which, broadly speaking, certain organisations must buy annual allowances to enable them to encourage the more efficient use of energy in their business for certain purposes. Where the landlord is to be a participant in the CRC scheme and is reselling energy supplies (e.g. electricity) to its tenants, the landlord may wish to recover a contribution towards the cost of buying the CRC allowance as well as the cost of the energy supplied. The proportion of the CRC allowance attributable to the building may prove to be difficult to calculate. This situation is most likely to arise with multi-let buildings and the sum is likely to be recovered by means of specific clauses in the lease (see further B25.1.3).

1.8.7.   Provision for the tenants to contribute to a reserve fund or sinking fund will assist in the financing of major works and eliminate the burden of imposing a very large service charge in one particular year when major items such as a central heating system need to be renewed.

1.8.8.   The landlord's expenditure on bank interest and bank charges can only be recovered if the lease so permits.[6] Management charges need only be included where either the landlord will be carrying out his obligations himself or employing independent managing agents to do so. Professional fees are only recoverable under a service charge clause where they are properly incurred in respect of items which are chargeable under the service charge provisions.[7] The Royal Institution of Chartered Surveyors (RICS) has published a code of practice, *RICS Code of Practice: Service Charges in Commercial Property*, for surveyors practising in England and Wales.[8] The code was designed to set best practice for commercial service charges. Its objectives are stated to:

- remove service charges as an area of conflict;

- deliver a budgetable and forecastable part of occupiers' overheads;

- ensure service charges are 'not for profit, not for loss';

- encourage transparency and communication in the relationship between landlords and tenants.

The code came into force on 1 April 2007 for service charges commencing on or after that date.

1.8.9.   RICS has also updated its *Code of Practice for Service Charge Management for Residential Properties* in April 2009. This voluntary code:

(a)   aims to promote good practice in the management of residential lease-hold property;

(b)   applies to leasehold properties in England where the landlord is not a registered social landlord or a local authority; and

(c)   has been approved by the Secretary of State.[9]

1.   Tribunals, Courts and Enforcement Act 2007, s.71.
2.   *Ibid.*, s.72.
3.   For an example of the consequences of such a situation see *Morshead MansionsLtd* v. *Leon Di Marco* [2008] EWCA 1371.
4.   Where the clause sets out a procedure for submission of the service charge accounts this must be followed by the landlord otherwise the tenant may not be obliged to pay the charge. See *Leonora Investment Company* v. *Mott MacDonald* [2008] EWCA Civ 857.
5.   See, e.g. *Mullaney* v. *Maybourne Grange (Croydon) Management Co. Ltd* (1986) 277 EG 1350.

6. *Frobisher (Second Investments) Ltd* v. *Kiloran Trust Co. Ltd* [1980] 1 All ER 488.
7. *Holding & Management Ltd* v. *Property Holding & Investment Trust plc* [1988] 2 All ER 702.
8. This can be downloaded from **www.servicechargecode.co.uk**.
9. The Code is available for purchase from RICS. Approval is by virtue of Approval of Code of Management Practice (Residential Management) (Service Charges) (England) Order 2009 (SI 2009/ 512).

1.9.   Proviso for forfeiture or re-entry

1.9.1.   The landlord's right to forfeit the lease for the tenant's breach of covenant is a valuable remedy which must be expressly included in the lease, since such a right is not implied by the common law unless, exceptionally, the lease is made conditional on the due observance of the covenants.[1] The landlord will be unable to remove the tenant from the premises during the currency of the lease term without such a clause. It is usual to include a clause which gives the landlord the right to forfeit the lease on non-payment of rent by the tenant after a stated period (e.g. 21 days) and for breach of any other covenant in the lease. Forfeiture for the tenant's insolvency[2] is common in non-residential leases but should not be included in the long lease of a dwelling house since such a provision is unacceptable to most mortgagees.[3] Forfeiture for breach of a covenant other than to pay rent must generally be preceded by the service of a notice under Law of Property Act 1925, s.146 and may in certain cases be affected by Leasehold Property (Repairs) Act 1938. Repossession of an occupied dwelling house requires a court order.[4] In other cases a court order will be required if re-entry cannot be made peaceably, otherwise an offence may be committed under Criminal Law Act 1977, s.6 (see also K1.9.5). There are further restrictions on the landlord's right to forfeit long residential leases set out in Commonhold and Leasehold Reform Act 2002; see further K6.9.2.

1.9.2.   Forfeiture may also occur (even in the absence of an express proviso) where the tenant denies the landlord's title to the property. If a tenant makes a specific allegation that the landlord does not own the property or that a third party has better rights to the property than the landlord, this may be construed as a denial of the landlord's title and result in forfeiture.[5] A general denial of the landlord's title contained in a defence to proceedings brought by the landlord will not have this effect.[6]

1.9.3.   A landlord may expressly or by implication waive his right to forfeit. The intention of the landlord does not matter and the position is judged objectively from the landlord's actions. An unequivocal act done by the landlord or his agent that recognises the existence of the lease after the landlord knows of the grounds of forfeiture will result in waiver of the right to forfeit.[7]

1.9.4.   A tenant may not apply for relief against forfeiture for breach of covenant other than for non-payment of rent after a landlord has forfeited a lease by court proceedings and entry into possession of the property pursuant to the judgment obtained in those proceedings. Where, however, entry is regained peaceably, the tenant retains his right to apply for equitable relief against forfeiture even after the landlord has taken possession of the property.[8] An equitable assignee from a tenant may claim relief against forfeiture.[9]

1.9.5. Great care must be taken where a landlord chooses to exercise his right to forfeit premises other than a dwelling by peaceable re-entry. If possession is resisted by the tenant when the landlord seeks to re-enter, there is a risk that a criminal offence under Criminal Law Act 1977, s.6 may be committed by the landlord.

1.9.6. Where the landlord seeks to forfeit following breach of a covenant against alienation by the tenant, any section 146 notice should be served on both the assignor (tenant) of the lease and on the purported assignee (person currently in possession).[10]

1.9.7. A notice under Law of Property Act 1925, s.146 is not required before forfeiting for non-payment of rent, and no formal demand for rent need be made if the re-entry clause states that the landlord can re-enter if rent is in arrears 'whether or not formally demanded' or there is wording to similar effect. Where the tenant is in breach of a repairing covenant and the landlord (acting under a power expressly given to him by the lease) effects the repairs himself and then seeks to recover the cost of the repairs from the tenant, it is not necessary to serve a section 146 notice and Leasehold Property (Repairs) Act 1938 does not apply. The action is for recovery of a liquidated sum only.[11]

1.9.8. If the landlord forfeits by legal proceedings, he can include a claim for arrears of rent, mesne profits, and interest.

1.9.9. Where the landlord is forfeiting by action (i.e. legal proceedings) in the county court for non-payment of rent,[12] the tenant can apply to the court for relief against forfeiture under County Courts Act 1984, ss.138–140. In outline, these provisions provide:

    (a)   for automatic relief if the tenant pays all arrears and costs of the action into court not less than five clear days before the return day of the landlord's proceedings;

    (b)   that if relief is not obtained as above then the court will make an order for possession on a future date suspended for not less than four weeks. If the tenant pays the arrears and costs within the period of suspension the lease is reinstated;

    (c)   that even if a possession order is made and the landlord re-enters, the tenant or any person with an interest under the lease derived from the tenant's interest can apply to the court for relief within six months from the landlord's recovery of possession and the court may grant relief on terms it thinks fit.

1.9.10. Where the landlord is forfeiting by action in the High Court the tenant can apply to the court for relief against forfeiture. If there is at least six months' rent in arrears the tenant will obtain automatic relief by paying all arrears and costs to the landlord or to the court before judgment.[13] The tenant's application must be made before the expiration of six months from execution of the judgment for possession.[14] Otherwise relief is still obtainable[15] so that if all the arrears and costs are paid, save in exceptional cases relief will normally be granted. If the tenant owes less than six months' rent he can apply for relief at any time after the possession order has been made. The court has an equitable jurisdiction and will take any delay into account.

1.9.11. The above rules only apply to forfeiture for non-payment of rent and the court has a wider discretion in cases of other breaches of covenant.[16]

1. Law Commission Report, *Termination of Tenancies for Tenant Default* (Law Com No.303) proposed that the law of forfeiture should be abolished and replaced by a new statutory scheme allowing for termination of tenancies by landlords following a breach of covenant or condition by the tenant.
2. Leave of the court may be required for forfeiture or before pursuing other remedies where the tenant is insolvent under the provisions of Insolvency Act 1986 and Enterprise Act 2002.
3. The requirements of the CML Lenders' Handbook are considered at K6.6.
4. Protection from Eviction Act 1977, s.2. This includes property which is a mixed residential and commercial letting; see *Pirabakaran* v. *Patel* [2006] EWCA Civ 685.
5. *WG Clarke (Properties) Ltd* v. *Dupre Properties Ltd* [1992] Ch 297.
6. *Warner* v. *Sampson* [1959] 1 QB 297. Note also *Abidogun* v. *Frolan Health Care Ltd* [2001] 45 EGCS 138.
7. A common example of waiver is the acceptance of rent by the landlord following knowledge of an act permitting forfeiture, despite being an error or being accepted 'without prejudice', see *Central Estates (Belgravia) Limited* v. *Woolgar* [1972] 1 WLR 1048. However, it has been held that waiver did not apply where a cheque in payment of other debts as well as rent was cashed and the rent element returned, see *Osibanjo* v. *Seahive Investments Ltd* [2008] EWCA Civ 1282.
8. *Billson* v. *Residential Apartments* [1992] 1 AC 494, HL.
9. *High Street Investments* v. *Bellshore* [1996] NPC 20.
10. *Fuller* v. *Judy Properties* [1992] 1 EGLR 75 but see *Old Grovebury Manor Farm Ltd* v. *W Seymour Plant Sales & Hire Ltd (No.2)* [1979] 3 All ER 504; and note *Brown & Root Technology* v. *Sun Alliance & London Assurance Co. Ltd* [1997] 18 EG 123.
11. *Jervis* v. *Harris* [1995] NPC 171.
12. Law of Property Act 1925, s.146(2); see, e.g. *Crown Estate Commissioners* v. *Signet Group plc* [1996] 2 EGLR 200.
13. Common Law Procedure Act 1852, s.212.
14. *Ibid.*, s.210.
15. Supreme Court Act 1981, s.38.
16. Law of Property Act 1925, s.146(2); *Crown Estate Commissioners* v. *Signet Group plc* [1996] 2 EGLR 200; also note *Shiryama Shokusan Co.* v. *Danovo* [2005] EWHC 2589.

1.10. Insurance

1.10.1. If the landlord is to insure the property (as would generally be the case in a lease of commercial premises) he should ensure that he is able to recover the amount of the premiums from the tenant, see, for example, Law Society Standard Business Lease (Whole of Building) (Registered) 2008, clause 1.4(d).

1.10.2. The Law Society's Standard Business Leases of Part provide for reimbursement of the insurance premiums paid by the landlord through the service charge payments. Where the landlord is to insure, the tenant should ensure that the lease specifies the risks against which the landlord should insure. If the tenant is responsible for repairing all or any part of the property he would also want to ensure that the repairing covenant excepts liability for damage by insured risks. If the tenant is to insure, the covenant should specify the risks against which the landlord wishes the policy to be effected and should give the landlord the right to inspect the policy, to see the receipt for the last premium due, and to insure in the case of the tenant's default.

1.10.3. Where the premises comprise part of a building the lease must provide for both the unit and the common parts of the building to be properly insured. Normally the landlord covenants to insure all the units and the common parts together under a block policy, with a right to recover a proportionate part of the premium from each tenant. Incidental costs are sometimes also recoverable from tenants including the costs of regular valuations for insurance cover. Occasionally the lease may make provision for each tenant to insure his individual unit and for the landlord to insure the common parts of the building, but such an arrangement is not popular since it can lead to situations where not all tenants are insured for the same amounts or against the same risks with consequent difficulties in enforcing claims where it has become necessary for one tenant to claim against another.

1.10.4. The insurance covenant in the lease should provide for an adequate level of cover and of risk to be maintained over the units and common parts, including the full costs of rebuilding or reinstatement and related professional fees, with reputable insurers. Consideration should be given to limiting liability where cover is unavailable in the open market at reasonable rates. Damage caused by certain risks, e.g. terrorist activities is sometimes excluded from cover in which case liability will fall on the party responsible for repair in the event of damage being caused by uninsured losses. In such cases it may be appropriate for the tenant to be entitled to terminate the lease following substantial damage by uninsured risks, unless the landlord elects to reinstate at his own cost. Absolute covenants to insure are strictly construed so that, for example, where a landlord is under an absolute duty to insure against fire risks, he would have to reinstate the property even if the property burns down as a result of an excluded cause such as terrorist action.[1] The tenants should have the right to a copy of the insurance policy or reasonable evidence of its existence and validity, and to inspect the original policy and the receipt (or reasonable evidence of payment) for the last premium due.

1.10.5. A tenant will wish the lease to provide for the landlord to use the proceeds of the policy to reinstate the premises in the event of their damage or destruction by an insured risk. Provision should also be made for the application of the policy money in the event of reinstatement not being possible.

1.10.6. It is also desirable that the landlord should maintain an occupiers' liability insurance policy in a situation where the landlord retains the ownership of common parts of the building.

1.10.7. It is preferable for the landlord to obtain a policy which cannot be vitiated by act or default of the tenants.

1.10.8.   Landlords are sometimes able to secure the payment of commission for the placing of insurance cover with a particular insurance company. Except to the extent that the landlord provides services in respect of the insurance, this commission, in principle, belongs to the tenants.[2] Landlords may provide in the lease that they are to be permitted to retain this commission.

1.10.9.   If the solicitor is involved in insurance mediation services with regard to any insurance policy, care must be taken to ensure that the relevant rules relating to financial services are complied with (see A4).

1.   See *Enlayde Ltd* v. *Roberts* [1917] 1 Ch 109; *Moorgate Estates Ltd* v. *Trower* [1940] 1 All ER 195.
2.   *Williams* v. *Southwark London Borough Council* [2000] EGCS 44.

1.11.   Underleases

1.11.1.   Most of the matters which are relevant when acting for the seller or buyer on grant of a lease will also be applicable to the grant of a sub-lease.

1.11.2.   The head-tenant will be liable to his own landlord (the freeholder) on the covenants contained in his lease irrespective of whether the breach is committed by the head- or sub-tenant. To protect himself against liability for a breach committed by the sub-tenant, the head-tenant should impose on the sub-tenant obligations which are at least as onerous as those contained in the head-lease.

1.11.3.   A sub-tenant will be directly liable to the freeholder in respect of breach of restrictive covenants which are contained in the head-lease since he will be deemed to know of those covenants through his entitlement to call for the head-lease as part of the evidence of title. Apart from this, the freeholder may choose, as a term of the head-lease or by a condition attached to the grant of any necessary consent to the sub-lease, to require the sub-tenant to enter into a direct covenant with the freeholder. This will put the freeholder in a strong position in relation to the enforcement of covenants contained in the head-lease because it has the effect of establishing the relationship of privity of contract between the freeholder and the sub-tenant. In the case of leases to which Landlord and Tenant (Covenants) Act 1995 applies the landlord may, in any event, sue the sub-tenant directly for breach of certain restrictive covenants under section 3(5).

1.11.4.   The existence and validity of a sub-lease is dependent on the existence and validity of the head-lease out of which it is derived. If, therefore, the head-lease is forfeited, the sub-lease is also automatically forfeited[1] although the sub-tenant may have the right to apply directly to the freeholder for relief against forfeiture even in circumstances where the head-tenant is unable to apply for relief. A lender (of the tenant or sub-tenant) has the same right to apply for relief against forfeiture as a sub-tenant.[2]

1.11.5.   Where the head-lease requires the prior consent of the freeholder to the grant of a sub-lease, the head-tenant should seek such consent at an early stage in the transaction and should not enter a binding unconditional contract for the grant of the sub-lease until it is certain that such consent will be forthcoming. The head-tenant's lender's consent may also be required to the grant of the sub-lease and this too should be obtained at an early stage in the transaction. Obtaining a landlord's consent to a sub-lease or assignment is discussed in K11.

1.11.6. Standard Condition 8.3 and Standard Commercial Property Condition 10.3 require the seller to apply for and pay for any necessary licence, the buyer (subtenant) supplying references and other information. In certain circumstances either party may rescind the contract if the consent is not forthcoming.[3]

1.11.7. In relation to leases granted or entered into on or after 11 May 2000, Contracts (Rights of Third Parties) Act 1999 may allow direct enforcement of covenants between tenants and between a head-landlord and a sub-tenant. The Act can be excluded if required.

1. The sub-lease will also terminate (subject to any rights of continuation under Landlord and Tenant Act 1954) if a superior lease is terminated under a break right. See *Pennell* v. *Payne* [1995] 1 EGLR 6 (confirmed by the House of Lords in *Barrett* v. *Morgan* [2000] 1 All ER 481). See also *PW & Co.* v. *Milton Gate Investments Ltd* [2003] PLSCS 204. A sub-lease will, however, survive the surrender of a head-lease (Law of Property Act 1925, s.139).
2. See Law of Property Act 1925, s.146.
3. See for example *Aubergine Enterprises Ltd* v. *Lakewood International Ltd* [2002] PLSCS 50; *Alchemy Estates Limited* v. *Astor* [2008] EWHC 2675 (Ch).

1.12. Title

1.12.1. Under an open contract in relation to a title which is unregistered, unless the parties are contracting to grant a lease which will trigger first registration, the tenant is not entitled to call for deduction of the freehold reversionary title on the grant of a lease.[1] This rule is unsatisfactory, particularly where a premium is to be paid for the grant of the lease or where a tenant is paying a significant rent for commercial premises. However, where the reversionary title is registered these principles can have no application because the title is open to inspection. The rule has therefore been amended so as not to apply to registered land or to a lease to be derived out of registered land.[2] In a similar way it is disapplied where the contract is to grant a term of years which will require first registration (e.g. for a term of more than seven years).[3] The tenant in such cases is entitled to see the superior title.

1.12.2. These provisions can be varied by contractual provision and in the majority of cases the landlord will contract to deduce his freehold title to the tenant in exactly the same way as if he were selling the freehold and should include a condition in the contract to this effect.[4]

1.12.3. Under an open contract in relation to a title which is unregistered, unless the parties are contracting to grant a lease which will trigger first registration, the rights of a sub-tenant in relation to deduction of title are limited. In such a case the sub-tenant is entitled to call for the head-lease out of which his sub-lease is to be derived and all subsequent assignments under which the lease has been held for the last 15 years. In the absence of a contractual condition to the contrary he is not entitled to call for production of the freehold title.[5]

1.12.4. The sub-tenant's inability in these cases to call for the deduction of the freehold title may cause problems, e.g. if a premium is being demanded for the grant of the sub-lease, or the sub-lease is to be mortgaged. However, as explained in K1.12.1, either where the reversionary title is registered or where the contract is to grant a term of years which will require first registration (e.g. for a term of more than seven years), the tenant is entitled to see the superior title.

1.12.5. A sub-lease will not contain an implied covenant on the part of the landlord that any user clause in the sub-lease is either lawful or complies with a restriction on use in a superior title.[6] A solicitor who accepts a lease or sub-lease without checking the validity of the user clause would be liable to his client in negligence if, as a result, the client suffered loss.

1.12.6. The statutory provisions relating to deduction of title can be varied by contractual provision and in most cases the landlord will contract to deduce such title that will enable the sub-tenant to apply for registration of his lease with title absolute. Such a clause is contained in the Standard Conditions and the Standard Commercial Property Conditions, and these require the head-tenant to produce the title to the freehold reversion to the sub-tenant on grant of certain sub-leases.[7] A head-tenant who did not call for deduction of the freehold title when he took his own lease may not be able to comply with this standard condition and will have to exclude it by special condition in the contract.

1. Law of Property Act 1925, s.44(4A) inserted by Land Registration Act 2002, s.133, Sched.11, para.2(2).
2. See Law of Property Act 1925, s.44(12) inserted by Land Registration Act 2002, s.133, Sched.11, para.2(1), (4).
3. See Law of Property Act 1925, s.44(4A) inserted by Land Registration Act 2002, s.133, Sched.11, para.2(1), (2).
4. See, for example, Standard Conditions of Sale 8.2.4 and Standard Commercial Property Condition 10.2.4.
5. Law of Property Act 1925, s.44.
6. *Hill* v. *Harris* [1965] 2 QB 601.
7. Standard Conditions of Sale 8.2.4 and Standard Commercial Property Condition 10.2.4.

1.13. Registration

1.13.1. A lease for seven years or less is generally not capable of being registered with its own title at the Land Registry,[1] but the lease will normally take effect as an overriding interest under Land Registration Act 2002.[2] If there is concern about protecting the tenant's interest in the property an application for entry of a notice may be lodged against the landlord's title where the lease is for a term of more than three years from the date of the grant. Alternatively, such a lease may be noted against the landlord's title by the Land Registrar where its existence is disclosed on a dealing with the superior title as a 'disclosable overriding interest'.[3] A lease for a term of three years or less cannot be protected by notice.[4]

In unregistered land a purchaser of the reversion will take subject to leases as they are legal estates, but an agreement for a lease must be registered as an estate contract (Class C(iv) land charge) in order to bind purchasers.[5] Should a tenant wish to check that his lease has been noted against a reversionary title where title to the reversion becomes registered subsequent to the grant of a lease, the tenant can ensure that he receives notification of the registration by applying for the registration of a caution against first registration at the Land Registry.[6]

1.13.2. Following completion of the grant of a lease which requires registration the tenant will make application for registration of the lease with a separate title.[7] A notice in respect of the lease will be entered automatically in the register of the landlord's title.[8]

1.13.3. Where a Prescribed Clauses Lease (as to which see K1.20) has been properly completed and registered,[9] on completion of the lease by registration the registrar will (where appropriate and where all relevant title numbers are included in clause LR2) make entries in the relevant individual registers in respect of interests contained in that lease which are of the nature referred to in clauses LR9 (rights of acquisition), LR10 (restrictive covenants given in the lease in respect of land other than the property), LR11 (easements) or LR12 (estate rentcharges). It is also possible for an application to be made for the entry of a standard form of restriction in clause LR13. Otherwise an application is necessary for a restriction to be entered against the leasehold title; this should be made in Form RX1 (see G3.9.15).

Easements

1.13.4. On registration of a properly completed Prescribed Clauses Lease where the landlord's title is registered, the Land Registry will automatically enter the benefit and burden of any easements granted and reserved. Where the lease is not registrable, any easements granted do not operate at law until the burden is noted on the landlord's title.[10] The application to note the easements should be made in Form AP1.[11] For more information see Land Registry Practice Guide 62.

Exempt information documents

1.13.5. As a registered lease will be open to public inspection, consideration may need to be given as to whether an application should be made to designate the lease an exempt information document (see G3.12 and K2.3.6).

1. Except leases granted under Housing Act 1985, Part V, and see other exceptions in G3.
2. Land Registration Act 2002, Sched.1, para.1 and Sched.3, para.1.
3. See Land Registration Rules 2003, rr.28 and 57 and Form DI.
4. Land Registration Act 2002, s.33.
5. Such purchasers must fall into the category of those acquiring a legal estate for money or money's worth where a failure to register will render the interest void against them. See Land Charges Act 1972, s.4(6).
6. Where the grant of an underlease is subject to consent (absolute or qualified) of the landlord, the tenant will normally be registered with absolute title. However, if no evidence of the landlord's consent is

disclosed, the Land Registry will place a note on the title that none has been shown to the registrar. For further information see Land Registry Practice Guide 1.

7. Land Registration Act 2002, s.15. As to the need for the consent of any mortgagee of the reversion to the grant of the lease see K1.15.4.
8. Land Registration Act 2002, Sched.2, para.3(2)(b).
9. See Land Registration Rules 2003, rr.72A and 92 as amended by Land Registration (Amendment) (No.2) Rules 2005 (SI 2005/1982).
10. Land Registration Act 2002, s.27(1) and (2)(d) and Sched.2, para.7.
11. Land Registration Rules 2003, r.90.

1.14. Surety

1.14.1. The landlord may require a surety to the lease as a condition of its grant. Where the proposed tenant is a small private company it is common to find that the directors of the company are asked to guarantee the company's obligations under the lease. In other circumstances a parent company may be asked to guarantee the obligations of a subsidiary company tenant. This gives the landlord additional protection under the lease since the sureties' obligations will be co-extensive with those of the principal debtor. If it is intended to enter a contract prior to the grant of the lease, the sureties should be made parties to that contract.

1.14.2. A buyer's solicitor who is also acting for the sureties to the lease must consider whether any conflict of interests exists or is likely to arise between the interests of his buyer client and the interests of the sureties. It may be in the best interests of the buyer to obtain a lease of the premises, which he can only do if he provides sureties to the lease (a pre-condition imposed by the landlord), but it may not be in the best interests of the sureties to enter into covenants with the landlord to guarantee performance of the buyer's obligations under the lease, e.g. as to payment of rent, repairs, etc., where the enforcement of the sureties' covenants would put the sureties' personal assets, such as a matrimonial home, at risk. Where such a conflict exists or is likely to arise, the sureties should receive independent advice about their potential liability (see further K4).

1.15. Mortgages

1.15.1. If the freehold reversion is subject to a mortgage, the mortgage deed should be checked to see whether it requires the lender's consent to be obtained prior to the grant of a lease. If so, steps should be taken to obtain the lender's consent before a binding unconditional contract to grant the lease is created.

1.15.2. The borrower's powers of leasing can be extended by or excluded from the mortgage by agreement (Law of Property Act 1925, s.99) except in the case of a mortgage of an agricultural holding where they cannot be excluded (Law of Property Act 1925, s.99(13A)) and the mortgage cannot exclude the court's power to order a new tenancy of business premises under Part II Landlord and Tenant Act 1954, s.36(4).

1.15.3. Failure to obtain such consent, where necessary, will put the seller into breach of his mortgage covenants, with the consequence that the principal sum under the mortgage will become due immediately. If consent is not required it should be checked that the lease is within the borrower's powers.

1.15.4. Further, failure to obtain consent will affect the position regarding the tenant's application to register the lease, where applicable. The Land Registry's view is that any lease granted without the consent of a lender is vulnerable to being challenged by the lender. However, the Land Registry is prepared to grant title absolute even though no consent of the lender is lodged, where title absolute would have been granted had there been no charge. An entry pointing out that the title is subject to any rights that may have arisen in favour of the lender will be made in the Property Register of the leasehold title.[1]

1. However, this does not affect the need for specific consent if a restriction has been registered in favour of the lender requiring consent before a disposition may be registered. In these circumstances its consent will be required before registration can take place. For further information see Land Registry Practice Guide 1 and also the 'Important developments' section of Land Registry website at **www.landregistry.gov.uk**: 'Key changes in practice from 19 June 2006'.

1.16. Sub-sales

1.16.1. By Standard Condition 1.5 and Standard Commercial Property Condition 1.5.1 the buyer is not entitled to transfer the benefit of the contract. Standard Commercial Property Condition 1.5.2 provides that the seller may not be required to transfer the property in parts or to any person other than the buyer. A suitable special condition to this effect would need to be inserted in a contract drawn on the Standard Conditions. For the SDLT provisions which apply to sub-sales, see A14.9.

1.17. Searches and enquiries before contract

1.17.1. When acting for a tenant on a long lease for a premium or on a commercial lease the same searches and enquiries as are relevant to a freehold purchase should be made. Searches are discussed in B10. In the case of a complex commercial lease it may be convenient to use the Commercial Property Standard Enquiries. In the case of residential transactions suitable 'TransAction' forms are available from law stationers.

1.17.2. Where a commercial lease is for a very short term at a low rent, or on short-term lettings of residential property, it is not usual for searches and enquiries to be made since the low risk attached to these lettings does not justify the expense of making the searches. The tenant client should be warned of the potential risks involved in not undertaking these. In some cases, however, the prospective tenant may feel it is prudent to make enquiries about the prospective landlord's solvency, particularly where the property is mortgaged, to avoid the risk of the landlord's lender seeking a possession order against the tenant if the landlord does not pay the mortgage.

1.18. The contract

1.18.1. A contract for the grant of the lease is normally entered into in the case of a purchase for a premium of a long-term residential lease but is not generally entered into on short-term lettings of residential premises nor on some commercial leases where in both cases the parties directly enter into negotiations on the draft lease. In the case of commercial lettings contracts are used to give early possession on terms, to deal with building work that may be required prior to completion or where in order to achieve quickly a binding commitment a contract is entered into which is expressed to be subject to some contingency, e.g. landlord's consent or grant of planning permission.

1.19. Drafting the lease

1.19.1. A lease for a term of over three years must be granted by deed to vest the legal estate in the tenant. A lease for three years or less, taking effect in possession at the best rent without a fine, may be granted orally or in writing.[1] To ensure certainty of terms between the parties it is recommended that all leases, no matter how short the term, should be in writing (see B1.6).

1.19.2. The lease is normally drafted by the seller's (landlord's) solicitor and annexed to the draft contract submitted to the buyer's (tenant's) solicitor.[2] Except where the lease is to be for a term not exceeding three years, taking effect in possession and with no premium payable for its grant, the contract for the lease must satisfy Law of Property (Miscellaneous Provisions) Act 1989, s.2. Standard Condition 8.2 and Standard Commercial Property Condition 10.2 provide for the lease to be in the form annexed to the draft contract and for the seller to engross the lease and supply the buyer with the engrossment at least five working days before completion date. Law of Property (Miscellaneous Provisions) Act 1989, s.2, requires that the contract must incorporate all its terms (see B1.7). In the case of a contract for a lease the length of the term and its commencement date must be expressly stated on the draft lease which is attached to the contract in order to satisfy Law of Property (Miscellaneous Provisions) Act 1989, s.2, or either or both could be stated in the contract.[3]

1.19.3. Leases which are granted by the same landlord to different tenants of separate units all of which are in the common ownership of the landlord (e.g. flats within a block owned by the landlord) should be uniform in content. If this is not so, difficulty may subsequently be experienced in the management of the property and, where the leases provide for mutual enforceability between tenants, enforcement of covenants against individual tenants. Subject to this, given the diversity of circumstances in which leases are granted, no two leases will ever be identical. It is recommended that the seller's solicitor refers to a suitable precedent before embarking on the drafting of the lease.[4]

1.19.4. Where the lease is of business premises the Law Society Standard Business Leases for the whole or part of premises may be used.

1.19.5. Consideration should be given to whether the landlord should give covenants for title on the grant of the lease.[5]

1. Law of Property Act 1925, ss.52–54 and Law of Property (Miscellaneous Provisions) Act 1989, s.2.
2. A lease may describe the property to be let by reference to a plan. For the Land Registry requirements as to plans, see B21.
3. *Marshall* v. *Berridge* (1881) 19 ChD 233.
4. See, e.g. *Encyclopaedia of Forms and Precedents (Vol. 22)*; *Drafting and Negotiating Commercial Leases* by Murray Ross; *Practical Lease Precedents* by Trevor Aldridge.
5. Covenants can be given on the grant of a lease: Law of Property (Miscellaneous Provisions) Act 1994, and see M9.

1.20.   Prescribed Clauses Leases

1.20.1. A standard method for the presentation of certain information applies to registrable leases.[1] The reasons for this include the need to make leases easier to refer to and to use, to assist with the increasing numbers of leases being registered, and to facilitate the move towards e-conveyancing.

1.20.2. In essence, both the lease and counterpart lease must contain certain prescribed clauses and these must appear at the beginning of the document or immediately after any front cover sheet and/or front contents page.

1.20.3. The requirement for leases to contain these prescribed clauses applies to most leases that are granted out of registered land and which are compulsorily registrable, such as leases granted for more than seven years. These leases are called 'Prescribed Clauses Leases'.[2]

1.20.4. There are some exceptions. A lease does not have to be a Prescribed Clauses Lease if it is granted in a form expressly required by any of the following:

(a)   an agreement entered into before 19 June 2006;

(b)   a court order;

(c)   an enactment;

(d)   a consent or licence for the grant of the lease, e.g. a superior landlord's consent, given before 19 June 2006.

1.20.5. The prescribed clauses' provisions do not apply to a lease that comes into existence by virtue of a variation of a lease that is a deemed surrender and re-grant.

1.20.6. In many cases the prescribed clause allows a cross-reference to the relevant part of the lease where the provision appears.

1.20.7. One advantage of using a Prescribed Clauses Lease is that, provided the document has been properly drafted, a separate application to register certain matters against other titles affected is not necessary. The registrar is required (where appropriate and where all the relevant title numbers are included in clause LR2) to make entries in the relevant individual register in respect of interests contained in that lease, which are of the nature referred to in clause LR9 (rights of acquisition), LR10 (restrictive covenants), LR11 (easements) or LR12 (rentcharges).[3] In addition a standard form restriction may be applied for in LR13 without the need for a separate application.

The clauses

1.20.8. Set out below is an outline of the prescribed clauses:

(a) LR1. Date of lease;

(b) LR2. Title number(s);

(c) LR2.1. Landlord's title number(s);

(d) LR2.2. Other title numbers. Here it is necessary to insert any existing title numbers against which entries of matters referred to in LR9, LR10, LR11 and LR13 are to be made;

(e) LR3. Parties to the lease;

(f) LR4. Property. Note that in the event of discrepancy between the contents of LR4 and the rest of the lease, the Land Registry will rely solely on the contents of LR4 for registration purposes;

(g) LR5. Prescribed statements etc.:

    (i) LR5.1. Statements in leases required by certain statutes. It is necessary to insert here statements prescribed where dispositions are made to a charity,[4] by a charity[5] or where a lease is granted under Leasehold Reform, Housing and Urban Development Act 1993;[6]

    (ii) LR5.2. Lease made under certain statutes. Certain statements must be inserted where the lease is made under, or by reference to, provisions of Leasehold Reform Act 1967, Housing Act 1985, Housing Act 1988 or Housing Act 1996;

(h) LR6. Term for which the property is leased;

(i) LR7. Premium;

(j) LR8. Prohibitions or restrictions on disposing of the lease. It is only necessary to include a statement as to whether or not the lease contains a provision that prohibits or restricts dispositions;

(k) LR9. Rights of acquisition etc.:

    (i) LR9.1. Tenant's contractual rights to renew the lease, to acquire the reversion or another lease of the property, or to acquire an interest in other land;

    (ii)   LR9.2. Tenant's covenant to (or offer to) surrender the lease;

    (iii) LR9.3. Landlord's contractual rights to acquire the lease;

  (l)   LR10. Restrictive covenants given in this lease by the landlord in respect of land other than the property;

  (m) LR11. Easements. In the relevant sub-clause below a reference must be made to the relevant clause, schedule or paragraph of a schedule in the lease where easements are either granted or reserved as appropriate:

    (i)   LR11.1. Easements granted by this lease for the benefit of the property;

    (ii)   LR11.2. Easements granted or reserved by this lease over the property for the benefit of other property;

  (n)   LR12. Estate rentcharge burdening the property;

  (o)   LR13. Application for standard form of restriction. Note the full text of the standard form restriction must be entered;[7]

  (p)   LR14. Declaration of trust where there is more than one person comprising the tenant.

1.20.9.   Full details can be obtained from Land Registry Practice Guide 64.[8]

1.   See Land Registration (Amendment) (No.2) Rules 2005.
2.   For details see Land Registration Rules 2003, r.58A(4)(a) and (b), and Land Registry Practice Guide 64.
3.   Land Registration Rules 2003, r.72(A).
4.   *Ibid.*, r.179.
5.   *Ibid.*, r.180.
6.   *Ibid.*, r.196.
7.   See Land Registry Practice Guide 19 for the wording of the standard restrictions.
8.   Available from **www.landregistry.gov.uk**.

1.21.   Side letters

1.21.1.   Side letters may be issued at the contract stage to agree a term that is intended to apply between the parties in relation to the transaction without a formal re-engrossment or amendment to the draft contract for the lease. As the contract for the lease must comply with the requirements of Law of Property (Miscellaneous Provisions) Act 1989, s.2, it will need to refer to the side letter. Where the side letter is issued after exchange and is intended to vary the terms of the contract, this new agreement must comply with section 2 (see further B1 and B11).

1.21.2.   Side letters are also sometimes used to change the terms of a lease itself. This is sometimes done where the change to the clause in question is intended to be personal to the tenant and therefore intended not to affect assignees. It is important to appreciate that the provisions contained within these letters are likely to be landlord or tenant covenants within the meaning of Landlord and Tenant (Covenants) Act 1995 and will therefore have the same status as a covenant in the lease itself.[1] Such a letter may bind an assignee of the reversion, even if the assignee did not know of the letter or its contents.[2] Where a side letter has been used to vary the terms of a proposed sub-letting this should be disclosed to the landlord on an application for consent to the sub-letting.[3] Variation of leases is dealt with further at K14.

1. Landlord and Tenant (Covenants) Act 1995, s.28(1).
2. *System Floors Ltd* v. *Ruralpride Ltd* [1994] EGCS 162.
3. *Allied Dunbar Assurance plc* v. *Homebase Ltd* [2002] PLSCS 123.

1.22. Energy performance certificates

1.22.1 An energy performance certificate must usually be provided to the potential tenant where the property is to be let (see further A27).

K2. Acting for the landlord

2.1. Taking instructions

2.1.1. Much of the information required by the landlord's solicitor from his client will be similar to that required from the seller in the case of a freehold transaction. These matters are considered in A1 and K1.

2.2. Drafting the lease

2.2.1. The lease is normally drafted by the seller's (landlord's) solicitor and annexed to the draft contract submitted to the buyer's (tenant's) solicitor. Except where the lease is to be for a term not exceeding three years, taking effect in possession and with no premium payable for its grant, the contract for the lease must satisfy Law of Property (Miscellaneous Provisions) Act 1989, s.2. Standard Condition 8.2 and Standard Commercial Property Condition 10.2 provide for the lease to be in the form annexed to the draft contract and for the seller to engross the lease and supply the buyer with the engrossment at least five working days before completion date. Law of Property (Miscellaneous Provisions) Act 1989, s.2 requires that the contract must incorporate all its terms (see B1.6 and B1.7). In the case of a contract for a lease the length of the term and its commencement date must be expressly stated in the draft lease which is attached to the contract in order to satisfy Law of Property (Miscellaneous Provisions) Act 1989, s.2, or either or both could be stated in the contract.[1] Where any blanks or gaps have been left in the draft lease that is attached to the contract the court will do all it can to apply the rules of construction to avoid the contract being void for uncertainty.[2]

2.2.2. Where the lease is of business premises the Law Society Standard Business Leases for the whole or part of premises may be used.

1. *Marshall* v. *Berridge* (1881) 19 ChD 233.
2. *Westvilla Propertie Ltd* v. *Dow Properties Ltd* [2010] EWHC 30 (Ch).

2.3. Preparing the documents for the tenant

Energy performance certificate

2.3.1. In the vast majority of cases it will be necessary to provide an energy performance certificate where the property is to be let (see further A27).

The contract

2.3.2.   The particulars of sale must state that the property is leasehold and give details of the term to be vested in the tenant. The draft lease should be drafted and annexed to the contract. It is usual to include a condition requiring the tenant to accept the lease in the form annexed to the contract.[1] Incumbrances affecting the freehold title must be disclosed and indemnity taken from the tenant in respect of future breaches. The landlord's solicitor should consider whether or not it is appropriate for his client to offer covenants for title to the tenant (see M9).

Checklist

2.3.3.   The documents that the landlord's solicitor may send to the tenant's solicitor are likely to include some or all of the documents specified below. So far as commercial leases are concerned, the procedures for the grant of these vary depending on the circumstances of the matter and it may be that some of these documents are omitted or some may only be supplied following a request by the tenant's solicitor. Indeed in many commercial lettings, there may be no contract and the parties will directly enter into negotiations on the draft lease. In other cases involving commercial lettings, contracts are used to give early possession on terms, e.g. to deal with building work that may be required prior to completion. The usual documents are:

(a)   draft contract with draft lease annexed;

(b)   evidence of the freehold title;

(c)   any relevant planning and building regulation consents;

(d)   answers to pre-contract searches and enquiries (or, in the case of a complex commercial property, it may be convenient to send replies to the Commercial Property Standard Enquiries);[2]

(e)   where appropriate, evidence of the lender's consent to the grant of the lease;

(f)   the memorandum and articles of any management company;

(g)   an energy performance certificate: either send it or check that the prospective tenant has received it.

Exempt information documents

2.3.4.   A landlord who wishes to apply for the lease to be designated an exempt information document faces the practical difficulty that the application for registration of the lease will be made by the tenant. It is only when the tenant lodges the lease for registration that a leasehold title number is allocated against which the exemption application can be made. A landlord may want, therefore, to include a provision in the contract requiring the tenant to lodge the landlord's exemption application when registering the lease (see further G3.12.3).

1. See Standard Condition 8.2.3 and Standard Commercial Property Condition 10.2.3.
2. Commercial Property Standard Enquiries may be downloaded from **www.bpf.org.uk** or **www. practicallaw.com**.

2.4. Engrossment and execution of lease

2.4.1. The lease is normally prepared in two parts (lease and counterpart) both engrossed by the landlord's solicitor.[1] If the landlord requires the tenant to pay a fee for the preparation of the engrossment this must be dealt with by special condition in the contract.

2.4.2. The counterpart should be sent to the tenant's solicitor at least five days before contractual completion date[2] for execution by the tenant. The requirements for execution of a deed are dealt with in section E1.7. The practical difficulties that stem from the law relating to the execution and delivery of deeds are particularly problematic for landlords in relation to leases. Once the deed is executed by the landlord and delivered, which can happen by sending it to his solicitor in certain circumstances,[3] it may be impossible for the landlord to withdraw unilaterally from the transaction prior to completion even though there is no contract.[4] Although in most cases delivery will be conditional (or in escrow), the condition being payment of the purchase price or the handing over of a counterpart, the signatory will still, however, be bound on delivery unless the condition (escrow) fails. It is possible to show that the executed lease has been handed by the client to the solicitor for delivery at some later date, e.g. on the day of completion. In this case withdrawal is possible.[5] As evidence of this intention, wording is commonly inserted into the lease to show that delivery is not intended to take place (and therefore the deed is not to be binding) until completion takes place, or this may be presumed from the surrounding circumstances, e.g. the existence of 'subject to contract' negotiations.[6]

1. Standard Condition 8.2.5 and Standard Commercial Property Condition 10.2.5.
2. *Ibid.*
3. *Venetian Glass Gallery Ltd* v. *Next Properties Ltd* [1989] 2 EGLR 42; *Beesly* v. *Hallwood Estates Ltd* [1961] Ch 105; *Johnsey Estates (1990) Ltd* v. *Newport Marketworld Ltd* [1996] EGCS 87.
4. However, the tenant cannot be bound before he has executed the lease, merely because the landlord has delivered the lease in escrow and the escrow conditions are subsequently performed: *Dyment* v. *Boyden* [2004] EWCA 1586.
5. *Longman* v. *Viscount Chelsea* (1989) 58 P&CR 189.
6. *Bolton Metropolitan Borough Council* v. *Torkington* [2003] PLSCS 241; although note *Bank of Scotland plc* v. *King and Okoronkwo* [2007] EWHC 2747 (Ch).

2.5. Completion and post-completion

2.5.1. On completion in addition to or in substitution for the matters relevant to a freehold transaction the items which the landlord will receive include:

    (a)   the counterpart lease executed by the tenant;

    (b)   any premium payable for the grant (less any deposit paid on exchange of contracts);

(c) an apportioned sum representing rent payable in advance under the lease and interim service charge. If the date from which the length of the term is calculated precedes the date of the lease itself, no rent can be recovered for this reason alone in respect of the period between the two dates.

2.5.2. The items which the landlord should give to the tenant include:

(a) the lease executed by him;

(b) if not already done, properly marked or certified copies of the freehold title deeds (unregistered land);

(c) where relevant and if not already done, a certified copy of the consent of the landlord's lender to the transaction;

(d) where relevant, share certificate relating to the management company.

2.5.3. After completion the landlord may receive notice in duplicate from the tenant, in accordance with the tenant's covenant to do so in the lease, of the tenant's mortgage of the property. One copy of the notice should be placed with the landlord's title deeds, the other receipted on behalf of the landlord and returned to the tenant's solicitor.

2.6. Apportionment of rent

2.6.1. Where the rent reserved by the lease is an annual rent payable quarterly in advance on the usual quarter days and the rent commencement date does not coincide with either the term commencement date or the usual quarter days, it is suggested that the apportionment of rent on completion of the grant of the lease should be made in accordance with the recommended method of calculation set out in Appendix IV.2. The quarter days are 25 March, 24 June, 29 September and 25 December.

Recommended method of calculation

2.6.2. The Law Society's Conveyancing and Land Law Committee has produced a formula for the calculation of the apportionment of rent. This formula is set out in Appendix IV.2.

2.6.3. For consistency, where the term expires by effluxion of time on a date other than the last day of a term year, the amount of the tenant's final payment of rent should be calculated on a basis similar to the apportionment of his initial payment on the grant of the lease.

2.6.4. Apportionment of rent where the term date does not commence on a rent payment date cannot be made according to the formula explained in Appendix IV.2. In most cases the most appropriate method of calculation in this situation will be what is sometimes called the 'surveyor's method'. This involves simply counting the days to immediately before the next payment date, and applying a daily rate computed on a 365 day per year basis. This is the method provided by the Standard Commercial Property Conditions to apply in all cases unless varied by special condition.

2.6.5. However, a daily rate for rent payable by, e.g. equal quarterly instalments is, by this method, being calculated on a yearly basis and then applied to the residue of a particular quarter, which does not comprise exactly one-fourth of a year. A variation would be to calculate the daily rate for the particular quarter by reference to the total number of days in that quarter.

2.6.6. On either basis, it will be apparent that, should it be necessary to calculate an apportionment at a later date (e.g. when the lease is assigned or surrendered, or the reversion is transferred), to achieve a fair result it would be necessary to ascertain how much rent was actually paid under the apportionment at the grant of the lease and carry the calculation forward on that basis. This will usually be impractical, and the parties will have to be prepared to adopt each time a more rough and ready approach, such as the 'surveyor's method'.

2.6.7. However, since that method is entirely arbitrary and bears no logical relationship to the term/rent structure of the lease, it is recommended that leases should be drafted so that the term year commences on one of the recurring rent payment dates. Thus if rent is to be payable on the usual quarter days, the term year should commence on a quarter day. This will enable apportionments to be computed on a logical basis as set out in Appendix IV.2.

K3. Acting for the tenant

3.1. Before exchange

Taking instructions

3.1.1. The information required by the buyer's (tenant's) solicitor from his client will be similar to that required in a freehold transaction (see A1). The client should be advised about the effect of any security of tenure provisions which may be applicable in the circumstances.

The draft lease

3.1.2. The draft lease, prepared by the seller's (landlord's) solicitor, will be supplied to the tenant's solicitor with the draft contract. The contract will normally require the tenant to accept the draft in the form annexed to the contract (see Standard Condition 8.2.3 and Standard Commercial Property Condition 10.2.3); therefore any queries or observations which are to be raised in connection with the lease must be finalised before contracts are exchanged. Even where the lease appears to contain the 'usual' clauses appropriate to the particular transaction in hand, the document must be carefully examined by the tenant's solicitor to ensure that it does contain provisions which are adequate to protect his client's interests and contains no onerous clauses (e.g. in relation to repairing obligations or rent review) which may adversely affect the client. The amount of rent and the length of the term will affect the amount of SDLT payable on the lease by the tenant and this also should be considered.

Energy performance certificate

3.1.3. It will normally be necessary to provide an energy performance certificate where the property is to be let (see further A27).

Checking the lease

3.1.4. When checking the lease particular attention should be paid to the provisions relating to the following matters:

(a) the property to be demised;

(b) easements and reservations (particularly in the case of flats or other non-detached property: see K1);

(c)   repairing obligations;

(d)   rent and rent review provisions;

(e)   provisions relating to service charges (see K1);

(f)   insurance (who is to insure: landlord or tenant? Do the insurance provisions accord with the tenant's mortgagee's instructions? What is covered by the policy both in terms of premises, amount of cover and risks insured against?);

(g)   forfeiture clauses;

(h)   covenants restricting alienation of the property;

(i)   covenants restricting the use of the property;

(j)   provisions relating to a management company or residents' association (is the tenant required to become a member of a management company which is limited by guarantee? Will his liability to the management company terminate on assignment of the lease?);

(k)   requirements for a surety or rent deposit scheme;

(l)   are any of the covenants onerous?

(m)   do the covenants adequately protect the tenant and his lender?

(n)   are covenants for title being offered?

(o)   requirements of the lender (see K6.6);

(p)   the proper completion of the prescribed clauses where it is a Prescribed Clauses Lease.

A brief summary of the most common express covenants found in leases is contained in K1.

Searches

3.1.5.   In many cases the tenant's solicitor will usually undertake the same searches and enquiries as if he were buying the freehold (see B10 and E2). Exceptionally, where a short tenancy agreement is being granted, it may be considered unnecessary to do such searches.

Lender's requirements

3.1.6.   Where the lease provides security for a loan, the tenant's lender's requirements, contained in the instructions given to the solicitors acting for the lender, must be observed. The tenant's lender will frequently be concerned to see that the following conditions have been satisfied:

(a)   the consent of the landlord's lender to the transaction has been obtained (where relevant);

(b) the length of the term to be granted provides adequate security for the loan. The requirements of lenders are referred to at K6.6;

(c) the lease contains adequate insurance provisions relating both to the premises themselves and (where relevant) to common parts of the building and that the insurance provisions coincide with the lender's own requirements for insurance;

(d) normally title to the freehold reversion should be deduced. This will enable the lease to be registered with an absolute title at the Land Registry (where appropriate);

(e) the lease contains proper repairing covenants in respect both of the property itself and (where relevant) the common parts of the building;

(f) in the case of residential leases, that there is no provision for forfeiture on the insolvency of the tenant;

(g) where the lease is of part of a building or is, e.g. of one house on an estate comprising leasehold houses all owned by the same landlord, that the lease provides for enforceability of covenants as between the tenants (usually by the landlord following a request by a tenant);

(h) where appropriate the landlord is giving the relevant covenants for title.

3.1.7.   Lenders' requirements are referred to at K6.6.

Advising the client

3.1.8.   The tenant's obligations under the lease, which are often complex and extensive, should be clearly explained to him. In particular, where relevant, the tenant should be warned of his continuing liability on the covenants in the lease notwithstanding the subsequent sale of the residue of the term to a third party (see K10) and of the danger of losing the lease through forfeiture for breach of covenant. A pre-contract report may be prepared and given to the client (as in freehold transactions, see C1). The report should explain the main provisions of the terms of the lease and their effect on the tenant.

3.2.   **Pre-completion and completion**

3.2.1.   The engrossment of the lease and counterpart will usually be prepared by the landlord's solicitor. The tenant, if the contract so provides, may be required on completion to pay a fee to the landlord for the preparation of the engrossment. By Standard Condition 8.2.5 and Standard Commercial Property Condition 10.2.5 the landlord is to deliver the engrossment of the counterpart lease to the tenant at least five working days before completion and by Standard Condition 8.2.6 and Standard Commercial Property Condition 10.2.6 the tenant is to execute the counterpart lease and deliver it to the landlord on completion. Similar points apply in relation to execution of the counterpart as those relating to execution of the lease. This is discussed in K2.4.2 and section E.

3.2.2. The tenant's solicitor should make pre-completion searches in the same way as if he were buying the freehold (see section E2).

3.2.3. Apportionments on completion may include amounts in respect of rent and service charge payable in advance under the provisions of the lease.

3.2.4. On completion the tenant should give to the landlord, *inter alia*:

    (a)   the duly executed counterpart lease;

    (b)   any money due on completion, e.g. balance of premium (less deposit paid on exchange), apportioned sums payable in respect of rent and service charge, landlord's fee for engrossment of the lease.

3.2.5. The tenant should on completion receive from the landlord, *inter alia*:

    (a)   the duly executed lease;

    (b)   where the landlord's title is unregistered, a marked abstract of the freehold title;

    (c)   where appropriate, consent to the dealing given by the landlord's mortgagee;

    (d)   share certificate and management company documents.

3.3.   **Post-completion**

Stamp Duty Land Tax

3.3.1. For every notifiable transaction (see A14.4) which will include the grant of many leases, the tenant must deliver a land transaction return to HM Revenue and Customs within 30 days of the effective date of the transaction. This delivery must include a self-assessment of the liability and payment of the SDLT due (if any).

3.3.2. The general rule is that the effective date of a land transaction is the date of completion. There are, however, special rules where a contract is substantially performed before it is completed (e.g. where under an agreement for lease, occupation is taken by the tenant before completion).[1] See further A14.19.

3.3.3. Unless exempt from certification for SDLT purposes a lease cannot be registered or noted at the Land Registry without a certificate as to compliance with SDLT (see A14.30).

3.3.4. The SDLT payable on a premium and on the lease rent are calculated separately (see A14.15).

Registration of the lease

3.3.5. Where applicable the lease must be registered at the Land Registry within the relevant priority period, or on first registration within two months of completion. The requirements for registration of a lease are outlined in K1.13.

Notice to landlord

3.3.6. The lease will usually contain a covenant requiring the tenant to notify the landlord within a stated period of all dealings with the lease and to pay a fee to the landlord for registration of the notice. The creation of a mortgage by the tenant, depending on the wording of the covenant, may fall within this obligation. Where the tenant is obliged to give notice of dealings, this should be done by sending two copies of the notice, together with the appropriate fee, to the landlord's solicitor or other person named in the covenant. The landlord should be asked to sign one copy of the notice and to return it to the tenant so that the receipted notice may be placed with the tenant's title deeds as evidence of compliance with this requirement.

3.3.7. A tenant's lender may require a signed but otherwise blank stock transfer form and the tenant's share certificate to be lodged with him to ensure that the lender will be able to transfer the tenant's share in the management company in the event of the lender exercising his power of sale.

Registration of certain covenants

3.3.8. Where the landlord's title is registered, restrictive covenants between landlord and tenant which relate to the demised premises cannot be protected by registration.[2] It is, however, necessary to protect restrictive covenants contained in leases which relate to property other than that demised by means of a notice. If, for example, the landlord has covenanted not to allow another unit in a retail park to trade in competition with a tenant, the tenant should protect the covenant against the landlord's title in respect of land other than the property by means of a notice.[3]

1. Both the contract and the transaction effected on completion may be notifiable transactions; see further A14.19.
2. Land Registration Act 2002, s.33.
3. This may be done by the proper registration of a Prescribed Clauses Lease with details of the restrictive covenants set out in LR10 (see K1.20.8, item (l)) and where all relevant title numbers are included in clause LR2.

K4. Acting for both parties

4.1.   Conflict of interests

4.1.1.   A solicitor must not act where there is a conflict of interest between himself and his clients or between two of his clients (see A10 and A11).

4.2.   Rule 3 Solicitors' Code of Conduct 2007

4.2.1.   Specifically in relation to leasehold conveyancing Rule 3 Solicitors' Code of Conduct 2007 prohibits a solicitor from acting for both landlord and tenant in the grant or assignment of a lease at arm's length. This rule and its exceptions are further discussed in A10 and Rule 3 is reproduced at Appendix I.1.

4.3.   Acting for the client's lender

4.3.1.   Generally, a solicitor may act for his landlord or tenant client and that client's lender provided that no conflict of interests exists or is likely to arise. See A11.

4.3.2.   The CML Lenders' Handbook and the BSA Mortgage Instructions also preclude the same fee earner in the same firm acting for the lender and either the borrower or the seller, where the borrower or seller is either the fee earner or a member of his immediate family. Consent may be given by some lenders but in this case a separate fee earner of no less standing in the firm must act for the lender.

4.4.   Sureties

4.4.1.   A prospective tenant's solicitor who is also considering acting for the prospective surety to the lease must consider his obligations under Solicitors' Code of Conduct 2007 which provides in Rule 3.01(2) that there is a conflict of interests if:

> 'you owe, or your firm owes, separate duties to act in the best interests of two or more clients in relation to the same or related matters, and those duties conflict, or there is a significant risk that those duties may conflict ...'

However the Code also provides in Rule 3.02(1):

'You or your firm may act for two or more clients in relation to a matter in situations of conflict or possible conflict if:

(a)   the different clients have a substantially common interest in relation to that matter or a particular aspect of it; and

(b)   all the clients have given in writing their informed consent to you or your firm acting.'

Where this rule is being relied upon Rule 3.02(4) requires the solicitor to:

'(a)   draw all the relevant issues to the attention of the clients before agreeing to act or, where already acting, when the conflict arises or as soon as is reasonably practicable, and in such a way that the clients concerned can understand the issues and the risks involved;

(b)   have a reasonable belief that the clients understand the relevant issues; and

(c)   be reasonably satisfied that those clietns are of full capacity.'

For example, it may be in the best interests of a prospective tenant to obtain a lease of the premises, which he can only do if he provides a surety to the lease (a pre-condition imposed by the landlord), but, on the face of it, it is not in the best interests of the surety to enter into covenants with the landlord to guarantee performance of the tenant's obligations under the lease, as it is potentially liable for these liabilities of the tenant. However, if the surety is a parent company and the tenant is a wholly owned subsidiary they may have a 'substantially common interest' in the matter proceeding. The position may be completely different if the surety is an individual who becomes potentially liable for the tenant's obligations under the lease where the enforcement of the surety's covenants would put the surety's personal assets, such as a matrimonial home, at risk. It is a matter of judgement in each case whether the situation is one where the interests of both the tenant and the surety are sufficiently 'common' so as to outweigh the extent to which there is a realistic risk of their interests being in conflict. If, in the opinion of the solicitor, he feels able to act for both parties then written consent should be obtained in accordance with Rule 3.02. However, where the solicitor feels that there is not a sufficient 'substantial common interest' so as to outweigh the conflict that exists, or is likely to arise, between them, then the surety should be given independent advice about his potential liability.

4.4.2.   Where a solicitor does act for a surety or guarantor he owes a duty of care to the surety or guarantor to exercise reasonable skill and care in carrying out the terms of the retainer.[1]

4.4.3.   Under the terms of the CML Lenders' Handbook and the BSA Mortgage Instructions[2] the solicitor who is acting for the borrower cannot, generally, also act for a guarantor, any borrower who does not personally benefit from the loan or anyone intending to occupy the property who is to consent to the mortgage. They must be independently advised.

1.   *Woodward* v. *Wolferstans* [1997] NPC 51.
2.   See the CML Lenders' Handbook, Part 1, section 8 and BSA Mortgage Instructions, paragraph B.24.

K5. Short-term residential tenancies

5.1. **Grant of lease**
5.2. **Public sector tenants**
5.3. **Rent Act tenancies**
5.4. **Assured tenancies**

5.5. **Shorthold tenancies**
5.6. **Long tenancies at low rents**
5.7. **Agricultural employees**

5.1.   Grant of lease

5.1.1.   A lease for a term of over three years must be granted by deed to vest the legal estate in the tenant. A lease for three years or less, taking effect in possession at the best rent without a fine, may be granted orally or in writing.[1] To ensure certainty of terms between the parties it is recommended that all leases, no matter how short the term, should be in writing.

5.1.2.   A contract for the grant of the lease is not generally entered into on short-term lettings of residential premises.

5.1.3.   On short-term lettings of residential property it is not usual for searches and enquiries to be made since the low risk attached to these lettings does not justify the expense of making the searches. However, the prospective tenant may feel it is prudent to make enquiries about the prospective landlord's solvency, particularly where the property is mortgaged, to avoid the risk of the landlord's lender seeking a possession order against the tenant if the landlord does not pay the mortgage. No SDLT will normally be payable, nor will such a transaction normally be notifiable (see A14.4).

5.1.4.   Where the lease is to be granted for a short term some of the considerations outlined in K1, K2 and K3 will not be relevant. Frequently a formal contract for the grant of the lease is dispensed with and the landlord's solicitor simply submits a draft lease (sometimes referred to as a tenancy agreement) for approval by the tenant's solicitor. When the form of the lease or agreement is finalised and signed, the tenant will take possession of the premises. No premium is normally taken. In some cases a premium is not permitted by law[2] but, in these cases, a deposit which must not exceed one-sixth of the annual rent may be taken as security against damage to fixtures and fittings.[3] Deposits in relation to assured shorthold tenancies are governed by the tenancy deposit scheme (see K5.5.45).

5.1.5.   Where the premises are furnished, an inventory of the contents should be prepared by the landlord and agreed by the tenant.

5.1.6.   If the rent is to be payable weekly, a rent book must be provided to the tenant.[4]

5.1.7. The tenant's solicitor will not normally investigate title on his client's behalf, but the risks of omitting this step must be considered in each individual case. The terms of the tenancy agreement must be carefully scrutinised and their effect explained to the client. Particular attention should be paid to the effects of any security of tenure legislation on the tenancy.[5]

5.1.8. A lease of seven years or less is generally not capable of being registered with its own title at the Land Registry,[6] but takes effect as an overriding interest.[7] If there is concern about protecting the tenant's interest in the property a notice may be entered against the landlord's title where the lease is for a term of more than three years from the date of the grant.[8] A lease for a term of three years or less cannot be protected by notice.[9]

5.1.9. Where the title to the reversionary estate is unregistered a purchaser of the reversion will take subject to a lease. An agreement for a lease must be registered as an estate contract (C(iv) land charge) and a caution against first registration may be registered at the Land Registry.

5.1.10. It will usually be necessary to provide an energy performance certificate to the prospective tenant where the property is to be let (see further A27.8).

Licences of houses in multiple occupation

5.1.11. Regulations have been introduced in order to improve the standard of rented accommodation in larger houses which contain tenants who share the facilities of the property, e.g. large nineteenth-century buildings that have been converted into bedsits. This type of property may be classified as a house in multiple occupation (HMO) if it meets the criteria set out in Housing Act 2004, s.77 and ss.254–260.

5.1.12. Part 2 Housing Act 2004 and the regulations made thereunder require the mandatory licensing of certain HMOs.[10]

5.1.13. HMOs are subject to the mandatory licensing scheme, broadly, if the HMO satisfies the following criteria:

    (a) the HMO or any part of it comprises three storeys[11] or more;

    (b) it is occupied by five or more persons; and

    (c) it is occupied by persons living in two or more single households.[12]

However, an HMO may be exempt from mandatory licensing in certain circumstances.[13] One type of HMO is a converted block of flats to which Housing Act 2004, s.257 applies. This applies to a building or part of a building which has been converted into and consists of self-contained flats if the building work undertaken in connection with the conversion did not comply with appropriate building standards and still does not comply with them, and less than two-thirds of the self-contained flats are owner-occupied. Specific regulations apply to the licensing regime of these types of HMOs.[14]

5.1.14. Further regulations make provision for related matters such as:

(a) application forms and the information to be held on public registers;[15]

(b) the minimum management standards for HMOs;[16]

(c) the circumstances in which a local authority may be authorised to take over the management of individual private rented properties that give rise to significant anti-social behaviour problems.[17]

5.1.15. Where universities and colleges of higher and further education manage and control student accommodation, they are required to comply with a code of management practice in order to secure exception from HMO licensing.[18]

5.1.16. Planning permission is required when changing the use of a property to an HMO and Town and Country Planning (Use Classes) Order 1987 has been amended with effect from April 2010. This applies to England only.[19]

Selective licensing of certain private rented property

5.1.17. Due to concerns about the activities of some private landlords in areas of declining housing demand who have been offering homes to anti-social tenants,[20] Housing Act 2004, Part 3 enables a local authority to designate an area for licensing of private rented accommodation, subject to certain exemptions.[21] Broadly, the local authority will have to be satisfied that the area is, or is likely to become, one of low housing demand and is experiencing a significant problem caused by anti-social behaviour which private sector landlords are failing to address properly.[22]

1. Section 54(2) Law of Property Act 1925. A legal easement must be created by deed (*Mason* v. *Clarke* [1954] 1 QB 460). Therefore if an easement is contained in a lease of three years or less the lease should be created by a deed.
2. As in the case of tenancies protected under Rent Act 1977, see Rent Act 1977, Part IX, Sched.1, Pt. II; and K5.3.9.
3. Rent Act 1977, s.128(1) and see further K5.5.45.
4. Landlord and Tenant Act 1985, s.4. See *R (on the application of Dewa)* v. *Marylebone Magistrates Court* [2004] EWHC 1002 (Admin), where the section was considered.
5. The Law Commission has issued a report proposing an entirely new scheme to cover short term residential lettings. This proposes that all these lettings would be controlled by statute and be called 'occupation contracts'. Although there is no immediate proposal to introduce any such legislation, the report may be of interest to anyone advising generally in this area. See Law Com No.297.
6. Except leases granted under Housing Act 1985, Part V, see K9.1.6. See exceptions in G3.2.
7. Land Registration Act 2002, Sched.1, para.1 and Sched.3, para.1.
8. Note that any easements granted to the tenant should be noted against the landlord's title as these do not operate at law until the burden is noted on the landlord's title; see Land Registration Act 2002, s.27(1) and (2)(d) and Sched.2, para.7. For more information see Land Registry Practice Guide 62.
9. Land Registration Act 2002, s.33(b).
10. For further details on the licensing scheme see **www.communities.gov.uk/housing/rentingandletting/privaterenting/selectivelicensing/**.
11. Licensing of Houses in Multiple Occupation (Prescribed Descriptions) (England) Order 2006 (SI 2006/371); Licensing of Houses in Multiple Occupation (Prescribed Descriptions) (Wales) Order 2006 (SI 2006/1712). Paragraph 3(3) of the Orders sets out the conditions to determine which storeys are taken into account depending on their use.
12. A single household is defined, for the purposes of determining whether a building is an HMO under s.254, by Housing Act 2004, s.258.

13. If, for example, the property is subject to a temporary exemption notice under Housing Act 2004, s.62, or if it is subject to an interim or final management order under Chapter 1 of Part 4 Housing Act 2004. There is power to extend the licensing regime in certain circumstances under Housing Act 2004, s.257 to certain blocks of self-contained flats.

14. Licensing and Management of Houses in Multiple Occupation (Additional Provisions) (England) Regulations 2007 (SI 2007/1903); Houses in Multiple Occupation (Certain Converted Blocks of Flats) (Modifications to the Housing Act 2004 and Transitional Provisions for section 257 HMOs) (England) Regulations 2007 (SI 2007/1904); Houses in Multiple Occupation (Certain Blocks of Flats) (Modifications to the Housing Act 2004 and Transitional Provisions for section 257 HMOs) (Wales) Regulations 2007 (SI 2007/3231); Licensing and Management of Houses in Multiple Occupation (Additional Provisions) (Wales) Regulations 2007 (SI 2007/ 3229).

15. Licensing and Management of Houses in Multiple Occupation and Other Houses (Miscellaneous Provisions) (England) Regulations 2006 (SI 2006/373); Licensing and Management of Houses in Multiple Occupation and other Houses (Miscellaneous Provisions) (Wales) Regulations 2006 (SI 2006/1715).

16. Management of Houses in Multiple Occupation (England) Regulations 2006 (SI 2006/372); Management of Houses in Multiple Occupation (Wales) Regulations 2006 (SI 2006/1713).

17. Housing (Interim Management Orders) (Prescribed Circumstances) (England) Order 2006 (SI 2006/ 369); Housing (Interim Management Orders) (Prescribed Circumstances) (Wales) Order 2006 (SI 2006/1706).

18. Houses in Multiple Occupation (Specified Educational Establishments) (England) Regulations 2010 (SI 2010/607); Houses in Multiple Occupation (Specified Educational Establishments) (Wales) Regulations 2006 (SI 2006/1707); Housing (Approval of Codes of Management Practice) (Student Accommodation) (England) Order 2006 (SI 2006/646); Housing (Approval of Codes of Management Practice) (Student Accommodation) (Wales) Order 2006 (SI 2006/1709).

19. Town and Country Planning (Use Classes) (Amendment) (England) Order 2010 (SI 2010/653).

20. See the housing green paper, *Quality And Choice: A Decent Home For All* (December 2000) available on **www.communities.gov.uk**.

21. Selective Licensing of Houses (Specified Exemptions) (England) Order 2006 (SI 2006/370); Selective Licensing of Houses (Specified Exemptions) (Wales) Order 2006 (SI 2006/2824); Selective Licensing of Houses (Additional Conditions) (Wales) Order 2006 (SI 2006/2825).

22. Housing Act 2004, s.80.

5.2. Public sector tenants

5.2.1. Security for public sector tenants is provided by Part IV Housing Act 1985 (as amended by Housing Act 1988) under what are called 'secure tenancies'.

5.2.2. Subject to:

(a) a number of exceptions set out in Schedule 1. Examples include:

(i) tenancies granted for over 21 years;

(ii) generally those tenancies granted pursuant to a local housing authority's duties to the homeless;

(iii) business tenancies within Part II Landlord and Tenant Act 1954; and

(iv) family intervention tenancies (see K5.2.7);

(b) tenancies ceasing to be secure tenancies after the death of the tenant subject to certain limited succession rights;[1] and

(c) tenancies ceasing to be secure tenancies in consequence of an assignment or sub-letting other than one permitted by the Act;[2]

a tenancy under which a dwelling house is let as a separate dwelling is a secure tenancy at any time when the 'landlord condition' and the 'tenant condition' are both satisfied.

5.2.3. The provisions apply to most licences as well as to tenancies.[3]

The 'landlord condition'

5.2.4. The 'landlord condition' is that the interest of the landlord belongs to one of a number of bodies specified in Housing Act 1985, s.80, as modified by Housing Act 1988, s.35. These include local authorities, development corporations and certain housing co-operatives.

The 'tenant condition'

5.2.5. The 'tenant condition' is that the tenant is an individual and occupies the house as his only or principal home or, where the tenancy is a joint tenancy, that each of the joint tenants is an individual and at least one of them occupies the house as his only or principal home.

5.2.6. Where a secure tenancy for a term certain ends by effluxion of time or by an order terminating the tenancy in pursuance of a right of forfeiture, a periodic tenancy arises. A secure tenancy which is either a periodic tenancy or for a term certain but subject to termination by the landlord cannot usually be brought to an end by the landlord except by obtaining a court order for possession. The grounds for possession are set out in Schedule 2 Housing Act 1985.[4] These have been extended by Anti-social Behaviour Act 2003.[5] It is also possible for most landlords[6] of secure tenancies to apply to a county court for a demotion order, which can be made if the tenant or a person residing in or visiting the dwelling house has, broadly, either engaged in anti-social behaviour or used the premises for unlawful purposes.[7] If the tenant remains in occupation, a new demoted tenancy will begin on the same date. The terms of a demoted tenancy are set out in the legislation and this may be terminated by the court, provided a prescribed procedure is followed by the landlord.[8]

5.2.7. Family intervention tenancies[9] are tenancies designed to enable the provision of behavioural support services to tenants. They can be offered to secure tenants against whom a possession order for anti-social behaviour has been made or against whom such an order could have been made (whether or not they have such a tenancy).[10] The landlord must serve prescribed information on the tenant at the outset. There is, effectively, no security of tenure available to these tenancies, although they can be converted into secure tenancies on notice by the landlord. They can be terminated by a notice to quit providing certain procedures are followed.[11] In outline, these require a written notice of intent to be served on the tenant and the tenant to be given the opportunity of a review.[12]

5.2.8. A secure tenancy ends on the death of the tenant, although provisions for succession to the tenancy after the death of the tenant are contained in Housing Act 1985, ss.87–90.

5.2.9. A secure tenancy cannot generally be assigned, but there are limited exceptions to this rule, e.g. an assignment with the landlord's consent by way of exchange. A secure tenant cannot, without the landlord's consent, sub-let or part with the possession of part only of the house. In this case, the landlord must not unreasonably withhold his consent to the alienation and, if consent is unreasonably withheld, it is treated as having been given. If, however, the tenant sub-lets the whole, the tenancy ceases to be a secure tenancy.[13]

Introductory tenancies

5.2.10. A local housing authority or housing action trust is empowered by Housing Act 1996, s.124 to operate an introductory tenancy regime.

5.2.11. Where the scheme has been adopted by the local authority, the majority of all new periodic tenancies or licences, which would otherwise be secure, granted by the authority will, instead, be 'introductory tenancies'. A new tenancy is one granted to a person (or persons) who immediately before its grant was not a secure tenant of the same or different premises and was not an assured tenant of a registered social landlord of the same or another dwelling house.

5.2.12. An introductory tenancy, broadly, remains such for a trial period of one year subject to certain earlier termination provisions contained in Housing Act 1996, s.125. If no proceedings are brought within the one-year period, the tenancy will normally automatically become a secure tenancy.[14]

5.2.13. The landlord can bring an introductory tenancy to an end, after serving notice on the tenant, by obtaining a court order under Housing Act 1996, s.127. The tenant has the right to ask for a review of the landlord's decision to end the tenancy within 14 days of notice of possession proceedings being served on him.[15] Subject to this, the possession ground is mandatory.

5.2.14. Provisions for succession to an introductory tenancy are contained in Housing Act 1996, ss.131–133. An introductory tenancy is not capable of assignment except under certain provisions of the Act which are similar to those for secure tenancies (e.g. assignments under the Matrimonial Causes Act 1973, s.24).

Non-secure tenants of local authorities

5.2.15. Where the occupier is a non-secure tenant it is unlikely that Article 8 European Convention on Human Rights will provide a further defence to applications for possession orders by local authorities (as a public authority). This Article provides, *inter alia*, that there is a right to a home and that there shall be no interference by a public authority with the exercise of this right except such as is in accordance with the law and as is there further provided.

5.2.16. The House of Lords has held[16] that for such a defence to succeed it would be necessary to argue either, exceptionally, that the law giving the right to possession was incompatible with Article 8; or that the decision to exercise the right to possession was one that no reasonable person would consider justifiable. For example, where the authority had not considered any alternatives to eviction, this was held to be a situation where no reasonable authority would have sought an order for possession.[17]

Unfair Terms in Consumer Contracts Regulations 1994

5.2.17. These regulations (despite their title) have been held to apply to certain tenancy agreements entered into by local authorities[18] and registered social landlords[19] with individual tenants. The regulations apply to contracts between a supplier or seller and a consumer.

5.2.18. If a term in such a contract is 'unfair' it will be void, although the rest of the contract will subsist. A term will be unfair, broadly, if it causes a significant imbalance in the parties' rights and obligations arising from the contract to the detriment of the consumer. The regulations also require contracts to be drafted in plain English.[20]

1. Housing Act 1985, ss.87–90.
2. *Ibid.*, ss.91, 93.
3. *Ibid.*, s.79.
4. If the tenant is permitted to remain in occupation once his secure tenancy is terminated by court order he becomes a 'tolerated trespasser'; see *Burrows* v. *London Borough of Brent* [1996] 1 WLR 1448; *Newham LBC* v. *Hawkins* [2005] EWCA 451. As to the consequences of a suspended possession order see *Knowsley Housing Trust* v. *White* [2008] UKHL 70. Housing and Regeneration Act 2008, s.299 and Sched. 11 prevent the future creation of tolerated trespassers by providing that the secure tenancy will only end on execution of the court possession order. It also contains provisions to deal with the position of current tolerated trespassers. These provisions substantially came into force in May 2009. See Housing and Regeneration Act 2008 (Commencement No.5) Order 2009 (SI 2009/1261), Housing (Replacement of Terminated Tenancies) (Successor Landlords) (England) Order 2009 (SI 2009/1262), and Housing (Replacement of Terminated Tenancies) (Successor Landlords) (Wales) Order 2009 (SI 2009/1260).
5. Section 16(1) inserts a new section 85A into Housing Act 1985. The effect of this is that where the court is considering making a possession order under one of the nuisance grounds for possession, the court must consider the effect of the anti-social behaviour on others.
6. The landlord must be either a local housing authority, a housing action trust (or a registered social landlord in respect of an assured tenancy – see K5.4.47); see Housing Act 1985, s.82A(1).
7. Housing Act 1985, s.82A(1), (2) and Housing Act 1996, ss.153A or 153B.
8. Anti-social Behaviour Act 2003, s.14(5) and Sched.1 amend Housing Act 1996 and Housing Act 1985 and set out the legal position regarding demoted tenancies.
9. Housing and Regeneration Act 2008, s. 297, inserting new provisions into Schedules 1 Housing Acts 1985 and 1988. See also 'Guidance on the use of Family Intervention Tenancies' available from: **www.communities.gov.uk/publications/housing/familyinterventionguide**.
10. The rules in Housing Act 1996 which apply to the allocation of housing do not apply to allocations made to a person who occupies accommodation let on a family intervention tenancy. See Allocation of Housing (England) (Amendment) (Family Intervention Tenancies) Regulations 2008 (SI 2008/3015).
11. Housing and Regeneration Act 2008, s. 298.
12. Regulations provide for the procedure to be followed on review of a decision by a local authority to end a family intervention tenancy. See Family Intervention Tenancies (Review of Local Authority Decisions) (England) Regulations 2008 (SI 2008/3111).
13. Housing Act 1985, s.95.
14. As to the calculation of this period see *Salford County Council* v. *Garner* [2004] EWCA Civ 364. This period may be extended by a further six months where there are concerns about the conduct of an introductory tenant, including in cases of anti-social behaviour.

15. Should the review lead to the local authority deciding not to proceed, but subsequently there are further breaches, the local authority does not have to serve a second notice: *R (on the application of Stone)* v. *Cardiff City Council* [2003] All ER (D) 379 (Jan), unless the first notice was withdrawn: *R (on the application of Forbes)* v. *Lambeth LBC* [2003] All ER (D) 236 (Feb).
16. *Leeds City Council* v. *Price; Kay* v. *London Borough of Lambeth* [2006] UKHL 10.
17. *Barber* v. *London Borough of Croydon* [2010] EWCA Civ 51.
18. *Khatun* v. *Newham London Borough Council* [2004] 3 WLR 417.
19. *Governors of the Peabody Trust* v. *Reeve* [2008] EWHC 1432 (Ch).
20. See further B11.10. The Office of Fair Trading has published various guides to what it believes are unfair terms in various types of contracts, including potentially unfair terms in assured and assured shorthold tenancy agreements. See **www.oft.gov.uk/shared_oft/reports/unfair_contract_terms/ oft356.pdf**.

5.3.   Rent Act tenancies

5.3.1.   A tenancy under which a dwelling house (including part of a house) was let as a separate dwelling before 15 January 1989 was (and will until termination of the tenancy continue to be) a protected tenancy under Rent Act 1977, unless that tenancy was excluded from the Act (see K5.3.3). Since 14 January 1989 no new Rent Act tenancies, subject to some minor exceptions, have come into being because on that date Rent Act 1977 was superseded by Housing Act 1988 (see K5.4).

5.3.2.   On the termination of a protected tenancy (e.g. by forfeiture or notice to quit), the person who at that time was the protected tenant will become a statutory tenant if and so long as he occupies the house as his residence. Although the terms of the protected tenancy apply to the statutory tenancy so far as they are consistent with the nature of the statutory tenancy, there are a number of differences between the two types of tenancy, such differences deriving from the fact that a protected tenancy is a proprietary right, while a statutory tenancy is merely a personal right of residence. A protected tenancy will vest in a tenant's trustee in bankruptcy and can be disclaimed by him (so ending the tenant's right of residence as against his landlord) but a statutory tenancy does not vest in a trustee in bankruptcy.

Exclusions from protection

5.3.3.   These include:[1]

    (a)   tenancies of high value dwellings;

    (b)   tenancies at low rents;

    (c)   holiday lettings;

    (d)   lettings by resident landlords;

    (e)   lettings by local authorities and housing associations;

    (f)   business tenancies within Part II Landlord and Tenant Act 1954; and

    (g)   licences.

Rent control[2]

5.3.4. Unless a rent is registered with the rent officer, a landlord who granted a protected tenancy can initially lawfully recover whatever amount of rent has been agreed between the parties. Such rent can be increased provided that the conditions in the Act relating to the making of a rent agreement are followed.[3] It is open to the tenant to apply to the rent officer for the determination and registration of a 'fair rent', in which case the fair rent will be the maximum legally recoverable amount. An application for revision of the fair rent cannot normally be made within two years of the previous registration.

Recovery of possession

5.3.5. A court order is necessary in order to recover possession from a tenant who has security of tenure under Rent Act 1977.[4] Such an order can only be made where the court[5] is satisfied either that suitable alternative accommodation is available to the tenant or that one or more of the grounds for possession set out in Schedule 15 Rent Act 1977 has been established. Some of the grounds under Schedule 15 are mandatory and others are discretionary, i.e. the landlord must not only prove the existence of the ground, he must also satisfy the court that it is reasonable in all the circumstances to make an order for possession.

Protected shorthold tenancies

5.3.6. These were introduced by Housing Act 1980, enabling landlords to grant fixed-term tenancies for a minimum period of one year and a maximum period of five years giving the landlord the guaranteed right to possession at the end of the term provided certain conditions were satisfied. The fair rent provisions of Rent Act 1977 apply to such tenancies. No new protected shorthold tenancies have come into existence since 14 January 1989 when these provisions were superseded by Housing Act 1988.

Death of tenant

5.3.7. On the death of the tenant a statutory tenancy may pass to a spouse or civil partner who occupies the property as his or her residence.[6] Otherwise it may pass to a family member who has lived there for at least two years prior to the death,[7] but in this case it is converted to an assured tenancy (see K5.4).

Assignment and sub-letting

5.3.8. Whether or not a protected tenant can assign or sub-let the house or part of it depends on the terms of the tenancy. A statutory tenant cannot assign the lease unless he follows a prescribed statutory procedure.[8] The requirements of this procedure include the need for the assignment to be in writing and for the landlord to be a party to it. The tenant may sub-let in theory, unless the terms of the protected tenancy prohibited this. However, he cannot sub-let in whole without the risk of terminating the statutory tenancy due to cessation of occupation.[9] In a similar way a sub-letting of part risks terminating the statutory tenancy of that part.[10]

Premiums

5.3.9.   There is a general prohibition on the taking of a premium as a condition of or in connection with the grant, renewal, continuance, assignment or underletting of a protected tenancy. In relation to long tenancies, these rules are substantially modified by Rent Act 1977, s.127, as amended by Housing Act 1980, s.78 and Housing Act 1988, s.115.

1. See Rent Act 1977, ss.4–16.
2. Parts III and IV Rent Act 1977, as amended by Housing Act 1980.
3. Rent Act 1977, ss.51 and 54.
4. *Ibid.*, s.98.
5. The county court has jurisdiction over all matters under Rent Act 1977.
6. This includes a person living with the tenant as if they were either a spouse or a civil partner; Rent Act 1977, Sched.1, para.2(2) (as amended).
7. Rent Act 1977, Sched.1, para.3. Where more than one person is qualified to succeed they may agree who the successor is to be (*ibid.*). See *Clore* v. *MacNicol* [2004] EWCA Civ 1055.
8. Rent Act 1977, s.3(5), Sched.1, paras.13 and 14.
9. *Smith's Charity Trustees* v. *Wilson* [1983] QB 316. Also note *Moreland Properties (UK) Ltd* v. *Dhokia and Others* [2003] All ER (D) 348 (Oct).
10. *Baron* v. *Phillips* (1979) 28 P&CR 9.

5.4.   Assured tenancies

Introduction

5.4.1.   The definition of an assured tenancy is set out in Housing Act 1988, s.1. A tenancy under which a dwelling house is let as a separate dwelling will be an assured tenancy, if and so long as all of the following requirements are met:

    (a)   the tenant or each of joint tenants is an individual; and

    (b)   the tenant or at least one of joint tenants occupies the dwelling house as his only or principal home; and

    (c)   the tenancy is not specifically excluded by other provisions of the Act.

5.4.2.   Most new lettings will actually be assured shorthold tenancies (see K5.5) and not assured tenancies. This applied from the commencement date of the relevant provisions of the Housing Act 1996 (28 February 1997). However, a shorthold is merely a type of assured tenancy and so must comply with the definition of an assured tenancy as well as the extra requirements which make it a shorthold.

5.4.3.   Tenancies which do not satisfy the definition of an assured tenancy (and so cannot be shortholds either) will not be subject to the provisions of Housing Act

1988. Instead, ordinary common law rules as to termination, etc., will apply. They will, however, be subject to Protection from Eviction Act 1977 (see K12.5.1).

Constituent elements of an assured tenancy

Tenancy

5.4.4. There must be a 'tenancy'; licences to occupy dwelling houses are excluded from protection. This distinction is dealt with in K12.

Dwelling house

5.4.5. Housing Act 1988, s.45(1) merely provides that a dwelling house may be a house or part of a house. Therefore it will be a question of fact whether premises can be considered to be a house or not, but any building designed or adapted for living in is capable of forming a dwelling house for these purposes.

Let as a separate dwelling

5.4.6. The premises, as well as being a dwelling house, must be let as a dwelling. So the purpose of the letting is relevant; thus if a building that would otherwise qualify as a dwelling house is let for business purposes, the tenant cannot claim that it is let on an assured tenancy merely because he decides to move in and live there.

5.4.7. There must be a letting as a dwelling. It has been established that this only permits of a singular construction (notwithstanding Interpretation Act 1978).[1] So if the let property comprises two or more residential units, each intended for separate occupation (e.g. the letting of the whole of a house converted into several flats), that tenancy cannot be an assured tenancy. The sub-letting of each of the individual flats could, however, be within the definition.

5.4.8. There must be a separate dwelling. This is intended to exclude lettings of accommodation which lacks some essential feature of a dwelling. The House of Lords has held that the presence of cooking facilities is not an essential feature of a dwelling.[2] However, Housing Act 1988, s.3 makes special provision for the situation where the tenant shares some of the essential features of a dwelling with others. Such a letting is deemed to be an assured tenancy (assuming that all the other conditions are met) even though the absence of essential facilities in the demised property would normally prevent the tenancy from fulfilling the statutory requirements. The tenant must, however, have the exclusive occupation of at least one room (otherwise it cannot be a tenancy), and if the other accommodation is shared with the landlord, the tenancy will be excluded from the definition of an assured tenancy for different reasons. Arrangements where each tenant is given exclusive occupation of his own bed-sitting room, but shares bathroom and kitchen with other tenants, will be deemed to be capable of being assured tenancies.

'If and so long as'

5.4.9.   The status of the tenancy is not to be determined once and for all at the commencement of the letting. Whether a tenancy is an assured tenancy can fluctuate according to changed circumstances. For example, one requirement of the definition is that the tenant must be occupying the house as his only or principal home. This may have been the case at the start of the tenancy, and so the tenancy would be assured, but if subsequently the tenant ceases to reside at the premises, the tenancy will no longer be assured. The tenant will thus lose his security of tenure.

The tenant must be an individual

5.4.10.   Lettings to companies are excluded from the definition, even though an individual (e.g. a director or employee of the company) may be in occupation of the house. Any sub-letting by a company tenant could, however, qualify as an assured tenancy.

The tenant must occupy as his 'only or principal home'

5.4.11.   It is possible for a person to have more than one 'home'. Therefore it is a question of fact as to which is the tenant's principal home. Only a tenancy of the principal home can be an assured tenancy. Although the provision requires 'occupation', this does not mean continuous occupation. A mere temporary absence will not deprive a tenancy of its status as an assured tenancy.

Tenancies excluded from the definition

Tenancies entered into before the commencement of Housing Act 1988

5.4.12.   Only lettings entered into on or after 15 January 1989 can be assured tenancies. Any pre-existing tenancy will, if it has any protection at all, still remain subject to the provisions of Rent Act 1977.[3] There are, however, exceptions to this rule in some cases where a succession has taken place in relation to a pre-existing tenancy.

High value properties

5.4.13.   For tenancies granted before 1 April 1990, a tenancy of a dwelling house with a rateable value in excess of £750 (£1,500 in Greater London) cannot be an assured tenancy. If the tenancy was granted on or after 1 April 1990, it cannot be an assured tenancy if the rent payable is £25,000 or more per annum. This figure is increased to £100,000 from 1 October 2010 in relation to England only. This change affects both existing tenancies which have been entered into before this date and new tenancies granted after that date.[4] There may be problems therefore for pre-existing tenancies that have become assured shorthold tenancies by virtue of this change.[5]

Tenancies at a low rent

5.4.14. Lettings made before 1 April 1990 cannot be assured if the annual rent is less than two-thirds of the rateable value of the property. For tenancies granted on or after 1 April 1990, the exclusion applies to tenancies in which the rent does not exceed £250 per annum (£1,000 per annum in Greater London).

Business tenancies

5.4.15. A tenancy to which Part II Landlord and Tenant Act 1954 applies cannot be an assured tenancy.[6]

Licensed premises

5.4.16. Premises licensed for the sale of alcohol for consumption on the premises, e.g. a public house, are excluded from the definition of an assured tenancy even if the tenant is residing on the premises.

Tenancies of agricultural land

5.4.17. A tenancy under which agricultural land exceeding two acres is let together with the house cannot be an assured tenancy (Housing Act 1988, Sched.1, para.6).

Tenancies of agricultural holdings

5.4.18. A tenancy under which a dwelling house is comprised in an agricultural holding (within the meaning of Agricultural Holdings Act 1986) or in a farm business tenancy under Agricultural Tenancies Act 1995, and is occupied by the person responsible for the control of the farming of the holding cannot be an assured tenancy (Housing Act 1988, Sched.1, para.7).

Lettings to students

5.4.19. Lettings to students by specified educational bodies are outside the definition of an assured tenancy. This exception does not apply to lettings to students by landlords other than the specified universities and colleges.

Holiday lettings

5.4.20. A letting to confer on the tenant the right to occupy the dwelling house for a holiday cannot be an assured tenancy.

Lettings by resident landlords

5.4.21. A letting by a resident landlord is excluded from the definition of an assured tenancy provided that certain conditions are satisfied.

Crown, local authority and housing association lettings

5.4.22. Crown, local authority and certain housing association lettings cannot be assured tenancies.

Rents under assured tenancies

The initial rent

5.4.23. There is no restriction on the amount of rent which can initially be charged on the grant of an assured tenancy. However, if the landlord subsequently wishes to increase the rent, he may not be able to do so unless he follows the correct procedure.

Statutory increases for assured periodic tenancies

5.4.24. Statutory increases for assured periodic tenancies are governed by Housing Act 1988, ss.13 and 14 which lay down a complicated procedure requiring the landlord to serve a notice (in the prescribed form) on the tenant. This can then be referred to the Rent Assessment Committee for determination if agreement as to the new rent cannot be reached between the parties.[7] The Rent Assessment Committee must determine the rent at which the premises might reasonably be let in the open market. If there is an express term in the tenancy agreement permitting rent increases, this avoids the need to rely on the statutory procedure.

Rent increases for fixed-term assured tenancies

5.4.25. There are no statutory provisions allowing an increase for fixed-term assured tenancies. In the absence of any express provision in the tenancy agreement, the landlord will be unable to increase the rent during the fixed term without the agreement of the tenant.[8] Once the fixed term has ended and the tenant continues in possession as a statutory periodic tenant, then the above provisions of Housing Act 1988, ss.13 and 14 will apply to enable the landlord to increase the rent, even if there is no express provision on the lease.

Prohibition of assignment without consent

5.4.26. If there is no such express provision against assignment in the lease, Housing Act 1988, s.15 may assist the landlord. The section only applies to periodic assured tenancies (including statutory periodic tenancies). It does not apply to fixed-term assured tenancies (including shortholds).

5.4.27. The term implied into a periodic assured tenancy is that the tenant must not without the consent of the landlord:

    (a)   assign the tenancy (in whole or in part); or

    (b)   sub-let or part with possession of all or part of the property.

Landlord and Tenant Act 1927, s.19 does not apply to this implied term and therefore the covenant is not subject to an implied proviso that consent will not be unreasonably withheld.

5.4.28. In the case of a periodic tenancy which is not a statutory periodic tenancy, these prohibitions do not apply if a premium was paid on the grant or renewal of the tenancy. 'Premium' is defined to include any pecuniary consideration in addition to rent and also includes returnable deposits exceeding one-sixth of the annual rent.[9]

Succession on death

5.4.29. On the death of one of joint tenants, the tenancy will vest in the survivor(s). On the death of a sole tenant the tenancy will pass under his will or intestacy. Housing Act 1988, however, contains specific provisions in section 17 dealing with the succession to an assured periodic tenancy on the death of a sole tenant which will override these normal rules.

5.4.30. On the death of a sole periodic tenant the tenancy will vest in the tenant's spouse or civil partner, notwithstanding the terms of the deceased's will, provided that immediately before the deceased tenant's death the spouse or civil partner was occupying the dwelling house as his or her only or principal home. 'Spouse or civil partner' is defined to include a person who was living with the tenant as his or her spouse or civil partner.[10] This provision will not apply if the deceased tenant was himself a 'successor', as defined, i.e. the tenancy became vested in him:

(a) by virtue of this section; or

(b) under the will or intestacy of a former tenant; or

(c) he is the sole survivor of joint tenants; or

(d) he succeeded to the tenancy under the provisions of Rent Act 1977.

5.4.31. Only one statutory succession is possible. If there is no statutory succession, e.g. because there is no qualifying 'spouse or civil partner', or there has already been a succession, or the tenancy is for a fixed term, the tenancy will then pass under the will or intestacy of the deceased in the normal way. However, on the death of a periodic assured tenant in such a situation, the landlord would be able to make use of one of the mandatory grounds in order to obtain possession.

Sub-lettings

5.4.32. Housing Act 1988, s.18 provides that in the case of a house lawfully sub-let on an assured tenancy, on the ending of the head lease the sub-tenancy will still continue. The assured sub-tenant will then become the direct tenant of the head landlord with full security of tenure. However, this only applies to lawful sub-lettings. In the case of an unlawful sub-letting, the sub-tenant will have no security once the head lease has been determined and the head landlord will thus have an absolute right to possession.

Lettings by resident landlords

Qualifying conditions

5.4.33. Under Part 1 Housing Act 1988, certain tenancies granted by resident landlords are excluded from statutory protection. In order to fall within this category the following conditions must apply to the tenancy:

(a) the dwelling house which is let forms only part of a building; and

(b) the building is not a purpose-built block of flats; and

(c) the tenancy was granted by an individual (i.e. not a limited company) who at the time of the grant occupied another part of the same building as his only or principal home; and

(d) at all times since the tenancy was granted, the interest of the landlord has continued to belong to an individual who continued so to reside.

Continuity of residence

5.4.34. It is not sufficient for the landlord merely to have been in residence at the commencement of the tenancy; he must be in occupation throughout the tenancy. If he ceases to reside then the exception will cease to apply and the letting will once again be capable of being an assured tenancy with full security of tenure.

5.4.35. But if the tenancy was entered into on or after the commencement date of Housing Act 1996, the letting will become an assured shorthold tenancy. However, if the interest of the landlord is vested in two or more individuals, only one of those persons need be in residence at any one time.

Periods of absence disregarded

5.4.36. Certain periods of absence will be disregarded when deciding whether the landlord's occupation has been continuous:

(a) a period of 28 days beginning with the date on which the interest of the landlord becomes vested at law and in equity in a new owner. If, during this 28 days, the new owner notifies the tenant in writing of his intention to occupy another part of the building as his only or principal home, the disregard will be extended up to six months from the change of ownership; and

(b) any period not exceeding two years during which the interest of the landlord becomes and remains vested in:

(i) trustees as such; or

       (ii)   the Probate Judge under Administration of Estates Act 1925, s.9; or

       (iii) personal representatives of a deceased person acting in that capacity.

5.4.37. Throughout any period during which absence is disregarded (except in a situation where the house is vested in personal representatives), no order for possession can be made except one which might have been made if the tenancy were an assured tenancy. In other words, during these periods of deemed residence the letting becomes a quasi-assured tenancy and possession can only be obtained against the tenant if assured tenancy grounds can be established. However, as an exception to that rule, personal representatives of a deceased resident landlord will be able to recover possession without proving assured tenancy grounds, provided that the contractual term can be terminated.

Purpose-built blocks of flats

5.4.38. The resident landlord exception does not apply if the building is a purpose-built block of flats and the landlord occupies one flat in the block and lets one (or more) of the others. Such lettings are therefore capable of being assured tenancies.

5.4.39. A building is a purpose-built block of flats if *as constructed* it contained, and still contains, two or more flats.

5.4.40. 'Flat' means a dwelling house which forms only part of a building and is separated horizontally from another dwelling house which forms part of the same building.

5.4.41. Housing Act 1988 makes it clear, however, that if the landlord occupies one flat in a purpose-built block and lets part of that flat, then the resident landlord exception can still apply.

Exceptions

5.4.42. A tenancy will be excluded from the resident landlord provisions if two conditions are both fulfilled:

       (a)   it was granted to a person who immediately before the grant was an assured tenant of the same house or of another house in the same building; and

       (b)   the landlord under the new tenancy and under the former tenancy is the same person. If either of the tenancies was granted by two or more persons, it is sufficient for this condition that the same person is the landlord or one of the landlords under each tenancy.

5.4.43. This is an anti-avoidance provision designed to ensure that a landlord does not deprive existing tenants of their protection as assured tenants by taking up possession himself and then granting a new tenancy to those existing tenants.

Security of tenure

Restriction on termination by landlord

5.4.44. An assured tenancy cannot be brought to an end by the landlord otherwise than by obtaining a court order for possession. Thus, in the case of a periodic assured tenancy, a notice to quit is of no effect. On the ending of a fixed-term assured tenancy (including a shorthold) otherwise than by an order of the court or by surrender, the tenant is entitled to remain in possession as a statutory periodic tenant. This statutory periodic tenancy will be on the same terms as the previous fixed-term tenancy.[11]

Obtaining a court order

5.4.45. The landlord will only obtain a court order for possession[12] if he follows the correct procedure and can establish one or more of the grounds for possession set out in Schedule 2 Housing Act 1988. Although some of these grounds are mandatory grounds, i.e. the court must order possession if the ground is established, many of them are discretionary grounds. With these, the court, on proof of the ground, may order possession only if it considers it reasonable to do so. The landlord must serve a notice on the tenant (a 'section 8 notice') in the prescribed form specifying the ground(s) upon which the landlord intends to rely and must give two weeks' notice of the landlord's intention to commence possession proceedings. (Sometimes two months' notice has to be given.) However, if ground 14[13] is specified (whether or not with any other ground), then the proceedings can be commenced as soon as the section 8 notice has been served. The proceedings must then be commenced not earlier than the date specified and not later than 12 months from the date of service of the notice. It is possible for the court to dispense with the requirement for a section 8 notice (unless ground 8 is being relied upon), but only if it considers it just and equitable to do so.[14]

5.4.46. Ground 14 has been extended by Anti-social Behaviour Act 2003. When considering whether it is reasonable to make an order for possession the court is required to consider the effect of anti-social behaviour by the tenant on other people.[15]

5.4.47. A registered social landlord may apply to a county court for a demotion order,[16] which can be made if the tenant or a person residing in or visiting the dwelling house has, broadly, either engaged in anti-social behaviour or used the premises for unlawful purposes.[17] A demotion order will terminate the assured tenancy and, if the tenant remains in occupation of the dwelling house, a demoted tenancy is created.[18] A demoted assured shorthold tenancy can be ended at any time during the demotion period.[19]

5.4.48. A family intervention tenancy can be offered to the tenant of an assured tenancy where the landlord is a registered social landlord or a registered provider of social housing. These are tenancies designed to enable the provision of behavioural support services to tenants. They can be offered to tenants against whom a possession order for anti-social behaviour has been made in relation to an assured tenancy or against whom such an order could have been made (whether or not they have such a tenancy). Family intervention tenancies in the context of secure tenancies are considered further at K5.2.7.[20]

5.4.49. In the case of a fixed-term assured tenancy, the landlord cannot normally obtain possession until after the end of the contractual fixed term (assuming that a ground for possession can then be established). However, as an exception to this, certain of the grounds for possession will be available to the landlord during the fixed term provided that the tenancy agreement contains a provision for it to be brought to an end on the ground in question. This provision can take any form at all, including a proviso for re-entry or a forfeiture clause. The grounds on which the landlord can obtain possession in this way during the fixed term are grounds 2, 8 and 10 to 15.

1. *Horford Investments Ltd* v. *Lambert* [1976] Ch 39.
2. *Uratemp Venture Ltd* v. *Collins* [2001] 3 WLR 806.
3. However, a tenant will lose his status as a tenant protected under Rent Act 1977 if he surrenders his existing tenancy and, after a short gap, takes a new tenancy; see *Truro Diocesan Board of Finance Ltd* v. *Foley* [2008] EWCA Civ 1162.
4. Assured Tenancies (Amendment) (England) Order 2010 (SI 2010/908). For the background to this see the explanatory memorandum to the statutory instrument.
5. The government is of the opinion that there are consequences for tenants' deposits in relation to pre-existing tenancies that are to be brought within the scheme after 1 October 2010. Where these tenancies were entered into after 6 April 2007, the deposit money should be paid into a recognised tenancy deposit scheme (see explanatory memorandum referred to in footnote 4 above). For a contrary view see comments at: **www.nearlylegal.co.uk**. For other consequences see K5.5.8.
6. See *Brewer* v. *Andrews* [1997] EGCS 19.
7. A tenant's application to challenge the landlord's notice of increase does not take effect until the Rent Assessment Committee has actually received it: *R (on the application of Lester)* v. *London Rent Assessment Committee* [2003] EWCA Civ 319.
8. Unless the increase is to a very high level designed to be a device to avoid security of tenure: *Bankway Properties* v. *Dunsford* [2001] 1 WLR 1369.
9. Housing Act 1988, s.15(4).
10. *Ibid.*, s.17 (as amended).
11. The type of periodic tenancy will depend on the period of the tenancy for which rent was 'last' payable: Housing Act 1988, s.5(3)(d); see *Church Commissioners for England* v. *Meya* [2006] EWCA Civ 821.
12. The court may make a suspended possession order, which may provide for its discharge if the tenant complies with its terms. During the period of this order the tenant remains an assured tenant, see *Knowsley Housing Trust* v. *White* [2008] UKHL 70.
13. Ground 14 relates to the tenant being a nuisance or annoyance or there being illegal or immoral use. This can apply where an offence was committed before the commencement of the tenancy: see *Raglan Housing Association Ltd* v. *Fairclough* [2007] EWCA Civ 1087.
14. As in *Knowsley Housing Trust* v. *Revell* [2003] All ER (D) 137 where possession proceedings were commenced against a tenant who was a secure tenant but who became an assured tenant during the proceedings on the transfer of the landlord's interest to a registered social landlord.
15. Housing Act 1988, s.9A added by Anti-social Behaviour Act 2003, s.16(2). See *London Quadrant Housing Trust* v. *Root* [2005] EWCA Civ 43.
16. Housing Act 1988, s.6A(1), (2).
17. Housing Act 1988, s.6A and Housing Act 1996, s.153A or s.153B.
18. Housing Act 1988, s.6A added by Anti-social Behaviour Act 2003, s.15.

19. Housing Act 1988, s.20B added by Anti-social Behaviour Act 2003, s.15
20. Note that one key difference between the two regimes is that it is only local authorities who are subject to the termination process requirements under Housing and Regeneration Act 2008, s.298. However, it appears that the Tenant Services Authority would expect registered social landlords to operate a similar termination and review procedure. See further 'Guidance on the use of Family Intervention Tenancies' available from **www.communities.gov.uk/publications/housing/familyinterventionguide**.

5.5. Shorthold tenancies

Introduction

5.5.1. It is important to distinguish between the two types of shortholds. 'Old' shortholds were entered into before the commencement of section 96 Housing Act 1996 (28 February 1997). 'New' shortholds are those entered into on or after this date unless made pursuant to a contract made before that date.

5.5.2. In the case of an old shorthold, before the grant of the tenancy the landlord was required to serve a warning notice on the tenant in a prescribed form. An old shorthold was required to be for a fixed term for a minimum duration of at least six months. Providing these criteria were satisfied the landlord had an absolute right to recover possession, provided that he complied with the correct procedure.

5.5.3. From the commencement of section 96 Housing Act 1996, however, all new lettings (with certain exceptions) are deemed to be shortholds. The old conditions need no longer be complied with; the letting need not be for a fixed term, there is no need for a warning notice, etc. However, the landlord still has the same absolute right to possession as in an old shorthold.

5.5.4. Note, that 'old' shortholds continue as before and if one fails due to the conditions not having been complied with, e.g. no warning notice was served, the tenancy will still become a fully protected assured tenancy. This means that the conditions for the grant of an old shorthold are still of considerable practical importance even after the introduction of new shortholds.

5.5.5. The only disadvantage of a shorthold (whether new or old) from a landlord's point of view is the right given to the tenant to refer the rent initially payable to the Rent Assessment Committee. However, this Committee can only reduce the rent if it is 'significantly higher' than the rents under other comparable assured tenancies.

An assured tenancy

5.5.6. An assured shorthold tenancy must comply with all the requirements of an assured tenancy as it is merely a type of assured tenancy (see K5.4). It is therefore necessary for there to be a letting of a dwelling house to an individual who occupies the house as his only or principal home. In the same way none of the specific exclusions from the definition of an assured tenancy must apply.

For example, high rental tenancies and lettings by resident landlords cannot be assured shortholds as they fall outside the definition of an assured tenancy.

5.5.7. A shorthold cannot be granted to an existing tenant under an ordinary assured tenancy (or to one of joint tenants) if it is granted by the landlord under that existing tenancy. This is so even if the lettings are not of the same premises.

Old shortholds

5.5.8. The qualifying conditions for shortholds entered into before the commencement date of Housing Act 1996 (28 February 1997) were set out in section 20 Housing Act 1988. It provides that an assured shorthold tenancy is an assured tenancy which:

(a) is a fixed-term tenancy granted for a term of not less than six months; and

(b) contains no power for the landlord to terminate it during the first six months; and

(c) was preceded by giving the tenant the prescribed shorthold notice.[1]

One of the consequences of the increase to the upper rent limits for assured tenancies (see K5.4.13) is that some tenants with tenancies that were entered into before 28 February 1997 will become assured tenants, but not assured shorthold tenants, as the protected shorthold notice was not served before the start of the tenancy.[2]

Minimum six-month fixed term

5.5.9. The initial grant of an old shorthold could not be for a periodic term. It was required to be for a fixed term and for a minimum duration of six months. A letting for 'six months and then from month to month' is not a letting for a term certain and so cannot be an old shorthold, even though it is for longer than the minimum six months. There is, however, no maximum length. Many shortholds were granted for the minimum six-month period and, in such a case, care must be taken to ensure that the tenant is given a right to occupy for the minimum period. The six-month period will run from the date on which the tenancy is entered into; it cannot be backdated. So a tenancy granted 'from and including 1 January 1994 until 30 June 1994' but not actually executed until 15 January 1994 would not give the tenant the requisite six months' occupation from the date of grant and so could not be a shorthold.

5.5.10. Problems are likely to arise where a tenancy agreement was drawn up containing a fixed termination date and there was then a delay in the agreement being executed so that by the time that it was executed there then remained less than six months until the prescribed termination date. Such a letting would amount to an ordinary assured tenancy giving the tenant full security of tenure.

No power for landlord to terminate during first six months

5.5.11. Even if a minimum period of six months was granted, any power, however expressed, which would or might allow the landlord to terminate the tenancy within the first six months of the tenancy will prevent the tenancy from amounting to a shorthold. Break clauses exercisable outside that period are not prohibited, but care must be taken with such clauses to ensure that they were only exercisable outside the initial six months; otherwise an ordinary assured tenancy will have been created giving the tenant full security of tenure. Note, however, that a forfeiture clause or a clause allowing termination on assured tenancy grounds 2, 8 and 10 to 15 will not breach this requirement even though it is exercisable during the first six months of the term. A term allowing the tenant to terminate during the first six months could have been validly included. Such a provision, however, will not be implied. A tenant entering into an old shorthold will, therefore, normally be contractually bound to pay the rent and perform the other obligations under the tenancy agreement for the full term entered into.

Preceded by the giving of the prescribed shorthold notice

5.5.12. As the tenant under an assured shorthold has no security of tenure, he had to be served with a notice prior to the grant of the tenancy warning him of this fact. This notice must have been in the prescribed form.

5.5.13. The notice must have been served before the tenancy agreement was entered into and not at the same time. Thus, it could not be included in the tenancy agreement itself. It was best to ensure that there was an adequate interval between the service of the notice and the signing of the tenancy agreement to give the tenant the opportunity of digesting the contents of the notice. However, it appears that an interval of a few hours between the service of the section 20 notice and the tenancy agreement being entered into would be sufficient.[3] In the case of joint tenants, all of the prospective tenants should have been served. Common law rules as to service will apply (and not section 196 Law of Property Act 1925) and so it is necessary to show that the notice actually came into the tenant's hands. It was advisable for a landlord to serve the notice in duplicate and to require all the prospective tenants to endorse one copy with an acknowledgement of receipt, and the date and time of receipt, and return this to the landlord before the tenancy agreement was entered into. Correct service of the current version of the shorthold notice was vital. The court has no power to dispense with these notice requirements even though it might be just and equitable to do so.

New shortholds

Definition

5.5.14. Shortholds entered into on or after 28 February 1997 (otherwise than pursuant to a contract made before that date) are governed by Housing Act 1988, s.19A (as inserted by Housing Act 1996). This provides that any assured tenancy entered into on or after the commencement date will be a shorthold unless it falls within one of the specified exceptions.

5.5.15. There is no need for a shorthold to be for a fixed term and therefore it can be periodic. There is no longer any need for a shorthold to be preceded by a prescribed form of notice. There is also no prohibition on the landlord being able to terminate during the first six months. However, no order for possession using the shorthold ground can be made earlier than six months from the start of the tenancy, whether the tenancy is for a fixed term or is a periodic tenancy. This does not stop possession being obtained during the first six months using an assured tenancy ground because a new shorthold, like an old shorthold, is merely a type of assured tenancy.

Exceptions

5.5.16. All new assured tenancies granted on or after 28 February 1997 (other than those granted pursuant to a contract made before that date) will be shortholds subject to certain exceptions,[4] which will take effect as ordinary assured tenancies. These include:

(a) tenancies excluded by notice. The landlord may serve a notice on the tenant either before or after the grant of the tenancy stating that the letting is not to be a shorthold;[5]

(b) tenancies containing a provision stating that the tenancy is not to be a shorthold;

(c) lettings to existing assured tenants.

5.5.17. Where the landlord (or one of the landlords) under the existing assured tenancy grants a letting to an existing assured (i.e. not shorthold) tenant (whether alone or with others) the new letting will not be a shorthold. However, it is possible for the tenant to serve notice on the landlord before the new tenancy is entered into that he wants it to be a shorthold. This notice must be in a prescribed form.

Duty of landlord to provide a statement of the terms of a shorthold tenancy

5.5.18. Under Housing Act 1988, s.20A (as inserted by Housing Act 1996), the landlord is placed under a duty in certain circumstances to provide a tenant with written details of the following terms provided that they are not already evidenced in writing:

(a) the commencement date of the tenancy;

(b) the rent payable and the dates on which it is payable;

(c) any terms providing for rent review;

(d) the length of a fixed term tenancy.

The tenant must make a request to the landlord in writing for this information.

5.5.19. It is a criminal offence to fail to provide the information within 28 days, unless the landlord has reasonable excuse.

5.5.20. The right only exists where the terms are not already evidenced in writing. The provision will only apply to tenancies granted orally, or those granted in writing which makes no reference to one or more of the specified matters.

5.5.21. A statement provided by the landlord is not to be regarded as conclusive evidence as to what was agreed between the parties. The statement is the landlord's version of what was agreed; it is still open to the tenant to allege that any particular term was not agreed to by him.

5.5.22. These provisions only apply to new shortholds, i.e. those to which Housing Act 1988, s.19A applies. They do not apply to old shortholds. However, on the ending of an old shorthold any new letting between the same parties will be a new shorthold, and these provisions will then apply.

Rent control

5.5.23. The general principles are the same for both new or old shorthold, but the details differ.

5.5.24. Any existing registration of a 'fair rent' under the provisions of Rent Act 1977 can be ignored, as can any rental figure previously determined by the Rent Assessment Committee under these provisions. Therefore on the granting of the tenancy, the landlord can charge such rent for the premises as the tenant will agree to pay. There is no statutory restriction on the amount of rent chargeable. However, an assured shorthold tenant can apply to the local Rent Assessment Committee for the determination of the rent which, in the Committee's opinion, the landlord might reasonably be expected to obtain under the shorthold tenancy.

5.5.25. If the tenant has an old shorthold, he can apply at any time within the fixed term of the tenancy.

5.5.26. If the tenant has a new shorthold, whether for a fixed term or a periodic letting, he cannot apply if more than six months have elapsed since the beginning of the tenancy. If the tenancy is a 'replacement tenancy', i.e. a second or subsequent shorthold between the same parties and of the same property, the application cannot be made if more than six months have elapsed from the commencement of the first shorthold between the parties.

The effect of a determination by the Rent Assessment Committee

5.5.27. If a rent is determined by the Committee, the effect again differs between old and new shortholds.

5.5.28. The rent assessed will become the maximum rent chargeable for the property throughout the remainder of the fixed term in the case of old shortholds and fixed-term new shortholds, despite anything to the contrary in the tenancy agreement. No matter how long the unexpired term of the tenancy there is no provision for this figure to be increased during the fixed term.

5.5.29. Where a new shorthold is a periodic tenancy, the rent remains fixed throughout the tenancy. Once 12 months have expired, the landlord will be able to make an application under Housing Act 1988, ss.13 and 14 to increase the rent.[6]

5.5.30. With both old and new shortholds, once the rent has been determined by the Committee no further application for the fixing of a different figure can be made by either landlord or tenant. However, the rent determined by the Committee only has relevance to the particular tenancy in question. It will not limit the amount of rent chargeable under any subsequent letting, even if this is between the same parties. Further, in the absence of a further grant, on the ending of a fixed-term shorthold (whether old or new), a statutory periodic tenancy will arise and the provisions of Housing Act 1988, ss.13 and 14 will again apply to allow the landlord to increase the rent. Any rent review clause in the original assured tenancy purporting to provide for a rent review once the statutory periodic tenancy has come into existence is of no effect and the statutory scheme will apply.[7]

When is an application to the Rent Assessment Committee not possible?

5.5.31. The restrictions on tenants with new shortholds applying have been dealt with in K5.5.26.

5.5.32. As far as old shorthold tenants are concerned, it is not possible for the tenant to refer the rent to the Rent Assessment Committee once the original term of the shorthold has expired. This is the case even if a new letting is entered into between the same parties and irrespective of whether an application was made during the original shorthold.

5.5.33. With both old and new shortholds, only one application to the Committee can be made. Once the rent has been determined by the Committee, it cannot be resubmitted for a further determination, even if the original determination was many years before and open market rents have fallen in the meantime.

What happens when a shorthold expires?

5.5.34. The tenant is allowed to remain in possession as a statutory periodic tenant when a fixed-term tenancy expires. However, the tenant will have no security of tenure. Under Housing Act 1988, s.21(1) the court must still make an order for possession if the landlord follows the correct procedure. This involves the service on the tenant of not less than two months' notice stating that the landlord requires possession.

What happens if a new tenancy is granted?

5.5.35.   Although there are differences between new and old shortholds, the basic principle remains the same; if the parties are the same, any new tenancy of the same (or substantially the same) premises will be deemed to be a shorthold unless the landlord serves notice on the tenant that the new letting is not to be a shorthold.

5.5.36.   In the case of an old shorthold, the effect of this deeming provision is that the new tenancy will be a shorthold even though it does not comply with the normal requirements for an old shorthold. So no shorthold notice need have been served, the letting need not be for a fixed term, i.e. a periodic shorthold is permissible, and any fixed term need not be for a minimum period of six months. However, the new tenancy must still comply with the normal requirements for an assured tenancy, e.g. the tenant must still be occupying the house as his only or principal home.

5.5.37.   A further feature of a deemed shorthold following an old shorthold is that there is no right to refer the rent to the Rent Assessment Committee. This is the case whether or not an application was made to the Committee during the initial shorthold term. In the case of a tenancy following a new shorthold, the second tenancy will be a 'replacement tenancy' and an application to the Rent Assessment Committee cannot be made more than six months from the commencement of the original tenancy. So in the unlikely event of a new shorthold granted for three months, followed by a replacement tenancy granted for (say) six months, an application to the Rent Assessment Committee could be made during the first three months of that replacement tenancy.

5.5.38.   In any event, if a rent was determined by the Rent Assessment Committee during the initial term this will not limit the amount of rent chargeable by the landlord under the new tenancy agreement.

How does the landlord obtain possession?

5.5.39.   The landlord must apply to the court and obtain an order for possession unless the tenant leaves voluntarily. The court must order possession provided that the landlord follows the correct procedure. This involves the landlord serving a notice on the tenant (the 'section 21 notice') giving the tenant at least two months' notice that he requires possession.

5.5.40.   Possession cannot be obtained using this shorthold procedure during the continuance of a fixed term; possession is only available after its expiry (although the procedure can be set in motion during the fixed term so that possession can be obtained as soon as it has ended). Note also that in the case of a new shorthold possession cannot be obtained within six months of the commencement of the term using the shorthold procedure. This is so whether the tenancy is a fixed-term tenancy or is periodic.

Grounds for possession

5.5.41. A shorthold is a type of assured tenancy and so, during the term, the mandatory and discretionary grounds which apply to ordinary assured tenancies can also apply. However, in the case of a fixed-term letting, as with other assured tenancies, only certain grounds can be used during the fixed term and only if the tenancy agreement so provides (see K5.4.49).

5.5.42. In the case of a shorthold which is a periodic tenancy, the ordinary assured tenancy grounds will be available to a landlord without the need for any such provision in the tenancy agreement.

5.5.43. In the case of a fixed-term shorthold, however, it is always sensible to insert a provision allowing the landlord to terminate the tenancy on the specified grounds. In the case of an old shorthold, this is permissible despite the usual rule that there must be no power for the landlord to terminate within the first six months of the tenancy. This rule does not apply to termination because of a breach of the terms of the tenancy, e.g. non-payment of rent. Similarly, in the case of new shorthold, although possession cannot be obtained using the shorthold procedure within six months of the commencement, possession can be obtained during that period using the ordinary assured grounds provided that they are satisfied.

5.5.44. When the landlord is seeking to obtain possession on one of the ordinary assured grounds, then the procedure relevant to an ordinary assured tenancy should be followed, and not the shorthold procedure. In particular, this will mean that a section 8 notice will have to be served on the tenant before proceedings can be commenced, and not a section 21 notice.

Deposits

5.5.45. A landlord may not take a deposit in respect of an assured shorthold tenancy unless he joins, and complies with the requirements of, a 'tenancy deposit scheme'. Where a landlord fails to do this he will be unable to regain possession of the property using the 'section 21 notice' procedure. There are additional penalties for failing to comply, so that on application by a tenant the county court may impose financial penalties on the landlord and it may order the return of the deposit to the tenant.[8] There are two types of schemes: a single custodial scheme (where deposits are paid into and held in a separate account); and insurance-based schemes (where any failure to repay the deposit to the tenant is covered by insurance).[9] The legislation does not deal specifically with the position relating to a deposit held in such a scheme where there is a sale of the landlord's interest in the property. Therefore the buyer and seller will need to make appropriate arrangements between themselves. It will also be necessary to contact the relevant scheme provider to find out if any arrangements have been made in relation to this situation in that scheme.

1.   In some circumstances the notice may be given to the tenant's agent; see *Yenula Properties Ltd* v. *Naida* [2002] EWCA Civ 719. The absence of details of the landlord may not be fatal if the details of the agent are given: *Osborn and Co. Ltd* v. *Dior* [2003] All ER (D) 185.

2. See the Explanatory Memorandum to Assured Tenancies (Amendment) (England) Order 2010 (SI 2010/908).
3. See *Bedding* v. *McCarthy* [1994] 41 EG 151.
4. See Housing Act 1988, Sched.2A as inserted by Housing Act 1996.
5. The words 'assured tenancy' on the cover of a rent book have been held not to constitute a notice which complied with the statutory requirements and therefore the tenancy was held to be an assured shorthold tenancy and not an assured tenancy (see *Andrews* v. *Cunningham* [2007] EWCA Civ 762).
6. Rules now enable landlords to specify a date for annual increases; see Regulatory Reform (Assured Periodic Tenancies) (Rent Increases) Order 2003 (SI 2003/259) and Assured Tenancies and Agricultural Occupancies (Forms) (Amendment) (England) Regulations 2003 (SI 2003/260).
7. See *London District Properties Management Ltd* v *Goolamy and another* [2009] EWHC (Admin) 1367.
8. There is also a requirement to provide prescribed information to tenants, and to do so within 14 days. However, if this deadline is not met payments required in Housing Act 2004, s.214 do not apply; see *Harvey* v. *Bamforth* [2008] 46 EG 119 (county court). Failure to comply with the same time limit for lodging the deposit also may not trigger liability for these payments: *Draycott* v. *Hannells Letting Limited* [2010] EWHC 217 (QB).
9. Housing Act 2004, ss.212–215; Housing (Tenancy Deposit Schemes) Order 2007 (SI 2007/796) and Housing (Tenancy Deposits) (Prescribed Information) Order 2007 (SI 2007/797); Housing (Tenancy Deposits) (Specified Interest Rate) Order 2007 (SI 2007/798). For further information including details of the providers, see **www.direct.gov.uk/en/TenancyDeposit/DG_066383**.

5.6.   Long tenancies at low rents

5.6.1.   Rent Act 1977 (as with previous Rent Acts) gave no protection to the tenant where the rent payable under the tenancy was less than two-thirds of the rateable value of the dwelling on the appropriate day (as defined in the Act), with the result that most tenants of dwellings under long tenancies at ground rents had no security of tenure when their contractual tenancies expired. Part I Landlord and Tenant Act 1954 extended to many such tenants the protection of Rent Act 1977 (and its predecessors) when their tenancies expired. Part I applied to a tenancy granted for over 21 years at a rent of less than two-thirds of the rateable value of the property where 'the circumstances (as respects the property comprised in the tenancy, the use of the property, and all other relevant matters) are such that on the coming to an end of the tenancy ... the tenant would, if the tenancy had not been one at a low rent, be entitled by virtue of the Rent Acts to retain possession of the whole or part of the property comprised in the tenancy'.

Security of tenure

5.6.2.   The current security of tenure provisions for tenants under long leases are contained in Schedule 10 Local Government and Housing Act 1989. This provides that tenants of dwellings who were granted certain long tenancies at a low rent have a right to stay in possession after the end of their leases as assured tenants.

5.6.3.   Local Government and Housing Act 1989 applies where the long tenancy was granted after 1 April 1990, and to those granted before this date but which expired after 15 January 1999. Tenants holding under long leases had previously been entitled to security of tenure under Part I Landlord and Tenant Act 1954 (see K5.6.1).

5.6.4. The detailed eligibility criteria are similar to those referred to in K5.6.1. Thus a tenancy is 'long' if, broadly, it is granted for a term of more than 21 years and is at a 'low rent' if the rent is so low that, in effect, it would prevent it being an assured tenancy.[1]

5.6.5. The drawback of these provisions is that the tenant will have to pay a full market rent at the end of the lease.[2] For these reasons other rights of long leaseholders, e.g. to acquire a new long lease or to enfranchise, are often more attractive for such tenants. These are considered in more detail at K9.

1. Housing Act 1988, Sched.1, para.3 and Local Government and Housing Act 1989, Sched.10, para.3.
2. For an example of the consequences of the operation of this provision see *Hughes* v. *Borodex Ltd* [2010] EWCA Civ 425.

5.7. **Agricultural employees**

5.7.1. Security of tenure for farm workers living in accommodation provided by their employers and who are outside the other security of tenure regimes, e.g. because they pay a low rent, is governed by either Rent (Agriculture) Act 1976 or Housing Act 1988, depending on the date of the grant of the tenancy.

5.7.2. To gain the protection of the 1976 Act, the employee must generally have spent two years whole time in agriculture; he then becomes a protected occupier of the house. If as a result of a notice to quit or otherwise he ceases to be a protected occupier, he becomes a statutory tenant of the house under terms laid down by the Act.

5.7.3. The court cannot make an order for possession of a house subject to a protected occupancy or statutory tenancy under the 1976 Act except on the grounds set out in the Act. Special provisions apply to the rehousing of agricultural employees. The provisions for rent control in the Act apply only to statutory tenancies.

5.7.4. Farm workers who enjoyed the protection of Rent Act 1977 (e.g. because they were tenants paying an economic rent) were equated to those protected by the 1976 Act by Rent Act 1977, s.99.

5.7.5. Farm workers with tenancies or licences granted before 15 January 1989 retain their protection under the 1976 Act. Tenancies or licences granted on or after that date are governed by Housing Act 1988. However, those tenants who were previously protected under the 1976 Act will, broadly, continue to enjoy the same regime of protection.[1] This Act introduced the assured agricultural occupancy, which qualifies for protection if it is an assured tenancy or would be such except for the fact that the rent (outside London) is less than £250 per annum or the fact that the house forms part of an agricultural holding and is occupied by the person responsible for the control of the farming. A licence to occupy which confers exclusive occupation and which fulfils the requisite conditions will also qualify. An assured shorthold is excluded from the definition, thus enabling the owner to create a tenancy giving a mandatory right to possession.

5.7.6.   In the case of tenancies or licences governed by Housing Act 1988, the main change is in regard to rent. The provisions of the Act in regard to the increase of rents under assured tenancies apply to assured agricultural occupancies, so that on a reference of a notice of increase of rent to a Rent Assessment Committee an open market rent can be fixed.

5.7.7.   An occupier of agricultural land may apply to the housing authority concerned (i.e. the local housing authority as defined by Housing Act 1985) to rehouse a tenant on the ground that the land occupier requires the dwelling house to provide accommodation for an agricultural employee, the land occupier being unable to provide the present tenant with suitable alternative accommodation. The housing authority in reaching its decision on whether to rehouse the tenant must have regard to the advice tendered to them by the Agricultural Dwelling House Advisory Committee.[2]

1. Housing Act 1988, s.34(4).
2. See Rent (Agriculture) Act 1976, ss.27–29.

K6. Long-term residential tenancies

6.1. Grant of lease

6.1.1. The grant or assignment of a long lease of a house or flat is similar to the grant or assignment of a lease of other premises. The matters to which particular attention needs to be paid when dealing with this type of lease are merely highlighted here.

6.1.2. The lease of a flat is frequently a complex document which should be specifically drafted to suit the individual requirements of the site. Except in the most straightforward cases, copying a precedent directly from a book or the reuse of a lease drafted for another development will not suffice. The client's attention should be directed to the need for a site inspection before drafting of the lease is commenced so that the following points can be correctly dealt with in the lease:

(a) what is the structure of the building composed of? Repairing covenants must be drafted appropriately so that a covenant, e.g. 'to repair main walls and timbers' will be inappropriate where the building is of concrete construction;

(b) access: the lease must deal with easements of access, e.g. is there a right of way over the drive from the public highway to the entrance of the flats, how does each tenant get from the door of the building to the door of his own flat, is there to be a lift, does each tenant require access to the dustbin area, etc.?

(c) where do the mains services run? Which tenants need easements for pipes, cables, etc., to pass through another flat or common parts on the way to or from their own flat?

(d) amenities: who is to have a garage or parking space, are these to be a part of the demise (i.e. a specific allocated space) or is there to be just a licence to use a garage/parking space (with no guarantee that a space will actually be available), use of gardens, is there communal central heating, is there an entry-phone system, is there a communal television or satellite aerial, are individual aerials to be permitted, is there a caretaker's flat?

(e) service charges: what services are to be included in the charge, will all tenants have the benefit of all the services supplied, should the service charge be split equally between all the tenants or should some pay a greater proportion than others or should different proportions apply to different services?

(f) check site and floor plans against the physical extent of the building both in relation to the whole building and individual flats, are they accurate, which tenants need which plans, and do they comply with Land Registry requirements?[1]

1. See B21 and Land Registry Practice Guide 40.

6.2. Enforcement of covenants in flats

6.2.1. The landlord for the time being can almost always enforce covenants in the lease against the tenant for the time being of each flat, because he enjoys privity of estate and in many cases also privity of contract with each tenant. Prima facie there is neither privity of contract nor of estate between the tenants and, although they will each be bound by identical covenants in their leases, without some device in the leases they cannot sue each other directly for breach of the tenants' covenants in their respective leases. It is advisable that the lease contains some method of allowing enforceability of covenants between the tenants, particularly in relation to restrictive covenants concerning use and noise and, in appropriate cases, positive covenants concerning tenant's repairs.

6.2.2. This can be achieved by taking a covenant in each lease that the landlord will if so requested by a tenant take action to enforce a breach of covenant committed by another tenant in the same block. Such a covenant usually requires the requesting tenant to provide a complete indemnity to the landlord against the costs of the action and provides an effective although cumbersome method of mutual enforceability of covenants. There are other schemes of varying complexity which attempt to ensure that one tenant can sue another. However, in practice none are now considered wholly satisfactory. Where the tenants are responsible for maintenance, insurance and repair of common parts, the CML Lenders' Handbook and the BSA Mortgage Instructions require the key clauses in a lease to be enforceable by the landlord (or the management company) at the request of the tenant (see K6.6). However, these requirements do not apply where the landlord or a management company is responsible for those repairs.

6.3. Management schemes

6.3.1. Any management scheme must ensure that the rights and obligations of both the landlord and the tenants under the lease are always enforceable. The landlord's objectives in setting up such a scheme are to provide for the maintenance and repair of the block. The type of scheme employed will depend on the landlord's particular requirements in relation to the flats concerned. It should be borne in mind that tenants have statutory rights in relation to management under Commonhold and Leasehold Reform Act 2002, which are considered in K6.11.

6.3.2. If the landlord is to retain the reversion of the block he may choose to carry out the landlord's functions personally or through a managing agent. From the landlord's point of view this arrangement has the disadvantage of the work involved and from the tenants' point of view it has the disadvantage that the tenants have only limited control over the way in which their block is managed. As a result tenants may have recourse to their rights under Commonhold and Leasehold Reform Act 2002, which are considered in K6.11.

6.3.3. Another type of arrangement is for the tenants to covenant with each other by separate deed of covenant to perform the obligations of repairing, etc., the common parts. Such a scheme is not binding on future assignees unless the lease obliges them to enter into similar deeds of covenant as a condition of their assignment.[1] Alternatively, limited use may be made of a letting scheme which can be created to enable tenants to sue each other for breach of restrictive covenants provided the conditions for a development scheme are fulfilled.[2]

6.3.4. Alternatively, the landlord may vest the reversion (with its obligations) in trustees (who would be representatives of the tenants) on trust for the tenants as a whole. This type of scheme is only suitable for the management of small blocks and saves the expense in that situation of setting up and running a management company.

6.3.5. Most larger blocks have schemes which entail the use of a management company. The landlord may transfer his reversion to the management company which will then assume the responsibility for performance of the landlord's covenants in the lease. Until transfer the landlord will be responsible for the management company's duties and should ideally expressly covenant to this effect in the lease. A management company can either be limited by shares or guarantee and is commonly purchased as a ready-made company. The management company may be a party to the lease and enter into direct covenants with the tenant for the performance of the maintenance obligations. Each tenant must be required to become a member of the company and to transfer his share in the company to an assignee on sale of the lease. Such a scheme allows the tenants to have absolute control over the management of their block, but carries with it the responsibility of performance of the maintenance obligations and duties in relation to the company itself under the Companies Acts. The landlord may reserve the right to take over the management company's responsibilities in the event of default by the company.

6.3.6. If maintenance is to be carried out by a maintenance trustee company, the tenant's solicitor should be satisfied as to the integrity of the trustee company. If this has been set up by a third party, the tenant will have no control over the company, and thus needs to be assured that the trustees (and any potential successors to the original trustees) are sound and responsible.

6.3.7. In relation to leases granted on or after 11 May 2000, direct enforcement of the benefit of covenants between tenants may be possible without the device of a management scheme through the operation of Contracts (Rights of Third Parties) Act 1999. However, the Act does not enable the burden of covenants to be passed to successors and is therefore unable to provide a satisfactory solution.

1. Such an obligation may be enforced by means of an appropriate restriction on the land register.
2. See *Williams* v. *Kiley (t/a CK Supermarkets Ltd)* [2003] 06 EG 147.

6.4. Other matters to be considered

6.4.1. The landlord may wish to reserve the right to prepare the engrossment of the lease himself. Such right is expressly reserved by the Standard Conditions of Sale.[1]

6.4.2. Where the landlord is to retain the reversion (and the liability for performance of the landlord's covenants in the lease) consideration may be given by the landlord to the appointment of reliable managing agents to carry out the landlord's duties under the lease.

6.4.3. On completion apportionments of the rent and service charge will have to be made. Apportionments of service charge will at this stage have to be made on an estimated basis and settled at the end of the first accounting period.

6.4.4. Where a management company is to perform the landlord's covenants under the lease, the company must be set up and share certificates (except where limited by guarantee) and the company books prepared in readiness for completion.

6.4.5. The term dates of all the leases in a block should commence on the same date (irrespective of the dates of completion of the various leases) otherwise it becomes very difficult to know precisely when performance of some covenants is due, e.g. to decorate.

Apportionment of rent

6.4.6. The Law Society's Conveyancing and Land Law Committee has prepared a formula for the calculation of the apportionment of rent. See Appendix IV.2.

1. See Standard Conditions of Sale 8.2.5; Standard Commercial Property Condition 10.2.5.

6.5.   Maisonettes

6.5.1.   Where a maisonette is being purchased, particular care needs to be exercised to ensure that the lease is quite specific as to the ownership and rights over the various parts of the property (especially common parts). Each tenant may be the freeholder of the other tenant's property; they will thus be jointly responsible for the maintenance and upkeep of the structure and common parts. A maintenance trustee company may be set up to deal with maintenance and repair. The CML Lenders' Handbook and BSA Mortgage Instructions set out specific requirements where there is a freehold flat or where one of the flat owners in the block owns the freehold in whole or in part. In many situations these arrangements may be acceptable to the lender where a building has been converted into not more than four flats (see CML Lenders' Handbook, para.5.5.3; BSA Mortgage Instructions, para. D.26).

6.6.   Lenders' requirements

6.6.1.   The lenders' requirements may be found in a combination of documents depending on the nature of the transaction and whether the lender is a member of the Council of Mortgage Lenders or the Building Societies Association. These documents are: the CML Lenders' Handbook England and Wales, the Building Societies Association Mortgage Instructions England and Wales, the mortgage offer, and instructions to the solicitor.

6.6.2.   Part 1 of the CML Lenders' Handbook is a set of universal instructions to which all CML lenders adhere. Individual lenders issue their own supplemental general instructions to their solicitors by use of Part 2 instructions. Part 1 and Part 2 are available online at **www.cml.org.uk**. Solicitors are also recommended to check the website for the latest version of both Parts.

6.6.3   The Building Societies Association has published a similar set of instructions (BSA Mortgage Instructions) with effect from 1 January 2010. These can only be accessed online (see **www.bsa.org.uk**). It is not mandatory for building societies to use the BSA Mortgage Instructions. The instructing building society lender will advise conveyancers in the mortgage offer whether they are instructed on the basis of the BSA Mortgage Instructions or the CML Lenders' Handbook. The provisions of the BSA Mortgage Instructions are very similar to those of the CML Lenders' Handbook. To avoid unnecessary duplication, in what follows reference is only made to the relevant provisions in the CML Lenders' Handbook.

6.6.4.   A lender is usually concerned with the following matters:

(a)   to ensure that the lease contains proper provision for the enforceability of certain covenants between tenants (CML Lenders' Handbook, para. 5.10.6);

(b)   to ensure that the property is leasehold and that the lease contains adequate repairing covenants relating to the flat itself, the exterior structure and the common parts of the building (CML Lenders' Handbook, para.5.10.4);

(c)   that the lease contains adequate provision for the insurance of the whole building (CML Lenders' Handbook, paras.5.10.4. and 5.10.5);

(d)   that the length of the term of the lease (or unexpired residue in the case of an assignment) is sufficient to permit a resale of the premises on the open market. A common period required by lenders is 55 years unexpired from completion and 30 years unexpired at the end of the mortgage term. Notification may be required if the minimum period is less than 70 years. A term which will have less than 20 years unexpired after the end of the mortgage term may be considered inadequate in the context of normal residential conveyancing;

(e)   that the lease contains no provision for forfeiture on the insolvency of the tenant (CML Lenders' Handbook, para.5.10.2);

(f)   that the lease contains no restrictions on alienation which may hinder a sale on the open market (CML Lenders' Handbook, para.5.10.3);

(g)   that the lease is, or will be, registered at the Land Registry with an absolute leasehold title, although a lesser title, e.g. good leasehold title, may be acceptable in certain circumstances (CML Lenders' Handbook, para.5.4);

(h)   where the tenant is to become a member of a management company, the mortgagee sometimes requires that a blank form of share transfer (signed by the mortgagor) and the tenant's share certificate is deposited with the lender to enable the lender to transfer that share to a buyer should he need to exercise his power of sale. A copy of the management company's memorandum and articles may also have to be deposited with the lender (CML Lenders' Handbook, para.5.11.2);

(i)   that notices have been given to the landlord of the mortgage (CML Lenders' Handbook, para.5.10.11);

(j)   that the lease reserves an appropriate ground rent and that receipts are provided for rent and service charge payments (CML Lenders' Handbook, paras.5.10.7 and 5.10.10);

(k)   if the property being purchased is held under a sub-lease (so that the landlord's own interest is leasehold), it is desirable that the aggregate ground rents payable by the flats in the block should exceed the amount of rent payable by the landlord to the freeholder. If this is not the case the landlord will have little incentive to pay his own rent, and thus the sub-tenants of the flats would be put at risk from forfeiture of the head-lease. For this reason it is desirable that in any situation where sub-letting is permitted the tenant should be required to enter a covenant with his landlord not to sub-let the whole at a rent lower than that payable under his own lease.

6.7.   Energy performance certificate

It will usually be necessary to provide an energy performance certificate where the property is to be let (see further A27).

6.8.   Service charges

6.8.1.   Service charge accounts must be examined carefully and the buyer advised as to his potential liability under the lease.

6.8.2.   Statutory provisions relating to service charges are now contained in Landlord and Tenant Act 1985, ss.18–30, as amended. The amendments made to these provisions by Commonhold and Leasehold Reform Act 2002 have significantly enhanced tenants' rights in this respect. For the purposes of these provisions, a service charge is an amount payable by a tenant as part of or in addition to rent:

(a)   which is payable, directly or indirectly, for services, repairs, maintenance, improvements or insurance or the landlord's costs of management; and

(b)   the whole or part of which varies or may vary according to the relevant costs.

Note that some management companies (for example, where the tenants are all members) may make a charge for services to properties by requiring members to pay contributions into a company management fund under the terms of its articles of association. In some cases this appears to be done to avoid tenants' statutory rights. It has been held that such payments are not 'service charges' within the meaning of Landlord and Tenant Act, s.18.[1] There are also provisions in Landlord and Tenant Act 1985, s.35 to enable an application to be made to vary certain leases in relation to the computation of a service charge (see further K14.2).

6.8.3.   Provisions in relation to payments to a reserve fund (which allow 'savings' against future expenditure) are contained in Landlord and Tenant Act 1987, ss.42–42B (as amended). These require such payments to be paid into a designated bank account and for the money to be held on trust for the tenants.[2]

6.8.4.   The statutory provisions apply to a lease of any dwelling (including houses as well as flats) except that they do not apply to lettings by certain bodies such as local authorities unless the tenancy is a long tenancy as defined in Landlord and Tenant Act 1985, s.26(2).

6.8.5.   The statutes impose certain limitations and obligations on landlords which are not set out in detail here but which relate to the following:

(a)   limitations on the amount recoverable. The landlord can only recover the costs of providing services to the extent that they are 'reasonable' and only if they are of a 'reasonable standard';[3]

(b)   consultations with tenants. Broadly, the obligation to consult applies where the landlord proposes to incur expenditure on works of repair, maintenance or improvement that would cost an individual service charge payer more than £250. Also there is a requirement to consult before entering into contracts for the provision of long term contracts for services lasting more than 12 months. This is necessary where the cost per tenant is £100 per year. Failure to consult or to obtain a dispensation[4] from a Leasehold Valuation Tribunal will limit a tenant's service charge contributions;[5]

(c)   estimates for work to be done and the giving of notices;

(d)   time limits on making demands for service charges;[6]

(e)   the tenant's right to receive a statement of account for costs incurred, an accountants certificate and to inspect the landlord's accounts;[7]

(f)   the landlord's duty to pass on requests for a summary of the relevant costs to a superior landlord;[8]

(g)   the right, in certain circumstances, to withhold a service charge;[9]

(h)   service charge contributions to be held in trust;[10]

(i)   a demand for service charges, which must be accompanied by a summary of the rights and obligations of the tenant.[11]

Tenants and landlords also have rights to apply to a leasehold valuation tribunal for an order varying the lease where an administration charge as specified in the lease is unreasonable.[12]

6.8.6.   A buyer of the reversion on a lease reserving a service charge and a buyer of a lease subject to such a charge should be aware of the following matters:

(a)   the statutory provisions outlined above;

(b)   that the obligation to pay a service charge can arise only from an express provision in the lease and the extent of the obligation depends on the wording of such provision.[13] Whether or not the landlord can recover from non-defaulting tenants his legal costs incurred in recovering rent and service charge contributions depends on the wording of the tenant's covenant, and the same is true in respect of a landlord's interest payments on money borrowed to finance the provision of works and services;

(c)   ideally the landlord's obligation should match with the service charge provisions. If the obligations are not matched the landlord may find that he is obliged to provide more services than he can charge for or conversely that the tenants cannot force the landlord to provide them, e.g. carry out repairs because the landlord's covenant does not extend to this matter;

(d) the manner in which the total service charge is to be apportioned between the various tenants;

(e) whether or not the landlord can require payment of a charge in advance of expenditure;

(f) the statutory provisions apply to contribution covenants concerned with improvements as well as repairs;[14]

(g) where premises are let wholly or mainly as a dwelling for less than seven years, a service charge provision cannot cast on the tenant the cost of matters falling within the landlord's repairing obligation under Landlord and Tenant Act 1985, ss.11–16;

(h) a provision in the lease enabling the landlord to make an interim service charge is desirable. In the absence of such a provision a landlord may be disinclined to carry out expensive repairs or to provide services since he would have to bear the cost of these matters himself before seeking recovery of the sums from the tenants at a later date.

6.8.7. The amount of service charge payable will be of particular concern to the buyer of a lease. A substantial sum recently spent on repairs and redecoration of the exterior of a building may indicate that a similar item should not recur for some time. In each case enquiry should be made of the particular circumstances relating to the building.

6.8.8. The apportionment of a service charge on a sale may create a problem as the amounts payable may not be determined at the time of completion. Standard Condition 6.3.5 provides that when any sums to be apportioned are not known or easily ascertainable a provisional apportionment is to be made on completion according to the best estimate available. As soon after completion as the amount is known, a final apportionment is to be made and notified to the other party and any resulting balance paid no more than 10 working days later, interest calculated at the contract rate being chargeable for late payment. The Standard Commercial Property Conditions also provide for the seller to provide the buyer with documentation that the buyer will need in order to claim from the tenants the service costs which the seller incurred.

6.8.9. Sections 45–51 Housing Act 1985 (as amended by Landlord and Tenant Act 1987, s.41) contain restrictions on service charges where a house has been disposed of by a public sector authority other than under a long lease.

6.8.10. A landlord may not forfeit the lease of a dwelling house for failure to pay a service charge unless the amount of the service charge is agreed or admitted by the tenant or has been determined by a court or tribunal.[15]

6.8.11. Where the tenant of a flat is having difficulty in paying a service charge and the landlord is a housing authority, the landlord has a discretionary power to give the tenant a loan or to buy an equitable interest in the flat. In the majority of cases, the tenants of these flats will have bought them originally under the 'right to buy' scheme.[16]

1. *Morshead Mansions Limited* v. *Leon Di Marco* [2008] EWCA Civ 1371.
2. These provisions are not yet wholly in force. See also *St. Mary's Mansions Ltd* v. *Limegate Investment Co. Ltd*, *The Times*, 13 November 2002, CA.
3. Landlord and Tenant Act 1985, ss.19 and 27A. As to the interpretation of these provisions in the context of a mixed use development, see *Southern Rent Assessment Panel* v. *Rowner Estates Ltd* [2007] LRX/3/2006 (Lands Tribunal).
4. As to the approach of the Leasehold Valuation Tribunal when considering an application for dispensation see *Daejan Investments* v. *Benson* [2009] UKUT 233 (LC).
5. Landlord and Tenant Act 1985, ss.20 and 20ZA; Service Charges (Consultation Requirements) (England) Regulations 2003 (SI 2003/1987); and Service Charges (Consultation Requirements) (Amendment) (No.2) (England) Regulations 2004 (SI 2004/2939) as amended by Commonhold and Leasehold Reform Act 2002, s.170; and see Commonhold and Leasehold Reform Act 2002 (Commencement Order No.5 and Saving and Transitional Provisions) (England) Order 2004 (SI 2004/3056). Also Service Charges (Consultation Requirements) (Wales) Regulations 2004 (SI 2004/684/W.72) as amended by Service Charges (Consultation Requirements) (Amendment) (Wales) Regulations 2005 (SI 2005/1357). As an example of the operation of this provision see *Paddington Basin Developments Ltd* v. *West End Quay Estate Management Ltd* [2010] EWHC 833 (Ch).
6. Where the relevant costs were incurred more than 18 months before a demand for payment of the service charge is served on the tenant, then they are not recoverable unless the tenant had been previously notified within 18 months from when the costs were incurred: see Landlord and Tenant Act 1985, s.20B.
7. Landlord and Tenant Act 1985, ss.21–22. Amendments to s.21, which are not yet in force, require the landlord to provide accounts to tenants automatically. There are amendments to these provisions contained in the Housing and Regeneration Act 2008, Sched.12, which are not yet in force.
8. *Ibid.*, s.23 (there are prospective amendments to this section, which are not yet in force).
9. *Ibid.*, s.21A (not yet in force). There are amendments to these provisions contained in the Housing and Regeneration Act 2008, Sched.12, which are not yet in force.
10. When the amendments to Landlord and Tenant Act 1987, ss.42–42B come into force these monies will have to be paid into a separate designated bank account. There are amendments to these provisions contained in the Housing and Regeneration Act 2008, Sched.12, para.12, which are not yet in force.
11. See Commonhold and Leasehold Reform Act 2002 (Commencement No.6) (England) Order 2007 (SI 2007/1256); Commonhold and Leasehold Reform Act 2002 (Commencement No.4) (Wales) Order 2007 (SI 2007/3161); Service Charges (Summary of Rights and Obligations, and Transitional Provision) (England) Regulations 2007 (SI 2007/1257); Service Charges (Summary of Rights and Obligations, and Transitional Provisions) (Wales) Regulations 2007 (SI 2007/3160); Administration Charges (Summary of Rights and Obligations) (England) Regulations 2007 (SI 2007/1258); and Administration Charges (Summary of Rights and Obligations) (Wales) Regulations 2007 (SI 2007/3162).
12. Commonhold and Leasehold Reform Act 2002, s.158 and Sched.11. Note that a charge for entering into a deed of variation is not an adminstration charge for these purposes. There is no power for the Leasehold Valuation Tribunal to consider the reasonableness of such a charge. See *Mehson Property Co. Ltd* v. *Pellegrino* [2009] UKUT 119 (LC).
13. See, e.g. *St Modwen Developments (Edmonton) Ltd* v. *Tesco Stores Ltd* [2006] EWHC 3177 (Ch).
14. Commonhold and Leasehold Reform Act 2002, s.150 and Sched.9.
15. Housing Act 1996, s.81.
16. Housing (Purchase of Equitable Interests) (England) Regulations 2009 (SI 2009/601); Housing (Service Charge Loans) (Amendment) (England) Regulations 2009 (SI 2009/602).

6.9.   Limitations on landlords' remedies

6.9.1.   Landlords of long leases as defined in Commmonhold and Leasehold Reform Act 2002 – generally over 21 years[1] – are required to send the leaseholder a notice requiring payment of ground rent before the sum can be due.[2] Regulations set out the form and content of notices requiring the payment of ground rent.[3]

6.9.2. There are restrictions on the landlord's rights to forfeit long leases. Thus a landlord under a long lease of a dwelling may not forfeit for failure by a tenant to pay an amount consisting of rent, service charges or administration charges (or a combination of them) unless the unpaid amount exceeds a figure prescribed by regulations or where the amount has been owing for more than a prescribed period.[4] The current prescribed amount is £350 and the prescribed period is three years.[5]

6.9.3. A landlord of a long lease may not serve a forfeiture notice in respect of a breach of covenant unless the tenant admits the breach, or a court or tribunal has determined that the breach has occurred.[6]

6.9.4. There are restrictions on the landlord's rights to enforce certain insurance covenants in long leases. Where a long lease of a house requires the tenant to insure it with an insurer nominated or approved by the landlord, a tenant may avoid this if he gives a statutory notice of cover to the landlord and meets certain conditions relating to the insurer, the interests and risks covered and the amount of the cover.[7] Regulations prescribe the information that is to be included in a notice of cover.[8]

1. Commonhold and Leasehold Reform Act 2002, ss.76 and 77.
2. *Ibid.*, s.166.
3. Landlord and Tenant (Notice of Rent) (England) Regulations 2004 (SI 2004/3096); Landlord and Tenant (Notices of Rent) (Wales) Regulations 2005 (SI 2005/1355).
4. Commonhold and Leasehold Reform Act 2002, s.167.
5. Rights of Re-entry and Forfeiture (Prescribed Sum and Period) (England) Regulations 2004 (SI 2004/3086); Rights of Re-entry and Forfeiture (Prescribed Sum and Period) (Wales) Regulations 2005 (SI 2005/1352).
6. Commonhold and Leasehold Reform Act 2002, ss.168 and 169; and see Commonhold and Leasehold Reform Act 2002 (Commencement Order No.5 and Saving and Transitional Provisions) (England) Order 2004 (SI 2004/3056); Commonhold and Leasehold Reform Act 2002 (Commencement No.3 and Saving and Transitional Provisions) (Wales) Order 2005 (SI 2005/1353).
7. Commonhold and Leasehold Reform Act 2002, s.164.
8. Leasehold Houses (Notice of Insurance Cover) (England) Regulations 2004 (SI 2004/3097), as amended by Leasehold Houses (Notice of Insurance Cover) (England) (Amendment) Regulations 2005 (SI 2005/177); Leasehold Houses (Notice of Insurance Cover) (Wales) Regulations 2005 (SI 2005/1354).

6.10. Appointment of manager

6.10.1. Where a landlord has not complied with his obligations under the terms of the lease, a tenant of a flat may, after serving a preliminary notice on his landlord (and the landlord's lender where relevant), apply to the Leasehold Valuation Tribunal under Part II Landlord and Tenant Act 1987 (as amended) for the appointment of a manager to carry out the landlord's management functions.

These provisions apply to premises[1] where the building or part of a building consists of two or more flats except *inter alia* where the landlord is an exempt or resident landlord.

1. The order may relate to premises which are not comprised in the buildings containing the leasehold flats and their curtilages, e.g. amenity land: see *Cawsand Fort Management Company Ltd* v. *Stafford* [2007] EWCA Civ 1187.

6.11. **The right to manage**

6.11.1. Commonhold and Leasehold Reform Act 2002 creates a right to manage in favour of the tenants of flats. This right enables tenants to take over the management of their building without having to prove fault on the part of the landlord and without having to pay compensation. The right is exercised through a specific company which must be created in order to manage property, known as an RTM company.

RTM companies[1]

6.11.2. These are defined by the Act in some detail but are essentially private companies limited by guarantee and all qualifying tenants are entitled to be members. Regulations prescribe the content and form of the memorandum and articles of association of these companies.[2]

6.11.3. There are a number of qualifying conditions for exercising the right.

Qualifying conditions

The premises

6.11.4. The premises must, broadly, consist of a self contained building or part,[3] contain two or more flats held by qualifying tenants and the total number of flats held by such tenants must be not less than two-thirds of the total number of flats in the premises.[4]

Excluded premises[5]

6.11.5. In outline this right to manage does not apply to premises if the internal floor area of non-residential parts exceeds 25% of the whole internal floor area.[6] It also does not apply if there is a resident landlord and the premises do not contain more than four units. It does not apply if the local authority is the immediate landlord of any of the qualifying tenants.

Qualifying tenants[7]

6.11.6. A qualifying tenant must be a tenant of a flat under a long lease. However there are some exceptions so that, for example, the right does not apply to tenants of business premises. A long lease is again defined by the Act[8] and is essentially one granted for a term of more than 21 years.

Claiming the right to manage[9]

6.11.7. The right to manage is claimed by the RTM company giving notice inviting participation to those qualifying tenants who are not members of the RTM company. A 'claim notice' is then served on a specified number of interested parties including the landlord. On the date on which the claim notice is served the membership of the RTM company must include a number of qualifying tenants which is not less than half the number of flats.[10] A counter notice may then be served and if the claim is contested an application may be made to a leasehold valuation tribunal for a determination.

1. Commonhold and Leasehold Reform Act 2002, ss.73 and 74.
2. RTM Companies (Memorandum and Articles of Association) (Wales) Regulations 2004 (SI 2004/675); RTM Companies (Model Articles) (England) Regulations 2009 (SI 2009/2767).
3. A part of a building can only be self-contained if 'it constitutes a vertical division of the property': see Commonhold and Leasehold Reform Act 2002, s.72(3)(a). The question of whether the division is of a material extent is irrelevant, although truly *de minimis* parts can probably be ignored: see *In the matter of Holding & Management (Solitaire) Ltd* (2007) LRX/138/2006, available from **www.landstribunal. gov.uk**.
4. Commonhold and Leasehold Reform Act 2002, s.72(1).
5. *Ibid.*, Sched.6.
6. In calculating the percentage of the property used for residential purposes, any part used as such even though part of premises let under a separate commercial lease is included. See *Gaingold Ltd* v. *WHRA RTM Company Ltd* [2006] 1 EGLR 81, Lands Tribunal (LRX/19/2005) available from **www. landstribunal.gov.uk**.
7. Commonhold and Leasehold Reform Act 2002, s.75.
8. *Ibid.*, s.76.
9. *Ibid.*, ss.78–87.
10. *Ibid.*, s.79(5).

6.12. Leasehold Advisory Service

6.12.1. LEASE, the Leasehold Advisory Service, provides free legal advice to professional advisers, tenants, landlords, and others on the law affecting residential leasehold and commonhold properties.

6.12.2. LEASE is funded by the government and does not act for any party. The areas on which it provides free advice and assistance include service charges and the right to manage. It will also advise on commonhold, applications to the Leasehold Valuation Tribunal, rights to information, extending the lease and buying the freehold.

6.12.3. LEASE provides a mediation service as an alternative to proceedings before the Leasehold Valuation Tribunal or the court.[1]

1. For further details visit **www.lease-advice.org**.

K7. Business premises

7.1. Business tenancies

7.1.1. Part II Landlord and Tenant Act 1954 (as amended) established a comprehensive code of security of tenure for business tenants. The following paragraphs provide only an introduction to this very complex subject.

7.1.2. The Act applies to a tenancy where the property comprised in the tenancy is or includes premises which are occupied by the tenant and are so occupied for the purposes of a business carried on by him or for those and other purposes.[1] It therefore will not apply to a licence (the distinction between licences and tenancies is dealt with in K12).

7.1.3. The word 'business' is widely defined to include a trade, profession or employment and includes any activity carried on by a body of persons, whether corporate or unincorporate.[2]

1. The degree of occupation by the tenant may be minimal. There is no need for a tenant to be physically present provided the tenant is using the premises for a purpose incidental to the ordinary course of a business; see *Pointon York Group plc* v. *Poulton* [2006] EWCA Civ 1001.
2. Landlord and Tenant Act 1954, s.23(2). See *Hawkesbrook Leisure Ltd* v. *The Reece-Jones Partnership* [2003] EWHC 3333. As to mixed use premises see *Broadway Investments Hackney Ltd* v. *Grant* [2006] EWCA Civ 1709.

7.2. Exclusions from the Act

7.2.1. These include:

(a) agricultural holdings;

(b) mining leases;

(c) written service tenancies;

(d) tenancies at will;

(e) fixed term tenancies not exceeding six months unless the tenancy contains provisions for renewing the term or for extending it beyond six months from its beginning. This exception also does not apply if the tenant has been in occupation for a period which, together with any period during which any predecessor in the carrying on of the business carried on by the tenant was in occupation, exceeds twelve months;[1]

   (f)   tenancies for a term certain where the statutory procedure has been followed to exclude the security of tenure provisions of the Act prior to the commencement of the tenancy.[2]

7.2.2.   The procedure referred to in K7.2.1(f) is as follows:[3]

   (a)   a notice in prescribed form containing a warning must be served on the tenant before the tenant 'enters into the tenancy to which it applies, or (if earlier) becomes contractually bound to do so'. This procedure must therefore be followed before a contract to enter into an excluded lease is made;

   (b)   either:

       (i)   not less than 14 days must elapse before the tenant enters into the tenancy. The tenant must then sign a simple, prescribed declaration that he has received the required warning notice and has accepted the consequences of entering into the agreement;[4] or alternatively

       (ii)   the tenant, or a person duly authorised by him to do so, must, before the tenancy or contract is entered into, make a prescribed statutory declaration;[5]

   (c)   a reference to the notice and the simple declaration or (if applicable) the statutory declaration must be contained in or endorsed upon the instrument creating the tenancy; and

   (d)   the agreement to exclude the security of tenure provisions of the Act must be contained in or endorsed upon the instrument creating the tenancy.[6]

7.2.3.   Subject to K7.2.1(f), where a tenancy is within the provisions of the Act it is not possible to exclude the operation of the security of tenure provisions of the Act by agreement between the parties.[7]

1.   Landlord and Tenant Act 1954, s.43. Considered in *Cricket Ltd* v. *Shaftesbury* [1999] 28 EG 127.
2.   This does not include a tenancy for a fixed period 'and thereafter from year to year determinable by the landlord on twelve months written notice', see *Nicholls* v. *Kinsey* [1994] 16 EG 145, nor for a fixed period and thereafter 'any period of holding over or extension of it whether by statute or at common law or by agreement', see *Newham LBC* v. *Staden* [2008] EWCA Civ 1414.
3.   Prior to 1 June 2004, the procedure required a court order to be obtained. Transitional provisions required this still to be done where there was a contract in existence before this date to grant a lease on condition that the parties first obtained a court order excluding security of tenure, see Regulatory Reform (Business Tenancies) (England and Wales) Order 2003, Art. 29.
4.   It does not matter if a statutory declaration is used when a simple declaration would have been sufficient: see *Chiltern Railway Co. Ltd* v. *Patel* [2008] EWCA Civ 178.
5.   The forms of notice and declaration are set out in schedules to Regulatory Reform (Business Tenancies) (England and Wales) Order 2003.

6. For a series of articles discussing differing views of some detailed issues relating to this procedure, see A. Colby, A. Wallis and K. Fenn, 'Follow the letter of the law', *Estates Gazette* 29 May 2004, 132; K. Fenn, 'Mind the traps', *Estates Gazette* 5 June 2004, 116; K. Fenn, A. Colby and S. Highmore. 'A procedure guaranteed to confuse', *Estates Gazette* 19 June 2004, 166; and A. Colby and K. Fenn, 'No semblance of order', *Estates Gazette* 26 June 2004, 187.
7. Landlord and Tenant Act 1954, s.38.

7.3. Termination of tenancy

7.3.1. A tenancy within the Act can only be determined by one of the methods prescribed by the Act. These include:

    (a) forfeiture;

    (b) notice to quit given by the tenant;

    (c) immediate surrender;[1]

    (d) service by the landlord of a notice under Landlord and Tenant Act 1954, s.25;

    (e) a tenant's request for a new tenancy under Landlord and Tenant Act 1954, s.26;

    (f) notice served under section 27 of the Act.

7.3.2. Where the tenant has a periodic tenancy, his notice to quit will be of the length appropriate to the period of his tenancy (e.g. one month's notice for a monthly tenancy). In the case of a fixed-term tenancy, the tenant may serve a three-month notice under section 27 of the Act to expire on the term date or at any time after the term date. Alternatively, the tenant may vacate before the end of the tenancy.[2]

7.3.3. A tenancy which is not determined by one of the above methods continues to run (despite expiry of a fixed term) on the same terms until terminated by one of these methods.[3]

1. An agreement for the tenant to surrender his tenancy at some future time is void under Landlord and Tenant Act 1954, s.38 except if authorised under the Act. This requires a similar procedure to that authorising contracting out of the security of tenure provisions of the 1954 Act considered in K7.2.1(f).
2. See Landlord and Tenant Act 1954, s.27(1A).
3. In the case of a business lease which was subject to the SDLT regime, further SDLT returns may have to be filed following the extension of the lease by the 1954 Act: see further A14.16.

7.4. Landlord's notice

7.4.1. A notice to terminate a tenancy served by a landlord under Landlord and Tenant Act 1954, s.25 must be in a prescribed form and must specify a date (not earlier than the term date and not less than six nor more than 12 months ahead) on which the tenancy is to end.[1] If the landlord does not wish to oppose the grant of a new tenancy, he must state in the notice his proposals for the premises, duration, rent and other terms of the new tenancy. If he wishes to oppose the grant of a new tenancy, he must set out which ground or grounds he intends to use (see K7.4.3).

7.4.2. If the tenant wants a new tenancy, he should apply to the court for a new tenancy by the date specified in the landlord's section 25 notice. A tenant's application to the court is a pending land action and should be protected by an entry in the register of pending land actions in the case of unregistered land. Where the land is registered a pending land action should be protected by a notice.[2] Note that even if the tenant is in occupation of registered land his pending land application will not be an overriding interest.[3]

7.4.3. The landlord's grounds for opposing the grant of a new tenancy are contained in Landlord and Tenant Act 1954, s.30 and are briefly as follows:

    (a)   breach of repairing obligations by the tenant;

    (b)   persistent delay in paying rent;

    (c)   substantial breaches of other obligations under the tenancy;

    (d)   alternative accommodation;

    (e)   possession of whole property required where tenant has a sub-tenancy of part;

    (f)   landlord's intention to demolish or reconstruct the property;

    (g)   landlord requires possession for his own occupation.[4]

7.4.4. The time limits specified in the Act for service of notices and application to the court are construed strictly and in general no extension of those limits is permitted. Thus if a tenant fails to apply to the court within the prescribed period he will lose his right to a new tenancy unless the landlord has made an application to the court by that date. This period cannot be extended by the court. However, the parties may agree in writing to extend the deadline for making an application to court, providing this agreement is made before the expiry of the statutory period. The agreement cannot be made retrospectively.[5]

1.   The form of notice is contained in Landlord and Tenant Act 1954, Part 2 (Notices) Regulations 2004. The methods of service are prescribed by Landlord and Tenant Act 1954, s.66(4), applying to Landlord and Tenant Act 1927, s.23 (as amended by Recorded Delivery Service Act 1962). The most common method used is recorded delivery under which the date of service is deemed to be the date of posting; see *CA Webber (Transport) Ltd* v. *Network Rail Infrastructure Ltd* [2003] All ER (D) 250.
2.   Land Registration Act 2002, s.87(1)(a).
3.   *Ibid.*, s.87(3).
4.   This ground is not available to a landlord whose interest was purchased or created within the five years preceding the termination date of the tenancy as specified in the notice terminating the tenancy (provided that the tenancy or series of tenancies was existing at the time of creation and has continued uninterrupted since that time).
5.   Landlord and Tenant Act 1954, s.29.

7.5. Tenant's request for a new tenancy

7.5.1. A tenant's request for a new tenancy can be made only if the tenant originally had a tenancy for a term of years certain exceeding one year. It must be in prescribed form and must specify a date (not earlier than the term date and not less than six nor more than 12 months ahead) for the start of the new tenancy. If the landlord wishes to oppose the grant of a new tenancy, he must notify the tenant within two months, stating on which ground(s) he will rely (see K7.4.3). The tenant must then apply to the court for a new tenancy not later than the day before the date specified in the tenant's request[1] (see K7.4.4). A tenant's application to the court is a pending land action and should be protected by an entry in the register of pending land actions in the case of unregistered land. Where the land is registered a pending land action should be protected by a notice. Even if the tenant is in occupation of the land, his application cannot be an overriding interest (see Land Registration Act 2002, s.87(3)).

1. Landlord and Tenant Act 1954, s.29A(2). The form of request is contained in Landlord and Tenant Act 1954, Part 2 (Notices) Regulations 2004.

7.6. Identifying the parties

7.6.1. The procedure to terminate the lease by landlord's notice or tenant's request must be carried out between the tenant and the relevant or 'competent' landlord as defined in Landlord and Tenant Act 1954, s.44. The competent landlord is the person who is the owner of that interest in the property that is either the fee simple or a tenancy that will not come to an end within 14 months by effluxion of time.

7.6.2. To enable the parties to discover the identity of the relevant individuals on whom they should serve notice, the Act contains a provision in section 40 to permit the service of a notice requesting information. This requires the other party to provide information in relation to others who may have an interest in the property. This enables landlords to discover if the tenant has created sub-tenancies, and tenants to discover the nature and extent of their landlord's and superior landlord's and their lender's interests. The section requires the recipient of such a notice to reply within a month, to keep the information up to date for six months and imposes a specific remedy for failing to comply with such a notice. The provision also deals with transfer of ownership of the landlord's or the tenant's interest taking place during the period in which a section 40 notice remains current.

7.7. Application to the court

7.7.1. Either the landlord or the tenant can apply to the court for an order determining the terms of the new tenancy. Alternatively, where the landlord is opposing a new tenancy he can apply to the court for an order terminating the current tenancy without the order for a new tenancy.

7.7.2. Unless the landlord can establish one or more of the grounds for possession within section 30(1) Landlord and Tenant Act 1954 (see K7.4.3), a new tenancy must be ordered by the court comprising such holding (i.e. the part of the property that is occupied by the tenant), at such rent and on such other terms as the court orders (in the absence of agreement between the parties), although the new tenancy cannot, in the absence of agreement, exceed 15 years in length (see ss.32–35 of the Act).

7.8. Compensation

7.8.1. If the landlord succeeds in obtaining possession, based on grounds (e), (f), or (g) in K7.4.3, the tenant is entitled to compensation for giving up his tenancy.

7.8.2. In certain circumstances a tenant of business premises may also be entitled to compensation for improvements effected by him under Part I Landlord and Tenant Act 1927. This provision enables a tenant to make improvements if they fall within the classification set out in the Act, which include, for example, certain improvements which add to the letting value of the property, provided, broadly, the tenant serves notice of his intention to do so on the landlord. The landlord then has three months to object when the matter is referred to the county court. If there is no objection or the court consents, the tenant can make the improvement and on leaving he is entitled to compensation equivalent to the increase in value of the premises.[1]

7.8.3. The court may order the landlord to pay the tenant compensation for loss or damage where the court refuses to grant a new tenancy and it subsequently appears that this was due to misrepresentation or concealment of material facts. The court may also award the tenant compensation where the tenant has quit the premises after failing to apply for renewal, or after withdrawing an application for renewal, by reason of misrepresentation or the concealment of material facts.[2]

1. See, for example, *Norfolk Capital Group Ltd* v. *Cadogan Estates Ltd* [2004] 1 WLR 1458.
2. Landlord and Tenant Act 1954, s.37A. See, for example, *Inclusive Technology* v. *Williamson* [2009] EWCA Civ 718.

7.9. Rent control

7.9.1. There are no statutory limitations on the rent recoverable on the original grant of a tenancy of business premises, but on a renewal the court can fix a new rent failing agreement by the parties. The court also has power, on application by either party, to fix an interim rent pending the outcome of proceedings.[1] The interim rent is calculated on a valuation based on a tenancy from year to year under the principles laid down in Landlord and Tenant Act 1954, s.24A. As a crude yardstick, it is generally considered that these principles will lead to an interim rent somewhere between 10% to 15% less than the open market valuation. This method of valuation applies where the renewal application is opposed. However, where renewal is uncontested, subject to certain exceptions, the interim rent will simply be the same as the rent for the tenancy once it is renewed.

1. Landlord and Tenant Act 1954, s.24A.

7.10.   **Buying a business lease**

7.10.1.   A prospective assignee (purchaser) of a lease of business premises should (in addition to the usual matters to be considered on the assignment of a lease) pay careful attention to the following matters:

     (a)   the rent review provisions contained in the lease;

     (b)   the repairing obligations imposed by the lease;

     (c)   any service charge provisions in the lease;[1]

     (d)   the VAT implications of the transaction;

     (e)   whether the existing tenant has committed any breach of covenant which would give the landlord the right to determine the lease or to refuse a renewal of it;

     (f)   the likelihood of a lease renewal being opposed by a landlord on other grounds, e.g. redevelopment;

     (g)   the provisions relating to alienation of the lease.

1. Note the *RICS Code of Practice: Service Charges in Commercial Property*. The code is designed to indicate best practice for commercial service charges; see K1.8.8.

7.11.   **Covenants restricting assignment**

7.11.1.   It is common for a business lease to prohibit an assignment without the landlord's consent.

7.11.2.   Where a lease contains a covenant prohibiting assignment without the landlord's consent, that consent is not to be unreasonably withheld (section 19(1) Landlord and Tenant Act 1927). Guidelines for testing reasonableness were set out in the Court of Appeal decision in *International Drilling Fluids Ltd* v. *Louisville Investments (Uxbridge) Ltd*.[1] The Supreme Court broadly approved these guidelines , whilst pointing out that the three overriding principles are:

     •   that consent must not be withheld on grounds that have nothing to do with the relationship of landlord and tenant;

     •   that the issue is one of fact; and

     •   that the landlord's obligation is to show his conduct was reasonable.[2]

The guidelines are summarised below, updated to take account of subsequent developments:

(a) the purpose of the covenant is to protect the landlord from an undesirable tenant or from an undesirable use being made of the premises;

(b) a landlord cannot, therefore, refuse consent on grounds which have nothing to do with the relationship of landlord and tenant;

(c) as long as the landlord's conclusions were those which a reasonable man might reach he does not have to prove they were justified;

(d) it may be reasonable for a landlord to withhold consent on the grounds of the proposed use of the premises;[3]

(e) normally a landlord need have regard only to his own interests but it may be that the detriment caused to the tenant by withholding consent so outweighs the advantage to the landlord that it is unreasonable for consent to be withheld.

7.11.3. Subject to these considerations, whether a landlord is acting reasonably is a question of fact in each case. A lease which is an 'old tenancy', i.e. one to which Landlord and Tenant (Covenants) Act 1995 does not apply, cannot set out what is to be considered reasonable, although a condition precedent can be imposed.[4] Under Landlord and Tenant Act 1988, a landlord must give consent within a reasonable time unless there is a reason for withholding it. Written reasons for refusal must be given within a reasonable time.[5] A landlord has only a very short time in which to reach a decision once possessed of all the necessary information. What period will be regarded as unreasonable is a question of fact in each case, but it may be a matter of weeks rather than months.[6] The burden of proving that the withholding of consent is reasonable is on the landlord. In appropriate cases a landlord may be penalised for undue delay by an award of exemplary damages.[7]

7.11.4. The above provisions have been amended[8] in relation to assignments of 'new tenancies', i.e. ones to which Landlord and Tenant (Covenants) Act 1995 applies; broadly those granted on or after 1 January 1996 of commercial premises.[9] Paragraphs K7.11.5 to K7.11.8 set out the new provisions.

7.11.5. A landlord may agree in advance with his tenant:

(a) any circumstance in which he may withhold consent to a proposed assignment; or

(b) any conditions subject to which his consent will be granted;

and if he withholds consent for these reasons he is not acting unreasonably. The agreement has to be made before the application for consent but does not have to be contained in the lease nor made at the same time as the lease.

7.11.6. The 1995 Act distinguishes between factual matters, for example:

(a) the assignee must be a plc;

(b)   the assignee must have net assets equal to a specified multiplier of the rent;

(c)   the assignee must provide a rent deposit; or

(d)   the assignor must enter an authorised guarantee agreement;

and discretionary matters, e.g. that the assignee is, in the landlord's opinion, of equal financial standing to the assignor. In the latter case, the landlord's decision has to be arrived at reasonably, or the tenant must have the right to have the decision reviewed by an independent third party who is identifiable from the agreement and whose decision is conclusive.

7.11.7.   The imposition of stringent conditions may have an adverse effect on the assessment of a revised rent or a subsequent review and/or may make it difficult for the tenant to assign the lease. In considering what conditions to impose, landlords are encouraged to have regard to the Code for Leasing Business Premises 2007.[10]

7.11.8.   'Virtual assignments' have been developed to deal with the need to 'assign' a tenant's interest speedily for commercial reasons, particularly where obtaining a landlord's consent to assign may be problematic. A virtual assignment is an arrangement whereby all the benefit and burdens of a lease are passed to a third party but without the leasehold legal estate passing to the assignee. This device is normally employed where the premises are an investment (so they are occupied by an under-tenant). This means that there will be no change in occupancy of the premises. A virtual assignment will not normally be in breach of any of the common covenants in a lease precluding dealing with the premises.[11] If the landlord wishes to prevent a virtual assignment then appropriate covenants must be included in the lease, for example to prevent assignment of the right to receive the rent.[12]

1.   [1986] 1 All ER 321.
2.   *Ashworth Frazer Ltd* v. *Gloucester City Council* [2001] 46 EG 180.
3.   This principle was considered by the House of Lords in *Ashworth Frazer Ltd* v. *Gloucester City Council* [2001] 46 EG 180.
4.   See *Bocardo SA* v. *S & M Hotels* [1980] 1 WLR 17; *Vaux Group plc* v. *Lilley* [1991] 04 EG 136.
5.   Once the landlord has made a decision this is final and he cannot reconsider this decision within the 'reasonable time' period: *Go West Ltd* v. *Spigarolo* [2003] 07 EG 136.
6.   In one case involving an application for consent to underlet, a week after receiving the final piece of information was held to be sufficient: *Blockbuster Entertainment Ltd* v. *Barnsdale Properties Ltd* [2003] EWHC 2912. Note also *NCR Ltd* v. *Riverland Portfolio No.1 Ltd (No.2)* [2004] EWCA Civ 312; [2005] 13 EG 135.
7.   *Design Progression Ltd* v. *Thurloe Properties Ltd* [2004] 10 EGCS 184.
8.   Landlord and Tenant (Covenants) Act 1995 inserting a new section 19(1A) into Landlord and Tenant Act 1927.
9.   This provision applies to leases apart from leases of residential premises or those of agricultural property, see Landlord and Tenant Act 1927, s.19.
10.   See K1.1.4.
11.   *Clarence House Ltd* v. *National Westminster Bank plc* [2009] EWCA 1311.
12.   If this approach is adopted, care will be needed to ensure that any such provision is not in conflict with the tenant's need to satisfy the requirement of any lender, if the lease might be offered as security.

7.12. **Professional arbitration on court terms (PACT)**

7.12.1. The Royal Institution of Chartered Surveyors (RICS) and the Law Society have jointly agreed to offer a service providing private determination of lease renewals under the provisions of Landlord and Tenant Act 1954. This is claimed to provide a faster, cheaper and more efficient method of settling lease renewal disputes than in the courts, by professionals who have the expertise to make decisions on technical matters.

7.12.2. The scheme is voluntary with referral by mutual agreement of the landlord and the tenant. Appointments of arbitrators and experts, experienced in landlord and tenant matters, are made by the President of the RICS or the President of the Law Society. Once an application has been made to the court the parties can apply for an agreed adjournment in order to deal with the matter under PACT. Model consent orders are provided to be adapted to cover the needs of the particular case.

7.12.3. The nature of the dispute will dictate the expertise required. Sufficient information on the issue in dispute will be requested from the parties to enable the appropriate President to determine whether the services of a surveyor or solicitor or indeed both are required.

7.12.4. The primary aim is to settle rents where other terms have already been agreed. Other disputes can be referred to the scheme on matters of principle or drafting of a lease.

7.12.5. The tenant will retain the right to reject the tenancy which at present exists under the Act.

7.12.6. Parties will have the option of excluding or retaining a right of appeal to the court from the arbitrator's decision.

7.12.7. The system is designed to be flexible, giving the parties the right to settle their own procedure for determination of a dispute in a way not open to them in litigation.

7.12.8. A summary of the key issues follows:

    (a) Decide with the other party whether it would be advantageous to refer aspects of the lease renewal to a third party solicitor or arbitrator rather than a judge.

    (b) Identify which aspects of the renewal (if any) are agreed.

    (c) Decide which aspects to refer to the third party:

        (i)   the interim rent;

        (ii)   the new rent;

        (iii) other terms of the lease;

         (iv)   the detailed drafting of terms;

         (v)   a combination of these.

(d)   Choose which aspects are to be resolved by a third party solicitor and which by a third party surveyor.

(e)   Choose the third party's capacity – arbitrator or expert?

(f)   Draft court application making use of or adapting PACT model orders.

(g)   Apply to court for consent.

(h)   Apply for appointment of person adjudicating (if not agreed).

(i)   Proceed with adjudication.

(j)   Receive award subject only to 'cooling off' rights and, in arbitration, any right of appeal.

7.12.9.   There have been relatively few referrals to PACT so information as to the effectiveness of the scheme is unavailable. For further information see **www.rics.org**.

K8. Agricultural tenancies

8.1. Definitions

8.1.1. Many tenants of agricultural holdings which were created before 1 September 1995 enjoy security of tenure under Agricultural Holdings Act 1986. As from 1 September 1995, it is no longer possible to create a new agricultural tenancy which has the protection of the 1986 Act, unless it is a succession tenancy or a contracted in tenancy falling within the limited scope of section 4 Agricultural Tenancies Act 1995 as amended by Regulatory Reform (Agricultural Tenancies) (England and Wales) Order 2006 (SI 2006/2805) which is relevant to minor boundary changes to the let area, assessed in terms of either area or value. K8.2–8.4 only apply to tenancies which are regulated by Agricultural Holdings Act 1986.

8.1.2. The expression 'agricultural holding' is defined as the aggregate of land (whether agricultural land or not) comprised in a contract of tenancy which is a contract for an agricultural tenancy (not being a service tenancy).

8.1.3. In general, 'agricultural land' means land used for agriculture and so used for the purpose of a trade or business.

8.1.4. 'Contract of tenancy' means a letting of land or an agreement for letting land, for a term of years or from year to year. This can be oral or in writing.

8.2. Protection of short-term tenants and licensees

8.2.1. Under Agricultural Holdings Act 1986, s.2 an agreement under which any land was let to a person for use as agricultural land for an interest less than a tenancy from year to year, or under which a person was granted a licence to occupy land for use as agricultural land (in circumstances such that if his interest were a tenancy from year to year he would be the tenant of an agricultural holding), took effect (with the necessary modifications) as an agreement for the letting of land for a tenancy from year to year. The licence must not have been gratuitous and must have conferred occupation on the licensee.

8.3.　Security of tenure

8.3.1.　Subject to a provision dealing with the death of the tenant before the term date[1] a tenancy of an agricultural holding for two years or more continues as a tenancy from year to year unless written notice to quit is given by either party at least one year and not more than two years before the end of the tenancy.[2]

8.3.2.　In consequence of Agricultural Holdings Act 1986, ss.2 and 3, a notice to quit is normally necessary to determine an agricultural letting for an interest less than a tenancy from year to year, a licence to occupy agricultural land, and a tenancy for two years or more. The importance of this is that the security of tenure provisions of Agricultural Holdings Act 1986 come into operation where notice to quit (the method of determination of periodic tenancies) is given to the tenant.

8.3.3.　In general, if a notice to quit an agricultural holding or part of a holding is given to the tenant he has the right to serve a counter-notice on the landlord, requiring the landlord to obtain the consent of the Agricultural Land Tribunal to the operation of the notice to quit, which consent can only be given on certain grounds. The tenant's right to serve a counter-notice is excluded if the notice to quit is given and is expressed to be given on one of a number of limited grounds specified in Schedule 3 Agricultural Holdings Act 1986.

1.　Agricultural Holdings Act 1986, s.4.
2.　*Ibid.*, s.3.

8.4.　Other matters dealt with by Agricultural Holdings Act 1986

8.4.1.　Agricultural Holdings Act 1986 deals with a large number of matters regulating the relationship between landlord and tenant, including the right of succession on the death or retirement of the tenant, the tenant's right to compensation for improvements, and arbitration as to rent. Arbitration procedures under the 1986 Act are now regulated by Arbitration Act 1996.

8.5.　Agricultural Tenancies Act 1995

8.5.1.　Agricultural Tenancies Act 1995 applies to all agricultural tenancies granted after the commencement of the Act on 1 September 1995 (excepting those mentioned at K8.1.1). It is not retrospective in effect and does not affect existing tenancies (or successions to those tenancies) granted under Agricultural Holdings Act 1986.

8.5.2.　The words 'agriculture' and 'agricultural' have the same meaning as under the 1986 Act.

8.5.3. Tenancies created under the 1995 Act are called 'farm business tenancies'. Certain conditions must be satisfied for a tenancy to fall within this definition:

(a) **Business**: all or part of the land is farmed for the purposes of a trade or business and has been so farmed since the start of the tenancy.

(b) **Agriculture**: having regard to a number of matters specified in the Act, the character of the tenancy is primarily or wholly agricultural.

(c) **Notice**: as an alternative to the agriculture condition, the parties can, before the grant of the tenancy, exchange written notices identifying the land and stating that the person giving the notice intends that the proposed tenancy is to be and remain a farm business tenancy. Even where such notices are exchanged, the character of the tenancy must be primarily or wholly agricultural at the start of the tenancy.

8.5.4. To be a farm business tenancy, condition (a) above must be satisfied, together with either (b) or (c). If (c) is used, the tenancy will remain a farm business tenancy so long as some part of the land is farmed, but other parts of the land may later be used for other business and non-agricultural purposes.

Exclusions

8.5.5. The following tenancies are excluded:

(a) tenancies granted before the commencement of the Act;

(b) tenancies granted under the succession on death or retirement provisions of the 1986 Act;

(c) tenancies granted to an existing tenant who is protected under the 1986 Act where a variation of the previous tenancy has the effect of an implied surrender and regrant;

(d) contracted in tenancies referred to in K8.1.1.

Security of tenure

8.5.6. There is no security of tenure or right of renewal given to the tenant under the 1995 Act (other than as provided for in the agreement itself), although note the termination requirements set out in K8.5.15.

Preparation of the agreement

8.5.7. If the tenancy agreement is to be for a fixed term of three years or more, it must be made by deed (under Law of Property Act 1925, s.52) and can only be prepared by 'accredited persons' – a barrister, solicitor, notary public, licensed conveyancer, a full member of the Central Association of Agricultural Valuers, or an Associate or Fellow of ISVA or RICS (Agricultural Tenancies Act 1995, s.35).

Rent and rent review

8.5.8. There are no statutory controls on rent other than its review. In relation to rent review, section 10 of the 1995 Act provides for a rent review to take place in accordance with the provisions of that section except where the provisions of section 9 are complied with. Section 9 applies to a tenancy which:

(a) expressly states that the rent is not to be reviewed during the term of the tenancy; or

(b) provides for a rent review at specified times, either:

    (i) by or to a specified amount; or

    (ii) in accordance with a specified formula (not upwards only) assessed by objective criteria; or

(c) expressly states that Part II of the 1995 Act does not apply and there is nothing that precludes a reduction in the rent; or

(d) provides for an independent expert to make a final determination of the revised rent and there is nothing that precludes a reduction in the rent.[1]

8.5.9. Statutory review under section 10:

(a) either party can call for a review by notice to the other;

(b) the review date must not be less than 12 nor more than 24 months from service of a 'statutory review notice';

(c) if the parties have agreed a specified review date, the review date must be a date as from which rent could be varied under the agreement;

(d) if the parties have agreed in writing that the review date is to be a specified date, the review must be on that date;

(e) if there is no agreement as to the date of the review, the date is the anniversary of the beginning of the tenancy;

(f) subject to any agreement to the contrary, rent reviews may not take place at less than three-yearly intervals.

8.5.10. An independent expert or arbitrator is to be appointed to fix the reviewed rent. In default of agreement, the President of the RICS is to appoint the arbitrator. If the tenancy agreement requires determination by an independent expert, arbitration is excluded.

8.5.11. The reviewed rent on a statutory review is assessed on an open market formula (section 13). Tenant's improvements are broadly disregarded.

Assignment

8.5.12. The 1995 Act does not restrict assignment but section 19 Landlord and Tenant Act 1927 does not apply to these tenancies.

Agricultural covenants

8.5.13. No agricultural covenants are implied by the 1995 Act. Such covenants must be expressly included in the agreement if required.

Repairs and insurance

8.5.14. The 1995 Act does not deal with these matters, thus appropriate clauses to deal with them must be included in the agreement.

Termination

8.5.15. The following apply to termination:

(a) a fixed-term agreement for two years or less will expire automatically;

(b) common law rules apply to periodic tenancies except that a yearly tenant needs to be given not less than one year's notice, expiring at the end of a year;

(c) for a fixed-term tenancy of more than two years, not less than 12 months' notice to terminate on the term day must be given (otherwise the tenancy continues as a tenancy from year to year);

(d) notices must be in writing.

Compensation

8.5.16. Compensation is payable for the tenant's improvements. These provisions cannot be excluded by agreement although consideration can be given to a restriction on alterations which do not fall within the statutory definition of an improvement. Improvements are categorised as follows:

(a) **Intangible advantages**

something which attaches to the holding and which the tenant has brought to the holding at his own expense, e.g. unimplemented planning permission or a water abstraction licence;

(b) **Physical improvements**

(i) non-routine, e.g. building a shed;

(ii) routine (section 19(10) of the 1995 Act), e.g. 'tenant's right' (growing crops, etc.).

Conditions for claiming compensation

8.5.17. The landlord's consent must have been obtained (generally before or after the improvement was made). Appeal against the landlord's refusal of consent lies to an arbitrator (but in respect of non-routine physical improvements an appeal can only be lodged before the improvement has been made). There is no appeal against the landlord's refusal of consent to an application by the tenant for planning permission. The arbitrator cannot vary any conditions imposed by the landlord.

Amount of compensation (sections 20–27 of the 1995 Act)

8.5.18. The amount of compensation is the amount attributable to the improvement in the value of the holding at the termination of the tenancy. Appeal lies to an arbitrator under section 22 of the 1995 Act. The landlord and tenant are free to agree an upper limit to the amount of compensation payable at the time consent is given to an improvement. If the concept of a limit is agreed but not the amount of compensation payable, then the amount is the cost to the tenant of making the improvement.

Fixtures

8.5.19. Tenant's fixtures can be removed by the tenant at the end of the tenancy. The tenant is under an obligation not to cause damage and to rectify any damage caused. The tenant need not give notice to the landlord of his intention to remove fixtures. If consent to an improvement was obtained, the tenant could alternatively claim compensation for the fixture as an improvement. The agreement should specify which fixtures are/are not tenant's fixtures.

Dispute resolution

8.5.20. The 1995 Act contains specific provisions for arbitration on rent review, improvements and compensation. Other disputes are to be referred to arbitration unless the parties agree to a different procedure. The arbitrator is appointed with the consent of the parties (either on a joint reference or four weeks' notice by one party unchallenged by the other). In default of agreement, the President of the RICS is to appoint the arbitrator. The court's jurisdiction is not excluded. Arbitration Act 1996 applies to arbitrations under the 1995 Act.

Stamp Duty Land Tax

8.5.21. Under the provisions of section 5 of the 1995 Act landlords and tenants are able to create a rolling tenancy agreement from year to year. The tenant in these circumstances needs to be aware of the ongoing liability to account to HM Revenue and Customs for any Stamp Duty Land Tax that may be payable under the terms of the transaction (see A14).

Single farm payment

8.5.22. The parties to the tenancy agreement will need to include appropriate clauses to cover the transfer and ownership of any entitlement held by the tenant at the end of the term. Where entitlements are to be leased to the tenant as part of the transaction, consideration should be given to the timing of such transfer. See B8.3.10.

1. Exceptions (c) and (d) were introduced under Regulatory Reform (Agricultural Tenancies) (England and Wales) Order 2006 (SI 2006/2805).

8.6. Taxation consequences

8.6.1. Farmland as well as woodland and buildings associated with it is often eligible for Inheritance Tax reliefs in the form of either Agricultural Property Relief or Business Property Relief or both. As a result, if those reliefs are required, those considering acquiring an agricultural tenancy or letting agricultural land should give careful thought as to how these reliefs will be affected before any arrangement or tenancy structure is formally documented.

K9. Right to buy

9.1.   Public sector

9.1.1.   Subject to certain conditions, a secure tenant normally has a right to buy.[1]

9.1.2.   'Right to buy' means:

(a)   if the dwelling is a house, and the landlord or a public sector head-landlord owns the freehold, the right to acquire the freehold;

(b)   if the landlord does not own the freehold or the dwelling is a flat, the right to be granted a lease of the premises.

9.1.3.   To qualify, the tenant must usually have occupied the house or flat as a secure tenant for two years, although there are special provisions in Schedule 4 Housing Act 1985 relating to spouses, civil partners and children. This provision is amended in relation to wholly new tenancies which begin on or after 18 January 2005. In these cases the relevant period of occupation is extended to five years.[2] Schedule 5 Housing Act 1985 (as amended) contains a number of exceptions to the right to buy.

9.1.4.   The price payable on exercise of the right is the price which the house would realise if sold on the open market by a willing seller, less any discount to which the buyer is entitled. The amount of the discount depends on the length of occupation of the secure tenant, but cannot usually be less than 32% nor more than 60% in the case of a house, or less than 44% or more than 70% in the case of a flat. This is subject to a maximum amount of the discount imposed by Housing Act 1985, s.131 and related costs incurred in respect of the house.[3] These provisions are amended in relation to wholly new tenancies which begin on or after 18 January 2005. These amendments are consequential to the extension of the initial qualifying period of occupation. Therefore in these cases the amount of the discount previously referred to in this paragraph is amended so that it cannot usually be less than 35% in the case of a house, or less than 50% in the case of a flat.[4]

9.1.5.   The Housing Act 2004 enables landlords of secure tenants to seek a court order suspending the right to buy for a specified period in respect of the tenancy on the grounds of anti-social behaviour.[5] In certain circumstances, where an application is pending for a demotion order, a suspension order or a possession order sought on the grounds of anti-social behaviour, a tenant is prevented from being able to enforce his right to buy.[6]

9.1.6. If a tenant who has received a discount sells the property within five years, he will (except in certain specified cases) be required to repay to the landlord a proportionate part of the discount.[7] This liability takes effect as a legal charge on the property. In addition, the purchase deed must grant a right of first refusal to the landlord if the property is sold within 10 years.[8] There are provisions in the legislation governing the form and effect of the conveyance/transfer or lease. There are service charge limits which the buyer can expect to see set out in the conveyance/transfer or lease. Where the title to the landlord's property is unregistered, the tenant does not need to examine a landlord's title as the landlord is required to supply the tenant with a certificate of title in the prescribed form, which the Land Registry is bound to accept for the purposes of registration of the tenant's title. A lease taken by a tenant under the right to buy provisions needs to be registered even if for a term of seven years or less since Land Registration Act 2002, s.4(1)(e) applies to it. If application for first registration is not made within two months, the lease will be void as regards the grant of the legal estate.[9] It takes effect as a contract made for valuable consideration to grant the lease concerned.[10] The contract may be protected as an overriding interest if the intended tenant is in occupation.[11]

1. Housing Act 1985, as amended.
2. Housing Act 1985, s.119(1) as amended by Housing Act 2004, s.180.
3. The maximum discount is subject to regulation by Housing (Right to Buy) (Limits on Discount) Order 1998 (as amended).
4. See footnote 2 above.
5. See Housing Act 1985, s.121 as amended by Housing Act 2004, s.192.
6. Housing Act 1985, s.138(2A) to (2D), as inserted by Housing Act 2004, s.193. Note also that an amendment to the provisions dealing with the position in relation to possession orders is to be inserted by the Housing and Regeneration Bill, clause 303, should this be enacted and come into force as currently drafted.
7. There is a sliding scale which applies to the amount of the discount which must be repaid on early sale which is proportional to the years of occupation at the rate of one-fifth per year; see Housing Act 1985, s.155A, as inserted by Housing Act 2004, s.185.
8. Housing Act 1985, s.156A inserted by Housing Act 2004, s.188(1). Note also: Housing (Right of First Refusal) (England) Regulations 2005 (SI 2005/1917) and Housing (Rights of First Refusal) (Wales) Regulations 2005 (SI 2005/2680).
9. Land Registration Act 2002, s.7(1).
10. *Ibid.*, s.7(2)(b).
11. *Ibid.*, Sched.1, para.2.

9.2. Leasehold Reform Act 1967

9.2.1. Part I Leasehold Reform Act 1967 gives certain tenants the right compulsorily to buy out the landlord's freehold interest (enfranchisement) or to take an extended lease for an additional 50 years. The right to enfranchise can still be exercised after the grant of an extended lease. These provisions have been modified by Leasehold Reform, Housing and Urban Development Act 1993, Housing Act 1996 and Commonhold and Leasehold Reform Act 2002 (see K9.3).

Qualifying conditions

9.2.2.   For the tenant to qualify, broadly the following factors must be considered:

(a)   his tenancy must be a long tenancy;[1]

(b)   the house must fall within the definition of that word in the 1967 Act;

(c)   the tenant must have held the lease for the last two years;

(d)   the value of the property may be relevant.[2]

Long tenancy

9.2.3.   A long tenancy is one granted for a term certain exceeding 21 years; but there are certain exceptions where shorter leases which have been extended beyond 21 years through renewal will qualify.

House

9.2.4.   A 'house' within the Act is one where it is a building designed or adapted for living in where it is reasonable to call it a house.[3] The House of Lords has held that where a house has become dilapidated so as to be uninhabitable the property can still be regarded as being 'designed or adapted for living in'.[4] However, where a property that was originally constructed for residential purposes has come to be used as offices it may not be 'reasonable to call it a house'.[5] Where a building has been converted into flats or maisonettes, it depends on the structure of the conversion as to whether the converted units fall within the scope of the Act. If the result of the conversion is to produce a building which is divided horizontally, so that each tenant occupies the whole or part of one floor of the building, the units will be classed as flats which do not enjoy the benefit of the Act. If, however, the conversion has been made vertically, so that each tenant occupies a part of each floor of the building from the ground upwards, the individual units will be classed as houses, each of which may utilise the provisions of the Act. This will apply where parts of one overhang the other so that the division is not entirely vertical, providing this is not to a material extent.[6] Flats, whether purpose built or otherwise, are not within the Act.

Value of house

9.2.5.   Originally a tenant was precluded from the right to enfranchise if the house was of high value as defined by the legislation. For the purposes of enfranchisement this requirement has, broadly, been abolished.[7] However, the terms on which the compensation is calculated will be different dependent on the value of the property on certain dates.[8] In the case of the right to a lease extension, the value of the property is still required to be within certain limits set out in Leasehold Reform Act 1967 (as amended).[9]

Residence qualification

9.2.6. The former residence qualification has essentially been abolished. However, it may be relevant in other circumstances. So, for example, a person may be treated as having been the tenant of a house for two years if it was vested in trustees and he was beneficially entitled and permitted to occupy under the trust.[10] A residence test also exists in order to deal with a situation where a non-resident head-tenant of a house, which is sub-let in parts, might be able to enfranchise and then make a profit if the sub-lessees subsequently exercise their rights under the Leasehold Reform, Housing and Urban Development Act 1993 (see K9.3). In this case the head-tenant of the house must, broadly, have been in occupation of part of the house as his only or main residence for at least two years in the previous ten years.[11] Also there are special residency rules if the Landlord and Tenant Act 1954, Part II applies to the tenancy.[12]

Registration of notice

9.2.7. A notice served by a qualifying tenant on his landlord of his desire to purchase the freehold or to take an extended lease creates a contract between the parties capable of registration as a notice in registered land or a Class C(iv) land charge in unregistered land. The tenant's rights under the contract, even though he is in occupation, do not constitute an overriding interest in registered land.[13]

Assignment of notice

9.2.8. The benefit of a notice served by a tenant under a lease within the Act can be assigned, but only with the lease itself. Such a provision must be dealt with by special condition in the contract to purchase the lease.[14]

Procedure

9.2.9. Details of the rights and obligations of the parties under the notice and of the procedures to be followed (e.g. form of transfer, etc.) are set out in the Act,[15] which also contains provisions dealing with the acquisition of intermediate reversions where the immediate landlord is not the freeholder.[16] In many cases, however, the strict procedures under the Act are not followed and the procedure following service of the desire notice follows the ordinary steps in a normal purchase transaction. The payment of a deposit is often dispensed with although by written notice the landlord can demand a deposit not exceeding three times the annual rent or £25 whichever is greater. Since the service of notice by the tenant creates a contract between the parties[17] it is not open to the landlord subsequently to draw up a contract on, e.g. the Standard Conditions of Sale Form and to require the tenant to agree to the terms included in the landlord's contract. Where not agreed by the parties the terms of the contract are governed by Leasehold Reform (Enfranchisement and Extension) Regulations

1967.[18] Section 10 of the Act regulates the terms of the conveyance to the tenant. The tenant will take the property subject to legal easements and restrictive covenants of which he has notice, e.g. by registration. The general words implied by Law of Property Act 1925, s.62 cannot be excluded without the tenant's consent and certain more extensive rights as to support and access are implied.[19] The purchase deed must also make reasonable provision for rights of way over and for the benefit of other property belonging to the landlord (where relevant).[20] The landlord is only obliged to give one covenant for title; namely that he has not himself incumbered the property and must give the statutory acknowledgement relating to retained title deeds (in unregistered land) but need not give an undertaking for safe custody (see M9).

Price formula

9.2.10.   The price payable on enfranchisement is the subject of one of two formulae, depending on the rateable/rental value of the property. Failing agreement between the parties the price is settled by the Lands Tribunal. Where premises have been brought into the Act by virtue of Leasehold Reform Housing and Urban Development Act 1993, the tenant must pay compensation to the landlord for loss of development value. Further amendments have been made to the calculation of the value of the property by Commonhold and Leasehold Reform Act 2002. These amendments require the tenant to pay one half of the marriage value except that if the unexpired term of the tenancy is more than 80 years there will be no marriage value.

Rent under extended lease

9.2.11.   Where an extended lease is taken, the rent under the extended term represents a ground rent for the property and may be subject to upwards revision after 25 years of the extension.

Costs

9.2.12.   The tenant is responsible for payment of the landlord's costs, e.g. of valuation, deduction of title and the purchase deed.

Mortgage

9.2.13.   Where the landlord's interest is subject to a mortgage, the lender must, on payment of the purchase price to him, release the property from the mortgage.

Redevelopment

9.2.14.   Where the Act applies it is non-excludable, although in certain limited circumstances a landlord may be able to defeat a tenant's claim to an extended lease because he intends to redevelop the premises, or to defeat a claim to enfranchise or to take an extended lease on the ground that he reasonably requires the property for occupation as the only or main residence of himself or an adult member of his family. In each case compensation is payable to the tenant by the landlord.

1. Leasehold Reform Act 1967, s.1 also required that the rent had to be a 'low rent' for certain properties in designated rural areas. However, Housing and Regeneration Act 2008, s.300 removed the low rent requirement completely in the case of enfranchisement claims.
2. Certain properties are excluded; see, e.g. Sched.4A which relates to certain shared ownership leases. This has been amended to restrict further the right of tenants under shared ownership schemes to enfranchise by Housing and Regeneration Act 2008, ss.301 and 302.
3. *Tandon* v. *Trustees of Spurgeons Homes* [1982] AC 755; and see *Hareford Ltd* v. *Barnet LBC* [2005] EG 122. Note also *Hosebay* v. *Day* [2009] PLSCS 318, CC.
4. *Boss Holdings Ltd* v. *Grosvenor West End Properties Ltd and another* [2008] UKHL 5.
5. *Grosvenor Estates Ltd* v. *Prospect Estates Ltd* [2008] EWCA Civ 1281: also note K9.2.6.
6. See *Malekshad* v. *Howard de Walden* [2002] All ER (D) 68. Note also *Collins* v. *Howard de Walden Estates Ltd* [2003] EWCA Civ 545.
7. Leasehold Reform Act 1967, s.1A, although there are some exceptions; see s.1AA and, e.g. *Neville* v. *Cowdray Trust Ltd* [2006] EWCA Civ 70. Also see K9.3.1.
8. *Ibid.*, s.1(1), (5) and (6).
9. *Ibid.*
10. *Ibid.*, s.7(3) and (4) as amended by Commonhold and Leasehold Reform Act 2002, s.138(6).
11. Leasehold Reform Act 1967, s.1(1ZB). See *Cadogan* v. *Search Guarantees plc* [2004] EWCA Civ 969 where this provision was interpreted.
12. In this case Leasehold Reform Act 1967 will only apply in these circumstances: broadly, if the tenancy is for a term certain exceeding 35 years and the tenant has occupied part as his only or main residence for the last 2 years or for periods amounting to 2 years in the last 10 (Leasehold Reform Act 1967, s.1(1ZC)). This test cannot be satisfied if the tenant is a company. If Landlord and Tenant Act 1954, Part II does not apply to a commercial letting then the tenant is not subject to this residence requirement; see also *Hosebay* v. *Day* [2009] PLSCS 318, CC.
13. Leasehold Reform Act 1967, s.5(5) as amended by Land Registration Act 2002, Sched.11, para.8(2).
14. Leasehold Reform Act 1967, s.5(2).
15. A form should be used by landlords to reply to claims. See Leasehold Reform (Notices) (Amendment) (No.2) (England) Regulations 2002 (SI 2002/3209).
16. Leasehold Reform Act 1967, Sched.1.
17. The tenant has a right to withdraw on ascertaining the purchase price: Leasehold Reform Act 1967, s.9(3)(b), as amended.
18. SI 1967/1879 as amended by Leasehold Reform (Enfranchisement and Extension) Regulations 2003 (SI 2003/1989); and Leasehold Reform (Enfranchisement and Extension) (Amendment) (Wales) Regulations 2004 (SI 2004/699/W.74).
19. For an example of how implied rights existing prior to enfranchisement survive, see *Kent* v. *Kavanagh* [2006] EWCA Civ 162.
20. See, for example, *Higgs* v. *Nieroba*, Lands Tribunal (2005) 24 October (LRA/2/2005).

9.3. Leasehold Reform, Housing and Urban Development Act 1993

Introduction

9.3.1. This Act, as amended by Commonhold and Leasehold Reform Act 2002, extends the rights to enfranchise/acquire an extended lease to the owners of flats and removes the rateable value limits which previously applied to houses under Leasehold Reform Act 1967. The Act also deals with some matters relating to public sector housing which are not dealt with in this book.

9.3.2.   The majority of the amendments to the 1993 Act are now in force.[1] However the provisions in relation to RTE companies are not yet in force.[2] This text sets out the new law and includes the provisions relating to RTE companies so that these can be dealt with. It therefore assumes that the RTE company provisions are in force. Until that happens the procedure is followed by a group of qualifying tenants known as a 'nominee purchaser'. In most cases this will, in fact, be a company formed by the tenants.[3]

Collective enfranchisement

The right

9.3.3.   The right is given to the tenants of a block of flats collectively to acquire the freehold of the block. The freehold is to be conveyed into the name of a company created by the tenants to buy the freehold known as an RTE company. The RTE company (a company limited by guarantee under section 122 Commonhold and Leasehold Reform Act 2002) must be formed before any further steps towards enfranchisement are taken. The RTE company must give notice to all the qualifying tenants under section 12A of the 1993 Act and invite their participation in the proposed enfranchisement. The conveyance can take place without the landlord's consent (subject to certain defences – see K9.3.7). Certain qualifying conditions must be fulfilled (see K9.3.21). Not all the flats in the block need to be let on long leases, nor need all the premises be let exclusively for residential purposes for the Act to apply.

Nature of the collective right

9.3.4.   The nature of the collective right is for the tenants to have the premises' freehold acquired on behalf of the participating qualifying tenants by the nominated RTE company at a price to be determined in accordance with the Act.

Exercise of the collective right

9.3.5.   Notice must be served on the reversioner by the RTE company as provided by section 13 of the 1993 Act.

9.3.6.   To be entitled to give this notice the RTE company must have members who include a number of qualifying tenants which is not less than one-half of the total number of flats in the premises. Prior to the RTE company provisions being brought into force, in essence, the notice must be given by a number of qualifying tenants which is not less than one-half of the total number of flats.

Landlord's grounds of opposition

9.3.7.   The landlord can oppose the tenants' bid to enfranchise if the qualifying conditions are not met by the tenants. He may also oppose on the grounds that he wants to redevelop the whole or a substantial part of the premises but this ground is only available where not less than two-thirds of the long leases in the block are due to terminate within five years and the landlord cannot reasonably carry out the redevelopment without gaining possession.

Qualifications

9.3.8. To qualify, the tenant must be a 'tenant' of a 'flat' under a 'long lease'. However, a tenant who owns three or more of the flats cannot be a qualifying tenant of any of them.

9.3.9. Tenant includes a person holding a lease or tenancy, or an agreement for a lease or tenancy, and includes sub-leases/tenancies. Joint leaseholders are treated as one tenant.

9.3.10. A flat is defined as a separate set of premises but need not necessarily be all on the same floor level. The premises must form part of a building and be constructed or adapted for use as a dwelling. Additionally, either the whole or some material part of the premises must lie above or below some other part of the building. This definition includes flats above shops, but may not apply to extensions, e.g. granny flats.[4]

9.3.11. A long lease is one which is granted for a term of years certain exceeding 21 years. Provisions for determination within that period by either party do not affect this. The definition also includes most perpetually renewable leases, leases terminable by death or marriage, and leases granted under right to buy provisions and shared ownership leases where the tenant's total share is 100%, and new leases (of whatever length) granted on the expiry of an old long (i.e. 21 years plus) lease, and continuations under Landlord and Tenant Act 1954, Part 1 or Local Government and Housing Act 1989, Sched.10. Leases for less than 21 years which have been renewed without payment of a premium, taking the total term over 21 years, are also included within this definition.

Excluded tenants

9.3.12. The following tenancies are excluded from the Act:[5]

    (a)   business tenancies;

    (b)   where the immediate landlord is a charitable housing trust;

    (c)   unlawful sub-lease out of non-qualifying superior lease.

Interests included in the collective right

9.3.13. Tenants who enfranchise will obtain the freehold of the premises in which the flats are situated and:

    (a)   certain other property owned by the same freeholder ('appurtenant property'), e.g. garage, garden;

    (b)   intermediate leasehold interests of those premises (but not of any non-residential parts of the building).

Interests excluded from the collective right

9.3.14. Mineral rights owned by the freeholder are excluded from the collective right.

Interests to be leased back

9.3.15. The Act contains provisions relating to certain interests which may (or in certain cases must) be leased back to the reversioner. They include the following:

    (a) flats let by the freeholder on secure tenancies;

    (b) flats let by housing associations on tenancies other than secure tenancies;

    (c) units which are not flats let to qualifying tenants (e.g. commercial parts of the building);

    (d) flat occupied by a resident landlord.

9.3.16. The items in (a) and (b) above are subject to mandatory leaseback; (c) and (d) need only be leased back if the freeholder requires them. Schedule 9, Part IV of the Act contains detailed provisions dealing with the terms of the leaseback. Broadly this is to be a 999-year term at a peppercorn rent and will include the usual covenants but there will be no restrictions on alienation where the premises are residential.

Price

9.3.17. The price which the tenants are to pay for the freehold comprises three elements:

    (a) market value;

    (b) where the unexpired length of the leases held by participating members of the RTE company is 80 years or less, one-half of marriage value;

    (c) compensation;

plus landlord's reasonable costs. Where intermediate leases are also to be acquired, the price of each interest has to be separately calculated. A valuer's advice must be sought in relation to this matter.

Market value

9.3.18. Market value is the price which might reasonably be expected to be paid if the property was sold on the open market by a willing seller to an arm's length buyer. The following assumptions also apply:

    (a) the seller is selling the freehold subject to any leases subject to which the freeholder's interest is to be acquired by the buyer, but subject to any intermediate or other leases which are to be acquired by the buyer;

   (b)   that the Act does not apply;

   (c)   any increase in value caused by the participating tenant's improvements to the premises are to be disregarded.

Marriage value

9.3.19. Marriage value is the increase in the value of the unencumbered freehold over the aggregate values of the freehold and any intermediate leasehold interest when held by the persons from whom they are to be acquired.

Compensation

9.3.20. Compensation is payable to the freeholder for any loss or damage he may suffer as a result of the enfranchisement. It includes any diminution in the value of any other property owned by the landlord, including loss of development value. Schedule 11 Housing Act 1996 also provides for the tenant to pay compensation to the landlord if an unsuccessful claim is made within two years of the original term date of the lease.

Premises

9.3.21. The flat must be in premises which either consist of a self-contained building or a self-contained part of a building whether or not the freehold of the whole building or of that part is owned by the same person. Self-contained means structurally detached. Buildings which are divided vertically may qualify under the Act.[6] Premises where more than 25% is occupied or intended to be occupied for non-residential purposes are excluded.[7] This last exclusion means that many flats above shops will not qualify under the Act. Resident landlords are excluded only if there are fewer than four flats in the block and they have owned the premises since their conversion or the block is not a purpose-built block.[8] Further, the building must contain two or more flats held by qualifying tenants; and the total number of flats held by qualifying tenants must be not less than two-thirds of the total number of flats in the building.

Advising in relation to collective enfranchisement

9.3.22. The first step is for the solicitor to find out whether the tenants and the building qualify under the Act. Information relating to these matters can be obtained by the service of various notices under section 11 of the Act:

   (a)   on the immediate landlord (or person receiving rent on his behalf) to obtain the name and address of the freeholder and any superior leasehold interest;

   (b)   on the freeholder to obtain the name and address of every person who is a tenant of the whole or any part of the building;

(c) on the freeholder and/or other tenants to acquire information reasonably required in relation to the enfranchisement claim (e.g. as to how many other tenants qualify).

9.3.23. Service of these notices does not commit the tenant(s) to proceed and apart from payment for copies of documents the tenants are not required to pay for the provision of this information by the landlord. The landlord must respond to this request for information within 28 days. The tenants have a right to inspect and take copies of documents which might reasonably be required in connection with the enfranchisement claim (e.g. the landlord's title deeds). The landlord is obliged to disclose to the tenant(s) whether he has received initial notices under the Act from any other person.

9.3.24. Having established that the tenants do qualify under the Act an RTE company must be formed and notice served by that company to all the tenants inviting their participation in the enfranchisement.

Costs of enfranchisement

9.3.25. Taking any further steps towards enfranchisement is inevitably going to commit the tenants to the payments of their own solicitor's costs and also the reasonable costs of the landlord. Other expenses, e.g. in connection with the preparation of plans, valuation of the premises, the setting up of a company to purchase the freehold and possibly the expense of a court action to enforce the tenants' rights, will also be incurred. The tenants should be fully advised of the potential liability to costs and an arrangement for the payments of these costs by the qualifying tenants should be made before the matter proceeds further.

Plans

9.3.26. If the tenants decide to proceed with their claim, a plan of the premises will be needed to accompany their initial notice. It may be necessary to have this plan prepared by a surveyor.

Valuation

9.3.27. The provisions for assessment of the price which the tenants have to pay for the freehold are complex and advice will be needed from a surveyor. An estimate of the price which the tenants may have to pay to acquire the freehold should be obtained from a suitably qualified surveyor at an early stage in the transaction to ensure that the tenants collectively will be able to afford to proceed with the transaction.

The initial notice

9.3.28. To exercise rights under the Act the RTE company must serve an initial notice on the reversioner under section 13 of the Act (as revealed in answer to the enquiries noted in K9.3.22). In practice the reason many tenants seek to pursue their rights under the Act is because the landlord fails to carry out its responsibilities and upon enquiry it cannot be located (or identified). The Act contains provisions which enable tenants to apply to the court for a declaration that the reversioner (or one or more of the reversioners) need not be served with a purchase notice and to apply for a vesting order.[9] The section 13 initial notice must be in writing and may be served by post. Where the tenant is a limited company it is important to ensure that the notice must be signed in a way that complies with the Companies Act 2006, s.44.[10] The Act prescribes the contents of the notice but not its form. Printed forms are available from law stationers. The notice must:

(a) specify the premises with a plan;

(b) contain a statement of the grounds on which eligibility rests;

(c) specify other freehold or leasehold interests (if any) to be acquired;

(d) state which flats (if any) are subject to mandatory leaseback provisions;

(e) specify the proposed purchase price of the freehold and any other interest specified in the notice;

(f) give the full names of all the qualifying tenants together with details of their leases;

(g) specify which tenants satisfy the residence qualification and how this is achieved;

(h) give the name and address of the RTE company;

(i) specify a date by which the landlord must respond with his counter-notice (not less than two months).

9.3.29. The initial notice must be registered as an estate contract against the reversioner's title. The right arising under the notice cannot be an overriding interest under Land Registration Act 2002, Scheds.1 and 3 (interests of persons in actual occupation). A second notice cannot be served while a previously served notice is in force. If the notice is withdrawn (or is deemed to be withdrawn) no further notice can be served for 12 months. Once given, the notice remains in force until a binding contract is entered into or the notice is withdrawn or deemed to be withdrawn. Schedule 3, para.15 of the Act contains provisions to overcome technical defects in the notice.

RTE company

9.3.30. The initial notice must specify the name and address of an RTE company through which negotiations for the acquisition of the freehold interest will be conducted and in whose name the freehold interest will ultimately be vested.

Landlord's rights and obligations when an initial notice is served

9.3.31. Once notice has been served on the reversioner he has the immediate right of access to the premises for the purposes of valuation and to require evidence from the RTE company of title to the qualifying tenants' leases. The RTE company must respond to this request from the landlord within 21 days in default of which the notice is deemed to be withdrawn. The landlord is required to serve a counter-notice on the RTE company within the time limit specified in the initial notice (not less than two months).[11] The counter-notice must comply with section 21 of the Act and must, broadly, either admit or deny the tenants' claim and, if the claim is denied, give the grounds of opposition.[12] It should also contain any lease-back proposals of the landlord.[13]

Subsequent procedure

9.3.32. After service of the landlord's counter-notice, and assuming that the matter is to proceed, negotiations will then ensue between the RTE company and the reversioner for the contract and then for completion of the acquisition. The form of the conveyance is prescribed by section 34 and Schedule 7. Provided the purchase price is paid to the landlord's lender, the property is discharged from the landlord's mortgage.[14] If the landlord fails to serve a counter-notice within the time limit stated in the initial notice (being not less than two months), the tenants may apply to the court within six months for the terms of the acquisition to be determined. If a counter-notice is served and agreement cannot be reached on the terms of the acquisition, an application can be made for a leasehold valuation tribunal to determine the matters in dispute. Any such application must be made not later than the period of six months beginning with the date on which the counter-notice was given to the nominee purchaser.[15] The Act contains no provisions enabling the time limits prescribed within it to be extended.

Individual acquisition of a long lease

Nature of the right

9.3.33. The tenant has the right to be granted a new lease to expire 90 years after expiry of the existing lease. The rent under the new lease is to be a peppercorn. A premium is payable for the grant.[16] The new lease takes effect immediately in substitution for the tenant's existing lease. This right is available irrespective of the rights to collective enfranchisement.

Entitlement to extension

9.3.34. The right to an extension applies to a qualifying tenant (as defined above) who has had the lease vested in him for at least the previous two years.[17] Tenants who own three or more flats are not excluded in this case.[18]

Landlord's defences

9.3.35. The landlord can oppose the tenant's request on the following grounds:

(a) that the tenant's existing lease is due to expire within five years; and

(b) that the landlord intends to demolish/reconstruct the property and would be unable to do so without being given possession of the premises.[19]

Terms of new lease

9.3.36. The terms of the new lease will be the same as the existing lease except that the new rent is a peppercorn. The new lease takes effect immediately and is for a period which comprises the residue remaining on the old lease plus a further 90 years. Service charge provisions are to be included. The new lease will also contain a statement that the lease has been granted under the Act. Options which were included in the original lease will not be included in the new lease. The new lease will also contain a modification of the landlord's liability under his covenants and modifications to reflect defects in the existing lease. The new lease will include the landlord's right to apply to the court for possession for redevelopment purposes during the last 12 months of the original term or the last five years of the extension, subject to compensation being payable to the tenant.

Premium

9.3.37. The amount of the premium payable by the tenant is the aggregate of:

(a) the diminution in the value of the landlord's interest;

(b) where the unexpired term of the tenant's existing lease does not exceed 80 years, 50% of the marriage value;

(c) compensation to landlord.

Effect of grant of new lease

9.3.38. The grant of a new lease does not preclude a later application for collective enfranchisement. A further claim for another new lease can be brought in relation to any lease granted; subject to this, no security of tenure provisions apply once the original term date has passed.

Acting for a buyer of an individual flat

9.3.39. When acting for a buyer who is buying an existing lease which potentially qualifies under the Act, consideration should be given to raising enquiries of the seller to establish:

(a) whether the flat and the lease qualify under the Act;

(b) how many qualifying flats and qualifying tenants there are in the block;

(c) whether and when any initial notice has been served by an RTE company and if so how far negotiations have reached (a copy of the notice should be requested if not already supplied by the seller's solicitor);

(d) whether any steps have been taken by the seller to acquire an extension of his lease under the Act.

1. See the various commencement orders: SI 2002/1912; 2002/3012; 2003/1986; 2003/2377.
2. In 2009 the government consulted on whether the provisions realting to RTE companies should be implemented or repealed. The consultation paper is available from **www.communities.gov.uk**.
3. One consequence of this is that SDLT relief under Finance Act 2003, s.74 that would otherwise be available on a purchase by an RTE company (when this provision is brought into force) cannot be claimed by a nominee purchaser in the meantime: see *Elizabeth Court (Bournemouth) Ltd* v. *Revenue & Customs Commissioners* [2008] EWHC 2828 (Ch). The Finance Bill 2009 (clause 79) contains provisions to resolve this problem so that the relief can be claimed by any nominee purchaser.
4. Leasehold Reform, Housing and Urban Development Act 1993, s.101. Considered in *Cadogan* v. *McGirk* [1996] 3 EG 175 in which a room on the 6th floor was not held to be part of a flat on the 2nd floor.
5. Leasehold Reform, Housing and Urban Development Act 1993, s.5.
6. It has been held that in determining the question of whether there is a vertical division there is no scope for importing a test of materiality (*Re Holding & Management (Solitaire) Ltd*, Lands Tribunal (LRX/138/2006)). This is in the context of a claim to the right to manage (see K6.11). However the same phrase is used in Leasehold Reform, Housing and Urban Development Act 1993.
7. As to the correct approach to this calculation, see *Indiana Investments Ltd* v. *Taylor* [2004] 50 EG 86.
8. See Leasehold Reform, Housing and Urban Development Act 1993, s.4. As to the interpretation of this provision with respect to a trust, see *Slamon* v. *Planchon* [2004] EWCA Civ 799.
9. Leasehold Reform, Housing and Urban Development Act 1993, ss.26 and 27.
10. It cannot be signed by an agent. Therefore it must be sealed with the common seal of the company, be signed by two authorised signatories or by a director of the company and properly witnessed (see *Hilmi & Associates Ltd* v. *20 Pembridge Villas Freehold* [2010] EWCA Civ 314). Note this also applies to a notice under Leasehold Reform, Housing and Urban Development Act 1993, s.42 (the tenant's notice used to start a claim for lease extension).
11. The counter-notice must comply with the requirements of Leasehold Reform, Housing and Urban Development Act 1993, s.21. Where it contains an alternative proposed purchase price this must be made in good faith but does not necessarily have to be a realistic price. See *9 Cornwall Crescent London Ltd* v. *Kensington and Chelsea LBC* [2005] EWCA Civ 324.
12. Failure to specify one of these options will render the counter-notice invalid; see *Burman* v. *Mount Cook Land* [2001] 48 EG 128, CA. Failure to give a counter-notice will entitle the RTE company to apply to the court and acquire the freehold (s.25(1)) and see *Willingale* v. *Globalgrange* [2000] 18 EG 152, CA. The form of notice is specified by Leasehold Reform (Collective Enfranchisement) (Counter-notices) (England) Regulations 2002 (SI 2002/3208). Failure to adhere to the form of counter-notice will not always be fatal, e.g. failure to declare there was no estate management scheme affecting the property; see *7 Strathray Gardens* v. *Pointstar Shipping & Finance Ltd and another* [2004] EWCA Civ 1669. It is possible for the tenant to waive the requirement for a counter-notice to be served. See *Latifi* v. *Colherne Freehold Ltd* [2003] 12 EG 130.
13. See *Cawthorne and Others* v. *Hamdan* [2007] EWCA Civ 6.
14. Leasehold Reform, Housing and Urban Development Act 1993, Sched.8, para.2.
15. For details see Leasehold Reform, Housing and Urban Development Act 1993, s.24. As to the calculation of time limits see *Goldeagle Properties Ltd* v. *Thornbury Court Ltd* [2008] EWCA 864.
16. A tenant must serve a notice specifying the premium he proposes to pay which must be genuine and not just a nominal figure: *Cadogan* v. *Morris* [1999] 1 EGLR 59; *Mount Cook Land Ltd* v. *Rosen* [2003] 10 EG 165.
17. A tenant of a block of flats (each underlet on short leases) may be the 'qualifying tenant' of each flat and therefore entitled to new long leases in respect of all the individual flats. See *Maurice* v. *Holloware Products Ltd* [2005] EWHC 815.

18. Note that a head tenant is entitled to an extended lease of an individual flat comprising part of the headlease demise: see *Cadogan* v. *26 Cadogan Square Ltd*; *Howard de Walden Estates* v. *Aggio* [2008] UKHL 44.
19. Leasehold Reform, Housing and Urban Development Act 1993, s.47. See, e.g. *Majorstake Ltd* v. *Curtis* [2008] UKHL 10.

9.4. Landlord and Tenant Act 1987

9.4.1. Landlord and Tenant Act 1987 (as amended) gives the tenants of certain premises the right of first refusal where the landlord intends to dispose of his interest in the premises. The Act applies where the landlord of premises which contain two or more flats held by qualifying tenants proposes to make a relevant disposal of the premises and provides that the landlord must first offer to make a disposal to a nominee of the qualifying tenants.

Premises

9.4.2. The provisions of the Act apply to premises consisting of the whole or part of a building which contains two or more flats held by qualifying tenants provided that the number of such flats exceeds 50% of the total number of flats in the building. Since the Act defines a tenancy as including an agreement for a tenancy, it seems that the Act can apply to new blocks as soon as the landlord has exchanged agreements for lease in relation to 50% of the flats. The definition of a flat includes maisonettes and houses which have been converted into flats as well as purpose-built blocks. Premises which are used partly for non-residential purposes may be within the Act subject to a measurement limit. Thus premises which consist of a shop on the ground floor with two or more flats on the upper floors may qualify under the Act provided that the internal floor area of the shop represents less than 50% of the internal area of the whole building[1] and a nominee of the qualifying tenants who purchased the reversion of the flats would also therefore become the landlord of the shop. Where a landlord owns several blocks of flats with communal grounds on an estate development, each block may or may not be a separate building depending on the circumstances.[2]

Landlord

9.4.3. For the purposes of the Act a landlord is the immediate landlord of the qualifying tenants, or the superior landlord if the immediate landlord is himself a tenant under a tenancy for less than seven years or one terminable by his landlord within the first seven years.[3] Certain landlords are exempt and the provisions of the Act do not apply to, e.g. local authorities, urban development corporations or registered housing associations.[4] Resident landlords are also exempted from the provisions of the Act where the three following conditions are satisfied:

(a) the premises are not a purpose-built block of flats;

(b) the landlord occupies a flat in the premises as his only or principal residence;

(c) the landlord has been in occupation for the last 12 months.

Qualifying tenants

9.4.4. A tenant of a flat (including a company tenant) is a qualifying tenant unless his tenancy is:

(a) a protected shorthold tenancy;

(b) a business tenancy within Part II Landlord and Tenant Act 1954;

(c) an assured tenancy or an assured agricultural occupancy;

(d) a tenancy terminable on the cessation of the tenant's employment;

(e) of the flat and by virtue of one or more non-excluded tenancies he is also the tenant of at least two other flats contained in the same building;

(f) a sub-tenancy and his landlord is a qualifying tenant of the flat in question.

Relevant disposal

9.4.5. The word 'disposal' is defined in Landlord and Tenant Act 1987, s.4(3) as meaning a disposal whether by the creation or the transfer of an estate or interest. It includes the surrender of a tenancy and the grant of an option or right of pre-emption but excludes a disposal by will or under the intestacy rules.

9.4.6. A 'relevant disposal' is defined by Landlord and Tenant Act 1987, s.4(1) as a disposal by the landlord of any estate or interest (legal or equitable) in premises to which the Act applies, including a disposal of an interest in any common parts of the premises,[5] other than the grant of a tenancy of a single flat with or without any appurtenant premises and subject to certain exceptions which are listed in K9.4.8.

9.4.7. A contract to sell is itself a relevant disposal. Further a disposal includes a disposal by the landlord's lender in selling or leasing the property, but not the creation of a mortgage. A conditional contract which is subject to the notice provisions being complied with at a later date is not valid.

Exceptions to 'relevant disposal'

9.4.8. By Landlord and Tenant Act 1987, s.4, the following are excluded from the definition of a relevant disposal:

(a) a disposal:

(i) of an interest of a beneficiary in settled land;

(ii) by way of the creation of a mortgage;

(iii) of any incorporeal hereditament;

(b) a disposal to a trustee in bankruptcy or liquidator;

(c) a disposal in pursuance of an order under Matrimonial Causes Act 1973, ss.24 or 24A, or Inheritance (Provision for Family and Dependants) Act 1975, s.2 or similar legislative provisions;

(d) a disposal in pursuance of a compulsory purchase order or agreement in lieu;

(e) a disposal of any interest by virtue of Leasehold Reform, Housing and Urban Development Act 1993;

(f) a gift to a member of the landlord's family as defined in section 4(5) or to a charity;

(g) a disposal of functional land by one charity to another as defined in section 60;

(h) a disposal of trust property in connection with the appointment or discharge of a trustee;

(i) a disposal between members of the same family provided that at least one of the original owners still retains an interest;

(j) a disposal in pursuance of a contract, option or right of pre-emption binding on the landlord (subject to exceptions);[6]

(k) a surrender of a tenancy in pursuance of any obligation contained in it;

(l) a disposal to the Crown;

(m) where the landlord is a body corporate, a disposal to an associated company which has been an associated company of that body for at least two years.

The landlord's offer

9.4.9. Where a landlord proposes to make a relevant disposal of premises to which the Act applies, he must follow the procedure set out in section 5 of the Act which requires him to serve notice on the qualifying tenants of the flats in the premises. Different types of proposed disposals require different prescribed information to be inserted into the notice as set out in s.5A (normal sale by contract), s.5B (sale at auction), s.5C (grant of options and pre-emption rights), s.5D (sale proceeding to completion without contract), and s.5E (wholly or partly for non-monetary consideration). In outline, a notice served under s.5A must:

(a) set out the principal terms proposed including the property and the estate or interest to be disposed of (the 'protected interest') and the consideration required;

(b) state that it constitutes an offer to dispose of the property on those terms which may be accepted by the requisite number of qualifying tenants (the offer is deemed by the Act to be 'subject to contract');

(c) specify a period for acceptance being at least two months beginning with the date of service; and

(d) specify a further period of at least two months beginning with the end of the period of acceptance within which a person or persons may be nominated to take the landlord's interest.

The tenant's acceptance

9.4.10. A tenant's acceptance may take the following forms:

(a) The landlord's offer can be accepted by a simple majority of the qualifying tenants on the basis of one vote per flat let to qualifying tenants in the building. The tenants must nominate a person to deal with the landlord within the periods for acceptance and nomination specified in the landlord's notice.

(b) If a management company structure run by the tenants is already in place in the building, the management company may be nominated to purchase the landlord's interest. In other cases the tenants may consider forming a new company for this purpose.

(c) Acceptance by the qualifying tenants must be by written notice served on the landlord within the period specified in the offer. A single notice is served on behalf of all the accepting tenants which specifies the names and addresses of all the persons serving the notice. If no acceptance notice is served within the acceptance period the landlord is free, for a period of 12 months, to sell to any person at not less than the price offered and on the same terms.[7]

Effects of acceptance

9.4.11. Once the acceptance notice has been served the landlord cannot dispose of the interest described in his offer to anyone other than the tenants' nominees during the 'protected period'. The procedure by which the tenants acquire their landlord's interest is covered by the Act and depends on the nature of the proposed disposal, e.g. sale by auction or not. There are further provisions to deal with the situation where the consideration did not consist wholly or partly of money and to deal with the situation where the landlord requires the consent of a third party to the disposal.[8] The 'protected period' is, in outline, the period beginning with the date of service of the acceptance notice and expiring at the end of the period for nominating a transferee specified in the offer notice (plus a further period covering the subsequent procedure if a transferee is nominated).[9] If no nomination is made the landlord may dispose of his interest during the 12 months following expiry of the nomination period provided that the price is not less than that stated in the offer notice and the other terms of the disposal correspond with the terms of the offer to the tenants. If no disposal occurs within this 12-month period, the landlord must serve a new offer notice on the tenants before attempting to dispose of the property. Acceptance of the offer does not create a binding contract since the offer itself is only subject to contract.

Rejection

9.4.12. If the tenants do not serve an acceptance notice within the period specified for acceptance in the landlord's offer notice or such longer period as may be agreed, the landlord may dispose of his interest during the 12 months following the expiry of that period subject to the same conditions outlined in K9.4.11.

Disposals in breach of the Act

9.4.13. A new landlord who acquires a reversionary interest in flats from a seller who is in breach of the provisions of the Act can be required (on request made by a majority of the qualifying tenants) to supply details of the transaction to a nominee of the qualifying tenants. The qualifying tenants, by serving a purchase notice on the new landlord, can require him to dispose of his interest to a nominee of the qualifying tenants on the same terms as he acquired his interest.[10] If the new landlord's interest is mortgaged, the property is discharged from the mortgage provided that the nominee pays the purchase price to the lender (even if the purchase price is less than the amount of the mortgage). A landlord who disposes of provisions in breach of the Act is also guilty of a criminal offence.[11]

Advice to proposed buyers of reversionary interests

9.4.14. A person who intends to purchase a reversionary interest direct from a landlord must before exchange of contracts check:

    (a)   whether or not the premises fall within the scope of the Act; and if they do

    (b)   whether the landlord and any relevant previous owners[12] have served notice on the qualifying tenants as required by the Act; and if so

    (c)   that either the tenants have rejected the landlord's offer or that the time limits for acceptance have expired and the purchase transaction to the buyer can be completed within 12 months of the expiry of the acceptance period; and

    (d)   the terms on which the buyer is buying are similar to the terms of the offer which was made to the tenants.

The Standard Commercial Property Conditions contain optional provisions in Part 2 section C providing for warranties covering some of these points (see Appendix III.6).

9.4.15. Section 18 Landlord and Tenant Act 1987 enables a prospective buyer to serve notice on tenants to ensure that rights of first refusal do not arise where it appears to the buyer that the disposal might be a relevant disposal of premises to which the Act applies. The notice must:

(a)   set out the principal terms of the proposed disposal;

(b)   invite the recipient to serve a notice stating:

    (i)   whether an offer notice has been served;

    (ii)   if not, whether he is aware of any reason why he is not entitled to such a notice; and

    (iii)   whether he would wish to exercise any right of first refusal; and

(c)   set out the effect of section 18(3) which says that, provided notices have been served on at least 80% of the tenants, and not more than 50% have replied within two months, or more than 50% have indicated that they do not regard themselves as entitled to an offer notice or would not wish to exercise a right of first refusal, the premises shall be treated as premises to which the Act does not apply.

Auctions

9.4.16.   The notice procedures set out in K9.4.9 are modified where the landlord intends to dispose of the property at auction. In outline, such notice must be served on the tenants between four to six months before the auction, giving the tenants at least two months to respond to the notice.[13] The tenants' nominee then has the opportunity to take over the auction contract, after the auction takes place, from the successful bidder. The Standard Commercial Property Conditions contain optional provisions in Part 2 section C covering this (see Appendix III.6).

1.   This percentage is subject to alteration by Landlord and Tenant Act 1987, s.1.
2.   A 'building' can comprise more than one structure if the occupants of the qualifying flats share the use of the same appurtenant premises; see *Long Acre Securities Ltd* v. *Karet* [2004] 11 EG 138.
3.   Landlord and Tenant Act 1987, s.2.
4.   *Ibid.*, s.58.
5.   This includes the air space above a block of flats: see *Dartmouth Court Blackheath Ltd* v. *Berisworth Ltd* [2008] EWHC 350 (Ch), in which the court was also of the opinion that the disposal of part of a block, e.g. the grant of a lease of the whole first floor, would potentially trigger rights under the Act. This has implications for landlords of mixed use buildings who are considering granting leases of part, e.g. business leases of commercial units within the building.
6.   It is, in effect, the entry into the contract, option or right of pre-emption that triggers the Act rather than the disposal following this. Therefore, if, e.g. a contract is entered into before the premises come within the Act, e.g. prior to the construction of a block of flats, then no relevant disposal will take place when the reversion is transferred pursuant to that contract, even though by then the flats are built and occupied and the premises come within the Act. Note there are exceptions to this in s.8D.
7.   *Ibid.*, s.7.
8.   *Ibid.*, ss.8A–8E.
9.   *Ibid.*, s.8A.
10.   *Ibid.*, ss.12A, 12B and 12C. Care must be taken to serve the correct form of purchase notice on the right party. This can be particularly problematic in relation to a surrender: see *Kensington Heights Commercial Co. Ltd* v. *Campden Hill Developments Ltd* [2007] EWCA Civ 245.
11.   Landlord and Tenant Act 1987, s.10A
12.   Tenants have broadly six months from receiving notice from the landlord in respect of a disposal to serve a notice triggering their rights under the Act. If no such notice has been served time will not have

started to run. Therefore, a purchaser of premises to which the Act potentially applies is concerned with all relevant disposals since the Act came into force (1 February 1988). See Landlord and Tenant Act 1987, s.12B. See also *Green* v. *Westleigh Properties* [2008] EWHC 1474.

13. *Ibid.*, s.5B.

9.5. Compulsory acquisition by tenants of landlord's interest

9.5.1.   Where a receiver or manager has been appointed under Part II Landlord and Tenant Act 1987 (see K6.10.1) but this remedy proves to be inadequate, the majority of the qualifying tenants may in certain circumstances apply to the court under Part III Landlord and Tenant Act 1987 for an acquisition order which allows them to acquire their landlord's interest without his consent.[1]

1.   An application can also be made if the landlord is in breach of, broadly, his management obligations in respect of the premises under the leases. See Landlord and Tenant Act 1987, s.29.

9.6. Registered providers of social housing

9.6.1.   Certain tenants of registered providers of social housing (formerly known as a registered social landlord)[1] have the right to acquire the dwelling of which they are tenants under Housing Act 1996, s.16. The purchase price may be discounted by the landlord and similar provisions relating to the repayment of discount apply as to public sector tenants (K9.1).

1.   Housing and Regeneration Act 2008 (Consequential Provisions) Order 2010 (SI 2010/866) made provision for registered social landlords to become registered providers of social housing. They must register with the Tenant Services Authority along with local authorities and other social housing providers.

K10. Liability on covenants in leases

10.1. Introduction

10.1.1. The general rule that an original tenant remains liable under his covenants throughout the term of the lease has been abolished by Landlord and Tenant (Covenants) Act 1995 but only in respect of new tenancies (as defined by the 1995 Act). The principle that only a party to a contract can sue or be sued on it has also been abrogated by Contracts (Rights of Third Parties) Act 1999 which affects leases and assignments made on or after 11 May 2000.

New tenancies

10.1.2. A new tenancy is one which is granted on or after 1 January 1996, except those tenancies granted pursuant to:

(a) an agreement made before 1 January 1996; or

(b) a court order made before 1 January 1996; or

(c) an option granted before 1 January 1996.

10.1.3. An overriding lease granted under section 19 Landlord and Tenant (Covenants) Act 1995 (e.g. granted to a former tenant who has discharged the liability of a subsequent assignee) takes its status from that of the original lease.

10.1.4. Some leases granted on or after 1 January 1996 will not be new tenancies. Such a lease should make this clear by including a statement that the lease is not a new lease within the provisions of the 1995 Act.

10.1.5. A variation of a lease sometimes results in a deemed surrender and re-grant, e.g. where:

    (a)   extra land is included in the tenancy in return for additional rent;[1] or

    (b)   there is an extension of the term.[2]

The date of the surrender and re-grant will determine whether the lease deemed to be re-granted is a new one.

10.1.6. K10.2–K10.5 inclusive deal with old tenancies (i.e. those to which the 1995 Act does not apply). K10.6 applies to all leases whenever granted. K10.7–K10.12 inclusive deal with new tenancies to which the provisions of the 1995 Act apply.

1.   *Jenkin R Lewis* v. *Kerman* [1971] Ch 477.
2.   *Baker* v. *Merckel* [1960] 1 QB 657. See also *Friends Provident Life Office* v. *British Railways Board* [1996] 1 All ER 336.

10.2. Old tenancies – liability of original landlord and tenant

10.2.1. Unless released by the landlord the original tenant is liable on all the express and implied covenants in the lease for breaches committed at any time during the term of the lease. His liability is to the landlord for the time being since on a transfer of the reversion all rights of action attached to the reversion pass to the transferee including the right to sue for an existing breach of covenant.[1] The liability of the original tenant to the transferee of the reversion exists even though the tenant assigned the lease before the transfer of the reversion.[2]

10.2.2. The continuing liability of the original tenant may have serious consequences for him if an assignee of the lease cannot meet his obligations to the landlord. The original tenant remains liable for rent due after disclaimer of the lease on an assignee's insolvency,[3] and the release by the landlord of an assignee's surety does not release the original tenant since the latter has primary liability.[4] Although the landlord will normally only pursue the original tenant when the current assignee is unable to fulfil his commitments under the lease, the landlord's right of action against the original tenant is not confined to this situation.[5] The original tenant's liability does not, however, extend to arrears of rent accrued by an assignee during a statutory continuation of the term under Landlord and Tenant Act 1954, Pt. II unless the original tenant's covenant is expressed widely enough to cover this liability.[6]

10.2.3. The original landlord remains contractually bound to the original tenant throughout the term of the lease.[7] If an original landlord is unable through his own act or default (e.g. by transferring the reversion to a third party) to carry out an obligation imposed on him by the lease the landlord may be liable in damages to the tenant.[8]

1.   Law of Property Act 1925, s.141 and see *Re King* [1963] Ch 459; *London and County (A & D) Ltd* v. *Wilfred Sportsman Ltd* [1971] Ch 764.

2.   *Arlesford Trading Co. Ltd* v. *Servansingh* [1971] 3 All ER 113.
3.   *Warnford Investments* v. *Duckworth* [1979] Ch 127; *Hindcastle Ltd* v. *Barbara Attenborough Associates Ltd* [1996] 2 WLR 262; and *Active Estates Ltd* v. *Parness* [2002] 36 EG 147.
4.   *Allied London Investments Ltd* v. *Hambro Life Assurance Ltd* (1985) 50 P&CR 207.
5.   *Norwich Union Life Insurance Society* v. *Low Profile Fashions Ltd* [1992] 21 EG 104.
6.   *London City Corporation* v. *Fell; Herbert Duncan* v. *Cluttons (A Firm)* [1992] NPC 150, CA.
7.   *Stuart* v. *Joy* [1904] 1 KB 362.
8.   See, e.g. *Eagon* v. *Dent* [1965] 3 All ER 334 where a landlord sold the reversion to a third party and the original tenant who failed in his attempt to exercise an unregistered option against the buyer of the reversion recovered damages from the original landlord for breach of covenant.

10.3.   Old tenancies – landlord and tenant for the time being

10.3.1.   The relationship between a transferee of the reversion and the tenant for the time being and between an assignee of the lease and the landlord for the time being rests on the doctrine of privity of estate. Liability under this doctrine extends to breaches of covenants which touch and concern the land committed by a transferee of the reversion while he holds the reversion and by an assignee of the lease while the lease is vested in him. This means that an assignee may be liable to the landlord for a breach of covenant giving rise to continuing liability, committed by the assignor.

10.3.2.   The doctrine embraces those covenants in the lease which affect the land demised and which also govern the landlord and tenant relationship as such, e.g. payment of rent or repairing covenants. While most covenants in leases will fall within the doctrine, including an option to renew the lease, it does not extend to purely personal obligations or to collateral obligations such as an option to purchase the reversion.[1]

10.3.3.   An assignee of the lease will not be liable to the landlord for breaches of covenant committed after the date of an assignment of the lease by him to a third party unless, as is commonly required, he has entered into direct covenants with the landlord, in which case his liability will continue throughout the remainder of the term. In this respect the liability of an assignee is no different from that of an original tenant.

Indemnity

10.3.4.   Irrespective of K10.3.3, an assignee of the lease may be called upon to indemnify his assignor in respect of any breach of covenant committed after the date of the assignment to him regardless of whether he has parted with the lease. On the transfer of a registered lease such an indemnity covenant is implied whether or not value was given for the assignment.[2] A similar indemnity provision is implied on the assignment of an unregistered lease, but only where value has been given for the assignment.[3] If the assignment of an unregistered lease is to be made for no valuable consideration an express indemnity covenant will be required by the assignor. At common law an original tenant who is sued by the landlord for a breach of covenant committed by an assignee can pursue a direct claim against that assignee.[4] Standard Condition 4.6.4 and Standard Commercial Property Condition 6.6.4 require the purchase deed to contain an express indemnity covenant except where one is implied by law. A contractual exclusion of Law of Property Act 1925, s.77 does not negate the underlying common law obligation to reimburse.[5]

1. The benefit of an option to purchase the reversion may, however, pass to an assignee of the lease by assignment (see K13).
2. Land Registration Act 2002, Sched.12, para.20. The nature of the liability of the transferee is one of indemnity, not guarantee: *Scottish & Newcastle plc* v. *Raguz* [2008] UKHL 65; and note comments by the Court of Appeal in this case at [2007] EWCA Civ 150.
3. Law of Property Act 1925, s.77.
4. *Moule* v. *Garrett* (1872) LR & Exch 101.
5. *Re Healing Research Trustee Co. Ltd* [1992] 2 All ER 481.

10.4.   Old tenancies – liability between head-landlord and sub-tenant

10.4.1.   No privity of estate exists between a head-landlord and a sub-tenant although a contractual relationship will exist between them if the sub-tenant has entered into direct covenants with the head-landlord (e.g. in a licence to sub-let). The sub-tenant will in any event be directly liable to the head-landlord on restrictive covenants in the head-lease of which the former had notice when he took his sub-lease.[1] The sub-tenant is entitled to call for production of the head-lease on grant of the sub-lease to him.[2] Also the head-landlord may have the right to sue under Contracts (Rights of Third Parties) Act 1999 (see K1.11).

1. In the case of new tenancies a restrictive covenant is enforceable against a sub-tenant by virtue of Landlord and Tenant (Covenants) Act 1995, s.3(5).
2. The rules relating to deduction of title are set out in K1.12.

10.5.   Old tenancies – guarantors and sureties

10.5.1.   The liability of a person who guarantees the performance of the tenant's obligations under the lease only arises if the original debtor defaults, but that liability may be extended by the terms of the guarantee to primary liability. The guarantor will have a continuing liability even though the lease has been disclaimed and the tenant's obligations terminated.[1]

10.5.2.   The benefit of a tenant's surety's covenant passes automatically to a buyer of the reversion,[2] as does the benefit of a surety's covenant to accept a lease to replace one disclaimed on the tenant's insolvency.[3]

10.5.3.   Where an assignee of the lease goes into liquidation and the landlord sues the original tenant for arrears of rent, the latter can pursue an action against the assignee's surety for reimbursement. Although both are liable to the landlord the surety's obligation is prior to that of the original tenant.[4] However, there is no obligation on the landlord to take action against the other parties before proceeding against the original tenant.[5]

1. *Hindcastle Ltd* v. *Barbara Attenborough Associates Ltd* [1996] 2 WLR 262; and *Active Estates Ltd* v. *Parness* [2002] 36 EG 147. Note also *Shaw v. Doleman* [2009] EWCA Civ 279.
2. *P & A Swift Investments (a firm)* v. *Combined English Stores Group plc* [1989] AC 643. This applies even after the lease is disclaimed following insolvency: *Scottish Widows plc* v. *Tripipatkul* [2003] NPC 106.
3. *Coronation Street Industrial Properties* v. *Ingall Industries plc* [1989] 1 All ER 979.
4. *Becton Dickinson UK Ltd* v. *Zwebner* [1989] QB 208.
5. *Norwich Union Life Insurance Society* v. *Low Profile Fashions Ltd* [1992] 1 EGLR 86.

10.6.   Old and new tenancies – restriction on liability of former tenant or guarantor for rent or service charge

10.6.1.   Where a landlord seeks to recover a 'fixed charge' from a former tenant or guarantor he must serve a written notice[1] on the tenant or guarantor under section 17 Landlord and Tenant (Covenants) Act 1995 within six months of the charge becoming due and in it inform the tenant or guarantor that the charge is now due, and that the landlord intends to recover the sum specified in the notice plus, where payable, interest. Depending on the terms of the lease, where there is an outstanding rent review the amount will not be due until the amount of the increase has been determined. Therefore, in such a case no notice need be served on former tenants or guarantors until there is actually a payment outstanding and recoverable.[2]

Fixed charge

10.6.2.   A fixed charge is rent, or a service charge as defined by section 18 Landlord and Tenant Act 1985 (but without the statutory restrictions applicable to residential property) or any other liquidated sum payable in the event of a breach of covenant.

Effect of failure to comply

10.6.3.   A landlord who fails to serve proper notice will not be able to recover the amounts from either the former tenant or a guarantor.

Restriction of liability of former tenant or his guarantor where tenancy subsequently varied

The effect of variations at common law

10.6.4.   A variation may not bind the original tenant following the decision in *Friends Provident Life Office* v. *British Railways Board*.[3] If an assignee agrees a variation with the landlord, the variation does not alter the terms of the contract between the original parties to the lease. The original tenant is not released from liability, but the liability remains governed by the terms of the contract which he entered when he was granted the lease.

Section 18 Landlord and Tenant (Covenants) Act 1995

10.6.5.   Section 18 relieves a former tenant of liability for any amount which is referable to a relevant variation made on or after 1 January 1996. A relevant variation need not be contained in a deed. It is a variation which occurs where either a landlord has an absolute right to refuse it, or the lease has been altered after the assignment so as to deprive the landlord of a right of absolute refusal (e.g. a lease which prohibits a change of use without consent). To the extent that a guarantor remains liable despite the variation he will nevertheless not be liable to pay any amount referable to a relevant variation.

Right of former tenant to overriding lease

10.6.6.   A person discharging a fixed charge has a right to require the landlord to grant him an overriding lease under Landlord and Tenant (Covenants) Act 1995, s.19. An overriding lease is a reversionary lease granted for the remainder of the term usually plus a short term (e.g. a few days). Its terms are broadly identical to those of the relevant tenancy. It does not contain personal covenants or covenants which are spent, and covenants framed by reference to the beginning of the tenancy, e.g. repairing covenants, should be adjusted.

10.6.7.   To obtain an overriding lease the tenant must serve on the landlord a written request specifying the payment and claiming the right to the lease. The request must be made at the time of making the payment or within 12 months. The landlord must grant the lease within a reasonable time. The tenant has to deliver a counterpart and is liable for the landlord's reasonable costs. There is no obligation to grant an overriding lease if the original tenancy has been determined, or if an overriding lease has been granted or a request for one is still outstanding. Two or more requests for overriding leases made on the same day are dealt with in the sequence in which the liability was incurred with a tenant having prior right to a guarantor. A tenant may withdraw his request or may fail to respond to a request from the landlord to take a lease within a reasonable time. In either case, the tenant will be liable for the landlord's costs. A request may be protected by the entry of a notice in registered land (or as an estate contract in unregistered land).

10.6.8.   It is possible to have tiers of overriding leases. Whether an overriding lease is a new lease or an old one depends upon the status of the original lease. It should state that it is an overriding lease granted under section 19 Landlord and Tenant (Covenants) Act 1995 and whether or not it is a new tenancy for the purpose of section 1. Any right arising from such a request cannot be an overriding interest.[4] A landlord who fails to grant a reversionary lease may face a claim in tort for breach of statutory duty. A tenant who fails to deliver a counterpart lease cannot exercise rights under the overriding lease. These provisions are binding on mortgagees.

1.   The form of notice is prescribed by Landlord and Tenant (Covenants) Act 1995 (Notices) Regulations 1995.
2.   *Scottish & Newcastle plc* v. *Raguz* [2008] UKHL 65. The need to specify in the notice that the amount may increase and, in which case, to serve a second notice as apparently required by Landlord and

Tenant (Covenants) Act 1995, s.17(4) was doubted by the House of Lords. See further article by Ben Baruch in *Landlord and Tenant Review* (2009) 13(1), 31–32.
3.   [1996] 1 All ER 336; and *Beegas Nominees* v. *BHP Petroleum Ltd* [1998] 31 EG 96.
4.   Landlord and Tenant (Covenants) Act 1995, s.20(6) as amended by Land Registration Act 2002, Sched.11, para.33(4).

10.7.   New tenancies – covenants to which Landlord and Tenant (Covenants) Act 1995 applies

10.7.1.   The 1995 Act applies to all covenants whether they are express, implied or imposed by law and whether or not they 'touch and concern the land'.[1] Most covenants in a lease do touch and concern the land, but not, for example, a covenant by a landlord to repay a deposit to the tenant.[2]

Transmission of the benefit and burden

10.7.2.   An assignee under a new tenancy acquires the benefit and takes the burden of all the covenants. The assignor remains liable, and can sue, for breaches occurring before the assignment is made. However, the assignee is not liable in relation to any time prior to the assignment to him, so he is not liable for once-and-for-all breaches of covenant committed by the assignor. An assignor may, however, assign the benefit of a right.[3] The covenants are enforceable by and against any person entitled to the rents and profits and also by and against a mortgagee in possession.

10.7.3.   The exceptions are:

(a)   personal covenants;

(b)   a covenant which does not bind the assignor immediately before the assignment, for example, one that is of limited duration or which has been released;

(c)   a covenant which relates to a part of the demised premises which is not included in the assignment;

(d)   a covenant which needs to be protected by registration and has not been so protected (e.g. an option).

The landlord's right of re-entry

10.7.4.   A landlord's right of re-entry attaches to the reversion and passes on an assignment of it.[4]

1.   But not to those imposed pursuant to Housing Act 1985, ss.35, 155 or Sched.6A, para.1, or Housing Associations Act 1985, Sched.2, paras.1 or 3.
2.   *Hua Chiao Commercial Bank Ltd* v. *Chiaphua Industries Ltd* [1987] AC 99, PC.
3.   Landlord and Tenant (Covenants) Act 1995, s.23(2).
4.   *Ibid.*, s.4.

10.8. New tenancies – tenant's release from covenants

10.8.1. A tenant who assigns the lease will be released from the burden and deprived of the benefit of the covenants from the moment the assignment is made by virtue of Landlord and Tenant (Covenants) Act 1995, s.5. The release is only from future observance of the covenants. The tenant's guarantor is also released to the same extent by virtue of section 24(2). Where the lease contains an obligation that the outgoing tenant's guarantor must enter into an authorised guarantee agreement (as to which see K10.9) to guarantee the assignee's liability, such a provision has been held to be void as being contrary to the provisions of section 24(2).[1] It appears that this may also be the case if the tenant's guarantor voluntarily guarantees the assignee's liability. There is no settled view on whether a tenant's guarantor may lawfully guarantee the outgoing tenant's liability under the authorised guarantee agreement.

10.8.2. The exceptions are:

(a) an assignment in breach of covenant or by operation of law (e.g. devolution to PRs) is an 'excluded assignment'. The assignor is not released until the next assignment as long as it is not another excluded one;[2]

(b) a tenant who has entered an authorised guarantee agreement is similarly not released until the next non-excluded assignment (see K10.9).

1. *Good Harvest Partnership* v. *Centaur Services* [2010] EWHC 330. The court held that the guarantee was void and unenforceable by virtue of the anti-avoidance provision in Landlord and Tenant (Covenants) Act 1995, s.25.
2. *Ibid.*, s.11(2).

10.9. New tenancies – authorised guarantee agreements

10.9.1. Where a lease contains a restriction on assignment, the landlord can, as a condition of his granting consent to the assignment, require the tenant to enter into an agreement which guarantees the performance of the lease covenants by the immediate assignee (called an 'authorised guarantee agreement'). The terms of the proposed authorised guarantee agreement may be set out in the lease.

10.9.2. The agreement:

(a) can only guarantee the liability of the assignee;

(b) must cease when that assignee assigns the lease;

(c) may impose a primary liability;

(d) is void to the extent that it imposes obligations beyond those permitted;[1]

(e) may require the tenant to accept a new lease where the old one is disclaimed as long as the tenancy is for no longer a period than the original term and its covenants are no more onerous.

Effect of disclaimers, vesting orders and reversionary leases

10.9.3. Where a tenant is granted a lease following disclaimer, or has a vesting order made in his favour under Insolvency Act 1986, or is granted an overriding lease, he may be required to enter a further authorised guarantee agreement on its assignment.

1. Landlord and Tenant (Covenants) Act 1995, s.16(4)(a) and (b), and s.25.

10.10. New tenancies – landlord's release from covenants

Need to serve notice

10.10.1. The landlord who assigns the reversion may apply for a release by serving a notice on the tenant either before or within four weeks beginning with the date of the assignment.[1] In the absence of a release under the statutory procedure the landlord will remain bound by the landlord covenants of the lease but will continue to be entitled to the benefit of the tenant covenants.[2] Note that it is possible to agree in the lease that a landlord will be automatically released from liability on assignment.[3] In default of such agreement the statutory notice procedure must be followed.

Contents of notice

10.10.2. The tenant must be told about the proposed assignment or the fact that it has occurred and that the landlord is seeking a release from his covenants.

Tenant's response

10.10.3. A tenant may object to the landlord's release by serving a notice on the landlord within four weeks beginning with the date of service of the landlord's notice.

Role of the court

10.10.4. Unless the objection is withdrawn, the county court will decide whether it is reasonable for the landlord to be released.

Date of release

10.10.5. A landlord's release takes effect from the date of the assignment. Section 3(3A) Landlord and Tenant Act 1985 still applies: therefore the liability of an assigning landlord is preserved until the tenant is notified of the change of landlord.

Subsequent release

10.10.6. A landlord who has not been released may make a fresh application on the next assignment of the reversion. He should, therefore, take an indemnity covenant from his buyer together with a covenant that the buyer will notify the landlord of his intention to re-sell the reversion.

10.10.7. Notices must comply with the Notices Regulations made pursuant to Landlord and Tenant (Covenants) Act 1995.[4]

1. Landlord and Tenant (Covenants) Act 1995, ss.6–8. Careful consideration needs to be given before taking this step in the case of multi-let properties as obtaining the release by only some of the tenants will leave the landlord in an exposed position.
2. *Wembley National Stadium Ltd* v. *Wembley (London) Ltd* [2007] EWHC 756 (Ch).
3. *Avonridge Property Co. Ltd* v. *Mashru* [2005] UKHL 70. Such an agreement does not fall foul of the anti-avoidance provisions of Landlord and Tenant (Covenants) Act 1995, s.25.
4. SI 1995/2964.

10.11. New tenancies – assignment of part

10.11.1. The release of the assignor is only in respect of covenants which relate to the part sold except where the assignment is an excluded assignment.

Apportionment of liability

10.11.2. The assignor and the assignee remain bound by 'non-attributable' covenants, e.g. a covenant to pay rent or a service charge which is charged on the whole property, but they can agree between them how the liability is to be borne. The apportionment may bind the other party to the lease if a notice[1] is served either before or within four weeks beginning with the date of the assignment in question on the other party to the lease. The notice must inform him of the proposed assignment or the fact that it has occurred, the prescribed particulars of the agreement, and the request that the apportionment becomes binding on him. The apportionment will be binding if the recipient fails to serve a written notice of objection within four weeks. If he does object, the parties to the agreement may apply to the county court for a declaration that it is reasonable for the apportionment to bind the other party to the lease. The recipient may also indicate consent to the apportionment or may withdraw a notice of objection. An apportionment which becomes binding does so from the date of the assignment.

Forfeiture or disclaimer limited to part only of demised premises

10.11.3. Where the landlord has a right to forfeit or there is a right for a liquidator or trustee in bankruptcy to disclaim a lease and where part only of the demised premises is affected, the forfeiture or disclaimer relates only to that part vested in the defaulting or insolvent tenant and not to the whole lease.[2]

1. The notices must comply with Landlord and Tenant (Covenants) Act 1995 (Notices) Regulations 1995 (SI 1995/2964).
2. Landlord and Tenant (Covenants) Act 1995, s.21.

10.12.   New tenancies – exclusion of the 1995 Act

10.12.1. An agreement to exclude, modify or otherwise frustrate the operation of provisions in the 1995 Act is void.[1]

1. Landlord and Tenant (Covenants) Act 1995, s.25.

10.13.   Contracts (Rights of Third Parties) Act 1999

10.13.1. Contracts (Rights of Third Parties) Act 1999 affects leases and assignments made on or after 11 May 2000 and provides that where a contract made between A and B is intended to benefit C (e.g. a sub-tenant or assignee) C may sue on that contract as if he was an original contracting party. C, the third party, must be identified in the contract made between A and B by name, class or description.[1] This will mean that covenants in a head lease may be directly enforceable as between tenants and as between a head-landlord and sub-tenant or head-landlord and an assignee where previously direct enforcement was not possible because of the doctrines of privity of contract and of estate.[2] The right of enforcement is not for the whole contract but just those terms which are made for the benefit of a third party. In practice the Act is commonly disapplied by the terms of the lease.

1. See e.g. *Avraamides* v. *Colwill* [2006] EWCA Civ 1533.
2. In the case of new tenancies a restrictive covenant is enforceable against a sub-tenant by virtue of Landlord and Tenant (Covenants) Act 1995, s.3(5).

K11. Assignment of leases

11.1. **Taking instructions**
11.2. **Covenants against alienation**
11.3. **Preparing the package**
11.4. **Energy performance certificates**

11.5. **Title**
11.6. **Preparing for completion**
11.7. **Completion**
11.8. **Post-completion**

NB: In this section the word 'lease' should be read to include the word 'sub-lease' where appropriate to the context.

11.1. Taking instructions

11.1.1. The information required by the seller's solicitor and buyer's solicitor will be similar to that needed in a freehold transaction (see A1) with the addition of details of the lease to be sold or bought. Of particular importance is the question of whether the landlord's consent to the transaction will be required (see K11.2). The seller's solicitor should check his own title, in particular to ensure that no outstanding breaches of covenant exist, before drafting the contract for sale. An energy performance certificate will usually be required. (See further A27.)

11.1.2. The length of the residue of the term should be checked. Where the buyer is to obtain a mortgage on the property his lender will usually require that a minimum stated length of the term remains unexpired at the date of acquisition of the buyer's interest in order to provide the lender with adequate security for his loan (see K6.6). A lease with only a few years left unexpired is a wasting asset in the hands of the tenant and particularly in the case of residential property may prove difficult to sell unless the lease can be extended or enfranchised (see K9).

Seller's solicitor

11.1.3. The seller's solicitor should obtain from his client or, if not available from the client, from the landlord:

(a) the receipt for the last rent due under the lease;

(b) where relevant, evidence of payment of service charge over the past three years including the receipt for the last payment due;

(c) details of the insurance of the property including the receipt for the last premium due;

(d) details of any fee payable to a management company on the transfer of the lease (mainly applicable to retirement schemes);

(e) a copy of the memorandum and articles of association of any management company together with a copy of the seller's share certificate;

(f) copies of any side letters made between landlord and tenant which affect the terms of the lease.

11.1.4. Does the seller's solicitor have in his possession:

(a) evidence of the freehold title?

(b) licence permitting the current assignment and/or use of the property?

(c) insurance policy?

(d) latest rent review memo?

11.1.5. What consents are needed:

(a) from landlord?

(b) from lender?

11.1.6. Consider what statutes affect the current letting and the proposed sale. What impact does this legislation make on the proposed transaction?

11.1.7. Consider the terms of the existing lease, e.g. as to repairs, user, alterations, alienation, forfeiture, because the buyer's solicitor may raise points on these clauses.

11.1.8. Will it be necessary to obtain a release of the current sureties' liability from the landlord, or to obtain a deed of variation of the lease to reflect the current situation as between landlord and tenant?

11.1.9. If the lease to be assigned commenced before 1 January 1996, the assignor should be reminded of his continuing liability under the covenants in the lease.

11.1.10. If the lease to be assigned was granted after 1 January 1996, its terms should be checked to see whether the landlord requires the outgoing tenant to enter into an authorised guarantee agreement on assignment.

Buyer's solicitor

Checking the lease

11.1.11. On receipt of a copy of the lease from the seller's solicitor, the buyer's solicitor should check the lease and lease plan carefully and advise his client about his responsibility under the various covenants in the lease. The lease may require an assignee to enter into direct covenants with the landlord which will create a contractual relationship between the landlord and the assignee and, in the case of 'old tenancies' (as defined by the Landlord and Tenant (Covenants) Act 1995), will make the assignee liable on all of the lease covenants for the remainder of the term, notwithstanding subsequent assignment of the lease to a third party (see K10). The solicitor will also need to check whether the lease, or rights granted by it, have been registered at the Land Registry (e.g. a lease for over seven years, or a lease of part for less than seven years but that grants an easement) where registration was required. The buyer's solicitor should also check whether the circumstances surrounding the payment of SDLT by the original tenant may require the buyer to file a subsequent return during the term, e.g. on a rent review within five years from the grant (see A14.16).

Landlord's consent

11.1.12. If the landlord's consent to the transfer or assignment will be needed the buyer should be asked to supply his solicitor with the names and addresses of potential referees so that this information may be passed on to the seller's solicitor as quickly as possible in order to avoid any delay in obtaining the licence. References are commonly required from all or some of the following sources:

(a) a current landlord;

(b) the buyer's bankers;

(c) the buyer's employer;

(d) a professional person, e.g. accountant or solicitor;

(e) a person or company with whom the buyer regularly trades;

(f) three years' audited accounts in the case of a company or self-employed person.

11.1.13. A solicitor should only give a reference on behalf of his client if he knows the client well and trusts him. The landlord will rely on the information given in the reference in assessing the suitability of the buyer as a potential tenant and a misstatement made by a solicitor in the course of giving a reference may lead to liability to the landlord under the principles in *Hedley Byrne & Co. Ltd* v. *Heller & Partners Ltd* [1964] AC 465. It is thus common practice for a reference given by a solicitor to exclude liability or responsibility for its contents.

Surety

11.1.14. The landlord may also require a surety to the lease as a condition of the grant of a licence to assign. Consideration should be given as to who should stand surety under the lease. Where the proposed assignee is a company it is common to find that the directors of the company are asked to guarantee the company's obligations under the lease. Although the directors may be happy to do this since, unless they agree, they are unlikely to secure the landlord's consent to the assignment, they should be advised of the considerable personal liability which they are assuming by accepting such a role. This is particularly so if the assignee, by entering direct covenants with the landlord, will be assuming a contingent liability under the lease since the sureties' obligations will be co-extensive with those of the principal debtor. In this situation there may be a conflict between the interests of the company client (the prospective assignee)

and those of the sureties (the company directors) and it may be advisable for the sureties to receive independent advice about their responsibilities in relation to the guarantee of the lease obligations. (See further K4.)

Buyer's lender

11.1.15. The terms of the lease should be checked to ensure that it will be acceptable to the buyer's lender (see further K6.6).

11.2.   Covenants against alienation

11.2.1. Covenants against alienation take many forms; they may restrict all or any of the following acts: assignment of the lease, sub-letting, sharing, parting with possession of the whole or any part of the property and creating a mortgage over the property. Such covenants are construed strictly by the courts so that when drafting a covenant it is essential that the covenant is worded to cover precisely the acts which it is intended to restrict, e.g. a covenant which prevents assignment will not restrict sub-letting and vice versa.

Long residential leases

11.2.2. A covenant which restricts assignment of a long lease of a house or flat, except during the final years of its term (e.g. during the last seven years of a 99-year lease), is not generally favoured by either buyers or their lenders since it unnecessarily restricts the saleability of the property and thus has an adverse effect on its market value. See K6.6 for the lenders' requirements. For this reason such a covenant is uncommon in such a lease and a buyer's solicitor should seek to remove such a restriction from the lease on grant.

11.2.3. Except in long residential leases the inclusion of some type of covenant against alienation is usual and acceptable and provides the landlord with some measure of control over the occupiers of his property. The precise effect of any covenant depends on its wording. The effect of Landlord and Tenant Act 1927, s.19(1)(*b*) on building leases should be noted.[1]

Absolute covenants

11.2.4. If the covenant is absolute, e.g. 'the tenant shall not assign or part with possession of the property', any assignment (or other dealing depending on the wording of the restriction), although effective, will be a breach of covenant by the tenant and may lead to forfeiture of the lease. Although a landlord may be prepared to waive the covenant, such provisions are not popular with tenants since there is no guarantee that the tenant will be able to sell the lease should the need or desire to do so arise. The presence of an absolute covenant may therefore have a deflationary effect on the rent obtainable for the property. Where an absolute covenant exists, there is no objection to the tenant asking the landlord's permission to grant him a variation of the lease to permit assignment (or as the case may be), but there is no obligation on the landlord to accede to the tenant's request or to give reasons for his refusal.

Qualified covenants

11.2.5. A qualified covenant permits the tenant to assign provided that the tenant obtains the prior consent of the landlord to the dealing. This type of covenant is more acceptable to prospective tenants than an absolute covenant but does not give the landlord total control over the occupiers of his property since his discretion to refuse consent to a proposed assignee may be tempered by the application of statutory provisions which, where they apply, are non-excludable.

Consent not to be unreasonably withheld

11.2.6. In the case of a qualified covenant contained in a lease, Landlord and Tenant Act 1927, s.19 adds to the covenant the non-excludable proviso that consent shall not be unreasonably withheld by the landlord.[2] The question of whether a landlord in refusing consent is acting 'unreasonably' presents problems for the tenant. If the tenant does apply for consent and the landlord unreasonably withholds his consent, the tenant may go ahead and assign (or as the case may be) without consent and the dealing will not constitute a breach of covenant by the tenant. The difficulty lies in knowing what is 'unreasonable' since a refusal which may appear to be unreasonable from the tenant's point of view may look very different when considered from the landlord's side.[3] If the landlord does refuse consent the prospective assignee (or as the case may be) is unlikely to wish to proceed with the transaction without consent because he runs the risk of the lease being forfeited against him. One solution is for the tenant to seek a declaration from the court to the effect that the landlord is being unreasonable in withholding his consent but such a course of action is costly and time-consuming. Landlord and Tenant Act 1988 attempts to resolve some of the problems associated with the application of section 19 by providing that the landlord must, after having received a written request for consent, give his consent within a reasonable time unless it is reasonable for him to withhold his consent. He must serve written notice of his decision on the tenant within a reasonable time stating what conditions (if any) are attached to the consent or, if consent is refused, stating his reasons for withholding his consent. Breach of the landlord's duty under the Act is actionable in tort as a breach of statutory duty, giving a remedy to the tenant in damages (see K7.11).

11.2.7. Note that various statutory provisions provide that a refusal to consent based on the grounds of race,[4] sex,[5] disability,[6] religion or sexual orientation[7] will be unlawful in most circumstances.[8]

Offer to surrender

11.2.8. Attached to some covenants against assignment is a proviso that should the tenant wish to assign he should first offer to surrender his lease to the landlord.

Such a proviso (variously known as a surrender-back, offer-back or an 'Adler clause' after the case of that name)[9] was held to be valid in *Bocardo S.A.* v. *S. & M. Hotels*,[10] but the effect of such a clause and the terms of any surrender need to be considered carefully by the tenant, especially since, in the case of business tenancies within Landlord and Tenant Act 1954, Pt. II, section 38 makes void an agreement which has the effect of precluding the tenant from making an application for a new tenancy under the Act. It may therefore be necessary in a commercial lease for landlord and tenant to follow the statutory procedure to 'contract out' of an agreement to surrender.[11] Since Law of Property (Miscellaneous Provisions) Act 1989, s.2 requires a contract for the disposal of an interest in land to be in writing, it is arguable that to create an effective contract for surrender landlord and tenant must both sign a single document incorporating all the terms of the surrender or otherwise comply with the terms of the Act.[12]

11.2.9. This right is a pre-emption right in favour of the landlord and should be registered against the tenant's title. Where the title is unregistered, it should be registered as a C(iv) land charge. Where the title is registered it should be protected by a notice,[13] or in the case of a Prescribed Clauses lease by referring to the right in clause LR9.3.

11.2.10. A pre-emption right may be subject to the rule against perpetuities where it was granted prior to 6 April 2010 (although the position is unclear).[14] Where Perpetuity and Accumulations Act 1964 applies, the relevant period is assumed to be 21 years from the grant of the lease.

11.2.11. Where the right is granted on or after 6 April 2010, Perpetuities and Accumulations Act 2009 will apply. This provides, broadly, that the rule against perpetuities only applies where a new instrument creates one or more interests from a very limited class of interests, which are generally trust interests. Therefore the rule against perpetuities does not apply, *inter alia*, to new pre-emption rights.

Landlord and Tenant (Covenants) Act 1995

11.2.12. In relation to new tenancies (i.e. generally those granted on or after 1 January 1996) of commercial property (section 19(1A) does not apply to residential or agricultural tenancies) the provisions of section 19 Landlord and Tenant Act 1927 are modified so that a landlord may agree in advance with his tenant:

(a)   any circumstances in which the landlord may withhold his licence or consent to a proposed assignment; or

(b)   any conditions subject to which such licence or consent may be granted.

11.2.13. A landlord who withholds consent because of the existence of any such circumstance or who imposes any such condition is not acting unreasonably.

11.2.14. The 1995 Act distinguishes between factual matters, for example:

(a)   the assignee must be a plc;

(b)   the assignee must have net assets equal to a specified multiplier of the rent;

(c)   the assignee must provide a rent deposit; or

(d)   the assignor must enter an authorised guarantee agreement;

and discretionary matters, for example, the assignee is, in the opinion of the landlord, of equal financial standing to the assignor.

11.2.15.   In discretionary matters, the landlord's decision has to be arrived at reasonably, or the tenant must have the right to have the decision reviewed by an independent third party, who is identifiable from the agreement, and whose decision is conclusive.

Demanding a premium for consent

11.2.16.   Unless the lease specifically allows the landlord to charge a premium for giving his consent (an uncommon provision in modern leases) the landlord may not attach a condition to his consent requiring a premium to be paid by the tenant.[15]

Undertaking for landlord's costs

11.2.17.   The landlord is entitled to ask the tenant to pay the landlord's solicitor's reasonable charges in connection with the preparation of the deed of consent (licence) but may not demand a premium. When the tenant's solicitor approaches the landlord's solicitor asking for consent to be given he should require the landlord's solicitor to provide a firm estimate of the costs of the application which should indicate whether or not VAT and disbursements are included in the estimate and should give a maximum fee which will be charged by the landlord in any event (see A8). A tenant paying the landlord's solicitor's costs is entitled to apply for these costs to be taxed.[16] In any event, deliberate overcharging is professional misconduct. The Solicitors' Code of Conduct 2007[17] states that solicitors must not 'use their position as solicitors to take unfair advantage either for themselves or another person'.

11.2.18.   It may be difficult for the landlord's solicitor to quote a fixed figure at the outset of the transaction, but he should try to give the tenant's solicitor an accurate estimate of the likely costs and there is no objection to his qualifying the estimate by saying that it is given on the understanding that the matter proceeds to completion without any unforeseen difficulties or delays. The estimate should make it clear whether the tenant is to be responsible for the landlord's costs in any event, i.e. whether or not consent is forthcoming and whether or not the proposed assignment (or as the case may be) proceeds to completion. To assist the landlord in giving an accurate estimate the tenant's solicitor should be prepared to supply the landlord with such information as he requires, e.g. references about the proposed assignee (or as the case may be) as quickly as possible and preferably at the time when the application for consent is first made.

11.2.19. A tenant's solicitor must advise his client of his potential liability to meet the landlord's costs and should not give an unqualified undertaking to meet the landlord's solicitors' costs of preparing the consent since he may be committing his client to an unquantified sum.

11.2.20. An undertaking should only be given if the landlord has provided an estimate of costs, and subject to the prior approval of the tenant client (see B16.1). It is undecided as to whether it is reasonable for a landlord to insist on an undertaking from the tenant's solicitors to pay its reasonable costs before dealing with the application for consent, although it is standard practice for this to be done. Certainly, it is likely to be unreasonable for the landlord to insist on an unlimited undertaking as a precondition for dealing with the application for consent for an indemnity as to costs.[18] Where an undertaking has been given, the tenant's solicitor should obtain money on account from his client to ensure that he will be able to fulfil the undertaking. However, since Landlord and Tenant Act 1988 renders the landlord liable to the tenant in damages if an application for consent is not dealt with within a reasonable time, the landlord's solicitor should be wary of refusing to deal with the matter until such time as he receives an undertaking in respect of his costs.

Standard Conditions of Sale

11.2.21. Standard Condition 8.3 and Standard Commercial Property Condition 10.3 require the seller to apply for the landlord's consent at his own expense and to use his best endeavours to obtain such consent, the buyer providing all information and references reasonably required. Either party may rescind the contract by notice if the consent has not been obtained within a certain time. In the case of the Standard Commercial Property Conditions this period is (broadly) four months after the original completion date. In the case of the Standard Conditions the period is (broadly) three working days before the original completion date. The Standard Conditions do not require the assignee to enter into a direct covenant with the landlord (reversioner). If the lease provides for the assignee to enter into a direct covenant, the contract should contain a condition to this effect.

11.2.22. In view of the difficulties attached to covenants against alienation, it is advisable that contracts for a disposition which is dependent on consent being obtained should not be exchanged until it is certain that the landlord's consent will be forthcoming.

1. The effect of this is, broadly, that if the lease is for more than 40 years and made partly in consideration for construction work, no consent to a dealing is required if this is done more than seven years before the end of the term. See *Vaux Group plc* v. *Lilley* [1991] 04 EG 136.
2. Section 19 does not apply to lettings of certain types of property, e.g. agricultural holdings: see s.19(4).
3. The principles of law which apply to determining the question of reasonableness in these circumstances were set out by the Court of Appeal in *International Drilling Fluids Ltd* v. *Louisville Investments (Uxbridge) Ltd* [1986] Ch 513.
4. Race Relations Act 1976, s.24.
5. Sex Discrimination Act 1975, s.31.
6. Disability Discrimination Act 1995, s.22.

7. Equality Act 2006, s.47. See also Equality Act (Sexual Orientation) Regulations 2007 (SI 2007/1263).
8. The Equality Act 2010 contains equivalent provision to those in footnotes 4–6. It is anticipated that this Act will come into force in October 2010.
9. *Adler* v. *Upper Grosvenor Street Investments* [1957] 1 All ER 229.
10. [1980] 1 WLR 17.
11. Landlord and Tenant Act 1954, s.38A(2) and Regulatory Reform (Business Tenancies) (England and Wales) Order 2003, Scheds.1 and 2.
12. *Proudreed Ltd* v. *Microgen Holdings plc* (1995) 72 P&CR 388, CA.
13. In the case of Prescribed Clauses Leases a reference should be made to this in clause LR9. See K1.20 and Land Registry Practice Guide 64.
14. See *Halsbury's Laws of England*, vol 42, Sale of Land, 1(3)(i) paragraph 28.
15. Law of Property Act 1925, s.144.
16. Solicitors Act 1974, s.71.
17. Solicitors' Code of Conduct 2007, r.10.01.
18. *Dong Bang Minerva* v. *Davina* [1996] 31 EG 87.

11.3. Preparing the package

11.3.1. The seller's solicitor should generally supply the buyer's solicitor with the following documents or information:

(a) the draft contract;

(b) a copy of the lease/sub-lease being purchased;

(c) a plan of the property (where appropriate);

(d) evidence of the seller's title;

(e) replies to pre-contract searches;

(f) details of the insurance of the property (including the receipt for the last premium due);

(g) details of any management company, including copies of the memorandum and articles of association;

(h) service charge accounts for the last three years including the receipt for the last sum payable (where appropriate);

(i) information about what steps have been taken to obtain the landlord's consent to the transaction (where appropriate);

(j) a request for references or such other information about the buyer as the landlord has indicated that he requires (where appropriate);

(k) answers to pre-contract enquiries. In residential cases suitable forms are available from law stationers: e.g. TA7 (Leasehold information form), TA6 (Property information form) and TA11 (Additional property information form). In the case of complex commercial property, replies to the Commercial Property Standard Enquiries should be supplied.[1]

1. The enquiries may be downloaded from **www.bpf.org.uk** or **www.practicallaw.com**. Also see K1.17.1.

11.4.   Energy performance certificates

11.4.1.   An energy performance certificate will usually be required. (See further A27.)

11.5.   Title

Lease registered with absolute title

11.5.1.   By Standard Condition 4.1.2 and Standard Commercial Property Condition 6.1.2, copies supplied must be official copies of the title. Since the title to the lease is guaranteed by the Land Registry there is no need for the buyer to investigate the title to the freehold or superior leases.

Lease registered with good leasehold title

11.5.2.   By Standard Condition 4.1.2 and Standard Commercial Property Condition 6.1.2 copies supplied must be official copies of the title. Registration with a good leasehold title provides no guarantee of the soundness of the title to the reversion(s) and thus the buyer should insist on deduction of the freehold and any intermediate leasehold titles to him. Without deduction of the reversionary title(s) the lease may be unacceptable to the buyer and/or his lender. See G3.5 and note the special requirements in relation to good leasehold title contained in the CML Lenders' Handbook and the BSA Mortgage Instructions. The reversionary title(s) will be deduced by the appropriate method applicable to unregistered land (see section D). As the register of title is open to public inspection a prospective tenant will in practice be able to find out a great deal about his proposed landlord's title, assuming it is registered (see G3.12).

Unregistered lease

11.5.3.   A special condition should in appropriate cases be added to the contract requiring the seller to deduce the reversionary title to the buyer by the method appropriate to unregistered land (see section D). The Standard Conditions of Sale do not require the seller to deduce a reversionary title in these circumstances.

11.6.   Preparing for completion

The purchase deed

11.6.1.   The purchase deed (an assignment in unregistered land or a transfer in registered land) will be prepared by the buyer's solicitor. Even where the lease was granted informally the assignment must be by deed in order to transfer the legal estate in the land to the buyer.[1] An assignment of an unregistered lease will normally recite the brief history of the lease and the granting of any necessary consent to the present transaction, but is otherwise similar to a conveyance of freehold land. The form of transfer is the same as that used in freehold transactions. Execution of the purchase deed is discussed in E1.

Indemnity

11.6.2. If the assignor is to remain liable on the covenants in the lease after completion of the assignment, the purchase deed should include an express indemnity covenant from the buyer. Where Landlord and Tenant (Covenants) Act 1995 applies so as to release the assignor from future liability, no indemnity covenant is necessary; however, liability is commonly continued by an authorised guarantee agreement. (See also K15.4.7.)

Modification of covenants for title

11.6.3. If a seller is in breach of a repairing covenant in the lease, the lack of repair could involve him in liability to the buyer after completion under the covenants for title which will be implied in the purchase deed.[2] Since liability under the covenants is strict, and it is usual for the contract to contain a provision requiring the buyer to accept the property in its existing state of repair,[3] the contract should also provide for modification of the covenants for title in this respect. Such a contractual condition must be reflected by an express modification of the covenants in the purchase deed itself. A buyer who accepts a condition which restricts the seller's liability under the covenants for title must ensure that he is fully aware of the actual state of repair of the property (e.g. by inspection or survey) before contracts are exchanged since the effect of such a contractual condition is to take away the buyer's right to sue the seller in respect of a breach of repairing covenant.

Pre-completion searches

11.6.4. Where the lease is registered with an absolute title the buyer will make a pre-completion search at the Land Registry in the same way as if buying the freehold. Any other searches which would be appropriate to the purchase of a registered freehold should also be undertaken (see E2). Where the title to the lease is unregistered, a Land Charges Department search against the names of the estate owners of the leasehold title should be made together with any other searches appropriate to the circumstances of the transaction (see E2). Where the freehold or other reversionary title has been deduced the names revealed through investigation of that title should also be included in the land charges search application. If the lease is registered with a good leasehold title, a search at the Land Registry must be made in respect of the registered title and a Land Charges Department search against the estate owners of an unregistered reversion. A company search should be carried out as necessary, e.g. against the management company.

Landlord's consent

11.6.5.   The landlord's solicitor will supply the engrossment of the licence which must be by deed if it is to contain covenants. If the licence requires the buyer to enter into a direct covenant with the landlord (and/or a management company) to observe and perform the covenants in the lease, the licence is usually drawn up in two parts, the landlord executing the original licence which will be given to the seller on completion for onwards transmission to the buyer, the buyer executing the counterpart which will be given to the landlord on completion.

Apportionments

11.6.6.   Since it is unlikely that completion will take place on a day when rent and/or service charge become due under the lease it will be necessary for these sums to be apportioned on completion and the seller should supply the buyer with a completion statement which shows the amounts due and explains how they have been calculated. Copies of the rent and service charge receipts or demands should be supplied to the buyer with the completion statement so that the buyer can check the apportioned sums. In many cases it will not be possible to make an exact apportionment of service charge since the figures required in order to make this calculation will not be available. In such a case a provisional apportionment of the sum should be made on a 'best estimate' basis in accordance with Standard Condition 6.3.5 or Standard Commercial Property Condition 8.3.5. These conditions, although of most relevance to the apportionment of service charges, are not confined in their application to service charges alone and can be used to make a provisional apportionment of any sums where the amount to be apportioned is not known or easily ascertainable. Where the seller's liability for unascertained service charges may be substantial and there is concern about enforcing his obligation to pay (e.g. where the seller is emigrating), it may be appropriate to negotiate a retention to be held by his solicitors pending the ascertainment of the service charge.

11.6.7.   The Law Society's Conveyancing and Land Law Committee has prepared a formula for calculating the apportionment of rent on assignment of a lease. The formula is given at Appendix IV.2.

Shares in management company

11.6.8.   Where appropriate the solicitor for the buyer should prepare a stock transfer form to be signed by the seller before completion in order to transfer the seller's management company share(s) to the buyer. If the management company is limited by guarantee (not shares) there will be no share certificate to transfer to the buyer but the buyer will need to write to the company and apply for membership after completion. If the amount of the guarantee is more than nominal the seller's liability under the guarantee continues for a year after he ceases to be a member and he should in such a case take an appropriate indemnity from the buyer.

1. Short leases do not have to be made by deed (Law of Property Act 1925, s.54), but the transfer of a legal estate in land must be by deed by Law of Property Act 1925, s.52. This includes the assignment of a short lease. See *Crago* v. *Julian* [1992] 1 All ER 744.
2. Land Registration Act 2002, Sched.12, para.20; Law of Property Act 1925, s.76; and B7.
3. See Standard Condition 3.2 and Standard Commercial Property Condition 3.2.

11.7.   Completion

11.7.1.   The procedure on completion follows closely that in a freehold transaction.

11.7.2.   The seller will hand to the buyer such of the following documents as are relevant to the transaction in hand:

(a)   the lease/sub-lease;

(b)   the purchase deed;

(c)   the landlord's licence;

(d)   marked abstract or other evidence of superior titles in accordance with the contract (lease not registered or not registered with absolute title);

(e)   Form DS1 or an appropriate undertaking in respect of the seller's mortgage and a certificate of non-crystallisation (where appropriate);

(f)   copies of duplicate notices served by the seller and his predecessors on the landlord in accordance with a covenant in the lease requiring the landlord to be notified of any dispositions;

(g)   insurance policy (or copy if insurance is effected by the landlord) and receipt (or copy) relating to the last premium due;

(h)   rent and service charge receipts;

(i)   management company memorandum and articles;

(j)   seller's share certificate and completed stock transfer form.

11.7.3.   The buyer should hand to the seller such of the following items as are appropriate to the transaction:

(a)   money due in accordance with the completion statement;

(b)   duly executed counterpart licence to assign;

(c)   a release of deposit.

Rent receipts

11.7.4.   Law of Property Act 1925, s.45(2) provides that on production of the receipt for the last rent due under the lease or sub-lease which he is buying a buyer must assume, unless the contrary appears, that the rent has been paid and the covenants performed under that and all superior leases. The buyer's solicitor should inspect the receipts on completion and also, where appropriate, receipts for payment of service charge. Standard Condition 6.6 and Standard Commercial Property Condition 8.6 entitle a buyer to assume that the correct person gave the receipt.

11.8.   **Post-completion**

Stamp Duty Land Tax

11.8.1.   Following the assignment of many leases, the tenant must deliver a land transaction return to HM Revenue and Customs within 30 days of the effective date of the transaction. This delivery must include a self-assessment of the liability and where appropriate payment of the SDLT due (see A14.2).

11.8.2.   The general rule is that the effective date of a land transaction is the date of completion. There are, however, special rules where a contract is substantially performed before it is completed and in relation to options and rights of pre-emption. These points and matters generally relating to SDLT are dealt with in A14.

11.8.3.   If the lease is a notifiable land transaction, unless exempt from certification, the lease cannot be registered or noted (if relevant) at the Land Registry without a certificate as to compliance with SDLT. See further A14.30.

11.8.4.   Tax is chargeable on any premium, and is in addition to any tax charged on the rent, and is computed according to the details set out in A14.15.

Registered lease

11.8.5.   Where the lease is already registered at the Land Registry with separate title an application for registration of the transfer to the buyer should be made within the priority period afforded by the buyer's pre-completion search.[1]

Unregistered lease

11.8.6.   An unregistered lease or sub-lease which, at the date of the transfer to the buyer, still has over seven years unexpired will need to be registered at the Land Registry within two months of the assignment. An application for first registration of title should therefore be made within this time limit. An absolute title can be granted where:

    (a)   the registrar is of the opinion that the applicant's title to the lease is such as a willing buyer could properly be advised by a competent professional adviser to accept; and

    (b)   the registrar approves the lessor's title to grant the lease.[2]

11.8.7.   In order to satisfy the Land Registry requirements as to the identification of the premises being assigned, a plan of the premises may be required (see B21). This may be a particular problem where the lease being assigned does not contain an existing plan that meets the Land Registry's criteria (see B21.2.3). In these circumstances a new plan will have to be prepared to meet these criteria and submitted with the application for registration. The parties will need to consider the additional cost implications of obtaining such a plan.

11.8.8. If the title to the reversion is already registered, the lease will be noted against the superior title. In other cases the buyer may consider lodging a caution against first registration against the unregistered superior title in order to protect his interests against a subsequent buyer of the reversion. If the lease has seven years or less unexpired it is generally incapable of registration with separate title but will take effect as an overriding interest.[3] It may be prudent to protect a term for more than three years by the entry of notice in the register of a superior title which is itself registered. A lease for three years or less cannot be so protected.[4]

Notice to landlord

11.8.9. The buyer's solicitor should give notice of the transfer (and of the buyer's mortgage if required) in accordance with any covenant to that effect in the lease. Two copies of the notice together with the appropriate fee should be sent to the landlord's solicitor (or other person specified in the covenant) and the landlord's solicitor should be asked to sign one copy of the notice as an acknowledgement of its receipt and to return the signed copy to the buyer's solicitor. The receipted notice should be kept with the buyer's title deeds as evidence of compliance with this covenant. The fee payable for service of the notice should have been included in the statement of account sent by the buyer's solicitor to his client before completion.

Share transfer

11.8.10. The duly stamped stock transfer form and seller's share certificate should be sent by the buyer's solicitor to the management company who will register the transfer of the share and issue a new share certificate in the buyer's name. The new share certificate should be kept with the buyer's title deeds. It will be necessary to check the requirements of the lender, where appropriate by means of the CML Lenders' Handbook or the BSA Mortgage Instructions, to see if the share certificate and other relevant documents should be sent to the lender. Where the management company is limited by guarantee the buyer should write to the company and apply for membership.

Outstanding apportioned sums

11.8.11. As soon as the figures are available the parties' solicitors should make an adjustment of the provisional apportionments which were made on completion. By Standard Condition 6.3.5 and Standard Commercial Property Condition 8.3.5 such outstanding sums must be settled within 10 working days of notification by one party to the other of the adjusted figures. The liability to account for the apportioned sums remains outstanding despite completion having taken place under Standard Condition 7.4 and Standard Commercial Property Condition 9.4 (see also K11.6.6).

1. The Land Registry's early completion policy will apply in appropriate circumstances. See Land Registry Practice Bulletin 16 and the Law Society's Practice Note 'Land Registry early completion' issued 9 July 2009. See also G1.5.2.
2. Land Registration Act 2002, s.10(2).
3. *Ibid.*, Sched.1, para.1 and Sched.3, para.1.
4. *Ibid.*, s.33.

K12. Licence or tenancy

12.1. Importance of the distinction

12.1.1. The principal reason for distinguishing between a licence and a tenancy is that in general a licensee will not enjoy the benefit of security of tenure, whereas a tenant may be protected from eviction at the end of his contractual term by the operation of some statutory provision. It will be a misrepresentation to describe a property as being sold subject to a licence, where in fact the occupier has a business tenancy.[1] A licensee is not protected under:

    (a)   Rent Act 1977;

    (b)   Housing Act 1988 (assured tenancies);

    (c)   Landlord and Tenant Act 1954, Pt. I (long tenancies);

    (d)   Local Government and Housing Act 1989, Sched.10 (assured tenancies arising after long tenancies, see K5.6.2);

    (e)   Landlord and Tenant Act 1954, Pt. II (business tenancies).

12.1.2. Conversely, licensees do enjoy protection from eviction in the following situations:

    (a)   where the licensee would otherwise be a secure tenant under Housing Act 1985, s.79;

    (b)   under Rent (Agriculture) Act 1976; and

    (c)   generally where a person is granted a licence to occupy land for use as agricultural land under Agricultural Holdings Act 1986, s.2.

1. *Pankhania* v. *Hackney London Borough Council* [2002] All ER (D) 22; and for the decision in relation to quantum of damages see *Pankhania* v. *Hackney London Borough Council and Metropolitan Police Authority* [2004] 1 EGLR 135.

12.2. Licences

12.2.1. It is not always easy to determine whether an arrangement between two parties constitutes a licence or a tenancy. The modern starting point is usually accepted to be *Street* v. *Mountford*[1] where it was held as a general rule that if exclusive possession is given for a term at a rent (although the reservation of a rent is not essential to a tenancy),[2] a tenancy may well come into being, whatever the parties chose to call the arrangement. However, sometimes the surrounding circumstances may show that the right to exclusive possession is due to a legal relationship other than a tenancy, for example occupancy under a contract for the sale of the land.[3]

12.2.2. The giving of exclusive possession is essential to the creation of a tenancy, so that if the agreement genuinely denies this to the grantee, no tenancy will come into being. If, therefore, a clause is inserted into an agreement for the occupation of business premises, enabling the grantor to move the location of the grantee's occupied space or stall, such a right, being inconsistent with the creation of a tenancy, would generally ensure that the grantee became a licensee and not a tenant.[4]

12.2.3. The ability of the grantor to move the location of the grantee has more realism in the case of a business arrangement than in the context of residential premises, but in residential cases grantors have sometimes succeeded in denying the existence of a tenancy by using the device of requiring the grantee to share the accommodation either with other tenants or with the grantor himself (i.e. denying exclusive possession to the grantee). The courts will, however, not accept these devices at their face value, and will look into the reality of the situation; thus if a sharing arrangement is patently a sham in order to deprive the grantee of security of tenure, it is unlikely to succeed.[5]

1. [1985] AC 809.
2. *Ashburn Anstalt* v. *Arnold* [1989] Ch 1.
3   See, e.g. *Cameron Ltd* v. *Rolls-Royce plc* [2007] EWHC 546.
4. *Dresden Estates Ltd* v. *Collinson* (1988) 55 P&CR 47. Note also *Clear Channel UK Ltd* v. *Manchester City Council* [2005] EWCA Civ 1304.
5. See *Dellneed* v. *Chinn* [1987] 1 EGLR 75; *Antoniades* v. *Villiers* [1988] 3 All ER 1058; *Aslan* v. *Murphy (No.1) and (No.2)* [1989] 3 All ER 130; *Duke* v. *Wynne* [1989] 3 All ER 130; *AG Securities* v. *Vaughan* [1988] 3 All ER 1058; *Mikeover Ltd* v. *Brady* [1989] 3 All ER 618; *Westminster City Council* v. *Clarke* [1992] 2 AC 288, HL.

12.3. Lodgers

12.3.1. A genuine lodger is likely to be a licensee and (apart from the denial of exclusive possession) special circumstances such as a family arrangement may negate a tenancy.

12.4. Possession before completion

12.4.1. In most circumstances a buyer who is let into occupation of the property before completion would be treated as a licensee.[1] This appears to apply to a prospective tenant allowed into occupation under an agreement for lease before the completion of the lease.[2] Standard Condition 5.2 provides that the buyer takes occupation as a licensee and not as a tenant.

1. But see *Bretherton* v. *Paton* [1986] 1 EGLR 172.
2. *Cameron Ltd* v. *Rolls-Royce plc* [2007] EWHC 546 (Ch).

12.5. **Notice to terminate**

12.5.1. The length of notice necessary to determine a licence which is not protected by statute will normally be settled by agreement between the parties. In the absence of such agreement, reasonable notice must be given. Notice should always be given in writing so that it will be possible, if a dispute arises, to prove the existence and contents of the notice. Some record of posting or delivery should for the same reason be kept. No notice by a landlord or a tenant to quit any premises let as a dwelling or by a licensor or a licensee to determine a periodic licence to occupy premises as a dwelling, is valid unless it is in writing and contains certain prescribed information[1] and it is given not less than four weeks before the date on which it is to take effect.[2] This does not apply if the premises are held on an 'excluded tenancy' or an 'excluded licence'. Protection from Eviction Act 1977 (as amended) sets out a number of situations where a tenancy or licence will be excluded. They principally relate to situations where the licensee or tenant shares accommodation with the landlord or where it is a hostel.[3] Even where the licensee does not have the benefit of security of tenure, it may still be necessary to obtain a court order if the grantor seeks to regain possession.[4]

1. Notices to Quit (Prescribed Information) Regulations 1988 (SI 1988/2201).
2. Protection from Eviction Act 1977, s.5(1), (1A).
3. *Ibid.*, s.3A; Housing Act 1985, s.322 and *Rogerson* v. *Wigan MBC* [2004] EWHC 1677.
4. See, e.g. Protection from Eviction Act 1977, s.2 in the case of residential premises and Housing Act 1988, s.32. This includes property which is a mixed residential and commercial letting. The phrase 'let as a dwelling' in the Protection from Eviction Act 1977, s.2 has been held to mean 'let wholly or partly as a dwelling' and so applied to premises that were let for mixed residential and business purposes. See *Pirabakaran* v. *Patel* [2006] EWCA Civ 685.

K13. Options

13.1. Introduction

13.1.1. An option for the tenant to renew the lease or to purchase the reversion may be included in some leases or may be granted to the tenant independently of the grant of the lease.

13.1.2. It is important that the price or rent to be paid on the exercise of the option is either fixed by the lease itself or is otherwise ascertainable by the operation of some effective formula (e.g. by reference to 'open market value at the time of the exercise of the option') in the absence of which the option may fail for uncertainty.

13.1.3. An option contained in a registrable lease should be protected by the entry of a notice in the register. If the option is protected as an overriding interest by virtue of the tenant's occupation,[1] the option will need to be disclosed on the application to register the reversion.[2] Notice of the option would then be entered in the register.[3]

13.1.4. If a lease out of a registered title is an overriding interest and is not registrable,[4] the option should be protected on the landlord's title by notice. If the tenant is in occupation, the option may be protected as an overriding interest.[5] It would be unwise to rely on protection as an overriding interest in case the tenant went out of occupation for any reason.

13.1.5. A specific application to enter notice of the option in the register of the landlord's title is usually required whether the option is contained in a lease that is being registered or in a separate document. The Land Registry will only automatically note an option in the landlord's title where the option is expressly referred to (usually in form DI as a disclosable overriding interest) on either an application for first registration of the landlord's title or an application to register a registrable disposition in relation to the landlord's title. Where a Prescribed Clauses Lease is used, the option may be automatically noted in the title affected. See K1.20.7.

13.1.6. In unregistered land an option will not bind the buyer of the landlord's reversionary interest unless registered as an estate contract under Land Charges Act 1972. Where an option cannot be enforced against a buyer of the reversion through lack of registration, the tenant may be able to sue the original landlord for damages for breach of contract,[6] who in turn may seek indemnity from the buyer under a contractual provision, e.g. Standard Condition 3.3.2. To protect his own interests the tenant should ensure that his option is registered as soon as possible after completion of its grant (the priority notice procedure may be used to ensure the date of registration is backdated to the date of grant). A landlord may choose to draft the option so that its validity is dependent on its registration within a stated period. Where a lease is granted out of an unregistered reversion, the option must be protected by registration under Land Charges Act 1972 even if the lease granted will itself be registered under Land Registration Act 2002.

13.1.7. The grant of an option is a disposition of an interest in land within Law of Property (Miscellaneous Provisions) Act 1989, s.2 and so must satisfy the requirements for writing specified by that section.[7]

13.1.8. It is unusual to find options contained in long leases of dwellings which are granted at a low rent because, provided the qualifying conditions are satisfied, Leasehold Reform Act 1967 (as amended) or Leasehold Reform Housing and Urban Development Act 1993 will frequently give the tenant the right to an extended lease and/or to purchase the freehold reversion (see K9).

1. Land Registration Act 2002, Sched.1, para.2 and Sched.3, para.2.
2. Land Registration Rules 2003, rr.28 and 57.
3. *Ibid.*, rr.28(4) and 57(5).
4. Land Registration Act 2002, Sched.1, para.1 and Sched.3, para.1.
5. *Ibid.*, Sched.1, para.2 and Sched.3, para.2.
6. *Wright* v. *Dean* [1948] Ch 686.
7. See B11; and note *Spiro* v. *Glencrown Properties Ltd* [1991] 02 EG 167.

13.2. Options to purchase the reversion

13.2.1. The perpetuity rule does not apply to an option to purchase the reversion to which Perpetuities and Accumulations Act 1964, s.9(1) applies. This requires the option to be contained in the lease itself and its exercise is restricted to the tenant and his successors in title either during the term of the lease or no later than one year after the end of the term. Any option which does not satisfy these requirements will fail for perpetuity unless confined within or exercised within 21 years from the date of the grant.[1] Where the right was granted after 6 April 2010, Perpetuities and Accumulations Act 2009 will apply. This provides, broadly, that the rule against perpetuities only applies where a new instrument creates one or more interests from a very limited class of interests, which are generally trust interests. Therefore the rule against perpetuities does not normally apply, *inter alia*, to new options.

13.2.2. An option to purchase the reversion is not within the doctrine of privity of estate, so that the mere fact that such a relationship exists between the landlord and an assignee of the lease does not automatically mean that the assignee can enforce the option. However, unless the lease restricts the assignability of the option, its benefit may be assigned to a third party.[2]

13.2.3. Although the benefit of such an option can be expressly assigned to an assignee of the lease (even after the assignment of the lease itself) and may pass to him by operation of law without express words of assignment,[3] it is recommended that in order to avoid doubt express words assigning the benefit of the option should be included in the document under which the benefit of the lease is transferred to the assignee.

1. Different rules apply to leases granted before Perpetuities and Accumulations Act 1964 came into force.
2. *Re Button's Lease* [1964] Ch 263.
3. *Griffith* v. *Pelton* [1958] Ch 205.

13.3. Options to renew

13.3.1. An option to renew a lease is not subject to the rule against perpetuities[1] but a contract to renew a lease for a term exceeding 60 years is invalidated by Law of Property Act 1922.[2]

13.3.2. Care must be taken in drafting such an option to ensure that it does not create a perpetually renewable lease, such leases being converted by Law of Property Act 1922 into terms for 2,000 years which are not terminable by a landlord's notice. To avoid the creation of a perpetually renewable lease, the option to renew should be drafted in order to permit the tenant to renew 'on terms identical to those contained in the present lease *with the exception of the covenant to renew*'. Unless the words which are italicised in the previous sentence are included in the option clause, the new lease will also have to contain a further option to renew, thus creating a perpetually renewable lease.

13.3.3. An option to renew is within the doctrine of privity of estate so that provided the terms of exercise are complied with it can be enforced by the assignee who is in possession of the lease at the date when the option becomes exercisable.

13.3.4. If the exercise of the option is conditional on the tenant's performance of his covenants under the lease, the landlord can insist on strict compliance with the covenants and can refuse to grant the renewal even where the tenant's breach of covenant is merely technical and causes no loss to the landlord.[3] It is common for tenants to limit the strict application of this principle by providing that the breach must be 'material' before it would prevent an option being exercised. 'Material' must be assessed by reference to the ability of the landlord to re-let or sell the property without delay or additional expenditure.[4]

1. *Woodall* v. *Clifton* [1905] 2 Ch 257.
2. Schedule 15, para 7(2). Also, a lease cannot be granted for a term that will start more than 21 years after the date of lease completion, see Law of Property Act 1925, s.149(3). A contract to grant such a lease will also be void.
3. See *West Country Cleaners (Falmouth) Ltd* v. *Saly* [1966] 3 All ER 210. See also *Little Ltd* v. *Courage Ltd*, *The Times*, 6 January 1995, CA. When construing the meaning of pre-conditions to the exercise of an option, in appropriate cases, reference can be made to the background situation that applied when the option was granted, see *William Page Co. Ltd* v. *BNP Paribas Securities Custody Bank Ltd* [2008] EWHC 2462.
4. *Fitzroy House Epworth Street (No.1) Ltd* v. *The Financial Times Ltd* [2006] EWCA Civ 329.

13.4. **Exercise of option**

13.4.1.   Unless there is provision to the contrary, time is automatically of the essence of the exercise of an option.[1]

13.4.2.   Following initial uncertainty Law of Property (Miscellaneous Provisions) Act 1989, s.2 has been interpreted as permitting the exercise of an option by a single document signed by the grantee only.[2]

13.4.3.   Exercise of an option or even holding-over at the end of a lease term may amount to a further grant for SDLT liability, in which case a return should be made within 30 days and tax paid (see A14.16).

1.   *United Scientific Holdings Ltd* v. *Burnley Borough Council* [1977] 2 All ER 62.
2.   *Spiro* v. *Glencrown Properties Ltd* [1991] 1 All ER 600; referred to in *Active Estates Ltd* v. *Parness* [2002] 36 EG 147.

K14. Variation of leases

14.1. Variation of lease

14.1.1. In practice most variations of leases are effected by deed. However, in some cases an informal variation of the terms of the lease (e.g. as to user) is only intended to be effective as between the landlord and tenant for the time being. Such a variation is commonly effected by a side letter or informal agreement.

14.1.2. Where a variation is made to a contract for the lease the variation may fall within the definition of a contract for the disposition of an interest in land within Law of Property (Miscellaneous Provisions) Act 1989, s.2. In essence, in this case the variation agreement must be in writing and signed by both parties and must contain all the terms of the contract between the parties or incorporate the document containing the terms by reference.[1] It is possible for the agreement to be in two identical parts each of which is signed by one of the parties.

14.1.3. In certain circumstances a side letter may be construed as creating a separate collateral agreement binding on the parties either by way of estoppel or as a contractual waiver. So that, for example, it may state that the tenant will only enter into a lease if the landlord agrees not to enforce some provision of it against the tenant. If this letter contains, in reality, a contractual term of a contract for the grant of the lease it will be unenforceable unless it complies with the requirements of Law of Property (Miscellaneous Provisions) Act 1989, s.2. However, if it can be shown that it was intended to have contractual effect separate from the contract for the grant of the lease[2] then, in this case, the collateral agreement will not have to comply with s.2, and in appropriate cases the collateral agreement may be enforced by the courts.[3]

14.1.4. Where a side letter varies the terms of a lease after it has been granted it may not have to comply with Law of Property (Miscellaneous Provisions) Act 1989, s.2.[4] In practice it is common for a variation effected by side letter to be personal to the tenant. In any event, the side letter should state whether the variation is to be for the benefit only of the signatories to the letter or is intended to bind and benefit their successors in title. Where the covenant is not personal the benefit and burden may run with the respective landlord and tenant interests.[5]

14.1.5. Where the landlord's title is registered, it is important to register any variation of a registered lease[6] (or one noted against the landlord's title), as otherwise it appears that the variation may not be binding on a purchaser. Although the point is unsettled, the effect of Land Registration Act 2002, s.29 appears to be that a variation must be registered in order to secure its priority and thus bind subsequent purchasers of the reversion and the tenant's estate. It may be, however, that the effect of section 29 only requires deeds of variation to be registered where they deal with 'an interest affecting the estate', i.e. a right affecting the title. Therefore a distinction could be drawn between amendments to what might be called general landlord and tenant covenants, which would not require registration, and those which create further interests in land, e.g. easements where the deed must be registered.[7] However, in many cases the tenant will be in actual occupation of the demised premises. Any interest he has as a result of a variation is presumably capable of having overriding status by virtue of his occupation and therefore it will be binding on purchasers of the reversion. In any event, the most prudent course of action is to register all deeds of variation, but when acquiring an interest under the lease or reversion to assume that not all variations may require registration to be binding, until the point is settled by case law.

1. See *Record* v. *Bell* [1991] 1 WLR 853; *McCausland* v. *Duncan Lawrie* [1996] NPC 94. Note generally *Jones* v. *Forest Fencing* [2001] PLSCS 249 and *Grossman* v. *Hooper* [2001] 2 EGLR 82. See also B11.2.3.
2. For the distinguishing features of a collateral agreement, see *Inntrepreneur Pub Company Ltd* v. *East Crown Ltd* [2000] 2 Lloyd's Rep 611.
3. See further *Business Environment Bow Lane Ltd* v. *Deanwater Estates Ltd* [2007] EWCA Civ 622.
4. *Tootal Clothing Ltd* v. *Guinea Properties Management Ltd* [1992] 41 EG 117.
5. See *Lotteryking Ltd* v. *AMEC Properties Ltd* [1995] 2 EGLR 13; *System Floors Ltd* v. *Ruralpride Ltd* [1995] 1 EGLR 48. Personal covenants do not appear to run with the respective landlord and tenant interests. As to this and the effect of Landlord and Tenant (Covenants) Act 1995, see *BHP Petroleum (Great Britain) Ltd* v. *Chesterfield Properties Ltd* [2002] 1 All ER 821.
6. See Land Registry Practice Guide 68 on amending deeds that effect dispositions of registered land, paras.5.4 and 5.5, for further details.
7. For an article discussing the issues, see 'Off the register' by Alan Riley, *SJ*, 26 March 2004. Also for an argument based on the fact that some landlord and tenant covenants are merely 'incidental to the estate' and therefore variations of them do not need registration as provided by Land Registration Act 2002, s.29(2)(b), see the article by Guy Fetherstonhaugh QC in *Estates Gazette*, 28 February 2008.

14.2. **Flats**

14.2.1. Any party to a long lease of a flat may apply to the Leasehold Valuation Tribunal under Part IV Landlord and Tenant Act 1987 as amended by Commonhold and Leasehold Reform Act 2002 for an order for the variation of the lease where the lease fails to make satisfactory provision for:

(a)   repair or maintenance of the flat or building;

(b)   insurance of the premises;

(c)   repair or maintenance of installations;

(d)   the provision of services;

(e)   recovery by one party to the lease from another party of expenditure incurred for the benefit of the other party;

(f)   computation of service charges under the lease.[1]

14.2.2.   The list of provisions which can be varied seemingly only applies to applications under section 35 of the 1987 Act, i.e. individual applications. It appears
that applications under section 37, made by a majority of tenants, are not
restricted to the items listed above.

14.2.3.   Similar but more limited provisions apply to leases of dwellings other than flats
in relation to insurance provisions only.

1.   This allows the Leasehold Valuation Tribunal to adjust the service charge only where it does not amount
to 100% of the cost of the services. It does not permit adjustment where the proportionate contributions
of different tenants are unfair. See *Morgan* v. *Fletcher* [2009] UKUT 186 (LC).

14.3.   Surrender and re-grant

Where the variation of the lease extends the premises contained in the original
demise or extends the length of the original term, it may be deemed to be a
surrender of the original lease and a re-grant of a new lease on the varied terms.[1]
The new lease created by the variation will be a 'new' tenancy and will therefore
be subject to the provisions of Landlord and Tenant (Covenants) Act 1995, even
though the former lease was not. It is preferable in these circumstances to
execute a new lease rather than a deed of variation. In the new lease the landlord
may need to consider whether he should include provisions (in a lease of
commercial premises) dealing with a range of matters including the terms on
which he will be prepared to consent to an assignment of the lease (including
provision for an authorised guarantee agreement) by the tenant.[2] He may also
wish to consider whether to exclude the new lease from the renewal provisions
of Part II Landlord and Tenant Act 1954.

1.   See *Friends Provident Life Office* v. *British Railways Board* [1995] 38 EG 106 and K10.1.5. For further
details concerning registered titles see Land Registry Practice Guides 28 (on extending leases) and 68
(on amending deeds that effect dispositions of registered land).
2.   See Landlord and Tenant (Covenants) Act 1995 and K10.

14.4.   Effect of variation on former tenant

14.4.1.   Where there has been a variation of a lease which variation the landlord has an
absolute right to refuse or where the lease has been altered after an assignment
so as to deprive the landlord of an absolute right of refusal (called a 'relevant
variation' under section 18 Landlord and Tenant (Covenants) Act 1995), a
former tenant is not liable to pay any amounts under the covenants in the lease
which are referable to the relevant variation. If, for example, a lease is varied
after an assignment and the rent payable under the lease is increased, a former
tenant who is sued by the landlord for rent unpaid by the assignee will only be
liable for the amount of rent which was payable by the tenant before the
variation and the former tenant cannot be held liable for the whole of the
increased rent. A guarantor's liability under a variation is co-extensive with that
of the tenant whose liability is being guaranteed (see K10.6.5).

14.5.   **Stamp Duty Land Tax**

14.5.1.   A variation of a lease may be notifiable and may give rise to liability to Stamp Duty Land Tax, particularly where the variation increases the rent but also in other circumstances.[1]

1. Finance Act 2003, Sched.17A paras.13–15A. The SDLT provisions relating to lease variations have been amended on a number of occasions to introduce anti-avoidance measures; see also A14.16.2.

K15. Sale of tenanted property

15.1.   Introduction

15.1.1.   Where a sale is subject to a tenancy, the procedure and steps to be taken equate with those of a vacant possession transaction, but a number of additional matters need to be considered. An energy performance certificate will usually have to be supplied to a potential buyer. See further A27.

15.2.   Disclosure of tenancies

15.2.1.   It is an implied (and frequently expressed) term of a contract for the sale of land that vacant possession will be given to the buyer on completion. As this will not be the case where the sale is of tenanted property, the contract must include an express term saying that the sale is subject to a tenancy or tenancies, and a copy of the relevant lease or leases (sometimes called tenancy agreements) should be supplied to the buyer with the draft contract. An express condition will also provide that the buyer, having been supplied with copies of the relevant agreements, shall be deemed to purchase with full knowledge of their contents. Standard Condition 3.3.2(a) and Standard Commercial Property Condition 4.1.2 contain provisions to this effect.

15.3.   Tenancy terminates before completion

15.3.1.   If the tenancy to which the sale is subject comes to an end between contract and completion, the seller should not re-let the property without first consulting the buyer and obtaining his instructions. To re-let the property without the buyer's permission would frequently put the seller in breach of his fiduciary duty to the buyer. Standard Condition 3.3.2(b) provides that the seller is to inform the buyer without delay if any tenancy ends; the seller is then to act as the buyer directs, provided the latter agrees to indemnify the seller against all loss and expense. Standard Condition 3.3.2(c) provides that after the contract is made, the seller is to inform the buyer without delay of any change in the tenancy terms. Standard Commercial Property Conditions 4.1.3 and 4.1.4 contain similar provisions.

15.4.   Buyer's solicitor

15.4.1.   The matters the buyer's solicitor should check include:

(a) the terms of the lease(s) or agreement(s) supplied by the seller's solicitor;

(b) the effect of any security of tenure legislation on the tenant(s);

(c) details of the landlord's obligations under the lease(s) or agreement(s), and in particular whether or not the seller has complied with such obligations;

(d) whether the tenant has complied with all his obligations under the lease or agreement (e.g. as to payment of rent and service charge) and, if not, what steps the seller has taken to enforce the agreement against the tenant;

(e) what variations have been made to the agreements and/or licences granted;

(f) details of any renewal applications or the exercise of an option made by the tenant;

(g) whether the tenants have a right of first refusal (see K9.4). This is also an important consideration for the seller's solicitor, since it is the seller who will be guilty of an offence if he fails to comply with the 1987 Act.

15.4.2. The buyer should be informed of the matters listed above and advised accordingly. If it is discovered that the landlord is in breach of any of his obligations (e.g. breach of a repairing covenant) the buyer's solicitor should require the seller to remedy the breach before completion. Alternatively the buyer may insist that the contract contains an express term providing that the seller will indemnify the buyer against liability for such breach since, on completion, the buyer will assume the seller's role as landlord and will thus be liable to the tenant for breaches of the landlord's covenants, even though such breach was committed before the buyer became the owner of the property.

15.4.3. If the tenant has the benefit of security of tenure legislation, consideration should be given to the question of whether the buyer, on termination of the contractual tenancy, would be able to recover vacant possession of the property if he so wished. In certain circumstances the buyer may be precluded from relying on some of the statutory grounds for possession, e.g. a landlord who purchases premises which are subject to a business tenancy within Landlord and Tenant Act 1954, Pt. II will be unable to regain possession under section 30(1)(*g*) of that Act until he has owned his interest in the property for a period of five years (see K7.4.3). On termination of some tenancies the landlord may also be liable to pay compensation to the outgoing tenant, and this contingency should also be discussed with the buyer (see K7.8).

15.4.4. Full enquiries must be made in relation to the amount of rent payable by the tenant, any statutory restrictions on the amount of rent recoverable, and the provisions for review or increase of that rent. Enquiries should also be made to ensure that the rent payable under the lease or agreement has been paid to the date of completion and that no arrears exist. Standard Condition 3.3.2(f) provides that the seller takes no responsibility for whether and how any legislation affects any tenancy and what rent is legally recoverable.

15.4.5. In certain circumstances a landlord who wishes to dispose of his reversionary interest in a block of flats must, before contracting to sell to a third party, first offer the reversion to the 'qualifying tenants'. Where these provisions apply, the buyer must ensure that the seller has correctly fulfilled his obligation to notify the qualifying tenants of their right to purchase the reversion, and that the time limit for the tenants' right to exercise this option has elapsed. See further K9.4.

15.4.6. Where a tenancy is of a dwelling, and the lease is for a term not exceeding seven years, the landlord may be responsible for repairing the structure and exterior of the premises under Landlord and Tenant Act 1985, ss.11–14. Where these sections apply, they are generally non-excludable and in appropriate cases the buyer should be advised of his potential liability under these provisions (see K1.7.2).

15.4.7. If on an assignment of the reversion the assignor is not to be released from his covenants by the tenant (or there is a possibility that the tenant may refuse to give consent to the landlord's release), the assignor may wish to consider taking an express indemnity covenant from the buyer together with a covenant by the buyer to notify the assignor of the buyer's sale of the reversion to a third party within a specified time of completion of that further sale. This is to enable the first assignor to serve notice on the tenant renewing his request to be released from liability under the landlord's covenants in the lease. The assignor must serve notice on the tenant before or within four weeks after completion of an assignment if he wishes to be released from the landlord's covenants in the lease. The buyer should therefore be required to notify the assignor within seven days of completion of a further sale in order to give the assignor sufficient time to serve his notice on the tenants within the four-week period. It may be possible for a restriction to be entered on the register to prevent registration of a purchase until this has been done. In practice this solution is likely to be impractical (see K10.10).

15.5. Completion

15.5.1. In addition to the usual requirements on completion of the purchase of a freehold property, the buyer should receive:

(a) the original lease(s) or tenancy agreement(s);

(b) an authority signed by the seller and addressed to the tenant(s), authorising the tenant(s) to pay future rent to the buyer.

15.6. After completion

15.6.1. Where the premises which have been purchased consist of a dwelling, Landlord and Tenant Act 1985, s.3 requires the new landlord (the buyer) to give written notice of the assignment and of his name and address to the tenant not later than the next day on which rent is payable, or if that is within two months of the date of the assignment, the end of the period of two months. The seller remains liable for breaches of covenant occurring until written notice of the assignment is given to the tenant by either the seller or the buyer.[1]

15.6.2. Landlord and Tenant Act 1987, s.48 also requires the landlord to provide the tenant with an address in England and Wales for service of notices. This section applies where the premises consist of or include a dwelling (including an agricultural holding)[2] but not to premises to which Landlord and Tenant Act 1954, Pt. II applies.[3] Further, until such notice is given, any rent or service charge under the lease is treated as not being due, and is thus not recoverable by action by the buyer. It is therefore in the interests of both seller and buyer to ensure that such notice is given promptly after completion. Notice should be given to the tenant in duplicate, the tenant being requested to sign one copy and return it to the landlord who will, on receipt of the tenant's signed copy notice, have evidence of compliance with this provision.

15.6.3. Section 47 Landlord and Tenant Act 1987 requires the landlord's name and address to be given on all demands for rent or any other sums payable under the tenancy. This will not satisfy the requirements of section 48.

15.6.4. However, the Act does not make it clear to whom and at what point the notice should be given. The safest course is to give a section 48 notice to the original tenant on the grant of a new lease and to the assignee following every assignment of the lease.

15.6.5. Since most leases contain a covenant by the tenant to give the landlord a notice of assignment within a specified time after the disposition, the section 48 notice should be given to the new assignee as soon as the change of tenant becomes known. Alternatively managing agents or landlords should print the notice on every rent or service charge demand.

15.6.6. Section 48 notices do not have to be served personally on the tenant; delivery by post is sufficient.[4]

---

1. This notice must also state whether the disposal is one to which the Landlord and Tenant Act 1987 applies (see K9). Failure to do so is a criminal offence; see Landlord and Tenant Act 1985, s.3A.
2. *Dallhold Estates (UK) Pty Ltd* v. *Lindsey Trading Properties Inc.*, *The Times*, 15 December 1993, CA.
3. See Landlord and Tenant Act 1987, s.46.
4. Landlord and Tenant Act 1987, s.54.

15.7.   Apportionment on sale of a reversion

15.7.1. The Law Society's Conveyancing and Land Law Committee has prepared a formula for the apportionment of rent on sale of a reversion (see Appendix IV.2).

L. COMMONHOLD

L1. Commonhold

1.1. Introduction

1.1.1.   Commonhold is a new form of freehold land ownership. It was introduced by Commonhold and Leasehold Reform Act 2002 ('the Act'), Part 1. The commonhold provisions of the Act came into force on 27 September 2004. Commonhold Regulations 2004 ('the Regulations') include the prescribed documentation. Commonhold (Land Registration) Rules 2004 (SI 2004/1830) ('the Rules') are also relevant.

1.1.2.   Commonhold is a system under which land is divided into separate freehold units, with common property owned by a company limited by guarantee, of which the unit owners are members.

1.1.3.   The Act overcomes the need to create a leasehold structure for buildings with multiple ownership by permitting the enforceability of positive obligations in a freehold environment.

1.1.4.   Commonhold was created principally as an alternative for blocks of flats, but it can be applied to various types of schemes. In other jurisdictions similar title systems are used for apartments, offices, industrial and retail parks and hotels.

1.1.5.   Commonhold land may only be created out of land registered with freehold title absolute. Certain land may not be registered as commonhold land, namely certain types of agricultural land, flying freeholds (except where being added to land which is already registered as commonhold) and land which is a contingent estate.

1.2. Standard documents

1.2.1.   The key document that creates the rights and obligations of unit-holders and the commonhold association is the commonhold community statement (CCS), which is registered against the title of each unit and the common parts of the commonhold and binds unit-holders, the commonhold association and in some respects tenants. The CCS sets out *inter alia* the percentage of commonhold assessment (service charge) and voting rights allocated to each unit, local rules regarding the use of commonhold units and common parts, and the permitted use for each unit.

1.2.2. The Regulations prescribe a form of CCS and the memorandum and articles of association for commonhold associations. Changes from the standard document must be clearly delineated, and the Regulations set out the requirements in this respect. Certain parts of the documents may not be changed.

1.2.3. The Act prohibits certain types of provisions being included in a CCS. For example, a CCS may not prevent or restrict the transfer of a unit. Some changes require special resolutions or the consent of specific persons: for example, an amendment to the permitted use of a commonhold unit requires a special resolution and the prior written consent of the unit-holder.

1.2.4. Any amendment to the CCS will not take effect until the amended CCS is registered at the Land Registry.

1.3. Creating a commonhold

1.3.1. The steps involved in creating a commonhold are:

- incorporation of the commonhold association;
- applying for registration of the land as commonhold land; and
- activation of the commonhold.

1.4. Incorporation of a commonhold association

1.4.1. A commonhold association is a company limited by guarantee. Each association must have a unique name, which must end with 'Commonhold Association Ltd' or the Welsh equivalent.

1.4.2. The liability of members on a winding up is capped at £1.

1.4.3. On applying for incorporation, the applicant must produce the following to Companies House:

(a) a statutory declaration that the requirements of Companies Act 1985 have been complied with in regard to registration;

(b) the memorandum and articles of association; and

(c) a completed Form 10 – this form sets out the details of the first directors and secretary and the registered office of the commonhold association.

1.4.4. The memorandum of association must specify the land in respect of which the association is to exercise functions. This should include any land to be brought into the commonhold under phased development.

1.5. Applying for registration at the Land Registry

1.5.1. The application to the Land Registry to register land as commonhold land must be made in Form CM1 and must be accompanied by the documents referred to in the form. These include a certified copy of the certificate of incorporation of the commonhold association, and two certified copies of the CCS with the relevant plans. The plans must comply with the Land Registry's technical requirements. The Land Registry offers a free service to have plans approved prior to formal registration.

1.5.2. The consent of the following parties is required to register land as commonhold land:

(a) the freeholder;

(b) any registered mortgagees of the freehold;

(c) any leaseholders with leases of more than 21 years;

(d) any mortgagees of such leases; and

(e) any other prescribed persons.

1.5.3. The consent of the holder of a lease of 21 years or less is required unless the tenant is given a replacement lease on the same terms. It is necessary to protect the interest of the tenant at the Land Registry by notice as the original lease will be extinguished on registration.

1.5.4. Consent is required to be given in prescribed form.

1.5.5. Consent may be dispensed with by court order in limited circumstances, namely where a person:

(a) cannot be identified after all reasonable efforts have been made to ascertain the identity of the person required to give consent;

(b) cannot be traced after all reasonable efforts have been made to trace him; or

(c) has been sent the request for consent and all reasonable efforts have been made to obtain a response but the person has not responded.

There is no right to challenge the reasonableness of refusal to give consent.

1.5.6. Consents may be given subject to conditions and will lapse if no application is made within 12 months of the giving of consent.

1.5.7. Compensation is payable to a tenant where a lease is extinguished without the consent of the holder of the lease. The liability rests with the person whose interest is most proximate to the extinguished lease.

1.5.8. Deregistration is possible where land is improperly registered as commonhold land. This requires a court order. The registered proprietor may also deregister commonhold land during the transitional period. The consent of any party required to register the land as commonhold land must be obtained.

Types of registration

1.5.9. There are two types of registration, registration without unit-holders and registration with unit-holders.

1.5.10. A registration without unit-holders is appropriate where a commonhold is set up for a new development and sales are to be completed following registration of the commonhold. It is also appropriate for the conversion of a property to commonhold where the land is owned by a single person.

1.5.11. A registration with unit-holders is appropriate where a property is already owned or occupied by separate parties and following registration each of those parties is to own one or more units, or for a joint venture where one party provides the land and the intention is that the property will be subdivided in separate ownership immediately on registration.

1.6. **Activation**

1.6.1. For a registration without unit-holders, the commonhold will enter a transitional period on registration. During this time the applicant will remain the registered proprietor of the whole of the freehold estate in the commonhold land and the rights and duties conferred and imposed by the CCS do not apply. The transitional period will come to an end once one (but not all) of the units is transferred to a third party, and when it does the common parts will vest in the commonhold association.

1.6.2. For a registration with unit-holders, the common parts will vest in the commonhold association and the provisions of the commonhold community statement will apply immediately on registration.

1.6.3. In either case, a separate title for each of the units and the common parts will be created on registration of the land as commonhold land.

1.7. **Conversion**

1.7.1. Tenants who wish to convert to a commonhold scheme will first have to enfranchise and subsequently register the land as commonhold land.

1.8. Effect of registration on existing dealings

1.8.1. All leases affecting the land will be extinguished on activation of the commonhold. In the case of a registration without unit-holders this will occur at the end of the transitional period. For a registration with unit-holders this will occur immediately on registration.

1.8.2. Charges over the common parts will be extinguished (to the extent that they relate to the common parts) once the commonhold association is registered as proprietor of the common parts. A charge over the whole of a commonhold unit will survive registration of the commonhold in so far as it relates to the unit. A charge which relates to part of a commonhold unit will however be extinguished on registration to the extent that it relates to that part of the unit.

1.8.3. Other entries such as notices, cautions or easements will continue on registration.

1.9. Acting for the buyer

1.9.1. The buyer's solicitor should review the commonhold documentation, namely the commonhold community statement, and the memorandum and articles of association of the commonhold association. These documents may be obtained from the Land Registry.

1.9.2. If the property is being acquired in joint names, the buyer's solicitor should advise the buyer that only one of them may be recorded as a member of the commonhold association. If no nomination is made, the secretary of the commonhold association will enter as a member the person whose name first appears on the proprietorship register of the commonhold unit.

1.9.3. Within 14 days of completion, the buyer's solicitor should give the secretary of the commonhold association notice of the transfer. Form 10 should be used if the transfer is of the whole of a unit, Form 11 if the transfer is of part of a unit and Form 12 if the transfer occurs by operation of law.

1.9.4. The buyer's solicitor should review the commonhold community statement in detail. Relevant matters for consideration are:

(a) the description/identification of the unit;

(b) any rights which benefit or burden the unit;

(c) the proportion of commonhold assessment and reserve fund assessments allocated to the unit;

(d) the votes allocated to the unit;

(e) any restrictions on use and duties in respect of maintenance and repair;

(f) rules relating to the use of the common parts;

(g)   insurance provisions; and

(h)   any development rights.

1.9.5.   The buyer's solicitor should raise enquiries in relation to the operation of the commonhold, and the common parts. Relevant enquiries would include:

(a)   Financial affairs of the commonhold association:

- What have the previous assessments been? (The buyer's solicitor should note whether there have been any unusually small or large assessments.)

- Are there are outstanding assessments in relation to the unit, or other units? (Outstanding assessments for other units could cause cash flow problems for the association.)

- Have reserve funds been set up? If so, when and what is the balance of these funds? Have these funds been called upon?

(b)   The administration of the commonhold association:

- Have meetings been held as required by the articles of association?

- Do the minutes identify any disputes?

- Have there been any amendments made to the CCS which are yet unregistered?

- Is there a management agreement in place? If so, what are the terms?

(c)   Management of the common parts:

- Do the records of the commonhold association identify any defects in the common parts, or necessary repairs?

- What are the terms of the insurance for the common parts? Have there been any claims in relation to the insurance?

1.9.6.   The buyer's solicitor should also ensure that the contract requires the seller to procure a commonhold unit information certificate. The standard CCS permits a unit-holder to give a notice to the commonhold association to provide a commonhold unit information certificate in respect of his unit. This certificate (in Form 9) sets out the arrears of commonhold assessment, reserve fund levies and interest due in respect of the unit. The benefit of the certificate is that the commonhold association may only recover from the buyer the amount specified in the certificate for the period up to and including the date of the certificate.

1.9.7.   The buyer's solicitor should ensure that any outstanding monies due to the commonhold association are paid on completion, as subject to the comments above regarding the commonhold unit information certificate, the incoming unit-holder will become liable.

1.10. Acting for the seller

1.10.1. The seller's solicitor should ensure that the seller provides all information necessary to answer any enquiries raised by the buyer's solicitor regarding the commonhold. The articles of association permit (subject to any contrary resolution of the commonhold association) a member of the commonhold association to inspect and be provided with a copy of any relevant documents and record of the association upon payment of a reasonable charge for copying.

1.10.2. The seller's solicitor should also ensure that any outstanding monies due to the commonhold association are paid on completion, as the seller will not be released from liability for such arrears on transfer of the unit.

1.11. Acting for the lender

1.11.1. Not all members of CML are prepared to lend on commonhold units. Part 2 of the CML Lenders' Handbook which sets out the requirements of individual lenders specifies whether a particular member of CML is prepared to accept part of a commonhold as security.

1.11.2. The commonhold specific requirements of the CML Lenders' Handbook which the solicitor will have to comply with include ensuring that the commonhold association has obtained insurance in accordance with the lender's requirements; a commonhold unit information certificate is obtained; the commonhold assessment is paid to the date of completion; and that the CCS does not include any material restrictions on occupation or use.

1.11.3. The CCS must also contain a provision requiring, in the event of voluntary termination of the commonhold, the termination statement to provide that the unit-holders will ensure that any mortgage secured on the unit is repaid on termination. This provision is not included in the model CCS so solicitors will need to ensure that it has been added.

1.11.4. A company search should be carried out to verify the existence of the commonhold association, that it has not been wound up and that there is no registered indication that it is to be wound up.

1.11.5. Notice of transfer of the commonhold unit and notice of the mortgage should be given to the commonhold association within 14 days of completion.

1.12. Leasing

1.12.1. Restrictions can apply to the letting of commonhold units.

1.12.2. A residential commonhold unit (i.e. one which the CCS requires to be used only for residential or for residential and incidental purposes) may not be leased at a premium, for a term longer than seven years, or under an option or agreement which would result in a term of longer than seven years. An exception applies for the grant of a lease of up to 21 years to the holder of a lease which has been extinguished on registration of the land as commonhold land. The lease must be on the same terms as the extinguished lease.

1.12.3. No restrictions are imposed on lettings of non-residential units. However it is open for a CCS to impose restrictions, such as restrictions on the permitted use.

1.12.4. A lease of a commonhold unit may not require the tenant to make payments to the commonhold association in discharge of payment due to be made by the unit-holder under the CCS. However, the model CCS includes provisions permitting the diversion of rent where an owner has failed to pay commonhold assessments or reserve fund assessments.

Acting for the landlord

1.12.5. Before granting a lease of a commonhold unit, the prospective landlord must give the tenant a copy of the CCS (including plans relevant to the unit) and a notice in Form 13 informing the tenant that he will be required to comply with provisions in the CCS on grant of the lease. If the landlord fails to do so, and the tenant suffers loss as a result of an obligation in the CCS being enforced against the tenant, the landlord can be liable to reimburse the tenant unless the obligation is reproduced in the lease.

1.12.6. A solicitor acting for a landlord should therefore get an acknowledgement from the tenant that the tenant has received these documents before the lease is entered into.

1.12.7. A solicitor acting for a landlord should also ensure that notice of the tenancy (in Form 14) is given to the commonhold association within 14 days of the grant of the lease.

Acting for the tenant

1.12.8. A solicitor acting for a tenant should review the terms of the CCS to identify whether:

(a) the CCS imposes any conditions in respect of letting;

(b) there are any rights attaching to the unit which should be included in the tenancy (for example, limited use rights);

(c) there are any rights granted to the commonhold association in relation to the unit (for example rights of entry, or rights to connect to services in the unit);

(d) there are restrictions on use in the CCS which may interfere with the use permitted under the lease; and

(e)   the CCS contains any other provisions which could interfere with the beneficial use and occupation of the property (for example, restrictions on signage or alterations).

1.12.9.   The solicitor should in particular bring to the tenant's attention the dispute resolution provisions of the CCS and the provisions dealing with the diversion of rent.

1.12.10.   The solicitor should also consider imposing restrictions on the landlord's right to consent to variations to the CCS (for example, amendments to the permitted use) without the consent of the tenant.

Assignment of a lease

1.12.11.   Before assigning a tenancy in a commonhold unit, a tenant must give the prospective assignee a copy of the CCS (including plans relevant to the unit) and a notice in Form 15 informing the assignee that he will be required to comply with the provisions in the CCS on assignment of the lease. If the outgoing tenant fails to comply with this and the assignee suffers loss as a result of an obligation in the CCS being enforced against the assignee, the outgoing tenant can be liable to reimburse the assignee unless the obligation is reproduced in the lease.

1.12.12.   A solicitor acting for an assignor should therefore obtain an acknowledgement from the assignee that the assignee has received these documents before the assignment is entered into.

1.13.   **Running a commonhold**

1.13.1.   A commonhold is managed by the commonhold association, although it will primarily be managed by the board. Some issues must be dealt with by the commonhold association in general meeting. Certain types of transactions and particular amendments require resolutions of the commonhold association in general.

1.13.2.   Each commonhold association must hold an annual general meeting each year unless dispensed with under Companies Act 1985. The quorum required for a meeting will be set out in the articles of association.

1.13.3.   Members vote either by a show of hands or a poll. A resolution is decided by show of hands unless a poll is demanded before the declaration of the result of the show of hands. On a poll each member has the number of votes allocated in the CCS in respect of the unit. Flying resolutions can be made, without the need for a meeting. Most matters require ordinary resolutions, but some matters require special or unanimous resolutions or special majorities.

1.13.4.   A commonhold association has a duty to manage the common parts of its commonhold. It is required to keep the common parts in good repair (including decorating them and putting them into sound condition), and insure them.

1.14. Dealing with the common parts

1.14.1. The commonhold association is free to sell or deal with its interest in the common parts. It may grant easements or leases over common parts. Charges over common parts are not permitted save for legal mortgages approved by unanimous resolution prior to the grant of the mortgage.

1.14.2. Alterations to common parts require the approval of the commonhold association by ordinary resolution.

1.14.3. The commonhold association must insure the common parts to their full rebuilding and reinstatement costs against loss or damage by fire and such other risks specified in paragraph 5 of Annexe 4 of the CCS. The CCS may impose obligations in respect of insurance of commonhold units.

1.15. Financial management

1.15.1. The commonhold association will raise income in the form of commonhold assessments and reserve fund levies. Other sources of income may include rental derived from the letting of common property.

1.15.2. Before raising a commonhold assessment, the directors must give the unit-holders a notice of the proposed commonhold assessment in Form 1. Unit-holders are entitled to make representations to the commonhold association regarding the amount of the assessment within one month of when the notice is given. The directors are required to consider the representations, and are then to issue a notice specifying the payment due.

1.15.3. Reserve funds may be set up to finance the repair and maintenance of common parts. The directors must try to ensure that unnecessary reserves are not accumulated.

1.16. Administration

1.16.1. The commonhold association is required to retain various records including minutes of meetings, a register of members and other registers. Subject to other statutory requirements, the records are required to be kept for a minimum of three years. A commonhold association must maintain financial records in accordance with the requirements of Companies Act 1985. In most cases commonhold associations will not have to have their accounts audited as they will qualify as small companies under Companies Act 1985.

1.16.2. Commonhold associations have to lodge annual returns and lodge notices of any change to the directors or secretary or registered office of the commonhold association. Normal company law rules regarding notice of certain types of resolution also apply.

1.17. **Commonhold units**

1.17.1. A commonhold must consist of at least two commonhold units. The extent of each unit is defined by the CCS and the plans annexed. A commonhold unit may not include the structure and exterior of a building where a building contains all or part of more than one commonhold unit. Therefore in a block of flats the structure and exterior of the building must form part of the common parts. However for a scheme consisting of a series of stand alone buildings, the structure and exterior of the buildings may constitute part of a commonhold unit.

1.17.2. A CCS may not prevent a unit-holder from transferring his unit or place restrictions on such transfer.

1.18. **Further information**

1.18.1. The former Department for Constitutional Affairs has published:

- a guidance paper on the drafting of a commonhold community statement: the paper includes specimen local rules and is intended to promote uniformity in the drafting of provisions for individual commonholds;

- non-statutory guidance on Commonhold Regulations 2004.

These are available on the archive of the Department's website at **www.dca.gov.uk**.

1.18.2. Land Registry Practice Guide 60 provides more information on the requirements relating to the registration of commonhold and dealings in commonhold land.

1.18.3. Form TA9 Commonhold Information may be used to supplement the normal pre-contract enquiries.

M. DELAY AND REMEDIES

M1. Delayed completion

1.1.	Breach of contract	1.4.	Compensation for delay
1.2.	Time of the essence	1.5.	Service of a notice to
1.3.	Anticipating delay		complete

1.1. Breach of contract

1.1.1. Any delay in completion beyond the contractual date will be a breach of contract entitling the innocent party to damages for his loss, but will not entitle him immediately to terminate the contract unless time was of the essence of the completion date.[1]

1. *Raineri* v. *Miles* [1981] AC 1050.

1.2. Time of the essence

1.2.1. At common law time is impliedly of the essence of the completion date where the subject matter of the contract makes it so, e.g. on the sale of a business as a going concern, or the sale of a wasting asset.[1] In such cases time will therefore be of the essence unless this implication is expressly negatived by a condition to the contrary in the contract.

1.2.2. By Standard Condition 6.1 and Standard Commercial Property Condition 8.1 time is not of the essence of the contract (but can be made so by express contractual condition) unless a notice to complete has been served.

1. See *Pips (Leisure Productions) Ltd* v. *Walton* (1982) 43 P&CR 415 (sale of a 21-year lease). It was also stated *obiter* in *Raineri* v. *Miles* [1981] AC 1050 that time might be considered to be of the essence in chain transactions.

1.3. Anticipating delay

1.3.1. Delay may occur owing to events outside the immediate control of the parties and their solicitors, e.g. postal delays or late receipt of funds from a lender. In such cases there is usually little doubt that completion will take place but it may be postponed for a few days beyond the contractual completion date.

1.3.2. Where delay is anticipated the client, his lender and the other party's solicitor should be informed of the anticipated delay as soon as possible, and of its likely duration and, subject to the solicitor's duty of confidentiality, of the reason for the delay. This is particularly important in chain transactions where the delay in completion of one link in the chain may have serious consequences on the remainder of the transactions in the chain.

1.3.3.   Any delay in completion may result in an adjustment being made to the repayment figure due on a seller's existing mortgage. This matter must, therefore, be resolved with the solicitors acting for the lender or the lender himself. Similarly, an advance cheque issued by the buyer's lender is usually delivered subject to the condition that it is used to complete the transaction within a stated number of days of its issue, failing which it must be returned to the lender and a fresh advance cheque issued in time for the rearranged completion date. Such an instruction must be observed by the solicitor acting for the buyer's lender.

1.3.4.   Delay in completing one transaction may affect the client's ability to complete a related sale or purchase. If, e.g. completion of the client's sale becomes delayed, he will not have the necessary funds available with which to complete his synchronised purchase transaction, and failure to complete that purchase on the contractual date for completion will be a breach of contract involving the client at the very least in the payment of compensation for the delay. The client should be advised of the delay and of its consequences.

1.3.5.   Although the solicitor should do his best to ensure that any breach of contract is avoided, e.g. by arranging bridging finance so that the purchase transaction can be completed on time, he is also under a duty to act in his own client's best interests, and in these circumstances completion of the purchase with the assistance of bridging finance may not always represent the best course of action for the client to take. In the example under discussion, the client would probably not be able to utilise the advance cheque from his new mortgage to complete the purchase since there will commonly be a condition attached to it that the advance is conditional on the client's existing mortgage first being discharged. Not being able to utilise the new mortgage advance may result in a large sum being needed by way of bridging finance with a possible consequent heavy commitment to interest on the loan. Alternatively the client may choose to use bridging finance to pay off his first mortgage, thus releasing the mortgage funds for his purchase. Secondly, the client will be in the position of owning two houses until the sale of the first is completed, and if the sale transaction is not completed within a short space of time, this too will represent an onerous commitment for the client.

1.3.6.   The reason for the delay on the sale transaction and the likely period of delay in its completion must be taken into account when advising the client whether to complete the purchase on time, or to delay completion of the purchase thereby putting himself into breach of that contract. In the converse situation, where the sale can proceed but the purchase is delayed, completion of the sale transaction on the due date will result in the client becoming homeless for an uncertain length of time with consequent problems relating to alternative accommodation for the period of the delay, storage of furniture and other similar problems.

1.3.7.   Any delay in completion will be a breach of contract for which the innocent party could recover damages but, where the delay is short, the amount of loss sustained by the breach is unlikely to justify the time and expense of an action for breach of contract. Compensation provisions under the contract may provide adequate redress for the innocent party in these circumstances. If not, an action for breach may be brought, but the amount of compensation received under the contract has to be credited against the amount claimed as damages.

1.4. Compensation for delay

1.4.1. The application of the common law provisions relating to payment of compensation for delay might not provide the innocent party with sufficient financial compensation for his loss and are usually replaced by specific contractual provisions providing for compensation. In default of a specific contractual clause dealing with the matter, the common law provisions as set out below would apply.

Common law provisions

1.4.2. In addition to any action for damages, where the delay is the buyer's fault:

(a) the buyer pays the outgoings on the property from the contractual date for completion;

(b) the buyer is entitled to keep the income from the property (if any) from the date of completion;

(c) from the contractual date of completion, the buyer pays interest to the seller on the balance of the purchase price at the general equitable rate.[1]

1.4.3. Where the delay is the seller's fault:

(a) the seller remains responsible for the outgoings on the property;

(b) he is entitled to keep whichever sum is the lesser of:

(i) the net income of the property; or

(ii) the amount of interest payable by the buyer, calculated as under (c) in M1.4.2.

1.4.4. Since there will be no income generated by a property which is being sold with vacant possession, the application of these rules effectively means that the buyer has to pay interest when the delay is his fault, but not when the delay is caused by the seller.

1.4.5. Standard Condition 7.3 provides for the payment of compensation at the 'contract rate' which is defined by Condition 1.1.1(e) as being 'the Law Society's interest rate from time to time in force' (see Appendix V.1), although the parties are free to substitute a different rate by special condition if they so wish.

1.4.6.   Under this condition, compensation is assessed using the 'concept of relative fault', so that whoever is most at fault for the delay pays the compensation; it is not simply a matter of the party who delayed in actual completion being liable to pay compensation. To calculate the liability for compensation, it is necessary to refer to the timetable of events contained in Conditions 4.3.1 and 4.3.2 in order to establish whether the delay in completion has been caused by a delay in carrying out a procedural step earlier in the transaction. Delay occurring before completion is assessed by reference to the definition of a 'working day' contained in Condition 1.1.1(m) but this definition ceases to apply once completion date has passed, after which every day's delay counts towards the liability for compensation. Having apportioned the delay between the parties, the party who is most at fault for the delay pays compensation to the other for the period by which his delay exceeds the delay of the other party. Compensation under this provision is neither additional to nor in substitution for common law damages, but merely on account.

1.4.7.   By Standard Conditions 6.1.2 and 6.1.3, where the sale is with vacant possession and the money due on completion is not paid by 2 pm on the day of actual completion (or such other time as may have been agreed by the parties), for the purposes of the compensation provisions only, completion is deemed to have taken place on the next following working day unless the seller had not vacated the property by 2 pm (or other agreed time). If this time limit is not complied with the buyer may find himself liable to pay compensation to the seller under Standard Condition 7.3.

1.4.8.   Condition 7.3.4 provides for cases in which the property is tenanted. It allows the seller to recover the income from the property in addition to any compensation to which it may be entitled under condition 7.3.1. While a provision to this effect is commonly encountered in contracts for the sale of commercial property, there is thought to be a risk that, if challenged, it would be struck down as a penalty. A particular source of difficulty is that the object of the compensation is to place the seller in the position it would have been in if the contract had been completed on time: if, however, the contract had been completed on time, the seller would not have received any income from the property following completion date. The seller may, therefore, need to satisfy the court that the inclusion of the provision is justified by the particular circumstances of the sale.

1.4.9.   Standard Commercial Property Condition 9.3 contains the compensation provisions under this form of contract. Condition 9.3 does not operate on the concept of relative fault and effectively only the buyer can be called upon to pay compensation for delayed completion. Where the seller is at fault the buyer is left to his remedy at common law, i.e. an action for damages.

1.4.10.   The seller is not entitled to compensation if he exercises his right to rescind the contract following the buyer's failure to comply with a notice to complete, but may be entitled to forfeit the deposit.[2]

1. According to *Esdaile* v. *Stephenson* (1822) 1 Sim & St 122, the general equitable rate is a mere 4% per annum, but more recently in *Bartlett* v. *Barclays Bank Trust Co. Ltd* [1980] Ch 515 interest was awarded based on the rate allowed on the court's short-term investment account under Administration of Justice Act 1965.
2. *Ng* v. *Ashley King (Developments) Ltd* [2010] EWHC 456.

1.5. Service of a notice to complete

1.5.1. Where it appears that the delay in completion is not likely to be resolved quickly (or at all), consideration may be given to the service of a notice to complete which will have the effect of making time of the essence of the contract so that if completion does not take place on the new completion date specified in the notice the aggrieved party may then terminate the contract forthwith, forfeit or recover his deposit (as the case may be) with accrued interest and commence an action for damages to recover his loss. This then gives the aggrieved party the certainty of knowing that on a stated date he can make a definite decision either to look for a new property to purchase (if a buyer), or resell the property elsewhere (as a seller). It must, however, be remembered that making time of the essence imposes a condition which binds both parties. If, therefore, between the date of service and new date for completion as specified by the notice, unforeseen events occur which result in the previously aggrieved party being unable to complete on the new date, the previously defaulting party could turn round and terminate the contract, leaving the aggrieved party in breach of contract himself. For this reason a notice to complete should never be served as an idle threat. The server must be sure that he will be able to comply with the new completion date himself before serving the notice.[1]

1.5.2. At common law, the service of a valid notice to complete can only be achieved where the notice specifies a 'reasonable time' for the new completion date, and the party serving the notice is himself ready, able and willing to complete. Both of these conditions present considerable difficulties for the server since it is difficult to assess the 'reasonable time' for the new completion date – a few days ahead may seem quite reasonable to a seller who is anxious to complete the sale, but a few weeks may seem more reasonable to a buyer whose mortgage arrangements have just fallen through. A seller may not be 'ready, able and willing' to complete if he has not discharged his subsisting mortgage over the property.[2] Since it is common practice for a seller to discharge his mortgage after completion, using part of the proceeds of sale with which to make repayment, this condition presents particular difficulties for a seller who wishes to serve a notice on a defaulting buyer. However, a seller will be 'ready, able and willing' to complete even though some of the administrative arrangements have yet to be made.[3] Since the decision in *Behzadi* v. *Shaftesbury Hotels Ltd*[4] it seems that a notice to complete (making time of the essence) can be served immediately contractual completion date passes – there is no need for there to have been 'unreasonable delay'.

1.5.3. The contract normally provides specifically for the service of a notice to complete, such clause being drafted to circumvent the common law problems outlined in the preceding paragraph. Standard Condition 6.8 and Standard Commercial Property Condition 8.8 are such conditions, and provided that the notice expressly refers to the fact that it is served under the provisions of the relevant condition, its service will be valid, the common law requirements being ousted by the specific contractual provisions.

1.5.4.　　Standard Condition 6.8.2 and Standard Commercial Property Condition 8.8.2 provide that on service of a notice to complete, completion must take place within 10 working days (exclusive of the date of service) and makes time of the essence of the contract.[5]

1.5.5.　　Standard Condition 6.8.3 requires a buyer who has paid less than a 10% deposit to pay the balance of the full 10% immediately on receipt of a notice to complete. No equivalent provision is contained in the Standard Commercial Property Conditions.

1.5.6.　　The parties' rights and obligations where a valid notice has been served but not complied with are governed by Standard Conditions 7.5 and 7.6 and Standard Commercial Property Conditions 9.5 and 9.6.

1.5.7.　　Once served, a notice to complete cannot be withdrawn.

1.5.8.　　If compliance with a first notice to complete is waived there is no reason why a second notice to complete, specifying an extended period for compliance, should not be served on expiry of the initial notice, or why the period for compliance with a first notice should not be extended by mutual agreement (provided it is done in writing so as to comply with Law of Property (Miscellaneous Provisions) Act 1989), but there is some doubt whether time would remain of the essence in such circumstances.

1.5.9.　　Non-compliance with a notice to complete gives the aggrieved party the right to terminate the contract, but is not in itself an automatic termination of the contract.

1.5.10.　　If it is necessary to serve a notice in a situation where the delay is caused by the death of one of the contracting parties, the notice should be addressed to the deceased and his personal representatives at the deceased's last known address. A further copy of the notice should be served on the Public Trustee.

1.　See *Northstar Land Ltd* v. *Maitland Brooks and Jacqueline Brooks* [2006] EWCA Civ 756.
2.　*Cole* v. *Rose* [1978] 3 All ER 1121.
3.　*Aero Properties Holdings Ltd* v. *Citycrest Properties Ltd* [2002] All ER (D) 77 (Feb) and *Midill (97PL) Ltd* v. *Park Lane Estates Ltd and Gomba International Investments Ltd* [2008] EWHC 18 (Ch).
4.　[1992] Ch 1.
5.　In *Northstar* v. *Brooks* an issue was raised as to whether, following the service of a notice to complete, the parties had to complete by the end of normal office hours or had until midnight on the tenth working day. The judge at first instance concluded that, in the absence of a special arrangement, the deadline was 'at 5.30 pm or 6.00 pm or perhaps a few minutes later' (*Northstar Land Ltd* v. *Maitland Brooks and Jacqueline Brooks* [2005] EWHC 1919 (Ch)). In the Court of Appeal, Ward LJ reserved his position on this, stating that he was 'anxious not to give a judgment of this Court which might be taken as a judgment of general and inflexible application to all conveyancing transactions'.

M2. Rescission

2.1.   Introduction

2.1.1.   The word rescission is used here in the context of contracts which involve a vitiating element, e.g. misrepresentation, fraud, mistake, and refers to the remedy which is available in these circumstances.

2.1.2.   Rescission denotes the restoration of the parties to their pre-contract position by 'undoing' the contract and balancing the position of the parties with the payment of compensation by one party to the other. Damages in the conventional sense of that word are not payable since there will have been no breach of contract.

2.1.3.   Since rescission is an equitable remedy, its operation is subject to the general equitable bars which are set out in more detail in M4.2.

2.2.   Contractual right to rescind

2.2.1.   No right to rescind exists except where there is a vitiating element in the contract or a specific contractual right to rescind. Therefore, unless there is a breach of contract entitling one party to terminate his obligations under it, the contract must be performed.

2.2.2.   A right to rescind may be given by a specific contractual condition which will specify the circumstances in which the right is to operate and the parties' rights and obligations in the event of rescission taking place. Such a right may be granted, e.g. where the contract is conditional on the fulfilment of a condition.

2.2.3.   Under the Standard Conditions of Sale, the right to rescind is available in four situations:

(a)   where risk in the property remains with the seller and the property is rendered unusable between contract and completion (Condition 5.1.2);

(b)   for misrepresentation (Condition 7.1.3);

(c)   where a licence to assign is not forthcoming (Condition 8.3.3);

(d)   where either the buyer or the seller has failed to comply with a notice to complete (Condition 7.5 and 7.6).

2.2.4.   The Standard Commercial Property Conditions contain similar provisions with the exception of (a) above (see Conditions 9.1, 10.3 and 9.5 and 9.6 respectively).

2.2.5.   Where the right to rescind is exercised under one of the Conditions referred to in M2.2.3 or M2.2.4, the parties' rights on rescission are governed by Standard Condition 7.2 and Standard Commercial Property Condition 9.2 which provide for the repayment of the deposit to the buyer with accrued interest, the return of documents to the seller and the cancellation of any registration of the contract at the buyer's expense. The seller is not entitled to compensation under Standard Condition 7.3 or Standard Commercial Property Condition 9.3, although interest may be awarded under section 35A Senior Courts Act 1981.[1]

1. *Ng* v. *Ashley King (Developments) Ltd* [2010] EWHC 456.

2.3.   Restrictions on the use of contractual rescission clauses

2.3.1.   A commonly encountered type of contractual rescission clause is one which gives the seller the right to rescind if he is unable or unwilling to answer a requisition raised by the buyer. This type of clause is narrowly construed by the courts who will only permit the seller to rescind where the requisition reveals an incumbrance of which the seller was previously unaware and which he is unable to discharge. They thus provide an emergency escape route for a seller in the event that an unforeseen difficulty with the title arises, and cannot be relied on by a seller who had not taken proper care to investigate his own title before drafting the contract, nor where the seller changes his mind after exchange and decides not to go ahead with the contract.[1] Neither the Standard Conditions of Sale nor the Standard Commercial Property Conditions, however, contain this type of clause.

2.3.2.   This type of clause was examined by the court in *Selkirk* v. *Romar Investments*[2] from which case it appears that the conditions set out below must be satisfied before the court will allow the seller to rely on the clause:

   (a)   the seller can show some title; if he can show no title at all his withdrawal from the contract will be a breach entitling the buyer to damages;

   (b)   at the date of the contract the seller was unaware of the defect of which the buyer complains;

   (c)   the defect is either irremovable or only removable at disproportionate expense;

   (d)   the seller relies on the condition definitely and within a reasonable time;

   (e)   the seller is reasonable in exercising his right to withdraw.

2.3.3.   The right to rescind under this type of clause can only be exercised in response to requisitions which are raised on the title itself and not in relation to, e.g. the form of the purchase deed or administrative matters relating to completion. Law of Property Act 1925, ss.42, 45 and 125 give the buyer non-excludable rights to raise requisitions about certain matters affecting the title and a contractual rescission clause would not be effective in circumstances affected by one of these sections (see D2).

1. See *Day* v. *Singleton* [1899] 2 Ch 320.
2. [1963] 3 All ER 994.

2.4. Misrepresentation

2.4.1. In certain circumstances rescission may be available for misrepresentation. This remedy is further discussed in M5.

2.5. Misdescription

2.5.1. Misdescription results from an error in the particulars of sale, e.g. misdescribing the tenure of the property or the physical extent of the land to be sold.

2.5.2. If the misdescription is substantial the buyer may ask for rescission of the contract and compensation. A misdescription is substantial if its effect is substantially to deprive the buyer of his bargain.[1]

2.5.3. If the misdescription is not substantial the buyer can be forced to complete but may seek compensation by way of an abatement from the purchase price.

2.5.4. A misdescription of the property will usually also amount to a misrepresentation and it is more common nowadays to pursue a remedy under Misrepresentation Act 1967 than for misdescription.

1. See generally *Watson* v. *Burton* [1957] 1 WLR 19.

2.6. Non-disclosure

2.6.1. Non-disclosure arises out of the seller's failure to comply with his duty of disclosure. The seller's duty of disclosure is discussed in B5.

2.6.2. Where the effect of the non-disclosure is substantial, i.e. its effect is substantially to deprive the buyer of his bargain, the buyer may seek rescission of the contract.

2.6.3. If the non-disclosure is not substantial the buyer can be forced to complete but may seek compensation by way of an abatement to the purchase price.

2.7.   **Mistake**

2.7.1.   Where the parties have entered a contract under a fundamental mistake of fact, the contract is void at common law. The transaction will be set aside by the court and the buyer is entitled to recover any money paid. This principle has been applied where the subject matter of the contract had been destroyed before the contract was made,[1] where the buyer unknowingly contracts to buy property which he already owns,[2] where the parties misunderstood the legal effect of the transaction,[3] and where both parties were mistaken as to the meaning of the contract.[4]

2.7.2.   A mistake as to the quality of the subject matter of the contract will not normally have the effect of making the contract void at common law, although equity may in such circumstances refuse specific performance. If the effect of the mistake is to make the subject matter of the contract something entirely different from that which the parties thought it to be, the contract may be avoided.[5]

2.7.3.   A mistake as to the identity of the contracting parties seems not to affect a written contract for the sale of land. The court treats the parties named in the contract as being the correct parties to it and will enforce the contract on that basis.[6]

1.   *Res extincta*: see, e.g. *Hitchcock* v. *Giddings* (1817) 4 Price 135.
2.   *Res sua*: see, e.g. *Cooper* v. *Phibbs* (1865) 17 I Ch R 73.
3.   *Wolff and another* v. *Wolff and others* [2004] All ER (D) 28.
4.   *George Wimpey UK Ltd* v. *VI Components Ltd* [2004] EWHC 1374 (Ch), BLD (2506024771).
5.   See generally *Bell* v. *Lever Bros Ltd* [1932] AC 161.
6.   *Hector* v. *Lyons* (1988) 58 P&CR 156. The principles relating to mistaken identity outlined in *Lewis* v. *Averay (No.2)* [1973] 2 All ER 229 are inapplicable in this situation.

2.8.   **Limitation periods**

2.8.1.   Where the right to rescind arises out of a contractual provision, it must be exercised within the time limits given within the condition, or if no time is specified within a reasonable time.[1] An action based on a contractual rescission clause is subject to the normal six-year limitation period under Limitation Act 1980 unless the contract was by deed when a 12-year limitation period would be available.

2.8.2.   Actions for rescission arising out of the general law principles, e.g. for misdescription are subject to the equitable doctrine of laches (see M4.3).

1.   *Alchemy Estates Ltd* v. *Astor* [2008] EWHC 2675 (Ch).

M3. Breach of contract

3.1.   Introduction

3.1.1. This section is intended as a brief overview of the subject under discussion. It is not intended to be used as a substitute for the advice of an experienced litigation solicitor. Prompt action by someone knowledgeable in the area of litigation is often required where problems arise in relation to a breach of contract.

3.1.2. Remedies for breach of contract depend on whether the breach is of a condition in the contract, entitling the aggrieved party to terminate the contract and/or claim damages, or of a warranty, entitling the aggrieved party to claim damages only.

3.1.3. A term of the contract will be a 'condition' if it is a major or fundamental term. Minor terms are classified as 'warranties'. In some cases it is not possible to classify a term as specifically falling into one or other of these categories until the consequences of the breach can be seen. Where the consequences are serious or far reaching, the unclassified term will be treated as a condition. In the converse situation it will be a warranty only. The terminology or labelling which the parties themselves have attached to the various terms of the contract is not conclusive as to their classification. In conveyancing contracts all terms are usually called 'conditions', but in law some of those terms would only have the status of warranties.[1]

3.1.4. An action on a simple contract, i.e. one not made by deed, has a limitation period under Limitation Act 1980 of six years running from the date of the breach. A limitation period of 12 years applies where the contract was made by deed. A three-year limitation period applies where the amount claimed includes damages for personal injury or death. In some cases, Latent Damage Act 1986 may extend the limitation period.

3.1.5. On completion the terms of the contract merge with the purchase deed in so far as the two documents cover the same ground, and an action on the contract is no longer sustainable after completion except where it is based on a contract term which remains extant despite completion taking place. For this to happen the contract would generally have to contain a non-merger clause (such as Standard

Condition 7.4 or Standard Commercial Property Condition 9.4) which expressly allowed a particular clause or clauses to remain alive after completion,[2] although sometimes the court may imply such an intention from the subject matter of the clause. If an action on the contract cannot be maintained, the buyer may have to attempt to pursue a remedy under the covenants for title or title guarantee (see M9).

3.1.6.   In any situation where the buyer suspects that the seller will or may default, consideration should be given to protecting the buyer's contract by entry of a notice (in registered land) or as a Class C(iv) land charge (if the seller's title is unregistered).

1. See *Cehave NV* v. *Bremer Handelgesellschaft mbH* [1976] QB 44.
2. See Standard Condition 7.4 and Standard Commercial Property Condition 9.4.

3.2.   Specific performance

3.2.1.   In sale of land cases an action for specific performance may provide an alternative remedy to an action for damages. This remedy is discussed in M4.

3.3.   Exclusion clauses

3.3.1.   An exclusion clause which purports to exclude liability under the contract must be incorporated in the contract if it is to be valid. In the case of a written contract, an exclusion clause contained within the writing is deemed to be incorporated whether or not the parties have read the document or were capable of reading it. In such circumstances illiteracy or inability to read English is no defence.[1]

3.3.2.   Exclusion clauses must be specifically drafted to fit the breach which has occurred; thus a clause which excludes liability for breach of condition will not protect against a breach of warranty and vice versa.[2]

3.3.3.   Any ambiguity in the wording of the clause will be construed against the party who is seeking to rely on the clause.

3.3.4.   The clause normally only affords protection to the parties to the contract. Therefore an action in tort may be brought against a third party who caused the loss of which the claimant complains. He will be unable to shelter behind the protection of the clause since he does not enjoy privity of contract with the claimant.[3]

3.3.5.   Standard Condition 7.1 and Standard Commercial Property Condition 9.1 restrict the remedies available for breach of contract. A buyer is only entitled to damages if there is a material difference in the tenure or value of the property and is only entitled to treat the contract as at an end if the error or omission results from fraud or recklessness, or where he would otherwise be obliged to accept a property differing substantially in quality, quantity or tenure from what he had been led to expect.

3.3.6. Exclusion clauses contained in contracts for the sale of land (except those relating to the exclusion of liability for misrepresentation) are not subject to the reasonableness test in Unfair Contract Terms Act 1977.

1. See *L'Estrange* v. *F Graucob Ltd* [1934] 2 KB 394; *Thompson* v. *London, Midland & Scottish Railway* [1930] 1 KB 41.
2. See *Curtis* v. *Chemical Cleaning and Dyeing Co.* [1951] 1 KB 805.
3. See *Adler* v. *Dickson* [1955] 1 QB 158.

3.4. Delayed completion

3.4.1. Unless time was of the essence of the completion date, or had been made so by service of a notice to complete, a completion which takes place later than the date specified in the contract does not of itself entitle the aggrieved party to terminate the contract.

3.4.2. Late completion will, however, be a breach of warranty entitling the aggrieved party to recover damages for any loss suffered as a result of the delay.[1]

1. *Raineri* v. *Miles; Wiejski (Third Party)* [1981] AC 1050 and see M1.4.

3.5. Damages for breach

3.5.1. Damages for breach of a contract for the sale of land are assessed under the normal contractual principles established in *Hadley* v. *Baxendale*.[1] Thus, subject to establishing causation, damages for losses naturally flowing from the breach may be claimed and in addition reasonably foreseeable consequential loss.

3.5.2. The quantum of damages under the consequential loss head are limited to loss which was reasonably foreseeable by the defaulting party in the light of the facts known by him (or by his agent) at the date when the contract was made (not at the date of the breach of contract).

3.5.3. The starting point for damages for breach of a contract for the sale of land is the difference between the contract and market prices of the property at the date of the breach. To this may be added actual financial loss suffered as a result of the breach, e.g. wasted conveyancing costs, legal costs involved in the purchase of another property, interest payable on a mortgage or bridging loan, costs of removal or storage of furniture, costs of alternative accommodation pending purchase of another property.[2]

3.5.4. Loss of development profit, or loss of profit on a sub-sale, can only be claimed if the defendant was aware of the claimant's proposals for the property at the time the contract was made.[3]

3.5.5.   Where the buyer defaults and the seller makes a loss on the resale, that loss can be claimed as damages but, if the seller makes a profit on the resale, he would have to give credit for the amount of the profit in his action since he is only entitled to recover his financial loss and is not entitled to benefit from the buyer's breach. The purpose of contractual damages is to place the parties in the position in which they would have been had the contract been duly performed. There is no punitive element in the assessment of damages.

3.5.6.   As a general principle of contractual damages, it is only possible to recover for financial loss, and no claim can be made in respect of mental distress suffered as a result of the defendant's breach. The practice of awarding a nominal sum in respect of damages for mental distress established by *Jarvis* v. *Swans Tours*[4] seems to be confined to leisure and pleasure contracts, e.g. holiday contracts and contracts for leisure activities.

3.5.7.   Damages can normally only be claimed in respect of losses which have occurred since the contract was made; thus there is generally no possibility of recovering expenses incurred at the pre-contract stage of the transaction, e.g. for a wasted surveyor's report or search fees.[5]

3.5.8.   The claimant must have attempted to mitigate his loss, e.g. by trying to purchase another similar property (as disappointed buyer) or by attempting to resell the property (as disappointed seller). The attempt to mitigate should be made; otherwise the award of damages may be reduced because of the failure to mitigate. If the claimant attempts to mitigate and in so doing increases his loss, the defendant will be liable for the increased loss.

3.5.9.   Credit must be given in the claim for damages for any compensation received under Standard Condition 7.3 or Standard Commercial Property Condition 9.3 or for any deposit forfeited by the seller (see M1) (whether the property is resold or not).[6]

3.5.10.   Actions claiming a sum under £50,000 will be brought in the county court; above that limit, the High Court has jurisdiction. Actions brought in the county court for sums not exceeding £1,000 may be referred to arbitration (but not if there is a dispute over a point of law) in which case no costs are normally awarded in the action. In other county court cases, a successful litigant may be penalised as to costs if he does not recover more than £1,000 in his judgment, or does not recover more than the amount paid into court by the defendant prior to the hearing. The question of costs must be fully discussed with the client before the decision to start proceedings is taken, since in some cases the action for breach of contract may not be cost effective for the client.

1. (1854) 9 Exch 341.
2. See, e.g. *Beard* v. *Porter* [1948] 1 KB 321.
3. *Diamond* v. *Campbell-Jones* [1961] Ch 22; *cf. Cottrill* v. *Steyning & Littlehampton Building Society* [1966] 2 All ER 295.
4. [1973] QB 233; and see *Bliss* v. *South-East Thames Regional Health Authority* [1987] ICR 700.
5. But see *Lloyd* v. *Stanbury* [1971] 2 All ER 267 where pre-contract expenditure including money spent on repairs to the property was recovered.
6. *Ng* v. *Ashley King (Developments) Ltd* [2010] EWHC 456.

3.6. Action in tort

3.6.1. If an action in contract is not possible, e.g. a valid exclusion clause prevents the claim, an action in tort may be considered. The limitation period for such an action will usually be six years from the time the tort was committed, but a three-year limitation period applies where the claim includes damages for personal injury or death. Actions in tort may also be considered where it is desired to sue a third party who was not privy to the contract. Most actions of this type will lie in negligence which imposes a fairly onerous burden of proof on the claimant. The quantum of damages is assessed using different principles and in general damages for pure economic loss cannot be claimed.[1]

1. Damages are awarded following the principles laid down in *The Wagon Mound* [1961] AC 388. See *Junior Books* v. *Veitchi Co. Ltd* [1983] 1 AC 520 and *Murphy* v. *Brentwood District Council* [1991] 1 AC 398 relating to economic loss.

3.7. Misrepresentation

3.7.1. Where an action on the contract cannot be sustained an action in misrepresentation may still be viable. This remedy is further discussed in M5.

3.8. Freezing order

3.8.1. Although not a conventional sale of land remedy, a freezing order could be obtained if it was suspected that the defendant was intending to remove his assets from the jurisdiction in order to avoid liability. Such an order would not provide a direct remedy but would protect the claimant's position as an interim measure. Prompt action is required. Where the land is registered, a freezing order should be reflected in the register by the entry of a restriction in Form AA.[1] A person who has applied to the court for a freezing order can apply for a restriction in Form CC.[2]

1. Land Registration Rules 2003, r.93 and Sched.4.
2. *Ibid.*

3.9. Frustration

3.9.1. Where the contract has become impossible of performance due to an unforeseen act which is beyond the control of both parties, the contract is frustrated and the parties' rights and obligations are terminated without there being liability for breach on either side. The parties' rights in this situation are, in the absence of specific contractual provision, governed by Law Reform (Frustrated Contracts) Act 1943 which aims to restore the parties to their pre-contract position without imposing penalties. Frustration is usually raised as a defence to an action for breach of contract and, if successfully pleaded, provides an absolute defence to the defendant.

3.9.2.   Although the general view is that the doctrine of frustration does not apply to contracts for the sale of land, *dicta* from the House of Lords in *National Carriers Ltd* v. *Panalpina (Northern) Ltd*[1] suggest otherwise. It is therefore possible that the defence of frustration might be allowed in a situation where, e.g. the land which was the subject of the sale was totally destroyed by landslip into the sea between the dates of contract and completion. If the land was destroyed before the date of the contract, the contract would be void for common mistake. Frustration would not apply where the property burned down between contract and completion. Neither does it apply where the property is subject to a compulsory acquisition order.[2]

1.   [1981] AC 675.
2.   *E Johnson & Co. (Barbados) Ltd* v. *NSR Ltd* [1996] EGCS 133.

3.10.   Return of deposit

3.10.1.   Where the buyer defaults on completion, the seller will wish to forfeit the deposit, but Law of Property Act 1925, s.49(2) gives the court an absolute discretion to order the return of the deposit to the buyer. A contractual clause attempting to negate the provisions of section 49 is of no effect.[1] There is a presumption that the seller will have the right to forfeit the deposit which will only be overridden in special or exceptional circumstances: these do not include, on its own, the fact that the seller achieves a higher price on the subsequent resale.[2] However, if the deposit is more than 10% the buyer may be able to argue that it is not a reasonable amount and is a penalty, in which case the court may order its return to the buyer.[3]

3.10.2.   Where the seller defaults on completion the buyer will have to bring an action under Law of Property Act 1925, s.49(2) to recover his deposit.[4]

3.10.3.   Under section 49, the court appears to have power to return all of the deposit or none of it to the buyer. There is no discretion to order the return of part of the deposit even where this course of action would represent the most equitable way of dealing with the position between the parties. It seems, however, that the court may be prepared to order the return of the whole deposit to the buyer on condition that the buyer reimburse certain expenses to the seller, which would seem to be a fair way round the restrictions imposed by section 49.[5]

1.   *Aribisala* v. *St James Homes (Grosvenor Dock) Ltd* [2007] EWHC 1694 (Ch).
2.   *Midill (97PL) Limited* v. *Park Lane Estate Ltd and another* [2008] EWCA Civ 1227 and *Aribisala* v. *St James Homes (Grosvenor Dock) Ltd* [2008] EWHC 456 (Ch).
3.   *Workers Trust & Merchant Bank Ltd* v. *Dojap Investments Ltd* (1993) 42 WIR 253, PC.
4.   *Midill (97PL) Ltd* v. *Park Lane Estates Ltd and Gomba International Investments Ltd* [2007] EWHC 18 (Ch).
5.   See *Universal Corporation* v. *Five Ways Properties* [1979] 1 All ER 552; *James Macara Ltd* v. *Barclay* [1945] KB 148; *cf. Dimsdale Developments (South East) Ltd* v. *De Haan* (1983) 47 P&CR 1. See also *Tennero Ltd* v. *Majorarch Ltd* [2003] EGCS 154 which provides guidance on when the court will exercise its discretion to order the return of the deposit.

3.11. Trade Descriptions Act 1968

3.11.1. Under Trade Descriptions Act 1968, it is an offence to make a false statement in a contract for the supply of services (including land). The Act applies where the seller is acting in the course of a business and so would be applicable where, e.g. a buyer was purchasing land from a builder, but not in an ordinary residential purchase between private individuals. If an action in contract or misrepresentation cannot for some reason be sustained, it may be worth considering reporting a 'false statement', e.g. a misrepresentation about the quality of the property, to the local trading standards office and asking them to pursue a prosecution under the Act. Such a prosecution does not afford a direct remedy for the client. On conviction for the offence it would, however, be possible for the client to ask the court for a compensation order under Powers of Criminal Courts Act 1973, s.35. Where the conviction is obtained in the magistrates' court, the compensation order cannot exceed £2,000 in respect of each offence.[1]

1. See *Breed* v. *Cluett* [1970] 2 QB 459 where such an order was obtained following a builder's conviction under this Act for making false statements about the availability of NHBC protection on a new house.

3.12. Property Misdescriptions Act 1991

3.12.1. This Act which came into force on 4 April 1993 creates a criminal offence which is committed where a false or misleading description is applied to certain aspects of the property as listed in regulations made under the Act in the course of an estate agency or property development business. The offence is of strict liability and can be committed by publishing a misleading photograph of property as well as by misdescribing property orally or in writing.[1] An action must generally be brought within three years of the alleged offence. Enforcement of the Act is through criminal proceedings brought by the Trading Standards Department for the area. Some estate agents are now seeking an indemnity from the seller in respect of liability under this Act. The seller should be advised not to accept such a clause.

1. In *Lewin* v. *Barratt Homes Ltd* [1999] EGCS 139 the defendants were held liable under this Act in relation to 'statements' made in photographs and through the display of a show house.

3.13. MIG policies

3.13.1. A lender who benefits from the proceeds of a MIG policy does not need to give credit for this sum when quantifying damages.[1]

1. *Europe Mortgage* v. *Halifax Estate Agencies* [1996] NPC 68.

3.14. Checklist

3.14.1. A client who is encountering problems with a property transaction will probably first seek the advice of the person who is advising him in the sale or purchase. A checklist of the main points to be considered when discussing the client's problems is set out below. These matters should be taken into consideration when deciding whether and how to pursue a remedy for breach of contract and cover the main points of information which will be needed by the litigation department if the matter is handed to them for further action. In addition to the matters listed below, the person taking instructions should obtain a complete history of the conveyancing transaction from the client, including a detailed timetable of the events leading to the present dispute, and should obtain from the client either the original documents relevant to the matter, or copies of them.

3.14.2.   The following is a checklist of the main points to be considered:

    (a)   Has there been a breach of contract?

    (b)   If so, what type of breach, i.e. of condition or warranty?

    (c)   What remedy does the client want, e.g. damages or specific performance?

    (d)   Is there a valid exclusion clause which might prevent the claim?

    (e)   When did the limitation period start to run?

    (f)   What (approximately) is the total of the client's financial loss?

    (g)   How much of that loss would be recoverable, bearing in mind the rules on remoteness of damage?

    (h)   Would the costs of an action be justified?

    (i)   Who should be sued, e.g. other party to the contract, solicitor, surveyor?

    (j)   If a claim cannot be made in contract, is there a viable alternative action, e.g. in tort or for misrepresentation?

M4. Specific performance

4.1.   Introduction

4.1.1.   Although this is an equitable remedy which is granted at the discretion of the court, an order for specific performance is not uncommon in sale of land cases where, since no two pieces of land are identical, an award of damages would be inadequate compensation for the injured party's loss.[1]

4.1.2.   The claim can be made either on its own, or in conjunction with a claim for damages or rescission, depending on the circumstances.

4.1.3.   Specific performance cannot generally be awarded for breach of a contract to grant a loan (whether secured or unsecured).[2] It would not therefore be available where a lender, in breach of contract, withdrew his offer of mortgage.

1. *Hall* v. *Warren* (1804) 9 Ves 605.
2. *Rogers* v. *Challis* (1859) 27 Beav 175.

4.2.   General bars to the award

4.2.1.   As an equitable remedy, the award of a decree of specific performance is subject to the usual principles of equity. It will not therefore be awarded where:

   (a)   an award of damages would adequately compensate for the loss sustained by the breach;

   (b)   one of the contracting parties lacks full contractual capacity;

   (c)   the contract contains a vitiating element, e.g. mistake, fraud, illegality;

   (d)   the enforcement of the order would require the constant supervision of the court;

   (e)   a third party has acquired an interest for value in the property;

   (f)   the award would cause exceptional hardship to the guilty party;

   (g)   the seller cannot make good title.

4.3.   Delay

4.3.1.   The Limitation Acts do not usually apply to equitable remedies, but the doctrine of laches (lapse of time) does. The remedy may therefore be barred if the innocent party is dilatory in seeking an award.[1]

4.3.2. Unlike a common law action for breach of contract, the injured party can apply for a decree before a breach of contract has actually occurred (i.e. before contractual completion date) provided that he can show that a serious breach is likely to take place if the court does not intervene.[2]

4.3.3. Laches will not bar the application where the buyer is already in possession of the property.[3]

1. *Lazard Brothers & Co. Ltd* v. *Fairfield Properties Co. (Mayfair) Ltd* (1977) 121 SJ 793.
2. *Marks* v. *Lilley* [1959] 2 All ER 647; *Hasham* v. *Zenab* [1960] AC 316, PC.
3. *Williams* v. *Greatrex* [1957] 1 WLR 31.

4.4. Damages in lieu

4.4.1. Subject to the above principles the injured party always has the right to apply for a decree of specific performance, but there is no guarantee that an award will be forthcoming in any given circumstances. If, in a situation where specific performance would otherwise be available to the injured party, the court decides not to make such an order, it may award damages in lieu of specific performance under Supreme Court Act 1981, s.50. Such damages are assessed using normal contractual principles as outlined in M3.

4.4.2. Where an award of specific performance has been made but has not been complied with, the injured party may return to the court asking the court to withdraw the order and to substitute the decree of specific performance with an award of damages.[1]

1. *Johnson* v. *Agnew* [1980] AC 367.

4.5. Standard Conditions of Sale and Standard Commercial Property Conditions

4.5.1. Where a notice to complete has been served by the seller under Standard Condition 6.8 or Standard Commercial Property Condition 8.8 and is not complied with, by Standard Condition 7.6 and Standard Commercial Property Condition 9.5, the innocent party's right to apply for a decree of specific performance is not excluded.

M5. Misrepresentation

5.1.   Definition

5.1.1.   A misrepresentation is an untrue statement of fact which is relied on by the aggrieved party, which induces him to enter the contract, and as a result of which he suffers loss.

5.1.2.   The statement must be of fact, not law.[1] A statement of opinion is not actionable unless it can be proved that the opinion was never genuinely held.[2]

5.1.3.   A misrepresentation may be fraudulent, i.e. deliberately dishonest within the definition of fraud laid down in *Derry* v. *Peek*,[3] negligent, i.e. made carelessly without having checked the facts, but not necessarily negligent within the tortious meaning of that word, or innocent, i.e. a genuine and innocently made mistake.

5.1.4.   The representation can be made by the seller's conduct. In *Taylor* v. *Hamer*[4] the seller was guilty of misrepresentation because her conduct had led the buyer to believe that certain items would be included in the sale. The items were present when the buyer inspected the property but were removed before exchange of contracts.

1.   The distinction between fact and law is not always clear; see *Solle* v. *Butcher* [1950] 1 KB 671; and *Pankhania* v. *Hackney London Borough Council* [2002] All ER (D) 22.
2.   *Edgington* v. *Fitzmaurice* (1885) 29 Ch 459.
3.   (1889) 14 App Cas 337.
4.   *Taylor* v. *Hamer* [2002] EWCA Civ 1130.

5.2.   Fraudulent misrepresentation

5.2.1.   Where the misrepresentation has been made fraudulently, the aggrieved party may bring an action in tort for deceit which may result in rescission of the contract and damages.[1]

5.2.2.   The party who alleges fraud must prove fraud. This places a very onerous burden of proof on the claimant in the action and, except where the evidence of fraud is indefeasible, it is more usual to treat the misrepresentation as having been made negligently and to pursue a remedy under Misrepresentation Act 1967.

5.2.3. A fraudulent misrepresentation may also be a criminal offence under Fraud Act 2006.

1. *Ross River Ltd and another* v. *Cambridge City Football Club Ltd* [2007] EWHC 2115 (Ch).

5.3. Actions under Misrepresentation Act 1967

5.3.1. The claimant must show that he has an action in misrepresentation as defined in M5.1, after which the burden of proof shifts to the defendant who, in broad terms, has to disprove negligence.

5.3.2. A misrepresentation is negligent if the defendant cannot prove that he had grounds for belief and did believe the statement he made was true up to the time the contract was made. There is therefore a duty to correct a statement which, although being true at the time when it was made, subsequently becomes untrue.

5.3.3. The remedies for a negligent misrepresentation are rescission of the contract and damages.

5.3.4. If the defendant successfully establishes the defence of grounds and belief outlined in M5.3.2, thus showing that the misrepresentation was truly innocent, rescission is available, but not damages.

5.3.5. Although Misrepresentation Act 1967 allows a party to ask for rescission of the contract, the award of the remedy remains within the equitable jurisdiction of the court and is thus discretionary and subject to the equitable bars.[1]

5.3.6. If none of the equitable bars applies, but nevertheless the court decides not to grant rescission, it may instead award damages in lieu of rescission to the claimant.[2]

5.3.7. Damages under Misrepresentation Act 1967 are awarded on a tortious basis[3] under Misrepresentation Act 1967, s.2(2).

5.3.8. An award of damages can be made under both the subsections of section 2, i.e. an award in lieu of rescission and an award to compensate the claimant for his loss, subject to the overriding principle that the claimant cannot recover more than his actual loss; thus the awards under the two subsections are not cumulative.

5.3.9. Rescission is only likely to be awarded where the result of the misrepresentation is substantially to deprive the claimant of his bargain.[4]

5.3.10. An action in misrepresentation does not arise out of the contract, since the misrepresentation is a non-contractual statement which has the effect of inducing the contract. Neither does it arise out of tort. The limitation periods prescribed by Limitation Act 1980 do not therefore apply in this situation and it seems that the limitation period for an action based on misrepresentation relies on the equitable doctrine of laches.

5.3.11. Where a misrepresentation has become incorporated as a minor term of the contract it is possible by Misrepresentation Act 1967, s.1 to treat the statement as a mere representation and to pursue a remedy under Misrepresentation Act 1967. This option would benefit the claimant by giving him the right to ask for rescission of the contract as well as damages. If his action were confined to breach of a minor contractual term his only available remedy would be damages.

1. The equitable bars are listed in M4.2.
2. Misrepresentation Act 1967, s.2(1).
3. *Chesneau* v. *Interhome*, *The Times*, 9 June 1983, CA; and see *Royscott Trust* v. *Rogerson* [1991] 2 QB 297.
4. See *Gosling* v. *Anderson*, *The Times*, 8 February 1972; *cf. Museprime Properties Ltd* v. *Adhill Properties Ltd* (1990) 61 P&CR 111.

5.4. Imputed knowledge

5.4.1. Knowledge gained by a solicitor in the course of a transaction is deemed to be known by the solicitor's client whether or not this is in fact the case. Thus where a solicitor makes an incorrect reply to pre-contract enquiries, basing his reply on an erroneous assessment of the title deeds, the solicitor's knowledge and also his misstatement is attributable to the client who will be liable to the buyer in misrepresentation.[1] In such a situation the solicitor would be liable to his own client in negligence.

5.4.2. The converse situation is also true. If, for example, the seller makes a misrepresentation to the buyer personally, but the misrepresentation is later corrected in correspondence between the seller's solicitors and the buyer's solicitors, the buyer is deemed to know of the correction (even if not actually told by his solicitor) and would not in these circumstances be able to sustain an action for misrepresentation against the seller.[2]

1. *Cemp Properties* v. *Dentsply* [1989] 35 EG 99.
2. *Strover* v. *Harrington* [1988] Ch 390.

5.5. Exclusion clauses

5.5.1. By Misrepresentation Act 1967, s.3, as amended by Unfair Contract Terms Act 1977, s.8, any clause which purports to limit or exclude liability for misrepresentation is only valid in so far as it satisfies the reasonableness test laid down in section 11 and Schedule 2 Unfair Contract Terms Act 1977.

5.5.2. The reasonableness test is applied subjectively, in the light of the circumstances which were known to the parties at the time when the contract was made. It therefore depends on the circumstances of each particular case as to whether the exclusion clause is valid in that situation. There is no guarantee that any given form of wording will satisfy the test unless and until the clause is subjected to the scrutiny of the court. Such clauses therefore require great care in drafting. Fraudulent misrepresentation should (if required) be excluded by express wording to this effect.

5.5.3.   Standard Condition 7.1 and Standard Commercial Property Condition 9.1 purport to limit the seller's liability for, *inter alia*, misrepresentation. The validity of this clause is subject to its satisfying the reasonableness test on the facts of each particular case.

5.5.4.   The majority of misrepresentation actions arising out of property transactions appear to result from erroneous replies to pre-contract enquiries. Some standard forms of pre-contract enquiries have an exclusion clause printed on them. This exclusion clause is also subject to the reasonableness test.[1]

1.   See *Walker* v. *Boyle* [1982] 1 All ER 634 where an exclusion clause contained in a then current edition of a standard form of pre-contract enquiries failed the reasonableness test. In the same case, the exclusion clause contained in the 19th edition of the National Conditions of Sale was held to be invalid for the same reason.

M6. Other causes of action

6.1. Introduction

6.1.1. In certain circumstances it may be possible or necessary to seek a remedy from someone other than a party to the contract. Such action will normally have to be brought in tort since no privity of contract will exist between the potential parties to the action.

6.1.2. A non-exhaustive list of suggestions of alternative sources of action which might be relevant if an action on the contract was unavailable is included here.

6.2. Solicitor's liability

6.2.1. A solicitor who is guilty of providing inadequate professional services may be reprimanded by the Legal Complaints Service which additionally may order the solicitor to rectify a mistake at his own expense or to waive his costs or repay costs to the client. The Legal Complaints Service can also order the solicitor to pay compensation of up to £15,000 to the client. For further information, see **www.legalcomplaints.org.uk**.

6.2.2. A solicitor who has been negligent in the conduct of a client's affairs can be sued in negligence (see M10).

6.2.3. If a client has suffered loss as a result of default by a solicitor which loss cannot be recovered from any other source, the Solicitors Regulation Authority's Compensation Fund may be able to assist.

6.2.4. A solicitor's duty of care is owed not only to his own client, but in certain circumstances to third parties as well.[1] It may therefore be possible in some circumstances for an aggrieved buyer to sue his seller's solicitor in negligence[2] although the court has held that in a normal conveyancing transaction the seller's solicitor does not owe a duty of care to the buyer.[3]

6.2.5. Where the solicitor's own client had been held liable for, e.g. breach of contract in circumstances where the breach was caused by the party's solicitor, the solicitor can be required to indemnify the client against his liability for damages.[4]

1. See *Ross* v. *Caunters* [1980] 1 Ch 297 but see *Murphy* v. *Brentwood District Council* [1991] 1 AC 398.
2. See, e.g. *Wilson* v. *Bloomfield* (1979) 123 SJ 860, CA.
3. *Gran Gelato Ltd* v. *Richcliff Ltd* [1992] Ch 560.
4. E.g. *Cemp Properties* v. *Dentsply* [1989] 35 EG 99.

6.3. Breach of warranty of authority

6.3.1. Where an agent acts outside the scope of his authority he will be liable to the third party for breach of warranty of authority.[1]

6.3.2. A solicitor or estate agent who exceeds his client's authority may thus be sued by a third party.[2]

1. *Yonge* v. *Toynbee* [1910] 1 KB 215.
2. *Suleman* v. *Shahsavari* [1989] 2 All ER 460; *Penn* v. *Bristol & West Building Society* [1997] 3 All ER 470.

6.4. Estate agents

6.4.1. Estate agents are regulated by Estate Agents Act 1979 which sets out the duties agents owe to clients and third parties. The Act also gives the Office of Fair Trading power to issue warning or prohibition notices against persons whom it considers unfit to carry on estate agency work. For further information, contact the Trading Standards Department for the relevant area or the Office of Fair Trading (**www.oft.gov.uk**).

6.4.2. Liability may also exist if the agent exceeds his authority as under M6.3.

6.4.3. An estate agent who is authorised to *sell* the property (but not one who is merely empowered to procure a buyer) may have authority to receive the contract deposit.[1]

6.4.4. As far as pre-contract deposits are concerned, unless there is express authority from the seller to take and hold a pre-contract deposit, such sum must be held on behalf of the buyer. If the pre-contract deposit is lost, e.g. where an estate agent absconds with the money, the loss falls on the buyer except where the agent was expressly authorised to take the pre-contract deposit.[2]

6.4.5. The estate agent's duty to the seller is similar to the common law duties which exist between an agent and his principal.[3]

6.4.6. The estate agent's duty is owed to his principal, i.e. the seller client, and generally he owes no duty to the buyer.[4] There may also in some circumstances be a liability in relation to the pre-contract deposit, or in negligence under *Hedley Byrne* v. *Heller* principles.[5]

6.4.7. Similar remedies to those afforded under Trade Descriptions Act 1968 lie under Property Misdescriptions Act 1991 against an estate agent (including a solicitor who is acting as an estate agent) who misdescribes a property which he is selling. This Act creates a criminal offence which is committed where a false or misleading description is applied to property in the course of an estate agency or property development business. The offence is of strict liability and can be committed by publishing a misleading photograph of property as well as by misdescribing property orally or in writing. An action must generally be brought within three years of the alleged offence. Enforcement of the Act is through criminal proceedings brought by the Trading Standards Department for the area or the Office of Fair Trading.

6.4.8. Anyone engaging in residential estate agency work is required to join an approved redress scheme to deal with disputes between member agencies and consumers who are buyers or sellers of residential property. The scheme administrator will consider complaints that a member agency has infringed a consumer's legal rights, failed to comply with the relevant code of practice, acted unfairly or been guilty of maladministration.[6] Details of every approved scheme are available on the Office of Fair Trading website (**www.oft.gov.uk**).

1.   *Boote* v. *RT Shiels & Co.* [1978] 1 NZLR 445.
2.   *Sorrell* v. *Finch* [1977] AC 728.
3.   But see *Luxor* v. *Cooper* [1941] AC 108; *cf. Prebble (PG) & Co.* v. *West* (1969) 211 EG 831.
4.   *McCulloch* v. *Lane Fox, The Times*, 22 December 1995, CA.
5.   [1964] AC 465.
6.   Estate Agents (Redress Scheme) Order 2008 (SI 2008/1712); Estate Agents (Redress Scheme) (Penalty Charge) Regulations 2008 (SI 2008/1713).

6.5.   Surveyors

6.5.1. A surveyor owes his client a duty to perform his contract with reasonable skill and care. This common law duty has been replaced by the implied term to the same effect under Supply of Goods and Services Act 1982, s.13, but the duty of the surveyor, and thus his liability, are necessarily limited by the extent of the instructions given to him.

6.5.2. If the problem with the survey stems from the results of a valuation report, the surveyor will generally have been instructed by the client's lender, and so there will probably be no contractual relationship between the client and the surveyor; thus any liability which does exist will necessarily be in tort. If however the contract between the lender and the valuer contemplates that the buyer will have the benefit of the valuation report, it may be possible for the buyer to sustain an action against the valuer in contract under Contracts (Rights of Third Parties) Act 1999.

6.5.3. In other cases a contractual relationship between the client and the surveyor will or may exist, giving the choice of action under either contract or tort.

6.5.4. An exclusion clause purporting to exclude liability for the survey will be construed narrowly against the party seeking to rely on it and will only be valid in so far as it is fair and reasonable in the context of the particular contract in which it is included.[1]

6.5.5. A surveyor who prepares a valuation report for a lender in the knowledge (express or implied) that the buyer will see the report and may rely on it in deciding whether or not to proceed with his purchase owes a duty of care to the buyer.[2] This duty will not, however, apply in every case. Where, for example, it is reasonable for the surveyor to assume that the buyer would be obtaining his own independent survey – which may be a fair assumption for him to make where the property is at the top end of the property market – or where the buyer is experienced in property matters, the surveyor may be entitled to shelter behind the protection of his exclusion clause and thus avoid liability.[3]

6.5.6. Where a surveyor is sued, the quantum of damages is usually limited to the difference between what the property was actually worth at the date of the contract and what it would have been worth if the survey report had been accurate (not what the client paid for the property, or the cost of repairs). Thus, in some circumstances, the amount of damages recoverable will not equate with the client's loss. For example, the difference in value may be only a few thousand pounds, but the cost of repairs to put the property right at the date of the action may be huge, and the client can only recover the smaller sum representing the difference in value.[4] Loss in value to the property which is attributable to the fall in value of the property market is not generally recoverable as a head of loss.[5] The lender's contributory negligence (e.g. in relying on the valuation without checking it) may reduce the award made against the surveyor.[6]

6.5.7. There is no doubt that a valuer owes a duty to the seller to provide a valuation which is as accurate as circumstances allow – a duty of skill and care is owed to the seller. If the valuer's error results in there being an undervalue of the property, the measure of damages will usually be the difference between the sale price and the market value of the property. If on the other hand an over-valuation is given, full contractual damages within *Hadley* v. *Baxendale*[7] principles will be payable to the seller, including loss caused by his inability to sell the property within a reasonable time, if this has been a consequence of the over-valuation.

6.5.8. The cause of action by a lender in respect of a negligent valuation arises when the loss crystallises, i.e. at the date when the security is sold.[8]

6.5.9. The RICS appraisal and valuation manual ('The Red Book') contains mandatory guidelines for surveyors to follow when undertaking surveys and valuations of all types of property. Non-observance of these guidelines may be evidence of negligence.

1. The reasonableness test in Unfair Contract Terms Act 1977, s.11 must be satisfied.
2. *Smith* v. *Eric S Bush (a firm)* [1990] 1 AC 831; and see *Qureshi* v. *Liassides* (unreported) (1995) EG 123 (case comment).
3. *Stevenson* v. *Nationwide Building Society* (1984) 272 EG 663.
4. *Philips* v. *Ward* [1956] 1 All ER 874; and see *Watts* v. *Morrow, The Independent,* 20 August 1991.
5. *Banque Bruxelles Lambert SA* v. *Eagle Star Insurance* [1995] 12 EG 144, CA reversed on appeal to the House of Lords *sub nomine South Australia Asset Management (Pty) Ltd* v. *York Montague* [1996] NPC 100 and see *Platform Home Loans* v. *Oyston* [1999] EGCS 26, HL.
6. *Ibid.*
7. (1854) 9 Exch 341.
8. *First National Commercial Bank* v. *Humberts, The Times,* 27 January 1995, CA.

6.6.   Dangerous substances

6.6.1.   There may be heavy liability (in financial terms) to third parties in tort, in negligence[1] or under Environmental Protection Act 1990 if, e.g. untreated sewage escapes into a waterway and pollutes the water.

6.6.2.   Anyone who is responsible for maintaining or repairing a non-domestic building has a duty to ascertain whether there is asbestos in the building and, if so, to put a risk management process in place. If a tenant is under a covenant to repair the property, the tenant will carry this liability, not the landlord.[2]

1. Subject to foreseeability: *Cambridge Water Co.* v. *Eastern Counties Leather plc* [1994] 1 All ER 53.
2. Control of Asbestos at Work Regulations 2006 (SI 2006/2739).

6.7.   Local searches

6.7.1.   In certain circumstances compensation may be claimed under Local Land Charges Act 1975, s.10, where there has been an error in an official search (see B10).

6.8.   The Land Registry

6.8.1.   In certain circumstances compensation may be claimed from the Land Registry where a person suffers loss by reason of a mistake in the register or in an official search (see M7).

6.9.   Covenants in freehold land

6.9.1.   Where restrictive covenants have been validly annexed to land, the person with the benefit of those covenants (who may be a successor in title of the original covenantee) will be able to enforce the covenants by injunction and/or damages against either the present estate owner of the land which bears the burden of the covenants or the original covenantor. The original covenantor may, in turn, be able to recover his loss from his immediate successor in title through an indemnity covenant.

6.9.2.   In certain circumstances it may be possible to make an *ex parte* application to the Lands Tribunal under Law of Property Act 1925, s.84 for the modification or release of an obsolete restrictive covenant and so remove the potential liability under it.

6.9.3.   The burden of positive covenants does not run with freehold land and can only be enforced directly between the original contracting parties.[1] An original covenantor who is held liable in this way may seek to recoup his own loss if an indemnity covenant was taken from his immediate successor in title.

6.9.4.   Covenants entered into on or after 11 May 2000 and which are clearly expressed to be taken for the benefit of successors in title to the land may be enforceable by successors under Contracts (Rights of Third Parties) Act 1999. This Act applies to both positive and negative covenants.

1.   *Rhone* v. *Stephens*, *The Times*, 18 March 1994, HL.

6.10.   Covenants in leasehold land

6.10.1.   Although both positive and restrictive covenants are enforceable, liability is limited by the doctrines of privity of contract and of estate. It may not therefore always be possible for a head-landlord to take direct action against a sub-tenant since neither privity of contract nor of estate exist in this situation. However, covenants entered into on or after 11 May 2000 may benefit from Contracts (Rights of Third Parties) Act 1999 which amends the law relating to privity of contract and will allow direct enforcement between e.g. a head-landlord and a sub-tenant.

6.10.2.   Similarly, in the absence of special provisions in the lease, it is not generally possible for one tenant directly to sue a fellow tenant for breach of one of the covenants contained in their leases, and the enforcement of the covenant against the offending tenant frequently has to be brought by the landlord at the request of the injured tenant. However, covenants entered into on or after 11 May 2000 may benefit from Contracts (Rights of Third Parties) Act 1999 which amends the law relating to privity of contract and will allow direct enforcement between tenants.

6.10.3.   Liability on leasehold covenants is further discussed in K6 and K10.

6.11.   Estate agent's commission

6.11.1.   The following points are relevant to the estate agent's entitlement to his commission and when it becomes payable.

6.11.2. The contract between the agent and the seller must be absolutely clear as to what is included in the price. For example does the fee quoted include, e.g. advertising, valuation, agent's expenses, VAT, or are these to be added to the bill?

6.11.3. In the absence of express provision in the contract no charge can be made for abortive work.[1]

6.11.4. As a general principle, an agent's entitlement to his fee depends on his introduction of a ready, able and willing buyer. This means someone who is prepared and able to go ahead to completion not merely a 'subject to contract' offer.[2]

6.11.5. It is in the estate agent's interests to ensure that the contract is quite specific as to the time when his fee for the estate agency work becomes due, and that the fee becomes payable as soon as a binding contract is entered into with the buyer – not on condition that completion takes place. This type of provision (commonly found in estate agent's contracts) ensures that the commission is still payable even if the contract is terminated between exchange and completion or completion fails to take place.[3]

6.11.6. The courts interpret the expressions 'the agent is to find a buyer' or 'the agent is to introduce a buyer' as meaning that the buyer must actually sign the contract before the commission becomes due.[4]

6.11.7. Three conditions must all be satisfied before the agent can claim his commission:

    (a) the agent must introduce a person who enters into a valid binding contract. This means a contract which satisfies the requirements of Law of Property (Miscellaneous Provisions) Act 1989, s.2 and the contract is not otherwise voidable for mistake, fraud, etc.;

    (b) the buyer must be willing and able (financially) to complete. The buyer's ability in this respect is judged at contractual date for completion, so if there is a dispute about the agent's entitlement to his fee the contractual completion date must be allowed to pass before proceedings for the commission are commenced. This is so even if, under the contract with the seller, commission became payable on exchange of contracts;

    (c) the agent must be the effective cause of the sale. This means that he must be able to show that his introduction of the buyer led to the formation of the contract of sale between the seller and buyer. An 'introduction' may be nothing more than bringing the property to the buyer's attention (see *Christie, Owen and Davies plc* v. *Rylance* [2005] 18 EG 148 (CS), *Pettigrew* v. *George Wimpey UK Ltd* [2007] EWHC 2559, QB and *Foxtons Ltd* v. *Pelkey Bicknell* [2008] EWCA Civ 419).

6.11.8. If the buyer fails to complete the contract and is in breach of his contract with the seller, unless commission was expressly due on exchange, no completion means no commission. If, however, the seller successfully claims damages from the buyer for breach, the agent may be entitled to recover a *quantum meruit* out of the seller's damages.[5]

6.11.9. Where two agents are instructed by the seller, there is frequently an argument about which of the agents is entitled to the commission for the sale. The principle here is that commission is payable to the first agent to secure a buyer who enters a binding contract.[6]

6.11.10. If it is the seller who withdraws from the sale, no contract means no commission, unless the contract contains express provision to the contrary. It makes no difference in this situation if the seller rescinds after the contract is made (even if the seller is in breach).

6.11.11. If a sole agency is agreed with the client, it is important that the terms of that agreement are fully and clearly explained to the client so he cannot complain of being misled if things go wrong. The danger as far as the client is concerned is that he does not understand what a sole agency means, instructs a second agent who sells the property and then feels aggrieved because both agents claim to be entitled to commission. If a sole agency agreement is expressed in terms using the phrase 'sole agent', the seller is not entitled to instruct another agent to sell the property, but there is nothing to prevent him from contracting a private sale and in that way depriving the agent of his commission. On the other hand, if the expression 'sole right to sell' is used this prohibits the seller from contracting a private sale on his own initiative. This latter phrase is therefore much more restrictive of the seller's rights than the former and would merit explicit explanation of its implications to the client. The term 'sole selling agent' is construed as meaning 'sole agent', so the seller is not prevented from contracting a private sale if this phrase is used.

6.11.12. If the seller withdraws his instructions from the agent before a sale contract is entered into, this is not a breach of the sole agency contract (the seller is entitled to change his mind and this is a normal and acceptable risk attached to estate agency) but a *sale* contracted elsewhere will be and the sole agent can then claim damages for the breach.

6.11.13. An agent who is himself in breach of his duty to his client may forfeit his right to commission.

6.11.14. Estate Agents (Provision of Information) Regulations 1991 require estate agents to inform their clients in writing of the terms of the agreement between themselves and their clients including, where appropriate, the meaning of 'sole agency' and 'sole selling rights'. The Regulations have adopted definitions of these two phrases which are similar to the explanations contained in M6.11.11.

1. *Lott* v. *Outhwaite* (1893) 10 TLR 76.
2. *Luxor* v. *Cooper* [1941] AC 108.
3. *Poole* v. *Clarke & Co.* [1945] 2 All ER 445; *cf. Midgley Estates Ltd* v. *Hand* [1952] QB 432. See also *Foxtons Ltd* v. *Thesleff* [2005] EWCA Civ 514; [2005] 21 EG 140.
4. *Jones* v. *Lowe* [1945] KB 73.

5. *Boots* v. *E Christopher & Co.* [1952] 1 KB 89.
6. *AA Dickson & Co.* v. *O'Leary* (1979) 254 EG 731 suggests that the seller cannot be made liable to pay commission twice over.

6.12. Timeshare properties

6.12.1. Timeshare Act 1992 gives the prospective buyer of a timeshare property a 14-day 'cooling off' period during which he has the right to cancel the contract.[1] The Act only applies where the buyer is buying from the developer and not to 'second-hand' timeshares.

6.12.2. Notice of the buyer's right to cancel must be given by the seller in prescribed form. Failure to give the correct notice renders the contract unenforceable and the seller is guilty of a criminal offence punishable by a fine. Enforcement of the Act is the responsibility of the local weights and measures office.

6.12.3. Timeshare Regulations 1997 (SI 1997/1081) extend Timeshare Act 1992 to rights acquired as the result of share ownership and rights under collective investment schemes. The Act is also extended to cover properties within the EU, Iceland, Norway, Liechtenstein and Switzerland, where the buyer is a private individual (not acting in the course of a business) who is normally resident in the UK.

6.12.4. A seller is required to provide any person on request with a document containing information on the property. This information will form part of the contract if a contract is subsequently entered into by an individual buyer acting in a private (i.e. non-business) capacity.

6.12.5. The contract must contain certain minimum information relating to the nature of the property, the price and recurring cover and charges. A buyer who is resident in the UK is entitled to have a copy of the contract in English.

1. This period may be extended to 3 months and 10 days if certain information is not provided to the buyer.

6.13. Squatters

6.13.1. A summary procedure for the eviction of squatters exists under Order 24 County Court Rules or under Criminal Justice and Public Order Act 1994, ss.72–75. The 1994 Act applies to both residential and commercial property.

6.14. Energy performance of buildings

6.14.1. Energy Performance of Buildings (Certificates and Inspections) (England and Wales) Regulations 2007 (SI 2007/991)[1] ('the regulations') amend the Building Regulations and place sellers, landlords and builders under an obligation to provide an energy performance certificate (EPC) to prospective buyers and tenants (see A27 for further details).

6.14.2. The local Weights and Measures Authority is responsible for the enforcement of the duties. An authorised officer of such an Authority has power to require the production of documents for inspection (reg.39) and, in the event of a breach of duty, has the power to issue a penalty charge notice (reg.40). The amount of the penalty charge is determined according to the category of building and the breach concerned (reg.43). An appeal against such a penalty charge notice lies to the County Court (reg.45).

6.14.3. An energy assessor must be a member of an accreditation scheme approved by the Secretary of State. Such schemes must contain adequate provision for indemnity arrangements and for facilitating the resolution of complaints (reg. 25).

6.14.4. Regulation 14 creates an offence for the unauthorised disclosure of an EPC, recommendation report or any data collected by an energy assessor for the purposes of preparing such a document.

1. As amended, most recently by Energy Performance of Buildings (Certificates and Inspection) (England and Wales) (Amendment) Regulations 2010 (SI 2010/1456).

6.15. Consumer Code for Home Builders

6.15.1. A redress scheme exists for complaints about non-compliance with the Consumer Code for Home Builders (see I1.2) arising and made within two years of completion of the purchase of the home.

6.15.2. Disputes are resolved using an adjudication process. Awards of up to a maximum of £15,000 inclusive of VAT can be made and home builders who are in serious breach of the Code could be removed from the registers of the home warranty providers. See **www.consumercodeforhomebuilders.com** for further information.

M7. Rectification

7.1.   Rectification of the contract

7.1.1.   Where the parties have reached agreement over a particular matter, but in error that matter is either omitted from the written contract, or is wrongly recorded in the written agreement, an application for rectification of the contract in order to correct the error can be made.[1] Under Law of Property (Miscellaneous Provisions) Act 1989, s.2(4) where rectification is ordered the court has a discretion to determine the date on which the contract comes into operation. If a term is missing from the contract, there is no contract.

1.   See *Wright* v. *Robert Leonard Developments Ltd* [1994] EGCS 69.

7.2.   Rectification of the purchase deed

7.2.1.   Where a term of the contract is either omitted from, or inaccurately represented in, the purchase deed an application for rectification of the deed may be made to the court. Rectification relates back to the date when the original document was executed and there is no need to draw up an amended deed. The order granting rectification is often endorsed on the affected deed.[1] Rectification is an equitable remedy and is thus subject to the equitable bars.

1.   For examples of the court's discretion to rectify see, e.g. *Craddock Bros* v. *Hunt* [1923] 2 Ch 136; *Wilson* v. *Wilson* [1969] 3 All ER 945; *Riverlate Properties Ltd* v. *Paul* [1975] Ch 133.

7.3.   Rectification of documents by the Adjudicator

7.3.1.   The Adjudicator to HM Land Registry[1] has power, on application, to make any order which the High Court could make for the rectification or setting aside of a document which:

(a)   effects a qualifying disposition of a registered estate or charge;

(b)   is a contract to make such a disposition; or

(c)   effects a transfer of an interest which is the subject of a notice in the register.[2]

A qualifying disposition is a registrable disposition or one which creates an interest which may be the subject of a notice in the register.[3]

1. See G3.13 as to other functions of the Adjudicator and the website at **www.ahmlr.gov.uk** for appropriate application forms and guidance notes.
2. Land Registration Act 2002, s.108(2).
3. *Ibid.*, s.108(3).

7.4.   Rectification of the register and indemnity

7.4.1.   Rectification in Land Registration Act 2002 has a narrower definition than in the previous law. It is limited to an alteration in the register which involves the correction of a mistake and prejudicially affects the title of a registered proprietor.[1] When such rectification occurs, the proprietor may be entitled to indemnity.

7.4.2.   The court has power to make an order for rectification of the register:

       (a)   to correct a mistake;

       (b)   to bring the register up to date; or

       (c)   to give effect to any estate, right or interest excepted from the effect of registration.[2]

7.4.3.   Rectification cannot be ordered against a proprietor without his consent in relation to land in his possession unless:

       (a)   the proprietor has by fraud or lack of proper care caused or substantially contributed to the mistake; or

       (b)   it would for any other reason be unjust for the alteration not to be made.[3]

Land is in the possession of a proprietor if it is physically in his possession. A proprietor is treated as being in possession of land which is physically in the possession of certain other people, for example, the proprietor's tenant or licensee.[4]

7.4.4.   Where the court has power to make an order for rectification it must do so unless there are exceptional circumstances which justify its not doing so.[5]

7.4.5.   The registrar has power to rectify the register without the need for the matter to be considered by the court. He can rectify the register for the same purposes, and subject to the same limitations, as the court has power to order it. He also has power to remove a superfluous entry, for example cancellation of a Form A restriction when its terms have been complied with.[6]

1. Land Registration Act 2002, Sched.4, para.1 and see Land Registry Practice Guide 39.
2. Land Registration Act 2002, Sched.4, para.2.
3. *Ibid.*, Sched.4, para.3(2).
4. *Ibid.*, s.131.

5. *Ibid.*, Sched.4, para.3(3).
6. *Ibid.*, Sched.4, paras.5 and 6.

7.5.   **Indemnity**

7.5.1.   Subject to the exceptions contained in Land Registration Act 2002 a person is entitled to be indemnified by the registrar if he suffers loss by reason of:

    (a)   a rectification of the register;

    (b)   a mistake whose correction would involve rectification of the register;

    (c)   a mistake in an official search;

    (d)   a mistake in an official copy;

    (e)   a mistake in a document kept by the registrar which is not an original and is referred to in the register;

    (f)   the loss or destruction of a document lodged at the registry for inspection or safe custody;

    (g)   a mistake in the cautions register; or

    (h)   failure by the registrar to perform his duty under section 50 Land Registration Act 2002 (duty of notification of overriding statutory charges).[1]

7.5.2.   Indemnity is not payable for any loss suffered by a claimant wholly or partly as a result of his own fraud or lack of proper care.[2]

7.5.3.   No indemnity is payable on account of any mines or minerals, or the existence of any right to work or get mines or minerals, unless it is noted in the register that the title to the registered estate concerned includes the mines or minerals.[3]

7.5.4.   Indemnity may be claimed for costs or expenses reasonably incurred by the claimant with the consent of the registrar.[4]

7.5.5.   For limitation purposes, the claim must be made within six years of the time when the claimant knows, or but for his own default might have known, of the existence of his claim.[5]

7.5.6.   A claim for indemnity should initially be made to the registrar. However, a person may apply to the court for the determination of any question as to whether he is entitled to an indemnity and its amount.[6]

7.5.7.   Where the register is not rectified, the amount of indemnity payable cannot exceed the value of the estate or interest at the time when the mistake which caused the loss was made. Where the register is rectified, the amount of indemnity is limited to the value of the estate or interest immediately before rectification of the register (but as if there were to be no rectification).[7]

7.5.8.   There are provisions for the payment of interest on the amount of any indemnity so paid.[8]

7.5.9.   Where an indemnity is paid the registrar is entitled either to recover the amount paid from any person who caused or substantially contributed to the loss by his fraud or to enforce any rights of action for the purpose of recovering the amount paid.[9]

1.   Land Registration Act 2002, Sched.8, para.1 and see Land Registry Practice Guide 39.
2.   Land Registration Act 2002, Sched.8, para.5.
3.   *Ibid.*, Sched.8, para.2 and see Land Registry Practice Guide 65.
4.   Land Registration Act 2002, Sched.8, para.3 and see Land Registry Practice Guide 38.
5.   Land Registration Act 2002, Sched.8, para.8.
6.   *Ibid.*, Sched.8, para.7.
7.   *Ibid.*, Sched.8, para.6.
8.   Land Registration Rules 2003, r.195.
9.   Land Registration Act 2002, Sched.8, para.10.

M8. Liens

8.1.	**Seller's lien**	8.3.	**Solicitor's lien**
8.2.	**Buyer's lien**	8.4.	**Abortive transactions**

8.1. Seller's lien

8.1.1. The seller has an equitable lien over the property being sold to the extent of the unpaid purchase price.[1]

8.1.2. The lien arises immediately there is a binding contract for sale and is discharged on completion to the extent that the purchase price is paid at that time.[2]

8.1.3. By Law of Property Act 1925, s.68 the presence of a receipt clause in the purchase deed is evidence (but not conclusive evidence) of the discharge of the seller's lien. In registered land, in the absence of an adverse entry on the register of the title (or protection of the lien as an overriding interest) a subsequent purchaser of the land will take free from the lien.[3]

8.1.4. To protect the lien it should be registered as a notice in the register of the title in registered land, or as a Class C(iii) land charge in unregistered land pursuant to a priority notice. The lien may take effect as an overriding interest in registered land if (unusually) the person with its benefit is in occupation of the land.[4] An unpaid seller who is in actual occupation may be estopped from claiming that the lien is an overriding interest if he has warranted, in answer to pre-contract enquiries, that vacant possession will be given on completion.[5]

8.1.5. The lien is enforceable by foreclosure[6] or by a court order for sale of the property.[7]

8.1.6. If the seller has agreed to permit the buyer to leave part of the purchase price outstanding on mortgage, the purchase deed should not contain a receipt clause. The buyer should enter a covenant to pay the money to the seller and to enter a formal mortgage if required. If the seller has taken a mortgage to secure the outstanding moneys, this will displace the lien. Where it appears from the transfer that further moneys are payable by the buyer to the seller but it is intended that the seller should not have a lien on the property, it is desirable for an express waiver to be included in the transfer. Where the buyer is entering another mortgage to assist with his purchase of the property, care needs to be exercised to ensure that the priorities of the lender's and seller's charges are correctly maintained; a lender will not normally cede priority to the seller's lien. It may be preferable to include a receipt clause in the document and to execute a formal mortgage in the seller's favour.

8.1.7. If the transfer cites the non-payment and contains a provision for a charge over the land, this charge may take priority over a formal mortgage created by the buyer in favour of a third party immediately after completion, but this will depend on priorities and registration.

8.1.8.   By Standard Condition 6.5.1 and Standard Commercial Property Condition 8.5.1 the seller is not entitled to a lien over the title deeds after completion. If the seller wishes to reserve such a lien this provision must be expressly excluded by contractual condition.

1. *Mackreth* v. *Symmons* (1808) 15 Ves 329.
2. *London and Cheshire Insurance Co. Ltd* v. *Laplagrene Property Co. Ltd* [1971] Ch 499.
3. Land Registration Act 2002, s.29.
4. *Ibid.*, Sched.1, para.2 and Sched.3, para.2.
5. *UCB Finance* v. *France* [1995] NPC 144.
6. *Hughes* v. *Griffin* [1969] 1 All ER 460.
7. *Williams* v. *Aylesbury & Buckingham Rail Co.* (1874) 9 Ch App 684.

8.2.   Buyer's lien

8.2.1.   The buyer has a similar lien over the property to the extent of any deposit paid by him. This lien can be registered as a notice in registered land or as a Class C(iii) land charge in unregistered land (see B17.12).

8.3.   Solicitor's lien

8.3.1.   At common law a solicitor has a lien over his client's property until his costs are paid. He may also ask the court to direct that property recovered by the solicitor in an action brought on the client's behalf should be retained by the solicitor as security against the solicitor's costs.

8.3.2.   The common law lien attaches to all deeds, papers and other personal property of the client which come into the solicitor's possession with the client's consent. Such property must have been received by the solicitor in his capacity as solicitor. No lien attaches to a client's will. A buyer's solicitor must have received documents over which he exercises his lien in his capacity as buyer's solicitor and not, e.g. as lender's solicitor.

8.3.3.   The lien is restricted to costs due to the solicitor in respect of work done on the client's instructions. The solicitor is entitled to retain the client's property until his costs are paid in full.

8.3.4.   The existence of the lien does not entitle the solicitor to sell or otherwise dispose of the client's property.

8.3.5.   Despite the existence of a lien the Law Society has power to order a solicitor to hand over papers to one of its officers where there is an intervention in a solicitor's practice under Solicitors Act 1974, Sched.1 and the court also has power to order papers to be delivered.[1]

8.3.6. On termination of the retainer where the client has instructed another solicitor to act for him, the first solicitor should hand over papers and documents to the second solicitor, subject to obtaining a satisfactory undertaking from the second solicitor in respect of payment of the first solicitor's costs.

8.3.7. A solicitor has no lien against the official receiver or a trustee in bankruptcy.[2]

8.3.8. A further type of lien exists by virtue of Solicitors Act 1974, s.73 which empowers the court to make a charging order over real or personal property belonging to the client as security for the solicitor's taxed costs (see N1).

8.3.9. No lien can be exercised over property which is held by the solicitor in the capacity of stakeholder.[3]

8.3.10. Under the terms of the CML Lenders' Handbook the lender's solicitor is not entitled to exercise a lien over the title deeds.

1. Solicitors Act 1974, s.68.
2. See *Re Toleman and England, ex p. Bramble* (1880) 13 Ch 885.
3. *Rockeagle Ltd* v. *Alsop Wilkinson* [1992] Ch 47.

8.4. Abortive transactions

8.4.1. A draft contract and other papers supplied by the seller's solicitor to the buyer's solicitor belong to the seller until contracts for the transaction are exchanged. If therefore the transaction is aborted before exchange takes place the buyer's solicitor should comply with a request for return of those papers made by the seller's solicitor. This is notwithstanding any contrary instructions issued by the buyer to his own solicitor. For the avoidance of doubt the seller's solicitor may choose to indicate in his covering letter to the buyer's solicitor that he expects such papers to be returned to him on request if the transaction does not proceed to exchange.

M9. Covenants for title

9.1. Introduction

9.1.1. On completion of the transaction the contract merges with the purchase deed in so far as the two documents cover the same ground, and in general an action arising out of the contract is not possible after completion has taken place. The principal post-completion remedy available to the buyer will be an action for breach of the title guarantee which was introduced by Law of Property (Miscellaneous Provisions) Act 1994. This applies to all transactions completed on or after 1 July 1995.

9.1.2. As an exception to the general rule outlined in the preceding paragraph, an action arising out of the contract is sustainable after completion in circumstances where a clause or clauses of the contract have been expressed in such a way that they do not merge with the purchase deed on completion.[1] In appropriate circumstances an action in misrepresentation would also be available since this action does not derive from the contract itself.

9.1.3. For transactions completed before 1 July 1995 the principal post-completion remedy is an action for breach of the covenants for title. The exact nature of the covenants implied into the purchase deed depends upon the capacity in which the seller transferred the land. The appropriate law is contained in Law of Property Act 1925, s.76 (as modified by Land Registration Act 1925, s.24). If a seller purported to convey in a capacity other than that which he in fact possessed, e.g. a trustee purported to sell as a beneficial owner, it is likely that no covenants of title will have passed in the purchase deed. The benefit of a covenant for title is annexed to and passes with the land. So if A sells to B, B's successor in title can enforce the covenant for title given by A provided the action is brought within the appropriate limitation period of 12 years.

1. See Standard Condition 7.4 and Standard Commercial Property Condition 9.4.

9.2. Title guarantee

9.2.1. The seller can sell with either full or limited title guarantee. The guarantees apply to the sale of both freehold and leasehold property and on the grant of a lease. They can also be used on the transfer of personal property including intellectual property and rights in shares.

9.2.2. On the front of the Standard Contract form the seller should specify whether he sells with full or limited title guarantee. Should the seller fail to specify the nature of the title guarantee, Standard Condition 4.6.2 and Standard Commercial Property Condition 6.6.2 provide that the seller will sell with full title guarantee.

9.2.3. The warranties given under the full and limited guarantees can be amended in the agreement. If the seller is concerned about incumbrances he should disclose them in the contract and ensure that the buyer agrees to take the property subject to them. See also Standard Condition 4.6.3. Under section 6 of the 1994 Act (as amended by Land Registration Act 2002) the sale of a registered title will also be subject to any matters entered in the register of title at the time of the disposition. As a result any such matters will not be covered by the title guarantee.

9.2.4. If the seller is a beneficial owner, he will usually provide full title guarantee. If the seller is a trustee, personal representative or mortgagee, he will usually provide a limited title guarantee.

Full title guarantee

9.2.5. Where the full guarantee is given the seller warrants that:

(a) he has the right to dispose of the property in the manner purported;

(b) he will at his own cost do all he reasonably can to give his transferee the title he purports to give;

(c) he disposes of his whole interest where that interest is registered;

(d) he disposes of the whole lease where the interest is leasehold;

(e) he disposes of a freehold where it is unclear from the face of the documents whether the interest is freehold or leasehold;

(f) in the case of a subsisting lease he covenants that the lease is still subsisting and that there is no subsisting breach which might result in forfeiture;

(g) in the case of a mortgage of a property which is subject to a rentcharge or lease, that the mortgagor will observe and perform the obligations under the rentcharge or lease;

(h) that the person giving the disposition is disposing of it free from all charges and encumbrances (whether monetary or not) and from all other rights exercisable by third parties, not being rights which the transferor does not and could not reasonably be expected to know about.

9.2.6. Under (b) the seller is promising to put right any defects in title, for example, he will execute any further documents needed to ensure that the buyer receives the title he contracted to buy.

9.2.7. As a result of the warranty in (e) a seller who is selling a leasehold estate must expressly state in the contract that the estate is leasehold. The seller can do this on the front page of the Standard Conditions of Sale form. The warranty in (f) applies on the sale of an existing lease. The seller should modify this covenant to ensure that he will not be liable to the buyer for any breach of any of the tenant's covenants relating to the physical state and condition of the property. Standard Condition 3.2.2 and Standard Commercial Property Condition 3.2.2 modify this implied warranty by providing that the property is sold subject to any subsisting breach of a condition or tenant's obligation relating to the physical state of the property which renders the lease liable to forfeiture. Standard Condition 3.2.3 and Standard Commercial Property Condition 3.2.3 contain a similar provision on the grant of a sub-lease.

9.2.8.   The warranty in (h) applies to any encumbrances created by the seller or by his predecessors unless the encumbrances are disclosed in the contract or on the title of a registered property.

Limited title guarantee

9.2.9.   Where limited title guarantee is given, all the above warranties apply except for (h), which is replaced with the following:

> (h)   that the transferor has not charged or encumbered the property by a charge or encumbrance which still exists, that he has not granted any third party rights which still subsist and that he is not aware that anyone else has done so since the last disposition for value.

9.2.10.   The seller therefore warrants that he has not encumbered the property but he does not warrant that his predecessor has not done so.

Assignment of the guarantee

9.2.11.   The title guarantee runs with the land and is enforceable by the buyer's successors in title.

Remedies

9.2.12.   A breach of title guarantee is actionable as a breach of contract. However, the remedies available may be restricted. Once completion has taken place, or a third party has acquired an interest in the property, e.g. a lender, it is unlikely that rescission will be granted. Damages will therefore be the usual remedy although the seller may be ordered to execute documents to perfect a defective title.

M10. Solicitor's negligence

10.1.   **Introduction**

10.2.   **Action to be taken by solicitor**

10.1.   Introduction

10.1.1.   Where a solicitor has been negligent the client must seek redress through a civil action against the solicitor.

10.1.2.   Where a client or third party makes a claim against a solicitor (or gives notice of intention to make such a claim) and the claim is one in respect of which indemnity is provided by the solicitor's insurance the solicitor must as soon as practicable notify his insurers and co-operate with them in order to enable the claim to be dealt with in the appropriate manner. Where top-up indemnity cover is maintained the terms of that policy should also be considered.

10.1.3.   The Legal Complaints Service can take action against a solicitor who provides inadequate professional services (see M6.2).

10.2.   Action to be taken by solicitor

10.2.1.   If a solicitor discovers an act or omission which would justify a claim by a client (or third party) against him he should:

   (a)   contact his insurers;

   (b)   inform the client (or third party) in order to enable him to take independent legal advice;

   (c)   seek the advice of his insurers as to any further communication with the client (or third party); and

   (d)   confirm any oral communication in writing.

10.2.2.   If a client makes a claim against his solicitor or notifies his intention of doing so, or if the solicitor discovers an act or omission which would justify such a claim, the solicitor is under a duty to inform his client that he should seek independent advice.

10.2.3.   If the client refuses to seek independent advice the solicitor should decline to act further for the client unless he is satisfied that no conflict of interest exists.

10.2.4.   The solicitor should not admit liability or settle a claim without the consent of his insurers.

10.2.5. Where the solicitor is asked to hand papers over to another solicitor who is giving independent advice to the client about the claim, the solicitor should keep copies of the original documents for his own reference. If the first solicitor has a lien over the client's papers he may, as an alternative to taking copies, ask the second solicitor to give an undertaking for the production of the papers should they be required.

N. COSTS

N1. Costs

1.1. The basis of charging

1.1.1. Costs in non-contentious matters including conveyancing are governed by Solicitors' (Non-Contentious Business) Remuneration Order 2009 (see Appendix VIII.3).

1.1.2. Solicitors' (Non-Contentious Business) Remuneration Order 2009 provides that the remuneration shall be 'such sum as may be fair and reasonable having regard to all the circumstances of the case'. The following matters must be taken into account:

(a) the complexity of the matter or the difficulty or novelty of the questions raised;

(b) the skill, labour, specialised knowledge and responsibility involved;

(c) the time spent on the business;

(d) the number and importance of the documents prepared or perused, without regard to length;

(e) the place where and the circumstances in which the business or any part thereof is transacted;

(f) the amount or value of any money or property involved;

(g) whether any land involved is registered land;

(h) the importance of the matter to the client; and

(i) the approval (express or implied) of the entitled person or the express approval of the testator to:

(i) the solicitor undertaking all or any part of the work giving rise to the costs; or

(ii) the amount of the costs.

1.1.3.   On taking instructions the solicitor should give his client the best information he can about the likely cost of the matter including when costs will be charged and whether or not such costs will be deducted from money held by the solicitor on the client's behalf. Where possible an estimate should be given to the client; in other cases the solicitor should give the client a general forecast of the approximate costs to be incurred. Where no estimate has been given and the solicitor has not arranged an agreed fee for the work, the client must be told how the solicitor's charges are to be calculated, e.g. on an hourly rate basis or as a percentage of the value of the transaction. Information should also be given to the client about the nature and cost of disbursements.

1.1.4.   Rule 2.03 (information about the cost) and Rule 2.05 (complaints handling) Solicitors' Code of Conduct 2007 and the Law Society's Practice Management Standards should also be followed. Failure to observe these standards is regarded as inadequate professional services by the Legal Complaints Service.

1.1.5.   By Supply of Goods and Services Act 1982, s.15 the contract between solicitor and client contains an implied term that the client will pay the solicitor a reasonable sum for his services; however, the matter of costs should be dealt with expressly. It is the solicitor's duty to raise the issue of costs if the client does not enquire.

1.1.6.   When confirming the client's instructions the solicitor should record whether a fee has been agreed, and if so what it covers and whether it includes VAT and disbursements.

1.1.7.   Where the client has imposed an upper limit on costs, a solicitor who exceeds that limit without the client's authority will not be able to recover his costs in so far as they exceed the agreed maximum sum. The client must be informed as soon as possible if it appears that the limit imposed on the costs will be insufficient and instructions obtained as to whether the client wishes the solicitor to continue with the matter. If the solicitor continues to act and exceeds the limit imposed by the client on the costs to be incurred the amount of the bill in excess of the agreed amount will be disallowed if the client applies for a remuneration certificate or taxation. The solicitor may also be guilty of professional misconduct in these circumstances.

1.1.8.   The amount of costs being incurred on a client's behalf should be reviewed regularly. It is recommended that the client should be informed at least every six months of the amount of costs incurred to date and where appropriate an interim bill should be delivered.

1.1.9.   A solicitor may, at the outset of the retainer, require the client to make a payment on account of costs and disbursements to be incurred. The solicitor must make his acceptance of the instructions conditional on the client's advance payment. Unless he does this the solicitor will not be able to justify the termination of the retainer if the client does not make the interim payment.

1.1.10. A solicitor may charge interest on the whole or outstanding part of an unpaid bill with effect from one month after delivery of the bill, provided that notice has been given to the client informing him of his right to apply for a remuneration certificate and taxation of the bill. The rate of interest chargeable is that which is payable on judgment debts.

1.1.11. A solicitor must not take advantage of the client by overcharging for work done or to be done. Overcharging the client may be professional misconduct. If a taxing officer allows less than one-half of the sum charged he is under a duty to report the matter to the Law Society. The solicitor is responsible for ensuring that the amount of the bill is fair and reasonable and cannot escape liability by delegating the preparation of the bill to a costs draftsman.

1.1.12. Unless there is an agreement to the contrary, a solicitor is personally responsible for paying the proper costs of any professional agent or other person whom he instructs on behalf of his client, whether or not he receives payment from his client.

1.1.13. If a solicitor wishes to recover costs by way of deduction from money which the solicitor is holding on the client's behalf, he must first give or send the client a bill of costs. Once this has been done, the costs element of the money being held by the solicitor becomes office money and must be transferred from clients' account to office account within 14 days.

1.1.14. At the end of the transaction, any surplus funds no longer required (or received after the solicitor has accounted to the client) must be returned to the client promptly.[1] If there is to be an ongoing retainer, the solicitor must promptly (and at least annually thereafter) inform the client of the amount retained and the reason for the retention.[2] If the solicitor has made adequate attempts to return unclaimed residual balances of £50 or less to the rightful owner, they may be withdrawn from client account and paid to charity subject to proper records being maintained. The withdrawal of larger sums and any amounts not being paid to charity require the prior authorisation of the Solicitors Regulation Authority.[3]

1.1.15. In the absence of agreement to the contrary a solicitor will charge on a *quantum meruit* basis (or for a reasonable sum under Supply of Goods and Services Act 1982, s.15) for abortive work.

1.1.16. Solicitors who terminate their retainer for good reason and on reasonable notice as permitted by Rule 2.01(2) Solicitors' Code of Conduct 2007 are entitled to recover from the client costs and disbursements for the work done before termination of the retainer.[4]

1.1.17. For practical advice, see also 'Non-contentious costs', published online by the Practice Advice Service of the Law Society (see **www.lawsociety.org.uk**).

1. Solicitors' Accounts Rules 1998, r.15(3).
2. *Ibid.*, r.15(4).

3. *Ibid.*, r.22.
4. *Richard Buxton (Solicitors)* v. *Huw Llewelyn Paul Mills-Owens and the Law Society (Intervener)* [2010] EWCA Civ 122.

1.2.   **Agreements for charges**

1.2.1.   Solicitors Act 1974, s.57 allows a solicitor to make an agreement with a client for costs in a non-contentious matter.

1.2.2.   In order to be enforceable under the Act, the agreement must fully comply with the provisions of section 57. Thus the agreement must be in writing and be signed by the party to be charged or his agent, i.e. the client.

1.2.3.   Remuneration may be by a gross sum, by reference to an hourly rate, or a commission, percentage, salary or otherwise, and should state whether the agreed remuneration is to be inclusive of disbursements and VAT. The agreement should specifically set out the method by which the remuneration is to be calculated.

1.2.4.   An agreement which complies with section 57 is enforceable under the ordinary principles of contract law and can be referred for assessment by the court.

1.2.5.   If the costs are ultimately assessed by the court and the client raises an objection to the agreement on the grounds that it is unfair or unreasonable, the taxing officer may enquire into the facts and the court may set the agreement aside or reduce the amount payable and give such consequential directions as it thinks fit.

1.3.   **VAT**

1.3.1.   When giving an estimate or quotation for costs the solicitor should make it clear to the client whether or not VAT is included in the quoted sum.

1.3.2.   If VAT is not mentioned it is presumed that the quotation or estimate is VAT inclusive.

1.3.3.   Where an individual or firm is registered for VAT the firm's VAT registration number must appear on the bills issued by the firm or, if a separate tax invoice is issued, on the tax invoice.

1.3.4.   The VAT registration number is also required to appear on any bill or fee note produced on a taxation of costs *inter partes*.

1.3.5.   Stamp duties and other statutory charges are not liable to VAT (see A14 and A16).

1.3.6. Where the client's bill is reduced by the amount of commission which a solicitor has earned, e.g. on an endowment policy taken out by the client, VAT should be charged on the gross amount of the bill but in practice is sometimes only charged on the net sum (see A8.8).

1.3.7. Costs and expenses incurred by a solicitor in performing his own services, such as fees for telegraphic transfers or travel costs, must bear VAT at the standard rate when passed on by a solicitor to his or her client. In order to be a true disbursement for VAT purposes, and therefore not be subject to VAT when recharged, the solicitor must meet stringent conditions set by HM Revenue and Customs. The Law Society's VAT on Disbursements Practice Note (19 February 2009) provides clarification on the VAT treatment of disbursements.

1.4. Delivery of bill

1.4.1. A solicitor is under a duty to render a bill of costs to his client within a reasonable time of concluding the matter to which the bill relates.

1.4.2. It is recommended practice to submit a bill to the client as soon as possible after the conclusion of the transaction and it is particularly important to do so where the solicitor is already holding sums of money on his client's behalf and has chosen to wait for the client's approval of the bill before deducting his costs and accounting to the client for the balance, or where the client has asked for the papers and the solicitor is claiming a lien over them until his costs are met.

1.4.3. In residential conveyancing purchase transactions the bill is usually submitted to the client before completion on the understanding that the solicitor's charges are paid in full before completion. In sale transactions, the solicitor's costs are usually deducted from money held by the solicitor on the client's behalf after completion before the balance is remitted to the client.

1.4.4. A solicitor's bill of costs should contain sufficient information to identify the matter to which it relates and the period covered.

1.4.5. The form of the bill should comply with Solicitors Act 1974, s.69 and must be signed by the solicitor personally or on his behalf by an employee authorised by him to do so. The bill may be in electronic form as the signature may be an electronic signature. Alternatively the letter which accompanies and refers to the bill should be so signed. Unless this provision is complied with the solicitor will be unable to sue on the bill. A form of signature such as, e.g. 'signed A. Smith, a partner in A. Smith & Co.' is recommended to ensure that it can be proved in evidence (should it be necessary to sue) that the bill was signed by a solicitor and not merely by an unqualified assistant. Disbursements should be separately itemised in the bill.

1.5. Remuneration certificate

1.5.1. The remuneration certificate procedure was abolished with effect from 11 August 2009.[1]

1.5.2. The client may however apply to have his bill assessed by the Supreme Court Costs Office.

1. See Solicitors (Non-Contentious Business) Remuneration Order 2009 (SI 2009/1931).

1.6. Client information on costs

1.6.1. Before bringing proceedings to recover non-contentious costs, or where costs (other than disbursements) are to be deducted from money held on behalf of a client in satisfaction of a bill and if an entitled person objects in writing to the amount of the bill within the prescribed time, the solicitor must inform the client or other entitled person in writing of their right to have the bill assessed by the court under Solicitors Act 1974, ss.70–72. The client or other entitled person must also be informed in writing that the solicitor is entitled to charge interest on the outstanding amount of the bill in accordance with Article 5 Solicitors (Non-Contentious Business) Remuneration Order 2009 (SI 2009/1931).[1]

1.6.2. The 'prescribed time' is either three months after delivery of the bill or rectification to the client or entitled third party; or a lesser term (not less than one month) specified in writing to the client or entitled third party at the time of delivery of the bill or notification.

1. Solicitors' Code of Conduct 2007, r.2.08. Note that this is an 'emergency' rule and consultation on the contents of a definitive new rule is currently taking place. See also SRA Consultation Paper 19 at **www.sra.org.uk** and the Law Society's Repeal of Remuneration Certificates Practice Note (6 August 2009).

1.7. Assessment of costs

1.7.1. The client has the right to assessment of the bill by the High Court. The costs of an application for assessment must be borne by the client.

1.7.2. If in a non-contentious matter a taxing officer allows less than one-half of the sum charged to the client by the bill, he is under a duty to bring the facts of the case to the attention of the Law Society.

1.7.3. A third party who is responsible for paying the costs of another can apply for a third party taxation within three months of delivery of the bill.

1.8. Lender's costs

1.8.1. The solicitor should consider making a separate charge for legal work carried out on behalf of the lender client.

1.8.2. The solicitor should agree his charges with the lender client at the outset of the transaction.

1.8.3.   Under the terms of the CML Lenders' Handbook the borrower client is responsible for the lender's solicitor's costs.

1.9.   Commissions, discounts, rebates on disbursements and telegraphic transfer fees

1.9.1.   Under Rule 2.06 Solicitors' Code of Conduct 2007, a solicitor must normally account to his client for any commission received by him which exceeds £20. Thus where the solicitor introduces a client to an insurance company for the purposes of the client obtaining an insurance policy, and as a result of that introduction the solicitor receives commission from the insurance company, that commission will be subject to Rule 2.06. The solicitor is only entitled to keep a commission which exceeds £20 if, having disclosed the amount to the client, the client agrees that the solicitor may keep the money. If the amount is not known, the solicitor must have disclosed an approximate amount or the basis of the calculation of the commission to the client.

1.9.2.   The rule does not apply where the solicitor acts as agent for a building society or other financial institution and a member of the public, whom the solicitor has not advised as a client about the investment of the money, deposits money with the solicitor.

1.9.3.   Stock Exchange commissions fall within the scope of the rule.

1.9.4.   The amount of any commission earned by the solicitor should be shown on the client's bill.

1.9.5.   Any discount or rebate offered to a solicitor on a search fee or other disbursement reduces the cost of that disbursement and must be passed on to the client (it is not a commission falling within Rule 2.06). See guidance paragraph 55 to Rule 2.

1.9.6.   The fee charged to the solicitor's firm by a financial institution for executing a telegraphic transfer is a disbursement and may be charged to the client as such. Any additional sum, such as an administrative fee charged by the firm to cover internal staff costs or the fixed monthly fee payable by the firm for having an in-house terminal, is a profit cost for the firm and should not be charged to the client as a disbursement: see the Law Society's Telegraphic Transfer Fees Practice Note (30 July 2008).

1.10.   Recovery of charges

1.10.1.   A solicitor may sue a client who does not pay his solicitor's bill provided that the conditions in the following paragraphs have been complied with.

1.10.2.   A bill of costs in the proper form must have been delivered to the client.

1.10.3. In a non-contentious matter, a solicitor may not sue the client until the expiration of one month from the delivery of the bill, unless the solicitor had been given leave to do so on the grounds set out in Solicitors Act 1974, s.69. A solicitor must not sue or threaten to sue unless he has first informed the client in writing of his right to seek assessment of the bill or, in the case of a bill delivered on or before 11 August 2009, to require a remuneration certificate. A statutory demand in bankruptcy can, however, be made within one month of an unpaid bill being presented.[1]

1.10.4. A lien exists by virtue of Solicitors Act 1974, s.73 which empowers the court to make a charging order over real or personal property belonging to the client as security for the solicitor's taxed costs.

1. *Re A Debtor (No.88 of 1991)* [1992] 3 All ER 301.

1.11. Court of Protection work

1.11.1. Fixed costs are payable for all conveyancing matters authorised by the Office of the Public Guardian.

1.11.2. Two elements will be allowable, as follows:

(a) a fixed sum in every case to cover correspondence with the Office of the Public Guardian, the preparation of the certificate or affidavit of value, and all other work solely attributable to the Court of Protection; together with

(b) a value element of a percentage of the consideration.[1]

1.11.3. As well as a fee for both the above elements, VAT and disbursements will be allowed.

1.11.4. Fixed costs will apply to conveyancing of all types of property.

1.11.5. If solicitors wish, they may choose to have their costs assessed by the Supreme Court Costs Office, rather than to accept fixed costs. It should, however, be emphasised that agreed costs will not be an option, save in exceptional circumstances.

1. For details of the fees, see **www.publicguardian.gov.uk**.

APPENDICES

I. Solicitors Regulation Authority

I.1. Solicitors' Code of Conduct 2007 [extracts][1]

[This appendix contains selected rules from the Solicitors' Code of Conduct 2007. The rules are as stated on 6 October 2010.

The guidance that accompanies the rules is not reproduced here, with the exception of selected guidance to rules 2 and 3.

The full text of the Solicitors' Code of Conduct 2007 as amended is available at **www.sra.org.uk**.]

RULE 1 – CORE DUTIES

1.01   Justice and the rule of law

You must uphold the rule of law and the proper administration of justice.

1.02   Integrity

You must act with integrity.

1.03   Independence

You must not allow your independence to be compromised.

1.04   Best interests of clients

You must act in the best interests of each client.

1.05   Standard of service

You must provide a good standard of service to your clients.

1.06   Public confidence

You must not behave in a way that is likely to diminish the trust the public places in you or the legal profession.

RULE 2 – CLIENT RELATIONS

2.01   Taking on clients

(1)   You are generally free to decide whether or not to take on a particular client. However, you must refuse to act or cease acting for a client in the following circumstances:

   (a)   when to act would involve you in a breach of the law or a breach of the rules of professional conduct;

1.   © The Law Society 2007, with consolidated amendments to 6 October 2010.

(b)   where you have insufficient resources or lack the competence to deal with the matter;

(c)   where instructions are given by someone other than the client, or by only one client on behalf of others in a joint matter, you must not proceed without checking that all clients agree with the instructions given; or

(d)   where you know or have reasonable grounds for believing that the instructions are affected by duress or undue influence, you must not act on those instructions until you have satisfied yourself that they represent the client's wishes.

(2)   You must not cease acting for a client except for good reason and on reasonable notice.

2.02   Client care

(1)   You must:

(a)   identify clearly the client's objectives in relation to the work to be done for the client;

(b)   give the client a clear explanation of the issues involved and the options available to the client;

(c)   agree with the client the next steps to be taken; and

(d)   keep the client informed of progress, unless otherwise agreed.

(2)   You must, both at the outset and, as necessary, during the course of the matter:

(a)   agree an appropriate level of service;

(b)   explain your responsibilities;

(c)   explain the client's responsibilities;

(d)   ensure that the client is given, in writing, the name and status of the person dealing with the matter and the name of the person responsible for its overall supervision; and

(e)   explain any limitations or conditions resulting from your relationship with a third party (for example a funder, fee sharer or introducer) which affect the steps you can take on the client's behalf.

(3)   If you can demonstrate that it was inappropriate in the circumstances to meet some or all of these requirements, you will not breach 2.02.

2.03   Information about the cost

(1)   You must give your client the best information possible about the likely overall cost of a matter both at the outset and, when appropriate, as the matter progresses. In particular you must:

(a)   advise the client of the basis and terms of your charges;

(b)   advise the client if charging rates are to be increased;

(c)   advise the client of likely payments which you or your client may need to make to others;

(d)   discuss with the client how the client will pay, in particular:

(i)   whether the client may be eligible and should apply for public funding; and

(ii)   whether the client's own costs are covered by insurance or may be paid by someone else such as an employer or trade union;

(e) advise the client that there are circumstances where you may be entitled to exercise a lien for unpaid costs;

(f) advise the client of their potential liability for any other party's costs; and

(g) discuss with the client whether their liability for another party's costs may be covered by existing insurance or whether specially purchased insurance may be obtained.

(2) Where you are acting for the client under a conditional fee agreement, (including a collective conditional fee agreement) in addition to complying with 2.03(1) above and 2.03(5) and (6) below, you must explain the following, both at the outset and, when appropriate, as the matter progresses:

(a) the circumstances in which your client may be liable for your costs and whether you will seek payment of these from the client, if entitled to do so;

(b) if you intend to seek payment of any or all of your costs from your client, you must advise your client of their right to an assessment of those costs; and

(c) where applicable, the fact that you are obliged under a fee sharing agreement to pay to a charity any fees which you receive by way of costs from the client's opponent or other third party.

(3) Where you are acting for a publicly funded client, in addition to complying with 2.03(1) above and 2.03(5) and (6) below, you must explain the following at the outset:

(a) the circumstances in which they may be liable for your costs;

(b) the effect of the statutory charge;

(c) the client's duty to pay any fixed or periodic contribution assessed and the consequence of failing to do so; and

(d) that even if your client is successful, the other party may not be ordered to pay costs or may not be in a position to pay them.

(4) Where you agree to share your fees with a charity in accordance with 8.01(h) you must disclose to the client at the outset the name of the charity.

(5) Any information about the cost must be clear and confirmed in writing.

(6) You must discuss with your client whether the potential outcomes of any legal case will justify the expense or risk involved including, if relevant, the risk of having to pay an opponent's costs.

(7) If you can demonstrate that it was inappropriate in the circumstances to meet some or all of the requirements in 2.03(1) and (5) above, you will not breach 2.03.

2.04   Contingency fees

(1) You must not enter into an arrangement to receive a contingency fee for work done in prosecuting or defending any contentious proceedings before a court of England and Wales, a British court martial or an arbitrator where the seat of the arbitration is in England and Wales, except as permitted by statute or the common law.

(2) You must not enter into an arrangement to receive a contingency fee for work done in prosecuting or defending any contentious proceedings before a court of an overseas jurisdiction or an arbitrator where the seat of the arbitration is overseas except to the extent that a lawyer of that jurisdiction would be permitted to do so.

2.05 Complaints handling

(1) If you are a recognised body, a manager of a recognised body or a recognised sole practitioner, you must ensure:

(a) that the firm has a written complaints procedure and that complaints are handled promptly, fairly and effectively in accordance with it;

(b) that the client is told, in writing, at the outset (or in the case of existing clients, at the next appropriate opportunity):

(i) that, in the event of a problem, the client is entitled to complain; and

(ii) how to and to whom the client should complain;

(iii) that this could include a complaint about the firm's bill;

(iv) that the firm has a complaints procedure, a copy of which is available on request;

(v) of their right to complain to the Legal Ombudsman at the conclusion of your complaint process, the timeframe for doing so and full details of how to contact the Legal Ombudsman;

(vi) that there may also be a right to object to the bill by applying to the court for an assessment of the bill under Part III of the Solicitors Act 1974; and

(vii) that if all or part of a bill remains unpaid the firm may be entitled to charge interest;

(c) that the client is given a copy of the complaints procedure on request; and

(d) that once a complaint has been made, the person complaining is told in writing:

(i) how the complaint will be handled; and

(ii) within what timescales they will be given an initial and/or substantive response;

(e) that at the conclusion of the firm's complaints process the client is told of their right to complain to the Legal Ombudsman, the timeframe for doing so and full details of how to contact the Legal Ombudsman.

(2) If you can demonstrate that it was inappropriate in the circumstances to meet some or all of these requirements, you will not breach 2.05.

(3) You must not charge your client for the cost of handling a complaint.

2.06 Commissions

If you are a recognised body, a manager of a recognised body or a recognised sole practitioner, you must ensure that your firm pays to your client commission received over £20 unless the client, having been told the amount, or if the precise amount is not known, an approximate amount or how the amount is to be calculated, has agreed that your firm may keep it.

2.07 Limitation of civil liability by contract

If you are a recognised body or a recognised sole practitioner, you must not exclude or attempt to exclude by contract all liability to your clients. However, you may limit your liability, provided that such limitation:

(a) is not below the minimum level of cover required by the Solicitors' Indemnity Insurance Rules for a policy of qualifying insurance;

(b) is brought to the client's attention; and

(c) is in writing.

RULE 3 – CONFLICT OF INTERESTS

3.01   Duty not to act

(1)   You must not act if there is a conflict of interests (except in the limited circumstances dealt with in 3.02).

(2)   There is a conflict of interests if:

(a) you owe, or your firm owes, separate duties to act in the best interests of two or more clients in relation to the same or related matters, and those duties conflict, or there is a significant risk that those duties may conflict; or

(b) your duty to act in the best interests of any client in relation to a matter conflicts, or there is a significant risk that it may conflict, with your own interests in relation to that or a related matter.

(3)   For the purpose of 3.01(2), a related matter will always include any other matter which involves the same asset or liability.

3.02   Exceptions to duty not to act

(1)   You or your firm may act for two or more clients in relation to a matter in situations of conflict or possible conflict if:

(a) the different clients have a substantially common interest in relation to that matter or a particular aspect of it; and

(b) all the clients have given in writing their informed consent to you or your firm acting.

(2)   Your firm may act for two or more clients in relation to a matter in situations of conflict or possible conflict if:

(a) the clients are competing for the same asset which, if attained by one client, will make that asset unattainable to the other client(s);

(b) there is no other conflict, or significant risk of conflict, between the interests of any of the clients in relation to that matter;

(c) the clients have confirmed in writing that they want your firm to act in the knowledge that your firm acts, or may act, for one or more other clients who are competing for the same asset; and

(d) unless the clients specifically agree, no individual acts for, or is responsible for the supervision of, more than one of those clients.

(3)   When acting in accordance with 3.02(1) or (2) it must be reasonable in all the circumstances for you or your firm to act for all those clients.

(4)   If you are relying on the exceptions in 3.02(1) or (2), you must:

(a) draw all the relevant issues to the attention of the clients before agreeing to act or, where already acting, when the conflict arises or as soon as is reasonably practicable, and in such a way that the clients concerned can understand the issues and the risks involved;

(b)   have a reasonable belief that the clients understand the relevant issues; and

(c)   be reasonably satisfied that those clients are of full capacity.

3.03   Conflict when already acting

If you act, or your firm acts, for more than one client in a matter and, during the course of the conduct of that matter, a conflict arises between the interests of two or more of those clients, you, or your firm, may only continue to act for one of the clients (or a group of clients between whom there is no conflict) provided that the duty of confidentiality to the other client(s) is not put at risk.

[Rules 3.04–3.06 are not reproduced here.]

3.07   Acting for seller and buyer in conveyancing, property selling and mortgage related services

(1)   Rules 3.07 to 3.15 apply to the transfer of land for value, and the grant or assignment of a lease or some other interest in land for value. Both commercial and residential conveyancing transactions are covered. The terms 'seller' and 'buyer' include a lessor and lessee. 'You' is defined in 23.01, but is to be construed in 3.07 to 3.15 as including an associated firm (see rule 24 (Interpretation) for the meaning of 'associated firms').

(2)   You must not act for more than one party in conveyancing, property selling or mortgage related services other than as permitted by, and in accordance with, 3.08 to 3.15. 'Property selling' means negotiating the sale for the seller. 'Mortgage related services' means advising on or arranging a mortgage, or providing mortgage related financial services, for a buyer. 'Mortgage' includes a remortgage.

3.08   Conveyancing transactions not at arm's length

Subject to the prohibition in 10.06(3) and 10.06(4), you may act for seller and buyer when the transaction between the parties is not at arm's length, provided there is no conflict or significant risk of conflict.

3.09   Conveyancing transactions at arm's length

Subject to the prohibition in 10.06(3) and (4), you may act for seller and buyer if the conditions set out in 3.10 below are satisfied and one of the following applies:

(a)   both parties are established clients;

(b)   the consideration is £10,000 or less and the transaction is not the grant of a lease; or

(c)   seller and buyer are represented by two separate offices in different localities.

3.10   Conditions for acting under 3.09

In order to act for seller and buyer under 3.09 above, the following conditions must be met:

(a)   the written consent of both parties must be obtained;

(b)   no conflict of interests must exist or arise;

(c)   the seller must not be selling or leasing as a builder or developer; and

(d)   when the seller and buyer are represented by two separate offices in different localities:

(i) different individuals authorised to do the work, who normally work at each office, conduct or supervise the transaction for seller and buyer; and

(ii) no office of the firm (or an associated firm) referred either client to the office conducting the transactions.

3.11 Property selling and mortgage related services

Subject to the prohibition in 10.06(3) and (4), you may act for seller and buyer if the conditions set out in 3.13 below are satisfied and one of the following applies:

(a) the only way in which you are acting for the buyer is in providing mortgage related services; or

(b) the only way in which you are acting for the seller is in providing property selling services through a Solicitors' Estate Agency Limited (SEAL).

3.12 SEALs and participating firms

A SEAL means a recognised body which:

(a) is a company;

(b) does not undertake conveyancing;

(c) is owned jointly by at least four participating firms which are not associated firms;

(d) has no participating firm with majority control;

(e) has at least one participating firm which is a recognised body or recognised sole practitioner; and

(f) is conducted from accommodation physically divided from, and clearly differentiated from that of any participating firm.

A 'participating firm' means a recognised sole practitioner, recognised body or authorised non-SRA firm which is a manager or owner of the SEAL, or one or more of whose managers or owners is a manager or owner of the SEAL.

3.13 Conditions for acting under 3.11

In order to act for seller and buyer under 3.11 above, the following conditions must be met:

(a) the written consent of both parties must be obtained;

(b) no conflict of interests must exist or arise;

(c) the seller must not be selling or leasing as a builder or developer;

(d) different individuals must conduct the work for the seller and the work for the buyer and, if these individuals need supervision, they must be supervised by different individuals who are authorised to do the work;

(e) you must inform the seller in writing, before accepting instructions to deal with the property selling, of any services which might be offered to a buyer, whether through the same firm or any associated firm; and

(f) you must explain to the buyer, before the buyer gives consent to the arrangement:

(i) the implications of a conflict of interests arising;

(ii) your financial interest in the sale going through; and

(iii)   if you propose to provide mortgage related services to the buyer through a SEAL which is also acting for the seller, that you cannot advise the buyer on the merits of the purchase.

3.14   Special circumstances in property selling and conveyancing

If any of the circumstances set out in 3.09 apply (established clients; consideration of £10,000 or less; representation by two separate offices), you may sell the property, provide mortgage related services, and act for seller and buyer in the conveyancing, subject to the prohibition in 10.06(3) and (4) and compliance with the conditions set out in 3.10 and 3.13 as appropriate.

3.15   Conflict arising when acting for seller and buyer

If a conflict arises during the course of a transaction in which you are acting for more than one party, you may continue to act for one of the parties only if the duty of confidentiality to the other party is not at risk.

3.16   Acting for lender and borrower in conveyancing transactions

(1)   Rules 3.16 to 3.22 cover the grant of a mortgage of land and are intended to avoid conflicts of interests. 'Mortgage' includes a remortgage. Both commercial and residential conveyancing transactions are covered. 'You' is defined in 23.01, but is to be construed in 3.16 to 3.22 as including an associated firm (see rule 24 (Interpretation) for the meaning of 'associated firms').

(2)   You must not act for both lender and borrower on the grant of a mortgage of land:

(a)   if a conflict of interests exists or arises;

(b)   on the grant of an individual mortgage of land at arm's length;

(c)   if, in the case of a standard mortgage of property to be used as the borrower's private residence only, the lender's mortgage instructions extend beyond the limitations contained in 3.19 and 3.21, or do not permit the use of the certificate of title required by 3.20; or

(d)   if, in the case of any other standard mortgage, the lender's mortgage instructions extend beyond the limitations contained in 3.19 and 3.21.

3.17   Standard and individual mortgages

(1)   A mortgage is a 'standard mortgage' where:

(a)   it is provided in the normal course of the lender's activities;

(b)   a significant part of the lender's activities consists of lending; and

(c)   the mortgage is on standard terms.

An 'individual mortgage' is any other mortgage.

(2)   A mortgage will not be on standard terms if material terms in any of the documents relating to the mortgage transaction are negotiated between the lender's and borrower's lawyers contemporaneously with effecting the mortgage. In commercial transactions, the element of negotiation will often relate to the facility letter or facility agreement rather than the mortgage deed itself.

(3)   Provided there has been no contemporaneous negotiation of material terms between the parties' lawyers, a mortgage will be on standard terms where the lender uses a prescribed form of

mortgage deed. Minor variations, such as the usual clause limiting the liability of trustee mortgagors, are not regarded as material and do not alter the nature of these terms as standard.

(4)   In addition to its normal standard terms, a lender may have a different set or sets of standard terms applicable to specialised types of borrower, such as registered social landlords. Provided these terms are applied by the lender to all equivalent specialist borrowers or have been agreed between the lender and a specialist borrower as applicable to all transactions between them, they will constitute standard terms for the purposes of 3.16 to 3.22.

(5)   The lender and the borrower must be separately represented on the grant of an individual mortgage at arm's length (see 3.16(2)(b)). Rules 3.16 to 3.22 are not then applicable.

(6)   You may act for both lender and borrower in a standard mortgage (see 3.16(2)(c) to (d)), provided:

    (a)   there is no conflict of interests;

    (b)   the mortgage instructions do not go beyond the limits set out in 3.19; and

    (c)   in the case of a property to be used solely as the borrower's private residence, the approved certificate of title set out in the annex to rule 3 is used.

(7)   The limitations of 3.19 also apply to a standard mortgage where the lender and the borrower are separately represented (see 3.22(1) which includes certificates of title). However, 3.22(2) allows the borrower's lawyer, in a transaction where the property is not to be used solely as the borrower's private residence, to give a certificate of title in any form recognised by the Solicitors Regulation Authority Board. You also remain free to give any other form of certificate which complies with this rule.

(8)   There may be cases where the lapse of time between the mortgage offer and completion (for example, when new properties are added) results in use of an earlier edition of a recognised certificate. That is acceptable.

3.18   Notification of certain circumstances to lender

(1)   If you wish to act for both lender and borrower on the grant of a standard mortgage of land, you must first inform the lender in writing of the circumstances if:

    (a)   the prospective borrower is:

        (i)   the firm or any of its managers or owners, or a member of their immediate family;

        (ii)   an associated firm, any of its managers or owners, or a member of their immediate family; and/or

        (iii)   the individual conducting or supervising the transaction, or a member of their immediate family; or

    (b)   you propose to act for seller, buyer and lender in the same transaction.

(2)   'Immediate family' means spouse, children, parents, brothers and sisters.

3.19   Types of instruction which may be accepted

If acting for both lender and borrower in a standard mortgage, you and the individual conducting or supervising the transaction may only accept or act upon instructions from the lender which are limited to the following matters:

(a)   (i)   taking reasonable steps to check the identity of the borrower (and anyone else required to sign the mortgage deed or other document connected with the mortgage) by reference to a document or documents, such as a passport, precisely specified in writing by the lender;

      (ii)   following the guidance given by the Law Society or the Solicitors Regulation Authority on property fraud and on money laundering;

      (iii)   checking that the seller's conveyancers (if unknown to you) appear in a current legal directory or hold practising certificates issued by their professional body; and

      (iv)   in the case of a lender with no branch office within reasonable proximity of the borrower, carrying out the money laundering checks precisely specified in writing by the lender;

(b)   making appropriate searches relating to the property in public registers (for example, local searches, commons registration searches, mining searches), and reporting any results specified by the lender or which you consider may adversely affect the lender; or effecting search insurance;

(c)   making enquiries on legal matters relating to the property reasonably specified by the lender, and reporting the replies;

(d)   reporting the purchase price stated in the transfer and on how the borrower says that the purchase money (other than the mortgage advance) is to be provided; and reporting if you will not have control over the payment of all the purchase money (other than a deposit paid to an estate agent or a reservation fee paid to a builder or developer);

(e)   reporting if the seller or the borrower (if the property is already owned by the borrower) has not owned or been the registered owner of the property for at least six months;

(f)   if the lender does not arrange insurance, confirming receipt of satisfactory evidence that the buildings insurance is in place for at least the sum required by the lender and covers the risks specified by the lender; giving notice to the insurer of the lender's interest and requesting confirmation that the insurer will notify the lender if the policy is not renewed or is cancelled; and supplying particulars of the insurance and the last premium receipt to the lender;

(g)   investigating title to the property and appurtenant rights; reporting any defects revealed, advising on the need for any consequential statutory declarations or indemnity insurance, and approving and effecting indemnity cover if required by the lender; and reporting if you are aware of any rights needed for the use or enjoyment of the property over other land;

(h)   reporting on any financial charges (for example, improvement or repair grants or Housing Act discounts) secured on the property revealed by your searches and enquiries which will affect the property after completion of the mortgage;

(i)   in the case of a leasehold property:

      (i)   confirming that the lease contains the terms stipulated by the lender and does not include any terms specified by the lender as unacceptable;

      (ii)   obtaining a suitable deed of variation or indemnity insurance if the terms of the lease are unsatisfactory;

      (iii)   enquiring of the seller or the borrower (if the property is already owned by the borrower) as to any known breaches of covenant by the landlord or any superior landlord and reporting any such breaches to the lender;

    (iv)   reporting if you become aware of the landlord's absence or insolvency;

    (v)   making a company search and checking the last three years' published accounts of any management company with responsibilities under the lease;

    (vi)   if the borrower is required to be a shareholder in the management company, obtaining the share certificate, a blank stock transfer form signed by the borrower and a copy of the memorandum and articles of association;

    (vii)   obtaining any necessary consent to or prior approval of the assignment and mortgage;

    (viii)   obtaining a clear receipt for the last payment of rent and service charge; and

    (ix)   serving notice of the assignment and mortgage on the landlord;

(j)   in the case of a commonhold unit:

    (i)   confirming receipt of satisfactory evidence that common parts insurance is in place for at least the sum required by the lender and covers the risks specified by the lender;

    (ii)   confirming that the commonhold community statement contains the terms specified by the lender and does not include any restrictions on occupation or use specified by the lender as unacceptable;

    (iii)   enquiring of the seller (or the borrower if the property is already owned by the borrower) and the commonhold association as to any known breaches of the commonhold community statement by the commonhold association or any unit-holder, and reporting any such breaches to the lender;

    (iv)   making a company search to verify that the commonhold association is in existence and remains registered, and that there is no registered indication that it is to be wound up;

    (v)   obtaining the last three years' published accounts of the commonhold association and reporting any apparent problems with the association to the lender;

    (vi)   obtaining a commonhold unit information certificate; and

    (vii)   serving notice of the transfer and mortgage of the commonhold unit on the commonhold association;

(k)   if the property is subject to a letting, checking that the type of letting and its terms comply with the lender's requirements;

(l)   making appropriate pre-completion searches, including a bankruptcy search against the borrower, any other person in whom the legal estate is vested and any guarantor;

(m)   receiving, releasing and transmitting the mortgage advance, including asking for any final inspection needed and dealing with any retentions and cashbacks;

(n)   procuring execution of the mortgage deed and form of guarantee as appropriate by the persons whose identities have been checked in accordance with any requirements of the lender under (a) above as those of the borrower, any other person in whom the legal estate is vested and any guarantor; obtaining their signatures to the forms of undertaking required by the lender in relation to the use, occupation or physical state of the property; and complying with the lender's requirements if any document is to be executed under a power of attorney;

(o)   asking the borrower for confirmation that the information about occupants given in the mortgage instructions or offer is correct; obtaining consents in the form required by the lender from existing or prospective occupiers of the property aged 17 or over specified by the lender, or of whom you are aware;

(p) advising the borrower on the terms of any document required by the lender to be signed by the borrower;

(q) advising any other person required to sign any document on the terms of that document or, if there is a conflict of interests between that person and the borrower or the lender, advising that person on the need for separate legal advice and arranging for them to see an independent conveyancer;

(r) obtaining the legal transfer of the property to the mortgagor;

(s) procuring the redemption of:

    (i) existing mortgages on property the subject of any associated sale of which you are aware; and

    (ii) any other mortgages secured against a property located in England or Wales made by an identified lender where an identified account number or numbers or a property address has been given by the lender;

(t) ensuring the redemption or postponement of existing mortgages on the property, and registering the mortgage with the priority required by the lender;

(u) making administrative arrangements in relation to any collateral security, such as an endowment policy, or in relation to any collateral warranty or guarantee relating to the physical condition of the property, such as NHBC documentation;

(v) registering the transfer and mortgage;

(w) giving legal advice on any matters reported on under 3.19, suggesting courses of action open to the lender, and complying with the lender's instructions on the action to be taken;

(x) disclosing any relationship specified by the lender between you and the borrower;

(y) storing safely the title deeds and documents pending registration and delivery to or as directed by the lender; and

(z) retaining the information contained in your conveyancing file for at least six years from the date of the mortgage.

3.20 Using the approved certificate of title

In addition, if acting for both lender and borrower in a standard mortgage of property to be used as the borrower's private residence only:

(a) you must use the certificate of title set out in the annex to rule 3 (below) ('the approved certificate'); and

(b) unless the lender has certified that its mortgage instructions are subject to the limitations contained in 3.19 above and 3.21 below, you must notify the lender on receipt of instructions that the approved certificate will be used, and that your duties to the lender are limited to the matters contained in the approved certificate.

3.21 Terms of rule to prevail

The terms of 3.16 to 3.20 above will prevail in the event of any ambiguity in the lender's instructions, or discrepancy between the instructions and 3.19 above or the approved certificate.

3.22   Anti-avoidance

(1)   Subject to (2) below, if acting only for the borrower in a standard mortgage of property you must not accept or act upon any requirements by way of undertaking, warranty, guarantee or otherwise of the lender, the lender's lawyer or other agent which extend beyond the limitations contained in 3.19.

(2)   Provided the property is not to be used solely as the borrower's private residence, (1) above does not prevent you from giving any form of certificate of title recognised from time to time by the Solicitors Regulation Authority Board (a 'recognised certificate'). Additions or amendments which arise from the individual transaction may be made to the text of a recognised certificate but, to the extent to which they create an increased or additional obligation, must not extend beyond the limitations contained in 3.19.

3.23   Waivers

In spite of 22.01(1) (Waivers), the Solicitors Regulation Authority Board shall not have power to waive any of the provisions of 3.01 to 3.05.

ANNEX

Certificate of title

Details box

TO: (Lender)
Lender's Reference or Account No:
The Borrower:
Property:
Title Number:
Mortgage Advance:
Price stated in transfer:
Completion Date:
Conveyancer's Name & Address:
Conveyancer's Reference:
Conveyancer's bank, sort code and account number:
Date of instructions:

WE THE CONVEYANCERS NAMED ABOVE CERTIFY as follows:

(1)   If so instructed, we have checked the identity of the Borrower (and anyone else required to sign the mortgage deed or other document connected with the mortgage) by reference to the document or documents precisely specified in writing by you.

(2)   Except as otherwise disclosed to you in writing:

    (i)   we have investigated the title to the Property, we are not aware of any other financial charges secured on the Property which will affect the Property after completion of the mortgage and, upon completion of the mortgage, both you and the mortgagor (whose identity has been checked in accordance with paragraph (1) above) will have a good and marketable title to the Property and to appurtenant rights free from prior mortgages or charges and from onerous encumbrances which title will be registered with absolute title;

(ii) we have compared the extent of the Property shown on any plan provided by you against relevant plans in the title deeds and/or the description of the Property in any valuation which you have supplied to us, and in our opinion there are no material discrepancies;

(iii) the assumptions stated by the valuer about the title (its tenure, easements, boundaries and restrictions on use) in any valuation which you have supplied to us are correct;

(iv) if the Property is leasehold the terms of the lease accord with your instructions, including any requirements you have for covenants by the Landlord and/or a management company and/or by a deed of mutual covenant for the insurance, repair and maintenance of the structure, exterior and common parts of any building of which the Property forms part, and we have or will obtain on or before completion a clear receipt for the last payment of rent and service charge;

(v) if the Property is a commonhold unit, the commonhold community statement contains the terms specified by you and does not include any restrictions on occupation or use specified by you as unacceptable, and we have or will obtain on or before completion a commonhold unit information certificate;

(vi) we have received satisfactory evidence that the buildings insurance is in place, or will be on completion, for the sum and in the terms required by you;

(vii) if the Property is to be purchased by the Borrower:

    (a) the contract for sale provides for vacant possession on completion;

    (b) the seller has owned or been the registered owner of the Property for not less than six months; and

    (c) we are not acting on behalf of the seller;

(viii) we are in possession of:

    (a) either a local search or local search insurance; and

    (b) such other searches or search insurance as are appropriate to the Property, the mortgagor and any guarantor, in each case in accordance with your instructions;

(ix) nothing has been revealed by our searches and enquiries which would prevent the Property being used by any occupant for residential purposes; and

(x) neither any principal nor any other individual in the firm giving this certificate nor any spouse, child, parent, brother or sister of such a person is interested in the Property (whether alone or jointly with any other) as mortgagor.

WE:

(a) undertake, prior to use of the mortgage advance, to obtain in the form required by you the execution of a mortgage and a guarantee as appropriate by the persons whose identities have been checked in accordance with paragraph (1) above as those of the Borrower, any other person in whom the legal estate is vested and any guarantor; and, if required by you:

    (i) to obtain their signatures to the forms of undertaking required by you in relation to the use, occupation or physical state of the Property;

(ii)   to ask the Borrower for confirmation that the information about occupants given in your mortgage instructions or offer is correct; and

(iii)   to obtain consents in the form required by you from any existing or prospective occupier(s) aged 17 or over of the Property specified by you or of whom we are aware;

(b)   have made or will make such Bankruptcy, Land Registry or Land Charges Searches as may be necessary to justify certificate no. (2)(i) above;

(c)   will within the period of protection afforded by the searches referred to in paragraph (b) above:

(i)   complete the mortgage;

(ii)   arrange for the issue of a stamp duty land tax certificate if appropriate;

(iii)   deliver to the Land Registry the documents necessary to register the mortgage in your favour and any relevant prior dealings; and

(iv)   effect any other registrations necessary to protect your interests as mortgagee;

(d)   will despatch to you such deeds and documents relating to the Property as you require with a list of them in the form prescribed by you within ten working days of receipt by us of the title information document from the Land Registry;

(e)   will not part with the mortgage advance (and will return it to you if required) if it shall come to our notice prior to completion that the Property will at completion be occupied in whole or in part otherwise than in accordance with your instructions;

(f)   will not accept instructions, except with your consent in writing, to prepare any lease or tenancy agreement relating to the Property or any part of it prior to despatch of the title information document to you;

(g)   will not use the mortgage advance until satisfied that, prior to or contemporaneously with the transfer of the Property to the mortgagor, there will be discharged:

(i)   any existing mortgage on property the subject of an associated sale of which we are aware; and

(ii)   any other mortgages made by a lender identified by you secured against a property located in England or Wales where you have given either an account number or numbers or a property address;

(h)   will notify you in writing if any matter comes to our attention before completion which would render the certificate given above untrue or inaccurate and, in those circumstances, will defer completion pending your authority to proceed and will return the mortgage advance to you if required; and

(i)   confirm that we have complied, or will comply, with your instructions in all other respects to the extent that they do not extend beyond the limitations contained in the Solicitors' Code of Conduct 2007, 3.19 (Conflict of interests – types of instruction which may be accepted).

OUR duties to you are limited to the matters set out in this certificate and we accept no further liability or responsibility whatsoever. The payment by you to us (by whatever means) of the mortgage advance or any part of it constitutes acceptance of this limitation and any assignment to you by the Borrower of any rights of action against us to which the Borrower may be entitled shall take effect subject to this limitation.

Signature box

SIGNED on behalf of THE CONVEYANCERS	....
NAME of Authorised Signatory	....
QUALIFICATION of Authorised Signatory	....
DATE of Signature	....

Guidance to rule 3 – Conflict of interests

[The following notes to rule 3 most pertinent to conveyancing are reproduced below (1–22, 39–54, and 70–88).]

Conflict is defined – 3.01

1.   Conflict is defined as a conflict between the duties to act in the best interests of two or more different clients, or between your interests and those of a client. The definition appears in 3.01(2). This will encompass all situations where doing the best for one client in a matter will result in prejudice to another client in that matter or a related matter.

2.   The definition of conflict in 3.01(2) requires you to assess when two matters are 'related'. Rule 3.01(3) makes it clear that if the two matters concern the same asset or liability, then they are 'related'. Accordingly, if you act for one client which is negotiating with publishers for the publication of a novel, an instruction from another client alleging that the novel is plagiarised and breaches copyright would be a related matter.

3.   However, there would need to be some reasonable degree of relationship for a conflict to arise. If you act for a company on a dispute with a garage about the cost of repairs to a company car, your firm would not be prevented from acting for a potential bidder for the company, even though the car is a minor asset of the company and would be included in the purchase. If you act for a client selling a business, you might conclude that your firm could also act for a prospective purchaser on the creation of an employee share scheme which would cover all the entities in the purchaser's group, this work perhaps requiring the future inclusion of the target within the scheme and consideration as to whether this raised any particular issues.

4.   In each case, you will need to make a judgement on the facts. In making this judgement, you might want to consider the view of your existing client where you are professionally able to raise the issue with him or her. You should also take care to consider whether your firm holds any confidential information from your existing client which would be relevant to the new instructions and if so, to ensure that you comply with rule 4 (Confidentiality and disclosure).

You are or your firm is permitted to act with clients' consent in defined circumstances of conflict subject to suitable safeguards

5.   This reflects the fact that there may be circumstances in which, despite peripheral or potential conflict, the clients' best interests are served by you, or your firm, being able to act for two or more

clients who are able to give informed consent. The circumstances in which you could act despite a conflict are set out in 3.02.

6.   Two different situations are defined. These are in 3.02(1) and (2):

   (a)   (i)   Rule 3.02(1) deals with the situation where the clients have a 'common interest', they all want to continue to instruct you and it would be disproportionate, for example, in terms of cost and general disruption to their matter, to require them to instruct separate solicitors.

        (ii)   For there to be a 'common interest' there must be a clear common purpose and a strong consensus on how it is to be achieved. However, it will be for you to decide objectively on the facts in each case whether there is a 'common interest' and it is appropriate to act. In making this decision, you should always consider whether the clients will be represented even-handedly with equal weight being given to the instructions from each.

       (iii)   The 'common interest' might arise, for example, where you are acting for several members of a family in relation to their affairs or acting for various individuals in the setting up of a company. Any areas of conflict must be substantially less important to all the clients than their common purpose and may, for example, relate to slightly different views on how the common purpose is to be achieved. It will be your duty to keep the differences under review with the clients and to decide if the point has been reached when it would be untenable to continue to represent all of them in a fair and open manner or without any of them being prejudiced.

       (iv)   There exist some multi-party complex commercial transactions, where sophisticated users of legal services, who have a common purpose, may expect a firm to act for two or more parties, because this will facilitate efficient handling of the matter (taking into account amongst other things the desire to complete the transaction quickly, the availability of necessary experience/expertise and the overall costs). Indeed in many cases it may already be accepted business practice for firms to act in this manner. An example is acting for different tiers of lenders (for example senior lenders and mezzanine lenders) and/or different parties (for example arrangers/underwriters and bond/security trustees) in entering into a financing transaction where there is already an agreed or commonly understood structure with regard to the ranking of their respective claims, the content of their respective obligations and associated commercial issues.

       (v)   While accepted business practice can be considered as a factor in determining whether an appropriate common purpose exists, you and your firm should always exercise caution when proposing to act in accordance with 3.02 and should be mindful of the residual test of reasonableness referred to in 3.02(3).

       (vi)   In some situations it might be possible for you to consider whether the retainer could be limited to those areas where there is no conflict with the clients seeking separate advice on any areas of conflict. This could only be done where the conflict did not undermine the overriding common purpose (see below for further guidance on limiting retainers).

      (vii)   In some circumstances it might be possible that, while a conflict would prevent you from acting for another party on all aspects of a matter, a mandate limited to a specific issue where there is common purpose might be accepted. For example, you may be retained by the owner of a company to advise on its disposal. In that case you would not generally be able to advise another party on the purchase of the company. However, in the hope and anticipation of a successful sale a seller client which is a sophisticated user of legal services might agree that you should also accept a limited retainer to provide competition law advice to the prospective purchaser regarding the filings for competition law purposes that would be required in the event that the two businesses were combined.

(viii) When acting under this exception, especially in family situations, you need to consider the developing legal position. Courts are likely to make a presumption of undue influence where one of the parties who is considered vulnerable through age or other circumstances places trust and confidence in the other party. In any situation of doubt it may well be in the best interests of the clients that they are separately represented.

(b)　(i)　Rule 3.02(2) is intended to apply to specialised areas of legal services where the clients are sophisticated users of those services and conclude that rather than seek out new advisers they would rather use their usual advisers in the knowledge that those advisers might also act for competing interests. An 'asset' is not necessarily physical, and can include a contract or a business opportunity. Examples where this exception might apply include:

(A)　acting on insolvencies so that a firm can act for more than one creditor;

(B)　acting for competing bidders, and/or for those involved with the funding of bidders, for a business being sold by auction; and

(C)　acting for competing tenderers submitting tenders to perform a contract.

(ii)　The wording of 3.02(2) is sufficiently wide to permit other transactional work in the commercial field where clients can give consent. Solicitors and their firms should exercise considerable caution when proposing to act in accordance with 3.02(2) in categories of work where to do so is not already accepted business practice.

(iii)　Rule 3.02(2) should not be applied to disputes over assets other than in the context of corporate restructurings and insolvencies.

7.　Reasonableness is an important rider to 3.02. There may be situations where, despite compliance with 3.02, it would still not be reasonable to act. The apparent unequal bargaining position of the parties, concerns about the mental stability of one of the parties, a family arrangement where an elderly parent is providing security for their son's or daughter's business loan, and the importance of one of the clients to the firm may all be situations where instructions to act for both or all parties should be declined. Having accepted instructions you must be satisfied that you can act even-handedly for both or all clients and that, taking into account any limitations in a specific retainer, you do not favour one at the expense of the other(s).

8.　The criterion against which reasonableness will be judged is whether one client is at risk of prejudice because of the lack of separate representation. In relation to all situations where you are proposing to act for two or more clients under the provisions of 3.02, the onus will be on you to demonstrate why it was reasonable to act for all the clients at the time the instructions were accepted. Above all, you must be satisfied that unfettered advice can be given, without fear or favour, to the clients. You must also keep under review whether it remains reasonable to continue to act for them. You should also have regard to 1.04 (Best interests of clients) which requires you to act in the best interests of each of your clients.

9.　(a)　Rule 3.02(4) places obligations on you to discuss with the clients the implications of you, or your firm, continuing to act for all of them. You must be satisfied that the clients understand the issues and that their consent is independently and freely given. You should consider setting out in your initial terms of business letter the issues discussed in relation to the conflict of interests and how that might affect your ability to represent both or all of the clients as the matter progresses. Extreme caution will be required where one of the clients is particularly vulnerable due to mental health, language or other problems affecting their understanding of the issues, although where a litigation friend acts for a person who lacks capacity they will be able to consent on that person's behalf. Similarly, you must always be alert to situations where a client might be consenting under duress or undue influence and in those circumstances must insist on separate representation. For the avoidance of doubt, and for evidential purposes, you should always keep a written record of all discussions with the clients about the implications of your acting for them. You must always obtain all the clients' written consent on each occasion when acting under either of the exceptions.

(b) Where seeking informed consent under 3.02(1)(b) you should identify by name the other clients you or your firm propose(s) to act for, or be able to do so when their identities are known. Provided that you do this and comply with the requirements of 3.02(4), the obligation to obtain 'informed' consent in 3.02(1)(b) will have been satisfied. Where consent is sought under 3.02(2), you need to comply with the requirements of 3.02(4) but you need not identify by name the other clients you or your firm propose(s) to act for.

10. When acting for two or more clients on a matter, or a related matter, there may be circumstances where you will have to cease acting for one or both clients. This may be in circumstances where no conflict was apparent when accepting instructions but a conflict subsequently arose or when acting under one of the exceptions and it becomes impossible to fulfil the conditions set out in 3.02. In these circumstances it is important to try and limit the disruption that will inevitably be caused for the clients. One way of doing this is to discuss and agree with the clients at the outset what will happen if a conflict arises and agree which client the firm would continue to represent where this is possible.

11. The rule does not specifically deal with potential or future conflict, although it does make clear that a significant risk of conflict should prevent a solicitor from acting. You should always be cautious, therefore, about accepting instructions where the possibility of future conflict is evident. The risks should be explained to the clients about the problems and expense which the requirement for future separate representation could bring.

Limited/defined retainers

12. There may be situations where, when acting for two or more clients, it is appropriate to continue to advise them but necessary to make clear that there are defined areas of conflict on which you cannot advise, and one or more of them may need separate advice. Your retainer with your clients will, when these situations arise, need to be limited to exclude those areas of work or advice. Care must always be taken, however, to ensure that the clients understand:

(a) exactly what you are proposing to deal with on their behalf; and

(b) those contested areas which are to be excluded from the retainer.

13. A limited retainer would be unlikely to be appropriate in any situation where one of the clients was disadvantaged in some way as against the other. This might be because of an unequal bargaining position or because one had some form of disability. In any situation where you agree to act for two or more clients by limiting the retainer it is important that you keep all developments under review to ensure that it remains appropriate to continue to act.

Professional embarrassment

14. There may be some circumstances in which you should refuse instructions when, although there is no actual conflict of interests as defined in rule 3, you might feel unable to do your best for a client because of some form of professional embarrassment. It may be, for example, that if you have acted for a client in the past and accept instructions to act against that client you may feel inhibited in doing your best for the new client because of the past relationship with the former client. If so, the instructions from the new client should be refused as you would, otherwise, be in breach of core duties 1.03 (Independence) and 1.04 (Best interests of clients).

15. There may also be situations where you and your firm are asked to act with consent, using an information barrier in accordance with rule 4 (Confidentiality and disclosure), but the information you hold and which you cannot disclose to your client is of such a nature that it would cause severe embarrassment to your firm if, or when, it later came to light that your firm held such information. It may be, for example, that you are asked to act for a client on the acquisition of a business in circumstances where confidential information is held by your firm that the business has a serious problem with its accounts. Similarly, it may be that you are asked to prepare an employment contract for a company which is planning to recruit an individual who is known, confidentially, to be under investigation for fraud. In those circumstances you and your firm would be seriously embarrassed acting for a client who you knew was wasting legal fees on an outcome the client would not want to pursue if in possession of the knowledge held by your firm. It could be argued that you are not acting in the best interests of the client (see 1.04 (Best interests of clients)) or that you are damaging public confidence in the profession (see 1.06 (Public confidence)).

16. Where professional embarrassment is not a factor and the circumstances which would otherwise prevent you from acting in 4.03 (duty not to put confidentiality at risk by acting) do not arise, it will be a purely commercial decision as to whether you should act against the interests of another client or former client, provided there is no conflict as defined in 3.01 or 3.02.

In-house practice

17. If you are employed as an in-house lawyer your employer is your client. The nature of this relationship may cause problems because you do not have the same freedom as a firm would have to decline instructions. There may be occasions, for example, when you are asked to advise your employer in situations where conflict or potential conflict arises between your interests and the interests of your employer. These include:

(a) where your personal interests as an employee may conflict with the interests of your employer who wants advice on a course of action which could be detrimental to you as an employee where, for example, a merger could lead to your redundancy;

(b) where your employer asks you to do something which would place you in breach of your professional obligations, for example, to file a document with the court which you know contains false information; or

(c) where your employer may act against your advice and, for example, engage in criminal activity which may require you to take action against your employer.

18. In relation to situations where your personal interests may conflict with a course of action proposed by your employer you need not necessarily be excluded from advising your employer. Your employer will usually be aware of exactly how you will be affected by its proposals, and if you are able to give objective advice on the legal issues where your expertise is required you would normally be free to do so. There may, however, be situations where you are so affected by the advice you are asked to give that you feel your objectivity and independence are impaired and in those

situations you would have to ask your employer to seek other advice, either internally or externally. What is important in these situations is that there is transparency about your interests. Beyond that, you will have to make a judgement about whether you feel you have the necessary objectivity to advise.

19.   If your employer was unaware of your interests – and, therefore, the potential for conflict – the position would be different. If, for example, you had a large shareholding in another company and your employer's proposed action could adversely affect the value of those shares then you would either have to disclose your interest or explain that a conflict prevented you from advising on that issue.

20.   In situations where you are asked to act contrary to your professional obligations then you should not compromise your position and you must refuse to carry out instructions which would have this result, even if ultimately this led to the loss of your job.

21.   There may be situations where there is a positive legal obligation on you to take action against your employer where, for example, your employer is engaging in money laundering or where there are 'whistle blowing' obligations. Legal issues of this nature are beyond the remit of this guidance. They are situations where your relationship with your employer has reached the stage where you would need to consider the advisability of seeking legal advice on your own position.

22.   Finally, as an in-house lawyer you are, under rule 13 (In-house practice), able to act for a limited number of other bodies and individuals. For example, if employed by a company, you may act for a holding, associated or subsidiary company of that company employer. If you do so you must ensure that you do not act in any situation where there would be a conflict between the interests of your employer and the other company for whom you are also acting (see 13.01 and 13.03). Similarly, if employed in local government you may act, for example, for local councillors in certain circumstances, provided you can comply with rule 3.

[Guidance notes 23–38 are not reproduced in this book. For the full text of the Solicitors' Code of Conduct 2007 and accompanying guidance notes, see **www.sra.gov.uk**.]

Your interests conflicting with the client's – 3.01(2)(b)

39.   There are no circumstances where you can act for a client whose interests conflict with your own interests. The situations outlined in 3.02 where you can act for two or more clients whose interests conflict have no application in this situation. This is because of the fiduciary relationship which exists between you and your client which prevents you taking advantage of the client or acting where there is a conflict or potential conflict of interests between you and your client. Examples appear below.

40.   In conduct there is a conflict of interests where you in your personal capacity sell to, or buy from, or lend to, or borrow from, your client. In all these cases you should insist the client takes independent legal advice. If the client refuses you must not proceed with the transaction.

41.   You should never enter into any arrangement or understanding with a client or prospective client prior to the conclusion of a matter under which you acquire an interest in the publication rights with respect to that matter. This applies equally to non-contentious business.

42.   Whilst you are entitled to take security for costs you should be aware of the risk of the court finding undue influence. Before you do take a charge over a client's property it is advisable, therefore, to suggest the client consider seeking independent legal advice. Such advice would not normally be essential unless the terms of the proposed charge are particularly onerous or would give

you some unusual benefit or profit. It is, however, important always to ensure that the client understands that a charge is being taken and the effect of such a charge.

43.   You are not able to secure costs by a first legal charge over your client's property if this means that you are entering into a regulated mortgage contract as a lender. A regulated mortgage contract is an investment which is regulated by the Financial Services Authority (FSA). It arises where the lender provides credit to an individual or trustee, and it is secured by a first legal mortgage on land which is in the United Kingdom, and at least 40% of the land is, or is to be, used as a dwelling by the borrower or, where the borrower is a trustee, by a beneficiary of the trust or by a related person. You must be authorised by the FSA in order to secure your costs in this way. Detailed guidance on this is in the booklet 'Financial Services and Solicitors' available from the Professional Ethics Guidance Team.

44.   You must always disclose with complete frankness whenever you have, or might obtain, any personal interest or benefit in a transaction in which you are acting for the client. In such circumstances, you must insist that the client receives independent advice.

45.   Independent advice means both legal advice and, where appropriate, competent advice from a member of another profession, e.g. a chartered surveyor.

46.   Your interests referred to in this rule may be direct (for example, where you seek to sell to or buy property from the client or lend to, or borrow from, the client), or indirect (for example, where your business interests lead you to recommend the client to invest in a concern in which you are interested).

47.   This rule applies, therefore, not only where you are personally interested in a transaction, but equally where another person working in your firm has an interest of which you are aware and it impairs your ability to give independent and impartial advice.

48.   The interests envisaged by this rule are not restricted to those of a primarily economic nature only. For example, if you become involved in a sexual relationship with a client you must consider whether this may place your interests in conflict with those of the client or otherwise impair your ability to act in the best interests of the client.

49.   If you are a director of a company for which you act, or own shares in the company, you must consider whether you are in a position of conflict when asked to advise the company upon steps it has taken or should take. It may sometimes be necessary to resign from the board or for another solicitor (including a solicitor from the same firm if appropriate) to advise the company in a particular matter where your own interests conflict, or are likely to conflict. If acting for a company in which you have a personal interest you should always ensure that your ability to give independent and impartial advice is not, for that reason, impaired.

50.   If you hold a power of attorney for a client you must not use that power to gain a benefit which, if acting as a professional adviser to that client, you would not be prepared to allow to an independent third party. This applies regardless of the legal position, for example, as to whether you could lend the donor's money to yourself.

51.   You are free to negotiate your terms of business, including costs, with your clients. This includes negotiating conditional fees which are subject to statutory regulation. In all these negotiations you are not acting for the client. There may be situations, however, where the terms of business are particularly unusual and it would be prudent for you to suggest the client seeks independent advice. It would be advisable to do so if, for example, as part, or all, of your remuneration you are to receive shares in a company you are setting up on behalf of your client.

52.   You need to consider whether the conditional fee agreement involves you in insurance mediation activities, such as arranging and/or advising on after the event insurance contracts, etc. Solicitors who carry on insurance mediation activities either need to be able to comply with the Solicitors' Financial Services (Scope) Rules 2001 or be authorised by the FSA. Detailed guidance is in the booklet *Financial Services and Solicitors* available from the Professional Ethics Guidance Team.

53.   You must always be careful to ensure that any settlement achieved for a client, or any advice given in a non-contentious matter conducted on a contingency fee basis, is in the client's best interests and not made with a view to your obtaining your fee.

54.   Where you discover an act or omission which would justify a claim against you, you must inform the client, and recommend they seek independent advice. You must also inform the client that independent advice should be sought in cases where the client makes a claim against you, or notifies an intention to do so. If the client refuses to seek independent advice, you should not continue to act unless you are satisfied that there is no conflict of interest. See 20.09 (Dealing with claims).

[Guidance notes 55–69 are not reproduced in this book. For the full text of the Solicitors' Code of Conduct 2007 and accompanying guidance notes, see **www.sra.gov.uk**.]

Acting for seller and buyer in conveyancing, property selling and mortgage related services

70.   Rules 3.07 to 3.15 set out the limited circumstances in which you may act for more than one party in conveyancing, property selling or mortgage related services. They apply to all types of conveyancing transaction, commercial and residential.

71.   The general rule is that separate representation is required because conveyancing is an area where the risk of a conflict arising between two parties is high and where any conflict may affect a conveyancing chain.

72.   When judging whether or not a transaction is 'at arm's length', you need to look at the relationship between the parties and the context of the transaction. A transaction may be regarded as not 'at arm's length', even if it is at market value or is stated to be on arm's length terms. A transaction would not usually be at arm's length, for example, if the parties are:

(a)   related by blood, adoption or marriage, or living together;

(b)   the settlor of a trust and the trustees;

(c)   the trustees of a trust and its beneficiary or the beneficiary's relative;

(d)   personal representatives and a beneficiary;

(e)   the trustees of separate trusts for the same family;

(f)   a sole trader or partners and a limited company set up to enable the business to be incorporated;

(g)   associated companies (i.e. where one is a holding company and the other is its subsidiary within the meaning of the Companies Act 1985, or two associated companies); or

(h)   a local authority and a company within the meaning of 13.08(c).

73.   Rules 10.06(3) and 10.06(4) deal with the prohibition on acting for more than one prospective buyer, or for seller and buyer where there is more than one prospective buyer. These provisions

recognise the inevitable conflict of interests which makes it impossible to act for more than one prospective buyer, or for the seller and one of several prospective buyers. If you were already acting for seller and buyer (for example, both are established clients), you would be unable to continue acting for both if another prospective buyer were introduced during the course of the transaction. There is a significant inherent conflict in these circumstances. It would be impossible, for example, to reconcile the interests of both clients if it were in the seller's best interests to exchange with the other prospective buyer.

74.   The test of whether a person is an 'established client' is an objective one – is it reasonable to regard the person as an established client? A seller or buyer who instructs you for the first time is not an established client. A former client is not necessarily the same as an established client. There needs to be a degree of permanence in the solicitor–client relationship as exemplified by some continuity of instruction over time and the likelihood of future instruction. An individual related by blood, adoption or marriage to an established client, or who is living with an established client, counts as an established client. A person also counts as an established client if selling or buying jointly with an established client.

75.   The consideration will only count as £10,000 or less if the value of any property given in exchange or part exchange is taken into account.

76.   A builder or developer who acquires a property in part exchange, and sells it on without development, is not selling 'as a builder or developer' within the meaning of 3.10(c) and 3.13(c).

77.   If acting for seller and buyer under the provisions of 3.07 to 3.15, you would have to stop acting for at least one of the clients if a conflict were to arise during the course of the transaction. Clients should be made aware of the consequent disruption and additional expense involved in such circumstances, and of the advantages of separate representation, before giving their written consent.

78.   An RFL cannot undertake conveyancing. RELs may undertake conveyancing only if they are entitled to do so under regulation 12 of the European Communities (Lawyer's Practice) Regulations 2000 (SI 2000/1119).

79.   The effect of 3.11 is as follows:

(a)   if providing mortgage related services to the buyer (either through your own firm or a SEAL – see 3.12 for the definition of a SEAL which allows participating authorised non-SRA firms but requires at least one participating firm to be a recognised body or recognised sole practitioner), you may also provide property selling services to the seller (either through your own firm or a SEAL) and do the seller's conveyancing; and

(b)   if providing property selling services to the seller through a SEAL (not your own firm), you may also provide mortgage related services to the buyer (either through your own firm or the SEAL) and do the buyer's conveyancing.

80.   A SEAL may act for the seller and provide mortgage related services to the buyer; one of the participating firms may do the seller's conveyancing, and another participating firm may do the buyer's conveyancing.

Acting for lender and borrower in conveyancing transactions

81.   There will be no breach of 3.16(2)(c) to (d) or 3.19 if the lender has certified that its mortgage instructions and documents sent pursuant to those instructions are subject to the limitations set out in 3.19 and 3.21, and certifies any subsequent instructions and documents in the same way. If there

is no certification, when acting in a transaction involving the charge of property to be used solely as the borrower's private residence you must notify the lender that the approved certificate of title will be used and that your duties to the lender will be limited accordingly (see 3.20(b)). In other types of transaction, you should draw the lender's attention to the provisions of 3.19 and 3.21 and state that you cannot act on any instructions which extend beyond the matters contained in 3.19.

82.   As an alternative to printing the approved certificate for each transaction, it is acceptable for a lender to use a short form certificate of title which incorporates the approved certificate by reference. The form must include, in the following order:

    (a)   the title 'Certificate of Title';

    (b)   the contents of the details box in the order set out in the approved certificate (use of two columns is acceptable) but with details not required shaded out or stated not to be required; and

    (c)   the wording 'We, the conveyancers named above, give the Certificate of Title set out in the annex to rule 3 of the Solicitors' Code of Conduct 2007 as if the same were set out in full, subject to the limitations contained in it.'

Administrative details, such as a request for cheque, may follow the Certificate of Title.

83.   The approved certificate is only required for a transaction where the property is to be used solely as the borrower's private residence. The approved certificate need not, therefore, be used for investment properties such as blocks of flats, business premises such as shops (even if living accommodation is attached), or 'buy to let mortgages' on properties which are not intended for owner-occupation.

84.   You must inform the lender of the circumstances, in accordance with 3.18, so that the lender can decide whether or not to instruct you.

85.   A lender's instructions (see 3.19(x)) may require a wider disclosure of your circumstances than 3.18 requires; and you must assess whether the circumstances give rise to a conflict. For example, there will be a conflict between lender and borrower if you become involved in negotiations relating to the terms of the loan. A conflict might arise from the relationship you have or your firm has with the borrower – for example, if you are, or your firm is, the borrower's creditor or debtor or the borrower's business associate or co-habitant.

86.   In relation to 3.22(2), the limitations contained in 3.19 will not apply to the insertion into a recognised certificate of any information required by that certificate. For example, where the recognised certificate requires details of the parties' repairing obligations under a lease of the property, you may provide a summary of the relevant terms of the lease despite the general limitation contained in 3.19(i). However, any additions or amendments to the text of a recognised certificate to suit a particular transaction must not, to the extent to which they create an increased or additional obligation, extend beyond the limitations contained in 3.19.

87.   Many lenders require their lawyer or licensed conveyancer to check the vires of corporate borrowers and that the correct procedures have been followed to ensure the validity of the mortgage. Rule 3.19(n) enables lenders to impose duties on their lawyer or licensed conveyancer in relation to the execution of the mortgage and guarantee. Within this context it is perfectly proper for a lender to require you to obtain such information as the circumstances may require in relation to the capacity of, or execution of documents by, the borrower, third party mortgagor or guarantor; for instance, by way of certified copy minutes or an opinion from a lawyer of the relevant jurisdiction as to the validity and enforceability of the security or guarantee given by a foreign registered company. There is no reason why you should not assist corporate clients by drafting minutes or board resolutions.

You should not, however, certify the validity or passing of resolutions unless you were present at the meeting and have verified that it was convened and held strictly in accordance with all relevant requirements.

88. Rule 3.19(u) allows you to accept instructions from a lender to carry out administrative arrangements in relation to any collateral security. This expression includes associated debentures, collateral warranties, second charges, rent assignments, charges over rent income and deeds of priority. The administrative arrangements necessarily include the preparation and execution of the relevant documents and subsequent registration.

RULE 5 – BUSINESS MANAGEMENT IN ENGLAND AND WALES

5.01 Supervision and management responsibilities

(1) If you are a recognised body, a manager of a recognised body or a recognised sole practitioner, you must make arrangements for the effective management of the firm as a whole, and in particular provide for:

(a) compliance by the firm and its managers with the duties of a principal, in law and conduct, to exercise appropriate supervision over all staff, and ensure proper supervision and direction of clients' matters;

(b) compliance with the money laundering regulations, where applicable;

(c) compliance by the firm and individuals with key regulatory requirements such as certification, registration or recognition by the Solicitors Regulation Authority, compulsory professional indemnity cover, delivery of accountants' reports, and obligations to co-operate with and report information to the Authority;

(d) the identification of conflicts of interests;

(e) compliance with the requirements of rule 2 (Client relations) on client care, costs information and complaints handling;

(f) control of undertakings;

(g) the safekeeping of documents and assets entrusted to the firm;

(h) compliance with rule 6 (Equality and diversity);

(i) the training of individuals working in the firm to maintain a level of competence appropriate to their work and level of responsibility;

(j) financial control of budgets, expenditure and cashflow;

(k) the continuation of the practice of the firm in the event of absences and emergencies, with the minimum interruption to clients' business; and

(l) the management of risk.

(2) If you are a solicitor or REL employed as the head of an in-house legal department, you must effect supervision and management arrangements within your department to provide for:

(a) adequate supervision and direction of those assisting in your in-house practice;

(b) control of undertakings; and

(c) identification of conflicts of interests.

5.02   Persons who must be 'qualified to supervise'

(1)   The following persons must be 'qualified to supervise':

    (a)   a recognised sole practitioner;

    (b)   one of the lawyer managers of a recognised body or of a body corporate which is a manager of the recognised body;

    (c)   one of the solicitors or RELs employed by a law centre; or

    (d)   one in-house solicitor or in-house REL in any department where solicitors and/or RELs, as part of that employment:

        (i)   do publicly funded work; or

        (ii)   do or supervise advocacy or the conduct of proceedings for members of the public before a court or immigration tribunal.

(2)   To be 'qualified to supervise' under this paragraph a person:

    (a)   must have completed the training specified from time to time by the Solicitors Regulation Authority for this purpose; and

    (b)   must have been entitled to practise as a lawyer for at least 36 months within the last ten years; and must be able to demonstrate this if asked by the Solicitors Regulation Authority.

5.03   Supervision of work for clients and members of the public

(1)   If you are a recognised body, a manager of a recognised body or a recognised sole practitioner, you must ensure that your firm has in place a system for supervising clients' matters.

(2)   If you are an in-house solicitor or in-house REL and you are required to be 'qualified to supervise' under 5.02(1)(c) or (d) above, you must ensure that your law centre or in-house legal department has in place a system for supervising work undertaken for members of the public.

(3)   The system for supervision under 5.03(1) and (2) must include appropriate and effective procedures under which the quality of work undertaken for clients and members of the public is checked with reasonable regularity by suitably experienced and competent persons within the firm, law centre or in-house legal department.

RULE 7 – PUBLICITY

7.01   Misleading or inaccurate publicity

Publicity must not be misleading or inaccurate.

7.02   Clarity as to charges

Any publicity relating to your, or your firm's, charges must be clearly expressed. In relation to practice from an office in England and Wales it must be clear whether disbursements and VAT are included.

7.03   Unsolicited approaches in person or by telephone

(1)   You must not publicise your firm or practice by making unsolicited approaches in person or by telephone to a member of the public.

(2)   'Member of the public' does not include:

    (a)   a current or former client;

    (b)   another firm or its manager;

    (c)   an existing or potential professional or business connection; or

    (d)   a commercial organisation or public body.

7.04   International aspects of publicity

Publicity intended for a jurisdiction outside England and Wales must comply with:

    (a)   the provisions of rule 7 (and 15.07, if applicable); and

    (b)   the rules in force in that jurisdiction concerning lawyers' publicity.

Publicity intended for a jurisdiction where it is permitted will not breach 7.04 through being incidentally received in a jurisdiction where it is not permitted.

7.05   Responsibility for publicity

You must not authorise any other person to conduct publicity for your firm or practice in a way which would be contrary to rule 7 (and 15.07, if applicable).

7.06   Application

(1)   Rule 7 applies to any publicity you or your firm conduct(s) or authorise(s) in the course of setting up or carrying on the practice in relation to:

    (a)   the firm or your practice;

    (b)   any other business or activity carried on by you or your firm; or

    (c)   any other business or activity carried on by others.

(2)   Rules 7.01 to 7.05 apply to all forms of publicity including the name or description of your firm, stationery, advertisements, brochures, websites, directory entries, media appearances, promotional press releases, and direct approaches to potential clients and other persons, and whether conducted in person, in writing, or in electronic form.

7.07   Letterhead, website and e-mails

(1)   The letterhead, website and e-mails of a recognised body or recognised sole practitioner must show the words 'regulated by the Solicitors Regulation Authority', and either

    (a)   the firm's registered name and number if it is an LLP or company, or

    (b)   if the firm is a partnership or sole practitioner, the name under which it is recognised by the Solicitors Regulation Authority, and the number allocated to it by the Authority.

(2)   (a)   The letterhead of a recognised sole practitioner must include the name of the sole practitioner.

    (b)   The letterhead of a recognised body which is a partnership of 20 or fewer partners, must include a list of the partners.

    (c)   The letterhead of a recognised body which is a partnership of more than 20 partners, must include either

        (i)   a list of the partners; or

(ii)   a statement that a list of the partners is open to inspection at the office.

(d)   The letterhead of a recognised body which is an LLP must include either

(i)   a list of the members, identified as members; or

(ii)   a statement that a list of the members is open to inspection at the office,

unless the LLP is practising under a name other than its corporate name and has 20 or fewer members, in which case the list must be on the letterhead.

(e)   The letterhead of a recognised body which is a company with a sole director must include the name of the director, identified as director.

(f)   The letterhead of a recognised body which is a company with more than one director must include either

(i)   a list of the directors, identified as directors; or

(ii)   a statement that a list of the directors is open to inspection at the office.

(3)   In a recognised body, if the managers include persons other than solicitors, any list referred to in this rule must:

(a)   identify any solicitor as a solicitor;

(b)   in the case of any lawyer or notary of an Establishment Directive state other than the UK:

(i)   identify the jurisdiction(s) – local or national as appropriate – under whose professional title the lawyer or notary is practising;

(ii)   give the professional title(s), expressed in an official language of the Establishment Directive state(s) concerned; and

(iii)   if the lawyer is an REL, refer to that lawyer's registration with the Solicitors Regulation Authority;

(c)   indicate the professional qualification(s) of any other lawyer and the country or jurisdiction of qualification of any RFL not included in (b) above;

(d)   identify any individual non-lawyer as a non-lawyer; and

(e)   identify the nature of any body corporate, if this is not clear from its name.

(4)   Whenever an REL is named on the letterhead used by any firm or in-house practice, there must be compliance with 7.07(3)(b).

(5)   In 7.07 'letterhead' includes a fax heading.

RULE 8 – FEE SHARING

8.01   Fee sharing with lawyers and colleagues

Except as permitted under 8.02 below, you may only share or agree to share your professional fees with the following persons:

(a)   practising lawyers, and businesses carrying on the practice of lawyers;

(b)   non-lawyer managers or owners within your firm;

(c) a retired manager, member, owner or predecessor, or the dependants or personal representatives of a deceased manager, member, owner or predecessor;

(d) your genuine employee (this does not allow you to disguise as 'employment' what is in fact a partnership which rule 12 prohibits);

(e) your non-lawyer employer, if you are practising in-house and acting in accordance with rule 13 (In-house practice, etc.) or 15.13 (In-house practice overseas);

(f) a law centre or advice service operated by a charitable or similar non-commercial organisation if you are working as a volunteer and receive fees or costs from public funds or recovered from a third party;

(g) an estate agent who is your sub-agent for the sale of a property; or

(h) a charity (as defined in rule 24 (Interpretation)), provided:

   (i) you remain in compliance with 1.02 (Integrity), 1.03 (Independence) and 1.04 (Best interests of clients);

   (ii) if requested by the Solicitors Regulation Authority to do so, you supply details of all agreements to share fees with a charity;

   (iii) the operation of any such agreement does not result in a partnership;

   (iv) any such agreement does not involve a breach of rule 9 (Referrals of business); and

   (v) if you are employed in-house, you remain in compliance with 13.04 (Pro bono work).

8.02 Fee sharing with other non-lawyers

(1) You may share your professional fees with another person or business ('the fee sharer') if:

(a) the purpose of the fee sharing arrangement is solely to facilitate the introduction of capital and/or the provision of services to your firm;

(b) neither the fee sharing agreement nor the extent of the fees shared permits any fee sharer to influence or constrain your professional judgement in relation to the advice which you give to any client;

(c) the operation of the agreement does not result in a partnership prohibited by rule 12 (Framework of practice);

(d) if requested by the Solicitors Regulation Authority to do so, you supply details of all agreements which you have made with fee sharers and the percentage of your firm's annual gross fees which has been paid to each fee sharer; and

(e) your fee sharing agreement does not involve a breach of rule 9 (Referrals of business) or 15.09 (Overseas practice – referrals of business).

(2) 'Fee sharer' means a person or business who or which shares your fees in reliance on (1) above and the expression includes any person or business connected to or associated with the fee sharer.

RULE 9 – REFERRALS OF BUSINESS

9.01   General

(1)   When making or receiving referrals of clients to or from third parties you must do nothing which would compromise your independence or your ability to act and advise in the best interests of your clients.

(2)   You must draw the attention of potential introducers to this rule and to the relevant provisions of rule 7 (Publicity).

(3)   This rule does not apply to referrals between lawyers (including businesses carrying on the practice of lawyers).

(4)   You must not, in respect of any claim arising as a result of death or personal injury, either:

    (a)   enter into an arrangement for the referral of clients with; or

    (b)   act in association with,

any person whose business, or any part of whose business, is to make, support or prosecute (whether by action or otherwise, and whether by a solicitor or agent or otherwise) claims arising as a result of death or personal injury, and who, in the course of such business, solicits or receives contingency fees in respect of such claims.

(5)   The prohibition in 9.01(4) shall not apply to an arrangement or association with a person who solicits or receives contingency fees only in respect of proceedings in a country outside England and Wales, to the extent that a local lawyer would be permitted to receive a contingency fee in respect of such proceedings.

(6)   In 9.01(4) and (5) 'contingency fee' means any sum (whether fixed, or calculated either as a percentage of the proceeds or otherwise howsoever) payable only in the event of success in the prosecution or defence of any action, suit or other contentious proceedings.

9.02   Financial arrangements with introducers

The following additional requirements apply when you enter into a financial arrangement with an introducer:

    (a)   The agreement must be in writing and be available for inspection by the Solicitors Regulation Authority.

    (b)   The introducer must undertake, as part of the agreement, to comply with the provisions of this rule.

    (c)   You must be satisfied that clients referred by the introducer have not been acquired as a result of marketing or publicity or other activities which, if done by a person regulated by the Solicitors Regulation Authority, would be in breach of any of these rules.

    (d)   The agreement must not include any provision which would:

        (i)   compromise, infringe or impair any of the duties set out in these rules; or

        (ii)   allow the introducer to influence or constrain your professional judgement in relation to the advice given to the client.

    (e)   The agreement must provide that before making a referral the introducer must give the client all relevant information concerning the referral, in particular:

(i)   the fact that the introducer has a financial arrangement with you; and

(ii)   the amount of any payment to the introducer which is calculated by reference to that referral; or

(iii)   where the introducer is paying you to provide services to the introducer's customers:

    (A)   the amount the introducer is paying you to provide those services; and

    (B)   the amount the client is required to pay the introducer.

(f)   If you have reason to believe that the introducer is breaching any of the terms of the agreement required by this rule, you must take all reasonable steps to ensure that the breach is remedied. If the introducer continues to breach it you must terminate the agreement.

(g)   Before accepting instructions to act for a client referred under 9.02 you must, in addition to the requirements contained in 2.02 (Client care), 2.03 (Information about the cost) or 2.05 (Complaints handling), give the client, in writing, all relevant information concerning the referral, in particular:

(i)   the fact that you have a financial arrangement with the introducer;

(ii)   the amount of any payment to the introducer which is calculated by reference to that referral; or

(iii)   where the introducer is paying you to provide services to the introducer's customers:

    (A)   the amount the introducer is paying you to provide those services; and

    (B)   the amount the client is required to pay the introducer;

(iv)   a statement that any advice you give will be independent and that the client is free to raise questions on all aspects of the transaction; and

(v)   confirmation that information disclosed to you by the client will not be disclosed to the introducer unless the client consents; but that where you are also acting for the introducer in the same matter and a conflict of interests arises, you might be obliged to cease acting.

(h)   You must not enter into a financial arrangement with an introducer for the referral of clients in respect of criminal proceedings or any matter in which you will act for the client with the benefit of public funding.

(i)   For the purpose of this rule:

(i)   'financial arrangement' includes:

    (A)   any payment to a third party in respect of referrals; and

    (B)   any agreement to be paid by a third party introducer to provide services to the third party's customers; and

(ii)   'payment' includes any other consideration but does not include normal hospitality, proper disbursements or normal business expenses.

9.03   Referrals to third parties

(1)   If you recommend that a client use a particular firm, agency or business, you must do so in good faith, judging what is in the client's best interests.

(2)   You must not enter into any agreement or association which would restrict your freedom to recommend any particular firm, agency or business.

(3)   Paragraph (2) above does not apply to arrangements in connection with any of the following types of contracts:

    (a)   regulated mortgage contracts;

    (b)   general insurance contracts; or

    (c)   pure protection contracts.

(4)   The terms 'regulated mortgage contracts', 'general insurance contracts' and 'pure protection contracts' in (3) above have the meanings given in 19.01(4).

(5)   Where you refer a client to a firm, agency or business that can only offer products from one source, you must notify the client in writing of this limitation.

(6)   If a client is likely to need an endowment policy, or similar life insurance with an investment element, you must refer them only to an independent intermediary authorised to give investment advice.

RULE 10 – RELATIONS WITH THIRD PARTIES

10.01   Not taking unfair advantage

You must not use your position to take unfair advantage of anyone either for your own benefit or for another person's benefit.

10.02   Agreeing costs with another party

When negotiating the payment of your client's costs by another firm's client or a third party, you must give sufficient time and information for the amount of your costs to be agreed or assessed.

10.03   Administering oaths

You can administer oaths or affirmations or take declarations if you are authorised to do so. You must not do so where you or your firm is acting for any party in the matter.

10.04   Contacting other party to a matter

You must not communicate with any other party who to your knowledge has retained a lawyer, or a business carrying on the practice of lawyers, to act in a matter, except:

    (a)   to request the name and address of the other party's lawyer;

    (b)   where it would be reasonable to conclude that the other party's lawyer has refused or failed for no adequate reason either to pass on messages to their client or to reply to correspondence, and has been warned of your intention to contact their client direct;

    (c)   with that lawyer's consent; or

    (d)   in exceptional circumstances.

10.05   Undertakings

(1)   You must fulfil an undertaking which is given in circumstances where:

    (a)   you give the undertaking in the course of practice;

    (b)   you are a recognised body, a manager of a recognised body or a recognised sole practitioner, and any person within the firm gives the undertaking in the course of practice;

    (c)   you give the undertaking outside the course of practice, but as a solicitor; or

    (d)   you are an REL based at an office in England and Wales, and you give the undertaking within the UK, as a lawyer of an Establishment Directive profession, but outside your practice as an REL.

(2)   You must fulfil an undertaking within a reasonable time.

(3)   If you give an undertaking which is dependent upon the happening of a future event, you must notify the recipient immediately if it becomes clear that the event will not occur.

(4)   When you give an undertaking to pay another's costs, the undertaking will be discharged if the matter does not proceed unless there is an express agreement that the costs are payable in any event.

10.06   Dealing with more than one prospective buyer in a conveyancing transaction

(1)   Each time a seller of land, other than in a sale by auction or tender, either:

    (a)   instructs you to deal with more than one prospective buyer; or

    (b)   to your knowledge:

        (i)   deals directly with another prospective buyer (or their conveyancer); or

        (ii)   instructs another conveyancer to deal with another prospective buyer;

you must, with the client's consent, immediately inform the conveyancer of each prospective buyer, or the prospective buyer if acting in person.

(2)   If the seller refuses to agree to such disclosure, you must immediately stop acting in the matter.

(3)   You must not act for both the seller and any of the prospective buyers.

(4)   You must not act for more than one of the prospective buyers.

10.07   Fees of lawyers of other jurisdictions

(1)   If in the course of practice you instruct a lawyer of another jurisdiction you must, as a matter of professional conduct, pay the lawyer's proper fees unless the lawyer is practising as a lawyer of England and Wales; or

    (a)   you have expressly disclaimed that responsibility at the outset, or at a later date you have expressly disclaimed responsibility for any fees incurred after that date;

    (b)   the lawyer is an REL or is registered with the Bar of England and Wales under the Establishment Directive; or

    (c)   the lawyer is an RFL based in England and Wales and practising in a firm.

(2)   If in the course of practice you instruct a business carrying on the practice of a lawyer of another jurisdiction you must, as a matter of professional conduct, pay the proper fees for the work that lawyer does, unless:

(a)   you have expressly disclaimed that responsibility at the outset, or at a later date you have expressly disclaimed responsibility for any fees incurred after that date; or

(b)   the business is a firm.

RULE 18 – PROPERTY SELLING

18.01   Standards of property selling services

(1)   When providing property selling services through your firm, you must:

(a)   ensure that you, or the relevant staff, are competent to carry out the work;

(b)   not seek from any prospective buyer a pre-contract deposit in excess of any prescribed limit; and

(c)   promptly send to your client written accurate details of any offer you have received from a prospective buyer in respect of an interest in the property (other than those of a description which your client has indicated in writing that they do not want to receive).

(2)   If you are the person who is responsible for marketing a residential property you must comply with any Home Information Packs Regulations made under the Housing Act 2004.

(3)   (a)   In 18.01(1) above:

(i)   'competent' includes meeting any standards of competence set by the Secretary of State under section 22 of the Estate Agents Act 1979; and

(ii)   'prescribed limit' means any limit prescribed by the Secretary of State under section 19 of the Estate Agents Act 1979.

(b)   In 18.01(2) 'the person who is responsible for marketing a residential property' has the meaning used in sections 151–153 of the Housing Act 2004.

18.02   Statement on the cost

(1)   When accepting instructions to act in the sale of a property, you must, at the outset of communication between you and the client, or as soon as is reasonably practicable, and before the client is committed to any liability towards you, give the client a written statement setting out your agreement as to:

(a)   the identity of the property;

(b)   the interest to be sold;

(c)   the price to be sought;

(d)   the amount of your fee or the method of its calculation;

(e)   the circumstances in which your fee is to become payable;

(f)   regarding any payments to be made to others, and charged separately:

(i)   the amount, or the method by which they will be calculated; and

(ii)   the circumstances in which they may be incurred; and

(g)   the incidence of VAT.

(2)   You must also, within the written statement:

(a)   state whether or not you are to have 'sole agency' or 'sole selling rights'. The statement must also include a clear explanation of the intention and effect of those terms, or any similar terms used; and

(b)   if the statement refers to a 'ready, willing and able' buyer (or similar term), include a clear explanation of the term.

18.03   Conflict of interests

(1)   In addition to your duties under rule 3 (Conflict of interests), when selling property you must comply with the following requirements.

(a)   If you or any connected person has, or is seeking to acquire, a beneficial interest in the property or in the proceeds of sale of any interest in the property, you must promptly inform your client in writing.

(b)   If you act in the sale of property, even if not in the conveyancing, you must not act for the buyer in the negotiations.

(c)   If a prospective buyer makes an offer for a client's property, you must promptly inform the client in writing if, to your knowledge, you or any connected person has been instructed, or is to be instructed by the buyer to sell an interest in land, and that sale is necessary to enable the buyer to buy from the client or results from that prospective purchase.

(d)   If you have, or to your knowledge any connected person has, a beneficial interest in a property or in the proceeds of sale of any interest in it, you must promptly inform in writing any person negotiating to acquire or dispose of any interest in that property. You must make this disclosure before entering into any negotiations with a prospective buyer.

(e)   You must not discriminate against a prospective buyer because they are unlikely to instruct you to sell an interest in land, which sale is necessary to enable the buyer to buy from your client or results from that prospective purchase.

(f)   When acting for a seller, you must restrict communication with the buyer to your property selling function. In particular:

(i)   you must communicate about legal matters so far as possible only through the buyer's solicitor; and

(ii)   you must not lead the buyer to believe that they are receiving legal advice from you.

(g)   When acting for a seller, if you arrange for a mortgage to be available on the property in order to facilitate the sale, you may inform prospective buyers of the availability of the mortgage (subject to the buyer's status) but, unless exempted by rule 3 (Conflict of interests) you must also inform prospective buyers in writing:

(i)   that you cannot advise or act for the prospective buyer in respect of the mortgage;

(ii)   that the mortgage may not be the only one available; and

(iii)   that the prospective buyer should consult their own lawyer.

(2)   In 18.03(1) above:

(a)   'connected person' means:

(i)   spouse, former spouse, reputed spouse, brother, sister, uncle, aunt, nephew, niece, direct descendant, parent or other direct ancestor;

(ii)   any employee of your firm, and any member of your employee's family;

(iii) any owner or employee of an associated firm defined in rule 24 (Interpretation) or any member of their families;

(iv)   any company of which you are a director or employee, or any LLP of which you are a member or employee, or any company in which you, either alone or with any other connected person or persons are entitled to exercise, or control the exercise of, one-third or more of the voting power at any general meeting;

(v)   any company of which any of the persons mentioned in (i) to (iii) above is a director or employee, or any LLP of which any of them is a member or employee, or any company in which any of them, either alone or with any other connected person or persons, is entitled to exercise, or control the exercise of, one-third or more of the voting power at any general meeting; and

(vi)   any other 'associate' as defined in section 32 of the Estate Agents Act 1979; and

(b) 'you' includes anyone with whom you carry on a joint property selling practice, and owners of an associated firm as defined in rule 24 (Interpretation).

18.04   Waivers

In spite of 22.01(1) (Waivers), the Solicitors Regulation Authority Board shall not have power to waive any of the provisions of this rule.

RULE 19 – FINANCIAL SERVICES

19.01   Independence

(1) You must not, in connection with any regulated activity:

(a) be an appointed representative; or

(b) have any arrangement with other persons under which you could be constrained to recommend to clients or effect for them (or refrain from doing so) transactions:

(i)   in some investments but not others;

(ii)   with some persons but not others; or

(iii) through the agency of some persons but not others; or

(c) have any arrangement with other persons under which you could be constrained to introduce or refer clients or other persons with whom you deal to some persons but not others.

(2) You must not have any active involvement in a separate business which is an appointed representative, unless it is the appointed representative of an independent financial adviser.

(3) Paragraph (1)(b) and (c) above shall not apply to arrangements in connection with any of the following types of investments:

(a) regulated mortgage contracts;

(b) general insurance contracts; or

(c) pure protection contracts.

(4) In this rule:

(a)　'appointed representative' has the meaning given in the Financial Services and Markets Act 2000;

(b)　'general insurance contract' is any contract of insurance within Part 1 of Schedule 1 to the Financial Services and Markets Act 2000 (Regulated Activities) Order 2001 (SI 2001/544);

(c)　'investment' means any of the investments specified in Part III of the Financial Services and Markets Act 2000 (Regulated Activities) Order 2001 (SI 2001/544);

(d)　'pure protection contract' has the meaning given in rule 8(1) of the Solicitors' Financial Services (Scope) Rules 2001;

(e)　'regulated activity' means an activity which is specified in the Financial Services and Markets Act 2000 (Regulated Activities) Order 2001 (SI 2001/544); and

(f)　'regulated mortgage contract' has the meaning given by article 61(3) of the Financial Services and Markets Act 2000 (Regulated Activities) Order 2001 (SI 2001/544).

RULE 21 – SEPARATE BUSINESSES

21.01　General

(1)　If you are practising from an office in England and Wales as a solicitor, REL, RFL or recognised body, or if you are a manager or employee of a recognised body, or an employee of a recognised sole practitioner, you must comply with the provisions of this rule in relation to:

(a)　services which may not be provided through a separate business;

(b)　services which may be provided through a separate business or (subject to these rules) through a firm or in-house practice; and

(c)　services which fall outside the scope of a solicitor's practice but which may be provided in conjunction with a firm or in-house practice.

(2)　This rule applies to your involvement in any separate business whether the separate business is in England and Wales or outside the jurisdiction.

(3)　For the avoidance of doubt, in this rule 'practising' includes practising as an in-house solicitor or an in-house REL.

21.02　Services which may not be provided through a separate business

(1)　Subject to (2) below, you must not provide any of the following services through a separate business:

(a)　the conduct of any matter which could come before a court, tribunal or inquiry, whether or not proceedings are started;

(b)　advocacy before a court, tribunal or inquiry;

(c)　instructing counsel in any part of the UK;

(d)　immigration advice or immigration services;

(e)　any activity in relation to conveyancing, applications for probate or letters of administration, or drawing trust deeds or court documents, which is reserved to solicitors and others under the Solicitors Act 1974;

(f)　drafting wills;

(g)   acting as nominee, trustee or executor in England and Wales;

(h)   legal advice not included above; or

(i)   drafting legal documents not included above.

Exceptions

(2)   The provisions of (1) above do not apply to prohibit you from providing services through a separate business:

(a)   which carries on your practice as a lawyer of another jurisdiction;

(b)   which carries on your business as a parliamentary agent;

(c)   which is a wholly owned nominee company operated as a subsidiary but necessary part of the work of a separate business providing financial services; or

(d)   which provides legal advice and/or drafts legal documents within (1)(h) and/or (i) above, as a subsidiary but necessary part of some other service which is one of the main services of the separate business.

However, you must comply with the requirements of 21.05 in relation to any such separate business.

21.03   Services which may be provided in conjunction with a firm or in-house practice

(1)   The following services extend beyond, or fall outside, the scope of a solicitor's practice but you may provide such services in conjunction with a firm or in-house practice:

(a)   educational and training activities; and

(b)   authorship, journalism and publishing.

(2)   Such services are not provided through a separate business for the purpose of this rule.

21.04   Services which may be provided (subject to these rules) either through a firm or in-house practice, or through a separate business

(1)   You may provide the following services either (subject to these rules) through a firm or in-house practice, or through a separate business:

(a)   alternative dispute resolution;

(b)   financial services (except those that cannot form part of a solicitor's practice);

(c)   estate agency;

(d)   management consultancy;

(e)   company secretarial services;

(f)   acting as a parliamentary agent;

(g)   practising as a lawyer of another jurisdiction;

(h)   acting as a bailiff;

(i)   acting as nominee, trustee or executor outside England and Wales; or

(j)   providing any other business, advisory or agency service which could be provided (subject to these rules) through a firm or in-house practice but is not included in 21.02.

(2)   If you provide any service listed in (1) above through a separate business you must comply with 21.05.

21.05   Safeguards in relation to a separate business

(1)   If you provide services through a separate business you must do nothing in the course of practice, or in the course of making referrals to the business or accepting referrals from the business, which would breach rule 1 (Core duties).

(2)   You must ensure that the following safeguards are in place in relation to a separate business which offers or provides any of the services listed in 21.04(1):

(a)   the separate business must not be held out or described in such a way as to suggest that the separate business is carrying on a practice regulated by the Solicitors Regulation Authority or another approved regulator, or that any lawyer connected with your firm is providing services through the separate business as a practising lawyer regulated by the Solicitors Regulation Authority or another approved regulator;

(b)   all paperwork, documents, records or files relating to the separate business and its customers must be kept separate from those of any firm or in-house practice, even where a customer of the separate business is also a client of the firm or in-house practice;

(c)   the client account or other account used to hold money for the clients of any firm or in-house practice must not be used to hold money for the separate business, or for customers of the separate business in their capacity as such;

(d)   if the separate business shares premises, office accommodation or reception staff with any firm or in-house practice:

(i)   the areas used by the firm or in-house practice must be clearly differentiated from the areas used by the separate business; and

(ii)   all customers of the separate business must be informed that it is not regulated by the Solicitors Regulation Authority and that the statutory protections attaching to clients of a lawyer regulated by the Authority are not available to them as customers of that business;

(e)   if you or your firm refer a client to the separate business, the client must first be informed of your interest in the separate business, that the separate business is not regulated by the Solicitors Regulation Authority, and that the statutory protections attaching to clients of a lawyer regulated by the Authority are not available to them as customers of the separate business; and

(f)   if the separate business is an estate agency, then without prejudice to the provisions of these rules regarding conflicts of interests, neither you nor any firm through which you practise may act in the conveyance for the buyer of any property sold through the estate agency unless:

(i)   the firm shares ownership of the estate agency with at least one other business in which neither you nor the firm have any financial interest;

(ii)   neither you nor anyone else in the firm is dealing with or has dealt with the sale of the seller's property for the separate business; and

(iii) the buyer has given written consent to you or the firm acting, after your financial interest in the sale going through has been explained to the buyer.

I.2. Property Fraud Warning Card[1]

The Solicitors Regulation Authority will not tolerate property fraud.

If in doubt – refuse to act

You must ensure that you do not facilitate dubious property transactions. Failure to observe our warnings could lead to disciplinary action or criminal prosecution.

If you doubt the propriety of a transaction you should refuse to act. Ensure you verify and question instructions to satisfy yourself that you are not facilitating a dubious transaction.

What is property fraud?

Mortgage fraud occurs when a loan is obtained on the basis of untrue statements to the lender, such as when a lender is led to believe that a property is worth more than its true value and therefore lends more than it would if it knew the true position. Always focus on informing the lender of the true price and other relevant facts, while taking into account confidentiality and legal professional privilege.

Some frauds do not involve a mortgage – only the deception of buyers.

Warning signs

- Back to back transactions where a property is bought and then sold quickly, apparently at a higher price. The lender advances money based on the higher price

- Misrepresentation or changes to the purchase price including sellers or developers providing incentives, allowances or discounts unless these are clearly and fully disclosed to the lender

- A representation to you that a deposit or part of the purchase price is paid direct

- 'Gifted deposit' or 'deposit paid' by the seller amounting to a reduction in the price paid by the buyer but distorting the value disclosed to the lender

- Unusual or suspicious instructions such as transactions controlled or funded by a third party; a client using an alias; sales and purchases between associates; parties using the same legal adviser; a request that net proceeds be sent to a third party

- Properties sold between related offshore or corporate companies that are commonly controlled by the same individuals, particularly where the properties are mortgaged at an inflated value

Be aware that variations of these warning signs exist and fraudsters change their methods. You do not need to act for the lender to become implicated. If you are not satisfied of the propriety of the transaction you should refuse to act.

Money laundering

Bear in mind that you may also have legal obligations to report your suspicions to the Serious Organised Crime Agency.

---

1. © The Law Society 2009. Last updated by the Solicitors Regulation Authority April 2009.

To report to us on a confidential basis, contact our Fraud and Confidential Intelligence Bureau on **01926 439673 / 0845 850 0999** or email **redalert@sra.org.uk**.

For advice, call the Ethics Helpline **0870 606 2577**, 9am–5pm Monday to Friday or email **professional.ethics@sra.org.uk**

For best practice advice, refer also to **www.lawsociety.org.uk/mortgagefraud**

Your obligations are set out in rules 1, 2, 3, 4 and 18 of the Solicitors' Code of Conduct 2007 and its guidance

You can get help from our website: **www.rules.sra.org.uk**

Or you can call the Ethics Helpline: **0870 606 2577** 9am–5pm Monday to Friday email: **professional.ethics@sra.org.uk**

Take care of all your clients – including lenders

Act independently and in their best interests

Put your clients first – but never assist impropriety

If you don't pay attention to these warnings, you may be liable to disciplinary action

I.3. Undertakings Warning Card[1]

The SRA takes breaches of undertakings very seriously.

Many transactions depend on the use of undertakings enabling you to negotiate and conduct your client's business successfully.

Where you give an undertaking

Those placing reliance on it will expect you to fulfil it. Ensure your undertakings are:

- Specific
- Measurable
- Agreed
- Realistic
- Timed

A breach of undertaking can lead to a disciplinary finding and costs direction.

Undertakings you give are also summarily enforceable by the High Court. Be aware that you do not become exposed to a liability within the excess of your firm's insurance.

Where you accept an undertaking

Ensure that in doing so your client's position is protected and you are not exposed to a breach.

If you are a regulated person or firm

- Be clear about who can give undertakings
- Ensure all staff understand they need your client's agreement
- Be clear about how compliance will be monitored
- Maintain a central record to ensure and monitor compliance
- Prescribe the manner in which undertakings may be given
- Prepare standard undertakings, where possible, with clear instructions that any departure be authorised in accordance with supervision and management responsibilities
- Adopt a system that ensures terms are checked by another fee-earner
- Confirm oral undertakings (given or received) in writing
- Copy each undertaking and attach it to the relevant file; label the file itself
- Ensure all staff understand the undertakings they give when using the Law Society's formulae for exchange of contracts and its code for completion by post.

To report to us on a confidential basis, contact our Fraud and Confidential Intelligence Bureau on **01926 439673 / 0845 850 0999** or email redalert@sra.org.uk.

---

1. © The Law Society 2009. Last updated by the Solicitors Regulation Authority April 2009.

For advice, call the Ethics Helpline **0870 606 2577**, 9am–5pm Monday to Friday or email **professional.ethics@sra.org.uk**

Your obligations are set out in rules 1, 5.01 and 10.05 of the Solicitors' Code of Conduct 2007 and its guidance

You must ensure that you act with complete integrity at all times

You can get help from our website: **www.rules.sra.org.uk**

Or you can call the Ethics Helpline: **0870 606 2577** 9am–5pm Monday to Friday email: professional.ethics@sra. org.uk

Take care of your clients

Act independently and in their best interests

Put your clients first – but never assist impropriety

If you don't pay attention to these warnings, you may be liable to disciplinary action

I.4. Money Laundering Warning Card[1]

The Solicitors Regulation Authority is determined to pursue those it regulates who are involved in money laundering.

You must ensure that you do not facilitate laundering even when money does not pass though your firm's accounts. Failure to observe our warnings can lead to disciplinary action, criminal prosecution, or both.

Warning Signs

Unusual payment requests

- Payments from a third party where you cannot verify the source of the funds
- Receipts of cash and requests for payments by cash
- Money transfers where there is a variation between the account holder/signatory
- Payments to unrelated third parties
- Litigation settlements which are reached too easily.

Unusual instructions

- Instructions outside the normal pattern of your business
- Instructions changed without a reasonable explanation
- Transactions that take an unusual turn
- Movement of funds between accounts, institutions or jurisdictions without reason.

Use of your client account

- Never accept instructions to act as a banking facility, particularly if you do not undertake any related legal work – be aware of note (ix) to rule 15 of the Solicitors' Accounts Rules 1998
- Be wary if you are instructed to do legal work, receive substantial funds into your client account, but the instructions are later cancelled and you are asked to send the money to a third party or perhaps to your client.

Suspect territory

- Check official sources about suspect territories and sanctions
- Be wary of funds moved around without a logical explanation.

Loss making transaction

- Instructions potentially leading to financial loss without logical explanation, particularly where your client seems unconcerned.

1. © The Law Society 2009. Last updated by the Solicitors Regulation Authority April 2009.

Legislation may require you to make an official disclosure to the Serious Organised Crime Agency (SOCA), PO Box 8000, London, SE11 5EN, call **020 7238 8282**, or send an email by registering on the secure site at www.ukciu.gov.uk/saroline.aspx. You will not commit the offence of 'tipping off' by reporting a matter to the SRA. To report to us on a confidential basis, contact our Fraud and Confidential Intelligence Bureau on **01926 439673 / 0845 850 0999** or email **redalert@sra.org. uk**.

For advice, call the Ethics Helpline **0870 606 2577**, 9am–5pm Monday to Friday or email **professional.ethics@sra.org.uk**

For general queries about anti-money laundering compliance, contact the Law Society's Practice Advice Service on 0870 606 2522, 9am- 5pm Monday to Friday, or refer to guidance on the website at **www.lawsociety.org.uk/antimoneylaundering**

Your obligations are set out in the Solicitors' Code of Conduct, particularly rules 1 and 4 and their guidance, the Solicitors' Accounts Rules, the Proceeds of Crime Act 2002, the Terrorism Act 2000, and the Money Laundering Regulations 2007

You can get help from our website: **www.rules.sra.org.uk**

For advice on professional conduct, call the Ethics Helpline on 0870 606 2577, 9am–5pm Monday to Friday or email **professional.ethics@sra.org.uk**.

For general queries about best practice anti-money laundering compliance, contact the Law Society's Practice Advice Service on 0870 606 2522, 9am–5pm Monday to Friday, or refer to guidance on the website at **www.lawsociety.org.uk/antimoneylaundering**

Take care of your clients

Act independently and in their best interests

Put your clients first – but never assist impropriety

If you don't pay attention to these warnings, you may be liable to disciplinary action

II. LAW SOCIETY'S PRACTICE NOTES

II.1. Telegraphic Transfer Fees Practice Note[1]

1. INTRODUCTION

1.1 Who should read this practice note?

All solicitors who arrange telegraphic transfers of funds on behalf of clients in the course of their business.

1.2 What is the issue?

A recent Solicitors Disciplinary Tribunal (SDT) decision found against the partners of a practice for concealing profit costs from their clients by referring to a telegraphic transfer fee as a disbursement.

1.3 Professional conduct

The following sections of the Solicitors' Code of Conduct 2007 (code of conduct) are relevant:

1.01	Justice and the rule of law
1.02	Integrity
1.04	Best interests of clients
1.05	Standard of service
1.06	Public confidence
2.03	Information about the cost

1.4 Status of this practice note

Practice notes are issued by the Law Society for the use and benefit of its members. They represent the Law Society's view of good practice in a particular area. They are not intended to be the only standard of good practice that solicitors can follow. You are not required to follow them, but doing so will make it easier to account to oversight bodies for your actions.

Practice notes are not legal advice, nor do they necessarily provide a defence to complaints of misconduct or of inadequate professional service. While care has been taken to ensure that they are accurate, up to date and useful, the Law Society will not accept any legal liability in relation to them.

For queries or comments on this practice note contact the Law Society's Practice Advice Service: **www.lawsociety.org.uk/practiceadvice**

---

1. © The Law Society. This Practice Note is as stated on 30 July 2008. Practice Notes are updated by the Law Society from time to time. Solicitors are advised to check **www.lawsociety.org.uk** for the latest version.

1.5   Terminology in this practice note

Must – a specific requirement in the Solicitors' Code of Conduct or legislation. You must comply, unless there are specific exemptions or defences provided for in the code of conduct or relevant legislation.

Should – good practice for most situations in the Law Society's view. If you do not follow this, you should be able to justify to oversight bodies why the alternative approach you have taken is appropriate, either for your practice, or in the particular retainer.

May – a non-exhaustive list of options for meeting your obligations. Which option you choose is determined by the risk profile of the individual practice, client or retainer. You must be able to justify why this was an appropriate option to oversight bodies.

SDT – Solicitors Disciplinary Tribunal.

TT – Telegraphic transfer.

2. CHARGING FOR TELEGRAPHIC TRANSFERS

2.1   What is a disbursement?

The Solicitors Accounts Rules define a disbursement as 'an expense'.

2.2   Is a telegraphic transfer fee a disbursement?

A TT fee is an expense but some practices charge more than the cost of the transfer under the heading disbursement, thereby concealing profit costs from clients.

The SDT has found that this clearly breaches rule 1 of the code of conduct, particularly in relation to the solicitor's duty to act with integrity and in the best interests of the client.

This conduct is also likely to be in breach of rule 2, client care, if any amount over the cost of the transfer is not explicitly declared to the client as profit costs.

2.3   How should telegraphic transfers be charged?

You must advise the client of the basis and terms of your charges.

You should tell your client that you are charging them the fee that has been charged to the practice by the financial institution executing the telegraphic transfer, and that this fee is a disbursement.

You must charge VAT on the fee that has been charged to the practice by the financial institution executing the telegraphic transfer, even if no VAT is charged to you. For more information see VAT on incidental expenses to clients; disbursements on the HM Revenue and Customs website.

You must not include any profit cost element as a disbursement. For example, you must not include a fixed monthly charge by the bank for having an in-house terminal, or any internal staff costs.

If you charge the client an administration fee for arranging the telegraphic transfer you must inform the client and charge it as profit cost.

3. THE SOLICITORS DISCIPLINARY TRIBUNAL (SDT) RULING

An SDT case reported in June 2008 clearly demonstrates the implications of referring to a mixed charge partially comprising a profit costs element and including a telegraphic transfer fee as 'a disbursement'.

3.1   The facts

The practice charged the client £30 plus VAT for a TT as a disbursement. The practice only paid £10 to its bank for each TT.

The client care letter sent to clients under rule 15 (now rule 2) of the code of conduct did not explain that the practice would only pay on £10 and that the balance amounted to profit costs for the practice.

It did not explain that the additional fee related to work undertaken in arranging the TT.

3.2 The allegations

Claiming the TT fee as a disbursement of £30 was misleading to the client. The balance over the actual disbursement was additional income and profit to the practice.

3.3 The findings

The respondents had acted in breach of rule 1 and rule 2 of the code of conduct.

The practice's invoices did not reflect the telegraphic transfer fee and the true position was not addressed in the letters addressed to the clients. The clients had therefore been misled.

A fee charged to the client by the practice had been described as a disbursement met by the practice which was inaccurate. This hid the fee for handling a transfer in addition to the bank's charges.

In all of the circumstances of the case, the STD considered it appropriate and proportionate to fine each respondent £1,500.

II.2. Execution of Documents by Virtual Means Practice Note[1]

1. INTRODUCTION

1.1 Who should read this practice note?

Solicitors who deal with execution of documents at virtual signings or closings where some or all of the signatories involved are not physically present at the same meeting.

1.2 What's the issue?

R (on the application of Mercury Tax Group and another) v. *HMRC* [2008] EWHC 2721 (*Mercury*) has led to discussion about the effectiveness in English law of using:

- pre-signed signature pages, and

- virtual signings and closings where signature pages are exchanged by e-mail.

This practice note gives suggestions on good practice in light of the Mercury case and suggests different options for virtual signings/closings. The options suggested are not exhaustive as it is not implied that virtual signings and closings cannot or should not be conducted in other ways.

It is considered that:

- the Court of Appeal decision in *Koenigsblatt* v. *Sweet* [1923] 2 Ch 314 (*Koenigsblatt*) remains the leading authority on the applicability of the principles of authority and ratification to the creation of legally binding written agreements

- the first instance decision in Mercury should be viewed as limited to its particular facts

- the decision in Koenigsblatt should prevail where there is inconsistency between the two.

This practice note is intended to assist parties who nevertheless wish to take a cautious approach, in the light of Mercury, where it is more convenient to have a virtual signing or closing and wet ink documents are not required for registration.. This is an evolving area of law and you should keep abreast of any relevant developments.

2. SUMMARY OF OPTIONS

Your options depend on the type of document in question, because of statutory and legal arrangements surrounding the formality of their creation. The options can be summarised as:

1. returning by e-mail the entire document and the signed signature page
2. returning by e-mail only the signed signature page
3. creating a pre-signed signature page in advance of finalising the document

---

1. © The Law Society 2010. The Practice Note is as stated on 16 February 2010. Practice Notes are updated by the Law Society from time to time. Solicitors are advised to check **www.lawsociety.org.uk** for the latest version.

Type of Document	Option 1 – Return entire PDF/Word document plus signature page	Option 2 – Return signature page only	Option 3 – Advance pre-signed signature pages
Deeds	Yes	No	No
Real estate contracts	Yes	No	No
Guarantees (stand-alone or contained in simple contracts)	Yes	Yes	Yes
Simple contracts (not incorporating any of the above)	Yes	Yes	Yes

3. STATUTORY AND OTHER LEGAL REQUIREMENTS

3.1 Deeds

The judge in Mercury took the view that section 1(3) of the Law of Property (Miscellaneous Provisions) Act 1989 (LPMPA) requires a deed to be executed by an individual in its final version. Section 1(3) LPMPA provides:

'An instrument is validly executed as a deed by an individual if, and only if –

    (a)   it is signed –

        (i)   by him in the presence of a witness who attests the signature; or

        (ii)   at his direction and in his presence and the presence of two witnesses who each attest the signature; and

    (b)   it is delivered as a deed by him or a person authorised to do so on his behalf.'

The judge's approach in Mercury could also apply to the execution of a deed by a company. See section 74A Law of Property Act 1925 and sections 44 and 46 Companies Act 2006 which also use the word 'it' in relation to the document being executed.

Whilst a different view of the judge's interpretation in Mercury of section 1(3) LPMPA may be taken, it is recognised that this is a question of statutory interpretation that was not addressed in Koenigsblatt. If you wish to take a prudent approach in relation to the execution of deeds (whether by an individual or on behalf of a company) at a virtual signing or closing, you should use option 1.

3.2 Real estate contracts

For real estate contracts section 2 of the LPMPA provides:

    '(1)   A contract for the sale or other disposition of an interest in land can only be made in writing and only by incorporating all the terms which the parties have expressly agreed in one document or, where contracts are exchanged, in each.

    (2)   The terms may be incorporated in a document either by being set out in it or by reference to some other document.

    (3)   The document incorporating the terms or, where contracts are exchanged, one of the documents incorporating them (but not necessarily the same one) must be signed by or on behalf of each party to the contract.'

Some contracts for the sale or other disposition of an interest in land may be included in a contract that is primarily about something else, e.g. an asset sale agreement may include:

(i)   an agreement to transfer properties, along with other assets, or

(ii) an agreement to share a site temporarily, by granting a lease on closing.

Another example would be a mortgage, trust deed, mortgage debenture or other security document creating any security interest in real estate that might be acquired in the future.

By analogy, the judge's approach in relation to section 1(3) LPMPA could apply also to section 2 LPMPA. For this reason, you should use option 1 where you decide to execute a real estate contract or contracts containing real estate provisions 'virtually', rather than by using traditional methods of executing 'wet ink' signatures.

3.2.1 *Informing other parties*

Many real estate contracts will be subject to an exchange using Law Society Formulae for exchanging contracts by telephone. In such cases you should: make clear to the other party that the contract in your possession does not

- have traditional 'wet ink' signature and

- obtain prior approval to its use from all relevant parties.

3.2.2 *'Wet-ink' originals for registration purposes*

You should also take account of any need for the future availability of documents with 'wet ink' signatures for registration purposes. Examples include transfers, leases, charges or other deeds that have to be registered at the Land Registry or Companies Registry in order to take effect or to have legal protection. In such cases, appropriate undertakings may be required, to ensure that such documents with 'wet-ink' signatures are available for those purposes.

However, where the parties are unwilling to rely on the other parties' undertakings or contractual obligations to produce 'wet-ink' signed originals, a virtual signing or closing may not be appropriate. In particular, a virtual signing or closing is very unlikely to be suitable for property documents that require registration, because solicitors responsible for carrying out the relevant registration will require the other parties' solicitors, on closing, to undertake to send them the 'wet-ink' signed parts of the documents. Those solicitors should give such undertakings only when they are actually holding the 'wet-ink' signed documents, not when they have merely seen electronic images of them.

3.3   Guarantees

Section 4 of the Statute of Frauds 1677 requires a guarantee (or a memorandum or note thereof) to be in writing and signed by or on behalf of the guarantor. Guarantees include undertakings by a party to procure that other parties such as subsidiaries perform their obligations.

Signature, for this purpose, has a relatively wide meaning. In *N Mehta* v. *J Pereira Fernandes SA* [2006] EWHC 813 (Ch), (*Mehta*), the judge said that an e-mail can be a sufficient memorandum or note of the guarantee, for purposes of section 4. This is true as long as the e-mail:

- shows an intention to contract as opposed to being a mere statement of expectation and

- contains the name of the guarantor, with the intention that it constitutes a signature (which is contained within the body of the e-mail, as in *Orton* v. *Collins* [2007] 1 WLR 2953, and not just information in an email header inserted automatically, as in Mehta).

Attaching a signature page to a final approved version of a document with the specific authority of the signatory is a signature within the wider meaning and test above.

3.3.1 *Guarantees executed as a deed*

If your guarantee is to be executed as a deed, you should follow the steps described in 3.1 above.

3.3.2 *Guarantees included in simple contracts*

Frequently, guarantees are included in simple contracts such as credit agreements; in such cases, you may follow any of the three options. However, option 3 is only available where there is clear evidence that the signatories or their lawyers or someone else authorised by the signatory have authorised the attachment of their signatures to the final version of the relevant guarantee. This can include an exchange of e-mails.

3.3.3 *Legal opinions on a guarantee*

If you are issuing a legal opinion in relation to a guarantee, you should consider the distinction between a guarantee and a memorandum or note thereof. When using option 2 or 3, the legal opinion could refer to the guarantee as a 'legally binding guarantee', rather than a 'contract of guarantee'.

3.4   Simple contracts

A simple contract which does not include a contract for the sale or other disposition of land or a guarantee can generally be formed without any signature, for example by an exchange of e-mails, provided the essential elements of a contract are present.

The judge's remarks in Mercury about the need for a 'discrete physical entity/existing authoritative version of the contractual document' seem to relate to an understanding in that case that a party is not bound until it has signed a final version of the contract, if the contract provides for signature.

You may follow options 1, 2 or 3 for simple contracts, signed at a virtual signing or closing.

However, each option has a different level of risk which you should balance against any potential evidential problems. For option 3, the use of pre-signed signature pages, you should have clear evidence, such as an exchange of e-mails, that the signatories, their lawyers or someone else authorised by the signatory have authorised the attachment of their signatures to the final version of the relevant contract. This will avoid any evidential concerns and show an intention to be legally bound, as well as ensuring the certainty of contractual terms.

4. SIGNATORIES – AVAILABILITY AND AUTHORISATION

Where a contracting party cannot attend the signing/closing meeting in person, you should ensure that such party is aware of the need for someone suitably authorised to be available remotely such as online, at the time of the virtual signing/closing. This authorised person would be available in order to:

- receive or otherwise be made aware of the content of and approve final versions of the documents
- sign the relevant documents under options 1 and 2
- authorise the release of the pre-signed signature pages under option 3.

For options 1 and 2, you should ensure that signatories have access to a PDF scanner.

5. DECIDING WHICH OPTION TO FOLLOW

You should choose which option to follow at your own discretion and according to the facts of each transaction.

Before choosing one of the options, you should:

- have prior approval and co-operation of all the parties
- consider relevant regulatory and tax implications, such as stamp duty, before deciding
- avoid conflict with procedures or restrictions particular to certain documents, such as notarisation or escrow conditions.

Factors you may consider include:

- countries of incorporation of the parties
- each party's domestic rules and internal procedures for execution of contracts
- the content of board resolutions
- whether individual contracts must take effect in a particular sequence
- whether a legal opinion is being issued on a party's due execution of the documents.

6. PERFORMING OPTION 1

This option is to return the entire PDF or MS Word document plus a signed signature page. It applies to deeds, real estate contracts, guarantees and simple contracts.

For option 1, you should perform the following steps:

1. Ensure all parties' lawyers have agreed to the proposed arrangements for the virtual signing/closing before execution.

2. Ensure the final execution copies of the documents are e-mailed as a PDF or Word attachment to all absent parties and/or their lawyers, as agreed. You may attach a separate PDF or Word document containing the relevant signature page for convenience.

3. Each absent signatory prints and signs the signature page only (there is no need to print off the full document).

4. Each absent party then returns a single e-mail to their lawyer or to the lawyers co-ordinating the signing/closing, as agreed, and attaches both the final version of the PDF or Word document and a PDF copy of the signed signature page. For a deed, you must either make clear when delivery is to take place or that it has not been delivered merely because it has been signed and the steps set out above followed.

5. At or shortly after signing/closing, you may wish to evidence the execution of the final document. A final version of the document, together with copies of the executed signature pages, may be circulated by one of the law firms.

The PDF or Word final version of the document and the PDF of the signed signature page will constitute an original signed document and equate to the 'same physical document' referred to in Mercury.

You may create one or more additional originals by printing off the final execution copy of the document and attaching it to the PDF copy of the signed signature page.

7. PERFORMING OPTION 2

This option is to print off and sign only the signature page from the final document. It is available for guarantees (other than those executed as deeds) and simple contracts.

For option 2, you should perform the following steps:

1. Ensure all parties' lawyers have agreed to the proposed arrangements for the virtual signing/closing before execution.

2. Ensure the final execution copies of the documents are e-mailed as a PDF or Word attachment to all absent parties and/or their lawyers, as agreed. You may attach a separate PDF or Word document containing the relevant signature page for convenience.

3. Each absent signatory prints and signs the signature page only (there is no need to print off the full document).

4. Each absent party then e-mails its signed signature page as a PDF attachment to their lawyers or to the lawyers co-ordinating the signing/closing, giving authority to attach it to the final approved version of the document. The degree of formality you require for this authority will depend on the circumstances. Where the authority is to a firm that is not acting for the party represented by the signatory, a greater degree of formality may be appropriate.

5. You may evidence the final execution of the final document at or shortly after signing/closing by providing a final version of the document, together with copies of the executed signature pages. This may be circulated by one of the law firms.

A print-off of the executed version of the document together with the attached signed signature page will constitute an original signed document.

The only difference between options 1 and 2 is step 4.

8. PERFORMING OPTION 3

This option is to use a pre-signed signature page. It is an alternative option for guarantees (other than those executed as deeds) and simple contracts.

For option 3, you should perform the following steps:

1. Ensure all parties' lawyers have agreed to the proposed arrangements for the virtual signing/closing before execution.

2. Allow enough time before signing/closing for the law firm co-ordinating the signing/ closing to e-mail or circulate hard copies of the signature pages relating to the documents still being negotiated, to each person who will not be present at the signing/closing or their lawyers. Each signature page should clearly identify the document to which it relates such as 'Credit Agreement – signature page'.

3. The signature page is executed by each of the signatories and returned to their lawyers or to the law firm co-ordinating the signing/closing, as agreed, by email (as a PDF attachment) or by courier, to be held to the order of the signatory or their lawyers, until authority is given for it to be attached to the document to be signed.

4. When each document has been finalised, the law firm co-ordinating the signing/ closing, should e-mail the final version of the document to each absent party and/or their lawyers and obtain confirmation from them or their lawyers, that they have agreed the final version of the document and authorising the relevant law firm to attach the pre-signed signature page to the final version and to date and release the document. The degree of formality required for this authority to be given will depend on the circumstances. Where the authority is to a firm that is not acting for the party represented by the signatory, a greater degree of formality may be appropriate.

5.　The final approved version of the document with the pre-signed signature pages, that have been attached with the prior approval of the parties or their lawyers, will constitute an original signed document.

9. MORE INFORMATION

9.1　Legal and other requirements

9.1.1 *Case law and rulings*

- *R (on the application of Mercury Tax Group and another)* v. *HMRC* [2008] EWHC 2721
- *Koenigsblatt* v. *Sweet* [1923] 2 Ch 314
- *N Mehta* v. *J Pereira Fernandes SA* [2006] EWHC 813 (Ch)
- *Orton* v. *Collins* [2007] 1 WLR 2953

9.1.2 *Acts and statutes*

- Section 1(3) of the Law of Property (Miscellaneous Provisions) Act 1989
- Section 2 of the Law of Property (Miscellaneous Provisions) Act 1989
- Section 74A Law of Property Act 1925
- Section 44 Companies Act 2006
- Section 46 Companies Act 2006
- Section 4 of the Statute of Frauds 1677

9.2　Further products and support

9.2.1 *Practice Advice Service*

The Law Society's practice advice service provides support for solicitors on a wide range of areas of practice. Practice Advice can be contacted on 0870 606 2522 from 09.00 to 17.00 on weekdays.

www.lawsociety.org.uk/practiceadvice

9.2.2 *City of London Paper*

This paper is based upon a more detailed paper that can be found on the City of London Law Society website.

9.2.3 *Execution of Documents 2nd Edition*

This Law Society guide covers deeds, contracts, powers of attorney, and documents used in litigation. The new edition includes expanded information on notarisation, electronic signatures, and covers changes in regulatory reform and the Companies Act 2006.

9.2.4 *Companies House Guidance on document signatures*

Guidance information is available at the Companies House website.

9.3　Status of this practice note

Practice notes are issued by the Law Society for the use and benefit of its members. They represent the Law Society's view of good practice in a particular area. They are not intended to be the only standard of good practice that solicitors can follow. You are not required to follow them, but doing so will make it easier to account to oversight bodies for your actions.

Practice notes are not legal advice, nor do they necessarily provide a defence to complaints of misconduct or of inadequate professional service. While care has been taken to ensure that they are accurate, up to date and useful, the Law Society will not accept any legal liability in relation to them.

For queries or comments on this practice note contact the Law Society's Practice Advice Service.

9.4   Terminology in this practice note

Must – a specific requirement in the Solicitor's Code of Conduct or legislation. You must comply, unless there are specific exemptions or defences provided for in the code of conduct or relevant legislation.

Should – good practice for most situations in the Law Society's view. If you do not follow this, you must be able to justify to oversight bodies why this is appropriate, either for your practice, or in the particular retainer.

May – a non-exhaustive list of options for meeting your obligations. Which option you choose is determined by the risk profile of the individual practice, client or retainer. You must be able to justify why this was an appropriate option to oversight bodies.

9.5   Acknowledgements

The Society acknowledges the contributions of the Joint Working Party of the Law Society Company Law Committee and the City of London Law Society Company Law Committee and Financial Law Committee in developing this practice note. The Society also acknowledges the contribution of the Conveyancing and Land Law Committee in the production of this practice note.

II.3. Cancellation of Contracts Practice Note[1]

1. INTRODUCTION

1.1 Who should read this practice note?

Solicitors who enter into contracts with clients, including conditional fee agreements or client care agreements, away from the solicitor's own place of business, or following discussions that take place away from their own place of business.

1.2 What is the issue?

The Cancellation of Contracts made in a Consumer's Home or Place of Work etc Regulations 2008 ('the Regulations') came into force on 1st October 2008.

The Regulations are likely to apply to a wide range of contracts made between solicitors and their clients. Whether they apply will depend on the nature of the client and the circumstances in which the contract was made.

Where the Regulations apply then the client has a right to cancel the contract within a 7 day period. The solicitor must give the client written notice of this right, setting out various prescribed information. Failure to do so is a criminal offence.

This practice note considers in what circumstances the Regulations will apply to contracts between solicitors and their clients, and explains the consequences if the Regulations apply.

2. THE REGULATIONS

The scope of the Regulations is governed by regulation 5. This provides that the Regulations apply to a contract between a consumer and a trader:

1. which is for the supply of goods or services to the consumer by a trader and

2. which is made:

    - during a visit by the trader to the consumer's home or place of work, or to the home of another individual;

    - during an excursion organised by the trader away from his business premises; or

    - after an offer made by the consumer during such a visit or excursion.

Under regulation 5, the Regulations apply to contracts for the supply of goods or services to the consumer by a trader. Contracts for the provision of legal advice or other legal services would therefore come within the Regulations.

---

1. © The Law Society 2010. The Practice Note is as stated on 2 March 2010. Practice Notes are updated by the Law Society from time to time. Solicitors are advised to check **www.lawsociety.org.uk** for the latest version.

2.1   Regulation 2(1): Definitions

A solicitor entering into a contract with a client is a 'trader' within the meaning of the Regulations. A 'trader' is defined in regulation 2(1) as 'a person who, in making a contract to which these Regulations apply, is acting in his commercial or professional capacity and anyone acting in the name or on behalf of a trader'.

A 'consumer' is defined in regulation 2(1) as 'a natural person who in making a contract to which these Regulations apply is acting for purposes which can be regarded as outside his trade or profession'. So not all clients will be consumers; but many clients will be caught by the Regulations.

2.2   Regulation 6: Exemptions

Regulation 6 sets out a number of contracts to which the Regulations do not apply. Where your contract consists wholly of exempt activities, you will not be subject to the Regulations. As a brief summary, the exemptions relate to:

- a cancellable agreement
- consumer credit agreements
- certain contracts made after a solicited visit
- immovable property
- foodstuffs or beverages
- supply of goods or services based on a trader's catalogue
- insurance
- credit provided which does not exceed £35 other than a hire purchase or
- conditional sale agreement and
- regulated activity relating to investments.

In most cases, these exemptions are unlikely to be relevant to contracts between solicitors and their clients. However you must refer to Regulation 6 and Schedule 3 of the Regulations for the full list of exempt contracts.

Work undertaken on the basis of legal aid funding is not excluded, and may fall within the scope of the Regulations. Whether or not it will do so depends on the matters discussed in the next section. The relevant contract, for the purposes of the Regulations, would be between the consumer (i.e the client) and the trader (i.e. the solicitor), notwithstanding that the solicitor receives payment from a third party funder. Thus where the Regulations apply written notice of the right to cancel must be provided to the client. Any legal aid client care letter should point out the potential difficulties in re-applying for legal aid for the same issue, if the contract is terminated. The Regulations do not affect the rights and liabilities of the solicitor and the funder under any separate funding agreement between them.

3.   SITUATIONS IN WHICH THE REGULATIONS APPLY

The Regulations only apply if the contract is made in one of the three situations described in limbs (a)–(c) of Regulation 5. The following text describes how those provisions may apply as between a solicitor and their client.

3.1   First situation: Contracts made in homes or workplaces

Limb (a) specifies situations in which the contract is made during a visit by the solicitor to:

- the client's home or place of work or
- the home of another individual.

Other than in respect of those agreements outside the scope of the regulations (see regulation 6), it does not matter whether the solicitor made the visit at the client's request; the relevant factor is whether the visit is to one of the places specified in (a), and whether the contract is made during that visit.

3.2 Second situation: contracts made during excursions

Limb (b) specificies situations in which the contract is made during an excursion organised by the solicitor away from their business premises.

This only applies if:

- the contract was made during an excursion organised by the solicitor and
- the excursion was away from the solicitor's normal business premises.

For example, if a contract is made over dinner at a restaurant, and the meal was organised by your client, then limb (b) does not apply. However, if you organised the meal then limb (b) would apply.

If the contract is made during a drinks party at your office then limb (b) would not apply; but if the drinks party took place at some other venue, and you organised it, limb (b) would apply.

The precise scope of limb (b) is, however, unclear. Until it is clarified by case-law, it is prudent to assume that limb (b) would apply to any situation where a solicitor arranged to meet a client away from his business premises. Therefore, if you arrange to meet a client in hospital you should assume that this falls within limb (b), even though the meeting would not be social in nature and the client and solicitor would not go anywhere or do anything together.

3.3 Distinguishing between situations 1 and 2

In order to determine whether the contract falls within (a) or (b), you must be aware of the point in time when a contract is made with your client. Difficult questions may arise where discussions take place with your client in your business office, either face to face or on the telephone, and then those discussions are continued during a visit falling within (a) or an excursion falling within (b). Determining when and where a contract was made will depend on the facts of the particular case.

In some cases it will be clear at which point the contract came into effect. For example, if a client telephones you and you orally run through the terms of the agreement and inform them of costs, and a client care letter is sent to the client with their agreement prior to any visit or excursion, then the situation would be unlikely to fall within (a) or (b). However, caution must be exercised if a subsequent agreement is made during a follow up visit; such an agreement may be a new contract, and caught by the Regulations. In general, where there is doubt you should assume that the Regulations do apply, to avoid criminal penalties for any breach.

3.4 Third situation: contracts made after a visit or excursion

Limb (c) of Regulation 5 will apply if the contract is made after an offer made by the consumer during:

- a visit (falling within limb (a)); or
- an excursion (falling within limb (b)).

A contract may fall within limb (c) even if it is made in your office, if it is made after an offer of the relevant kind made by the client.

For example, if you visit a client at home, the client offers to engage you to carry out legal work, and you then accept the offer by telephoning the client from your office the following day, then the Regulations will apply.

In order for limb (c) to apply, it is not necessary for the contract to be made by your acceptance of the client's offer. For instance, it may be that the client makes an offer, and that you subsequently make a counter-offer which the client accepts. In this case the contract would be made after the client's offer. However, if the client's offer was not part of the negotiations leading to the contract, but was a wholly separate matter, then limb (c) would be unlikely to apply.

For example: you visit a client at home and the client offers to engage you to perform work at an hourly rate of £80 but you refuse. After returning to your office you write a letter offering to do the work for £100 an hour, and the client accepts. The contract is made after an offer made by the client during a home visit: it therefore comes within (c) and the Regulations would apply.

If, however the client refuses your intial offer but telephones you at your office six months later to request that you do other work for £100 an hour, and you agree, the client's initial offer is wholly separate from the contract that has come into existence, and limb (c) is therefore unlikely to apply.

You should bear in mind that regulation 5(c) applies where a contract is made after an offer made by the consumer in certain circumstances. The word offer probably bears its normal contractual meaning; i.e. a communication that would be capable, if accepted, of giving rise to a binding contract. Not every request as to whether a solicitor would be willing to carry out work will be an offer in this sense.

3.5   In practice: determining where regulations apply

The following are hypothetical examples of how the Regulations may apply in practice:

Example 1

A client phones you and during this call you take oral instructions to prepare a Will for the client. You later visit the client's home with the drafted Will based on the oral instructions provided over the phone and the client signs the Will without any amendments.

In this situation the Regulations probably do not apply as the contract was probably made during the telephone conversation and prior to the visit. If however the contract did not come into existence until the visit itself then limb (a) of regulation 5 would apply, and the contract would come within the Regulations.

If the Will was subsequently amended during the visit to the client's home then this would probably make no difference to the above analysis. If the contract was made before the home visit, the work done in amending the Will will almost certainly fall within the scope of that contract, rather than being the subject of a fresh contract.

Example 2

A relative of one of your clients, acting on behalf of your client, visits your office and provides you with instructions on the preparation of a personal welfare lasting power of attorney (LPA). Based on these instructions you prepare the LPA and visit the client who is critically ill in hospital. The client agrees to the LPA.

Again, if the contract is made during the visit to your office then the Regulations probably do not apply. In order to establish whether the contract was made at your office, you would need to consider carefully the content of what was said in your office, and whether the relative had authority to enter into a contract on the client's behalf.

If the contract was made during the hospital visit then limb (a) of regulation 5 would not apply; the visit was not to the client's home or place or work or to the home of another individual. However, there would be a question as to whether limb (b) would apply. This depends on whether the hospital visit amounted to an 'excursion' organised by you away from your business premises.

As a matter of construction, this is not wholly clear. However, what you have done here is to make arrangements to travel to a place other than your business premises (i.e. the hospital), for the purpose of meeting a client or potential client.

This situation may fall within limb (b) of regulation 5. In the absence of any case-law on the question, it may be wise to treat the Regulations as applicable to any contract with the client that you make during the hospital visit.

Example 3

At the request of a client you visit the client's work place. During this visit a contractual agreement is made that you will undertake work for the client. The client has asked this work to be done urgently and provides you with a request in writing for work to commence before the 7 day cancellation period expires. You commence work but receive a cancellation notice from the client 6 days after the agreement is reached.

In this situation the Regulations apply to the contract: it falls within regulation 5(a). The client is entitled to cancel the contract, despite the written request. However, you are entitled to claim payment in accordance with the reasonable requirements of the contract for services that were supplied before the cancellation: regulation 9(2). If the client had not provided a written request to start work before the cancellation period expired, then the solicitor would not be entitled to payment: regulation 9(3). See section 5 below for discussion of regulation 9.

Example 4

A Solicitor organises for a client to accompany him/her to a trade conference and during this conference the consumer makes an offer for work to be done by the solicitor. The solicitor goes back to his/her business premises and then informs the client that the offer has been accepted.

The Regulations apply to this situation. The client's offer was made during an excursion falling within regulation 5(b). The contract was made following that offer, and so would fall within regulation 5(c).

If the offer was made at the home of one of the client's friends, then the offer would be made during a visit falling within regulation 5(a); hence, if the contract was made following that offer, again, it would fall within regulation 5(c).

4. ACTIONS REQUIRED WHERE THE REGULATIONS APPLY

If the Regulations apply then the client has a right to cancel the contract during the cancellation period (regulation 7(1)). The cancellation period is the period of 7 days starting with the date of receipt by the client of a notice of the right to cancel (regulation 2(1)).

4.1 Providing written notice

Under regulation 7(2) you must give the client a written notice of his right to cancel the contract.

Notice must be given as follows:

- In the first and second situations described in section 3 above, notice must be given at the time the contract is made.

- In situation three (as detailed in limb (c) of regulation 5), the notice must be given at the time the offer is made by the client.

Regulations 7(3) and 7(5) set out what the notice must contain.

Regulation 7(4) stipulates that you must incorporate the notice in the contract where the contract is wholly or partly in writing

If incorporated in the contract or another document the notice of the right to cancel must be set out in a separate box with the heading 'Notice of the Right to Cancel'. It must have as much prominence as any other information in the contract or document apart from the heading and the names of the parties to the contract and any information inserted in handwriting: see regulation 7(5).

Draft example templates have been provided in section 6 to assist in the preparation of a standardised notice.

4.2 Failure to provide notice

If you enter into a contract to which the Regulations apply, and you do not give the client a notice of the right to cancel and the information required by regulation 7, then you will not be able to enforce the contract against the client: see regulation 7(6).

For instance, you will not be able to sue under the contract for fees for work done. But the contract will not be void, and so it will still be enforceable against you by the client.

4.3 Current contracts

You may have entered into a contract to which these Regulations apply, since 1 October 2008, without advising your client of the right to cancel under the Regulations. If so and all fees remain outstanding in such a matter, you should consider advising the client of the right to cancel.

You may consider entering into a new agreement that meets the requirements, to ensure that you are entitled to payment of any fees or costs due for future work.

Even if you enter into a new contract, you may be unable to recover fees for work already done, if you ought to have given notice of the right to cancel but failed to do so.

This matter is not free of doubt and is likely to remain so until an opportunity presents itself for the court to provide further guidance. Until then, to minimise the risk of potential difficulties an alternative option may be to offer to vary the terms of the agreement where this is a possibility and is appropriate in the circumstances. However, when inviting the client to agree to any variation you must explain clearly what is proposed and the full implications of any agreement to vary the contract.

If you have entered into a conditional fee agreement (CFA) without giving notification of the right to cancel, then where applicable, you may consider entering into a retrospective CFA which provides notification of this right.

You must, however, fully explain to the client the reason for the new contract and the consequences of such an agreeement.

With regard to CFAs, the courts do appear to have recognised that inviting a client to agree a retrospective CFA is an acceptable means of remedying certain failures to comply with the legislative requirements to provide prescribed information to clients prior to entering a CFA to which those requirements would apply. It therefore seems likely that entering a retrospective CFA with a client in order to comply with the Cancellation of Contracts Regulations is a realistic option to consider in respect of any client whose CFA came into existence after 1 October 2008 but without the requisite notice.

With regard to any amendments to CFAs you should ensure that you take into account the Civil Procedure Rules 1998 (Parts 43–45), and in particular the requirement under 44.15 to provide information regarding the existence of the CFA to the court and other parties to the litigation, and inform them within 7 days of any amendments that may lead to additional liabilities. Failure to do so may result in additional liabilities being irrecoverable.

5. CRIMINAL OFFENCES

It is a criminal offence to fail to provide written notice of the right to cancel the contract: regulation 17. The offence is one of strict liability and carries up to the maximum penalty for a summary offence.

The duty of enforcing regulation 17 is placed on weights and measures authorities (i.e. local trading standards departments): see regulation 21(1). They have various powers of investigation, including powers to require the production of documents: regulation 22. However, you cannot be required to produce a document which you would be entitled to refuse to produce in High Court litigation on grounds of legal professional privilege: regulation 22(6).

There are various offences in connection with obstructing, or failing to co-operate with, officers of enforcement authorities. On summary conviction these carry a fine not exceeding level 3 on the standard scale: see regulation 23.

6. THE COOLING-OFF PERIOD

The cancellation period lasts for 7 days, beginning with the date when the client receives notice of the right to cancel: see regulation 2(1).

During that period the client can cancel the contract by serving a written notice indicating that s/he wishes to cancel it. The notice does not have to be in any specific form.

If a client exercises their right to cancel, then s/he is not liable to pay for work done before the cancellation, unless s/he has made a written request for the performance of the contract to begin before the end of the cancellation period: regulation 9(1)–(3).

6.1   Receiving notice

Notice of cancellation can be given by e-mail (see regulation 8(6)), and you must inform clients of this fact in your written notification of your right to cancel.

In practical terms this means that you must be able to deal with notices sent by e-mail, even if you do not usually conduct correspondence by e-mail or accept service of documents by this means.

A cancellation notice sent by e-mail is taken to have been served on the day on which it is sent: regulation 8(6). It is unclear whether an e-mail notice that is not actually received by you is an effective notice of cancellation under the Regulations.

A cancellation notice sent by post is taken to have been served at the time of posting, whether or not it is actually received: regulation 8(5).

There is some risk that a client will serve an effective notice of cancellation, without you becoming aware that this has been done. To avoid this situation you may wish to check with clients, shortly after the end of the cancellation period, that they have not exercised their right to cancel.

6.2   Dealing with urgent requests

If your client wishes you to do work urgently, your client can request in writing that you commence work before the cancellation period expires. This request means the client must pay for services provided such as the instructions, even if the contract is later cancelled. This request does not mean that the client has waived the right to cancel the contract within the cancellation period.

Absent such a written request, you are not legally obliged to start work on performing the contract before the end of the cancellation period: regulation 9(3)(a). However, see also section 6.3 below.

6.3 Vulnerable clients

You must ensure that the client fully understands the nature, effect, benefits, risks and foreseeable consequences of requesting work to commence before the cancellation period expires, in order to enable them to form a view as to the wisdom of the proposed transaction.

Assessing your client's understanding of the implications of commencing work straight away may help you to determine whether they have the capacity to make the decision, or whether they are subject to undue influence from family, beneficiaries or others.

Where you are requested to attend a weak or seriously ill client it may be impracticable or inappropriate either to obtain a written request, or to wait for the cancellation period to expire before you start work.

These situations are very difficult. You will need to balance your interest in securing payment for work done, with your professional duty to act in the best interests of the client.

6.4 Payment taken before the cooling-off period expires

Unless there is a request to commence work before the cooling-off period expires, any payment taken before the end of the cooling off period will be repayable under regulation 10 should the client cancel the contract under regulation 8.

7. TEMPLATES: PROVIDING WRITTEN NOTICE

Template 1: contracts made in homes or workplaces or during excursions

Suggested template for written Notice of right to cancel, for use in cases falling within regulation 5(a) or (b) of the Cancellation of Contracts made in a Consumer's Home or Place of Work etc Regulations 2008 ('the Regulations').

Notice of the right to cancel

This Notice has been provided to you because you have entered into a contract to which the Cancellation of Contracts made in a Consumer's Home or Place of Work Regulations 2008 ('the Regulations') apply. The contract is for the supply to you of goods or services. The person providing the goods or services is referred to in the Regulations as 'the trader'.

Under the Regulations, you have the right to cancel this contract if you wish to do so. This Notice explains how to exercise this right. It also gives you other information that is required by the Regulations.

In order to exercise your right to cancel the contract, you need to deliver or send a cancellation notice, that is, a written notice that you wish to cancel the contract. You can use the cancellation form provided below if you wish, but you do not have to do so. You can send your notification by e-mail if you prefer.

Any cancellation notice should be delivered or sent to [*name of person*] at [*postal address*] or at [*e-mail address*].

You have 7 days in which to serve a cancellation notice. The period of 7 days begins with the date when you receive this Notice. This 7 day period is referred to in the Regulations as 'the cancellation period'.

Under the Regulations, a cancellation notice is treated as being served as soon as it is sent or posted to the trader. A cancellation notice sent by electronic communication is treated as being served from the day when it is sent to the trader.

If you agree in writing that the performance of this contract should begin before the end of the cancellation period, then even if you cancel the contract you may still be required to pay for goods or services supplied before the cancellation.

If you enter into a related credit agreement, then that agreement will be automatically cancelled if the contract is cancelled. A 'related credit agreement' means an agreement under which fixed sum credit which fully or partly covers the price under the contract is granted to you by the trader, or by another person under an arrangement made between that person and the trader.

The identity of the trader providing goods or services under this contract is [*insert name of solicitor or firm that is party to the contract, including any trading name*].

The reference number, code or other details to enable the contract to be identified is [*insert details*].

This Notice is dated [*insert date when the Notice is given to the client*].

[*You must include with the written Notice a cancellation form as a detachable slip, in accordance with the form set out in Schedule 4 Part II to the Regulations. Schedule 4 Part II is reproduced at Template 3 below. You must complete the cancellation form in accordance with the notes in Schedule 4 Part II, before you give the written notice to the client.*]

NOTES ON THE USE OF THE ABOVE TEMPLATE

The Template is designed to meet the requirement that, where a contract between you and your client falls within the Regulations, you must give your client written notice of their right to cancel under the Regulations. Regulation 7, and Schedule 4, set out strict requirements as to the form of the notice. You are strongly advised to read the Regulations yourself in their entirety in order to understand the duties that they impose. **Remember that failure to give a written notice complying with the requirements of regulation 7 and Schedule 4 is a criminal offence.**

The above Template is designed to be used in cases falling within regulation 5(a) or (b) of the Regulations. In these cases, written notice of the right to terminate must be given to the client at the time when the contract is made. There is a separate Template for cases falling within regulation 5(c): see Template 2.

Note that the written notice must include a cancellation form. This must be in the form set out in Schedule 4 Part II to the Regulations, reproduced at Template 3 below.

Note that where the contract is wholly or partly in writing the notice of the right to cancel must be incorporated in the same document: regulation 7(4).

Note that if incorporated in the contract or another document the Notice of the right to cancel must –

- be set out in a separate box with the heading 'Notice of the Right to Cancel'; and
- have as much prominence as any other information in the contract or document apart from the heading and the names of the parties to the contract and any information inserted in handwriting. See regulation 7(5).

Template 2: contracts made after a visit or excursion

Suggested template for written Notice of right to cancel, for use in cases falling within regulation 5(c) of the Cancellation of Contracts made in a Consumer's Home or Place of Work etc Regulations 2008 ('the Regulations')

Notice of the right to cancel

This Notice has been provided to you because you have offered to enter into a contract to which the Cancellation of Contracts made in a Consumer's Home or Place of Work Regulations 2008 ('the Regulations') would apply. The contract would be for the supply to you of goods or services. The person who would provide the goods or services is referred to in the Regulations as 'the trader'.

Under the Regulations, you have the right to cancel this contract if you wish to do so. This Notice explains how to exercise this right. It also gives you other information that is required by the Regulations.

In order to exercise your right to cancel the contract, you need to deliver or send a cancellation notice, that is, a written notice that you wish to cancel the contract. You can use the cancellation form provided below if you wish, but you do not have to do so. You can send your notification by e-mail if you prefer.

Any cancellation notice should be delivered or sent to [*name of person*] at [*postal address*] or at [*e-mail address*].

You have 7 days in which to serve a cancellation notice. The period of 7 days begins with the date when you receive this Notice. This 7 day period is referred to in the Regulations as 'the cancellation period'.

Under the Regulations, a cancellation notice is treated as being served as soon as it is sent or posted to the trader. A cancellation notice sent by electronic communication is treated as being served from the day when it is sent to the trader.

If you agree in writing that the performance of this contract should begin before the end of the cancellation period, then even if you cancel the contract you may still be required to pay for goods or services supplied before the cancellation.

If you enter into a related credit agreement, then that agreement will be automatically cancelled if the contract is cancelled. A 'related credit agreement' means an agreement under which fixed sum credit which fully or partly covers the price under the contract is granted to you by the trader, or by another person under an arrangement made between that person and the trader.

The identity of the trader providing goods or services under this contract is [*insert name of solicitor or firm that is party to the contract, including any trading name*].

The reference number, code or other details to enable the contract to be identified is [*insert details*].

This Notice is dated [*insert date when the Notice is given to the client*].

[*You must include with the written Notice a cancellation form as a detachable slip, in accordance with the form set out in Schedule 4 Part II to the Regulations. Schedule 4 Part II is reproduced at Template 3 below. You must complete the cancellation form in accordance with the notes in Schedule 4 Part II, before you give the written notice to the client.*]

NOTES ON THE USE OF THE ABOVE TEMPLATE

The Template is designed to meet the requirement that, where a contract between you and your client falls within the Regulations, you must give your client written notice of their right to cancel under the Regulations. Regulation 7, and Schedule 4, set out strict requirements as to the form of the notice. You are strongly advised to read the Regulations yourself in their entirety in order to understand the duties that they impose. **Remember that failure to give a written notice complying with the requirements of regulation 7 and Schedule 4 is a criminal offence.**

The above Template is designed to be used in cases falling within regulation 5(c) of the Regulations. In these cases, written notice of the right to terminate must be given to the client at the time when the client makes an offer falling within regulation 5(c). There is a separate Template for cases falling within regulation 5(a) or (b): see Template 1.

Note that the written notice must include a cancellation form. This must be in the form set out in Schedule 4 Part II to the Regulations, reproduced at Template 3 below.

Note that where the contract is wholly or partly in writing the notice of the right to cancel must be incorporated in the same document: regulation 7(4).

Note that if incorporated in the contract or another document the Notice of the right to cancel must –

- be set out in a separate box with the heading 'Notice of the Right to Cancel'; and
- have as much prominence as any other information in the contract or document apart from the heading and the names of the parties to the contract and any information inserted in handwriting. See regulation 7(5).

Template 3: Schedule IV Part II to the Cancellation of Contracts made in a Consumer's Home or Place of Work etc Regulations 2008.

If you wish to cancel the contract you MUST DO SO IN WRITING and deliver personally or send (which may be by electronic mail) this to the person named below. You may use this form if you want to but you do not have to.

....

(Complete, detach and return this form ONLY IF YOU WISH TO CANCEL THE CONTRACT.)

To: .... [trader to insert name and address of person to whom notice may be given.]

I/We (delete as appropriate) hereby give notice that I/we (delete as appropriate) wish to cancel my/our (delete as appropriate) contract .... [trader to insert reference number, code or other details to enable the contract or offer to be identified. He may also insert the name and address of the consumer.]

Signed

Name and Address

Date

8. MORE INFORMATION

8.1 Professional conduct

The following section of the Solicitors' Code of Conduct 2007 is relevant to this practice note:

- Rule 2: Client relations

8.2 Legal and other requirements

- Consumer Protection (Cancellation of Contracts made in a Consumer's Home or Place of Work etc) Regulations 2008
- Civil Procedure Rules 1998

8.3 Status of this information

Practice Notes are issued by the Law Society as a professional body for the benefit of its members. They represent the Law Society's view of good practice in a particular area. They are not intended to be the only standard, nor do they necessarily provide a defence to complaints of misconduct or of inadequate professional service. Solicitors are not required to follow them.

They do not constitute legal advice and, while care has been taken to ensure that they are accurate, up-to-date and useful, the Law Society will not accept any legal liability in relation to them.

For queries or comments on this practice note contact the Law Society's Practice Advice Service.

8.4 Terminology in this practice note

Must – a specific requirement in the Solicitor's Code of Conduct or legislation. You must comply, unless there are specific exemptions or defences provided for in the code of conduct or relevant legislation.

Should – good practice for most situations in the Law Society's view. If you do not follow this, you must be able to justify to oversight bodies why this is appropriate, either for your practice, or in the particular retainer.

May – a non-exhaustive list of options for meeting your obligations. Which option you choose is determined by the risk profile of the individual practice, client or retainer. You must be able to justify why this was an appropriate option to oversight bodies.

8.5 Further products and support

8.5.1 *Department for Business Enterprise and Regulatory Reform*

The Department has provided explanatory notes on the regulation [see **www.legislation.gov.uk/ uksi/2008/1816/pdfs/uksiem_20081816_en.pdf**].

8.5.2 *Practice Advice Line*

The Law Society provides support for solicitors on a wide range of areas of practice. Practice Advice can be contacted on 0870 606 2522 from 09:00 to 17:00 on weekdays.

8.5.3 *Solicitors Regulation Authority Contact Centre*

Assists solicitors with enquiries relating to practising certificates, continuing professional development (CPD) and other general enquiries. Telephone 0870 606 2555, **www.sra.org.uk**.

II.4. Mortgage Fraud Practice Note[1]

1. INTRODUCTION

1.1 Who should read this practice note?

All solicitors who do conveyancing work involving a mortgage.

1.2 What is the issue?

Criminals will exploit weaknesses in lending and conveyancing systems to gain illegitimate financial advantage from the UK property market. This can be either:

- opportunistic action using misrepresentation of income or property value to obtain greater loans than a person is entitled to

- organised crime syndicates overvaluing properties, using false identities and failing to make any mortgage repayments

A solicitor will be involved in most property transactions undertaken in the UK. You can find yourself criminally liable if your client commits mortgage fraud, because of the extension of the definition of fraud in the Fraud Act 2006 and the anti-money laundering regime in the UK. You can be liable even if you were not aware of the fraud or actively participated in it.

Courts will assume a high level of knowledge and education on your part. They will often be less willing to accept claims that you were unwittingly involved if you have not applied appropriate due diligence.

This practice note highlights the warning signs of mortgage fraud and outlines how you can protect yourself and your firm from being used to commit mortgage fraud.

1.3 Professional conduct

The following sections of the Solicitors' Code of Conduct 2007 (code of conduct) are relevant to mortgage fraud:

- Rule 1.01 Justice and the Rule of Law

- Rule 3.16 Acting for lender and borrower in conveyancing transactions

- Rule 4.01 Duty of confidentiality

- Rule 4.02 Duty of disclosure

1.4 Legal and other requirements

Several pieces of legislation impose obligations on you with respect to property transactions. If these obligations are breached, criminal sanctions can follow.

- Fraud Act 2006

---

1. © The Law Society. This Practice Note is as stated on 15 April 2009. Practice Notes are updated by the Law Society from time to time. Solicitors are advised to check **www.lawsociety.org.uk** for the latest version.

- Proceeds of Crime Act 2002 (as amended)
- Money Laundering Regulations 2007

All links to legislation in this practice note will take you to the Statute Law Database website. The legislation contained in this database may not contain the most current amendments and you should take your own action to ensure you have the most up-to-date version of the legislation.

1.5 Status of this practice note

Practice notes are issued by the Law Society for the use and benefit of its members. They represent the Law Society's view of good practice in a particular area. They are not intended to be the only standard of good practice that solicitors can follow. You are not required to follow them, but doing so will make it easier to account to oversight bodies for your actions.

Practice notes are not legal advice, nor do they necessarily provide a defence to complaints of misconduct or of inadequate professional service. While care has been taken to ensure that they are accurate, up to date and useful, the Law Society will not accept any legal liability in relation to them.

For queries or comments on this practice note contact the Law Society's Practice Advice Service. **www.lawsociety.org.uk/practiceadvice**.

1.6 Terminology in this practice note

Must – a specific requirement in the Solicitors' Code of Conduct or legislation. You must comply, unless there are specific exemptions or defences provided for in the code of conduct or relevant legislation.

Should – good practice for most situations in the Law Society's view. If you do not follow this, you should be able to justify to oversight bodies why the alternative approach you have taken is appropriate, either for your practice, or in the particular retainer.

May – a non-exhaustive list of options for meeting your obligations. Which option you choose is determined by the risk profile of the individual practice, client or retainer. You must be able to justify why this was an appropriate option to oversight bodies.

1.7 More information and products

- best practice training
- the Law Society's anti-money laundering practice note
- the Council of Mortgage Lenders' Handbook – what's expected of you when working with lenders
- the Law Society's Property Section – join for support and training
- other Law Society publications – order from our bookshop
  - Solicitors and Money Laundering
  - Conveyancing Handbook
- the Solicitors Regulation Authority's Professional Ethics Helpline for advice on conduct issues

2. HOW DOES MORTGAGE FRAUD OCCUR?

2.1 What is mortgage fraud?

Mortgage fraud occurs where individuals defraud a financial institution or private lender through the mortgage process.

The definition of fraud in the Fraud Act 2006 covers fraud by false representation and by failure to disclose information where there is a legal duty to disclose. False representations can be made explicitly or implicitly and may occur even where you know only that the representation might be misleading or untrue.

The value of a mortgage obtained through fraud is the proceeds of crime. Under the Proceeds of Crime Act 2002, you risk committing a money laundering offence if you acquire, use, have possession of, enter into an arrangement with respect to, or transfer this criminal property.

Read the relevant legislation and the anti-money laundering practice note, Chapter 5.

2.2 Opportunistic mortgage fraud

2.2.1 *General methodology*

Individual purchasers can commit mortgage fraud by obtaining a higher mortgage than they are entitled to by providing untrue or misleading information or failing to disclose required information. This may include providing incorrect information about:

- identity
- income
- employment
- other debt obligations
- the sources of funds other than the mortgage for the purchase
- the value of the property
- the price to be paid and whether any payments have been, or will be made, directly between the seller and the purchaser

2.2.2 *Use of professionals*

Opportunistic fraudsters will not usually attempt to include their solicitor in the original fraud. However, you may become aware of information conflicting with that provided to the lender as you progress the conveyance.

Clients engaged in opportunistic fraud may be evasive when questioned on the conflict and may try to dissuade you from conducting relevant checks or advising the lender.

2.3 Large scale mortgage fraud

2.3.1 *General methodology*

Large scale mortgage fraud is usually more sophisticated and involves several properties. It may be committed by criminal groups or individuals, referred to hereon as fraudsters. The buy-to-let market is particularly vulnerable to mortgage fraud, whether through new-build apartment complexes or large scale renovation projects. Occasionally commercial properties will be involved. The common steps are:

- The nominated purchasers taking out the mortgage often have no beneficial interest in the property, and may even be fictitious.

- The property value is inflated and the mortgage will be sought for the full inflated valuation.

- Mortgage payments are often not met and the properties are allowed to deteriorate or used for other criminal or fraudulent activities, including drug production, unlicensed gambling and prostitution.

- When the bank seeks payment of the mortgage, the fraudsters raise mortgages with another bank through further fictitious purchasers and effectively sell the property back to themselves, but at an even greater leveraged valuation.

- Because the second mortgage is inflated, the first mortgage and arrears are paid off, leaving a substantial profit. This may be repeated many times.

- Eventually a bank forecloses on the property, only to find it in disrepair and worth significantly less than the current mortgage and its arrears.

2.3.2 *Use of non-bank lenders*

Fraudsters may use private sources of funding such as property clubs, especially when credit market conditions tighten. These lenders often have lower safeguards than institutional lenders, leaving them vulnerable to organised fraud. Property clubs can be targeted particularly in relation to overseas properties where the property either does not exist, or it is a vacant piece of land, not a developed property.

2.3.3 *Use of corporate structures*

Sometimes fraud is achieved by selling the property between related private companies, rather than between fictitious individuals. The transactions will involve inflated values, and will not be at arm's length.

Increasingly, off-shore companies are being used, with the property sold several times within the group before approaching a lender for a mortgage at an inflated value.

You may be asked to act for both the seller and the purchaser in these transactions.

2.3.4 *Flipping and back-to-back transactions*

Investors will always look to re-sell a property at a profit. However, fraudsters may seek to re-sell a property very quickly for a substantially increased price. This process is called flipping, and will usually involve back-to-back sales of the property to limit the time between sales. Variations on this fraud include:

- The first mortgage is not registered against the property, and not redeemed upon completion of the second sale.

- The second purchaser may be fictitious, using a false identity or be someone vulnerable to pressure from the fraudster.

- A mortgage may only be obtained by the second purchaser and for an amount significantly higher than the value of the property. The profit goes to the fraudster.

2.3.5 *Use of professionals*

Fraudsters will usually use at least one professional at the core of the fraud, to direct and reassure other professionals acting at the periphery. Mortgage brokers and introducers have been used in this role in the past.

Mortgage lenders often rely on other professionals to verify the legitimacy of a transaction and safeguard their interests. Lenders may not extensively verify information they receive, especially in a rising market. Institutional lenders will subscribe to the Council of Mortgage Lenders' Handbook and expect solicitors to comply with these guidelines. Private investors will rely on compliance with the Solicitors' Code of Conduct to protect their lending.

You may be approached in any of the following ways:

- You may be asked to complete the transaction and simply transfer the title in accordance with already exchanged contracts. A lender who has received the loan applications and already approved the loan may approach you with packaged transactions and completed paper work.

- You may be encouraged to alter the value on the Certificate of Title given to the lender.

- You may be encouraged not to comply with obligations in the CML Handbook.

- You may be offered continued work at a higher margin to encourage less diligent checks.

- Fraudsters may attempt to recruit you into the fraud, especially if you have unwittingly assisted previously, or have developed an especially close relationship with other participants in the scheme.

2.4   Other methodologies

Fraud methodologies regularly evolve, particularly in changing economic circumstances.

2.4.1 *Equity release fraud*

In difficult economic times, clients may struggle to meet mortgage repayments, and turn to an equity release scheme, to be able to remain in their homes. This scheme sees home owners receiving an offer from a third party to purchase the property while the home owner is allowed to rent the property. The home owner is given the option to purchase the property back when their financial position improves.

However, criminal involvement can result in the following:

1. The home owner sells the property to someone who is actually a member of the criminal syndicate, a mortgage mule, or an entirely fictitious person.

2. A mortgage will be taken out by this investor for an inflated value against the property.

3. The original loan will be paid out and the money representing the equity in the home will be taken by the criminal syndicate. No payments will be made towards the mortgage.

4. The original home owner will be unaware of the lack of payments being made until the bank seeks to repossess the property and evicts them a mere tenant.

5. The value of the mortgage will be far greater than the original mortgage and it will be impossible for the original owner to purchase the property back.

2.4.2 *Application hijack*

Application hijacking involves criminals intervening before completion of a mortgage, falsely claiming to be the new representatives for the purchaser. They thereby obtain the mortgage advance in place of the real purchaser.

The lender is contacted later by the real representatives looking to complete the transaction, only to find the funds have already been paid away and have now disappeared.

The criminals will generally pose as solicitors or conveyancers, taking the details of someone who is on the professional register. They will then use fake or cloned letterhead to write to the lender as the representative, providing their own account details for the client account.

Solicitors who have unknowingly undertaken work for criminal syndicates previously may find that they are at greater risk of this type of fraud as the syndicate will have access to their genuine letter head and standard mortgage correspondence.

2.4.3 *After the event mortgaging*

While re-mortgaging and re-financing may be common during an economic downturn, the use of apparent equity to access mortgage funds is an avenue also exploited by criminals.

1. Fraudsters will use private funds, often of criminal origin, to purchase a property. Often the purchase will be through an auction and may involve repossessed properties, to ensure a discounted purchase price.

2. After the purchase is completed, and usually within 12 months, the fraudster will seek external funding against the property.

3. They then take the mortgage advance and disappear, failing to make any payments.

Another variation on this methodology is that the fraudster will pose as a property developer and will seek bridging loans to cover the purchase of a number of properties. These may be properties which the fraudsters previously used as part of a flipping scheme and have finally been repossessed by the bank. The bridging loan is only sought after the purchase has been registered and possession has been taken of the property.

2.4.4 *Claiming deceased estates*

Criminals will make use of the notices section of their local papers to identify deceased estates that can be exploited for criminal gain, either because there are no known heirs or probate has been delayed. They will seek to either falsely establish their identity as a long lost heir or will pose as the deceased person. In both scenarios they will seek a mortgage over the existing equity in the property and then disappear with the funds.

2.4.5 *Court orders for sale*

In an economic downturn, more properties are repossessed or are unable to be sold. They are then left unoccupied and boarded up.

- Criminals will seek out these properties and details of the owners.

- They will then apply to the County Court for a judgment against the owner over a non-existent debt.

- They will not actually give the owner notice of this application.

- Once obtained, this judgment is converted into an order for sale.

- The property is sold either directly to the person claiming the debt or to one of their associates at an inflated price, using criminal money.

- A mortgage will be obtained over the property at the inflated value.

- The mortgage advance will be taken and no payments will be made.

3. WARNING SIGNS

Criminal methodologies are continually changing. However, there are several known warning signs, which may be indicators of mortgage fraud.

You should remain alert to warning signs in the information and documentation which are in your possession. You should pay particular attention to transactions which exhibit a number of warning signs.

3.1　Identity and ownership

- The client or the property involved is located a long distance from your firm. If bulk long distance instructions are not in your normal work, you may ask why they chose your firm, especially if they are a new client.

- The client seems unusually uninterested in their purchase. You should look for other warning signs suggesting they are not the real purchaser.

- The seller is a private company or they have recently purchased the property from a private company. You should consider whether the office holders or shareholders of the private company are otherwise connected with the transaction you are undertaking, and whether this is an arm's length commercial transaction.

- The client does not usually engage in property investment of this scale. You should ask why they are undertaking this new venture and where they are getting the financial backing from.

- The current owner has owned the property for under six months. You should ask them to explain why they are selling so quickly.

- The client's credit history is shorter than you would expect for their age, when you run an electronic identity check, which may include credit history information. Fraudsters will often run a fake identity for a few months to give it legitimacy. You should ask your client about this.

- There are plans for a sub-sale or back-to-back transactions. You should ask your client why they are structuring the transaction this way and seek information on the identities of the second purchaser, their solicitor and the lender.

- There is a last minute change of representative on the other side.

- The property has a history of being re-sold quickly or mortgages settled quickly.

- A transfer of title to land is requested with respect to only some of the seller's holdings and the properties are not grouped together.

- Finance is sought after the property has been registered in the buyer's name.

- The property has been registered to an owner for a significant period of time and the person claiming to be the owner does not appear to be of an age to have held the land for that length of time.

- The other conveyancer or solicitor allegedly involved in the transaction has an e-mail address from a large-scale web based provider.

- There is a County Court judgment against the property.

- The land is transferred following a court order, but the mortgage is sought some time later.

3.2 Value

- The property value has significantly increased in a short period of time out of line with the market in the area
- The mortgage is for the full property value. While this is less likely in tighter credit conditions, you should consider it in light of the other warning signs.
- The seller or developer have provided incentives, allowances or discounts. These may include cash back, free holidays, household fittings, payment of legal fees, help with mortgage repayments or rental guarantees, among others. You should consider whether this information has been properly disclosed to the lender.
- The deposit is being paid by someone other than the purchaser. You should ask why, where the money is coming from, and whether this information has been properly disclosed to the lender.
- The purchaser has paid the deposit directly to the seller or a developer. You should ask for evidence of the payment and consider whether this information has been properly disclosed to the lender.
- There is money left over from the mortgage after the purchase price has been paid, and you are asked to pay this money to the account of someone you do not know, or to the introducer. You should ask why, and remember that you must not use your client account as a mere banking facility. See note ix to Rule 15 of the Solicitors Accounts Rules 1998.
- You are asked to enter a price on the title that is greater than you know was paid for the property. You should ask why the prices are different. Read more about recording property value in the anti-money laundering practice note, Chapter 4.6.
- There has been a recent transfer of land where no money has changed hands or the price was significantly less than the full market value.

4. PROTECTING YOUR FIRM

4.1 Ask questions

You should ask questions if you receive unusual instructions from your client, if any of the warning signs are present or there are inconsistencies in the retainer. You will better understand your instructions and be able to effectively assess the risk of the retainer to your firm.

Criminal methodologies change constantly, so you should remain alert to transactions that are unusual for a normal residential or commercial conveyance.

4.2 Identify and verify the client

You must find out and verify the identity of your client and where relevant, any beneficial owners. This is important whether you are acting for the purchaser or the seller. You are not expected to be experts in forged documents, but you should ensure the identities you have been given correspond with the information on the mortgage documents and the bank accounts relating to the transaction.

If you have concerns about a person's identity, you should consider checking whether the person is listed on a negative database, such as the register of deaths or a list of known fraudsters.

Where a private company is the seller, or the seller has purchased from a private company in the recent past, and you are concerned that the sale may not be an arm's length transaction, you should conduct a search of the Companies Register. You should find out the names and addresses of the office holders and the shareholders, which can be cross referenced with the names of those connected with the transaction, the seller and the buyer.

You should consider the anti-money laundering practice note, the identity evidence for land registry practice note and the CML Handbook when deciding what information needs to be obtained to identify and verify the client and others.

4.2.1 *Enhanced due diligence*

Many mortgage fraudsters provide only paperwork and try to avoid meetings, particularly with the named purchasers. If you do not meet your client in a property transaction, you must undertake enhanced due diligence, as required under the Money Laundering Regulations 2007.

Read about enhanced due diligence in our anti-money laundering practice note, Chapter 4.9.

4.2.2 *Reliance*

Fraudsters will try to limit scrutiny of their identity and the transaction. They may ask you to use the reliance provisions under the Money Laundering Regulations 2007 to minimise the number of due diligence checks that you conduct.

You should consider reliance as a potential risk in itself. You remain liable for any breach of the regulations if the checks you rely on have not been conducted properly. To protect your firm, you should ask the following questions of the firm or individual you are being asked to rely on:

- Are they regulated for anti-money laundering purposes? Mortgage brokers are currently not regulated under the Money Laundering Regulations 2007.

- Have you done business with them previously?

- Are they from an established firm?

- What is their reputation? A general web search may reveal this.

- Are they able to provide you with the client due diligence material they have?

You should ask for copies of the due diligence conducted, so that you can cross reference documents within the retainer and satisfy yourself as to the identity of the purchaser and, where relevant, beneficial owners.

Read more about reliance in our anti-money laundering practice note, Chapter 4.3.4.

4.3 Identify other solicitors or conveyancers

Fraudsters may pose as a solicitor or a conveyancer acting for either party to add greater legitimacy to the transaction. If you do not know them, you should check the recognised directory of their professional body.

- The Law Society (**www.lawsociety.org.uk/choosingandusing/findasolicitor.law**)

- Council for Licensed Conveyancers (**www.theclc.gov.uk/directory.asp**)

You can also check a solicitor's details with the SRA over the telephone. Their contact number is 0870 606 2555.

Some fraudsters will try to assume the identity of professionals who actually exist. You should check that both the details and the final destination of documents match the details in the directory. You may consider contacting the firm directly by the contact details on the registry if you have concerns about the bona fides of the representatives on the other side to the transaction, particularly if there is a last minute change of representative.

4.4 Consider all information on the retainer

4.4.1 *Sources of information*

The following information may be relevant in assessing the risk of a retainer, in monitoring of the retainer, and in resolving concerns when mortgage fraud risks appear:

- documents involved in the retainer
- comments by the client in interviews
- correspondence or telephone conversations
- comments by other parties to the transaction or their representatives
- previous retainers for the client

4.4.2 *Does it all add up?*

You should consider whether the property and mortgage are consistent with what you know about the financial position and sources of income available to the client.

EXAMPLE

You may have prepared a will for a client and done conveyancing on the purchase of a modest family home. If, a few years later, they then instruct you in the purchase of a holiday home that appears to be beyond their means according to earlier retainers, this would warrant closer inspection of the mortgage application. You should ask questions of the client to verify this information.

You should check all mortgage and contractual documentation carefully. Seek explanations from the client for any discrepancies in the document. It may be a simple misunderstanding of the documents or an inadvertent error needing correction.

You should consider whether the identity you have been given is consistent with the actual presentation of the client and the transaction as a whole.

4.4.3 *Ensure documents are fully completed*

You may receive contract documents that are not fully completed. For example, dates may be missing, the identities of parties not fully described, or financial details not fully stated. You should ensure all relevant sections of documents are completed before your client signs them, to avoid incorrect or fraudulent information being added later.

4.5 Signatures

You must ensure that you and your staff only witness signatures where you have actually seen the person signing the document. If any contract or mortgage documents have been pre-signed, you must either:

- verify it was pre-signed in the presence of a witness
- have the documents re-signed in your presence

You should take note of all signatures on transaction documents and consider examining and comparing signatures with other available documentation if:

- you notice a discrepancy between signatures on the documentation

- you have concerns about the identity of any of the parties to the transaction
- the transaction is higher risk because it exhibits a number of the warning signs of mortgage fraud

4.6 Recording the property value

You should ascertain the true net cash price to be paid, to comply with the CML Handbook and Land Registry requirements. You should consider any direct payments, allowances, incentives or discount in ascertaining this price.

You should state this amount as the consideration in all of the following documents:

- contract
- transfer documents
- mortgage instructions
- certificate on title to the lender
- Land Registry forms

You should seek to understand any discrepancy between the value recorded in any of these documents, or if you are asked to enter a different value.

If you discover discrepancies in the valuation of the property between any of the relevant documents, you should consider your obligations to disclose this information to the lender.

Part one of the CML Handbook says you must report such changes to the lender. However, individual lenders may vary this obligation, either by using part two of the handbook, or through the specific instructions they provide.

Also consider your obligation to the lender to disclose any direct payments between the buyer and seller either already made, or proposed, that are not included in the mortgage instructions.

4.7 Changes to the retainer

You should stay alert to any changes in the circumstances of the retainer that may affect the agreed basis of the mortgage provision. These may include changes to the purchase price or previously undisclosed allowances, incentives or discounts.

Such arrangements may mean that the purchase price is different to that in the lender's instructions. In general, lenders will reasonably expect to receive such information, as it may affect their decision to grant the mortgage, or the terms of granting the mortgage.

You should ask questions to understand any changes. You should consult the lenders instructions or the CML Handbook part two, to assess your obligations to disclose this information to the lender.

5. CONFIDENTIALITY AND DISCLOSURE

5.1 Code of conduct obligations

5.1.1 *Rule 3.16*

You must not act for a buyer and a lender if a conflict of interest exists or arises between them. You have a conflict of interest if you have information about the conveyance that the lender would consider relevant to granting the loan, but the client does not want you to tell the lender.

5.1.2 *Rule 4.02*

You must disclose relevant information to the lender client. Any change to the purchase price, or information reasonably expected to be important to the decision to grant the mortgage, will be relevant to the lender.

However this obligation of disclosure to the lender client is overridden by your duty of confidentiality to the purchaser client in Rule 4.01. This duty of confidentiality can only be waived with the consent of the purchaser client, or if it is required or permitted by law.

While you should always seek clarification from your client if you discover any discrepancies in relevant information, you may wish to streamline the consent process. You may include a section in your standard terms and conditions for conveyancing clients, which provides that you will advise the lender client of any relevant information arising during the retainer. To rely on this approach for consent, you should:

- specifically bring this term to the client's attention at the outset of the retainer
- have them sign to signify acceptance of the terms and conditions

5.2   When can you tell the lender?

Where you believe a purchaser client has provided incorrect or incomplete information to a lender during the mortgage process, you must seek consent from them to provide the correct information to the lender. If your purchaser client refuses, you must refuse to continue to act for them and the lender.

You must still consider legal professional privilege and your duty of confidentiality before passing information to the lender, even after you have ceased to act for a client.

You are only released from your duty of confidentiality where you are satisfied of a strong prima facie case that the client, or third party, was using you to further a fraud or other criminal purpose. This test may be satisfied if a client has made deliberate misrepresentations on their mortgage application.

If you are not released from the duty of confidentiality, you should simply return the mortgage documents to the lender and advise that you are ceasing to act due to professional reasons, without providing any further information.

For further advice on whether you need to cease to act in a matter and whether you can provide information to the lender, contact the SRA's Professional Ethics Helpline, or seek independent legal advice.

5.3   When can you tell law enforcement?

You must consider the money laundering risk if you discover or suspect that a mortgage has been obtained fraudulently, and the funds have been received by the client, either into their account, or your client account.

You must consider making a disclosure to the Serious Organised Crime Agency. You must also consider your duty of confidentiality and legal professional privilege before you do so.

Importantly, making a disclosure to SOCA is merely a defence to money laundering offences. It is not a crime report. You may also make a report to your local police if you feel an investigation is warranted.

For further information on money laundering offences and making disclosures to SOCA, see the anti-money laundering practice note.

For further information on whether legal professional privilege prevents you from making a disclosure to either SOCA or the lender you may take legal advice. You can find a list of solicitors offering such advice in the Law Society's AML directory.

For further advice on whether you need to cease to act in a matter, contact the SRA's Professional Ethics Helpline.

5.4 Alerting your insurer

Banks are increasingly trying to recover mortgage fraud losses from professionals involved in conveyancing. If you suspect mortgage fraud has occurred, you should consider your obligations to your professional indemnity insurer. For further information on possible civil liability see the anti-money laundering practice note, Chapter 10.

5.5 Tipping off

You may be concerned about tipping off offences under the Proceeds of Crime Act 2002, in talking to the lender, insurer, or your purchaser client.

A key element of these offences is the likelihood of prejudicing an investigation. The risk of this is small when disclosing to a reputable lender or your insurer. They are also regulated for the purposes of anti-money laundering and subject to the same obligations. There is also a specific defence of making a disclosure for the purposes of preventing a money laundering offence.

In relation to asking further questions of your client and discussing the implications of the Proceeds of Crime Act 2002, there is a specific defence for tipping off for legal advisors who are seeking to dissuade their client from engaging in a money laundering offence.

For further advice on tipping off, see anti-money laundering practice note, Chapter 5.8.

For further information about avoiding tipping off in a particular case, contact SOCA's Financial Intelligence Helpdesk on 020 7238 8282.

II.5. Land Registry Early Completion Practice Note[1]

1. INTRODUCTION

1.1 Who should read this practice note?

Solicitors dealing with conveyancing matters for buyers, sellers and lenders.

1.2 What is the issue?

From 3 August 2009, Land Registry (LR) will introduce 'early completion'. The early completion policy will apply to any situation involving a discharge of whole and another application. This new process relates to the procedure for, and the order in which LR will process multiple applications including discharge of a seller's charge.

Applications containing such multiple requests will be treated as separate applications. For example this means that where applications to discharge a seller's charge, transfer title to the buyer, then register the buyer's charge are made together, but evidence of discharge does not accompany the application and has not already been received by LR, LR will complete registration of the other applications, where possible.

This will leave the entries relating to existing charge(s) subsisting in the register. A transfer to a buyer and the buyer's charge might be registered before a seller's charge is removed from the title. Early completion may apply regardless of the method of discharge being used by the seller's lender.

Crucially, LR early completion does not mean legal or physical completion of the transaction. It simply means acceleration of when LR will make the first changes to the register in connection with the applications received. This practice note gives advice on:

- how early completion will operate
- handling applications where the registered proprietor's charge contains a restriction
- how to proceed with the different applications
- undertakings
- discharges
- identification
- fees.

2 THE ESTABLISHED PROCEDURE ON SALE

LR currently treat applications to discharge the seller's charge, transfer to the buyer and add the buyer's charge as linked and conditional upon each other. They are dealt with in that order.

So until evidence of discharge of the seller's charge is available to LR and has been registered, all of the applications are held over, except where the discharge takes place by ED or eDS1.

---

1. © The Law Society. This Practice Note is as stated on 9 July 2009. Practice Notes are updated by the Law Society from time to time. Solicitors are advised to check **www.lawsociety.org.uk** for the latest version.

LR allow applications like this to be held over several times, awaiting proof of satisfaction of a charge if you do all of the following:

- make a request for an extension of time
- keep LR informed as to progress
- show that you are actively pursuing the matter
- show that the lender is causing the delay.

LR consider requests for further extensions of time beyond an initial 20 business day period on their merits. Such extensions are granted largely when LR think it is realistic that the discharge will be produced in a reasonable time.

The applications to discharge, transfer and charge are likely to be cancelled, if:

- it appears unlikely that the discharge will be produced in a reasonable time
- you are not able to explain the reason for the delay or what is being done to obtain proof of satisfaction of the charge.

Provided that LR receive your application before 3 August 2009 it will be processed under the established procedure; LR will requisition for a discharge if this is not lodged before or with the application.

3 EARLY COMPLETION FROM 3 AUGUST 2009

Early completion will apply when you make an application to register (for example, for a sale remortgage or lease) that accompanies an application to discharge an existing charge of whole, and proof of satisfaction of that charge does not accompany or precede the application.

When you make an application like this, LR will reject the application for discharge, but will complete the other applications, where possible. The entries relating to the existing charge will be left on the register until LR receive proof of satisfaction of repayment of the mortgage.

How LR deal with the application will depend upon whether or not a restriction is registered in favour of the existing chargee.

3.1 Sellers' charges without restrictions

Early completion will operate immediately where the seller's charge does not contain matters on which requisitions need to be raised. The registrations will happen in the order that complete applications are received by LR, subject to the effect of any priority search. Complete applications are those that are ready to be processed with no documents missing or to follow.

If there are matters on which requisitions need to be raised LR will include a reminder about the missing discharge in their requisition but the missing discharge will not be a point on which a requisition is raised.

This may result in the transfer and the new charge being registered without the prior charge being removed.

3.2 Sellers' charges containing a restriction

When acting for a buyer, you should establish any relevant restrictions early in the transaction from the proprietorship register. This is prudent because the content of the restriction on the register will determine how LR will apply the new policy.

Restrictions in favour of a proprietor's chargees may prevent the registration of any further charge or in most cases of any disposition without the chargee's written consent. In such cases, the LR will requisition for either:

- proof of satisfaction of the charge
- evidence of compliance with the restriction.

If the lender does not provide evidence of the discharge within twenty business days, you will not be able to address the requisition within that time. In these circumstances, the LR will allow a further twenty business day extension if you do all of the following:

- make a written request for the extension
- demonstrate that you are actively pursuing the matter
- show that the existing lender is causing the delay.

LR has not given further formal guidance on these requirements. We assume that they will operate as before 3 August 2009 if you are unable to satisfy the requisition within the time limit.

LR will cancel both your application for discharge and applications to register the transfer and charge, where there is a restriction against the registration of any disposition. This time limit is up to forty business days if you have successfully applied for an extension. At the expiration of the time limit the application will be cancelled. LR will allow less time for satisfying any requisitions under early completion.

It may be of some benefit to make an additional priority search immediately prior to legal completion to extend the initial time available within which to obtain the evidence of discharge.

In the rarer case of a restriction only against the registration of charges, LR will complete the registration of the transfer, and cancel the application for discharge, which will leave the existing charge entries on the register. LR will also cancel the application for the new charge. The face of the register will then show the buyer as registered proprietor and the seller's lender as the mortgagee.

3.3 If your application is cancelled

As now, if your application is cancelled, you might lose priority for the application, unless you resubmit it within the priority period and it is subsequently registered.

Unless the further application is made within any existing priority period, priority for the interest will be lost if there is any competing application and/or search made before you made a further application to register the disposition, or received a further clear search. Making a further search will give you a new priority period, not extend the original one. The new search cannot act retrospectively and attach itself to the substantive application already lodged.

As is the case currently, the application will be subject to any other application or search made in respect of the property before your new search takes effect. If, for example, a further search is made at the time an extension is requested, whilst it will remain in the LR day list for thirty business days, it will not provide protection for the pending application. The application will have priority by virtue of it having been lodged at LR and entered in the day list. This means that from day thirty, when your search expires, to day 40, when your extension expires, the application will have priority by virtue of its entry in the day list and not by virtue of your search.

The new search may provide priority for any renewed application but this will depend on whether any other search and/or applications have been lodged before the search is received by LR.

Where there is a restriction and either early completion has been applied or LR has cancelled applications because of failure to satisfy a requisition, any official search protecting the cancelled application will remain in effect until its expiry.

Early completion matrix – evidence of discharge not lodged with application(s)

Restriction in favour of existing charge[1]	Discharge only	Application or combination of applications		
		DC (Discharge and new charge)	DTC (Discharge, new transfer and new charge)	DT (Discharge and new transfer)

Restriction against registration of any disposition	Reject	– Requisition[2] for discharge or compliance with restriction.
		– If not lodged:
		  – Both applications cancelled.
		  – Existing charge entries and restriction remain.
		  – Official search (if any) protecting the charge remains on the day list until expiry.
		– If discharge lodged:
		  – Both applications completed[3].
		  – Charge entries, related restriction and protecting search removed.
			– Requisition[2] for discharge or compliance with restriction.
			– If not lodged:
			  – All applications cancelled.
			  – Existing charge entries and restriction remain.
			  – Official search (if any) protecting the charge remains on the day list until expiry.
			– If discharge lodged:
			  – All applications completed[3].
			  – Charge entries, related restriction and protecting search removed.
				– Requisition[2] for discharge or compliance with restriction.
				– If not lodged:
				  – Both applications cancelled.
				  – Existing charge entries and restriction remain.
				  – Official search (if any) protecting the transfer remains on the day list until expiry.
				– If discharge lodged:
				  – All applications completed[3].
				  – Charge entries, related restriction and protecting search removed.

Restriction against registration of charge	Reject	– Requisition[2] for discharge or compliance with restriction.
		– If not lodged:
		  – Both applications cancelled.
		  – Existing charge entries and restriction remain.
		  – Official search (if any) protecting the charge remains on the day list until expiry.
		– If discharge lodged:
		  – Both applications completed[3].
		  – Charge entries, related restriction and protecting search removed.
			– Requisition[2] for discharge or compliance with restriction.
			– If not lodged:
			  – Early completion of transfer.
			  – Discharge and registration of new charge cancelled. Existing charge entries and restriction remain.
			  – Official search (if any) protecting the charge remains on the day list until expiry.
			– If discharge lodged:
			  – All applications completed[3].
			  – Charge entries, related restriction and protecting search removed.
				– Early completion of new transfer.
				– Existing charge entries and restriction remain.
				– Removal from the day list of official search (if any) protecting the transfer.

No restriction	Reject	– Early completion of new charge. – Existing charge entries remain. – Removal from the day list of official search (if any) protecting the charge.	– Early completion of new charge and transfer. – Existing charge entries remain. – Removal from the day list of official search (if any) protecting the charge.	– Early completion of new transfer. – Existing charge entries remain. – Removal from the day list of official search (if any) protecting the transfer.

[1] This refers only to a restriction expressly related to the registered charge intended to be discharged.

[2] The usual 20-day requisition timescale applies. One extension of 20 days can be requested, and will be granted provided it is made in writing and shows that the matter is being actively pursued and the lender is causing the delay. Further extensions are unlikely to be given. This matrix assumes that no requisitions arise on other aspects of the application, or that if they do they are satisfactorily dealt with.

[3] In the event that a consent is supplied in response to the requisition, the discharge application will be cancelled.

3.4 Following the first part of the registration process

To avoid early completion leaving sellers' or outgoing charges on the register for a long time after completion of other parts of the registration, you should do both of the following:

1   Check the Registration Completion Sheet (RCS) letter you receive from LR to understand the status of the registration and to establish whether you should make further applications to conclude the necessary registration, particularly in relation to cancelling the seller's charge.

2   Establish office procedures to monitor the status of recently made and completed applications.

LR will make it very clear on the RCS where registration has been completed on the basis of early completion, and what other steps should be taken depending on the nature of the application. LR is currently developing the proposed wording.

3.5 The further application for registration of the discharge

3.5.1 *Discharge by DS1*

Where you are awaiting a paper DS1 you should make your subsequent application for registration of the discharge when you receive the DS1 from the seller's lender or seller's solicitor.

3.5.2 *Discharge by Electronic Notification of Discharge (END)*

ENDs do not incorporate an application to register, so you will need to establish if the END is available before making your second application in form AP1 or DS2E for the charge entries to be cancelled.

Lenders should notify the seller's solicitor, who will usually be redeeming the seller's charge, when they have sent an END to LR. The seller's solicitors in most cases will not be making application to redeem the seller's charge. You, the buyer's solicitor, will usually be making this application. This is why it is important that the sellers' solicitors immediately pass such information or notification as they receive from the lender to you. Some lenders, in relation to some electronic methods of discharge, provide no further notification following the redemption statement.

You can make a day list enquiry of LR to find out if an END transmitted by the lender is awaiting registration or view the register to find out whether the charge has been removed electronically.

Alternatively you can phone the relevant local LR office to establish that :

- the charge entries have been cancelled following receipt of an ED or eDS1

- an END, ED or e-DS1 has been received, or

- no END, ED or e-DS1 has been received.

This is a free service.

You can also contact LR telephone services centre to make an END enquiry. Call 0844 892 0307 for properties in England and 0844 892 0308 for properties in Wales and for the Welsh speaking service.

3.5.3 *Restrictions against the registration of charges*

In the case of a restriction against the registration of charges rather than against any disposition, LR will register the transfer and then requisition as set out in 3.2 above. If LR then receive the discharge LR will register this and subsequently register the buyer's charge which will be part of the application they are already holding provided that time limits have not been exceeded and the application has not been cancelled. This applies to discharges by both DS1 and END.

3.5.4 *Discharge by ED and E-DS1*

Both of these kinds of electronic discharge incorporate an application to LR to discharge the charge. You therefore do not need to make any further application to LR to register the discharge but to comply with your obligations you do need to monitor the status of the original application.

3.6   Title Information Documents (TIDs)

A TID will be issued as usual following completion of a registration. LR will issue the RCS and the TID which includes an official copy of the register.

LR will issue a TID and an official copy of the register after the subsequent application.

LR are considering the following issues:

- whether and how notification should be sent to you when a charge left on the register after early completion is subsequently discharged by an ED or a e-DS1

- whether any such notification should also include an updated official copy of the register.

3.7   Lenders' checking of the register

Lenders are likely to continue to make checks to establish when applications for registrations have been made following a purchase and whether they were they made within the priority period. Once early completion is introduced, lenders are likely to want to know whether they have a registered first charge and whether any former charges have been removed from the register. The fact that lenders may be carrying out these checks does not relieve you of your duty to the lender to make your own checks.

4   COUNCIL OF MORTGAGE LENDERS (CML) HANDBOOK

The CML Handbook states that on completion of the instructions in a retainer, the lender will require a fully enforceable first legal charge. The CML say this requirement remains unchanged by LR's early completion processes. The CML's view is that early completion is not an issue substantially affecting the current process. Accordingly they do not propose to amend the Handbook.

The CML states:

'The order of events may in some cases be reversed but the stages of the process remain exactly the same.

Lenders regard completion as having taken place once the retainer is complied with. It is not relevant that the Land Registry has imposed an intervening stage in the transaction as this does not change the overall position'.

By 'completion', the CML means completion of the instructions from a lender, not legal or physical completion.

In connection with the CML Handbook LR states that:

'Completing the applications to register the transfer and new charge subject to the existing charge would not appear to affect the obligations of any party in relation to that existing charge. If the existing charge has been repaid then the requirement on the lender to provide evidence of proof of satisfaction of that charge will remain. The obligation of the seller's conveyancer arising from any undertaking given to the buyer's conveyancer in relation to the charge will not change.

Early completion will not prevent the new charge taking effect as a first legal charge; it can never become a first charge until the existing charge is discharged. This is so whether or not the new charge is entered in the register. The entry of the new charge under early completion simply protects the priority of that new charge as against any other interest whose priority is not protected at the time of registration.'

The CML states that the changes will not alter the requirements set out in paragraph 14.1.1.1 of the CML Lenders Handbook which require the conveyancer to register the mortgage as a first legal charge at the Land Registry. Lenders do not regard the retainer as being complied with until this is achieved.

By implication this suggests that lenders will not regard the temporary situation, of the buyer's mortgagee having a second mortgage whilst the seller's mortgage is awaiting discharge, as being in breach of the provisions of the CML Handbook. This is so because lenders will not regard completion as having taken place until the retainer has been completed by the lender being registered with a first legal charge. It is upon completion of, and not during, the retainer, that lenders require a first legal charge.

5 UNDERTAKINGS AND ASSURANCES

Early completion is a policy change that does not directly affect the existing advice in the Conveyancing Handbook and Rule 10 of the Code of Conduct in relation to undertakings.

The changes in practice arising from early completion may make you, as a buyer's solicitor, want to seek further assurances from the seller's solicitor. You may seek these by way of representations, contractual obligations and/or undertakings.

Where you seek a further or extended undertaking to meet the requirements of the early completion policy, the seller's solicitor will need to consider whether any such extended undertaking can properly be given. It may not be possible, or proper for the seller's solicitor to give such extended undertaking.

In order to attempt to meet the requirements of early completion you may instead seek pre-contract representations or warranties from the seller's solicitors that they will:

- pay over the money required to discharge the charge on completion
- press the lender for the discharge
- endeavour to obtain from the lender and will supply to the buyer
- information about the likely method of discharge to be used
- in the absence of DS1, DS3 or END notices continue to press for such information and supply such information as is available to them as to the status and likely issue time of the release.

Note carefully that a 'representation' or 'warranty' to do something could well amount to an undertaking (see Solicitors Code of Conduct rule 10.05 and the associated guidance).

These assurances may assist in providing you with the necessary information to enable you to apply to the LR for extensions of time or to make further priority searches. However, even if the seller's solicitor provides full information this will not resolve the problem. If the discharge is not available within the extended time limits the application is likely to be rejected, but the information you receive may assist you in assessing the risk of this occurring in any transaction.

Making a further priority search does not guarantee protection. Making a further search will give you a new priority period; it will not extend the original one. The search result will be subject to any other application or search made in respect of the property before your new search takes effect. In these circumstances you will be acting in your clients' interest by requesting and obtaining such assurances from the seller's solicitor to ensure that priority for the buyer's registration of ownership and the lenders registration of charge is protected.

Solicitors acting for sellers can reasonably be expected to co-operate in affording such information and assurances as are reasonable as this will, in most cases, be in their clients' 'best interests'.

For further information on conveyancing undertakings to discharge mortgages see both:

1   rule 10.05 of the Solicitors' Code of Conduct

2   the *Conveyancing Handbook*, 15th edition. The relevant sections are section E.3, F.4 and the guidance on accepting undertakings after *Patel* v. *Daybells* [2001] EWCA Civ 1229 in appendix IV.7.

See also the SRA warning card on undertakings updated in April 2009.

This provides that 'you must ensure that your undertakings are specific, measurable, agreed, realistic and timed.'

6 DISCHARGES

Lenders may use any of a variety of methods available to them for effecting a discharge. This brings uncertainty because the nature of the form of discharge used affects the timing of the availability of the discharge for registration.

The discharge may be evidenced by a DS1, an ED, an END or an e-DS1.

A buyer's solicitor may attempt to establish from the seller's solicitor the nature of the discharge that will be used in the transaction. However this is unlikely to provide certainty as to the method that will ultimately be used.

The reasons for this are:

● The seller's solicitor may not know the form of discharge that the seller's lender is proposing to use until quite a late stage in the transaction.

● The nature of discharge may change during the course of a transaction. For example, some electronic methods of discharge revert to paper if they cannot be processed electronically for some reason.

In addition, some lenders:

● operate different methods of discharge for different members within the same group

● use multiple methods of discharge that change according to the nature of the mortgage product.

Nonetheless as set out in paragraph 4 above it may assist you to request from the seller's solicitor information about the likely method of discharge to be used. It is factor that may help you to assess the risks.

From 27 July 2009, LR will make available an updated version of [Practice Guide 31 'Discharge of charges' – see **www.landreg.gov.uk/publications/?pubtype=309**].

7 IDENTIFICATION REQUIREMENTS (ID)

When making the second application to register the paper discharge of the seller's discharge you will not need to provide a new ID form if LR has retained form ID1 or ID2 in respect of the lender for a charge being discharged by a paper DS1. This is so long as the evidence of identity is no more than three months old at the time the further application is made after early completion.

You should add a note to panel 13 of form AP1 to refer LR to the ID form you have already provided.

This is only relevant where the solicitor is not representing the discharging lender. This should already have been established in replies to TA13 Completion arrangements and requisitions, if not earlier.

You may make provision in the contract for when evidence of identity becomes more than three months old, because it will be difficult to establish, in advance, cases in which evidence is likely to be or may be more than three months old. You can provide that such provisions do not merge on completion. See Standard Conditions of Sale (4th edition) condition 7.4.

This also applies to evidence of identity for the borrower or lender for a new charge in respect of which the LR has cancelled an application.

8   APPLICATION OF EARLY COMPLETION

8.1   Transfers of part

LR will not complete applications to register transfers of part on the basis of early completion but say they will keep the position under review. LR will requisition for a discharge of part if one is required and not lodged with an application to register a transfer of part. However LR will continue to operate the process as now without implementing early completion.

8.2   Charges of part

Early completion does not apply to applications that only comprise an application for a discharge of part of a charge to be registered.

8.3   Remortgages

Early completion presents fewer concerns when applied to remortgages where the borrower in relation to the incoming and outgoing charges will be the same, as there will be no undertaking between sellers and buyers solicitors. However the status of the application needs to be monitored to ensure that the new lender obtains a first legal charge.

8.4   Leases

LR states that it already applies a form of early completion when dealing with applications to register a dispositionary first lease where there is a charge registered against the landlord's title. Although the charge is not usually discharged when a lease is granted, the absence of the chargee's consent to the grant of a lease by the landlord does not prevent the lease from being registered with absolute title.

In relation to the transfer or assignment of leases subject to a mortgage, rather than the grant of a lease, early completion will apply as at 3 above.

8.   DISCHARGES

Where the application to remove the registered charge is the only application made, and the evidence is not available to LR when the application is received LR will reject it as being substantially defective under rule 16(3) of the Land Registration Rules 2003, regardless of the method of discharge. This is because the new early completion procedures relate to applications to remove the entries relating to a registered charge where evidence of discharge is not supplied with, or prior to, the application. This is the only circumstance in which the LR will reject, rather than cancel an application.

See the following for further information:

- LR Practice Guide 50 'Requisition and cancellation procedures'
- LR Practice Guide 49 'Return and rejection of applications for registration'.

9 FEES

9.1 LR fees

No further fee is payable if you need to make a further application to remove the charge entries that remain after early completion. This remains true if your further application also includes the registration of a new charge rejected under early completion, provided that you lodge a copy of the Registration Completion Sheet (RCS) sent following completion of your original application.

9.2 Your fees

When estimating your charges at the start of the retainer, you may wish to give advance notice of any additional work that you may have to carry out as a result of early completion. These may include likely additional LR fees, additional priority search fees and/or lodgement of restriction fees in addition to your professional charges as the operation of this policy is likely to involve you in spending additional time on each matter.

10 MORE INFORMATION

10.1 Professional conduct

The following sections of the Solicitors' Code of Conduct 2007 are relevant.

- Rule 1.01 (Justice and the rule of law)
- Rule 2 (Client relations)
- Rule 3 (Conflict of interests)
- Rule 3.07 (Acting for lender and borrower in conveyancing transactions)
- Rule 4.01 (Duty of confidentiality)
- Rule 4.02 (Duty of disclosure)
- Rule 10 (Relations with third parties)

10.2 Legal and other requirements

- Land Registration Amendment Rules 2008 (as amended) (LRR)
- Land Registration Act 2002 (as amended) (LRA) various but see sections 16, 27(2)(a) and (f)
- Land Registration Rules 2003 (as amended) (LRR) various but see rule 114 and 115
- Fraud Act 2006
- Money Laundering Regulations 2007
- Proceeds of Crime Act 2002 (as amended)
- CML Handbook

10.3　Further products and support

10.3.1_Practice Advice Line_

The Law Society provides support for solicitors on a wide range of areas of practice. Practice Advice can be contacted on 0870 606 2522 from 09:00 to 17:00 on weekdays.

10.3.2_Other practice notes and Law Society materials_

- Mortgage Fraud Practice Note
- Anti-Money Laundering Practice Note
- Property Section [**www.propertysection.org.uk**]
- Identity Evidence for Land Registry Practice Note
- Home Information Packs [**www.lawsociety.org.uk/areasoflaw.law** (see 'Conveyancing residential/Hot topics]
- The Law Society's _Conveyancing Handbook_ (16th Edition)
- Land Registry Practice Bulletin 16 Early Completion
- Land Registry Early Completion FAQs [**www1.landregistry.gov.uk/early_completion**]

10.3.3_Council of Mortgage Lenders_

The CML is the trade association for the mortgage lending industry and represents first charge lenders. Not all lenders are members of the CML.

- CML handbook [**www.cml.org.uk/handbook**]
- CML FAQs [**www.cml.org.uk/cml/handbook/faqs**]

10.4　Status of this practice note

Practice notes are issued by the Law Society for the use and benefit of its members. They represent the Law Society's view of good practice in a particular area. They are not intended to be the only standard of good practice that solicitors can follow. You are not required to follow them, but doing so will make it easier to account to oversight bodies for your actions.

Practice notes are not legal advice, nor do they necessarily provide a defence to complaints of misconduct or of inadequate professional service. While care has been taken to ensure that they are accurate, up to date and useful, the Law Society will not accept any legal liability in relation to them.

For queries or comments on this practice note contact the Law Society's Practice Advice Service.

10.5　Terminology in this practice note

'Completion' – LR in the context of 'early completion' use this to mean acceleration of when they will make the first changes to the register in connection with the applications received.

'You' – the solicitor making the application to LR – the applicant's solicitor.

'Charge' – may refer to more than one charge that is it includes first, second and third charges.

'Held over' – the process whereby LR puts incomplete applications to one side pending receipt of the information necessary to complete the application.

'Registration Completion Sheet (RCS)' – the new form that LR will use in place of the completion of registration letter that accompanies an application completed on the basis of early completion.

'Title Information Document' (TID) – issued by LR following completion of an application for registration with an official copy of the register. The TID explains why the official copies have been issued.

Must – a specific requirement in the Solicitor's Code of Conduct or legislation. You must comply, unless there specific exemptions or defences provided for in the code of conduct or relevant legislation.

Should – good practice for most situations in the Law Society's view. If you do not follow this, you must be able to justify to oversight bodies why this is appropriate, either for your practice, or in the particular retainer.

May – a non-exhaustive list of options for meeting your obligations. Which option you choose is determined by the risk profile of the individual practice, client or retainer. You must be able to justify why this was an appropriate option to oversight bodies.

10.6 Acknowledgements

- Law Society Conveyancing and Land Law Committee
- Law Society E-Conveyancing Task Force
- Law Society Property Section

II.6. Making Gifts of Assets Practice Note[1]

1 INTRODUCTION

1.1 Who should read this practice note

This practice note is for solicitors who advise clients about transferring their assets to family and friends before they die.

1.2 What is the issue?

Clients may ask about transferring property or investments to their next of kin, family members, or friends in order to mitigate large tax bills after their death, or as a means of providing funding for their future care. Whether they wish to gift assets or offer them at significant undervalue, you must advise your client about the benefits and risks of doing so, and clarify your role and responsibilities in the process.

Some clients may have received advice from non-solicitor legal advice services that included unjustified claims about gifting of assets to avoid the assets being considered for inheritance tax or care fees liability.

2 TAKING ON A CLIENT

2.1 New clients

Before taking on a new client, you should check whether they retained another solicitor or adviser before you, and find out why they decided to change. If you are concerned, you should ask your client if you can contact their previous adviser so that you can establish all the facts of the case.

You should also satisfy yourself that your client is making the gift freely and has not been unduly influenced, especially where someone else purports to be giving instructions on behalf of the client. If indirect instructions are being given, you should confirm the instructions with the client, ideally in person without anyone else being present.

2.2 Conflict of interest

You should clarify who you will be acting for and who you will be receiving instructions from. You must consider any possible conflict of interest where you receive instructions from a donee, especially if you already act for the donor. Rule 3.01 of the Solicitors' Code of Conduct 2007 indicates when instructions must be refused.

If you are asked to act for both parties, you must make them both aware of the possible conflict of interest, and should advise one of them to take independent advice. You should explain you may be unable to disclose all that you know to each of them. You may also be unable to give advice to one of them which conflicts with the interests of the other. Both parties must give their consent to the arrangement in writing. If you remain in any doubt, you should not act for both parties.

---

1. © The Law Society 2009. This Practice Note is as stated on 16 July 2009. Practice Notes are updated by the Law Society from time to time. Solicitors are advised to check **www.lawsociety.org.uk** for the latest version.

2.3   Money laundering

There is a risk that clients seeking to transfer assets may be involved in money laundering or fraud. The Law Society's anti-money laundering practice note will help you to spot warning signs and gives information on what to do if, for example, your client attempts a transaction involving criminal property.

When you accept instructions from a client, you enter into a binding contract with them and you are obliged to follow their instructions. However, Rule 2.01 of the Solicitors' Code of Conduct creates an exception to this. Rule 2.01 requires that you do not act for a client if it would involve you in a breach of law or your professional obligations.

2.4   Professional negligence and file retention

To protect yourself in the event of a subsequent dispute or a professional negligence claim, you must retain evidence of the advice you give your client. Your file notes and correspondence will normally be covered by legal professional privilege or the duty of confidentiality. A court will not usually order discovery of a solicitor's file unless there is prima facie evidence of fraud, but has done so where there are public policy considerations – see *Barclays Bank plc* v. *Eustice* [1995] 1 WLR 1238. It is possible that a trustee in bankruptcy, or a local authority bringing proceedings under the Insolvency Act 1986, section 423-425, may persuade the court to override privilege.

3 ADVISING YOUR CLIENT

Your role is more than just drawing up and registering the necessary deeds and documents to effect the making of a gift. You must ensure that the client fully understands the nature, effect, benefits, risks and foreseeable consequences of making the gift, in order to enable them to form a view as to the wisdom of the proposed transaction.

Assessing your client's understanding of the implications of making the gift may help you to determine whether they have the capacity to make the decision, or whether they are subject to undue influence from family or other beneficiaries.

Since your advice will depend to a large extent on your client's motivations for disposing of their assets, you must first find out:

- what they are seeking to achieve
- who they wish to receive the gift
- what types of assets are involved

You should spend time with your client to enable you to:

- evaluate their instructions
- clarify their domestic and financial circumstances
- establish that they own the assets they wish to dispose of, and
- assess whether they have the mental capacity to make the gift.

The Mental Capacity Act 2005 (MCA) and MCA code of practice state that your client should be able to understand relevant information, use it to make a decision, and communicate that decision to you. The leading case of *Re Beaney (Deceased)* [1978] 1 WLR 770 sets out the test of capacity to make a gift, and states that capacity to make a gift will vary depending on the size, nature and circumstances of the gift.

Further, you should stress to your client that your advice is the best possible advice at the time it is given. You should point out that the unexpected can and often does occur and that the best laid plans can go wrong, so donors should always adopt a cautious approach.

In many cases, your client will be the person intending to make the gift, but you may be approached by a next of kin acting on their behalf. In this case, you should confirm your instructions with the client in person, preferably in private, so as to ensure that they are capable of making the decision and that they have not been unduly influenced by the donee or next of kin.

3.1 Establish your client's objectives and understanding

To enable you to provide relevant advice, you should do both of the following:

1. ensure that you receive full instructions

2. ensure that your client fully understands the implications of their proposed transaction.

3.1.1 *Why the client is considering a gift*

You should ask why your client has decided to make the gift, as you may be able to suggest more effective ways of achieving the same objective, for example: does your client wish to ensure that a particular person inherits an asset? This objective could be achieved simply by making a will.

Other points to consider could be:

- Is your client seeking peace of mind by making the gift? Do they think it provides certainty for the future or satisfies a moral obligation?

- Will the gift affect others who might have expected to eventually inherit a share of the asset?

If the intention in making the gift is to avoid tax, you should ensure that your client is aware of all tax implications, including Inheritance Tax, Capital Gains Tax and Pre-Owned Asset Tax. There are additional considerations if your client retains the benefit of an asset after giving it away. For instance, if the recipient of the gift dies before the donor, the asset may be subject to Inheritance Tax.

If your client is seeking relief from the worry and responsibility of owning an asset, granting a lasting power of attorney to a family member may be a better way of dealing with this issue.

If your client wants to avoid the value of their assets being taken into account for means testing, such as when they foresee the need to pay for long-term care, your advice must deal with the consequences of such an action, including tax implications and the risks in relation to deprivation of assets.

3.1.2 *Issues involved in the clients decision*

There may be other issues involved in your client's decision which you should be aware of, including where:

- Your client is infirm or disabled, and an adult child or other relative has given up a paid job or the chance of career advancement to provide full-time live-in care in the expectation of inheriting the home on their death.

- Your client is no longer able to pay for the upkeep or improvement of their home, and their child or children have been funding these in the expectation of inheriting the property.

- The home or other asset is a part of a family business which would no longer be viable if the asset were not included. For instance, a farm might not be able to function without the farmhouse.

- The asset was vested in the name of your client but was funded in whole or in part by their son or daughter.

3.1.3 *Nature and extent of the assets*

You should request details from your client regarding the nature and extent of the assets being disposed of, and whether your client expects to receive anything in return, including:

- whether the asset is the family home, or an interest in a property or business

- whether the gift will include art, antiques, jewellery or investments

- whether the gift is a one-off or one of a series

- the extent of the gift in relation to the rest of your client's assets, including assets held on their behalf or in trust by others, and the impact on their standard of living

- if they are making an outright gift, offering a loan, setting up a trust, or acquiring a share in a business or property owned by the donee

- whether your client expects to receive anything in return for their gift and, if so, what is the magnitude of their expectation? For instance, they may propose to give their house to a family member and in return remain there for the rest of their life. In this case, you would need to talk to your client about rent, insurance and maintenance of or alterations to the property

- the age, health and circumstances of the donee, including if they are reliant on means-tested benefits or local authority funded care, noting that a donee may die first or become involved in divorce, civil partnership dissolution or bankruptcy proceedings

- whether they expect the donee to provide care or financial assistance

- whether they intend the gift to take effect immediately or later, for example perhaps on your client's death or if they go into a care home

- whether your client has already made gifts to the donee or others.

A proper assessment of the implications of making a gift of the asset both for your client and the donee is best achieved by listing the benefits and risks, and thinking about other issues such as tax and future care. You should also tell your client that if the gift is made outright, they cannot assume that the asset would be returned to them upon request.

3.2   Benefits of transferring assets

If your client transfers assets to a family member or carer:

- There may be savings in relation to Inheritance Tax and administration costs upon the death of the client.

- The client may avoid the need to sell assets to pay for care fees.

- The asset may not be taken into account if your client has to undergo means-testing for benefits or publicly funded services.

- Your client may be relieved of the burden of responsibility for the asset.

- It may reduce delays in processing their estate on their death.

- There may be savings in both time and expense in applying for a court order from the Court of Protection in the event your client loses mental capacity and there is no relevant power of attorney in force.

3.3   Risks in transferring assets

Among the risks involved are the following:

- The value of the home may still be taken into account for funding long-term care as there are anti-avoidance measures in relation to means-testing. This is set out further at 5.1.2 Means testing.

- If your client subsequently needs to move into a home but does not have the resources to pay for their care themselves because of the gift, the local authority may only pay for the basic level of care, leaving your client to rely upon the financial support of others to enable them to move into a home of their choice.

- The donee may not provide the support expected, resulting in suffering for your client – for example, by not topping up care fees, or by moving your client prematurely into residential care home in order to occupy or sell the family home.

- If the donee dies or runs into financial difficulties and the donor continues to live in the gifted home, your client may be made homeless.

- The relationship between the donor and donee, since parties can and often do fall into dispute and even become quite hostile to one another.

- The donee may later put pressure on your client to liquidate the gifted assets.

- If your client transfers their home, they may be deprived of opportunities to adapt to changing circumstances – for example by downsizing, or releasing equity to pay for adaptations or care at home, so the donor may be left with no option but to move into a care home.

- The person to whom the assets have been gifted may lose their entitlement to benefits and/or services based on personal means testing.

- If the arrangement is challenged, there could be additional legal fees.

3.4 Tax implications

There are many issues arising in relation to tax as a direct result of transferring assets. For example:

- There may be no Inheritance Tax saving as long as your client receives benefit from the asset – for example, if they continue to live in the home after transferring it to a child.

- There may be an Inheritance Tax liability if the donee dies before the donor, or if the donor dies within seven years of making the gift.

- The Capital Gains Tax main residence exemption will be lost unless the donee lives in the property.

- There may be no automatic uplift to the market value for Capital Gains Tax on the donor's death.

- Stamp Duty Land Tax and additional administrative burdens may be payable.

- Under the pre-owned assets rules, your client may be subject to an Income Tax charge after the transfer.

3.5 Other consequences

As well as the more practical issues, you should ask your client to think about their general approach to their future once they have transferred assets including:

- What effect making the gift could have on their future standard of living?

- If a main motivator in gifting assets was to avoid means-testing for future care provision, how would your client feel if this situation didn't arise? Does the benefit outweigh the risk?

- What effect would transferring an asset have on others who might have expected to inherit a share of it?

- What might happen if relations between your client and the donee deteriorate?

4 SPECIAL CONSIDERATIONS

4.1 Joint donors

Where your clients are seeking to make a joint gift, you should consider the position of each donor separately. Where the donors may have children from previous relationships, you should consider their obligations to those children. You must also make your clients aware of any potential conflict of interest between the two of them in terms of your advice.

You must establish whether both donors have capacity to make the gift and whether either donor is exerting undue influence on the other.

Where the gift to a third party is the home in which the couple are living, there will be the same risks as with individuals providing the gift, however if the gift is of a share in the home by one of the donors to a third party, you should fully explore the implications for the potential survivor.

It is common for spouses, civil partners or cohabitees to contemplate a gift of their home to avoid its value being taken into account in relation to means-testing for care home fees. You should tell the donors that if only one of them goes into care, there are circumstances in which the value of the share of that donor will not be taken into account, where the other donor remains in the home. However, the value of the resident's home is disregarded in the following circumstances:

- during a temporary stay

- if it is occupied by a spouse, civil partner, person living with the resident as a spouse or civil partner or relative who is aged sixty or over or is incapacitated

- if it is occupied by someone else and the local authority exercises its discretion

- for the first twelve weeks of a permanent stay in a care home.

4.1.1 *Establish the nature of the donors' relationship*

You should ascertain the relationship of the donors because different considerations apply for marriage, civil partnership, cohabitation or living together on a non-sexual basis.

For married couples and civil partners, you should make your clients aware that they benefit from the inheritance tax exemption on the transfer of assets between them both on death and during their lifetime. So a gift of an asset to a third party during their lifetime may not result in any tax saving on the first death of the couple. The survivor's expenses may increase due to living alone at the time as income is reduced because of lost pensions. To ensure that the survivor is left with sufficient assets following the first death, it may be preferable to retain assets, either absolutely or in an interest in possession trust until the death of the survivor. The survivor's estate will then benefit from the transferable nil rate band if it is still in force at that time.

For cohabitees, there is no inheritance tax exemption on gifts between them so a lifetime gift to a third party may appear to have a tax saving advantage. However, you should explore the implications for the survivor. As with a married couple, the survivor may well have increased living expenses or have a fall in income following the first death. It may still be better to choose a gift of the nil rate band to a discretionary trust of which the surviving cohabitant is a beneficiary.

It is not uncommon for joint donors to be living together on a non-sexual basis, for example children and parents, or siblings or for a parent to make a gift of the property to their children.

In these circumstances, you should remember that there is an automatic presumption of undue influence in the making of lifetime gifts where the donor is a child and donee a parent. This will necessitate separate advice for the donor(s) and the donee as a means of rebutting such a presumption.

You should also establish whether the donor(s) have taken into account the needs and expectations of each other and any other children. However unlikely it may appear to be, the consequences of the death of the donee before the donor(s) needs to be considered both from the point of view of inheritance tax and of succession to the property. The donor may be at risk of losing the property.

4.2 Multiple donees

Often, the gift will be to more than one donee, such as to multiple children, including where joint donors have children from different relationships.

These situations greatly increase the potential problems and risks. For example, the death of a donee before the donor is more likely, as is divorce, financial hardship, bankruptcy or incapacity of one or more of the donees. There is also the possibility that in the future the donees may disagree about issues concerning the donor(s) and the assets.

It is unlikely to be appropriate for one person to act for both the donor(s) and all the donees. Each party is likely to need separate legal representation to ensure their particular interests are considered.

5 GIFTING ASSETS TO FUND FUTURE CARE

Many clients will be motivated to transfer assets because they fear they will have to sell their home to pay for care and wish to protect their family's inheritance.

To advise your clients properly, you should familiarise yourself with:

- the eligibility criteria for NHS-funded continuing health care
- charging and funding arrangements by local authorities for residential and continuing health care
- when care must be provided free of charge
- any means-testing criteria applied by local authorities which charges for care.

There is no foolproof way of avoiding the value of assets being taken into account for means-testing. Anti-avoidance measures in the law allow some gifts to be ignored by the authorities, and even set aside by the court. The measures are subject to periodic change, might apply retrospectively, and are pursued more vigorously by some authorities than others.

5.1 Local authority care provision

Local authorities are not allowed to take responsibility for a person who is an NHS responsibility, but they must assess anyone who appears to it to be in need of community care services. These include residential accommodation for those who by reason of age, illness or disability are in need of care and attention which is not otherwise available to them, and domiciliary and community-based services enabling people to continue to live in the community. Relevant legislation:

- National Health Service and Community Care Act 1990, section 47
- National Assistance Act 1948, section 21

- National Assistance Act 1948, section 29, including functions under the Chronically Sick and Disabled Persons Act 1970, section 2

On the results of their assessment, they must decide whether there is a need to provide community care services. If that is the case, the person in need of care is likely to be subject to the financial means test.

5.1.1 *Paying for care*

If your client can afford to pay for a place in a care home, they can arrange this independently, though they should have a needs assessment to consider all their care options including whether and how much financial assistance would be available from their local authority. The assessment of need for care provision does not depend on the need for funding. Some care homes do not provide accommodation for local authority-funded residents.

Where the local authority pays or contributes to the cost of care:

- A standard weekly charge is fixed which represents the true economic cost of providing the accommodation, or a weekly charge is agreed for a place in an independent home which should represent the cost of the place to the authority.

- Residents must generally contribute in accordance with their resources up to the weekly charge, but no one should be required to pay more.

- The local authority will either pay the full weekly charge to the care home and collect the resident's contribution or, with the agreement of all parties, pay the home net of the person's assessed contribution, with the resident paying this to the care home direct.

- The contract should state what is included in the charge and what are extras.

If your client wishes to move to a care home which is more expensive than the local authority will pay on the basis of their assessed needs, and if the local authority can show that there are suitable homes with vacancies in the local area, you should note that the cost difference will need to be topped up by a third party such as a family member.

5.1.2 *Means testing*

For those who cannot afford the standard charge for their care, local authorities will make an assessment of their ability to pay. This is reviewed annually, though a reassessment can be requested at any time.

The assessment applies to both permanent and temporary care, and is based on the means only of the person in need of care: a partner's or spouse's resources are not taken into account, though jointly owned assets may be assessed. The National Assistance (Assessment of Resources) Regulations 1992 (as amended) and the Charging for Residential Accommodation Guide set out how fees are calculated. Half the occupational and private pensions of a resident can be disregarded if they are paid to a non-resident spouse or civil partner.

The basis of assessments for care provision is largely in line with that for income support, but there are some significant differences:

Some capital is disregarded, and everyone is allowed to keep a set level of capital. The level is set each year in the National Assistance (Assessment of Resources and Sums for Personal Requirements) (Amendments) (England) Regulations and the National Assistance (Assessment of Resources and Sums for Personal Requirements) (Amendments) (Wales) Regulations.

Notional capital and notional income rules may apply where the local authority believes there has been deliberate deprivation of assets.

A small amount of income is disregarded if it would have been incorporated into the assessment for the Savings Credit element of Pension Credit. This is to ensure that pensioners who save still see some benefit of this when they are resident in a care home.

The local authority may agree to defer payment by means of a legal charge on the resident's property, so that the resident does not have to sell their home during their lifetime. The resident must contribute to their care fees from available resources, making up any shortfall through the legal charge. Interest starts to accrue 56 days after the resident's death. A deferred payment option will not be provided where the resident's income or capital is assessed as being above the upper capital limit outlined in the National Assistance (Assessment of Resources) Regulations.

All residents retain an allowance for personal expenditure on toiletries, stationery and treats, etc. This is set each year in:

- the National Assistance (Assessment of Resources and Sums for Personal Requirements) (Amendments) (England) Regulations, and

- the National Assistance (Assessment of Resources and Sums for Personal Requirements) (Amendments) (Wales) Regulations.

The local authority has discretion to increase the allowance, but it should not be used as top-up towards more expensive accommodation.

Local authorities should offer to carry out a benefits check on residents' behalf, since it is in their interests to ensure that people in care homes are receiving maximum state benefits.

5.1.3 *Anti-avoidance measures and deprivation of assets*

In most cases, the intention behind making gifts of assets is the most important factor. If a local authority believes that an asset has been given away with the intention of creating or increasing entitlement to means-tested benefits, it may decide that the donor has notional capital of equivalent value to that of the asset given away.

Your client will be particularly vulnerable if they are deemed to have notional capital since, although the local authority is obliged to provide care, this does not have to be in a residential home. Moreover, your client may not be entitled to financial assistance towards the fees. The local authority may still be obliged to provide care, but the local authority could seek payment using debt recovery methods, as in the case of *Robertson* v. *Fife* [2002] UKHL 35.

A local authority financial assessment must follow the needs assessment. There is a question mark regarding whether *Robertson* v. *Fife* would stand up in England because of the slightly different wording of the legislation, such that the local authority would refuse to provide the care because the notional capital makes it otherwise unavailable (see 'Community Care and the Law' from paragraph 8.91), and as such are arguably under no obligation to provide residential accommodation under s.21 National Assistance Act 1948. However, the person might qualify as a vulnerable adult, regardless of notional capital, where they are in need of such accommodation because they cannot arrange their care or no longer has any resources to fund their care.

If the local authority believed that a significant part of the intention to transfer an asset was to increase entitlement to financial assistance, they could impose a charge on the asset after it had been gifted, or even recover the asset. For a local authority to pursue a claim they would have to show what the donor's intention was at the time of disposal. It may be difficult for the donor or donee to give evidence as to the donor's intentions and if another purpose of the gift cannot be established or indicated, the judge may conclude that it must have been to avoid means-testing.

One way to establish the intention is the foreseeability or immediacy of the need for care. Any decision to reject or accept the evidence requires an overall assessment of that evidence by the local authority – see *Beeson* v. *Dorset County Council* [2002] HRHR 15. If, for example, your client was fit and healthy and could not have foreseen the need for residential care, it would be unreasonable for the local authority to treat the transfer of assets as deliberate deprivation. However, *Yule* v. *South Lanarkshire Council* [1999] 1 CCLR 546, states that there was no time limit on local authorities when deciding whether a person had deprived themselves of assets for the purposes of avoiding residential care fees.

If a local authority were to pursue a claim for care funding, your client could challenge that decision but would bear the burden of proof that the authority's decision was Wednesbury unreasonable – *Associated Provincial Picture Houses Ltd* v. *Wednesbury Corporation* [1948] 1 KB 233). This process could be protracted, involving local authority complaints and ombudsman procedures, and this could be very stressful for your client and expensive if it involves court proceedings.

5.1.4 *Enforcement of fees for care*

Local authorities can take steps to recover contributions towards care charges, and their assessment of ability to pay may take into account property that has been given away for the purpose of avoiding means-testing. Their enforcement options include:

- taking proceedings in the Magistrates' Court to recover sums due as a civil debt (section 56, National Assistance Act 1948)

- imposing a charge on any property belonging to the resident, with interest chargeable from the day after death (sections 22 and 24 of the Health and Social Services and Social Security Adjudication's (HASSASSA) Act 1983)

- imposing a charge on property transferred by the resident, within six months of going to residential care or while in care, on property transferred by the resident with the intention of avoiding contributions (section 21, HASSASSA Act 1983)

If the debt for unpaid contributions reaches £750, the local authority could start insolvency proceedings to declare the resident bankrupt. Transactions at an undervalue may be set aside within two years, or within five years if the person made bankrupt was insolvent at the time of the transaction, which is unlikely. See sections 339–341 Insolvency Act 1986. A gift may be set aside without time limit and without bankruptcy if the court is satisfied that the transfer was made for the purpose of putting assets beyond the reach of a potential creditor or otherwise prejudicing the creditor's interests. See sections 423–425, Insolvency Act 1986.

This provision is exceptionally wide, and the court has extensive powers to restore the position to that which it would have been had the gift not been made. The Court of Appeal in *Derbyshire CC* v. *Akrill* [2005] EWCA Civ 308, considered the application of section 423, concluding that the section could apply where a person transferred his house by deed of gift to his children for the purposes of putting it beyond the reach of those who might have a claim in respect of the costs of his imminent residential care.

Although some local authorities have threatened to use insolvency proceedings, few have actually done so, perhaps because of lack of expertise, cost or the prospect of bad publicity. However, with increasing pressures on local authority resources to provide community care services, the incidence of this may rise in the future. There is evidence that families can be placed under considerable pressure to pay for care, even where the gift was entirely innocent.

5.2 National Health Service-funded care

You may be asked by clients who are already in receipt of care for advice on mitigating the cost of this. You may consider whether the National Health Service (NHS) should fund care, whether wholly or in part.

Section 1 of the National Health Service Act 2006 requires the Secretary of State to promote a comprehensive health service in England with the aim of improving people's physical and mental health, and effectively preventing, diagnosing and treating those who are ill. Section 3 sets out the duty to provide services for the care of those suffering from illness to the extent necessary to meet reasonable requirements. This includes accommodation for the purposes of health services provided under the act. Similar provision applies in Wales under the NHS (Wales) Act 2006.

Strategic health authorities and primary care trusts carry out this function on behalf of the Secretary of State in England, and local health boards have the responsibility in Wales.

NHS fully funded care is provided in this context, defined in the NHS Continuing Healthcare (Responsibilities) Directions 2007 as 'a package of care that can be arranged and funded by the NHS to meet both physical and mental health which have arisen because of illness'. Thus, the NHS would fund the full cost of care for eligible people in care homes, including accommodation and board, and those in their own homes would receive the cost of their both their health care and any social care funded by the NHS.

5.2.1 *Extent of NHS-funded care provision*

Where someone's care is primarily one of health, the full cost of care is the responsibility of the NHS. However, the distinction between care services that can and cannot be provided as part of a package of services is one of degree, and in borderline cases it depends on a careful appraisal of the facts of the individual case.

The Court of Appeal considered whether a local authority could lawfully provide nursing care for a chronically ill patient in the case of *R* v. *North & East Devon Health Authority ex p Coughlan* [2000] 3 All ER 850. In that case her care included nursing care but was not confined to it. A very general indication as to where the line is to be drawn between lawfully providing care or not is dependent on whether the nursing services were either:

1.   Merely incidental or ancillary to the provision of the accommodation which a local authority is under a duty to provide.

2.   Of a nature which it can be expected that a local authority could be expected to provide.

The judge confirmed that where the individual's care was primarily one of health, the full cost of care was the responsibility of the NHS. Until recently, in England it was the local NHS body's responsibility to determine what they meant by a primary health care need, whereas in Wales it remains up to the local health board. In any event, the NHS body must publish guidance on how eligibility for continuing NHS health care is determined, based on a full assessment of the relevant facts such as the quantity and/or quality of care need and how this is weighed to determine the person's eligibility. See *R (Grogan)* v. *Bexley NHS Care Trust* [2006] EWHC 44 (admin).

5.2.2 *Eligibility for NHS-funded care in England*

Eligibility is determined following a full multidisciplinary assessment of the individual's needs which indicate a primary health care need. Certain characteristics of need and their impact on the care required to manage them may help determine eligibility. These characteristics are:

●   Nature – the types of need, and the overall effect of those needs on the individual, including the type (quality) of interventions required to manage them

●   Intensity – both the extent (quantity) and severity (degree) of the needs, including the need for sustained care (continuity)

●   Complexity – how the needs arise and interact to increase the skill needed to monitor and manage the care

●   Unpredictability – the degree to which needs fluctuate, creating difficulty in managing needs, and the level of risk to the person's health if adequate and timely care is not provided

Eligibility and ineligibility should not be based on:

- the setting of care
- the ability of the care provider to manage care: only where the successful management of a health care need has permanently reduced or removed an ongoing need will this have a bearing on eligibility
- the use, or not, of NHS-employed staff to provide care
- the individual's financial position
- the need for/presence of specialist staff in care delivery
- the existence of other NHS-funded care
- any other input-related, rather than needs-related, rationale.

The National Framework for NHS Continuing Healthcare and NHS Funded Nursing Care in England came into operation in October 2007. The framework is accompanied by a decision support tool, screening tool and fast -track tool for those with apparent and immediate needs.

5.2.3 *Eligibility for NHS-funded care in Wales*

Eligibility in Wales is based on satisfying one of the following criteria:

- The nature or complexity or intensity or unpredictability of the individual's health care needs (and any combination of these needs) requires regular supervision by a member of the NHS multidisciplinary team, such as the consultant, palliative care, therapy or other NHS member of the team.
- The individual's needs require the routine use of specialist health care equipment under supervision of NHS staff.
- The individual has a rapidly deteriorating or unstable medical, physical or mental health condition and requires regular supervision by a member of the NHS multidisciplinary team such as a consultant, palliative care, therapy or other NHS member of the team.
- The individual is in the final stages of a terminal illness and is likely to die in the near future.

Guidance for Wales is contained in WHC (2004) 54: NAFWC 41/2004, which is supported by *All Wales Continuing NHS Health Care: Framework for Implementation in Wales*, published in 2004. Further advice to the NHS and local authorities on continuing NHS health care (NAFWC32/06) was given in 2006 following the Grogan judgment.

5.2.4 *Registered nursing care funding*

Your client may receive financial support, even if not eligible for continuing NHS health care, if they live in a care home registered for nursing care, and receive registered nursing care by a registered nurse. This includes any service provided by a registered nurse which involves the provision of care, or the planning, supervision or delegation of the provision of care, other than services which, having regard to their nature and the circumstances in which they are provided, do not need to be provided by a registered nurse. See section 49(2) of the Health and Social Care Act [2001]. Nursing home residents in both England and Wales are now eligible for a contribution of a flat rate towards their care fees.

5.2.5 *Transitional arrangements for those in a nursing home before 1 October 2007*

Before 1 October 2007, the level of need for residents was assessed as low, moderate or high, with a different financial contribution at each level. Those residents who were on the former high band

(£139/week) continue to be funded at the higher level (uprated annually) as the change would otherwise put them in a worse financial position. They can continue to remain on the high band until either:

- their care needs decrease to what would be the middle of low band level and they become entitled to the single rate
- they move from the nursing home
- they no longer need nursing care but choose to continue to reside in a nursing home
- they qualify for continuing NHS health care
- they die.

5.2.6 *Aftercare under section 117 of the Mental Health Act 1983*

The Mental Health Act 1983 at s.117(2) creates a joint duty on the NHS body and social services to provide, in cooperation with relevant voluntary agencies, after-care services for certain mentally ill people, until such time as they are both satisfied that the aftercare service is no longer required.

Section 117 of the act applies to those who have been detained under:

- Section 3 (which provides for the compulsory admission of a patient suffering from any mental disorder to hospital for treatment)
- Section 37 (a hospital or guardianship order made by the Crown or Magistrate Court)
- Section 45A (a hospital direction made by the Crown Court), or those who have been subject to a transfer direction made by the Secretary of State under sections 47 or 48.

NHS bodies and social services should not charge for services provided under section 117.

See *R* v. *Redcar & Cleveland BC ex p Armstrong*: *R* v. *Manchester City Council ex p Stennett R: Harrow London BC ex p Cobham* [2002] 4 All ER 124.

The act does not define what is meant by aftercare services, but in *Clunis* v. *Camden and Islington Health Authority* [1998] QB 978, 992 Beldam LJ commented that these 'include social work support, support in helping the ex-patient with problems of employment, accommodation or family relationships, the provision of domiciliary services and the use of day centre and residential facilities'.

It is up to the appropriate authority to determine which aftercare services, within the framework of the care plan, should occur before discharge.

Aftercare services should continue until, after a joint assessment, the NHS body and local authority are satisfied that the person no longer needs them. It is for the authority providing the services to take the lead in deciding when aftercare is no longer required. Funding can end if the patient is no longer in need of mental health care, though in practice this point is unlikely to affect many people. See *R* v. *Richmond Upon Thames LBC ex p Watson*, *The Times*, October 15, 1999/ LGO complaint into Bath and North East Somerset Council No 06/B/16774.

6 MORE INFORMATION

6.1 Solicitors' Code of Conduct

- Rule 2.01: Taking on clients
- Rule 3.01: Duty not to act

6.2 Law Society products and support

6.2.1 *Practice Advice Service*

The Law Society's Practice Advice Service provides support for solicitors on a wide range of areas of practice. The Practice Advice team can be contacted on 0870 606 2522 from 09:00 to 17:00 on weekdays.

6.2.2 *Law Society publications*

- Anti-money laundering practice note
- *Conveyancing Handbook*, 16th Edition
- The *Elderly Client Handbook*, 3rd Edition
- *Health and Social Care Handbook*
- *Mental Capacity Act 2005: A Guide to the New Law*, 2nd Edition
- *Solicitors' Code of Conduct 2007*, June 2009 Edition
- *Solicitors and Money Laundering*, 3rd Edition

6.3 Further reading and reference

6.3.1 *Client capacity to give instructions*

- Mental Capacity Act 2005
- Mental Capacity Act code of practice
- *Re: Beaney (Deceased)* [1978] 1 WLR 770: test of capacity to make a gift

6.3.2 *Publicly funded care*

- National Framework for NHS continuing healthcare and NHS-funded nursing care
- Age Concern advice about continuing care
- *Robertson* v. *Fife* [2002] UKHL 35: local authority recovery of care fees
- Department of Health continuing care website
- NHS Continuing Healthcare (Responsibilities) Directions 2007
- Delayed Discharges (Continuing Care) Directions 2007
- National Health Service (Nursing Care in Residential Accommodation) (England) Directions 2007
- Nursing Guide Handbook October 2007
- Health Service Ombudsman's (HSO) Second Report for sessions 2002–2003 – NHS funding for long term care
- HSO's NHS funding for Long term care follow up report 2004–2005
- HSO case no E.22/02/02–03 (The Pointon Case)
- Health Committee Report on NHS Continuing Care Sixth Report of Session 2004–2005 (April 2005)
- The Parliamentary and Health Service Ombudsman's report *Retrospective Continuing Care Funding and Redress* – 13 March 2007

- National Assistance (Assessment of Resources) Regulations 1992 as amended

- Circular LAC (99)9 *Charging for Residential Accommodation Guide* (CRAG) (copies available from the Department of Health, PO Box 777, London SE1 6XH. Fax: 01623 724 524. E-mail: doh@prologistics.co.uk).

- Department of Health website

6.4   Status of this practice note

Practice notes are issued by the Law Society for the use and benefit of its members. They represent the Law Society's view of good practice in a particular area. They are not intended to be the only standard of good practice that solicitors can follow. You are not required to follow them, but doing so will make it easier to account to oversight bodies for your actions.

Practice notes are not legal advice, nor do they necessarily provide a defence to complaints of misconduct or of inadequate professional service. While care has been taken to ensure that they are accurate, up to date and useful, the Law Society will not accept any legal liability in relation to them.

For queries or comments on this practice note, contact the Law Society's Practice Advice Service.

6.5   Terminology in this practice note

Must – a specific requirement in the Solicitor's Code of Conduct or legislation. You must comply, unless there are specific exemptions or defences provided for in the code of conduct or relevant legislation.

Should – good practice for most situations, in the Law Society's view. If you do not follow this, you must be able to justify to oversight bodies why this is appropriate, either for your practice or in the particular retainer.

May – a non-exhaustive list of options for meeting your obligations. Which option you choose is determined by the risk profile of the individual practice, client or retainer. You must be able to justify why this was an appropriate option to oversight bodies.

III. LAW SOCIETY'S FORMS

III.1. CON 29R Enquiries of Local Authority (2007)[1]

PLANNING AND BUILDING REGULATIONS

1.1. Planning and building decisions and pending applications

Which of the following relating to the property have been granted, issued or refused or (where applicable) are the subject of pending applications?

    (a)   a planning permission

    (b)   a listed building consent

    (c)   a conservation area consent

    (d)   a certificate of lawfulness of existing use or development

    (e)   a certificate of lawfulness of proposed use or development

    (f)   building regulations approval

    (g)   a building regulation completion certificate and

    (h)   any building regulations certificate or notice issued in respect of work carried out under a competent person self-certification scheme

1.2. Planning designations and proposals

What designations of land use for the property or the area, and what specific proposals for the property, are contained in any existing or proposed development plan?

ROADS

2. Roadways, footways and footpaths

Which of the roads, footways and footpaths named in the application for this search (via boxes B and C) are:

    (a)   highways maintainable at public expense

    (b)   subject to adoption and, supported by a bond or bond waiver

    (c)   to be made up by a local authority who will reclaim the cost from the frontagers

    (d)   to be adopted by a local authority without reclaiming the cost from the frontagers

1.© The Law Society 2007. Reproduced with the kind permission of Oyez Straker.

CON 29R Enquiries of local authority (2007)

The Law Society

A duplicate plan is required for all searches submitted directly to a local authority.
If submitted manually, this form must be submitted in duplicate. Please type or use **BLOCK LETTERS**

A.

Local authority name and address	Search No:...
	Signed:..
	On behalf of: ....
	Local authority/private search company/ member of the public (indicate as applicable)
	Dated: ....

B.

Address of the land/property

UPRN(s):

Secondary name/number:

Primary name/number:

Street:

Locality/village:

Town:

Postcode:

C.

Other roadways, footways and footpaths in respect of which a reply to enquiry 2 is required

D.

Fees

£_____ is enclosed/is paid by NLIS transfer (delete as applicable)

Signed:

Dated:

Reference:

Telephone No:

Fax No:

E-mail:

E. (For HIPs regulations compliance only)

Names of those involved in the sale (this box is only completed when the replies to these enquiries are to be included in a Home Information Pack)

Name of vendor:

Name of estate agents:

Name of HIP provider:

Name of solicitor/conveyancer:

Your personal data – name and address – will be handled strictly in accordance with the requirements of the Data Protection Act. It is required to pass on to the relevant authority(ies) in order to carry out the necessary searches.

Notes

A.   Enter name and address of appropriate Council. If the property is near a local authority boundary, consider raising certain enquiries (e.g. road schemes) with the adjoining Council.

B.   Enter address and description of the property. Please give the UPRN(s) (Unique Property Reference Number) where known. **A duplicate plan is required for all searches submitted directly to a local authority**. The search may be returned if land/property cannot easily be identified.

C.   Enter name and/or mark on plan any other roadways, footways and footpaths abutting the property (in addition to those entered in Box B) to which a reply to enquiry 2 is required.

D.   Details of fees can be obtained from the Council, your chosen NLIS channel or search provider.

E.   Box E is only to be completed when the replies to these enquiries are to be included in a Home Information Pack. Enter the name of the individual(s) and firms involved in the sale of the property.

F.   Enter the name and address/DX address of the person or company lodging or conducting this enquiry.

F.

Reply to

DX address:

Oyez 7 Spa Road, London SE16 3QQ   © Law Society 2007   4.2007 F7618   5033382

Conveyancing 29R (Enquiries)

OTHER MATTERS

3.1. Land required for public purposes

Is the property included in land required for public purposes?

3.2. Land to be acquired for road works

Is the property included in land to be acquired for road works?

3.3. Drainage agreements and consents

Do either of the following exist in relation to the property?

(a) an agreement to drain buildings in combination into an existing sewer by means of a private sewer

(b) an agreement or consent for (i) a building, or (ii) extension to a building on the property, to be built over, or in the vicinity of a drain, sewer or disposal main

3.4. Nearby road schemes

Is the property (or will it be) within 200 metres of any of the following?

(a) the centre line of a new trunk road or special road specified in any order, draft order or scheme

(b) the centre line of a proposed alteration or improvement to an existing road involving construction of a subway, underpass, flyover, footbridge, elevated road or dual carriageway

(c) the outer limits of construction works for a proposed alteration or improvement to an existing road involving

  (i)   construction of a roundabout (other than a mini roundabout), or

  (ii) widening by construction of one or more additional traffic lanes;

(d) the outer limits of

  (i)   construction of a new road to be built by a local authority,

  (ii) an approved alteration or improvement to an existing road involving construction of a subway, underpass, flyover, footbridge, elevated road or dual carriageway,

  (iii) construction of a roundabout (other than a mini roundabout) or widening by construction of one or more additional traffic lanes

(e) the centre line of the proposed route of a new road under proposals published for public consultation

(f) the outer limits of

  (i)   construction of a proposed alteration or improvement to an existing road involving construction of a subway, underpass, flyover, footbridge, elevated road or dual carriageway,

  (ii) construction of a roundabout (other than a mini roundabout),

  (iii) widening by construction of one or more additional traffic lanes, under proposals published for public consultation

3.5. Nearby railway schemes

Is the property (or will it be) within 200 metres of the centre line of a proposed railway, tramway, light railway or monorail?

3.6. Traffic schemes

Has a local authority approved but not yet implemented any of the following for the roads, footways and footpaths (named in Box B) which abut the boundaries of the property?

- (a) permanent stopping up or diversion
- (b) waiting or loading restrictions
- (c) one way driving
- (d) prohibition of driving
- (e) pedestrianisation
- (f) vehicle width or weight restriction
- (g) traffic calming works including road humps
- (h) residents parking controls
- (i) minor road widening or improvement
- (j) pedestrian crossings
- (k) cycle tracks
- (l) bridge building

3.7. Outstanding notices

Do any statutory notices which relate to the following matters subsist in relation to the property other than those revealed in a response to any other enquiry in this form?

- (a) building works
- (b) environment
- (c) health and safety
- (d) housing
- (e) highways
- (f) public health

3.8. Contravention of building regulations

Has a local authority authorised in relation to the property any proceedings for the contravention of any provision contained in Building Regulations?

3.9. Notices, orders, directions and proceedings under Planning Acts

Do any of the following subsist in relation to the property, or has a local authority decided to issue, serve, make or commence any of the following?

- (a) an enforcement notice
- (b) a stop notice

    (c)   a listed building enforcement notice

    (d)   a breach of condition notice

    (e)   a planning contravention notice

    (f)   another notice relating to breach of planning control

    (g)   a listed building repairs notice

    (h)   in the case of a listed building deliberately allowed to fall into disrepair, a compulsory purchase order with a direction for minimum compensation

    (i)   a building preservation notice

    (j)   a direction restricting permitted development

    (k)   an order revoking or modifying planning permission

    (l)   an order requiring discontinuance of use or alteration or removal of building or works

    (m) a tree preservation order

    (n)   proceedings to enforce a planning agreement or planning contribution

3.10.   Conservation area

Do the following apply in relation to the property?

    (a)   the making of the area a conservation area before 31st August 1974

    (b)   an unimplemented resolution to designate the area a conservation area

3.11.   Compulsory purchase

Has any enforceable order or decision been made to compulsorily purchase or acquire the property?

3.12.   Contaminated land

Do any of the following apply (including any relating to the land adjacent to or adjoining the property which has been identified as contaminated land because it is in such a condition that harm or pollution of controlled waters might be caused on the property)?

    (a)   a contaminated land notice

    (b)   in relation to a register maintained under section 78R of the Environmental Protection Act 1990

        (i)   a decision to make an entry

        (ii) an entry

    (c)   consultation with the owner or occupier of the property conducted under section 78G(3) of the Environmental Protection Act 1990 before the service of a remediation notice

3.13.   Radon gas

Do records indicate that the property is in a 'Radon Affected Area' as identified by the Health Protection Agency?

NOTES:

(1) References to the provisions of particular Acts of Parliament or Regulations include any provisions which they have replaced and also include existing or future amendments or re-enactments.

(2) The replies will be given in the belief that they are in accordance with information presently available to the officers of the replying Council, but none of the Councils or their officers accept legal responsibility for an incorrect reply, except for negligence. Any liability for negligence will extend to the person who raised the enquiries and the person on whose behalf they were raised. It will also extend to any other person who has knowledge (personally or through an agent) of the replies before the time when he purchases, takes a tenancy of, or lends money on the security of the property or (if earlier) the time when he becomes contractually bound to do so.

(3) This Form should be read in conjunction with the guidance notes available separately.

(4) Area means any area in which the property is located.

(5) References to the Council include any predecessor Council and also any council committee, sub-committee or other body or person exercising powers delegated by the Council and their approval includes their decision to proceed. The replies given to certain enquiries cover knowledge and actions of both the District Council and County Council.

(6) Where relevant, the source department for copy documents should be provided.

III.2. CON 290 Optional Enquiries of Local Authority (2007)[1]

ROAD PROPOSALS BY PRIVATE BODIES

4.   What proposals by others, still capable of being implemented, have the Council approved for any of the following, the limits of construction of which are within 200 metres of the property?

   (a)   the construction of a new road

   (b)   the alteration or improvement of an existing road, involving the construction, whether or not within existing highway limits, of a subway, underpass, flyover, footbridge, elevated road, dual carriageway, the construction of a roundabout (other than a mini roundabout) or the widening of an existing road by the construction of one or more additional traffic lanes

This enquiry refers to proposals by bodies or companies (such as private developers) other than the Council (and where appropriate the County Council) or the Secretary of State. A mini roundabout is a roundabout having a one-way circulatory carriageway around a flush or slightly raised circular marking less than 4 metres in diameter and with or without flared approaches.

PUBLIC PATHS OR BYWAYS

5.1.   Is any footpath, bridleway, restricted byway or byway open to all traffic which abuts on, or crosses the property, shown in a definitive map or revised definitive map prepared under Part IV of the National Parks and Access to the Countryside Act 1949 or Part III of the Wildlife and Countryside Act 1981?

5.2.   If so, please mark its approximate route on the attached plan.

ADVERTISEMENTS

Entries in the register

6.1.   Please list any entries in the register of applications, directions and decisions relating to consent for the display of advertisements.

6.2.   If there are any entries, where can that register be inspected?

Notices, proceedings and orders

6.3.   Except as shown in the official certificate of search:

   (a)   has any notice been given by the Secretary of State or served in respect of a direction or proposed direction restricting deemed consent for any class of advertisement

---

1.   © The Law Society 2007. Reproduced with the kind permission of Oyez Straker.

CON 290 Optional enquiries of local authority (2007)

A duplicate plan is required for all searches submitted directly to a local authority.
If submitted manually, this form must be submitted in duplicate. Please type or use BLOCK LETTERS

The Law Society

A.

Local authority name and address	Search No:...
	Signed:...
	On behalf of: Local authority/private search company/ member of the public (indicate as applicable)
	Dated:...

B.

Address of the land/property

UPRN(s):

Secondary name/number:

Primary name/number:

Street:

Locality/village:

Town:

Postcode:

C.

Optional enquiries (please tick as required)

☐ 4. Road proposals by private bodies

☐ 5. Public paths or byways

☐ 6. Advertisements

☐ 7. Completion notices

☐ 8. Parks and countryside

☐ 9. Pipelines

☐ 10. Houses in multiple occupation

☐ 11. Noise abatement

☐ 12. Urban development areas

☐ 13. Enterprise zones

☐ 14. Inner urban improvement areas

☐ 15. Simplified planning zones

☐ 16. Land maintenance notices

☐ 17. Mineral consultation areas

☐ 18. Hazardous substance consents

☐ 19. Environmental and pollution notices

☐ 20. Food safety notices

☐ 21. Hedgerow notices

☐ 22. Common land, town and village greens

D.

Fees

£_____ is enclosed/is paid by NLIS transfer (delete as applicable)

Signed:

Dated:

Reference:

Telephone No:

Fax No:

E-mail:

Notes

A. Enter name and address of appropriate Council. If the property is near a local authority boundary, consider raising certain enquiries (e.g. road schemes) with the adjoining Council.

B. Enter address and description of the property. Please give the UPRN(s) (Unique Property Reference Number) where known. **A duplicate plan is required for all searches submitted directly to a local authority.** The search may be returned if land/property cannot easily be identified.

C. Questions 1-3 appear on CON 290 Enquiries of local authority (2007).

D. Details of fees can be obtained from the Council, your chosen NLIS channel or search provider.

E. Enter the name and address/DX address of the person or company lodging or conducting this enquiry.

E.

Reply to

DX address:

Conveyancing 290 (Optional Enquiries)

(b) have the Council resolved to serve a notice requiring the display of any advertisement to be discontinued

(c) if a discontinuance notice has been served, has it been complied with to the satisfaction of the Council

(d) have the Council resolved to serve any other notice or proceedings relating to a contravention of the control of advertisements

(e) have the Council resolved to make an order for the special control of advertisements for the area

COMPLETION NOTICES

7.   Which of the planning permissions in force have the Council resolved to terminate by means of a completion notice under s.94 of the Town and Country Planning Act 1990?

PARKS AND COUNTRYSIDE

Areas of outstanding natural beauty

8.1.   Has any order under s.82 of the Countryside and Rights of Way Act 2000 been made?

National Parks

8.2.   Is the property within a National Park designated under s.7. of the National Parks and Access to the Countryside Act 1949?

PIPELINES

9.   Has a map been deposited under s.35 of the Pipelines Act 1962, or Schedule 7 of the Gas Act 1986, showing a pipeline laid through, or within 100 feet (30.48 metres) of the property?

HOUSES IN MULTIPLE OCCUPATION

10.   Is the property a house in multiple occupation, or is it designated or proposed to be designated for selective licensing of residential accommodation in accordance with the Housing Act 2004?

NOISE ABATEMENT

Noise abatement zone

11.1.   Have the Council made, or resolved to make, any noise abatement zone order under s.63 of the Control of Pollution Act 1974 for the area?

Entries in register

11.2.   Has any entry been recorded in the noise level register kept pursuant to s.64 of the Control of Pollution Act 1974?

11.3.   If there is any entry, how can copies be obtained and where can that register be inspected?

URBAN DEVELOPMENT AREAS

12.1. Is the area an urban development area designated under Part XVI of the Local Government, Planning and Land Act 1980?

12.2. If so, please state the name of the urban development corporation and the address of its principal office.

ENTERPRISE ZONES

13. Is the area an enterprise zone designated under Part XVIII of the Local Government, Planning and Land Act 1980?

INNER URBAN IMPROVEMENT AREAS

14. Have the Council resolved to define the area as an improvement area under s.4 of the Inner Urban Areas Act 1978?

SIMPLIFIED PLANNING ZONES

15.1. Is the area a simplified planning zone adopted or approved pursuant to s.83 of the Town and Country Planning Act 1990?

15.2. Have the Council approved any proposal for designating the area as a simplified planning zone?

LAND MAINTENANCE NOTICES

16. Have the Council authorised the service of a maintenance notice under s.215 of the Town and Country Planning Act 1990?

MINERAL CONSULTATION AREAS

17. Is the area a mineral consultation area notified by the county planning authority under Schedule 1 para 7 of the Town and Country Planning Act 1990?

HAZARDOUS SUBSTANCE CONSENTS

18.1. Please list any entries in the register kept pursuant to s.28 of the Planning (Hazardous Substances) Act 1990.

18.2. If there are any entries:

    (a) how can copies of the entries be obtained

    (b) where can the register be inspected

ENVIRONMENTAL AND POLLUTION NOTICES

19. What outstanding statutory or informal notices have been issued by the Council under the Environmental Protection Act 1990 or the Control of Pollution Act 1974? (This enquiry does not cover notices under Part IIA or Part III of the EPA, to which enquiries 3.12 or 3.7 apply.)

FOOD SAFETY NOTICES

20.   What outstanding statutory notices or informal notices have been issued by the Council under the Food Safety Act 1990 or the Food Hygiene Regulations 2006?

HEDGEROW NOTICES

21.1.   Please list any entries in the record maintained under regulation 10 of the Hedgerows Regulations 1997.

21.2.   If there are any entries:

   (a)   how can copies of the matters entered be obtained

   (b)   where can the record be inspected

COMMON LAND, TOWN AND VILLAGE GREENS

22.1.   Is the property, or any land which abuts the property, registered common land or town or village green under the Commons Registration Act 1965 or the Commons Act 2006?

22.2.   If there are any entries, how can copies of the matters registered be obtained and where can the register be inspected?

NOTES:

(1)   References to the provisions of particular Acts of Parliament or Regulations include any provisions which they have replaced and also include existing or future amendments or re-enactments.

(2)   The replies will be given in the belief that they are in accordance with information presently available to the officers of the replying Council, but none of the Councils or their officers accept legal responsibility for an incorrect reply, except for negligence. Any liability for negligence will extend to the person who raised the enquiries and the person on whose behalf they were raised. It will also extend to any other person who has knowledge (personally or through an agent) of the replies before the time when he purchases, takes a tenancy of, or lends money on the security of the property or (if earlier) the time when he becomes contractually bound to do so.

(3)   This form should be read in conjunction with the guidance notes available separately.

(4)   Area means any area in which the property is located.

(5)   References to the Council include any predecessor Council and also any council committee, sub-committee or other body or person exercising powers delegated by the Council and their approval includes their decision to proceed. The replies given to certain enquiries cover knowledge and actions of both the District Council and County Council.

(6)   Where relevant, the source department for copy documents should be provided.

III.3. CON 29DW Standard Drainage and Water Enquiries (2007)[1]

Public sewer map

1   Where relevant, please include a copy of an extract from the public sewer map.

Foul water

2   Does foul water from the property drain to a public sewer?

Surface water

3   Does surface water from the property drain to a public sewer?

Public adoption of sewers and lateral drains

4   Are any sewers or lateral drains serving or which are proposed to serve the property the subject of an existing adoption agreement or an application for such an agreement?

Public sewers within the boundaries of the property

5   Does the public sewer map indicate any public sewer, disposal main or lateral drain within the boundaries of the property?

Public sewers near to the property

6   Does the public sewer map indicate any public sewer within 30.48 metres (100 feet) of any buildings within the property?

Building over a public sewer, disposal main or drain

7   Has a sewerage undertaker approved or been consulted about any plans to erect a building or extension on the property over or in the vicinity of a public sewer, disposal main or drain?

Map of waterworks

8   Where relevant, please include a copy of an extract from the map of waterworks.

Adoption of water mains and service pipes

9   Is any water main or service pipe serving or which is proposed to serve the property the subject of an existing adoption agreement or an application for such an agreement?

Sewerage and water undertakers

10   Who are the sewerage and water undertakers for the area?

1. © The Law Society 2007.

CON 29DW Standard drainage and water enquiries (2007)

This search form must be submitted with the appropriate fee and a copy of the location plan.

A. Name and address of water company

(For use by water company only)

B. Address of the land/property

UPRN(s)

House name/number

Street

Locality

Town

County

Postcode

If the enquiries are made of a plot of land or of a property less than 5 years old:

Name of developer

Plot no.

Site name and phase

C. Your details

Signed ....

Name/contact name

Company name

Date

Your reference

Telephone

Fax

Email

Account no.

D. Fees

Search	Fee
CON 29DW Standard drainage and water enquiries 2007	
Total	

E. Reply to

DX

Notes

The standard drainage and water enquiries are listed on page 2 of this form. These enquiries comply with the Home Information Pack (No.2) Regulations 2007.

Completing and submitting this form to a water company indicates an acceptance of that water company's terms and conditions. Terms and conditions may vary between water companies. Request a copy of the terms and conditions from the water company or see its website for details.

A. Ensure that search forms are sent to the correct water company, see www.drainageandwater.co.uk for details.

B. Enter the address of the property. Please give the Unique Property Reference Number if known. If the enquiries are made of a plot of land or the property is less than 5 years old, please give the developer's details.

C. Sign, date and enter your details. Account customers of water companies may enter their account number.

D. Enter the fee for the enquiries. Fees may differ between water companies. Consult the water company or see www.drainageandwater.co.uk for the current fees.

E. Enter the name and address/DX address of the person or company conducting this enquiry.

Connection to mains water supply

11   Is the property connected to mains water supply?

Water mains, resource mains or discharge pipes

12   Are there any water mains, resource mains or discharge pipes within the boundaries of the property?

Current basis for sewerage and water charges

13   What is the current basis for charging for sewerage and water services at the property?

Charges following change of occupation

14   Will the basis for charging for sewerage and water services at the property change as a consequence of a change of occupation?

Surface water drainage charges

15   Is a surface water drainage charge payable?

Water meters

16   Please include details of the location of any water meter serving the property.

Sewerage bills

17   Who bills the property for sewerage services?

Water bills

18   Who bills the property for water services?

Risk of flooding due to overloaded public sewers

19   Is the dwelling-house which is or forms part of the property at risk of internal flooding due to overloaded public sewers?

Risk of low water pressure or flow

20   Is the property at risk of receiving low water pressure or flow?

Water quality analysis

21   Please include details of a water quality analysis made by the water undertaker for the water supply zone in respect of the most recent calendar year.

Authorised departures from water quality standards

22   Please include details of any departures –

   (a)   authorised by the Secretary of State under Part 6 of the 2000 Regulations from the provisions of Part 3 of those Regulations; or

   (b)   authorised by the National Assembly for Wales under Part 6 of the 2001 Regulations from the provisions of Part 3 of those Regulations.

Sewage treatment works

23   Please state the distance from the property to the nearest boundary of the nearest sewage treatment works.

NOTES

(i)   The terms used in these enquiries have the meaning given to them by the Home Information Pack (No.2) Regulations 2007, Sched.8, Part 1.

(ii)   The report prepared by a water company in response to these enquiries will include those enquiries and replies which are relevant to the property. The numbering and order of enquiries may differ between this form and a report.

III.4. CON 29M (2006) Coal Mining and Brine Subsidence Claim Search (including Guidance Notes)[1]

LAW SOCIETY GUIDANCE NOTES 2006

1. Introduction

1.1   A coal mining and brine subsidence claim search should be made by solicitors when acting on the occasion of any dealing with land in coal mining and brine subsidence claim areas ('affected areas'), including purchase, mortgage, further advance or before any development takes place.

1.2   For those solicitors not using the National Land Information Service (NLIS) or other electronic means, the enquiry should be made using form CON 29M which has been extended to include enquiries covering brine subsidence claims. This revised CON 29M (2006) is approved by the Law Society, the Coal Authority and the Cheshire Brine Subsidence Compensation Board ('the Brine Board'). The search should be made before the exchange of contracts or any binding obligation is entered into.

1.3   Whilst the Brine Board will retain control, liability and responsibility for the accuracy of the Brine data and be available to deal with any technical non-service related follow-up enquiries, the combined CON 29M coal and brine report service will be provided by the Coal Authority.

1.4   Where reports are provided by the Coal Authority on its own and on behalf of the Brine Board following a CON 29M search, there is no need for the applicant to supply evidence of the authority from the seller or seller's solicitor to the release of the information (if any) on the brine register. However, where a property is purchased that is subject of a pending brine claim, clients need to complete a notice of purchase. These are available from the Brine Board on 0845 002 0562.

1.5   Solicitors are recommended to submit a plan of the property with every postal search enquiry. Plans should be marked with the full boundary of the property and not just the property building footprint or other lesser area. Solicitors should retain a copy of the search form and plan.

1.6   These Guidance Notes should be read in conjunction with the Coal Authority and Brine Board's Terms and Conditions 2006 and User Guide 2006.

2. Preliminary enquiries

2.1   If the property is in an affected area (see User Guide 2006, paragraph 2), a solicitor should make a search on form CON 29M and raise an additional preliminary enquiry of the seller. The enquiry should ask whether during the ownership of the seller, or to the seller's knowledge his predecessors in title, the property has sustained subsidence damage related to coal mining or brine

---

1. © The Law Society 2006.

CON 29M (2006) COAL MINING AND BRINE SUBSIDENCE CLAIM SEARCH

A cheque with the appropriate fee MUST be sent with the printed form unless charged to an appropriate account. A location plan should be included with all search requests to avoid delay. Users should retain a copy of the form and the location plan.

	(For Coal Authority Use Only)
The Coal Authority Mining Reports 200 Lichfield Lane Mansfield Nottinghamshire NG18 4RG **DX 716176 MANSFIELD 5**	

Complete each applicable box below. Use type or BLOCK LETTERS.

	Notes
Reply to:	Enter the name, firm/organisation and DX number to which the report is to be returned. If you are not a member of the DX system please enter your name, firm/organisation and the full address, including postcode, to which the report is to be returned.
DX	
Email (if applicable):	Only insert your email address when you wish the report to be returned by email in a secure PDF file.
Telephone number:	Insert your telephone number so that the Authority may contact you if necessary regarding this search.
Account number (if applicable):	See the User Guide 2006
Report type requested (tick box): Residential Property Search Non-Residential Property or Site Search	Please tick the appropriate box and ensure that the correct fee is enclosed for the report type requested (see Notes overleaf). It is inappropriate to request a Residential Property Search for non-residential property or development sites and any such requests will be returned for resubmission and the correct fee. A Residential Property Search includes enquiries 1-12 overleaf. A Non-Residential or Site Search includes enquiries 1-15 overleaf.
Expedited Search required (delete as applicable): YES/NO	Expedited Search Reports can be ordered and returned by fax within 48 hours. The full fee, including the expedite element, is payable in advance (see Notes overleaf).
Fax number:	Only insert your fax number when you wish the report to be returned by fax or you are requesting an expedited search.
Request date:	Insert the date on which this search form is sent.
Address of the land/site/property:	The Address field may be used for house and flat names and numbers.
Address	Include the complete address if possible.
Street	Always include the postcode where the property has a postal address.
Locality	
Town/Village	Where the land, site or property does not have a postal address, use any fields provided to include a description sufficient for the property to be identified.
County	
Postcode	
Location plan enclosed (delete as applicable): YES/NO	Searches may be returned unanswered or delayed if a plan is not enclosed (see Notes overleaf).
Customer reference:	Insert your own file reference number.

TERMS AND CONDITIONS – These enquiries are made and the replies prepared in accordance with the Coal Authority's and the Cheshire Brine Subsidence Compensation Board's Terms and Conditions 2006, User Guide 2006 and Law Society's Guidance Notes 2006. These are available to view at www.miningreports.co.uk or by contacting the Coal Authority's Mining Reports Helpline on 0845 762 6848 or by email to miningreports@coal.gov.uk. These terms and conditions apply regardless of the method used to order and receive reports.

CON 29M (2006) COAL MINING AND BRINE SUBSIDENCE CLAIM SEARCH

RESIDENTIAL PROPERTY SEARCH ENQUIRIES

1. Past underground coal mining

Is the property within the zone of likely physical influence on the surface of past underground coal workings? If yes, indicate the number of seams involved, their depth and approximate last date of working.

For the purpose of this enquiry "zone of likely physical influence" will be based on the principle of 0.7 times the depth of the working allowing for seam inclination.

2. Present underground coal mining

Is the property within the zone of likely physical influence on the surface of present underground coal workings? If yes, indicate the seams involved.

3. Future underground coal mining

(a) Is the property within any geographical area for which the Coal Authority is determining whether to grant a licence to remove coal by underground methods?

(b) Is the property within any geographical area for which a licence to remove coal by underground methods has been granted? If yes, when was the licence granted?

(c) Is the property within the zone of likely physical influence on the surface of planned future underground coal workings? If yes, indicate the seams involved and approximate date of working.

(d) Has any notice of proposals relating to underground coal mining operations been given under section 46 of the Coal Mining Subsidence Act 1991? If yes, supply the date and details of that such notice.

For the purpose of this enquiry "geographical area" means the surface area directly above a licence being determined or granted.

4. Shafts and adits (mine entries)

Are there any shafts and adits or other entries to underground coal mine workings within the property or within 20 metres of the boundary of the property? If yes, supply a plan showing the approximate recorded location and any relevant information, where available, regarding any treatment carried out to such shafts, adits or entries.

5. Coal mining geology

Is there any record of any fault or other line of weakness due to coal mining at the surface within the boundary of the property that has made the property unstable?

6. Past opencast coal mining

Is the property situated within the geographical boundary of an opencast site from which coal has been removed in the past by opencast methods?

7. Present opencast coal mining

Is the property within 200 metres of the boundary of an opencast site from which coal is being removed by opencast methods?

8. Future opencast coal mining

(a) Is the property within 800 metres of the boundary of an opencast site for which the Coal Authority are determining whether to grant a licence to remove coal by opencast methods?

(b) Is the property within 800 metres of the boundary of an opencast site for which a licence to remove coal by opencast methods has been granted? If yes, when was the licence granted?

9. Coal mining subsidence claims

(a) Has any damage notice or claim for alleged coal mining subsidence damage to the property been given, made or pursued since 1 January 1984? If yes, supply the date of such notice or claim.

(b) In respect of any such notice or claim has the responsible person given notice agreeing that there is a remedial obligation or otherwise accepted that a claim would lie against him?

(c) In respect of any such notice or acceptance has the remedial obligation or claim been discharged? If yes, state whether such remedial obligation or claim was discharged by repair or payment, or a combination thereof.

(d) Does any current "Stop Notice" delaying the start of remedial works or repairs affect the property? If yes, supply the date of the notice.

(e) Has any request been made under section 33 of the 1991 Act to execute preventive works before coal is worked, which would prevent the occurrence or reduce the extent of subsidence damage to any buildings, structures or works? If yes, has any person withheld consent or failed to comply with any such request to execute preventive works?

10. Mine gas emissions

Does the Coal Authority have record of any mine gas emission within the boundary of the property being reported that subsequently required action by the Authority to mitigate the effects of the mine gas emission?

11. Emergency Surface Hazard Call Out incidents

Have the Coal Authority carried out any work on or within the boundaries of the property following a report of an alleged hazard related to coal mining under the Authority's Emergency Surface Hazard Call Out procedures?

12. Cheshire brine subsidence compensation claims

(a) Is the property situated within the Cheshire Brine Compensation District prescribed by the Cheshire Brine Pumping (Compensation for Subsidence) Act 1952?

(b) If yes, is the property situated within a Consultation Area prescribed by the Cheshire Brine Board under the provisions of section 38(1) of the 1952 Act?

(c) Has a Notice of Damage been filed in respect of the property? If yes, was the claim accepted and how was the claim discharged?

(d) Have any claims in respect of the property been commuted by a once and for all payment of compensation?

(e) Would the compensation provisions of the Cheshire Brine Pumping (Compensation for Subsidence) Acts of 1952 and 1964 apply should the property be affected at some future date by subsidence due to brine pumping?

ADDITIONAL ENQUIRIES FOR NON-RESIDENTIAL PROPERTY OR SITE SEARCH IN COAL MINING AREAS

13. Withdrawal of support

(a) Does the land lie within a geographical area in respect of which a notice of entitlement to withdraw support has been published? If yes, supply the date of the notice.

(b) Does the land lie within a geographical area in respect of which a revocation notice has been given under section 41 of the Coal Industry Act 1994? If yes, supply the date of the notice.

14. Working facilities orders

Is the property within a geographical area subject to an order in respect of the working of coal under the Mines (Working Facilities and Support) Acts of 1923 and 1966 or any statutory modification or amendment thereof? If yes, supply the date and title of the order.

15. Payments to owners of former copyhold land

(a) Has any relevant notice, which may affect the property, been given?

(b) If yes, has any notice of retained interests in coal and coal mines been given?

(c) If yes, has any acceptance notice or rejection notice been served?

(d) If any such acceptance notice has been served, has any compensation been paid to a claimant?

NOTES

(A) Advice and information on coal mining and brine subsidence searches

For information on procedure, turnaround and current fees, account facilities or further to a specific search, contact the Coal Authority Mining Reports Helpline on 0845 762 6848 or by email to miningreports@coal.gov.uk or visit www.miningreports.co.uk There is a higher fee for the Non-Residential Property or Site Search and an additional fee for Expedited Searches. Searches having incorrect fees will be returned uncompleted.

(B) Refunds

No refund or transfer of any fee (or part of a fee) will be made once a search has been logged onto the Authority's MRSDS computer systems for report production.

(C) Expedited searches

Select 'YES' against Expedited Search and add your fax number in full. This service is only available to credit account customers or where the full fee, including the expedite element, is paid in advance by credit/debit card (over the telephone 0845 762 6848) or by cheque (postal enquiries).

(D) Affected areas

A directory of places where a CON 29M (2006) search is required can be found on the Authority's website at www.miningreports.co.uk together with a useful search by postcode facility.

(E) Ordering CON 29M reports

Reports can be ordered by telephone, and ordered and returned by post, fax or electronically via the internet and email (www.miningreports.co.uk). A fully electronic link to the National Land Information Service (NLIS) provides a further channel for customers to order and receive searches.

(F) Terms and Conditions, User Guide and Law Society's Guidance

These Notes should be read in conjunction with the Coal Authority's and the Cheshire Brine Board's Terms and Conditions 2006, User Guide 2006, and the Law Society's Guidance Notes 2006, under which all replies to these enquiries are made. These terms apply regardless of the method used to order and receive reports. The Terms and Conditions and User Guide have been approved by the Law Society following consultation with key stakeholders including the CML and RICS, and apply to all searches made including those using the CON 29M search form. Copies of these documents can be found on the Coal Authority's website at www.miningreports.co.uk

(G) Plans

If a plan is not submitted there may be difficulties and delays in identifying the property and its extent, in which case the Coal Authority may request that a plan be supplied before the search can be completed.

© The Law Society 2006

pumping and if so how any claim was resolved (by repair or payment in respect of the cost of remedial, merged or redevelopment works or otherwise).

2.2   If the report discloses a current 'Stop Notice' concerning the deferment of remedial works or repairs affecting the property, or the withholding of consent to a request for preventive works affecting the property, it is recommended that a solicitor should ask preliminary enquiries of the seller as to the present position.

3.   Reproduction of forms

3.1   Copyright in the form CON 29M and enquiries belong to the Law Society, which has granted to solicitors a non-exclusive licence to reproduce them. Any such form must follow precisely and in all respects the printed version.

3.2   The Coal Authority (as operator of the service) will reject any reproduction of the CON 29M enquiry form which does not comply with these requirements.

4.   Mining surveys and site investigation

4.1   Disclosure of a disused mine shaft or mine adit in a report, the existence of recorded shallow coal workings or possible unrecorded coal workings reported as believed to be at or close to the surface (such that future ground movement may still subsequently occur) and/or any other coal mining related hazard identified within the report, should be brought to the attention of the client. If further information or advice is required in addition to that available from the Coal Authority (e.g. further to that contained within a Coal Authority Interpretive Report, see paragraph 19 of the User Guide 2006), then solicitors should in these circumstances explain to clients that there are experienced mining surveyors and structural engineers able to advise as to what further enquiries, surveys or investigation should be made.

4.2   If a lender is involved in the transaction, solicitors should establish that the surveyor or engineer selected is acceptable to the lender and make arrangements to provide a copy of the search to them.

4.3   In most cases, but not all, the Coal Authority and not the adjacent surface landowner will own any coal shaft or adit. Clients should be advised accordingly and reminded that in these cases the permission of the Coal Authority must be sought before carrying out any works to locate, treat or in any other way interfere with former coal workings including disused coal mine shafts or adits.

5.   Dealing with lenders

5.1   If domestic property which is the subject of a CON 29M search is to be charged as security for a loan, a copy of the report should be sent to the lender as soon as received. Whether or not this is appropriate depends on the result of the search and the lender's instructions. The solicitor should not comment substantively on the replies within the report but should recommend that they be referred to the lender's valuer for review and information.

5.2   Provided that a copy of the mining report has been so provided, solicitors are not obliged to make any other reference to the replies in any report on title to a lender save to refer to the existence of the CON 29M search and the report.

5.3   With regard to non-domestic property a similar procedure should be adopted. Solicitors should, however, refer to the replies to the additional enquiries included in the mining reports for non-residential, commercial or development sites as these deal with legal matters (namely the withdrawal of support, the existence of working facilities orders and payments to owners of former copyhold land).

5.4   When also acting for the lender it is suggested that solicitors should, in all cases, check whether the instructions from that lender require the solicitor to deal with the replies to the CON 29M report in any other manner. If so, it is suggested that the solicitor should explain to the lender the basis upon which the solicitor is recommended by these paragraphs to proceed. It is important that solicitors should not attempt to perform the function of the client's valuer or surveyor with regard to the replies to the CON 29M report.

6.   Implementation of Form CON 29M (2006)

6.1   Form CON 29M (2006) will be available from 31 October 2006. The Coal Authority will continue to accept the 2003 form until 31 December 2006.

6.2   From 31 October 2006, all CON 29M reports requested from the Coal Authority will be prepared in accordance with the Law Society's Guidance Notes 2006, the User Guide 2006 and the Coal Authority's and the Brine Board's Terms and Conditions 2006.

III.5. Standard Conditions of Sale (fourth edition) (including Explanatory Notes)[1]

CONTRACT

(Incorporating the Standard Conditions of Sale (Fourth Edition))

Date	:
Seller	:
Buyer	:
Property (freehold/leasehold)	:
Title Number/root of title	:
Specified incumbrances	:
Title guarantee (full/limited)	:
Completion date	:
Contract rate	:
Purchase price	:
Deposit	:
Chattels price (if separate)	:
Balance	:

The seller will sell and the buyer will buy the property for the purchase price.

WARNING	**Signed**
This is a formal document, designed to create legal rights and legal obligations. Take advice before using it.	Seller/Buyer

1. © Oyez (The Solicitors' Law Stationery Society Ltd) and the Law Society 2003.

STANDARD CONDITIONS OF SALE (FOURTH EDITION)
(NATIONAL CONDITIONS OF SALE 24TH EDITION, LAW SOCIETY'S CONDI-
TIONS OF SALE 2003)

1 GENERAL

1.1 Definitions

1.1.1   In these conditions:

(a)   'accrued interest' means:

    (i)   if money has been placed on deposit or in a building society share account, the interest actually earned

    (ii)   otherwise, the interest which might reasonably have been earned by depositing the money at interest on seven days' notice of withdrawal with a clearing bank

less, in either case, any proper charges for handling the money

(b)   'chattels price' means any separate amount payable for chattels included in the contract

(c)   'clearing bank' means a bank which is a shareholder in CHAPS Clearing Co. Limited

(d)   'completion date' has the meaning given in condition 6.1.1

(e)   'contract rate' means the Law Society's interest rate from time to time in force

(f)   'conveyancer' means a solicitor, barrister, duly certified notary public, licensed conveyancer or recognised body under sections 9 or 23 of the Administration of Justice Act 1985

(g)   'direct credit' means a direct transfer of cleared funds to an account nominated by the seller's conveyancer and maintained by a clearing bank

(h)   'lease' includes sub-lease, tenancy and agreement for a lease or sub-lease

(i)   'notice to complete' means a notice requiring completion of the contract in accordance with condition 6

(j)   'public requirement' means any notice, order or proposal given or made (whether before or after the date of the contract) by a body acting on statutory authority

(k)   'requisition' includes objection

(l)   'transfer' includes conveyance and assignment

(m)   'working day' means any day from Monday to Friday (inclusive) which is not Christmas Day, Good Friday or a statutory Bank Holiday.

1.1.2   In these conditions the terms 'absolute title' and 'official copies' have the special meanings given to them by the Land Registration Act 2002.

1.1.3   A party is ready, able and willing to complete:

(a)   if he could be, but for the default of the other party, and

(b)   in the case of the seller, even though the property remains subject to a mortgage, if the amount to be paid on completion enables the property to be transferred freed of all mortgages (except any to which the sale is expressly subject).

1.1.4   These conditions apply except as varied or excluded by the contract.

1.2 Joint parties

If there is more than one seller or more than one buyer, the obligations which they undertake can be enforced against them all jointly or against each individually.

1.3 Notices and documents

1.3.1 A notice required or authorised by the contract must be in writing.

1.3.2 Giving a notice or delivering a document to a party's conveyancer has the same effect as giving or delivering it to that party.

1.3.3 Where delivery of the original document is not essential, a notice or document is validly given or sent if it is sent:

(a) by fax, or

(b) by e-mail to an e-mail address for the intended recipient given in the contract.

1.3.4 Subject to conditions 1.3.5 to 1.3.7, a notice is given and a document is delivered when it is received.

1.3.5 (a) A notice or document sent through a document exchange is received when it is available for collection

(b) A notice or document which is received after 4.00 pm on a working day, or on a day which is not a working day, is to be treated as having been received on the next working day

(c) An automated response to a notice or document sent by e-mail that the intended recipient is out of the office is to be treated as proof that the notice or document was not received.

1.3.6 Condition 1.3.7 applies unless there is proof:

(a) that a notice or document has not been received, or

(b) of when it was received.

1.3.7 A notice or document sent by the following means is treated as having been received as follows:

(a) by first-class post: before 4.00 pm on the second working day after posting

(b) by second-class post: before 4.00 pm on the third working day after posting

(c) through a document exchange: before 4.00 pm on the first working day after the day on which it would normally be available for collection by the addressee

(d) by fax: one hour after despatch

(e) by e-mail: before 4.00 pm on the first working day after despatch.

1.4 VAT

1.4.1 An obligation to pay money includes an obligation to pay any value added tax chargeable in respect of that payment.

1.4.2 All sums made payable by the contract are exclusive of value added tax.

1.5   Assignment

The buyer is not entitled to transfer the benefit of the contract.

2   FORMATION

2.1   Date

2.1.1   If the parties intend to make a contract by exchanging duplicate copies by post or through a document exchange, the contract is made when the last copy is posted or deposited at the document exchange.

2.1.2   If the parties' conveyancers agree to treat exchange as taking place before duplicate copies are actually exchanged, the contract is made as so agreed.

2.2   Deposit

2.2.1   The buyer is to pay or send a deposit of 10 per cent of the total of the purchase price and the chattels price no later than the date of the contract.

2.2.2   If a cheque tendered in payment of all or part of the deposit is dishonoured when first presented, the seller may, within seven working days of being notified that the cheque has been dishonoured, give notice to the buyer that the contract is discharged by the buyer's breach.

2.2.3   Conditions 2.2.4 to 2.2.6 do not apply on a sale by auction.

2.2.4   The deposit is to be paid by direct credit or to the seller's conveyancer by a cheque drawn on a solicitor's or licensed conveyancer's client account.

2.2.5   If before completion date the seller agrees to buy another property in England and Wales for his residence, he may use all or any part of the deposit as a deposit in that transaction to be held on terms to the same effect as this condition and condition 2.2.6.

2.2.6   Any deposit or part of a deposit not being used in accordance with condition 2.2.5 is to be held by the seller's conveyancer as stakeholder on terms that on completion it is paid to the seller with accrued interest.

2.3   Auctions

2.3.1   On a sale by auction the following conditions apply to the property and, if it is sold in lots, to each lot.

2.3.2   The sale is subject to a reserve price.

2.3.3   The seller, or a person on his behalf, may bid up to the reserve price.

2.3.4   The auctioneer may refuse any bid.

2.3.5   If there is a dispute about a bid, the auctioneer may resolve the dispute or restart the auction at the last undisputed bid.

2.3.6   The deposit is to be paid to the auctioneer as agent for the seller.

3   MATTERS AFFECTING THE PROPERTY

3.1   Freedom from incumbrances

3.1.1   The seller is selling the property free from incumbrances, other than those mentioned in condition 3.1.2.

3.1.2   The incumbrances subject to which the property is sold are:

(a)   those specified in the contract

(b)   those discoverable by inspection of the property before the contract

(c)   those the seller does not and could not reasonably know about

(d)   entries made before the date of the contract in any public register except those maintained by the Land Registry or its Land Charges Department or by Companies House

(e)   public requirements.

3.1.3   After the contract is made, the seller is to give the buyer written details without delay of any new public requirement and of anything in writing which he learns about concerning a matter covered by condition 3.1.2.

3.1.4   The buyer is to bear the cost of complying with any outstanding public requirement and is to indemnify the seller against any liability resulting from a public requirement.

3.2   Physical state

3.2.1   The buyer accepts the property in the physical state it is in at the date of the contract unless the seller is building or converting it.

3.2.2   A leasehold property is sold subject to any subsisting breach of a condition or tenant's obligation relating to the physical state of the property which renders the lease liable to forfeiture.

3.2.3   A sub-lease is granted subject to any subsisting breach of a condition or tenant's obligation relating to the physical state of the property which renders the seller's own lease liable to forfeiture.

3.3   Leases affecting the property

3.3.1   The following provisions apply if any part of the property is sold subject to a lease.

3.3.2   (a)   The seller having provided the buyer with full details of each lease or copies of the documents embodying the lease terms, the buyer is treated as entering into the contract knowing and fully accepting those terms.

(b)   The seller is to inform the buyer without delay if the lease ends or if the seller learns of any application by the tenant in connection with the lease; the seller is then to act as the buyer reasonably directs, and the buyer is to indemnify him against all consequent loss and expense.

(c)   Except with the buyer's consent, the seller is not to agree to any proposal to change the lease terms nor to take any step to end the lease.

(d)   The seller is to inform the buyer without delay of any change to the lease terms which may be proposed or agreed.

(e) The buyer is to indemnify the seller against all claims arising from the lease after actual completion; this includes claims which are unenforceable against a buyer for want of registration.

(f) The seller takes no responsibility for what rent is lawfully recoverable, nor for whether or how any legislation affects the lease.

(g) If the let land is not wholly within the property, the seller may apportion the rent.

3.4 Retained land

Where after the transfer the seller will be retaining land near the property:

(a) the buyer will have no right of light or air over the retained land, but

(b) in other respects the seller and the buyer will each have the rights over the land of the other which they would have had if they were two separate buyers to whom the seller had made simultaneous transfers of the property and the retained land.

The transfer is to contain appropriate express terms.

4. TITLE AND TRANSFER

4.1 Proof of title

4.1.1 Without cost to the buyer, the seller is to provide the buyer with proof of the title to the property and of his ability to transfer it, or to procure its transfer.

4.1.2 Where the property has a registered title the proof is to include official copies of the items referred to in rules 134(1)(a) and (b) and 135(1)(a) of the Land Registration Rules 2003, so far as they are not to be discharged or overridden at or before completion.

4.1.3 Where the property has an unregistered title, the proof is to include:

(a) an abstract of title or an epitome of title with photocopies of the documents, and

(b) production of every document or an abstract, epitome or copy of it with an original marking by a conveyancer either against the original or an examined abstract or an examined copy.

4.2 Requisitions

4.2.1 The buyer may not raise requisitions:

(a) on the title shown by the seller taking the steps described in condition 4.1.1 before the contract was made

(b) in relation to the matters covered by condition 3.1.2.

4.2.2 Notwithstanding condition 4.2.1, the buyer may, within six working days of a matter coming to his attention after the contract was made, raise written requisitions on that matter. In that event, steps 3 and 4 in condition 4.3.1 apply.

4.2.3 On the expiry of the relevant time limit under condition 4.2.2 or condition 4.3.1, the buyer loses his right to raise requisitions or to make observations.

4.3   Timetable

4.3.1   Subject to condition 4.2 and to the extent that the seller did not take the steps described in condition 4.1.1 before the contract was made, the following are the steps for deducing and investigating the title to the property to be taken within the following time limits:

Step		Time limit
1.	The seller is to comply with condition 4.1.1	Immediately after making the contract
2.	The buyer may raise written requisitions	Six working days after either the date of the contract or the date of delivery of the seller's evidence of title on which the requisitions are raised whichever is the later
3.	The seller is to reply in writing to any requisitions raised	Four working days after receiving the requisitions
4.	The buyer may make written observations on the seller's replies	Three working days after receiving the replies

The time limit on the buyer's right to raise requisitions applies even where the seller supplies incomplete evidence of his title, but the buyer may, within six working days from delivery of any further evidence, raise further requisitions resulting from that evidence.

4.3.2   The parties are to take the following steps to prepare and agree the transfer of the property within the following time limits:

Step		Time limit
A.	The buyer is to send the seller a draft transfer	At least twelve working days before completion date
B.	The seller is to approve or revise that draft and either return it or retain it for use as the actual transfer	Four working days after delivery of the draft transfer
C.	If the draft is returned the buyer is to send an engrossment to the seller	At least five working days before completion date

4.3.3   Periods of time under conditions 4.3.1 and 4.3.2 may run concurrently.

4.3.4   If the period between the date of the contract and completion date is less than 15 working days, the time limits in conditions 4.2.2, 4.3.1 and 4.3.2 are to be reduced by the same proportion as that period bears to the period of 15 working days. Fractions of a working day are to be rounded down except that the time limit to perform any step is not to be less than one working day.

4.4   Defining the property

4.4.1   The seller need not:

    (a)   prove the exact boundaries of the property

    (b)   prove who owns fences, ditches, hedges or walls

    (c)   separately identify parts of the property with different titles further than he may be able to do from information in his possession.

4.4.2   The buyer may, if it is reasonable, require the seller to make or obtain, pay for and hand over a statutory declaration about facts relevant to the matters mentioned in condition 4.4.1. The form of the declaration is to be agreed by the buyer, who must not unreasonably withhold his agreement.

4.5   Rents and rentcharges

The fact that a rent or rentcharge, whether payable or receivable by the owner of the property, has been, or will on completion be, informally apportioned is not to be regarded as a defect in title.

4.6   Transfer

4.6.1   The buyer does not prejudice his right to raise requisitions, or to require replies to any raised, by taking any steps in relation to preparing or agreeing the transfer.

4.6.2.   Subject to condition 4.6.3, the seller is to transfer the property with full title guarantee.

4.6.3   The transfer is to have effect as if the disposition is expressly made subject to all matters covered by condition 3.1.2.

4.6.4   If after completion the seller will remain bound by any obligation affecting the property which was disclosed to the buyer before the contract was made, but the law does not imply any covenant by the buyer to indemnify the seller against liability for future breaches of it:

(a)   the buyer is to covenant in the transfer to indemnify the seller against liability for any future breach of the obligation and to perform it from then on, and

(b)   if required by the seller, the buyer is to execute and deliver to the seller on completion a duplicate transfer prepared by the buyer.

4.6.5   The seller is to arrange at his expense that, in relation to every document of title which the buyer does not receive on completion, the buyer is to have the benefit of:

(a)   a written acknowledgement of his right to its production, and

(b)   a written undertaking for its safe custody (except while it is held by a mortgagee or by someone in a fiduciary capacity).

5   PENDING COMPLETION

5.1   Responsibility for property

5.1.1   The seller will transfer the property in the same physical state as it was at the date of the contract (except for fair wear and tear), which means that the seller retains the risk until completion.

5.1.2   If at any time before completion the physical state of the property makes it unusable for its purpose at the date of the contract:

(a)   the buyer may rescind the contract

(b)   the seller may rescind the contract where the property has become unusable for that purpose as a result of damage against which the seller could not reasonably have insured, or which it is not legally possible for the seller to make good.

5.1.3   The seller is under no obligation to the buyer to insure the property.

5.1.4   Section 47 of the Law of Property Act 1925 does not apply.

5.2   Occupation by buyer

5.2.1.   If the buyer is not already lawfully in the property, and the seller agrees to let him into occupation, the buyer occupies on the following terms.

5.2.2.   The buyer is a licensee and not a tenant. The terms of the licence are that the buyer:

    (a)   cannot transfer it

    (b)   may permit members of his household to occupy the property

    (c)   is to pay or indemnify the seller against all outgoings and other expenses in respect of the property

    (d)   is to pay the seller a fee calculated at the contract rate on a sum equal to the purchase price and the chattels price (less any deposit paid) for the period of the licence

    (e)   is entitled to any rents and profits from any part of the property which he does not occupy

    (f)   is to keep the property in as good a state of repair as it was in when he went into occupation (except for fair wear and tear) and is not to alter it

    (g)   is to insure the property in a sum which is not less than the purchase price against all risks in respect of which comparable premises are normally insured

    (h)   is to quit the property when the licence ends.

5.2.3   On the creation of the buyer's licence, condition 5.1 ceases to apply, which means that the buyer then assumes the risk until completion.

5.2.4   The buyer is not in occupation for the purposes of this condition if he merely exercises rights of access given solely to do work agreed by the seller.

5.2.5   The buyer's licence ends on the earliest of: completion date, rescission of the contract or when five working days' notice given by one party to the other takes effect.

5.2.6   If the buyer is in occupation of the property after his licence has come to an end and the contract is subsequently completed he is to pay the seller compensation for his continued occupation calculated at the same rate as the fee mentioned in condition 5.2.2(d).

5.2.7   The buyer's right to raise requisitions is unaffected.

6. COMPLETION

6.1   Date

6.1.1   Completion date is twenty working days after the date of the contract but time is not of the essence of the contract unless a notice to complete has been served.

6.1.2   If the money due on completion is received after 2.00 pm, completion is to be treated, for the purposes only of conditions 6.3 and 7.3, as taking place on the next working day as a result of the buyer's default.

6.1.3   Condition 6.1.2 does not apply and the seller is treated as in default if:

    (i)   the sale is with vacant possession of the property or any part of it, and

(ii) the buyer is ready, able and willing to complete but does not pay the money due on completion until after 2.00 pm because the seller has not vacated the property or that part by that time.

6.2 Arrangements and place

6.2.1 The buyer's conveyancer and the seller's conveyancer are to co-operate in agreeing arrangements for completing the contract.

6.2.2 Completion is to take place in England and Wales, either at the seller's conveyancer's office or at some other place which the seller reasonably specifies.

6.3 Apportionments

6.3.1 Income and outgoings of the property are to be apportioned between the parties so far as the change of ownership on completion will affect entitlement to receive or liability to pay them.

6.3.2 If the whole property is sold with vacant possession or the seller exercises his option in condition 7.3.4, apportionment is to be made with effect from the date of actual completion; otherwise, it is to be made from completion date.

6.3.3 In apportioning any sum, it is to be assumed that the seller owns the property until the end of the day from which apportionment is made and that the sum accrues from day to day at the rate at which it is payable on that day.

6.3.4 For the purpose of apportioning income and outgoings, it is to be assumed that they accrue at an equal daily rate throughout the year.

6.3.5 When a sum to be apportioned is not known or easily ascertainable at completion, a provisional apportionment is to be made according to the best estimate available. As soon as the amount is known, a final apportionment is to be made and notified to the other party. Any resulting balance is to be paid no more than ten working days later, and if not then paid the balance is to bear interest at the contract rate from then until payment.

6.3.6 Compensation payable under condition 5.2.6 is not to be apportioned.

6.4 Amount payable

The amount payable by the buyer on completion is the purchase price and the chattels price (less any deposit already paid to the seller or his agent) adjusted to take account of:

(a) apportionments made under condition 6.3

(b) any compensation to be paid or allowed under condition 7.3.

6.5 Title deeds

6.5.1 As soon as the buyer has complied with all his obligations on completion the seller must hand over the documents of title.

6.5.2 Condition 6.5.1 does not apply to any documents of title relating to land being retained by the seller after completion.

6.6 Rent receipts

The buyer is to assume that whoever gave any receipt for a payment of rent or service charge which the seller produces was the person or the agent of the person then entitled to that rent or service charge.

6.7 Means of payment

The buyer is to pay the money due on completion by direct credit and, if appropriate, an unconditional release of a deposit held by a stakeholder.

6.8 Notice to complete

6.8.1   At any time on or after completion date, a party who is ready, able and willing to complete may give the other a notice to complete.

6.8.2   The parties are to complete the contract within ten working days of giving a notice to complete, excluding the day on which the notice is given. For this purpose, time is of the essence of the contract.

6.8.3   On receipt of a notice to complete:

    (a)   if the buyer paid no deposit, he is forthwith to pay a deposit of 10 per cent

    (b)   if the buyer paid a deposit of less than 10 per cent, he is forthwith to pay a further deposit equal to the balance of that 10 per cent.

7. REMEDIES

7.1 Errors and omissions

7.1.1   If any plan or statement in the contract, or in the negotiations leading to it, is or was misleading or inaccurate due to an error or omission, the remedies available are as follows.

7.1.2   When there is a material difference between the description or value of the property, or of any of the chattels included in the contract, as represented and as it is, the buyer is entitled to damages.

7.1.3   An error or omission only entitles the buyer to rescind the contract:

    (a)   where it results from fraud or recklessness, or

    (b)   where he would be obliged, to his prejudice, to accept property differing substantially (in quantity, quality or tenure) from what the error or omission had led him to expect.

7.2 Rescission

If either party rescinds the contract:

    (a)   unless the rescission is a result of the buyer's breach of contract the deposit is to be repaid to the buyer with accrued interest

    (b)   the buyer is to return any documents he received from the seller and is to cancel any registration of the contract.

7.3 Late completion

7.3.1 If there is default by either or both of the parties in performing their obligations under the contract and completion is delayed, the party whose total period of default is the greater is to pay compensation to the other party.

7.3.2 Compensation is calculated at the contract rate on an amount equal to the purchase price and the chattels price, less (where the buyer is the paying party) any deposit paid, for the period by which the paying party's default exceeds that of the receiving party, or, if shorter, the period between completion date and actual completion.

7.3.3 Any claim for loss resulting from delayed completion is to be reduced by any compensation paid under this contract.

7.3.4 Where the buyer holds the property as tenant of the seller and completion is delayed, the seller may give notice to the buyer, before the date of actual completion, that he intends to take the net income from the property until completion. If he does so, he cannot claim compensation under condition 7.3.1 as well.

7.4 After completion

Completion does not cancel liability to perform any outstanding obligation under this contract.

7.5 Buyer's failure to comply with notice to complete

7.5.1 If the buyer fails to complete in accordance with a notice to complete, the following terms apply.

7.5.2 The seller may rescind the contract, and if he does so:

    (a) he may

        (i) forfeit and keep any deposit and accrued interest

        (ii) resell the property and any chattels included in the contract

        (iii) claim damages

    (b) the buyer is to return any documents he received from the seller and is to cancel any registration of the contract.

7.5.3 The seller retains his other rights and remedies.

7.6 Seller's failure to comply with notice to complete

7.6.1 If the seller fails to complete in accordance with a notice to complete, the following terms apply.

7.6.2 The buyer may rescind the contract, and if he does so:

    (a) the deposit is to be repaid to the buyer with accrued interest

    (b) the buyer is to return any documents he received from the seller and is, at the seller's expense, to cancel any registration of the contract.

7.6.3 The buyer retains his other rights and remedies.

8   LEASEHOLD PROPERTY

8.1   Existing leases

8.1.1   The following provisions apply to a sale of leasehold land.

8.1.2   The seller having provided the buyer with copies of the documents embodying the lease terms, the buyer is treated as entering into the contract knowing and fully accepting those terms.

8.1.3.   The seller is to comply with any lease obligations requiring the tenant to insure the property.

8.2   New leases

8.2.1   The following provisions apply to a contract to grant a new lease.

8.2.2   The conditions apply so that:

> 'seller' means the proposed landlord
>
> 'buyer' means the proposed tenant
>
> 'purchase price' means the premium to be paid on the grant of a lease.

8.2.3   The lease is to be in the form of the draft attached to the contract.

8.2.4   If the term of the new lease will exceed seven years, the seller is to deduce a title which will enable the buyer to register the lease at the Land Registry with an absolute title.

8.2.5   The seller is to engross the lease and a counterpart of it and is to send the counterpart to the buyer at least five working days before completion date.

8.2.6   The buyer is to execute the counterpart and deliver it to the seller on completion.

8.3   Consent

8.3.1   (a)   The following provisions apply if a consent to let, assign or sub-let is required to complete the contract

   (b)   In this condition 'consent' means consent in the form which satisfies the requirement to obtain it.

8.3.2   (a)   The seller is to apply for the consent at his expense, and to use all reasonable efforts to obtain it

   (b)   The buyer is to provide all information and references reasonably required.

8.3.3   Unless he is in breach of his obligation under condition 8.3.2, either party may rescind the contract by notice to the other party if three working days before completion date (or before a later date on which the parties have agreed to complete the contract):

   (a)   the consent has not been given, or

   (b)   the consent has been given subject to a condition to which a party reasonably objects. In that case, neither party is to be treated as in breach of contract and condition 7.2 applies.

9. COMMONHOLD LAND

9.1   Terms used in this condition have the special meanings given to them in Part 1 of the Commonhold and Leasehold Reform Act 2002.

9.2   This condition applies to a disposition of commonhold land.

9.3   The seller having provided the buyer with copies of the current versions of the memorandum and articles of the commonhold association and of the commonhold community statement, the buyer is treated as entering into the contract knowing and fully accepting their terms.

9.4   If the contract is for the sale of property which is or includes part only of a commonhold unit:

    (a)   the seller is to apply for the written consent of the commonhold association at his expense and is to use all reasonable efforts to obtain it

    (b)   either the seller, unless he is in breach of his obligation under paragraph (a), or the buyer may rescind the contract by notice to the other party if three working days before completion date (or before a later date on which the parties have agreed to complete the contract) the consent has not been given.

In that case, neither party is to be treated as in breach of contract and condition 7.2 applies.

10. CHATTELS

10.1   The following provisions apply to any chattels which are included in the contract, whether or not a separate price is to be paid for them.

10.2   The contract takes effect as a contract for sale of goods.

10.3   The buyer takes the chattels in the physical state they are in at the date of the contract.

10.4   Ownership of the chattels passes to the buyer on actual completion.

SPECIAL CONDITIONS

1   (a)   This contract incorporates the Standard Conditions of Sale (Fourth Edition).

    (b)   The terms used in this contract have the same meaning when used in the Conditions.

2   Subject to the terms of this contract and to the Standard Conditions of Sale, the seller is to transfer the property with either full title guarantee or limited title guarantee, as specified on the front page.

3   The chattels which are on the property and are set out on any attached list are included in the sale and the buyer is to pay the chattels price for them.

4   The property is sold with vacant possession.

(or)

4   The property is sold subject to the following leases or tenancies:

Seller's conveyancers*:

Buyer's conveyancers*:

*Adding an e-mail address authorises service by e-mail: see condition 1.3.3(b).

EXPLANATORY NOTES

General

The fourth edition of the Standard Conditions of Sale (the SCS) takes effect on 13 October 2003, being the date on which the main provisions of the Land Registration Act 2002 come into force. The fourth edition takes account of the changes made by that Act, and also anticipates the coming into force in early 2004 of the provisions relating to commonhold in Part I of the Commonhold and Leasehold Reform Act 2002.

The SCS are intended primarily for use in residential sales and in the sale of small business premises. For more complex commercial transactions, conveyancers are likely to find the Standard Commercial Property Conditions (the SCPC) better suited to their needs. A second edition of the SCPC is planned for later in 2003.

The fourth edition of the SCS represents the 24th Edition of the National Conditions of Sale and the Law Society's Conditions of Sale 2003.

'Contract'

Previous editions of the SCS have distinguished between 'the agreement' (meaning the contractual document which contains the individually negotiated terms and incorporates the SCS) and 'the contract' (meaning the whole bargain, including the SCS). Some users of the SCS have found this distinction confusing, and it has been abandoned in the present edition, which refers only to 'the contract'.

It should, however, be noted that condition 1.1.4 of the SCS embodies a new general provision to the effect that the SCS apply except as varied or excluded by the contract, so ensuring that, where there is a conflict, the individually negotiated terms will prevail over the SCS.

Condition 1.1.4 will also ensure that the general provisions of the SCS which determine the completion date (conditions 1.1.1(d) and 6.1.1), the contract rate (condition 1.1.1(e)) and the title guarantee to be given in the transfer (condition 4.6.2) will automatically take effect subject to any individually negotiated terms which deal with these matters. For that reason, these provisions no longer include words making them expressly subject to the particular terms of the agreement.

Front and back pages: specified incumbrances

The back page no longer contains a special condition stating that the property is sold subject to the incumbrances set out on the front page. However, condition 3.1.2(a) provides that the property is sold subject to the incumbrances specified in the contract, and the front page includes space for specifying any incumbrances to which the sale is expressly made subject. The sale will, therefore, continue to take effect subject to any incumbrances there set out.

Chattels

The SCS now make fuller provision for cases in which a separate price is agreed for any chattels included in the sale. In such a case, the 'purchase price' will refer to the price agreed for the property and the 'chattels price' (as defined in condition 1.1.1(b)) will refer to the price separately agreed for the chattels. The SCS provide for the deposit to be 10 per cent of the total of the purchase price and the chattels price (condition 2.2.1). They also provide for the chattels price to be taken into account in calculating any licence fee payable where the buyer goes into occupation before completion (condition 5.2.2(d)), in working out the amount payable on completion (condition 6.4) and in working out any compensation payable on late completion (condition 7.3.2).

It should, however, be noted that condition 10 will apply to any chattels included in the sale whether or not a separate price is payable for them.

'Conveyancer'

In this edition, 'conveyancer' has replaced 'solicitor' as the defined term used to refer to the various categories of persons who may lawfully carry out conveyancing work for reward (condition 1.1.1(f)). Note, however, that, in a case where the property is being sold otherwise than at auction and the deposit is paid by cheque, the cheque may be drawn only on a solicitor's or licensed conveyancer's client account (conditions 2.2.3 and 2.2.4). This requirement reflects the fact that solicitors and licensed conveyancers (in contrast, for example, to barristers) hold money on client account and can be expected to have taken steps to comply with their obligations under the general law and professional rules to ensure that their client accounts are not being used for money-laundering purposes.

Payment by direct credit

In the light of developments in conveyancing practice, the present edition of the SCS no longer gives the buyer the option of paying the deposit by banker's draft, or of paying the money due on completion by banker's draft or legal tender. The current position is that, unless the property is being sold by auction, the deposit must be paid either by direct credit or (as noted above) by cheque drawn on a solicitor's or licensed conveyancer's client account (conditions 2.2.3 and 2.2.4). The money due on completion may now be paid only by direct credit, coupled where appropriate with the release of any deposit held by a stakeholder (condition 6.7). For these purposes, 'direct credit' is defined in condition 1.1.1(g) as meaning a direct transfer of cleared funds to an account nominated by the seller's conveyancer and maintained by a 'clearing bank', that is to say, a bank which is a shareholder in CHAPS Clearing Co. Ltd (condition 1.1.1(c)).

Ready, able and willing to complete

Condition 1.1.3 contains a new general provision stating when a party is ready, able and willing to complete. The provision is relevant in applying conditions 6.1.3 and 6.8.1.

Notices and documents

Condition 1.3.6 now makes it clear that the presumed times of receipt set out in condition 1.3.7 may be displaced not only by proof of the actual time at which a notice or document was received, but also by proof that the notice or document was not received at all.

Condition 1.3.3(b) is a new provision, which enables a notice or document to be sent by e-mail where delivery of the original is not essential. It is important to appreciate that condition 1.3.3(b) permits notices or documents to be sent in this way if, but only if, an e-mail address for the intended recipient is given in the contract. Thus, a party's conveyancers should not include their e-mail address in the contract unless they are prepared to accept service by e-mail at that address.

Two further provisions relevant to the use of e-mail should be noted. First, condition 1.3.5(c) provides that, where a notice or document sent by e-mail prompts an automated response that the intended recipient is out of the office, the response (while in reality establishing that the message has reached its intended destination) is to be treated as proof that the notice or document has not been received. The sender may, therefore, need to consider other means for sending the notice or document to its intended recipient (e.g., hand delivery or fax). Secondly, condition 1.3.7(e) provides that (in the absence of proof to the contrary under condition 1.3.6) a notice or document sent by e-mail is treated as having been received before 4.00 pm on the first working day after dispatch. It will be noted that this is later than the time of receipt presumed by condition 1.3.7(d) for a notice or document sent by fax (one hour after despatch). The reason for this is that the receipt of an e-mail may on occasion be delayed for several hours without the delay in transmission being readily apparent to the sender.

Assignment

Condition 1.5 now contains a general prohibition on the transfer by the buyer of the benefit of the contract. The specific prohibitions which formerly applied to the transfer of contracts for the grant or assignment of a lease or sub-lease have accordingly been deleted.

Auctions

Condition 2.3.6 now follows the SCPC in providing that, on a sale by auction, the deposit is to be paid to the auctioneer as agent for the seller.

Proof of title

Condition 4.1.1 requires the seller to provide the buyer with proof of his title to the property and of his ability to transfer it or to procure its transfer (the latter alternative applying, for example, to a sub-sale).

Where the title is registered, the effect of condition 4.1.2 is that the proof must include official copies of the individual register and any title plan referred to in it, and of any document referred to in the register and kept by the registrar (unless the document is to be discharged or overridden at or before completion).

Requisitions

Previous editions of the SCS have allowed the buyer to raise requisitions after the making of the contract, whether or not title was deduced beforehand. The fourth edition recognises that where the seller deduces title before the contract is made (as he normally will, at least where the title is registered), the buyer should ensure that any concerns about the title so shown are raised before contract and, where necessary, appropriately provided for in the special conditions. Accordingly, condition 4.2.1(a) now bars the buyer from raising any requisitions on the title shown by the seller before the making of the contract. The buyer, however, retains the right to raise requisitions on matters coming to his attention for the first time after the contract is made (condition 4.2.2).

In cases where the seller deduces title (either in whole or in part) after the contract is made, condition 4.3.1 continues to allow the buyer to raise requisitions within six working days of the date of the contract or delivery of the seller's proof of title on which the requisitions are raised.

Completion after 2.00 pm

Conditions 6.1.2 and 6.1.3 clarify the position where the money due on completion is received after 2.00 pm. Condition 6.1.2 states the normal rule that, in such a case, apportionments are to be worked out as if completion had taken place on the next working day, and compensation is to be calculated as if completion had been deferred to that day as a result of the buyer's default. It would, however, be unfair to adopt that approach where completion has been delayed because the seller has failed to vacate the property by 2.00 pm. Condition 6.1.3 therefore disapplies condition 6.1.2 in a case where the sale is with vacant possession and the buyer is ready, able and willing to complete (as to which, see condition 1.1.3(a)) but does not pay the money due on completion because the seller has not vacated the property by 2.00 pm. In such a case, condition 6.1.3 provides that the seller is to be treated as in default, so that compensation will be calculated on that basis under condition 7.3.

Consent

Condition 8.3.1(a) ensures that condition 8.3 now applies not only in cases where the landlord's consent is required for the assignment of an existing lease or the creation of a sub-lease but also in cases where consent is required for the creation of a new lease of freehold land.

Two changes to condition 8.3 have been made in the light of the decision of the Court of Appeal in *Aubergine Enterprises Ltd* v. *Lakewood International Ltd* [2002] 1 WLR 2149. First, condition 8.3.1(b) confirms that any necessary consent must be in the form which satisfies the requirement to obtain it. Secondly, condition 8.3.3 now provides that, where the parties agree to complete the contract after the contractual completion date, the right to rescind will not arise unless the consent has not been obtained by three working days before the later date agreed for completion.

Commonhold

The new commonhold regime is made the subject of express provision in two ways. First, the seller is required to provide the buyer with current copies of the memorandum and articles of the commonhold association and the commonhold community statement. If the buyer then enters into the contract, he is treated as doing so knowing and accepting their terms (condition 9.3, and cf. condition 3.3.2(a), which makes similar provision with regard to the terms of leases affecting the property). Secondly, cases in which the consent of the commonhold association is required to the sale of part only of a commonhold unit are dealt with (in condition 9.4) in a way which parallels the provision made in conditions 8.3.2(a) and 8.3.3 for cases in which a consent to let, assign or sub-let is required to complete the contract.

III.6. Standard Commercial Property Conditions of Sale (second edition) (including Explanatory Notes)[1]

CONTRACT

(Incorporating the Standard Commercial Property Conditions (Second Edition))

Date	:
Seller	:
Buyer	:
Property (freehold/leasehold)	:
Title Number/Root of title	:
Specified incumbrances	:
Completion date	:
Contract rate	:
Purchase price	:
Deposit	:

The seller will sell and the buyer will buy:

(a) the property, and

(b) any chattels which, under the special conditions, are included in the sale for the purchase price

WARNING	Signed
This is a formal document, designed to create legal rights and legal obligations. Take advice before using it.	Authorised to sign on behalf of Seller/Buyer

---

1. © Oyez (The Solicitors' Law Stationery Society Ltd) and the Law Society 2004.

STANDARD COMMERCIAL PROPERTY CONDITIONS
(SECOND EDITION)

Part 1

1. GENERAL

1. Definitions

1.1.1   In these conditions:

    (a)   'accrued interest' means:

        (i)   if money has been placed on deposit or in a building society share account, the interest actually earned

        (ii)   otherwise, the interest which might reasonably have been earned by depositing the money at interest on seven days' notice of withdrawal with a clearing bank

  less, in either case, any proper charges for handling the money

    (b)   'apportionment day' has the meaning given in condition 8.3.2

    (c)   'clearing bank' means a bank which is a shareholder in CHAPS Clearing Co. Limited

    (d)   'completion date' has the meaning given in condition 8.1.1

    (e)   'contract rate' is the Law Society's interest rate from time to time in force

    (f)   'conveyancer' means a solicitor, barrister, duly certified notary public, licensed conveyancer or recognised body under sections 9 or 23 of the Administration of Justice Act 1985

    (g)   'direct credit' means a direct transfer of cleared funds to an account nominated by the seller's conveyancer and maintained at a clearing bank

    (h)   'election to waive exemption' means an election made under paragraph 2 of Schedule 10 to the Value Added Tax Act 1994

    (i)   'lease' includes sub-lease, tenancy and agreement for a lease or sublease

    (j)   'notice to complete' means a notice requiring completion of the contract in accordance with condition 8

    (k)   'post' includes a service provided by a person licensed under the Postal Services Act 2000

    (l)   'public requirement' means any notice, order or proposal given or made (whether before or after the date of the contract) by a body acting on statutory authority

    (m)   'requisition' includes objection

    (n)   'transfer' includes conveyance and assignment

    (o)   'working day' means any day from Monday to Friday (inclusive) which is not Christmas Day, Good Friday or a statutory Bank Holiday.

1.1.2   In these conditions the terms 'absolute title' and 'official copies' have the special meanings given to them by the Land Registration Act 2002.

1.1.3   A party is ready, able and willing to complete:

    (a)   if it could be, but for the default of the other party, and

(b)   in the case of the seller, even though a mortgage remains secured on the property, if the amount to be paid on completion enables the property to be transferred freed of all mortgages (except those to which the sale is expressly subject).

1.1.4 (a)   The conditions in Part 1 apply except as varied or excluded by the contract.

    (b)   A condition in Part 2 only applies if expressly incorporated into the contract.

1.2   Joint parties

If there is more than one seller or more than one buyer, the obligations which they undertake can be enforced against them all jointly or against each individually.

1.3   Notices and documents

1.3.1   A notice required or authorised by the contract must be in writing.

1.3.2   Giving a notice or delivering a document to a party's conveyancer has the same effect as giving or delivering it to that party.

1.3.3   Where delivery of the original document is not essential, a notice or document is validly given or sent if it is sent:

    (a)   by fax, or

    (b)   by e-mail to an e-mail address for the intended recipient given in the contract.

1.3.4   Subject to conditions 1.3.5 to 1.3.7, a notice is given and a document delivered when it is received.

1.3.5 (a)   A notice or document sent through the document exchange is received when it is available for collection

    (b)   A notice or document which is received after 4.00 p.m. on a working day, or on a day which is not a working day, is to be treated as having been received on the next working day

    (c)   An automated response to a notice or document sent by e-mail that the intended recipient is out of the office is to be treated as proof that the notice or document was not received.

1.3.6   Condition 1.3.7 applies unless there is proof:

    (a)   that a notice or document has not been received, or

    (b)   of when it was received.

1.3.7   Unless the actual time of receipt is proved, a notice or document sent by the following means is treated as having been received as follows:

    (a)   by first class post: before 4.00 pm on the second working day after posting

    (b)   by second-class post: before 4.00 pm on the third working day after posting

    (c)   through a document exchange: before 4.00 pm on the first working day after the day on which it would normally be available for collection by the addressee

    (d)   by fax: one hour after despatch

    (e)   by e-mail: before 4.00 pm on the first working day after despatch.

1.3.8   In condition 1.3.7, 'first class post' means a postal service which seeks to deliver posted items no later than the next working day in all or the majority of cases.

1.4   VAT

1.4.1   The seller:

    (a)   warrants that the sale of the property does not constitute a supply that is taxable for VAT purposes

    (b)   agrees that there will be no exercise of the election to waive exemption in respect of the property, and

    (c)   cannot require the buyer to pay any amount in respect of any liability to VAT arising in respect of the sale of the property, unless condition 1.4.2 applies.

1.4.2   If, solely as a result of a change in law made and coming into effect between the date of the contract and completion, the sale of the property will constitute a supply chargeable to VAT, the buyer is to pay to the seller on completion an additional amount equal to that VAT in exchange for a proper VAT invoice from the seller.

1.4.3   The amount payable for the chattels is exclusive of VAT and the buyer is to pay to the seller on completion an additional amount equal to any VAT charged on that supply in exchange for a proper VAT invoice from the seller.

1.5   Assignment and sub-sales

1.5.1   The buyer is not entitled to transfer the benefit of the contract.

1.5.2   The seller may not be required to transfer the property in parts or to any person other than the buyer.

2.   FORMATION

2.1   Date

2.1.1   If the parties intend to make a contract by exchanging duplicate copies by post or through a document exchange, the contract is made when the last copy is posted or deposited at the document exchange.

2.1.2   If the parties' conveyancers agree to treat exchange as taking place before duplicate copies are actually exchanged, the contract is made as so agreed.

2.2   Deposit

2.2.1   The buyer is to pay a deposit of 10 per cent of the purchase price no later than the date of the contract.

2.2.2   Except on a sale by auction the deposit is to be paid by direct credit and is to be held by the seller's conveyancer as stakeholder on terms that on completion it is to be paid to the seller with accrued interest.

2.3 Auctions

2.3.1   On a sale by auction the following conditions apply to the property and, if it is sold in lots, to each lot.

2.3.2   The sale is subject to a reserve price.

2.3.3   The seller, or a person on its behalf, may bid up to the reserve price.

2.3.4   The auctioneer may refuse any bid.

2.3.5   If there is a dispute about a bid, the auctioneer may resolve the dispute or restart the auction at the last undisputed bid.

2.3.6   The auctioneer is to hold the deposit as agent for the seller.

2.3.7   If any cheque tendered in payment of all or part of the deposit is dishonoured when first presented, the seller may, within seven working days of being notified that the cheque has been dishonoured, give notice to the buyer that the contract is discharged by the buyer's breach.

3. MATTERS AFFECTING THE PROPERTY

3.1 Freedom from incumbrances

3.1.1   The seller is selling the property free from incumbrances, other than those mentioned in condition 3.1.2.

3.1.2   The incumbrances subject to which the property is sold are:

   (a)   those specified in the contract

   (b)   those discoverable by inspection of the property before the contract

   (c)   those the seller does not and could not reasonably know about

   (d)   matters, other than monetary charges or incumbrances, disclosed or which would have been disclosed by the searches and enquiries which a prudent buyer would have made before entering into the contract

   (e)   public requirements.

3.1.3   After the contract is made, the seller is to give the buyer written details without delay of any new public requirement and of anything in writing which he learns about concerning a matter covered by condition 3.1.2.

3.1.4   The buyer is to bear the cost of complying with any outstanding public requirement and is to indemnify the seller against any liability resulting from a public requirement.

3.2 Physical state

3.2.1   The buyer accepts the property in the physical state it is in at the date of the contract unless the seller is building or converting it.

3.2.2   A leasehold property is sold subject to any subsisting breach of a condition or tenant's obligation relating to the physical state of the property which renders the lease liable to forfeiture.

3.2.3   A sub-lease is granted subject to any subsisting breach of a condition or tenant's obligation relating to the physical state of the property which renders the seller's own lease liable to forfeiture.

3.3   Retained land

Where after the transfer the seller will be retaining land near the property:

    (a)   the buyer will have no right of light or air over the retained land, but

    (b)   in other respects the seller and the buyer will each have the rights over the land of the other which they would have had if they were two separate buyers to whom the seller had made simultaneous transfers of the property and the retained land.

The transfer is to contain appropriate express terms.

4.   LEASES AFFECTING THE PROPERTY

4.1   General

4.1.1   This condition applies if any part of the property is sold subject to a lease.

4.1.2   The seller having provided the buyer with full details of each lease or copies of documents embodying the lease terms, the buyer is treated as entering into the contract knowing and fully accepting those terms.

4.1.3   The seller is not to serve a notice to end the lease nor to accept a surrender.

4.1.4   The seller is to inform the buyer without delay if the lease ends.

4.1.5   The buyer is to indemnify the seller against all claims arising from the lease after actual completion; this includes claims which are unenforceable against a buyer for want of registration.

4.1.6   If the property does not include all the land let, the seller may apportion the rent and, if the lease is a new tenancy, the buyer may require the seller to apply under section 10 of the Landlord and Tenant (Covenants) Act 1995 for the apportionment to bind the tenant.

4.2   Property management

4.2.1   The seller is promptly to give the buyer full particulars of:

    (a)   any court or arbitration proceedings in connection with the lease, and

    (b)   any application for a licence, consent or approval under the lease.

4.2.2   Conditions 4.2.3 to 4.2.8 do not apply to a rent review process to which condition 5 applies.

4.2.3   Subject to condition 4.2.4, the seller is to conduct any court or arbitration proceedings in accordance with written directions given by the buyer from time to time (for which the seller is to apply), unless to do so might place the seller in breach of an obligation to the tenant or a statutory duty.

4.2.4   If the seller applies for directions from the buyer in relation to a proposed step in the proceedings and the buyer does not give such directions within 10 working days, the seller may take or refrain from taking that step as it thinks fit.

4.2.5   The buyer is to indemnify the seller against all loss and expense resulting from the seller's following the buyer's directions.

4.2.6   Unless the buyer gives written consent, the seller is not to:

(a)   grant or formally withhold any licence, consent or approval under the lease, or

(b)   serve any notice or take any action (other than action in court or arbitration proceedings) as landlord under the lease.

4.2.7   When the seller applies for the buyer's consent under condition 4.2.6:

(a)   the buyer is not to withhold its consent or attach conditions to the consent where to do so might place the seller in breach of an obligation to the tenant or a statutory duty

(b)   the seller may proceed as if the buyer has consented when:

(i)   in accordance with paragraph (a), the buyer is not entitled to withhold its consent, or

(ii)   the buyer does not refuse its consent within 10 working days.

4.2.8   If the buyer withholds or attaches conditions to its consent, the buyer is to indemnify the seller against all loss and expense.

4.2.9   In all other respects, the seller is to manage the property in accordance with the principles of good estate management until completion.

4.3   Continuing liability

At the request and cost of the seller, the buyer is to support any application by the seller to be released from the landlord covenants in a lease to which the property is sold subject.

5.   RENT REVIEWS

5.1   **Subject to condition 5.2, this condition applies if**:

(a)   the rent reserved by a lease of all or part of the property is to be reviewed,

(b)   the seller is either the landlord or the tenant,

(c)   the rent review process starts before actual completion, and

(d)   no reviewed rent has been agreed or determined at the date of the contract.

5.2   The seller is to conduct the rent review process until actual completion, after which the buyer is to conduct it.

5.3   Conditions 5.4 and 5.5 cease to apply on actual completion if the reviewed rent will only be payable in respect of a period after that date.

5.4   In the course of the rent review process, the seller and the buyer are each to:

(a)   act promptly with a view to achieving the best result obtainable,

(b)   consult with and have regard to the views of the other,

(c)   provide the other with copies of all material correspondence and papers relating to the process,

(d)   ensure that its representations take account of matters put forward by the other, and

(e)   keep the other informed of the progress of the process.

5.5   Neither the seller nor the buyer is to agree a rent figure unless it has been approved in writing by the other (such approval not to be unreasonably withheld).

5.6   The seller and the buyer are each to bear their own costs of the rent review process.

5.7   Unless the rent review date precedes the apportionment day, the buyer is to pay the costs of a third party appointed to determine the rent.

5.8   Where the rent review date precedes the apportionment day, those costs are to be divided as follows:

(a)   the seller is to pay the proportion that the number of days from the rent review date to the apportionment day bears to the number of days from that rent review date until either the following rent review date or, if none, the expiry of the term, and

(b)   the buyer is to pay the balance.

6. TITLE AND TRANSFER

6.1   Proof of title

6.1.1   Without cost to the buyer, the seller is to provide the buyer with proof of the title to the property and of his ability to transfer it, or to procure its transfer.

6.1.2   Where the property has a registered title the proof is to include official copies of the items referred to in rules 134(1)(a) and (b) and 135(1)(a) of the Land Registration Rules 2003, so far as they are not to be discharged or overridden at or before completion.

6.1.3   Where the property has an unregistered title, the proof is to include:

(a)   an abstract of title or an epitome of title with photocopies of the documents, and

(b)   production of every document or an abstract, epitome or copy of it with an original marking by a conveyancer either against the original or an examined abstract or an examined copy.

6.2   Requisitions

6.2.1   The buyer may not raise requisitions:

(a)   on the title shown by the seller taking the steps described in condition 6.1.1 before the contract was made

(b)   in relation to the matters covered by condition 3.1.2.

6.2.2   Notwithstanding condition 6.2.1, the buyer may, within six working days of a matter coming to his attention after the contract was made, raise written requisitions on that matter. In that event steps 3 and 4 in condition 6.3.1 apply.

6.2.3   On the expiry of the relevant time limit under condition 6.2.2 or condition 6.3.1, the buyer loses his right to raise requisitions or to make observations.

6.3 Timetable

6.3.1   Subject to condition 6.2 and to the extent that the seller did not take the steps described in condition 6.1.1 before the contract was made, the following are the steps for deducing and investigating the title to the property to be taken within the following time limits:

Step	Time limit
1. The seller is to comply with condition 6.1.1	Immediately after making the contract
2. The buyer may raise written requisitions	Six working days after either the date of the contract or the date of delivery of the seller's evidence of title on which the requisitions are raised whichever is the later
3. The seller is to reply in writing to any requisitions raised	Four working days after receiving the requisitions
4. The buyer may make written observations on the seller's replies	Three working days after receiving the replies

The time limit on the buyer's right to raise requisitions applies even where the seller supplies incomplete evidence of its title, but the buyer may, within six working days from delivery of any further evidence, raise further requisitions resulting from that evidence.

6.3.2   The parties are to take the following steps to prepare and agree the transfer of the property within the following time limits:

Step	Time limit
A. The buyer is to send the seller a draft transfer	At least twelve working days before completion date
B. The seller is to approve or revise that draft and either return it or retain it for use as the actual transfer	Four working days after delivery of the draft transfer
C. If the draft is returned the buyer is to send an engrossment to the seller	At least five working days before completion date

6.3.3   Periods of time under conditions 6.3.1 and 6.3.2 may run concurrently.

6.3.4   If the period between the date of the contract and completion date is less than 15 working days, the time limits in conditions 6.2.2, 6.3.1 and 6.3.2 are to be reduced by the same proportion as that period bears to the period of 15 working days. Fractions of a working day are to be rounded down except that the time limit to perform any step is not to be less than one working day.

6.4 Defining the property

6.4.1   The seller need not, further than it may be able to do from information in its possession:

    (a)   prove the exact boundaries of the property

    (b)   prove who owns fences, ditches, hedges or walls

    (c)   separately identify parts of the property with different titles.

6.4.2   The buyer may, if to do so is reasonable, require the seller to make or obtain, pay for and hand over a statutory declaration about facts relevant to the matters mentioned in condition 6.4.1. The form of the declaration is to be agreed by the buyer, who must not unreasonably withhold its agreement.

6.5   Rents and rentcharges

The fact that a rent or rentcharge, whether payable or receivable by the owner of the property, has been or will on completion be, informally apportioned is not to be regarded as a defect in title.

6.6   Transfer

6.6.1   The buyer does not prejudice its right to raise requisitions, or to require replies to any raised, by taking steps in relation to the preparation or agreement of the transfer.

6.6.2   Subject to condition 6.6.3, the seller is to transfer the property with full title guarantee.

6.6.3   The transfer is to have effect as if the disposition is expressly made subject to all matters covered by condition 3.1.2.

6.6.4   If after completion the seller will remain bound by any obligation affecting the property and disclosed to the buyer before the contract was made, but the law does not imply any covenant by the buyer to indemnify the seller against liability for future breaches of it:

(a)   the buyer is to covenant in the transfer to indemnify the seller against liability for any future breach of the obligation and to perform it from then on, and

(b)   if required by the seller, the buyer is to execute and deliver to the seller on completion a duplicate transfer prepared by the buyer.

6.6.5   The seller is to arrange at its expense that, in relation to every document of title which the buyer does not receive on completion, the buyer is to have the benefit of:

(a)   a written acknowledgement of the buyer's right to its production, and

(b)   a written undertaking for its safe custody (except while it is held by a mortgagee or by someone in a fiduciary capacity).

7.   INSURANCE

7.1   Responsibility for insuring

7.1.1   Conditions 7.1.2 and 7.1.3 apply if:

(a)   the contract provides that the policy effected by or for the seller and insuring the property or any part of it against loss or damage should continue in force after the exchange of contracts, or

(b)   the property or any part of it is let on terms under which the seller (whether as landlord or as tenant) is obliged to insure against loss or damage.

7.1.2   The seller is to:

(a)   do everything required to continue to maintain the policy, including the prompt payment of any premium which falls due

(b)   increase the amount or extent of the cover as requested by the buyer, if the insurers agree and the buyer pays the additional premium

(c)   permit the buyer to inspect the policy, or evidence of its terms, at any time

   (d)   obtain or consent to an endorsement on the policy of the buyer's interest, at the buyer's expense

   (e)   pay to the buyer immediately on receipt, any part of an additional premium which the buyer paid and which is returned by the insurers

   (f)   if before completion the property suffers loss or damage:

        (i)   pay to the buyer on completion the amount of policy moneys which the seller has received, so far as not applied in repairing or reinstating the property, and

        (ii)   if no final payment has then been received, assign to the buyer, at the buyer's expense, all rights to claim under the policy in such form as the buyer reasonably requires and pending execution of the assignment, hold any policy moneys received in trust for the buyer

   (g)   on completion:

        (i)   cancel the insurance policy

        (ii)   apply for a refund of the premium and pay the buyer, immediately on receipt, any amount received which relates to a part of the premium which was paid or reimbursed by a tenant or third party. The buyer is to hold the money paid subject to the rights of that tenant or third party.

7.1.3   The buyer is to pay the seller a proportionate part of the premium which the seller paid in respect of the period from the date when the contract is made to the date of actual completion, except so far as the seller is entitled to recover it from a tenant.

7.1.4   Unless condition 7.1.2 applies:

   (a)   the seller is under no obligation to the buyer to insure the property

   (b)   if payment under a policy effected by or for the buyer is reduced, because the property is covered against loss or damage by an insurance policy effected by or for the seller, the purchase price is to be abated by the amount of that reduction.

7.1.5   Section 47 of the Law of Property Act 1925 does not apply.

8. COMPLETION

8.1 Date

8.1.1   Completion date is twenty working days after the date of the contract but time is not of the essence of the contract unless a notice to complete has been served.

8.1.2   If the money due on completion is received after 2.00 pm, completion is to be treated, for the purposes only of conditions 8.3 and 9.3, as taking place on the next working day as a result of the buyer's default.

8.1.3   Condition 8.1.2 does not apply if:

   (a)   the sale is with vacant possession of the property or a part of it, and

   (b)   the buyer is ready, willing and able to complete but does not pay the money due on completion until after 2.00 pm because the seller has not vacated the property or that part by that time.

8.2   Place

Completion is to take place in England and Wales, either at the seller's conveyancer's office or at some other place which the seller reasonably specifies.

8.3   Apportionments

8.3.1   Subject to condition 8.3.6 income and outgoings of the property are to be apportioned between the parties so far as the change of ownership on completion will affect entitlement to receive or liability to pay them.

8.3.2   The day from which the apportionment is to be made ('apportionment day') is:

    (a)   if the whole property is sold with vacant possession or the seller exercises its option in condition 9.3.4, the date of actual completion, or

    (b)   otherwise, completion date.

8.3.3   In apportioning any sum, it is to be assumed that the buyer owns the property from the beginning of the day on which the apportionment is to be made.

8.3.4   A sum to be apportioned is to be treated as:

    (a)   payable for the period which it covers, except that if it is an instalment of an annual sum the buyer is to be attributed with an amount equal to 1/365th of the annual sum for each day from and including the apportionment day to the end of the instalment period

    (b)   accruing –

        (i)   from day to day, and

        (ii)   at the rate applicable from time to time.

8.3.5   When a sum to be apportioned, or the rate at which it is to be treated as accruing, is not known or easily ascertainable at completion, a provisional apportionment is to be made according to the best estimate available. As soon as the amount is known, a final apportionment is to be made and notified to the other party. Subject to condition 8.3.8, any resulting balance is to be paid no more than ten working days later, and if not then paid the balance is to bear interest at the contract rate from then until payment.

8.3.6   Where a lease of the property requires the tenant to reimburse the landlord for expenditure on goods or services, on completion:

    (a)   the buyer is to pay the seller the amount of any expenditure already incurred by the seller but not yet due from the tenant and in respect of which the seller provides the buyer with the information and vouchers required for its recovery from the tenant, and

    (b)   the seller is to credit the buyer with payments already recovered from the tenant but not yet incurred by the seller.

8.3.7   Condition 8.3.8 applies if any part of the property is sold subject to a lease and either:

    (a)   (i)   on completion any rent or other sum payable under the lease is due but not paid

        (ii)   the contract does not provide that the buyer is to assign to the seller the right to collect any arrears due to the seller under the terms of the contract, and

        (iii) the seller is not entitled to recover any arrears from the tenant, or

(b)   (i)   as a result of a rent review to which condition 5 applies a reviewed rent is agreed or determined after actual completion, and

      (ii)   an additional sum then becomes payable in respect of a period before the apportionment day.

8.3.8 (a)   The buyer is to seek to collect all sums due in the circumstances referred to in condition 8.3.7 in the ordinary course of management, but need not take legal proceedings or distrain.

     (b)   A payment made on account of those sums is to be apportioned between the parties in the ratio of the amounts owed to each, notwithstanding that the tenant exercises its right to appropriate the payment in some other manner.

     (c)   Any part of a payment on account received by one party but due to the other is to be paid no more than ten working days after the receipt of cash or cleared funds and, if not then paid, the sum is to bear interest at the contract rate until payment.

8.4   Amount payable

The amount payable by the buyer on completion is the purchase price (less any deposit already paid to the seller or its agent) adjusted to take account of:

    (a)   apportionments made under condition 8.3

    (b)   any compensation to be paid under condition 9.3

    (c)   any sum payable under condition 7.1.2 or 7.1.3.

8.5   Title deeds

8.5.1   As soon as the buyer has complied with all its obligations on completion the seller must hand over the documents of title.

8.5.2   Condition 8.5.1 does not apply to any documents of title relating to land being retained by the seller after completion.

8.6   Rent receipts

The buyer is to assume that whoever gave any receipt for a payment of rent which the seller produces was the person or the agent of the person then entitled to that rent.

8.7   Means of payment

The buyer is to pay the money due on completion by direct credit and, if appropriate, by an unconditional release of a deposit held by a stakeholder.

8.8   Notice to complete

8.8.1   At any time on or after completion date, a party who is ready, able and willing to complete may give the other a notice to complete.

8.8.2   The parties are to complete the contract within ten working days of giving a notice to complete, excluding the day on which the notice is given. For this purpose, time is of the essence of the contract.

9. REMEDIES

9.1 Errors and omissions

9.1.1   If any plan or statement in the contract, or in the negotiations leading to it, is or was misleading or inaccurate due to an error or omission, the remedies available are as follows.

9.1.2   When there is a material difference between the description or value of the property as represented and as it is, the buyer is entitled to damages.

9.1.3   An error or omission only entitles the buyer to rescind the contract:

(a)   where the error or omission results from fraud or recklessness, or

(b)   where the buyer would be obliged, to its prejudice, to accept property differing substantially (in quantity, quality or tenure) from that which the error or omission had led it to expect.

9.2 Rescission

If either party rescinds the contract:

(a)   unless the rescission is a result of the buyer's breach of contract the deposit is to be repaid to the buyer with accrued interest

(b)   the buyer is to return any documents received from the seller and is to cancel any registration of the contract

(c)   the seller's duty to pay any returned premium under condition 7.1.2(e) (whenever received) is not affected.

9.3 Late completion

9.3.1   If the buyer defaults in performing its obligations under the contract and completion is delayed, the buyer is to pay compensation to the seller.

9.3.2   Compensation is calculated at the contract rate on the purchase price (less any deposit paid) for the period between completion date and actual completion, but ignoring any period during which the seller was in default.

9.3.3   Any claim by the seller for loss resulting from delayed completion is to be reduced by any compensation paid under this contract.

9.3.4   Where the sale is not with vacant possession of the whole property and completion is delayed, the seller may give notice to the buyer, before the date of actual completion, that it will take the net income from the property until completion as well as compensation under condition 9.3.1.

9.4 After completion

Completion does not cancel liability to perform any outstanding obligation under the contract.

9.5 Buyer's failure to comply with notice to complete

9.5.1   If the buyer fails to complete in accordance with a notice to complete, the following terms apply.

9.5.2   The seller may rescind the contract, and if it does so:

(a) it may

        (i)   forfeit and keep any deposit and accrued interest

        (ii)   resell the property

        (iii) claim damages

    (b) the buyer is to return any documents received from the seller and is to cancel any registration of the contract.

9.5.3   The seller retains its other rights and remedies.

9.6   Seller's failure to comply with notice to complete

9.6.1   If the seller fails to complete in accordance with a notice to complete, the following terms apply:

9.6.2   The buyer may rescind the contract, and if it does so:

    (a) the deposit is to be repaid to the buyer with accrued interest

    (b) the buyer is to return any documents it received from the seller and is, at the seller's expense, to cancel any registration of the contract.

9.6.3   The buyer retains its other rights and remedies.

10. LEASEHOLD PROPERTY

10.1   Existing leases

10.1.1   The following provisions apply to a sale of leasehold land.

10.1.2   The seller having provided the buyer with copies of the documents embodying the lease terms, the buyer is treated as entering into the contract knowing and fully accepting those terms.

10.1.3   The seller is to comply with any lease obligations requiring the tenant to insure the property.

10.2   New leases

10.2.1   The following provisions apply to a contract to grant a new lease.

10.2.2   The conditions apply so that:

        'seller' means the proposed landlord

        'buyer' means the proposed tenant

        'pufchase price' means the premium to be paid on the grant of a lease.

10.2.3   The lease is to be in the form of the draft attached to the contract.

10.2.4   If the term of the new lease will exceed seven years, the seller is to deduce a title which will enable the buyer to register the lease at the Land Registry with an absolute title.

10.2.5   The seller is to engross the lease and a counterpart of it and is to send the counterpart to the buyer at least five working days before completion date.

10.2.6   The buyer is to execute the counterpart and deliver it to the seller on completion.

10.3   Consents

10.3.1(a)   The following provisions apply if a consent to let, assign or sub-let is required to complete the contract

(b)   In this condition 'consent' means consent in a form which satisfies the requirement to obtain it.

10.3.2(a)   The seller is to:

(i)   apply for the consent at its expense, and to use all reasonable efforts to obtain it

(ii)   give the buyer notice forthwith on obtaining the consent

(b)   The buyer is to comply with all reasonable requirements, including requirements for the provision of information and references.

10.3.3   Where the consent of a reversioner (whether or not immediate) is required to an assignment or sub-letting, then so far as the reversioner lawfully imposes such a condition:

(a)   the buyer is to:

(i)   covenant directly with the reversioner to observe the tenant's covenants and the conditions in the seller's lease

(ii)   use reasonable endeavours to provide guarantees of the performance and observance of the tenant's covenants and the conditions in the seller's lease

(iii)   execute or procure the execution of the licence

(b)   the seller, in the case of an assignment, is to enter into an authorised guarantee agreement.

10.3.4   Neither party may object to a reversioner's consent given subject to a condition:

(a)   which under section 19(1A) of the Landlord and Tenant Act 1927 is not regarded as unreasonable, and

(b)   which is lawfully imposed under an express term of the lease.

10.3.5   If any required consent has not been obtained by the original completion date:

(a)   the time for completion is to be postponed until five working days after the seller gives written notice to the buyer that the consent has been obtained or four months from the original completion date whichever is the earlier

(b)   the postponed date is to be treated as the completion date.

10.3.6   At any time after four months from the original completion date, either party may rescind the contract by notice to the other, if:

(a)   consent has still not been given, and

(b)   no declaration has been obtained from the court that consent has been unreasonably withheld.

10.3.7   If the contract is rescinded under condition 10.3.6 the seller is to remain liable for any breach of condition 10.3.2(a) or 10.3.3(b) and the buyer is to remain liable for any breach of condition 10.3.2(b) or 10.3.3(a). In all other respects neither party is to be treated as in breach of contract and condition 9.2 applies.

10.3.8   A party in breach of its obligations under condition 10.3.2 or 10.3.3 cannot rescind under condition 10.3.6 for so long as its breach is a cause of the consent's being withheld.

11. COMMONHOLD

11.1   Terms used in this condition have the special meanings given to them in Part 1 of the Commonhold and Leasehold Reform Act 2002.

11.2   This condition applies to a disposition of commonhold land.

11.3   The seller having provided the buyer with copies of the current versions of the memorandum and articles of the commonhold association and of the commonhold community statement, the buyer is treated as entering into the contract knowing and fully accepting their terms.

11.4   If the contract is for the sale of property which is or includes part only of a commonhold unit:

    (a)   the seller is, at its expense, to apply for the written consent of the commonhold association and is to use all reasonable efforts to obtain it

    (b)   either the seller, unless it is in breach of its obligation under paragraph (a), or the buyer may rescind the contract by notice to the other party if three working days before completion date (or before a later date on which the parties have agreed to complete the contract) the consent has not been given. In that case, neither party is to be treated as in breach of contract and condition 9.2 applies.

12. CHATTELS

12.1   The following provisions apply to any chattels which are included in the contract.

12.2   The contract takes effect as a contract for the sale of goods.

12.3   The buyer takes the chattels in the physical state they are in at the date of the contract.

12.4   Ownership of the chattels passes to the buyer on actual completion but they are at the buyer's risk from the contract date.

Part 2*

*The conditions in Part 2 do not apply unless expressly incorporated. See condition 1.1.4(b).

A. VAT

A1   Standard rated supply

A1.1   Conditions 1.4.1 and 1.4.2 do not apply.

A1.2   The seller warrants that the sale of the property will constitute a supply chargeable to VAT at the standard rate.

A1.3   The buyer is to pay to the seller on completion an additional amount equal to the VAT in exchange for a proper VAT invoice from the seller.

A2   Transfer of a going concern

A2.1   Condition 1.4 does not apply.

A2.2   In this condition 'TOGC' means a transfer of a business as a going concern treated as neither a supply of goods nor a supply of services by virtue of article 5 of the Value Added Tax (Special Provisions) Order 1995.

A2.3   The seller warrants that it is using the property for the business of letting to produce rental income.

A2.4   The buyer is to make every effort to comply with the conditions to be met by a transferee under article 5(1) and 5(2) for the sale to constitute a TOGC.

A2.5   The buyer will, on or before the earlier of:

  (a)   completion date, and

  (b)   the earliest date on which a supply of the property could be treated as made by the seller under this contract if the sale does not constitute a TOGC, notify the seller that paragraph (2B) of article 5 of the VAT (Special Provisions) Order 1995 does not apply to the buyer.

A2.6   The parties are to treat the sale as a TOGC at completion if the buyer provides written evidence to the seller before completion that it is a taxable person and that it has made an election to waive exemption in respect of the property and has given a written notification of the making of such election in conformity with article 5(2) and has given the notification referred to in condition A2.5.

A2.7   The buyer is not to revoke its election to waive exemption in respect of the property at any time.

A2.8   If the parties treat the sale at completion as a TOGC but it is later determined that the sale was not a TOGC, then within five working days of that determination the buyer shall pay to the seller:

  (a)   an amount equal to the VAT chargeable in respect of the supply of the property, in exchange for a proper VAT invoice from the seller; and

  (b)   except where the sale is not a TOGC because of an act or omission of the seller, an amount equal to any interest or penalty for which the seller is liable to account to HM Customs and Excise in respect of or by reference to that VAT.

A2.9   If the seller obtains the consent of HM Customs and Excise to retain its VAT records relating to the property, it shall make them available to the buyer for inspection and copying at reasonable times on reasonable request during the six years following completion.

B.   CAPITAL ALLOWANCES

B1   To enable the buyer to make and substantiate claims under the Capital Allowances Act 2001 in respect of the property, the seller is to use its reasonable endeavours to provide, or to procure that its agents provide:

  (a)   copies of all relevant information in its possession or that of its agents, and

    (b)   such co-operation and assistance as the buyer may reasonably require.

B2.1   The buyer is only to use information provided under condition B1 for the stated purpose.

B2.2   The buyer is not to disclose, without the consent of the seller, any such information which the seller expressly provides on a confidential basis.

B3.1   On completion, the seller and the buyer are jointly to make an election under section 198 of the Capital Allowances Act 2001 which is consistent with the apportionment in the Special Conditions.

B3.2   The seller and the buyer are each to submit the amount fixed by that election to the Inland Revenue for the purposes of their respective capital allowance computations.

C. REVERSIONARY INTERESTS IN FLATS

C1   No tenants' rights

C1.1   In this condition, sections refer to sections of the Landlord and Tenant Act 1987 and expressions have the special meanings given to them in that Act.

C1.2   The seller warrants that:

    (a)   it gave the notice required by section 5,

    (b)   no acceptance notice was served on the landlord or no person was nominated for the purposes of section 6 during the protected period, and

    (c)   that period ended less than 12 months before the date of the contract.

C2   Tenants' right of first refusal

C2.1   In this condition, sections refer to sections of the Landlord and Tenant Act 1987 and expressions have the special meanings given to them in that Act.

C2.2   The seller warrants that:

    (a)   it gave the notice required by section 5, and

    (b)   it has given the buyer a copy of:

        (i)   any acceptance notice served on the landlord and

        (ii)   any nomination of a person duly nominated for the purposes of section 6.

C2.3   If the sale is by auction:

    (a)   the seller warrants that it has given the buyer a copy of any notice served on the landlord electing that section 8B shall apply,

    (b)   condition 8.1.1 applies as if 'thirty working days' were substituted for 'twenty working days',

    (c)   the seller is to send a copy of the contract to the nominated person as required by section 8B(3), and

    (d)   if the nominated person serves notice under section 8B(4):

    (i)   the seller is to give the buyer a copy of the notice, and

    (ii)   condition 9.2 is to apply as if the contract had been rescinded.

SPECIAL CONDITIONS

1.   This contract incorporates the Standard Commercial Property Conditions (Second Edition).

2.   The property is sold with vacant possession.

(or)

2.   The property is sold subject to the leases or tenancies set out on the attached list but otherwise with vacant possession on completion.

3.   The chattels at the Property and set out on the attached list are included in the sale. [The amount of the purchase price apportioned to those chattels is £[…]]

4.   The conditions in Part 2 shown against the boxes ticked below are included in the contract:

- Condition A1 (VAT: standard rate)

[or]

- Condition A2 (VAT: transfer of a going concern)
- Condition B (capital allowances). The amount of the purchase price apportioned to plant and machinery at the property for the purposes of the Capital Allowances Act 2001 is £
- Condition C1 (flats: no tenants' rights of first refusal)

[or]

- Condition C2 (flats: with tenants' rights of first refusal).

Seller's Conveyancers*:

Buyer's Conveyancers*:

*Adding an e-mail address authorises service by e-mail: see condition 1.3.3(b).

EXPLANATORY NOTES

General

The second edition of the Standard Commercial Property Conditions (the SCPC) takes effect on 1 June 2004. It takes account of the Land Registration Act 2002 and also anticipates the coming into force in the summer of 2004 of the provisions relating to commonhold in Part I of the Commonhold and Leasehold Reform Act 2002. In addition, it covers a number of other developments.

The SCPC are intended primarily for use in more complex commercial transactions. Conveyancers are likely to find that, for residential sales and the sale of small business premises, the Standard Conditions of Sale (the SCS) are better suited to their needs.

The fourth edition of the SCS came into effect on 13 October 2003 and represents the 24th Edition of the National Conditions of Sale and the 2003 revision of the Law Society's Conditions of Sale. It should be noted that the second edition of the SCPC does not represent a further edition or revision of either of those sets of conditions. References in existing legal documents to 'the current' edition of the National Conditions of Sale or the Law Society Conditions of Sale accordingly continue to have effect as references to the fourth edition of the SCS.

Front page and special conditions

In contrast to the first edition of the SCPC (which provided for any amount payable for chattels to be stated separately from the purchase price for the property), the purchase price to be entered on the front page is now the total sum payable both for the property and for any chattels which are included in the sale. Special condition 3 makes provision for chattels included in the sale to be set out on an attached list, and, if part of the purchase price has been apportioned to the chattels, for that amount to be stated.

The special conditions no longer provide that the property is sold subject to the incumbrances set out on the front page. Instead, condition 3.1.2(a) provides that the property is sold subject to the incumbrances specified in the contract, and the front page includes space for specifying any incumbrances to which the sale is expressly made subject. The sale will, therefore, continue to take effect subject to any incumbrances there set out.

'Conveyancer'

In this edition, 'conveyancer' has replaced 'solicitor' as the defined term used to refer to the various categories of persons who may lawfully carry out conveyancing work for reward (condition 1.1.1(f)).

Ready, able and willing to complete

Condition 1.1.3 contains a new general provision stating when a party is ready, able and willing to complete. The provision is relevant in applying conditions 6.1.3 and 6.8.1.

Part 1 and Part 2

The new edition is in two parts. Part 1 is an updated and expanded version of the first edition. Part 2 is new, and contains a number of optional further conditions which the parties may wish to incorporate in particular cases.

As is apparent from condition 1.1.4, the conditions in Part 1 apply except as varied or excluded by the contract, whereas a condition in Part 2 will not apply unless expressly incorporated into the contract by a special condition.

A particular effect of condition 1.1.4(a) is that the general provisions in Part 1 which determine the completion date (conditions 1.1.1(d) and 8.1.1), the contract rate (condition 1.1.1(e)) and the title guarantee to be given in the transfer (condition 6.6.2) will automatically take effect subject to any individually negotiated terms which deal with these matters. For that reason, these provisions no longer include words making them expressly subject to the particular terms of the agreement.

Notices and documents

Condition 1.3.6 now makes it clear that the presumed times of receipt set out in condition 1.3.7 may be displaced not only by proof of the actual time at which a notice or document was received, but also by proof that the notice or document was not received at all.

Condition 1.3.3(b) is a new provision, which enables a notice or document to be sent by e-mail where delivery of the original is not essential. It is important to appreciate that condition 1.3.3(b) permits notices or documents to be sent in this way if, but only if, an e-mail address for the intended recipient is given in the contract. Thus, a party's conveyancers should not include their e-mail address in the contract unless they are prepared to accept service by e-mail at that address.

Two further provisions relevant to the use of e-mail should be noted. First, condition 1.3.5(c) provides that, where a notice or document sent by e-mail prompts an automated response that the intended recipient is out of the office, the response (while in reality establishing that the message has reached its intended destination) is to be treated as proof that the notice or document has not been received. The sender may, therefore, need to consider other means for sending the notice or document to its intended recipient (e.g., hand delivery or fax). Secondly, condition 1.3.7(e) provides that (in the absence of proof to the contrary under condition 1.3.6) a notice or document sent by e-mail is treated as having been received before 4.00 pm on the first working day after dispatch. This is later than the time of receipt presumed by condition 1.3.7(d) for a notice or document sent by fax (one hour after despatch), because the receipt of an e-mail may on occasion be delayed for several hours without the delay in transmission being readily apparent to the sender.

VAT

Condition 1.4 now includes a warranty by the seller that the sale of the property (as distinct from any chattels) is exempt from VAT and an agreement by the seller not to elect to waive that exemption before completion. In a case where it is intended either that the sale is to be standard rated for VAT, or that it is to be treated as the transfer of a going concern, condition 1.4 should be excluded, either partly or completely, by special condition. In such cases, users may wish to adopt condition A1 or A2 in Part 2 (see below), which have the effect of partly or wholly excluding condition 1.4, as appropriate.

Leases affecting the property

Condition 4 corresponds to condition 3.3 in the first edition, but has been expanded and rationalised. Condition 4.1, preserves the former condition 3.3.1 and 3.3.2, which specified the circumstances in which the condition applied and provided that the seller should provide the buyer with details of leases affecting the property before exchange and the buyer should then be treated as knowing and accepting the terms of each lease. It expands the terms previously found in condition 3.3.6 by providing not only that the seller is debarred from serving a notice to end the lease but also that it must not accept a surrender (condition 4.1.3). It is then provided that the seller is to inform the buyer if the lease ends (condition 4.1.4). Conditions 4.1.5 and 4.1.6 adopt the previous conditions 3.3.7 and 3.3.8 relating to the indemnity to be given by the buyer to the seller and the apportionment of the rent.

Provisions relating to the management of the property are then gathered together in condition 4.2. The information which the seller must give the buyer now extends to court or arbitration proceedings as well as to applications, and relevant applications are identified as applications for a licence, consent or approval (condition 4.2.1). Conditions 4.2.3 to 4.2.8 (which do not, however, apply to a rent review process governed by condition 5) distinguish between the conduct of court or arbitration proceedings and the taking of other steps in connection with the lease.

As regards court or arbitration proceedings, condition 4.2.3 requires the seller to conduct the proceedings in accordance with the buyer's directions (for which the seller must apply), unless the seller might thereby be placed in breach of an obligation to the tenant or a statutory duty. If the buyer fails to give directions with regard to a proposed step in the proceedings within 10 working days, the seller can decide for itself whether or not to take that step (condition 4.2.4). Where directions are given, the buyer must indemnify the seller against all loss or expense which it incurs by following those directions (condition 4.2.5).

As regards other steps in connection with the lease, condition 4.2.6 provides that the written consent of the buyer is required before the seller may grant or formally withhold any licence, consent or approval under the lease or take any other action as landlord under the lease. The previous provision prohibiting a buyer from refusing consent or attaching conditions where to do so might place the seller in breach of an obligation or statutory duty is now in condition 4.2.7(a), and additionally the seller is entitled to proceed as if the buyer has consented when the buyer is not entitled to refuse consent or, if so entitled, has not in fact refused consent within 10 working days. The buyer must indemnify the seller against loss and expense resulting from the refusal of consent or the attaching of conditions to consent (condition 4.2.8).

The general obligation to manage the property in accordance with the principles of good estate management is retained and now appears in condition 4.2.9.

A new condition (condition 4.3) has been included obliging the buyer, at the request and cost of the seller, to support any application by the seller to be released from the landlord covenants in the lease (see sections 6 to 8 of the Landlord and Tenant (Covenants) Act 1995).

Rent reviews

Condition 5 is new, and makes specific provision for cases in which a rent review is in progress during some or all of the period between the date of the contract and actual completion. As will be apparent from condition 5.1(a), the condition applies whether the seller's position is that of landlord or tenant: condition 5.4(a) will normally oblige the parties to press for the highest rent in the former case and the lowest rent in the latter.

The general rule is that condition 5 will continue to apply after actual completion if the rent review process has not been concluded by then. If the reviewed rent will be payable only in respect of a period which will begin after actual completion (so that the seller has no interest in the amount of the reviewed rent), the obligation to conduct the review in accordance with conditions 5.4 and 5.5 will cease to apply on actual completion (condition 5.2). Accordingly, the buyer will be a free agent in conducting the review process from then on.

The seller and buyer will each bear their own costs of the rent review process (condition 5.6). Where a third party is appointed to determine the rent, the buyer is to pay the third party's costs, except that, if the rent review date precedes the apportionment date, those costs are to divided between the buyer and seller in accordance with condition 5.8.

Where the seller is the landlord and a new rent is not agreed or determined until after actual completion, conditions 8.3.7(b) and 8.3.8 make provision for any additional rent which becomes due in respect of the period before the completion date to be collected by the buyer and paid to the seller.

Proof of title

Condition 6.1.1 requires the seller to provide the buyer with proof of its title to the property and of its ability to transfer it or to procure its transfer (the latter alternative applying, for example, to a sub-sale).

Where the title is registered, the effect of condition 6.1.2 is that the proof must include official copies of the individual register and any title plan referred to in it, and of any document referred to in the register and kept by the registrar (unless the document is to be discharged or overridden at or before completion).

Requisitions

The first edition of the SCPC allowed the buyer to raise requisitions after the making of the contract, whether or not title was deduced beforehand. The present edition recognises that where the seller deduces title before the contract is made (as it normally will, at least where the title is registered), the buyer should ensure that any concerns about the title so shown are raised before contract and, where necessary, appropriately provided for in the special conditions. Accordingly, condition 6.2.1(a) now bars the buyer from raising any requisitions on the title shown by the seller before the making of the contract. The buyer, however, retains the right to raise requisitions on matters coming to its attention for the first time after the contract is made (condition 6.2.2). The prohibition in condition 6.2.1(a) will not prevent the buyer from making enquiries about the seller's arrangements for discharging any mortgages because these enquiries relate to matters of conveyance rather than matters of title and are not, strictly speaking, requisitions.

In cases where the seller deduces title (either in whole or in part) after the contract is made, condition 6.3.1 continues to allow the buyer to raise requisitions within six working days of the date of the contract or delivery of the seller's proof of title on which the requisitions are raised.

Insurance

The old condition 5, which was entitled 'Pending completion' has been radically amended by the removal of the provisions relating to the occupation of the property by the buyer. The view was taken that in the commercial context such occupation would be upon terms specifically negotiated and the general provisions of condition 5.2 were unlikely to be used to a significant extent. The material then remaining in the condition related to the insurance of the property, and so condition 7 (as it is now) has been re-titled 'Insurance'. The provisions themselves have also been considerably revised.

Condition 7.1.4 maintains the general principle that the seller is under no obligation to the buyer to insure the property. However, in the circumstances specified in condition 7.1.1 (namely, where the contract provides for the seller's policy to continue after exchange or where the seller is obliged by the terms of a lease to continue to insure), the general rule is displaced and the position is governed by conditions 7.1.2 and 7.1.3. The obligations in relation to insurance which the seller then comes under are generally similar to those which previously applied, but it is now expressly provided that to the extent that the policy proceeds are applied in repairing or reinstating insured property which has been damaged, the seller is not obliged to pay the proceeds to the buyer (condition 7.1.2(f)). The provisions for the situation on completion which were formerly contained separately in condition 5.1.3 are now incorporated in condition 7.1.2 as paragraph (g). The buyer is still obliged to pay the seller a proportionate part of the premium paid by the seller for the period between contract and completion, but an exception has been introduced for the case in which the seller is entitled to recover the premium from a tenant (condition 7.1.3).

Section 47 of the Law of Property Act 1925 continues to be excluded, now by condition 7.1.5.

Completion after 2.00 pm

Conditions 8.1.2 and 8.1.3 clarify the position where the money due on completion is received after 2.00 pm. Condition 8.1.2 states the normal rule that, in such a case, apportionments and compensation are to be worked out as if completion had taken place on the next working day as a result of the buyer's default. It would, however, be unfair to adopt that approach where completion has been delayed because the seller has failed to vacate the property by 2.00 pm. Condition 8.1.3 therefore disapplies condition 8.1.2 in a case where the sale is with vacant possession and the buyer is ready, able and willing to complete (as to which, see condition 1.1.3(a)) but does not pay the money due on completion because the seller has not vacated the property by 2.00 pm.

Apportionments

Condition 8.3.2 identifies the day (called the 'apportionment day') from which income and outgoings are to be apportioned. That day will be the date of actual completion where the whole property is being sold with vacant possession or where (in a case where completion of tenanted property is delayed through the buyer's default) the seller opts to take the net income from the property until completion as well as compensation from the buyer. In any other case, the apportionment day will be the completion date.

Condition 8.3.4 explains how the apportionment is to be carried out. For these purposes, condition 8.3.4(a) provides that a sum to be apportioned is to be treated as payable for the period which it covers (so that, for example, a monthly rent will be treated as paid for the relevant month, however many days it may contain, and not as an equal twelfth part of the rent that would be payable over a complete year). Where, however, the sum is an instalment of an annual sum (e.g. a yearly rent payable by twelve monthly instalments), condition 8.3.4(a) will require the buyer to be credited or debited with 1/365th of the annual sum for each day from and including the apportionment day to the end of the instalment period. Thus, where, for example, the seller receives a quarterly instalment of rent and the apportionment day falls 10 days before the end of the relevant quarter, the buyer will be treated as entitled to so much of the instalment as corresponds to 10/365ths of the annual rent. It is thought that this accords with normal commercial practice. Condition 8.3.4(b) provides that sums are to be treated as accruing from day to day and at the rate applicable from time to time. Accordingly, changes in the daily rate occurring at any time during the period covered by the payment will need to be taken into account.

Condition 8.3.6 is no longer limited to service charge payments, but covers any expenditure on goods or services incurred, or to be incurred, by the seller in its capacity as landlord under a lease of the property. Under condition 8.3.6(a), the buyer's obligation to reimburse the seller for expenditure already incurred but not yet due from the tenant is dependent on the provision by the seller of the information and vouchers which the buyer will need to recover the expenditure from the tenant.

Seller's right to net income and compensation

Condition 9.3.4 (formerly condition 7.3.4) provides for cases in which the property is tenanted. It allows the seller to recover the income from the property in addition to any compensation to which it may be entitled under condition 9.3.1. While a provision to this effect is commonly encountered in contracts for the sale of commercial property, there is thought to be a risk that, if challenged, it would be struck down as a penalty. A particular source of difficulty is that the object of the compensation is to place the seller in the position it would have been in if the contract had been completed on time: if, however, the contract had been completed on time, the seller would not have received any income from the property following the completion date. The seller may, therefore, need to satisfy the court that the inclusion of the provision is justified by the particular circumstances of the sale.

Consent

The consent provisions of condition 10.3 (formerly condition 8.3) have undergone some significant amendment. Condition 10.3.1(a) ensures that condition 10.3 now applies not only in cases where the landlord's consent is required for the assignment of an existing lease or the creation of a sub-lease but also in cases where consent is required for the creation of a new lease of freehold land (e.g. from a mortgagee). In the light of the decision of the Court of Appeal in *Aubergine Enterprises Ltd* v. *Lakewood International Ltd* [2002] 1 WLR. 2149, condition 10.3.1(b) confirms that any necessary consent must be in a form which satisfies the requirement to obtain it.

Condition 10.3.2(b) now obliges the buyer to comply with all reasonable requirements, including requirements for the provision of information and references (thereby slightly rephrasing the obligation under the old condition 8.3.3(a) to use reasonable endeavours to provide promptly all information and references). This obligation applies whether the consent is required for a new lease or for an assignment or for a sub-letting. The further obligations which applied to the buyer in the case of an assignment or sub-letting under the previous edition are now included in condition 10.3.3. As regards the seller's obligations, these remain unchanged in content, but the seller's obligations in connection with applying for consent and giving notice to the buyer apply in all cases (condition 10.3.2(a)), whereas condition 10.3.3(b) now expressly provides that an authorised guarantee agreement may be required only in cases of assignment.

The remaining provisions of the old condition 8.3 appear in the new condition 10.3, subject to minor drafting amendments and a change in the order of the provisions.

Commonhold

The new commonhold regime is made the subject of express provision in two ways. First, the seller is required to provide the buyer with current copies of the memorandum and articles of the commonhold association and the commonhold community statement. If the buyer then enters into the contract, it is treated as doing so knowing and accepting their terms (condition 11.3, and cf. condition 4.1.2, which makes similar provision with regard to the terms of leases affecting the property). Secondly, in cases in which the consent of the commonhold association is required to the sale of part only of a commonhold unit, condition 11.4 places the onus on the seller to apply for the association's consent and to use all reasonable efforts to obtain it; a right of rescission will normally be available to either party if the association's consent has not been given three working days before completion date.

Part 2

As already noted, Part 2 consists of optional provisions which the parties may wish to incorporate by special condition in particular cases.

Conditions A1 and A2 offer two alternatives to the provision for VAT made in condition 1.4 of Part 1 (which assumes that the sale will be exempt from VAT). Condition A1 is designed for cases where the purchase price will attract VAT at the standard rate (either because exemption is not available or because it has been waived). Condition A2 is designed for cases where (i) the seller is using the property for the business of letting to produce a rental income, (ii) the seller has waived the exemption from VAT or for some other reason the sale attracts VAT (e.g. where the property consists of a newly constructed building) and (iii) it is intended that the sale should be treated as the transfer of a going concern (so that it will not be treated as the supply of either goods or services for VAT purposes).

Condition B is offered for use in cases where the seller has claimed capital allowances in respect of plant and machinery at the property and it is intended that, on completion, the parties will make an election under section 198 of the Capital Allowances Act 2001 which will determine the amount of the sale price which is to be treated as expenditure incurred by the buyer on the provision of the plant and machinery. It should be noted that condition B3.1 assumes that the special conditions will include an apportionment of part of the total price to plant and machinery.

Condition C contains two alternative provisions which may be relevant if the seller is selling a reversionary interest in a building which contains flats held by tenants who qualify for the right of first refusal conferred by the Landlord and Tenant Act 1987. Condition C1 is intended for use in cases where the seller, having served an offer notice on the tenants under section 6 of the Act, is free to proceed with the sale to the buyer (i.e. because the tenants did not accept the offer, or failed to nominate a person to take a transfer of the property, within the relevant time limits). Condition C2 is intended for use in cases where, at the date of the contract, the qualifying tenants have exercised, or may yet exercise, the right of first refusal conferred by the 1987 Act. Condition C2.3 makes provision for cases in which the sale is by auction. Among other things, it caters for the possibility that, following the auction, a person nominated by the tenants exercises the right under section 8B(4) to take over the contract: should that happen, the consequences as between the seller and the buyer will be the same as if the contract had been rescinded.

Error on first print of SCPC 2nd edition

Condition 10.3.4 should refer to section 19(1A), not section 19A, of the Landlord and Tenant Act 1927.

III.7. Report on proposed purchase (domestic)[1]

Of the property known as
15 High Hill, Harkley, Herts

prepared for Mr and Mrs Harvey Hart

1. The Property

The Property is known as 15 High Hill, Harkley, Herts HH1 2ZZ. A copy of the Land Registry entries and title plan is attached [*not produced in this book*] showing the extent of the property edged in red.

Land Registry title plans are to a small scale and are not intended to show the precise location of each boundary; these should be checked on site and any significant discrepancies referred to us so that we can seek clarification from the sellers.

2. Title

The Property is freehold. The title number is HH123456. It is registered at the Land Registry with 'absolute' title, which means that ownership is guaranteed by the Registry. You should inspect the property to ensure that it is only occupied by the seller and his immediate family and let us know if this is not the case. The property is being sold to you with full vacant possession on completion.

3. Rights passing with the Property

The Property has the benefit of a right of way over the alleyway at the rear of the Property, marked in brown on the Land Registry plan, leading to the road known as Hall Hollow. This right is on foot only, so there is no right to drive vehicles (or ride bicycles or horses) along it. The deeds do not make provision for any person to be responsible for maintaining or clearing the alleyway but do provide for the owner of the Property to pay a fair contribution towards any expenditure on such matters. The sellers state that they are not aware of anyone carrying out such works and have not been asked to pay anything in this regard. If the alleyway needs maintaining so that you can walk along it, as a matter of general law the right of way would give you the right to do necessary maintenance, but wholly at your own cost.

4. Rights over the Property

The owner of the property known as 13 High Hill has a right of way on foot across the south-west corner of the rear garden of the Property, to enable him to pass between the end of his garden and the alleyway. The route is marked in blue on the Land Registry plan. This right was apparently granted because the alleyway stops level with the west boundary of the Property and does not run behind the garden of number 13. The sellers state that the neighbour has never exercised this right during their 8 years of ownership of the Property; however, this does not mean that the right has legally lapsed.

5. Covenants

A number of restrictive covenants were imposed on the owner of the Property when the plot was sold to the original house builder in 1898. It appears that similar covenants were imposed on all the

---

1. This Report has been written by Frances Silverman and the Editorial Board of the Conveyancing Handbook.

plots in the street, and these covenants may still be enforceable by one house owner against another; if you purchase the Property, you may be obliged to observe them, and you may be entitled to require the neighbouring owners to observe them. The following is a summary of those that may still be relevant:

(1) not to park any caravan or similar vehicle on the Property;

(2) not to erect more than one single house on the Property, apart from a greenhouse or other usual outbuilding;

(3) not to use any house for business use but only as a private dwelling;

(4) not to cause nuisance or annoyance to neighbours.

Even if these covenants are not strictly enforceable in law, planning restrictions imposed by the local authority may in practice have a similar effect.

A positive covenant was also imposed in 1898, requiring the owner of the Property to maintain the fence on the east boundary of the Property. We have marked this fence with the letter 'T' on the attached copy of the Land Registry plan. Whilst it is unlikely that anyone could legally enforce compliance with this covenant, in practice you should be prepared to maintain this fence, and the other fences bounding the Property, at your own cost.

6. Information from the Sellers

The solicitors acting for the sellers, Henry and Hetty Hodgson, have supplied us with a package of information under the Law Society TransAction scheme. We attach copies of the following items supplied to us in that package:

(a) Property Information Form

This gives information about boundaries, disputes, notices, guarantees, services, rights and other matters. Our comments are:

(1) the information on boundaries must be read subject to our comment about the eastern fence, in paragraph 5 of this Report;

(2) the building work mentioned in reply to question 10.3 of the Form did not need planning permission, but future enlargement of the building might.

(b) List of Fittings and Contents

This indicates which items at the Property are included in the sale and which are not. Please let us know if anything stated to be excluded was in fact supposed to be included, or if you reach agreement with the sellers to buy any of the excluded items.

We understand that this sale is dependent upon the sellers buying another property, but their solicitors tell us that this is progressing well and they hope to be in a position to exchange contracts on both transactions at the end of next month.

7. Information from the Local Authority, etc.

We have made a search in the Register of Local Land Charges and have raised enquiries with the local council, and have obtained the following information which relates to the property which you are intending to buy. A separate search would be needed to obtain information relating to neighbouring properties:

(1) High Hill and Hall Hollow are publicly maintained roads, but the rear alleyway is not;

(2) there are no current plans for road improvements or new roads within 200 metres of the Property;

(3) foul drainage is believed to be connected to the public sewer but the means of connection is not known (a drain running between a house and the public sewer is not maintained at public expense and you should consult your surveyor as to the likelihood of your having to repair or maintain any drain connected to the property).

None of the other replies by the council to our enquiries need to be drawn to your attention.

Because of the location of the Property, we have also made a search with the Coal Authority in order that you or your surveyor can assess the risk of future subsidence due to coal extraction beneath the Property. A statutory compensation scheme is available if you suffer damage as a result of mining works. The Coal Authority has given the following response:

(1) Two seams of coal have been mined at an approximate depth of 200 metres under or near the Property, the last working being in 1990.

(2) There are presently no workings taking place within influencing distance of the Property.

(3) Although coal exists unworked, the Coal Authority states that the possibility of future working is considered unlikely.

8. Outgoings

The Property is in band F for council tax purposes. The annual water charge (currently £XXX) is payable to Hartford Water Company. The water supply at the Property is not metered.

9. The Purchase Contract

This is in a form incorporating the Standard Conditions of Sale, which are widely used for this type of transaction. The main provisions of the contract are:

(1) The purchase price is £XXX,XXX. (No VAT will be payable on this.) The price includes the items shown on the list attached to the contract, which corresponds with the list of Fittings and Chattels mentioned above.

(2) On exchange of contracts, you must pay a deposit of £XX,XXX. If we cannot complete your purchase of the Property due to the Hodgsons' default, you will become entitled to the return of the deposit (and may be able to claim damages for your loss). However, under the Standard Conditions of Sale, all or part of the deposit money can be used by Mr and Mrs Hodgson to pay the deposit on their new property, and only the remainder, if any, will be retained by their solicitors as 'stakeholder' until we satisfactorily complete the purchase. Whilst this arrangement has become common practice, we must warn you that in the event of the matter not completing, it may be more difficult to obtain repayment of deposit money which has been used by the Hodgsons in that way, than if the whole deposit was retained by their solicitors until completion; on the other hand, very few house purchases totally fail to complete (though completion is occasionally delayed), and you may be prepared to take this risk rather than insisting that the Hodgsons incur the expense of obtaining separate bridging finance for the deposit on their new property. Please discuss this with us if you are concerned about it.

(3) The completion date will be inserted just before contracts are exchanged. We will discuss it with you at that time so that a date acceptable to both you and the Hodgsons can be fixed. This date will then be the date on which the transaction is to be completed: the Hodgsons must vacate the Property on that date, if they do not vacate earlier, and we must send the completion money to their solicitors to reach their bank account by 2 pm that afternoon. You will be liable to pay daily interest at X% per year above bank base rate if cleared funds are not made available to us in time to remit the completion money

early enough, so we will need to receive the funds (other than the loan from your Building Society, mentioned below) from you either by cheque in favour of this firm reaching us at least five working days before the completion date, or by bank transfer into this firm's bank account preferably on the day before the completion date. Nearer the time, we will let you know how much we require; this will include a sum to cover our fees, disbursements paid or payable by us (including stamp duty of £X,XXX and registration fees of £XXX) and VAT.

(4)   You are buying the Property in its actual state and condition. You must be satisfied about this from your own inspection of the Property and from your surveyor's report. If you expect the sellers to remedy (or pay for the remedy of) any defects, this will have to be agreed with them before contracts are exchanged and special provisions added to the contract. Your lender has asked us to point out to you that the valuation undertaken by their surveyor may not reveal all the defects in the Property.

(5)   The Property remains at the sellers' risk until completion, and the sellers must hand it over in its present condition, except for fair wear and tear. You would be entitled to withdraw from the transaction, with the return of your deposit, if the Property was so badly damaged before the completion date as to make it unusable, and the sellers would have a similar right if the damage was caused by a risk against which they could not have been expected to insure.

10.   Mortgage

We have received instructions from the Highland Building Society to act for them on a mortgage loan to assist you in buying the Property. We have to report to them on the result of our investigations about the Property and also on any discrepancies between the details of the transaction known to us and the details you gave the Society with your mortgage application (e.g. as to the purchase price). So far, the documents supplied to us do not show any such discrepancies.

The main terms of the proposed mortgage are:

(1)   The loan will be £XX,XXX.

(2)   Interest is variable at the discretion of the Society, but will initially be at the rate of X% per year.

(3)   The loan is repayable, with interest, over XX years, by monthly instalments comprising a mixture of capital and interest. Initially the instalments will be £XXX per month, but this is variable and the Society will recalculate the amount as a result of changes in the rate of interest. You will be required to pay the instalments by bank standing order. Failure to pay any instalments will entitle the Society to call for immediate repayment of the entire loan.

(4)   The loan will be to both of you, and you will both be individually legally responsible for ensuring that the instalment payments are duly made and that the other provisions of the mortgage, mentioned below, are observed.

(5)   The loan and interest will be secured on a first legal mortgage over the Property. This will give the Society various rights if you fail to pay the instalments, including the right to apply to the court to evict you and your family so that the Society can sell the Property in order to recoup the outstanding loan and any unpaid interest. If the sale proceeds exceed the amount due to the Society, the surplus will be paid to you (or to any second lender), but if there is a shortfall the Society can sue you for it.

(6)   The mortgage will impose a number of standard obligations and restrictions, the most important being:

(a)   you must keep the Property in good repair;

(b)   you must insure the Property with insurers agreed between you and the Society;

(c)   you must not alter the Property, or change its use, without the Society's prior consent;

(d)   you must not let any part of the Property without the Society's prior consent;

(e)   no second or subsequent mortgage must be taken out without the Society's prior consent.

(7)   The mortgage will be security for any future loans you may borrow from the Society, as well as for the loan mentioned above.

The full text of the mortgage terms are set out in the enclosed book from the Society, and we recommend that you read them.

11.   Environmental matters

We have/have not made enquiries relating to environmental matters affecting the property. [Our enquiries revealed the following information [*set out details*].]

Please ask us if you have any queries about this report or on any other aspect of this transaction.

12.   Joint purchase

[*Where there are two or more buyers explain the difference between joint tenancy and tenancy in common and request the buyers to confirm their choice to you.*]

[*Name of solicitors*]

IV. LAW SOCIETY'S PRACTICE INFORMATION

IV.1. Contaminated Land Warning Card[1]

Warning – To All Solicitors – Contaminated Land Liabilities

The advice contained on this Card is not intended to be a professional requirement for solicitors. Solicitors should be aware of the requirements of Part IIA of the Environmental Protection Act 1990 but they themselves cannot provide their clients with conclusive answers. They must exercise their professional judgement to determine the applicability of this advice to each matter in which they are involved and, where necessary, they should suggest to the client obtaining specialist advice. In the view of the Law Society the advice contained in this Card conforms to current best practice.

Solicitors should be aware that environmental liabilities may arise and consider what further enquiries and specialist assistance the client should be advised to obtain.

Contaminated land

1. The contaminated land regime was brought into effect in England on 1 April 2000. It applies to all land, whether residential, commercial, industrial or agricultural. It can affect owners, occupiers, developers, and lenders. The legislation, which is contained in Part IIA, Environmental Protection Act 1990 and in regulations and statutory guidance issued under it (see Contaminated Land (England) Regulations 2000 SI 2000/227 and DETR Guidance on Contaminated Land April 2000) is retrospective. It covers existing and future contamination.

The National Assembly is expected shortly to introduce similar regulations regarding contaminated land in Wales.

2. Local authorities must inspect and identify seriously contaminated sites. They can issue remediation notices requiring action to remediate contamination, in the absence of a voluntary agreement to do so. In certain cases ('Special Sites') responsibility for enforcement lies with the Environment Agency.

A negative reply to the standard local authority enquiries from the local authority may merely mean the site has not been inspected. It does not necessarily mean there is no problem.

Compliance can be costly, and may result in expenditure which could exceed the value of the property.

Liability falls primarily on those who 'cause or knowingly permit' contamination (a Class A person). If the authority cannot identify a Class A person, liability falls on a Class B person, the current owner, or occupier of the land. Class B persons include lenders in possession. There are complex exclusion provisions for transferring liability from one party to another. Some exclusions

---

1.© The Law Society June 2001.

apply only on the transfer of land, or the grant of a lease. The applicability of any relevant exclusion needs to be considered before entering such transactions.

In every transaction you must consider whether contamination is an issue.

Conveyancing transactions

In purchases, mortgages and leases, solicitors should:

1. Advise the client of potential liabilities associated with contaminated land.

Generally clients should be advised of the possibility and consequences of acquiring interests in contaminated land and the steps that can be taken to assess the risks.

2. Make specific enquiries of the seller.

In all commercial cases, and if contamination is considered likely to be a risk in residential cases (e.g. redevelopment of brown field land):

3. Make enquiries of statutory and regulatory bodies.

4. Undertake independent site history investigation, e.g. obtaining site report from a commercial company.

In commercial cases, if there is a likelihood that the site is contaminated:

5. Advise independent full site investigation.

6. Consider use of contractual protections and the use of exclusion tests.

This may involve specific disclosure of known defects, possibly coupled with price reduction, requirements on seller to remedy before completion, and in complex cases the use of warranties and indemnities.

Unresolved problems, consider

7. Advising withdrawal, and noting advice;

8. Advising insurance (increasingly obtainable for costs of remediation of undetected contamination and any shortfall in value because of undisclosed problems).

Specific transactions

1. Leases

Consider if usual repair and statutory compliance clauses transfer remediation liability to tenant, and advise.

2. Mortgages

Advise lender, if enquiries reveal potential for or existence of contamination, and seek instructions.

In enforcement cases, consider appointment of receivers, rather than steps resulting in lender becoming mortgagee in possession, and so treated as a Class B person.

3. Share sales and asset purchases

Consider recommending the obtaining of specialist technical advice on potential liabilities, use of detailed enquiries, warranties and indemnities.

Other relevant legislation

Other legislation and common law liabilities (e.g. nuisance) may also be relevant when advising on environmental matters including:

Water Resources Act 1991
Groundwater Regulations 1998
Pollution Prevention and Control (England and Wales) Regulations 2000

Further information

Law Society's *Environmental Law Handbook*
DETR's Website **www.detr.gov.uk**

IV.2. Apportionment of rent

1. APPORTIONMENT OF RENT FORMULA[1]

The method of calculation is based on the view that, where a lease or tenancy agreement reserves an annual rent, the usual direction to pay the rent by equal quarterly payments will have been inserted for estate management convenience only and will not have been intended to convert the annual rent into a quarterly rent. This is important because the traditional quarters are of unequal duration and hence the daily amount of rent would differ between one quarter and another if it were calculated quarter by quarter.

The example used below to illustrate the methods is for a lease dated 8 March [20—] expressed to grant a term of 'ten years commencing on 29 September [20— (the previous year)]' and expressed to reserve 'a rent of £36,500 per annum payable by equal quarterly payments in advance on the usual quarter days (the first payment being a due proportion thereof for the period from the date hereof to the following quarter day to be paid on the execution hereof)'.

Initial payment

Step 1: Ascertain the 'term year'. In the example, the term year will begin on 29 September in one year and end on 28 September in the following year. If, instead, the term had been expressed as 'a term commencing on the date hereof and expiring on 28 September [in ten years time]', the 'term year' would probably (although it is a matter of intention evidenced by the wording used in the lease) commence on 8 March in one year and end on 7 March in the following year. If the term was expressed to run 'from' a particular date, it would be necessary to consider whether under the particular lease the term began on that date or on the next day, a question discussed in most of the reference books on leases.

Step 2: Count the number of days for which the tenant is liable to pay rent during the first term year. In the example, this would be from 8 March to 28 September inclusive, namely 205 days.

Step 3: Calculate the rent payable for that number of days on an annual basis. In our example, this would be

$$205/365 \times £36,500 = £20,500$$

Step 4: Calculate the rent that the tenant will have to pay on those rent payment days which will fall between the grant of the lease and the end of the first term year. In our example, there would be two such rent payment days, 25 March and 24 June, on each of which the tenant will have to pay one quarter's rent (£9,125) and therefore the total rent payable on those days will be

$$2 \times £9,125 = £18,250$$

Step 5: Deduct the sum calculated at step 4 from the sum calculated at step 3. The difference is the amount that the tenant must pay on the grant of the lease. In our example, this is

$$£20,500 - £18,250 = £2,250$$

1. © The Law Society. This article by Philip Freedman, [1990] *Gazette*, 3 October, 35, gives the method of calculation for the apportionment of rent formulated by the Law Society's Conveyancing and Land Law Committee.

. (Contrast this with the figure of £1,700 that would have been calculated by simply taking the number of days from 8 March to 24 March inclusive at a daily rate of £100 (calculated on an annual basis) or the figure of £1,723.61 that would have been calculated by taking those days as a fraction of the current quarter.)

Assignment of lease

Assume that the lease is assigned on 31 March [in the second year of the term]. The apportionment as between the assignor and the assignee is to be calculated as follows:

Step 1: Ascertain the term year.

Step 2: Count the number of days for which the present tenant is liable to pay the rent during the current term year down to the date of the assignment. In our example, this is from 29 September [in year 1] to 31 March [in year 2], namely 184 days.

Step 3: Calculate the rent payable for that number of days on an annual basis. In our example, this would be

$$184/365 \times £36,500 = £18,400.$$

Step 4: Ascertain the amount of rent that will have been paid by the present tenant in respect of the current term year. In our example, the present tenant will have paid rent for the current year on 29 September [in year 1], 25 December [in year 1] and 25 March [in year 2], namely

$$3 \times £9,125 = £27,375$$

Step 5: Compare the figures calculated at steps 3 and 4. If the former exceeds the latter, the present tenant must make an allowance of the difference to the assignee. If the latter exceeds the former, the assignee must make an allowance in favour of the present tenant. In our example, the present tenant has paid more rent than relates to his period of occupation during the current term year by the figure

$$£27,375 - £18,400 = £8,975$$

. This is the amount for which he is to be reimbursed by his assignee. (Contrast this with the sum of £8,400 that would have been calculated by simply applying the daily rate of £100 to the number of days between 31 March and the end of that quarter.)

On sale of reversion

Using our example, suppose that the landlord's interest was transferred to a new landlord on 30 April [in the second year of the term]. The apportionment of rental income between the old landlord and the new landlord is to be calculated as follows:

Step 1: Ascertain the term year.

Step 2: Count the number of days for which the old landlord is entitled to retain the rent received from the tenant in respect of the current term year. In our example, the old landlord is entitled to the rent for the period from 29 September [in year 1] to 30 April [in year 2], namely 214 days.

Step 3: Calculate the rent receivable for that number of days on an annual basis. In our example, this would be

$$214/365 \times £36,500 = £21,400$$

Step 4: Calculate the amount of rent actually received by the old landlord from the tenant in respect of the current term year. In our example, this rent should have been received on 29 September [in year 1], 25 December [in year 1] and 25 March [in year 2], namely

$$3 \times £9,125 = £27,375$$

Step 5: Compare the figures calculated at steps 3 and 4. If the former exceeds the latter, the new landlord must make an allowance of the difference to the old landlord. If the latter exceeds the former, the old landlord must make an allowance of the difference to the new landlord. In our example, the old landlord has received more rent than relates to his period of ownership by the sum of

$$£27,375 - £21,400 = £5,975$$

. This is the amount which the old landlord must allow to the new landlord on transferring the reversion. (Contrast that with the sum of £5,400 that would have been calculated simply by taking the number of days between 30 April and the end of the current quarter and applying the daily rate of £100.)

For consistency, where the term expires by effluxion of time on a date other than the last day of a term year, the amount of the tenants' final payment of rent should be calculated on a basis similar to the apportionment of his initial payment on the grant of the lease.

2. APPORTIONMENT OF RENT – FURTHER GUIDANCE[1]

In [1990] *Gazette*, 3 October, 35, an article was published setting out the land law committee's recommended formula ('the standard formula') for the calculation of apportionment of rent.

The application of the standard formula depends on being able to ascertain from the lease a 'term year', and for that term year to commence on a rent payment date (e.g. a quarter day where the rent is payable on quarter days).

To avoid doubt the committee wishes to emphasise that the standard formula cannot be properly applied where the term year runs from a date which is not a rent payment date. Attempting to apply the concept behind the standard formula in that situation usually produces manifestly wrong results. This is because there is a logical nexus where the payment dates for yearly rent are geared to the term year (since this enables one to identify the period to which particular rent payments relate), but not where the rent payment dates bear no relationship to the term year.

For example, take a lease granted for 25 years starting on 11 November 1992 at an initial rent of £365,000 per annum, payable in advance by equal quarterly payments on the usual quarter days. The first 'term year' runs from 11 November 1992 to 10 November 1993 inclusive. How should the first rent payment, payable on the grant of the lease, be calculated? The standard formula cannot be sensibly applied unless it is adjusted on the basis that the payment will fall due on 29 September 1993 (the last rent payment date in the first term year) will only take the rent up to 10 November 1993. That cannot be right, since part of that payment would then have to relate to a period prior to 29 September 1993, in which event the payment would not be 'in advance'.

Therefore in cases where the term is not calculated from a calendar date which is also a recurring rent payment date, the apportionment will have to be made on some other basis. While this may vary according to the precise facts, it is likely that the most appropriate alternative would be what is sometimes called the 'surveyor's method'. This involves simply counting the days to immediately before the next payment date, and applying a daily rate computed on a yearly basis. In this example, the period from 11 November to 24 December 1992 (inclusive) is 44 days, and applying it to the daily rate (calculated by the year) or £1,000 per day produces a figure of £44,000.

---

1. © The Law Society. This article by the Law Society's Conveyancing and Land Law Committee, [1992] *Gazette*, 10 June, 22, gives further guidance from the Committee on the formula in no.1 above.

This illogicality of this common approach is obvious. A daily rent for rent payable by quarterly instalments is being calculated on a yearly basis and then applied to the residue of a particular quarter, which does not comprise exactly one-fourth of a year. A variation would be to calculate the daily rate for the particular quarter by reference to the total number of days in that quarter, and in this example the daily rate for the September quarter would be £1,061.05, which produces a figure of £46,686.20.

On either basis, it will be apparent that, should it be necessary to calculate an apportionment at a later date (e.g. when the lease is assigned or surrendered, or the reversion is transferred), to achieve a fair result it would be necessary to ascertain how much rent was actually paid under the apportionment at the grant of the lease and carry the calculation forward on that basis. This will usually be impractical, and the parties will have to be prepared to adopt each time a more rough and ready approach, such as the 'surveyor's method'.

However, since that method is entirely arbitrary and bears no logical relationship to the term/rent structure of the lease, the conveyancing and land law committee recommends that leases should be drafted so that the term year commences on one of the recurring rent payment dates. Thus if the rent is to be payable on the usual quarter days, the term year should commence on a quarter day. This will enable apportionments to be computed on a logical basis set out in the standard formula.

IV.3. Insolvency (No.2) Act 1994: counsel's opinion[1]

Section 339 of the 1986 Act gives the court power, on the application of the trustee in bankruptcy, to set aside an undervalue transaction, i.e. a gift or transfer for significantly low consideration, should the maker of the gift or transfer become bankrupt within five years after the date of the undervalue transaction. Section 342 provides protection, in certain conditions, against the use of section 339 powers. However, in its 1986 form, it was too restrictive. It left exposed to the risk of section 339 proceedings not only those who had benefited from undervalue transactions, but also those who had subsequently acquired, in good faith and for value, by way of genuine open market purchases, any property which had previously been the subject of an undervalue transaction. The 1994 Act overcame this problem by removing the 1986 Act's requirement that a buyer of – or, strictly, the acquirer of an interest in – property had to acquire not only in good faith and for value, but also without notice of the previous undervalue transaction, in order to get a title unchallengeable under section 339. With most types of property, a subsequent good faith buyer is unlikely to have notice of a previous undervalue transaction affecting it, and this generally applies to land as long as its title is registered. However, where title is unregistered, a buyer will inevitably have notice of a previous undervalue transaction. There is still a substantial amount of unregistered land in the UK and difficulties caused by section 339 are common. To the extent that the 1994 Act brought about protection for the good faith and for value acquirer, its effect was wholly beneficial. Unfortunately, as the price paid for removing the 'without notice' requirement, section 2(2) of the Act (which inserted new subsection (2A) into section 342 of the 1986 Act) made two exceptions to the improved protection. One of these is of little significance since it applies to an acquirer who is an 'associate of', or is 'connected with' (both terms are defined by the 1986 Act) either the undervalue transferor or transferee. However, the other exception, the 'dual notice' exception, gives rise to the main question which has been raised about the 1994 Act. These are counsel's views on this and other questions about the Act's effect.

Question 1

What is the effect of the 'dual notice' exception on the person who will for convenience be called the 'subsequent acquirer' (i.e. a person acquiring on the open market from the undervalue transferee, and also any further person who later acquires on the open market from that person)? The dual notice exception (section 342(2A) of the 1986 Act as amended by the 1994 Act) says that, where a subsequent acquirer of an interest in property has notice both of a previous undervalue transaction and of bankruptcy proceedings (i.e. a petition which leads to a bankruptcy order; or an actual bankruptcy order) against the undervalue transferor, the acquirer will be presumed to acquire other than in good faith, until he or she shows otherwise. The problem which this exception causes arises thus: A transfers a property at an undervalue to B; B sells on the open market to C who buys in good faith; C, some time later, wants to sell to D, another open market and good faith buyer. C knew of the undervalue transaction between A and B (though, with current land registration rules, this is perhaps unlikely to happen very often) but, at the time when he or she bought, there were no bankruptcy proceedings against A, so C acquired an unquestionably good title. However, by the time C sells to D, bankruptcy proceedings have begun against A, and D knows of the previous undervalue transaction (though this is even more unlikely under the current land registration

1. © The Law Society. In 1995 the Law Society obtained the opinion of leading counsel, Gabriel Moss QC. These paragraphs set out his views.

regime). What is D's position as to possible section 339 proceedings? Counsel's view is that D is, in practice, at no risk if he acquires in these circumstances (provided that, in reality, he acts in good faith). Counsel says that this is an issue which must be looked at in context.

The underlying purpose of the legislation is to protect the *bona fide* buyer in good faith and for value, i.e. the buyer in the ordinary course of buying and selling property, while preventing creditors being cheated. Counsel is also confident that no court would deprive D of an interest bought in good faith and for value, for the benefit of the creditors of A, since it would be outrageously unfair to do so. Counsel is also confident that the courts would be concerned to interpret the legislation so as to achieve a fair result. He refers to the observation of Sir Donald Nicholls V-C in *Paramount Airways Ltd (No.2)* [1992] 3 All ER 1 (CA) in support of the view that 'the court will ensure that it does not seek to exercise oppressively or unfairly the very wide jurisdiction conferred by the sections' (in that case, sections 238 to 241). In fact, counsel thinks it highly unlikely that, in practice, any trustee in bankruptcy would even consider trying to challenge D since it would be a waste of the assets of the bankrupt's estate to do so. However, should this unlikely situation occur, counsel's view is that there are three bases on which an application should be resisted.

(i) Under the 'shelter' rule: this rule, which is not widely known, is illustrated in *Wilkes* v. *Spooner* [1911] 2 KB 473 (CA). It says, broadly, that a person who acquires property in good faith and for value can pass on as good a title as he or she has to another person who also acquires in good faith. In *Wilkes* v. *Spooner*, a person acquired land which was subject to various covenants. However, as he had acquired without notice of them, but in good faith and for value, he was not bound by them. By the time he came to sell, the covenants had come to light, but he claimed that, because of the 'shelter' principle, he could sell free of them to another good faith buyer. The Court of Appeal agreed. In counsel's view, this principle applies equally to property in the undervalue transaction context – and, indeed, some of the drafting of section 342 may, he thinks, be a somewhat clumsy attempt to reflect the 'shelter' rule.

(ii) On the grounds that D's title is 'derived' from that of C section 342(2)(a) of the 1986 Act (as amended) says that no order made under section 339 shall prejudice an interest acquired in good faith and for value, nor any interest 'derived' from that interest. What 'derived' means in this context is unclear, but counsel thinks that its use may have been intended to replicate the 'shelter' rule. If this is the effect of the term, D's interest would be protected by reason of being 'derived' from that of C. It is possible, however, that interests such as those of subsequent buyers were not intended to be treated as 'derived' interests and that the term was meant to cover only interests such as those acquired by inheritance.

(iii) On the grounds, simply, that he or she had acquired in good faith and for value. In a normal open market transaction, there would be no question that the buyer had acquired his or her interest in this way. However, new subsection (2A) of section 342 (inserted by the 1994 Act) creates an artificial presumption against good faith where the dual notice exception applies, even in relation to such a transaction. Counsel's view, however, is that a court would ask no more of D, in order to displace this presumption, than to show that his purchase was at arm's length and for value, i.e. that it was a normal, open market purchase. Thus, in the highly unlikely event of a challenge, the presumption against good faith would be easily rebutted. Only where there was actual evidence calling D's good faith into question could there be any prospect of a serious challenge by a trustee. If D had bought on the open market, this would be a highly unusual situation – indeed, it is difficult to imagine its arising.

Question 2

What does 'notice' mean in this context (i.e. as to notice of a previous undervalue transaction but, in particular, notice of bankruptcy proceedings)? Counsel's view is that actual notice is notice in this context, both as to bankruptcy proceedings and previous undervalue transactions. As to statutory notice of bankruptcy proceedings, an acquirer of an interest in unregistered land will have notice of any information recorded either in the register of pending actions or in the register of writs and orders – sections 5 and 6 Land Charges Act 1972. Although there is some question (because of the wording of sections 5 and 6, and also of section 198 Law of Property Act 1925) as to whether this notice would be effective against an acquirer, because it would not be recorded against the name of a bankrupt with any present connection with the property concerned, the prudent view is to assume that it would do so. As to registered land, the acquirer will have notice only of what appears on the land register. Section 59 Land Registration Act 19[2]5 says that a writ, order, etc. has effect against registered land only if lodged as provided by that Act, so that it is shown on the registered title; and section 14 Land Charges Act 1972 excludes that Act's effect as to any matter relating to registered land. Nevertheless, counsel suggests that, where a prospective buyer of registered land has notice of an undervalue transaction – but only then – it would be prudent to carry out a bankruptcy search against the undervalue transferor, if known, as failure to do so might cause difficulties in rebutting the presumption against good faith (section 342(2A)) should the issue arise.

Question 3

What is the effect of the 1994 Act on mortgagees? In counsel's view, exactly the same as on the acquirer of any other kind of interest. A mortgagee acquires an interest in property. In a normal mortgage of domestic property to a bank or building society, the mortgagee clearly acquires its interest in good faith and gives value. The mortgagee's interest is thus protected by section 342(2)(a) as amended. This applies regardless of whether the mortgagor is B, the undervalue transferee; or C, the first subsequent good faith and for value buyer; or D, the next subsequent good faith and for value buyer. Similarly, a mortgagee exercising its power of sale would be able to pass good title to a subsequent acquirer, for the same reasons that a subsequent freehold buyer (C or D) can do so. The Law Society has received queries about the effect of section 339 and the 1994 Act where property which is the subject of an undervalue transaction is transferred subject to an existing mortgage. In this situation, no section 339 issue arises at all, as far as the mortgaged interest is concerned, because the mortgage agreement was entered into before the undervalue transaction took place. Though the trustee in bankruptcy could apply under section 339 for the return of the property itself – in practice, the equity which would have been the subject of an undervalue transaction – the mortgagee's interest would remain intact (as it would have had the mortgage been created after the undervalue transaction, in the event of section 339 proceedings).

Question 4

Where A transfers property at an undervalue to A (self) and B jointly or in common; or A and B transfer jointly either to A or B alone, does the section 342(2)(a) protection operate in relation to C, the subsequent acquirer, or is it disapplied by the exclusion contained in section 342(2)(a) of an interest acquired from 'that individual', i.e. the undervalue transferor. Counsel's view is that C is not excluded from the protection given by section 342(2)(a) because of having acquired from 'that individual'. Where A, as sole owner, transfers to himself and B jointly, what happens is that A transfers the whole of the legal estate in the property, but only that part of his beneficial interest which passes to B. In this context, what Insolvency Act 1986 is concerned with is the beneficial, not the legal, interest in the property which is the subject of an undervalue transaction. Thus, when A and B then sell to C (a good faith and for value buyer), what C acquires is A's beneficial interest which has not been the subject of an undervalue transaction, and B's beneficial interest which has been but which C obviously does not acquire from 'that individual'). Thus, the interest acquired by C comes within the section 342(2)(a) protection to the extent that it is acquired from B, and is outside section 339 altogether to the extent that it is acquired from A. Similarly, when A and B transfer jointly owned property to B, and B then sells to C, the same principle applies. That is, since the only transfer to which section 339 and section 342(2)(a) are material is that of A's beneficial interest to B and, as C is acquiring from B and not A, he or she is not affected by the 'other than that individual' exclusion.

IV.4. Dealing with unqualified conveyancers[1]

Effect of section 22 of the Solicitors Act 1974

1.   Section 22 of the Solicitors Act 1974 (see Annex 2A at p.45 in the Guide) makes it an offence for an unqualified person to draw or prepare, *inter alia*, a contract for sale or a transfer, conveyance, lease or mortgage relating to land in expectation of fee, gain or reward. Qualified persons under this section are solicitors, barristers, notaries public, licensed conveyancers, some public officers and, for unregistered conveyancing, Scottish solicitors.

2.   It is inevitable that an unqualified person who undertakes a conveyancing transaction in the course of a conveyancing business will commit an offence under section 22, unless the drawing or preparation of the relevant documents is undertaken by a qualified person. In such circumstances, the unqualified conveyancer's client is likely, albeit unwittingly, to be guilty of aiding and abetting the offence. The solicitor acting for the other party could also be guilty of procuring the commission of an offence by inviting or urging the unqualified person to provide a draft contract or transfer or to progress the transaction.

3.   Solicitors should therefore refuse to have any dealings with any unqualified person carrying on a conveyancing business unless there is clear evidence that offences under section 22 will not be committed.

4.   It is recommended that, at the outset of any transaction, the solicitor should write to the unqualified conveyancer drawing attention to this guidance and saying that the solicitor cannot enter into any dealings with him or her unless there is clear evidence that no offences will be committed. An example of satisfactory evidence would be a letter from a qualified person confirming that he or she will prepare the relevant documents. The solicitor should also immediately report to his or her own client and explain why he or she cannot deal with the unqualified conveyancer unless clear evidence is forthcoming.

Draft letter to unqualified conveyancer

'We are instructed to act for the seller/buyer in connection with the above transaction and understand that you have been instructed by the buyer/seller. Please confirm that you are a solicitor or licensed conveyancer. If not, please state who will prepare the contract/conveyance/transfer for you; we need to receive written confirmation from a qualified person that he or she will personally settle the contract/conveyance/transfer.

As you know, it is an offence for an unqualified person to prepare a contract for sale or a transfer, conveyance or mortgage relating to land in expectation of fee, gain or reward. We have been advised by the Law Society that we should not deal with an unqualified person carrying on a conveyancing business unless clear evidence is provided that offences under section 22 of the Solicitors Act 1974 will not be committed. The written confirmation referred to above, if explicit and unequivocal, could provide such evidence.

---

1. © The Law Society. The following text was previously published as Annex 25A in *The Guide to the Professional Conduct of Solicitors 1999*. Cross references to paragraphs in the *Guide* include page references from the *Guide*.

We regret that unless you are a solicitor or licensed conveyancer, we cannot deal with you until the evidence required above is provided.'

Draft letter to client of solicitor

'Thank you for your instructions relating to the above transactions. There is unfortunately a problem. The buyer/seller appears to have instructed an unqualified conveyancer to act for him/her and this could lead to the conveyancer, his/her client and myself being involved in the commission of criminal offences under the Solicitors Act 1974. The Law Society, my professional body, has advised solicitors not to deal with unqualified conveyancers because of the possibility of committing criminal offences.

I have therefore written to the firm acting for the buyer/seller asking for confirmation whether or not they are unqualified conveyancers and, if they are, whether they will be making arrangements to prevent the commission of such offences. If they cannot satisfy me about this, the buyer/seller will have to instruct a solicitor or licensed conveyancer, or deal with me direct.'

Further help

1.   Solicitors should first check with the Council for Licensed Conveyancers whether a person is a licensed conveyancer, since a licensed conveyancer can normally be dealt with as if a solicitor (see **25.06**, p.472 in the Guide).

2.   The Society can help practitioners dealing with unqualified conveyancers if the above guidance and the practice notes below do not cover the situation. Telephone calls and written requests for guidance should be made to the Practice Advice Service – for contact details see p.xv.

3.   The Professional Adviser (for contact details, see p.xv) has responsibility for investigating and prosecuting non-solicitors who appear to be in breach of the Solicitors Act 1974. Solicitors are asked to report (without submitting their files) any case where there is *prima facie* evidence of breaches of the Solicitors Act.

4.   For assistance in those cases where the solicitor has clear evidence that no offences under section 22 will be committed, there is set out below a series of practice notes relating to the problems which might arise in a transaction in which the other party is represented by an unqualified conveyancer. These practice notes give advice only and it is for solicitors to decide for themselves what steps should properly be taken in any particular situation.

PRACTICE NOTES

(applicable only where evidence is provided of compliance with section 22)

General

1.   Any undertaking which unqualified agents may offer in the course of a transaction is not enforceable in the same way as an undertaking given by a solicitor or licensed conveyancer. Solicitors should therefore never accept such undertakings.

2.   Solicitors are under no duty to undertake agency work by way of completions by post on behalf of unqualified persons, or to attend to other formalities on behalf of third parties who are not clients, even where such third parties offer to pay the agent's charges.

3.   The Council also suggests that in cases where a solicitor is dealing with an unqualified conveyancer, the solicitor should bear in mind the line of decisions starting with *Hedley Byrne* v.

Heller [1964] AC 465, which extends the duty of care owed by a solicitor to persons who are not clients, but who rely and act on the solicitor's advice to his or her knowledge.

4. Solicitors must decide in each case whether special provisions should be incorporated in the draft contract to take account of the problems which arise by reason of the other party having no solicitor or licensed conveyancer, e.g. that the seller should attend personally at completion if represented by an unqualified agent. All such matters must be considered prior to exchange of contracts since contractual conditions cannot, of course, be imposed subsequently.

5. The protection provided by section 69 of the Law of Property Act 1925 only applies when a document containing a receipt for purchase money is handed over by a solicitor or licensed conveyancer or the seller himself or herself. Thus it should be considered whether the contract should provide either for the seller to attend personally at completion, or for an authority signed by the seller, for the purchase money to be paid to his or her agent, to be handed over on completion.

Acting for the seller: buyer not represented by a solicitor or licensed conveyancer

Completion

6. It is important to ensure that the deeds and keys are passed to the person entitled to receive them, i.e. the buyer. If an authority on behalf of the buyer is offered to the seller's solicitor, it is for the solicitor to decide whether or not to accept it, bearing in mind that no authority, however expressed, can be irrevocable. Again it is worth considering at the outset whether the point should be covered by express condition in the contract (see practice note 4 above).

Acting for the buyer: seller not represented by a solicitor or licensed conveyancer

Preliminary enquiries and requisitions on title

7. It may be prudent to require and ensure that replies to all preliminary enquiries and requisitions are signed by the seller.

Payment of deposit

8. Difficulties may arise in connection with payment of the deposit where there is no estate agent involved to whom the deposit may be paid as stakeholder in the ordinary way. The deposit may be paid direct to the seller, but this cannot be recommended since it is equivalent to parting with a portion of the purchase money in advance of investigation of the title and other matters.

9. Some unqualified agents insist that the deposit be paid to them. The Council does not recommend this. If a solicitor is obliged to pay the deposit to unqualified agents, he or she should inform the client of the risks involved, and obtain specific instructions before proceeding.

10. An alternative is for the deposit to be paid to the buyer's solicitor as stakeholder. The buyer's solicitor should insist on this where possible. If the seller will not agree to this, it may be possible to agree to place the deposit in a deposit account in the joint names of the buyer's solicitor and the seller, or in a deposit account in the seller's name, with the deposit receipt to be retained by the buyer's solicitor.

Payment of purchase money

11. As referred to in practice note 5 above, the buyer's solicitor should ensure that all the purchase money, including any deposit, is paid either to the seller or to the seller's properly authorised agent.

Matters unresolved at completion

12.   Whilst it is unusual to leave any issues revealed by searches and other enquiries outstanding at completion, undertakings relating to their discharge or resolution may on occasions be given between solicitors or licensed conveyancers. Such undertakings should not be accepted from unqualified agents for the reason mentioned in practice note 1 above.

Power of attorney

13.   Unqualified agents sometimes obtain a power of attorney to enable themselves or their employees to conduct certain aspects of the transaction. It is clearly important to ensure that such powers are valid, properly granted, and effective for all relevant purposes.

Acting for the lender: borrower not represented by a solicitor or licensed conveyancer

14.   The lender's solicitor often finds himself or herself undertaking much of the work which a borrower's solicitor would do. Whilst the client's interests are paramount, the solicitor must ensure that he or she does not render the unqualified agent additional assistance in a way which might establish a solicitor/client relationship either with the unqualified conveyancer or with the borrower, or leave the solicitor open to a negligence claim either from the solicitor's lender client or from the borrower.

Advances

15.   As regards the drafting and preparation of the instrument of transfer by the borrower's representative, the lender's solicitor is not obliged to undertake work which would normally be done by the borrower's solicitor. Solicitors are reminded, however, that it is of paramount importance to their lender client that good title is conveyed to the borrower.

16.   The importance of paying mortgage advances only to those properly entitled to receive them is a reason for insisting either that the borrower attends personally on completion, or that a signed authority from the borrower in favour of his or her agent is received on completion. Section 69 of the Law of Property Act 1925 is a relevant consideration in this context (see practice note 5 above).

Redemptions

17.   On completion, cheques or drafts should be drawn in favour of solicitors or licensed conveyancers or their clients, and not endorsed over to some intermediate party. The deeds should normally be handed over to the borrower personally, unless he or she provides a valid authority for them to be handed to a third party.

18.   Any issues of doubt or difficulty must be referred to the lender/client for detailed instructions. Where the lender is a building society and its solicitor considers that the totality of the work involved justifies a charge in excess of the building society's guideline fee, he or she should seek the approval of the lender/client, supported if necessary by a bill of costs containing sufficient detail of the work and the time spent on it.

16th March 1988, revised December 1995

IV.5. Tax on bank and building society interest – practice information[1]

Since April 1996, savings income received by an individual, the estate of a deceased person or an interest in possession trust has been taxable at the lower rate (20%), unless in the case of an individual his or her total income makes him or her liable to higher rate tax, rather than the basic rate of tax (section 73 of the Finance Act 1996 inserting a new section 1A into the Income and Corporation Taxes Act 1988). This is relevant to the tax treatment of bank and building society interest received by solicitors.

The Solicitors' Accounts Rules 1998, Part C

Under this part of the rules ('the interest provisions'), a solicitor who is required to account for interest to a client may do so by either of two methods. He or she may:

(a)   account to the client for the interest earned on the client's money in a separate designated client account; or

(b)   pay to the client a sum in lieu of interest when the money is held in a general client account.

These two procedures are referred to as Method A and Method B respectively.

Deduction of tax at source

The tax deduction at source rules apply, broadly, to separate designated client accounts, e.g. accounts held for individuals who are ordinarily resident in the UK.

Interest on general client accounts, whether with a bank or a building society, is paid gross.

When opening any separate designated client account the solicitor must provide the necessary information for the bank or building society to decide whether or not deduction of tax at source is appropriate.

Tax treatment of interest – Method A

Method A applies to separate designated client accounts. Where tax is deducted at source by the bank or building society interest will be received by the solicitor net, and he or she will simply pass it on to the client net – no tax deduction certificate is required. Interest from separate designated client accounts is taxable as savings income. The client, when making his or her tax return, will declare the interest as having been received under deduction of tax, and will only be liable to be assessed in relation to higher rate tax in respect of it (since he or she will have a tax credit for the lower rate of tax). If the client is for any reason not liable to income tax, he or she can recover any tax deducted from the interest. In those circumstances the solicitor must, on being required by the client, obtain a certificate of deduction of tax from the bank or building society and deliver this to the client. The client's position is, therefore, for practical purposes, the same as that which arises where he or she receives interest from a building society or bank on a deposit of his or her own.

---

1. © The Law Society. This information was previously published in Annex 28D in *The Guide to the Professional Conduct of Solicitors 1999*.

Where the client is not liable to tax or is not ordinarily resident (NOR) in the UK the bank or building society will pay the interest gross provided that it holds the relevant declaration. Declarations of non-ordinary residence can be completed by either the solicitor or the client but declarations of non-liability by UK residents will normally be completed by the client. However, in view of the difficulty of obtaining complete information about an overseas client, solicitors may feel that it is more appropriate for the client concerned to make the declaration, especially since it contains an undertaking to notify the bank or building society should circumstances change.

Where the tax deduction at source rules do not apply, the solicitor will receive interest from the bank or building society gross and may account to the client for it gross, even if the client is non-resident. The client will be assessed on the gross receipt (but a non-resident client may, by concession, not be assessed) and (unless the solicitor has been acting as the client's agent for tax purposes – see below under 'Solicitors as agents') the solicitor himself or herself will not be assessed in respect of the interest.

Tax treatment of interest – Method B

Where Method B is used, deduction of tax at source does not apply to the solicitor's general client account at either a bank or building society, and interest is therefore paid to the solicitor gross. When making a payment to the client of a sum in lieu of interest under the interest provisions, the solicitor should make the payment gross even if the client is not ordinarily resident. The Revenue's view is that such payments may be treated as within Case III of Schedule D, so that the lower rate of tax on savings income may apply where appropriate. The client will be assessed to income tax on his or her receipt, but a non-resident may, by concession, not be assessed.

Wherever payments are made by solicitors to clients under Method B they can, in practice, be set off against the solicitor's Case III assessment on gross interest received on general client account deposits; if the payments exceed the interest received, a Case II deduction can be claimed for the excess.

Stake money

Since 1st June 1992, stake money has been included in the definition of 'client money'. Interest will be payable to the person to whom the stake is paid using either Method A or B above. But there will still be circumstances in which payment is not possible until a later tax year. Where this situation looks likely to arise, e.g. if the stake is held pending the outcome of litigation, the deposit would normally be placed in a general client account until it is established to whom the stake is to be paid. Because, in the meantime, interest will be included in the solicitor's Case III assessment, it is again important to make provision for the tax liability to be met out of the interest as it arises.

Tax treatment of interest – money paid into court

The position of money paid into court is covered by the Supreme Court Funds Rules as amended. Where any order for payment out of money paid into court is made, the order should provide for the disposal of any interest accrued to the date of the judgment or order, and for interest accruing thereafter up to the date the money is paid out in accordance with the order. In the absence of such provision, interest accruing between the date of the payment into court, and its acceptance or the judgment or order for payment out, goes to the party who made the payment in, and interest from the date of the judgment or order follows the capital payment.

Where interest is paid to a party to proceedings in respect of money held in court, it should be paid to the client gross, even if he or she is non-resident. The client will normally be assessable under Case III, but the solicitor will not, unless exceptionally he or she is assessable as the client's agent.

Solicitors as agents

Where a solicitor acts for tax purposes as agent for a non-resident client, the solicitor will remain liable to be assessed on behalf of the client in relation to interest earned in a separate designated client account, where Method A is used, unless he or she is an agent without management or control of the interest, in which case, under Extra Statutory Concession B13, no assessment will be made on him or her. Where the solicitor is assessable, the charge may, if appropriate, be to higher rate tax, so the solicitor will need to retain tax at the client's marginal rate of income tax from interest received gross from a bank or building society before remitting it to the client. This is the case even though the account would not be subject to deduction of tax at source since the client would have completed a declaration of non-liability due to his or her non-residence. No question of the solicitor being taxed as an agent will arise where the interest in question has been earned in a general client account, or on stake money, but it could very exceptionally do so in relation to money held in court.

Determination of whether a solicitor has management or control for the purposes of the extra statutory concession will depend on the nature of the solicitor's relationship with the client. Under the Finance Act 1995, a person not resident in the UK is assessable and chargeable to income tax in the name of an agent if the agent has management or control of the interest. Acting as a solicitor in giving advice or in conducting a transaction on the client's instructions will not of itself give management or control nor usually would the holding of a power of attorney on behalf of the client for a specific purpose, e.g. concluding a specified purchase or sale. If a client had no fixed place of business in the UK, and his or her solicitor had, and habitually exercised, an authority to conclude contracts on behalf of the client, this would give rise to the client having a permanent establishment in the UK, and accordingly the client would be taxable. In essence, the solicitor would be deemed to have management and control if he or she were effectively carrying on the client's business in the UK, rather than merely acting as a solicitor, even regularly. Therefore, in order for the agency principle to apply, the solicitor/client relationship would normally have to go beyond a solicitor's usual representative capacity. It should be noted that where interest arises in connection with the receipt of rents on behalf of the non-resident, the solicitor would be chargeable as agent in relation to the rent.

For a more detailed analysis of when solicitors can be taxed as agents, see [1991] *Gazette*, 1 May, 15 (article by John Avery Jones).

If a solicitor is assessable on behalf of the client, he or she has a general right to reimbursement, out of the client's money coming into his or her hands, for any tax for which the client is liable and in respect of which the solicitor has been charged. For the exercise of this right see the Finance Act 1995.

Trusts

Deduction of tax at source may apply depending upon the type of trust and where the investment is held. But it can only apply where money is held in a separate designated client account. The income of trusts where none of the beneficiaries is ordinarily resident in the UK will not be subject to deduction of tax at source, even if a separate designated client account is used, provided that the appropriate declaration has been made.

Administration of estates

Interest on money held for UK resident personal representatives will, if placed in a separate designated client account, be subject to deduction of tax at source unless a declaration is made by the solicitor or the personal representatives that the deceased was not resident in the UK immediately before his death.

AIDE-MEMOIRE OF NORMAL SITUATIONS

Type of account	Payment of interest by bank or building society	Consequences
A Designated – where subject to tax deduction	Net	Pay net to client, who gets basic rate tax credit. No further tax deductions for residents (unless solicitor is assessable as an agent).
B Designated – where paid gross (client money generally)	Gross	Pay gross to client who is assessable on payment as gross income. No deduction of tax for non-residents (unless the solicitor is assessable as agent).
C Bank and building society general client account – always paid gross (client money generally and stake money)	Gross	Pay gross to client who in turn is assessable on payment as gross income; in practice solicitor assessed on interest after setting-off this payment. No deduction of tax for non-residents.

4th March 1992, revised February 1999

IV.6. Accepting undertakings on completion following the Court of Appeal decision in Patel v. Daybells[1]

Accepting undertakings on completion

The first instance decision in *Patel* v. *Daybells* [2000] All ER(D) 1004 caused consternation among conveyancers. It held that it was negligent for a buyer's solicitor to accept an undertaking for Form 53 (now DS1), save in exceptional circumstances. The Court of Appeal ([2001] EWCA Civ 1229) has now upheld the decision that the solicitor in the case was not negligent, but reversed the reasoning – the acceptance of a solicitor's undertaking for a DS1 will not normally be negligent. But does this mean a return to business as usual?

The Court of Appeal held that 'conformity to a common (or even universal) professional practice is not an automatic defence against liability; the practice must be demonstrably reasonable and responsible'. This involves considering the risks involved and how to avoid them. The Court of Appeal was satisfied that the legal profession had considered the risks of accepting an undertaking and that in the standard case it was reasonable to rely on the existence of compulsory insurance, the Compensation Fund and the summary procedure for enforcing undertakings when assessing the extent of that risk. Other relevant factors were: the Council of Mortgage Lenders' advice to its members to discharge a mortgage even where insufficient funds were sent, if this was due to the lender's error; and the problems which would ensue if the buyer's solicitor had to communicate directly with the seller's lender.

Exceptional cases

The 'exceptional circumstances' in which it might be negligent for a buyer's solicitor to accept an undertaking were not specified by the Court of Appeal, although the court made it clear that the fact that the seller's solicitor was a sole practitioner did not make the transaction exceptional.

The court referred in detail to the expert evidence on behalf of the buyer's solicitor that it would not be normal or advisable to rely on an undertaking in two situations, but did not expressly endorse these as the relevant 'exceptional circumstances'. The two situations mentioned are:

- Where the amount required to redeem the seller's mortgage exceeds the minimum level of solicitors' indemnity insurance (currently [£2m] per claim); or

- Where the mortgagee is not a member of the Council of Mortgage Lenders.

Minimising the risks in exceptional cases

The risk of accepting an undertaking for a DS1 is that it might not be forthcoming (e.g. because of the fraud or negligence of the seller's solicitor or because of problems in identifying the amount required to redeem the mortgage). Default by the seller's solicitor is dealt with by the requirement for compulsory insurance and, ultimately, the Compensation Fund. Only where the figures exceed

---

1. © The Law Society. Prepared by the Law Society's Conveyancing and Land Law Committee in May 2002.

the compulsory level of insurance might the buyer's solicitor need to take additional steps to deal with that risk. The risk of a dispute with the lender should not normally be a problem where the lender is a member of the CML. Even disputes not covered by the CML's advice may not put the buyer's solicitor at risk: the Law Society's recommended form of undertaking puts an absolute obligation on the seller's solicitor to discharge the relevant mortgage. It is therefore the seller's solicitor who is at risk if the DS1 is not forthcoming: his obligations can be summarily enforced and are backed by compulsory insurance and in certain cases, the Compensation Fund.

In each of the exceptional cases mentioned in *Patel* v. *Daybells* the matter comes back to the safeguards put in place by the profession. The only variable is the level of insurance cover and that is only relevant in the case of large mortgages. Normally the buyer's solicitor does not know the amount of the debt (and the Court of Appeal disapproved of the idea that the buyer's solicitor should have to make such enquiries). It is common to ask in preliminary enquiries for confirmation that the sale price exceeds the amount secured on the mortgage. Provided the sale price is not more than [£2m], such confirmation should give the buyer's solicitor the necessary comfort to accept an undertaking from the seller's solicitor. In larger transactions the buyer's solicitor may wish to take additional steps before or instead of accepting an undertaking.

- The buyer's solicitor could ask the seller's solicitor to get express written confirmation from the lender that he has been appointed the lender's agent for the receipt of the redemption money. This places the risk of default or dispute with the lender and avoids the buyer having to investigate either the details of the mortgage or the seller's solicitor's insurance.

- The buyer's solicitor could insist on sending the redemption money direct to the lender. The buyer's solicitor should ask to see the redemption statement as independent evidence of the figure. The Court of Appeal disapproved of the buyer making such enquiries in the standard case but in an exceptional case, where large sums are involved, this may be inevitable. As this information is confidential to the seller, the seller's solicitor should get instructions before revealing it. However, this solution does not deal with the problem of a dispute over the amount required to redeem. It may also be difficult to arrange in the case of an 'all moneys' mortgage. If this course is followed, Standard Condition 6.7 should be amended (or, if using the Standard Commercial Property Conditions, expand condition 6.7). In either case, the issue must be addressed before exchange (or if using the Standard Commercial Property Conditions, expand condition 8.7).

- Where the amount of the mortgage debt exceeds the minimum indemnity insurance (as will often be the case in commercial transactions), a buyer's solicitor might only accept an undertaking for DS1 if coupled with a warranty from the seller's solicitor that his insurance cover exceeds the amount required to redeem the mortgage.

- Finally, there is no obligation to accept an undertaking in place of performance of the obligation. Indeed, solicitors have often been unwilling to accept an undertaking for the DS1 in the case of a mortgage to a non-institutional or overseas lender or in the case of a private loan. However, if that is the buyer's solicitor's position, a contract condition that the DS1 must be available on completion will be necessary. In many cases this will not be a realistic option as institutional lenders' procedures do not include issuing the DS1 in escrow.

Before the buyer's solicitor accepts an undertaking where the expert evidence in *Patel* v. *Daybells* stated it would not be normal practice to do so, it is essential to explain the risks to the buyer and get clear instructions that the buyer is willing to take them.

Even where the lender is separately represented, the buyer's solicitor should consider whether there are any exceptional circumstances making it unwise (or potentially negligent) to accept an undertaking (or at least without evidence of the lender's solicitor's authority to accept the redemption money).

ENDs

The use of Electronic Notifications of Discharge (END) presents a particular problem as there is never a paper DS1 to be handed over: the buyer's solicitor is always reliant on an undertaking by the seller's solicitor to forward the redemption money and the END form to the lender, who then sends the discharge notification directly to the Land Registry. Even where the transaction might fall into the category of exceptional cases the buyer's solicitor will ultimately have no choice but to accept the undertaking and will have to take such steps as are available (e.g. split payments, evidence of the seller's solicitor's authority, evidence of sufficient insurance cover).

IV.7. Undue influence – solicitors' duties post Etridge[1]

Introduction

Many negligence claims have arisen as a result of solicitors viewing their role in the execution of third party charge documentation as little more than a formality. The important House of Lords decision in *Royal Bank of Scotland* v. *Etridge* was delivered on 11th October 2001 and as a result all conveyancing lawyers should consider carefully their procedures when faced with a transaction where a third party provides security for another person's borrowing. The risk to solicitors' professional indemnity cover remains acute. *Etridge* involved a wife claiming that she had charged her interest in the matrimonial home as a result of the undue influence of her husband. Whilst the decision has to some extent clarified the scope of the solicitors' duties and set out what is required of the lender this arrangement does still present all parties with exposure to risk and this has not in any way been reduced following the House of Lords decision.

Can you advise?

Whilst *Etridge* does contemplate that the same solicitor can act for both parties and the lender in an administrative capacity, the first decision for the solicitor is whether he or she should be acting at all. The risk of conflict is extreme when attempting to reconcile Lord Nicholls' comments concerning the provision of full information with a client who in many cases may not wish for the documentation to be fully explained. When the third party realises that the home will be at risk to secure the other person's borrowing, there may be some reluctance to sign.

If advising the third party the solicitor will be acting for the third party alone and so must consider carefully whether there is a conflict of duty or interest and whether it would be in the best interests of that client to accept the instructions. If the third party is a wife she may well have an interest in supporting the husband's business as it is the source of the family's income. In such cases the wife may, despite the risks, have a good reason to sign the charge.

Many solicitors will, however, be reluctant to advise in such circumstances. The Law Lords stressed the importance of bank finance in the business world and stated that 'finance raised by second mortgages on the principal's home is a significant source of capital for the start up of small businesses'. So in order to facilitate the development of embryonic businesses, solicitors will no doubt still be asked to witness charge documentation. What steps should the solicitor take to ensure that the obligation of independent advice is properly discharged?

Who is your client?

The solicitor must ensure that the client wishes and intends to instruct the solicitor. It must be established that there is no conflict of interest and that it is the third party (and not the borrower) who is the client.

---

1. © The Law Society. Prepared by the Law Society's Conveyancing and Land Law Committee in May 2002.

Full financial information

The solicitor must obtain full financial information concerning the borrower's account. This will normally include (para 79 of Lord Nicholls' judgment) information on the purpose for the new facility, the current indebtedness, the amount of the current overdraft facility, and the amount and terms of any new borrowing together with a copy of any application form. Lord Nicholls stated that:

> '...it should become routine practice for banks if relying on confirmation from a solicitor for their protection to send to the solicitor the necessary financial information'.

Expertise

The solicitor must be satisfied that he or she has the necessary expertise to interpret or advise on the detailed financial information.

Advice

The solicitor must explain to the client the purpose for which the solicitor has become involved and that the bank, should it ever become necessary, will rely upon the solicitor's involvement to counter any suggestion that the client did not properly understand the implications of the transaction (para 64). After explaining the documents, it is the client's rather than the solicitor's decision as to whether or not to proceed.

Core Minimum Requirements

Lord Nicholls summarised at paragraph 65 of the judgment the core minimum requirements for advice which typically will include:

- the nature of the documents and the risk that the client will lose the home if the borrower's business does not prosper, and even the possibility that the client could be made bankrupt;

- the seriousness of the risks involved by reference to the purpose, amount and terms of the new facility and whether the client understands the value of the property being charged and if there are any other assets out of which repayment could be made if the business fails;

- the fact that the lender may alter the terms of the loan including increasing the amount borrowed without reference to the client;

- asking whether the client is content for the solicitor to write to the bank confirming that the solicitor has explained the nature of the documents to the client and the practical implications they may have;

- discussing whether the client wishes the solicitor to negotiate with the bank on the terms of the transaction (e.g. limitation on the amount borrowed);

- providing the advice at a face to face meeting in the absence of the borrower and giving the advice using non-technical language;

- explaining that the client does have a choice on whether to sign the charge/guarantee or to consent to mortgage with the decision being up to the client alone.

However, it must be appreciated that additional requirements may become appropriate depending on the specific facts of the case. It should be appreciated by the solicitor that 'the solicitor's task is an important one. It is not a formality' (Lord Nicholls, para 65). To comply properly with the House of Lord's judgment guidance is likely to take several chargeable hours.

Confirmation

The advice given should be recorded in a full attendance note and confirmed in detail in writing in a letter sent promptly after the meeting. A draft letter is available on the Law Society website [and is reproduced in Appendix IV.8].

Summary

All conveyancing solicitors should be certain that before advising on third party charges:

(1)   they have the necessary expertise.

(2)   there is no conflict.

(3)   there is no suspicion of undue influence or impropriety.

(4)   the bank provides full financial information.

(5)   the advice covers, at the very least, the core minimum requirements.

(6)   the advice is confirmed in writing.

In addition the solicitor should check if the firm's indemnity insurers have any additional requirements or have issued any guidance.

Finally it is up to the solicitor to exercise his or her skill and judgement in each individual case to decide whether to act. A solicitor who is acting for the borrower should not agree to advise the third party if there is a real possibility that the advice would be that the third party should not execute the charge/guarantee or consent to mortgage.

IV.8. Model letter to wife where charging home to secure loan to husband or his business[1]

To be amended as necessary

Dear […]

This letter confirms the advice that [I] [we] gave you at our meeting [today] in respect of the proposal that your [freehold][leasehold] property known as […] (the Property) is to be mortgaged to […] (the Lender) to secure a loan from the Lender to […] (the Borrower).

The Lender requires that you are given this advice so that, if you sign [the mortgage] [and related documents] [a consent to mortgage] you will not be able to claim afterwards that you are not legally bound by [it] [them].

(1)   The Property is owned [in your sole name] [in the Borrower's sole name] [in the joint names of yourself and […]] and you [both] will be required to sign [the mortgage] [and related documents] [the consent to mortgage] in favour of the Lender.

(2)   Enclosed is a copy of the form of mortgage [and the mortgage conditions that are incorporated into it] [and related documents], which please read carefully and ask [me] [us] if you have any questions. The following is a summary of the main provisions and implications, but does not cover everything.

(3)   The mortgage is [initially] required to give the Lender security for a loan [of £…] [a loan facility of up to £…] to be provided to the Borrower.

[However, the mortgage will be on 'all monies' terms and will also give the Lender security over the Property for:

  (1)   any further loan or increased facility that the Borrower (individually or jointly with you or anyone else) may in future obtain from the Lender while the mortgage remains in existence, even if this is done without your knowledge or consent;

  (2)   any existing loans from the Lender to the Borrower (individually or jointly with you or anyone else), even if you do not know about them;

  (3)   any existing or future loans that you yourself may obtain (individually or jointly with anyone else) from the Lender while the mortgage remains in existence;

  (4)   any sums owing to the Lender, at any time while the mortgage remains in existence, by any other person or company if you or the Borrower has already given, or shall in future give, a guarantee for those sums to the Lender, and even if the Borrower has given or shall give such a guarantee without your knowledge and consent;

---

1. © The Law Society. This model letter was issued by the Law Society's Conveyancing and Land Law Committee in May 2002. It was first published as an appendix to the guidance – 'Undue influence – solicitors' duties post *Etridge*', which is reproduced here as Appendix IV.7.

(5)   interest on all such sums as charged by the Lender;

(6)   [*anything else*].]

According to the terms of the loan the Lender can demand repayment at [any time,] [on fixed dates,] [by instalments,] [*set out repayment requirements*] .

(4)   During the subsistence of the mortgage, [you] [the Borrower] must:

(1)   keep the Property insured in accordance with the Lender's requirements;

(2)   keep the Property in good repair;

(3)   not make any structural alterations or changes of use without the Lender's consent;

(4)   not let the Property or take in lodgers without the Lender's consent;

(5)   comply with all covenants and restrictions affecting the Property ;

(6)   [*anything else*].

(5)   The mortgage will give the Lender a [first] charge over the Property as security for all the sums mentioned in paragraph (3) above. You could lose the Property if the Borrower's business does not prosper, or if the borrowing is increased unwisely. This is because, if any loan repayment or interest charge is not paid on time, the Lender would be entitled to enforce the mortgage by taking court proceedings to evict you and any other occupiers from the Property and sell the Property in order to obtain repayment. Alternatively the Lender could appoint a receiver to take possession of the Property from you and any other occupiers.

(6)   [The Lender reserves the right to transfer the benefit of the mortgage to another lender.]

(7)   [In addition, the mortgage will contain a covenant by you to pay all sums falling within paragraph (3) above if the Borrower fails to pay them [up to a maximum of £[…] plus interest charged by the Lender]. This means that [up to that level] you will be a guarantor for the liabilities of the Borrower to the Lender, you will be personally liable for those sums, you could be sued by the Lender for them and, if the value of the Property and your other assets is insufficient to meet those sums, you could be made bankrupt as well as losing the Property.]

(8)   [*Any other features of the mortgage needing comment?*]

The above legal advice relates to the effect of the proposed mortgage documents and the types of risks that arise. [However, [I am] [we are] not qualified to assess the likelihood of those risks actually materialising. That depends largely on the financial standing and prospects of the Borrower [and his business], although you should also consider whether the sums secured could be repaid from the sale value of the Property and your other assets. Therefore, before you decide whether to agree to sign [the mortgage] [the consent to mortgage], you should get help on assessing the risks by taking advice on those important financial aspects from a chartered accountant or other qualified professional financial adviser who should be independent of the Borrower.]

You do not have to agree to these arrangements at all if you consider that the risks are too great or if you think that these arrangements are of no advantage to you. If you are generally willing but find particular terms unacceptable, it may be possible to negotiate variations of those terms with the Lender in order to make them acceptable to you. These decisions are yours and yours alone.

[As you know, [I am] [my firm is] also acting for the Borrower in this matter [and also for the Lender in an administrative capacity] but I have given you this advice independently. Nevertheless you should consider whether you want further legal advice from a completely separate solicitor before you make a final decision in connection with the mortgage.]

Please sign paragraph (A) at the end of the enclosed copy of this letter to acknowledge that you have been given, and have understood, this advice.

If and when you decide that you will enter into the mortgage and will not require the Lender to vary any of the terms, please also sign paragraph (B) to confirm that decision and to allow the Lender to be told that you have received this advice.

Yours […]

ACKNOWLEDGEMENTS

(A)   I confirm that I have read this letter and have received and understood the advice given in it.

Signed: .... Date: ....

(B)   I confirm that that I have decided, of my own free will, to enter into the mortgage, I do not require the Lender to vary any of the terms, [I do not require any further legal advice,] and I agree that the Lender may be told that I have received the advice in this letter.

Signed: .... Date: ....

IV.9. Form of undertaking agreed with banks[1]

FORM NO. 4 (BRIDGING FINANCE)

Undertaking by solicitor (with form of authority from client) to account to bank for net proceeds of sale of the existing property, the bank having provided funds in connection with the purchase of the new property.

Authority from client(s)

[*Date*]

To [*name and address of solicitors*]

I/We hereby irrevocably authorise and request you to give an undertaking in the form set out below and accordingly to pay the net proceeds of sale after deduction of your costs to [...] Bank plc [...] Branch.

Signature of client(s) ....

Undertaking

[*Date*]

To [...] Bank plc

If you provide facilities to my/our client [...] for the purchase of the freehold/leasehold property (the new property) [*description of property*] pending the sale by my/our client of the freehold/leasehold property (the existing property) [*description of property*]

I/we undertake:

1.   That any sums received from you or your customer will be applied solely for the following purposes:

   (a)   in discharging the present mortgage(s) on the existing property [*delete if not applicable*];

   (b)   in acquiring a good marketable title to the new property, subject to the mortgage mentioned below [*delete if not applicable*];

   (c)   in paying any necessary deposit, legal fees, costs and disbursements in connection with the purchase.

The purchase price contemplated is £[...] gross.

---

1. © The Law Society 1999.

I/We are informed that a sum of £[...] is being advanced on mortgage by [...] [*delete if not applicable*]. The amount required from my/our client for the transaction including the deposit and together with costs, disbursements and apportionments is not expected to exceed £[...]

2.   To hold to your order when received by me/us the documents of title of the existing property pending completion of the sale (unless subject to any prior mortgage(s)) and of the new property (unless subject to any prior mortgage(s)).

3.   To pay to you the net proceeds of sale of the existing property when received by me/us. The sale price contemplated is £[...] and the only deductions which will have to be made at present known to me/us are:

   (i)   the deposit (if not held by me/us),

   (ii)   the estate agents' commission,

   (iii)   the amount required to redeem any mortgages and charges, which so far as known to me/us at present do not exceed £[...],

   (iv)   the legal fees, costs and disbursements relating to the transaction.

4.   To advise you immediately of any subsequent claim by a third party upon the net proceeds of sale of which I/we have knowledge.

   Notes:

   (1)   If any deductions will have to be made from the net proceeds of sale other than those shown above, these must be specifically mentioned.

   (2)   It would be convenient if this form of undertaking were presented in duplicate so that a copy could be retained by the solicitor.

IV.10. Recommended form of undertaking for discharge of building society mortgages

'In-consideration of your today completing the purchase of […] WE HEREBY UNDERTAKE forthwith to pay over to the […] Building Society the money required to redeem the mortgage/legal charge dated […] and to forward the receipted mortgage/legal charge to you as soon as it is received by us from the […] Building Society.'[1]

---

1. © The Law Society. Previously published in *The Guide to the Professional Conduct of Solicitors 1999* as Annex 25B.

IV.11. The Law Society's formulae for exchanging contracts by telephone, fax or telex[1]

Introduction

It is essential that an agreed memorandum of the details and of any variations of the formula used should be made at the time and retained in the file. This would be very important if any question on the exchange were raised subsequently. Agreed variations should also be confirmed in writing. The serious risks of exchanging contracts without a deposit, unless the full implications are explained to and accepted by the seller client, are demonstrated in *Morris* v. *Duke-Cohan & Co.* (1975) 119 SJ 826.

As those persons involved in the exchange will bind their firms to the undertakings in the formula used, solicitors should carefully consider who is to be authorised to exchange contracts by telephone or telex and should ensure that the use of the procedure is restricted to them. Since professional undertakings form the basis of the formulae, they are only recommended for use between firms of solicitors and licensed conveyancers.

Law Society telephone/telex exchange – Formula A (1986)

(for use where one solicitor holds both signed parts of the contract):

A completion date of […] is agreed. The solicitor holding both parts of the contract confirms that he or she holds the part signed by his or her client(s), which is identical to the part he or she is also holding signed by the other solicitor's client(s) and will forthwith insert the agreed completion date in each part.

Solicitors mutually agree that exchange shall take place from that moment and the solicitor holding both parts confirms that, as of that moment, he or she holds the part signed by his or her client(s) to the order of the other. He or she undertakes that day by first class post, or where the other solicitor is a member of a document exchange (as to which the inclusion of a reference thereto in the solicitor's letterhead shall be conclusive evidence) by delivery to that or any other affiliated exchange, or by hand delivery direct to that solicitor's office, to send his or her signed part of the contract to the other solicitor, together, where he or she is the purchaser's solicitor, with a banker's draft or a solicitor's client account cheque for the deposit amounting to £… .

Note:

1. A memorandum should be prepared, after use of the formula, recording:

(a) date and time of exchange;

(b) the formula used and exact wording of agreed variations;

---

1. © The Law Society. Formulae A and B: 9 July 1986, revised January 1996. Formula C: 15 March 1989, revised January 1996. The formulae were previously published in *The Guide to the Professional Conduct of Solicitors 1999* as Annex 25D.

(c)   the completion date;

(d)   the (balance) deposit to be paid;

(e)   the identities of those involved in any conversation.

Law Society telephone/telex exchange – Formula B (1986)

(for use where each solicitor holds his or her own client's signed part of the contract):

A completion date of [...] is agreed. Each solicitor confirms to the other that he or she holds a part contract in the agreed form signed by the client(s) and will forthwith insert the agreed completion date.

Each solicitor undertakes to the other thenceforth to hold the signed part of the contract to the other's order, so that contracts are exchanged at that moment. Each solicitor further undertakes that day by first class post, or, where the other solicitor is a member of a document exchange (as to which the inclusion of a reference thereto in the solicitor's letterhead shall be conclusive evidence) by delivery to that or any other affiliated exchange, or by hand delivery direct to that solicitor's office, to send his or her signed part of the contract to the other together, in the case of a purchaser's solicitor, with a banker's draft or a solicitor's client account cheque for the deposit amounting to £....

> *Notes:*
>
> 1.   *A memorandum should be prepared, after use of the formula, recording:*
>
>> (a)   *date and time of exchange;*
>>
>> (b)   *the formula used and exact wording of agreed variations;*
>>
>> (c)   *the completion date;*
>>
>> (d)   *the (balance) deposit to be paid;*
>>
>> (e)   *the identities of those involved in any conversation.*
>
> 2.   *Those who are going to effect the exchange must first confirm the details in order to ensure that both parts are identical. This means in particular, that if either part of the contract has been amended since it was originally prepared, the solicitor who holds a part contract with the amendments must disclose them, so that it can be confirmed that the other part is similarly amended.*

9 July 1986, revised January 1996

Law Society telephone/fax/telex exchange – Formula C (1989)

Part I

The following is agreed:

Final time for exchange: [...] pm

Completion date:

Deposit to be paid to:

Each solicitor confirms that he or she holds a part of the contract in the agreed form signed by his or her client, or, if there is more than one client, by all of them. Each solicitor undertakes to the other that:

(a) he or she will continue to hold that part of the contract until the final time for exchange on the date the formula is used, and

(b) if the vendor's solicitor so notifies the purchaser's solicitor by fax, telephone or telex (whichever was previously agreed) by that time, they will both comply with part II of the formula.

The purchaser's solicitor further undertakes that either he or she or some other named person in his or her office will be available up to the final time for exchange to activate part II of the formula on receipt of the telephone call, fax or telex from the vendor's solicitors.

Part II

Each solicitor undertakes to the other henceforth to hold the part of the contract in his or her possession to the other's order, so that contracts are exchanged at that moment, and to despatch it to the other on that day. The purchaser's solicitor further undertakes to the vendor's solicitor to despatch on that day, or to arrange for the despatch on that day of, a banker's draft or a solicitor's client account cheque for the full deposit specified in the agreed form of contract (divided as the vendor's solicitor may have specified) to the vendor's solicitor and/or to some other solicitor whom the vendor's solicitor nominates, to be held on formula C terms.

'To despatch' means to send by first class post, or, where the other solicitor is a member of a document exchange (as to which the inclusion of a reference thereto in the solicitor's letterhead is to be conclusive evidence) by delivery to that or any other affiliated exchange, or by hand delivery direct to the recipient solicitor's office. 'Formula C terms' means that the deposit is held as stakeholder, or as agent for the vendor with authority to part with it only for the purpose of passing it to another solicitor as deposit in a related property purchase transaction on these terms.

Notes:

1.   Two memoranda will be required when using formula C. One needs to record the use of part I, and a second needs to record the request of the vendor's solicitor to the purchaser's solicitor to activate part II.

2.   The first memorandum should record:

(a)   the date and time when it was agreed to use formula C;

(b)   the exact wording of any agreed variations;

(c)   the final time, later that day, for exchange;

(d)   the completion date;

(e)   the name of the solicitor to whom the deposit was to be paid, or details of amounts and names if it was to be split; and

(f)   the identities of those involved in any conversation.

3.   Formula C assumes the payment of a full contractual deposit (normally 10%).

4.   The contract term relating to the deposit must allow it to be passed on, with payment direct from payer to ultimate recipient, in the way in which the formula contemplates. The deposit must ultimately be held by a solicitor as stakeholder. Whilst some variation in the formula can be agreed this is a term of the formula which must not be varied, unless all the solicitors involved in the chain have agreed.

5.   If a buyer proposes to use a deposit guarantee policy, formula C will need substantial adaptation.

6.   It is essential prior to agreeing part I of formula C that those effecting the exchange ensure that both parts of the contract are identical.

7.   Using formula C involves a solicitor in giving a number of professional undertakings. These must be performed precisely. Any failure will be a serious breach of professional discipline. One of the undertakings may be to arrange that someone over whom the solicitor has no control will do something (i.e. to arrange for someone else to despatch the cheque or banker's draft in payment of the deposit). An undertaking is still binding even if it is to do something outside the solicitor's control.

8.   Solicitors do not as a matter of law have an automatic authority to exchange contracts on a formula C basis, and should always ensure that they have the client's express authority to use formula C. A suggested form of authority is set out below. It should be adapted to cover any special circumstances:

I/We [...] understand that my/our sale and purchase of [...] are both part of a chain of linked property transactions, in which all parties want the security of contracts which become binding on the same day.

I/We agree that you should make arrangements with the other solicitors or licensed convey-ancers involved to achieve this.

I/We understand that this involves each property-buyer offering, early on one day, to exchange contracts whenever, later that day, the seller so requests, and that the buyer's offer is on the basis that it cannot be withdrawn or varied during that day.

I/We agree that when I/we authorise you to exchange contracts, you may agree to exchange contracts on the above basis and give any necessary undertakings to the other parties involved in the chain and that my/our authority to you cannot be revoked throughout the day on which the offer to exchange contracts is made.

15 March 1989, revised January 1996

IV.12. The Law Society's code for completion by post[1]

Preamble

The code provides a procedure for postal completion which practising solicitors may adopt by reference. It may also be used by licensed conveyancers.

Before agreeing to adopt this code, a solicitor must be satisfied that doing so will not be contrary to the interests of the client (including any mortgagee client).

When adopted, the code applies without variation, unless agreed in writing in advance.

PROCEDURE

General

1.　To adopt this code, all the solicitors must expressly agree, preferably in writing, to use it to complete a specific transaction.

2.　On completion, the seller's solicitor acts as the buyer's solicitor's agent without any fee or disbursements.

Before completion

3.　The seller's solicitor will specify in writing to the buyer's solicitor before completion the mortgages or charges secured on the property which, on or before completion, will be redeemed or discharged to the extent that they relate to the property.

4.　The seller's solicitor *undertakes*:

    (i)　to have the seller's authority to receive the purchase money on completion; and

    (ii)　on completion to have the authority of the proprietor of each mortgage or charge specified under paragraph 3 to receive the sum intended to repay it,

BUT if the seller's solicitor does not have all the necessary authorities then:

    (iii)　to advise the buyer's solicitor no later than 4pm on the working day before the completion date that they do not have all the authorities or immediately if any is withdrawn later; and

    (iv)　not to complete until he or she has the buyer's solicitor's instructions.

5.　Before the completion date, the buyer's solicitor will send the seller's solicitor instructions as to any of the following which apply:

    (i)　documents to be examined and marked;

1.　© The Law Society 1984, revised 1998. This code was previously published in *The Guide to the Professional Conduct of Solicitors 1999* as Annex 25E. The Warning Card referred to in note 9 has since been replaced by the Property Fraud Warning Card issued in May 2009 by the Solicitors Regulation Authority (see Appendix I.2).

    (ii)   memoranda to be endorsed;

   (iii)   undertakings to be given;

   (iv)   deeds, documents (including any relevant undertakings) and authorities relating to rents, deposits, keys, etc. to be sent to the buyer's solicitor following completion; and

    (v)   other relevant matters.

In default of instructions, the seller's solicitor is under no duty to examine, mark or endorse any document.

6.   The buyer's solicitor will remit to the seller's solicitor the sum required to complete, as notified in writing on the seller's solicitor's completion statement or otherwise, or in default of notification as shown by the contract. If the funds are remitted by transfer between banks, the seller's solicitor will instruct the receiving bank to telephone to report immediately the funds have been received. Pending completion, the seller's solicitor will hold the funds to the buyer's solicitor's order.

7.   If by the agreed date and time for completion the seller's solicitor has not received the authorities specified in paragraph 4, instructions under paragraph 5 and the sum specified in paragraph 6, the seller's solicitor will forthwith notify the buyer's solicitor and request further instructions.

Completion

8.   The seller's solicitor will complete forthwith on receiving the sum specified in paragraph 6, or at a later time agreed with the buyer's solicitor.

9.   When completing, the seller's solicitor *undertakes*:

    (i)   to comply with the instructions given under paragraph 5; and

   (ii)   to redeem or obtain discharges for every mortgage or charge so far as it relates to the property specified under paragraph 3 which has not already been redeemed or discharged.

After completion

10.   The seller's solicitor *undertakes*:

    (i)   immediately completion has taken place to hold to the buyer's solicitor's order every item referred to in (iv) of paragraph 5 and not to exercise a lien over any such item;

   (ii)   as soon as possible after completion, and in any event on the same day,

        (a)   to confirm to the buyer's solicitor by telephone or fax that completion has taken place; and

        (b)   to send written confirmation and, at the risk of the buyer's solicitor, the items listed in (iv) of paragraph 5 to the buyer's solicitor by first class post or document exchange.

Supplementary

11.   The rights and obligations of the parties, under the contract or otherwise, are not affected by this code.

12.   (i)   References to the seller's solicitor and the buyer's solicitor apply as appropriate to solicitors acting for other parties who adopt the code.

(ii)   When a licensed conveyancer adopts this code, references to a solicitor include a licensed conveyancer.

13.   A dispute or difference arising between solicitors who adopt this code (whether or not subject to any variation) relating directly to its application is to be referred to a single arbitrator agreed between the solicitors. If they do not agree on the appointment within one month, the President of the Law Society may appoint the arbitrator at the request of one of the solicitors.

NOTES TO THE CODE

1.   This code will apply to transactions where the code is adopted after 1st July 1998.

2.   The object of this code is to provide solicitors with a convenient means for completion on an agency basis when a representative of the buyer's solicitor is not attending at the office of the seller's solicitor.

3.   As with the Law Society's formulae for exchange of contracts by telephone and fax, the code embodies professional undertakings and is only recommended for adoption between solicitors and licensed conveyancers.

4.   Paragraph 2 of the code provides that the seller's solicitors will act as agents for the buyer's solicitors without fee or disbursements. The convenience of not having to make a specific appointment on the date of completion for the buyer's solicitors to attend to complete personally will offset the agency work that the seller's solicitor has to do and any postage payable in completing under the code. Most solicitors will from time to time act for both sellers and buyers. If a seller's solicitor does consider that charges and/or disbursements are necessary in a particular case this would represent a variation in the code and should be agreed in writing before the completion date.

5.   In view of the decision in *Edward Wong Finance Company Limited* v. *Johnson, Stokes and Master* [1984] AC 1296, clause 4(ii) of the code requires the seller's solicitors to undertake on completion to have authority of the proprietor of every mortgage or charge to be redeemed to receive the sum needed to repay such charge.

6.   Paragraph 11 of the code provides that nothing in the code shall override any rights and obligations of the parties under the contract or otherwise.

7.   The buyer's solicitor is to inform the seller's solicitor of the mortgages or charges which will be redeemed or discharged (see paragraph 3 above) and is to specify those for which an undertaking will be required on completion (paragraph 5(iii)). The information may be given in reply to requisitions on title. Such a reply may also amount to an undertaking.

8.   Care must be taken if there is a sale and sub-sale. The sub-seller's solicitor may not hold the title deeds nor be in a position to receive the funds required to discharge the seller's mortgage on the property. Enquiries should be made to ascertain if the monies or some part of the monies payable on completion should, with either the authority of the sub-seller or the sub-seller's solicitor, be sent direct to the seller's solicitor and not to the sub-seller's solicitor.

9.   Care must also be taken if there is a simultaneous resale and completion and enquiries should be made by the ultimate buyer's solicitor of the intermediate seller's solicitor as to the price being paid on that purchase. Having appointed the intermediate seller's solicitor as agent the buyer's

solicitor is fixed with the knowledge of an agent even without having personal knowledge (see the Society's 'green card' warning on property fraud at Annex 25G, p.501).

10.   If the seller's solicitor has to withdraw from using the code, the buyer's solicitor should be notified of this not later than 4pm on the working day prior to the completion date. If the seller's solicitor's authority to receive the monies is withdrawn later the buyer's solicitor must be notified immediately.

These notes refer only to some of the points in the code that practitioners may wish to consider before agreeing to adopt it. Any variation in the code must be agreed in writing before the completion date.

IV.13. Mortgage redemption statements[1]

The guidance set out below has been issued jointly by the Law Society and Council of Mortgage Lenders in connection with problems arising out of incorrect redemption statements supplied by lenders.

GUIDANCE NOTES

Problems relating to mortgage redemption statements have caused difficulties for lenders and solicitors (this expression to include licensed conveyancers) for a number of years. In 1985 the Building Societies Association and the Law Society issued detailed advice to their respective members on this subject because of the difficulties which were apparent at that time.

The advice comprised paras. 9 to 13 of BSA circular No. 3155. Those paragraphs are now replaced by the new guidance set out below.

In recent months, the Council of Mortgage Lenders (CML) has received a number of enquiries in respect of redemption statements provided by lenders to solicitors acting for the lender (who will often also act for the seller). This guidance refers to some of the circumstances which can produce errors and problems, and the consequences which this can have for the solicitor in the conveyancing transaction. It also suggests certain practical measures designed to reduce problems in this area. Accordingly, it is of importance to all lenders and covers:

  (a) the function and importance of solicitors' undertakings;

  (b) the general principle that lenders should seal a discharge where a redemption statement was incorrect;

  (c) ways in which lenders might overcome the difficulty caused when the borrower prematurely stops payments;

  (d) similar proposals as to the problem of dishonoured cheques;

  (e) suggestions for overcoming difficulties sometimes presented by multiple mortgage accounts;

  (f) information to be provided to banks for inclusion in telegraphic transfers; and

  (g) the importance of returning the sealed discharge promptly.

Terms of reference

This guidance applies to England and Wales; separate guidance for Scotland and Northern Ireland will follow, if necessary.

Redemption on sale

The guidance applies primarily to redemption of a mortgage on sale of the security and, consequently, the lender's/seller's solicitor is required to give an undertaking to the buyer's solicitor that the charge will be discharged.

---

1. Joint guidance from the Law Society and the Council of Mortgage Lenders issued on 29 April 1992.

Remortgages

It is appreciated that an undertaking will also be given on a remortgage and that, accordingly, the guidance should be interpreted as including this situation.

Simple redemption

Much of the guidance is inapplicable to a straightforward redemption (without sale or remortgage) as no undertaking is given. However, even in redemption per se, solicitors and lenders will no doubt wish to provide accurate information and deal promptly with their respective responsibilities.

Solicitors' undertakings

The solicitor acting for the seller will need, on completion, to satisfy the buyer's solicitor that the mortgage on the property being sold has been or will be discharged. In theory the buyer's solicitor will wish to see the mortgage discharged before the purchase money is paid. However, where the monies to repay the mortgage are being provided wholly or partly by the proceeds of sale, then the mortgage cannot be paid off until after completion.

Most lenders will not seal the discharge (this expression to include sealing the vacating receipt on a mortgage deed or sealing of Form DS1) until they receive the redemption money. This leaves the buyer's solicitor with a problem in that he or she has to be satisfied that the mortgage will be discharged and that he or she will obtain the receipted mortgage or Land Registry Form DS1 or END1. This problem is solved by the use of the solicitor's undertaking.

On completion, the seller's/lender's solicitor will provide the buyer's solicitor with a written undertaking to redeem the mortgage(s) in a form recommended by the Law Society similar to that set out below:

'In consideration of your today completing the purchase of [...] we hereby undertake forthwith to pay over to [...] [*the lender*] the money required to redeem the mortgage/legal charge dated [...] and to forward the receipted mortgage/legal charge to you as soon as it is received by us from [...] [*the lender*].'

Incorrect redemption statements

Before completion of a sale, the lender's seller's solicitor will obtain a redemption statement calculated to the date of redemption. He or she will sometimes request the daily figure for interest which will be added if completion is delayed. If the lender supplies an incorrect redemption statement, the solicitor is likely to forward insufficient money to redeem the mortgage. The lender might be unwilling to discharge the mortgage and, if the solicitor is not holding more funds on behalf of the borrower, the solicitor would be in breach of his or her undertaking.

Problem areas

Problems with redemption statements can arise for a number of reasons:

(a)   a lender might simply make a mistake in calculating the redemption figure;

(b)   difficulties could be caused by the cancellation of standing orders or direct debit payments or by borrowers' cheques being dishonoured; and

(c)   there might be misunderstanding between a lender and the solicitor.

Some of the more common practical problems are outlined below.

Cancellation

A difficulty arises if the mortgage payments are made by standing order and, shortly before completion, the borrower stops the payments without notice to the lender. There will be a shortfall if the lender assumed, without making this assumption clear, that the next payment would be paid and made the redemption figure calculation accordingly.

If this is the case, and the solicitor has acted in good faith and with no knowledge that a payment has been or is likely to be cancelled, the view of the CML is that the lender should seal the discharge. This is to avoid the solicitor being in breach of his or her undertaking to the buyer's solicitor. (The lender would then have to recoup the money from the borrower.)

This difficulty is less likely to arise where payments are made by direct debit because the lender is the originator of the debit and therefore has control over the raising of any future direct debits from the borrower's bank account.

However, there is no guarantee that direct debits will be honoured and they may be returned on the grounds of insufficient funds or that the customer has closed his or her account or instructed his or her bank to cancel the direct debit.

Some lenders overcome this problem by excluding any future payments due when calculating the redemption figure. In other words, they 'freeze' the account balance at the day of the redemption calculation. The disadvantages of this are that (if the payment has not been cancelled) the borrower has to pay a higher redemption figure and the lender has to make a refund to the borrower after redemption.

An alternative is for the lender on the redemption statement to make it clear to the solicitor that it is assumed that the next payment will be made and that, if it is not paid, the mortgage will not be discharged until the balance is received. This gives the solicitor an early chance to address his or her and his or her borrower client's mind to this situation and to ensure that sufficient monies will be available to redeem the mortgage. Indeed, this would also serve as a reminder to the solicitor to warn the borrower client of the importance of continuing the payments in the normal way up to completion.

Uncleared cheques

This is a very similar situation to that of standing orders and direct debits. The CML's view is that if the lender does not notify the solicitor that it is assumed that the borrower's cheque will clear then, provided that the solicitor acts in good faith and without knowledge that the cheque would be or is likely to be dishonoured, the lender should seal the discharge. Exceptions to this are if the lender:

(a) prepares the redemption statement on the assumption that the cheque will not clear and informs the solicitor of this, probably, in a note on the statement. This has the disadvantages described above, or

(b) notifies the solicitor that a cheque has been received and that, if it does not clear by the date of redemption, the mortgage will not be discharged until the balance is received.

Separate loan account

The lender may have more than one loan secured on the property. For example, in addition to the principal mortgage, there could be a secured personal loan which is a regulated agreement under Consumer Credit Act 1974 and/or a further advance conducted on a separate account basis. In such cases, there will be more than one account number.

On a sale, as all mortgage accounts will be repaid, multiplicity of accounts should not present a problem unless the solicitor does not know and is unable to specify every account and has no notice or cause to query the matter and the lender fails to cross-check the matter internally.

However, it is possible, for example, on certain remortgages, that it is the intention of the borrower and the lender that not all mortgages will be discharged and replaced. If so, when requesting the redemption statement, the solicitor should make it clear to the lender which mortgages the borrower wishes to redeem. The solicitor should inform the lender of any mortgages of which he or she is aware which are outstanding with the lender but which are not being redeemed. The solicitor should also quote all relevant account numbers if known as far as possible and ensure that the redemption statement received from the lender includes all the mortgages which are intended to be redeemed.

The lender should have its own internal cross-checking system but it is vital that the solicitor (who will, after all, be acting for the lender in most cases) is as clear as possible about the mortgage account(s) being redeemed. It is suggested that the solicitor should if possible, and time permits, send a copy of the redemption statement to the borrower to check agreement on the amount shown as due to the lender. Solicitors should be encouraged to ask for a statement at the earliest possible date.

Telegraphic transfers

Lenders could request that solicitors adopt procedures to assist in the identification of telegraphic transfers. When mortgages are being redeemed the telegraphic transfer which a lender receives is often difficult to identify and to match to a particular account.

The administrative difficulties which are caused by the inability to identify the money would be overcome if solicitors provided to the bank the information to be included in the telegraphic transfer, i.e. the borrower's mortgage account number and the firm's name and address.

Delay

Lenders are sometimes criticised for delay in providing a form of discharge after redemption of the mortgage. It is recognised that most lenders can and do return the receipted mortgage or Form DS1 promptly and that solicitors can apply for registration to protect priority. However, unless there is good reason for the delay, e.g. a solicitor sending the form to the wrong office of the lender, lenders will no doubt deal promptly with this important procedure.

It is suggested that lenders should aim to return the receipted mortgage or Form DS1 within seven days, and if there is likely to be a delay beyond that period they should notify the seller's solicitor. This would enable the buyer's solicitor to lodge an application with the Land Registry pending receipt of receipted mortgage or sealed Form DS1, although it is hoped that this would only be necessary in exceptional circumstances.

The CML view

Many of the difficulties described above would be reduced if as a matter of course solicitors gave lenders correct information about the borrower, the property, the account number(s), etc., and lenders, in turn, operated internal cross-checking systems and provided accurate and complete redemption statements showing clearly the last payment to be taken into account and, systems permitting, details of all the borrower's accounts relating to the property which represent mortgages to be discharged.

If the solicitor, relying on an incorrect redemption statement provided by the lender, sends insufficient money to redeem a mortgage, the lender should discharge the mortgage. (However, the lender might wish to make it clear that the release was not intended to discharge the borrower from his or her outstanding personal liability. This might prevent the borrower from successfully claiming estoppel against the lender.)

Such cases do not occur frequently; when they do, it is generally because of a clerical or administrative error on the part of the lender, such as by omitting one month's interest or an insurance premium, and the amount is usually small. Nevertheless, where it appears that there has been an error, the solicitor should immediately draw this to the lender's notice and should pursue his or her borrower client actively for any shortfall.

Very rare cases could arise where general guidance of this kind is inapplicable, for example, if there is such a major discrepancy in the redemption figure that the borrower, and, perhaps, his or her solicitor, could not reasonably have believed in the accuracy of the statement.

Conclusion

Where there is an incorrect redemption statement, which is clearly due to an error by the lender or lack of clarification, it is unreasonable that a solicitor should be put in breach of his or her undertaking. The undertaking given to the buyer's solicitor is a vital part of the conveyancing process. It is the CML's view, in such cases, that the lender should seal the discharge.

The Law Society and the Council for Licensed Conveyancers agree with the views expressed in these paragraphs. It is hoped that some of the practical measures referred to above will be implemented to avoid difficulties on redemption.

V. LAW SOCIETY INTEREST RATE

V.1. The Law Society interest rate

The Law Society interest rate is the 'contract rate' in the Standard Conditions of Sale first published in 1990. The Law Society interest rate is 4% above Barclays Bank base rate. Rates are as at close of business on the day indicated.

This information is provided for your use and it is your responsibility to check its accuracy and application. No liability is accepted to third parties.

Please note: For the current rate ring the Library Enquiry Line on 0870 606 2511. A message giving the current rate is accessible even when the Library is closed.

05 March 2009	4.50%	10 May 2001	9.25%
05 February 2009	5.00%	05 April 2001	9.50%
08 January 2009	5.50%	08 February 2001	9.75%
04 December 2008	6.00%	10 February 2000	10.00%
06 November 2008	7.00%	13 January 2000	9.75%
08 October 2008	8.50%	04 November 1999	9.50%
10 April 2008	9.00%	08 September 1999	9.25%
07 February 2008	9.25%	10 June 1999	9.00%
06 December 2007	9.50%	08 April 1999	9.25%
05 July 2007	9.75%	04 February 1999	9.50%
10 May 2007	9.50%	07 January 1999	10.00%
11 January 2007	9.25%	11 December 1998	10.25%
09 November 2006	9.00%	05 November 1998	10.75%
03 August 2006	8.75%	09 October 1998	11.25%
04 August 2005	8.50%	04 June 1998	11.50%
05 August 2004	8.75%	06 November 1997	11.25%
10 June 2004	8.50%	07 August 1997	11.00%
06 May 2004	8.25%	10 July 1997	10.75%
05 February 2004	8.00%	06 June 1997	10.50%
06 November 2003	7.75%	06 May 1997	10.25%
10 July 2003	7.50%	30 October 1996	10.00%
06 February 2003	7.75%	06 June 1996	9.75%
08 November 2001	8.00%	08 March 1996	10.00%
04 October 2001	8.50%	18 January 1996	10.25%
18 September 2001	8.75%	13 December 1995	10.50%
02 August 2001	9.00%	02 February 1995	10.75%

07 December 1994	10.25%	05 May 1992	14.00%
12 September 1994	9.75%	04 September 1991	14.50%
08 February 1994	9.25%	12 July 1991	15.00%
23 November 1993	9.50%	24 May 1991	15.50%
26 January 1993	10.00%	12 April 1991	16.00%
13 November 1992	11.00%	22 March 1991	16.50%
16 October 1992	12.00%	27 February 1991	17.00%
22 September 1992	13.00%	13 February 1991	17.50%
17 September 1992	14.00%	08 October 1990	18.00%
16 September 1992	16.00%	30 April 1990	19.00%

VI. HM REVENUE AND CUSTOMS

VI.1. Stamp Duty Form 22: Apportionment of consideration under agreement for sale[1]

	A		B
Amount of consideration payable in Cash or Bills	£	Legal Estates in Freehold Property	£
Amount of consideration payable in Shares, Debentures etc.	£	Fixed Plant and Machinery in Freehold Property	£
Liabilities assumed by the Purchaser:		Legal Estates in Leasehold Property	£
Amounts due on mortgages of Freeholds and/or Leaseholds, including interest to date of sale	£	Fixed Plant and Machinery in Leasehold Property	£
Hire Purchase Debts for Goods acquired	£	Equitable interests in Freehold or Leasehold Property	£
Other liabilities of the Vendor	£	Loose Plant and Machinery, Stock-in-Trade and other Chattels	£
		(Only Plant and Machinery in an actual state of severance, i.e. not fixed to the premises at the date of the Agreement for Sale, must be included in this figure)	
Any other consideration	£	Goods, Wares and Merchandise subject to Hire Purchase Agreements (Written Down Value)	£
		Goodwill and Benefit of Contracts	£
		Patents, Designs, Trade Marks, Licences, etc.	£
		Book Debts	£
		Cash in Hand and at Bank on Current Account	£
		Cash on Deposit	£
		Shares, Debentures and other investments	£
Please note that Column A should equal Column B.		Other property viz	£
	£		£

1. Crown copyright.

I hereby certify that the particulars shown in this form are in every respect fully and truly stated according to the best of my judgment and belief, and that the Loose Plant and Machinery included in the above apportionment were in a state of severance at the date of the sale agreement.

This certificate should be signed by the Vendor or Purchaser (the Secretary in the case of a Company) or by an Accountant or Solicitor acting in the sale.

Signed .... Address ....

Date ....

VI.2. HM Revenue and Customs SDLT Manual – SDLTMO4010 Fixtures and fittings[1]

For an item to be regarded as a fixture or part of the land and therefore chargeable to tax, as opposed to a chattel or moveable in Scotland which is not chargeable, it must be annexed to the property.

The issue will then turn on the degree and purpose of the annexation, with emphasis being placed in many cases to purpose.

Where a purchaser agrees to buy a property for a price that includes an amount properly attributed to chattels or moveables, that amount will not be charged to stamp duty land tax.

Under stamp duty land tax a purchaser is responsible for the accurate completion of their land transaction return, including the entry for the consideration of the land transaction at box 10 in form SDLT1.

By virtue of FA03/SCH4/PARA4 a just and reasonable apportionment is required where a price is paid partly for a land transaction and partly for a non-land transaction such as the purchase of chattels.

It does not matter that the parties to a transaction may agree a particular apportionment which is then documented in the contract. The apportionment will not be correct unless it was arrived at on a just and reasonable basis.

HM Revenue and Customs has the right to make enquiries into the accuracy of a land transaction return. See SDLTM80800+.

The apportionment of the purchase price may well be one aspect on which an enquiry may be opened.

Similarly it is quite possible that we will also undertake enquiries into cases where a deduction has been made for chattels to confirm that those items properly fall within the definition of chattels.

HM Revenue and Customs is unable to provide a comprehensive list of items that are accepted as chattels or moveables. This is because each case must be considered on its own merits and because this is an area of the law that continues to evolve.

The following items are, however, confirmed as being assets that will normally be regarded as chattels

- carpets (fitted or otherwise)
- curtains and blinds
- free standing furniture
- kitchen white goods
- electric and gas fires (provided that they can be removed by disconnection from the power supply without causing damage to the property)

---

1. Crown copyright.

- light shades and fittings (unless recessed)

On the other hand, the following items will not normally be regarded as chattels

- fitted kitchen units, cupboards and sinks
- agas and wall mounted ovens
- fitted bathroom sanitary ware
- central heating systems
- intruder alarm systems

Externally, any plants, shrubs or trees growing in the soil which forms part of the land, are not to be regarded as chattels.

A deduction would, however, be appropriate for amounts properly apportioned to any plants growing in pots or containers.

The above guidance is written primarily in the context of sales of residential property.

HM Revenue and Customs is advised that the same principles will apply when considering the purchase of industrial or commercial property in which the sale may also involve the acquisition of plant, machinery or equipment.

Tenants fixtures

The question of whether plant or machinery is a fixture or a chattel is determined in the same way as for any other asset.

In particular tenants fixtures in England, Wales and Northern Ireland are fixtures and therefore part of the land, notwithstanding that a tenant may have a right to sever them.

The tenant's right of severance is also a chargeable interest within the meaning of FA03/S48(1).

While each case depends on its own facts it is unlikely that plant or machinery that can be relatively easily severed from the property to which it is fixed, for example by the simple expedient of removing some bolts securing it to the floor or walls, will be a fixture.

Alternatively heavy plant or machinery that is integral to a building, or plant or machinery whose removal would damage the building or land, is likely to be a fixture.

It follows therefore that escalators and elevators, boilers, furnaces, walk-in refrigerators and restaurant cooking stations are likely to be fixtures.

VI.3. HM Customs Statement of Practice: variations of leases of commercial property[1]

HM Customs and Excise have published the following revised Statement of Practice which will apply in circumstances where a deemed surrender and re-grant occur by operation of law.

'(A) Where there is no monetary consideration passing from lessor to lessee as a result of or in connection with the variation, then Customs Policy is that there is no surrender of the old lease for non-monetary consideration when:

    (i) the new lease is for the same building (or the same part of the building) but the new lease is for an extended term; or

    (ii) the new lease is for a larger part of the same building than the old lease but the term is for the same or an extended term; or

    (iii) the new lease is for the same land and for an extended term.

However, (i)–(iii) above do not embrace 'new for old' ground leases or building leases, i.e. leases granted on condition that the lessee will undertake development. Very often, the negotiations between the parties will result in agreement for demolition of an old building and the construction of a new one, or partial demolition and reconstruction or enlargement. In the case of these ground/building leases and in any other cases not covered above, Customs would expect to find that the terms of the new lease will be more favourable to the lessee as a result of the surrender of the old lease. They would be likely to rule that the old lease was being surrendered in consideration of the grant of the new on favourable terms and that the surrender supply by the lessee should be valued at its open market value. Where there is doubt, the position should be discussed with Customs.

(B) Where the surrender and re-grant involves ground leases or building leases, i.e. leases granted on condition that the lessee will undertake development, very often the negotiations between the parties will result in demolition of an old building and the construction of a new one, or partial demolition and reconstruction or enlargement. Customs may find that the terms of the new lease will be more favourable to both the lessee and the lessor but do not consider this in itself indicates that the old lease was surrendered in consideration of the grant of the new one. However, if the lessee receives a direct benefit in return for undertaking the construction works (e.g. a rent-free period, or reduced rent for a period) Customs are likely to see a consideration passing from the lessee to the lessor in return for the benefit. In cases where there is doubt you should agree the position with Customs.

(C) Where monetary consideration passes from lessor to lessee, Customs would normally regard the monetary consideration as the sole consideration for the surrender.

---

1. Crown copyright. First published [1991] *Gazette*, 1 May, 16, and revised version published as A16.9.3 in the Law Society's *Conveyancing Handbook*, seventh edition.

Where monetary consideration passes to the lessor from the lessee Customs would normally see this as consideration for the grant of the new lease which would be exempt subject to the lessor's election to waive exemption (option to tax). However, the circumstances may indicate that the payment is consideration for the lessor's supply of the acceptance of the surrender of an onerous lease from the lessee (sometimes known as a reverse surrender). From 1 March 1995, we say these payments are for an exempt supply, with the option to tax. When the payment received by the lessor is seen as consideration for the grant of a new lease, there would be no surrender by the lessee.'

VII. STATUTE LAW

VII.1. Stamp Duty (Exempt Instruments) Regulations 1987 (SI 1987/516)[1]

1987 No. 516

TAXES

The Stamp Duty (Exempt Instruments) Regulations 1987

Made 24th March 1987
Laid before the House of Commons 26th March 1987
Coming into force 1st May 1987

Note. – FA 1985, s. 87 (2) provides that instruments which would otherwise be chargeable with stamp duty of a fixed amount under any provision specified in regulations shall not be so charged if they are of a kind specified in regulations and certified to be instruments of that kind.

These regulations specify the provisions under which, subject to conditions, that duty shall not be charged; specify the instruments (executed on or after 1 May 1987) in relation to which the exemption is available; and provide for the certification requirements.

Regulation 1 provides the title and commencement date.

Regulation 2 provides the conditions for the exemption.

Regulation 3 provides for the requirements for the certificate and the conditions which have to be fulfilled.

Regulation 4 introduces the Schedule which specifies the instruments which may qualify for the exemption provided by regulation 2.

Regulation 5 dispenses with the requirement of adjudication in accordance with the Stamp Act 1891, s. 12 as required by FA 1985, ss. 82(5) and 84(9).

The Treasury, in exercise of the powers conferred on them by section 87(2) of the Finance Act 1985, hereby make the following regulations:

1. These regulations may be cited as the Stamp Duty (Exempt Instruments) Regulations 1987 and shall come into force on 1st May 1987.

In these Regulations 'life policy' means –

    (a) any policy of insurance on a human life, or on the happening of a contingency dependent upon a human life, except a policy of insurance for a payment only upon the death of a person otherwise than from a natural cause, or

1. Crown copyright. Incorporating amendments made by Stamp Duty (Exempt Instruments) (Amendments) Regulations 1999 (SI 1999/2539) and Tax and Civil Partnership (No.2) Regulations 2005 (SI 2005/3230).

(b)   a grant or contract for the payment of an annuity upon a human life.

2.   (1)   An instrument which –

(a)   is executed on or after 1st May 1987,

(b)   is of a kind specified in the Schedule hereto for the purposes of this regulation, and

(c)   is certified by a certificate which fulfils the conditions of regulation 3 to be an instrument of that kind,

shall be exempt from duty under the provisions specified in paragraph (2) of this regulation.

(2)   The provisions specified are –

(a)   the following paragraphs of Part III of Schedule 13 to the Finance Act 1999 –

(i)   paragraph 16 (conveyance or transfer otherwise than on sale),

(ii)   paragraph 17 (declaration of use or trust),

(iii)   paragraph 18 (dispositions in Scotland);

(b)   sections 83(2) and 84(8) of the Finance Act 1985.

3.   The certificate –

(a)   shall be in writing and –

(i)   be included as part of the instrument, or

(ii)   be endorsed upon or, where separate, be physically attached to the instrument concerned;

(b)   shall contain a sufficient description of –

(i)   the instrument concerned where the certificate is separate but physically attached to the instrument, and

(ii)   the category in the Schedule hereto into which the instrument falls;

(c)   (i)   shall be signed by the transferor or grantor or by his solicitor or duly authorised agent, and

(ii)   where it is not signed by the transferor or grantor or by his solicitor, it shall contain a statement by the signatory of the capacity in which he signs, that he is authorised so to sign and that he gives the certificate from his own knowledge of the facts stated in it.

4.   The Schedule to these regulations shall have effect for the specification of instruments for the purposes of regulation 2.

5.   An instrument which is certified in accordance with these regulations shall not be required under section 82(5) or section 84(9) of the Finance Act 1985 to be stamped in accordance with section 12 of the Stamp Act 1891 with a particular stamp denoting that it is duly stamped or that it is not chargeable with any duty.

SCHEDULE

Regulation 4

An instrument which effects any one or more of the following transactions only is an instrument specified for the purposes of regulation 2 –

A.   The vesting of property subject to a trust in the trustees of the trust on the appointment of a new trustee, or in the continuing trustees on the retirement of a trustee.

B.   The conveyance or transfer of property the subject of a specific devise or legacy to the beneficiary named in the will (or his nominee).

C.   The conveyance or transfer of property which forms part of an intestate's estate to the person entitled on intestacy (or his nominee).

D.   The appropriation of property within section 84(4) of the Finance Act 1985 (death: appropriation in satisfaction of a general legacy of money) or section 84(5) or (7) of that Act (death: appropriation in satisfaction of any interest of surviving spouse or civil partner and in Scotland also of any interest of issue).

E.   The conveyance or transfer of property which forms part of the residuary estate of a testator to a beneficiary (or his nominee) entitled solely by virtue of his entitlement under the will.

F.   The conveyance or transfer of property out of a settlement in or towards satisfaction of a beneficiary's interest, not being an interest acquired for money or money's worth, being a conveyance or transfer constituting a distribution of property in accordance with the provisions of the settlement.

G.   The conveyance or transfer of property on and in consideration only of marriage to a party to the marriage (or his nominee) or to trustees to be held on the terms of a settlement made in consideration only of the marriage.

GG.   The conveyance or transfer of property on and in consideration only of the formation of a civil partnership to a party to the civil partnership (or his nominee) or to trustees to be held on the terms of a settlement made in consideration only of the civil partnership.

H.   The conveyance or transfer of property within section 83(1) or (1A) of the Finance Act 1985 (transfers in connection with divorce or dissolution of civil partnership etc.).

I.   The conveyance or transfer by the liquidator of property which formed part of the assets of the company in liquidation to a shareholder of that company (or his nominee) in or towards satisfaction of the shareholder's rights on a winding-up.

J.   The grant in fee simple of an easement in or over land for no consideration in money or money's worth.

K.   The grant of a servitude for no consideration in money or money's worth.

L.   The conveyance or transfer of property operating as a voluntary disposition inter vivos for no consideration in money or money's worth nor any consideration referred to in section 57 of the Stamp Act 1891 (conveyance in consideration of a debt etc.).

M.   The conveyance or transfer of property by an instrument within section 84(1) of the Finance Act 1985 (death: varying disposition).

N.   The declaration of any use or trust of or concerning a life policy, or property representing, or benefits arising under, a life policy.

VII.2. Land Charges Fees Rules 1990 (SI 1990/327)[1]

1990 No. 327

LAND CHARGES

The Land Charges Fees Rules 1990

Made 21st February 1990
Coming into force 2nd April 1990

The Lord Chancellor, with the concurrence of the Treasury, in exercise of the powers conferred on him by sections 9(1), 10(2), 16(1) and 17(1) of the Land Charges Act 1972 hereby makes in the following rules:

1.   (1)   These Rules may be cited as the Land Charges Fees Rules 1990 and shall come into force on 2nd April 1990.

      (2)   In these Rules, unless the context otherwise requires –

         'the Act' means the Land Charges Act 1972;

         'credit account' means an account authorised by the Registrar for the purpose of providing credit facilities for the payment of fees;

         'fee' means a fee specified in Schedule 1;

         'Schedule' means a schedule to these Rules;

         'written application' in Schedule 1 does not include an application made by teleprinter or facsimile transmission.

2.   The fees specified in Schedule 1 shall be payable under the Act.

3.   Every fee which accompanies an application is to be paid in money in accordance with the Land Charges (Fees) Order 1990 and shall, except as mentioned in Rule 4 or as the Registrar may otherwise allow, be paid in cash or by means of a postal order crossed and made payable to HM Land Registry.

4.   (1)   Any person or firm having a credit account may request the Registrar, on any application, to debit the requisite fee to that account.

      (2)   When a person or firm having a credit account makes an application which is not accompanied by any fee and does not contain a request for the fee to be debited to that account, the Registrar may, if he thinks fit, nevertheless accept the application and debit the fee to that person's or that firm's account.

      (3)   If the Registrar debits a fee to a credit account, this shall be treated as due payment of that fee.

---

1. Crown copyright. Incorporating amendments made by the Land Charges Fees (Amendment) Rules 1994 (SI 1994/286).

(4)   Credit accounts shall be authorised and maintained in accordance with the provisions set out in Schedule 2.

5.   The Land Charges Fees Order 1985 so far as made under powers conferred by the Act is hereby revoked.

Mackay of Clashfern, C.
Dated 16th February 1990

We concur

David Lightbown
Stephen Dorrell
Two of the Lord Commissioners of Her Majesty's Treasury
Dated 21st February 1990

SCHEDULE 1

Rule 2

Service		Amount of Fee
1. Registration, renewal, rectification or cancellation of an entry in any register	per name	£1
2. Certificate of cancellation	per name	£1
3. Entry of priority notice	per name	£1
4. Inspection of an entry in the register	per entry	£1
5. Office copy of an entry in the register (including any plan) whether the application is made in writing or by telephone or teleprinter or facsimile transmission or to the registrar's computer system by means of the applicant's remote terminal	per copy	£1
6. Official search in the index (including issue of printed certificate of result):–		
written application	per name	£1
telephone application	per name	£2
teleprinter application	per name	£2
facsimile transmission application	per name	£2
application made to the registrar's computer system by means of the applicant's remote terminal	per name	£2
7. Official search in the index (including visual display of result of search and issue of printed certificate of such result)	per name	£2

SCHEDULE 2

Provision of credit accounts

Rule 4(4)

1.   The Registrar may, as he thinks fit, authorise any person or firm to use a credit account for the purpose of the payment of fees but may withdraw or suspend any such authorisation at any time without giving any reason therefor.

2.   The Registrar may also at any time terminate or suspend all credit accounting facilities generally.

3.   A statement of account shall be sent by the Registrar to each account holder at the end of each calendar month or at such other period as the Registrar shall direct either in any particular case or generally.

4.   On receipt of the statement and if no question arises thereon the account holder shall pay by cheque any sum due on his account promptly, and in any event within ten days of its receipt.

5.   Cheques shall be made payable to HM Land Registry and sent to the Accounts Section, Land Charges Department, Burrington Way, Plymouth, PL5 3LP or at such other address as the Registrar shall direct.

VII

VII.3. Solicitors' (Non-Contentious Business) Remuneration Order 2009 (SI 2009/1931)[1]

2009 No. 1931

LEGAL PROFESSION, ENGLAND AND WALES

The Solicitors' (Non-Contentious Business) Remuneration Order 2009

Made 16th July 2009
Laid before Parliament 20th July 2009
Coming into force 11th August 2009

The Lord Chancellor, the Lord Chief Justice, the Master of the Rolls, the President of the Law Society, the president of Surrey law society and the Chief Land Registrar (in respect of business done under the Land Registration Act 2002), together constituting the committee authorised to make orders under section 56 of the Solicitors Act 1974, in exercise of the powers conferred on them by that section and having complied with the requirements of section 56(3), make the following Order:

Citation, commencement and revocation

1.   (1)   This Order may be cited as the Solicitors' (Non-Contentious Business) Remuneration Order 2009.

(2)   This Order shall come into force on 11th August 2009 and applies to all non-contentious business for which bills are delivered on or after that date.

(3)   The Solicitors' (Non-Contentious) Business Remuneration Order 1994 is revoked except in its application to non-contentious business for which bills are delivered before this Order comes into force.

Interpretation

2.   In this Order–

'client' means the client of a solicitor;

'costs' means the amount charged in a solicitor's bill, exclusive of disbursements and value added tax, in respect of non-contentious business;

'entitled person' means a client or an entitled third party;

1. Crown copyright

'entitled third party' means a residuary beneficiary absolutely and immediately (and not contingently) entitled to an inheritance, where a solicitor has charged the estate for his professional costs for acting in the administration of the estate and the only personal representatives are:

(a)   solicitors (whether or not acting in a professional capacity);

(b)   solicitors acting jointly with partners, managers or employees in a professional capacity;

(c)   employees of a solicitor sole practitioner acting in that capacity; or

(d)   managers or employees of a recognised body acting in that capacity;

'manager' has the same meaning as in the Legal Services Act 2007 (see section 207 of that Act);

'paid disbursements' means disbursements already paid by the solicitor;

'recognised body' means a body recognised by the Law Society under section 9 of the Administration of Justice Act 1985;

'registered European lawyer' means a registered European lawyer within the meaning of the European Communities (Lawyer's Practice) Regulations 2000 who is registered with the Law Society;

'residuary beneficiary' includes a person entitled to all or part of the residue of an intestate estate; and

'solicitor' includes a registered European lawyer and a recognised body.

Solicitors' costs

3.   A solicitor's costs must be fair and reasonable having regard to all the circumstances of the case and in particular to–

(a)   the complexity of the matter or the difficulty or novelty of the questions raised;

(b)   the skill, labour, specialised knowledge and responsibility involved;

(c)   the time spent on the business;

(d)   the number and importance of the documents prepared or considered, without regard to length;

(e)   the place where and the circumstances in which the business or any part is transacted;

(f)   the amount or value of any money or property involved;

(g)   whether any land involved is registered land within the meaning of the Land Registration Act 2002;

(h)   the importance of the matter to the client; and

(i)   the approval (express or implied) of the entitled person or the express approval of the testator to–

(i)   the solicitor undertaking all or any part of the work giving rise to the costs; or

(ii)   the amount of the costs.

Security for costs

4.   A solicitor may take from his client security for the payment of any costs, including the amount of any interest to which the solicitor may become entitled under article 5.

Interest

5. (1) A solicitor may charge interest on the unpaid amount of his costs plus any paid disbursements and value added tax, subject to the remainder of this article.

    (2) Where an entitlement to interest arises under paragraph (1), and subject to any agreement made between a solicitor and client, the period for which interest may be charged runs from one month after the date of delivery of a bill.

    (3) Subject to any agreement made between a solicitor and client, the rate of interest must not exceed the rate for the time being payable on judgment debts.

    (4) Interest charged under this article must be calculated, where applicable, by reference to—

       (a) the amount specified in a determination of costs by the Law Society under Schedule 1A to the Solicitors Act 1974;

       (b) the amount ascertained on taxation if an application has been made for the bill to be taxed.

Judge, C.J.
Sir Anthony Clarke, M.R.
Paul Marsh
John Perry
Peter Collis

Jack Straw
Lord Chancellor

16th July 2009

VII.4. Land Registration Fee Order 2009 (SI 2009/845)[1]

2009 No. 845

LAND REGISTRATION, ENGLAND AND WALES

The Land Registration Fee Order 2009

Made 1st April 2009
Laid before Parliament 2nd April 2009
Coming into force 6th July 2009

The Lord Chancellor makes the following Order in exercise of the powers conferred on him by sections 102 and 128(1) of the Land Registration Act 2002.

In accordance with section 102 of that Act, he has received the advice and assistance of the Rule Committee, appointed under section 127 of that Act.

Also in accordance with section 102 of that Act, the Treasury has consented to the making of this Order.

PART 1

General

Citation, commencement and interpretation

1.   (1)   This Order may be cited as the Land Registration Fee Order 2009 and shall come into force on 6 July 2009.

        (2)   In this Order –

'account holder' means a person holding a credit account,

'the Act' means the Land Registration Act 2002,

'CLRA' means the Commonhold and Leasehold Reform Act 2002,

'charge' includes a sub-charge,

'common parts' has the same meaning as in the CLRA,

'a commonhold' has the same meaning as in the CLRA,

'commonhold association' has the same meaning as in the CLRA,

'commonhold community statement' has the same meaning as in the CLRA,

---

1. Crown copyright.

'commonhold land' has the same meaning as in the CLRA,

'commonhold unit' has the same meaning as in the CLRA,

'credit account' means an account authorised by the registrar under article 14(1),

'developer' has the same meaning as in the CLRA,

'large scale application' has the same meaning as in article 6(1)(b),

'monetary consideration' means a consideration in money or money's worth (other than a nominal consideration or a consideration consisting solely of a covenant to pay money owing under a mortgage),

'premium' means the amount or value of any monetary consideration given by the lessee as part of the same transaction in which a lease is granted by way of fine, premium or otherwise, but, where a registered leasehold estate of substantially the same land is surrendered on the grant of a new lease, the premium for the new lease shall not include the value of the surrendered lease,

'profit' means a profit à prendre in gross,

'remote terminal' means a remote terminal communicating with the registrar's computer system in accordance with a notice given under Schedule 2 to the rules,

'rent' means the largest amount of annual rent the lease reserves within the first five years of its term that can be quantified at the time an application to register the lease is made,

'the rules' means the Land Registration Rules 2003 and a rule referred to by number means the rule so numbered in the rules,

'Scale 1' means Scale 1 in Schedule 1,

'Scale 2' means Scale 2 in Schedule 2,

'scale fee' means a fee payable in accordance with a scale set out in Schedule 1 or 2 whether or not reduced in accordance with article 2(6),

'scale fee application' means an application which attracts a scale fee, or which would attract such a fee but for the operation of article 6,

'share', in relation to land, means an interest in that land under a trust of land,

'surrender' includes a surrender not made by deed,

'termination application' has the same meaning as in the CLRA,

'unit-holder' has the same meaning as in the CLRA,

'voluntary application' means an application for first registration (other than for the registration of title to a rentcharge, a franchise or a profit) which is not made wholly or in part pursuant to section 4 of the Act (when title must be registered).

(3) Expressions used in this Order have, unless the contrary intention appears, the meaning which they bear in the rules.

PART 2

Scale fees

Applications for first registration and applications for registration of a lease by an original lessee

2. (1) The fee for an application for first registration of an estate in land is payable under Scale 1 on the value of the estate in land comprised in the application assessed under article 7, unless the application is –

   (a) for the registration of title to a lease by the original lessee or his personal representative, where paragraph (2) applies,

   (b) a voluntary application, where either paragraph (6) or article 6(3) applies, or

   (c) a large scale application, where article 6 applies.

   (2) The fee for an application by the original lessee or his personal representative for the registration of title to a lease, or for the registration of the grant of a lease, is payable under Scale 1 –

   (a) on an amount equal to the sum of the premium and the rent, or

   (b) where

      (i) there is no premium, and

      (ii) either there is no rent or the rent cannot be quantified at the time the application is made,

   on the value of the lease assessed under article 7 subject to a minimum fee of £50,

   unless either of the circumstances in paragraph (3) applies.

   (3) Paragraph (2) shall not apply if the application is –

   (a) a voluntary application, where paragraph (6) applies, or

   (b) a large scale application, where article 6 applies.

   (4) The fee for an application for the first registration of a rentcharge is £50.

   (5) The fee for an application for the first registration of a franchise or a profit is payable under Scale 1 on the value of the franchise or the profit assessed under article 7.

   (6) The fee for a voluntary application (other than a large scale application, where article 6(3) applies) is the fee which would otherwise be payable under paragraph (1) or (2) reduced by 25 per cent and, where the reduced fee would be a figure which includes pence, the fee must be adjusted to the nearest £10.

   (7) In paragraph (2) 'lease' means –

   (a) a lease which grants an estate in land whether or not the grant is a registrable disposition, or

   (b) a lease of a franchise, profit or manor the grant of which is a registrable disposition.

Transfers of registered estates for monetary consideration, etc.

3. (1) Subject to paragraphs (2), (3) and (4), the fee for an application for the registration of –

   (a) a transfer of a registered estate for monetary consideration,

    (b)   a transfer for the purpose of giving effect to a disposition for monetary consideration of a share in a registered estate, or

    (c)   a surrender of a registered leasehold estate for monetary consideration, other than a surrender to which paragraph (3) of Schedule 4 applies,

is payable under Scale 1 on the amount or value of the consideration.

(2)   Paragraph (1) shall not apply if the application is –

    (a)   a large scale application, where article 6 applies, or

    (b)   for the registration of a transfer of a registered estate made pursuant to an order of the Court under the Matrimonial Causes Act 1973 or the Civil Partnership Act 2004, where article 4(1)(h) applies.

(3)   Where a sale and sub-sale of a registered estate are made by separate deeds of transfer, a separate fee is payable for each deed of transfer.

(4)   Where a single deed of transfer gives effect to a sale and a sub-sale of the same registered estate a single fee is assessed upon the greater of the monetary consideration given by the purchaser and the monetary consideration given by the sub-purchaser.

(5)   The fee for an application to cancel an entry in the register of notice of an unregistered lease which has determined is payable under Scale 1 on the value of the lease immediately before its determination assessed under article 7.

Transfers of registered estates otherwise than for monetary consideration, etc.

4.   (1)   Unless the application is a large scale application (where article 6 applies), the fee for an application for the registration of –

    (a)   a transfer of a registered estate otherwise than for monetary consideration (unless paragraph (2) applies),

    (b)   a surrender of a registered leasehold estate otherwise than for monetary consideration,

    (c)   a transfer of a registered estate by operation of law on death or bankruptcy, of an individual proprietor,

    (d)   an assent of a registered estate (including a vesting assent),

    (e)   an appropriation of a registered estate,

    (f)   a vesting order or declaration to which section 27(5) of the Act applies,

    (g)   an alteration of the register, or

    (h)   a transfer of a registered estate made pursuant to an order of the Court under the Matrimonial Causes Act 1973 or the Civil Partnership Act 2004,

is payable under Scale 2 on the value of the registered estate which is the subject of the application, assessed under article 7, but after deducting from it the amount secured on the registered estate by any charge subject to which the registration takes effect.

(2)   Where a transfer of a registered estate otherwise than for monetary consideration is for the purpose of giving effect to the disposition of a share in a registered estate, the fee for an application for its registration is payable under Scale 2 on the value of that share.

Charges of registered estates or registered charges

5. (1) The fee for an application for the registration of a charge is payable under Scale 2 on the amount of the charge assessed under article 8 unless it is an application to which paragraph (2), (3) or (4) applies.

    (2) No fee is payable for an application to register a charge lodged with or before the completion of either a scale fee application or an application to which paragraph (17) in Part 1 of Schedule 3 applies ('the primary application') that will result in the chargor being registered as proprietor of the registered estate included in the charge unless –

        (a) the charge includes a registered estate which is not included in the primary application, where paragraph (4) applies, or

        (b) the primary application is a voluntary application, in which case this paragraph shall apply only if the application to register the charge accompanies the primary application.

    (3) No fee is to be paid for an application to register a charge made by a predecessor in title of the applicant that is lodged with or before completion of an application for first registration of the estate included in the charge.

    (4) Where a charge also includes a registered estate which is not included in the primary application ('the additional property') any fee payable under Scale 2 is to be assessed on an amount calculated as follows:

$$\frac{\text{Value of the additional property}}{\text{Value of all the property included in the charge}} \times \text{Amount secured by the charge}$$

    (5) The fee for an application for the registration of –

        (a) a transfer of a registered charge for monetary consideration, or

        (b) a transfer for the purpose of giving effect to a disposition for monetary consideration of a share in a registered charge,

    is payable under Scale 2 on the amount or value of the consideration.

    (6) The fee for an application for the registration of the transfer of a registered charge otherwise than for monetary consideration is payable under Scale 2 on –

        (a) the amount secured by the registered charge at the time of the transfer, or

        (b) where the transfer relates to more than one charge, the aggregate of the amounts secured by the registered charges at the time of the transfer.

    (7) The fee for an application for the registration of a transfer for the purpose of giving effect to a disposition otherwise than for monetary consideration of a share in a registered charge is payable under Scale 2 on –

        (a) the proportionate part of the amount secured by the registered charge at the time of the transfer, or

        (b) where the transfer relates to more than one charge, the proportionate part of the aggregate of the amounts secured by the registered charges at the time of the transfer.

    (8) This article takes effect subject to article 6 (large scale applications).

Large scale applications, etc.

6.   (1)   In this article –

      (a)   'land unit' means –

         (i)   the land registered under a single title number other than, in the case of an application to register a charge, any estate under any title number which is included in a primary application within the meaning of article 5(2), or

         (ii)   on a first registration application, a separate area of land not adjoining any other unregistered land affected by the same application.

      (b)   'large scale application' means a scale fee application which relates to 20 or more land units, other than an application to register a disposition by the developer affecting the whole or part of the freehold estate in land which has been registered as a freehold estate in commonhold land, or a low value application,

      (c)   'low value application' means a scale fee application, other than an application for first registration, where the value of the land or the amount of the charge to which it relates (as the case may be) does not exceed £30,000.

   (2)   Subject to paragraphs (3) and (4), the fee for a large scale application is the greater of –

      (a)   the scale fee, and

      (b)   a fee calculated on the following basis –

         (i)   where the application relates to not more than 500 land units, £12 for each land unit, or

         (ii)   where the application relates to more than 500 land units, £6,000 plus £6 for each land unit in excess of 500.

   (3)   If a large scale application is a voluntary application, the fee payable under paragraph (2) is reduced by 25 per cent and, where the reduced fee would be a figure which includes pence, the fee must be adjusted to the nearest £10.

   (4)   The maximum fee payable for a large scale application for first registration is £52,000 unless the application is a voluntary application in which case the maximum fee is £39,000.

PART 3

Valuation

Valuation (first registration and registered estates)

7.   (1)   The value of the estate in land, franchise, profit, manor or share is the maximum amount for which it could be sold in the open market free from any charge –

      (a)   in the case of a surrender, at the date immediately before the surrender, and

      (b)   in any other case, at the date of the application.

   (2)   As evidence of the amount referred to in paragraph (1), the registrar may require a written statement signed by the applicant or his conveyancer or by any other person who, in the registrar's opinion, is competent to make the statement.

   (3)   Where an application for first registration is made on –

(a)   the purchase of a leasehold estate by the reversioner,

(b)   the purchase of a reversion by the leaseholder, or

(c)   any other like occasion,

and an unregistered interest is determined, the value of the land is the combined value of the reversionary and determined interests assessed in accordance with paragraphs (1) and (2).

Valuation (charges)

8.   (1)   On an application for registration of a charge, the amount of the charge is –

(a)   where the charge secures a fixed amount, that amount,

(b)   where the charge secures further advances and the maximum amount that can be advanced or owed at any one time is limited, that amount,

(c)   where the charge secures further advances and the total amount that can be advanced or owed at any one time is not limited, the value of the property charged,

(d)   where the charge is by way of additional or substituted security or by way of guarantee, an amount equal to the lesser of –

(i)   the amount secured or guaranteed, and

(ii)   the value of the property charged, or

(e)   where the charge secures an obligation or liability which is contingent upon the happening of a future event ('the obligation'), and is not a charge to which subparagraph (d) applies, an amount equal to –

(i)   the maximum amount or value of the obligation, or

(ii)   if that maximum amount is greater than the value of the property charged, or is not limited by the charge, or cannot be calculated at the time of the application, the value of the property charged.

(2)   Where a charge of a kind referred to in paragraph (1)(a) or (1)(b) is secured on unregistered land or other property as well as on a registered estate or registered charge, the fee is payable on an amount calculated as follows –

$$\frac{\text{Value of the registered estate or registered charge}}{\text{Value of all the property charged}} \times \frac{\text{Amount secured by the}}{\text{charge}}$$

(3)   Where one deed contains two or more charges made by the same chargor to secure the same debt, the deed is to be treated as a single charge, and the fee for registration of the charge is to be paid on the lesser of –

(a)   the amount of the whole debt, and

(b)   an amount equal to the value of the property charged.

(4)   Where one deed contains two or more charges to secure the same debt not made by the same chargor, the deed is to be treated as a separate single charge by each of the chargors and a separate fee is to be paid for registration of the charge by each chargor on the lesser of –

(a)   the amount of the whole debt, and

(b)   an amount equal to the value of the property charged by that chargor.

(5)   In this article 'value of the property charged' means the value of the registered estate or the amount of the registered charge or charges affected by the application to register the charge, less the amount secured by any prior registered charges.

PART 4

Fixed fees and exemptions

Fixed fees

9.   (1)   Subject to paragraph (2) and to article 10, the fees for the applications and services specified in Schedule 3 shall be those set out in that Schedule.

(2)   Where an application is one specified in paragraphs (1), (2) or (10) in Part 1 of Schedule 3 affecting the whole or part of the freehold estate in land which has been registered as a freehold estate in commonhold land registered in the name of the developer under more than one title number, the fee is to be assessed as if the application affects only one title.

Exemptions

10.   No fee is payable for any of the applications and services specified in Schedule 4.

PART 5

General and administrative provisions

Cost of surveys, advertisements and special enquiries

11.   The applicant is to meet the costs of any survey, advertisement or other special enquiry that the registrar requires to be made or published in dealing with an application.

Applications not otherwise referred to

12.   The fee payable for an application in respect of which no other fee is payable under this Order shall be £50.

Method of payment

13.   (1)   Except where the registrar otherwise permits, every fee shall be paid by means of a cheque or postal order crossed and made payable to Land Registry.

(2)   Where there is an agreement with the applicant, a fee may be paid by direct debit to such bank account of the land registry as the registrar may from time to time direct.

(3)   Where the amount of the fee payable on an application is immediately quantifiable, the fee shall be payable on delivery of the application.

(4)   Where the amount of the fee payable on an application is not immediately quantifiable, the applicant shall pay the sum of £50 towards the fee when the application is made and shall lodge at the same time an undertaking to pay on demand the balance of the fee due, if any.

(5)   Where an outline application is made, the fee payable shall be the fee payable under paragraph (9) of Part 1 of Schedule 3 in addition to the fee otherwise payable under this Order.

Credit accounts

14.   (1)   Any person may, if authorised by the registrar, use a credit account in accordance with this article for the payment of fees for applications and services of such kind as the registrar shall from time to time direct.

(2)   To enable the registrar to consider whether or not a person applying to use a credit account may be so authorised, that person shall supply the registrar with such information and evidence as the registrar may require to satisfy him of that person's fitness to hold a credit account and the ability of that person to pay any amounts which may become due from time to time under a credit account.

(3)   To enable the registrar to consider from time to time whether or not an account holder may continue to be authorised to use a credit account, the account holder shall supply the registrar, when requested to do so, with such information and evidence as the registrar may require to satisfy him of the account holder's continuing fitness to hold a credit account and the continuing ability of the account holder to pay any amounts which may become due from time to time under the account holder's credit account.

(4)   Where an account holder makes an application where credit facilities are available to him, he may make a request, in such manner as the registrar directs, for the appropriate fee to be debited to the account holder's credit account, but the registrar shall not be required to accept such a request where the amount due on the account exceeds the credit limit applicable to the credit account, or would exceed it if the request were to be accepted.

(5)   Where an account holder makes an application where credit facilities are available to him, and the application is accompanied neither by a fee nor a request for the fee to be debited to his account, the registrar may debit the fee to his account.

(6)   The registrar shall send a statement of account to each account holder at the end of each calendar month or such other interval as the registrar shall direct.

(7)   The account holder must pay any sums due on his credit account before the date and in the manner specified by the registrar.

(8)   The registrar may at any time terminate or suspend any or all authorisations given under paragraph (1).

(9)   In this article 'credit limit' in relation to a credit account authorised for use under paragraph (1) means the maximum amount (if any) which is to be due on the account at any time, as notified by the registrar to the account holder from time to time, by means of such communication as the registrar considers appropriate.

Revocation

15.   The Land Registration Fee Order 2006 is revoked.

Signed by the authority of the Lord Chancellor

Michael Wills
Minister of State
Ministry of Justice
31st March 2009

We consent

Tony Cunningham
Frank Roy
Two of the Lord Commissioners of Her Majesty's Treasury
1st April 2009

SCHEDULE 1

Articles 2 and 3

SCALE 1

NOTE 1: Where the amount or value is a figure which includes pence, it must be rounded down to the nearest £1.

NOTE 2: The third column, which sets out the reduced fee payable where article 2(6) (voluntary registration: reduced fees) applies, is not part of the scale.

Amount or value £	Fee £	Reduced fee where article 2(6) (voluntary registration: reduced fees) applies £
0–50,000	50	40
50,001–80,000	80	60
80,001–100,000	130	100
100,001–200,000	200	150
200,001–500,000	280	210
500,001–1,000,000	550	410
1,000,001 and over	920	690

SCHEDULE 2

Articles 4 and 5

SCALE 2

NOTE: Where the amount or value is a figure which includes pence, it must be rounded down to the nearest £1.

Amount or value £	Fee £
0–100,000	50
100,001–200,000	70
200,001–500,000	90
500,001–1,000,000	130

Amount or value £	Fee £
1,000,001 and over	260

SCHEDULE 3

Articles 9 and 13

PART 1

Fixed fee applications

	Fee
(1) To register:	
(a) a standard form of restriction contained in Schedule 4 to the rules, or	
(b) a notice (other than a notice to which section 117(2)(b) of the Act applies), or	
(c) a new or additional beneficiary of a unilateral notice	
– total fee for up to three registered titles affected	£50
– additional fee for each subsequent registered title affected	£25
Provided that no such fee is payable if, in relation to each registered title affected, the application is accompanied by a scale fee application or another application which attracts a fee under this paragraph.	
(2) To register a restriction in a form not contained in Schedule 4 to the rules – for each registered title	£100
(3) To register a caution against first registration (other than a caution to which section 117(2)(a) of the Act applies)	£50
(4) To alter the cautions register – for each individual cautions register	£50
(5) To close or partly close a registered leasehold or a registered rentcharge title other than on surrender – for each registered title closed or partly closed	£50
Provided that no such fee is payable if the application is accompanied by a scale fee application.	
(6) To upgrade from one class of registered title to another	£50
Provided that no such fee is payable if the application for upgrading is accompanied by a scale fee application.	
(7) To cancel an entry in the register of notice of an unregistered rentcharge which has determined – for each registered title affected	£50
Provided that no such fee is payable if the application is accompanied by a scale fee application.	
(8) To enter or remove a record of a defect in title pursuant to section 64(1) of the Act	£50

	Fee
Provided that no such fee is payable if the application is accompanied by a scale fee application.	
(9) An outline application made under rule 54:	
(a) where delivered from a remote terminal	£3
(b) where delivered by any other permitted means	£6
Such fee is payable in addition to any other fee which is payable in respect of the application.	
(10) For an order in respect of a restriction under section 41(2) of the Act – for each registered title affected	£50
(11) To register a person in adverse possession of a registered estate – for each registered title affected	£150
(12) For registration as a person entitled to be notified of an application for adverse possession	
– for each registered title affected	£50
(13) For the determination of the exact line of a boundary under rule 118 – for each application	£100
(14) To register a freehold estate in land as a freehold estate in commonhold land which is not accompanied by a statement under section 9(1)(b) of the CLRA:	
(a) up to 20 commonhold units	£50
(b) for every 20 commonhold units, or up to 20 commonhold units, thereafter	£15
(15) To add land to a commonhold:	
(a) adding land to the common parts title	£50
(b) adding land to a commonhold unit	£50
(c) adding commonhold units – up to 20 commonhold units	£50
– for every 20 commonhold units, or up to 20 commonhold units, thereafter	£15
(16) To apply for a freehold estate in land to cease to be registered as a freehold estate in commonhold land during the transitional period, as defined in the CLRA	£50
(17) To register a freehold estate in land as a freehold estate in commonhold land, which is accompanied by a statement under section 9(1)(b) of the CLRA – for each commonhold unit converted	£50
(18) To register an amended commonhold community statement which changes the extent of the common parts or any commonhold unit:	
(a) for the common parts	£50
(b) for up to three commonhold units	£50
(c) for each subsequent commonhold unit	£25
Provided that no such fee shall be payable if, in relation to each registered title affected, the application is accompanied by a scale fee application or another application that attracts a fee under this Part.	

		Fee
(19)	To register an amended commonhold community statement, which does not change the extent of a registered title within the commonhold	£50
	Provided that no such fee shall be payable if, in relation to each registered title affected, the application is accompanied by a scale fee application or another application that attracts a fee under this Part.	
(20)	To register an alteration to the Memorandum or Articles of Association of a commonhold association	£50
(21)	To make a termination application – for each registered title affected	£50
(22)	To note the surrender of a development right under section 58 of the CLRA	£50

PART 2

Services – inspection and copying

Note: In this Part 'lease' means a lease or a copy of a lease.

			Fee
(1)		Inspection, from a remote terminal:	
	(a)	for each individual register	£4
	(b)	for each title plan	£4
	(c)	for any or all of the documents (other than leases) referred to in an individual register – for each registered title	£6
	(d)	for each lease kept by the registrar which is referred to in an individual register or which relates to an application to him	£12
	(e)	for the individual register and title plan of a commonhold common parts title – for each registered title	£4
	(f)	for each individual caution register	£4
	(g)	for each caution plan	£4
	(h)	for any other document kept by the registrar which relates to an application to him	
		– for each document	£6
(2)		Inspection (otherwise than under paragraph (1)):	
	(a)	for each individual register	£8
	(b)	for each title plan	£8
	(c)	for any or all of the documents (other than leases) referred to in an individual register	
		– for each registered title	£12
	(d)	for each lease kept by the registrar which is referred to in an individual register or which relates to an application to him	£24

		Fee
(e)	for the individual register and title plan of a commonhold common parts title – for each registered title	£8
(f)	for each individual caution register	£8
(g)	for each caution plan	£8
(h)	for any other document kept by the registrar which relates to an application to him	
	– for each document	£12

(3) Official copy in respect of a registered title:

    (a) for each individual register

        (i) where an official copy in electronic form is requested from a remote terminal — £4

        (ii) where an official copy in paper form is requested by any permitted means — £8

    (b) for each title plan:

        (i) where an official copy in electronic form is requested from a remote terminal — £4

        (ii) where an official copy in paper form is requested by any permitted means — £8

    (c) for each commonhold common parts individual register and title plan:

        (i) where an official copy in electronic form is requested from a remote terminal — £4

        (ii) where an official copy in paper form is requested by any permitted means — £8

(4) Official copy in respect of the cautions register

    (a) for each individual caution register:

        (i) where an official copy in electronic form is requested from a remote terminal — £4

        (ii) where an official copy in paper form is requested by any permitted means — £8

    (b) for each caution plan

        (i) where an official copy in electronic form is requested from a remote terminal — £4

        (ii) where an official copy in paper form is requested by any permitted means — £8

(5) Official copy of any or all of the documents (other than a lease) referred to in an individual register – for each registered title:

    (a) where an official copy in electronic form is requested from a remote terminal — £6

    (b) where an official copy in paper form is requested by any permitted means — £12

			Fee
(6)		Official copy of a lease kept by the registrar which is referred to in an individual register or which relates to an application to him – for each lease	
	(a)	where an official copy in electronic form is requested from a remote terminal and a copy of the lease is held in electronic form by the registrar	£12
	(b)	where an official copy in electronic form is requested from a remote terminal and a copy of the lease is not held in electronic form by the registrar	£24
	(c)	where an official copy in paper form is requested by any permitted means.	£24
(7)		Official copy of any other document kept by the registrar which relates to an application to him – for each document	
	(a)	where an official copy in electronic form is requested from a remote terminal and a copy of the document is held in electronic form by the registrar	£6
	(b)	where an official copy in electronic form is requested from a remote terminal and a copy of the document is not held in electronic form by the registrar	£12
	(c)	where an official copy in paper form is requested by any permitted means	£12
(8)		Copy of an historical edition of a registered title (or of part of the edition where rule 144(4) applies) – for each title	£10

PART 3

Services – searches

			Fee
(1)		An official search of an individual register or of a pending first registration application made to the registrar from a remote terminal – for each title	£4
(2)		An official search of an individual register by a mortgagee for the purpose of section 56(3) of the Family Law Act 1996 made to the registrar from a remote terminal	£4
(3)		An official search of an individual register or of a pending first registration application other than as described in paragraphs (1) and (2) – for each title	£8
(4)		The issue of a certificate of inspection of a title plan	£8
(5)		An official search of the index map	
	(a)	where no or not more than five registered titles are disclosed	£5

	Fee
(b) where more than five registered titles are disclosed	
(i) for the first five titles	£5
(ii) for every ten titles, or up to ten titles, thereafter	£3
(6) Search of the index of proprietors' names – for each name	£12
(7) An official search of the index of relating franchises and manors – for each administrative area:	
(a) where the application is made from a remote terminal	£4
(b) where the application is made by any other permitted means	£8

PART 4

Services – Other information

	Fee
(1) Application for return of a document under rule 204	£10
(2) Application that the registrar designate a document an exempt information document	£26

SCHEDULE 4

Article 10

Exemptions

No fee is payable for:

(1)   reflecting a change in the name, address or description of a registered proprietor or other person referred to in the register, or in the cautions register, or changing the description of a property,

(2)   giving effect in the register to a change of proprietor where the registered estate or the registered charge, as the case may be, has become vested without further assurance (other than on the death or bankruptcy of a proprietor) in some person by the operation of any statute (other than the Act), statutory instrument or scheme taking effect under any statute or statutory instrument,

(3)   registering the surrender of a registered leasehold estate where the surrender is consideration or part consideration for the grant of a new lease to the registered proprietor of substantially the same premises as were comprised in the surrendered lease and where a scale fee is paid for the registration of the new lease,

(4)   registering a discharge of a registered charge,

(5)   registering a home rights notice, or renewal of such a notice, or renewal of a home rights caution under the Family Law Act 1996,

(6)   entering in the register the death of a joint proprietor,

(7)   cancelling the registration of a notice (other than a notice in respect of an unregistered lease or unregistered rentcharge), caution against first registration, caution against dealings, including a withdrawal of a deposit or intended deposit, inhibition, restriction, or note,

(8)   the removal of the designation of a document as an exempt information document,

(9)   approving an estate layout plan or any draft document with or without a plan,

(10)   an order by the registrar (other than an order under section 41(2) of the Act),

(11)   deregistering a manor,

(12)   an entry in the register of a note of the dissolution of a corporation,

(13)   registering a restriction in Form A in Schedule 4 to the rules,

(14)   an application for day list information on any one occasion from a remote terminal,

(15)   an application to lodge a caution against first registration or to make a register entry where in either case the application relates to rights in respect of the repair of a church chancel.

VIII. DIRECTORY

VIII.1. Land Registry addresses

The Land Registry will reject applications that are sent to the wrong office. To determine which area is served by which office, see Land Registry Practice Guide 51 (**www.landregistry.gov.uk**).

Following consultation, the Land Registry has announced several changes of address to occur during 2011. The offices affected are: Head Office, Peterborough, Portsmouth, Stevenage, and Tunbridge Wells.

Land Registry Head Office

32 Lincoln's Inn Fields
London WC2A 3PH

Tel: 020 7917 8888
Fax (for correspondence only): 020 7955 0110
DX: 1098 London/Chancery Lane
(*Due to move to Croydon by March 2011*)

Birkenhead

Land Registry
Birkenhead Office
Rosebrae Court
Woodside Ferry Approach
Birkenhead
Merseyside CH41 6DU

Tel: 0151 472 6666
Fax: 0151 472 6789
DX: 24270 Birkenhead (4)

Coventry

Land Registry
Coventry Office
Leigh Court
Torrington Avenue
Tile Hill
Coventry CV4 9XZ

Tel: 024 7686 0860
Fax: 024 7686 0021
DX: 18900 Coventry (3)

Croydon

Land Registry
Croydon Office
Trafalgar House
1 Bedford Park
Croydon CR0 2AQ

Tel: 020 8781 9100
Fax: 020 8781 9110
DX: 2699 Croydon (3)

Durham (Southfield)

Land Registry
Durham (Southfield) Office
Southfield House
Southfield Way
Durham DH1 5TR

Tel: 0191 301 3500
Fax: 0191 301 0020
DX: 60200 Durham (3)

Fylde

Land Registry
Fylde Office
Wrea Brook Court
Lytham Road
Warton
Lancashire PR4 1TE

Tel: 01772 836700
Fax: 01772 836970
DX: 721560 Lytham St Annes (6)

VIII

Gloucester

Land Registry
Gloucester Office
Twyver House
Bruton Way
Gloucester GL1 1DQ

Tel: 01452 511111
Fax: 01452 510050
DX: 7599 Gloucester (3)

Kingston Upon Hull

Land Registry
Kingston Upon Hull Office
Earle House
Colonial Street
Hull HU2 8JN

Tel: 01482 223244
Fax: 01482 224278
DX: 26700 Hull (4)

Leicester

Land Registry
Leicester Office
Westbridge Place
Leicester LE3 5DR

Tel: 0116 265 4000
Fax: 0116 265 4008
DX: 11900 Leicester (5)

Nottingham

Land Registry
Nottingham Office
Chalfont Drive
Nottingham NG8 3RN

Tel: 0115 935 1166
Fax: 0115 935 0038
DX: 10298 Nottingham (3)

Peterborough

Land Registry
Peterborough Office
Touthill Close
City Road
Peterborough PE1 1XN

Tel: 01733 288288
Fax: 01733 280022
DX: 12598 Peterborough (4)

Plymouth

Land Registry
Plymouth Office
Plumer House
Tailyour Road
Crownhill
Plymouth PL6 5HY

Tel: 01752 636000
Fax: 01752 636161
DX: 8299 Plymouth (4)

Portsmouth

Land Registry
Portsmouth Office
St Andrew's Court
St Michael's Road
Portsmouth
Hampshire PO1 2JH

Tel: 023 9276 8888
Fax: 023 9276 8768
DX: 83550 Portsmouth (2)
(*Due to close by February 2011*)

Stevenage

Land Registry
Stevenage Office
Brickdale House
Swingate
Stevenage
Hertfordshire SG1 1XG

Tel: 01438 788888
Fax: 01438 785460
DX: 6099 Stevenage (2)
(*Due to close by June 2011*)

Telford

Land Registry
Telford Office
Parkside Court
Hall Park Way
Telford TF3 4LR

Tel: 01952 290355
Fax: 01952 290356
DX: 28100 Telford (2)

Tunbridge Wells

Land Registry
Tunbridge Wells Office
Forest Court
Forest Road
Tunbridge Wells
Kent TN2 5AQ

Tel: 01892 510015
Fax: 01892 510032
DX: 3999 Tunbridge Wells (2)
(*Due to close by June 2011*)

Wales/Cymru

Land Registry
Wales Office
Ty Cwm Tawe
Phoenix Way
Llansamlet
Swansea SA7 9FQ

Tel: 01792 355000
Fax: 01792 355055
DX: 82800 Swansea (2)

Weymouth

Land Registry
Weymouth Office
Melcombe Court
1 Cumberland Drive
Weymouth
Dorset DT4 9TT

Tel: 01305 363636
Fax: 01305 363646
DX: 8799 Weymouth (2)

VIII

VIII.2. All other addresses

BRB (Residuary) Ltd (formerly British Railways Board)

4th Floor
One Kemble Street
London WC2B 4AN

Tel: 020 7904 5079
www.brbr.co.uk

British Gas

PO Box 4805
Worthing
BN11 9QW

Tel: 0800 048 0202
www.britishgas.co.uk

British Geological Survey

Kingsley Dunham Centre
Keyworth
Nottingham NG12 5GG

Tel: 0115 936 3100
Fax: 0115 936 3200
www.bgs.ac.uk

British Sugar plc

Sugar Way
Peterborough PE2 9AY

Tel: 01733 563 171
Fax: 01733 422 967
www.britishsugar.co.uk

British Waterways

Head Office

64 Clarendon Road
Watford
Herts WD17 1DA

Tel: 01923 201 120
Fax: 01923 201 304
www.britishwaterways.co.uk

Regional Offices

Central Shires Office
Peel's Wharf

Lichfield Street
Fazeley
Tamworth
Staffordshire B78 3QZ

Tel: 01827 252 000
Fax: 01827 288 071

East Midlands Office
The Kiln
Mather Road
Newark NG24 1FB

Tel: 01636 704 481
Fax: 01636 705 584

Kennet & Avon Office
The Locks
Bath Road
Devizes
SN10 1QR

Tel: 01380 722 859

London Office
British Waterways London
1 Sheldon Square
Paddington Central
London W2 6TT

Tel: 020 7985 7200
Fax: 020 7985 7201

Manchester & Pennine Office
Red Bull Yard
Congleton Road South
Church Lawton
Stoke on Trent
ST7 3AP

Tel: 01782 785 703

North East Office
Fearns Wharf
Neptune Street
Leeds LS9 8PB

Tel: 0113 281 6860
Fax: 0113 281 6886

North Wales and Borders Office
Navigation Road
Northwich

Cheshire CW8 1BH

Tel: 01606 723800

North West Office
Waterside House
Waterside Drive
Wigan WN3 5AZ

Tel: 01942 405700

South East Office
510–524 Elder House
Elder Gate
Milton Keynes MK9 1BW

Tel: 01908 302500
Fax: 01908 302510

The Charity Commission

Charity Commission Direct
PO Box 1227
Liverpool L69 3UG

Tel: 0845 3000 218
Fax: 0151 7031 555
www.charity-commission.gov.uk

Cheshire Brine Subsidence Compensation Board

Sir Henry Doulton House
Forge Lane
Etruria
Stoke on Trent
ST1 5BD

Tel: 0845 002 0562
Fax: 0845 111 8888
www.cheshirebrine.com

Church Commissioners for England

Church House
Great Smith Street
Westminster
London SW1P 3AZ

Tel: 020 7898 1000
www.churchcommissioners.org

Coal Authority

200 Lichfield Lane
Mansfield
Nottinghamshire NG18 4RG

Tel: 01623 637 000
www.coal.gov.uk

Companies House

Companies House
Crown Way
Maindy
Cardiff CF14 3UZ

Tel: 0303 1234 500
DX: 33050 Cardiff
www.companieshouse.gov.uk

Cornish Mines and Property Surveys Ltd

22 New Bridge Street
Truro
Cornwall TR1 2AA

Tel/Fax: 01872 272 720

Cornwall Consultants Ltd

Parc Vean House
Coach Lane
Redruth
Cornwall TR15 2TT

Tel: 01209 313 511
Fax: 01209 313 512
www.cornwallconsultants.co.uk

Council for Licensed Conveyancers

16 Glebe Road
Chelmsford
Essex CM1 1QG

Tel: 01245 349 599
DX: 121925 Chelmsford (6)
www.conveyancer.org.uk

Council of Mortgage Lenders

Bush House
North West Wing
Aldwych
London WC2B 4PJ

Tel: 0845 373 6771 (switchboard)
Fax: 0845 373 6778
www.cml.org.uk

VIII

Court of Protection

Archway Tower
2 Junction Road
London N19 5SZ

Tel: 0300 456 4600
DX: 141150 Archway 2
www.hmcourts-service.gov.uk

Crown Estate

Headquarters
16 New Burlington Place
London W1S 2HX

Tel: 020 7851 5000
www.crownestate.co.uk

Drinking Water Inspectorate

Room M03
55 Whitehall
London SW1A 2EY

Tel: 030 0068 6400
Fax: 030 0068 6401
www.dwi.gov.uk

Duchy of Cornwall

10 Buckingham Gate
London SW1E 6LA

Tel: 020 7834 7346
www.duchyofcornwall.org

Duchy of Lancaster

1 Lancaster Place
Strand
London WC2E 7ED

Tel: 020 7269 1700
Fax: 020 7269 1710
www.duchyoflancaster.org.uk

Electricity – Distribution Network Operator Companies

Central Networks – E.ON
3rd Floor
Toll End Road
Tipton
DY4 0HH

Tel: 0845 072 7270
www.eon-uk.com

CE Electric UK
Cargo Fleet Lane
Middlesbrough
TS3 8DG

Tel: 0845 070 2703
www.ceelectricuk.com

EDF Energy Networks
FREEPOST RRYZ-BRTT-CBJS
Osprey House
Osprey Road
Exeter
EX2 7WN

Tel: 0800 096 9000
www.edfenergy.com

Scottish and Southern Energy plc
Inveralmond House
200 Dunkeld Road
Perth PH1 3AQ

Tel: 01738 456 000
www.scottish-southern.co.uk

Scottish Power Energy Networks (Cheshire, Merseyside and North Wales)
SP Energy Networks
PO Box 168
Prenton CH26 9AY

Tel: 0845 273 4444
www.spenergynetworks.co.uk

Western Power Distribution
Lostwithiel Road
Bodmin
Cornwall PL31 1DE

Tel: 0845 601 2989
Fax: 01208 892292
www.westernpower.co.uk

Avonbank
Feeder Road
Bristol BS2 0TB

Tel: 0845 601 2981/3341
www.westernpower.co.uk

Electricity – domestic supply companies

Atlantic Electric and Gas
PO Box 7506
Perth
PH1 3QR

Tel: 0845 073 3030
www.atlanticeg.co.uk

British Gas
PO Box 3055
Eastbourne
BN21 9FE

Tel: 0800 048 0202
www.britishgas.co.uk

Countrywide Energy
Defford Mill
Earls Croome
Worcestershire
WR8 9DF

Tel: 0800 328 0011
www.countrywidefarmers.co.uk

Ecotricity
Axiom House
Station Road
Stroud
Gloucestershire
GL5 3AP

Tel: 08000 302 302
www.ecotricity.co.uk

Ebico Ltd
PO Box 354
Witney
OX29 7WN

Tel: 0800 096 6344
www.ebico.co.uk

EDF Energy
FREEPOST RRYZ-BRTT-CBJS
Osprey House, Osprey Road
Exeter
EX2 7WN

Tel: 0800 096 9000
www.edfenergy.com

E.ON
PO Box 7750
Nottingham
NG1 6WR

Tel: 0845 303 3020
www.eonenergy.com

First Utility
Athena House
Athena Drive

Tachbrook Park
Warwick
CV34 6RL

Tel: 0845 215 5000
www.first-utility.com

Green Energy
Marsh Lane
Ware
Herts
SG12 9QL

Tel: 0800 954 0675
www.greenenergyuk.com

LoCO2 Energy Ltd
1st Floor,
Batchworth Lock House,
99 Church Street,
Rickmansworth,
Hertfordshire,
WD3 1JJ

Tel: 0845 074 3601
www.loco2energy.com

NPower
PO Box 93
Peterlee
SR8 2XX

Tel: 0845 078 2925
www.npower.com

Opus Energy Limited
Royal Pavilion
2 Summerhouse Road
Northampton
NN3 6BJ

Tel: 0845 330 2655
www.opusenergy.com

Scottish and Southern Energy Group
PO Box 7506
Perth
PH1 3QR

Tel: 01738 456 000
www.scottish-southern.co.uk

Scottish Power
Customer Services
Cathcart Business Park
Spean Street
Glasgow G44 4BE

VIII

Tel: 0845 2700 700
www.scottishpower.co.uk

Spark Energy
Ettrick Riverside
Dunsdale Road
Selkirk
TD7 5EB

Tel: 0845 034 7474
www.sparkenergy.co.uk

Telecom Plus (Utility Warehouse)
Network HQ
333 Edgware Road
London
NW9 6TD

Tel: 0844 815 7777
www.utilitywarehouse.co.uk

Utilita Services Ltd
PRI House
Moorside Road
Winchester
Hampshire
SO23 7RX

Tel: 0845 450 4357
www.utilita.co.uk

Energy Assessor Accreditation Schemes

Building Engineering Services Competence Accreditation Ltd (BESCA)

www.besca.org.uk

Building Research Establishment Ltd (BRE)

www.bre.co.uk

Chartered Institute of Architectural Technologists (CIAT)

www.ciat.org.uk

Chartered Institution of Building Services Engineers (CIBSE)

www.cibse.org

ECMK Ltd

www.ecmk.co.uk

Elmhurst Energy Systems Ltd

www.elmhurstenergy.co.uk

Heating and Ventilation Certificated Associates

www.hicertification.co.uk

Knauf

www.knauf.co.uk

National Association of Professional Inspectors and Testers (NAPIT)

www.napit.org.uk

National Energy Services Ltd (NES)

www.nesltd.co.uk

Northgate Information Solutions UK Ltd

www.northgate-dea.com

Quidos Ltd

www.quidos.co.uk

Royal Institution of Chartered Surveyors

www.rics.org

Sterling Accreditation

www.sterlingaccreditation.com

Stroma

www.stroma.com

Energy Performance Certificate Register

www.hcrregister.com

Environment Agency

National Customer Contact Centre (NCCC)
PO Box 544
Rotherham S60 1BY

Tel: 08708 506 506
www.environment-agency.gov.uk

GroundSure Ltd

Lees House
Brighton BN1 3FE

Tel: 08444 159 000
www.groundsure.com

Health Protection Agency (HPA)

Central Office
7th Floor
Holborn Gate
330 High Holborn
London WC1V 7PP

Tel: 020 7759 2700
Fax: 020 7759 2733
www.hpa.org.uk

HM Revenue and Customs (Inheritance Tax)

Ferrers House
PO Box 38
Castle Meadow Road
Nottingham NG2 1BB

Tel: 0845 302 0900
www.hmrc.gov.uk

HM Revenue and Customs Stamp Offices

Land Transaction Returns

HMRC Stamp Taxes
Comben House
Farriers Way
Netherton
Merseyside L30 4RN

DX: 725593 Bootle (9)
www.hmrc.gov.uk (online returns)

Stamp Taxes General Correspondence

Customer Service Manager
Birmingham Stamp Office
9th Floor
City Centre House
30 Union Street
Birmingham B2 4AR

Tel: 0845 603 0135

Imerys Minerals Ltd

Par Moor Centre
Par Moor Road
Par
St Austell
Cornwall PL24 2SQ

Tel: 01726 811 311
www.imerys.com

Insolvency Practitioners Unit

The Insolvency Service
Cannon House
18 Priory Queensway
Birmingham B4 6BS

Tel: 0121 698 4000
www.insolvency.gov.uk

Kaolin and Ball Clay Association Ltd

See: Imerys and Sibelco UK Ltd for the property search.
Par Moor Centre
Par Moor
Par
Cornwall PL24 2SQ

Tel: 01726 811 328
Fax: 01726 811 200
www.kabca.org

Land Charges Department (the Land Registry)

Plumer House
Tailyour Road
Crownhill
Plymouth PL6 5HY

Tel: 01752 636 666
DX: 8249 Plymouth (3)
www.landregistry.gov.uk

Landmark Information Group Ltd

5–7 Abbey Court
Eagle Way
Sowton Industrial Estate
Exeter EX2 7HY

Tel: 01392 441 700
Fax: 01392 441 709
DX: 149460 Exeter (23)
www.landmark.co.uk

VIII

Land Registry, Independent Adjudicator

The Adjudicator to HM Land Registry
7th Floor
Victory House
34 Kingsway
London WC28 6EX

Tel: 020 3077 5800
Fax: 020 3077 5836
www.ahmlr.gov.uk

Lands Tribunal (Lands Chamber of the Upper Tribunal)

43–45 Bedford Square
London WC1B 3AS

Tel: 020 7612 9710
Fax: 020 7612 9723
www.landstribunal.gov.uk

Law Society of England and Wales

113 Chancery Lane
London WC2A 1PL

Tel: 020 7242 1222 (switchboard)
Tel: 0870 606 2522 (practice advice)
DX: 56 London/Chancery Lane
www.lawsociety.org.uk

Legal Complaints Service

Victoria Court
8 Dormer Place
Leamington Spa
Warwickshire CV32 5AE

Tel: 01926 820 082
Fax: 01926 431 435
Tel: 0845 608 6565 (helpline)
www.legalcomplaints.org.uk

Legal Ombudsman

Tel: 0121 503 2930
www.legalombudsman.org.uk

Local Government Association

Local Government House
Smith Square
London SW1P 3HZ

Tel: 020 7664 3131
Fax: 020 7664 3030
www.lga.gov.uk

Mutual Societies Registration

Financial Services Authority
25 The North Colonnade
Canary Wharf
London E14 5HS

Tel: 0845 606 9966 (option 3)
www.fsa.gov.uk

National Archives

Kew
Richmond
Surrey TW9 4DU

Tel: 020 8876 3444
www.nationalarchives.gov.uk

National Association of Estate Agents

Arbon House
6 Tournament Court
Edgehill Drive
Warwick CV34 6LG

Tel: 01926 496 800
Fax: 01926 808 182
www.naea.co.uk

Network Rail

King's Place
90 York Way
London N1 9AG

Tel: 020 7557 8000
www.networkrail.co.uk

National Channels

MDA SearchFlow
42 Kings Hill Avenue
Kings Hill
West Malling
Kent ME19 4AJ

Tel: 0870 787 7625
Fax: 0870 990 9949
www.searchflow.co.uk

Thames Water Property Insight
PO Box 3189
Slough
SL1 4WW

Tel: 0118 925 1504
www.twpropertyinsight.co.uk

Office of the Public Guardian

PO Box 15118
Birmingham B16 6GX

Tel: 0845 330 2900
Fax: 020 7664 7705
DX: 744240 Birmingham 79
www.publicguardian.gov.uk

Ordnance Survey

Customer Service Centre
Romsey Road
Southampton SO16 4GU

Tel: 08456 05 05 05
Fax: 023 8079 2615
www.ordnancesurvey.co.uk

Probate Service

London Probate Department
PFRD, First Avenue House
42–49 High Holborn
London WC1V 6NP

Tel: 0845 302 0900
www.hmcourts-service.gov.uk (for list of probate registries)

Residential Property Tribunal Service

Corporate Unit
10 Alfred Place
London WC1E 7LR

Tel: 020 7446 7740
Fax: 020 7580 5684
www.rpts.gov.uk

Eastern Rent Assessment Panel
Unit 4c Quern House
Mill Court, Great Shelford
Cambridge CB22 5LD

Tel: 0845 100 2616
Fax: 01223 843 224

London Rent Assessment Panel
10 Alfred Place
London WC1E 7LR

Tel: 020 7446 7700
Fax: 020 7637 1250

Midlands Rent Assessment Panel
2nd Floor
Louisa House
92–93 Edward Street
Birmingham B1 2RA

Tel: 0121 236 7837/0845 100 2615
Fax: 0121 236 9337

Northern Rent Assessment Panel
First Floor
5 New York Street
Manchester M1 4JB

Tel: 0845 100 2614
Fax: 0161 237 3656

Southern Rent Assessment Panel
1st Floor
1 Market Avenue
Chichester PO19 1JU

Tel: 01243 779 394/0845 100 2617
Fax: 01243 779 389

Royal Courts of Justice

The Strand
London WC2A 2LL

Tel: 020 7947 6000
www.hmcourts-service.gov.uk

Rural Payments Agency

Headquarters
Kings House
33 Kings Road
Reading RG1 3BU

Tel: 0118 958 3626
Fax: 0118 959 7736
www.rpa.gov.uk

Milk Quotas
PO Box 277
Exeter EX5 1WB

Tel: 01392 266466
Fax: 01392 266489

Serious Organised Crime Agency (SOCA)

PO Box 8000
London SE11 5EN

Tel: 0370 396 7622
www.soca.gov.uk

Sibelco UK Ltd

Lovering Lodge
Kingsteignton Road
Newton Abbot
Devon TQ12 2PA

Tel: 01626 322331
Fax: 01626 322388

Solicitors Regulation Authority (SRA)

Ipsley Court
Berrington Close
Redditch B98 0TD

Tel: 0870 606 2555
Fax: 01527 510 213
www.sra.gov.uk

Tenancy deposit protection schemes

The Deposit Protection Service (The DPS)
The Pavilions
Bridgwater Road
Bristol BS99 6AA

Tel: 0844 4727 000
www.depositprotection.com

The Dispute Service Ltd
PO Box 1255
Hemel Hempstead
Herts HP1 9GN

Tel: 0845 226 7837
Fax: 01442 253 193
www.thedisputeservice.co.uk

Mydeposits
Ground Floor
Kingmaker House
Station Road
New Barnet
Hertfordshire EN5 1NZ

Tel: 0844 980 0290
Fax: 08456 34 34 03
www.mydeposits.co.uk

TM Group (UK) Ltd
200 Delta Business Park
Swindon
Wiltshire SN5 7XD

Tel: 0844 249 9200
www.tmgroup.co.uk

Treasury Solicitor's Department

1 Kemble Street
London WC2B 4TS

Tel: 020 7210 3000
DX: 123242 Kingsway
www.tsol.gov.uk

Water and Sewerage Companies (address for CON 29DW enquiries)

Anglian Water (trading as Geodesys)
Property Information Centre
PO Box 485
Huntingdon PE29 6YB

Tel: 01480 323889
Fax: 01480 323890
DX: 123730 Huntingdon 6
www.geodesys.com

Northumbrian Water Property Solutions
PO Box 338
Durham
DH1 9ZR

Tel: 0870 241 7408
Fax: 0870 241 7409
DX: 717042 Durham 15
www.nwpropertysolutions.co.uk

Severn Trent Searches
PO Box 6187
Nottingham NG5 1LE

Tel: 0115 962 7269
Fax: 0115 962 7132
DX: 723860 Nottingham 43
www.severntrentsearches.com

South West Water Conveyancing Services
Peninsula House
Rydon Lane
Exeter
Devon EX2 7HR

Tel: 08453 303 401
Fax: 01392 433 008

DX: 119851 Exeter 10
www.southwestwater.co.uk

Southern Water Land Search Team
The Land Search Team
Southern House, Capstone Road
Chatham
Kent ME5 7QA

Tel: 0845 270 0212
Fax: 01634 844514
DX 400450 Chatham 5
www.southernwater.co.uk

Thames Water
PO Box 3189
Slough SL1 4WW

Tel: 0118 925 1504
Fax: 0118 923 6655/57
DX: 151280 Slough 13
www.twpropertyinsight.co.uk

United Utilities
Stephens Way
Goose Green
Wigan WN3 6PJ

Tel: 0870 751 0101
Fax: 0870 751 0102
DX 719690 Wigan 8
www.unitedutilities.com

Welsh Water NDC
PO Box 10
Treharris CF46 6XZ

Tel: 01443 331 155
Fax: 01443 331 161
www.dwrcymrusearches.com

Wessex Water
Searches Team
Operations Centre
Claverton Down Road
Bath BA2 7WW

Tel: 01225 526206
Fax: 01225 528994
DX 146200 Bath 6
www.wessexsearches.co.uk

Yorkshire Water (trading as Safe-Move)
PO Box 99
Bradford BD3 7YB

Tel: 08001 385 385
Fax: 01274 804 086

DX 723 020 Bradford 20
www.safe-move.co.uk

Water Only Companies (Head Offices)

Bournemouth & West Hampshire Water plc
George Jessel House
Francis Avenue
Bournemouth BH11 8NX

Tel: 01202 590 059
Fax: 01202 597 022
www.bwhwater.co.uk

Bristol Water plc
1 Clevedon Walk
Nailsea
Bristol BS48 1WW

Tel: 0117 966 5881
www.bristol-water.co.uk

Cambridge Water Company plc
90 Fulbourn Road
Cambridge CB1 9JN

Tel: 01223 706 050
www.cambridge-water.co.uk

Cholderton & District Water Company Ltd
Estate Office
Cholderton
Nr Salisbury
Wiltshire SP4 0DR

Tel: 01980 629 203
www.choldertonwater.co.uk

Dee Valley Water plc
Packsaddle
Wrexham Road
Rhostyllen
Wrexham LL14 4EH

Tel: 01978 846 946
Fax: 01978 846 888
www.deevalleygroup.com

Essex & Suffolk Water Company
Hall Street
Chelmsford
Essex CM2 0HH

Tel: 01245 491 234
www.eswater.co.uk

VIII

Hartlepool Water plc
3 Lancaster Road
Hartlepool TS24 8LW

Tel: 01429 858 050
www.hartlepoolwater.co.uk

Portsmouth Water Ltd
PO Box 8
West Street
Havant PO9 1LG

Tel: 023 9249 9888
www.portsmouthwater.co.uk

South East Water Ltd
Snodland
Kent
ME6 5AH

Tel: 01634 242 764
www.southeastwater.co.uk

South Staffordshire Water plc
PO Box 63
Walsall WS2 7PJ

Tel: 0845 60 70 456
www.south-staffs-water.co.uk

Sutton & East Surrey Water plc
London Road
Redhill RH1 1LJ

Tel: 01737 772 000
www.waterplc.com

Veolia Water Central
Tamblin Way
Hatfield
Herfordshire AL10 9EZ

Tel: 0845 782 3333
www.veoliawater.co.uk/central

Veolia Water East
Mill Hill
Manningtree
Essex CO11 2AZ

Tel: 0845 148 9288
Fax: 01206 399 212
www.veoliawater.co.uk/east

Veolia Water South East
Cherry Garden Lane
Folkestone CT19 4QB

Tel: 0845 888 5888
Fax: 01303 276 712
www.veoliawater.co.uk/southeast

Index

INDEX

THE LAW SOCIETY'S CONVEYANCING HANDBOOK 17TH EDITION